THE ENCYCLOPEDIA OF AGING

A Comprehensive Resource in Gerontology and Geriatrics

Fourth Edition

THE ENCYCLOPEDIA OF AGING

A Comprehensive Resource in Gerontology and Geriatrics

Fourth Edition

RICHARD SCHULZ, PhD
EDITOR-IN-CHIEF

Linda S. Noelker, PhD
Kenneth Rockwood, MD, FRCPC
Richard L. Sprott, PhD
ASSOCIATE EDITORS

Springer Publishing Company, Inc.
11 West 42nd Street
New York, NY 10036

Managing Editor: Sheri W. Sussman
Assistant Managing Editor: Alana Stein
Cover Designer: Mimi Flow
Production: Chernow Editorial Services, Inc.
Composition: TechBooks

06 07 08 09 10/ 5 4 3 2 1

Library of Congress Cataloging-in-Publication Data

Encyclopedia of aging.—4th ed. / Richard Schulz . . . [et al.].
p. ; cm.
Includes bibliographical references and index.
ISBN 0–8261–4843–3
1. Gerontology—Encyclopedias. 2. Older people—Encyclopedias.
[DNLM: 1. Geriatrics—Encyclopedias—English. 2. Aged. WT 13 E56 2006]
I. Schulz, Richard, 1947–
HQ1061 .E53 2006
305.2603—dc22

2006003769
CIP

Printed in the United States of America by Bang Printing.

CONTENTS

THE EDITORS

Richard Schulz, PhD, is Professor of Psychiatry, Psychology, Epidemiology, Sociology, and Health and Rehabilitation Sciences, and Director of the University Center for Social and Urban Research at the University of Pittsburgh. He is also Associate Director of the Institute on Aging at the University of Pittsburgh. He received his AB in Psychology from Dartmouth College and his PhD in Social Psychology from Duke University. He is the recipient of several honors, including the Kleemeier Award for Research on Aging from the Gerontological Society of America and the Developmental Health Award for Research on Health in Later Life from the American Psychological Association. He also served as Editor of the *Journal of Gerontology: Psychological Sciences*. He has spent his entire career doing research and writing on adult development and aging. Funded by numerous NIH institutes for more than two decades, his research has focused on the social-psychological aspects of aging, including the role of control as a construct for characterizing life-course development and the impact of disabling late life disease on patients and their families. This body of work is reflected in publications, which have appeared in major medical (*JAMA, NEJM*), psychology (*Psychological Review, Psychological Bulletin, JPSP*), and aging (*Journal of Gerontology, Psychology and Aging, JAGS, AJGS*) journals.

Linda S. Noelker, PhD, joined Benjamin Rose in 1974 as an applied aging researcher and is currently the Senior Vice President for Planning and Organizational Resources. In that capacity, she oversees the Research Institute and the Institutional Advancement and the Advocacy and Public Policy Departments. She received her MA and PhD from Case Western Reserve, where she is an Adjunct Professor of Sociology. She also is the Editor-in-Chief of *The Gerontologist*, the leading journal in applied aging research, practice, and policy. Dr. Noelker holds leadership positions in the American Society on Aging and the Gerontological Society of America and recently received the 2005 American Society on Aging Award for exemplary contributions to the field of aging. Throughout her career, she has conducted research on the nature and effects of family care for frail aged, patterns of service use by older adults and their family caregivers, and sources of stress and job satisfaction among the direct care workforce. She has published widely on the support networks of older adults, quality of life, the well-being of family caregivers, predictors of service use, and the nature of social relationships in nursing homes.

Kenneth Rockwood, MD, FRCPC, Professor of Medicine (Geriatric Medicine & Neurology) and Kathryn Allen Weldon Professor of Alzheimer Disease Research, is the Director of the Geriatric Medicine Research Unit at Dalhousie University. He is a Canadian Institute of Health Research (CIHR) Investigator and a member of the CIHR Institute of Aging Advisory Board. He has a long-standing interest in delirium, dementia, and frailty.

Professor Rockwood is author of more than 200 peer-reviewed scientific publications, and five books. He is a staff physician in the Department of Medicine at the Queen Elizabeth II Health Sciences Centre, Halifax, Nova Scotia, Canada

Currently, he is the principal investigator in the Video Imaging Synthesis of Treating Alzheimer's disease (VISTA) study, an investigator-initiated national, multicenter project to identify and track novel treatment effects in patients with mild to moderate Alzheimer's disease who are treated with galantamine, an antidementia medication.

Kenneth Rockwood is a native of Newfoundland and became a Doctor of Medicine at Memorial University in 1985. He is married to an internationally recognized scientist in the Faculty of Medicine—Susan Howlett, Professor of Pharmacology, and together they have two teenage sons, Michael and James.

Richard L. Sprott, PhD, Executive Director of the Ellison Medical Foundation, began his undergraduate studies at Franklin and Marshall College in Lancaster, Pennsylvania. He completed them at the University of North Carolina at Chapel Hill, earning a BA with honors in Psychology. After receiving his PhD in Experimental Psychology (Behavior Genetics) at the University of North Carolina, he went on to a postdoctoral fellowship in Behavior Genetics at the Jackson Laboratory in Bar Harbor, Maine. Following two years of teaching at Oakland University, Dr. Sprott returned to the Jackson Laboratory where he conducted a research program on single gene influences on behavior and the interaction of aging variables with those genes.

After a decade in Maine, Dr. Sprott moved to the National Institute on Aging where he directed the Institute's programs on the Biology of Aging. A major focus of his career has been the development of animal models for aging research. He developed a nationwide research program on biomarkers of aging and the effects of dietary restriction on longevity. He is the author of a large number of books and articles. He is an internationally recognized expert on animal model development and plays an active role in model development in countries around the world. He is the Past President of the International Biogerontological Resource Institute (IBRI) in Friuli, Italy.

Dr. Sprott left the National Institute on Aging in 1998 to become the first Executive Director of the Ellison Medical Foundation, created to support basic biological and biomedical research on aging and recently expanded to provide similar support for basic research on infectious diseases of importance in the developed and developing worlds. The Ellison Medical Foundation is the largest private foundation source of funding for research on the biology of aging, providing about $28,000,000 per year in grant funds for aging research, and $12,000,000 for infectious disease research.

FOREWORD
TO THE FOURTH EDITION

The Fourth Edition of the *Encyclopedia of Aging* marks the 20th anniversary of what has become the authoritative, comprehensive, and multidisciplinary introduction to gerontology and geriatrics. Originally proposed by Ursula Springer, PhD, and edited by George L. Maddox, PhD, the *Encyclopedia* serves as the gateway to the world of aging and the aged. The vision and hard work of these pioneers have established the *Encyclopedia* as a leading resource in the field. With the Fourth Edition of the *Encyclopedia,* we hope to continue this tradition by providing the most up-to-date and comprehensive introduction to gerontology and geriatrics currently available.

Knowledge about adult development and aging is advancing at an incredibly rapid pace. This is particularly true in the medical, biological, and social sciences, where new information becomes available almost daily. Keeping abreast of new developments in multiple disciplines requires expertise that far exceeds the capabilities of any one individual. Thus, the team of associate editors assembled for this project represents cutting edge expertise in biology (Richard Sprott), medicine and health (Ken Rockwood), and sociology (Linda Noelker). Advances in psychological aspects of aging were covered by the editor-in-chief. Together we commissioned, reviewed, and edited well more than 400 entries, and while previous editions of the *Encyclopedia* provided a firm foundation for this one, almost every entry has been updated and many new ones have been added. As with previous editions, our goal has been to explain complex issues in plain English that can be understood by educated laypersons.

The structure of the *Encyclopedia* remains the same. A comprehensive index is provided in both volumes, and extensive cross-referencing within the text provides readers with links among entries, enabling a comprehensive, in-depth view of topics. Sheri W. Sussman, the veteran Managing Editor of previous editions of the *Encyclopedia*, and her assistant, Alana Stein, provided the logistic support, guidance, and encouragement to keep this project on track. My able assistant at the University of Pittsburgh, Anna Aïvaliotis, stepped in when needed to solve emerging problems and more importantly keep me on track throughout this project.

Of course, the most essential ingredients to the success of this volume are the several hundred authors who contributed their expertise to write the entries for this edition. The quality of their work is outstanding. Without them, this *Encyclopedia* would not be possible.

RICHARD SCHULZ, PHD
Editor-in-Chief

CONTRIBUTORS

W. Andrew Achenbaum, PhD
College of Humanities, Fine Arts, and Communication
University of Houston
Houston, Texas

Jonathan D. Adachi, MD
McMaster University
Hamilton, Ontario, Canada

Ronald H. Aday, PhD
Middle Tennessee State University
Murfreesboro, Tennessee

George J. Agich, PhD
The Cleveland Clinic
Cleveland, Ohio

Judd M. Aiken, BS, MS, PhD
Department of Animal Health and Biomedical Sciences
University of Wisconsin, Madison
Madison, Wisconsin

Marilyn Albert, PhD
Gerontology Research Unit
Harvard Medical School
Charlestown, Massachusetts

Steven M. Albert, PhD, MSc
Department of Sociomedical Science
Columbia University
New York, New York

James E. Allen, PhD, MSPH
School of Public Health
University of North Carolina at Chapel Hill
Chapel Hill, North Carolina

Philip A. Allen, PhD
Department of Psychology
University of Akron
Akron, Ohio

Rebecca S. Allen, PhD
Department of Psychology
Center for Mental Health and Aging
University of Alabama
Tuscaloosa, Alabama

Robert G. Allen, PhD
Lankenau Institute for Medical Research
Wynnewood, Pennsylvania

Susan Allen, PhD
Center for Gerontology and Health Care Research
Brown University
Providence, Rhode Island

Keith A. Anderson, MSW
Graduate Center in Gerontology College of Public Health
The University of Kentucky
Lexington, Kentucky

Melissa Andrew, MD, MSc (Public Health), BSc
Division of Geriatric Medicine
Dalhousie University
Halifax, Nova Scotia, Canada

Jacqueline Angel, PhD
School of Public Affairs
University of Texas at Austin
Austin, Texas

Joaquin A. Anguera, PhD (c)
Division of Kinesiology
University of Michigan
Ann Arbor, Michigan

Toni C. Antonucci, PhD
Department of Psychology
University of Michigan
Ann Arbor, Michigan

Robert A. Applebaum, PhD
Scripps Foundation Gerontology Center
Miami University
Oxford, Ohio

Patricia A. Areán, PhD
Department of Psychiatry
University of California, San Francisco
San Francisco, California

Robert Arking, PhD
Department of Biological Sciences
Wayne State University
Detroit, Michigan

Wilbert S. Aronow, MD
Divisions of Cardiology and Geriatrics
New York Medical College
Valhalla, New York

Robert C. Atchley, PhD
Department of Gerontology
The Naropa Institute
Boulder, Colorado

Alejandro R. Ayala, MD
Clinical Endocrinology Branch NIDDK/NIH
Bethesda, Maryland

Lodovico Balducci, MD
Department of Interdisciplinary Oncology
University of South Florida College of Medicine
Tampa, Florida

Beverly A. Baldwin, PhD (deceased)
School of Nursing
University of Maryland
Baltimore, Maryland

Arthur K. Balin, MD, PhD, FACP
Medical Director
The Sally Balin Medical Center
Media, Pennsylvania

Ashley S. Bangert, PhD (c)
Department of Psychology
University of Michigan
Ann Arbor, Michigan

John C. Barefoot, PhD
Duke University Medical Center
Durham, North Carolina

Jane Barratt, PhD
Secretary General
International Federation on Ageing
Montreal, Quebec, Canada

Nir Barzilai, MD
Albert Einstein College of Medicine
Bronx, New York

Scott A. Bass, PhD
Dean of the Graduate School
Vice Provost for Research and Planning
University of Maryland
Baltimore, Maryland

John W. Baynes, PhD
University of South Carolina
Columbia, South Carolina

William Bechill, MSW
Former U.S. Commissioner on Aging
Current Chair of the Board for the Center on Global Aging at Catholic University
Washington, DC

Nigel Beckett, MB, ChB, MRCP
Imperial College Faculty of Medicine
Hammersmith Campus
London, UK

François Béland, PhD
Co-Director, Solidage Research Group
Department of Health
University of Montreal
Montreal, Quebec, Canada

Ann Benbow, PhD
SPRY Foundation
Washington, DC

Vern L. Bengtson, PhD
Ethel Percy Andrus Gerontology Center
Social and Behavioral Sciences Division
University of Southern California
Los Angeles, California

Karen McNally Bensing, MSLS
The Benjamin Rose Institute
Cleveland, Ohio

Edit Beregi, MD, DMSci
Retired Director of the Gerontology Center
Budapest, Hungary

Howard Bergman, MD
Department of Geriatric Medicine
McGill University
Montreal, Quebec, Canada

David E. Biegel, PhD
Mandel School of Applied Social Sciences
Case Western Reserve University
Cleveland, Ohio

Robert H. Binstock, PhD
Department of Epidemiology and Biostatistics
Case Western Reserve University
Cleveland, Ohio

Kira S. Birditt, PhD
Institute for Social Research
University of Michigan
Ann Arbor, Michigan

Fredda Blanchard-Fields, PhD
Georgia Institute of Technology
Atlanta, Georgia

Dan G. Blazer, MD, PhD
Department of Psychiatry
Duke University Medical Center
Durham, North Carolina

Avrum Z. Bluming, MD, MACP
Department of Medicine
University of Southern California
Los Angeles, California

Cory R. Bolkan, MS, PhD (c)
Human Development and Family Sciences
Oregon State University
Corvallis, Oregon

Enid A. Borden, BA, MA
CEO, Meals on Wheels Association of America
Alexandria, Virginia

Kevin Borders, PhD
Kent School of Social Work
University of Louisville
Louisville, Kentucky

Hayden B. Bosworth, PhD
Senior Health Scientist
Duke University Medical Center
Durham, North Carolina

Meg Bourbonniere, PhD, RN
Yale University School of Nursing
New Haven, Connecticut

Susan K. Bowles, PharmD
College of Pharmacy
Centre for Health Care of the Elderly
Capital District Health Authority
Halifax, Nova Scotia, Canada

Dana Burr Bradley, PhD
University of North Carolina at Charlotte
Charlotte, North Carolina

Lawrence G. Branch, PhD
College of Public Health University of South Florida
Tampa, Florida

Joshua R. Bringle, MS
University of Massachusetts at Amherst
Amherst, Massachusetts

Harold Brody, MD, PhD
Department of Anatomy
State University of New York School of Medicine
Buffalo, New York

G.A. Broe, AM, BA, MBBS, FRACP
Prince of Wales Medical Research Institute and
University of New South Wales
Randwick, NSW, Australia

Susan V. Brooks, PhD
The University of Michigan
Ann Arbor, Michigan

W. Ted Brown, MD, PhD
Chairman, Department of Human Genetics
NYS Institute for Basic Research in Developmental Disabilities
Staten Island, New York

Winifred Brownell, PhD
College of Arts and Sciences
University of Rhode Island
Kingston, Rhode Island

Entela Bua, MD, PhD
Department of Animal Health and Biomedical Sciences
University of Wisconsin, Madison
Madison, Wisconsin

Barbara Bucur, PhD
Center for the Study of Aging and Human Development
Duke University Medical Center
Durham, North Carolina

Elisabeth O. Burgess, PhD
Department of Sociology
Georgia State University
Atlanta, Georgia

Louis D. Burgio, PhD
Department of Psychology
Center for Mental Health and Aging
University of Alabama
Tuscaloosa, Alabama

Robert N. Butler, MD
President and CEO
International Longevity Center USA, Ltd.
New York, New York

Kevin E. Cahill, PhD
Tinari Economics, Inc.
Livingston, New Jersey

Margaret P. Calkins, PhD
IDEAS Institute
Kirtland, Ohio

Richard T. Campbell, PhD
Department of Sociology
University of Illinois at Chicago
Chicago, Illinois

Elizabeth Capezuti, RN
New York University
New York, New York

Gregory D. Cartee, PhD
Department of Kinesiology
University of Wisconsin, Madison
Madison, Wisconsin

Neil Charness, PhD
Department of Psychology
Florida State University
Tallahassee, Florida

Yung-Ping Chen, PhD
Gerontology Institute
University of Massachusetts
Boston, Massachusetts

Judith G. Chipperfield, PhD
Health, Leisure, and Human Performance Research Institute
Winnipeg, Manitoba, Canada

Victor G. Cicirelli, PhD
Department of Psychological Sciences
Purdue University
West Lafayette, Indiana

Giovanni Cizza, MD, PhD
Clinical Endocrinology Branch
NIDDK/NIH
Bethesda, Maryland

A. Mark Clarfield, MD, FRCPC
Ben-Gurion University of the Negev Beersheva, Israel and
Division of Geriatric Medicine
McGill University
Montreal, Quebec, Canada

Robert L. Clark, PhD
Department of Business Management
North Carolina State University
Raleigh, North Carolina

Carl I. Cohen, MD
Division of Geriatric Psychiatry
State University of New York
Brooklyn, New York

Harvey Jay Cohen, MD
Department of Medicine
Duke University Medical Center
Durham, North Carolina

Nathan S. Consedine, PhD
Department of Psychology
Long Island University
Brooklyn, New York

Constance L. Coogle, PhD
Virginia Center on Aging and
Department of Gerontology
Virginia Commonwealth University Medical Center
Richmond, Virginia

Fay Lomax Cook, PhD
School of Education and Social Policy
Northwestern University
Evanston, Illinois

Susan G. Cooley, PhD
U.S. Department of Veterans Affairs
West Palm Beach, Florida

Germaine Cornélissen, PhD
Halberg Chronobiology Center
University of Minnesota
Minneapolis, Minnesota

Joseph F. Coughlin, PhD
MIT Age Lab
Massachusetts Institute of Technology
Cambridge, Massachusetts

Vincent J. Cristofalo, PhD
Lankenau Institute for Medical Research
Wynnewood, Pennsylvania

Stephen Crystal, PhD
Institute for Health, Health Care Policy, and Aging Research
New Brunswick, New Jersey

Ana Maria Cuervo, MD, PhD
Albert Einstein College of Medicine
Bronx, New York

Leslie Curry, PhD, MPH
University of Connecticut Health Center
Farmington, Connecticut

Stephen J. Cutler, PhD
Departments of Sociology and Gerontology
University of Vermont
Burlington, Vermont

Sara J. Czaja, PhD
Department of Psychiatry and Behavioral Sciences
University of Miami School of Medicine
Miami, Florida

Elizabeth M. Dax, MD, PhD
National Institute on Aging and
The Johns Hopkins School of Medicine
Baltimore, Maryland

Howard B. Degenholtz, PhD
Center for Bioethics and Health Law
University of Pittsburgh
Pittsburgh, Pennsylvania

Sharon A. DeVaney, PhD
Purdue University
West Lafayette, Indiana

Samantha Devaraju-Backhaus, MA
Center for Psychological Studies
Nova Southeastern University
Fort Lauderdale, Florida

Roger A. Dixon, PhD
Department of Psychology
University of Alberta
Edmonton, Alberta, Canada

Elizabeth B. Douglas, MA
Executive Director
Association for Gerontology in Higher Education
Washington, DC

Elizabeth Dugan, PhD
Division of Geriatric Medicine
University of Massachusetts Medical School
Worcester, Massachusetts

David Dupere, MD, FRCPC
Division of Palliative Medicine
Queen Elizabeth II Health Sciences Center
Dalhousie University
Halifax, Nova Scotia, Canada

Tzvi Dwolatzky, MD, MBBCh
Beersheva Mental Health Center and
Ben-Gurion University of the Negev
Beersheva, Israel

Rita B. Effros, PhD
Department of Pathology and Laboratory Medicine
University of California
Los Angeles, California

David J. Ekerdt, PhD
Gerontology Center
University of Kansas
Lawrence, Kansas

Glen H. Elder, Jr., PhD
University of North Carolina at Chapel Hill
Chapel Hill, North Carolina

Bernard T. Engel, PhD
School of Medicine
Johns Hopkins University
Raleigh, North Carolina

Joan T. Erber, PhD
Department of Psychology
Florida State University
Miami, Florida

Carroll L. Estes, PhD
Institute for Health and Aging
University of California, San Francisco
San Francisco, California

J. Grimley Evans, MD
Division of Clinical Gerontology
University of Oxford
Oxford, UK

Lois K. Evans, DNSc, RN, FAAN
School of Nursing
University of Pennsylvania
Philadelphia, Pennsylvania

John A. Faulkner, PhD
University of Michigan
Ann Arbor, Michigan

John Feightner, MD, MSc, FCFPC
University of Western Ontario
London, Ontario, Canada

Patrick J. G. Feltmate, MD
Dalhousie University
Halifax, Nova Scotia, Canada

Christine Ferri, PhD
Center for Aging
UMDNJ-School of Osteopathic Medicine
Stratford, New Jersey

Luigi Ferrucci, MD
Division of Epidemiology and Clinical Applications
National Heart, Lung, and Blood Institute
Baltimore, Maryland

Gerda G. Fillenbaum, PhD
Center for the Study of Aging and Human Development
Duke University Medical Center
Durham, North Carolina

David B. Finkelstein, PhD
Director, Pathobiology Program
National Institute on Aging
Bethesda, Maryland

Joseph H. Flaherty, MD
Geriatric Research, Education and Clinical Center
St. Louis VA Medical Center
Division of Geriatrics
St. Louis University School of Medicine
St. Louis, Missouri

Jerome L. Fleg, MD
Division of Epidemiology and Clinical Applications
National Heart, Lung, and Blood Institute
Baltimore, Maryland

Leon Flicker, MB, BS, PhD, FRACP
Geriatric Medicine Unit at Royal Perth Hospital
The University of Western Australia
Perth, Australia

Anne Foner, PhD
Department of Sociology
Rutgers University
New Brunswick, New Jersey

Barry Fortner, PhD
Rush-Presbyterian-St. Luke's Medical Center
Chicago, Illinois

Susan Freter, MD, FRCPC
Department of Medicine
Dalhousie University
Halifax, Nova Scotia, Canada

Alexandra M. Freund, PhD
Departments of Human Development and Social Policy and Psychology
Northwestern University
Evanston, Illinois

Robert B. Friedland, PhD
Center on an Aging Society
Georgetown University
Washington, DC

Brant E. Fries, PhD
University of Michigan and
Ann Arbor VA Medical Center
Ann Arbor, Michigan

James F. Fries, MD
Department of Medicine
Stanford University School of Medicine
Stanford, California

Christine L. Fry, PhD
Department of Anthropology
Loyola University of Chicago
Chicago, Illinois

Terry T. Fulmer, RN, PhD, FAAN
Division of Nursing
New York University
New York, New York

Ari Gafni, PhD
Institute of Gerontology and Biophysics Research Division
University of Michigan
Ann Arbor, Michigan

Mary Ganguli, MD, MPH
University of Pittsburgh
Pittsburgh, Pennsylvania

Joseph E. Gaugler, PhD
Department of Behavioral Science
College of Medicine
University of Kentucky
Lexington, Kentucky

Serge Gauthier, MD, FRCPC
Departments of Neurology and Neurosurgery, Psychiatry, and Medicine
Director, Alzheimer Disease and Related Disorders Research Unit
McGill University
Montreal, Quebec, Canada

Louise E. Gelwicks
Gerontological Planning Association
Santa Monica, California

Linda K. George, PhD
Department of Sociology
Duke University
Durham, North Carolina

Scott Miyake Geron, PhD
Faculty of Medicine, Dentistry and Nursing
University of Manchester
Manchester, UK

Lora Giangregorio, PhD
Lyndhurst Centre
Toronto Rehabilitation Institute
Toronto, Ontario, Canada

Roseann Giarrusso, PhD
Andrus Gerontology Center
University of Southern California
Los Angeles, California

Laura N. Gitlin, PhD
Center for Applied Research on Aging and Health
Thomas Jefferson University
Philadelphia, Pennsylvania

Stephen M. Golant, PhD
University of Florida
Gainesville, Florida

Charles J. Golden, PhD
Center for Psychological Studies
Nova Southeastern University
Fort Lauderdale, Florida

Barry J. Goldlist, MD, FRCPC, FACP, AGSF
Director, Division of Geriatric Medicine
University of Toronto and
Director, General Medicine and Geriatrics
University Health Network/Mt. Sinai Hospital
c/o Toronto Rehab Institute
Toronto, Ontario, Canada

Judith G. Gonyea, PhD
School of Social Work
Boston University
Boston, Massachusetts

Michael Gordon, MD, MSc, FRCPC, FRCP Edin
Vice President, Medical Services and
Head, Geriatrics and Internal Medicine Baycrest Centre for Geriatric Care
University of Toronto
Toronto, Ontario, Canada

Elise Gould, PhD
Economy Policy Institute
Washington, DC

David C. Grabowski, PhD
Department of Health Care Policy
Harvard Medical School
Boston, Massachusetts

Edward M. Gramlich, PhD
Board Member
Board of Governors of the Federal Reserve System
Washington, DC

Aubrey de Grey, PhD
Department of Genetics
University of Cambridge
Cambridge, UK

Janet D. Griffith, PhD
Research Triangle Institute
Research Triangle Park, North Carolina

Francine Grodstein, ScD
Brigham and Women's Hospital
Harvard Medical School
Cambridge, Massachusetts

Murray Grossman, MD
Department of Neurology
University of Pennsylvania School of Medicine
Philadelphia, Pennsylvania

Gordon Gubitz, MD, FRCPC
Department of Medicine
Dalhousie University
Halifax, Nova Scotia, Canada

Juan J. Guiamet, PhD
Instituto de Fisiologia Vegetal
Universidad Nacional de La Plata
La Plata, Argentina

ZhongMao Guo, PhD
Department of Physiology
University of Texas Health Science Center at San Antonio
San Antonio, Texas

Franz Halberg, MD
Director, Halfberg Chronobiology Center
University of Minnesota
Minneapolis, Minnesota

Calvin B. Harley, PhD
Chief Scientific Officer
Geron Corporation
Menlo Park, California

Charles R. Harrington, PhD
Department of Mental Health
Institute of Medical Sciences
University of Aberdeen
Fosterhill, Aberdeen, UK

Alan A. Hartley, PhD
Department of Psychology
Scripps College
Claremont, California

Lynn Hasher, PhD
University of Toronto
Toronto, Ontario, Canada

Betty Havens, DLitt (deceased)
University of Manitoba
Brandon, Manitoba, Canada

Robert J. Havighurst, PhD
Department of Education
University of Chicago
Chicago, Illinois

Catherine Hawes, PhD
Department of Health Policy and Management
School of Rural Public Health
Texas A&M University System Health Science Center
College Station, Texas

Lara Hazelton, MD, FRCPC (Psychiatry)
Department of Psychiatry
Dalhousie University
Nova Scotia Hospital
Dartmouth, Nova Scotia, Canada

Robert P. Heaney, MD
Creighton University
Omaha, Nebraska

Randy S. Hebert, MD, MPH
Division of General Medicine
University of Pittsburgh Medical Center
Pittsburgh, Pennsylvania

Jutta Heckhausen, PhD
University of California, Irvine
Irvine, California

Franz Hefti, PhD
Vice President
Merck Sharp & Dohme
Essex, United Kingdom

Jenifer Heidorn, MA, PhD (c)
Purdue University
West Lafayette, Indiana

Margaret L. Heidrick, PhD
College of Medicine
University of Nebraska
Omaha, Nebraska

L. Carson Henderson, PhD, MPH
College of Public Health
Department of Health Promotion Sciences
University of Oklahoma
Oklahoma City, Oklahoma

Jon G. Hendricks, PhD
University Honors College
Oregon State University
Corvallis, Oregon

John G. Hennon, EdD
University of Pittsburgh
Pittsburgh, Pennsylvania

Christopher Hertzog, PhD
School of Psychology
Georgia Institute of Technology
Atlanta, Georgia

Thomas M. Hess, PhD
Department of Psychology
North Carolina State University
Raleigh, North Carolina

Nancy Hikoyeda, MPH
Stanford Geriatric Education Center
University of California, Los Angeles
San Jose, California

Franklin G. Hines, PhD (c)
Department of Psychology
Florida State University
Tallahassee, Florida

Gregory A. Hinrichsen, PhD
Director of Psychology Training
The Zucker Hillside Hospital and
Professor of Psychiatry
Albert Einstein College of Medicine
Glen Oaks, New York

David Hogan, MD
Department of Geriatric Medicine
University of Calgary
Calgary, Alberta, Canada

Heidi H. Holmes, PhD (c)
Graduate Center for Gerontology
University of Kentucky
Lexington, Kentucky

Karen Hooker, PhD
Director, Program on Gerontology
Human Development and Family Sciences
Oregon State University
Corvallis, Oregon

Michelle Horhota, MS
Georgia Institute of Technology
Atlanta, Georgia

Darlene V. Howard, PhD
Georgetown University
Washington, DC

Shafter Cristina Howard
Institute for Health and Department of Psychology
Rutgers University
New Brunswick, New Jersey

Susan E. Howlett, PhD
Department of Pharmacology
Faculty of Medicine
Dalhousie University
Halifax, Nova Scotia, Canada

William J. Hoyer, PhD
Department of Psychology
Syracuse University
Syracuse, New York

Ruth Huber, PhD
Kent School of Social Work
University of Louisville
Louisville, Kentucky

Robert B. Hudson, PhD
School of Social Work
Boston University
Boston, Massachusetts

Mary Elizabeth Hughes, PhD
Department of Sociology
Duke University
Durham, North Carolina

Linnae L. Hutchison, MBA
Department of Health Policy and Management
School of Rural Public Health
Texas A&M University System Health Science Center
College Station, Texas

Bradley T. Hyman, PhD
Department of Neurology Research
Massachusetts General Hospital
Boston, Massachusetts

Margaret B. Ingraham, BA, MA
Director of Policy and Legislation
Meals on Wheels
Association of America
Alexandria, Virginia

Donald K. Ingram, PhD
Gerontology Research Center
National Institutes of Health
Baltimore, Maryland

James S. Jackson, PhD
Institute for Social Research
University of Michigan
Ann Arbor, Michigan

Susan T. Jackson, PhD, CCC-SLP
Department of Hearing and Speech
University of Kansas Medical Center
Kansas City, Kansas

Cynthia R. Jasper, PhD
Department of Consumer Science
University of Wisconsin, Madison
Madison, Wisconsin

Tiffany Jastrzembski, PhD (c)
Department of Psychology
Florida State University
Tallahassee, Florida

S. Michal Jazwinski, PhD
Department of Biochemistry and Molecular Biology
Louisiana State University Health Science Center
New Orleans, Louisiana

Nancy S. Jecker, PhD
Department of Medical History and Ethics
University of Washington
Seattle, Washington

Susan J. Jelonek, MBA
Andrus Gerontology Center
University of Southern California
Los Angeles, California

Lori Jervis, PhD
University of Colorado at Denver Health Sciences Center
Denver, Colorado

Megan M. Johnson, PhD (c)
Department of Sociology
University of Vermont
Burlington, Vermont

Shanthi Johnson, PhD, PDt
School of Nutrition and Dietetics
Acadia University
Wolfville, Nova Scotia, Canada

Thomas E. Johnson, PhD
Department of Integrative Physiology Institute for Behavioral Genetics
University of Colorado
Boulder, Colorado

Steven Jonas, MD, MPH, MS, FNYAS
Department of Preventive Medicine
Stony Brook University School of Medicine
Stony Brook, New York

Lyndon J. O. Joseph, PhD
Division of Gerontology
Baltimore VA Medical Center
Baltimore, Maryland

Boaz Kahana, PhD
Department of Psychology
Case Western Reserve University
Cleveland, Ohio

Eva Kahana, PhD
Director, Elderly Care Research Center
Department of Sociology
Case Western Reserve University
Cleveland, Ohio

Arnold Kahn, PhD
Department of Cell and Tissue Biology
University of California, San Francisco
San Francisco, California

Rosalie A. Kane, DSW
Division for Health Services, Research and Policy
School of Public Health
University of Minnesota
Minneapolis, Minnesota

Marshall B. Kapp, JD, MPH
Office of Geriatric Medicine and Gerontology
Wright State University School of Medicine
Dayton, Ohio

Cary S. Kart, PhD
Scripps Gerontology Center
Miami University
Oxford, Ohio

Sathya Karunananthan, MS (c)
Canadian Initiative on Frailty and Aging Solidage Research Group
Lady Davis Institute
Montreal, Quebec, Canada

Julia Kasl-Godley, PhD
VA Hospice Care Center
VA Palo Alto Health Care System
Palo Alto, California

Robert J. Kastenbaum, PhD
Department of Communication
Arizona State University
Tempe, Arizona

Sharon R. Kaufman, PhD
Institute for Health and Aging
University of California, San Francisco
San Francisco, California

Melanie E. M. Kelly, PhD
Department of Pharmacology
Dalhousie University
Halifax, Nova Scotia, Canada

Joseph W. Kemnitz, PhD
Director, National Primate Research Center
University of Wisconsin, Madison
Madison, Wisconsin

Susan J. Kemper, PhD
University of Kansas
Lawrence, Kansas

Gary M. Kenyon, PhD
Gerontology Program
St. Thomas University
Fredericton, New Brunswick, Canada

Leslie Dubin Kerr, MD
Department of Medicine and Geriatrics
Mount Sinai Medical Center
New York, New York

Anne-Marie Kimbell, PhD
Texas A&M University System Health Science Center
College Station, Texas

Douglas C. Kimmel, PhD
Professor Emeritus, Department of Psychology
City College, City University of New York
New York, New York

Thomas B. L. Kirkwood, PhD
Co-Director, Institute for Ageing and Health
University of Newcastle
Newcastle upon Tyne, UK

Paul Kleyman
Aging Today, American Society on Aging
San Francisco, California

Donald Kline, PhD
Departments of Psychology and Surgery (Ophthalmology)
University of Calgary
Calgary, Alberta, Canada

Leon W. Klud, PhD
Congressional Joint Committee on Taxation
Washington, DC

Thomas Kornberg, PhD
Department of Biochemistry
University of California, San Francisco
San Francisco, California

Suzanne R. Kunkel, PhD
Scripps Gerontology Center Miami University
Oxford, Ohio

Ute Kunzmann, PhD
International University of Bremen
Bremen, Germany

Claudia K. Y. Lai, RN, PhD
School of Nursing
The Hong Kong Polytechnic University
Hong Kong SAR, China

Kenneth M. Langa, MD, PhD
Department of Internal Medicine and Institute for Social Research
University of Michigan
Ann Arbor, Michigan

Melinda S. Lantz, MD
Director of Psychiatry
The Jewish Home and Hospital
New York, New York

Felissa R. Lashley, RN, PhD, ACRN, FAAN, FACMG
College of Nursing
Rutgers University
Newark, New Jersey

Nicola T. Lautenschlager, MD
School of Psychiatry & Clinical Neurosciences
Royal Perth Hospital
Perth, Australia

Barry D. Lebowitz, PhD
National Institute of Mental Health
Bethesda, Maryland

Chin Chin Lee, MPH (c)
Center on Aging
University of Miami School of Medicine
Miami, Florida

Makau Lee, MD, PhD
University of Mississippi Medical Center
Jackson, Mississippi

Bruce Leff, MD
The Johns Hopkins University School of Medicine
Department of Health Policy and Management
The Johns Hopkins University Bloomberg School of Public Health
Baltimore, Maryland

Eric J. Lenze, MD
Western Psychiatric Institute and Clinic
University of Pittsburgh
Pittsburgh, Pennsylvania

Howard Leventhal, PhD
Institute for Health and Department of Psychology
Rutgers University
New Brunswick, New Jersey

Jeff Levin, PhD
Valley Falls, Kansas

Sue E. Levkoff, ScD, SM, MSW
Brigham and Women's Hospital
Department of Psychiatry
Harvard Medical School
Boston, Massachusetts

Phoebe S. Liebig, PhD
Andrus Gerontology Center
University of Southern California
Los Angeles, California

Robert D. Lindeman, MD
University of New Mexico School of Medicine
Albuquerque, New Mexico

Charles F. Longino Jr., PhD
Department of Sociology
Wake Forest University
Winston-Salem, North Carolina

Oscar L. Lopez, MD
Departments of Neurology and Psychiatry
University of Pittsburgh School of Medicine
Pittsburgh, Pennsylvania

Antonello Lorenzini, PhD
Lankenau Institute for Medical Research
Wynnewood, Pennsylvania

Jonathan D. Lowenson, PhD
Department of Chemistry and Biochemistry
University of California, Los Angeles
Los Angeles, California

Judith A. Lucas, EdD, APN, BC
Institute of Health Care Policy and Aging Research
Rutgers University
New Brunswick, New Jersey

Cindy Lustig, PhD
University of Michigan
Ann Arbor, Michigan

Stephen Lyle, MD, PhD
Harvard Medical School
Boston, Massachusetts

Thomas R. Lynch, PhD
Director, Cognitive Behavioral Research and Treatment Program
Duke University
Durham, North Carolina

J. Beth Mabry, PhD
Department of Sociology
Indiana University of Pennsylvania
Indiana, Pennsylvania

Chris MacKnight, MD, MSc, FRCPC
Department of Medicine
Dalhousie University
Halifax, Nova Scotia, Canada

George L. Maddox, PhD
Long Term Care Resources Program
Duke University Center for the Study of Aging
Durham, North Carolina

Carol Magai, PhD
Department of Psychology
Long Island University
Brooklyn, New York

Kevin J. Mahoney, PhD
Graduate School of Social Work
Boston College
Chestnut Hill, Massachusetts

James Malone-Lee, MD, FRCP
Head, Department of Medicine
Archway Campus
University College London
London, UK

P. K. Mandal, PhD
Department of Psychiatry
University of Pittsburgh School of Medicine
Pittsburgh, Pennsylvania

Ronald J. Manheimer, PhD
North Carolina Center for Creative Retirement
University of North Carolina at Asheville
Asheville, North Carolina

Spero M. Manson, PhD
University of Colorado
Denver Health Sciences Center
Denver, Colorado

Kenneth G. Manton, PhD
Center for Demographic Studies
Duke University
Durham, North Carolina

Jennifer A. Margrett, PhD
Department of Psychology
West Virginia University
Morgantown, West Virginia

Kyriakos S. Markides, PhD
Department of Psychiatry
University of Texas Medical Branch
Galveston, Texas

Lori N. Marks, PhD
University of Maryland College Park
HLHP-Public & Community Health
College Park, Maryland

Elizabeth W. Markson, PhD
Associate Director, Gerontology Center
Boston University
Boston, Massachusetts

Sandy Markwood
CEO, National Association of Area Agencies on Aging
Washington, DC

George M. Martin, MD
Director Emeritus, Alzheimer's Disease Research Center
University of Washington
Seattle, Washington

Anne Martin-Matthews, PhD
Scientific Director
School of Social Work and Family Studies
University of British Columbia
Vancouver, British Columbia, Canada

Lynn M. Martire, PhD
Department of Psychiatry
University of Pittsburgh
Pittsburgh, Pennsylvania

Meredith Masel, LMSW
Department of Preventive Medicine and Community Health
University of Texas Medical Branch
Galveston, Texas

Edward J. Masoro, PhD
Department of Physiology
University of Texas Health Science Center
San Antonio, Texas

Emad Massoud, MB, MSc, FRCSC
Program Director
Otolaryngology-Head & Neck Surgery
Dalhousie University
Halifax, Nova Scotia, Canada

Roger J. M. McCarter, PhD
Department of Physiology
University of Texas
San Antonio, Texas

Gerald E. McClearn, MS, PhD
Center for Developmental and Health Genetics
Pennsylvania State University
University Park, Pennsylvania

R. J. McClure, PhD
Department of Psychiatry
University of Pittsburgh School of Medicine
Pittsburgh, Pennsylvania

Richard W. McConaghy, PhD
University of Massachusetts
Boston, Massachusetts

Anna M. McCormick, PhD
Biology of Aging Program
National Institute on Aging
Bethesda, Maryland

Peter N. McCracken, MD, FRCPC
Division of Geriatric Medicine
University of Alberta
Edmonton, Alberta, Canada

Robert R. McCrae, PhD
Gerontology Research Center
National Institute on Aging
Baltimore, Maryland

Ian McDowell, PhD
Department of Epidemiology
University of Ottawa
Ottawa, Ontario, Canada

Debbie McKenzie, BS, PhD
Department of Animal Health and Biomedical Sciences
University of Wisconsin, Madison
Madison, Wisconsin

Mary McNally, MSc, DDS, MA
Faculty of Dentistry
Dalhousie University
Halifax, Nova Scotia, Canada

Christina McNamara, RN, MN, GNC
Queen Elizabeth II Health Sciences Center
Dalhousie University
Halifax, Nova Scotia, Canada

Shelly McNeil, MD, FRCPC
Dalhousie University
Halifax, Nova Scotia, Canada

Michelle L. Meade, PhD
Beckman Institute
University of Illinois at Urbana-Champaign
Urbana, Illinois

Kate de Medeiros, MS
University of Maryland
Baltimore, Maryland

Zhores A. Medvedev, PhD
National Institute for Medical Research
London, UK

Kimberly M. Meigh, PhD (c)
Communication Science and Disorders
University of Pittsburgh
Pittsburgh, Pennsylvania

Heather Menne, MGS
Margaret Blenkner Research Institute
The Benjamin Rose Institute
Cleveland, Ohio

E. Jeffrey Metter, MD
Division of Epidemiology and Clinical Applications
National Heart, Lung, and Blood Institute
Baltimore, Maryland

Mathy D. Mezey, RN, EdD, FAAN
Director, The John A. Hartford Foundation Institute for Geriatric Nursing
New York University
New York, New York

Jean-Pierre Michel, MD
Geriatric Department
Geneva University
Geneva, Switzerland

Richard B. Miller, PhD
Brigham Young University
Provo, Utah

Alexandra Minicozzi, PhD
Department of Economics
University of Texas at Austin
Austin, Texas

Arnold B. Mitnitski, PhD
Department of Medicine and Faculty of Computer Science
Dalhousie University
Halifax, Nova Scotia, Canada

Ethel L. Mitty, EdD, RN
Steinhardt School of Education
Division of Nursing
New York University
New York, New York

Charles V. Mobbs, PhD
Mount Sinai School of Medicine
New York, New York

Frank J. Molnar, MSc, MDCM, FRCPC CIHR
CanDRIVE Research Team
Elisabeth-Bruyere Research Institute
Ottawa, Ontario, Canada

Timothy H. Monk, DSc
Clinical Neuroscience Research Center
Western Psychiatric Institute and Clinic
University of Pittsburgh Medical Center
Pittsburgh, Pennsylvania

Harry R. Moody, PhD
Brookdale Center on Aging of Hunter College
The City University of New York
New York, New York

James T. Moore, MD
Halifax Psychiatry Center
Daytona Beach, Florida

Vincent Mor, PhD
Center for Gerontology and Health Care
Brown University School of Medicine
Providence, Rhode Island

Pablo A. Mora, PhD
Institute for Health and Department of Psychology
Rutgers University
New Brunswick, New Jersey

Russell E. Morgan Jr., DrPh
President, SPRY Foundation
Washington, DC

John E. Morley, MB, MCh
Department of Gerontology
St. Louis University Health Sciences Center
St. Louis, Missouri

Roger W. Morrell, PhD
The Practical Memory Institute
Silver Spring, Maryland

Nancy Morrow-Howell, PhD
Warren Brown School of Social Work
Washington University
St. Louis, Missouri

Penelope A. Moyers, EdD, OTR, FAOTA
Department of Occupational Therapy
University of Alabama at Birmingham
Birmingham, Alabama

Katrin Mueller-Johnson, PhD
Institute of Criminology
University of Cambridge
Cambridge, UK

Benoit H. Mulsant, MD, MS
University of Pittsburgh School of Medicine
Pittsburgh, Pennsylvania

Joanne Mundorf
Department of Communication Studies
University of Rhode Island
Kingston, Rhode Island

Norbert Mundorf, PhD
Department of Communication Studies
University of Rhode Island
Kingston, Rhode Island

Martin D. Murphy, PhD
Department of Psychology
The University of Akron
Akron, Ohio

Ganesh C. Natarajan, MD
Boston University Medical Center
Boston, Massachusetts

H. Wayne Nelson, PhD
Department of Health Science
Towson University
Towson, Maryland

F. Ellen Netting, PhD
Virginia Commonwealth University School of Social Work
Richmond, Virginia

Nancy E. Newall, MA
Health, Leisure, and Human Performance Research Institute
Winnipeg, Manitoba, Canada

Nancy R. Nichols, PhD
Department of Physiology
Monah University
VIC, Australia

Robert A. Niemeyer, PhD
Department of Psychology
University of Memphis
Memphis, Tennessee

Katherina A. Nikzad
Graduate Center for Gerontology
University of Kentucky
Lexington, Kentucky

Christy M. Nishita, PhD
Andrus Gerontology Center
University of Southern California
Los Angeles, California

Linda S. Noelker, PhD
The Benjamin Rose Institute
Cleveland, Ohio

Soo Rim Noh, PhD
University of Illinois at Urbana-Champaign
Champaign, Illinois

Larry D. Noodén, PhD
Department of Biology
University of Michigan
Ann Arbor, Michigan

Dawn D. Ogawa, BA
Institute for Health and Aging
University of California, San Francisco
San Francisco, California

Jiro Okochi, MD
University of Occupational and Environmental Health
Kitakyushu City, Japan

Morris A. Okun, PhD
Department of Educational Psychology
Arizona State University
Tempe, Arizona

S. Jay Olshansky, PhD
School of Public Health
University of Illinois at Chicago
Chicago, Illinois

Angela M. O'Rand, PhD
Department of Sociology
Duke University
Durham, North Carolina

Erdman B. Palmore, PhD
Departments of Psychiatry and Sociology
Duke University Medical Center
Durham, North Carolina

K. Panchalingam, PhD
Department of Psychiatry
University of Pittsburgh School of Medicine
Pittsburgh, Pennsylvania

Alexandra Papaioannou, MD
McMaster University
Hamilton, Ontario, Canada

Denise C. Park, PhD
Department of Psychology
University of Illinois at Urbana-Champaign
Champaign, Illinois

Scott L. Parkin
Vice President, Communications
The National Council on the Aging
Washington, DC

Christopher Patterson, MD, FRCPC
McMaster University
Hamilton, Ontario, Canada

Nancy L. Pedersen, PhD
Department of Medical Epidemiology and Biostatistics
Karolinska Institute
Stockholm, Sweden

M. Kristen Peek, PhD
Department of Preventive Medicine and Community Health
University of Texas Medical Branch
Galveston, Texas

Adam T. Perzynski, PhD (c)
Department of Sociology
Case Western Reserve University
Cleveland, Ohio

Ruth Peters, BSc, MSc
Imperial College Faculty of Medicine
Hammersmith Campus
London, UK

J. W. Pettegrew, MD
Departments of Psychiatry and Neurology Health Service Administration
University of Pittsburgh School of Medicine
Pittsburgh, Pennsylvania

John P. Phelan, PhD
The Biological Laboratories
Harvard University
Cambridge, Massachusetts

Charles D. Phillips, PhD, MPH
Department of Health Policy and Management
School of Rural Public Health
Texas A&M University System Health Science Center
College Station, Texas

Amy Mehraban Pienta, MA, PhD
University of Michigan
Ann Arbor, Michigan

Russell I. Pierce, MD, MPH
Honolulu, Hawaii

Robert J. Pignolo, MD, PhD
Division of Geriatric Medicine
University of Pennsylvania
Philadelphia, Pennsylvania

Karl Pillemer, PhD
Department of Human Development and
Cornell Institute for Translational Research on Aging
Cornell University
Ithaca, New York

Brenda L. Plassman, PhD
Department of Psychiatry
Duke University Medical Center
Durham, North Carolina

Leonard W. Poon, PhD
Gerontology Center
University of Georgia
Athens, Georgia

Linda Farber Post, JD, BSN, MA
Bioethicist and Clinical Ethics Consultant
Saddle River, New Jersey

Michael J. Poulin
Department of Social Ecology
University of California, Irvine
Irvine, California

Colin Powell, MB, FRCP
Queen Elizabeth II Health Sciences Center
Dalhousie University
Halifax, Nova Scotia, Canada

Pat Prinz, PhD
University of Washington
Seattle, Washington

Jon Pynoos, PhD
Andrus Gerontology Center
University of Southern California
Los Angeles, California

Sara Honn Qualls, PhD
Department of Psychology
Gerontology Center
University of Colorado at Colorado Springs
Colorado Springs, Colorado

Christine M. Quinn-Walsh, PhD (c)
Neuroscience Program and Institute of Gerontology
University of Michigan
Ann Arbor, Michigan

Paul E. Rafuse, PhD, MD, FRCSC
Department of Ophthalmology
Dalhousie University
Halifax, Nova Scotia, Canada

William L. Randall, EdD
Department of Gerontology
St. Thomas University
Fredericton, New Brunswick, Canada

Arati V. Rao, MD
Department of Medicine
Duke University Medical Center
Durham, North Carolina

G. William Rebeck, PhD
Neurology Service
Massachusetts General Hospital
Boston, Massachusetts

Russel J. Reiter, PhD
Department of Cellular and Structural Biology
University of Texas Health Science Center
San Antonio, Texas

Sandra L. Reynolds, PhD
School of Aging Studies
University of South Florida
Tampa, Florida

Arlan Richardson, PhD
Department of Physiology
Geriatric Research, Education, and Clinical Center
University of Texas Health Science Center at San Antonio
San Antonio, Texas

Virginia Richardson, PhD
College of Social Work
Ohio State University
Columbus, Ohio

Brad A. Rikke, PhD
Institute for Behavioral Genetics
University of Colorado
Boulder, Colorado

Sara E. Rix, PhD
Senior Policy Advisor
Public Policy Institute
AARP
Washington, DC

Jay Roberts, PhD
Department of Pharmacology
Medical College of Pennsylvania
Philadelphia, Pennsylvania

Cynthia K. Robinson, MLS
Director of Library and Information Services
National Primate Center
University of Wisconsin, Madison
Madison, Wisconsin

Kenneth Rockwood, MD, FRCPC
Department of Medicine
Queen Elizabeth II Health Sciences Centre
Dalhousie University
Halifax, Nova Scotia, Canada

Peter R. Rockwood, MD
Newfoundland Medical Board
St. John's, Newfoundland & Labrador, Canada

Ekaterina Rogaeva, PhD
Centre for Neurodegenerative Diseases
Department of Medicine
University of Toronto
Toronto, Ontario, Canada

Darryl B. Rolfson, MD, FRCPC
Division of Geriatric Medicine
University of Alberta
Edmonton, Alberta, Canada

James C. Romeis, PhD
School of Public Health
St. Louis University
St. Louis, Missouri

Sarah F. Roper-Coleman, PhD
University of California, Irvine
Irvine, California

Debra J. Rose, PhD
Division of Kinesiology and Health Science
Co-Director of the Center for Successful Aging
California State University, Fullerton
Fullerton, California

J. B. Ross, MB, BS, FRCPC D Obst RCOG
Division of Dermatology
Dalhousie University
Halifax, Nova Scotia, Canada

John Rother
AARP
Washington, DC

Graham D. Rowles, PhD
Graduate Center for Gerontology
University of Kentucky
Lexington, Kentucky

Laurence Rubenstein, MD, MPH
Director, Geriatric Research, Education and Clinical Center
Sepulveda, California

David C. Rubin, PhD
Department of Psychology
Duke University Medical Center
Durham, North Carolina

Robert L. Rubinstein, PhD
Department of Sociology and Anthropology
University of Maryland
Baltimore, Maryland

Eric Rudin, MD
Albert Einstein College of Medicine
Bronx, New York

Laura Rudkin, PhD
Department of Preventive Medicine and Community Health
University of Texas Medical Branch
Galveston, Texas

Alice S. Ryan, PhD
Division of Gerontology
Baltimore VA Medical Center
Baltimore, Maryland

Bruce Rybarczyk, PhD, ABPP (RP)
Rush University Medical Center
Chicago, Illinois

Mark Sadler, MD, FRCP (c)
Dalhousie University
Halifax, Nova Scotia, Canada

Judith Saxton, MD
Departments of Neurology and Psychiatry
University of Pittsburgh School of Medicine
Pittsburgh, Pennsylvania

K. Warner Schaie, PhD, ScD (hon), Dr Phil.h.c
Department of Human Development and Psychology
Pennsylvania State University
State College, Pennsylvania

Victoria L. Scharp, MS, PhD (c)
Communication Science and Disorders
University of Pittsburgh
Pittsburgh, Pennsylvania

Susan S. Schiffman, PhD
Department of Psychiatry
Duke University Medical School
Durham, North Carolina

Kristin Grace Schneider, PhD (c)
Department of Psychology Social and Health Sciences
Duke University
Durham, North Carolina

Lawrence Schonfeld, PhD
Department of Aging and Mental Health
Louise de la Parte Florida Mental Health Institute
University of South Florida
Tampa, Florida

Richard Schulz, PhD
University of Pittsburgh
Pittsburgh, Pennsylvania

Carol A. Schutz
Executive Director, Gerontological Society of America
Washington, DC

Jori Sechrist, MS
Purdue University
West Lafayette, Indiana

Daniel L. Segal, PhD
Department of Psychology
University of Colorado at Colorado Springs
Colorado Springs, Colorado

Rachael D. Seidler, PhD
Department of Psychology
Division of Kinesiology Neuroscience Program
and
Institute of Gerontology
University of Michigan
Ann Arbor, Michigan

Julie F. Sergeant, PhD (c)
University of Kansas
Lawrence, Kansas

Matthew C. Shake, PhD
University of Illinois at Urbana-Champaign
Champaign, Illinois

Amy R. Shannon, Esq.
Legislative Representative
Federal Affairs Department
AARP
Washington, DC

Katherine Shear, MD
University of Pittsburgh
Pittsburgh, Pennsylvania

Tarek M. Shuman, EdD
United Nations World Assembly on Aging
New York, New York

Felipe Sierra, PhD
National Institute on Aging
Bethesda, Maryland

Merril Silverstein, PhD
Andrus Gerontology Center
University of Southern California
Los Angeles, California

Lori Simon-Rusinowitz, PhD
University of Maryland, College Park
HLHP-Center on Aging
College Park, Maryland

Eleanor M. Simonsick, PhD
National Institute on Aging
and
The Johns Hopkins School of Medicine
Baltimore, Maryland

Dean Keith Simonton, PhD
Department of Psychology
University of California
Davis, California

Marilyn McKean Skaff, PhD
Department of Family and Community Medicine
University of California, San Francisco
San Francisco, California

Max J. Skidmore, PhD
Department of Political Science
University of Missouri
Kansas City, Missouri

Anderson D. Smith, PhD
College of Sciences
Georgia Institute of Technology
Atlanta, Georgia

Jacqui Smith, PhD
Max Planck Institute for Human Development
Berlin, Germany

Matthew J. Smith, PhD
Department of Physiology
University of Kentucky
Lexington, Kentucky

Michael A. Smyer, PhD
Dean, Graduate School of Arts and Sciences
and
Associate Vice President for Research
Boston College
Chestnut Hill, Massachusetts

David L. Snyder, PhD
Department of Pharmacology
Medical College of Pennsylvania
Philadelphia, Pennsylvania

Jay H. Sokolovsky, PhD
Department of Anthropology
University of South Florida
St. Petersburg, Florida

Nina S. Sonbolian, BS
Clinical Endocrinology Branch
NIDDK/NIH
Bethesda, Maryland

William E. Sonntag, PhD
Department of Physiology and Pharmacology
Wake Forest University School of Medicine
Winston-Salem, North Carolina

Dara H. Sorkin, PhD
Center for Health Policy Research
University of California, Irvine
Irvine, California

David W. Sparrow, DSc
Department of Medicine
Boston University School of Medicine
Brookline, Massachusetts

Avron Spiro III, PhD
Department of Epidemiology
Boston University School of Public Health
Boston, Massachusetts

Sara Staats, PhD
Ohio State University at Newark
Newark, Ohio

Bernard D. Starr, PhD
Gerontology Program
Marymount Manhattan College
New York, New York

Derek D. Stepp
Director, Association for Gerontology in Higher Education
Washington, DC

Anthony A. Sterns, MA
Creative Action, Inc.
Akron, Ohio

Harvey L. Sterns, PhD
Department of Psychology
The University of Akron
Akron, Ohio

Ronni S. Sterns, PhD
Institute for Life-Span Development and Gerontology
The University of Akron
Akron, Ohio

Alan B. Stevens, PhD
Director, Dementia Care Research Program
Division of Gerontology and Geriatric Medicine
University of Alabama
Birmingham, Alabama

Judy A. Stevens, PhD
National Center for Injury Prevention and Control
Atlanta, Georgia

David G. Stevenson, PhD
Department of Health Care Policy
Harvard Medical School
Boston, Massachusetts

Peter St George-Hyslop, MD, DSc
Centre for Research in Neurodegenerative Diseases
Department of Medicine
Division of Neurology
Toronto Western Hospital Research Institute
University of Toronto
Toronto, Ontario, Canada

Elizabeth A. L. Stine-Morrow, PhD
Department of Educational Psychology
University of Illinois at Urbana-Champaign
Champaign, Illinois

Leroy O. Stone, PhD
University of Montreal
and
Statistics Canada
Ottawa, Ontario, Canada

Neville E. Strumpf, PhD, RN, C, FAAN
Director of the Center for Gerontologic Nursing Science
University of Pennsylvania School of Nursing
Philadelphia, Pennsylvania

J. Jill Suitor, PhD
Purdue University
West Lafayette, Indiana

Robert J. Sullivan Jr., MD
Department of Community and Family Medicine
Duke University Medical Center
Durham, North Carolina

Emiko Takagi, MA, PhD (c)
Andrus Gerontology Center
University of Southern California
Los Angeles, California

Jeanette C. Takamura, MSW, PhD
U.S. Department of Health and Human Services
Washington, DC

Alvin V. Terry Jr., PhD
Director, Small Animal Behavior Core
Medical College of Georgia
Augusta, Georgia

David R. Thomas, MD, FACP, AGSF, GSAF
Division of Geriatric Medicine
St. Louis University Health Sciences Center
St. Louis, Missouri

Vince S. Thomas, PhD
Department of Community and Family Medicine
Dartmouth Medical School
Hanover, New Hampshire

Constance Todd, MPA
The National Council on the Aging
Washington, DC

Catherine J. Tompkins, PhD
Center for the Neural Basis of Cognition
University of Pittsburgh
Pittsburgh, Pennsylvania

Connie A. Tompkins, PhD
Communication Science and Disorders
Center for the Neural Basis of Cognition
University of Pittsburgh
Pittsburgh, Pennsylvania

Edgar A. Tonna, PhD, FRMS
Institute for Dental Research
New York University Dental Center
New York, New York

Maria Tresini, PhD
Lankenau Institute for Medical Research
Wynnewood, Pennsylvania

John A. Turner
AARP
Washington, DC

Peter Uhlenberg, PhD
University of North Carolina
Chapel Hill, North Carolina

R. Alexander Vachon III, PhD
President, Hamilton PPB
Washington, DC

Kimberly S. Van Haitsma, PhD
Polisher Research Institute
Madlyn and Leonard Abramson Center for Jewish Life
North Wales, Pennsylvania

James W. Vaupel, PhD
Founding Director, The Max Planck Institute for Demographic Research
Rostock, Germany

Paul Verhaeghen, PhD
Department of Psychology
Syracuse University
Syracuse, New York

Ronald T. Verrillo, PhD
Institute for Sensory Research
Syracuse University
Syracuse, New York

Jan Vijg, PhD
Basic Research Laboratory
Cancer and Therapy Research Center
San Antonio, Texas

Michael M. Vilenchik, PhD
Senior Scientist
Longevity Achievement Foundation
Media, Pennsylvania

Dennis T. Villareal, MD, FACE, FACP
Division of Geriatrics and Nutritional Science
Washington University School of Medicine
St. Louis, Missouri

Pantel S. Vokonas, MD
Boston University School of Medicine
Boston, Massachusetts

Heather M. Wallace
University of Kentucky
Lexington, Kentucky

Robert B. Wallace, MD, MSc
Department of Epidemiology
University of Iowa College of Public Health
Iowa City, Iowa

Edith Walsh, PhD
RTI International
Washington, DC

Christi A. Walter, PhD
Department of Cellular and Structural Biology
University of Texas Health Science Center
San Antonio, Texas

Eugenia Wang, PhD
Bloomfield Centre for Research in Aging
Sir Mortimer B. Davis Jewish General Hospital
Montreal, Quebec, Canada

Huber R. Warner, PhD
Biochemistry and Metabolism Branch
National Institute on Aging
Bethesda, Maryland

Debra K. Weiner, MD
Pain Medicine at Centre Commons
University of Pittsburgh Medical Center
Pittsburgh, Pennsylvania

Carlos Weiss, MD
Division of Geriatric Medicine and Gerontology
The Johns Hopkins University School of Medicine
Baltimore, Maryland

Tracy Weitz, MPA
Institute for Health and Aging
University of California, San Francisco
San Francisco, California

Chris Wellin, PhD
Department of Sociology and Gerontology
Scripps Gerontology Center
Miami University
Oxford, Ohio

David G. Wells, PhD
Department of Molecular Cellular and Developmental Biology
Yale University
New Haven, Connecticut

Jennie L. Wells, BSc, MSc, MD, FRCPC
St. Joseph's Health Care Parkwood Hospital
and
The University of Western Ontario
London, Ontario, Canada

Susan Krauss Whitbourne, PhD
University of Massachusetts at Amherst
Amherst, Massachusetts

Heidi K. White, MD, MHS
Department of Medicine
Duke University Medical Center
Durham, North Carolina

Monika White, PhD
President/CEO, Center for Healthy Aging
Santa Monica, California

J. Frank Whittington, PhD
Department of Sociology
Georgia State University
Atlanta, Georgia

Darryl Wieland, PhD, MPH
Research Director, Geriatrics Services Palmetto Health Richland
and
Professor of Medicine
University of South Carolina School of Medicine
Columbia, South Carolina

Joshua M. Wiener, PhD
RTI International
Washington, DC

Kathleen H. Wilber, PhD
Andrus Gerontology Center
University of Southern California, University Park
Los Angeles, California

Monique M. Williams, MD
Department of Medicine
Washington University School of Medicine
St. Louis, Missouri

Sherry L. Willis, PhD
Department of Human Development
Pennsylvania State University
University Park, Pennsylvania

Arthur Wingfield, PhD
Brandeis University
Waltham, Massachusetts

Phyllis M. Wise, PhD
Department of Physiology
University of Kentucky
Lexington, Kentucky

Christina Wolfson, PhD
Department of Epidemiology and Biostatistics
McGill University
and
Director of Centre for Clinical Epidemiology and Community Studies
Jewish General Hospital
Montreal, Quebec, Canada

Fredric D. Wolinsky, PhD
College of Publish Health
University of Iowa
Iowa City, Iowa

Carsten Wrosch, PhD
Department of Psychology
Centre for Research in Human Development
Concordia University
Montreal, Quebec, Canada

Hans Christian Wulf, MD, DSc
Department of Dermatology
Bispebjerg Hospital
University of Copenhagen
Copenhagen, Denmark

Frances M. Yang, PhD
Brigham and Women's Hospital
Department of Psychiatry
Harvard Medical School
Boston, Massachusetts

F. Eugene Yates, MD
Department of Medicine/Gerontology
University of California
Los Angeles, California

Gwen Yeo, PhD
Stanford Geriatric Education Center
Stanford University School of Medicine
Palo Alto, California

Laurie Young
Executive Director
Older Women's League
Washington, DC

Steven H. Zarit, PhD
Department of Human Development and Family Studies
Pennsylvania State University
University Park, Pennsylvania

Zachary Zimmer, PhD
Population Council
New York, New York

David Zitner, MD
Director of Medical Informatics
Faculty of Medicine
Dalhousie University
Halifax, Nova Scotia, Canada

LIST OF ENTRIES

Italics indicate that this subject is covered under a different title.

THE ENCYCLOPEDIA OF AGING

A Comprehensive Resource in Gerontology and Geriatrics

Fourth Edition

AARP (THE AMERICAN ASSOCIATION OF RETIRED PERSONS)

With more than 35 million members, *AARP* is the leading not-for-profit, nonpartisan membership organization for people who are 50 years of age and older in the United States. It is dedicated to making life better, not only for its members, but for all Americans. The AARP vision is a society in which all can age with independence, dignity, and purpose.

Mission

AARP provides information and resources; engages in legislative, regulatory, and legal advocacy; assists members in serving their communities; and offers a wide range of benefits, products, and services. These include *AARP The Magazine*, which is published every two months and is the highest circulation magazine in the United States; the *AARP Bulletin*, a monthly newspaper; *AARP Segunda Juventud*, a quarterly newspaper in Spanish; *NRTA Live & Learn*, a quarterly newsletter for 50+ educators; and www.aarp.org, the award-winning Web site. AARP has staff and offices in all 50 states, the District of Columbia, Puerto Rico, and the U.S. Virgin Islands. AARP is dedicated to enhancing the quality of life as people age by leading positive social change and delivering value to members. AARP recognizes that the phrase "quality of life" means different things to different people. Some need help coping with the basics of daily living. Others want to get involved in personally rewarding volunteer activities or health promotion programs. And, some members want to make the most of their leisure time with sports and travel opportunities. The range of connections to services, activities, and products possible through AARP's programs is so large that few are aware of all of them.

AARP serves the most rapidly growing portion of the population—an increasingly diverse segment—who are working full-time, part-time, and retired; married, widowed and single; urban, suburban, and rural; taking care of children, taking care of parents, or both, and empty nesters. The organization's goals include:

- Informing members and the public on issues important to older Americans and their families.
- Advocating on legislative, consumer, and legal issues before Congress, the state houses of all 50 states, the courts, and regulatory bodies at every level of government.
- Fostering community service and health promotion programs.
- Offering a wide range of special products and personal services to members.

Membership

Membership in AARP is open to any person who is 50 years of age or older. Almost one-third of the U.S. population falls into this age group and more than 45% of all people over the age of 50 are AARP members. U.S. citizenship, or even U.S. residence, is not a requirement for membership. More than 40,000 members live outside the United States. People also do not have to be retired to join. In fact, 44% of AARP members work part time or full time. For this reason, AARP shortened its name in 1999 from the American Association of Retired Persons to just four letters. AARP. The "median age" of AARP members is 65, so half are younger than 65 and half are older. Slightly more than half of members are women.

History

Ethel Percy Andrus, PhD, who retired as principal of a large Los Angeles high school, founded the *National Retired Teachers Association (NRTA)* in 1947 to promote her philosophy of active, productive aging and to respond to the need of retired teachers for health insurance. At that time, private health insurance was virtually unavailable to older Americans, for it was not until 1965 that the Congress enacted Medicare, which provides healthcare benefits to those 65 and older.

Dr. Andrus approached dozens of insurance companies until she found one willing to take the risk of insuring older persons. She then developed other benefits and programs for retired teachers, including a discount mail-order pharmacy service. Over the years NRTA heard from thousands of others who wanted to know how they could obtain insurance and other NRTA benefits without being retired teachers. In 1958, Dr. Andrus realized the time had come to create a new organization open to all Americans. Today, NRTA continues as a division within AARP.

In 1963, Dr. Andrus established an international presence for AARP by founding the Association of Retired Persons International (ARPI), with offices in Lausanne, Switzerland, and Washington, D.C. While ARPI disbanded as a separate organization in 1969, AARP has continued to develop networks and form coalitions abroad with its office of International Affairs (IA). IA is creating a growing presence in the worldwide aging community, promoting the well-being of older people everywhere through advocacy, education, and policy development. IA also functions as a clearinghouse for information on successful programs and possibilities for older people throughout the world, both learning from and mentoring those abroad.

Dr. Andrus's motto for AARP was "To serve, not to be served." Since 1958, AARP has grown and changed dramatically in response to societal changes; however, AARP has remained true to its founding principle.

Advocacy Efforts

For a number of years, *Fortune* magazine has named AARP the nation's foremost advocacy organization ("most powerful lobbying organization"). This is an extraordinary accomplishment given that AARP is a not-for-profit, nonpartisan organization that has no Political Action Committee (PAC), does not contribute any money to candidates or political parties, and does not endorse or oppose political candidates or parties. The strength comes from members choosing to be involved in policy issues that affect them and their families. Whether the issue is Social Security, Medicare, Medicaid, pension protection and reform, age discrimination, long-term care, work and retirement, or transportation, AARP volunteers make their presence count on Capitol Hill and in state capitals throughout the country.

AARP members are not only vocal on health and income security issues, but they are active advocates on consumer issues as well. AARP volunteers are fighting consumer fraud, including telemarketing, sweepstakes, and mail fraud. Issues range from the rights of grandparents to setting utility and telephone rates to safety standards for manufactured housing. AARP has had particular success in the courts opposing predatory lending, a practice by which older Americans are encouraged to remortgage homes that are paid off or nearly paid off for egregiously high interest rates and unfavorable payoff periods.

AARP backs up its advocacy efforts with quality policy research efforts. The AARP Public Policy Institute (PPI) was created in 1985 to conduct objective, relevant, and timely policy analyses to inform the development of AARP's public policy positions, and to contribute to public debate and discussion. Research findings are typically published in the form of detailed reports such as *Issue Papers, Issue Briefs*, and *Data Digests*. PPI also publishes numerous shorter *Fact Sheets, In-Briefs*, and "*FYIs*" each year. All are available on the Web site.

Volunteer Programs

AARP volunteers are the heart and soul of the Association. The members of its Board of Directors and its national officers are all unpaid volunteers, as are the state presidents and thousands of legislative and program volunteers and chapter leaders. Members can be involved in a number of innovative community service and education programs, including tax preparation assistance, driver training and re-education, grief and loss counseling, and independent living programs, if they choose. Through their involvement in national state, and local affairs, AARP volunteers are shaping the experience of aging positively for members and for society.

Special Services

Dr. Andrus was a pioneer in establishing group health insurance for older Americans. She recognized then, as AARP does today, that making such services available to—and affordable for—older Americans is essential to maintain the quality of life for all people as they grow older. From the beginning, AARP has responded to members' needs by making available products and services created especially for them. Through market innovation and leadership, AARP Services, Inc. (ASI), a wholly owned subsidiary of AARP created in 1999, manages the wide range of products and services offered as benefits to AARP's members. ASI also develops new products and services that reflect the changing expectations and needs of members. Developing good products means selecting quality business partners as providers, so ASI continually monitors each service's operation to make sure AARP's service-provider partners are meeting the Association's standards.

Among the programs ASI manages are Medicare supplemental insurance, automobile/homeowners insurance, a prescription drug program, long-term care insurance, a motoring plan, a credit card, and life insurance. ASI also oversees the AARP Privileges Program, designed to respond to the wide-ranging needs of the AARP traveler by providing discounts on hotels and motels, auto rentals, airlines, cruise lines, vacation packages, entertainment products, and consumer goods. Discounted legal fees are available from state Bar Association members of the AARP Legal Services Network. Profits from any of the services offered by ASI are rolled back into the activities of the non-profit AARP organization so that dues for members can be kept as low as possible and charitable services supported.

The Foundation

Through the AARP Foundation, AARP works to expand the understanding of aging with research and service. In its 30 years of grant making, the Foundation has supported more than 630 projects with grants totaling approximately $35 million. Foundation programs provide security, protection, and empowerment for older people in need. Low-income older workers receive the job training and placement they need to rejoin the workforce. Free tax preparation is provided for low- and moderate-income older individuals. The Foundation's litigation staff protects the legal rights of older Americans in critical health, long-term care, and consumer and employment court cases. Additional programs provide information, education, and services to ensure that people older than 50 lead lives with independence, dignity, and purpose.

Foundation programs are funded by grants, tax-deductible contributions from AARP members, the general public, and AARP. In 2004, the Foundation reorganized and greatly enlarged its capacity to raise additional funds from individuals, corporations, other foundations, and government agencies. The Foundation also strengthened its partnership with AARP by increasing support of AARP's charitable programs that advance the Foundation's mission. AARP members support the Foundation's charitable work through volunteerism, as well as through annual and long-term financial contributions.

Conclusion

AARP recognizes that aging is synonymous with living. As we progress along life's continuum, we find that what matters most is not age but experiences along the way. AARP's founder Dr. Ethel Percy Andrus once observed, "The stereotype of old age—increasingly costly and troublesome—is contradicted by the host of happy and productive older people participating and serving beyond the call of duty. Second only to the desire to live is the natural yearning to be wanted and needed, to feel that one's contribution to life is essential."

JOHN ROTHER

See also
Organizations in Aging

A-B-C MODEL

See
Behavior Management

ABSTRACT THINKING

Young children understand the relation between objects and events in a functional manner. They note that the first object is seen to go with or to operate on the second object. *Complementarity criteria* are integral components of their thinking. By contrast, older children and young adults tend to use *similarity criteria*. As one ages, however, the use of complementarity criteria increases once again (Reese & Rodeheaver, 1985). The reversal to complementarity as people age is thought to be caused by environmental factors rather than attributable to changes in competence. Young children as well as elderly people are rarely required to state their thoughts in a specifically prescribed way, and complementary categorization may therefore seem more natural since such categories are grouped naturally in time and space.

Older adults do not necessarily lose the ability to use more abstract criteria, but they are often willing to indulge in an alternative mode that offers greater imaginary scope. Complementarity as an aspect of thinking has been found to be more prevalent in nonprofessional than in professional men or women from age 25 to 69, with neither age nor gender differences found to be significant (Denney, 1974). Luria (1976) observed the same phenomena in a study in Central Asia, where uneducated workers were more likely to engage in concrete thought, while educated collective farm members were more prone to use abstract thought.

Abstract thinking and aging has also been investigated in the context of the crystallized-fluid ability model (cf. Cattell, 1963). Convergent fluid abilities that involve abstract thinking have shown an average decline somewhat earlier than was found for the more concrete information-based crystallized abilities. Paradoxically, abstract thinking may become more important as people age because many lifelong experiences must be reappraised. Even well-established everyday behaviors that previously could be performed in a routine and concrete manner may now require a modicum of abstract thought to evoke a novel response appropriate to changed circumstances (cf. Schaie & Willis, 1999; Willis & Schaie, 1993).

An alternate explanation for the reduction in abstract reasoning with increasing age might be sought in the reduction of cortical volume in brain areas essential for high levels of abstract thinking (cf. Gunning-Dixon & Raz, 2003).

The contention that the increased incidence of concrete thought in elderly people may be the result of experiential rather than neurological factors is further supported by positive results of training studies that involve persons who had not earlier used abstract classification principles (Denney, 1974), or who had had a lower performance rating on abstract ability measures (Schaie & Willis, 1986; Willis, 1996, 2001).

K. Warner Schaie

See also
Cognitive Processes
Intelligence
Metamemory
Problem Solving

References

Cattell, R. B. (1963). Theory of fluid and crystallized intelligence: A critical experiment. *Journal of Educational Psychology*, *54*, 1–22.

Denney, N. W. (1974). Classification ability in the elderly. *Journal of.*

Gunning-Dixon, F. M., & Raz, N. (2003). Neuroanatomical correlates of selected executive functions in middle-aged and older adults: A prospective MRI study. *Neuropsychologia*, *41*, 1929–1941.

Luria, A. R. (1976). *Cognitive development: Its cultural and social foundations*. Oxford, UK: Oxford University Press.

Reese, H. W., & Rodeheaver, D. (1985). Problem solving and complex decision making. In J. E. Birren & K. W. Schaie (Eds.), *Handbook of the psychology of aging* (2nd ed., pp. 474–499). New York: Van Nostrand Reinhold.

Schaie, K. W., & Willis, S. L. (1986). Can intellectual decline in the elderly be reversed? *Developmental Psychology*, *22*, 223–232.

Schaie, K. W., & Willis, S. L. (1999). Theories of everyday competence and aging. In V. L. Bengtson & K. W. Schaie (Eds.), *Handbook of theories of aging* (pp. 174–195). New York: Springer Publishing Co.

Willis, S. L. (1996). Everyday cognitive competence in elderly persons: Conceptual issues and empirical finding. *Gerontologist*, *36*, 595–601.

Willis, S. L. (2001). Methodological issues in behavioral intervention research with the elderly. In J. E. Birren & K. W. Schaie (Eds.), *Handbook of the psychology of aging* (5th ed., pp. 78–108). San Diego, CA: Academic Press.

Willis, S. L., & Schaie, K. W. (1993). Everyday cognition: Taxonomic and methodological considerations. In J. M. Puckett & H.W. Reese (Eds.), *Mechanisms of everyday cognition* (pp. 33–54). Hillsdale, NJ: Erlbaum.

ACID-BASE BALANCE

Hydrogen ion (H^+) is a highly reactive cation. For that reason it is essential that the concentration of Fr′ in the body fluids be tightly regulated. In healthy people the H^+ concentration of the blood plasma ranges from 36 to 43 nanomoles per liter (pH 7.45-7.35). H^+ is produced by acids and consumed by bases; thus, the regulation of the H^+ concentration is called acid-base balance.

The body is continuously producing acids and bases. The production of carbon dioxide, which is a major end product of metabolism, is equivalent to producing carbonic acid. Although large quantities of carbon dioxide are produced each day, they are eliminated from the body by the lungs through alveolar ventilation as quickly as they are produced. The important point is that the nervous system controls alveolar ventilation so that the concentration of carbon dioxide in the blood plasma is maintained at the level needed for the maintenance of an appropriate H^+ concentration in the body fluids. The body also produces fixed acids (i.e., acids not eliminated by the lungs) and produces bases. If fixed acid production is in excess of base production, the kidneys excrete the excess H^+ in the urine. It is also the case that if base production is in excess of the fixed acid production, the kidneys excrete the excess base in the urine. Although the finely regulated pulmonary and renal functions can sometimes transiently fail to do the job, no immediate problem occurs because the body is rich in chemical buffers that serve to blunt rapid change in H^+ concentration.

Do these exquisite systems for the control of H^+ concentration continue to function effectively at advanced ages? It has long been held that healthy elderly living in usual unchallenged conditions have no problem in maintaining normal acid-base balance (Lye, 1998). However, a careful meta-analysis of published data on acid-base balance and age has challenged this long-held view (Frassetto & Sebastian, 1996). This analysis indicates that a significant rise in steady-state blood I-i^+ concentration occurs with increasing adult age. Moreover, assessment of the concentration of blood carbon dioxide concentration revealed a decrease with age, and this would be expected because of the increase in alveolar ventilation by the respiratory system in response to a rising blood H^+ concentration. On the basis of these findings, plus the meta-analysis assessment that plasma bicarbonate concentration decreases with age, it is likely that the age-associated deterioration of kidney function is responsible for the increasing H^+ concentration. Of course, to be certain of the gerontological validity of the findings of this meta-analysis requires data from a welldesigned longitudinal study. The results of such a study have yet to be reported. However, if the conclusions from this meta-analysis are valid, an age-associated progressive increase of this magnitude in the near steady-state H^+ concentration could have negative consequences in regard to bone loss, muscle mass loss, and kidney function.

In contrast to uncertainty of the effect of age on unchallenged, near steady-state acid-base balance, the evidence is clear that healthy elderly people respond less well than the young to an acid-base challenge. In an early study, young and old were challenged by a load of ammonium chloride (Adler, Lindeman, Yiengst, Beard, & Shock, 1968). The body metabolizes ammonium chloride to hydrochloric acid. In that early study, it was found that increased blood levels of H^+ and decreased levels of bicarbonate ion persisted much longer in old than in young individuals. Altered kidney function appears to be the main reason for this difference between young and old. Indeed during the first 8 hours following ammonium chloride administration, a much greater percentage of the acid load is excreted in the urine by the young than by the old (Lubran, 1995). There is also evidence that the elderly cope less effectively with increased acid loads caused by exercise. This decrease in the ability of the kidney to excrete H^+ predisposes the elderly to the development of and delayed recovery from *metabolic acidosis* (Lindeman, 1995). Whether the respiratory change in alveolar ventilation is as effective in the elderly in compensating for changes in blood H^+ concentration is subject to debate; not all studies have found the response of the respiratory system to chemical stimuli to be blunted with increasing age (Rubin, Tack, & Cherniack, 1982).

Of course, the elderly have many age-associated diseases that predispose them to *acid-base disorders* (e.g., *chronic obstructive pulmonary disease* and *chronic renal disease*). Thus, acid-base disorders are commonly encountered in geriatric medicine.

EDWARD J. MASORO

See also
Kidney and Urinary System

References

Adler, S., Lindeman, R. D., Yiengst, M. J., Beard, E.S., & Schock, N. W. (1968). Effect of acute acid loading on urinary acid excretion by the aging human kidney. *Journal of Laboratory and Clinical Medicine, 72,* 278–289.

Lindeman, R. D. (1995). Renal and urinary tract function. In E. J. Masoro (Ed.), *Handbook of physiology:* See, 11, *Aging* (pp. 485–503). New York: Oxford University Press.

Lubran, M. M., (1995). Renal function in the elderly. *Annals of Clinical and Laboratory Science, 25,* 122–133.

Rubin, S., Tack, M., & Cherniack, N. S. (1982). Effect of aging on respiratory responses to CO_2 and inspiratory resistance loads. *Journal of Gerontology, 37,* 306–312.

ACQUIRED IMMUNE DEFICIENCY SYNDROME

See
AIDS/HIV

ACTIVITIES OF DAILY LIVING

The term *activities of daily living (ADL)* refers to a range of common activities whose performance is required for personal self-maintenance and to remain a participating member of society. As illustrated by the *International Classification of Functioning, Disability, and Health (ICF)* (WHO, 2001), ADL is a central aspect of human functioning, affected by and affecting health conditions, physiological and psychological functioning, and participation in life situations, while also interacting with environmental and personal factors (de Kleijn-de Vrankreijker, 2003). Intended for international use, ICF should provide a common language for gathering data and interdisciplinary communication. That, however, remains for the future. To date, the recoding of current disability survey questions to meet ICF criteria has proved to be difficult (Swanson et al., 2003). Nevertheless, the U.S. National Committee on Vital and Health Statistics identified ICF "as the only viable code set for consistently reporting functional status." (Iezzoni & Greenberg, 2003).

The theoretical model of ADL proposed by Katz (1983) suggests three areas: *mobility* (e.g., Rosow & Breslau, 1966); *instrumental (I) ADL,* which is concerned with complex activities needed for independent living (e.g., taking own medications, using the telephone, handling everyday finances, preparing meals, shopping, traveling, and doing housework (Lawton & Brody, 1969)); and *basic personal care tasks (BADL)* (e.g., toileting, dressing, eating, transferring, grooming, and bathing (Katz et al., 1959)).

More recent analyses, typically based on large representative samples of older persons, offer conflicting suggestions regarding the psychometric characteristics of IADL and BADL items. Some investigators have found that these items constitute not two, but three dimensions (Fillenbaum, 1985; Stump, Clark, Johnson & Wolinsky, 1997; Thomas, Rockwood & McDowell, 1998). Within each factor, the items have sometimes been found to constitute a hierarchical measure, but this is not invariable. In fact, a multiplicity of hierarchies have been identified for the Katz items (Lazaridis et al., 1994). While there is considerable agreement across studies in the items included in each of these groups, differences in the items present reflect the datasets from which information was drawn. Thus, the study of Thomas et al. (1998), based on data from the Canadian Study of Health and Aging, which used the Older Americans Resources and Services ADL scale (Fillenbaum, 1988), identifies toileting, dressing, eating, transferring, and grooming as Basic self-care. Intermediate self-care items include bathing, walking indoors, housework, meal preparation, shopping, and traveling alone, while Complex self-management (which is recognized as having a substantial cognitive component) includes handling money, using telephone, and handling own medicine.

Alternatively, BADL and IADL items have been found to constitute a hierarchy (Spector & Fleishman, 1998; Suurmeijer et al., 1994). Spector & Fleishman (1998) used a set of items which overlap considerably with those of Thomas et al. (1998)—the only differences are the absence of grooming and the inclusion of incontinence, laundry, and the specification that housework is light—yet have come to a different conclusion regarding multidimensionality. Possibly alternative statistical techniques and different samples of elders (nationally representative vs. disabled) account for the discrepant findings.

Standardized ADL assessments have increased in use, acceptance, and importance during the last 40 years, while the number of such assessments has proliferated. Current measures date back to the *Katz Index of Independence in Activities of Daily Living* (Katz et al., 1959) and to the *Barthel Index* (Mahoney & Barthel, 1965). Both were developed in rehabilitation settings to measure tasks basic to personal self-care, and include comparable items, such as feeding, continence, transferring, use of toilet, dressing, bathing, and for the Barthel, mobility.

Use of these scales has since diverged. Modifications of the Barthel permit increasingly specific focus on the type of rehabilitative intervention required and the impact of that intervention. Experience with this and related assessments used in rehabilitation have culminated in the *Functional Independence Measure* (FIM™, Linacre et al., 1994), which operationalizes the *Uniform Data System for Medical Rehabilitation (UDS)*. FIM™ is currently the basis for reimbursement in rehabilitation, where level of functioning, and not diagnosis, indicates service needs. (See Multidimensional Functional Assessment for further information on FIM™.)

The level of detail required in rehabilitation is inappropriate where assessment of the general older population is concerned, because the overwhelming majority can perform basic activities. To better discriminate within the general older population, inquiry is directed to more difficult tasks, including mobility and instrumental ADL (although not all of these tasks are more difficult to perform than BADL activities).

The multiplicity of measures that exist differ in several important regards. Some are intended for general use, others with a specific subgroup (e.g., persons with arthritis, cognitive impairment, dementia, multiple sclerosis, stroke, etc.; see e.g., Bowling, 2001, for measures intended for neurological and rheumatological conditions, and cardiovascular disease; Burns, Lawlor & Craig, 2004, for measures designed for psychiatric conditions, including dementia; and Spilker, 1996 for measures in multiple areas). Information may be sought from the individual, from a family member, or a service provider. Information from the three may not be equivalent (Dorevitch, Cossar, Bailey, Bisset, Lewis, Wise, & McLennon, 1992). Items may differ across measures. Inquiry may focus on whether the person *can* perform the task (i.e., capability) or *does* perform the task (actuality), with what level of difficulty, or pain, and whether problems are the result of particular health conditions. There may be inquiry into the type of help received (e.g., from an aid, a person, or both); help from a person is seen as indicating more dependence than the use of an aid. The time interval considered (current, past week, past month, past year) may vary. Possible responses may be dichotomous (e.g., can do unaided vs. not), trichotomous (e.g., can perform unaided, need some help, cannot perform at all), or polychotomous (e.g., FIM™ uses very clearly specified seven-point scales). Differences in wording have yielded estimates of disability prevalence differing by up to 60%, with potentially serious impact on service planning (Freedman & Martin, 2004; Wiener, Hanley, Clark, & van Nostrand, 1990). Statistical techniques are now being applied in an attempt to equate different measures (Jette, Haley & Ni, 2003).

While the majority of scales require self- (or proxy-) report, performance scales have also been developed. Information from the two sources are not identical, but may be complementary, with level of performance valuable in distinguishing among persons who self-report no problems (Hoeymans, Feskens, van den Bos, & Kromhout, 1996; Myers, Holiday, Harvey, & Hutchinson, 1993; Reuben et al., 2004; Young et al., 1996).

Although of extraordinary value, current ADL scales nevertheless have some drawbacks. Environmental factors that might affect performance are seldom considered (Freedman & Martin, 2004). Some activities are rarely included (e.g., sexual activities), and few measures have kept pace with technological advances (e.g., use of ATMs, microwaves, cell phones). In its initial wave the Health and Retirement Survey (Soldo, Hurd, Rodgers, & Wallace, 1997) included such items, but these were later dropped. ADL tasks may be affected by gender and culture. The manner in which various activities must be performed may vary from country to country. Tasks important in one country may not be as relevant in another. Some tasks may not be relevant at all in, say, a developing country (Fillenbaum et al., 1999), or may measure different abilities (Jitapunkul, Kamolratanakul & Ebrahim, 1998).

ADL is central to any assessment of personal independent functioning. Information on ADL capacity has been used more extensively and for a greater variety of purposes than has information from any other type of assessment. It has been used to indicate individual social, mental, and physical functioning, as well as for diagnosis; to determine service requirement and impact; to guide service inception and cessation; to estimate the level of qualification needed in a provider; to assess need for structural environmental support; to justify residential location; to provide a basis for personnel employment decisions; to determine service change and provide arguments for reimbursement; to calculate active and disabled life expectancy; and to estimate eligibility for specific services (e.g., attendant allowances). Accurate assessment of ADL is probably one of the most valuable of measures.

Excellent reviews, which provide information on psychometric characteristics, and some of which reproduce the ADL measures used in assessment of the elderly may be found in Bowling, 1997; 2001; Burns, Lawlor, & Craig, 2004; Israel, Kozarevic, & Sartorius, 1984; McDowell & Newell, 1996; Salek, 1998; and on the QOLID (Quality of Life Instruments Database) site (www.qolid.com). The latter lists 1000 quality-of-life instruments, including detailed information on more than 450 of these.

GERDA G. FILLENBAUM

See also
Disability
Mobility
Self-Care Activities

References

Bowling, A. (1997). *Measuring health: A review of quality of life measurement scales. Philadelphia*. Philadelphia: Open University Press.

Bowling, A. (2001). *Measuring disease: A review of disease-specific quality of life measurement scales* (2nd ed.) Philadelphia, Open University Press.

Burns, A., Lawlor, B., & Craig, S. (2004). *Assessment scales in old age psychiatry* (2nd ed.). New York: Martin Dunitz, Taylor & Francis Group.

de Kleijn-de Vrankreijker, M. W. (2003). The long way from the International Classification of Impairments, Disabilities and Handicaps (ICIDH) to the International Classification of Functioning, Disability and Health (ICF). *Disability and Rehabilitation*, *25*, 561–564.

Dorevitch, M. I., Cossar, R. M., Bailey, F. J., Bisset, T., Lewis, S. J., Wise, L. A., & McLennan, W. J. (1992). The accuracy of self and informant ratings of physical functional capacity in the elderly. *Journal of Clinical Epidemiology*, *45*, 791–798.

Fillenbaum, G. G. (1985). Screening the elderly: A brief instrumental activities of daily living measure. *Journal of the American Geriatrics Society*, *33*, 698–706.

Fillenbaum, G. G. (1988). *Multidimensional functional assessment of older adults: The Duke Older Americans Resources and Services Procedures*. Hillsdale, NJ: Erlbaum.

Fillenbaum, G. G., Chandra, V., Ganguli, M., Pandav, R., Gilby, J. E., Seaberg, E. L., Belle, S., Baker, C., Echemont, D. A., & Nath, L. M. (1999). Development of an activities of daily living scale to screen for dementia in an illiterate rural older population in India. *Age and Ageing*, *28*, 161–168.

Freedman, V. A., & Martin, L. G. (2004). Incorporating disability into population-level models of health change at older ages. *Journal of Gerontology*, *59A*, 602–603.

Hoeymans, N., Feskens, E. J. M., van den Bos, G. A. M., & Kromhout, D. (1996). Measuring functional status: Cross-sectional and longitudinal associations between performance and self-report (Zutphen Elderly Study 1900-1993). *Journal of Clinical Epidemiology*, *49*, 1103–1110.

Iezzoni, L. I., & Greenberg, M. S. (2003). Capturing and classifying functional status information in administrative databases. *Health Care Financing Review*, *24*(3), 61–76.

Israel, L., Kozarevic, D., & Sartorius, N. (1984). *Source book of geriatric assessment*. Basel: Karger.

Jette, A. M., Haley, S. M., & Ni, P. (2003). Comparison of functional status tools used in post-acute care. *Health Care Financing Review*, *24*(3), 13–24.

Jitapunkul, S., Kamolratanakul, P., & Ebrahim, S. (1998). The meaning of activity of daily living in a Thai elderly population: Development of a new index. *Age & Ageing*, *23*, 97–101.

Katz, S., Chinn, A. B., and the staff of the Benjamin Rose Hospital (1959). Multidisciplinary studies of illness in aged persons. Part II. New classification of functional status in activities of daily living. *Journal of Chronic Diseases*, *9*, 55–62.

Katz, S. (1983). Assessing self-maintenance: Activities of daily living, mobility and instrumental activities of daily living. *Journal of the American Geriatrics Society*, *31*, 721–727.

Lawton, M. P., & Brody, E. M. (1969). Assessment of older people: Self-maintaining and instrumental activities of daily living. *Gerontologist*, *9*, 179–186.

Lazaridis, E. N., Rudberg, M. A., Furner, S. E., & Cassel, C. K. (1994). Do activities of daily living have a hierarchical structure? An analysis using the Longitudinal Study of Aging. *Journal of Gerontology: Medical Sciences*, *49*, M47–M51.

Linacre, J. M., Heinemann, A. W., Wright, B. D., Granger, C. V., & Hamilton, B. B. (1994). The structure and stability of the Functional Independence Measure. *Archives of Physical Medicine and Rehabilitation*, *75*, 127–132.

Mahoney, F. I. & Barthel, D. W. (1965). Functional evaluation: The Barthel Index. *Maryland State Medical Journal*, *14*, 61–65.

McDowell, I., & Newell, C. (1996). *Measuring health: A guide to rating scales and questionnaires* (2nd ed.). New York: Oxford University Press.

Myers, A., Holiday, P. J., Harvey, K. A., & Hutchinson, K. S. (1993). Functional performance measures: Are they superior to self-assessments? *Journal of Gerontology: Medical Sciences*, *48*, M196–M206.

QOLID Quality of Life Instruments Database. www.qolid.com

Reuben, D. B., Seeman, T. E., Keeler, E., Hayes, R. P., Bowman, L., Sewall, A., Hirsch, S. H., Wallace, R. B., & Guralnik, J. M. (2004). The effect of self-reported and performance-based functional impairment on future hospital costs of community-dwelling older persons. *Gerontologist*, *44*, 401–407.

Rosow, I., & Breslau, N. (1966). A Guttman health scale for the aged. *Journal of Gerontology*, *21*, 556–559.

Salek, S. (1998). *Compendium of quality of life instruments*. Chichester, UK: John Wiley & Sons.

Soldo, B. J., Hurd, M. D., Rodgers, W. L., & Wallace, R. B. (1997). Asset and Health Dynamics among the Oldest Old: An overview of the AHEAD study. *Journals of Gerontology: Social Sciences*, *52B* (*Special Issue*), 1–20.

Spector, W. D., & Fleishman, J. A. (1998). Combining activities of daily living with instrumental activities of daily living to measure functional disability. *Journals of Gerontology: Psychological and Social Sciences*, *53B*, S46–S57.

Spilker, B. (Ed.). *Quality of life and pharmacoeconomics in clinical trials*. Philadelphia: Lippincott-Raven.

Stump, T. E., Clark, D. O., Johnson, R. J., & Wolinsky, F. D. (1997). The structure of health status among Hispanic, African American, and White older adults. *Journals of Gerontology: Psychological and Social Sciences*, *52B*, *Special No*., 49–60.

Swanson, G., Carrothers, L., & Mulhorn, K. A. (2003). Comparing disability survey questions in five countries: a study using ICF to guide comparisons. *Disability and Rehabilitation*, *25*, 665–675.

Suurmeijer, T. P., Doeglas, D. M., Moum, T., Braincon, S., Krol, B., Sanderman, R., Guillemin, F., Bjelle, A., & van den Heuvel, W. J. (1994). The Groningen Activity Restriction Scale for measuring disability: Its utility in international comparisons. *American Journal of Public Health*, *84*, 1270–1273.

Thomas, V. S., Rockwood, K., & McDowell, I. (1998). Multidimensionality in instrumental and basic activities of daily living. *Journal of Clinical Epidemiology*, *51*, 315–321.

Wiener, J. M., Hanley, R. J., Clark, R., & van Nostrand, N. F. (1990). Measuring the activities of daily living: Comparisons across national surveys. *Journal of Gerontology*, *45*(6), S229–237.

World Health Organization (2001). International classification of functioning, disability and health. Geneva, WHO. www.who.int/classification/icf

Young, N. L., Williams, J. I., Yoshida, K. K., Bombadier, C., & Wright, J. G. (1996). The context of measuring disability: Does it matter whether capability or performance is measured? *Journal of Clinical Epidemiology*, *49*, 1097–1101.

ACTIVITY THEORY

In the gerontology of the early 1960s, activity theory and disengagement theory became opposing grand metaphors for successful aging. In the case of activity theory, the archetype image portrayed an older person who had managed to maintain vigor and social involvement despite the vagaries of aging. For disengagement theory, the archetype image was of an older person who had voluntarily and gracefully disengaged from the hustle and bustle of midlife to a more serene and satisfying contemplation of life from a distance. These dualistic images of two very different paths of aging have been a part of Western civilization for a long time.

Robert Havighurst and his colleagues at the University of Chicago (Havighurst, 1963; Havighurst, Neugarten, and Tobin, 1963) were the early spokespersons for activity theory. Havighurst laid no claim to have invented activity theory; he simply put in writing what many practitioners of the day assumed: that keeping active was the best way to enjoy satisfying senior years. According to this view,

> except for the inevitable changes in biology and health, older people are the same as middle-aged people, with essentially the same psychological and social needs. In this view, the decreased social involvement that characterizes old age results from the withdrawal by society from the aging person; and the decrease in interaction proceeds against the desires of most aging men and women. The older person who ages optimally is the person who stays active and who manages to resist the shrinking of his [or her] social world. [She or] he maintains the activities of middle age as long as possible, and then finds substitutes for those activities he [or she]

> is forced to relinquish–substitutes for work when [she or] he is forced to retire; substitutes for friends or loved ones whom he [or she] loses by death. (Havighurst, Neugarten, and Tobin, 1963, p. 419)

In contrast to activity theory, disengagement theory (Cumming and Henry, 1961) held that successful aging involved growing older gracefully by gradually replacing the equilibrium system of social relations typical of midlife with a new equilibrium more appropriate to the interests of people approaching the end of life. This new equilibrium was presumed to involve a lower overall volume of social relations and a less psychological investment in the social affairs of the larger community.

Rosow (1963) picked up this theme of equilibrium in his rendition of activity theory, but his position was that the best course of action was to maintain the equilibrium of middle age. He argued that Americans do not want to grow old and that, by inference, their "basic premise in viewing older age is that the best life is the life that changes least." (Rosow, 1963, p. 216). He went on to argue that a "good adjustment" to older age involves maximum stability and minimum change in life pattern between late middle age and later years.

Activity theory assumed that activity produced successful aging through the relationship between activity and life satisfaction or subjective well-being. It was presumed that activity level was the cause and life satisfaction the effect.

Major Concepts of Activity Theory

Activity theory is built around four major concepts: activity, equilibrium, adaptation to role loss, and life satisfaction. Each of these very general concepts is open to a variety of interpretations, which has led to no small amount of confusion.

Activity. At its simplest, activity is any form of doing. But in Havighurst's original formulation of activity theory, activity was not just a level of doing but also a pattern of activity that formed the person's lifestyle. Activity theory predicted that maintaining both level and pattern of activities from middle age into old age would lead to the highest level of life satisfaction in older age.

Equilibrium. Activity theory makes the functionalist assumption that activity patterns arise to meet needs and that the needs of older people are no different from the needs of middle-aged people; therefore, whatever equilibrium the person has achieved in middle age should be maintained into one's senior years. Significant assaults to this midlife equilibrium are best resisted, and lost activities or roles should be replaced. Simply dropping out would not meet functional needs and would therefore be expected to lead to lowered life satisfaction.

Adaptation to Role Loss. Role loss was assumed to be a common experience for aging individuals because of the withdrawal of society from the aging person. Activity theory predicted that the most successful way to adapt to role loss was to find a substitute role to satisfy needs. The original formulation assumed that role substitutes should be roughly equivalent to the roles lost, so retirement would lead to a search for job substitutes, for example. Later, the concept of substitution was broadened by Maddox (1963) to include alternative activities of any kind.

Life Satisfaction. How do we know when a person has aged successfully? Both activity theorists and disengagement theorists agreed on one thing. Life satisfaction was the best criterion for measuring social and psychological adjustment. Havighurst and his colleagues' (1963) concept of life satisfaction was made up of five components: zest and enthusiasm, resolution and fortitude, a feeling of accomplishment, self-esteem, and optimism. This construct addressed the level of subjective well-being experienced by an individual, not his or her evaluation of specific objective circumstances. The Life Satisfaction Index B (Havighurst, 1963) was constructed to measure these attributes, and it has been most often used as the dependent variable in formal tests of activity theory.

Evolution of Activity Theory

In its original form, activity theory was a homeostatic, equilibrium theory of the relation between activity patterns and life satisfaction. However, the theoretical ties between activity theory and functional equilibrium theory were largely ignored, although they were made explicit by Rosow (1963).

Lemon, Bengtson, and Peterson (1972) reformulated activity theory into an interactionist theory. By interactionist, they meant both symbolic interactionist in the form of a relation between self and role and the use of reflected appraisals to bolster the self as well as social interactionist in the form of role supports going from others to the aging individual. Thus, for Lemon and colleagues, the motivation for maintaining activity was not the meeting of functional needs but the need to maintain a socially supported self-structure that was assumed to lead to optimal life satisfaction.

Lemon et al. (1972) developed a formal propositional theory that attempted to explain why high activity levels could be expected to produce high life satisfaction and declines in activity could be expected to result in lower life satisfaction. Their theory was based on a series of assumptions about the relationships among role loss, role supports (feedback from others about role performance), self-esteem, and life satisfaction. This reformulation of activity theory was essentially a domino theory in which role loss was presumed to lead to less role support and lower activity, which were presumed to lead to lower self-esteem, which in turn was presumed to cause lower life satisfaction. On the other hand, maintaining high activity levels by substituting for lost roles would maintain activity level and role support, which would maintain self-esteem, and thereby maintain life satisfaction. Further, they classified activities into informal, formal, and solitary, and they hypothesized that all three types would be associated with life satisfaction, but informal activity was expected to show the strongest association because of its greater likelihood of providing role support, followed by formal activity, and informal activity was expected to show the lowest association with life satisfaction because of its presumed lack of role support. Unfortunately, their test of the theory provided little support for this reformulation. The only significant association they found between activity and life satisfaction occurred for informal activities among married women. Longino and Kart (1982) retested Lemon, Bengtson, and Peterson's (1972) hypotheses and reported more support for the hypothesized relationships between types of activities and life satisfaction. They also suggested several additional hypotheses to be included in the interactionist activity theory:

- Formal activity damages self-concept and lowers morale. This hypothesis was based on the notion that service use is the most common type of formal activity in an older population and that service use results in negative role support.
- Lower life satisfaction leads to increased formal activity. Here they argued that the causal direction of activity theory may be wrong. Elders with low morale tend to be targeted by formal service providers; therefore low life satisfaction causes formal activity, not the reverse.
- Formal activity is a variable context and its effects on life satisfaction depend on the extent to which it offers opportunities for supportive human relationships.
- Role supports may not be substitutable. If confidants are lost, they may not be replaceable.
- Frequency of activity is as important as the type of activity. They found that any level of informal activity resulted in life satisfaction near the sample mean, whereas an absence of informal activity resulted in a significant deficit in life satisfaction compared to the sample mean.

Part of the difficulty with the interactionist version of activity theory may have been its simplistic assumptions about the relation of self and roles. Research evidence on the relationship between self and role in later life suggests that the linkage is neither as direct nor as simple as the interactionist formulations of activity theory indicate. For example, Markus and Herzog's (1991) review of the literature on aging and the self conceptualized the self as a dynamic, complex structure made up of past, current, and future images of the self arising from specific antecedents. Self-schema are used to organize and interpret experience, regulate affect, and motivate behavior. Life satisfaction is presumed to be one of the consequences of these self processes. In this formulation all roles are not equally important to the self, only those that are part of the set of core self-schema that persists over time. Likewise, the place of specific activities in the core self could be expected to be a significant intervening variable in the relations among activity patterns, activity change, the self, and life satisfaction.

Research on activity has addressed some of these concerns.

Larson, Zuzanek, and Mannell (1985) and Mannell (1993), for example, looked at the meaning of specific activities for the individual as a significant intervening variable in the relationship between activity and life satisfaction. Larson and colleagues reported that the retired adults in their study voluntarily spent almost half of their waking hours alone, but being alone was not a negative experience for the majority of them. When they were alone, they were engaged in activities that required concentration and challenge. Mannell probed this issue further and found that the link between specific activities and life satisfaction was the culmination of a complex string of contingencies. First, activities had to be available that had a high potential for attracting individual investment of time and energy. Second, activities had to be freely chosen, not obligatory, and accompanied by a sense of commitment. Third, activities had to produce the experience of flow, life experience transported to a higher level of quality by activities that focus attention, match challenges to capabilities, reduce self-consciousness, and increase feelings of control. If these contingent conditions were met, then we could expect activities to bolster life satisfaction.

Important Unaddressed Issues

Does activity theory apply equally to men and women as they age? To what reference point in the past should patterns of activity and life satisfaction in old age be compared? When does old age begin chronologically? Does activity influence some of the components of life satisfaction more than others? Does activity influence life satisfaction, or is it the other way around? Is activity level correlated with life satisfaction consistently?

Gender differences are very obvious in the findings of research on aging and activities. The number and types of activities and the frequency of participation in an array of activities have all been found to differ substantially by gender, with activity patterns of older men showing a stronger relation to life satisfaction than the activity patterns of older women. However, there has been no attempt to integrate these findings into activity theory, to explain why activities are more important to the life satisfaction of older men than to older women.

Activity theory might be further refined by looking at specific components of subjective well-being. It is likely that self-esteem is not the only mental construct that is influenced by the experiences gained from a person's activities. Lawton (1983) mapped a number of dimensions of subjective well-being that could profitably be used in research on activity theory.

Finally, activity level is not always correlated with life satisfaction. Indeed, in a meta-analysis of 10 predictors of subjective well-being among elders, Okun et al. (1984) found that activity level was only modestly related to life satisfaction when the effect of health was controlled. Health was by far the strongest predictor of life satisfaction. Research on activity theory should be sure to control the effects of health and life stage before coming to conclusions about the influence of activity level on life satisfaction.

Directions for Activity Theory

Current research using activity theory falls into two categories: research aimed at comparing activity theory with other theories as descriptions of typical patterns related to aging and research aimed at testing and extending the social psychological components of activity theory to better specify the causal relationships between activity and life satisfaction.

Researchers who focus primarily on activities tend to describe activity patterns and then compare their descriptions to the ideal descriptions presented in the homeostatic, functional version of activity theory. Because there is usually a good bit of change in the frequency of specific activities over time in later adulthood, the equilibrium hypothesis of activity theory is usually rejected.

However, researchers who focus primarily on life satisfaction are increasingly looking at the social psychological relation between specific activities and life satisfaction. These researchers have met with increasing success in identifying specific conditions under which activity is strongly related to life satisfaction. But as the list of specifications grows, the power of activity theory as a general theory of aging is diminished.

Despite the many difficulties with activity theory, its ties to the cultural conception of successful aging have made gerontologists reluctant to abandon it. Some of each new generation of gerontologists have been attracted to the basic ideas contained in activity theory. Instead of rejecting the theory out of hand, it is used as an ideal standard against which to compare actual activity patterns. For those more interested in activity theory as theory, the focus has shifted to understanding the conditions under which the kernel of truth contained in the cultural conception could be expected occur in its more obvious forms. As a result, activity theory has seldom been tested in recent research but instead is more often used as one element of a more complex theoretical argument.

ROBERT C. ATCHLEY

See also
Continuity Theory
Disengagement Theory
Social Gerontology: Theories

References

Cumming, E., & Henry, W. E. (1961). *Growing old: The process of disengagement*. New York: Basic Books.

Havighurst, R. J. (1963). Successful aging. In R. H. Williams, C. Tibbitts, & W. Donohue (Eds.), *Processes of aging: Social and psychological perspectives*, (Vol. 1, pp. 299–320). New York: Atherton.

Havighurst, R. J., Neugarten, B. L., & Tobin, S. S. (1963). Disengagement, personality and life satisfaction in the later years. In P. F. Hansen (Ed.), *Age with a future* (pp. 419–425). Copenhagen: Munksgaard.

Larson, R., Zuzanek, J., & Mannell, R. (1985). Being alone versus being with people: disengagement in the daily experience of older adults. *Journal of Gerontology, 40*, 375–381.

Lawton, M. P. (1983). Environment and other determinants of well-being in older people. *The Gerontologist, 23*, 349–357.

Lemon, B. W., Bengtson, V. L., & Peterson, J. A. (1972). An exploration of the activity theory of aging: Activity types and life satisfaction among in-movers to a retirement community. *Journal of Gerontology, 27*, 511–523.

Longino, C. F., Jr., & Kart, C. S. (1982). Explicating activity theory: A formal replication. *Journal of Gerontology, 37*, 713–722.

Maddox, G. L. (1963). Activity and morale: A longitudinal study of selected elderly subjects. *Social Forces, 42*, 195–204.

Mannell, R. C. (1993). High-investment activity and life satisfaction among older adults. In J. R. Kelly (Ed.), *Activity and aging* (pp. 125–145). Newbury Park, CA: Sage.

Markus, H. R., & Herzog, A. R. (1991). The role of the self-concept in aging. *Annual Review of Gerontology and Geriatrics, 11*, 110–143.

Okun, M. A., Stock, W. A., Haring, M. J., & Witter, R. A. (1984). Health and subjective well-being: A meta-analysis. *International Journal of Aging and Human Development, 19*, 111–132.

Rosow, I. (1963). Adjustment of the normal aged. In R. H. Williams, C. Tibbitts, & W. Donohue (Eds.), *Processes of aging: Social and psychological perspectives* (Vol. 2, pp. 195–233). New York: Atherton.

ADAPTIVE CAPACITY

A major characteristic of living things is the ability to adapt to environmental changes. For example, upon perceiving a threat mammals will incur an immediate activation of the *sympathetic nervous system* that will stimulate heart and breathing rate in preparation for the increased metabolic demands of fighting or fleeing. If the metabolic demand is actually activated (for example, by running), heart and breathing rate will be further activated as long as the metabolic demand from the muscles continues. Similarly, exposure to a novel antigen will produce a robust activation of the *immune system*, including the proliferation of immune cells that produce antibodies against the novel antigen, a process that is essential to survive infections. At the cellular level, many toxic insults produce a characteristic profile of molecular responses, called the heat shock response, that is highly protective.

However, there are limits to the extent to which organisms can adapt. For example, each individual can only sustain a maximum metabolic demand even at peak performance (such as during a sprint). In humans the maximum sustainable metabolic demand, constrained by a number of factors but especially by cardiovascular capacity, is often measured by the rate of oxygen consumed at maximum short-term effort on a treadmill (a parameter called VO_{2max}). Thus VO_{2max} constitutes a major indicator of the capacity of the cardiovascular system to adapt to short-term metabolic stress; thus VO_{2max} may be considered to reflect short-term adaptive capacity for metabolic demand. It is has been amply demonstrated that in healthy humans VO_{2max} decreases steadily during aging, approximately 9% per decade (Rosen et al., 1998). Similarly, immune responses to novel antigens (McGlauchlen, 2003) and the heat shock response (Shamovsky, 2004) are increasingly attenuated with age.

On the other hand, short-term adaptive capacity can be modified by chronic stimulation, a phenomenon which may be termed long-term adaptive capacity. For example, repetitive *aerobic exercise* (for example, endurance training at 70% VO_{2max} for 30 minutes 3 times per week for 12 weeks) enhances VO_{2max}, apparently by inducing remodeling of the cardiovascular system. The enhancement of VO_{2max} by chronic training appears to occur about as well in healthy elderly men as in younger men, and older master athletes exhibit higher VO_{2max} than healthy older nontrained humans. Nevertheless, VO_{2max} decreases about as fast in athletes who are in training as in age-matched controls (although trained athletes continue to exhibit higher VO_{2max} than nontrained healthy controls as they age). Furthermore, since the effect of age on VO_{2max} is substantially greater than the training effect on VO_{2max}, even though training can enhance VO_{2max} about as well in older as in younger individuals, this effect of training cannot completely reverse or prevent the reduction in VO_{2max} during aging (Trappe et al., 1996).

Short-term and long-term adaptive capacity occur in response to many perturbations, including changes in temperature, altitude, diet, and many other environmental factors. In general, short-term adaptive capacity decreases with age. For example, a cold environment causes many physiological responses, including shivering and enhanced heat production, which allow maintainance of normal body temperature; these adaptations to cold are enhanced after chronic exposure to low temperature. As with VO_{2max} (and possibly related to this parameter), the ability to adapt to a cold environment is impaired with age (Anderson et al., 1996). However, chronic exposure to cold enhances adaptation to cold about as well in older as in younger individuals. Nevertheless, as with VO_{2max}, because the effect of age on cold tolerance is greater than the effect of chronic exposure to cold, chronic exposure to cold cannot fully reverse the effects of age on cold tolerance. This pattern of greater impairments of short-term than long-term adaptive capacity is common for many responses to environmental perturbations.

An important but largely unresolved question is the physiological significance of adaptive capacity during aging under circumstances in which environmental fluctuations are minimal, as in the case of most human populations. The fact that the elderly are more likely to die of *hyperthermia* or *hypothermia* clearly indicates that in extreme circumstances impairments in short-term adaptive capacity can have profound effects. On the other hand, the vast majority of deaths during aging, either in human populations or in the laboratory, occur without major fluctuations in the environment. Nevertheless, VO_{2max} is closely related to cardiovascular health, suggesting that long-term adaptive capacity, which is less impaired during aging than short-term adaptive capacity, could play an important role in mediating effects of lifestyle on health and mortality during aging (Bortz and Bortz, 1996). Since long-term adaptive capacity is relatively intact during aging, and especially since short-term adaptive capacity seems to be intrinsically reduced during aging, training and other lifestyle changes may be at least as valuable in the elderly as in the young. Consistent with this principle, elderly individuals who maintain a lifelong engagement with *intellectual stimulation* exhibit fewer cognitive impairments than nonengaged controls. While a training effect on age-related cognitive deficits has not yet been rigorously demonstrated, this question obviously is of great practical interest.

Adaptive capacity may reflect a fundamental process of aging. For example, long-lived lines of fruitflies and nematodes not only live longer, but even when young are more resistant to the effects of numerous environmental stresses than shorter-lived strains (Lin et al., 1998). Thus genetic influences on longevity also influence short-term adaptive capacity, suggesting that adaptive capacity may play an important role in age-related mortality even in benign environments.

CHARLES V. MOBBS

See also

Stress Theory of Aging
Successful Aging

References

Anderson, G. S., Meneilly, G. S., & Mekjavic, I. B. (1996). Passive temperature lability in the elderly. *European Journal of Applied Physiology*, *73*, 278–286.

Bortz, W. M., IV, & Bortz, W. M., II. (1996). How fast do we age? Exercise performance over time as a biomarker. *Journal of Gerontology: A Biological and Medical Science, 51*, M223–225.

Fitzgerald, M. D., Tanaka, H., Tran, Z. V., & Seals, D.R. (1997). Age-related declines in maximal aerobic capacity in regularly exercising vs. sedentary women: a meta-analysis. *Journal of Applied Physiology, 83*, 160–165.

Lin, Y. J., Seroude, L., & Benzer, S. (1998). Extended lifespan and stress resistance in the Drosophila mutant methuselah. *Science 282*, 943–946.

Rosen, M. J., Sorkin, J. D., Goldberg, A. P., Hagberg, J. M., & Katzel, L. I. (1998). Predictors of age-associated decline in maximal aerobic capacity: a comparison of four statistical models. *Journal of Applied Physiology, 84*, 2163–2170.

Trappe, S. W., Costill, D.L., Vukovich, M. D., Jones, J., & Melham, T. (1996). Aging among elite distance runners: A 22-yr longitudinal study. *Journal of Applied Physiology, 80*, 285–290.

ADHERENCE

When a physician prescribes a medication for a patient, an implied contract is made between the two—one requiring specific behaviors by both doctor and patient. The doctor must prescribe the correct drug in the proper dose, provide the patient with adequate instructions for its use and warnings about possible adverse effects, and monitor the patient's use of the drug to ensure a therapeutic outcome. The patient is expected to purchase the medication, take it as directed, and report to the physician any untoward side effects—in other words, to adhere to the doctor's instructions. For elderly patients, adherence may be particularly difficult, given their greater risk of adverse effects from medication.

Types of *Nonadherence*

Nonadherence (or noncompliance, as it is still sometimes called) can be classified as overuse, underuse, erratic use, and contraindicated (or inappropriate) use. Patients who overuse drugs either take more types of drugs than necessary, take more than the prescribed amount of one drug, or take a "pm" (i.e., take as needed) drug when it is not actually needed. Underuse includes the failure to have the prescription filled ("initial noncompliance"), the premature discontinuation of the drug, and the consistent failure to take as much of the drug as the doctor ordered. Erratic use means that the patient generally fails to follow instructions. This type includes missed doses (underuse), double doses (overuse), and drug confusion, which is taking the wrong drug by mistake or taking doses at the wrong time, by the wrong route of administration, or with the wrong liquid. Contraindicated drug use occurs when the patient takes a drug that is inappropriate either because it is unnecessary or potentially harmful. This can occur when the older patient selfmedicates incorrectly or when the physician prescribes the wrong drug—one that is ineffective, produces a harmful or unwanted side effect, or interacts negatively with other medications being taken, food, or alcohol. Obviously, these four types of nonadherence are not mutually exclusive, and the older patient may engage in more than one at a time.

Most researchers agree that the failure to take medications (underuse) is by far the most common type of nonadherence, generally comprising over half of all reported instances (e.g., Gurwitz, Glynn, Monane, Everitt, Gilden, Smith, et al., 1993). Although underuse can have serious consequences for a person for whom the medication is necessary for control of a dangerous condition, it is probably the safest form of misuse for those who take psychotropic medications and many of those on multiple drug regimens. This behavior has been termed intelligent noncompliance.

Shimp and Ascione (1988) have differentiated between unintentional nonadherence, when the patient merely forgets a dose or gets confused about how or when to take it, and intentional nonadherence, which occurs when the patient deliberately alters the dose or the timing or chooses not take it at all. Evidence suggests that intentional nonadherence may be more common with up to 30% of prescriptions never even filled by the patient. A majority of older patients state that they would discontinue taking a drug that they felt was not working and self-medicators will stop using a drug or, use less because they do not like the drug, the dosage, the side effects, or the cost; or they get better results by taking it their way.

Extent of Nonadherence

It is extremely difficult to estimate how often physicians do not live up to their responsibilities under the doctor-patient contract; the consensus is that the failure rate is quite high (Simonson, 1994). We have somewhat better data on the patient's side of the bargain. Nonadherence is, of course, a problem in patients of all ages. Early researchers suggested that nonadherence is particularly likely among elderly persons, because it is known to correlate highly with several factors common to old age, including chronic illness, multiple prescription drugs, social isolation, and mental confusion. Later reviews of adherence studies, however (e.g., Simonson, 1984), concluded that no clear evidence exists of any relationship between age and adherence. Simonson (1984) reports that researchers have estimated that nonadherence by the elderly ranges from 2% to 95%. Most studies place the proportion of older people who admit some nonadherence in taking prescription drugs at around 40%–60% (Botelho & Dudrak, 1992), although many instances probably are not therapeutically significant.

Nevertheless, Ascione (1994) argues that nonadherence in an older person is likely to have much more serious consequences than in a younger individual because of the elder's greater likelihood of serious illness and comorbidity. The results of nonadherence in older persons include failure to recover, aggravation of the condition, hospitalization, and the addition of medications to treat the supposed intractable symptoms. So far, few investigators have attended to sex or race differences in adherence, though some findings suggest that they may exist (Bazargan, Barbre, & Hamm, 1993; Kail, 1992).

Causes of Nonadherence

Many factors can contribute to nonadherence among older persons. Simonson (1984) has organized them into three main groups: those related to the patient, to therapy, and to the health professional. Patient-related causes include failure to understand the importance of therapy; misunderstanding the doctor's instructions; self-medication; not feeling well; physical disabilities, including sensory losses; and lack of supervision. Factors associated with the therapy itself include the number of drugs prescribed, the frequency of doses, difficult dosage forms, adverse drug reactions, and the expense of medications. Health professionals, including physicians, nurses, and pharmacists, also can precipitate nonadherence in their elderly patients by failing to establish a good relationship with the patient, expressing doubt about the drug's efficacy, and being unwilling to spend time educating patients. Using a different organization scheme, Ascione (1994) lists the contributing factors as: (1) complexity of the drug regimen; (2) the patient's poor drug knowledge; (3) the patient's physical limitations (especially sensory losses); (4) poor communication between professional and patient; and (5) psychosocial characteristics of the patient, such as health beliefs and social isolation.

Some researchers (e.g., Morrell, Park, Kidder, & Martin, 1997) have suggested poor cognitive function, especially memory problems and the inability to understand complex medical instructions, as a possible cause of nonadherence in older people. Research so far seems to show that both memory and visual perception can affect adherence, at least among the oldest-old, and that various memory aids can improve adherence (Morrow, Hier, Menard, & Leirer, 1998). On the other hand, nonadherence is patient-initiated *and* represents a majority of older people's attempts to control their own therapy. Thus, it seems likely that cognitive deficits are a significant cause of nonadherence for older persons who suffer such losses but may have little or no effect on the vast majority of elders.

Older people are at risk of nonadherence due to many factors outside their control, including their own health status, the number and types of drugs they are prescribed, the failure of therapeutic instructions, health care organization costs, and social isolation. In fact, nonadherence can create significant problems for elderly persons (Ascione, 1994), but many writers (e.g., Simonson, 1994) agree that, "compared with the inability of health care professionals to prescribe and administer drugs properly and to monitor their use by older patients, nonadherence is relatively less troublesome."

Reducing Noncompliance

Ascione (1994) aptly summarizes what little is known about reducing nonadherence among older persons: "What appears most successful is a comprehensive approach that assesses the individual needs of the patient, uses multiple strategies and incorporates a medication monitoring system to give continual feedback to the patient." He groups the strategies developed so far as dissemination of drug information, simplification of the administration process, and teaching medication management skills.

FRANK J. WHITTINGTON

See also
Doctor-Patient Relationships

References

Ascione F. (1994). Medication compliance in the elderly. *Generations, 18,* 28–33.

Bazargan, M., Barbre, A. M., & Hamm, V., Failure to have prescriptions filled among Black elderly. *Journal of Aging and Health, 5,* 264–282.

Botelho M. B., & Dudrak R. (1992). Home assessment of adherence to long-term medication in the elderly. *Journal of Family Practice, 35,* 61–65.

Gurwitz, J. H., Glynn, R. J., Monane, M., Everitt, D. E., Gilden, D., Smith, N., & Avorn, J. (1993). Treatment for glaucoma: Adherence by the elderly. *American Journal of Public Health, 83,* 711–716.

Kail, B. L. (Ed.). (1992). *Special problems on non-compliance among elderly women of color*. Lewiston, NY: Academic Press.

Morrell, R. W., Park, D. C., Kidder, D. P., & Martin, M. (1997). Adherence to antihypertensive medications across the life span. *The Gerontologist, 37,* 609–619.

Morrow, D. G., Hier, C. M., Menard, W. E., & Leirer, V. O. (1998). Icons improve older and younger adults' comprehension of medication information. *Journal of Gerontology: Psychological Sciences, 53B,* P240–P254.

Shimp, L. A.., & Ascione, F. J. (1988). Causes of medication misuse and error. *Generations, 12,* 17–21.

Simonson, W. (1984). *Medications and the elderly: A guide for promoting proper use*. Rockville, MD: Aspen Systems Corporation.

Simonson, W. (1994). Geriatric drug therapy: Who are the stakeholders? *Generations, 18,* 7–12.

ADJUSTMENT

See
Adaptive Capacity

ADL/IDL

See
Activities of Daily Living

ADULT DAY CARE

Adult Day Care Services

Adult day services (ADS) are "community-based group programs designed to meet the needs of functionally and/or cognitively impaired adults through an individual plan of care" (*National Adult Day Services Association [NADSA]*, 2002). These programs provide a variety of health, social, and personal services in a protective setting. Most programs provide activities, meals, social services, personal assistance, and health services; others include nursing and medical services, rehabilitation therapies, counseling, and transportation. ADS vary greatly depending on whether they follow a medical, social, or combination model; whether they are dedicated to special populations (e.g., aged, disabled, Alzheimer's care, and developmentally disabled); or whether they are for persons of all ages. For example, dementia-care programs may provide cognitive stimulation, family counseling, and music therapy (Jarrott, Zarit, Berg, & Johansson, 1998). ADS goals include improving participant functioning and independence; delaying or preventing placement in residential care; and alleviating caregiver burden.

ADS regulations vary widely across states and funding sources. Some states require licensure or certification; some have voluntary standards; still others require nothing. The *Commission on Accreditation of Rehabilitation Facilities (CARF)* voluntarily accredits ADS programs as a way to maintain standards through an agreement with NADSA. No federal policy governs *adult day health services (ADHS)* apart from the *Program of All Inclusive Care for the Elderly (PACE)*, a model of acute and chronic care for elderly persons that is based on day health care and funded by Medicare and Medicaid. Medicaid also funds ADHS under 1915c HCBS waivers. Forty-five states report having waivers that include ADHS for persons meeting nursing home level-of-care criteria (http://www.cms.hhs.gov/medicaid/waivers). Federal funding of ADS comes through the Social Security Act including Medicaid (Title XIX), Social Services Block Grants-Title XX (SSBG), and the Older Americans Act (Title III). Other funding sources vary and include private pay, philanthropic support, other state programs, and private long-term care insurance. State programs vary widely for eligibility, program goals and standards, services, staffing, reimbursement, and monitoring (Howell-White, Scotto Rosato, & Lucas, 2003; Lucas, Scotto Rosato, Lee, & Howell-White, 2001). Adult day health care is not a Medicare reimbursable service, although Medicare reimburses for rehabilitative services (i.e., physical, occupational, and speech therapy) delivered in some adult day health settings. The recent Medicare Modernization Act of 2003 allows for a demonstration of ADHS as a substitute for Medicare reimbursable home health care.

A recent national survey of ADS conducted by *Partners in Caregiving* (Cox, 2003) reported that 3407 adult day centers are operating in the United States, which represents a 25% growth rate between 1997 and 2002. For-profit programs represented the greatest growth sector in new programs (44%). Characteristics of centers reported in this survey include the facts that 78% are not-for-profit; most (74%) are affiliated with a larger organization; most operate 5 days a week for an 8 to 10 hour day; 21% are based on the medical model, 37% are social, and 42% are combination programs; the average number of enrollees is 43, with an average daily attendance of 26; average cost is $56 per day. Participant average age is 72, 66% are women, and more than 50% have some cognitive impairment. Most participants attend 2 to 3 days a week for 5 to 6 hours, with participants enrolled for an average of 2 years.

NADSA is the national association for ADS providers. It serves as an important resource for ADS programs, providing "national program standards and guidelines," technical assistance, training, national conferences, newsletter, Web site, and advocacy with policymakers (NADSA, The National Adult Day Services Association, Inc. 772 Grant Street, Suite L, Herndon, VA 20170. www.nadsa.org).

Partners in Caregiving is another resource. This program is funded by RWJF and located at Wake Forest University. This program provides technical assistance to improve financial viability and quality with, teaching centers, a newsletter and Web site. Its work demonstrates that ADS can effectively serve people with chronic conditions (see http://www.rwjf.org/reports/npreports/partnerse.htm). (Partners in Caregiving, Wake Forest University School of Medicine, Medical Center Boulevard, Winston-Salem NC, 27157.)

Research in ADS

The seminal work by Weissert (1976; 1977) surveyed 10 adult day programs. Analysis resulted in conceptualizing the programs into the "medical" model (provides rehabilitative therapies) and "social" model (stresses social activities, client function, nutrition, and recreation). Using data from the National Adult Day Care Survey (Weissert et al., 1989) these prevailing models were expanded by Conrad and associates (1993) to include "special purpose" centers (i.e., serve single type of clientele). The *Dementia Care Respite Services Program* (Cox and Reifler, 1994; Reifler, Henry, Sherrill, Asbury, & Bodford, 1992) described dementia-specific adult day care. Their national survey of 240 centers found: 17% were social; 25% were medical; and the remaining were a combination medical-social model.

Program Effectiveness Research

Gaugler and Zarit (2001) provide a recent systematic review of ADS program effectiveness research. Their schema organizes program effectiveness research according to the ADS goals of client functioning, caregiver outcomes, and impact on institutionalization. A notable study by Weissert and colleagues (1980) used an experimental design to evaluate four programs (including On Lok) but found negligible effect on ADL functioning. Satisfaction was very high for 82.2% of clients (Weissert et al., 1990). This was followed by an evaluation of 24 California programs by Capitman (1982) which found 90% of enrollees maintained or improved ADL function. A large-scale study by Hedrick and associates (1993) determined the effect of adult day health care compared to usual care on health and psychosocial status at eight Veterans Affairs (VA) medical centers over one year. There were no differences in psychosocial, ADL functioning or health, but costs were significantly higher than for clients assigned to usual care. While large, their sample was 96% male and the effectiveness of social programs was not addressed. Gaugler (1999) in a quasi-experimental study of adult day services for dementia caregivers, did not find significant differences in frequency of behavior problems or ADL dependencies. Evaluations of ADS as part of integrated demonstration programs have also been conducted. Eng and colleagues (1997) found PACE clients had lower mortality rates when compared to nursing home residents.

Studies of impact on *family caregivers* have reported that ADS can be quite effective in providing caregivers with emotional and psychological relief from the daily demands of care with sustained and regular utilization. A noteworthy example is the *Adult Day Care Collaborative Study (ADCCS)* (Zarit et al., 1998) that found utilization of ADS for at least 8 hours per week over at least 3 months resulted in significantly lower feelings of role overload, worry, depression, and anger. Replicating these results in a large-scale study was attempted in the *Medicare Alzheimer's Disease Demonstration Evaluation (MADDE)* by Newcomer and colleagues (1998). Caregivers in the treatment group reported significantly less depression and burden, but effect sizes were small. Using longitudinal data from the ADCCS, Jarrott and colleagues (1999) found caregiver satisfaction to be high with ADS staff, program availability, and activities.

Experts have also been interested in whether ADS act as a substitute for or delay institutionalization. Weissert and colleagues' study (1980) found participation in ADS lowered nursing home use. California's evaluation, Capitman (1982) focused on nursing-home eligible clients and found ADS delayed placement about 15 to 22 months. For caregivers, Kosloski and Montgomery (1995) reported high respite use lowered probability of institutional care; however, Gaugler (1999) found that dementia clients using ADS were more likely to be placed in nursing homes. The large scale VA and MADDE studies (Hedrick et al., 1993; Newcomer et al., 1998) did not show significant effects on institutionalization. However, Weissert and associates (1997) in evaluating Arizona's Long-Term Care System (ALTCS) comprised of many HCBS, found nursing home days were reduced when eligibility was "targeted" to those who were screened most likely to need long-term nursing home care. In 2004, Dabelko explored ADHS length of stay and reported that those older, at higher nutritional risk, nonwhite, and receiving public funding, disenrolled at higher rates. Lack of social support, cultural issues, and higher disability levels for later enrolled publicly funded clients were seen as important to earlier disenrollment. ADS stays were both for short-term and long-term care, indicating ADS may provide multiple roles in the continuum of care for older adults.

Other recent ADS studies have focused on changing client characteristics (Cefalu, Ettinger, & Espeland, 1996; Travis, Steele, & Long, 2001), funding streams, and policy issues. For example, Bradsher, Estes, & Stuart (1995) identified program growth, rising demand, and higher levels and chronicity of disability among ADS clients and noted the barriers to access for persons with dementia or behavior problems. Dabelko and Balaswamy (2000) compared users of ADS and home health care (HHC) users. ADS users were younger, had greater cognitive impairment, needed more supervised assistance with ADLs, and had more social contacts than HHC users—suggesting the need for integrated models (physical, mental, and social services) for both settings.

The research so far implies that ADS does not affect functional outcomes consistently, but appears to exert positive effects on subjective aspects of well-being, such as satisfaction. Work with PACE suggests that ADHS programs may serve as an important setting that can provide the coordinating link in a continuum of long-term care services, when enhanced with case management and access to acute care and chronic care services. The models that integrate ADS with adult day care with a variety of services and case management, such as PACE and ALTCS, appear effective in delaying nursing home use.

JUDITH A. LUCAS

See also

Program of All-Inclusive Care for the Elderly (PACE)

References

Bradsher, J. E., Estes, C. L., & Stuart, M. H. (1995). Adult day care: A fragmented system of policy and funding streams. *Journal of Aging & Social Policy, 7*(1), 17–38.

Capitman, J. A. (1982). Evaluation of adult day health care programs in California pursuant to Assembly Bill 1611, Chapter 1066, Statutes of 1977. Sacramento: Office of Long-term Care and Aging, Department of Health Services.

Cefalu, C., Ettinger, W., & Espeland, M. (1996). A study of the characteristics of the dementia patients and caregivers in dementia-nonspecific adult day care programs. *The Journal of the American Geriatrics Society, 44*(6), 654–659.

Conrad, K. J., Hughes, S. L., Hanrahan, P., & Wang, S. (1993). Classification of adult day care: A cluster analysis of services and activities. *Journal of Gerontology: Social Sciences, 48*(3), S112–122.

Cox, N. J. (2003). *National Study of Adult Day Services 2001–2002.* Partners in Caregiving: The Adult Day Services Program, Winston-Salem, NC: Wake Forest University School of Medicine.

Cox, N. J., & Reifler, B. V. (1994). Dementia Care and Respite Services Program. *Alzheimer's Disease and Associated Disorders, 8*(3), 113–121.

Dabelko, H. I. (2004). Individual and environmental factors that influence length of stay in adult day care programs. *Journal of Gerontological Social Work, 43*(1), 83–105.

Dabelko, H. I. & Balaswamy, S. (2000). Use of adult day services and home health care services by older adults: A comparative analysis. *Home Health Care Services Quarterly, 18*(3), 65–79.

Eng, C., Padulla, J. Eleazer, G. P., McCann, R., & Fox, N. (1997). Program of All-Inclusive Care for the Elderly (PACE): An innovative model of integrated geriatric care and financing. *Journal of American Geriatrics Society, 45,* 223–232.

Gaugler, J. E. & Zarit, S. H. (2001). The effectiveness of adult day services for disabled older people. *Journal of Aging & Social Policy, 12*(2), 23–47.

Gaugler, J. E. (1999). *Evaluating community-based care for people with dementia: The cost-effectiveness of adult day services*. Unpublished PhD dissertation, The Pennsylvania State University, University Park.

Hedrick, S. C., Rothman, M. L., Chapko, M., Ehreth, J. Diehr, P. Inui, T. S., et al., (1993). Summary and discussion of methods and results of the Adult Day Health Care Evaluation Study. *Medical Care, 31,* SS94–103.

Howell-White, S., Scotto Rosato, N., & Lucas, J. A. (Nov., 2003). Adult Day Health Services Across States: Results from a 50 State Survey of State Health Policies. Slide Presentation available at http://www.cshp@rutgers.edu/presentations. Accessed 10/06/04.

Jarrott, S. E., Zarit, S. H., Berg, S., & Johansson, L. (1998). Adult day care for dementia: A comparison of programs in Sweden and the Unites States. *Journal of Cross-Cultural Gerontology, 13,* 99–108.

Jarrott, S. E., Zarit, S.H., Stephens, M.A., Townsend, A. & Greene, R. (1999). Caregiver satisfaction with adult day service programs. *American Journal of Alzheimer's Disease, 14*(4), 233–244.

Kosloski, K., & Montgomery, R. J. (1995). The impact of respite care use on nursing home placement. *The Gerontologist, 35,* 67–74.

Lucas, J.A., Scotto Rosato, N., Lee, J.A. & Howell-White, S. (Dec 10, 2001). Adult Day Health Services: A Review of the Literature. Report for the N. J. Department of Health and Senior Services, Rutgers University: Center for State Health Policy. Available at http://www.cshp@rutgers.edu/papers. Accessed 10/06/04.

National Adult Day Care Services Association (2002). Mission statement. Available at http://www.nadsa.org. Accessed 10/06/04.

Newcomer, R., Fox, P., Yordi, C., Wilkinson, A., Arnsberger, P., Donatonni, G., et al. (1998). *Medicare Alzheimer's Disease Demonstration Evaluation: Final Report.* San Francisco: Institute for Health and Aging, University of California.

Reifler, B. V., Henry, R. S., Sherrill, K. A., Asbury, C. H., & Bodford, J. S. (1992). A national demonstration program on dementia day centers and respite services: An interim report. *Behavioral Health & Aging, 2,* 199–205.

Travis, S., Steele, L., & Long, A. (2001). Adult day services in a frontier state. *Nursing Economics, 19*(2), 62–67.

Weissert, W. G. (1976). Two models of geriatric day care. *The Gerontologist, 16*(5) 420–427.

Weissert, W. G. (1977). Adult day care programs in the United States: Current research projects and a survey of 10 centers. *Public Health Reports, 92*(1), 49–56.

Weissert, W.G., Wan, T., Livieratos, B., & Katz, B. (1980). Effects and costs of day-care services for the chronically ill. *Medical Care, 18,* 567–584.

Weissert, W.G., Elston, J.M., Bolda, E.J., Cready, C.M., Zelman, W.N., Sloane, P.D., Kalsbeek, W.D., et al. (1989). Models of adult day care: Findings from a national survey. *The Gerontologist, 29,* 640–649.

Weissert, W.G., Elston, J.M., Bolda, E.J., Zelman, W.N., Mutran, E. & Mangum, A.B. (1990). *Adult day care: Findings from a national survey*. Baltimore, MD: John Hopkins University Press.

Weissert, W.G., Lesnick, T., Musliner, M., & Foley, K.A. (1997). Cost savings from home and community-based services: Cost savings from Arizona's Medicaid long-term care program. *Journal of Health Politics, Policy, & Law, 22*(6), 1329–1357.

Zarit, S. H., Stephens, M.A. Townsend, A., & Greene, R. (1998). Stress reduction for family caregivers: Effects of adult day care use. *Journal of Gerontology, 5,* S267–278.

ADULT DEVELOPMENT

Adult development refers to normative and non-normative changes in the physical, cognitive, and psychosocial domains, which occur between age 20 and 65 years. These physical, cognitive, and psychosocial *developmental changes* in adulthood are highly variable depending on which stage in adult development is being examined. For instance, while *early adulthood* is characterized by growth and vitality, *midlife* is a stage where some developmental domains reach their full potential and other domains have *developmental declines* that become more common and noticeable. In contrast, *later adulthood* is characterized by the challenges of physical and cognitive decline, as well as psychosocial loss. However, many of these changes are not universal, so any discussion of adult development must be conditioned upon significant, interindividual variability.

Traditionally, *developmental research* has largely ignored adulthood in favor of childhood and adolescence. With the rise of the *life-span* prospective (review in Baltes, Staudinger, & Lindenberger, 1999) there has been an increased attention to old age and more recently to midlife (Lachman, 2004; Ryff, Singer, & Seltzer, 2002) and *young adulthood*; however, the focus on adult development still does not reach the degree of focus on childhood and adolescence. The age boundaries of each stage of adult development are somewhat vague and arbitrary, but most would agree that young adulthood encompasses between ages 20 and 40; midlife at least the years between 40 and 55, and at most from 35 to 65 years (Staudinger & Bluck, 2001); and late adulthood begins at age 65.

Three pioneers in life-span developmental psychology have focused on development in adulthood and should be mentioned: Erikson, Loevinger, and Levinson. Erikson's (1985) stage theory of *psychosocial development* posits that as individuals move through life, they experience distinct crisis regarding a developmental issue important to the current phase of their life. According to Erikson, the normative crisis of early adulthood concerns "*intimacy versus isolation*," in which the individual seeks to make a commitment to another individual. The normative crisis of midlife concerns the topic of "*generativity versus stagnation*," which challenges the individual in the area of assisting and mentoring young people and thus guiding the next generation. In later life the individual is concerned with acceptance of their life and impending death. This stage is referred to as "*ego integrity versus despair*." If an individual does not successfully master each of these goals, he or she experiences psychological distress related to the developmental topic.

A second theory of adult development builds on the work by *Erikson* and focuses on *ego development* (Loevinger, 1997). According to *Loevinger*, adult ego development moves through stages pertaining to conformity, conscientiousness, individualism, autonomy, and finally, in late adulthood, integration. A third conceptual approach addressing development in adulthood is Levinson's "*seasons*" *of adulthood* (1986). The main goal of the season in early adulthood concerns the establishment of a family. During the midlife season, Levinson suggests that although biological capacities are decreasing, individuals are still able to maintain active and energetic lives. In addition, he also suggests that during this time of development, individuals are responsible for the current generation's development. Finally, the late adulthood season is characterized as a period of reflection of one's life and acceptance of impending death.

Physical, Sensory, and Cognitive Development in Adulthood

Adulthood is a time of life characterized mostly by growth and stability, but over the *adult life span* loss and decline begins (Heckhausen, 2001). Levels of stability or decline differ greatly in different areas of physical, sensory, and cognitive functioning. Although there is great interindividual variability, some of the most noticeable *signs of aging* across the life span include the loss of pigmentation leading to the *graying of hair*, *thinning of hair caused* by hair germination center destruction, rigidity of the skin's dermal layer leading to *wrinkling*, and changes in the strength and tone of voice (Whitbourne, 2001). Less noticeable signs of aging, which may affect many individuals in adulthood, include decrease in bone density, decline in muscle mass, visual and auditory deterioration, changes in cardiovascular fitness and respiratory functioning, and changes in body regulation (e.g. decreased basal metabolism rates, endocrine and immune function, and sexual changes) (Masoro & Austad, 2001).

In general, *cognitive changes in adulthood* are much more subtle than physical changes. Young adulthood is characterized as a time when cognitive abilities reach their peak levels (Lehman, 1945; Ericsson, 2000). Losses in midlife are primarily at the level of peak performances in that only at times when performance is pushed to its limits by optimizing training and performance conditions do declines in developmental reserve capacity become apparent (Lindenberger, Marsiske, & Baltes, 2000). A prominent theoretical perspective for interpreting cognitive developmental change is the distinction between fluid and crystallized intelligence (Horn & Cattell, 1966), or as in a more recent conceptualization between the pragmatics and mechanics of intelligence (Baltes, 1987). *Crystallized intelligence* refers to general knowledge developed through a lifetime of experiences (accumulated knowledge) (Sternberg, Grigorenko, & Oh, 2001). In contrast, *fluid intelligence* refers to "creative and flexible thinking" required to solve novel problems (e.g. anagrams, memory tests). In general, research examining age-related changes in fluid and crystallized intelligence has found that fluid intelligence declines with age, but crystallized intelligence remains stable or even increases (e.g. professional specialization) across the life span (Kaufman & Horn, 1996). However, in a more detailed examination of cognitive decline in fluid intelligence, it is important to distinguish between fluid intelligence pertaining to the solving of more practical problems and that pertaining to more traditional (academic) problem-solving tasks. Performance on traditional problem-solving tasks begins to decline around age 20 years and continues to decline throughout adulthood, whereas performance on practical *problem-solving tasks* peaks in midlife, suggesting that it is at this time that individuals are best at practical problem-solving (Sternberg, Grigorenko, & Oh, 2001).

In their related *dual-processing model*, Baltes and colleagues (1999) distinguish between the mechanics of intelligence that generally refer to processing abilities (information-processing strategies and problem-solving functions) independent of specific content, and the pragmatics of intelligence that typically refers to knowledge about facts and procedures, including *practical thinking*, *expertise*, *wisdom*, and knowledge accumulated across the life span. While the pragmatics of intelligence are expected to grow into adulthood and then remain stable into old age, there is abundant evidence of age-related decline in the mechanics of intelligence (Salthouse, 2003). The declines in mechanics of intelligence compromise individual capacities beginning in midlife only under conditions of multitasking and time pressure (Lindenberger, Marsiske, & Baltes, 2000). Thus, implications of these declines for everyday functioning in midlife are constrained to time-sensitive *multitasking* in everyday behavior (e.g., talking on the phone while merging into freeway traffic) and select professions (e.g., air traffic controllers). Strategies that are part of the *pragmatics of intelligence* (e.g., sequence activities to avoid multitask overload) in midlife can compensate for the weaknesses in the mechanics of intelligence (Baltes, 1993). However, such strategies may become increasingly insufficient as cognitive decline progresses in advanced old age.

Psychosocial Influences on Development in Adulthood

Adaptation to growth and resilience in managing losses are 2 key focuses in adult development (Heckhausen, 1999). Several developmental tasks and transitions represent important challenges for adaptation and resilience. First, adulthood is a period of continued growth but also of emerging decline and loss. In comparison to early adulthood, midlife into late adulthood (the 40s, 50s, 60s, and beyond) is marked by a dramatic increase in developmental changes that are loss-related. However, many developmental processes continue to advance in midlife (e.g., expertise) and even into old age (e.g. improved emotional balance). Thus, individuals have to cope with the co-occurrence of *growth and decline* (Heckhausen, 1999), perhaps more so during midlife than during any other phase of the life span. The individual needs to orchestrate the allocation of resources so that areas of functioning involving growth are optimized and other areas of impeding loss are protected.

Second, during adulthood the pronounced perspective on life shifts toward an increasing awareness of the "finitude of life." While in early adulthood the future is open and many paths seem viable, in midlife there is a focus shift from time lived from birth to time left before death. An aspect of Erikson's (1963) developmental theory concerns the acceptance that the time left until death is limited and it is only through acceptance that *ego integrity* can be achieved. Because of this change in perspective, individuals may begin to view goals as unattainable, which then may lead to *goal disengagement*. The passing of these "developmental deadlines" can result in strong needs for emotion regulation and goal readjustments (Heckhausen, Wrosch, & Fleeson, 2001). Goals that are now "off time" are sacrificed for goals that can still be obtained. For goals that must be abandoned (e.g. due to the "biological clock" for procreation running out) individuals may need to cope with the loss of the goal through *emotion regulation*. Losses in old age often require further disengagement and selective optimization (Baltes & Baltes, 1990) of most cherished and/or essential areas of functioning (Schulz & Heckhausen, 1996). Regret of the lost goals may lead to depression and rumination and an increased need to cope with the loss.

Finally, developmental challenges in adulthood can vary with regard to whether they are *age normative* and nonnormative. Changes in physical (e.g. menopause) and cognitive (e.g. decreases in fluid intelligence) functioning are considered to be age normative and as such may be easier to cope with because the individual can prepare for the change and disengage in the goals associated with the decline. In contrast, *nonnormative challenges* cannot be predicted, so the adaptation to the developmental change can be more challenging and as such, there may be higher regulatory demands. For example, a cancer diagnosis is unpredictable and as such it will be more challenging and require more resources to adapt to the change.

Because of the many age-specific burdens and challenges in various stages of adulthood, the conclusion might be reached that these challenges overwhelm individuals. Indeed, the notion of a midlife crisis suggests that developmental losses, rising awareness of the finitude of life, and opportunities lost result in *depression* and problem behavior in a majority of midlife adults (Whitbourne, 1986; Hunter & Sundel, 1989). Although Jacques (1965) suggested that the *midlife crisis* is a normative developmental milestone generally accepted by the greater public, there is little empirical evidence to suggest that the midlife crisis is either normative or widespread (Hunter & Sundel, 1989). In fact, most research on midlife development has found that midlife is a period with "continuous development, maintained well-being, adaptivity, and resilience" (Heckhausen, 2001).

For many of the challenges encountered during adulthood, individuals have appropriate strategies for mastering them or at least avoiding the socio-emotionally debilitating consequences. Specifically there are 3 types of regulatory resources available to deal with stressful situations: social support and social relations, general psychological resources, and specific control strategies for managing the stress of the loss. First, social support involves instrumental and emotional support from others in one's social network. Second, general psychological resources comprise such personality characteristics as ego resiliency (Block & Block, 1980) or generalized *self-efficacy* beliefs (Bandura, 1977). Finally, strategies for managing the challenges of midlife include control striving, experience and knowledge about adult development, and the existence of multiple roles and identities. Control strategies of developmental regulation help individuals to match their goal selections (e.g., whether to focus on career goals or have a child) to the opportunities available at the particular age and its developmental ecology. Thus, for example, an impeding deadline related to declining fertility might prompt a woman and/or her partner in early midlife to give priority to founding a family over pushing for advances in their career, whereas later in midlife other priorities take precedence (Heckhausen, Wrosch, & Fleeson, 2001). Sets of control strategies orchestrated for goal engagement or, for *goal disengagement*, can help the individual to address the transitions from better to worse opportunities in an organized and efficient manner.

Thus, during adulthood, each of its phases has its own set of challenges, opportunities, and risks for development. Many of these challenges involve the potential for disillusionment, decline, and loss. Growth and loss co-occur and confront the individual with converse regulatory challenges. It is most impressive to see how most individuals fare well across these transitions.

Sarah F. Roper-Coleman
Jutta Heckhausen

See also
- Life Course
- Life-Span Theory of Control
- Personality
- Selection, Optimization, and Compensation Model
- Successful Aging

References

Baltes, P. B. (1987). Theoretical propositions of life-span developmental psychology: On the dynamics between growth and decline. *Developmental Psychology, 23*, 611–626.

Baltes, P. B. (1993). The aging mind: Potential and limits. *Gerontologist, 33*, 580–594.

Baltes, P. B., & Baltes, M. M. (1990). Psychological perspectives on successful aging: The model of selective optimization with compensation. In P. B. Baltes & M. M. Baltes (Eds.), *Successful aging: Perspectives from the behavioral sciences* (pp. 1–34). New York: Cambridge University Press.

Baltes, P. B., Staudinger, U. M., & Lindenberger, U. (1999). Lifespan psychology: Theory and application to intellectual functioning. *Annual Review of Psychology, 50*, 471–507.

Bandura, A. (1977). Toward a unifying theory of behavioral change. *Psychological Review, 84*(2), 191–215.

Block, J. H., & Block, J. (1980). The role of ego-control and ego-resiliency in the organization of behavior. In W. A. Collins (Ed.), *Development of cognition, affect, and social relations* (pp. 39–101). Hillsdale, NJ: Erlbaum.

Ericsson, K. A. (2000). How experts attain and maintain superior performance: Implications for the enhancement of skilled performance in older individuals. *Journal of Aging and Physical Activity, 8*(4), 366–372.

Erikson, E. H. (1985). *The life cycle completed*. New York: Norton.

Heckhausen, J. (1999). *Developmental regulation in adulthood: Age-normative and sociostructural constraints as adaptive challenges*. New York: Cambridge University Press.

Heckhausen, J. (2001). Adaptation and resilience in midlife. In M. E. Lachman (Ed.), *Handbook of midlife development* (pp. 345–394). New York: John Wiley.

Heckhausen, J., Wrosch, C., & Fleeson, W. (2001). Developmental regulation before and after a developmental deadline: The sample case of "biological clock" for child-bearing. *Psychology and Aging, 16*, 400–413.

Horn, J. L., & Cattell, R. B. (1966). Refinement and test of the theory of fluid and crystallized intelligence. *Journal of Educational Psychology, 57*, 253–270.

Hunter, S., & Sundel, M. (1989). Introduction: An examination of key issues concerning midlife. In S. Hunter & M. Sundel (Eds.), *Midlife myths: Issues, findings, and practice implications* (pp. 8–28). Newbury Park, CA: Sage Publications.

Jacques, E. (1965). Death and the midlife crisis. *International Journal of Psychoanalysis, 46*, 502–514.

Kaufman, A. S., & Horn, J. L. (1996). Age changes on tests of fluid and crystallized ability for women and men on the Kaufman Adolescent and Adult Intelligence Test (KAIT) at ages 17–94 years. *Archives of Clinical Neuropsychology, 11*(2), 97–121.

Lachman, M. E. (2004). Development in midlife. *Annual Review of Psychology, 55*, 305–331.

Lehman, H. C. (1945). "Intellectual" vs. "physical peak" performance. *Scientific Monthly, 61*, 127–137.

Levinson, D. (1986). A conception of adult development. *American Psychologist, 41*, 3–13.

Lindenberger, U., Marsiske, M., & Baltes, P. B. (2000). Memorizing while walking: Increase in dual-task costs from young adulthood to old age. *Psychology and Aging, 15*, 417–436.

Loevinger, J. (1997). Stages of personality development. In R. Hogan & J. A. Johnson, et al. (Eds.), *Handbook of personality psychology*. St. Louis: Washing University, Department of Psychology.

Masoro, E. J., & Austad, S. N. (2001). *The handbook of the biology of aging*. San Diego: Academic Press.

Ryff, C. D., Singer, B. H., & Seltzer, M. M. (2002). Pathways through challenges: Implications for well-being and health. In L. Pulkkinen & A. Caspi (Eds.), *Pathways to successful development: Personality in the life course* (pp. 302–328). New York: Cambridge University Press.

Salthouse, T. A. (2003). Interrelations of aging, knowledge, and cognitive performance. In U. M. Staudinger & U. Lindenberger (Eds.), *Understanding human development: Dialogues with lifespan psychology* (pp. 265–287). Dordrecht, Netherlands: Kluwer Academic Publishers.

Schulz, R., & Heckhausen, J. (1996). A life-span model of successful aging. *American Psychologist, 51*, 702–714.

Staudinger, U. M., & Bluck, S. (2001). A view on midlife development from life-span theory. In M. E. Lachman (Ed.), *Handbook of midlife development* (pp. 345–394). New York: John Wiley.

Sternberg, R. J., Grigorenko, E. L., & Oh, S. (2001). The development of intelligence at midlife. In M. E. Lachman (Ed.), *Handbook of midlife development* (pp. 217–247). New York: John Wiley.

Whitbourne, S. K. (1986). *The me I know: A study of adult identity*. New York: Springer Publishing.

Whitbourne, S. K. (2001). The physical aging process in midlife: Interactions with psychological and sociocultural factors. In M. E. Lachman (Ed.), *Handbook of midlife development* (pp. 109–155). New York: John Wiley.

ADULT FOSTER CARE HOMES

Adult foster care (AFC) typically involves minimal assistance and around-the-clock supervision for several adults residing in a private community-based dwelling. Proprietors of such homes supply material and emotional support typical of "informal" caregiving. There are approximately 34,000 community residential facilities, including AFC homes, across the United States (Wildfire, Hawes, More, Lux, & Brown, 1998). More often than not, residents of AFC homes are unrelated and require some assistance with *activities of daily living*, such as housekeeping, personal care, and meal planning and preparation. The amount of assistance can vary greatly among AFC homes and among residents within an AFC home. Assistance provided is generally more than is received in a *board-and-care home* but less than is found in *assisted living* or *continuing care retirement communities* where transportation, assistance with medication administration, supportive services, and onsite professional medical staff are often provided.

Stark and colleagues (1995) described AFC homes as a cottage industry in which there are limited profits from the provision of care. Often care is provided by family members of the foster care provider with occasional paid helpers for peak hours. AFC homes are highly effective for older adults with early- to mid-stage *Alzheimer's disease* or other forms of *dementia* (Golant, 2003). Residents with complex medical conditions or who require extensive assistance are better suited to facilities equipped to provide higher levels of care, such as nursing homes. AFC homes are likely to increase in popularity in the coming years for several reasons: (1) fewer family members are available to care for older adults due to changes in family structure (Cantor, 1991); (2) people are living to older ages with chronic illnesses that necessitate assistance but not skilled care (Morgan, Eckert, & Lyon, 1995); and (3) the *Olmstead Act* encourages states to make available community-based housing options to all persons who are capable of living with minimum support (Pease, 2002; Centers for Medicaid and Medicare Services, 2005).

Oregon has made AFC homes one of the most viable support options for older adults by covering the cost of residence under home and community-based Medicaid waivers. As a testament to the appeal and affordability of AFC, 70% of AFC residents in Oregon are able to afford their own care. At present, Oregon has over 12,000 beds compared to fewer than 1,500 in Florida (Polivka, 2004). If Florida had the same proportion of AFC beds in comparison with nursing home beds, there would be over 60,000 AFC beds currently available. Kane (2001) has shown that residents of AFC homes fare better socially and psychologically than residents of other long-term care settings. Other studies have found higher levels of interpersonal and environmental satisfaction among residents of AFC (Curtis, Sales, Sullivan, Gray, & Hedrick, 2005).

History and Trends. The concept of adult foster care can be traced to Gheel, Belgium, in the year 600 A.D. when ill wanderers were taken into the homes of kind strangers and provided with care (Sherman & Newman, 1988). Although adult foster care for older adults in the United States is a fairly recent trend, board-and-care homes providing similar care can be traced to Colonial times (Reinardy & Kane, 1999; Sherman & Newman, 1979). English poor laws in the colonies provided reimbursement from public funds to unrelated families who provided food, shelter, and care to the elderly and the poor. Public foster family programs and boarding houses for mentally ill adults were also developed in the late 19th century. Boarding homes for older adults were established in the 1930s, and proprietary rest homes were common during the Depression.

Typically, AFC homes serve from 1 to 6 residents. The majority are older adults, often in an early or moderate stage of Alzheimer's disease or in frail or declining health. One-third have diagnoses of mental illness and/or developmental disabilities (Melcher, 2000). While designed to provide assistance, these homes were originally designed for the support of older adults in declining health, not adults with significant mental health problems striving for independent living. Thus, adult foster care homes are not entirely appropriate for those with mental illness or developmental disabilities. The *National*

Alliance for the Mentally Ill (NAMI) is working to find other similar resources for these populations.

Residents in AFC homes with more personal control over their lives and surroundings are more satisfied with their living arrangements (Polivka & Salmon, 2001; Reinardy & Kane, 1999). Compared with residents in nursing homes and assisted living facilities, AFC residents express a preference for their current placement, but report less satisfaction with their quality of life and personal control than do assisted living residents.

Management and Oversight. Proposed changes to long-term care policy in the United States through the 1970s and 1980s focused on alternatives to nursing home placement for older adults (Nyman, Finch, Kane, Kane, & Illston, 1997). Some states, such as Oregon, offer *Medicaid coverage for AFC* homes, while others are private pay only. AFC homes are not regulated by comparable standards or laws across the United States or abroad, a point of contention with the nursing home industry. Nursing homes are required to follow strict rules with heavy penalties for noncompliance, whereas in most states AFC homes are not subject to such oversight. With the advent of assisted living, the issue of governmental regulation for other types of congregate care, including AFC, is emerging as a significant public policy issue. Many states are developing recommendations, guidelines, and preliminary governance standards for the full range of congregate care settings between independent living and skilled nursing. Kentucky for example, with 265 AFC homes, requires state licensing and allows a maximum of 3 nonrelated residents per household (Pease, 2002). At issue with regulation and oversight are unannounced inspections of AFC homes, with the majority of residents in support of such measures to ensure quality of care and resident protection (Cummins, 2002).

Adult foster care homes, called by various titles but fitting the same description, are reported in 26 of the 50 states in the United States. Regulations and support services for such homes vary across the states (Hawes, Wildfire, & Lux, 1993; Folkemer, Jensen, Lipson, Stauffer, & Fox-Grage, 1996). Much of the oversight is at the state level, although federal regulations for board-and-care homes were established with an amendment to the Social Security Act in 1976 (Pease, 2002). The *Keys Amendment* required states to develop minimum standards for homes with 3 or more residents that receive federal monies. In 1981, the *Rinaldo Amendment* to the Older Americans Act required states to have ombudsman representation for each AFC or board-and-care home. At present, the states are still negotiating the types and levels of governmental regulation and oversight. Oregon, Minnesota, Ohio, and Washington, states with substantial numbers of AFC homes, are pioneers in developing standards of care and regulation.

Providers and Training. The majority of AFC homes are family-owned and managed, with little or no profits for providers. Many of the providers have previous health care experience and the majority are aged 50 and older. Pay for care and services can be from private sources, Medicaid, or other government vouchers, Social Security or through the Veterans Administration. Oregon and Minnesota are reporting an increase in homes run by not-for-profit and for-profit organizations (Pease, 2002; Kane, Baker, Salmon, & Veazie, 1998).

Currently, very little training is provided to the proprietors and personnel of AFC homes. Needed educational programs for providers include training on legal issues, budgeting and management strategies, home and fire safety, accident prevention, medical emergency procedures, nutrition counseling, medication, exercise, personal hygiene, and use of and/or linkages to local community resources.

Advantages and Disadvantages. Perhaps the greatest advantage of adult foster care homes is the potential for close familial relationships to be fostered among residents and providers. Care is provided in a comfortable home-like setting within a community where social and formal service networks are stable and familiar. Skruch & Sherman (1995) found that family relationships were reported more between resident and provider than among residents. Such relationships are beneficial not only to residents but also to providers who might otherwise be living alone and in social isolation. Residents of AFC homes who have more control over their lives and surroundings appear to fare better physically and psychosocially than residents of other more medically focused congregate settings such as nursing homes (Kane, 2001; Polivka & Salmon, 2001; Reinardy & Kane, 1999). Part of this may be attributed to the increased sense of privacy as compared to more institutionalized facility living, ability to retain significant personal possessions, freedom to structure ones physical and social environment, and compatibility among residents and staff (Kane, Baker, Salmon, & Veazie, 1998).

Provision of care within a community setting is beneficial to the community as well. The cost of AFC homes is much less than the provision of nursing home care and with increasing governmental funds covering the cost of adult foster care placements direct costs to individuals and their families are reduced. Residents of care homes are more likely to be involved in community organization activities and contribute to use of community resources. This type of symbiotic relationship is particularly valuable in small, rural communities and cities in which naturally occurring retirement communities are prevalent. Additionally, AFC community dwellings are also generally more architecturally attractive and able to blend into neighborhood environments than larger structures designed for congregate living.

Adult foster care also provides a bridge between independent living and fully supportive skilled care. Depending on the resident, community-based service offerings, and facility-based assistance, the possibility of aging-in-place or remaining in care until death is enhanced. The comfortable, home-like surroundings can be structured to challenge those who are more independent while supporting those in declining health. A one-size-fits-all approach, typical of the highly structured medical model of residential care, is not the standard. Indeed, AFC homes epitomize flexibility of care provision and client-focused care.

As with all situations involving care of the frail or cognitively impaired, the risk of victimization, neglect, and abuse is also present. The same characteristics that make the AFC homes so appealing are also the features that potentially contribute to the failure of this option. With limited oversight from a regulating body, there is limited assurance of quality care. Residents who are, or perceive themselves to be, neglected or abused may be fearful of retribution. They may not have access to authorities to which reports may be made. Lack of a central location, an invisible dispersion of AFC homes throughout communities, and the absence of centralized reporting mechanisms make it difficult for states to effectively monitor such facilities.

Conclusions. Variations of AFC have been demonstrated to be effective in providing care for the ill and frail for many centuries. Such options are especially beneficial in delaying or avoiding entry into skilled nursing care and allowing residents to have more control over their daily lives, feel part of the larger community, and retain a modicum of privacy and independence. AFC is cost-effective and affords both social and physical health benefits compared to other congregate care settings.

Heidi H. Holmes
Graham D. Rowles

See also
Long Term Care: Ethics
Long Term Care Ombudsman Program

References

Centers for Medicaid and Medicare Services. (2005). *Americans with Disabilities Act: The Olmstead Decision*. Available: http://www.cms.hhs.gov/olmstead/default.asp

Cantor, M. H. (1991). Family and community: Changing roles in an aging society. *Gerontologist, 31*(3), 337–346.

Cummins, R. (2002). *Hawaii care homes: An AARP survey*. Washington, DC: AARP.

Curtis, M. P., Sales, A. E. B., Sullivan, J. H., Gray, S. L., & Hedrick, S. C. (2005). Satisfaction with care among community residential care residents. *Journal of Aging and Health, 17*(1), 3–27.

Folkemer, D., Jensen, A., Lipson, L., Stauffer, M., & Fox-Grage, W. (1996). *Adult foster care for the elderly: A review of state regulatory and funding strategies* (Vols. 1 and 2). Washington, DC: AARP Public Policy Institute.

Golant, S. M. (2003). *The ability of U.S. assisted living facilities to accommodate impaired older persons with health care needs: A meta-analysis*. Gainesville, FL: University of Florida, Department of Geography and Institute on Aging.

Hawes, C., Wildfire, J. B., & Lux, L. J. (1993). *The regulation of board and care homes: Results of a survey in the*

50 states and the District of Columbia. Washington, DC: AARP Public Policy Institute.

Kane, R. A. (2001). Long-term care and a good quality of life: Bringing them closer together. *Gerontologist, 41*(3), 293–304.

Kane, R. A., Baker, M. O., Salmon, J., & Veazie, W. (1998). *Consumer perspectives on private versus shared accommodations in assisted living settings*. Washington, DC: AARP, Public Policy Institute.

Melcher, B. (2000). Presentation to the Mental Health Study Commission, NAMI, North Carolina. Available: http://www.naminc.org/presentationmhsc3.htm

Morgan, L. A., Eckert, J. K., & Lyon, S. M. (1995). *Small board-and-care homes: Residential care in transition*. Baltimore, MD: John Hopkins University Press.

Nyman, J. A., Finch, M., Kane, R. A., Kane, R. L., & Illston, L. H. (1997). The substitutability of adult foster care for nursing home care in Oregon. *Medical Care, 35*(8), 801–813.

Pease, R. M. (2002). The marginalization of family care homes in Kentucky. Unpublished doctoral dissertation. Lexington, KY: University of Kentucky.

Polivka, L. (2004). Community residential care for the frail elderly: What do we know, what should we do? Available: http://www.nga.org/center/divisions/1,1188,C_ISSUE_BRIEF^D_7176,00.html

Polivka, L., & Salmon, J. (2001). *Consumer-directed care: An ethical, empirical, and practical guide for state policymakers*. Tampa, FL: Florida Policy Exchange Center on Aging.

Reinardy, J., & Kane, R. A. (1999). Choosing an adult foster home or a nursing home: Residents' perceptions about decision making and control. *Social Work, 44*(6), 571–585.

Sherman, S. R., & Newman, E. S. (1979). Foster family care for the elderly: Surrogate family or mini institution? *International Journal of Aging and Human Development, 10*, 165–176.

Sherman, S. R., & Newman, E. S. (1988). *Foster families for adults: A community alternative in long-term care*. New York: Columbia University Press.

Skruch, M. K., & Sherman, S. R. (1995). Assessing the interpersonal environment in small residential care homes: A comparison of findings on family-likeness in New York and Maryland. *Adult Residential Care Journal, 9*(2), 67–79.

Stark, A., Kane, R. L., Kane, R. A., & Finch, M. (1995). Effect of physical functioning of care in adult foster homes and nursing homes. *Gerontologist, 35*(5), 648–655.

Wildfire, J. B., Hawes, V. L., More, L., Lux, L., & Brown, F. (1998). The effect of regulation on the quality of care in board and care homes. *Generations, 21*(4), 325–329.

ADULT PROTECTIVE SERVICES

Adult Protective Services (APS) protects vulnerable adults by investigating allegations of *elder abuse*, including abuse, neglect, abandonment, and *financial exploitation*. Based on the outcome of an investigation, APS may offer legal and/or social services. Adults who need APS tend to have *physical or mental impairments* that put them at risk for harming themselves (self-neglect) or being harmed by others.

Elder abuse or *mistreatment* is discussed in detail elsewhere in this encyclopedia, but indications are that factors placing older adults at risk for mistreatment include the presence of a brittle support system, loneliness, family conflict, alcohol abuse, psychiatric problems, social awkwardness, and short-term memory problems (Shugarman, Fries, Wolf, & Morris, 2003). In cases where elder abuse occurs in institutional settings, there are mechanisms set in place, flawed though they may be, to identify such abuse and manage the consequences. Such resources include *institutional review processes* and the *State Ombudsman* program adopted after the passage of the *Omnibus Budget Reconciliation Act of 1987*. When elder abuse occurs in the community, recourse is available through Adult Protective Services programs in each state.

Historical and Legislative Background

The need for APS has been acknowledged as a social problem since the early 1950s, but it was not until the 1960s that it was studied formally and incorporated into our public policies by passage of the 1962 amendments to the Social Security Act (Otto, 2000). By the end of the 1960s, there were only twenty community protective services programs in the country (Mixson, 1995). After the passage of the *Title XX amendment* to the Social Security Act (1974), federal funding was provided to the states through *Social Security Block Grants* (SSBG) that allowed states the flexibility to provide protective services to adults. SSBG funding reached a peak of $83.3 million spent on APS in 1980; since that time, funding has been reduced to just under $40 million (Otto, 2000).

In 1978, the *Select Committee on Aging* conducted the first intensive investigation on elder abuse and recommended that states enact laws to address this problem (U. S. Congress, 1981). Since that time, all 50 states have established APS programs that provide a system of preventative, supportive, and surrogate services to community-dwelling older adults to enable them to remain in their homes without fear of abuse or exploitation (Greenberg, McKibben, & Raymond, 1999).

Most states include *elder mistreatment* provisions in their existing APS legislation, while many use domestic violence statutes and/or elder abuse laws to protect the older adults from abuse. California has a special criminal statute that pertains to elder abuse. In addition, 42 states have mandatory reporting laws (Capezuti, Bush & Lawson, 1997) that require various health care professionals, paraprofessionals, and laypersons (including various privately employed health care providers and caregivers) to report known or suspected mistreatment to their state agency. Eleven states address *self-neglect* as a type of neglect that may warrant protection, and either designate it as a separate category of elder mistreatment or include it within their general abuse definitions (Velick, 1995). For information on state agencies charged with responsibility for APS, the *National Center on Elder Abuse* provides a list of weblinks that can be accessed at http://www.elderabusecenter.org/default.cfm?p=apsstate.cfm (NCEA, accessed 10-28-04). In addition, information on state statutes can be found at http://web2.westlaw.com (cited in Jogerst, Daly, Brinig, Dawson et al., 2003).

Service Philosophy and Delivery

APS workers are frequently called on to make critical, life changing decisions in complex situations. Statutes typically require APS investigations to be initiated within 24 hours of receiving a report with the appropriate actions taken as quickly as possible to ensure the safety of the victim. Many cases involve life and death medical problems, difficult issues surrounding the older adult's mental capacity to consent to or refuse services, undue influence, guardianship, powers of attorney, and the rights of victims to self-determination versus the state's *parens patriae* duty to protect helpless citizens (National Association of Adult Protective Services Administrators [NAAPSA], 2003).

Although many have criticized APS for being modeled inappropriately on the Child Protective Services paradigm, some basic tenets of service exist that are unique to older adults. These tenets include the client's *right to self-determination*, use of the least restrictive alternative, maintenance of the family unit whenever possible, use of community-based services rather than institutions, avoidance of ascription of blame, and the presumption that inadequate or inappropriate services are worse than none (Otto, 2000).

To protect and serve older adults subject to alleged abuse, APS receives reports, conducts investigations, evaluates risks to clients, assesses clients' ability to give consent, develops and implements case plans, counsels clients, arranges for a variety of services and benefits, and monitors ongoing service delivery (Otto, 2000). Services most likely to be recommended by APS for abused older adults include medical and social services, guardianship, psychological and/or family counseling, legal counsel, and institutional placement when necessary.

Prevalence of Abuse

Pillemer & Finkelhor (1989) conducted the first random sample survey of abuse, relying on interviews with 2,020 community-dwelling elderly persons in the Boston area. They reported that the overall rate of mistreatment was 32 persons per thousand. Using population estimates of 1987 and assuming that their results could be replicated nationwide, this would imply over 950,000 older adults mistreated.

Because it was believed that most cases of elder mistreatment go unreported, in 1996 the National Center on Elder Abuse (NCEA) conducted the *National Elder Abuse Incidence Study* (NEAIS) to estimate the number of older adults mistreated in the United States over a 12 month period within 20 representative counties, relying on two sources of data: APS investigations and reports from 1,150 trained "sentinels," that is, individuals employed by agencies that regularly provided services to elders (National Center on Elder Abuse [NCEA], 1998). Using probabilistic methods, the NEAIS investigators estimated that 551,011 older adults (or 16 in every 1000) were victims of abuse, neglect, exploitation, and/or self-neglect in 1996, with a range of the estimate being between 314,995 and 787,027.

Most cases of mistreatment (79%) were identified through the trained sentinels, while only 21% were substantiated reports through APS. However, in a more recent study, Jogerst et al. (2003) found abuse rates that ranged from 4.5 per 1000 in New Hampshire to 14.6 per 1000 in California, for a national range of between 160,000 and 520,000 victims of abuse. Estimates of the need for APS, thus, vary widely although all indicate a significant number of potentially abused older adults in our society.

APS Referrals

According to the National Elder Abuse Incidence Study, most substantiated reports to APS were from family members hospitals, law enforcement, in-home service providers, friend/neighbors, the victims themselves, and physicians, nurses, or medical clinics (NCEA, 1998). In a recent study of APS in Florida in the 1990s, Reynolds and Schonfeld (in press) found the most prevalent reasons for referrals to be medical neglect, conditions hazardous to health, inadequate supervision when a caregiver is present, inadequate food, bruises and/or welts, inadequate supervision when a caregiver is absent, and complaints of harassment, belittlement, or ridicule.

In the NEAIS (NCEA, 1998), researchers found that victims of abuse and neglect were women (57.6%), white (84%), and had low annual income (most had less than $14,000). The eldest victims, age 80 and older, were abused and neglected at the highest rate, two to three times their proportion of the older adult population. *Elder self-neglect* is a different category than those who are victims of acts perpetrated by others. Of those older adults who self-neglect, most were white (77.4% versus 20.9% black), female (65%), and age 75 or older (65%). Almost all (93.4%) have some difficulty caring for themselves, and have some form of confusion/disorientation (45.4% sometimes confused, 29.9% very confused).

In the same study, males were more often the perpetrators of mistreatment for abandonment (83.4%), physical abuse (62.6%), emotional/*psychological abuse* (60.1%), and exploitation (59.0%), while females were more likely to neglect an older adult (52.4%). More than three quarters of perpetrators (77.4%) were white, and most (66%) were under age 60. With respect to relationship with the victim, adult children were the most frequent perpetrators of all categories of abuse for abandonment (79.5%), exploitation (60.4%), emotional/psychological abuse (53.9%), physical abuse (48.6%), and neglect (48.6%—NCEA, 1998).

Ongoing Issues for APS

While it is commendable that all 50 states now address the need for Adult Protective Services in some formal manner, all APS programs are subject to a number of ongoing issues that threaten their ability to accomplish their missions. As noted in a survey of state APS administrators ($n = 42$ respondents), first and foremost are the issues of underfunding and understaffing, a problem that is rampant. Other problems include lack of emergency or alternative placements for victims, lack of public awareness, and insufficient community resources (NAAPSA, 2003).

Another issue is the outcome of APS referral for older adults and their families. In a recent study, Lachs, Williams, O'Brien, and Pillemer (2002) used the EPESE to examine older adults referred to APS in Connecticut, finding that referral to APS resulted in a five-time greater risk of nursing home placement compared to those not referred to APS. In spite of the stated desire to preserve the family unit and apply the least restrictive alternative interventions, Lachs and colleagues' findings (2002) indicate that these efforts are of questionable effect.

The Future of APS

To ensure the maintenance and enhancement of programs to assist older adults suspected of being victims of abuse, several improvements should be made. First, APS programs need increased federal funding, improvements in training, access to examples of best practice models, and a national public awareness campaign (National Association of Adult Protective Services Administrators, 2003). Second, we need to continue advocacy for the rights of elders, and push for greater involvement of the medical community (Kohn, 2003). In one study, Marshall, Benton, and Brazier (2000) found that physician referrals accounted for only 2% of cases of abuse. The implication is that physicians are either unable or unwilling to identify and report potential abuse. Recent efforts to devise expedient methods for physicians to screen older adults for further diagnostic assessment for abuse have been encouraging (Fulmer, Guadagno, Bitondo Dyer, & Connolly, 2004), but much more needs to be done.

APS provides a much needed service to older adults living in the community. Communities, large and small, must be encouraged to recognize the potential threat of elder abuse and the importance of APS in protecting potential victims of abuse. This will take a commitment of time, money, and advocacy to ensure that APS remains a viable source of comfort to abused older adults.

SANDRA L. REYNOLDS
LAWRENCE SCHONFELD

See also
Elder Abuse and Neglect
Elder Law
Guardianship/Conservatorship

References

Capezuti, E., Brush, B. L., & Lawson, W. T. (1997). Reporting elder mistreatment. *Journal of Gerontological Nursing, 23,* 24–32.

Fulmer, T., Guadagno, L., Bitondo Dyer, C., & Connolly, M. T. (2004). Progress in elder abuse screening and assessment instruments. *Journal of the American Geriatrics Society, 52,* 297–304.

Greenberg, J., McKibben, M., & Raymond, J. (1990). Dependent adult children and elder abuse. *Journal of Elder Abuse and Neglect, 2,* 73–86.

Jogerst, G. J., Daly, J. M., Brinig, M. F., Dawson, J. D., et al. (2003). Domestic elder abuse and the law. *American Journal of Public Health, 93,* 2131–2136.

Kohn, N. (2003). Second childhood: What child protection systems can teach elder protection systems. *Stanford Law & Policy Review, 14,* 175.

Lachs, M. S., Williams, C. S., O'Brien, S., & Pillemer, K. A. (2002). Adult Protective Service use and nursing home placement. *The Gerontologist, 42,* 734–739.

Marshall, C. E., Benton, D., & Brazier, J. M. (2000). Elder abuse. Using clinical tools to identify clues of mistreatment. *Geriatrics, 55,* 47–50, 53.

Mixson, P. M. (1995). An Adult Protective Services perspective. *Journal of Elder Abuse & Neglect, 7*(2/3).

National Association of Adult Protective Services Administrators, (2003). *Problems Facing State Adult Protective Services Programs and the Resources Needed to Resolve Them.* Washington, DC: NAAPSA.

National Center on Elder Abuse (1998). *The National Elder Abuse Incidence study. Final report.* Washington, DC: National Center on Elder Abuse.

Otto, J. M. (2000). The role of Adult Protective Services in addressing abuse. *Generations, Summer 2000,* 33–38.

Pillemer, K., & Finkelhor, D. (1988). The prevalence of elder abuse: A random sample survey. *The Gerontologist. 28,* 51–57.

Reynolds, S. L., & Schonfeld, L. (in press). Using Florida's Adult Protective Services data in research: Opportunities and challenges. *Journal of Elder Abuse & Neglect,* forthcoming.

Shugarman, L. R., Fries, B. E., Wolf, R. S., & Morris, J. N. (2003). Identifying older people at risk of abuse during routine screening practices. *Journal of the American Geriatrics Society, 51,* 24–31.

U. S. Congress, (1981). *Elder Abuse, an Examination of a Hidden Problem.* Report by the Senate Subcommittee on Aging. Washington, DC: 97th Congress. Com. Pub. 97–277.

Velick, M.M.R.S. (1995). A necessary yet underutilized response to elder abuse. *Elder Law Journal, 3,* 165.

ADVANCED GLYCATION END-PRODUCTS

As we age, the long-lived proteins in our body become gradually browner, more fluorescent, more highly crosslinked and less soluble. These changes are most apparent in the lens of the eye, which becomes visibly yellow and brown with age, interfering with the transparency of the lens and color vision. Similar changes occur in *collagen,* the major structural protein of the body, found in skin and tendons and in the basement membranes of the kidneys, arteries and other tissues. The gradual browning and *crosslinking* of arterial collagen is associated with the age-dependent decrease in elasticity and compliance of the arterial wall. These age-related changes in tissue proteins are thought to result, in part, from nonenzymatic reactions between proteins and reducing sugars in extracellular fluids. In 1984 *Anthony Cerami* introduced the term, advanced glycation end-product (AGE), to describe the class of compounds formed as a result of chemical reactions between sugars and proteins. The term AGE is a play on words—AGEs are involved in the *chemical aging* of tissue proteins and contribute to the

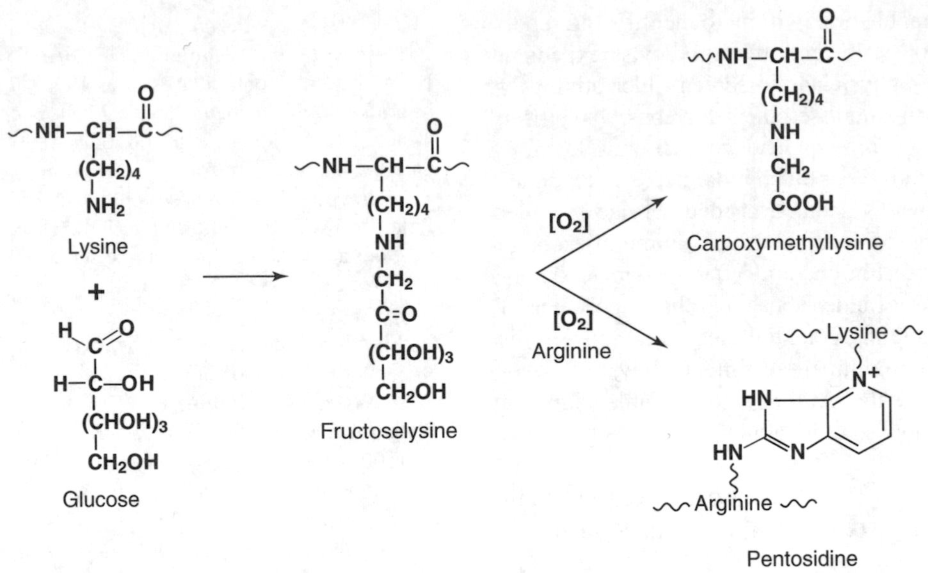

FIGURE 1 Reaction of lysine with glucose to form the Amadori compound, fructoselysine, the primary glucose adduct on glycated proteins. Fructoselysine is oxidized to form AGEs, e.g. by oxidative cleavage to form carboxymethyllysine, or by oxidative reaction with arginine to form pentosidine. (CML)

age-dependent increase in chemical modification and crosslinking of tissue proteins.

The chemistry of "*AGEing*" reactions in vivo is similar to that of Maillard or browning reactions that occur during the cooking and caramelization of foods and enhance food color, taste, and aroma. One of the first steps in this reaction is the condensation of a reducing sugar with an amino group in protein, yielding a Schiff base (imine) adduct, which then undergoes an *Amadori rearrangement* to form a relatively stable ketoamine adduct to the protein (Figure 1). This process of addition of a sugar to a protein is known as *nonenzymatic glycosylation*, or *glycation*, of protein. The Amadori product is not brown or fluorescent, nor is it a protein crosslink. It is a reversible modification of protein, but is a precursor to AGEs, which are irreversible chemical modifications and crosslinks in protein.

The Maillard reaction first attracted the interest of biomedical scientists in the mid-1970s when a modified form of hemoglobin, isolated from normal human blood, was shown to contain glucose as an Amadori adduct. During the 120 day lifespan of the red cell, less than 10% of human hemoglobin is converted to this glycated form, now known as *glycated hemoglobin* or HbA_{1c}. However, the concentration of glycated hemoglobin increases in the blood of diabetic patients and correlates strongly with mean blood glucose concentration during the previous one-month period. Measurements of glycated hemoglobin are widely used for monitoring long-term blood glucose control in diabetes.

Glycation is now recognized as a common chemical modification of body proteins, occurring mostly at the ε-amino group of lysine residues. The glycation of proteins in vivo suggested that the later, browning stages of the *Maillard reaction* also take place in the body, leading to the formation of AGEs. Indeed, more than a dozen structurally characterized AGEs are now known to accumulate with age in long-lived proteins, such as lens crystallins and tissue collagens—these same compounds are found in cooked foods, pretzels, and toasted bread. They include *lysine modifications* such as N^{ε}-carboxymethyllysine (CML), N^{ε}-carboxyethyllysine (CEL) and pyrraline; fluorescent and nonfluorescent crosslinks, such as pentosidine, crosslines, vesperlysines, and glucosepane; and imidazoles and imidazolones derived from glyoxal and methylglyoxal. Most of these AGEs increase in lens proteins with age, and, because of chronic *hyperglycemia*, are found at higher concentrations in collagen and other long-lived proteins (e.g., myelin and actomyosin from patients with diabetes). Increased age-adjusted levels of AGEs in tissue collagens are associated with the development of retinal, renal, neurological, and vascular complications of diabetes. AGEs are also detectable at high concentration in protein deposits in the brains of patients with *Alzheimer's disease*, in atherosclerotic plaque, in amyloid plaque of patients with hemodialysis-associated *amyloidosis*, and in articular collagen in arthritis. In these diseases, AGEs may have a role in recruitment of macrophages, enhancing inflammation, and tissue damage. AGEs may also chelate transition metal ions (iron and copper) in redox-active form, catalyzing oxidative stress, and may react with soluble proteins, contributing to deposition of plasma protein in the vascular wall and glomerular basement membrane in diabetes.

AGE-proteins are recognized by scavenger receptors on macrophages and by *AGE-specific receptors*, including RAGE (Receptor for AGE) on macrophages. AGE receptors and RAGE are also found on endothelial and neural cells, myocytes, and lymphocytes. The uptake of AGE-proteins by macrophages and endothelial cells is associated with generation of oxygen radicals and release of cytokines that promote collagen turnover and biosynthesis, cell proliferation, and tissue remodeling, suggesting that receptor-mediated binding of AGEs may trigger the rejuvenation of tissues.

The meaning of the term, AGE, has evolved over time. It is now used to refer to a broad range of carbohydrate-derived products formed during advanced stages of the Maillard reaction in vivo. Not all AGEs accumulate in tissue proteins with age, and some AGEs react with and form crosslinks with other proteins, so that they are not necessarily "end-products." AGEs may also be formed from a variety of carbohydrates other than blood sugar (glucose), including ascorbate, fructose, sugar phosphates, and even simpler molecules, such as methylglyoxal. Ascorbate is present at high concentrations in the lens and may be a major precursor of AGEs in lens proteins. There is increasing evidence that some circulation AGEs may also be derived from the diet, especially cooked foods, and that the dietary AGEs, known as *glycotoxins*, may affect renal and vascular function. Analogs of AGEs have also been detected in phospholipids and in DNA, and products similar to, and in some case identical to AGEs, known as *advanced lipoxidation end-products* (ALEs), are formed during peroxidation of lipids in plasma and membranes. More than 25 AGE/ALEs have been structurally characterized and have been measured in tissue proteins throughout the body by chemical analysis and immunological methods.

Oxygen and catalysts of oxidation reactions, such as copper and iron ions, accelerate the Maillard reaction. Oxygen and oxidative reactions are considered fixatives of the chemical modification of proteins by carbohydrates, and *glycoxidation* products are a subclass of AGEs formed by both glycation and oxidation reactions. All ALEs require oxygen and *peroxidation* reactions for their formation from lipids. *Antioxidants* and *AGE/ALE* inhibitors, such as *aminoguanidine* and *pyridoxamine*, which trap reactive sugars and *dicarbonyl* intermediates in formation of AGE/ALEs, are effective in preventing or retarding the development of complications in animal models of diabetes and are being tested in clinical trials. Other drugs used for treatment of diabetes and cardiovascular disease, such as *angiotensin converting enzyme (ACE) inhibitors*, *angiotensin receptor blockers* (ARBs) and *hypolipidemic agents*, also inhibit the accumulation of AGE/ALEs in collagen in experimental animals, suggesting that their beneficial effects may be attributed, in part, to inhibition of AGE/ALE formation. Although the relationship between AGE/ALEs and aging is still associative, caloric restriction, which extends the lifespan of rodents, also inhibits the accumulation of AGE/ALEs in tissue collagens, possibly through a combined effect on blood glucose and lipids and oxidative stress. Future research will continue to focus on the structure and mechanism of formation of AGE/ALEs, but especially on the AGE/ALE inhibitors for *treatment of aging* and chronic disease.

JOHN W. BAYNES

See also
Carbohydrate Metabolism
Diabetes

References

Baynes, J. W. (2003). Chemical modification of proteins by lipids in diabetes. *Clinical Chemical and Laboratory Medicine*, *41*, 1159–1165.

Monnier, V. M. (2003). Intervention against the Maillard reaction in vivo. *Archives of Biochemistry and Biophysics*, *419*, 1–15.

Peppa, M., Uribarri, J., Vlassara, H. (2004). The role of advanced glycation end products in the development of atherosclerosis. *Current Diabetes Reports*, *4*, 31–36.

Reddy, V. P., Obrenovich, M. E., Atwood, C. S., Perry, G., Smith, M. A. (2002). Involvement of Maillard reactions in Alzheimer disease. *Neurotoxin Research*, *4*, 191–209.

Thorpe, S. R., Baynes, J. W. (2003). Maillard reaction products in tissue proteins: new products and new perspectives. *Amino Acids*, *25*, 275–281.

Yan, S. F., Ramasamy, R., Naka, Y., Schmidt, A. M. (2003). Glycation, inflammation, and RAGE: a scaffold for the macrovascular complications of diabetes and beyond. *Circulation Research*, *93*, 1159–1169.

Web Sites

http://www.chemsoc.org/exemplarchem/entries/2001/caphane/maillard.html

http://teachhealthk-12.uthscsa.edu/pa/pa10/pa10pdf/10overview.pdf

http://food.oregonstate.edu/color/maillard/

http://maillard.sc.edu

AFRICAN AMERICAN ELDERS

In recent years, substantial progress continues to be made in social and psychological research on black older adults, and the research and scholarly literature is expanding (Curry & Jackson, 2003; Whitfield, 2004; Beech & Goodman, 2004). The title of this entry reflects the heterogeneity of the black population in the United States: with the increased growth of both the black Caribbean and African immigrant populations in the United States, the term "African American," denoting a native black heritage traced to slavery, is no longer as viable as in prior decades (Jackson, 2003; Jackson & Williams, 2003). Recent research continues to feature "racial" comparisons; however, more studies and analyses are being done, permitting greater attention to the heterogeneity among other racial and ethnic groups (Whitfield, 2004). Larger concerns with health disparities (Anderson, Bulatao, & Cohen, 2004; Beech & Goodman, 2004) are propelling greater focus on broader, more inclusive, and more heterogeneous concerns of both race and ethnicity among all groups, placing the previously strict comparison of black-white differences in a larger national and international context (Anderson, et al., 2004; Jackson, 2003).

While progress in research has been and can continue to be made with a focus within a race or ethnic group (Jackson, 1985; Whitfield, 2004), observed health morbidity and mortality differences among racial and ethnic groups have propelled research in a more strictly comparative framework. There is a need for more systematic, empirical research on aging within the black population, especially with a life-course focus (Brown, Jackson, & Faison, 2005). Continued improvement in the quality of data among race and ethnic groups, especially national survey data (for example, the *Health and Retirement Survey*, Jackson, Lockery, & Juster, 1996; and the *National Survey of American Life*, Jackson & Williams, 2003) is leading to greater use of more representative samples and the application of methodologically sophisticated data collection and analytic methods (Skinner, Teresi, Holmes, Stahl, & Stewart, 2001).

There is still not a great deal of support for a coherent field of *ethnogerontology* (Jackson, 1985). On the other hand, a growing emphasis on population aging worldwide (United Nations, 2002) is leading to greater concern with international issues and the immigration of older individuals (Jackson, 2003). The areas of socioeconomic status, health status, family and social support, psychological well being, and work and retirement are used below to sample progress over the last 5 years.

Socioeconomic Status

Older black Americans continue to lag behind older whites in all indicators of social and economic statuses (Anderson, et al., 2004; Federal Interagency Forum on Aging-Related Statistics, 2004; Friedland & Summer, 2005). Indicators of income, education, and poverty statuses reveal the continued poor position of older blacks relative to older whites. Belying a cohort replacement perspective, the continuing poor relative position of blacks suggests that entering new cohorts of children and adults are not faring appreciably better than prior ones (Brown, et al., 2005); unfortunately, recent data on the statuses of middle-aged and younger blacks, relative to whites, in housing, income, occupation, health, and education indicates only small expected gains as new cohorts enter older ages (Anderson, et al., 2004; Muhammad, Davis, Leondar-Wright, & Lui, 2004).

Again it is important to note that some improvements in socioeconomic status indicators have occurred. For example, in 2001 approximately 34% of the black elderly lived below the poverty level. Today approximately 24% (compared to 8% of whites) live at or below this level, though women (27.4%) far outstrip men (18.1%) in this regard. Some of this gender difference is accounted for by sex differences in mortality rates and living arrangements between black men and women. But it is true that older blacks are better fed, better housed, and in better health than in earlier eras, though the relative differences between racial groups persist (Anderson, et al., 2004). According to the author, most of this improvement is attributable to government assistance programs (Williams & Jackson, 2005), which are still the prime support of black Americans in older (and to some extent younger) age groups. A larger relative proportion of blacks, as compared to whites, because of histories of poor occupational opportunities, lack of wealth, and private retirement funds, are heavily dependent upon these government programs (Jackson, et al., 1996; Brown & Jackson, 2005; Williams & Jackson, 2005).

The figures on net worth or wealth perhaps best illustrate the nature of the problem. Since 1984, the net worth of households headed by older whites has improved 81% to $205,000. Reflecting the continuing gap, the net worth of households headed by blacks rose 61% from $25,600 to $41,000: the gap was larger in 2004 than in 1984 (Federal Interagency on Aging Related Statistics, 2004). Continuing attacks on state programs, a stagnant national economy, especially in the northeast, slow job creation, particularly those that provide sustainable incomes at low education levels, and simultaneous growth in low-paying service positions (e.g., fast food restaurants) that do not provide sustainable incomes, leave little room for black youth and young adults, or for their middle-aged cohorts, whose educational attainments and job preparation capital still lags significantly behind that of whites (Muhammad, et al., 2004; Williams & Jackson, 2005). It continues to be uncertain that future cohorts of older blacks will be generally as well off as their white counterparts, although the author foresees growing heterogeneity among older black cohorts themselves in social and economic well-being as a function of the growing status differences among younger aged black cohorts (Jackson & Williams, 2003). Thus, it is likely that a growing, but still small, group of older blacks will take adequate pensions and financial resources into older age; this proportion, though larger than in prior years, will still be relatively small in comparison to the proportion of older whites who enjoy these statuses (Friedland & Summer, 2005).

Health, Morbidity, and Mortality

Recent papers clearly document that at nearly every point across the life course black Americans have poorer morbidity and mortality than whites (Hayward & Heron, 1999; Whitfield & Hayward, 2003; Williams & Jackson, 2005). At age 65, whites can expect to live on average 2 years longer than blacks. As earlier publications have pointed out, this is because *black death rates* are higher in adulthood in the below-65 age groups (Gibson, 1994; Gibson, & Jackson, 1992). It is also well documented that there is increased longevity over that of whites among blacks who live to approximately the age of 85 or so (Federal Interagency Forum on Aging-Related Statistics, 2004). Many have suggested possible selection biases resulting in the survival of particularly robust and hardy individuals (e.g., Hayward & Heron, 2002; Whitfield & Hayward, 2003). Others have claimed that this supposed crossover is only an artifact of faulty reporting and exaggerated age claims. The effect has been firmly established (Preston, Elo, Rosenwaike, & Hille, 1996), although there continues to be no widely accepted explanations (Hummer, Benjamins & Rogers, 2004; Jackson, 1985). The *racial mortality crossover* appears to be a real phenomenon (Preston, et al., 1996), one that involves some type of "*survival of the fit*." More important than the work on the *race crossover phenomenon*, however, is the recent research on active life expectancy. Crimmins and colleagues (2004) have shown large race and ethnic differences in active life expectancy and complex relationships between longevity and health. For example, Asian Americans may live longer in relatively good health as compared to Native Americans and black Americans (Hayward & Heron, 1999).

Research on older blacks has long documented heterogeneity in social and psychological health indicators (Anderson, et al., 2004). Clark and colleagues (1993) have shown evidence for greater functional health, in comparison to whites, among older blacks. Recent work (Hayward & Heron, 1999) points to the need for more focused and detailed studies on the relationships among *race/ethnicity, mortality, and morbidity*.

The nature of differences in the structure of health, the processes of health, and the influence of service use on experienced health problems remain open questions (Gibson, 1994; Williams & Jackson, 2005). The growing heterogeneity among the *American black population*, especially due to immigration, is a phenomenon that will have important implications for health and mortality, but also for understandings of well-being more generally (Jackson, Antonucci & Brown, 2004; Jackson, 2003).

Family and Social Support

Two myths have characterized research on the black family and social support networks (Antonucci & Jackson, 2004; Mendes de Leon & Glass, 2004; Taylor, Jackson, & Chatters, 1997). The first is a view of older blacks cared for by loving and extended family members and kin. The other is a view of the impoverished lonely older black abandoned by a disorganized and incompetent family system. National and other large social surveys indicate a reality somewhere in between (Taylor, et al., 1997; Taylor, Chatters, & Levin, 2004; Chatter, Taylor, Lincoln, & Schroepfer, 2002). These recent research findings document the existence of extended families but also demonstrate that much of the assistance is reciprocal, that the black aged often provide help to younger family members and neighbors (Chatters, et al., 2002; Antonucci & Cantor, 1994). The importance of community institutions like the church as sources of physical and *emotional support to older blacks* has also been well documented (Taylor, et al., 1997; Taylor, Chatters, & Levin, 2004). Some recent data indicates possible changes in the structure of American families and more dispersed living patterns that may result in lowered possibilities of support in older ages (Jackson, Brown, & Antonucci, 2005).

Psychological Well-Being

Research on well-being has shown an increasing sophistication over the last few years (Brown, et al., 2005; Federal Interagency Forum on Aging-Related Statistics, 2004). Structural factors, like income and education, tend to show small but positive relationships to well-being (Brown, et al., 2005). Some recent evidence also suggests that younger cohorts of blacks may be less satisfied than older cohorts at comparable periods in the life span (Brown, et al., 2005; Chatters & Jackson, 1989). This is in sharp contrast to whites, who have shown the opposite pattern. This lowered satisfaction and happiness in younger blacks may be related to rising expectations and structural constraints that are likely to persist into older age, portending future cohorts of older blacks with lowered levels of subjective well-being (Brown, et al., 2005).

Work and Retirement

Little empirical research had been devoted to the study of work and *retirement in the black aged* (Jackson, et al., 1996). Some earlier work had speculated that the entire retirement process, viewed within a life-span context, may be very different for blacks. Since blacks often have long histories of dead-end jobs with poor benefits and bleak expectations, the advantages of retirement are lessened (Brown, et al., 2005). Thus, inadequate income, poor housing, and uncertain futures face many older blacks at retirement age (Brown, et al., 2005). Faced with limited retirement resources, many blacks may continue working past customary retirement ages out of desperation (Brown, et al., 2005). Some recent research indicates that these individuals are physically, psychologically, and socially worse off than their retired black counterparts (Brown, et al., 2005). As suggested earlier, even the relatively poor but stable government retirement support blacks may receive (if they are fortunate enough to qualify) may, in contrast, be better than sporadic and poor jobs in the regular labor market (Jackson, 2001). Thus, retirement may provide a small but secure government income, leading to increased psychological and social well-being (Brown, et al., 2005).

In contrast to 5 years ago, more research on the *social gerontology of the black aged* is being included within the general investigation of ethnicity and cultural factors in aging (Antonucci & Jackson, 2004; Jackson, et al., 2004, 2005; Brown, et al., 2005). The existence of new national datasets and more powerful analytical techniques is increasing the quality and quantity of research on African American aging in all areas (Whitfield, 2004). New national data collection efforts, like the Health and Retirement Survey and the new National Survey of American Life (Jackson, et al., 2004) are improving the available data on the *aging experience of African Americans* (Curry & Jackson, 2004; Whitfield & Hayward, 2003). While better data is always needed, especially longitudinal and panel studies, the improvement in a relatively few short years has been impressive. Similarly, the approach to research on the black elderly is continuing to include a greater recognition of the heterogeneity among elderly blacks, as well as other race and ethnic groups (Anderson, et al., 2004; Brown, et al., 2005). Research is more focused on the role of the life course, culture, socioeconomic status, and gender as important structures and processes related to potential process differences within and among older groups of color (Anderson, et al., 2004; Jackson, et al., 2004; Whitfield, 2004).

The field of ethnogerontology as an organizing theoretical framework in the study of the black aged seems to be a growing reality over the last few years, though it is not characterized as such (Jackson, 1985). Recent research continues to reverse past trends of poor data and impoverished theory; generalizable, high-quality findings are beginning to emerge concerning health, socioeconomic status, social support, family patterns, well-being, work, and retirement among black older populations (Anderson, et al., 2004; Brown, et al., 2005). Interestingly enough, research emphases on differences within race and ethnic groups is being reversed of late, especially in health-related research (Anderson, et al., 2004; Williams & Jackson, 2005). This is due in part to the acceleration of work on health inequalities and disparities, bringing a greater focus to *cross-ethnic group comparisons* (Anderson, et al., 2004; Whitfield & Hayward, 2003). While of vital importance in addressing real disparities in physical and psychological health, one perverse outcome of this theoretical and research attention may be to impede further development of theory and empirical research that focuses on differences in social, psychological, and health statuses and processes within race and ethnic groups (Brown, et al., 2005). As noted in the earlier volume, work on population genetics may hold some promise for focusing greater attention on intra-group, individual factors and processes related to observed population level disparities (Whitfield, 2004).

JAMES S. JACKSON

See also
Ethnicity
Minority Populations: Recruitment and Retention in Aging Research

References

Anderson, N. P., Rodolfo, R. A., & Cohen, B. (Eds.). (2004). *Critical perspectives on racial and ethnic differences in health in late life*. Panel on Race, Ethnicity, and Health in Later Life. Committee on Population, Division of Behavioral and Social Sciences and Education. Washington, DC: National Academies Press.

Antonucci, T. C., & Jackson, J. S. (2004). Ethnic and cultural differences in intergenerational social support. In V. L. Bengtson & A. Lowenstein (Eds.), *International perspectives on families, aging, and social support*. Aldine de Gruyter Publishing Co.

Beech, B. M., & Goodman, M. (2004). *Race and research: Perspectives on minority participation in health studies*. Washington, DC: America Public Health Association.

Brown, E., Jackson, J. S., & Faison, N. (in press, 2005). The work and retirement experiences of aging black Americans. In J. James & P. Wink (Eds.), *The crown of life: Dynamics of the early post-retirement period*.

Chatters, L. M., & Jackson, J. S. (1989). Quality of life and subjective well-being among black adults. In R. Jones (Ed.), *Black adult development and aging*, (pp. 191–214). Berkeley, CA: Cobb & Henry.

Chatters, L. M., Taylor, R. J., Lincoln, K. D., & Schroepfer, T. (2002). Patterns of informal social support from family and church members among African Americans. *Journal of Black Studies, 33*(1), 66–85.

Clark, D. O., Maddox, G. L., & Steinhauser, K. (1993). Race, aging, and functional health. *Journal of Aging and Health, 5*, 536–553.

Crimmins, E. M., Hayward, M. D., & Seeman, T. E. (2004). Race/ethnicity, socioeconomic status, and health. In N. P. Anderson, R. A. Rodolfo, & B. Cohen (Eds.), *Critical perspectives on racial and ethnic differences in health in late life. Panel on race,* ethnicity, and health in later life*. (pp. 310–352). Panel on Race, Ethnicity, and Health in Later Life. Committee on Population, Division of Behavioral and Social Sciences and Education. Washington, DC: National Academies Press.

Curry, L., & Jackson, J. S. (2003). The science of inclusion: Recruiting and retaining racial and ethnic elders in health research. Washington, D.C.: Gerontological Society of America.

Federal Interagency Forum on Aging-Related Statistics (2004).: Older Americans 2004: Key indicators on well being. Washington, DC: U.S. Government Printing Office.

Friedland, R. B., & Summer, L. (2005). *Demography is not destiny, revisited*. Washington, DC: Center on an Aging Society, Georgetown University.

Gibson, R. C. (1994). The age-by-race gap in health and mortality in the older population: A social science research agenda. *Gerontologist, 34,* 454–462.

Gibson, R. C., & Jackson, J. S. (1992). The black oldest old: Health, functioning, and informal support. In R. M. Suzman, D. P. Willis, & K. G. Manton (Eds.), *The oldest old* (pp. 321–340). New York: Oxford University Press.

Hayward, M. D., & Heron, M. (1999). Racial inequality in active life among adult Americans. *Demography, 36*(1), 77–91.

Hummer, R. A., Benjamins, M. R., & Rogers, R. G. (2004). Racial and ethnic disparities in health and mortality among the U.S. elderly population. In N. P. Anderson, R. A. Rodolfo, & B. Cohen (Eds.), *Critical perspectives on racial and ethnic differences in health in late life. Panel on race, ethnicity, and health in later life*. ((pp. 53–94). Committee on Population, Division of Behavioral and Social Sciences and Education. Washington, DC: National Academies Press.

Jackson, J. J. (1985). Race, national origin, ethnicity, and aging. In R. H. Binstock & E. Shanas (Eds.), *Handbook of aging and the social sciences* (pp. 264–303). New York: Van Nostrand Reinhold.

Jackson, J. S. (2001). Changes over the life-course in productive activities: Black and white comparisons. In N. Morrow-Howell, J. Hinterlong, & M. Sherraden (Eds.), *Productive aging: Perspectives and research directions* (pp. 214–241). Baltimore: Johns Hopkins University Press.

Jackson, J. S. (2003). Conceptual and methodological linkages in cross-cultural groups and cross-national aging research. *Journal of Social Issues, 58*(4), 825–835.

Jackson, J. S., & Williams, D. R. (2003). Surveying the Black American Population. In, J. S. House, F. T. Juster, R. L. Kahn, H. Schuman, & E. Singer (Eds.), *Telescope on society: Survey research and social science at the University of Michigan and beyond*. Ann Arbor: University of Michigan Press.

Jackson, J. S., Chatters, L. M., & Taylor, R. J. (1993). Status and functioning of future cohorts of African-American elderly: Conclusions and speculations. In J. S. Jackson, L. M. Chatters, & R. J. Taylor, *Aging in black America* (pp. 301–318). Newbury Park, CA: Sage Publications.

Jackson, J. S., Lockery, S. M., & Juster, F. T. (1996). Introduction: Health and retirement among ethnic and racial minority groups. *Gerontologist, 36*(3), 282–284.

Jackson, J. S., Antonucci, T. C., & Brown, E. (2004). A cultural lens on biopsychosocial models of aging. In P. T. Costa Jr., & I. C. Siegler, (Eds.), *Recent advances in psychology and aging*. Amsterdam: Elsevier B. V.

Jackson, J. S., Brown, E., & Antonucci, T. C. (in press, 2005). Ethnic diversity in aging, multicultural societies. In M. Johnson, V. L. Bengtson, P. Coleman, & T. Kirkwood (Eds.), *The Cambridge Handbook of Age and Ageing*. Cambridge, UK: Cambridge University Press.

Jackson, Torres, Caldwell, Neighbors, Nesse, Taylor, Trierweiler, & Williams. (2004). The national survey of American life: A study of racial, ethnic, and cultural influences on mental disorders and mental health. *International Journal of Methods in Psychiatric Research 13*(4), 196–207.

Mendes de Leon, C. F., & Glass, T. A. (2004). The role of social and personal resources in ethnic disparities in late-life health. In N. P. Anderson, R. A. Rodolfo, & B. Cohen (Eds.), *Critical perspectives on racial and ethnic differences in health in late life. Panel on race, ethnicity, and health in later life*. (pp. 353–405). Committee on Population, Division of Behavioral and Social Sciences and Education. Washington, DC: National Academies Press.

Muhammad, D., Davis, A., Lui, M. & Leondar-Wright, B. (2004). *The state of the dream 2004: Enduring disparities in black and white*. Boston: United for a Fair Economy.

Myers, H. F., & Hwang, W. (2004). Cumulative risks and resilience: A conceptual perspective on ethnic health disparities in late life. In N. P. Anderson, R. A. Rodolfo, & B. Cohen (Eds.), *Critical perspectives on racial and ethnic differences in health in late life. Panel on race, ethnicity, and health in later life*. (pp. 492–539). Committee on Population, Division of Behavioral and Social Sciences and Education. Washington, DC: National Academies Press.

Preston, S. H., Elo, I. T., Rosenwaike, I., & Hill, M. (1996). African American mortality at older ages: Results from a matching study. *Demography, 33,* 193–209.

Skinner, J. H., Teresi, J. A., Holmes, D., Stahl, S. M., & Stewart, A.L. (2001). Measurement in older ethnically diverse populations. *Journal of Mental Health and Aging, 7*(1), 5–200.

Taylor, R. J., Chatters, L. M., & Levin, J. (2004). *Religion in the lives of African Americans: Social, psychological, and health perspectives*. Thousands Oaks, CA: Sage Publications.

Taylor, J. T., Jackson, J. S., & Chatters, L. M. (Eds.). (1997). *Family life in black America*. Thousand Oaks, CA: Sage Publications.

United Nations. (2002). *World population ageing: 1950-2050*. New York: United Nations.

Whitfield, K. E. (2004a). *Closing the gap: Improving the health of minority elders in the new millennium*. Washington, DC: Gerontological Society of America.

Whitfield, K. E. (2004b). Sources of individual differences in indices of health disparities among older African Americans. *Phylon, 50*(1-2), 145–159.

Whitfield, K. E., & Hayward, M. (2003). The landscape of health disparities among older adults. *Public Policy and Aging Report, 13*(3), 1–7.

Williams, D. R., & Jackson, P. B. (2005). Social sources of racial disparities in health. *Health Affairs, 24*(2), 325–334.

AGE AND EXPERTISE

Two primary questions drive research on age and expertise. At what age do people typically reach peak *performance levels*? Do the same mechanisms support expert performance in early and late adulthood? Both lead to an intriguing issue: Can people develop and maintain expertise in later life?

Experts are usually defined as those who demonstrate consistently superior performance on representative tasks from a domain (Ericsson & Lehmann, 1996). It typically takes about 10 years (1000 hr–10,000 hr) of intense devotion to self-improvement activities, *deliberate practice*, to become a *world-class expert*.

Age and Peak Performance

Quetelet (1842/1969) and Lehman (1953) were among the first to identify the classic curvilinear function between *age and performance*, which showed a sharp rise in performance in young adulthood, a peak in the decade of the thirties, and gradual decline thereafter. *Peak performance* tends to occur in the mid-30s in intellectual domains, such as chess (Elo, 1965; Charness, Krampe, & Mayr, 1996) and in the 20s or early 30s in athletics (Schulz & Curnow, 1988; Schulz, Musa, Staszewski & Siegler, 1994; Stones & Kozma, 1995). According to Simonton (1997), the ability of aging elite artists and scientists to sustain exceptional performance is less the result of consistent success than consistent productivity. In both science and sports, individuals apparently past their prime have occasionally broken world records or won world championships, but not without several previous attempts. Also, a better predictor of the developmental trajectory is *professional age*, rather than chronological age. Several mechanisms have been proposed to account for such high-level performance in the face of expected age-related decline.

Mechanisms Supporting Expertise

General or specific abilities are usually assumed to underlie expert performance. By this logic, musicians who must memorize musical scores should have better memory for music notation than nonmusicians. Further, if aging degrades memory abilities, then older musicians ought to perform worse than younger ones in professional activities. The former assumption has proven accurate (e.g., Meinz & Salthouse, 1998) though the latter has not. Studies consistently fail to show much of a relationship between age and productivity in the work place (Salthouse & Maurer, 1996).

One explanation for the failure to find a link between *age and job performance* is that older experts may not rely on the same abilities as younger ones to perform the same task. They may compensate for a decline in one ability (e.g., speed of response) by honing another (e.g., working memory). Salthouse (1984) showed that older high-speed typists are slower at tapping tasks than their younger counterparts, but compensate by buffering more text (greater eye-hand span) to give them additional time to create efficient overlapping keystroke patterns. It also appears that experts can partially circumvent general age-related declines in physical and psychological capacities by deliberately engaging in counteractive measures. Krampe and Ericsson (1996) found minimal age-related declines in speeded *music-related performance* (tapping task) among older expert pianists who maintained rigorous maintenance practice schedules, despite finding declines in general psychomotor speed. Relative to the older experts, older amateur pianists exhibited significantly slower performance in both tasks. Both cumulative and current practice levels were positively related to performance.

Similarly, Tsang and Shaner (1998) reported that *age-related declines* among pilots in flight simulator tasks appear to be somewhat attenuated by experience. When older active pilots were asked to perform two aviation-relevant tasks at the same time, their performance was comparable to middle-aged and younger pilots. However, when the same individuals were asked to perform two general tasks, older active pilots performed substantially worse than their younger colleagues, suggesting that the positive effects of maintenance practice were restricted to the domain of expertise.

Older pilots' memory for air traffic control messages is normally inferior to that of younger pilots (Morrow et al., 2001). However, it becomes comparable to that of younger pilots when sufficient environmental support, in the form of note taking, is allowed (Morrow et al., 2003). Thus, storing information in the environment can be a useful compensatory strategy for older adults when task demands exceed *working memory* capabilities.

Computer simulations hint at how acquired knowledge may compensate for waning abilities. *Neural network models* with greater knowledge of opening chess positions were better protected against simulated age-related declines, such as degrading the signal-to-noise ratio in the nervous system, on a recall task (Mireles & Charness, 2002). This is consistent with the finding that extensive knowledge of rare words is strongly predictive of crossword puzzle solving proficiency, even in the case of older puzzlers who exhibit age-related declines in reasoning and problem solving ability (Hambrick, Salthouse, & Meinz, 1999). These results imply that acquired knowledge can mitigate declines in age-sensitive *fluid intelligence* abilities to allow for exceptional performance even at the far end of the age spectrum.

Conclusions

Recent studies of expert performance reveal mixed findings. Although there is a strong tendency for basic abilities and for some aspects of domain-specific performance to decline with age, critical skills in some domains may be sustained through practice and the accumulation of structured knowledge. Experts may compensate for, or adapt to changing abilities. However, the nature and potency of these compensatory mechanisms are not thoroughly understood and will continue to spur future investigations.

A question that remains to be explored is whether expert levels of performance in a new domain can be attained at a later stage of life. Older adults may have additional monetary resources and time at their disposal to engage in skill acquisition, though research indicates that they take about twice as long as younger counterparts to learn a new skill, such as word processing (Charness et al., 2001). Further, *deliberate practice* requires strong motivation and it remains to be seen under what circumstances older adults choose to forego more enjoyable activities for those needed to build expertise.

Neil Charness
Tiffany Jastrzembski
Franklin G. Hines

This work was supported by a grant from the National Institute on Aging (1 PO1 AG17211-05, CREATE) to the first author.

References

Charness, N., Kelley, C. L., Bosman, E. A., & Mottram, M. (2001). Word processing training and retraining: Effects of adult age, experience, and interface. *Psychology and Aging*, *16*, 110–127.

Charness, N., Krampe, R. Th., & Mayr, U. (1996). The role of practice and coaching in entrepreneurial skill domains: An international comparison of life-span chess skill acquisition. In K. A. Ericsson (Ed.), *The Road to Excellence* (pp. 51–80). Mahwah, NJ: Lawrence Erlbaum Associates, Inc.

Elo, A. E. (1965). Age changes in master chess performances. *Journal of Gerontology*, *20*, 289–299.

Ericsson, K. A., & Lehmann, A. C. (1996). Expert and exceptional performance: Evidence of adaptation to task constraints. *Annual Review of Psychology*, *47*, 273–305.

Hambrick, D. Z., Salthouse, T. A., & Meinz, E. J. (1999). Predictors of crossword puzzle proficiency and moderators of age-cognition relations. *Journal of Experimental Psychology: General*, *128*, 131–164.

Krampe, R. Th., & Ericsson, K. A. (1996). Maintaining excellence: Deliberate practice and elite performance in young and older pianists. *Journal of Experimental Psychology: General, 125*, 331–359.

Lehman, H. C. (1953). *Age and achievement*. Princeton, NJ: Princeton University Press.

Meinz, E. J. & Salthouse, T. A. (1998). The effects of age and experience on memory for visually presented music. *Journal of Gerontology: Psychological Science, 53B*, P60–P69.

Mireles, D. E., & Charness, N. (2002). Computational explorations of the influence of structured knowledge on age-related cognitive decline. *Psychology and Aging, 17*, 245–259.

Morrow, D., Menard, W. E., Stine-Morrow, E. A. L., Teller, T., & Bryant, D. (2001). The influence of expertise and task factors on age differences in pilot communication. *Psychology and Aging, 16*, 31–46.

Morrow, D. G., Ridolfo, H. E., Menard, W. E., Sanborn, A., Stine-Morrow, E. A. L., Magnor, C., Herman, K. L., Teller, T., & Bryant, D. (2003). Environmental support promotes expertise-based mitigation of age differences on pilot communication tasks. *Psychology and Aging, 18*, 268–284.

Quetelet, L. A. J. (1969). *A treatise on man and the development of his faculties*. Gainesville, Fl.: Scholars' Facsimiles and Reprints. (Original work published 1842).

Salthouse, T. A., & Maurer, J. J. (1996). Aging, job performance, and career development. In J. E. Birren & K. W. Schaie (Eds.). *Handbook of the psychology of aging* (4th ed., pp. 353–364). New York: Academic Press.

Salthouse, T. A. (1984). Effects of age and skill in typing. *Journal of Experimental Psychology: General, 13*, 345–371.

Schulz, R., & Curnow, C. (1988). Peak performance and age among superathletes: Track and field, swimming, baseball, tennis, and golf. *Journal of Gerontology: Psychological Sciences, 43*, P113–120.

Schulz, R., Musa, D., Staszewski, J., & Siegler, R. S. (1994). The relationship between age and major league baseball performance: Implications for development. *Psychology and Aging, 9*, 274–286.

Simonton, D. K. (1997). Creative productivity: A predictive and explanatory model of career trajectories and landmarks. *Psychological Review, 104*, 66–89.

Stones, M. J., & Kozma, A. (1995). Compensation in athletic sport. In R. A. Dixon & L. Bäckman (Eds.), *Compensating for psychological deficits and declines* (pp. 297–316). Mahwah, NJ: Lawrence Erlbaum Associates, Inc.

Tsang, P. S., & Shaner, T. L. (1998). Age, attention, expertise, and time-sharing performance. *Psychology and Aging, 13*, 323–347.

AGE DISCRIMINATION

See
Ageism
Age Stereotype
Aging, Images of

AGEISM

Ageism is defined as a process of systematic stereotyping and discrimination against people because they are old, just as racism and sexism accomplish this for skin color and gender. It is deeply engrained in society, categorizing old people as senile, rigid in thought and manner, and old fashioned in morality and skills. In medicine, terms like "crock" and "vegetable" are common (Shem, 1978). Ageism allows the younger generation to see older people as different from themselves; thus, they suddenly cease to identify with persons who grow old as human beings. This behavior serves to reduce their own sense of fear and dread of aging. Stereotyping and myths surrounding old age are explained in part by a lack of knowledge and insufficient contact with a wide variety of older people. But another factor comes into play—a deep and profound dread of growing old. Ageism is a broader concept than *gerontophobia*, which refers to a rarer, "unreasonable fear and/or irrational hatred of older people, whereas ageism is a much more comprehensive and useful concept" (Palmore, 1972). This concept and term was introduced in 1968 (Butler, 1969).

Age prejudice is a human rights violation that is exhibited in health care, employment, the media. Discrimination exists in the very definition of who is considered poor in the United States, in that people age 65 and older must be poorer than younger adults in order to be counted as poor (Muller, 2001).

Some of the myths of age include a lack of productivity, disengagement, inflexibility, senility, and loss of sexuality (Stone & Stone, 1997; Bytheway, 1995). There have been some advances in, and more attention to, the productive capabilities of older people, and a better understanding that older persons have desires, capabilities, and satisfaction with regard to sexual activities. The "write-off" of older persons as "senile" because of memory problems, for example, is being replaced by an understanding of the profound and most common forms of what is popularly referred to as "senility," namely, *Alzheimer's disease*. *Senility* is no longer seen as inevitable with age. Rather, it is understood to be a disease or group of diseases. When means of effectively treating dementia are available, ageism will also decline.

The underlying psychological mechanism of ageism makes it possible for individuals to avoid dealing with the reality of aging, at least for a time. It also becomes possible to ignore the social and economic plight of some older persons. Ageism is manifested in a wide range of phenomena (on both individual and institutional levels), stereotypes and myths, outright disdain and dislike, or simply subtle avoidance of contact; discriminatory practices in housing, employment, and services of all kinds; epithets, cartoons, and jokes. At times, ageism becomes an expedient method by which society promotes viewpoints about the aged in order to relieve itself from the responsibility toward them, and at other times ageism serves a highly personal objective, protecting younger (usually middle-aged individuals, often at high emotional cost), from thinking about things they fear (aging, illness, and death).

Ageism, like all prejudices, influences the behavior of its victims (Hausdorff and Levy, 1999). Older people tend to adopt negative definitions about themselves and to perpetuate the various stereotypes directed against them, thereby reinforcing societal beliefs. They may in a sense "collaborate" with the enemy, with stereotypes.

Ageism can apply to stages of life other than old age. Older persons have many prejudices against the young and the attractiveness and vigor of youth. Angry and ambivalent feelings may flow, too, between older and middle-aged people. Middle-aged people often bear many of the pressures of both young and older people, and they experience anger toward both groups. Some older people refuse to identify with their peers and may dress and behave inappropriately in frantic attempts to appear young. Others may underestimate or deny their age.

Since the introduction of the concept of ageism, there have been some gains on the part of older adults. The *Age Discrimination and Employment Act of 1967*, amended in 1978, ended mandatory retirement in the federal government and advanced it to age 70 in the private sector. *Mandatory retirement* at all ages was abolished in the United States in 1986 (with a few exceptions, such as police officers and fire fighters), and the European Commission has mandated that members of the European Union have laws making age discrimination illegal in place by 2006.

Although the underlying dread, fear and distaste for older persons remains, several trends may help reduce ageism in the future: (1) With the *aging of baby boomers* old age is in the process of being redefined as a more robust and contributory stage of life. (2) Increasing interest in aging in the general public, mass media, government, and academia will support increasing knowledge and fewer misconceptions about older persons. (3) Increasing scientific research on aging has reduced and will continue to reduce ageism by providing a realistic picture of older people and aging and by improving the health of older persons. (4) By 2000 persons over the age of 65 and younger adults had nearly attained the same education level, challenging the stereotype that older men and women were illiterate or poorly educated. (5) As people become more aware of racism and sexism they tend to become more aware of discrimination in general, and will be less likely to approve or practice ageism (Palmore, 2004).

Reminiscence or *life review* has helped focus attention on what can be learned from listening to the lives of the old. Indeed, the memoir has become, in the minds of some, the signature genre of our age.

ROBERT N. BUTLER

See also
Age Stereotype
Aging, Images of

References

Butler, R. N. (1969). Ageism: Another form of bigotry. *The Gerontologist*, *9*, 243–246.

Bytheway, B. (1995). *Ageism: Rethinking ageing series*. Buckingham, UK: Open University Press.

Hausdorff, J., Levey, B., & Wei, J. (1999). The power of ageism on physical function of older persons: Reversibility of age-related gait changes. *Journal of the American Geriatrics Society*, *47*, 1346–1349.

Muller, Charlotte, Nyberg James, & Estrine, Judith. (2001). *Old and poor in America*. International Longevity Center-USA.

Palmore, Leonard B. (2004). *The future of ageism*. International Longevity Center-USA.

Shem, S. (1978). *The house of God*. New York: Dell.

Stone, M., & Stone, L. (1997). Ageism: The quiet epidemic. *Canadian Journal of Public Health*, *88*, 293–294.

AGE STEREOTYPE

An age stereotype is a simplified, undifferentiated portrayal of an age group that is often erroneous, unrepresentative of reality, and resistant to modification. Although the word *stereotype* was first used in the technology of duplicate printing, where a metal plate (i.e., the stereotype) was first cast into a mold, the American journalist *Walter Lippmann* introduced its usage for both scholarly and popular audiences in his 1922 book *Public Opinion. Lippman* argues that seeing things freshly and in detail is exhausting and so people see a trait that marks a type and "fill in the rest of the picture by means of the stereotypes we carry about in our heads" (p. 89). Age stereotypes have to do with people "filling in the picture" of a person or group of people after knowing only one characteristic—age. In this way, age stereotypes are similar to other overgeneralized and oversimplified portrayals of groups sharing a social characteristic; gender and race are persistent bases for stereotyping.

Age stereotypes can be positive and negative. Hummert and colleagues (1994) used a checklist of positive and negative adjectives to identify traits commonly attributed to people of different age groups. By combing these traits, the researchers identified several stereotypes of older people. The negative stereotypes included "shrew/curmudgeon" and "despondent"; positive stereotypes included "perfect grandparent," "small-town neighbor," and "golden ager." Political scientist Robert Binstock (1983, 1994) makes a frequently cited argument that, since the 1960s and 1970s Americans have reversed their "compassionate stereotype" of the elderly as poor, frail, and dependent to a new stereotype of the elderly as prosperous, active, and politically powerful. Neither image is accurate. Is a *positive stereotype* better than a *negative stereotype*? Both are examples of overstated homogeneity and implicit creation of "other" or "*outgroup*." By stereotyping people, we assume that everyone in the other group (not our own group) is like each other and that they are not like us. The fact that our assumptions about the "outgroup" are often negative compounds the problems that arise from stereotyping.

One of the problems with stereotyping is that we sometimes act on these oversimplified assumptions; this leads to *age discrimination*. Older workers have been discriminated against on the basis of the stereotypes that they are unable to learn new things, less productive than younger workers, more likely to miss work because of sickness, and set in their ways. Even though all of these stereotypes have been disproven by research, they still persist. The extent of *age discrimination in the work place* that ensues from these stereotypes has been the impetus for continual changes to the *Age Discrimination in Employment Act*. A recent Supreme Court decision made it easier for older workers to sue their employer for age discrimination, allowing plaintiffs to use the same kind of evidence as is used in gender and race discrimination cases, and making it harder for employers to defend their actions on the basis that the age discrimination was not intentional (*New York Times*, April 1, 2005).

Recent research has examined additional consequences of stereotyping. Levy discusses a new line of research showing that older people internalize negative stereotypes and that these *aging self-stereotypes* can influence cognitive and physical health. Hess, Hinson, and Statham (2004) studied the ways in which positive and negative stereotypes influence the older adults' performance on a memory task. Participants who were exposed to negative stereotypes performed more poorly than those who were primed with positive stereotypes. The idea of "*stereotype threat*" is used to help explain the impact of stereotypes on memory, cognition, and health. This concept suggests that when individuals are afraid that their behavior will reinforce a negative stereotype about a group to which they belong, their performance is affected.

Age stereotypes are communicated in numerous ways. Television programs, advertisements in all media, the jokes we tell, and birthday cards are often full of age stereotypes. Stereotypes stem from our need to simplify our social world through the creation of categories and they are related to *age norms* which suggest that certain roles and behavior are appropriate at certain ages and not at other ages. From these benign or neutral starting points, age stereotypes can lead to age discrimination, *aging self-stereotypes*, and can thus affect both psychological and social quality of life for older people. Further research on the origins, perpetuation, and impact of age stereotypes will help us understand a complex array of factors that influence the experiences of aging in our society.

FAY LOMAX COOK
Updated by SUZANNE R. KUNKEL

See also
Ageism
Aging, Images of

References

Binstock, R. H. (1983). The aged as scapegoat. *The Gerontologist, 23,* 136–143.

Binstock, R. H. (1994). Changing criteria in old-age programs: The introduction of economic status and need for services. *The Gerontologist, 34,* 726–730.

Hummert, M. L., Garstka, T. A., Shaner, J. L., & Strahm, S. (1994). Stereotypes of the elderly held by young, middle-aged, and elderly adults. *Journal of Gerontology: Psychological Sciences, 49,* P240–P249.

AGING, ATTITUDES TOWARD

See
Ageism
Age Stereotype
Aging, Images of

AGING, IMAGES OF

Since the early 1970s, social scientists have been investigating the power of the media to influence *attitudes about aging* in the United States. The majority of research in assessing images of aging has been done in the realm of television. However, that may begin to change in the next decade as the pervasive influence of the Internet is explored with respect to images of aging.

Internet and Print

Internet and Aging. Using the Google search engine on the Internet in 2004, one can locate 9,220,000 links to Web sites that include reference to the aged, 8,520,000 to aging, 6,500,000 to elderly, and 985,000 just to images of aging. Many more sites are of interest to older adults, including those that provide information, products, and services, which may not have explicit references to aging or images of aging. The Internet features materials designed specifically for the Web as well as ready access to images first published through print and broadcast media.

Due to its interactive and highly segmented nature, it is difficult to generalize the *portrayal of older adults* on the Internet. However, due to the vast number of Web sites, those catering to the elderly are far more prevalent compared to television networks and programs. A recent study by Hilt and colleagues (2004) provide some insights on *elderly Internet use* patterns that may permit some inferences about Internet content related to older demographics. Email is one of the most common activities for older adults, and might aid in conveying a modern, upbeat image of older users. Web surfing tends to be targeted to sites that are useful (weather, health, travel, education) or entertaining (jokes, games, culture). Older adults often use Google.com and Yahoo.com to find these sites. The authors contend that currently local radio and television Web sites have limited usefulness to older viewers. But they recommend redesigning them to help *older users navigate the Web* and locate information and entertainment easily. Cody and colleagues (1999) found that training older adult learners in Internet use had a positive impact on their attitudes toward learning and perceived social support. As far as the content that is distributed via the Internet, Gerbner, and colleagues (2002) contend that the distortions found in the traditional media may be multiplied through additional channels, such as multichannel cable and satellite and Internet-delivered video. This is particularly significant, since levels of concentration in media ownership continue to increase.

Even the most popular Internet search engine, *Google*, has recently become the object of criticism because of *ageist hiring practices*. Recently, a 54-year-old director of operations was dismissed because he did not fit into the *youthful culture of the company*. The average age of Google's male workers is 29.7 years old, and 28.4 for women (Liedtke, 2004).

Print Media. Despite widespread access to information via the Internet, television still wields great power to influence millions of people and, therefore, commands considerable attention. In the print medium, some magazines promote the image of an active and healthy older consumer. *Older people are pictured* in association with products such as medications, including those used to address incontinence and impotence, dental and digestive aids, cosmetics to reduce the signs of aging, and assorted health products. In contrast, upscale business publications might present affluent seniors, advertising elegant automobiles, life insurance companies, upscale travel, and financial institutions. De Luce (2001) examined *images of aging in publications* and reported that *Forbes*, *Fortune*, and *Prevention* offered the most images of mature models and marketing aimed at readers older than age 50, clearly targeting the segment of older adults who have considerable *discretionary income*. Hilt and Lipschultz (2004) point out that Americans aged 50 and older control half the country's discretionary income and 75% of all personal assets. *Newspaper articles featuring older people* tend to focus on extremes: either the severely disadvantaged or those who are interesting because they accomplish feats contrary to *age stereotypes*, such as hang gliding or skydiving. One vivid recent example featured former President *George Bush skydiving* to celebrate his 80th birthday, a story that still appears on 6,690 Web sites to date.

Television and the Aging

The most pervasive mediated images of aging are projected by television. Often unrealistic expectations about life are encouraged when the world of television is confused with the real world. A major concern is not only what is shown, but also what is not shown, and what this lack of content teaches viewers. Older people are not seen on television in proportion to their numbers in real life (Signiorelli, 2004). Moreover, they appear to be marginalized and represented in negative stereotypes. In a review of 28 studies, Vasil and Wass (1993) found that older persons were underrepresented in both electronic and print media in terms of their presence in the United States population.

Although older adults are the group with the greatest exposure time to television (Hilt & Lipschultz, 2004), most research describes unfavorable portrayals of them on television. Studies of television programs and surveys of *older viewers* have demonstrated that television caters poorly to the needs of older adults. Powell and Williamson's (1985) review of the mass media revealed stereotypic *ageist* biases and a trend toward *learned helplessness*. Robinson and Skill (1995) report that only 2.8% in their study of the 1,228 adult speaking characters in primetime television were determined to be 65 years and older. Of those older characters, only 8.8% were in lead roles, a figure that is lower than studies reported in the 1970s. In a study of primetime network programs broadcast between 1993 and 2002, Signiorelli (2004) reports that "less than 3% of the characters, both male and female, white and minority, in major and supporting roles, are characterized as elderly." She also found that women aged 50 to 64 years are more often classified as elderly, while men in that age group are portrayed as middle-aged.

Negative images of older adults are not limited to fictional programs. In general, the television industry and advertisers have been obsessed with young viewers (Larson & Elkin, 1999). Numerous *older anchors* have become victims of the pressure to reach younger demographics. Reuven (2002) points to the average age of corporate (28 years) and advertising account representatives (31 years) as one of the factors that may play a role in the decline of older news personalities.

Gender and Aging on Television

Research since the 1970s has documented that women are less likely to be seen in television programs as they age than are men (Gerbner et al., 2002). Davis and Davis (1985) report that women appear on screen about one-third as often as do men. Men are more likely to be found populating dramas when they are in the 30 to 49 age bracket. Women are more likely to be in their 20s and early 30s. *Women on television* tend to be younger than men, and minority women tend to be younger than white women (Signiorelli, 2004). On television, for those older than age 50 men by far outnumber women. This picture is beginning to change, however. Robinson and Skill (1995) reported that the proportion of *female characters on primetime* aged 50 to 64 years has increased since 1975. They suggest that "this may be one of the reasons the public believes *TV portrayals of older Americans* has improved in recent years." Nevertheless, Signiorelli (2004) contends that men in the 50 to 64 age group tend to be portrayed as middle-aged, while women are more likely to appear elderly.

Although the predominant *image of older women on television* has been as a nurturer, followed by nags or adoring attendants, that pattern is beginning to change. Thanks to the expansion of cable, shows featuring older women in prominent roles are available in syndication as repeats long after episodes ceased production. In the 1980s, *Golden Girls* presented older women as attractive and sexually active; repeats of the series remain in syndication in 2004. With repeat episodes still broadcast via syndication, *Jessica Fletcher*, a murder mystery writer and amateur detective on *Murder She Wrote* appears as an attractive older woman who is intelligent, perceptive, courageous, and effective in her investigative skills. In science fiction series, characters that would be considered much older in human years are portrayed as *middle aged in various alien* species.

The popular Web site *Seniornet.org* recently requested reader input under the heading "What's worth watching?" and the mostly female respondents tended to focus on *soap operas* (*Days of Our Lives*, *As the World Turns*, and *Passion*), music programs, and a number of *PBS programs* targeted to older viewers, such as *Maggie Growl* and *Sweet Old Song*, but also the cable channel *Court TV*. Among popular programs *West Wing* attracted considerable attention.

In general, younger characters are portrayed in more prestigious positions. An interesting gender interaction was found for the 50 to 64 age group: white men in this age group are still shown in prestigious positions, while professional prestige for women and minorities has already declined. After age 65, white men are also cast in less prestigious job categories (Signiorelli, 2004).

One exception to the *negative portrayal of the elderly on TV* is advertising. In ads older persons are typically portrayed as vigorous and healthy. However, their gender distribution is contrary to demographic trends. While only 40% of adults older than 65 are male, in advertising between 62% and 70% of characters in this age group are males (Harris, 2004). Hajjar (1997) found similar effects in her content analysis of *television commercials*. Older than age 60 characterizations (8% of the total) were 70% male and 84% white. Positive characterizations tend to be clustered in the categories of food/beverage and financial/insurance, while negative ones focus on medical/pharmaceutical products.

Health and *Older Adults on Television*

The *medical show* remains a television staple, and *ER*, the most watched example in 2004, portrays older adults as patients, concerned family members, and health practitioners. The patients have suffered from various conditions ranging from acute illness and accidents to terminal illness and chronic problems associated with aging. Some have died, just as younger adults and children have on the same show.

Older people tend to have "multiple comorbid conditions and complicated prevention and treatment regiments" (Dishman et al., 2004). Poor health provides more drama than good health. It would be easy to assume that older people are going to be the ill people in the world of television drama. Characters in soap operas do not generally have diseases that viewers are likely to have. Often their health problems are so exotic that they are not threatening to the average viewer. In many continuing dramas, the ill get well. Death befalls only those who must be written out of the story. Thus, older people are not usually victims of illness on television.

Consequences of *Age Stereotyping*

The images of age presented on television tend to promote stereotypes. Stereotyping and simplistic portrayals are convenient shorthand for support characters in television programming. Older individuals are more likely to play supporting than central roles. As television educates viewers to see aging as a negative and undesirable experience, it perpetuates a *self-fulfilling prophecy*.

Gerbner and colleagues (2002) point out that the kinds of distortions discussed above can have considerable impact in shaping perceptions and attitudes, especially among heavy television viewers. Viewers older than age 65 are among the heaviest group of viewers. Grajczyk and Zöllner (1998) point out that it can be a lifeline and a window to the outside world, "a substitute for primary interpersonal communication, a tool for structuring time patterns and keeping up the rhythms of long-established every-day rituals." Hofstetter and Schultze (1993) found that *negative perceptions of aging* appear to be related to "*contextual aging*" (i.e. social interaction, health, living alone, economic status) rather than chronological age.

Expectations for the Future

Television viewing by adults increases with age (Mundorf & Brownell, 1990). The aging American populace and the increasing proportion of disposable income among those older than 50 years have lead advertisers and television producers to gradually discover the *gray market*. In the early 1980s, networks began to change their programming strategies in response to these demographic and economic shifts in the population. Presently, extensive programming on *cable channels* offers viewers contemporary images of older adults. This contrasts to stereotypical images of rebroadcast shows from the 1950s and silent era films.

In a study of viewing preferences, older adults made little reference to *cable programming* (Mundorf & Brownell, 1990). The potential of *cable TV* appears to be increasing as more access and programming options are provided. With the expansion of cable and the increase in programming opportunities, we should expect more targeting of market niches that feature an increased number of older adults and especially more in lead characters.

Television is slowly mirroring the changes occurring among American men and women. As adults are living higher quality lives at older ages, what is portrayed as "old" keeps changing. Women in their 50s and 60s are seen as attractive and sexually active. But the changes are not happening fast enough for many older adults. Chafetz and colleagues (1998) report that many older adults expressed serious reservations about the attitudes displayed toward the elderly as implied in negative or insufficient news coverage.

Movies made for television frequently use *older performers* as central characters. Age-related issues are often confronted in an era where social problems are seen as legitimate subjects for comedy as well as drama. Each season showcases at least 1 significant *film about aging* and being old ("What's worth watching," 2004). Series programs have not ignored the story potential of being old in American society. Confronting old age is no longer taboo. In addition, *images of aging on the Internet* may soon gain comparable influence to those on television as more adults who possess computer expertise reach their 60s.

WINIFRED BROWNELL
NORBERT MUNDORF
JOANNE MUNDORF

See also
Age Stereotype
Ageism

References

Chafetz, P. K., Holmes, H., Lande, K., Childress, E., & Glazer, H. R. (1998). Older adults and the news media: Utilization, opinions and preferred reference. *Gerontologist, 38*, 481–489.

Cody, M. J., Dunn, D., Hoppin, S., & Wendt, P. (1999). Silver surfers: Training and evaluating Internet use among older adult learners. *Communication Education, 48*, 269–286.

Davis, R. H., & Davis, J. A. (1985). *TV's image of the elderly*. Lexington, MA: Lexington Books.

Dishman, E., Matthews, J., & Dunbar-Jacob, J. (2004). Everyday Health: Technology for Adaptive Aging. In Pew and Van Hemel (Eds.), *Technology For Adaptive Aging*. Washington, D.C.: National Academy of Sciences Press.

Gerbner, G., Gross, L., Morgan, M., Signiorelli, N., & Shanahan, J. (2002). Growing up with television: Cultivation processes. In J. Bryant & D. Zillmann, *Media effects* (pp. 43–68). Mahwah, NJ: L. Erlbaum Associates.

Grajczyk, A., & Zöllner, O. (1998). How older people watch television. *Gerontology, 44*, 176–181.

Hajjar, W. (1997). The image of aging in television commercials: An update for the 1990s. In N. Al-Deen, *Cross-cultural communication and aging in the United States* (pp. 231–244). Hillsdale, NJ: Erlbaum.

Hofstetter, C. R., & Schultze, W. A. (1993). The elderly's perception of TV ageist stereotyping: TV or contextual aging? *Communication Reports, 6*, 92–100.

Harris, R. J. (2004). *A cognitive psychology of mass communication*. Mahwah, NJ: Erlbaum.

Hilt, M. L., & Lipschultz, J. H. (2004). Elderly Americans and the Internet: E-mail, TV news, information and entertainment Websites. *Educational Gerontology, 30*, 57–72.

Larson, C., & Elkin, T. (1999). Special report—upfront markets. *Media Week*, 44–48.

Liedtke, M. (2004). Google accused of elderly discrimination. Available: *Sitepoint.com.*

de Luce, J. (2001). Silence at the newsstands. *Generations, 25*, 39–43.

Mundorf, N., & Brownell, W. (1990). Media preferences of older and younger adults. *Gerontologist, 30*, 685–691.

Powell, L. A., & Williamson, J. B. (1985). The mass media and the aged. In H. Fox (Ed.), *Aging*. Guilford, CT: Dushkin Publishing Group.

Reuven, F. (2002). Eliminating the elderly. *New Leader, 85*(3), 47–49.

Robinson, J. D., & Skill, T. (1995). The invisible generation: Portrayals of the elderly on primetime television. *Communication Reports*, *8*, 111–119.

Signiorelli, N. (2004). Aging on television: Messages relating to gender, race, and occupation in primetime. *Journal of Broadcasting and Electronic Media*, *48*, 279–301.

Vasil, L., & Wass, H. (1993). Portrayal of the elderly in the media: A literature review and implications for educational gerontologists. *Educational Gerontology*, *19*, 71–85.

"What's worth watching." (2004). Available: *Seniornet.org*.

Web Sites

aarpmagazine.org
aoa.gov
aging.today.org
asaging.org
generationsjournal.org
gerontologist.gerontologyjournals.org
helptheaged.org
icaa.cc
isapa.org
ncoa.org
seniornet.org

AGING POLICY

See
Policy Analysis: Issues and Practices

AGING SERVICES

See
Adult Protective Services
Senior Centers
Senior Companion Program

AIDS/HIV

By the end of 2003, approximately 38 million people were living with HIV/AIDS, and 20 million had died since the recognition of the epidemic (Joint United Nations Program on HIV/AIDS, 2004). Infection with *human immunodeficiency virus (HIV)* eventually progresses to *HIV* disease and *acquired immunodeficiency syndrome (AIDS)*. *AIDS* can be thought of as one end of a spectrum of *HIV-related conditions* that may include acute infection, an asymptomatic period, and eventually certain opportunistic infections, neoplasias, and other conditions. The Centers for Disease Control and Prevention (CDC) has a still-current detailed surveillance definition and classification system for AIDS based on documentation of HIV infection, degrees of laboratory evidence of *immunosuppression* using *CD4+ lymphocyte counts*, and specified symptoms and AIDS indicator conditions (Centers for Disease Control and Prevention, 1992). The major result of HIV infection is both quantitative and qualitative immune impairment that largely affects the *T-helper lymphocytes* (T4, CD4+ cells), but macrophages, monocytes, glial cells, fibroblasts, and *antigen-presenting dendritic cells* also can become infected. This results in increased susceptibility to *opportunistic infections* and neoplasms. Major conditions resulting from opportunistic infections in the HIV-infected person include *Pneumocystis jiroveci* (formerly *carinii*) pneumonia (PCP); encephalitis due to *Toxoplasma gondii*, severe diarrhea and gastrointestinal problems due to *Cryptosporidium spp., Isospora belli*, and others; meningitis from *Cryptococcus neoformans*; *candidiasis* of the oral cavity, esophagus, and in women, the vagina; tuberculosis; herpes simplex virus lesions; retinitis due to *cytomegalovirus*; and disseminated infections due to cytomegalovirus, *Mycobacterium avium complex*, and others. Major neoplasms include *Kaposi sarcoma* and *non-Hodgkin lymphomas*.

HIV also affects certain cells and tissues directly, particularly in the central nervous system. The nervous system may be affected, even asymptomatically, in persons with HIV; effects such as *AIDS dementia complex* (ADC), *vacuolar myopathy*, and peripheral neuropathy are common (Peiperl, Coffey, & Volberding, 2004; Wormser, 2004). Medical treatment has been directed: (1) against HIV itself through the use of combinations of *antiretroviral drugs*, of which highly active antiretroviral therapy has been a mainstay, (2) toward immune system enhancement, and (3) toward the prevention and treatment of specific opportunistic infections and conditions. The latter includes nonpharmacological measures and the use of pharmacological and biological agents, including vaccines. Monitoring viral load and CD4+ cell counts as well as clinical status is integral to the treatment. Treatment in the older adult parallels that of other adult age groups, with the necessary adaptations in dosage and/or regimens to account for the physiological and psychosocial consequences of aging, the presence of non-HIV–related coexisting chronic illness, possible interactions with drugs used to treat these other conditions, and the increased adverse drug effects in older persons due to these issues.

Transmission of HIV

The major documented transmission modes for HIV are those in which persons are exposed to HIV-containing blood or body fluids: (1) through intimate homosexual or heterosexual contact, (2) through parenteral or blood-borne exposure via transfusions, needlesticks, injection drug use, or similar means, or (3) vertically from an infected mother to her infant in the prenatal, perinatal, or immediate postnatal period. Several factors influence the likelihood of HIV acquisition, including risky behaviors such as unprotected sexual encounters, sex with high-risk partners, engaging in receptive anal intercourse, and sharing apparatus to inject drugs. The modes of HIV transmission (except perinatal) apply to all age groups including the elderly. Currently, sexual transmission is the leading mode of HIV acquisition in older adults.

Exposure Categories

The CDC classifies U.S. AIDS cases by the major exposure categories in a hierarchical manner. These categories for all adults and their percentages are as follows: male-to-male sexual contact (48%); injection drug use (27.5%); male-to-male sexual contact and injection drug use (7%); heterosexual contact (15%); and other, including hemophilia, blood transfusion, perinatal, and risk not reported or identified (2.5%) (Centers for Disease Control and Prevention, 2003). In the past, *blood transfusion* and/or *tissue transplantation* was an important mode of HIV acquisition in those older than 55 years, at one time even accounting for the majority of cases in those aged 65 years and older (Ship, Wolff, & Selik, 1991). Because of the protective mechanisms now in place to screen the blood supply, this acquisition mode has decreased significantly. On the other hand, AIDS cases due to heterosexual transmission have increased in those 65 years and older.

AIDS Cases in Older Adults

The term "invisible" has been used to describe many groups affected by the AIDS epidemic, including the elderly. Relatively little attention has been paid to both the present and future aspects of HIV in the older adult. Although the mean age of a first diagnosis of HIV/AIDS is rising, many aspects of HIV/AIDS in older adults, such as response to therapy, drug interactions, and updated epidemiological and clinical data have not been studied in controlled trials in older adults (Manfredi, 2004). In its standard statistical reporting of AIDS cases, the CDC gives data by 10-year intervals until age 65, after which it lumps together cases among those aged 65 years and older. Through 2002, approximately 6% of cumulatively reported U.S. adult AIDS cases occurred in those aged 55 years and older, and about 1.5% occurred in those aged 65 years and older (Centers for Disease Control and Prevention, 2003).

The statistics described above report the age at the time of AIDS *diagnosis*. It is expected that an increased absolute number of cases of both HIV infection and AIDS will eventually be seen in the older population, as well as a greater relative proportion of cases due to a decrease in perinatal transmission. Reasons for the increased number include: (1) HIV-infected persons may progress to symptomatic states and AIDS over a longer period of time, in part due to early and increasingly effective therapy such as highly active retroviral therapy, and thus persons who were infected in the middle-aged group will move into the elderly age category; (2) persons in older age groups may continue to receive blood transfusions and tissue/organ transplantation at higher rates than younger persons, so a certain number of cases (although relatively few, and a decreasing number) will continue to arise from this source; (3) the ready availability of drugs such as Viagra (sildenafil citrate) to treat erectile dysfunction has led to increased sexual activity in older males; (4) older persons may engage in risky sexual behaviors such as not using condoms for sexual encounters, for reasons including lack of concern about birth control, lack of awareness about HIV risks, and difficulty manipulating protective devices due to conditions such as arthritis, and thus they become more vulnerable to infection with HIV and/or other sexually transmitted diseases; (5) the life expectancy for persons in the United States continues to increase, and older people enjoy better health and mobility, allowing them to pursue risky behaviors and activities; and (6) age-related changes in the body's immune function and protective barriers, such as the drying of vaginal mucosa in women, make older people more susceptible to the acquisition of HIV when they are exposed.

Sex, Drugs, and the Elderly

Since the majority of cases of HIV transmission involve unprotected sexual contact and/or drug abuse, these areas have been the focus of general HIV prevention, assessment, and educational efforts. Society still subscribes to many false beliefs and negative views of sexuality in the older adult. Often, older people are seen as relatively asexual or as secure in a monogamous relationship. Even with the advent of drugs to treat erectile dysfunction, little has been described in the literature about sexual practices of the elderly population, including risky behavior, multiple and/or same-sex sexual partners, and so on. Health care workers may not ask about sexual activity as part of an older person's health history. Most studies of sexuality among the elderly have concentrated on sexual dysfunction as opposed to sexual activity. Older persons may also believe they should hide their sexual activity, whether heterosexual, homosexual, or both, and they may not readily volunteer or discuss risk factors or exposures fearing the reaction of friends or family if they acknowledge sexual relationships, especially if those relationships are outside their usual partnership or marriage. Decades ago, sex-related activities were not openly discussed or displayed. "Gray" and "gay" were seen as antithetical terms, and men who had sex with other men were accustomed to being closeted to avoid discrimination. However, it is estimated that at least 1 million male homosexuals are older than 65 years (Ship, Wolff, & Selik, 1991). This may be an underestimate and may not consider cultural definitions of sexuality or occasional same-sex experiences.

Frequently sexual transmission of HIV occurs proportionately in the older population. More than 50% of all reported AIDS cases in those aged 55 years and older are classified in some exposure category pertaining to sexual transmission (Centers for Disease Control and Prevention, 2003). Probable heterosexual transmission of HIV was reported in a woman of 89 years (Rosenzweig & Fillit, 1992). Sexual relationships outside monogamous ones may be becoming increasingly common in the elderly. Examples include: (1) older men whose long-term partners have died may now have sexual contact with several other partners who may be younger, increasing the risk of exposure to HIV; (2) elderly women may seek sexual fulfillment with younger men in a non-monogamous relationship; and (3) elderly men (married or not) may pay for sexual relationships with prostitutes (male or female) or seek available sexual companionship, which, particularly in long-term care settings, may be with a male. All of these individuals may now be at risk for HIV infection but be reluctant to disclose this behavior unless the health care provider asks specific questions regarding sexual behavior. Primary care providers may not discuss topics related to HIV risk as frequently with older patients as with younger ones, and many fail to recommend HIV testing or consider HIV in the differential diagnosis.

A sentinel study examined risk factors and behaviors in a large national sample of adults older than 50 years. The prevalence of a known risk factor for HIV infection, such as being a transfusion recipient, having multiple sexual partners, or having a partner with a known risk for HIV infection, was 10%. Few of these respondents used condoms during sex or had HIV testing, particularly in comparison with a younger sample (Stall & Catania, 1994). In another study, few persons older than 50 years (11%) had discussed AIDS with their physician (Gerbert, Maguire, & Coates, 1990).

In addition to sexuality, drug abuse in the older adult is another topic that is often avoided in discussion. Few studies have addressed injection drug use for nonprescribed or nonmedical purposes in the elderly. Yet medical conditions that cause pain and discomfort might cause older adults to seek drugs, as might social conditions or other reasons. Furthermore, those who began using drugs at a younger age may continue this habit into old age. Thus, health care workers also need to consider drug use when assessing risk for HIV exposure in the older person, although currently AIDS attributed to this exposure category is infrequent in the elderly.

Clinical Aspects of HIV/AIDS and Survival in the Elderly

AIDS may mimic other conditions in the elderly, and it can be difficult to recognize HIV infection in this group. It can present with vague and nonspecific signs and symptoms, such as weight loss and wasting, aches and pains, fever, cough, or cognitive impairment and confusion. Symptoms in the elderly may present against a background of multiple actual or potential illnesses and medication side effects and interactions. Cases of HIV infection in the elderly have been described in which ADC was the presenting and/or sole feature. The symptoms of ADC can include forgetfulness, slow thought processes, personality changes, depression, loss of concentration, and apathy, among other features. Many of these are similar to problems seen in the elderly from other causes, including the dementia seen in Alzheimer's disease and in extrapyramidal disorders, as well as delirium. Because HIV infection can persist for years, with few manifestations, some persons acquiring it later in life may live their life span without showing major recognizable symptoms. Thus, clinicians must be ready to consider a differential diagnosis of HIV disease in the older adult regardless of gender.

In general, when compared to younger counterparts, older adults with HIV tend to have a shorter and more severe course, shorter AIDS-free intervals, a greater number of opportunistic infections which tend to be more severe, earlier development of neoplasms, and a shorter survival period (Stoff, Khalsa, Monjan, & Portegies, 2004). Other debilitating conditions of aging may complicate those due to HIV infection, compounding and/or accelerating disease progression and decreasing functional capabilities. For example, cognitive impairment may adversely affect adherence to therapy (Hinkin, et al., 2004). Alzheimer's disease is commonly associated with aging, and it has been suggested that there is interaction between the pathologies induced by Alzheimer's disease and HIV-associated disorders (Stoff, Khalsa, Monjan, & Portegies, 2004). Becker, Lopez, Dew, and Aizenstein (2004) noted that HIV-positive persons older than 50 years had a greater prevalence of cognitive disorder than younger persons, and dementia was a more common classification. Those with a higher HIV viral load were at greater risk to develop cognitive impairment.

Changed social networks and other conditions make the indirect consequences of AIDS significant for the older person.

Although some persons are still living who have been known to be HIV-infected for 20 years or more and who seem to have nonprogressive disease, the ultimate outcome of HIV infection is considered to be death. Yearly overall mortality rates remain high, although newer treatment regimens with highly active antiretroviral therapy have increased life spans. Since the advent of highly active antiretroviral therapy, it is questionable whether HIV progresses more rapidly in older people than in younger ones, but increased age was still found to be a factor shortening survival in older persons already HIV-infected (Porter et al., 2003).

Felissa R. Lashley

See also
Immune System

References

Becker, J. T., Lopez, O. L., Dew, M. A., & Aizenstein, H. J. (2004). Prevalence of cognitive disorders differs as a function of age in HIV virus infection. *AIDS, 18*(suppl 1), S11–S18.

Centers for Disease Control and Prevention. (2003). *HIV/AIDS Surveillance Report 2002, 14*, 1–47.

Centers for Disease Control and Prevention. (1992). 1993 revised classification system for HIV infection and expanded surveillance case definition for AIDS among adolescents and adults. *Morbidity and Mortality Weekly Report, 41*(RR-17), 1–19.

Gerbert, B., Maguire, B. T., & Coates, T. J. (1990). Are patients talking to their physicians about AIDS? *American Journal of Public Health, 80*, 467–468.

Hinkin, C. H., Hardy, D. J., Mason, K. I., Castellon, S. A., Durvasula, R. S., Lam, M. N., & Stefaniak, M. (2004). Medication adherence in HIV-infected adults: Effect of patient age, cognitive status, and substance abuse. *AIDS, 18*(suppl 1), S19–S25.

Joint United Nations Program on HIV/AIDS. (2004). *2004 report on the global AIDS epidemic*. Geneva: World Health Organization.

Manfredi, R. (2004). HIV infection and advanced age: Emerging epidemiological, clinical, and management issues. *Ageing Research Reviews, 3*, 31–54.

Peiperl, L., Coffey, S., & Volberding, P. (Eds). (2004). *HIV InSite Knowledge Base*. San Francisco: University of California San Francisco. Available: http://hivinsite.ucsf.edu/InSite

Porter, K., Babiker, A., Bhaskaran, K., Darbyshire, J., Pezzotti, P., Porter, K., Walker, A. S., & CASCADE Collaboration. (2003). *Lancet, 362*, 1267–1274.

Rosenzweig, R., & Fillit, H. (1992). Probable heterosexual transmission of AIDS in an aged woman. *Journal of the American Geriatric Society, 40*, 1261–1264.

Ship, J. A., Wolff, A., & Selik, R. M. (1991). Epidemiology of acquired immune deficiency syndrome in persons aged 50 years or older. *Journal of the Acquired Immune Deficiency Syndrome, 4*, 84–88.

Stall, R., & Catania, J. (1994). AIDS risk behaviors among late middle-aged and elderly Americans. The National AIDS Behavioral Surveys. *Archives of Internal Medicine, 154*, 57–63.

Stoff, D. M., Khalsa, J. H., Monjan, A., & Portegies, P. (2004). Introduction: HIV/AIDS and aging. *AIDS, 18*(suppl 1), S1–S2.

Wormser, G. (Ed). (2004). *AIDS and other manifestations of HIV infection*. 4th ed. San Diego, CA: Elsevier Academic Press.

ALCOHOL USE

Beverage alcohol (ethanol) has complex physiological and psychological effects on those who drink it, as well as a complex social history. Its use is ancient and almost universal, particularly in the development of Western civilization. Ancients often described alcohol as "the water of life"; they attributed magical significance to its effects in religious and social ceremonies and marked life-course transitions from birth to death with drinking behavior. Consuming alcohol in religious communion services and in convivial social toasts, such as "to your health," are well-known cultural celebrations. Alcohol as a beverage appears in a remarkable variety of tastes, smells, and colors. It is consumed in a variety of settings, often with elaborate attention to the aesthetics of presentation. In sum, beverage alcohol in Western societies has a long history and has become a domesticated drug whose addictive potential tends to be understated (Roueche, 1960).

Beverage alcohol has a darker side. It can be misused as well as used to produce intoxication, and for a persistently and significantly large minority of drinkers it results in addictive behavior, clinically recognized as *alcoholism*. The ambivalence toward beverage alcohol is dramatically illustrated by national prohibition of beverage alcohol in the United States (1917–1933), a country in which a large majority of adults historically have drunk alcohol and in which an estimated 5% of adult drinkers persistently exhibit serious problems associated with their drinking.

Interest in how drinking and abuse of alcohol relate to aging is relatively recent. Scholars who know the relevant scientific literature note that in the first 2 decades of the major journal in the field, *The Quarterly Journal of Studies on Alcohol* (1940–1960), only 1 article referred to aging, old age, or gerontology. In this journal's third decade (1960–1969), 13 articles referenced aging; only after 1970 did references to age and aging become common. By 1980 a comprehensive bibliography on aging and alcohol use listed 1,200 articles, over half of which had been published in the previous decade (Barnes, Abel, & Ernst, 1980). Also in that year, a monograph on alcohol and old age was published (Mishra & Kastenbaum, 1980). Increased interest in the *drinking behavior of older adults* in the 1980s, particularly abuse of alcohol, appeared to have 2 sources. One was the assumption that loss of status through retirement and the stresses of growing older would, particularly among men, increase the risk of abusive use of alcohol as an expression of frustration. A second source appears to have been the concern of social welfare agencies and administrators of long-term care facilities; they reported that the everyday problems of some older adults were in fact sometimes exacerbated by intoxication and apparent alcoholism.

Adequate evidence for characterizing the relationship between *drinking behavior and aging*, however, has continued to be somewhat sparse. Systematic comparisons of drinking behavior and alcohol abuse between societies are not available. But here, in general, is what the growing body of evidence indicates about drinking among older adults in the United States (Maddox, Robins, & Rosenberg, 1985; Midanik & Clark, 1994; Mishra & Kastenbaum, 1980):

1. A substantial majority of adults in the United States are not abstinent. At any point a minority of males (perhaps 20%) are abstinent or are ex-drinkers, and a larger minority of females are abstinent. A minority of males who drink and a smaller minority of females exhibit significant personal and social problems with their drinking. The usual estimate of alcoholism or serious problems with drinking among adults is 5%.

2. Among adults who drink, both the frequency and the quantity of alcohol consumed tend to decrease with age. Available cross-sectional evidence tends to be flawed as the basis for concluding that there is an age-related decrease in consumption; the same outcome could be explained by the different drinking patterns of earlier and later cohorts of adults. However, changing patterns of sociability with age, age-related health problems, and the complicated interaction of alcohol with prescribed medication appear to have a moderating effect on drinking behavior in later life.

   Earlier assumptions that abusive drinking in adulthood ensured an early death appear to be wrong. Adults with a lifetime history of abusive drinking are observed in long-term care institutions. The assumption that "*late-onset alcoholism*" (i.e., an adult with no history of abuse who develops problems late in life) is common is not supported by evidence. Problems with drinking in later life appear typically to be a continuation of drinking patterns established in the adult years.
3. When abusive drinking or alcoholism is observed in later life, therapeutic intervention is at least as effective with older adults as with adults generally. Trend analysis of drug use (Johnson, 1996) and research on alcohol use among community-dwelling older adults (LaKhani, 1997) continue to reinforce these conclusions.

Although recognition of possible cohort differences requires one to be cautious in making broad generalizations about future patterns of drinking behavior among older adults, no current evidence has established an increased risk of abusive drinking in later life. Evidence continues to suggest that social factors associated with aging tend to moderate drinking behavior.

George L. Maddox

See also
Substance Abuse and Addictions

References

Barnes, G., Abel, E., & Ernst, C. (1980). *Alcohol and the elderly*. Westport, CT: Greenwood Press.

Johnson, R. A. (1996). Trends in the incidence of drug use in the U.S., 1919-1992. Washington, DC: U.S. Department of Health and Human Services.

LaKhani, N. (1997). Alcohol use amongst community-dwelling elderly people: A review of the literature. *Journal of Advanced Nursing*, *25*, 1227–1232.

Maddox, G., Robins, L., & Rosenberg, N. (Eds.). (1985). *Nature and extent of alcohol problems among the elderly*. New York: Springer Publishing.

Midanik, L., & Clark, W. B. (1994). The demographic distribution of U.S. drinking patterns in 1990: Description and trends from 1984. *American Journal of Public Health*, *84*(8), 218–222.

Mishra, B., & Kastenbaum, R. (1980). *Alcohol and old age*. New York: Grune and Stratton.

Roueche, B. (1960). *Alcohol*. New York: Grove Press.

ALZHEIMER'S DISEASE: CLINICAL

Alzheimer's disease (AD) is a neurodegenerative condition of late adulthood with a characteristic pattern of progression that allows for an accurate clinical diagnosis during life (85% correlation with autopsy findings of *neuritic plaques* and *neurofibrillary tangles*). Early symptoms include decline in the memory of recent events, in executive abilities, and in word-finding. In AD's moderate stage, judgment is impaired in financial affairs, supervision is required for most instrumental day-to-day tasks, and hallucinations and false beliefs can emerge, although they are more common in moderated later stages. The moderate stage is defined by impairment in instrumental activities of daily living and requiring prompting to complete personal ADLs, which otherwise are largely done without assistance. In the late stage, the patient needs help for basic activities, such as dressing, eating, and using the toilet; agitation, especially after dark, and aggressivity may occur, imposing an additional burden on caregivers often leading to the patient's placement in a nursing home. The final stage is one of muscle rigidity leading to aspiration pneumonia. The life span of persons with AD is shorter than that for age-matched populations.

A diagnosis of *dementia* due to AD is made on the basis of a decline in two or more cognitive domains that interferes with a patient's social or occupational life, and which has no other neurological psychiatric or systemic cause. A new trend is to diagnose AD in its early, purely amnestic stage, labeled "*amnestic mild cognitive impairment*" (aMCI); sophisticated psychometric testing is required at this stage, and additional genetic and brain imaging testing may be needed. A pre-symptomatic stage of AD can be diagnosed in first-degree relatives of patients carrying *presenilin* or *amyloid precursor protein mutations*, using *serial psychometric testing* and brain imaging. Diagnosing AD in its pre-symptomatic or aMCI stages will be clinically meaningful once disease-modifying treatments become available.

A vascular component to dementia is frequently found in people aged 75 years and older, especially in those with a history of *transient ischemic attacks* (stroke-like symptoms lasting less than 24 hours), *vascular risk factors* (diabetes, high blood pressure, atrial fibrillation, high blood lipid levels), and evidence of strokes on brain imaging; the combination of AD and vascular components is referred to as "*mixed dementia*." Vascular risk factors (VRF) are so frequent in patients with late-onset AD that they likely play a role in the emergence of symptoms and are certainly worth treating at all stages of AD. Along with an active and socially integrated lifestyle, treating VRF is currently one of the best ways to prevent dementia in the population at large.

Management of AD includes accurate diagnosis, education of both patients and caregivers about the disease, referral to community resources and lay associations, and drug treatments for depression and other psychiatric symptoms, cognitive and functional decline, and associated VRF. Within 5 years, it is expected that there will be treatments to target the primary pathophysiology of AD, acting on brain amyloid metabolism, synaptic plasticity, or inflammatory responses. *Pharmacogenetic profiles* of individuals at risk or in early stages of AD will help select the best long-term therapy. Until then, *cholinesteraseinhibitors* (*donepezil*, *rivastigmine*, *galantamine*) and the *NMDA receptor antagonist memantine* are used to treat symptoms through the mild to moderately severe stages of AD. *Cognitive training* alone for aMCI, or as value added to pharmacotherapy in mild AD, is being studied. Structured caregiver education and support in mild to moderate AD may delay the need for the patient's placement in a nursing home.

For updates, consult:
www.alz.co.uk/adi/publications.html#gp
www.cnsforum.com

SERGE GAUTHIER

See also
Dementia
Dementia: Frontotemporal
Dementia: Lewy Body

ALZHEIMER'S DISEASE: GENETIC FACTORS

The majority of Alzheimer's Disease (AD) cases are sporadic (~95%), with onset after 65 years of age. Multiple studies suggest a complex etiology of AD, with both environmental and genetic factors influencing the pathogenesis of the disease. Twin studies found the concordance rate for AD among monozygotic twins to be 78% versus 39% among dizygotic twin pairs, indicating a strong genetic influence (Bergem, Engedal and Kringlen, 1997).

The earliest sign of AD brain pathology is the deposition of *extracellular amyloid plaques*, consisting mainly of $A\beta_{40/42}$ peptides generated by cleavage of the *β-amyloid precursor protein* (APP). The longer and more neurotoxic isoform ($A\beta_{42}$) appears to be elevated in the brains of individuals affected with either sporadic or familial AD, implying that they have a shared pathogenetic mechanism. The combination of genetic and biochemical data led to the formulation of the *amyloid cascade hypothesis* which suggested that Aβ deposition was the primary event in disease pathogenesis (Glenner and Wong, 1984; Selkoe, 1991; Hardy and Higgins, 1992). To date four genes responsible for AD have been identified (Figure 1). The common pathological effect imparted by all four AD-linked genes is to alter APP processing and promote Aβ deposition.

Approximately 5% of cases are associated with early onset AD. The disease in these families is often transmitted as a pure genetic, autosomal dominant trait. Genetic analyses of such pedigrees have found three causal genes: *APP* (Goate, Chartier-Harlin, Mullan, Brown, Crawford, et al., 1991); *presenilin 1* (PS1) (Sherrington, Rogaev, Liang, Rogaeva, Levesque, et al., 1995); and *presenilin 2* (PS2) (Rogaev, Sherrington, Rogaeva, Levesque, Ikeda, et al., 1995; Levy-Lahad, Wasco, Poorkaj, Romano, Oshima, et al. 1995). Another genetic locus for inherited susceptibility to AD was resolved to the *Apolipoprotein E* (APOE) gene that acts as a risk factor and age at onset modifier for the late

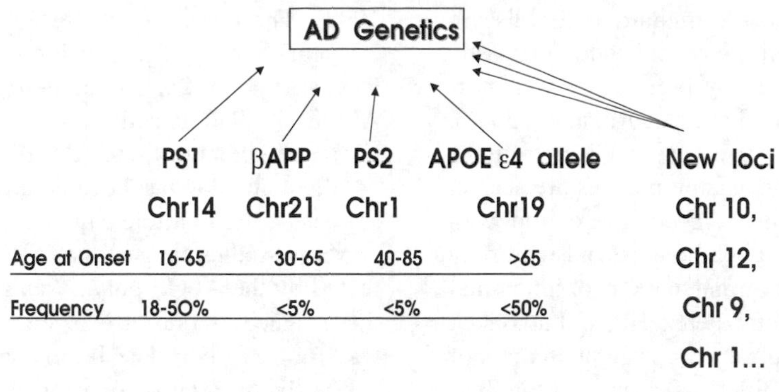

FIGURE 1 Genetic determinants of AD.

onset form of AD (Saunders, Strittmatter, Schmechel, George-Hyslop, Pericak-Vance, et al., 1993) (Figure 1).

APP Gene

To date 15 distinct AD-associated mutations have been published in the APP gene located on *chromosome 21q21* (http://molgen-www.uia.ac.be/ADMutations/). APP mutations affect at least 45 families in which the age at onset is ranging between 30 and 65 years. The Val717Ile is the most frequent substitution found in ~50% of APP families. Another five mutations either have a questionable pathogenic nature or are associated with a different stroke-related, but amyloid-dependant pathology (Levy, Carma, Fernandez-Madrid, Power, Lieberburg, et al., 1990; Van Broeckhoven, Haan, Bakker, Hardy, Van Hul, et al., 1990).

All known pathological APP mutations have a direct effect on APP processing. APP can be cleaved by at least two separate pathways. One involves *α-secretase cleavage* within the Aβ peptide sequence. The other pathway requires proteolysis by β- and γ-secretases to generate $A\beta_{40-42}$ peptides. AD mutations are clustered near the α-, β-, or *γ-secretase cleavage* sites (Hardy, 1997). The majority of the mutations either lead to an elevation of the *$A\beta_{42}$ peptide*, or to an increase of both short and long forms of Aβ. In contrast, the *Ala692Gly mutation* reduces α-secretase cleavage but increases the variety of the Aβ species (Haass, Hung, Selkoe and Teplow, 1994). Furthermore, Val715Met and Glu693Gly, reduce total Aβ production, indicating that the overall ratio of $A\beta_{42}$ to the other Aβ species may be a more relevant indicator of AD pathology than the absolute level of $A\beta_{42}$ or total Aβ(Ancolio, Dumanchin, Barelli, Warter, Brice, et al., 1999; Nilsberth, Westlind-Danielsson, Eckman, Condron, Axelman, et al., 2001).

PS1 and PS2 Genes

Mutations in the *PS1 gene*, located on chromosome 14q24.3, are responsible for the most aggressive form of familial AD cases (age at onset 16-65 years) and account for 18%-50% of all early-onset AD cases. To date 140 different fully penetrant PS1 mutations have been found in 278 AD families (http://molgen-www.uia.ac.be/ADMutations/). PS1 mutations (mainly missense substitutions) are not clustered in a particular region but broadly distributed throughout the gene and cumulatively affect ~25% of the coding region of the PS1 gene. The Gly206Ala is the most frequent PS1 mutation observed in 18 unrelated Caribbean Hispanic families (Athan, Williamson, Ciappa, Santana, Romas, et al., 2001).

Most of the PS1 mutations are associated with the classical presentation of AD. However, in 15 families with different PS1 mutations the disease (in addition to dementia) is associated with spastic paraplegia characterized by progressive weakness of the lower limbs (reviewed in Rogaeva, 2002). The brain pathology of these cases differs from the typical picture for AD. Mature plaques are scarce; instead, there are diffuse, Aβ-positive cotton wool plaques without a congophilic core and with only minor neuritic pathology and markers of inflammation (Crook, Verkkoniemi, Perez-Tur, Mehta, Baker, et al., 1998). Several observations argue in favor of the existence of a modifier in variant AD families. For example, an identical PS1 mutation has been found in a family with variant AD, as well as in a family with a typical AD.

PS1 shares amino acid and structural similarities with PS2 (chromosome 1q31-q42). However, AD that is associated with mutations in the *PS2 gene* is rare and variably penetrant (Sherrington, Froelich, Sorbi, Campion, Chi, et al., 1996). To date 10 distinct PS2 mutations have been reported in 45 families with age at onset ranging between 40 and 85 years (http://molgen-www.uia.ac.be/ADMutations/).

The concept that changes in APP processing are central to AD pathology won further support after the discovery that mutations in PS1 and PS2 genes cause the overproduction of the Aβ_{42} (Citron, Westaway, Xia, Carlson, Diehl, et al., 1997). Nevertheless, presenilins have a complex functional profile as integrators of several signaling pathways and it is possible that a dysfunction of these pathways can contribute to neurodegeneration in mutation carriers. In addition to APP processing, PS1 and PS2 are essential for the proteolytic cleavage of several proteins including Notch1 (De Strooper, Annaert, Cupers, Saftig, Craessaerts, et al., 1999).

APOE Gene

The three common isoforms of the APOE gene on chromosome 19q13.2 are encoded by alleles $\varepsilon 2$, $\varepsilon 3$ and $\varepsilon 4$. The $\varepsilon 4$ polymorphism is significantly over-represented in AD subjects (up to 40% from 15% in the general population), whereas the frequency of the $\varepsilon 2$ allele is reduced from 10% to 2% in AD (Saunders, Strittmatter, Schmechel, George-Hyslop, Pericak-Vance, et al, 1993; Corder, Saunders, Risch, Strittmatter, Schmechel, et al., 1994). The mean age of onset of AD is less than 70 years among the $\varepsilon 4/\varepsilon 4$ population, but over 90 years for the $\varepsilon 2/\varepsilon 3$ population (Roses, 1998). The APOE $\varepsilon 4$ allele is acting as a risk factor and may not be sufficient to cause AD. The link between the $\varepsilon 4$ allele and AD has been confirmed in numerous studies across multiple ethnic groups.

Many studies suggest that APP processing is affected by the APOE polymorphisms. For example, the absence or presence of one or two $\varepsilon 4$ alleles was found to correlate in a dose-dependent manner with the relative density of amyloid plaques (Schmechel, Saunders, Strittmatter, Crain, Hulette, et al., 1993). The APOE gene itself is not useful for pre-symptomatic testing since not all $\varepsilon 4$ carriers will develop the disease and $\varepsilon 4$-association is not entirely specific to AD. Nevertheless in the future APOE can be used in combination with other yet to be discovered AD risk factors. Notably, up to 68% of AD cases do not have an APOE-$\varepsilon 4$ allele indicating that additional factors are involved in late-onset form of the disease.

Search for Novel AD Risk Factors

There are two approaches to finding susceptibility loci: *linkage analysis* (*genome scans*) and *candidate gene studies*. To date, several complete genome screens have been published for late-onset AD and more than 20 distinct AD loci were reported, however many of them are likely to be false positive results and will have to be confirmed in independent data sets (Pericak-Vance, Bass, Yamaoka, Gaskell, Scott, et al., 1997; Kehoe, Wavrant-De Vrieze, Crook, Wu, et al., 1999; Blacker, Bertram, Saunders, Moscarillo, Albert, et al., 2003). The linkage support was obtained for chromosomes 1, 5, 6, 9, 10, 12 and 19.

A subsequent follow-up study confirmed the presence of AD susceptibility loci on chromosome 12 (Rogaeva, Premkumar, Song, Sorbi, Brindle, et al., 1998; Mayeux, Lee, Romas, Mayo, Santana, Williamson, et al., 2002) and on chromosome 10 (Myers, Holmans, Marshall, Kwon, Meyer, et al, 2000; Ertekin-Taner, Graff-Radford, Younkin, Eckman, Baker, et al., 2000; Bertram, Blacker, Mullin, Keeney, Jones, et al, 2000; Lee, Mayeux, Mayo, Mo, Santana, et al 2003). However, the linkage results support very broad intervals on both chromosomes

(~70 cM) and often point to distant chromosomal regions. Therefore, the chromosome 10 and 12 loci could harbor several distinct AD genes; so far none of the genes responsible for these linkages have been found.

In candidate gene studies, genes are selected based upon the known biology of the disease and assessed to determine whether variants in each candidate are associated with disease. In recent years, many genes have been reported to be associated to AD (reviewed in Rogaeva, Tandon and St. George-Hyslop, 2001). However, most of these findings have not received the same robust replication as the association between AD and the APOE $\varepsilon4$ allele. The conflicting results could be explained by the genetic and neuropathological heterogeneity of AD.

Conclusion

Genetic studies have proven to be an effective way to develop understanding of AD. Altered APP/Aβ metabolism is central to all known causes of AD. Treatment and diagnostic strategies based on genetic knowledge are now about to reach the clinic. This will entail the identification of individuals predisposed to AD before they are affected while the neuronal damage is still negligible. The future of AD research should include studying the genetic epidemiology of AD with the objective of investigating gene/environment interactions.

EKATERINA ROGAEVA
PETER ST. GEORGE-HYSLOP

References

Ancolio, K., Dumanchin, C., Barelli, H., Warter, J. M., Brice, A., Campion, D., Frebourg, T., & Checler, F. (1999). Unusual phenotypic alteration of beta amyloid precursor protein (betaAPP) maturation by a new Val-715 Met betaAPP-770 mutation responsible for probable early-onset Alzheimer's disease. *Proceedings of the National Academy of Sciences USA, 96,* 4119–4124.

Athan, E. S., Williamson, J., Ciappam, A., Santana, V., Romas, S. N., Lee, J. H., Rondon, H., Lantigua, R. A., Medrano, M., Torres, M., Arawaka, S., Rogaeva, E., Song, Y. Q., Sat, C., Kawarai, T., Fafel, K. C., Boss, M. A., Seltzer, W. K., Stern, Y., St George-Hyslop, P., Tycko, B., & Mayeux, R. (2001). A founder mutation in presenilin 1 causing early-onset Alzheimer disease in unrelated Caribbean Hispanic families. *Journal of the American Medical Association, 286,* 2257–2263.

Bergem, A. L. M., Engedal, K., & Kringlen, E. (1997). The role of heredity in late-onset Alzheimer disease and vascular dementia. *Archives of General Psychiatry, 54,* 264–270.

Bertram, L., Blacker, D., Mullin, K., Keeney, D., Jones, J., Basu, S., Yhu, S., McInnis, M. G., Go, R. C., Vekrellis, K., Selkoe, D. J., Saunders, A. J., & Tanzi, R. E. (2000). Evidence for genetic linkage of Alzheimer's disease to chromosome 10q. *Science, 290,* 2302–2303.

Blacker, D., Bertram, L., Saunders, A. J., Moscarillo, T. J., Albert, M. S., Wiener, H., Perry, R. T., Collins, J. S., Harrell, L. E., Go, R. C., Mahoney, A., Beaty, T., Fallin, M. D., Avramopoulos, D., Chase, G. A., Folstein, M. F., McInnis, M. G., Bassett, S. S., Doheny, K. J., Pugh, E. W., & Tanzi, R. E. (2003). NIMH Genetics Initiative Alzheimer's Disease Study Group. Results of a high-resolution genome screen of 437 Alzheimer's disease families. *Human Molecular Genetics, 12,* 23–32.

Citron, M., Westaway, D., Xia, W., Carlson, G., Diehl, T., Levesque, G., Johnson-Wood, K., Lee, M., Seubert, P., Davis, A., Kholodenko, D., Motter, R., Sherrington, R., Perry, B., Yao, H., Strome, R., Lieberburg, I., Rommens, J., Kim, S., Schenk, D., Fraser, P., St George, H. P., & Selkoe, D. J. (1997). Mutant presenilins of Alzheimer's disease increase production of 42-residue amyloid beta-protein in both transfected cells and transgenic mice. *Nature Medicine, 3,* 67–72.

Corder, E. H., Saunders, A. M., Risch, N. J., Strittmatter, W. J., Schmechel, D. E., Gaskell, P. C. Jr., Rimmler, J. B., Locke, P. A., Conneally, P. M., & Schmader, K. E. (1994). Protective effect of apolipoprotein E type 2 allele for late onset Alzheimer disease. *Nature Genetics, 7,* 180–184.

Crook, R., Verkkoniemi, A., Perez-Tur, J., Mehta, N., Baker, M., Houlden, H., Farrer, M., Hutton, M., Lincoln, S., Hardy, J., Gwinn, K., Somer, M., Paetau, A., Kalimo, H., Ylikoski, R., Poyhonen, M., Kucera, S., Haltia, M. (1998). A variant of Alzheimer's disease with spastic paraparesis and unusual plaques due to deletion of exon 9 of presenilin 1. *Nature Medicine, 4,* 452–455.

De Strooper, B., Annaert, W., Cupers, P., Saftig, P., Craessaerts, K., Mumm, J. S., Schroeter, E. H., Schrijvers, V., Wolfe, M. S., Ray, W. J., Goate, A., & Kopan, R. (1999). A presenilin-1-dependent gamma-secretase-like protease mediates release of Notch intracellular domain. *Nature, 398,* 518–522.

Ertekin-Taner, N., Graff-Radford, N., Younkin, L. H., Eckman, C., Baker, M., Adamson, J., Ronald, J.,

Blangero, J., Hutton, M., & Younkin, S. G. (2000). Linkage of plasma Abeta42 to a quantitative locus on chromosome 10 in late-onset Alzheimer's disease pedigrees. *Science*, *290,* 2303–2304.

Glenner, G. G., & Wong, C. W. (1984). Alzheimer's disease: initial report of the purification and characterization of a novel cerebrovascular amyloid protein. *Biochemical and Biophysical Research Communications*, *120,* 885–890.

Goate, A. M., Chartier-Harlin, M. C., Mullan, M. C., Brown, J., Crawford, F., Fidani, L., Giuffra, L., Haynes, A., Irving, N., James, L., Mant, R., Newton, P., Rooke, K., Roques, P., Talbot, C., Pericak-Vance, M., Roses, A., Williamson, R., Rossor, M. N., Owen, M., & Hardy, J. (1991). Segregation of a missense mutation in the amyloid precursor protein gene with familial Alzheimer's disease. *Nature*, *349,* 704–706.

Hardy, J. (1997). Amyloid, the presenilins and Alzheimer's disease. *Trends in Neuroscience*, *20,* 154–159.

Hardy, J. A., & Higgins, G. A. (1992). Alzheimer's disease: the amyloid cascade hypothesis. *Science*, *286,* 184–185.

Haass, C., Hung, A. Y., Selkoe, D. J., & Teplow, D. B. (1994). Mutations associated with a locus for familial Alzheimer's disease result in alternative processing of amyloid beta-protein precursor. *Journal of Biology and Chemistry*, *269,* 17741–17748.

Kehoe, P., Wavrant-De Vrieze, F., Crook, R., Wu, W. S., Holmans, P., Fenton, I., Spurlock, G., Norton, N., Williams, H., Williams, N., Lovestone, S., Perez-tur, J., Hutton, M., Chartier-Harlin, M. C., Shears, S., Roehl, K., Booth, J., Van Voorst, W., Ramic, D., Williams, J., Goate, A., Hardy, J., & Owen, M. J. (1999). A full genome scan for late onset Alzheimer's disease. *Human Molecular Genetics*, *8,* 237–245.

Lee, J. H., Mayeux, R., Mayo, D., Mo, J., Santana, V., Williamson, J., Flaquer, A., Ciappa, A., Rondon, H., Estevez, P., Lantigua, R., Kawarai, T., Toulina, A., Medrano, M., Torres, M., Stern, Y., Tycko, B., Rogaeva, E., St George-Hyslop, P., & Knowles, J. A. (2004). Fine mapping of 10q and 18q for familial Alzheimer's disease in Caribbean Hispanics. *Molecular Psychiatry*, *9,* 1042–1051.

Levy, E., Carman, M. D., Fernandez-Madrid, I. J., Power, M. D., Lieberburg, I., van Duinen, S. G., Bots, G. T., Luyendijk, W., & Frangione, B. (1990). eMutation of the Alzheimer's disease amyloid gene in hereditary cerebral hmorrhage, Dutch type. *Science*, *248,* 1124–1126.

Levy-Lahad, E., Wasco, W., Poorkaj, P., Romano, D. M., Oshima, J., Pettingell, W. H., Yu, C. E., Jondro, P. D., Schmidt, S. D., Wang, K., et al. (1995). Candidate gene for the chromosome 1 familial Alzheimer's disease locus. *Science*, *269,* 973–977.

Mayeux, R., Lee, J. H., Romas, S. N., Mayo, D., Santana, V., Williamson, J., Ciappa, A., Rondon, H. Z., Estevez, P., Lantigua, R., Medrano, M., Torres, M., Stern, Y., Tycko, B., & Knowles, J. A. (2002). Chromosome-12 mapping of late-onset Alzheimer disease among Caribbean Hispanics. *American Journal of Human Genetics*, *70,* 237–243.

Myers, A., Holmans, P., Marshall, H., Kwon, J., Meyer, D., Ramic, D., Shears, S., Booth, J., DeVrieze, F. W., Crook, R., Hamshere, M., Abraham, R., Tunstall, N., Rice, F., Carty, S., Lillystone, S., Kehoe, P., Rudrasingham, V., Jones, L., Lovestone, S., Perez-Tur, J., Williams, J., Owen, M. J., Hardy, J., & Goate, A. M. (2000). Susceptibility locus for Alzheimer's disease on chromosome 10. *Science*, *290,* 2304–2305.

Pericak-Vance, M. A., Bass, M. P., Yamaoka, L. H., Gaskell, P. C., Scott, W. K., Terwedow, H. A., Menold, M. M., Conneally, P. M., Small, G. W., Vance, J. M., Saunders, A. M., Roses, A. D., & Haines, J. L. (1997). Complete genomic screen in late-onset familial Alzheimer disease. Evidence for a new locus on chromosome 12. *Journal of the American Medical Association*, *278,* 1237–1241.

Rogaeva, E. (2002). The solved and unsolved mysteries of the genetics of early-onset Alzheimer's disease. *Neuromolecular Medicine*, *2,* 1–10.

Rogaeva, E., Premkumar, S., Song, Y., Sorbi, S., Brindle, N., Paterson, A., Duara, R., Levesque, G., Yu, G., Nishimura, M., Ikeda, M., O'Toole, C., Kawarai, T., Jorge, R., Vilarino, D., Bruni, A. C., Farrer, L. A., & George-Hyslop, P. H. (1998). Evidence for an Alzheimer disease susceptibility locus on chromosome 12 and for further locus heterogeneity. *Journal of the American Medical Association*, *280,* 614–618.

Rogaev, E. I., Sherrington, R., Rogaeva, E. A., Levesque, G., Ikeda, M., Liang, Y., Chi, H., Lin, C., Holman, K., Tsuda, T., et al. (1995). Familial Alzheimer's disease in kindreds with missense mutations in a gene on chromosome 1 related to the Alzheimer's disease type 3 gene. *Nature*, *376,* 775–778.

Rogaeva, E., Tandon, A., & St George-Hyslop, P. H. (2001). Genetic markers in the diagnosis of Alzheimer's disease. *Journal of Alzheimers Disease*, *3,* 293–304.

Roses, A. D. (1998). Apolipoprotein E and Alzheimer's disease. The tip of the susceptibility iceberg. *Annals of the New York Academy of Science*, *855,* 738–743.

Saunders, A. M., Strittmatter, W. J., Schmechel, D., George-Hyslop, P. H., Pericak-Vance, M. A., Joo, S. H., Rosi, B. L., Gusella, J. F., Crapper-MacLachlan, D. R., Alberts, M. J., et al. (1993). Association of apolipoprotein E allele epsilon 4 with late-onset familial and sporadic Alzheimer's disease. *Neurology*, *43,* 1467–1472.

Schmechel, D. E., Saunders, A. M., Strittmatter, W. J., Crain, B. J., Hulette, C. M., Joo, S. H., Pericak-Vance, M. A., Goldgaber, D., & Roses, A. D. (1993). Increased amyloid beta-peptide deposition in cerebral cortex as a consequence of apolipoprotein E genotype in late-onset Alzheimer disease. *Proceedings of the National Academy of Sciences USA, 90,* 9649–9653.

Selkoe, D. J. (1991). The molecular pathology of Alzheimer's disease. *Neuron, 6,* 487–498.

Sherrington, R., Froelich, S., Sorbi, S., Campion, D., Chi, H., Rogaeva, E. A., Levesque, G., Rogaev, E. I., Lin, C., Liang, Y., Ikeda, M., Mar, L., Brice, A., Agid, Y., Percy, M. E., Clerget-Darpoux, F., Piacentini, S., Marcon, G., Nacmias, B., Amaducci, L., Frebourg, T., Lannfelt, L., Rommens, J. M., & St. George-Hyslop, P. H. (1996). Alzheimer's disease associated with mutations in presenilin 2 is rare and variably penetrant. *Human Molecular Genetics, 5,* 985–988.

Sherrington, R., Rogaev, E. I., Liang, Y., Rogaeva, E. A., Levesque, G., Ikeda, M., Chi, H., Lin, C., Li, G., Holman, K., et al. (1995) Cloning of a gene bearing missense mutations in early-onset familial Alzheimer's disease. *Nature, 375,* 754–760.

Van Broeckhoven, C., Haan, J., Bakker, E., Hardy, J. A., van Hul, W., Wehnert, A., Vegter-Van der Vlis, M., & Roos, R. A. (1990). Amyloid beta protein precursor gene and hereditary cerebral hemorrhage with amyloidosis (Dutch). *Science, 248,* 1120–1122.

AMBULATORY AND OUTPATIENT CARE

For an increasing number of older adults, ambulatory and *outpatient care* constitute the nexus of health care across time and transitions in health status. A spectrum of care settings and providers delivers formal care for older individuals outside the hospital setting. *Ambulatory care* can take place in locations as varied as hospital-based procedural units and individual patients' homes. The rate of ambulatory care use continues to rise. In 2002, individuals aged 65 to 74 years made approximately 550 visits to office-based physician practices per 100 individuals in the United States. For individuals aged 75 years and older, this number was approximately 700 visits per 100 (Woodwell & Cherry, 2004). Family members often accompany patients to these visits and are integral in the care provided. *Geriatricians* provide but a small fraction of paid care; in the United States, only 9,000 of 650,000 licensed physicians have this added qualification (Mitka, 2002), and of those only approximately 10% had formal training in *geriatric medicine* in 1992 (Reuben & Beck, 1994). In ambulatory care, the complex interactions among social, health care system, psychological, and medical issues play out vividly, making collaboration across disciplines an essential facet of care for older adults.

Ideal ambulatory care would put the patient at the center of the health care system, acknowledge the heterogeneity and vulnerability of older persons from physiologic and social standpoints, and be continuous across care settings, in addition to being cost-effective. The obstacles to providing such care to older persons are substantial. The heterogeneity of health status in the elderly makes appropriate targeting of ambulatory care a major challenge. Compared to younger persons, a higher proportion of older individuals are not healthy. Sixty-two percent of older individuals have 2 or more chronic illnesses, compared with 21% in the general population. The result is that a small, ill subset of the population receives the majority of ambulatory care. For example, 66% of the Medicare budget is used for the care of individuals with 5 or more chronic illnesses, even though these individuals comprise approximately 1% of the U.S. population (Partnership for Solutions, 2002). Although the majority of health care spending is for hospital care, the chronically ill are the main focus of ambulatory care. The complex health status of older individuals often requires difficult decisions involving tradeoffs and the incorporation of personal preferences.

For healthy older persons, preventive services should be a major focus of care. The U.S. Preventive Services Task Force and the Canadian Task Force on Preventive Health Care have identified several conditions for which evidence supports *screening in the elderly* (Agency for Health Care Research and Quality, 2004; Canadian Task Force on Preventive Health Care, 2004). Growing evidence suggests that exercise can delay many adverse outcomes across the range of functional ability, if it is modified for the specific needs of the individual (Bean, Vora, & Frontera, 2004).

Practice guidelines based on small to moderate degrees of average benefit in younger persons who suffer from 1 chronic illness may not be applicable to people with multiple comorbidities (Kravitz, Duan, & Braslow, 2004; Tinetti, Bogardus, & Agostini, 2004). Older adults with multiple chronic illnesses are often unable to surmount the economic privation and social isolation which can threaten health. In addition, their care trajectories often wend through different formal health care sites, leading to fragmented care. One study found that 39% of Medicare beneficiaries do not go straight home upon hospital discharge (Coleman, Min, Chomiak, & Kramer, 2004). Efforts dedicated to communication across care settings are necessary. It is now more widely recognized that older individuals bear the brunt of inadequacies and errors in health care. For example, work in the prescribing rates of potentially inappropriate medications for older outpatients has led to increased awareness and measurement (Goulding, 2004).

Several trends in ambulatory care delivery and research are encouraging. *Health care for older people* is entering an age of process scrutiny, outcome assessment, and demand for improvement. Recognition that a new model of care for chronic disease is needed has led to growth in research and practices that focus on systems processes and span *silos* of care. For example, comprehensive *hospital discharge planning* with a built-in *ambulatory care bridge* has been studied in more than 8 countries, and findings show a reduction of adverse outcomes related to congestive heart failure (Phillips, Wright, Kern, Singa, Shepperd, & Rubin, 2004). In addition, there has been an increase in the number of home-based practices and other alternative models of ambulatory care. The *Program of All-inclusive Care for the Elderly (PACE) program*, which integrates primary care for high-risk, *nursing home–eligible persons* with other services including medication coverage and social support in a capitated fee structure, has matured from a demonstration project to a system with more than 25 sites (Gross, Temkin-Greener, Kunitz, & Mukamel, 2004). *Home-hospital care* models that either substitute entirely for hospital admission or facilitate early hospital discharge have been developed in several countries, including Australia, Israel, Italy, the United Kingdom, and the United States (Shepperd & Iliffe, 2001). There is also increased interest in care models and systems that incorporate care principles crucial to chronic disease management (Bodenheimer, Lorig, Holman, & Grumbach, 2002). However, widespread dissemination of these innovations remains a challenge.

Two mainstays of care for older individuals have matured further. The *comprehensive geriatric assessment* (CGA) is an interdisciplinary assessment of an individual's health and geriatric conditions. *Geriatric evaluation and management* (GEM) adds responsibility for implementation. Systematic review and meta-analysis of studies performed on 3 continents have shown that when targeted appropriately and with sufficient follow-up, home-based CGA reduces placement in nursing homes, functional decline, and mortality (Stuck, Egger, Hammer, Minder, & Beck, 2002). Outpatient GEM has also been shown to improve mental health scores without increasing cost (Cohen, Feussner, Weinberger, Carnes, Hamdy, Hsieh, et al., 2002). Nonetheless, not all trials have been consistent with benefit, and translating these results into practice has been a challenge (Rubenstein, 2004). The challenges have arisen in part because there is no single recipe for how CGA or GEM is performed. One example of an adapted CGA is a home-based intervention in which physical and occupational therapists implemented CGA and related principles to improve the function of older individuals (Tinetti, Baker, Gallo, Nanda, Charpentier, & O'Leary, 2002). Another challenge is that standard outcome measures may not capture changes important to many older individuals. This has led to research on how to use individualized responses in assessing program efficacy (Rockwood, Howlett, Stadnyk, Carver, Powell, & Stolee, 2003).

Recent growth in the area of *palliative care* has contributed to change in ambulatory care for older individuals. Strictly speaking, *palliation* refers to attention to the control of symptoms without regard for their cause. This field originated from care for dying patients, but it has now expanded to include many ill groups. Research and advocacy that prioritize *pain control* and incorporating the experiences of patients and their families have been combined with interdisciplinary and process-focused perspectives. Consensus regarding how palliative care can be targeted or reliably differentiated from other care has yet to be firmly established (Ahmedzai, Costa, Blengini, Bosch, Sanz-Ortiz, Ventafridda, & Verhagen, 2004).

Carlos Weiss
Bruce Leff

See also
Geriatric Assessment Programs

References

U.S. Department of Health and Human Services, Agency for Health Care Research and Quality. (2004). U.S. Preventive Services Task Force. Available: http://www.ahrq.gov/clinic/uspstfix.htm

Ahmedzai, S. H., Costa, A., Blengini, C., Bosch, A., Sanz-Ortiz, J., Ventafridda, V., & Verhagen, S. C. (2004). A new international framework for palliative care. *European Journal of Cancer, 40*(15), 2192–2200.

Bean, J. F., Vora, A., & Frontera, W. R. (2004). Benefits of exercise for community-dwelling older adults. *Archives of Physical Medicine and Rehabilitation, 85*(7 Suppl 3), S31-42; quiz S43–44.

Bodenheimer, T., Lorig, K., Holman, H., & Grumbach, K. (2002). Patient self-management of chronic disease in primary care. *Journal of the American Medical Association, 288*(19), 2469–2475.

Canadian Task Force on Preventive Health Care. (2004). Available: http://www.ctfphc.org

Cohen, H. J., Feussner, J. R., Weinberger, M., Carnes, M., Hamdy, R. C., Hsieh, F., Phibbs, C., Courtney, D., Lyles, K. W., May, C., McMurtry, C., Pennypacker, L., Smith, D. M., Ainslie, N., Hornick, T., Brodkin, K., & Lavori, P. (2002). A controlled trial of inpatient and outpatient geriatric evaluation and management. *New England Journal of Medicine, 346*(12), 905–912.

Coleman, E. A., Min, S. J., Chomiak, A., & Kramer, A. M. (2004). Posthospital care transitions: Patterns, complications, and risk identification. *Health Services Research, 39*(5), 1449–1465.

Goulding, M. R. (2004). Inappropriate medication prescribing for elderly ambulatory care patients. *Archives of Internal Medicine, 164*(3), 305–312.

Gross, D. L., Temkin-Greener, H., Kunitz, S., & Mukamel, D. B. (2004). The growing pains of integrated health care for the elderly: Lessons from the expansion of PACE. *Milbank Quarterly, 82*(2), 257–282.

Kravitz, R. L., Duan, N., & Braslow, J. (2004). Evidence-based medicine, heterogeneity of treatment effects, and the trouble with averages. *Milbank Quarterly, 82*(4), 661–687.

Mitka, M. (2002). As Americans age, geriatricians go missing. *Journal of the American Medical Association, 287*(14), 1792–1793.

Partnership for Solutions. (2002). *Chronic conditions: Making the case for ongoing care* (p. 48). Baltimore: Available: http://www.partnershipforsolutions.com/dms/files/chronicbook2002.pdf

Phillips, C. O., Wright, S. M., Kern, D. E., Singa, R. M., Shepperd, S., & Rubin, H. R. (2004). Comprehensive discharge planning with postdischarge support for older patients with congestive heart failure: a meta-analysis. *Journal of the American Medical Association, 291*(11), 1358–1367.

Reuben, D. B., & Beck, J. C. (1994). Training physicians to care for older Americans: Progress, obstacles, and future directions. In National Academies Press (Ed.). Washington, DC: Institute of Medicine.

Rockwood, K., Howlett, S., Stadnyk, K., Carver, D., Powell, C., & Stolee, P. (2003). Responsiveness of goal attainment scaling in a randomized controlled trial of comprehensive geriatric assessment. *Journal of Clinical Epidemiology, 56*(8), 736–743.

Shepperd, S., & Iliffe, S. (2001). Hospital at home versus in-patient hospital care. Cochrane Database of Systematic Reviews, *3*, CD000356.

Stuck, A. E., Egger, M., Hammer, A., Minder, C. E., & Beck, J. C. (2002). Home visits to prevent nursing home admission and functional decline in elderly people: Systematic review and meta-regression analysis. *Journal of the American Medical Association, 287*(8), 1022–1028.

Tinetti, M. E., Baker, D., Gallo, W. T., Nanda, A., Charpentier, P., & O'Leary, J. (2002). Evaluation of restorative care versus usual care for older adults receiving an acute episode of home care. *Journal of the American Medical Association, 287*(16), 2098–2105.

Tinetti, M. E., Bogardus Jr., S. T., & Agostini, J. V. (2004). Potential pitfalls of disease-specific guidelines for patients with multiple conditions. *New England Journal of Medicine, 351*(27), 2870–2874.

Woodwell, D. A., & Cherry, D. K. (2004). National Ambulatory Medical Care Survey: 2002 Summary. *Advance data from vital and health statistics*. Hyattsville, MD: U.S. Department of Health and Human Services, Centers for Disease Control and Prevention, National Center for Health Statistics. Available: http://www.cdc.gov/nchs/about/major/ahcd/adata.htm

AMERICAN ASSOCIATION OF HOMES AND SERVICES FOR THE AGING

The American Association of Homes and Services for the Aging (AAHSA), located in Washington, DC, serves 2 million people every day through mission-driven, not-for-profit organizations dedicated to providing the services people need, when they need them, in the place they call home. AAHSA members offer the continuum of aging services: assisted living residences, continuing care retirement communities, nursing homes, outreach programs, and senior housing. AAHSA is committed to creating the future of aging services through quality people can trust.

The AAHSA also houses the *Institute for the Future of Aging Services* (IFAS), a policy research center. The IFAS mission is twofold: (1) to create a bridge between the practice, policy, and research communities to advance the development of high-quality aging services and a high-quality long-term care workforce, and (2) to provide a forum for the health, supportive services, and housing communities to explore and develop policies and programs to meet the needs of an aging society. Through its connection with AAHSA, IFAS has access to untapped "*living laboratories*," where independent researchers can study real-world providers and their efforts to improve the lives of older adults and those who care for them. IFAS disseminates these provider-driven, evidence-based models to the aging services provider community and policy makers.

Recently, AAHSA also established the *Center for Aging Services Technology* (CAST), which brings together technology companies, university researchers, care providers, and the government to collaborate in the development and application of technologies that can help increase quality of care for older people while decreasing costs. CAST works to identify technology-based solutions to deal with the challenges the U.S. society will face as the population ages.

In addition to its national focus, AAHSA now sponsors the *International Association of Homes and Services for the Ageing* (IAHSA), a not-for-profit educational and charitable organization with members from more than 30 countries. In recognition of its leadership in the field of aging, recently IAHSA was granted special consultant status to the United Nations Economic and Social Council.

AAHSA offers a number of benefits to its members, such as group purchasing and insurance programs. AAHSA was established in 1961 by a group of 99 persons, who felt a need to critically examine services to the elderly and provide leadership to not-for-profit organizations seeking to provide quality care to current and future generations of elderly persons.

James E. Allen

See also
Organizations in Aging

AMERICAN FEDERATION FOR AGING RESEARCH

The American Federation for Aging Research (AFAR) is a not-for-profit organization that supports research and research training with the goal of enhancing healthy aging through improved knowledge of the basic mechanisms of biological aging and age-related disorders. While *AFAR* supports clinically relevant investigations, it especially encourages research on age-related diseases that emphasizes aging's underlying mechanisms.

AFAR has consistently directed its programs to the needs of beginning investigators, including students, postdoctoral fellows, and junior faculty members. More than 1,000 such scientists and physicians have launched their careers with the help of AFAR training and research grants. Information on its various programs, awardees, and corporate and foundation supporters can be found at www.afar.org/.

Recently, AFAR has been collaborating with the National Institute on Aging, the John A. Hartford Foundation, Atlantic Philanthropies, and the Starr Foundation in support of the Paul B. Beeson Career Development Awards in Aging Research, a program that sustains and promotes clinically trained individuals who are pursuing research careers in the *field of aging*. Another innovation has been the development of an AFAR-sponsored educational Web site at www.infoaging.org/. AFAR's educational activities also have been enhanced by the *Dorothy Dillon Eweson Lecture Series*, through its support of meetings of organizations such as the Gerontological Society of America and the American Geriatrics Society, and through a series of news conferences on recent developments in aging research. AFAR also honors distinguished scientists and citizens for their contributions to research on aging.

AFAR was founded in 1980, thanks largely to the visionary ideas of a New York City cardiologist, *Irving S. Wright*, and generous initial funding from New York philanthropists. Although the national headquarters remains in New York City, regional chapters are being developed, the first of which have opened in Ohio and upper New York state.

George M. Martin

See also
Organizations in Aging

AMERICAN GERIATRICS SOCIETY

Founded in 1942, the American Geriatrics Society (AGS) is a professional organization of health care providers dedicated to improving the health and well being of older adults. With an active membership of more than 6,800 health care professionals, AGS has a long history of effecting change in the provision of health care for older adults. In the last decade, it has become a pivotal force in shaping the attitudes, policies, and practices in health care for older people.

Current membership is comprised primarily of geriatrics health care professionals, including: physicians, nurses, medical educators, pharmacists, physician assistants, social workers, physical therapists, occupational therapists, health care administrators, and others. Historically, the society's members have been predominantly physicians. It also includes research scientists from different disciplines who are interested in the issues of aging and health.

The goals of the American Geriatrics Society are:

- To develop and promote quality, culturally sensitive, interdisciplinary geriatric clinical care and to support the practitioners providing such care.
- To increase the number of health care professionals who are knowledgeable about and participate in the clinical care of older adults, and who seek to improve their quality of life.
- To promote high-quality research that expands *knowledge of the aging process* and addresses the *health care problems of older people*.
- To conduct education programs for health professionals that promote better understanding of the aging process and its unique clinical challenges.
- To provide public education and information that addresses the health care concerns and needs of older people, their families, and their caregivers.
- To engage in public policy that focuses on the study, accessibility, and improvement of culturally sensitive health care and quality of life for older people, including preventive, rehabilitative, long-term, and end-of-life care.

As part of these goals, AGS disseminates numerous influential publications, including the *Journal of the American Geriatrics Society*, one of the leading geriatrics and gerontology publications reporting results or current research on aging and the care of older patients; *Annals of Long-term Care: Clinical Care and Aging*, which presents clinical reviews, analysis, and opinions that impact the present and future of long-term care, and provides information for professionals in the long-term care market; and *Clinical Geriatrics*, which serves as a resource on the care of the mature patient.

RICHARD SCHULZ

See also
Organizations in Aging

Reference

American Geriatrics Society. Available at: http://www.americangeriatrics.org

AMERICAN SOCIETY ON AGING

The American Society on Aging (ASA) is the largest professional organization in the field of aging, with more than 6,000 members, most in the United States. Its mission is to improve the *quality of life for older people* and their families by enhancing the capacity and strengthening the commitment of those who work with them and on their behalf. *ASA* serves its professional membership as well as other organizations in the field through a broad spectrum of activities in education, training, and information dissemination. It sponsors an annual joint conference with the *National Council on the Aging* that attracts approximately 4,000 professionals, who have access to more than 1,000 papers and presentations in 50 aging-related subject areas.

Other education and training events include more than 250 half-day and full-day workshops, either presented as pre-conference events to the joint conference or as part of its "*Summer Series on Aging*," which is held in several cities each year. ASA also sponsors and hosts international conferences on long-term care management and disability issues in aging, as well as on special topical areas.

The association publishes the quarterly, peer-reviewed journal *Generations* and the bimonthly newspaper *Aging Today*, as well as 8 quarterly newsletters on specific areas of interest to members. The extensive Web site (www.asaging.org) offers Web-delivered seminars and other forms of distance learning. Its Web-based learning modules have been developed in association with major organizations such as the Centers for Disease Control and Prevention.

ASA's multidisciplinary membership represents a broad range of individuals and organizations working with older adults. Members include health and social service professionals, educators, researchers, students, policy makers, planners, clergy, business executives, and administrators. They come from a variety of settings that include home-, community-, and institutionally-based long-term care services, residential settings, universities, lifelong learning programs, faith-based organizations, businesses, hospitals, medical centers and managed care organizations, mental health services, and many others.

The Society's Founding

The association was formed in 1954 as the *Western Gerontological Society* (WGS) by a small group of California professionals in the still-emerging field of gerontology. Initially it was conceived as a regional satellite group of the *Gerontological Society of America*, based in Washington, DC, according to James E. Birren, who served as WGS president in the late 1960s. In its early years, WGS was a volunteer-run organization, but it would spread its wings to eventually become the American Society on Aging in 1985.

According to *Gloria Cavanaugh*, president and CEO of ASA, early on WGS founders recognized that the people attending the meetings were practitioners, not the academics who formed the bulk of GSA's membership, and since then their professional needs—such as for best-practice models, or applied social research findings—have set the organization's tone. Tens of thousands of professionals who work with older adults came to WGS/ASA for training, education, and information, prompting the association to expand its regional focus, first to 18 Western states and then going nationwide in 1985.

Cavanaugh, who became the organization's first paid professional staff member in 1975, recalled that when she decided to base the group in San Francisco, the WGS leadership provided her with the society's archives and operating papers in a shoebox and there was barely enough money to reserve the hotel for the upcoming conference. However, a successful conference in San Diego in 1976 provided WGS with enough resources to hire 2 more staff members, and the organization began to blossom.

Diversity and Aging

One of ASA's primary contributions has been its initiatives in diversity. Today the association offers 5 programs in racial or ethnic diversity, such as the *Network of Multicultural Aging* (NOMA)—a national community of individuals and organizations that is concerned with diversity and working toward cultural competence among the health and service professionals who assist older adults, through conference, publications and professional networking activities. ASA's *New Ventures in Leadership* (NVL) also is especially notable. This yearlong program was created in the early 1990s to promote the leadership potential of professionals of color and their involvement in the field of aging on a national level. NVL participants, known as *Partners*, are professionals who continue working with their agencies or organizations in the field while they attend educational conferences, work with senior-level volunteer mentors, and focus their energies on special projects. Partners enhance their skills in areas aligned with their career objectives, such as leadership development, community building and advocacy, grant writing and fundraising, and applied research techniques.

ASA also addressed other issues of diversity in the late 1980s and early 1990s, such as through the establishment of the *Lesbian and Gay Aging Issues Network*. In the same period, the association diversified its membership by creating the *Business Forum on Aging* and the *Forum on Religion, Spirituality, and Aging*. Recognizing that the growing diversity of its professional disciplines represented a range of political views, in 1989 the board of directors decided to refrain from advocating for specific legislation, instead opting to educate members on all points of view while retaining a voice on the *Leadership Council of Aging Organizations*, a public policy consortium in Washington, DC. Public policy issues now are discussed and debated from all sides at ASA conferences and in its publications.

Other networks within ASA bring together professionals in health care, mental health, and older-adult learning, and those working to reduce the effects of disability and maximize the independence of older adults.

ASA has worked to develop strategic partnerships to educate, inform, and train those who serve older individuals and their families. One example is the ASA *MindAlert* program, created in association with the MetLife Foundation and Archstone Foundation to disseminate research and innovative practices that address the steps that older adults can take to maintain and enhance their cognitive and mental functions in their later years. In addition, the *Live Well, Live Long* program, which ASA developed with the Centers for Disease Control and Prevention, offers tools for professionals in stand-alone educational modules available for free on the Internet. Each module is designed to complement existing health promotion programs. A further example is ASA support of the *Institute for Geriatric Social Work* at Boston University, which aims to strengthen *gerontological teaching, research, and training* among social workers, the majority of whom have received little or no *geriatric education*.

ASA is continuing to look for new ways—including the use of CD-ROMs, Web sites, and online conferences—to expand on its core mission: bringing service providers, researchers, and members of the community together to share information and resources that ultimately benefit North America's growing older adult population.

PAUL KLEYMAN

See also
Organizations in Aging

AMERICANS WITH DISABILITIES ACT

The *Americans with Disabilities Act* (ADA) of 1990 (P.L. 101-336) is a *civil rights law* to promote equal opportunity and greater participation by people with disabilities in employment, services offered by state and local governments and private businesses, and telecommunications. *ADA* prohibits discrimination on the basis of disability, with remedies like those provided under civil rights laws for race, sex, national origin, and religion. However, unlike other civil rights laws, ADA requires various proactive measures to ensure access.

Given the positive correlation with *age and disability*, and the demographic trend of the aging of the U.S. population (a function of better public health and medical care), the benefits of ADA are significant for older Americans as well as the nation at large. The *disability rights movement*, of which ADA is a product, is in part an outgrowth of the increasing prevalence and complexity of disabling conditions—including the improved survival of individuals with once-fatal conditions, albeit with permanent impairments (Vachon, 1987).

History and Theory of Disability Rights Laws

Two historically unprecedented trends of the past 35 years underpin ADA: the evolution of *federal disability rights law*, and the *self-empowerment of people with disabilities*.

The *Architectural Barriers Act* of 1968 (P.L. 90-480) is the first modern *disability rights law*. Introduced in January 1967 by Senator *E. L. Bartlett*, its stated purpose was to "ensure that public buildings financed with federal funds are so designed and constructed as to be accessible to the physically handicapped." After hearings and amendments, it was signed into law in August 1968 (Katzmann, 1986).

The act was drafted by Bartlett's aide, *Hugh Gallagher*. His story not only illustrates a personal struggle against exclusion and for accessibility, but exemplifies other personal stories that later convinced Congress of the need for ADA. In 1952, while in college, Gallagher contracted polio, developed lower-body paralysis, and subsequently required lifelong use of a wheelchair. In 1963, he went to work for Senator Bartlett. On many occasions Gallagher wanted to visit public buildings in Washington, DC, but most were inaccessible to him. For example, to enter the National Gallery of Art, Gallagher needed a small ramp to climb the 2-step, 10-inch curb at the museum's entrance on Constitution Avenue.

Gallagher wrote to the National Gallery asking for a ramp to be built, but was told that it would "destroy the architectural integrity of the building" (H. Gallagher, personal communication, October 2, 1992). Gallagher thought his request was simple and reasonable, and that the National Gallery, as a *public and taxpayer-supported* museum, was the property of all Americans, not just those who could walk into it. Gallagher eventually got his wish when Senator Bartlett prevailed on the National Gallery's trustees to install a ramp—which turned out be barely noticeable.

To *remove physical barriers* in general, Gallagher drafted a bill with Senate legislative counsel, one that was "short and simple and that would put in a civil rights context," a mandate that "buildings constructed wholly or in part with federal funds be available to all citizens" (H. Gallagher, personal communication, July 27, 1992).

Although modest—only a page long, and with no enforcement provisions—the Barriers Act created a precedent, departing from existing laws for the disabled. While previous legislation involved social welfare measures (e.g., providing cash assistance or job training), the Barriers Act was a civil rights law, promoting integration and pointing to constitutional claims of equal protection and due process. It was the first law based on the theory that disability is not simply a function of an individual's impairment, but an interaction between *impairment and environment*. Environments—physical and otherwise—disable or enable a person with a disability. As a corollary, the act was the first disability law that did not require an individual to identify himself as disabled to benefit. Lastly, it expressed new aspirations for *public disability policy*.

The second important modern disability rights law was *Title V of the Rehabilitation Act* of 1973 (P.L. 93-112), in particular section 504. Section 504 provides a broad guarantee that "no otherwise qualified handicapped individual ... shall be excluded from the participation in, be denied the benefits of, or be subjected to discrimination under any activity or program receiving federal financial assistance. ..." Section 504 was drafted by Senate aides and used language from other civil rights laws (Scotch, 2001).

The second trend in the push for disability rights was the birth of the "*independent living movement*" in the late 1960s—a movement by and for people with disabilities. *Ed Roberts*, an early leader of the movement, also contracted polio and required the use of a ventilator and wheelchair. In the mid-1960s, he entered the University of California at Berkeley over the objections of school officials and later helped found the first *independent living center* (ILC) in Berkeley in 1972. Today, a nationwide network of ILCs provides peer support, advocacy, and services for people with disabilities. For a history of this movement, see Shapiro (1993).

Although these trends began independently, they came together with great force in the mid-1970s when the Carter administration delayed publishing federal regulations to implement section 504. *Disability advocates* responded with nationwide demonstrations, including sit-ins at federal office buildings. This event was perhaps the most important spark in coalescing a nationwide "disability community" and fostering its political education (Bowe, 1986; Scotch, 2001).

ADA was first proposed by a Reagan-appointed *National Council on Disability*, in a 1986 report entitled "*Toward Independence*." Created in 1979, the National Council on Disability is an independent federal agency charged with advising the president and Congress on disability policy. The first ADA bill was introduced in Congress in April 1988, but it died when the session ended. A substantially revised bill, modeled on section 504 and other civil rights laws, was introduced in May 1989. That bill passed Congress overwhelmingly in 1990 with broad bipartisan support and was signed into law on July 26, 1990, by President George H. W. Bush, who had spoken out strongly on disability rights issues as vice president (Shapiro, 1993).

Specific Provisions of ADA

Preamble. The opening sections describe congressional findings and purposes, including the historical segregation and exclusion experienced by people with disabilities, the nation's disability policy goals, and definitions, including the definition of who qualifies as disabled for purposes of the act.

Title I—Employment. Employers may not discriminate against an individual with a disability in hiring, promotion, or other employment benefits if that person is otherwise qualified for the job.

Employers must provide "*reasonable accommodations*" to assist an individual with a disability to meet job requirements, such as *job restructuring* and adaptive equipment, except where accommodations would be an "undue hardship." Title I only applies to employers with more than 15 employees and is enforced by the *Equal Employment Opportunity Commission* (www.eeoc.gov) and private lawsuit.

Title II—Public Services. Title II applies to state and local governments, and has two major subtitles. Subtitle A prohibits discrimination against individuals with disabilities and requires services to be accessible to them. Subtitle B applies to public transportation—requiring accessible buses and bus stations, or paratransit or comparable transportation services for individuals who cannot use fixed-route bus services, and accessible train cars and stations. Title II is enforced by the U.S. Departments of Justice and Transportation, and private lawsuit.

Title III—Public Accommodations and Services Operated by Private Entities. Private entities, such as restaurants, hotels, and retail stores, may not discriminate and must provide auxiliary aids and services to individuals with sensory impairments (hearing and vision), unless an undue burden. Physical barriers in existing facilities must be removed if "readily achievable;" if not, other means of providing services must be provided, again if readily achievable. All new construction and alterations to existing structures must be accessible. Title III is enforced by the U.S. Department of Justice and private lawsuit.

Title IV—Telecommunications. Title IV establishes a nationwide system of *telecommunications relay services* (TRS), which allow people with hearing impairments to talk with people without hearing impairments. Title IV is enforced by the Federal Communications Commission (FCC) (www.fcc.gov).

ADA Since Enactment and New Directions in Disability Policy

Although ADA concepts have had plenary effect on U.S. public policy, 2 specific changes inspired by ADA are of particular note. Beginning in 1993, at the behest of then Senate Majority Leader Bob Dole, the State Department has reported on discrimination against people with disabilities in foreign countries in its annual "*Country Reports on Human Rights Practices*." This report now provides an annual situation report of people with disabilities worldwide. (The report is available online on the U.S. Department of State Web site, at www.state.gov.) The ADA also has served as a model for similar legislation in other countries, including the United Kingdom's 1995 Disability Discrimination Act (see www.disability.gov.uk/drc).

ADA also prompted a provision in the *Telecommunications Act* of 1996 (P.L. 104-104), which requires telecommunications equipment manufacturers and service providers to ensure that equipment and services are usable by persons with disabilities, if readily achievable. This provision is intended to improve access to a broad range of products, such as telephones, cell phones, pagers, call-waiting, and operator services, as well as the Internet. The FCC is charged with enforcing this provision (www.fcc.gov).

Given the sweeping scope of ADA, naturally the question arises whether ADA has met expectations since its passage 14 years ago. The answer is complicated by important legal challenges, which have redefined, and in some cases limited, key portions of the act. Indeed, ADA law continues to evolve rapidly. Moreover, apart from providing specific remedies to discrimination and access, proponents of ADA often have broader goals, such as increasing employment. For an introduction to this literature with a review of Title I (employment), see Blanck et al. (2003).

Resources for Further Information

The U.S. Department of Justice is charged with overall coordination of federal government action on ADA. A copy of the ADA statute text, together with resource materials and links to other federal agencies, is available on the *Department of Justice* ADA home page at www.usdoj.gov/crt/ada. This Web site also includes a summary of all federal disability rights laws. The *National Council on Disability's Web site* provides in-depth information on ADA and disability public policy, which can be found at www.ncd.gov.

R. Alexander Vachon III

See also
Disability

References

Blanck, P., Schur, L., Kruse, D., Schwochau, S., & Song, C. (2003). Calibrating the impact of the ADA's employment provisions. *Stanford Law and Policy Review, 14*(2), 267–290. Available: http://disability.law.uiowa.edu/lhpdc/publications/documents/blancketaldocs/Stanford_Blancketal03.pdf.

Bowe, F. (1986). *Changing the rules*. Silver Spring, MD: T. J. Publishers.

Katzmann, R. A. (1986). *Institutional disability: The saga of transportation policy for the disabled*. Washington, DC: Brookings Institution.

Scotch, R. K. (2001). *From good will to civil rights: Transforming federal disability policy* (2nd ed.). Philadelphia: Temple University Press.

Shapiro, J. P. (1993). No pity: People with disabilities forging a new civil rights movement. New York: Times Books.

Vachon, R. A. (1987). Inventing a future for people with disabilities: The challenge of writing national disability policies. In D. E. Woods & D. Vandergoot (Eds.), *The changing nature of work, society, and disability: The impact of rehabilitation policy* (pp. 19–45). New York: World Rehabilitation Fund.

ANTI-AGING MEDICINE

What is anti-aging medicine? Scientists view *aging* as a process of accumulated damage to the building blocks of life that begins early in life, eventually leading to the malfunction and/or disregulation of the components of cells and of the tissues and organs they form—and ultimately the death of the whole organism (Olshansky, Hayflick, Carnes, et al., 2002). In this context, anti-aging medicine would be an intervention that reduces the rate and/or amount of accumulated damage that contributes to aging, and which also has been demonstrated to extend life. To date, no intervention has been scientifically demonstrated to slow, stop, or *reverse biological aging* in any species. This is not because it has not necessarily been accomplished, but because currently it is not possible to measure aging in such a way that scientists know with certainty whether experimentally induced *life extension* is occurring because of changes in disease pathology, or because of a modification to aging itself (Butler, Fossel, Harman, Heward, Olshansky, Perls, Rothman, Rothman, Warner, West, & Wright, 2002; Wick, 2002; Olshansky, Hayflick, & Carnes, 2002).

Physicians are trained to understand and diagnose the etiology of disease in patients, and then find ways to either eliminate the disease or its consequences. In addition, *evidence-based medicine* is increasingly focused on encouraging lifestyle changes in patients for purposes of disease prevention. This approach to medicine has led some to believe that aging itself can be postponed and even reversed by modulating the risk of chronic fatal diseases and disorders, such as heart disease and cancer, and non-fatal conditions such as sensory impairments (Klatz & Kahn, 1998). The rise of some *anti-aging* and *age management clinics* is based in part on this model. Although this approach to modern medicine is a repackaging of traditional preventive medicine that certainly has health and longevity benefits for some people, such interventions do not meet the criteria for a demonstrated modification to the underlying biology of aging. Distinguishing between the biological factors that contribute to aging and those related factors that contribute to pathology and disease is critical to understanding why some proponents of anti-aging medicine mistake preventive medicine for delayed aging (Hayflick, 2000).

Recently a third type of "anti-aging medicine" has resurfaced, involving the old claim that interventions exist which can stop or reverse the biological process of aging. A large and rapidly growing anti-aging industry has been built upon such false or exaggerated claims, and the Government Accounting Office (2001) and Senate Special Committee on Aging (2001)have aggressively pursued the protection of the U.S. population by exposing the fraudulent claims of this industry. The history of anti-aging movements of this sort, which are known to have surfaced numerous times in the past 3,000 years, has been well documented in scientific literature (Haber, 2004; Gruman, 2003).

Examples of Past Anti-Aging Medicine

Some 1,700 years ago, famous Chinese alchemist *Ko Hung* became the prophet of his day by resurrecting the ancient but popular cult known as *Hsien*, which was devoted to the idea that *physical immortality* is within our grasp (Haber, 2004). Ko Hung believed that animals could be changed from one species to another (the origin of evolutionary thought), that lead could be transformed into gold (the origin of *alchemy*), and that mortal humans could achieve physical *immortality* by adopting dietary practices based on moderation. He found arrogant and dogmatic the attitude that death was inevitable and immortality impossible. Ko Hung died at the age of 60 in 343 AD, which was a ripe old age for his time, but evidently Hsien did not enable its inventor to live forever.

The famous 13th century English philosopher and scientist *Roger Bacon* also believed there was no fixed limit to life and that physical immortality could be achieved by adopting the "secret arts of the past." According to Bacon, the human life span had been declining since the time of the ancient patriarchs because of increasingly decadent and unhealthy lifestyles. All that was needed to reacquire physical immortality, or at least much longer lives, was to adopt the ways of the past—at the time, this meant a lifestyle based on moderation and the ingestion of substances such as gold, pearl, and coral, which were thought to replenish the innate moisture or vital substance alleged to be associated with aging and death. Bacon died in 1292 in Oxford at the age of 78, also at a ripe old age for his time, but apparently the "*secret arts*" did not work quite as well as he thought they would.

Physical immortality has proven seductive, and countless stories of immortality have permeated popular literature. The ancient Hindus sought it, and Greek physician *Galen* in the 2nd century AD and Arabic philosopher/physician *Avicenna* in the 11th century AD also believed in it. Alexander the Great roamed the world searching for it, and *Ponce de Leon* discovered Florida in his quest for the *fountain of youth*. Although immortality may not be forthcoming anytime soon, individual and population aging are demographic certainties that will continue to generate interest in claims that anti-aging interventions exist—whether or not there is scientific proof to support such claims. Ironically, at a time when the modern prophets of the anti-aging industry claim that the secret to the fountain of youth has already arrived, the real science of aging is progressing rapidly toward a more complete understanding of how and why aging occurs.

The Future

It has yet to be determined whether it will ever be possible to develop interventions that can be proven to influence the biological process of aging in humans. What is known is that for the first time scientists now can demonstrate and empirically verify that the duration of life of a number of species can be experimentally extended in the laboratory. Although it is thought by some that such life extension is a result of *decelerated aging*, as yet this claim cannot be verified because of the difficulty in distinguishing between disease pathology and biological aging.

Both the future of *biogerontology* and the scientific pursuit of interventions that may decelerate aging are promising and exciting. Summaries of the literature in this area (Warner, 2004; Arking, Novoseltsev, & Novoseltseva 2004; Suresh, 2004) show that scientists have already made significant progress in identifying some of the genetic and physiological pathways that influence the duration of life. There is reason to be optimistic that research advances in this area will continue, and there is ample justification for continuing the pursuit of interventions that will decelerate the process of aging in humans and other species (Miller, 2002; Roth, Lane, Ingram, Mattison, Elahi, Tobin, Muller, & Metter, 2002).

S. Jay Olshansky

See also
Complementary and Alternative Medicine
Life Extension

ANXIETY

Anxiety is characterized by worry and/or fear in response to a situation or stressor; not unlike pain, it is part of the mental "alarm system" which alerts us to problems. All persons have symptoms of anxiety at times, which is considered normal and even adaptive. Clinically significant anxiety is that which is chronic (lasts well beyond a limited period of time during which a person is under acute stress) and uncontrollable (cannot be "set aside" and is disturbing for considerable periods of time during the day). In these cases, the person suffers from an *anxiety disorder*, although clinically significant anxiety also can be observed in persons with depression or other psychiatric diagnoses.

Anxiety in all persons tends to have 3 main components: (1) a feeling of *worry* or *fear*, sometimes only in specific situations, (2) *somatic symptoms*, such as palpitations in those who panic, or *gastrointestinal upset* in persons with generalized worry, and (3) *avoidance* (*of situations* that make one anxious or fearful). It is common for older persons to have symptoms of anxiety, and many have diagnoses. However, older adults are less likely than their younger counterparts to endorse anxiety terminology. Frequently, the term "anxious" is not endorsed, though terms such as worried, *nervous*, tense, or fretful are.

Anxiety disorders are thought to decline with aging. However, this does not seem to be the case for all of them. *Generalized anxiety disorder*, which is marked by chronic, uncontrollable worry about multiple topics, is possibly more common in older persons than young adults (Beekman, Bremmer, Deeg, van Balkom, Smit, de Beurs, et al., 1998). On the other hand, *panic disorder* and *obsessive-compulsive disorder* seem to become rarer with aging (Flint, 1994). In terms of phobias, *social phobia* (or *social anxiety disorder*) seems to be less common and less stigmatizing in older persons, while specific phobias (such as fear of heights, or fear of open spaces) neither increase nor decrease with age. Aging does not seem to be protective against having anxiety per se, although it may be protective against some anxiety-induced somatization symptoms, such as the palpitations seen in those who panic (Flint, Koszycki, Vaccarino, Cadieux, Boulenger, & Bradwejn, 1998).

Another unique aspect of *anxiety in older persons* is that it seems to cause some degree of impairment in memory, attention, and other aspects of neuropsychological (cognitive) status. Unlike in younger adults, in whom mild increases in anxiety can actually improve cognitive performance, older adults have decrements in *cognitive performance with anxiety* at any level (Deptula, Singh, & Pomara, 1993). It is not known whether standard treatments for anxiety disorders in older persons would improve cognitive status, although a study of *relaxation training produced memory improvement* in normal older persons with some degree of anxiety (Yesavage, et al., 1982). This neuropsychological finding may result from a bias in anxious persons toward threatening stimuli and future events, which could produce frank distractibility, and might explain why for example older persons with a fear of falling are paradoxically more likely to suffer a fall (Maki, 1997).

A final aspect of anxiety unique in older persons is its association with physical (or functional) disability. Older adults are subject to such disabling medical events as stroke, hip fracture, or heart attack; there is some evidence that anxiety increases this risk (Lenze, Rogers, Martire, Mulsant, Rollman, Dew, et al., 2001; Brenes, Guralnik, Williamson, Fried, Simpson, Simonsick, et al., 2005). Little is known about why anxious elderly persons would become more disabled over time than non-anxious ones, but increased risk for medical disease, poorer medication adherence, greater inappropriate use of pharmaceuticals, and cognitive impairments could mediate this relationship.

Despite the evidence that anxiety disorders are common and are associated with cognitive impairment and functional decline in older persons, few studies have been undertaken to demonstrate the benefit of treatments (Lauderdale & Sheikh, 2003). For example, although a recent study demonstrated that *antidepressant medication* was helpful for short-term symptomatic relief of *anxiety disorders in older persons* (Lenze, Mulsant, Shear, Dew, Miller, Pollock, et al., 2005), no studies have demonstrated long-term benefit in the course of *geriatric anxiety disorders* or in associated functional or cognitive impairment. There is some evidence for at least acute improvement of anxiety with psychotherapy (Stanley, Beck, & Glassco, 1996), and efforts are underway to adapt traditional psychotherapy for anxious older persons (Wetherell, Sorrell, Thorp, & Patterson, in press).

ERIC J. LENZE

See also
Depression

References

Beekman, A. T., Bremmer, M. A., Deeg, D. J., van Balkom, A. J., Smit, J. H., de Beurs, E., van Dyck, R., & van Tilburg, W. (1998). Anxiety disorders in later life: A report from the Longitudinal Aging Study Amsterdam. *International Journal of Geriatric Psychiatry, 13*, 717–726.

Brenes, G. A., Guralnik, J. M., Williamson, J. D., Fried, L. P., Simpson, C., Simonsick, E. M., & Penninx, B. W. (2005). The influence of anxiety on the progression of disability. *Journal of the American Geriatrics Society, 53*(1), 34–39.

Deptula, D., Singh, R., & Pomara, R. (1993). Aging, emotional states and memory. *American Journal of Psychiatry, 150*, 429–434.

Flint, A. J. (1994). Epidemiology and comorbidity of anxiety disorders in the elderly. *American Journal of Psychiatry, 151*, 640–649.

Flint, A. J., Koszycki, D., Vaccarino, F. J., Cadieux, A., Boulenger, J. P., & Bradwejn, J. (1998). Effect of aging on cholecystokinin-induced panic. *American Journal of Psychiatry, 155*, 283–285.

Lauderdale, S. A. & Sheikh, J. I. (2003). Anxiety disorders in older adults. *Clinics in Geriatric Medicine, 19*(4), 721–741.

Lenze, E. J., Rogers, J. C., Martire, L. M., Mulsant, B. H., Rollman, B. L., Dew, M. A., Schulz, R., & Reynolds, C. F. (2001). The association of late-life depression and anxiety with physical disability: A review of the literature and prospectus for future research. *American Journal of Geriatric Psychiatry, 9*, 113–135.

Lenze, E. J., Mulsant, B. H., Shear, M. K., Dew, M. A., Miller, M. D., Pollock, B. G., Houck, P., Tracey, B., & Reynolds, C. F. (2005). Efficacy and tolerability of citalopram in the treatment of late-life anxiety disorders: Results from an eight-week, placebo-controlled trial. *American Journal of Psychiatry, 162*, 146–150.

Maki, B. E. (1997). Gait changes in older adults: Predictors of falls or indicators of fear. *Journal of the American Geriatrics Society, 45*, 313–320.

Stanley, M. A., Beck, J. G., & Glassco, J. D. (1996). Treatment of generalized anxiety in older adults: A preliminary comparison of cognitive-behavioral and supportive approaches. *Behavior Therapy, 27*, 565–581.

Wetherell, J. L., Sorrell, J. T., Thorp, S. R., & Patterson, T. L. (in press). Psychological interventions for late-life anxiety: A review and early lessons from the CALM Study. *Journal of Geriatric Psychiatry and Neurology.*

APHASIA

Aphasia is an acquired, *neurologically-based language disorder* that results from damage to language processing systems in the brain. For the vast majority of individuals, these systems are represented predominantly in the left cerebral hemisphere, surrounding the *sylvian fissure*. Aphasia is most often caused by *cerebrovascular accident* (a *stroke* or brain attack). Stroke risk increases sharply with age, and stroke is the leading cause of disability among older adults. Aphasia can also result from other conditions that cause circumscribed damage to *peri-sylvian* regions of the *language-dominant hemisphere*, such as a relatively focal traumatic brain injury or tumor.

The *National Aphasia Association* (www.aphasia.org) estimates that about 1 million people are living with this devastating language disorder. The most common symptoms include difficulty in accessing vocabulary (sometimes denoted as *anomia*), in producing grammatical sentences, and in understanding questions, instructions, jokes, or other input, whether spoken or written. To appreciate the impact of aphasia, one must appreciate the scope of the construct of language and its central role in daily life vocation, avocation, and socialization.

Language is a symbol system used to represent, convey, and interpret ideas, thoughts, and feelings. A number of interactive subsystems are involved in language relative to its content (semantics), system of sound (phonology), form (morphology, syntax), and use (pragmatics). While many equate language with speech, speech is just one channel by which language is expressed. Other *expressive language modalities* include writing/typing and gesture/sign. Language is understood through reciprocal channels, such as listening, reading, and interpreting gesture/sign.

Depending on one's definition, aphasia may affect any or all such functions, processes, components, and/or channels of language. Aphasia also must be defined with reference to what it is not. For example, language changes that reflect sensory, perceptual, or motor deficits do not constitute aphasia. Aphasia manifests along a continuum of severity ranging from mild deficits—such as *word-finding difficulties* greater than expected with normal aging, and subtle problems with demanding texts or listening situations—to profound impairments that disrupt every aspect of the communicative process.

Theory and Definition

The operational definition of aphasia is conceptualized differently across and within the disciplines that diagnose and manage care for people with aphasia. These disciplines include but are not limited to neurology, *physiatry*, *speech-language pathology*, *linguistics*, psychology, neuroscience, cognitive science, gerontology, and rehabilitation science. Discrepancies in current views of aphasia derive from differing theoretical perspectives about intact and *disordered language*, and about the nature and importance of the rehabilitative process for aphasia.

One longstanding theoretical controversy is whether aphasia is defined with or without adjectives (Rosenbek, LaPointe, & Wertz, 1989). The prevailing view, with roots in the Wernicke-Lichtheim tradition (Caplan, 2004), is to classify aphasia into specific types or syndromes, such as *Broca* versus *Wernicke*—sometimes also referred to as motor versus sensory, syntactic versus semantic, expressive versus receptive, or fluent versus nonfluent. Syndrome classification is based on a constellation of signs and symptoms that reflect the diagnostician's judgment and/or the affected individual's performance on tasks that reflect global language parameters or behaviors, such as auditory comprehension, spoken expression, spoken repetition, and naming. *Aphasia syndromes* typically are related to the site of brain lesion, and lesion location thus is assumed to predict the presenting symptoms of individuals with aphasia. This symptom-syndrome-lesion assumption is so strong that in some descriptions aphasia is characterized in purely anatomical terms, such as anterior versus posterior (to the *rolandic fissure*). However, both current neuroimaging techniques and re-analyses of classic assumptions (Marie, 1906; Mohr, Pessin, Finkelstein, Funkenstein, Duncan, & Davis, 1978) make it evident that lesion site-to-symptom cluster mapping is neither consistent nor predictable across individuals with aphasia (Wertz, Dronkers, & Ogar, 2004).

Other challenges to the syndrome approach include: (1) the evolution of aphasia from one type to another as the brain recovers physiologically and/or with treatment (Wertz, Dronkers, & Ogar, 2004); (2) the often poor agreement by the various tests and procedures designed to make classifications (Wertz, Dronkers, & Ogar, 2004); (3) the fact that as many as 60% of people with aphasia cannot be classified unambiguously into traditional syndrome categories such as Broca, Wernicke, conduction, or *global aphasia*. Further, as implied above, these symptom profiles are based on patient performances at the task level, rather than on fine-grained psycholinguistic or cognitive neuropsychological assessments of spared and impaired language processes.

Those who define aphasia without adjectives follow in the footsteps of John Hughlings Jackson (1868), and later Hildred Schuell (Schuell, Jenkins, & Jimenez-Pabon, 1964) and Frederic Darley (1982). In this view, aphasia affects both the expression and comprehension of language, in all of the channels of language, at least to some degree. This perspective derives in part from factor analyses that demonstrate performance on aphasia test batteries to load primarily on a single factor (Rosenbek, LaPointe, & Wertz, 1989; Caplan, Waters, DeDe, Michaud, & Reddy, 2004), even for those tests that were developed to define particular aphasia types (e.g., the *Boston Diagnostic Aphasia Examination*, Goodglass & Kaplan, 1983). Individual differences occur because aphasia reflects a continuum of normal language performance (McNeil, 1988), varies in severity, reflects a performance deficit rather than a loss of language representations and processes, and can be complicated by co-existing problems, such as *motor speech disorders* (such as *apraxia* of speech; *see Communication Disorders*, this volume).

A different version of this "without adjectives" perspective is articulated by McNeil, who attributes aphasia to a deficit in the allocation of attention for language processing, rather than to a language disorder per se (McNeil, Doyle, Hula, Rubinsky, Fossett, & Matthews, 2004). This attention allocation difficulty is assumed to account for several hallmarks of aphasia, including performance variability and responsiveness to cues. Detractors of this perspective are concerned that it does not capture the true differences within the domain of aphasia, which may have important implications for continued investigation of its nature, phenomenology, treatment, and recovery.

Another controversy is whether the diagnostic label "aphasia," regardless of adjectives, should be used to characterize every acquired, neurologically based language disorder, including for example those found in people with neurodegenerative conditions such as Alzheimer's disease. Most medical professionals and many trained psychologists and linguists use the term in this all-encompassing manner, but most clinical *aphasiologists* explicitly reserve "aphasia" for language impairments that are disproportionate to, and cannot be explained by, other cognitive deficits. Lesion characteristics, prognoses, and treatment options differ dramatically for aphasia thus conceptualized and for a dementing condition such as Alzheimer's disease. For instance, language function would decline over time in patients with Alzheimer's disease, while patients with aphasia would evidence improvement (unless they had primary progressive aphasia, discussed next). Although overlooked in most quarters, this controversy has crucial implications for subject selection in aphasia research.

Primary progressive aphasia (PPA) is a poorly understood condition in which language performance deteriorates for at least 2 years, while other cognitive functions are retained (Rogers, 2004). Precise causal factors are unclear, but *focal cortical atrophy* underlies this condition (Mesulam, 2000). Time course and symptom presentation are varied in PPA, with the primary complaint involving *word-finding deficits*. Fluent and nonfluent variants have been proposed, but Rogers (2004) indicates that PPA rarely conforms easily to this distinction. Duffy and Avery (2004) warn that misdiagnosis is common, because of incomplete and insensitive diagnostic testing.

Recovery and Rehabilitation

As noted above, patients with aphasia improve. The acute aftermath of stroke involves physiologic processes that resolve with time, like neurotransmitter release and edema. An early period of relatively rapid physiologic improvement, which lasts anywhere from several weeks to several months, is called "*spontaneous recovery*," although at present brain cells do not regenerate and people with aphasia rarely recover completely. However, pharmaceutical interventions such as *t-PA* (Burger & Tuhrim, 2004) and *reperfusion techniques* (Hillis & Heidler, 2002) offer great promise for full recovery from stroke at the most early stage of symptom presentation. When delivered within hours of the stroke, these approaches can prevent further brain damage and reverse acute impairments.

Aphasia also improves with *language intervention*, and meta-analyses of aphasia treatment in general indicate its benefit (Robey, 1998; Robey, Schultz, Crawford, & Sinner, 1999). Specific treatment approaches based on linguistic theory (Thompson, 2001; Thompson, Shapiro, Kiran, & Sobecks, 2003) have been gaining an evidence base as well. The *Academy of Neurologic Communication Disorders and Sciences* (www.ancds.org) is expected to publish evidence-based practice guidelines for aphasia. Chapey (2001) offers more than 20 approaches to language treatment for aphasia.

Current Research and Research Needs

Advances in imaging technology combined with the enduring interest in *brain localization of language* processes and deficits have spurred a raft of *neuroplasticity* investigations (Fridriksson, 2004; Thompson, 2004). Some of these efforts focus on brain reorganization in relation to particular types of language treatment (Thompson, 2004), and all require increasingly more interdisciplinary investigation. In addition, cross-linguistic aphasia research has raised challenges to traditional theory and definitions that derive predominantly from investigations in North America, England, France, and Germany (Caramazza, 2004; Dronkers, 2004; Menn, 2004). *Psycholinguists* are working to integrate processing time considerations into theories of aphasic performance (Federmeier & Kutas, 2000; Shapiro, 2004), and *attentional allocation theories* of aphasia are being challenged and modified (Shuster, 2004).

At the clinical level, further investigation is needed, and in some cases is underway, to expand the behavioral treatment evidence base for aphasia (Friedman, 2004a,b; Schwartz, 2004a,b), to assess pharmacologic adjuncts to behavioral treatment (Small, 2004), to improve diagnosis (Ross & Wertz,

2004) and prognosis (de Riesthal & Wertz, 2004), and to address quality of life issues (Doyle, McNeil, Hula, & Mikolic, 2003; LaPointe, 2000). A significant challenge remains to determine how best to treat aphasia in light of ever-shrinking monetary reimbursement for the clinical management of this life-altering condition.

CONNIE A. TOMPKINS
VICTORIA L. SCHARP

See also
Communication Disorders
Language Comprehension
Language Production

References

Burger, K. M., & Tuhrim, S. (2004). Antithrombotic trials in acute ischaemic stroke: A selective review. *Expert Opinion on Emerging Drugs*, *9*(2), 303–312.

Caplan, D. (2004). Aphasic syndromes: Connectionist models. In R. D. Kent (Ed.), *The MIT encyclopedia of communication disorders* (pp. 262–265). Cambridge: The MIT Press.

Caplan, D., Waters, G., DeDe, G., Michaud, J., & Reddy, A. (2004). A study of syntactic processing in aphasia I: Behavioral (psycholinguistic) aspects. *Brain and Language*, *91*, 64–65.

Caramazza, A. (2004). Disorders of lexical access in speech production. CRISP. Available: http://crisp.cit.nih.gov

Chapey, R. (Ed). (2001). *Language intervention strategies in aphasia and related neurogenic communication disorders* (4th ed.). Philadelphia: Lippincott Williams and Wilkins.

Darley, F. L. (1982). *Aphasia*. Philadelphia: W. B. Saunders.

de Riesthal, M., & Wertz, R. T. (2004). Prognosis for aphasia: Relationship between selected biographical and behavioral variables and outcome and improvement. *Aphasiology*, *18*(10), 899–915.

Doyle, P. J., McNeil, M. R., Hula, W. D., & Mikolic, J. M. (2003). The burden of stroke scale (BOSS): Validating patient-reported communication difficulty and associated psychological distress in stroke survivors. *Aphasiology*, *17*(3), 291–304.

Dronkers, N. F. (2004). Cross-linguistic studies of aphasia. CRISP. Available: http://crisp.cit.nih.gov

Duffy, J., & Avery, A. (2004). *An uncommon speech disorder: Diagnosis and management*. Paper presented at 2004 Academy of Neurologic Communication Disorders and Sciences Annual Educational and Scientific Meeting, Philadelphia.

Federmeier, K. D., & Kutas, M. (2000). It's about time. *Brain and Language*, *71*, 62–64.

Fridriksson, J. (2004). Neurological predictors of aphasia recovery. CRISP. Available: http://crisp.cit.nih.gov

Friedman, R. B. (2004a). Cognitively based treatments of acquired dyslexias. CRISP. Available: http://crisp.cit.nih.gov

Friedman, R. B. (2004b). Learning paradigms in aphasia rehabilitation. CRISP. Available: http://crisp.cit.nih.gov

Goodglass, H., & Kaplan, E. (1983). *The Boston Diagnostic Aphasia Examination*. Philadelphia: Lea and Febiger.

Hillis, A. E., & Heidler, J. (2002). Mechanisms of early aphasia recovery. *Aphasiology*, *16*(9), 885–895.

Jackson, J. H. (1868). On the physiology of language. *Brain*, *38*, 59–64.

LaPointe, L. L. (2000). Quality of life with brain damage. *Brain and Language*, *71*, 135–137.

Marie, P. (1906). Revision de la question de l'aphasie: L'aphasie de 1861 á 1866: Essai de critique historique sur la genése de la doctrine de Broca. *La Simaine Médicale*, *26*, 565–571.

McNeil, M. R., Doyle, P. J., Hula, W. D., Rubinsky, H. J., Fossett, T. R. D., & Matthews, C. T. (2004). Using resource allocation theory and dual-task methods to increase the sensitivity of assessment in aphasia. *Aphasiology*, *18*(5/6/7), 521–542.

McNeil, M. R. (1988). Aphasia in the adult. In N. J. Lass, L. V. McReynolds, J. Northern, & D. E. Yoder, (Eds.), *Handbook of speech-language pathology and audiology* (pp. 738–786). Toronto: D.C. Becker, Inc.

Menn, L. (2004). Aphasiology, comparative. In R. D. Kent, (Ed.), *The MIT encyclopedia of communication disorders* (pp. 265–269). Cambridge: The MIT Press.

Mesulam, M. M. (2000). *Principles of behavioral and cognitive neurology* (2nd ed.). Oxford: Oxford University Press.

Mohr, J. P., Pessin, M. S., Finkelstein, S., Funkenstein, H. H., Duncan, G. W., & Davis, K. R. (1978). Broca aphasia: Pathological and clinical aspects. *Neurology*, *28*, 311–324.

Robey, R. R. (1998). A meta-analysis of clinical outcomes in the treatment of aphasia. *Journal of Speech, Language, and Hearing Research*, *41*, 172–187.

Robey, R. R., Schultz, M. C., Crawford, A. B., & Sinner, C. A. (1999). Single-subject clinical-outcome research: Designs, data, effect sizes, and analyses. *Aphasiology*, *13*, 445–473.

Rogers, M. A. (2004). Aphasia, primary progressive. In R. D. Kent, (Ed.), *The MIT encyclopedia of communication disorders* (pp. 245–249). Cambridge: The MIT Press.

Rosenbek, J. C., LaPointe, L. L., & Wertz, R. T. (1989). *Aphasia: A clinical approach.*

Ross, K. B., & Wertz, R. T. (2004). Accuracy of formal tests for diagnosing mild aphasia: An application of evidence-based medicine. *Aphasiology, 18*(4), 337–355.

Schuell, H. M., Jenkins, J. J., & Jimenez-Pabon, E. (1964). *Aphasia in adults: Diagnosis, prognosis and treatment* New York: Harper & Row.

Schwartz, M. F. (2004a). AAC processing support for spoken language in aphasia. CRISP. Available: http://crisp.cit.nih.gov

Schwartz, M. F. (2004b). Long-term aphasia rehabilitation: Groups, email, assisted communication. CRISP. Available: http://crisp.cit.nih.gov

Shapiro, L. P. (2004). Sentence processing in normal and aphasic populations. CRISP. Available: http://crisp.cit.nih.gov

Shuster, L. I. (2004). Resource theory and aphasia reconsidered: Why alternative theories can better guide our research. *Aphasiology, 18*(9), 811–830.

Small, S. L. (2004). A biological model of aphasia rehabilitation: Pharmacological perspectives. *Aphasiology, 18*(5/6/7), 473–492.

Thompson, C. K. (2004). Neurolinguistic investigations of aphasia and recovery. CRISP. Available: http://crisp.cit.nih.gov

Thompson, C. K. (2001). Treatment of underlying forms: A linguistic-specific approach for sentence production deficits in agrammatic aphasia. In R. Chapey, (Ed), *Language intervention strategies in aphasia and related neurogenic communication disorders* (4th ed., pp. 605–625). Philadelphia: Lippincott Williams & Wilkins.

Thompson, C. K., Shapiro, L. P., Kiran, S., & Sobecks, J. (2003). The role of syntactic complexity in treatment of sentence deficits in agrammatic aphasia: The complexity account of treatment efficacy (CATE). *Journal of Speech, Language, and Hearing Research, 46*(3), 591–607.

Wertz, R. T., Dronkers, N. F., & Ogar, J. (2004). Aphasia: The classical syndromes. In R. D. Kent, (Ed.), *The MIT encyclopedia of communication disorders* (pp. 249–251). Cambridge: The MIT Press.

APOE 4

See
Apolipoprotein Epsilon 4

APOLIPOPROTEIN EPSILON 4

Apolipoprotein E (ApoE) is one of the proteins that helps transport cholesterol and other lipids through the bloodstream. ApoE binds to the surface of lipid particles and interacts with receptors on cells, directing lipid uptake into cells that need lipid and cholesterol. It has been studied for many years by scientists interested in arteriosclerosis and heart disease because of its role in cholesterol transport. ApoE can be inherited in several different forms. The major types are designated ApoE2, ApoE3, and ApoE4. These differ from each other by single amino acid changes. Depending on which of these types of ApoE one inherits, the cholesterol-carrying abilities of the protein vary slightly. Inheritance of ApoE4 is associated with increased low-density lipoprotein (LDL) cholesterol and a 1.5–2.0-fold increased risk of coronary heart disease (Wilson, Myers, Larson, Ordovas, Wolf, & Schaefer, 1994).

Recently, ApoE's role in the brain, where it may contribute to lipid metabolism and neuronal regeneration after injury, has received attention (Mahley, 1988). In a surprising discovery in 1993, Roses and colleagues at Duke University found that inheritance of the ApoE4 type is associated with a very high incidence of developing Alzheimer's disease (Strittmatter, Saunders, Schmechel, Pericak-Vance, Enghild, Salvesen, et al., 1993). The term *allele frequency* describes the percentage of total genes that are of a certain type. In the general population the allele frequencies are ApoE2, 0.10; ApoE3,0.76; ApoE4, 0.14. In Alzheimer's disease, the ApoE4 allele frequency nearly triples to about 0.36 (Rebeck, Reiter, Strickland, & Hyman, 1993; Strittmatter et al., 1993).The overrepresentation of ApoE4 implies that inheritance of ApoE4 is a risk factor for Alzheimer's disease. In addition, some data now suggest that inheritance of the ApoE2 allele makes one less likely than average to develop Alzheimer's disease (Corder, Saunders, Risch, Strittmatter, Gaskel, Rimmler, et al., 1994; West, Rebeck, & Hyman, 1994).

These data also suggest that there is an influence of ApoE genotype on age of onset of dementia, with ApoE4 associated with a relatively younger average age of onset and ApoE2 with a later age of onset, compared to ApoE3 (Corder, Saunders, Strittmatter, Schmechel, Gaskell, Small, et al., 1993). However, it is important to note that some individuals inherit ApoE4 and live in good health to old age (90+) (Rebeck, Perls, West, Sodhi, Lipsitz, & Hyman, 1994).

These new observations about the inheritance of a risk factor for Alzheimer's disease have spawned intensive research to understand how ApoE4 could predispose individuals to developing Alzheimer's disease, and it is hoped that they will provide new insight into the causes of this illness. A review by St. George-Hyslop (1999) helps place ApoE in the overall context of the genetics of Alzheimer's disease. Two additional reviews (Finch & Sapolsky, 1999; Martin, 1999) illustrate the status and prospects of research on ApoE for research on aging.

BRADLEY T. HYMAN
G. WILLIAM REBECK

See also
Alzheimer's Disease: Genetic Factors
Cerebrovascular Disease: Stroke and Transient Ischemic Attack
Lipoproteins, Serum

APOPTOSIS

Cells, like organisms, are in general mortal, and their life span in host tissues is usually defined genetically. For some cells, such as neurons, this life span equals that of the organism; for others, such as the intestinal epithelium and hemopoietic systems, the *cellular life span* is only as long as their functional operation lasts. The *mortality of a cell*, then, is crucial to the total count of cell numbers in a given tissue. Too much will result in the loss of functional units, detrimental to the host system's optimal functionality, such as *neurode generation* associated neuronal cell loss; and too little will create excess baggage for the system to support, such as the *neoplastic growth* found in cancer. To achieve the proper number of healthy cells for any given tissue, nature provides an exquisitely controlled genetic mechanism called *apoptosis*, or *programmed cell death*, a process that, when activated, commits cells to undergo suicide (Ashkenazi & Dixit, 1998; Deveraux & Reed, 1999; Li, Nijhawan, Budhardio, Srinivasula, Ahmad, Alnemri, et al., 1997; Wang, 1997; White, 1996; Widmann, Gibson, & Johnson, 1998). This self-elimination is directed by the orchestration of hundreds of genes' function, and it is seen in many physiological events when an excess number of cells is produced or when cells are damaged via infection, toxin, oxidative damage, or UV-irradiation.

In general, most genes associated with apoptosis are classified into *pro-apoptotic*, or pro-survival, defined as to whether their action promotes or prevents death. Large families of genes have been discovered in the last few years whose members function in either the pro-life or pro-death camps of genetic function. Most noted of these are the families of CASPASE and Bcl-2 classes. The *CASPASE genes* uniformly act pro-apoptotically; their action is, in general, via proteolysis, mainly by cleaving other substrate proteins into fragments, thereby annulling their crucial function in the cells. This *proteolytic activity* is the culprit that performs the final act of death by severing vital cellular proteins into pieces. These protein victims include *actin*, *vimentin*, *DNA repair enzymes*, and RNA synthetic machinery members; the list of candidate CASPASE substrates increases as new proteins are identified daily in this category. The Bcl-2 family, on the other hand, initially acts as a pro-survival factor; the best-known member is the original *Bcl-2 gene*. Interestingly enough, not all members of this family are "good guys" for survival; many of them behave molecularly in the opposite fashion (i.e., they promote death). This change to the opposite function is due to the fact that the protective mode of the Bcl-2 family is composed of unique molecular domains. Some members of the Bcl-2 family can bind to their sisters' survival functional domains and therefore disable the sister's protective function. In other cases, genetic mutations occur and change the functional domain from protective to killing mode. In all, the balance between the *pro-* and *anti-apoptotic* molecular forces is always inaction at many checkpoints when an apoptotic event is activated, allowing the cell ample opportunity to change its mind on the road to self-inflicted death.

The genetic script dictating the regulation of apoptotic death was initially thought of as a duet-playing party of good guys *versus* bad guys. Since then, astounding discoveries show that there are many checkpoints within the cellular milieu to map out the apoptotic path. Individual checkpoints are identified by major players such as the CASPASE or Bcl-2 family genes; however, the completion of their function may involve dozens of other proteins, serving to help or block their action. Therefore, the clusters at each checkpoint serve largely as gatekeepers, to determine whether a signal to die ever passes through that particular checkpoint. Who are these helpers, and how do they function as the facilitators of apoptotic death? The answer is that, although any protein can play this role, they are mainly the members of the intertwining signal transduction pathways, and they act at the transcriptional, translational, and posttranslational modification steps to facilitate the passing or blocking of the signals through the checkpoints.

To a nonbiologist, these *signal transduction* pathways may make it seem that life is composed of dismantled telephone wires, with no clue as to how a cell can ever maintain its operation through this chaos. Nevertheless, there is method in this madness; in general, this method follows a simple rule, starting with the signal generators (visually at the plasma membrane), with hundreds of receptors as the antennae to receive stimuli from the extracellular environment. Once the signal is received, it generates a cascade of multiple reactions, in parallel and/or serially, eventually targeting the nucleus, mitochondria, or other cytoplasmic organelles as the final point. The final executive decision is then the sum of the many balanced biochemical actions to dictate whether the cell lives or dies. A complete picture of how this complex system works is possible only when we are able to know all the players' identities and their roles in this genetic symphonic dance.

As described above, apoptosis is mostly seen during development, as the way to get rid of extra cells that are not needed in the formation of a given organ. This molecular sculpturing act is essential to the production of a new organism, to make its tissue pattern of the designated function. For example, in the central nervous system (CNS), far more neurons than ultimately required are produced during development, but only those that can successfully generate a neuronal network survive; the rest of them are deleted by the cellular suicidal program of apoptosis. As CNS neurons possess no regenerative ability, the strategy is not to have apoptosis occur postdevelopmentally. The loss of any of them is a permanent loss to the organism. In contrast, for breast ductal epithelium, the cells lining the milk-producing ducts follow a precise menopausal cue to dispose of themselves in postmenopausal women. Intestinal epithelial cells are yet another example; each traverses a villus from the crypt to the tip in 8 days, and afterward die, via apoptosis, and the cell corpse is shed into the intestinal lumen. Therefore, strategies for the operation of *apoptosis signals* in different tissues are vastly different and unique to the functional and developmental path for each tissue.

Obviously, to maintain a successful aging process is to have neurons stay alive and healthy as long as possible by blocking the apoptotic process from ever happening and to have the *breast ductal epithelial cells* all gotten rid of by promoting apoptotic death, so that no cells will be left as the seed hotbed for cancer development in postmenopausal women. How can these programs ever be maintained for as long as an organism's life? For humans, this need may require a duration as long as 100 years in centenarians. The answers lie in the area of genetic and environmental elements, that is, the nature and nurture factors that influence individuals' lives. Age-dependent defects in maintaining the balance of apoptosis between tissues are contributed to by heritable traits working together with our environment in terms of oxidative stress, UV exposure, and so on.

The etiology of many *age-dependent diseases* is thought to be related to the cells' inability to maintain some intended program, either pro- or anti-apoptosis. Every tissue precisely regulates the critical cell mass needed for its specific function. The number of cells contributing to the composition of this critical mass is in general determined by the cell proliferation program. This number is largely determined during prenatal development for those tissues composed of permanently growth-arrested cells, such as neurons and cardiomyocytes; therefore, loss of such cells via excess apoptotic activity precipitates cardiovascular and neurological disorders. On the other hand, if the critical number of cells exceeds the tissue's needs because of too little apoptotic activity, this scenario creates an environment of too many cells or retaining cells that are no longer needed, a prelude to hyperplasia and eventually neoplastic growth. Thus, too little apoptosis causes cancer-related problems, and too much apoptosis in certain tissues creates neurode-generative disorders such as Alzheimer's disease; both are perils of the elderly.

The obvious connection to use drug- or gene-directed therapeutic treatment has been thought to be the next frontier of science to combat the old-age plague, largely by reducing or increasing apoptotic activity in tissues where too much or too little is observed. This simple logic is, however, complicated by the fact that the orchestration of the apoptotic process in a cell requires several dozen checkpoints, each controlled by yet other dozens of molecular players. The art of fine-tuning the molecular symphony to its optimal functional output in producing suicidal death or not doing so is a learned skill contributed to by both inherited traits and environmental influences. Moreover, the ultimate question remains: Wherever the pro- or anti-apoptotic phenotype is, why does it take a lifetime to develop, with time of onset differing among individuals? For some, this onset of *abnormal apoptosis* occurs at middle age; for others in the late 80s; and for yet others it never occurs. This fact speaks loudly of an individual genetic signature for apoptosis regulation. With the advent of high-throughput biochip technology, this *genetic signature* for individuals is within our grasp, and we look forward to the days when a *gene profile* for an individual's apoptosis regulation is the guideline for prognostic and diagnostic tools against age-dependent diseases. With this hope, we anticipate that age-dependent debility can be reduced via apoptosis regulation by therapeutic treatment, and then we can all aspire to a life such as that of the world's oldest individual, *Madame Calmette*, who died at the age of 122 in fairly good health.

EUGENIA WANG

See also

Cell Aging In Vitro

DNA

References

Ashkenazi, A., & Dixit, V. M. (1998). Death receptors: Signaling and modulation. *Science*, *281*, 1305–1308.

Deveraux, Q. L., & Reed, J. C. (1999). IAP family proteins. Suppressors of apoptosis. *Genes and Development*, *13*, 239–252.

Li, P., Nijhawan, D., Budhardio, I., Srinivasula, S. M., Ahmad, M., Alnemri, E. S., & Wang, X. (1997). Cytochrome c and dATP-dependent formation of Apaf-l/Casp[ase]-9 complex initiates an apoptopic protease cascade. *Cell*, *91*, 479–489.

Wang, E. (1997). Regulation of apoptosis resistance and ontogeny of age-dependent diseases. *Experimental Gerontology*, *32*, 471–484.

White, E. (1996). Life, death, and the pursuit of apoptosis. *Genes and Development*, *10*, 1–15.

Widmann, C., Gibson, S., & Johnson, G. L. (1998). Caspase-dependent cleavage of signaling proteins during apoptosis. *Journal of Biological Chemistry*, *273*, 7141–7147.

ARCHITECTURE

Architecture specifically designed for older adults has served as a catalyst in the past 40 years in the effort to enhance the quality as well as the quantity of life for the aging person.

Architects, possibly more than any other professionals, have been responsible for bringing together a multitude of disciplines and professions to address the problems associated with living to an advanced age. The individual's declining abilities to respond appropriately to his/her environment requires architecture that will contribute to, rather than detract from, the individual's maximum physical, mental, and emotional functioning.

The initial focus on designing better buildings for the elderly came in the late 1940s and early 1950s in response to the construction of a small but increasing number of facilities such as homes for the aging and nursing homes. Architects were soon to go beyond the boundary of their drawing boards to address the social and health needs of the elderly. They were required to create new building forms, including *housing for the elderly, congregate living facilities, personal care units, senior centers, retirement communities, life-care communities*, and *continuing-care retirement communities*.

The impetus behind this creative effort came in the early 1960s and shaped the field of *housing for the elderly* for the next 2 decades. Major governmental agencies, including the Federal Housing Administration, Public Housing Administration, Administration on Aging, Farmers Home Administration, and later the Department of Housing and Urban Development were among those that initiated programs, standards, and financing mechanisms for a wide variety of services and facilities for the elderly to which architecture and architects responded.

Private agencies and organizations such as the National Council on Aging and the American Association of Retired Persons supported research, training, and demonstration projects toward improving the design of environments for the elderly. The Gerontological Society of America established the *Aging and Environments* project directed by *Thomas Byerts*, AIA.

Early publications by architects having a major influence in the field were *Buildings for the Elderly* (Musson & Heusinkveld, 1963) and *Planning Housing Environments for the Elderly* (Gelwicks & Newcomer, 1974). The latter encouraged a multidisciplinary approach emphasizing the programming of housing to incorporate the psychosocial components of care. The purpose was to produce an environmental match between the resident and the architecture.

The research of psychologists and sociologists exerted an important influence on many architects. *M. Powell Lawton*, research psychologist at the *Philadelphia Geriatric Center* and *Leon Pastalan*, sociologist at the University of Michigan, engaged in many collaborative works with architects, and their research on the effect of physical environment on the behavior, life satisfaction, and health of older persons provided an important behavioral basis for design. Lawton's book, *Environment and Aging* (1980), addressed key interdisciplinary issues for architects.

Architectural schools committed to the generalist educational approach became increasingly aware of the role of buildings for the elderly as a useful medium to challenge students in the solving of interrelated physical, social, and psychological design problems. Major federal funding for such programs as the graduate program in *environmental design for the elderly* at the *Andrus Gerontology Center*, University of Southern California, encouraged many schools of architecture to develop courses and programs in the design of facilities for the elderly. The Andrus Center established the *Environmental Studies Laboratory*, directed by *Victor Regnier*, and has since 1976 offered a dual degree in gerontology and urban planning.

A major impact on architecture and architects has come from 3 distinguished women: *Ollie Randall*, *Wilma Donahue*, and *Marie McGuire Thompson*. Randall, a social worker and pioneer in the field of aging, encouraged and assisted many architects. In 1966 she shared her podium in Vienna with the first architect to present a paper at the International Congress of Gerontology. Her initiatives led to the founding of both the National Council on Aging and the *American Association of Homes for the Aging*.

Donahue, a sociologist at the University of Michigan, developed interdisciplinary programs involving both architecture and sociology and was instrumental in the development of a variety of housing projects for the elderly.

In 1961 Marie McGuire Thompson, Executive Director of the Housing Authority in San Antonio, Texas, which had just completed the first federally financed public housing high-rise building for the elderly, *Victoria Plaza*, addressed the first White House Conference on Aging as the keynote speaker. Her long and distinguished career includes her appointment as U.S. Commissioner of Public Housing. In that post she established regional programs for architects to promote better design in housing for low-income elderly persons.

The 1980s brought new interest and new players in the development of housing for older adults. These developments were triggered by the slump in the home building and multifamily housing market, a significant increase in the numbers of older people (as well as their retirement incomes), and health care legislation including changes in Medicare and Medicaid reimbursement. The latter changes encouraged hospitals to develop multiple levels of care and facilities to meet the needs of a rapidly expanding older population.

Developers and major national corporations, including hotel chains and hospitals, are currently developing housing linked to a continuum of care. Architects, desiring to serve these clients, in turn, are expanding their services to include planning and programming for the elderly. Planning firms specialize in the planning, programming, and marketing of facilities and services for the elderly.

To attract the elderly market many health care providers offer a full continuum of care ranging from acute to home care. Within the continuum, the development of congregate housing and continuing-care retirement communities has become an important option. The architectural design of each element of the continuum and their interrelationship plays an essential role in the older person's ability to negotiate the health care environment.

The current market is a new generation, which for the first time in history is composed of 2 generations of elderly. This population has an entirely new set of lifetime experiences and preferences. The future success of architecture for older adults will be determined by the professional response to the demands as well as the needs of the consumer.

Discussion of both design and policy issues of particular relevance for architects interested in the special requirements of frail and disabled adult populations are found in the American Institute for Architects Foundations (1985) and in Regnier and Pynoos (1987).

LOUIS E. GELWICKS

See also
Americans with Disabilities Act
Housing

References

American Institute for Architects Foundations. (1985). *Design for aging: An architect's guide*. Washington, DC: American Institute for Architects Foundations.

Gelwicks, L. E., & Newcomer, R. J. (1974). *Planning housing environments for the elderly*. Washington, DC: National Council on Aging.

Lawton, M. P. (1980). *Environment and aging*. Belmont, CA: Wadsworth.

Musson, N., & Heusinkveld, H. (1963). *Buildings for the elderly*. New York: Reinhold.

Regnier, V., & Pynoos, J. (1987). *Housing and the aged: Design directives and policy considerations*. New York: Elsevier.

ARTHRITIS

Arthritis is strictly defined as inflammation occurring within the confines of the joints. Joints are composed of the ends of 2 bones. These ends are covered with *hyaline cartilage*, lined by a layer of tissue known as synovium and bathed in a nutritive and lubricating fluid known as synovial fluid. When affected by arthritis, a joint will exhibit varying degrees of soft tissue swelling, redness, heat, and an increased amount of *synovial fluid*, as well as pain and limitation of motion. Although infection and trauma can both cause an immediate arthritis that completely resolves with treatment, most types of arthritis are chronic or recurring diseases, the causes of which are not well understood.

In older adults, the most common types of arthritis are *osteoarthritis*, *rheumatoid arthritis*, *gout*, and *pseudogout*. Osteoarthritis is a relatively *noninflammatory arthritis* characterized by the slow deterioration of the hyaline cartilage and underlying bone over time. As such, its prevalence increases with age (Hammerman, 1989). Prior injury to a joint as well as the unappreciated trauma involved in the *repetitive motions* of everyday life predisposes persons to the development of osteoarthritis, although genetic factors governing collagen composition also play a role. Osteoarthritis is not a systemic disease and occurs in only 1 or a few joints. The clinical presentation consists of pain, bony enlargement, and crepitation with motion of the joint—a palpable or even audible creaking of bone upon bone implying *cartilage loss*. Marked signs of inflammation such as redness, heat, and significant soft tissue swelling are absent in osteoarthritis. Pain due to osteoarthritis is increased by use of the joint and decreased by joint rest. The most commonly affected joints are the hips, knees, first toe, and the distal finger joints such as (DIPs, PIPs), the thumbs, neck, and lower spine. X-rays demonstrate increased bony thickness and extra bone known as *osteophytes*, as well as narrowing of the joint space indicative of cartilage loss. Treatment of osteoarthritis is directed at unloading the affected joint with weight reduction and/or supportive devices such as canes, corsets, and collars. *Physical therapy* is also useful to strengthen contiguous muscles (Slemenda, Brand, Heilman, et al., 1999). Pain control is achieved through analgesics, such as acetaminophen or low-dose *nonsteroidal anti-inflammatory drugs (NSAIDs)*. Local injections into the joints with long-acting steroids may be of short-term benefit, as is *viscosupplementation*, in which *hyaluronic acid*, a lubricating substance found in normal joints, is injected locally as replacement therapy to damaged joints (Raynauld, Buckland-Wright, Ward, et al., 2003; Brandt, Smith, & Simon, 2000). *Glucosamine* and *chondroitin* ingestion may provide pain control comparable to the use of low-dose NSAIDs, but as yet there is no convincing data of its ability to induce restoration of damaged cartilage (McAlindon,

Gulin, & Felson, 1998). When osteoarthritis symptoms begin to impair quality of life despite conservative therapy, the definitive treatment is joint replacement surgery.

Rheumatoid arthritis is the second most common arthritis found in older adults. Unlike osteoarthritis, rheumatoid arthritis is a systemic inflammatory disorder expressed predominantly as an inflammatory and potentially destructive disorder of multiple joints. Persons with rheumatoid arthritis feel systemically ill, with marked fatigue and a pervasive sense of overwhelming stiffness known as *morning stiffness*. Morning stiffness lasting greater than 1 hour is so characteristic of the disease that it is a major clinical diagnostic criteria. The other diagnostic features include involvement of multiple joints, a predilection for proximal hand joints such as the wrist, metacarpals, or proximal interphalangeal joints, symmetrical distribution of the arthritis, and chronicity (Arnett, 1989). Other joints such as the shoulders, elbows, knees, ankles, and toes are also inflamed, and in some persons with rheumatoid arthritis other organs of the body such as the eyes, lungs, skin, and nerves may also exhibit evidence of inflammation. Physical examination demonstrates marked soft tissue swelling around these joints, as well as increased heat, mild redness, and increased joint fluid. Marked tenderness and limitation of joint motion also occurs. Laboratory tests may demonstrate a mild anemia of chronic disease and an elevated sedimentation rate (indicative of *systemic inflammation*). In approximately three-quarters of persons with rheumatoid arthritis, an *autoantibody* known as *rheumatoid factor* is present. X-rays show a thinning of the ends of the bones known as *periarticular osteopenia*, as well as marked joint space narrowing and variable degrees of erosion in the cartilage and bone. Two patterns of rheumatoid arthritis are encountered in older persons (Kerr, 2003). The first is one of longstanding disease, because the person developed rheumatoid arthritis at the most common time of life, namely the late 20s or early 30s, and over time has had considerable damage to multiple joints and possibly toxicity from years of treatment. The second pattern of onset is the development of rheumatoid arthritis after age 65. Persons with this pattern of disease may have marked disability from joint pain and swelling, but are less likely to have destruction of their joints.

The treatment of rheumatoid arthritis has 2 objectives. The first objective is to control the symptoms caused by marked inflammation of the joints. This palliative strategy employs high-dose salicylates, high-dose NSAIDs, and/or low-dose steroids. The second component of treatment attempts to block the inflammation in the joints and thereby protect them from progressive autoimmune destruction. This remitted strategy employs potent medications known as *DMARDs*, or *disease modifying antirheumatic drugs* (Van der Heidea, Jacobs, Bijlsma, et al., 1996). Examples of commonly used DMARDs include *methotrexate*, *hydroxychloroquine*, *sulfasalazine*, *azathioprine*, and *leflunomide*. Newer therapies known as *biologics*, which consist of *tumor necrosis factor alpha inhibitors* (*etanercept*, *infliximab*, and *adalimumab*), also are used. DMARDs have the potential for protecting joints from progressive damage, but also possess potential toxicity (O'Dell, 2004). Physical therapy and judicious joint replacement surgery also are of therapeutic value in the treatment of rheumatoid arthritis.

Gout and pseudogout, 2 types of inflammatory arthritis highly prevalent in older adults, are caused by an immune response to the shedding of crystals into the joints. In gout, the crystal is monosodium *urate*, and in pseudogout the crystal is *calcium pyrophosphate dihydrate*. These diseases present as dramatic episodic attacks of severe localized joint pain and swelling. In gout, the most commonly affected joint is the *first toe*. Subsequent attacks can involve the forefoot, ankle, knee, and wrist. In pseudogout, the knee is most commonly affected, followed by the wrist, ankle, or shoulder.

For both diseases, the diagnosis is made by extracting a sample of synovial fluid and identifying the characteristic presence of these crystals. Treatment either consists of high-dose nonsteroidal anti-inflammatory drugs, steroids, *colchicine*, or judicious joint *injections of steroids* (Emmerson, 1996). In some persons with severe gout, agents such as *allopurinol* or *probenecid* to lower *uric acid* may also be used.

LESLIE DUBIN KERR

References

Arnett, F. C. (1989). Revised criteria for the classification of rheumatoid arthritis. *Bulletin of Rheumatic Diseases, 38*, 1–5.

Brandt, K. D., Smith, G. N., & Simon, L. S. (2000). Intra-articular injection of hyaluronan as treatment for knee osteoarthritis. *Arthritis/Rheumatism, 43,* 1192–1203.

Emmerson, B. T. (1996). The management of gout. *New England Journal of Medicine, 334,* 445–451.

Hammerman, D. (1989). The biology of osteoarthritis. *New England Journal of Medicine, 320,* 1322–1330.

Kerr, L. D. (2003). Inflammatory arthritis in the elderly. *Mount Sinai Journal of Medicine, 70,* 23–26.

McAlindon, T. E., Gulin, J., & Felson, D. T. (1998). Glucosamine and chondroitin therapy for osteoarthritis of the knee and hip; meta-analysis and quality assessment of clinical trials. *Arthritis/Rheumatism, 41,* 198.

O'Dell, J. R. (2004). Therapeutic strategies for rheumatoid arthritis. *New England Journal of Medicine, 350,* 591–602.

Raynauld, J. P., Buckland-Wright, C., Ward, R., et al. (2003). Safety and efficacy of long-term intra-articular steroid injections in osteoarthritis of the knee. *Arthritis/Rheumatism, 48,* 370–377.

Slemenda, C., Brandt, K. D., Heilman, D. C., et al. (1999). Quadriceps weakness and osteoarthritis of the knee. *Annals of Internal Medicine, 127,* 97–104.

Van der Heidea, Jacobs, J. W., Bijlsma, J. W., et al. (1996). The effectiveness of early treatment with "second line" antirheumatic drugs. *Annals of Internal Medicine, 124,* 699–704.

ASIAN AND PACIFIC ISLANDER AMERICAN ELDERS

Older Americans from Asian and Pacific Island (A/PI) backgrounds are the most rapidly growing of the federally recognized ethnic minority categories. In the 2000 U.S. census, over 900,000 people aged 65 years and older identified themselves as Asian or *Pacific Islander* (either alone or in combination with another race), an increase of 204% over 1990's 454,000. In 2000, they comprised 2.6% of all U.S. older persons and are projected to comprise 8% by 2050. The majority of A/PI elders in the United States live in California and Hawaii (Young & Gu, 1995). There are more than 30 national backgrounds represented among the A/PI elders, the largest of which are listed in Table 1, along with selected demographic characteristics.

Vast heterogeneity exists for older adults both between and within each A/PI ethnic group, including time in the United States, acculturation level, income, education, rural/urban background, and religion. Although the term "Asian" is limited in its usefulness, A/PI older adults are often lumped together in national statistics or excluded from analyses altogether because of their relatively small numbers. Compared with other racial/ethnic categories, cumulatively A/PI elders have been found to be less likely to live alone or in institutions (perhaps related to the traditions of filial piety in many Asian populations) and have longer life expectancy, although again there is considerable variation between and within the ethnic groups.

Data on most groups is very limited. Some known characteristics of the larger groups are summarized below.

Chinese American Elders

This largest group of A/PI elders is extremely diverse within itself. They may be second- or third-generation American-born or immigrants from mainland China, Hong Kong, Taiwan, or Vietnam. The first known *Chinese immigrants to the United States* were males in the 1850s who came to "Gold Mountain" (California). They were exposed to sometimes violent *anti-Chinese sentiment*, resulting in the *Chinese Exclusion Act of 1882*, which made immigration of laborers illegal until 1943. Many families were separated for decades until the laws changed, which allowed more than 9,000 wives to immigrate after World War II (Kitano & Daniels, 1988). Older adults of Chinese ancestry continue to come to the United States in large numbers, especially from Taiwan and Hong Kong, in most cases as "followers of children."

Some *Chinese American older persons* have done well economically, but the poverty rate exceeds that for older Americans in general. Many older immigrants do not receive pension income, and some are not eligible for Medicare.

Mortality rates for older cohorts of Chinese Americans are about two-thirds that of older whites, and higher for foreign-born than for American-born. Health risks are similar to that for other U.S. older adults, with the following exceptions: higher rates of liver, esophageal, and pancreatic cancers, and a 3 times higher *suicide rate* for *older Chinese women*. Depression among Chinese immigrant elders is frequently undiagnosed and untreated and has been attributed to factors such as migratory grief and low

TABLE 1 Asian and Pacific Islander Elders 65 & Over, 2000, Selected Characteristics

Ethnic Identification	Number 55+	Number 65+	% of Asians 65+	% 65+ Foreign Born*	% 65+ in Poverty	% 65+ with Education <9 Yrs.	Bachelor's+	% 65+ Linguistically Isolated**
Asian American Alone	**1,577,339**	**800,795**	**100%**	**NA**	**12.3%**	**30.9%**	**20.8%**	**30%**
Chinese	418,300	235,995	29.5%	84.2%	16.2%	38.0%	21.7%	46%
Filipino	334,022	164,768	20.6%	90.5%	8.4%	29.4%	26.6%	17%
Japanese	240,527	161,288	20.1%	20.0%	5.6%	11.3%	15.2%	19%
Korean	162,050	68,505	8.6%	90.2%	22.1%	31.7%	20.9%	53%
Asian Indian	176,793	66,834	8.3%	88.9%	9.1%	31.6%	31.9%	12%
Vietnamese	137,729	58,241	7.3%	92.1%	16.0%	47.3%	8.4%	46%
Cambodian	14,975	6,570	0.8%	100.0%	22.3%	73.7%	4.6%	54%
Pakistani	12,174	4,804	0.6%	96.7%	13.0%	30.7%	29.8%	NA
Hmong	9,056	4,698	0.6%	92.61%	29.3%	91.6%	2.0%	59%
Thai	13,198	2,954	0.4%	97.2%	11.7%	36.2%	21.4%	31%
Other Asian	58,515	26,138	3.2%	88.1%	8.6%	27.2%	24.3%	NA
Asian in combination with 1 or more other races	122,860	60,930						
Native Hawaiian and Other Pacific Islander (NHPI) American	**44,391**	**20,821**	**% of NHPI 65+ 100%**	NA	11.5%	24.6%	9.4%	NA
Native Hawaiian	21,581	10,451	50.2%	NA	9.3%	18.8%	9.1%	NA
Samoan	7,721	3,567	17.1%	NA	16.5%	32.4%	7.9%	NA
Guamanian or Chamorro	6,090	2,845	13.7%	NA	10.9%	25.0%	13.1%	NA
Tongan	2,418	1,030	4.9%	NA	12.8%	36.3%	2.6%	NA
Other Pacific Islander	6,581	2,928	14.1%	NA	NA		NA	NA
Native Hawaiian and other Pacific Islanders in combination with 1 or more races	90,793	43,802			12.5%	23.2%	11.5%	NA

Adapted from 2000 U.S. Census data provided to the authors by A. Locsin, Seattle: National Asian Pacific Center on Aging.
NOTES: NA = not available; **data on linguistically isolated are from 1990 since they were not available from the 2000 census.
It should be noted that some of the data is from very small samples so it may not be completely accurate.

English proficiency (Stokes, Thompson, Murphy, & Gallagher-Thompson, 2001; Casado & Leung, 2001). Preliminary data also indicates higher risk for diabetes and multi-infarct dementia but lower risk for Alzheimer's disease. Heart disease and colorectal cancer appear to be less common in the countries of origin but increase with acculturation. Although many Chinese American older adults accept Western biomedical health practices, many also accept aspects of classical *Chinese health beliefs*, such as the balance theory of health (*yin/yang*) and the importance of *chi* (McBride, Morioka-Douglas, & Yeo, 1996; Liu & Yu, 1985).

Japanese American Elders

Four historical periods have been identified for Japanese Americans: (1) immigration (1890–1924) of young male laborers and women, (2) prewar (1924–1941) era of growing hostility and *anti-Japanese discrimination*, (3) wartime evacuation (1941–1945) and internment of people of Japanese descent from the West Coast in relocation centers, and (4) postwar (1945-present). The current older cohort includes: a few *issei* (early immigrant pioneers), *nisei* (American-born children of *issei*), older *sansei* (*nisei* offspring), *kibei* (*niseis* sent to Japan to study when young); and *shin-issei* (post-1965 immigrants) (Kitano & Daniels, 1988).

Although generational, geographic, and socioeconomic variations are common, as a whole Japanese Americans are the most acculturated and assimilated Asian subgroup. *Japanese American older adults* are at lower risk for heart disease, but at higher risk for diabetes, multi-infarct dementia, stomach cancer, and suicide; men are at higher risk for esophageal and pancreatic cancers, and women for osteoporosis (McBride, Morioka-Douglas, & Yeo, 1996). To provide culturally competent long-term care, several Japanese American communities have developed ethnic-specific residences, including skilled nursing and assisted living facilities (Yeo & Hikoyeda, 1992).

Filipino American Elders

Large numbers of men from the Philippines were recruited to work in Hawaii and California from 1910 to 1930. As the U.S. economy worsened in the 1930s, severe discrimination and legal restrictions intensified, culminating in the *Tydings-McDuffie Act* of 1934, which set an annual quota of 50 Filipino immigrants. During World War II, the U.S. navy recruited residents of the Philippines with promises of U.S. citizenship; after the war, veterans and family members of U.S. residents immigrated in large numbers. Since quotas were relaxed in 1965, and continuing through the 1990s, there has been a dramatic increase in immigration of older adults from the Philippines, many times following adult children who have come as health care professionals. In 1990, *U.S. Immigration Act amendments* allowed naturalization of Filipino veterans of World War II who had not been given the promised U.S. citizenship. By 1994, over 2,000 older veterans had resettled in California, swelling the already large numbers of single older Filipino men living alone or in male-only rooming houses (Yeo, Hikoyeda, McBride, Chin, Edmonds, & Hendrix, 1998).

Mortality rates among older adults are roughly half that of their white counterparts, and higher for foreign born (Liu & Yu, 1985). High rates of diabetes, hypertension, and gout have been found in Filipino older adults (McBride, Morioka-Douglas & Yeo, 1996).

Korean American Elders

Waves of *Korean migration to the United States* include: (1) recruited migration (1903–1905) of farm workers and families to Hawaii, (2) restricted migration (1905–1924) of picture brides, students, and political exiles, (3) dependent immigrants (1952–1964), including war brides and war orphans, and (4) new waves of settlers (1965–present), over 20,000 annually, many well-educated, urban professionals, and their extended families (Yamato, Chin, Ng, & Franks, 1993).

Traditional Korean American characteristics emphasize a high regard for *filial piety*, clearly divided family roles, family collectivity and interdependence overriding individualism, and the importance of a good education (Chin, 1993; Kitano & Daniels, 1988). Christian churches are social and educational centers that provide group ties, identity, and acceptance. Many *Korean elders* own businesses unrelated to their professional training because of cultural or language barriers.

Korean Americans tend to underutilize health care and to seek care during later disease stages. The following conditions are reported to be higher among Korean Americans: depression, diabetes, and esophageal and stomach cancers, in men, liver cancer and cirrhosis, and in women cervical cancer. Rates of hypertension appear to be lower (Zane, Takeuchi, & Young, 1994).

Asian Indian American Elders

The minimal literature that exists on older adults who have immigrated to the United States from India describes a very heterogeneous population.

Some came as farmers from Punjab in the early 1900s and endured considerable discrimination; a more highly educated group has come since 1965, many as "followers of children." Depending on region of origin, they may refer to themselves *Indo-Americans*, *South Asians*, or *Asian Indians*. Hindi is the most common language, but there are 7 other major languages in addition, and hundreds of dialects. Most of these older adults practice Hinduism, but Sikhism and Islam are also common. *Familism* is still strong in Asian Indian communities in the United States, as is respect for elders.

Among older adults of this group, heart disease, diabetes, and hypertension are the most common chronic conditions. Better health is associated with having relatives nearby, and poorer health with high body mass index, longer residence in the United States, and being older and female (Diwan & Jonnalagadda, 2001). The traditional health beliefs and practices in India were founded on *Ayurvedic medicine*, which emphasizes balance of basic 5 elements and their analogues in the body (McBride, Morioka-Douglas, & Yeo, 1996).

Southeast Asian American Elders

Since 1975, nearly 2 million refugees have fled Vietnam, Cambodia, and Laos due to wars, politics, and famine; about half have settled in the United States in 2 waves of migration (Yamato, Chin, Ng, & Franks, 1993; Kitano & Daniels, 1988). The first group (1975–1977) followed the fall of Saigon, when 130,000 Vietnamese and Cambodians escaped by helicopter, sea lift, or self-evacuation. This more advantaged cohort included military personnel, civil servants, teachers, farmers, fishermen, and American employees (Kitano & Daniels, 1988). The second wave (post-1979) of Vietnamese, Cambodian, Hmong, and *Laotian refugees* were poor, rural, less educated, and survived harrowing escapes and refugee camps. Both waves included older adults who came with families, although individuals older than 65 years make up only 2–3% of the population.

The *Hmong* were forced to flee their Laotian tribal homelands because of mass exterminations. Hmong communities have developed primarily in California, Minnesota, and Wisconsin and tend to be characterized by clans as basic family/political units, large, male-dominated families, and strong spiritual influences on health beliefs and behaviors. No written language existed until 1953, and there was little exposure to formal education or Western culture prior to their forced migration (Fadiman, 1998). Immigration is continuing because of closure of the last remaining refugee camps in Thailand.

Over 1 million *Cambodians* were exterminated during the rule of the Khmer Rouge. Those who survived spent many years in refugee camps before immigrating to the United States. For these older adults, the most frequent chronic complaint is headache, many times with dizziness, which they frequently attribute to "thinking too much" (about the trauma and lost loved ones) (Handelman & Yeo, 1996).

Mental health problems are common among Southeast Asian refugees, who suffer from *survivor guilt*, *relocation depression*, and *posttraumatic stress disorder*. Health studies reveal that they may suffer from hepatitis B, liver disorders, tuberculosis, thalassemia, and malnutrition more than other U.S. older adults. They also encounter language and cultural barriers, high poverty rates, disrupted families, intergenerational conflict, loss of identity, and racial discrimination (Kagawa-Singer, Hikoyeda, & Tanjasiri, 1997; McBride, Morioka-Douglas, & Yeo, 1996; Zane, Takeuchi, & Young, 1994). Diagnosis and treatment of mental disorders may be hampered by cultural perceptions of conditions such as dementia, which caregivers may view as part of normal aging (Yeo, Tran, Hikoyeda, & Hinton, 2001).

Native Hawaiian and Pacific Islander Elders

The population of *Native Hawaiian and Pacific Islander* (NHPI) American older adults is relatively small, and research is extremely limited. The indigenous group includes more than 25 distinct cultures from 3 areas comprising thousands of *Pacific islands* and atolls: Polynesia (with cultural groups such as *Native Hawaiian*, *Samoan*, and *Tongan*), Micronesia (*Guamanian* and *Chamorro*), and Melanesia (*Fijian* and *Papua New Guinean*) (Braun, Yee, Browne, & Mokuau, 2004). The 3 largest subpopulations are Native Hawaiians, Samoans, and Chamorros. All of the populations in this group except Tongans have been influenced by their historical domination by colonial powers.

Overall, the NHPI population is relatively young. Thus, fewer older adults are heads of households or own their own homes, and they are less likely to live alone or to live in rural areas (U.S. Census Bureau, 2004). Life expectancy for NHPI men and women is lower than for whites and some of the larger Asian groups (U.S. Census, 2004). The leading causes of death and disability among NHPI older adults (heart disease, cancer, stroke, and diabetes) mirror those of other older Americans due to their adoption of western lifestyles.

In general, NHPI older adults have been found to believe in a spiritual source or power, respect nature, the land, and its resources, emphasize family over the individual, and maintain a strong sense of community (Braun, Yee, Browne, & Mokuau, 2004). Among the group, NHPI elders are highly respected for their wisdom and as cultural guides for future generations.

GWEN YEO
NANCY HIKOYEDA

See also
Ethnicity
Minority Populations: Recruitment and Retention in Aging Research

References

Braun, K. L., Yee, B. W. K., Browne, C. V., & Mokuau, N. (2004). Native Hawaiian and Pacific Islander elders. In *Closing the gap: A report on minority aging* (pp. 47–59). Washington, DC: Gerontological Society of America.

Casado, B. L., & Leung, P. (2001). Migratory grief and depression among elderly Chinese American immigrants. *Journal of Gerontological Social Work, 36*(1/2), 5–26.

Diwan, S., & Jonnalagadda, S. S. (2001). Social integration and health among Asian Indian immigrants in the United States. *Journal of Gerontological Social Work, 36*(1/2), 45–62.

Fadiman, A. (1998). *The spirit catches you and you fall down: A Hmong child, her American doctors, and the collision of two cultures*. New York: Farrar, Straus, & Giroux.

Handelman, L., & Yeo, G. (1996). Using explanatory models to understand chronic symptoms of Cambodian refugees. *Family Medicine, 28,* 271–276.

Kagawa-Singer, M., Hikoyeda, N., & Tanjasiri, S. P. (1997). Aging, chronic conditions, and physical disabilities in Asian and Pacific Islander Americans. In K. S. Markides & M. R. Miranda (Eds.), *Minorities, aging, and health* (pp. 149–180). Thousand Oaks, CA: Sage Publications.

Kim, P. K., & Kim, J-S. (1992). Korean elderly: Policy, program, and practice implications. In S. M. Furuto, R. Biswas, D. K. Chung, K. Murase, & F. Ross-Sheriff (Eds.), *Social work practice with Asian Americans* (pp. 227–239). Newbury Park, CA: Sage Publications.

Kitano, H. L., & Daniels, R. (1988). *Asian Americans: Emerging minorities*. Englewood Cliffs, NJ: Prentice Hall.

Liu, W. T., & Yu, E. (1985). Asian/Pacific American elderly: Mortality differentials, health status and use of health services. *Journal of Applied Gerontology, 4,* 35–64.

McBride, M., Morioka-Douglas, N., & Yeo, G. (1996). *Aging and health: Asian/Pacific Island American elders* (2nd ed.). SGEC Working Paper no. 3. Stanford, CA: Stanford Geriatric Education Center.

Stokes, S. C., Thompson, L. W., Murphy, S., & Gallagher-Thompson, D. (2001). Screening for depression in immigrant Chinese-American elders: Results of a pilot study. *Journal of Gerontological Social Work, 36*(1/2), 27–44.

U.S. Census Bureau. (2004). American FactFinder datasets. Available: http://factfinder.census.gov/servlet/datasetmainpaageservlet?)program-DEC&_langueng&.ts=

Yamato, S., Chin, S-W, Ng, W. L., & Franks, J. (Eds.) (1993). *Asian Americans in the United States,* Vol. 2, (pp. 83–87). Dubuque, IA: Kendall/Hunt.

Yeo, G., & Hikoyeda, N. (1992). *Characteristics of Asian-oriented residential long-term care*. Paper presented at the annual meeting of the Gerontological Society of America, Washington, DC.

Yeo, G., Hikoyeda, N., McBride, M., Chin, S-Y., Edmonds, M., & Hendrix, L. (1998). *Cohort analysis as a tool in ethnogeriatrics: Historical profiles of elders from eight ethnic populations in the United States*. SGEC Working Paper no. 3. Stanford, CA: Stanford Geriatric Education Center.

Yeo, G., Tran, J. N. U., Hikoyeda, N., & Hinton, L. (2001). Conceptions of dementia among Vietnamese American caregivers. *Journal of Gerontological Social Work, 36*(1/2), 131–152.

Young, J. J., & Gu, N. (1995). *Demographic and socioeconomic characteristics of elderly Asian and Pacific*

Island Americans. Seattle: National Asian Pacific Center on Aging.

Zane, N. S. W., Takeuchi, D. T., & Young, K. N. J. (Eds.). (1994). *Confronting critical health issues of Asian and Pacific Islander Americans* (pp. 148–173). Thousand Oaks, CA: Sage Publications, Inc.

ASSISTED LIVING

Although families continue to be the major source of long-term care, various types of residential long-term care settings have emerged to supplement their efforts or to meet the needs of older and disabled persons without family. A variety of factors have contributed to an increased demand for housing with supportive services for the *frail elderly*. First, the population of older persons is growing rapidly. Second, most elderly persons have a strong preference for receiving long-term care services outside of a nursing home. Third, private market factors have played a role, including consumer preferences, concerns about nursing home quality, and the availability of capital for the construction and conversion of facilities. Finally, public policies, such as the *Olmstead decision*, federal initiatives, and states' concern with containing spending on nursing homes have led to greater interest in community-based programs, including residential long-term care settings.

After nursing homes, the most common form of residential setting offering supportive long-term care services are *board and care homes* (Hawes, Mor, Wildfire, Lux, Greene, Iannacchione, et al., 1995). Such facilities are known by more than 30 different names across the country, including *shelter care homes*, *adult congregate living facilities*, adult *care homes*, *personal care homes*, *domiciliary care homes*, and residential care homes for the elderly (Hawes, Mor, Wildfire, Lux, Greene, Iannacchione, et al., 1995). Most states also have begun to include *assisted living facilities (ALFs)* among their residential care options.

During the 1990s, ALFs were the most rapidly expanding form of *senior housing* (American Seniors Housing Association, 1998), and the past 15 years have seen the emergence and growth of an industry known as assisted living. Indeed, 60% of facilities that call themselves assisted living had been in business for 10 or fewer years by the late 1990s (Hawes, Rose, & Phillips, 2000). Some observers have argued that this development represented a fundamental change for long-term care (Kane & Wilson, 1993). Advocates asserted that assisted living "represents a promising new model of residential long-term care, one that blurs the sharp and invidious distinction between receiving long-term care in one's own home and in an 'institution'" (Hawes, Rose, & Phillips, 2000, p. 1).

Estimates of the total number of assisted living facilities vary, in large measure because of differences in definitions of what constitutes an ALF. Moreover, there is no federal regulation of assisted living, so there is no national definition, or a list and count of facilities. Thus, one is left with a variety of sources for data on the total number of facilities and residents, since studies have used different definitions and produced different numbers. For example, a national study by Hawes et al. used a standard definition of assisted living, independent of various state categorizations, and identified 11,500 ALFs in 1998 with slightly more than 611,000 beds (Hawes, Phillips, Rose, Holan, & Sherman, 2003). This operational definition limited ALFs to those facilities that served the elderly, had 11 or more beds, had no rooms shared by 3 or more residents, and either advertised themselves as "assisted living" or provided key services, including 24-hour staff oversight, housekeeping, at least 2 meals a day, and assistance with 2 or more activities of daily living (ADLs) or with at least 1 ADL and medications.

By contrast, Mollica's 2002 survey of state licensing agencies allowed each state to individually define assisted living and provided an estimate of more than 36,000 ALFs with 910,000 beds. Indeed, according to Mollica, states reported a 30% increase in the number of ALFs between 1998 and 2000; in 2002, they reported a 14.5% growth in the number of ALFs over the preceding 2 years (Mollica, 2002). This growth represented a combination of new ALF construction, conversion of existing facilities to assisted living, and reclassification to ALF of some residential long-term care facilities, such as personal care homes, either voluntarily by the provider or as part of a state regulatory name change. Thus, this estimated number of places classified as assisted living by some states includes what are known as board and care homes, personal care homes, or residential care facilities in other states. But by any estimate, assisted living is a major segment of the *long-term care sector.*

Initially, the development and expansion of assisted living was largely an unregulated market response to both demographic trends and consumer preferences. The first licensure regulation specifically directed toward assisted living was in Oregon in 1989. In 1992 fewer than 10 states had such regulations in place, but by 1998 most states had expanded their definition of residential care to include a specific licensure category known as "assisted living" or simply had incorporated these facilities into their traditional concept of residential care. Further, more than half the states provided some type of Medicaid funding for services in ALFs by 1998 (Mollica, 1998). As of 2002, 32 states had a licensure category or a statute that used the term "assisted living," and 41 states reported that their Medicaid programs were serving 102,000 residents in such settings.

Despite the phenomenal growth in both public and private support for assisted living, no consensus has emerged on the appropriate regulatory model for assisted living. Models have varied from state policies that seek to create assisted living as a unique long-term care arrangement with distinctive environmental features (e.g., requiring apartments with kitchens and privacy in accommodations) to those that basically allow the same types of shared rooms and limited services typically found in traditional board and care homes. In addition, states differ on whether the features that ought to be subject to regulation should include the housing component or should be limited to the service component, in effect treating assisted living as a kind of home health service (Mollica, 1998).

This variability in public policy has been matched by diversity among providers, who differ in size, ownership, auspices, target population, physical environment, and services (Hawes, Rose, & Phillips, 2000; Hawes, Phillips, Rose, Holan, & Sherman, 2003; Zimmerman, Gruber-Baldini, Sloane, Eckert, Hebel, Morgan, et al., 2003). Thus, both public policies and private business decisions prompted different models of assisted living to emerge around the country, with a lack of uniformity in the environment, services, and policies.

Despite this lack of consensus about an appropriate regulatory model and the diversity in the assisted living industry, there has been a surprising consensus about the philosophy of assisted living. In the view of many observers, assisted living represents a promising new model of long-term care because of the philosophical principles underlying the conceptual model.

The key philosophical tenets of assisted living derive from the premise that the goal of assisted living is to meet consumers' needs and preferences, preserve independence or autonomy and dignity, and allow residents to age in one place, in a homelike environment. A useful definition has been provided by the *Assisted Living Quality Coalition*, a group representing the Alzheimer's Association, AARP, the *American Association of Homes and Services for the Aging*, the *Assisted Living Federation of America*, the *American Seniors Housing Association*, and the *American Health Care Association/National Center for Assisted Living*. According to the coalition, an assisted living setting is:

> A congregate residential setting that provides or coordinates personal services, 24-hour supervision and assistance (scheduled and unscheduled), activities, and health-related services; designed to minimize the need to move, designed to accommodate individual residents' changing needs and preferences, designed to maximize residents' dignity, autonomy, privacy, independence, and safety; and designed to encourage family and community involvement (Assisted Living Quality Coalition, 1998, p. 2).

Key elements of the philosophy of assisted living have typically been operationalized as an environment with single-occupancy units, shared only by choice, that contain specific areas for sleeping, living, and preparing food, as well as private baths. The philosophy also emphasizes flexible service arrangements that respond to both consumer preferences and changes in care needs over time. Such arrangements are intended to facilitate *aging-in-place* and support self-care in the performance of ADLs and instrumental activities of daily living (IADLs) such as managing medications, meals, and transportation.

During the last few years the volume of research on assisted living has grown. However, most studies have focused on assisted living in only 1 or in a few states. The only study that provides national-level estimates for assisted living uses data collected in

1998 (Hawes, Phillips, Rose, Holan, & Sherman, 2003; Hawes, Rose, & Phillips, 2000). As noted above, this study found an estimated 11,500 ALFs with a total of just over 600,000 beds housing more than 500,000 residents. The average ALF size was 53 beds; 67% of the ALFs had 11 to 50 beds, 21% had 51 to 100 beds; and 12% had more than 100 beds. Facility occupancy averaged 84% (Hawes, Rose, & Phillips, 2000). This research, A *National Study of Assisted Living for the Frail Elderly*, was conducted for the U.S. Department of Health and Human Services, Office of the Assistant Secretary for Planning and Evaluation.

This study was restricted to places that called themselves assisted living, or that provided a specified range of basic services common to most ALFs. Despite this restriction, the study still found tremendous variation among ALFs. Fewer than half the residential units were apartments; most accommodations were bedrooms. The vast majority of these accommodations (73%) were private, but a sizable proportion (27%) were accommodations shared by 2 or more unrelated individuals. Moreover, more than one-third (35%) of the accommodations had a shared bathroom (Hawes, Phillips, Rose, Holan, & Sherman, 2003; Hawes, Rose, & Phillips, 2000). Thus, the majority of ALFs offered considerably more privacy than that found in nursing homes or traditional board and care homes. This is particularly important, given the overwhelming preference of older persons for private accommodations (Jenkens, 1997; Kane, Baker, & Veazie, 1998). At the same time, a significant number of ALFs did not conform to what many view as a central element of the philosophy underlying assisted living.

Assisted living facilities also differed in the services they offered and how these were provided. Nearly all facilities provided or arranged for 24-hour staff, 3 meals a day, and housekeeping. More than 90% of the ALF administrators also reported that the facility provided medication reminders and assistance with bathing and dressing, while 88% of the ALFs provided or arranged for central storage of drugs or assistance with administration of medications. However, they varied with respect to care or monitoring by a licensed nurse. About half (52%) of the facilities provided some care or monitoring by a licensed nurse (RN or LPN) with their own staff, while one-quarter (25%) arranged for nursing care with an outside agency. However, 1 in 5 ALF administrators (21%) reported that the facility did not arrange for or provide any care or monitoring by a licensed nurse (Hawes, Phillips, Rose, Holan, & Sherman, 2003; Hawes, Rose, & Phillips, 2000).

In a smaller but well-defined study that compared care among nursing homes and 3 types of residential care or assisted living facilities (RC/AL) in 4 states, researchers also found significant differences among various types of RC/AL facilities (Zimmerman, Gruber-Baldini, Sloane, Eckert, Hebel, Morgan, et al., 2003). In this study, Zimmerman and her colleagues examined differences in process quality among RC/AL facilities with 16 or fewer beds and whether they embodied elements of "traditional" residential care or "*new model" assisted living*, finding statistically significant differences across these facilities in 10 different process care measures.

What was also striking about the 2 studies is that 59% of the places that called themselves assisted living in the national ASPE study were classified as offering a relatively low level of services and of private accommodations, a model that was similar to the "traditional" RC/ALs in the study by Zimmerman and her colleagues (Hawes, Phillips, Rose, Holan, & Sherman, 2003; Zimmerman, Gruber-Baldini, Sloane, Eckert, Hebel, Morgan, et al., 2003). Only 12% of the ALFs in the national study would be classified as offering a mixture of high-level services, including having a full-time registered nurse on staff and being willing to offer nursing care with their own staff, and high privacy in accommodations (more than 80% of the units were private) (Hawes, Phillips, Rose, Holan, & Sherman, 2003).

Admission and retention policies also varied among ALFs. In ASPE's national study, most ALFs reported a willingness to admit and retain residents who have moderate physical limitations, such as those using a wheelchair (71%) or needing help with locomotion (62%). But fewer than half the ALFs were willing to retain a resident who needed assistance with transfers (such as moving in or out of bed, or to a chair or wheelchair). More than half (55%) of the ALFs would not retain a resident with moderate to severe cognitive impairment, and 76% would not retain residents with behavioral symptoms (such as wandering). Seventy-two percent of the ALFs would not retain a resident who needed nursing care for more than 14 days (Hawes, Phillips, Rose, Holan,

& Sherman, 2003; Hawes, Rose, & Phillips, 2000). Zimmerman and her colleagues (2003) had similar findings for the "new model" RC/AL facilities in 4 states. The residents tended to have fewer limitations in activities of daily living than in other types of RC/ALs, and most RC/ALs had relatively few residents with behavioral symptoms. Both studies found that the vast majority of residents in new model or high-privacy ALFs were female, white, and among the "*oldest old*." Moreover, while some residents in ALFs were nursing-home eligible, the overall case mix in nursing homes is considerably more impaired than the resident population in the typical ALF, even the new model or high-privacy/high-service ALFs.

Two issues continue to represent a significant challenge for assisted living: aging-in-place and affordability. As a result of policies on retention and nurse staffing, the degree to which ALFs match the service-related philosophical tenets of assisted living is an open question. For example, the ability of ALFs to meet residents' health-related needs is unknown. Similarly, the ability of residents to age in place has been limited in many ALFs by policies that would lead to the discharge of residents whose physical or cognitive limitations progressed beyond a certain point. This was likely to be particularly troublesome for residents with conditions such as Alzheimer's disease, which is associated with progressive cognitive impairment and often with behavioral manifestations. The same is true in the average ALF for residents whose need for help progresses beyond light-care ADLs, such as dressing and bathing, or independently using a wheelchair. The result of these policies can be seen in resident discharges. First, the average length of stay is about 2 years. Second, a 6-month follow-up with a national probability sample of residents who had exited an ALF found that their main reason for leaving was a need for more care than the ALF was willing or able to provide (Phillips, Munoz, Sherman, Rose, Spector, & Hawes, 2003).

Assisted living is still a predominately private-pay phenomenon. While states have expanded the availability of *Medicaid waiver programs*, they also report serving only about 100,000 out of what they estimate to be more than 900,000 beds (Mollica, 2002). The same is true of other public and private efforts to expand affordable assisted living, such as that sponsored by the *Robert Wood Johnson Foundation* (see www.rwjf.org and www.ncbdc.org) and other state efforts using state and federal housing finance funds (Gulyas, 2002; Mollica & Jenkens, 2002). While important, they have had limited impact to date on the industry overall.

Not only is assisted living largely private pay, it is also costly relative to the income of most older persons. With an average annual cost of more than $21,000 in early 1998 for basic services plus any ancillary charges, assisted living was largely unaffordable for moderate- and low-income elderly—indeed, for about three-quarters of all persons aged 75 years and older. This group could only afford assisted living if they disposed of assets and used those funds to supplement their income and pay for care (U.S. Census Bureau, 1998).

To date, assisted living has offered a compelling philosophy, one that has the potential to inform and transform much of residential long-term care, including nursing homes. It certainly resonates with older adults and their families, who are trapped between their difficulties in remaining at home and despair at the idea of living in an "institution." At the same time, the current supply of facilities does not uniformly exhibit this compelling philosophy in their day-to-day operations. Thus, it is difficult to understand the real-world role of ALFs in meeting the long-term care needs of the frail elderly. This issue will become more crucial as the number of facilities expands and the acuity levels of their residents increase.

CATHERINE HAWES
CHARLES D. PHILLIPS
LINNAE L. HUTCHISON

See also
Housing
Nursing Homes

References

American Seniors Housing Association. (1998). *Seniors housing construction report—1998*. Washington, DC: American Seniors Housing Association.

Assisted Living Quality Coalition. (1998). *Assisted living quality initiative: Building a structure that promotes quality*. Washington, DC: Assisted Living Quality Coalition.

Gulyas, R. (2002). *How states have created affordable assisted living: what advocates and policy makers need to know*. Washington, DC: AARP. Available http://www.aarp.org.

Hawes, C., Phillips, C. D., Rose, M., Holan, S., Sherman, M. (2003). *A national survey of assisted living facilities*. *Gerontologist*, *43*, 875–882.

Hawes, C., Rose, M., & Phillips, C. D., (2000). *A national study of assisted living for the frail elderly: Results of a national survey of assisted living facilities*. Beachwood, OH: Myers Research Institute. Available: http://www.aspe.hhs.gov/daltcp/home.htm, under "Research Project."

Hawes, C., Mor, V., Wildfire, J., Lux, L., Greene, A., Iannacchione, V., Spore, D., & Phillips, C. D. (1995). *Analysis of the effect of regulation on the quality of care in board and care homes*. Research Triangle Park: Research Triangle Institute. Available: http://www.aspe.hhs.gov/daltcp/home.htm, under "Research Project Archives."

Jenkens, R. (1997). *Assisted living and private rooms: What people say they want*. Washington, DC: American Association of Retired Persons, Public Policy Institute.

Kane, R. A., & Wilson, K. B. (1993). *Assisted living in the United States: A new paradigm for residential care for frail older persons*? Washington, DC: American Association of Retired Persons.

Kane, R., Baker, M. O., & Veazie, W. (1998). *Consumer perspectives on private versus shared accommodations in assisted living settings*. Washington, DC: American Association of Retired Persons, Public Policy Institute.

Mollica, R. (1998). *State assisted living policy 1998*. Portland, ME: National Academy for State Health Policy.

Mollica, R. (2002). *State assisted living policy 2002*. Portland, ME: National Academy for State Health Policy. Available: http://www.nashp.org.

Mollica, R. & Jenkens, R. (2002). *State assisted living practices and options: A guide for state policy makers*. Princeton, NJ: Robert Wood Johnson Foundation. Available: http://www.rwjf.org.

Phillips, C. D., Munoz, Y., Sherman, M., Rose, M., Spector, W. & Hawes, C. (2003). Effects of facility characteristics on departures from assisted living: Results from a national study. *Gerontologist*, *43*, 690–696.

U.S. Census Bureau. (1997). *Current population survey* (P60-200, Table 8). Washington, DC: U.S. Government Printing Office.

Zimmerman, S., Gruber-Baldini, A. L., Sloane, P. D., Eckert, J. K., Hebel, J. R., Morgan, L. A., Stearns, S. C., Wildfire, J., Magaziner, J., Chen, C., & Konrad, T. R. (2003). Assisted living and nursing homes: Apples and oranges? *Gerontologist*, *43*(Spec. 2), 107–117.

ASSOCIATION FOR GERONTOLOGY IN HIGHER EDUCATION

The Association for Gerontology in Higher Education (AGHE), the educational unit of the *Gerontological Society of America*, was established in 1974 and remains the only national membership organization devoted primarily to gerontological education. Its basic goals are to improve the quality of gerontology and geriatrics programs in higher education, to provide gerontological educators with opportunities for personal fulfillment and professional growth, and to present students with opportunities to work with and on behalf of older adults. The association is sustained largely through the voluntary efforts of educators, researchers, students, administrators, health practitioners, policy makers, and business professionals from all 50 states and 14 foreign countries.

AGHE comprises more than 300 institutional members—colleges, universities, private businesses, and government organizations that provide education, training, and research programs in gerontology and/or geriatrics. Member institutions represent 47 states and 6 foreign countries (Australia, Canada, Israel, Jamaica, Japan, and Kenya) and range from small 2-year colleges to large research universities and organizations outside higher education as well. The *gerontology programs* of member schools vary from developing programs with only a few courses to major centers in the *field of aging in the United States* that offer credentials in gerontology and *geriatrics* and conduct *multidisciplinary aging research*. Although most members are colleges and universities, other organizations that have an interest in gerontological or *geriatrics education*, research, and training may join the association as non-voting organizational affiliates. Individuals not affiliated with a member institution but who are interested in AGHE's activities and services may be added to the association's mailing list for a modest fee.

AGHE carries out its purposes through the following services and programs:

Meetings. The AGHE Annual Meeting and Educational Leadership Conference is a national forum for discussing ideas and issues in gerontological and geriatrics education. The meeting provides an opportunity to network and discuss faculty and program development with others from across the nation and around the world. Participants represent a wide range of disciplines and professions in the field of aging.

Publications and Resources. AGHE offers many resources both for its members and the public, including the *AGHExchange* newsletter, the *Directory of Educational Programs in Gerontology and Geriatrics, Standards and Guidelines for Gerontology Programs, Brief Bibliographies in Aging Series*, and *Collection of Syllabi for Courses in Aging*. In addition, it offers information on various careers in the field of aging via 2 Web sites (www. *aghe.org* and www. *careersinaging.com*). These resources provide vehicles for sharing information about educational developments and opportunities, practical assistance, innovative programs, and research related to *gerontological education*.

Programs and Services. The central office in Washington, DC, serves as a clearinghouse for information about gerontology and geriatrics programs in higher education for students, faculty, and other interested persons. AGHE's *Expert Consultation Program* assists schools with developing new gerontology instruction and expanding or evaluating existing gerontology programs. The *Database of Gerontology and Geriatrics Programs in Higher Education* contains information on more than 1,000 programs of credit instruction at all educational levels across more than 500 campuses. The database can assist students seeking education in the field of aging, faculty seeking information on other aging studies programs, administrators and researchers interested in the scope of gerontological education, and policy makers interested in the training of gerontology and geriatrics professionals. In addition, the Program of Merit initiative establishes AGHE as the organizational body that evaluates and recognizes educational programs—certificate/specializations, minors, and undergraduate and graduate degrees—according to national standards and guidelines, and provides gerontology programs with an AGHE "stamp of approval." This designation is used to verify program quality to administrators, to lobby for additional resources to maintain a quality program, to market the program, and to recruit prospective students into the program.

Advocacy. AGHE advocates for education and research within the field of aging and for gerontology and geriatrics within higher education institutions. It monitors and advocates on behalf of appropriations for the various education and research programs of federal agencies, such as the Administration on Aging, the National Institute on Aging, the Aging branch of the National Institute of Mental Health, the Department of Veterans Affairs, and the Geriatric Initiative branch of the Bureau of Health Professions. The association also seeks to improve the capacity of its member institutions to serve as *advocates for gerontology education* and research on their own campuses, in their communities and states.

Research. The association regularly undertakes analyses, such as the *Core Principles and Outcomes of Gerontology, Geriatrics and Aging Studies Instruction* project co-sponsored with the *Andrus Gerontology Center* at the University of Southern California. Such analyses are designed help improve the character and quality of academic programs in gerontology and geriatrics.

AGHE is a not-for-profit organization, and the resources for its activities are derived from members' annual dues, conference registration revenues, sales of publications and resources, and grants and contracts. For further information, please visit the AGHE Web site: www.aghe.org.

ELIZABETH B. DOUGLASS
Updated by CATHERINE J. TOMPKINS (2001)
Updated by DEREK D. STEPP (2005)

See also
Organizations in Aging

ATTENTION

The mental landscape is a blooming, bustling confusion of sensory inputs, thoughts, and memories. We would be paralyzed by this confusion if we did not have some way to select out of it the information that is of importance to us, that is relevant to our actions, and that allows us to pursue our train of thought and behavior. Attention is the name given to those processes that allow us to carry out that selection. The central question here is whether advancing age is accompanied by changes in attention.

Casual observation suggests the answer to this question is yes. Older adults are more likely than younger adults to report that their *mind has wandered* from what they are reading and that they have to go back and reread, that they start doing one thing around the house and are unintentionally distracted into doing something else, that they forget why they went from one part of the house to another, or that they cannot locate what they want on a supermarket shelf even when it is there. There are many situations in which lapses of attention can have serious consequences. For example, older adults have more accidents per mile driven and are more likely to commit driving violations caused by inattention to relevant information.

Despite these findings, a review of empirical research shows that age-related differences in the basic processes of attention are far smaller and less uniform than might be expected. Since there are comprehensive reviews of this area that effectively document the basic findings (such as McDowd & Shaw, 1999), the present review will not list extensive citations for generally accepted conclusions, but will instead highlight the studies that are recent or that contradict or qualify those conclusions.

Attention has been thought of by some, following William James (1890), as a spotlight illuminating first one then another part of the mental landscape. Others have described attention as a distribution of processing resources, with *attended information* receiving more resources than unattended information. These theories are largely isomorphic and can provide a useful metaphor for thinking about attention and how it might change with advancing age. LaBerge (2002) provides a provocative review of contemporary *theories of attention*.

Externally Initiated Reallocation of Attention

In many cases, shifts in the spotlight or reallocation of resources are in response to external events, for example as when a flashing taillight warns a driver that the car ahead is about to turn, or when a road sign warns of "Trucks Entering from Left." The effect of *advance warnings about imminent events* has been studied in the laboratory by providing advance cues about upcoming information. The benefits of a correct cue and the costs of an incorrect cue have generally been found to be equivalent for younger and older adults, although overall older adults are slower to respond. This is true both for cues that appear at the location where the information will appear, known as *exogenous cues*, and for those that appear elsewhere but instruct the person where it will be, known as *endogenous cues*. The ability to spread attention over a wider area or to narrow it down also appears to be similar in older and younger persons. Some have found that the speed with which attention can be shifted or reallocated is unaffected by age, but others have found that the speed is slower in older adults, particularly when distracting information is present (McCarley, Mounts, & Kramer, 2004). Older adults are not always more susceptible to distraction. When the important information (the target) is in a known location and the distracting information is in other locations, older adults are no more distractible than younger adults. However, when the target location is unknown or unpredictable, or when the target and distracting information are confusable, older adults are disadvantaged compared to their younger counterparts (Little & Hartley, 2000).

Internally Initiated Reallocation of Attention

Shifts or *reallocation of attention* can also be internally generated, particularly when a person is searching for something, whether in their mind or in the visual environment. The goal, the target we are looking for, may be provided to us, but the process by which we seek out candidates, examine them, and evaluate them is controlled internally. Older adults almost always take longer to locate the goal than younger adults, and the difference increases strikingly as the number of distracting, non-goal items increases. An exception is when the goal is distinguished by a single feature—as when searching for the sole red-backed book among a shelf of blue-backed books. Extensive practice can, in some situations, erase the age differences. Why age differences in search occur is a question of both practical and theoretical importance, but it remains unanswered. It may be that older adults have difficulty in disengaging from a distractor once they have attended to it, or that they search inefficiently, returning to items they have already. Or it may be that the search is less well guided, and that younger adults select for examination locations where the target is more likely to be.

If attention has been directed to a location and if nothing appears at that location within about 800 milliseconds, or if attention is then deliberately redirected, an event at the original location is likely to be either missed or responded to more slowly. This is called the *inhibition of return* of attention. Researchers have found that the inhibition attaches both to the location where an object was and to the object itself, even if it moves to a new location. In old age, inhibition of return to the location appears to be preserved, but inhibition of return to the object appears to weaken (McCrae & Adams, 2001).

Attending to More Than One Task

People are often called upon to carry out more than one line of mental processing and action. This is true both in the laboratory (where it is called a *dual task situation*) and in real life, as when we drive and carry on a conversation. Whether we carry out the tasks at the same time or switch rapidly from one to another, it is clear that we require attention to the coordination of the two tasks that goes beyond the attention devoted to each of the tasks alone. Older adults are widely believed to be more challenged by handling 2 tasks at once than are younger adults, even when the demands of each task alone are carefully equated. Recent experiments have carefully controlled when the information about the second task arrives relative to the start of the first (Allen, Lien, Murphy, Sanders, Judge, & McCann, 2002; Glass, Schumacher, Lauber, Zurbriggen, Gmeindl, Kieras, et al., 2001; Hartley, 2001). In these studies, age differences are circumscribed and appear largely attributable to a general slowing with advancing age, and not to any specific difficulty with handling more than one task. It is interesting that older adults appear to benefit less than younger adults from practice at dual tasks (Maquestiaux, Hartley, & Bertsch, in press). In a broader review of many different types of *dual task studies*, Verhaeghen, Steitz, Sliwinski, and Cerella (2003) concluded that there are additional costs of managing 2 tasks and that these costs were slightly higher in older adults.

European researchers have led studies exploring a form of dual task processing in which there is more than one task and the individual must determine on each trial which task is to be carried out, a process known as *task switching*. For example, while driving I do not know until an event occurs whether I will need to brake or to swerve. There are general costs of maintaining more than one active task, as well as specific costs of shifting from one task to another. The basic finding is that specific costs of an immediate shift are no greater for older than younger adults, but the general costs are much higher (Kray & Lindenberger, 2000; Mayr, 2001; Meiran, Gotler, & Perlman, 2001). Even this conclusion must be qualified, however. Specific costs are higher in older adults when the number of possible tasks is large (Kray, Li, & Lindenberger, 2002), whereas when the task is a familiar one (such as looking toward a stimulus when it appears) the age difference in general costs disappears (Bojko, Kramer, & Peterson, 2004).

Generalizations and Explanations

In summary, the basic processes of allocating attention to relevant information, selecting that information, and filtering out surrounding information are little affected by age. In contrast, there are limited changes among older adults in managing more than one task at the same time, and substantial and reliable changes with age in searching through a number of possibilities for a target. A number of explanations have been offered for these facts. One is that *cognitive processing resources decline* with advancing age. This explanation has the disadvantages that it can be tautological if not carefully applied and that it is not readily falsifiable. Another explanation is that *inhibitory functioning* is impaired with aging, but this is simply inconsistent with the available evidence. Some argue that a generalized change, such as a slowing of central cognitive processes, could account for the results, although others contend that this, too, is inconsistent with available evidence. One promising explanation derives from recent advances in the neurosciences and neuropsychology: age differences will be substantial in attentional functions critically dependent on the integrity of the frontal lobes, while attentional functions dependent on posterior cortical and midbrain areas will be relatively well preserved in advanced age. This explanation, termed the *frontal lobe hypothesis* (West, 2000), accounts well for the data and is consistent with the evidence for reductions in cerebral blood flow and for tissue loss with age

(Gunning-Dixon & Raz, 2003). A number of researchers have demonstrated *hyperactivation of the prefrontal cortex* in older adults during cognitive tasks, activation that is more diffuse and less selective than that in younger adults (Cabeza, 2001). Future research will determine the value of the frontal lobe hypothesis as an explanation for the patterns of age-related sparing and impairment of function.

ALAN A. HARTLEY

See also
Cognitive Processes
Learning
Memory and Memory Theory

References

Allen, P. A., Lien, M.-C., Murphy, M. D., Sanders, R. E., Judge, K. S., & McCann, R. S. (2002). Age differences in overlapping task performance: Evidence for efficient parallel processing in older adults. *Psychology and Aging, 17,* 505–519.

Bojko, A., Kramer, A. F., & Peterson, M. S. (2004). Age equivalence in switch costs for prosaccade and antisaccade tasks. *Psychology and Aging, 19,* 226–234.

Cabeza, R. (2001). Cognitive neuroscience of aging: Contributions of functional neuroimaging. *Scandinavian Journal of Psychology, 42,* 277–286.

Glass, J. M., Schumacher, E. H., Lauber, E. J., Zurbriggen, E. L., Gmeindl, L., Kieras, D. E., & Meyer, D. E. (2000). Aging and the psychological refractory period: Task-coordination strategies in young and old adults. *Psychology and Aging, 15,* 571–595.

Gunning-Dixon, F. M., & Raz, N. (2003). Neuroanatomical correlates of selected executive functions in middle-aged and older adults: A prospective MRI study. *Neuropsychologia, 41,* 1929–1941.

Hartley, A. A. (2001). Age differences in dual-task interference are localized to response generation processes. *Psychology and Aging, 16,* 47–54.

James, W. (1890). *The principles of psychology* (Vols. 1 & 2). New York: Holt, Rinehart, & Winston.

Kray, J., & Lindenberger, U. (2000). Adult age differences in task switching. *Psychology and Aging, 15,* 126–147.

Kray, J., Li, K. Z. H., & Lindenberger, U. (2002). Age-related changes in task-switching components: The role of task uncertainty. *Brain & Cognition, 49,* 363–381.

LaBerge, D. (2002). Attentional control: Brief and prolonged. *Psychological Research, 66,* 220–233.

Little, D. M., & Hartley, A. A. (2000). Further evidence that negative priming using the Stroop color-word task is equivalent in younger and older adults. *Psychology and Aging, 15,* 9–17.

Maquestiaux, F., Hartley, A. A., & Bertsch, J. (in press). Can practice overcome age-related differences in the psychological refractory period effect? *Psychology and Aging.*

McCarley, J. S., Mounts, J. R. W., & Kramer, A. F. (2004). Age-related differences in localized attentional interference. *Psychology and Aging, 19,* 203–210.

McDowd, J. M., & Shaw, R. J. (1999). Attention and aging: A functional perspective. In F. I. M. Craik & T. A. Salthouse (Eds.), *Handbook of aging and cognition* (2nd ed). Hillsdale, NJ: Erlbaum.

Meiran, N., Gotler, A., & Perlman, A. (2001). Old age is associated with a pattern of relatively intact and relatively impaired task-set switching abilities. *Journals of Gerontology: Psychological Sciences & Social Sciences, 56B,* P88–P102.

Verhaeghen, P., Steitz, D. W., Sliwinski, M. J., & Cerella, J. (2003). Aging and dual-task performance: A meta-analysis. *Psychology and Aging, 18,* 443–460.

West, R. (2000). In defense of the frontal lobe hypothesis of cognitive aging. *Journal of the International Neuropsychological Society, 6,* 727–729.

ATTENTION SPAN

See
Attention

AUTOIMMUNITY

The term *autoimmunity* refers to the development of *immune responses* by an individual to self-constituents (constituents of that individual's own body) to which the immune system should not react. Immune reactions are mediated by *effector cells* such as *B-lymphocytes*, which differentiate into antibody-secreting plasma cells, by *T-lymphocytes*, which produce *lymphokines* and mediate cellular immunity, and by *monocytes* and *tissue macrophages*. These effector cells are regulated by an intricate network of control mechanisms that include specific receptors on lymphocyte surface membranes, secreted antibody and lymphokines, and specialized subpopulations of T-lymphocytes that modulate and regulate the effector cells. Autoimmunity is the result of abnormal or excessive activity on the part of immune effector cells. Autoimmune responses can include the production of *autoantibodies* by B-lymphocytes and infiltration or destruction of self-tissue by lymphocytes and macrophages. Evidence indicates that potentially *autoreactive lymphocytes* are present in the normal individual and sensitive assays usually reveal low levels of autoantibody in healthy individuals. In the healthy individual, however, the autoreactive lymphocytes are generally held in check by the control mechanisms, and development of autoimmune responses appears to be the result of a breakdown or deterioration of the control mechanisms (Hausman & Weksler, 1985).

Autoimmune Diseases

There are a number of diseases that clearly have autoimmune reactions as a component, and the term *autoimmune disease* is used for such diseases in which specific and relevant autoimmune responses (organ specific or systemic) can be demonstrated. Such diseases include: *systemic lupus erythematosus*, *rheumatoid arthritis*, *scleroderma*, *Sjogren's syndrome*, *autoimmune thyroid disease*, *Addison's disease*, *insulin-dependent diabetes*, *pernicious anemia*, *chronic active hepatitis*, *multiple sclerosis*, *autoimmune hemolytic anemia*, and *myasthenia gravis*. For some of these diseases the circumstantial evidence linking the development of autoimmune responses and the symptoms of the disease is so strong that a cause-and-effect relationship is evident, whereas in other diseases the relationship is less clear (Rose & MacKay, 1985).

Autoantibodies and Aging

The level of autoantibodies increases with age, and it is quite common to find older people whose sera test *positive for autoantibodies*, but who show no signs of any corresponding clinical disease.

Autoimmune Diseases and Aging

Although experimental animals and humans develop autoantibodies with age, autoimmune diseases do not increase in frequency. The most conspicuous autoimmune conditions are probably *thyrotoxicosis*, systemic lupus, myasthenia gravis, and autoimmune hemolytic anemias, none of which is commonly associated with old age. Thus, autoimmune diseases do not appear to be diseases characteristic of old age but are more likely due to a genetic predisposition to the autoimmune disease. There is evidence that diseases that are either generally accepted as autoimmune in character or have some other immunopathological quality show significant correlations with a given *histocompatibility antigen*. The major *histocompatibility complex* (MHC) (H-2 region in mice and the HLA gene cluster in the human) regulates immune responsiveness and the age-related rate of maturation and decline to different immunogenic stimuli. There is a correlation of many autoimmune conditions with a particular HLA group indicating an important genetic component, in the absence of which the disease cannot appear. The relevant antigens are HLA-8, W-27, and HLA-7. It is obvious that any genetic factor is only part of the etiology; environmental influences and accumulating genetic errors in lymphocyte lines must also be considered.

The most characteristic feature of *autoimmunity in old age*, then, is its common occurrence, but generally inconspicuous character. Genetic errors, involving both germ-line and somatic genomes, which interfere with the self-monitoring function of the immune system, are thought to be the principal cause of autoimmune disease. For a general discussion of issues, see Walford, Weindruch, Gottesman, and Tam (1981).

Recently, the theory has been advanced that *atherosclerosis* is an autoimmune disease (Wick & Xu, 1999). If this theory is correct, autoimmunity may play a major role in human aging because atherosclerosis is a common occurrence, progresses in severity with age, and is a major player in coronary heart disease and stroke.

MARGARET L. HEIDRICK

See also
Immune System

References

Hausman, P. B., & Weksler, M. W. (1985). Changes in the immune response with age. In C. E. Finch & E. L. Schneider (Eds.), *Handbook of the biology of aging* (pp. 414–432). New York: Van Nostrand Reinhold.

Rose, N. R., & MacKay, I. R. (Eds.) (1985). *The autoimmune diseases*. New York: Academic Press.

Walford, R. L., Weindruch, R. H., Gottesman, S. R., & Tam, C. F. (1981). Immunology of aging, In C. Eisdorfer (Ed.), *Annual review of gerontology and geriatrics* (pp. 3–48). New York: Springer Publishing.

Wick, G., & Xu, Q. (1999). Atherosclerosis: An autoimmune disease. *Experimental Gerontology, 34*, 559–566.

AUTONOMY AND AGING

Autonomy is a special concern in the context of aging. Improvements in health care and increases in the health status of older individuals have allowed older persons to maintain unprecedented levels of activity and control in economic, family, political, and social affairs. For many individuals in developed societies, growing old now involves a significant delay in the diminishment or loss of functional capacities that are traditionally associated with old age. As a result, this cohort of individuals who are old but still active and functionally intact has challenged traditional expectations about the types of personal and social activities that are appropriate for older persons, and has shifted political and social power. Unwilling to accept retirement as their defining function, older adults are confronting a wide range of choices unknown to their predecessors, making the problem of autonomous choice central to aging.

The large group of functionally capable old persons is balanced by a smaller cohort of the *old-old*, who have significant frailty and high rates of dependence on others for performing activities of daily living (ADLs). They typically have serious morbidities and their need for health care and social supports daunt policy makers (Baltes & Smith, 2003; Becker, 1994). Making health care decisions for these patients has proven to be difficult, because their frailty and incapacity complicates the bioethical principle of respect for the autonomy of patients. In addition, diseases associated with aging, like Alzheimer's and dementia, which involve manifest impairments in autonomy-related functions like cognition and decision making, make the everyday care of compromised individuals ethically problematic. How best to respect the autonomy of patients with cognitive and memory deficits is a nettlesome ethical question. Whether caregivers should respect the current preferences or values of these patients, or their wishes expressed in the past, such as in *advance directives*, has emerged as an important practical and theoretical issue (Dresser, 1994; Dresser & Astrow, 1998).

Contemporary medicine promises not just life extension, but the maintenance and enhancement of personal capacities. The emergence of *biogerontology* and so-called *anti-aging medicine* promises to alter patterns of aging and is already provoking debate about the legitimacy of these options (Juengst, Binstock, Mehlman, Post, & Whitehouse, 2003; Juengst, Binstock, Mehlman, & Post, 2003; Mackey, 2003). In the discussion and debate over anti-aging medicine, individual choice is pitted squarely against social regulation assuring that the link between aging issues and issues of autonomy will persist.

Assessing the function of autonomy in aging is theoretically complicated, because autonomy has such a broad range of meanings. Its dominant understanding, particularly in Western societies, is influenced by liberal theory that regards liberty—or freedom from external restraint—as the central feature of autonomy. This definition elevates the individual as the central focus of ethical and social concern. It assumes that persons have and are able to exercise rather high-level capacities—such as reflective self-awareness, the ability to understand the range of choices available, and one's own preferences, values, and beliefs, and to make choices based on the hierarchical interrelationship among one's values and beliefs. This somewhat idealized account has dominated social and political thought, and its influence on aging research and reform efforts in long-term care has been significant.

In liberal theory, the ideal of autonomy focuses on the individual as an isolated, atomistic center of action and choice. Relationships with others, including social institutions, are regarded as incidental to the definition of who the autonomous person truly is and what should be included within the focus of ethical regard. Family and social relationships are marginalized and seem to enter the picture primarily when they threaten the liberty of the individual. This view encourages a society composed of solitary, isolated individuals who lack significant relations with others and fail to appreciate the contribution that social relationships make toward their functioning and identity (Clark, 1991). It affiliates the concept of autonomy with personal self-interest and is often used to trump the competing interests of family or society. No wonder, then, that dependence or diminishment in capacity is regarded with such revulsion.

The influence of the ideal of individual autonomy is seen in the decision making surrounding choice of treatment at the end of–life, as well as in attitudes toward long-term care. The *patient rights movement* that began in the late 20th century led to the establishment of advance directives that recognized the right of individuals to make medical decisions for themselves without undue influence by health professionals. This right of decision making included whether and under what conditions life-sustaining medical interventions would be accepted. Standard advance directives almost universally empower individuals to refuse advance life support, on the presumption that a life dependent on supportive technologies violates the independence that is so integral to the liberal view of autonomy.

This devaluation of dependence extends beyond technologically advanced life-sustaining technologies to include everyday help with ADLs. Thus the need for long-term care is often seen as an assault on personal autonomy, because it validates the existence of dependence. Paradoxically, one response to problems or inadequacies in the care provided to *dependent older persons* involves attempts to increase autonomous choice in home care and nursing homes. These reformist tendencies initially focused on institutional long-term care, but increasingly have turned to problems associated with autonomy in the context of home care as well (Gallagher, Alcock, Diem, Angus, & Medves, 2002). In all of these settings, the stark realities of dependence that underlie the need for long-term care challenges the assumptions and approaches associated with the ideals of the liberal model of autonomy. Thus, a profound ambivalence permeates the topic of autonomy in aging, given the prominence of the liberal model. In long-term care, this ideal model of independent, atomistic decision making is seldom to be found, given the diminishment and loss of capacities that engender the need for long-term care. When dependence creates the need for continuous types of supportive care, autonomy seems to be threatened. From the view of liberal theory, then, aging represents a fundamental threat to the core values associated with autonomy.

Although attention to patient autonomy has been a powerful force in an emancipatory movement for older adults, especially those requiring long-term care, it runs squarely into conflict with the underlying expectations and ideas associated with standard views of autonomy, which assume that autonomous persons have robust capacities of action, decision making, and thought. Recognition of the limitations of autonomy for aging persons has led to work that attempts to reframe our understanding of it (Agich, 1990). Rather than independence and self-centered action and choice, personal autonomy is viewed in a developmental and social context where dependence and relationships with others are essential to what it means to be a mature person acting with autonomy (Agich, 2003). Viewed in these terms, *actual autonomy*, as opposed to the liberal ideal of *autonomy as independence*, becomes the focus of attention (Agich, 1995). This approach recognizes that persons grow old with others; they are psychologically and socially enmeshed with others in ways that contradict the independence so highly regarded by liberal theory. These accounts view individuals within their unique biographical and social setting and accept dependence as an ineliminable feature of becoming and being autonomous. Thus, from the perspective of *actual autonomy*, aging is transformed from a process representative of the deterioration of individual capacity to a process through which autonomy manifests an evolving set of relationships with others. The implications of this view for rethinking the ethical and psychosocial challenges associated with aging are significant.

Understanding the conditions that enhance or thwart the expression of autonomy consistent with dependence across the life span becomes an important research concern. If dependency is viewed as a necessary correlate of normal aging, rather than as a failure of aging, then it can be seen as a correlative feature of autonomy rather than as characteristic of its loss. In ethical terms, respecting autonomy has to be reinterpreted according to what autonomy actually involves, rather than some inflated ideal of autonomy as independence. Autonomy thus becomes an essential theme and challenge for any serious reflection on the meaning of aging (Fenech, 2003). To respect autonomy in aging involves far more than simply acknowledging the rights of persons at specific times in their lives. Instead, understanding the developmental, institutional, psychological, and social conditions that promote and sustain autonomy across the life span will be a central problem for future aging research.

Autonomy is therefore a concern for the field of aging not only when conflicts over the rights of older persons arise, but also in the complex social processes of everyday life, in which persons and institutions influence how individuals develop and express their personal identities. The psychosocial and institutional settings within which persons live and grow older are essential components of being and becoming autonomous, because they help define the conditions for personal meaning and dignity (Weiss & Bass, 2002). When the concept of autonomy in aging is thus understood in terms of the processes for its development, rather than as an ideal state of existence, the ethical questions associated with aging can be more adequately approached (Agich, 2003). More importantly, autonomy becomes a concern for any serious treatment of aging itself.

George J. Agich

See also
Life-Span Theory of Control

References

Agich, G. J. (1995). Actual autonomy and long-term care decision making. In L. B. McCullough & N. L. Wilson (Eds.), *Long-term care decisions: Ethical and conceptual dimensions* (pp. 15). Baltimore, MD: Johns Hopkins University Press.

Agich, G. J. (2003). *Dependence and autonomy in old age: An ethical framework for long-term care.* Cambridge, UK: Cambridge University Press.

Agich, G. J. (1990). Reassessing autonomy in long-term care. *Hastings Center Report,* 12–17.

Baltes, P. B., & Smith, J. (2003). New frontiers in the future of aging: From successful aging of the young old to the dilemmas of the fourth age. *Gerontology, 49,* 123–135.

Becker, G. (1994). The oldest old; autonomy in the face of frailty. *Journal of Aging Studies, 8,* 59–76.

Clark, P. G. (1991). Ethical dimensions of quality of life in aging: Autonomy versus collectivism in the United States and Canada. *Gerontologist, 31,* 631–639.

Dresser, R. (1994). Missing persons: Legal perceptions of incompetent patients. *Rutgers Law Review, 46,* 609–719.

Dresser, R., & Astrow, A. B. (1998). An alert and incompetent self. The irrelevance of advance directives. *Hastings Center Report, 28,* 28–30.

Fenech, F. F. (2003). Ethical issues in ageing. *Clinical Medicine, 3,* 232–234.

Gallagher, E., Alcock, D., Diem, E., Angus, D., & Medves, J. (2002). Ethical dilemmas in home care case management. *Journal of Healthcare Management, 47,* 85–96.

Juengst, E. T., Binstock, R. H., Mehlman, M., Post, S. G., & Whitehouse, P. (2003). Biogerontology, "anti-aging medicine," and the challenges of human enhancement. *Hastings Center Report, 33,* 21–30.

Juengst, E. T., Binstock, R. H., Mehlman, M. J., & Post, S. G. (2003). Aging. Anti-aging research and the need for public dialogue. *Science, 299,* 1323.

Mackey, T. (2003). An ethical assessment of anti-aging medicine. *Journal of Anti-Aging Medicine, 6,* 187–204.

Weiss, R. S., & Bass, S. A. (2002). *Challenges of the third age: Meaning and purpose in later life.* New York and Oxford: Oxford University Press.

B

BABY BOOM GENERATION

In the academic imagination as well as in public perception, particularly in the United States, the idea of the baby boom generation has had pervasive influence on thinking about the present and future of aging. This cohort, usually considered to include the 76 million persons born between 1946 and 1964, has been called the "most over-defined group of our time" (Helen O'Connor, cited in Bouvier & DeVita, 1991), serving as fodder for sweeping generalizations of all sorts despite its manifest diversity. Such overgeneralizations have led some demographers to question the utility of the whole concept of a distinct baby boom generation and the emphasis given to it in the United States. Clearly, however, the cohort born in the years following World War II has faced, at each stage of its life history, economic and social circumstances distinct from those encountered by their predecessors and successors at similar ages.

One important strand in debates over baby boomers emerged by the early 1960s; it concerns the extent to which this cohort's large size, relative to preceding and successive cohorts, would be critical in shaping its destiny (Easterlin, 1962). This argument was presented in extended form by Easterlin (1987), who stated that large cohorts such as the baby boom generation would face labor surpluses and hence encounter more competition for jobs, command lower wages, and face more economic uncertainty, and in consequence would delay or forgo marriage and family commitments. Such a view would imply discouraging prospects for *baby boomers' retirement* prospects, a concern augmented by evidence of wage stagnation during the 1970s and 1980s (Levy & Murnane, 1992). Indeed, some researchers concluded that baby boomers seemed to be doing less well economically than did their parents' cohort at similar ages (Levy & Michel, 1991). However, some studies have found otherwise (Baek & DeVaney, 2004). In an early study, Russell (1982) concluded that the *baby boomers' economic prospects* were at least comparable to those of previous generations. By the 1990s, with the oldest baby boomers well into their working lives, the Congressional Budget Office (1993) estimated that at ages 35 to 44, leading-edge boomers had an 82% advantage over their parents' generation in median household income adjusted for household size. Similarly, Crystal and Johnson (1998), using data from the National Longitudinal Surveys, found that at ages 40 to 44, women in the 1949–1953 birth cohort experienced 51% improvement in mean family income, adjusted for family size, compared with the cohort of women born in 1923–1927. These improvements in size-adjusted family income were largely achieved through changes in family economic behavior—a shift toward 2-earner families and smaller family sizes—rather than through improvements in earnings rates.

TABLE 1 Age Range of Baby-Boom Generation for Selected Years, 2000–2030

Year	*Age Range of Baby Boomers*
2000	36–54
2005	41–59
2010	46–64
2015	51–69
2020	56–74
2025	61–79
2030	66–84

Of course, these comparisons of averages mask enormous heterogeneity among baby boomers. Indeed, an important question concerns the impact of the process of cumulative advantage and disadvantage (Crystal & Shea, 1990; Crystal & Waehrer, 1996) on baby boomers' economic prospects. Will this cohort, whose careers have unfolded in an era of increasing income gaps between those with high education and skills and those without, experience very high income inequality in their later years? Crystal and Johnson (1998) found that the *Gini coefficient of inequality* among leading-edge baby boomers in their early 40s was comparable to that among earlier cohorts, but what will happen as this group nears retirement age is not yet known.

As with any simplifying scheme applied to complex realities, the notion of a distinct baby boom generation is to some extent a figment of the imagination. Americans born in the 2 decades following World War II are an extraordinarily diverse group.

Demography is not necessarily destiny, and cohort size alone is only one of a large number of economic, demographic, political, technological, and other circumstances that make each cohort's historical experience unique. Nevertheless, its pervasive use suggests that the idea of a distinct "baby boom generation" has been a compelling one.

STEPHEN CRYSTAL
Updated by Richard SCHULZ

References

Baek, E., & DeVaney, S. A. (2004). Assessing the baby boomers' financial wellness using financial ratios and a subjective measure. *Family and Consumer Sciences Research Journal*, *32*, 321–384.

Bouvier, L. F., & DeVita, C. J. (1991). The baby boom: Entering midlife. *Population Bulletin*, *46*(3).

Congressional Budget Office. (1993). *Baby boomers in retirement: An early perspective*. Washington, DC: Congressional Budget Office.

Crystal, S., & Johnson, R. (1998). *The changing retirement prospects of American families: Impact of labor market shifts on economic outcomes*. Public Policy Institute Publication No. 9801. Washington, DC: American Association of Retired Persons.

Crystal, S., & Shea, D. (1990). Cumulative advantage, cumulative disadvantage, and inequality among elderly people. *Gerontologist*, *30*, 437–443.

Crystal, S., & Waehrer, K. (1996). Later-life inequality in longitudinal perspective. *Journal of Gerontology: Social Sciences*, *51B*(6), S307–S318.

Easterlin, R. A. (1962). *The American baby boom in historical perspective*. New York: National Bureau of Economic Research.

Easterlin, R. A. (1987). *Birth and fortune: The impact of numbers on personal welfare* (2nd ed.). Chicago: University of Chicago Press.

Levy, F., & Michel, R. (1991). The economic future of American families. Washington, DC: Urban Institute Press.

Levy, F., & Murnane, R. J. (1992). U.S. earning levels and earnings in inequality: A review of recent trends and proposed explanations. *Journal of Economic Literature*, *30*, 1333–1381.

BALTIMORE LONGITUDINAL STUDY OF AGING

The Baltimore Longitudinal Study of Aging (BLSA) was started in 1958, largely thanks to the efforts of pioneer gerontologist *Nathan Shock*, with the goal of characterizing the physiological and *psychological aging processes* in normal individuals living in the community (Shock, Greulich, Andres, Arenberg, Costa, & Lakatta, et al., 1984). Prior to this, aging research consisted primarily of cross-sectional measurements made of older patients in hospitals or long-term care facilities. By studying healthy active individuals, it was thought that the confounding influences of disease and inactivity on the aging process could be minimized. Furthermore, performing serial measurements in the same individuals over time would allow a more precise determination of age-associated changes than the "snapshot" produced by a single measurement.

Initially recruits to the BLSA were well-educated men from the Baltimore-Washington area who volunteered to undergo extensive medical, physiological, and psychological testing for 2 days every 1 to 2 years for the rest of their lives. Beginning in 1978, women were recruited into the study, once expanded facilities for housing participants overnight became available. Although the recruitment of new participants from family members and friends of those already enrolled in the BLSA resulted in a predominantly Caucasian cohort of higher socioeconomic status, major efforts were made in the 1990s to increase the diversity of the sample.

As of March 2005, 1,806 men and 1,199 women aged 18 to 96 years on entry have been studied on at least 1 visit; the mean follow-up is 11.4 years, with some individuals followed over 40 years. The racial composition is now 80% Caucasian, 16% African-American, and 4% others. Three-quarters have at least 16 years of formal education. Although the visit frequency has varied over the years, the current interval between visits is yearly for those aged 80 years and older, 2 years for those aged 60 to 79 years, and 4 years for those aged less than 60 years. To encourage continued participation for those who have moved out of the area or are unable to drive to the testing facility, airfare or ground transportation is now provided for individuals older than 75 years with at least 4 prior BLSA visits.

On each visit, participants undergo a clinical examination to identify disease and to characterize their health status. Thus, the BLSA focuses on the progressive changes that occur over time in individual participants. In broad terms, the research agenda attempts to characterize and quantify normal aging changes, identify the transitions between healthy aging and the development of early disease, and unravel the mechanisms involved in both processes. This agenda allows investigators to separate usual aging from successful aging. In recent years, the search for genetic markers for successful aging as well as those associated with, or predictive of, age-related diseases has received heightened attention.

The BLSA can be envisioned as a series of nested longitudinal and cross-sectional studies oriented toward: (1) description of the anatomical, physiological, psychological and functional changes that occur with advancing age, (2) identification of the biological, behavioral, and environmental factors that account for these changes, (3) identification of the physiological pathways leading to frailty in older adults, conceptualized as increased susceptibility to disease and reduced ability to withstand stress, (4) identification of factors that predict successful aging and health-related outcomes, and (5) development of hypotheses concerning possible targets for interventions that may favorably affect the aging process and prevent or retard development of age-related diseases.

Over the past 5 decades, assessments of the following major areas have been performed: anthropometric measurements with estimates of body composition, blood and urine chemistries, glucose tolerance, renal function, pulmonary function, immunological competence, endocrine function, cardiovascular structure and resting function, maximal aerobic capacity, exercise electrocardiography, muscle strength, neuromotor function, hearing, and vision. Cognitive function is assessed via specially designed tests to measure learning, problem solving, memory, and reaction times. Personality responses to psychological stress and methods of coping with life stresses are assessed by written tests (now computerized) and structured interviews. Finally, questionnaires are administered to assess lifestyle habits.

Although testing in most of these areas has continued throughout the study, some methodologies used in their assessment have evolved over time. For example, the Master-2 step exercise test used to assess aerobic fitness and the presence of silent myocardial ischemia during the first decade of the study was replaced by treadmill exercise electrocardiography and maximal oxygen consumption measurement. In other areas, new technologies such as *dual photon x-ray absorptiometry* (DEXA) have been added to older ones like *anthropometry* to provide detailed information on body composition. Such methodological additions and substitutions must be introduced carefully and appropriately validated against older measures where possible, to avoid introducing a measurement bias that might affect the quantitation of longitudinal changes in the system under study.

New *longitudinal measures* can be initiated as new techniques and ideas develop in the medical community. For example, BLSA *prostate-specific antigen* (PSA) determinations were begun in the late 1980s, several years after initial reports that PSA could detect prostate cancer. Results from stored blood samples demonstrated greater longitudinal increases in PSA over a 25-year period among men who were diagnosed with prostate cancer compared to men with benign prostatic hyperplasia or normal prostate glands (Carter, Pearson, Metter, Brant, Chan, & Andres, et al., 1992). These findings established the concept of *PSA velocity*, which has become a commonly used approach in the diagnosis of prostate cancer.

In the medical research community, *cross-sectional studies*—in which a measurement is made at a single point in time across a broad range of individuals—are often used to characterize age-associated changes, because such studies are much less costly and time-consuming than longitudinal studies, in which repeated measurements are made on the same individuals over time. The BLSA also uses cross-sectional studies to investigate the aging process, particularly when a new technique or measurement is introduced into the study. Such cross-sectional studies, however, may not provide an accurate picture of true—that is, longitudinal—aging within an individual. In particular, the oldest participants in a cross-sectional study represent selective survivorship because some of the younger persons in the sample may not live to reach this age while remaining free of disease in the specific organ system being evaluated. As a result, cross-sectional studies may underestimate longitudinal aging changes at older ages, providing a falsely optimistic estimate of normative aging.

An example of this phenomenon is shown in Figure 1, which describes aging changes in *peak treadmill oxygen consumption* (VO_2) in 810 men and women free of cardiac disease (Fleg, Morrell, Bos, Talbot, Wright, & Lakatta, 2005). The figure describes the 10-year changes in peak VO_2 in 6 separate age-decade groups from the 20s through the 70s, separated by gender. In both sexes, the

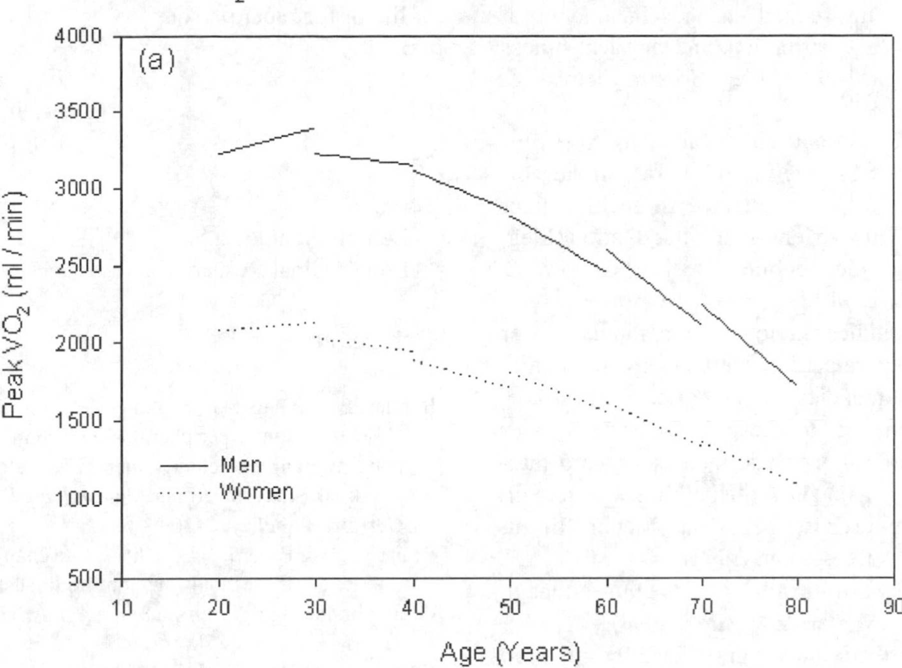

FIGURE 1 Cross-sectional and longitudinal changes in peak oxygen consumption (VO_2) in ml/min, by gender and age decade. The figure displays the 10-year longitudinal change in peak VO_2 for age groups from the 20s through the 70s, predicted from a mixed effects linear regression model. Note the progressively steeper decline in peak VO_2 with successive age decades, particularly in men. Cross-sectional estimates of peak VO_2 decline, derived by connecting the starting point for each of the 6 age-group lines, substantially underestimate longitudinal declines.

longitudinal decline in peak VO_2 becomes steeper as the initial age at observation increases. Cross-sectional estimates of the percent decline in peak VO_2 per decade, derived by connecting the left-hand points for each of the 6 age decade lines, average 8% to 10% in the older groups. However, the true longitudinal decline per decade in peak VO_2 approaches 30% in the elderly—approximately 3 times the projected cross-sectional decrease. It should be emphasized that given individuals may show remarkable variation from these group averages in their rates of VO_2 change with age.

Most physiological functions demonstrate a gradual decline over the adult life span. Examples include peak VO_2, creatinine clearance, glucose tolerance, pulmonary function, muscle strength, and reaction time. *Age-associated declines* are generally greater for complex tasks that require the integrated performance of multiple systems, such as maximal minute ventilation or muscular power, than for simple tasks like forced vital capacity or muscle strength. Thus, it appears that aging-related changes in function are the result of both changes within an organ system and less efficient cross talk between systems. It should also be emphasized that lifestyle factors such as physical activity, diet, and cigarette smoking can have profound effects on the starting values and measured rates of change in many functions. Finally, the correlations between aging-related changes in different physiological and psychological performance measures are relatively low, discounting the concept of a single aging process common to multiple systems.

In its nearly 5 decades of existence, BLSA investigators have published over 1,000 scientific manuscripts. A sampling of important findings includes the following:

1. Kidney function, indexed by creatinine clearance, declines—30% between ages 30 and 80 years (Rowe, Andres, Tobin, Norris, & Shock, 1976).

2. Glucose tolerance declines with age, independent of aging-related changes in amount of body fat, fat distribution, and physical fitness (Shimokata, Muller, Fleg, Sorkin, Ziemba, & Andres, 1991).
3. Although maximal cardiac output declines progressively with age in both sexes, stroke volume per beat is maintained in healthy older adults by greater left-ventricular dilation (Fleg, O'Connor, Gerstenblith, Becker, Clulow, & Schulman, et al., 1995).
4. Age-related hearing loss is more rapid at lower frequencies related to everyday speech than at higher frequencies (Brant, & Fozard, 1990).
5. Men destined to develop prostate cancer demonstrate more rapid increases in prostate-specific antigen (PSA) than those who remain cancer-free (Carter, Pearson, Metter, Brant, Chan, & Andres, et al., 1992).
6. Personality traits in adults change little after age 30 (Costa, Metter, & McCrae, 1994).
7. Early dementia may be predicted by impaired visual recall 6 to 15 years before clinical findings appear (Zonderman, Giambra, Arenberg, Resnick, & Costa, 1995).
8. Elevated serum cholesterol continues to be a risk factor for coronary heart disease in men aged 75 to 97 years. (Sorkin, Andres, Muller, D. C., Baldwin, H. L., & Fleg, J. L., 1992).
9. An accelerated longitudinal decline in forced expiratory volume on pulmonary function testing predicts excess mortality from coronary heart disease (Tochman, Pearson, Fleg, Metter, Kao, & Rampal, et al., 1995).
10. A decline in absolute peripheral blood lymphocyte count is observed within 3 years of death in healthy elderly men (Bender, Nagel, Adler, & Andres, 1986).

A major challenge for any longitudinal study is to introduce promising new areas of investigation while continuing core measurements. In recent years the BLSA has initiated or expanded its research in aging in such areas as inflammatory markers, oxidative stress, genetic markers/predictors of usual and successful aging, and racial and socioeconomic influences on the aging process. With the dramatic current and projected growth of the older population in the United States, the BLSA, now approaching its 50th year, has an unprecedented opportunity to contribute to the longevity and quality of life of the older persons.

Jerome L. Fleg
E. Jeffrey Metter
Luigi Ferrucci

See also
Longitudinal Data Sets
Longitudinal Research

References

Bender, B. S., Nagel, J. E., Adler, W. H., & Andres, R. (1986). Absolute peripheral blood count and subsequent mortality of elderly men. The Baltimore Longitudinal Study of Aging. *Journal of the American Geriatrics Society*, *34*, 649–654.

Brant, L. J., & Fozard, J. L. (1990). Age changes in pure-tone hearing thresholds in a longitudinal study of normal human aging. *Journal of the Acoustical Society of America*, *88*, 813–820.

Carter, H. B., Pearson, J. D., Metter, E. J., Brant, L. J., Chan, D. W., Andres, R., Fozard, J. L., & Walsh, P. C. (1992). Longitudinal elevation of prostate specific antigen levels in men with and without prostate disease. *Journal of the American Medical Association*, *267*, 2215–2220.

Costa, P. T., Metter, E. J., & McCrae, R. R. (1994). Personality stability and its contribution to successful aging. *Journal of Geriatric Psychiatry*, *27*, 41–59.

Fleg, J. L., Morrell, C. H., Bos, A. G., Talbot, L. A., Wright, J. G., & Lakatta, E. G. (2005, in press). Accelerated longitudinal decline of aerobic capacity in healthy older adults. *Circulation*.

Fleg, J. L., O'Connor, F., Gerstenblith, G., Becker, L. C., Clulow, J., Schulman, S. P., & Lakatta, E. G. (1995). Impact of age on the cardiovascular response to dynamic upright exercise in healthy men and women. *Journal of Applied Physiology*, *78*, 890–900.

Rowe, J. W., Andres, R., Tobin, J. D., Norris, A. H., & Shock, N. W. (1976). The effect of age on creatinine clearance in men: A cross-sectional and longitudinal study. *Journal of Gerontology*, *31*, 155–163.

Shimokata, H., Muller, D. C., Fleg, J. L., Sorkin, J., Ziemba, A. W., & Andres, R. (1991). Age as independent determinant of glucose tolerance. *Diabetes*, *40*, 44–51.

Shock, N. W., Greulich, R. C., Andres, R. A., Arenberg, D., Costa, P. T. Jr., Lakatta, E. G., & Tobin, J. D. (1984). *Normal human aging: The Baltimore Longitudinal Study of Aging*. Bethesda, MD: Washington DC: U.S. Government Printing Office.

Sorkin, J. D., Andres, R., Muller, D. C., Baldwin, H. L., & Fleg, J. L. (1992). Cholesterol as a risk factor for coronary heart disease in elderly men: The Baltimore Longitudinal Study of Aging. *Annals of Epidemiology*, *2*, 59–67.

Tochman, M. S., Pearson, J. D., Fleg, J. L., Metter, E. J., Kao, S. Y., Rampal, K. G., Cruise, L. J., & Fozard, J. L. (1995). Rapid decline in FEV1. A new risk factor for coronary heart disease mortality. *American Journal of Respiratory and Critical Care Medicine*, *151*, 390–398.

Zonderman, A. B., Giambra, L. M., Arenberg, D., Resnick, S. M., & Costa, P. T. (1995). Changes in immediate visual memory predict cognitive impairment. *Archives of Clinical Neuropsychology*, *10*, 111–123.

BEHAVIOR MANAGEMENT

Behavior management is an intervention strategy. It includes a collection of procedures based on the assumptions that behavior is influenced by stimuli, mostly in the environment, that precede the behavior (antecedents) and stimuli that immediately follow the behavior (consequences, also known as contingencies). This is often referred to as the *A-B-C model* (Teri, Borson, Kiyak, & Yamagishi, 1989).

Historically, the roots of behavior management go back to Skinner's (1974) deterministic *stimulus-response theory*, which posits that the organism (person) mechanistically responds (R) to stimuli (S) in the environment. Contemporary behavior management is more closely aligned to Bandura's (1969) *social learning theory*, which includes the organism in the loop (S-O-R) and considers the person's cognitions (thoughts) and emotions as mediators between S and R as well as causes of behavior in their own right. Bandura introduced the principle of *reciprocal determinism*, hypothesizing that the environment (antecedents and consequences) affects the person, but the person can, and often does, affect his or her environment.

Behavior—or, more commonly, a problematic behavior—can be changed by altering either the antecedent, the consequence, or the individual's cognition, or any combination of the 3. The degree to which cognitions are targeted depends on the cognitive status of the individual: individuals with moderate or severe dementia are almost always exposed to antecedent and/or consequent interventions.

Antecedent Interventions. Data suggests that various environmental stimuli can increase the probability of both adaptive and non-adaptive behaviors. For example, furniture arrangement, lighting level, room color and temperature, aromas, and, most important, how one is approached by another person can produce either pleasant or unpleasant responses in both cognitively intact older persons and those who are cognitively impaired (the latter have been found to be more vulnerable to environmental influence). Consequently, interventions have been developed to identify aromas and room colors that can calm *agitated nursing home residents* (Ballard, O'Brien, Reichelt, & Perry, 2002; Loew & Silverstone, 1971). Studies also have been conducted on increasing lighting in dim hallways to decrease aimless "wandering" (Cohen-Mansfield & Werner, 1998), and intense white light has been examined to "energize" lethargic residents and also to decrease agitation (Ancoli-Israel, Martin, Kripke, Marler, & Klauber, 2002; Lovell, Ancoli-Israel, & Gevirtz, 1995; Mishima, Okawa, Hishikawa, Hozumi, Hori, & Takahashi, 1994; Rheaume, Manning, & Harper, 1998; Van Someren, Kessler, & Mirmiran, 1997).

The most critical environmental influence in an older person's life is the people with whom they interact on a day-to-day basis. For this reason, much *research in nursing homes* has focused on teaching staff better communication skills (Burgio, Allen-Burge, Roth, Bourgeois, Dijkstra, & Gerstle, et al., 2001; McCallion, Toseland, & Lacey, 1999). For example, staff have been taught to interact more positively with residents; they have also learned the verbal and nonverbal approach behaviors that are least likely to elicit catastrophic responses from residents and most likely to result in resident cooperation (Burgio, et al., 2001).

Consequent Interventions (Contingency Management). An abundance of data indicates that behaviors that are followed by positive events are more likely to occur in the future, while those followed by negative events are less likely to occur in the future. Consequently, interventions have been developed (most frequently with older adults suffering from dementia) that deliver a positive stimulus (event) immediately after the person engages in an adaptive behavior, such as positive interaction. A simple example is a study that showed increased nursing home resident ambulation when staff praise "reinforced" the ambulation (Burgio, Burgio, Engel, & Tice, 1986).

A common syndrome shown by individuals with dementia is often referred to as "agitation," which includes problems ranging from disruptive vocalization to physical aggression and repeated questions. *Agitation* is a major known *stressor of family caregivers*, and for staff and the other residents in nursing homes. Clinical trials have shown that teaching family and nursing home caregivers (certified nursing assistants) behavior management skills can decrease agitation and, in turn, the amount of stress associated with these problems (Burgio, Stevens, Guy, Roth, & Haley, 2003; Burgio, et al., 2002).

Instituting *behavior management programs in nursing homes* produces a unique set of complications. To be effective, behavior management programs need to be performed consistently and accurately by the staff. Staff members are often overworked and inadequately supervised, resulting in inconsistent program application (poor quality control). In recent years researchers have recognized that behavior management programs work in these settings only if with a "systems approach", such as setting up a system of monitoring accurate and consistent application of the procedures by the staff. In essence, behavior management programs, or staff motivational systems, are created to ensure that the staff applies behavior management programs for the residents.

It should be noted that studies examining the application of negative events to change older adults' behavior are practically nonexistent (however, see Sanavio, 1981). The common practice of removing an agitated resident from a common area to his/her room could be interpreted as applying a negative event (being placed in one's room) as a consequence for an nonadaptive behavior (agitation); in childrearing literature, this is often referred to as a "time-out."

Altering Cognitions. As stated previously, these procedures are used almost exclusively with cognitively intact older persons. A prime example is the use of what has been called "mood management" or more broadly, "*cognitive behavior therapy*." In this procedure, the person is taught to identify thoughts or cognitions that are affecting their mood or behavior negatively. They then learn techniques to challenge these unhelpful thoughts, such as replacing the negative thought with a pleasant or neutral thought, or using a "*thought-stopping*" *strategy* in which the person shouts (internally) "NO!" each time the negative thought occurs (Dick, Gallaghher-Thompson, Coon, Powers, & Thompson, 1995; Thompson, Gallaghher-Thompson, & Dick, 1995). Sometimes the person is asked to wear a rubber band around his/her wrist and to snap the band along with the internal "NO!" (note that the latter is an example of applying a negative stimulus to decrease the future probability of a nonadaptive behavior).

The last examples contradict a commonly held belief that behavior management techniques are always imposed by a "behavior change agent" on others. Although this is often true when applied to persons with dementia, a host of techniques collectively referred to as behavioral self-management can be used by older adults to help them change nonadaptive behaviors (such as cigarette smoking, excessive eating). Behavioral self-management also can be used to increase adaptive behaviors, such as exercise or preventive health behaviors.

Behavior management techniques can be effective and have been designated "first-line therapy" for a host of problems, from agitation in older adults with dementia to weight control, treatment of urinary incontinence, and lack of exercise. Additional research is needed to increase their effectiveness and to widen their application to additional problems.

LOUIS D. BURGIO
REBECCA S. ALLEN

References

Ancoli-Israel, S., Martin, J. L., Kripke, D. F., Marler, M., & Klauber, M. R. (2002). Effect of light treatment on sleep and circadian rhythms in demented nursing home patients. *Journal of the American Geriatrics Society*, *50*, 282–289.

Ballard, C. G., O'Brien, J. T., Reichelt, K., & Perry, E. K. (2002). Aromatherapy as a safe and effective treatment for the management of agitation in severe dementia: The results of a double-blind, placebo-controlled trial with Melissa. *Journal of Clinical Psychiatry*, *63*, 553–558.

Bandura, A. (1969). *Principles of behavior modification*. New York: Holt, Rinehart and Winston.

Burgio, L., Stevens, A., Guy, D., Roth, D. L., & Haley, W. E. (2003). Impact of two psychosocial interventions on white and African American family caregivers of individuals with dementia. *Gerontologist, 43*, 568–579.

Burgio, L. D., Allen-Burge, R., Roth, D. L., Bourgeois, M. S., Dijkstra, K., Gerstle, J., et al. (2001). Come talk with me: Improving communication between nursing assistants and nursing home residents during care routines. *Gerontologist, 41*, 449–460.

Burgio, L. D., Burgio, K. L., Engel, B. T., & Tice, L. M. (1986). Increasing distance and independence of ambulation in elderly nursing home residents. *Journal of Applied Behavior Analysis, 19*, 357–366.

Burgio, L. D., Stevens, A., Burgio, K. L., Roth, D. L., Paul, P., & Gerstle, J. (2002). Teaching and maintaining behavior management skills in the nursing home. *Gerontologist, 42*, 487–496.

Cohen-Mansfield, J., & Werner, P. (1998). The effects of an enhanced environment on nursing home residents who pace. *Gerontologist, 38*, 199–208.

Dick, L. P., Gallaghher-Thompson, D., Coon, D. W., Powers, D. V., & Thompson, L. W. (1995). *Cognitive-behavioral therapy for late life depression: A client manual.* Palo Alto, CA: Older Adult and Family Center, Veterans Affairs Palo Alto Health Care System.

Loew, C. A., & Silverstone, B. M. (1971). A program of intensified stimulation and response facilitation for the senile aged. *Gerontologist*, 341–347.

Lovell, B. B., Ancoli-Israel, S., & Gevirtz, R. (1995). Effect of bright light treatment on agitated behavior in institutionalized elderly subjects. *Psychiatry Research, 57*, 7–12.

McCallion, P., Toseland, R. W., & Lacey, D. (1999). Educating nursing assistants to communicate more effectively with nursing home residents with dementia. *Gerontologist, 39*, 546–558.

Mishima, K., Okawa, M., Hishikawa, Y., Hozumi, S., Hori, H., & Takahashi, K. (1994). Morning bright light therapy for sleep and behavior disorders in elderly patients with dementia. *Acta psychiatrica Scandinavica, 89*(1).

Rheaume, Y. L., Manning, B. C., & Harper, D. G. (1998). Effect of light therapy upon disturbed behaviors in Alzheimer patients. *American Journal of Alzheimer's Disease, 13*, 291–295.

Sanavio, E. (1981). Toilet retraining psychogeriatric residents. *Behavior Modification, 5*, 417–427.

Skinner, B. F. (1974). *About behaviorism.* New York: Alfred A. Knopf.

Teri, L., Borson, S., Kiyak, H. A., & Yamagishi, M. (1989). Behavioral disturbance, cognitive dysfunction, and functional skill. Prevalence and relationship in Alzheimer's disease. *Journal of the American Geriatrics Society, 37*, 109–116.

Thompson, L. W., Gallaghher-Thompson, D., & Dick, L. P. (1995). *Cognitive-behavioral therapy for late life depression: A therapist manual.* Palo Alto, CA: Older Adult and Family Center, Veterans Affairs Palo Alto Health Care System.

Van Someren, E. J., Kessler, A., & Mirmiran, M. (1997). Indirect bright light improves circadian rest–activity rhythm disturbances in demented patients. *Biological Psychiatry, 41*, 955–963.

BEREAVEMENT

According to the 2003 U.S. census report approximately one-third of the 35 million people older than 65 years in the United States are widowed (www.census.gov/prod/2003pubs/c2kbr-30.pdf). *Rates of widowhood* for women are about twice that for men, and rates for both sexes are highest in those aged 85 years and older (72% of women, and 35% of men.) Rates of bereavement are higher still. Most widowed people also have lost their parents, many have lost siblings or close friends, and some have lost their children. The death of a loved one is among the most intense stressors a person can experience. Bereavement brings the deep anguish of *grief*, often accompanied by a need to reorient one's life. Nevertheless, recent data suggest that most people cope well with this difficult stressor. The majority of people are resilient following loss (Bonanno, et al., 2002), and intervention is unnecessary and may even worsen outcomes (Jordan & Neimeyer, 2003; Schut, Stroebe, van den Bout, & Terheggen, 2001). On the other hand, it is equally clear that a subgroup of bereaved individuals does suffer *bereavement-related health problems*, and that these can be chronic, serious, and debilitating.

Estimates suggest about 20% of the bereaved population (Zisook & Shuchter, 1991) experiences a major depressive episode, and a smaller percentage has the onset or worsening of a Diagnostic and Statistical Manual-IV anxiety disorder, with panic disorder, posttraumatic stress disorder, and generalized anxiety disorder being the most common. Additionally, there is growing consensus that bereavement can lead to a grief-specific condition called "*complicated grief*" (Lichtenthal, Cruess, & Prigerson, 2004). Bereaved people also appear to be at increased risk for cardiovascular, immune function, and neoplastic diseases (Zisook, & Shuchter, 1993; Goodkin, et al., 2001). People who have lost loved ones have higher rates of suicidality (Szanto, Prigerson, Houck, Ehrenpreis, & Reynolds, 1997), substance use, and insomnia (Chen, et al., 1999). Given the severity of the *stress of bereavement*, it is not surprising that it is a trigger for mental and physical health problems. Unfortunately, physicians may neglect bereaved family members of elderly people who die (Prigerson & Jacobs, 2001).

Recent theories of grief suggest that coping with loss progresses optimally when there is alternating attention to both the stresses created by the loss and to the need for restoration of a satisfying life (Stroebe & Schut, 1999). *Loss stresses* include those related to the emotional meaning of the loss and to the need to reconfigure the attachment to the deceased, while *restoration stresses* focus on doing new things, attending to life changes and tasks, and taking on new roles or identities. These dual processes of *coping* are thought to proceed in an oscillating manner, and there is some empirical evidence to support this model (Bisconti, Bergeman, & Boker, 2004). Inadequate coping increases the risk for a DSM-IV disorder and/or complicated grief. Studies are beginning to elucidate risk factors for these outcomes; for example, positive emotions (Bonanno & Keltner, 1997) and trait humor (Ong, Bergeman, & Bisconti, 2004) have been found to predict better outcomes. Another study (Boerner, Schulz, & Horowitz, 2004) found *loss of a spouse*, compared to another significant loss, and more positive caregiving benefits predicted more grief intensity but not higher levels of bereavement-related depression, while caregiver health was related to depression but not grief.

The high levels of distress related to bereavement in older adults have led some to propose intervention as a routine (Gilbar & Ben-Zur, 2002). *Widow-widow groups* (Silverman, 1988) are popular although not well studied. When support group attendance has been compared to a wait list (Tudiver, Hilditch, Permaul, & McKendree, 1993) results have indicated no differences. Nevertheless it is possible that subgroups of people do benefit from intervention. In meta-analyses those with high grief intensity and complicated grief appear to benefit most (Jordan & Neimeyer, 2003). Individuals with *bereavement-related depression* (Zisook, Shuchter, Pedrelli, et al., 2001) and other DSM-IV Axis I conditions should receive standard treatments for these conditions. Additionally, *complicated grief* is associated with considerable impairment and chronicity, and should be treated when present. The *Inventory of Complicated Grief* (Prigerson, et al., 1995) can be used to identify individuals with this condition; scores greater than 25 on this instrument 6 months after the death of a loved one predict negative outcomes over the next several years. This syndrome's core symptoms (Horowitz, et al., 1997) include: (1) a sense of disbelief or difficulty accepting the death, (2) anger or bitterness about the death, (3) frequent pangs of painful emotions, often accompanied by intense yearning and longing for the person who died, and (4) preoccupation with thoughts, memories, and images of the deceased loved one. These thoughts often include distressing, intrusive thoughts related to the death. Many individuals with complicated grief studiously avoid people, places, objects, or activities that remind them of their painful loss.

It is important to distinguish between depression, posttraumatic stress disorder, and complicated grief, since the treatment of these conditions is different. A recent study comparing the outcome of antidepressant medication, interpersonal psychotherapy, and placebo with medical management in older individuals with bereavement-related depression found that antidepressant treatment was superior to placebo in reducing the symptoms of depression, but not those for complicated grief (Reynolds, et al., 1999). Interpersonal psychotherapy also failed to produce substantial improvement in complicated grief symptoms. A targeted psychotherapy produced much better results for complicated grief symptoms (Shear, et al., 2001), and a randomized controlled trial has shown this treatment to be superior to interpersonal psychotherapy. An interesting approach to treating bereaved individuals has been developed by studying family functioning in *palliative care*. The results of a study of this intervention have not yet been published, but therapist adherence appears to be good (Chan, O'Neill, McKenzie, Love, & Kissane, 2004).

Cultural and social factors clearly play a role in bereavement course and outcomes. There is evidence that those who have strong religious faith can find comfort in their religion, although some who experience a difficult death of a loved one may instead lose faith in religion. Clearly there are important cultural differences in *bereavement practices* as well. For example, a recent study shows marked differences in coping in China compared to the United States (Bonanno, Papa, Lalande, Zhang,

& Noll, 2005). On average, loss of a child has a significantly more prolonged course in the United States than in China, compared to loss of a spouse. Additionally, Chinese individuals use *avoidant-type coping* more than U.S. participants. There has been a great increase in empirical studies of bereavement over the past decade, and it is likely that we will see this work continue to increase. Good empirical studies promise to do much to help us develop a better understanding of bereavement in older persons, and are needed to develop more effective and rational interventions for those whose grief is problematic.

KATHERINE SHEAR

See also
End-of-Life Care
Widowhood

References

Bisconti, T. L., Bergeman, C. S., & Boker, S. M. (2004). Emotional well-being in recently bereaved widows: A dynamical systems approach. *Journal of Gerontology: Psychological Sciences 59b*, 158–167.

Boerner, K., Schulz, R., & Horowitz, A. (2004). Positive aspects of caregiving and adaptation to bereavement. *Psychology and Aging, 19*, 668–675.

Bonanno, G. A., & Keltner, D. (1997). Facial expressions of emotion and the course of conjugal bereavement. *Journal of Abnormal Psychology, 106*, 126–137.

Bonanno, G. A. et al. (2002). Resilience to loss and chronic grief: A prospective study from pre-loss to 18-months post-loss. *Journal of Personality and Social Psychology, 83*, 1150–1164.

Bonanno, G. A., Papa, A., Lalande, K., Zhang, N., & Noll, J. G. (2005). Grief processing and deliberate grief avoidance: A prospective comparison of bereaved spouses and parents in the United States and the People's Republic of China. *Journal of Consulting and Clinical Psychology, 73*, 86–98.

Chan, E. K. H., O'Neill, I., McKenzie, M., Love, A., & Kissane, D. W. (2004). What works for therapists conducting family meetings: Treatment integrity in family-focused grief therapy during palliative care and bereavement. *Journal of Pain and Symptom Management, 27*, 502–512.

Chen, J. H. et al. (1999). Gender differences in the effects of bereavement-related psychological distress in health outcomes. *Psychological Medicine, 29*, 367–380.

Gilbar, O., & Ben-Zur, H. (2002). Bereavement of spouse caregivers of cancer patients. *American Journal of Orthopsychiatry, 72*, 422–432.

Goodkin, K. et al. (2001). *Handbook of bereavement research.* In M. S. Stroebe, R. O. Hansson, W. Stroebe, & H. Schut (Eds.), (pp. 705–738). Washington, DC: American Psychological Association.

Horowitz, M. J. et al. (1997). Diagnostic criteria for complicated grief disorder. *American Journal of Psychiatry, 154*, 905–910.

Jordan, J. R., & Neimeyer, R. A. (2003). Does grief counseling work? *Death Studies, 27*, 765–786.

Lichtenthal, W. G., Cruess, D. G., & Prigerson, H. G. (2004). A case for establishing complicated grief as a distinct mental disorder in DSM-V. *Clinical Psychology Review, 24*, 637–662.

Ong, A. D., Bergeman, C. S., & Bisconti, T. L. (2004). The role of daily positive emotions during conjugal bereavement. *Journal of Gerontology: Psychological Sciences, 59b*, 168–176.

Prigerson, H. G. et al. (1995). Inventory of complicated grief: A scale to measure maladaptive symptoms of loss. *Psychiatry Research, 59*, 65–79.

Prigerson, H. G., & Jacobs, S. C. (2001). Caring for bereaved patients: "All the doctors just suddenly go." *Journal of the American Medical Association, 286*, 1369–1376.

Reynolds, C. F. et al. (1999). Treatment of bereavement-related major depressive episodes in later life: A randomized, double-blind, placebo-controlled study of acute and continuation treatment with nortriptyline and interpersonal psychotherapy. *American Journal of Psychiatry, 156*, 202–208.

Schut, H., Stroebe, M. S., van den Bout, J., & Terheggen, M. (2001). Handbook of bereavement research. In M. S. Stroebe, R. O. Hansson, W. Stroebe, & H. Schut (Eds.), (pp. 705–738). Washington, DC: American Psychological Association.

Shear, M. K. et al. (2001). Traumatic grief treatment: A pilot study. *American Journal of Psychiatry, 158*, 1506–1508.

Silverman, P. R. (1988). *Fourteen ounces of prevention: A casebook for practitioners.* In R. H. Price, & E. L. Cowen (Eds.), (pp. 175–186). Washington, DC: American Psychological Association.

Stroebe, M., & Schut, H. (1999). The dual process model of coping with bereavement: Rationale and description. *Death Studies, 23*, 197–224.

Szanto, K., Prigerson, H. G., Houck, P. R., Ehrenpreis, L., & Reynolds, C. F. (1997). Suicidal ideation in elderly bereaved: The role of complicated grief. *Suicide and Life-Threatening Behavior, 27*, 194–207.

Tudiver, F., Hilditch, J., Permaul, J. A., & McKendree, D. J. (1993). Does mutual help facilitate newly bereaved widowers? Report of a randomized controlled trial. *Evaluation and the Health Professions, 15*, 147–162.

Zisook, S., & Shuchter, S. R. (1991). Depression through the first year after the death of a spouse. *American Journal of Psychiatry, 148*, 1346–1352.

Zisook, S., & Shuchter, S. R. (1993). Uncomplicated bereavement. *Journal of Clinical Psychiatry, 54*, 365–372.

Zisook, S., Shuchter, S. R., Pedrelli, P., et al. (2001). Bupropion sustained release for the bereavement: Results of an open trial. *Journal of Clinical Psychiatry, 62*, 227–230.

BERLIN AGING STUDY

The Berlin Aging Study (BASE) investigates questions about the young old and oldest old from the joint, collaborative perspectives of 4 disciplines: psychiatry, psychology, sociology, and internal medicine (Baltes & Mayer, 2001; Baltes, Mayer, Helmchen, & Steinhagen-Thiessen, 1993; Mayer & Baltes, 1996). The study was initiated in 1989 by the Berlin Academy of Sciences and Technology and its study group on aging and societal development. From 1994 to 1998, BASE was conducted with the support of the Berlin-Brandenburg Academy of Sciences. In addition to continuous funding by the *Max Planck Society*, from 1989 to 1998 BASE obtained substantial financial support from the German federal government. The institutions involved in BASE include the Free University Berlin, the Humboldt University of Berlin, and the Max Planck Institute for Human Development.

This multidisciplinary study is one of a few projects worldwide that collect extensive, face-to-face standardized interviews, test performances, and clinical data for a heterogeneous sample of men and women aged between 70 and more than 100 years. The baseline, cross-sectional intensive protocol involved at least 14 individual 90-minute sessions scheduled over 3 to 5 months and resulted in a databank of approximately 10,000 variables per participant (at all levels of aggregation). Detailed descriptions of the study design, recruitment, sample selectivity, and assessment procedures are published in Baltes and Mayer (2001; see also Baltes & Smith, 1997; Lindenberger, Gilberg, Little, Nuthmann, Pötter, & Baltes, 2001; Lindenberger, Singer & Baltes, 2002; Mayer & Baltes, 1996; Smith & Delius, 2003; Smith, Maas, Mayer, Helmchen, Steinhagen-Thiessen, & Baltes, 2002). As of 2005, the study involves 6 measurement occasions. In addition, subsamples have been recruited for intensive study. Mortality information is obtained regularly from the city registry.

Central Research Questions, Methods, and Publications

BASE researchers focus on questions about the antecedents, correlates, and consequences of normative age-related and death-related change, as well as subgroup and individual differences in aging. These topics are addressed at discipline-specific and interdisciplinary levels. Two sides of old age are portrayed in BASE findings: the *Third Age*, associated with relative functional stability and maintenance of well–being, and the *Fourth Age*, during which individuals appear to be more at risk for impairment and functional decline (Baltes & Smith, 2003).

In addition to a single-session, multidisciplinary interview, the 4 disciplines in BASE each contribute data on specific topics and measurement batteries. The BASE sociology unit deals with issues of social inequality, family life, and access to resources, using comprehensive social survey interviews to provide information about life history, generational experiences, and current life conditions. The psychology unit investigates 3 areas of functioning: intelligence and cognition, self and personality, and personal social networks. This discipline uses a computerized cognitive battery together with standard tests of self and personality and a structured interview about social networks. Psychiatric morbidity (in particular depression and dementia), neuropsychological functioning, and everyday competence are the central focus of the psychiatry unit, which derives diagnoses from clinical interviews and tests conducted in the field. The internal medicine unit concentrates on aspects of physical, functional, and subjective health, disability, and treatment. Data collected in the field by BASE physicians includes a medical anamnesis, a noninvasive full-body examination, medication details, dental examination, and blood and saliva samples for biochemical analyses. Information is also obtained from the participants' family doctors.

The project Web site (www.base-berlin.mpg.de) lists more than 430 publications reporting BASE data. Central resources include an edited book published with Cambridge University Press (Baltes & Mayer, 2001), a German monograph (Mayer & Baltes, 1996) as well as featured sections in the journals *Psychology and Aging* (volume 12, 1997) and *Journals of Gerontology: Psychological Sciences* (volume 57B, 2002). Initially more than 60 researchers were associated with the project; a core group of 10 remain active in 2005. At the end of 2004, there were 21 masters and 16 doctoral theses on BASE data. From 1998 to 2004, BASE research findings and data provided the foundation for a doctoral program on the Psychiatry and Psychology of Aging at the Free University Berlin.

The Initial Cross-Sectional Sample (1990–1993)

The goal at baseline was to achieve extensive multidisciplinary data from an age-by-sex stratified heterogeneous (locally representative) sample of individuals aged 70 to more than 100 years (mean age 85 years). Research resources permitted the study of about 500 persons. The final sample, recruited between 1990 and 1993 for 14 multidisciplinary 90-minute sessions of assessment, consisted of 516 men and women (258 aged 70 to 84 years, and 258 aged 85 to 103 years). Because planning for the study began before the reunification of Germany, the sample was drawn only from the districts of West Berlin. For age-related comparisons, the sample was divided into 6 age cohorts (each with 86 persons): 70 to 74 years (born 1922–1915), 75 to 79 years (1917–1910), 80 to 84 years (1913–1905), 85 to 89 years (1908–1900), 90 to 94 years (1902–1896), and 95 to 103 years (1897–1883).

Given the intensity and range of the initial assessment protocol and the age groups investigated, a high drop-out rate was expected in recruitment for the complete baseline assessment package. Therefore, procedures that allowed examination of response rates and selectivity were included from the outset. BASE commenced with a verified parent sample of 1,908 addresses obtained from the obligatory Berlin city registry. Demographic information was available for this entire sample. The initial participation rate was 78% (1,491 individuals): 22% of the parent sample volunteered no additional data beyond the registry information. After face-to-face clinical observations, 227 people (12%) were excluded from further participation for ethical and health-related reasons (90% of this group were older than age 85). In addition to the 516 individuals (27% of the parent sample) who completed the entire 14-session protocol, 412 people (21%) participated at the level of a single 90-minute multidisciplinary assessment, and 336 (18%) participated at the level of a 30-minute interview. Information from each of these subgroups of the parent sample is used to examine selectivity (Lindenberger et al., 2001). The selectivity analyses indicate that the core BASE sample of 516 was positively selected in terms of mean-level functioning (effect sizes were small) and subsequent mortality.

Longitudinal BASE Samples (1990–2005)

The longitudinal follow-up of BASE participants has taken 2 main routes: repeated assessment without replacement, and mortality analyses. As of early 2005, survivors of the 516 (T1) core sample have been recontacted on 5 occasions. These follow-ups, at intervals of 2 to 4 years, have involved different amounts of face-to-face assessment. A repetition of the single-session 90-minute multidisciplinary assessment was collected in 1993 to 1994 (T2). At this time, 431 of the 516 T1 core sample were still alive and 84% (359) of the survivors participated. This single-session protocol was repeated in combination with a reduced version of the multidisciplinary intensive protocol (6 sessions of individual testing) in the periods 1995 to 1996 (T3) and 1997 to 1998 (T4). At T3, 313 of the original participants survived; 78% took part in the single session and 66% (206 individuals) also completed the 6-session intensive protocol (Lindenberger, et al., 2002; Smith, et al., 2002). At T4, 239 of the core sample were still alive; 69% participated in a single session and 55% (132) completed the entire intensive protocol. Two subsequent follow-ups—in 2000 (T5, with 88 from 159 surviving individuals) and 2004 (T6, with 48 from 89 surviving individuals)—have involved a repetition of the 90-minute multidisciplinary assessment (including additional measures of dementia and well being), followed by a repetition of the psychology battery (2 sessions) and a clinical dental assessment (1 session). At T5, 82 individuals completed all sessions (Lövdén, Ghisletta, &

Lindenberger, 2004; Smith & Delius, 2003) and at T6 the total was 46 (age range 82 to 101 years).

The second longitudinal strategy in BASE involves following the sample for mortality: 83% of the 516-member sample survived 2 years after baseline, but only 61% at the 4-year interval (T3). The majority of the 109 individuals diagnosed with suspected dementia at T1 in the 516 sample were deceased at T3. At T6, 17% of the initial sample had survived. Mortality information is used to examine selectivity effects (Lindenberger, et al., 2002) and also to model death-related change.

On the one hand, it is essential to have repeated measures over time in order to gain insight into the nature of change and individual difference in change. On the other hand, the longitudinal BASE design highlights the complex implications of participant dropout over time for the interpretation of findings about very old age. For the most part, attrition in BASE is due to selective mortality. Participants in the various BASE longitudinal samples (followed over 2, 4, 6, 8 and more than 13 years) are a positive selection of the initial T1 cross-sectional sample in terms of physical and functional health, social status, cognitive functioning, openness to new experiences, outgoingness, age, and distance from death. This suggests that BASE findings likely underestimate functional change in the general population of older adults.

JACQUI SMITH

See also
Longitudinal Data Sets
Longitudinal Research

References

Baltes, P. B., & Mayer, K. U. (Eds.). (2001). *The Berlin Aging Study: Aging from 70 to 100*. New York: Cambridge University Press.

Baltes, P. B., Mayer, K. U., Helmchen, H., & Steinhagen-Thiessen, E. (1993). The Berlin Aging Study (BASE): Overview and design. *Ageing and Society, 13*, 483–515.

Baltes, P. B., & Smith, J. (1997). A systemic-wholistic view of psychological functioning in very old age: Introduction to a collection of articles from the Berlin Aging Study. *Psychology and Aging, 12*, 395–409.

Baltes, P. B., & Smith, J. (2003). New frontiers in the future of aging: From successful aging of the young old to the dilemmas of the Fourth Age. *Gerontology: Behavioral Science Section/Review, 49*, 123–135.

Lindenberger, U., Gilberg, R., Little, T. D., Nuthmann, R., Pötter, U., & Baltes, P. B. (2001). Sample selectivity and generalizability of the results of the Berlin Aging Study. In P. B. Baltes & K. U. Mayer (Eds.), *The Berlin Aging Study: Aging from 70 to 100* (pp. 56–82). New York: Cambridge University Press.

Lindenberger, U., Singer, T., & Baltes, P. B. (2002). Longitudinal selectivity in aging populations: Separating mortality-associated versus experimental components in the Berlin Aging Study (BASE). *Journal of Gerontology: Psychological Sciences, 57B*, 474–482.

Lövdén, M., Ghisletta, P., & Lindenberger, U. (2004). Cognition in the Berlin Aging Study (BASE): The first 10 years. *Aging, Neuropsychology, and Cognition, 11*, 104–133.

Smith, J., & Delius, J. (2003). Die längsschnittlichen Erhebungen der Berliner Altersstudie (BASE): Design, Stichproben und Schwerpunkte 1990-2002 [The longitudinal assessments in the Berlin Aging Study (BASE): Design, samples, and topics 1990-2002]. In F. Karl (Ed.), *Sozial-und verhaltenswissenschaftliche Gerontologie: Alter und Altern als gesellschaftliches Problem und individuelles Thema* (pp. 225–249). Weinheim: Juventa.

Smith, J., Maas, I., Mayer, K. U., Helmchen, H., Steinhagen-Thiessen, E., & Baltes, P. B. (2002). Two-wave longitudinal findings from the Berlin Aging Study: Introduction to a collection of papers. *Journal of Gerontology: Psychological Sciences, 57B*, 471–473.

BIOGRAPHY

The term *biography*, as it is employed in the field of aging, has at least 3 related meanings (Birren, Kenyon, Ruth, Schroots, & Svensson, 1996; Kenyon, Clark, & de Vries, 2001). First, it refers to the use of narratives, *life histories*, autobiographies, and *life stories* as sources of data in research. Second, biography refers to several forms of intervention in aging, such as *life review*, *reminiscence*, and *guided autobiography*. Third, biography refers to the life story of a person, expressed in either written or verbal form and told to oneself or another. It is important to note that literary forms of biography are also effective sources of knowledge of aging in these 3 areas (Cole, Kastenbaum, & Ray, 1999).

In research, *biographical approaches* provide an excellent medium for investigating both the idiosyncratic and shared aspects of human aging over the life span. For example, personal recollections of developmental tasks, turning points, stresses, and individual coping strategies can be analyzed. These sources of information facilitate insight into how a life *has been* lived, how it *is* lived, and how it *can be* lived. By employing biographical approaches it is also possible to describe how cultures, subcultures, or family patterns are reflected in individual lives, and how particular people adapt to or expand the possibilities and limits set by the historical period in which they live.

A particular research strength of biographical materials is that they provide data on both individual and societal levels. They give glimpses of the historical periods of the society that the narrator has lived through—that is, shared experiences such as wars and difficult economic times, as well as significant leaps forward in the development of a culture as evidenced in such things as the welfare state. Life stories thus can also be viewed as individual interpretations of cultural conditions of earlier times.

There are important aspects of biography in the field of aging that require further theoretical discussion as well as empirical inquiry (Kenyon, Ruth, & Mader, 1999; Kenyon, Clark, & de Vries, 2001). For example, there is the question as to whom stories are told and why. A narrative may be produced out of special concerns, such as to provide an authorized career biography, act as a research subject, enhance change in therapy, or lend consolation in spiritual counseling. The *storyteller* will present himself or herself in a specific way and different parts of his or her life story will emerge as a function of the intended audience: the reasons for telling the story, as well as the medium, partly form the message. Such issues as these also give rise to methodological concerns that are actively debated both from technical and philosophy of science perspectives.

Studies exploring the reality within stories are also receiving increased attention in research (Gubrium & Holstein, 1997, 1998; Kenyon & Randall, 1997). Questions concerning the presumed reader of the text, the relation between *storyteller and society*, culturally rooted expressions in life stories, and the role of *memory in biography* are considered fruitful topics of investigation. Nevertheless, the most important issue remains that of concentrating on the *subjective meaning* that is communicated concerning central issues and decisive situations in life, within the context of the larger story we live in, which co-authors our biography (Kenyon & Randall, 1997).

Biographical forms of intervention are increasingly being considered crucial to the field of aging, both in the context of assessment and diagnosis, in such areas as competence and community care, and in the context of therapy modalities such as life review, reminiscence, and narrative therapy. The understanding of *dementia stories* is also a growing area of interest, with the goal of providing a better quality of life for both clients and caregivers (Gubrium, 1993; Kenyon, Clark, & de Vries, 2001).

In addition to the foregoing, there are biographical forms of intervention that serve to enhance personal meaning and quality of life from a learning, in contrast to a therapeutic, perspective. *Guided autobiography* would be an example of this approach. Important *ethical issues* arise in connection with the distinction between therapy and learning, as they do in the area of aging and biography as a whole (Josselson, 1996).

The discussion of *biography and aging* from the point of view of a personal life story is significant because meaning is expressed through metaphors, which are the raw materials out of which one constructs one's narratives, life story, and autobiography. In other words, "the story of my life" is made up of images and perceptions, characters and plots, that are significantly figurative and creative in nature, rather than imprints of factual events. Consequently, the relationship between personal meanings of aging and biography is fundamental in that not only do people express or communicate meaning through stories of various kinds, but storytelling also is basic to the organization of experience.

From the viewpoint of "*narrative gerontology*" (Kenyon, Clark, & de Vries, 2001), human beings are always constructing stories that reflect an intersection of genetic predispositions, past experience (intrapersonal and interpersonal, and sociocultural), and personal choice. Further, biographies contain cognitive, affective, and motivational components. Our thoughts, feelings, and actions are influenced by the stories we tell ourselves about ourselves and the world. *Storytelling* (and story listening) is an ontological phenomenon in that not only do we *have* a life story but we are stories. Finally, our biographies may constitute a key to the further understanding of *wisdom*, including the "*ordinary wisdom*" in each of our lives (Randall & Kenyon, 2000).

GARY M. KENYON

See also
Narrative Analysis

References

Birren, J., Kenyon, G., Ruth, J. E., Schroots, H., & Svensson, T. (Eds.) (1996). *Aging and biography: Explorations in adult development*. New York: Springer Publishing.

Cole, T. R., Kastenbaum, R., & Ray, R. E. (Eds.) (1999). *Handbook of the humanities and aging*. New York: Springer Publishing.

Gubrium, J., & Holstein, J. (1997). *The new language of qualitative method*. New York: Oxford University Press.

Gubrium, J., & Holstein, J. (1998). Narrative practice and the coherence of personal stories. *Sociological Quarterly, 39*, 163–187.

Gubrium, J. F. (1993). *Speaking of life: Horizons of meaning for nursing home residents*. New York: Aldine de Gruyter.

Josselson, R. (Ed.) (1996). *Ethics and process in the narrative study of lives*. Thousand Oaks, CA: Sage Publications.

Kenyon, G., Clark, P., & de Vries, B. (Eds.) (2001). *Narrative gerontology: Theory, research, and practice*. New York: Springer Publishing.

Kenyon, G., & Randall, W. (1997). *Restoring our lives: Personal growth through autobiographical reflection*. Westport, CT: Praeger.

Kenyon, G., Ruth, J. E., & Mader, W. (1999). Elements of a narrative gerontology. In V. Bengtson & W. Schaie (Eds.), *Handbook of theories of aging* (pp. 40–58). New York: Springer Publishing.

Randall, W., & Kenyon, G. (2000). *Ordinary wisdom: Biographical aging and the journey of life*. Westport, CT: Praeger.

BIOLOGICAL AGING MODELS

See
Biological Models for the Study of Aging: Flies
Biological Models for the Study of Aging: Nematodes
Biological Models for the Study of Aging: Rhesus Monkeys and Other Primates
Biological Models for the Study of Aging: Rodents
Biological Models for the Study of Aging: Transgenic Mice/Genetically Engineered Animals
Biological Models for the Study of Aging: Yeast and Other Fungi

BIOLOGICAL MODELS FOR THE STUDY OF AGING: FLIES

There was once a time when the view that model organisms would actually lead us to informative views regarding human aging was but a pious hope. That time has passed. Much of what we now know or suspect about human aging is based on studies originally done in model organisms. It turns out that the major gene systems regulating aging are highly conserved public mechanisms; the characterization of the genetic and metabolic pathways involved in longevity regulation and the environmental conditions necessary for their expression required the integration of data from the 4 most commonly used species: yeast, worm, fly, and mouse. This sort of molecular homology validates the usefulness of *comparative animal research on aging*.

In fact, the laboratory experiments done over the past few decades have allowed the robust identification of 4 different—but intertwined—genetic and physiological pathways which seem to *regulate longevity* in all 4 of our model systems. These 4 major *public longevity processes* may be listed as follows: (1) metabolic control, (2) stress resistance, (3) genetic stability, and (4) reproductive effects. Information regarding different patterns of senescence is still sketchy, but we will deal with it under the fifth heading of *patterns of senescence* (Arking, 2005) (Table 1). Each of these categories should be regarded not as an autonomous set of metabolic reactions, but rather as sets of regulatory reactions which are more closely linked to one another than to any of the other categories. Such a view obviously permits the existence of crosstalk between these several network hubs. Much of the variation inherent in aging may stem from such cross-reactions. Table 1 contains an outline summary of these major processes which play an important role in bringing about differential longevity and senescence. These processes may be induced or repressed by a variety of stimuli, including pharmaceutical interventions. The evidence for this is discussed elsewhere

TABLE 1 Summary of Major Longevity and Senescence Regulatory Pathways in *Drosophila*

Type of Intervention & Pathway Effect	Major Genes or Pathway	
Metabolic Control		
via Caloric Restriction (CR)	*indy, rpd3, Sir2*	CR slows rate of gene expression change relative to WT. Downregulates synthesis, turnover, and reproduction. No consistent upregulation pattern. CR effect is relatively rapid.
via Insulin-like Signaling Pathway (ISP)	*InR, chico, forkhead*	ISP affects hormones which indirectly affect longevity by altering stress resistance levels (see below). Forkhead is key transcription factor which increases stress resistances.
via Nuclear-cytoplasmic Interactions	—	Cybrids show longevity intermediate between nuclear and mitochondrial donors.
Stress Resistance	*CuZnSOD, MnSOD, catalase, Gpx, hsp, other.*	Up-regulation of different ADS genes by various techniques usually leads to increased oxidative/other stress resistance. Likely basis of extended longevity; QTL confirmation of ADS basis in one strain. Tissue-specific protective effects. May use both JNK as well as ISS to activate dFOXO3 downstream genes.
Genetic Stability	—	Genome appears to be highly stable in normal flies. Large interacting complex of DNA repair genes necessary for longevity. No evidence for regional or overall genomic dysregulation.
Reproductive Effects	ISP, Juvenile Hormone (JH), Ecdysone, *EcR, DTS-3*	ISP induces JH synthesis which induces egg production and ecdysone synthesis. At high levels, ecdysone represses resistance to various stressors, and reduces lifespan. At moderate levels, longevity and stress resistance significantly increase.
Patterns of Senescence	—	Various sensory and locomotor abilities do not age in unison. Long-lived mutants do not delay the senescence of all their functions but retain some and lose others as do normal-lived animals.

in more detail (Arking, 2005). Here we will briefly summarize the metabolic control processes and their role in longevity regulation. It is the failure of these processes which triggers the onset of senescence in later life. This discussion will illustrate the complexity and interactions of this important regulatory network. In addition to the mechanistic summary, the reader should take away the notion that even these simple laboratory organisms demonstrate the existence of multiple related longevity pathways.

The metabolic control of *longevity in Drosophila* is modulated by at least 3 major pathways: *caloric restriction* (CR), the insulin-like signaling pathway (ISP), and nuclear-cytoplasmic interactions (NCI). Although CR was definitively demonstrated in rodents in 1934, it was not until 1996 that the first repeatable report appeared showing that CR was effective in altering the fly's lifespan (Chapman & Partridge, 1996). Raising adults on food containing only 33% of the calories contained in the standard food resulted in significant (~33 day) increases in the median and maximum lifespans (Pletcher, Macdonald, Marguerie, Certa, Stearns, Goldstein, et al., 2002). Analysis of the age-specific mortality rates showed that the extended longevity comes about because of a delay in the onset of senescence. Microarray analysis of the gene expression patterns of flies on a normal (ad libitum, AL) or CR diet showed that only 8.4% of the 14,028 gene probes assayed (essentially the entire fly genome) showed highly significant age-related changes in either or both of the control and CR cohorts. The genome is normally very stable; most genes do not change their expression very much until the onset of senescence. Our interest is focused on those few genes that do change with age. The 754 gene probes that increase with age in both sets comprise mostly genes involved with innate immunity and detoxification, enzyme inhibitors, and all sorts of genes involved in the response to various stresses. As a general rule, these gene probes increase in both cohorts but do so slower in the CR set than in the control set. These data suggest that *senescent animals*-regardless of their diet or chronological age—are under increasing stress from pathogens. The proximate cause of *death in old flies* is probably infection (Kim, Nam, Kim, Ryu, Lee, Arking, et al., 2001; Tower, 2004). Other stressors are also involved. The nature of the 458 gene probes down-regulated with age is consistent with a loss of mitochondrial function. Other data show that *oxidative stress* increases as mitochondrial efficiency decreases; the aging animals are probably under increasing oxidative stress. The loss of energy production associated with decreased mitochondrial function is a major factor in the loss of function characteristic of aging. The fact that the gene probes in the control and CR cohorts were qualitatively similar to one another suggested that CR extends lifespan in the fly by preventing the large-scale breakdown in homeostasis and concomitant disregulation of gene expression that normally occurs in older animals. Most interesting is the CR-induced down-regulation of at least 1 gene (*methuselah [mth]*) known to significantly extend longevity when mutated. Its down-regulation under CR conditions suggests that the wild type *mth* might act as a negative regulator of extended longevity. If so, then the breakdown may not be entirely stochastic.

What gene pathways are involved in the CR response? Two different *histone deacetylases* (the *rpd3* and the *Sir2* genes) are involved in mediating the CR response, and the data suggests that the former gene is located upstream of the latter (Rogina, Helfand, & Frankel, 2002). Mutations in either gene interfere with the CR response; it is reasonable to conclude that both these genes are components of the genetic pathway mediating CR expression. Another gene possibly involved in CR is the *indy gene* which encodes a metabolite transporter protein responsible for the uptake and transport of Krebs and citric acid cycle intermediates through the gut epithelium and into the appropriate organs (Knauf, Rogina, Jiang, Aronson, & Helfand, 2002). Flies carrying a mutation in this gene display a 90% increase in their mean lifespan and a 50% increase in their maximum lifespan (Rogina et al., 2002). In flies, the *indy* gene is normally expressed primarily in the midgut, fat body (liver equivalent), and *oenocytes* which are the main sites of intermediary metabolism. It is not unreasonable to assume that the mutant-induced down-regulation in the activity of this metabolite cotransporter protein brings about a lower effective concentration of essential metabolites in the cell, thus creating a metabolic state similar to that induced by CR.

AL-raised flies normally have a higher age-specific mortality rate than do CR-raised animals. But after an AL->CR shift, the animals rapidly adopt the age-specific mortality rate characteristic of animals who have been raised on a CR regime for their entire life (Mair, Gomeyer, Pletcher, & Partridge, 2003). A corresponding rapid upward shift in mortality rate is observed following a CR->AL shift. What this means is that aging has no cellular memory. Changing the nutritional environment induces the animal to shift its gene expression pattern from a pro-growth pattern to a pro-stress resistance pattern. The consequent change in damage patterns affects the mortality rate within a few days. The age-specific mortality rate is due mostly to the current levels of damage occurring in the organism. The animal's prior history does not directly play a determining role in its current mortality rate, although certainly the existence of prior unrepaired damage must have some effect. As we shall see below, there is some evidence that the CR response depends on the *insulin-like signaling pathway* (ISP), either in whole or in part. If so, then aging is an environmentally dependent, cell-level function.

Metabolic Control of Longevity via the Insulin-like Signaling Pathway

The generic structure of the ISP was initially investigated for its effects on growth and size of the fly, but it was soon realized that the ISP also affects blood sugar levels. The fly possesses 5 insulin-like proteins with significant homology to the mouse and human insulin proteins. These proteins are expressed in several tissues but most particularly in small clusters of insulin-producing cells (IPCs) in the brain (Rulifson, Kim, & Nusse, 2002). These workers showed that ablation of these IPCs caused retarded growth and elevated carbohydrate levels, and that a normal phenotype could be restored by expressing one of the *Drosophila* insulin-like proteins. Thus there is a remarkable conservation of the insulin based *glucoregulatory mechanisms in flies* and mammals with respect to its effects on growth and blood sugar. Once the experimental data allowed the concept of a conserved longevity regulation mechanism to become clear from the nematode work, then the fly's ISP was investigated to see if it regulated longevity.

As you might expect, flies with no ISP activity at all are lethal. But in rare cases, one can construct homozygous flies which contain 2 different mutations, each with a defect in a different part of the gene. Such unusual animals have a low but detectable level of ISP activity (~25% or less) and can survive through adulthood. These *"heteroallelic" homozygotes* contain 2 different *mutations in their insulin receptor gene* (*InR,* homologous to the *C. elegans daf-2* gene) and gave rise to dwarf adults, with different longevity effects on the 2 sexes (Tatar, Kopelman, Epstein, Tu, Yin, & Garofalo, 2001). Females expressed a delayed onset of senescence, with an 87% increase in the mean lifespan and a ~45% increase in their maximum lifespan. Flies heterozygous for a InR mutation would be expected to have about a 50% decrease in their ISP activity. Preliminary data suggests that such animals are both fertile and normal sized, but show a ~25% increase in their mean lifespan and a 10% increase in the maximum lifespan (Hwangbo & Arking, unpublished data). The longevity effect appears to be without obvious side effects, presumably because a ~50% decrease in ISP activity may be sufficient to alter lifespan but not to affect size or fertility. These flies were shown to be more resistant to oxidative stress relative to their normal controls and to live long due to a delayed onset of senescence.

Both heterozygous and homozygous InR mutants have an impaired synthesis of *ecdysone* (Tu, Yeng, & Tatar, 2002). (Ecdysone is a steroid hormone which plays a key role in development and metamorphosis.) This suggests that the increased longevity associated with the heterozygous InR mutants are likely dependent on a decreased level of juvenile hormone synthesis and the consequent reduction of ecdysone synthesis to levels which do not repress the animal's level of stress resistance (see Table 1).

Flies which are either heterozygous or homozygous for a certain mutation in their IRS proteins (associated with the cytoplasmic side of the InR) also yield long-lived females but not males (Clancy, Gems, Harshman, Oldhan, Stocker, Hafen et al., 2001), and these flies were also observed to be more resistant to oxidative stress than their controls. The disabling of the *InR* and/or IRS genes is sufficient to down-regulate the entire ISP.

Finally, flies heterozygous for a mutation in the *dFOXO gene* (homologous to the *C. elegans daf16* gene) are incapable of expressing the extended longevity otherwise resulting from a mutational down-regulation of the InR gene (Hwangbo, Gersham, Tu, & Tatar, 2004). This functional test demonstrates that the *dFOXO gene* is the functional equivalent of the *daf-16* gene.

The simplest conclusion of these several experiments is that the modulation of longevity via the ISP is highly conserved and seems to involve similar (but perhaps not completely identical) mechanisms in our several model organisms. The fact that longevity regulation in the fly is intertwined in the same system with the regulation of growth, cell size, and fertility suggests that the fly ISP has multiple specific regulatory functions compared to a nematode. This increased signaling complexity, which might have arisen as a consequence of the increased size and complexity of the fly, might well account for its apparent greater genetic complexity. It is consistent with the fact that the fly has at least 4 independent isoloci of the PI3K gene, each of which is apparently involved in controlling different sorts of processes.

What Triggers the *Onset of Senescence*?

Senescence is the stochastic and nonprogrammed loss of function which becomes obvious as the reproductive period ends. This is a time-independent process, occurring at about 2 years in a mouse but at about 55 years in a human. What triggers its onset? In the fly, it has been shown that the repression of the ISP results in the activation of the dFOXO gene, and in the activation or repression of a whole suite of downstream genes under its singular or joint control (Hsu et al., 2003). These downstream genes include a variety of *stress resistance genes*, including a number of molecular chaperones (heat shock protein [hsp] genes). Mutational inactivation of these downstream *hsp genes* reverses the extended longevity brought about by ISP repression. This leads to the emerging view that the beneficial effects of the ISP are mediated via these downstream hsps, which protect the cells in various ways against the accumulation of unrepaired damage to the cell's proteome. Up-regulation of the ISP, possibly via the increased production of the insulin-like peptides (ILPs) or growth factors such as IGF-1 under the control of the fly's glucoregulatory system, represses the expression of these downstream hsps. This results in the down-regulation of damage control systems, the accumulation of unrepaired damage, and the gradual onset of senescence as various critical thresholds within the cell are exceeded. The individual nature of aging may be explained by individual and environmental variations in gene product levels, damage rates, repair levels, and so forth; all of which may be the outcome of various gene epistatic effects.

An *Integrated Theory of Aging*

We may view the lifespan as being composed of the "health span" and the "senescent span." The former is the time during which the ISP is down-regulated and somatic stress resistance levels are high. The latter begins with the up-regulation of the ISP, and is characterized by increasing stochastic degradation of the individual's gene expression network. The transition between the two is thus a phase of great interest and potential. This concept is developed in more detail in Arking (2005). Details about specific genes of Drosophila may be found on the Flybase Web site (http://flybase.bio.indiana.edu/) although not within the context of aging per se. Their relationship to aging, and much more, is spelled out on the *Science of Aging-Knowledge Environment* (SAGE) Web site (http://sageke.sciencemag.org/index.dtl).

Robert Arking

References

Arking, R. (2005). *Biology of aging: Observations and principles.* (3rd ed.). Oxford: Oxford University Press.

Chapman, T., & Partridge, L. (1996). Female fitness in Drosophila melanogaster: An interaction between the effect of nutrition and of encounter rate with males. *Proceedings of the Royal Society of London, Series B, 263*, 755–759.

Clancy, D. J., Gems, D., Harshman, L. G., Oldhan, S., Stocker, H., Hafen, E., Leevers, S. J., & Partridge, L. (2001). Extension of life-span by loss of CHICO, a Drosophila insulin receptor substrate protein. *Science, 292*, 104–107.

Hwangbo, D. S., Gersham, B., Tu, M. P., & Tatar, M. (2004). Drosophila dFOXO controls lifespan and regulates insulin signaling in brain and fat body. *Nature*. Available: [doi:10.1038/nature02549] www.nature.com/nature

Kim, Y. S., Nam, H. J., Kim, N. O., Ryu, J. H., Lee, W. J., Arking, R., & Yoo, M. A. (2001). Role of xanthine dehydrogenase and aging on the innate immune response of Drosophila. *Journal of the American Aging Association, 24*, 187–194.

Knauf, F., Rogina, B., Jiang, Z., Aronson, P. S., & Helfand, S. L. (2002). Functional characterization and immunolocalization of the transporter encoded by the life-extending gene Indy. *Proceedings of the National Academy of Sciences of the U.S.A., 99*, 14315–14319.

Landis, G. N., Abdueva, D., Skortsov, D., Yang, J., Rabin, B. E., Carrick, J., Tavare, S., & Tower, J. (2004). Similar gene expression patterns characterize aging and oxidative stress in Drosophila melanogaster. *Proceedings of the National Academy of Sciences of the U.S.A., 101*, 7663–7668.

Mair, W., Gomeyer, P., Pletcher, S. D., & Partridge, L. (2003). Demography of dietary restriction and death in Drosophila. *Science, 301*, 1731–1733.

Pletcher, S. D., Macdonald, S. J., Marguerie, R. Certa, U., Stearns, S. C., Goldstein, D. B., & Partridge, L. (2002). Genome-wide transcript profiles in aging and calorically restricted Drosophila melanogaster. *Current Biology, 12*, 712–723.

Rogina, B., Helfand, S. L., & Frankel, S. (2002). Longevity regulation by Drosophila rpd3 deacetylase and caloric restriction. *Science, 298*, 1745–1747.

Rulifson, E. J., Kim, S. K., & Nusse, R. (2002). Ablation of insulin-producing neurons in flies: Growth and diabetic phenotypes. *Science, 296*, 1118–1120.

Tatar, M., Kopelman, A., Epstein, D., Tu, M. P., Yin, C. M., & Garofalo, R. S. (2001). A mutant Drosophila insulin receptor homolog that extends life span and impairs neuroendocrine function. *Science, 292*, 107–110.

Tu, M. P., Yeng, C. M., & Tatar, M. (2002). Impaired ovarian ecdysone synthesis of Drosophila melanogaster insulin receptor mutants. *Aging Cell, 1*, 158–160.

BIOLOGICAL MODELS FOR THE STUDY OF AGING: NEMATODES

Several species of nematodes have been used in *aging research*, but the most widely studied species is the *soil nematode*, *Caenorhabditis elegans* (Gems, 1999; Johnson, 1997; Johnson, Sinclair, & Guarente, 1997; Martin, Austad, & Johnson, 1996; Barton & Partridge, 2000). This is a self-fertilizing hermaphroditic species, about 1 mm long (producing facultative males), containing only 959 somatic cells as an adult. Genetic analysis in *C. elegans* is highly developed, and this is the first metazoan species to have its entire genome sequenced (Plasterk, 1999).

C. elegans provides an excellent model for the study of certain aspects of aging, especially genetics, molecular biology, and more recently pathology and responses to pharmacological agents (Gems, 1999; Johnson, 1997; Lithgow & Kirkwood, 1996; Herndon et al., 2002; Ishii, Senoo-Matsuda, Miyake, Yasuda, Ishii, Hartman et al., 2004; Melov, Ravenscroft, Malik, Gill, Walker, Clayton, Wallace, et al., 2000a). It has a 10- to 20-day life expectancy, depending on growth conditions. The first genetically long-lived strains ever created in any organism were obtained by intercrossing wild-type strains of *C. elegans*; in these strains increased longevity resulted from the action of many genes, called *quantitative trait loci*, or QTLs (Johnson, 1997). QTLs specifying a variety of life-history traits have been mapped in this species, including QTLs specifying life expectancy and *maximum lifespan* (Johnson, 1997).

Gerontogenes (genes that affect the rate of aging) can be defined operationally as genes that can be altered so that a longer than normal maximum lifespan is the result. We refer to this phenotype as age. *C. elegans* is also the first species in which single-gene mutants having extended lifespan were identified. The first age mutant identified was *age-1*, which was identified in 1983, mapped in 1988, shown to affect the rate of aging in 1990, and finally molecularly identified in 1996 (Johnson, 1997). In the past 10 years, hundreds of *age genes* have been identified either by mutation or by RNA interference (RNAi) (Gems, 1999; McElwee, Bubb, & Thomas, 2003); Murphy, Carroll, Bargmann, Fraser, Kamath, Ahringer, et al., 2003); Lee, Kennedy, Tolonen, & Ruvkun, 2003).

Classes of Mutants

Until more is known about the mechanisms of lifespan extension, the classification of age genes is somewhat arbitrary; however it is useful to recognize the various ways in which some age genes appear to affect worm physiology and aging. Age phenotype can result from *hypomorphic* or *nullomorphic* mutations. We will describe classes of age genes in the order in which they were identified and will name each class based on the first gene cloned in that class.

Polygenic Class. The first report of long-lived strains in *C. elegans* involved the segregation of multiple genes in recombinant-inbred (RI) strains. The life prolongation of these strains results from the combined action of many of the QTL genes (Shook & Johnson, 1999). Genes affecting survival characteristics and life-history traits in *C. elegans* have been mapped. Both life expectancy and maximum lifespan map to the same 3 genetic regions, suggesting common genetic determination of life expectancy and maximum longevity. However, different QTLs are observed in different environments, and there are significant epistatic interactions.

age-1 Class. The first gerontogene mutant identified was *age-1*. The *age-1(hx546)* reference allele has a life expectancy 70% longer than the wild type and a maximum lifespan that is 105% longer; *age-1 mutations* have little effect on fertility, length of reproduction, or rate of development but are dauer-constitutive (Daf-c) at the semilethal temperature of 27°C. (The dauer is an alternative developmental path taken by *C. elegans* under conditions of crowding or starvation.) The *age-I (hx546)* causes resistance to H_2O_2, paraquat, heat, and UV; the mutant also has reduced frequencies of deletions in mitochondrial DNA. Three other alleles of *age-1*, isolated by longevity alone, are also stress resistant (Str). Other *age-I* alleles have been isolated by selecting for increased thermotolerance. All *age-1* alleles are also Daf-c at 27°C. Mutations in another gene, previously called *daf-23*, also lead to age, Daf-c, and Str phenotypes; *daf-23* mutants are Daf-c at 25°C and fail to complement mutations previously called *age-1* that are wild type at 25°C. The *daf-23* locus was cloned and shown to encode a gene homologous to mammalian phosphatidylinositol-3-OH kinase (PI3K), but no mutations in alleles formerly assigned to *age-1* were found in the structural sequence of the gene (Gems, 1999; Johnson, 1997).

Another mutant in the *age-I* class is *daf-2*, which is Daf-c at 25.5°C and results in a more than twofold extension of life expectancy in the adult phase. Also included are 2 mutants *(daf-16, daf-I8)* that suppress the Daf-c phenotype and also suppress increased longevity. All of these genes are proposed to participate in the same molecular signaling pathway. The *daf-2* has structural homology with the human insulin and IGF-1 receptors. It has been proposed to encode an insulin-like receptor that interacts with the AGE-1 protein to convey an intracellular signal leading to altered transcription mediated by DAF-16. All of the effects (dauer formation, life extension, and stress resistance) of *age-1* and *daf-2* are suppressed by mutant alleles of *daf-16*, the last gene in the path, encoding a forkhead-type transcription factor (Gems, 1999; Johnson, Sinclair, & Guarente, 1999). The *daf 16* is also necessary for *dauer formation*. Many other genes in this pathway have been identified. Prompted by the longevity effects of this pathway in *C. elegans*, studies in *Drosophila*, mouse, and human populations suggest the pathway affects aging across very distinct groups of metazoans (Tatar et al., 2001; Clancy et al., 2001; Holzenberger, 2003; Bluher et al., 2003; van et al., 2005).

Despite the similarity of fertility rates and development times between many of the long-lived mutants and wild type worms, there is a considerable fitness cost to extended lifespan. In competition with wild types, the *age-1 (hx546)* allele is rapidly lost from the population under conditions of cyclical starvation (Walker, McColl, Jenkins, Harris, & Lithgow, 2000) and daf-2 mutants reach extinction under normal laboratory culturing conditions (Jenkins, McColl, & Lithgow, 2004). This is consistent with an antagonistic pleiotropic model for the evolution of aging.

spe-26 Class. Two of the 6 mutant alleles of *spe-26*, a gene specifying proper segregation of cellular components affecting sperm activation, result in life extensions of about 80% for the hermaphrodite and the mated male, although the details are contentious (Gems, 1999). The only other known long-lived fertility-deficient strain is *spe-10* (Gems, 1999).

clk-I Class. Some *clk-1* mutants, which have altered cell cycle and developmental timing, also have increased life expectancy (Gems, 1999). The *elk-1* gene encodes a 187 amino acid protein showing some homology with yeast *CoQ7/Cat5*, a gene required for coenzyme Q synthesis in yeast. The *elk-1* mutant alleles have reduced metabolic rates that may be responsible for the extended longevity (Gems, 1999). Other genes in the Clk class include *clk-2*, *clk-3*, and *gm-1*, all of which have modest (typically 20% to 30%) extensions of lifespan, but only for some alleles.

eat-6 Class. Seven mutants (*eat-1, -2, -3, -6, -13, -18*, and *unc-26*) that slow the consumption of food also result in life extension, presumably through a self-imposed dietary restriction.

old-1 Class. The final class of *gerontogene* that increases lifespan when overexpressed is typified by *old-1* (*overexpression longevity determinant*, formerly called *tkr-1*; Gems, 1999). The *old-1* encodes a predicted receptor, tyrosine kinase, and overexpression in transgenics increases longevity 40% to 100% (average, 65%), confers increased resistance to heat and ultraviolet light, and does not alter development or fertility. Unlike previously identified gerontogenes, which act negatively to modulate longevity, *old-1* positively modulates longevity, as well as stress resistance. These results are consistent with previous observations of apleiotropic relationship between increased stress resistance and increased longevity seen in all previously studied longevity mutants (Johnson, Sinclair, & Guarente, 1999; Martin, Austad, & Johnson, 1996). This transgenic system is an effective means for identifying overexpression gerontogenes.

There are several additional *gerontogene mutants* that complement all known age genes that have been identified.

Resistance to Environmental Stresses as a Concomitant of Increased Longevity

All of the gerontogene mutants in *C. elegans* that have been tested are more resistant to environmental stresses (Str) such as reactive oxygen species (ROS), high temperature, and UV radiation (Lithgow & Kirkwood, 1996; Martin, Austad, & Johnson, 1996; Lithgow & Walker, 2002). However, not all mutations conveying Str are long-lived, showing that Str may be necessary but not sufficient for increased longevity. The increased UV resistance (Uvr) of *age-1, daf-2, spe26, elk-1, spe-10,* and *old-1* is suppressed by *daf-16*, as are other Str traits tested. The increased resistance to a variety of environmental stressors and the putative roles of *age-1/daf-23*, *daf-2* and *daf-16* in a signal-transduction pathway are consistent with a model in which lifespan is determined as a result of increased resistance or repair capability after environmental damage. The insulin signaling pathway interacts with the transcriptional regulator *heat shock factor* (HSF) and regulates a range of stress genes including those encoding heat shock proteins (Walker, Thompson, Brawley, Scanlon, & Devaney, 2003; Morley, Brignull, Weyers, & Morimoto, 2002; Murphy, Carroll, Bargmann, Fraser, Kamath, Ahringer, et al., 2003; Garigan, Hsu, Fraser, Kamath, Ahringer, & Kenyon, 2002; Hsu, Murphy, & Kenyon, 2003). Overexpression of individual HSPs or HSF results in extended lifespan, pointing to a central role of stress response in aging (Yokoyama, Fukumoto, Murakami, Harada, Hosono, Wadhwa, et al., 2002;) Walker & Lithgow, 2003). All age alleles of *spe-26* and *clk-1* (but not the non-age alleles) have increased thermotolerance (Itt) and Uvr, consistent with Strs playing a causal role in the life extension of these mutants as well. It is important to note that these results suggest that the capacity to prevent or repair macromolecular damage has not been maximized by evolution (Lithgow & Kirkwood, 1996). Additional capabilities are latent within the animal and can be stimulated, leading to increased longevity.

At the molecular level, increased resistance to ROS has been associated with higher levels of *superoxide dismutatse* and *catalase*, both of which detoxify ROS. The molecular etiology of the increased Str to other stressors remains to be determined. Several life-shortening mutants (mev-1) and the life-shortening dauer suppressor (daf-16) have been shown to have higher levels of reactive oxidants than the wild type.

Pharmacological Interventions That Extend Lifespan

C. elegans longevity can be significantly increased by treatment with *synthetic catalytic mimetics* (SCMs) that exhibit superoxide dismutase and catalase activities (Melov Ravenscroft, Malik, Gill, Walker, Clayton, Wallace, et al., 2000b) under certain conditions (Keaney & Gems, 2003) In addition, SCMs protect against *oxidative stress* (Sampayo, Gill, & Lithgow, 2003a; Sampayo, Olsen, & Lithgow, 2003b). Other classes of compounds effect lifespan including the electron carrier *ubiquinol* and anticonvulsants (Evason, Huang, Yamben, Covey, & Kornfeld, 2005). It seems likely that new automated system of survival analysis will make screening compounds a reality for this organism (Gill, Olsen, Sampayo, & Lithgow, 2003).

Functional Changes over the Lifespan

Changes that occur during senescence include decreasing mobility, alterations in enzyme activity, changes in morphology, the accumulation of *lipofuscin*, alterations in morphology, and changes in muscle structure (Johnson, 1997). There are changes in the abundance of mRNA transcripts of functionally related groups over the lifespan, although there is probably considerable variation between individual worms. The *age-1* mutation does affect the rate of decline of mobility in aging nematodes; but, at almost all ages, *age-1* mutants are more active than wild type (Johnson, 1997). The *age-1* mutants have a reduction in the frequency of mitochondrial mutations (Johnson, 1997), a physiological indicator of aging that has been seen in many species. Many of these findings suggest that *age-1* and maybe other age mutants actually slow the rate of aging and make these long-lived animals healthier and physiologically younger than wild type, even at very advanced ages.

THOMAS E. JOHNSON

References

Barton, N., & Partridge, L. (2000). Limits to natural selection. *Bioessays*, *22*, 1075–1084.

Bluher, M., Kahn, B. B., & Kahn, C. R. (2003). Extended longevity in mice lacking the insulin receptor in adipose tissue. *Science*, *299*, 572–574.

Clancy, D. J., Gems, D., Harshman, L. G., Oldham, S., Stocker, H., Hafen, E., Leevers, S. J., & Partridge, L. (2001). Extension of life-span by loss of CHICO, a Drosophila insulin receptor substrate protein. *Science*, *292*, 104–106.

Evason, K., Huang, C., Yamben, I., Covey, D. F., & Kornfeld, K. (2005). Anticonvulsant medications extend worm life-span. *Science*, *307*, 258–262.

Garigan, D., Hsu, A. L., Fraser, A. G., Kamath, R. S., Ahringer, J., & Kenyon, C. (2002). Genetic analysis of tissue aging in Caenorhabditis elegans: A role for heat-shock factor and bacterial proliferation. *Genetics*, *161*, 1101–1112.

Gems, D. (1999). Nematode ageing: Putting metabolic theories to the test. *Current Biology*, *9*, R614–R616.

Gill, M. S., Olsen, A., Sampayo, J. N., & Lithgow, G. J. (2003). An automated high-throughput assay for survival of the nematode Caenorhabditis elegans. *Free Radical Biology and Medicine*, *35*, 558–565.

Herndon, L. A., Schmeissner, P. J., Dudaronek, J. M., Brown, P. A., Listner, K. M., Sakano, Y., Paupard, M. C., Hall, D. H., & Driscoll, M. (2002). Stochastic and genetic factors influence tissue-specific decline in ageing C. elegans. *Nature*, *419*, 808–814.

Hsu, A. L., Murphy, C. T., & Kenyon, C. (2003). Regulation of aging and age-related disease by DAF-16 and heat-shock factor. *Science*, *300*, 1142–1145.

Ishii, N., Senoo-Matsuda, N., Miyake, K., Yasuda, K., Ishii, T., Hartman, P. S., & Furukawa, S. (2004). Coenzyme Q10 can prolong C. elegans lifespan by lowering oxidative stress. *Mechanisms of Ageing and Development*, *125*, 41–46.

Jenkins, N. L., McColl, G., & Lithgow, G. J. (2004). Fitness cost of extended lifespan in Caenorhabditis elegans. *Proceedings of the Royal Society of London Series B Biological Sciences*, *271*, 2523–2526.

Johnson, T. E. (1997). Genetic influences on aging. *Experimental Gerontology*, *32*, 11–22.

Johnson, F. B., Sinclair, D. A., & Guarente, L. (1999). Molecular biology of aging. *Cell*, *96*, 291–302.

Keaney, M., & Gems, D. (2003). No increase in lifespan in Caenorhabditis elegans upon treatment with the superoxide dismutase mimetic EUK-8. *Free Radical Biology and Medicine*, *34*, 277–282.

Lee, S. S., Kennedy, S., Tolonen, A. C., & Ruvkun, G. (2003). DAF-16 target genes that control C. elegans life-span and metabolism. *Science*, *300*, 644–647.

Lithgow, G. J., & Kirkwood, R. B. L. (1996). Mechanisms and evolution of aging. *Science*, *273*, 80.

Lithgow, G. J., & Walker, G. A. (2002). Stress resistance as a determinate of C. elegans lifespan. *Mechanisms of Ageing and Development*, *123*, 765–771.

Martin, G. M., Austad, S. N., & Johnson, T. E. (1996). Genetic analysis of ageing: Role of oxydative damage and environmental stresses. *Nature Genetics*, *13*, 25–34.

McElwee, J., Bubb, K., & Thomas, J. H. (2003). Transcriptional outputs of the Caenorhabditis elegans forkhead protein DAF-16. *Aging Cell*, *2*, 111–121.

Melov, S., Ravenscroft, J., Malik, S., Gill, M. S., Walker, D. W., Clayton, P. E., Wallace, D. C., Malfroy, B., Doctrow, S. R., & Lithgow, G. J. (2000a). Extension of life-span with superoxide dismutase/catalase mimetics. *Science*, *289*, 1567–1569.

Melov, S., Ravenscroft, J., Malik, S., Gill, M. S., Walker, D. W., Clayton, P. E., Wallace, D. C., Malfroy, B., Doctrow, S. R., & Lithgow, G. J. (2000b). Extension of life-span with superoxide dismutase/catalase mimetics. *Science*, *289*, 1567–1569.

Morley, J. F., Brignull, H. R., Weyers, J. J., & Morimoto, R. I. (2002). The threshold for polyglutamine-expansion protein aggregation and cellular toxicity is dynamic and influenced by aging in Caenorhabditis elegans. *Proceedings of the National Academy of Sciences of the U.S.A.*, *99*, 10417–10422.

Murphy, C. T., McCarroll, S. A., Bargmann, C. I., Fraser, A., Kamath, R. S., Ahringer, J., Li, H., & Kenyon, C. (2003). Genes that act downstream of DAF-16 to influence the lifespan of Caenorhabditis elegans. *Nature*, *424*, 277–283.

Sampayo, J. N., Gill, M. S., & Lithgow, G. J. (2003a). Oxidative stress and aging—the use of superoxide dismutase/catalase mimetics to extend lifespan. *Biochemical Society Transactions*, *31*, 1305–1307.

Sampayo, J. N., Olsen, A., & Lithgow, G. J. (2003b). Oxidative stress in Caenorhabditis elegans: Protective effects of superoxide dismutase/catalase mimetics. *Aging Cell*, *2*, 319–326.

Tatar, M., Kopelman, A., Epstein, D., Tu, M. P., Yin, C. M., & Garofalo, R. S. (2001). A mutant Drosophila insulin receptor homolog that extends life-span and impairs neuroendocrine function. *Science*, *292*, 107–110.

van Heemst, D., Beekman, M., Mooijaart, S. P., Heijmans, B. T., Brandt, B. W., Zwaan, B. J., Slagboom, P. E., & Westendorp, R. G. (2005). Reduced insulin/IGF-1 signaling and human longevity. *Aging Cell*, *4*, 79–85.

Walker, D. W., McColl, G., Jenkins, N. L., Harris, J., & Lithgow, G. J. (2000). Evolution of lifespan in C. elegans. *Nature*, *405*, 296–297.

Walker, G. A., & Lithgow, G. J. (2003). Lifespan extension in C. elegans by a molecular chaperone dependent upon insulin-like signals. *Aging Cell*, *2*, 131–139.

Walker, G. A., Thompson, F. J., Brawley, A., Scanlon, T., & Devaney, E. (2003). Heat shock factor functions at the convergence of the stress response and developmental pathways in Caenorhabditis elegans. *FASEB Journal*, *17*, 1960–1962.

Walker, G. A., White, T. M., McColl, G., Jenkins, N. L., Babich, S., Candido, E. P., Johnson, T. E., & Lithgow, G. J. (2001). Heat shock protein accumulation is upregulated in a long-lived mutant of Caenorhabditis elegans. *Journals of Gerontology, Series A, Biological Sciences and Medical Sciences*, *56*, B281–B287.

Yokoyama, K., Fukumoto, K., Murakami, T., Harada, S., Hosono, R., Wadhwa, R., Mitsui, Y., & Ohkuma, S. (2002). Extended longevity of Caenorhabditis elegans by knocking in extra copies of hsp70F, a homolog of mot-2 (mortalin)/mthsp70/Grp75. *FEBS Letters*, *516*, 53–57.

BIOLOGICAL MODELS FOR THE STUDY OF AGING: RHESUS MONKEYS AND OTHER PRIMATES

The study of *aging in nonhuman primates* has progressed rapidly since the early 1990s (DeRoussseau, 1994; Colman & Kemnitz, 1999). Early work focused on age-related pathologies and was generally cross-sectional in nature (Bowden & Jones, 1979). This work was often hampered by the use of feral animals for which precise ages were not known. It is difficult to estimate the age of mature monkeys by their morphological and physiological characteristics, especially in their natural environment. Establishment of the *National Primate Research Center Program* (formerly Regional) and other *breeding programs for biomedical research* during the past 5 decades has enabled maintenance of relatively large numbers of nonhuman primates, particularly macaques, under stable conditions for longitudinal study. These animals typically have precisely known birth dates and complete clinical histories, which make them valuable for studies of aging. The rhesus monkey (Macaca mulatta) is the most studied nonhuman primates species in the area of *biogerontology* and in biomedical investigation in general and continues to be the predominant species maintained at the *National Primate Research Centers* (NPRC). In 2000 there were approximately 13,584 rhesus monkeys held at the 8 NPRCs. Of these, 482 were older than 20 years (Robinson & Beattie, 2003).

The rhesus monkey is a member of the phylogenetic superfamily Cercopithecoidea, or Old World (Asian and African) monkeys, which is the most closely related superfamily to Hominoidea, our own. They are indigenous to the Indian subcontinent, but their range extends into southern China and Southeast Asia. Rhesus monkeys are quite adaptable to different environments, a characteristic that makes them very suitable for laboratory study. Although they are largely herbivorous, they will eat a wide variety of foods and have been characterized as opportunistic omnivores.

The *life history of rhesus monkeys* makes them good models for studies of aging. They experience puberty at age 2.5 to 5 years and achieve peak bone mass by approximately age 11 years (Champ, Binkley, Havighurst, Colman, Kemnitz, & Roecker, 1996). Adult males typically weigh 8 to 12 kg, and adult females about 6 to 8 kg. Female rhesus monkeys have reproductive cycles that are similar in terms of endocrinology and physiology to those of women, and they go through menopause in their mid-20s, preceded by a phase of irregular menstrual cycles (Kemnitz, Holston, & Colman, 1998). Decline in reproductive performance of male rhesus monkeys is also evident by late in the second decade of life, with behavioral manifestations appearing to be independent of slowly declining androgen levels

(Phoenix & Chambers, 1982). Maximum lifespan in the laboratory is approximately 40 years.

The selective advantage, in evolutionary terms, of the potential for a long post-reproductive phase of life can be questioned. *Studies of rhesus monkey* society, however, show that males' status in the social hierarchy increases beyond the time of maximal reproductive performance, and that females continue to act protectively and supportively of their offspring well into the later phases of their lives. Their contribution to the success of their genes, therefore, is through intergenerational alliances with offspring, as well as total reproductive output (DeRousseau, 1994; Johnson & Kapsalis, 1995).

Monkeys maintained under laboratory conditions develop several pathologies and infirmities in later life that are similar to those of elderly people (Uno, 1997). These include certain malignant and nonmalignant tumors, senile plaques and small infarctions in the brain, lenticular cataracts, presbyopia, diabetes mellitus, arthritis, degenerative joint disease, muscle atrophy, drier skin, telangiectasias ("age spots"), and gingivitis. The incidence of all these conditions increases dramatically after age 15 (e.g., all monkeys older than age 30 years have cataracts). This growing descriptive data on older monkeys confirms their similarities to humans and hence their usefulness for studies of age-related disorders.

Free-ranging but provisioned colonies of rhesus monkeys have also been established and provide a valuable contrast to those maintained under typical laboratory conditions. One such semi-naturalistic colony is located on *Cayo Santiago*, Puerto Rico, a facility of the *Caribbean Primate Research Center* (Rawlins & Kessler, 1986). These monkeys have been directly compared to indoor-housed animals at the *Wisconsin National Primate Research Center*, revealing many similar age-related changes for monkeys at both sites. Few monkeys survive beyond their mid-20s, however, in the more naturalistic colony.

Studies of aging in the rhesus are entering a new era: the prospective evaluation of interventions designed to influence the basic processes of aging. One such intervention that has been shown to dramatically affect the course of aging in several nonprimate species is dietary restriction, also known as *caloric restriction*. Reducing caloric intake in rodents while maintaining adequate intake of essential nutrients decreases the incidence, delays the onset, and lessens the severity of many age-related diseases (Weindruch & Walford, 1988). Dietary restriction also extends maximal lifespan, suggesting that it slows the rate of aging. The possibility that *dietary restriction* exerts similar effects in primates is currently being assessed in rhesus monkeys (Ingram, et al., 1990; Kemnitz, et al., 1993; Lane, Tilmont, DeAngelis, Handy, Ingram, Kemnitz, et al., 1999). A Wisconsin study initiated in 1989 and a study by the National Institutes on Aging (NIA) begun in 1987 both examine the impact of dietary restriction in male and female rhesus monkeys (Ramsey, Colman, Binkley, Christensen, Gresl, Kemnitz, et al., 2000; Mattison, Lane, Roth, & Ingram, 2003). Results after several years suggest that dietary restriction may have a similar beneficial effect as that observed in rodents—in particular, improved glucose tolerance, protection from non-insulin-dependent diabetes mellitus, and the possible prevention of cardiovascular disease (Bodkin, Ortmeyer, & Hansen, 1995; Kemnitz, Roecker, Weindruch, Elson, Baum, & Bergman, 1994; Colman, Ramsey, Roecker, et al., 1999; Lane, 2000; Mattison, Lane, Roth, & Ingram, 2003). Because of the longitudinal nature of these studies, it will be several years before the effects of dietary restriction on maximum lifespan can be determined.

Because of their phylogenetic proximity to humans, rhesus monkeys have proven to be excellent models for the study of age-related disorders. As noted earlier, they are also the most widely used *nonhuman primate model* in biomedical research. Currently, demand for rhesus monkeys exceeds the supply (Demands for Rhesus Monkeys in Biomedical Research, 2003). As a result, alternative nonhuman primate models of aging are being explored, and a variety of other species have been used in age-related research. These include *cynomolgus* and *pig-tailed macaques*, chimpanzees and other great apes, squirrel monkeys, lemurs, and marmosets (Lane, 2000; Gilissen, Dhenain, & Alllman, 2001; Erwin, Nimchinsky, et al., 2001; Herndon & Tigges, 2001; Mahaney, 2002; Voytko, 2001; Williams, 2001). Although New World (Central and South America) monkeys, the cebids (e.g., squirrel monkeys) and callitrichids (e.g., marmosets), have been less well studied in the context of aging, and there is increased interest in using these species as a model for age-related disorders (National Research Council, 1981; Abbott, Colman, Saltzman, et al., 2001; Brady,

Watford, Massey, et al., 2003). New World monkeys are not as closely related to humans as are Old World species, and they differ markedly in several respects. Callitrichids, in particular, are much smaller, their levels of steroid hormones are much higher, and they are largely insectivorous. Lifespans of New World species are thought to be in the range of 15 to 25 years, and their relatively short lifespan enhances the feasibility of studying individuals throughout their lives.

The next several years hold promise for significant advances in the description of normative aging in nonhuman primates and in our understanding of fundamental processes of aging. This will be accomplished by the continued careful interdisciplinary, longitudinal study of well-defined populations of animals. New knowledge is likely to come in areas of reproductive senescence and its consequences (e.g., osteoporosis); metabolic changes and their impact on diseases of the elderly (e.g., insulin resistance); and in the effects of modulating caloric intake on processes of aging, including differential gene expression (Lee, Klopp, Weindruch, & Prolla, 1999; Black, Tilmont, Handy, et al., 2001).

JOSEPH W. KEMNITZ
CYNTHIA K. ROBINSON

References

Bodkin, N. L., Ortmeyer, H. K., & Hansen, B. C. (1995). Long-term dietary restriction in older-aged rhesus monkeys: Effects on insulin resistance. *Journals of Gerontology Series A, Biological Sciences and Medical Sciences, 50(3)*, B142–B147.

Bowden, D. M., & Jones, M. L. (1979). Aging research in nonhuman primates. In D. M. Bowden (Ed.), *Aging in nonhuman primates* (pp. 1–13). New York: Van Nostrand Reinhold.

Champ, J. E., Binkley, N., Havighurst, T., Colman, R. J., Kemnitz, J. W., & Roecker, E. B. (1996). The effect of advancing age on bone mineral content of the female rhesus monkey. *Bone, 19*, 485–492.

Colman, R., & Kemnitz, J. W. (1999). Aging experiments using nonhuman primates. In B. P. Yu (Ed.), *Methods in aging research* (pp. 249–267). Boca Raton, FL: CRC Press.

DeRousseau, C. J. (1994). Primate gerontology: An emerging discipline. In D. E. Crews & R. M. Garruto (Eds.), *Biological anthropology and aging* (pp. 127–153). New York: Oxford University Press.

Johnson, R. L., & Kapsalis, E. (1995). Ageing, infecundity and reproductive senescence in free-ranging female rhesus monkeys. *Journal of Reproduction and Fertility, 105*(2), 271–278.

Kemnitz, J. W., Holston, K. A., & Colman, R. J. (1998). Nutrition, aging and reproduction in rhesus monkeys. In W. Hansel, G. A. Bray, & D. H. Ryan (Eds.), *Pennington Center Nutrition Series: 4. Evolution of research methods in nutrition and reproduction* (pp. 180–195). Baton Rouge: Louisiana State University Press.

Kemnitz, J. W., Roecker, E. B., Weindruch, R., Elson, D. F. Baum, S. T., & Bergman, R. N. (1994). Dietary restriction increases insulin sensitivity and lowers blood glucose in rhesus monkeys. *American Journal of Physiology: Endocrinology and Metabolism, 29*, E540–E547.

Lee, C.-K., Klopp, R. G., Weindruch, R., & Prolla, T. A. (1999). Gene expression profile of aging and its retardation by caloric restriction. *Science, 285*, 1390–1393.

National Research Council, Committee on Animal Models for Research on Aging. (1981). In Institute of Laboratory Animal Resources, Division of Biological Sciences, Assembly of Life Sciences (Ed.), *Mammalian models for research on aging* (pp. 243–278). Washington, DC: National Academy Press.

Phoenix, C. H., & Chambers, K. C. (1982). Sexual behavior in aging male rhesus monkeys. In A. B. Chiarelli & R. S. Corruccini (Eds.), *Advanced views in primate biology* (pp. 95–104). Berlin: Springer-Verlag.

Rawlins, R. G., & Kessler, M. J. (Eds.). (1986). *The Cayo Santiago macaques*. Albany: State University of New York Press.

Uno, H. (1997). Age-related pathology and biosenescent markers in captive rhesus macaques. *Age, 20*, 1–13.

Weindruch, R., & Walford, R. L. (1988). *The retardation of aging and disease by dietary restriction*. Springfield, IL: Charles C Thomas.

BIOLOGICAL MODELS FOR THE STUDY OF AGING: RODENTS

A National Research Council Committee on Animal Models for Research on Aging (1981) summarized relevant gerontological research on mammals under the categories of rodents and lagomorphs, carnivores, and non-human primates, but the preponderant taxon was Rodentia and within that group, mice and rats were clearly the favored research species. The desirability of a broad phyletic representation in model systems of aging has been cogently argued (Austad, 1993). However, the advantages of relatively short lifespans, convenience, economy, available knowledge concerning husbandry, and the enormous accumulated database on aging processes make it likely that rats and mice will continue to be an important source of biogerontological knowledge for the foreseeable future.

An "animal model" comprises not only the animals themselves, but also includes the attendant circumstances of housing, nutrition, disease exposure, and detailed features of the measurement procedure. However, the animals are clearly a cardinal element of the model, and the genetic control and manipulation of relevant attributes of the animals has been of major concern in the design and application of rodent model systems. Historically, there has been heavy reliance on inbred strains and on the conceptual framework of quantitative genetics within which the strengths and limitations of inbred animals are to be understood (Falconer & Mackay, 1996). A large number of inbred strains of mice and of rats now exists (more than 200 rat strains and 400 mouse strains are listed by Festing, 1988; information on strain nomenclature is also available at the Jackson Laboratory at www.jacksonlab.com). The oldest of these strains were established nearly a century ago, and they have been major contributors to biomedical research ever since.

In the following discussion of the genetic nature of inbred strains, and the consequent strengths and limitations of their use, some terminological definitions are useful. A locus is a region of the chromosome that constitutes a "gene." There are many thousands of loci in rats, mice, and men (perhaps 20,000 to 25,000), and many genes exist in variant forms called alleles. The 2 alleles an individual has received, 1 from each parent, constitute the genotype for that locus. If the alleles are identical, the genotype is said to be homozygous; if they differ, the genotype is heterozygous.

Inbreeding is accomplished simply by mating of relatives. In the generation of inbred strains of rats and mice, sibling mating has been the usual mating regimen, with each successive generation being derived from a single sibling pair. (Numerous matings are required to provide sufficient animals for research purposes, but the nucleus stock is maintained as described). It is intuitively reasonable that sibling offspring of such matings will have a higher probability of possessing like alleles at any given locus than will offspring of unrelated parents. Once homozygosity has been attained at a particular locus, it remains fixed thereafter in that configuration (except for mutations). Overall, the probability that any locus will be in a homozygous state increases systematically, approaching 99% after 20 generations, and this is generally taken as the required level for a strain to be designated as inbred. At this level, an inbred strain approximates the condition that all members of the strain are homozygous in the same allelic state at all loci (females differing from males in respect to genes on the sex chromosome, of course). That this condition is not absolute is due principally to the occurrence of mutations, which add new genetic variation. Continued sib-mating will result in re-attainment of homozygosity within the strain, but perhaps for the new allele. Thus, the genotypes of substrains that have been derived from a common parent strain can gradually diverge. There are other subtleties (Falconer & Mackay, 1996), but as a working assumption, all of the animals within an inbred strain can be regarded as having the same genotype. The fundamental advantages of inbred strains are thus relative genetic uniformity and stability, providing the research community with the capability of observing an indefinite number of genetically replicate individuals. This capability has been an asset of great power: research questions can be addressed to different samples from the strain at different times and in different laboratories, with the confident expectation that the results pertain to the same basic biological material.

The research objective may be descriptive, as for example, in the characterization of life course changes of a particular age-related variable. Alternatively, it may be to evaluate a putative intervention to alter the phenotype, as in caloric restriction. A strain that displays an extreme value of an important trait—liability to develop a particular cancer, for example—can become a standard tool for diverse research on that trait. Insofar as there is genetic influence on the trait, the evidence from different laboratories and different times will accumulate, because all of the various studies will have dealt with the same genotype.

This powerful feature is accompanied, however, by an important limitation: in any of these usages, observations from a single strain simply show that the outcome is a possible one. In fact, the results may be highly idiosyncratic to the particular genotype of the strain. Generalizability cannot be assumed a priori but must be demonstrated by further observations. This situation can be appreciated by observing that each strain is a very small sample of the total genomic variability in the species. No more can a single inbred strain be regarded as representing all of its species' genetic range than a single human individual can be regarded as representing all of human genetic variability.

Not only does this constraint apply to means and variances. Because genetic variability has been essentially eliminated within an inbred strain, the only source for phenotypic variability is the environment. This fact limits the usefulness of correlations among variables within strains, because only covariance induced by environmental factors can be thus assessed. For certain purposes this may be acceptable or even desirable, but it is probably the case that most such correlational analyses are seeking co-relationships based upon a broad collectivity of influences, genetic as well as environmental.

The particularity of inbred strains derives largely from interactions among genes (epistasis) and between genes and environments (see McClearn, 2002). For example, a near century's accumulation of data has made clear that the effect of a specific difference in genotypes at a given locus is dependent upon "residual genotype"—i.e., the allelic configuration at other loci. These effects are sometimes dismissively labeled "genetic noise," but to do so is to overlook that they represent epistatic interactions and are indications of potentially powerful research directions.

Of many possible examples, one compelling result may be cited here. Coleman and Hummel (1975) explored the effects of homozygosity for the recessive allele (symbolized db) of a major locus affecting diabetes on the genetic backgrounds of 2 related inbred strains (C57BL/6 and C57BL/Ks). Respectively, the glucose level at age 4 months was 184 and 400 mg/100 ml respectively, and body weight at 12 months was 64.5 and 35.0 grams. The former experienced hypertrophy of the Islets of Langerhans, the latter developed Islet atrophy and had a severely shortened lifespan. These differences in effect of a particular "disease" gene on the backgrounds of 2 related strains suggest how extensive the effects might be on even more discrepant backgrounds.

Again, one example must represent many and varied instances of gene X environment interaction. Fosmire and colleagues (1993) investigated the effects of a diet with high aluminum levels (sometimes but inconsistently identified as a risk factor for the development of Alzheimer's disease) on brain aluminum levels in 5 different inbred strains of mice. One strain showed a three-fold increase, 1 showed marginal increase, and 3 showed no effect whatsoever.

As a general proposition, then, the observed effect of a particular gene may depend not just marginally, but in a major way, on the homogenized configuration of the "genetic noise" of the inbred background, and the effects of an environmental factor (risk factor or presumably beneficent intervention) may depend upon the genotype of the organism. What are the symptomatic consequences for an inbred mouse of having the genotype db/db? It depends on the other genes of the strain. Similarly, the effect of an environmental variable may depend upon the genetic background. What are the consequences of exposure to dietary aluminum? It depends on the strain. Similarly, what is the effect of strain on brain aluminum level? It depends on the aluminum content of the diet.

These dependencies clearly limit generalizations. From a different perspective, however, the particularity of inbred strains can be seen as a prime virtue; failure to obtain the same results in different strains can provide a golden opportunity. Indeed, the strongest applications of "inbred" research have been in exploiting the differences among strains. In gerontological research, differences among inbred strains have been described along the entire conceptual hierarchy from the molecular level to complex phenotypes such as longevity or of cognitive functioning in advanced age. Another virtue of inbred strains is that they provide stable resources for the generation of other genetically defined groups. Thus, crosses between different strains yield an F1 (first filial) generation that comprises a group that is genetically uniform, like its parents, but heterozygous at all loci for which the 2 parent strains differ in allelic configuration. Mating of F1 animals produces an offspring generation, the F2, in which each animal is a unique configuration of genes. Such matings provide the basic array of genetically defined samples that enable the quantitative characterization of the polygenic system and the relative contributions of that system, and of the environmental system underlying variation in the phenotype of interest. But the usefulness of genetically defined models ranges far beyond the specific opportunities to characterize the genetic and environmental components of variance. They are, in fact, pertinent to the whole spectrum of gerontological research issues that may be addressed by animal research.

Perhaps inevitably, favored strains have emerged from this research effort. These strains-of-choice were explicitly recognized by an initiative of the National Institute on Aging entitled "Development of Biomarkers of Aging" (Sprott, 1999), which provided for the maintenance of aging animals under barrier conditions until they could be provided to investigators for specific research projects. The chosen animal groups were the Brown Norway and Fischer 344 inbred rats and the F1 hybrid between them, and C57BL/6 and DBA/2 inbred mice, and F1 hybrids between these 2 strains and between C57BL/6 and C3H.

Groups derived from inbred strains offer models for examining complex systems that are in important respects less constrained than those provided by inbred strains. For example, by virtue of the genetic individuality of all of the animals in an F2, it is a valuable group for exploring the generalizability of results obtained from a single or a few inbred strains. Furthermore, for the same reason, it is advantageous for the study of correlations among variables. However, the genetic variability presented by the F2 is also constrained. F2 individuals can only be different from each other in respect to loci at which the original parental inbred strains had different alleles. An obvious response is to generate more diversity by mating unlike F1s. Thus various 4-way crosses, and by extension 8-way or other heterogeneous groups can be generated. None of these can escape the limitation that allelic differences can only be assessed if some of the parent strains differ from others in genotype, but in general genetic diversity can be expected to be greater, the larger the number of progenitor strains. The potential of these heterogeneous groups is presently underutilized (McClearn & Hofer, 1999; Miller, Austad, Burke, Chrisp, Dysko, Galecki, et al., 1999) but their use is increasing. By contrast to haphazardly derived and maintained stocks, the critically important feature of such stocks is that, although no F2 or 4-way cross individual can be duplicated genetically, the gene pools of these populations are replicable. Thus, a heterogeneous stock can be reconstituted at any time or place, given the availability of the progenitor strains.

In addition to the established uses of inbred strains and derived generations, new applications are arising in combinations of the classical with the modern methods deriving from molecular genetics. For example, a currently flourishing area of research utilizes recombinant inbred strains (RIs) in the search for quantitative trait loci (QTLs). RIs are generated by re-inbreeding from an F2 (or other intercross). The newly derived inbred strains can be seen as differently reshuffled configurations of the gene pool of the progenitor strains. Consider a quantitatively distributed phenotype influenced by a polygenic system. There may exist, in that polygenic set, some loci that have bigger effect sizes than others but insufficiently large to have been detected as major genes. Assume that a panel of RI strains displays mean differences in the phenotype and that, among the recombined alleles in the Ris, there are some loci of this intermediate effect size. If the chromosomes of the strains are characterized for the many DNA markers now known, associations can be sought between the level of the phenotype and the configuration of the markers. Significant associations indicate the general chromosomal location of a locus affecting the quantitative trait and provide the basis for subsequent functional genomics research, both in reductionist and integrationist contexts. Another illustration of the joint utilization of classical and recent genetics is to be found in the placement of the results of molecular genetic manipulations (knockouts, controlled expression, knock-ins, etc.) upon particular inbred backgrounds by successive backcrossing. The caution expressed above about the particularity of results from single strains due to "residual genotype" applies with full force in these circumstances, of course, as documented by the many inconsistent results that have been found in this research endeavor.

In conclusion, inbred strains have proven to be powerful tools in biogerontology, as in biomedical research in general. The limitation in their application does not deny their value, but simply indicates that, like all tools, they are more suited to some purposes than to others. In addition to their utility per se, inbred strains are a resource in generation of other genetically defined groups, each with special advantages. Particularly potent tools are in the merging of inbred strain and molecular genetic methodologies in combined animal model systems.

GERALD E. MCCLEARN

References

Austad, S. N. (1993). The comparative perspective and choice of animal models in aging research. *Aging Clinical and Experimental Research, 5*, 259–267.

Coleman, D. L, & Hummel, K. P. (1975). Influence of genetic background on the expression of mutations at the diabetes locus in the mouse. II. Studies on background modifiers. *Israeli Journal of Medical Science, 11*, 708–713.

Committee on Animal Models for Research on Aging. (1981). *Mammalian models for research on aging*. Washington, DC: National Academy Press.

Falconer, D. S. & Mackay, T. F. C. (1996). *Introduction to quantitative genetics* (4th ed.). London: Longman.

Fosmire, G. J., Focht, S. J., & McClearn, G. E. (1993). Genetic influences on tissue deposition of aluminum in mice. *Biological Trace Element Research, 37*, 115–121.

McClearn, G. E. (2002). Genetics of behavioral aging: Animal models and the human condition. *Experimental Aging Research, 28*, 453–476.

McClearn, G. E., & Hofer, S. M. (1999). Genes as gerontological variables: Genetically heterogeneous stocks and complex systems. *Neurobiology of Aging, 20*, 147–156.

Miller, R. A., Austad, S., Burke, D., Chrisp, C., Dysko, R., Galecki, A., Jackson, A., & Monnier, V. (1999). Exotic mice as models for aging research: Polemic and prospectus. *Neurobiology of Aging, 20*, 217–231.

Sprott, R. L. (1999). Biomarkers of aging. *Journal of Gerontology: Biological Sciences, 54A*, B464–B465.

BIOLOGICAL MODELS FOR THE STUDY OF AGING: TRANSGENIC MICE/GENETICALLY ENGINEERED ANIMALS

Transgenic animals are powerful model systems that facilitate the manipulation and investigation of one or a few genes in a whole mammal. Transgenic mice are made by microinjecting a *transgene* (an engineered piece of DNA) into a pronucleus of a one-cell embryo (Gordon & Ruddle, 1983). Afterward, the embryos are transferred into the oviducts of pseudopregnant females and allowed to develop to term. Soon after birth, DNA is prepared from each pup and tested for the presence of the transgene (genotyped) by the *polymerase chain reaction* (PCR) or *Southern blot analysis*. If the transgene does not compromise viability, a fraction of the pups will have integrated the transgene into their genome in a random manner and are typically referred to as founders (F_0). If the transgene was integrated into genomic DNA prior to the first cell division, every cell of the founder animal will carry the transgene as part of its genome; however, a proportion of injected embryos will not integrate the transgene until after the first cell division and will be mosaic for the transgene. A transgenic founder is then bred to nontransgenic animals to establish a *transgenic line*. The transgene is typically passed to offspring in a Mendelian manner, and lines can be bred to homozygosity for the transgene.

Inbred and hybrid strains have been used to make transgenic mice. The strain of mouse used is ultimately dependent upon what strain is most appropriate for the study. Consideration of spontaneous tumor burden, maximum lifespan, susceptibility to a particular phenotype, genetic drift, and genetic heterogeneity may all contribute to strain selection. In general, the efficiency of transgenic founder production is lower for inbred strains than for hybrid strains.

Multiple transgenic lines are established for each transgene because the transgenes integrate randomly into the genome and because the site of integration can affect the expression of the transgene and thereby the phenotype of the transgenic line. With multiple transgenic lines, the investigator can then distinguish phenotypes that are due to the transgene itself and those due to effects resulting from the site of transgene integration. It has been estimated that 10% of transgene integration events cause a mutation. When a transgene integrates into a genomic site and perturbs gene expression or protein function corresponding to the integration locus, an *insertional mutation* has occurred. Insertional mutagenesis can yield important information about the disrupted gene.

However, the majority of insertional mutations are undesirable. An approach to bypass random integration involves directing the integration of the transgene to a desired site in the genome via homologous recombination (Bronson, Plaehn, Kluckman,

Hagmaman, Maeda, & Smithies, 1996). *Embryonic stem (ES) cells* are most commonly employed, because they can be manipulated such that they retain pluripotency throughout the process of gene targeting and expansion for injection into mouse blastocysts. Alternatively, homologous recombination can be observed from microinjection of oocytes, but this process is low yield and the number of oocytes available becomes limiting. The investigator can select a site in the genome that is constitutively expressed and is presumably free of transcriptional silencing effects. The ES cells carrying targeted integrations are injected into blastocysts and the blastocysts subsequently transferred to a *pseudopregnant* female. A portion of the pups will be identified as *chimeric* based on a mixed coat color consisting of the coat color corresponding to the ES cell line and the color of the host blastocysts. This is an indication that some of the manipulated ES cells have contributed to cell lineages in the pup. The ES cells contribute to the germline in some of the *chimeric animals*, and animals capable of germline transmission are identified through matings and genotyping of resulting pups that have the coat color derived from the ES parental mouse strain. Thus, lines of mice carrying the genetic manipulation can be generated. This approach for generating transgenic animals has not become widely utilized.

Periodically, transgenes employed to analyze transcriptional control of a gene do not yield the same results in transgenic animals as they do in cultured cells. In these situations, a relatively small amount of 5′-flanking DNA appears to direct cell-type specific gene expression in transfected cell lines, but does not direct appropriate expression in the transgenic mice. However, when large fragments of genomic DNA (100 kilobases or more) are used to generate transgenic animals, appropriate tissue and developmental expression is often realized. An example is the human apolipoprotein B gene. Appropriate cell specific expression was directed in cultured cells by a few hundred base pairs of 5′-flanking DNA, but transgenic animals carrying transgenes of approximately 80 kbp did not display appropriate apolipoprotein B expression in intestine. Transgenic mice made with larger genomic regions displayed appropriate expression (Nielsen, McCormick, Pierotti, Tam, Gunn, Shizuya, et al., 1997). The efficiency of producing transgenic mice with large fragments of DNA has improved and often is equivalent to that for a typically smaller transgene. The larger fragments also are more likely to undergo rearrangements, and an effort must be made to determine if such events have occurred. Technology for visualizing fluorescent and chemiluminescent reporter transgenes in intact (live) animals (Yang, Baranov, Moossa, Penman, & Hoffman, 2000) has added another dimension to the experimental repertoire available to investigators to study the action of promoters during aging.

In the last few years, *viral-mediated transgenesis techniques* have been developed. Historically such vectors have lost expression over time. The newer *self-inactivating lentivirus vectors* are associated with a greater efficiency and apparently sustained expression. *Lentivirus-mediated transgenesis* has been successfully performed by injecting transgene-carrying lentivirus into the perivitelline space of zygotes yielding up to 80% transgenic founders, with 90% of the lines demonstrating transgene expression (Lois, Hong, Pease, Brown, & Baltimore, 2002). *Transgenic rodents* have also been made by transducing ES cells. Up to 95% of the ES cells were observed to express the transgene (Pfeifer, Ikawa, Dayn, & Verma, 2002). Cultures of rat spermatogenic stem cells have been transduced with transgene-carrying lentiviral vectors, transferred to colonize the testes and given rise to mature spermatozoa that successfully produced up to 70% transgenic offspring (Hamra, Gatlin, Chapman, Grellhesl, Garcia, Hammer, et al., 2002). This technique may be the most productive in terms of generating transgenic lines; each transduced spermatogonial stem cell would represent an independent transgenic line, since it would be rare for any stem cell to give rise to more than 1 line due to the large number of spermatozoa generated during spermatogenesis. Regardless, the offspring can be tested by Southern blot analysis to determine if any carry the same transgene integration pattern.

Gene targeting in ES cells (Thomas & Capecchi, 1987; Doetschman, Gregg, Maeda, Hooper, Melton, & Thompson, 1987) is another powerful genetic manipulation for the development of mouse models with defined genetic alterations. Several kilobases of genomic DNA corresponding to the gene of interest and a pluripotent ES cell line are required for this procedure. The design of the targeting vector determines whether an allele will be inactivated, duplicated, or modified in some manner. *Antibiotic resistance genes* for positive and negative selection can be incorporated into the targeting vector to facilitate screening clones for those potentially carrying targeted recombination events. The ES cells must be grown on a feeder layer of cells that are resistant to the antibiotic used for positive selection. Appropriately targeted clones are definitively identified by Southern blot analysis and expanded for transfer into mouse blastocysts obtained from a strain that has a coat color different from that of the strain corresponding to the ES cells. Resulting *chimeric mice* are bred to establish lines carrying the targeted integration event. Heterozygous animals can be mated to produce mice homozygous for the targeting event presuming the homozygous state does not impart embryonic lethality. *Homologous recombination* can be used to produce mice with 0 to 4 copies of a gene (Oliver, John, Purdy, Kim, Maeda, Goy, et al., 1998).

Genetic engineering via *targeted integration* is limited by the representation of only a few mouse strains among established ES cell lines with proven *germline transmission* capabilities. In aging research there is an additional concern that the animals may compensate for the inactivated gene during development through some unknown means. Exerting temporal control over the loss of gene expression can alleviate this problem to some extent. Systems that accommodate temporal *regulation of transgene expression* include *Cre-lox recombination*, the *tetracycline binary system of gene regulation*, and other similar systems. Finally, ES cells are not readily available for species other than mice, while transgenic technology can be and has been applied to several different species.

Alternatives to the laborious *gene knockout system* have recently been described. *RNA interference* (RNAi) has rapidly become a viable alternative to *gene knockouts*. *Lentiviral vectors* are typically used to generate transduced ES cells or zygotes. An *RNA polymerase III promote*r directs expression of the transgene such that a *short hairpin RNA* (shRNA) is produced. This shRNA mediates reduced (knockdown) expression of the target gene (Rubinson, Dillon, Kwiatkowski, Sievers, Yang, Kopinja, et al., 2003; Kunath, Gish, Lickert, Jones, Pawson, & Rossant, 2003). The *RNAi methodology* is faster and may be used to dramatically reduce expression without causing embryonic or neonatal lethality. RNAi is gaining in popularity and was first identified as a mechanism for *reducing gene expression* in C. elegans (Fire, Xu, Montgomery, Kostas, Driver, & Mello, 1998). RNAi is easily used in C. elegans to study gene function via gene knockdowns.

Transgenic mice have made a strong impact on aging research, however other *transgenic model systems* are also important. Historically, many studies in aging research have been performed using rats. While substantially fewer transgenic models have been developed in rats, they provide better continuity for historical reasons in some studies and provide another rodent model to assess the commonality of mechanisms implicated in aging.

Invertebrate transgenic models are considerably more affordable than rodents, and it is feasible to include much larger numbers of animals than in rodent studies. Studies using *transgenic Drosophila* have provided support for the *oxidative stress theory* of aging and served to reinforce efforts to perform similar experiments in transgenic mice. C. elegans has served as a *genetic model for aging research* in many regards, including transgenic manipulation. Indeed, the powerful new technique of gene expression knockdown was first well developed using C. elegans. The transgenic invertebrate models are subject to limitations and problems similar to those described for rodents.

In conclusion, genetically engineered animals are being used to study the molecular processes that may be involved in aging. The power of *genetically engineered models* is that the function and impact of a single or a few genes can be addressed in any tissue or cell type at all stages of life.

CHRISTI A. WALTER

References

Bronson, S. K., Plaehn, E. G., Kluckman, K. D., Hagmaman, J. R., Maeda, N., & Smithies, O. (1996). Single-copy transgenic mice with chosen-site integration. *Proceedings of the National Academy of Sciences, U.S.A.*, *98*, 9067–9072.

Doetschman, T. C., Gregg, R. G., Maeda, N., Hooper, M. L., Melton, D. W., Thompson, S., & Smithies, O. (1987). Targeted correction of a mutant HPRT gene in mouse embryonic stem cells. *Nature*, *330*, 576–578.

Fire, A., Xu, S., Montgomery, M. K., Kostas, S. A., Driver, S. E., & Mello, C. C. (1998). Potent and specific genetic interference by double-stranded RNA in Caenorhabditis elegans. *Nature, 391*, 806–811.

Gordon, J. W., & Ruddle, F. H. (1983). Gene transfer into mouse embryos: Production of transgenic mice by pronuclear injection. *Methods in Enzymology, 101*, 411–433.

Hamra, F. K., Gatlin, J., Chapman, K. M., Grellhesl, D. M., Garcia, J. V., Hammer, R. E., & Garbers, D. L. (2002). Production of transgenic rats by lentiviral transduction of male germ-line stem cells. *Proceedings of the National Academy of Sciences, U.S.A., 99*, 14931–14936.

Kunath, T., Gish, G., Lickert, H., Jones, N., Pawson, T., & Rossant, J. (2003). Transgenic RNA interference in ES cell-derived embryos recapitulates a genetic null phenotype. *Nature Biotechnology, 21*, 559–561.

Lois, C., Hong, E. J., Pease, S., Brown, E. J., & Baltimore, D. (2002). Germline transmission and tissue-specific expression of transgenes delivered by lentiviral vectors. *Science, 295*, 868–872.

Nielsen, L. B., McCormick, S. P. A., Pierotti, V., Tam, C., Gunn, M. D., Shizuya, H., & Young, S. G. (1997). Human apolipoprotein B transgenic mice generated with 207 and 145-kilobase pair bacterial artificial chromosomes. *Journal of Biological Chemistry, 272*, 29752–29758.

Oliver, P. M., John, S. W. M., Purdy, K. E., Kim, R., Maeda, N., Goy, M. F., & Smithies, O. (1998). Natriureic peptide receptor 1 expression influences blood pressures of mice in a dose-dependent manner. *Proceedings of the National Academy of Sciences, U.S.A., 95*, 2547–2551.

Pfeifer, A., Ikawa, M., Dayn, Y., & Verma, I. M. (2002). Transgenesis by lentiviral vectors: Lack of gene silencing in mammalian embryonic stem cells and preimplantation embryos. *Proceedings of the National Academy of Sciences, U.S.A., 99*, 2140–2145.

Rubinson, D. A., Dillon, C. P., Kwiatkowski, A. V., Sievers, C., Yang, L., Kopinja, J., Zhang, M., McManus, M. T., Gertler, F. B., Scott, M. L., & Van Parijs, L. (2003). A lentivirus-based system to functionally silence genes in primary mammalian cells, stem cells and transgenic mice by RNA interference. *Nature Genetics, 33*, 401–406.

Thomas, K. R., & Capecchi, M. T. (1987). Site-directed mutagenesis by gene targeting in mouse embryo-derived stem cells. *Cell, 51*, 503–512.

Yang, M., Baranov, E., Moossa, A. R., Penman, S., Hoffman, R. M. (2000). Visualizing gene expression by whole-body fluorescence imaging. *Proceedings of the National Academy of Sciences, U.S.A., 97*, 12278–12282.

BIOLOGICAL MODELS FOR THE STUDY OF AGING: YEAST AND OTHER FUNGI

Fungi have been used successfully to identify genes that determine life span and to elucidate molecular mechanisms of aging. These genes have mammalian homologues, and some of the mechanisms of aging possess apparent parallels in physiological processes implicated in aging in higher organisms. Thus, fungi are good models for the study of aging in humans. The genetic analysis of aging in fungi is particularly facile, both by virtue of the powerful genetics available and because of the very short life spans these organisms enjoy. The latter allows the use of life span as an endpoint assay, thus avoiding the pitfalls associated with the search for adequate biomarkers of aging. The genetic analysis of aging in fungi points to the significance of metabolic control, resistance to stress, gene dysregulation, and genetic stability in aging (Jazwinski, 1996).

Life span in the fungi can be measured in various ways. Although its measure can be time, the usual metric is connected to reproductive capacity. In baker's (*Saccharomyces cerevisiae*) and fission (*Schizosaccharomyces pombe*) yeast, this amounts to the number of cell divisions or daughter cells produced by an individual cell before death. In the filamentous fungi *Podospora* and *Neurospora*, it is usually measured by the length of the mycelium attained before its demise. The limited reproductive capacity of fission yeast has been described very recently (Barker & Walmsley, 1999), and it provides support for the hypothesis that asymmetric division is the foundation of the totipotency of germ cells and stem cells. The genetic analysis of aging in *Podospora anserina* has resulted in the identification and cloning of *grisea* as a longevity assurance gene (Borghouts & Osiewacz, 1998). Studies in bakers' yeast have identified over a dozen such genes (Table 1).

Metabolic Control

The importance of metabolic control in determining life span has been most thoroughly documented in *S. cerevisiae* (Kirchman, Kim, Lai, & Jazwinski,

TABLE 1 Yeast Longevity Genes

Cell cycle	Growth	Stress resistance	Transcriptional silencing	Spatial organization	Genetic stability
CDC7	*RAS1*	*RAS1*	*SIR2*	*RAS2*	*SGS1*
RAS2	*RAS2*	*RAS2*	*SIR4*	*BUD1*	*RAD52*
LAG1?	*RTG2*	*SIR4*	*CDC7*	*LAG1*?	*FOB1*
LAC1?	*FOB1*?	*UTH4*?	*RPD3*	*LAC1*?	
	PHB1?	*YGL023*?	*HDA1*		
	PHB2?	*PHB1*?	*RAS2*		
	LAG1?	*PHB2*?	*UTH4*?		
	LAC1?		*YGL023*?		
			FOB1?		

Yeast longevity assurance genes are tabulated according to their cellular functions. In some cases (?), these functions are putative. Some of the genes are pleiotropic, and they appear under more than one function.

1999). It has been demonstrated that an intracellular signaling pathway from the mitochondrion to the nucleus plays a role in baker's yeast longevity. This pathway is called the retrograde response, and it alerts the nucleus to the metabolic status of the mitochondria, resulting in a change in the expression of a wide array of nuclear genes. These genes include ones that encode a variety of metabolic enzymes, and the result is a realignment of cellular energy metabolism. The observed physiological changes resemble those seen in *Caenorhabditis elegans* mutants that show extended life span and in *Drosophila* strains selected for extended longevity. They also bear similarity to the alterations that occur as a result of caloric restriction in mammals. Caloric restriction is a proven method for the extension of life span and postponement of senescence in mammals. Both the retrograde response and caloric restriction represent an adjustment to life with fewer calories.

The retrograde response is modulated by *RAS2*, a homologue of mammalian c-H-*ras1*. *RAS2* is a longevity-assurance gene in its own right. It modulates a variety of cellular processes that have been implicated in baker's yeast longevity. In this sense, it can be considered a homeostatic device in yeast longevity. The retrograde response plays a special role in establishing life span. The increase in longevity afforded is directly proportional to the intensity of the retrograde signal. Thus, the retrograde response does not function as an on-off signal but rather as a rheostat. In addition to *RAS2*, the downstream effector of the retrograde response, *RTG2*, has been found to control life span.

Stress Resistance

The implication of stress resistance as a determinant of baker's yeast aging comes from studies of the genes *RAS1* and *RAS2* (Jazwinski, 1999). Chronic sublethal heat stress curtails yeast life span. The *RAS2* gene, but not *RAS1*, protects yeast from this stress. This effect appears to be mediated through the expression of stress resistance genes, which is modulated by *RAS2*. This includes genes that are important for resistance to heat and to oxidative stress. Indeed, oxidative stress also has a negative effect on yeast longevity. The role of *RAS2* resides in its downregulation of the expression of stress response genes following bouts of stress.

Stress can have a positive effect on longevity in baker's yeast. A transient sublethal heat stress results in an extension of life span, due to a marked reduction in mortality rate that persists for a good portion of the life span but is not permanent. Both *RAS* genes are essential for this effect, as is the major heat shock protein gene *HSP104* that is largely responsible for induced thermotolerance. Similar increases in longevity have been described in *C. elegans* and in *Drosophila* following induction of thermotolerance. Caloric restriction enhances survival of old rodents after heat stress, indicating an intersection of stress resistance and postponed aging in mammals.

Gene Dysregulation

During aging, there is a loss of transcriptional silencing at heterochromatic regions of the baker's yeast genome—subtelomeric chromatin and the silent mating type loci. This gene dysregulation has the potential for exerting negative effects on the cell through inappropriate expression of various activities. It has been postulated that this may be one cause of aging in this organism. Similar gene dysregulation processes have been observed in aging mammals.

Some indirect genetic evidence was available, indicating that this gene dysregulation in yeast may indeed cause aging, and stronger support has been obtained more recently (Kim, Benguria, Lai, & Jazwinski, 1999). The structure and transcriptional activity of chromatin is modulated by the acetylation status of the histones. The equilibrium between the acetylated and nonacetylated state of the histones is maintained by histone acetylases and deacetylases. It has been demonstrated that two histone deacetylase genes, *RPD3* and *HDA1*, are longevity assurance genes. The effects of these genes on the chromatin containing the ribosomal DNA repeats are associated with longevity. It is the relatively silent state of ribosomal DNA that extends life span.

As baker's yeast cells age, there is a loss of protein translational capacity. At the same time, there is an increase in the content of ribosomal RNA. It is possible that this increase is due to a loss of transcriptional silencing of the ribosomal DNA, similar to that which occurs at other heterochromatic regions of the yeast genome. If the increase in ribosomal RNA is not matched by an increase in ribosomal proteins, assembly of defective ribosomes may result, as well as loss of protein synthetic capacity. Maintenance of an appropriate level of silencing of ribosomal DNA can thus enhance longevity.

Genetic Stability

Two kinds of genetic stability are important in determining the life span of fungi. In the filamentous fungi (*Podospora* and *Neurospora*), it is the stability of mitochondrial DNA. The loss of mitochondrial DNA sequences or their rearrangement has dire consequences for these obligate aerobes. The mitochondrial DNA deficits occur in two different ways: In *Podospora* they result from the appearance of a circular DNA plasmid derived from mitochondrial DNA; in different species of *Neurospora*, the plasmid can be either circular or linear, and it is foreign rather than derived from the mitochondrial DNA. The loss of functional mitochondrial DNA in these filamentous fungi bears striking similarity to the accumulation of mitochondrial deletions in mitochondrial encephalopathies and cardiomyopathies, as well as to the accretion of such losses during aging in mammals. This has been determined to be a cause of aging and death in these fungi.

A mutation in either the *grisea* or the *vivax* gene in *Podospora* prevents the accumulation of the mitochondrial DNA plasmid and its recombination with intact mitochondrial DNA, which extends the life span of the organism. The double mutant displays the synergistic effect of immortality. The *grisea* gene has been cloned (Borghouts & Osiewacz, 1998). It is a homologue and an orthologue of the baker's yeast gene *MAC1*, which is a copper-responsive transcription factor. One of the genes regulated by *MAC1* is *CTR1*, a high-affinity copper transporter. In the absence of *grisea*, copper cannot accumulate in mitochondria, ameliorating the generation of reactive oxygen species. The studies on *grisea* point to the importance of mitochondrial metabolism and its relationship to oxidative stress in aging.

In baker's yeast, genetic stability is also an important factor in determining life span. However, this genetic stability involves nuclear DNA sequences. Specifically, the intramolecular recombination that occurs naturally among the 100 to 200 tandem ribosomal DNA repeats results in the appearance of ribosomal DNA circles that can amplify during the life span (Defossez, Prusty, Kaeberlein, Lin, Ferrigno, Silver, et al., 1999). The excessive accumulation of these circles causes cell death. It is accelerated by mutations in the *SGS1* gene, a DNA helicase homologous to the human *WRN* gene, which is mutated in a segmental progeroid syndrome. Mutations in the *FOB1* gene limit the accumulation of the circles and increase the life span. Double-stranded DNA breaks that are likely to be involved in the formation of the ribosomal DNA circles can themselves curtail yeast life span. It appears at present that the accumulation of ribosomal DNA circles is not a cause of mammalian aging. However, there are many other types of repeated DNA elements in mammals that could give rise to a similar sort of DNA instability.

S. Michal Jazwinski

References

Barker, M. G., & Walmsley, R. M. (1999). Replicative ageing in the fission yeast *Schizosaccharomyces pombe. Yeast, 15*, 1511–1518.

Borghouts, C., & Osiewacz, H. D., (1998). GRISEA, a copper-modulated transcription factor from *Podospora anserina* involved in senescence and morphogenesis, is an ortholog *of MAC1* in *Saccharomyces cerevisiae. Molecular and General Genetics, 260*, 492–502.

Defossez, P. A., Prusty, R., Kaeberlein, M., Lin, S. J., Ferrigno, P., Silver, P. A., Keil, R. L., & Guarente, L. (1999). Elimination of replication block protein Fobl extends the life span of yeast mother cells. *Molecular Cell, 3*, 447–455.

Jazwinski, S. M. (1996). Longevity, genes, and aging. *Science, 273*, 54–59.

Kim, S., Benguria, A., Lai, C.-Y., & Jazwinski, S. M. (1999). Modulation of life-span by histone deacetylase genes in *Saccharomyces cerevisiae. Molecular Biology of the Cell, 10*, 3125–3136.

Kirchman, P. A., Kim, S., Lai, C.-Y., & Jazwinski, S. M. (1999). Interorganelle signaling is a determinant of longevity in *Saccharomyces cerevisiae. Genetics, 152*, 179–190.

BIOLOGICAL THEORIES OF AGING

See
Stress Theory of Aging

BIOLOGY OF *FAT*

Aging is often associated with an increase in *adiposity*, particular *abdominal obesity*, which can occur without a significant increase in body mass index (the measure of body fat adjusted for height). This increased abdominal adiposity is largely due to an increase in *visceral fat*. Visceral fat may have important health implications, as it is linked to the development of poor health outcomes and has a central role in the *metabolic syndrome of aging*. The metabolic syndrome of aging includes a cluster of abnormalities such as *insulin resistance*, *dyslipidemia*, and *hypercoagulability* and is associated with an increased risk for cancer, Alzheimer's disease, type II diabetes, and atherosclerosis. As the population ages and the obesity epidemic grows, our understanding of the relationship between increased *adiposity and the poor health* outcomes associated with the metabolic syndrome becomes increasingly important.

Adipose tissue is not simply a reservoir for excess nutrients, but rather an active and dynamic organ capable of expressing biologically active fat-derived peptides. Macrophages contribute to the release of these peptides at times of acute injury and the term "*inflammatory markers*" is often applied, but in the basal state, adipose tissue is the predominant source of production. Some *fat-derived peptides* may have a role in development of the metabolic syndrome of aging and other obesity-related diseases.

Fat as a Biologically Active Endocrine Tissue

A growing number of fat-derived peptides are being described, many of which are measured in physiologically relevant levels in plasma. Examples include *interleukin-6* (IL-6), *leptin*, *tumor necrosis factor-alpha* (TNF-α), *plasminogen activator inhibitor-1* (PAI-1), *adiponectin*, and *resistin*. Recent advances in understanding fat-derived peptides lead to the hypothesis that adipose tissue itself may be an underlying link between *obesity and excess morbidity*.

TNF-α, previously known as *lymphotoxin* and *cachetin*, is believed to be involved in the wasting that occurs during illness and malignancy. In the basal stat, TNF-α is directly proportional to fat mass and has been shown experimentally to be involved in the development of insulin resistance. In vitro studies have demonstrated that TNF-α decreases the insulin receptor *tyrosine phosphorylation* and down-regulates several steps in the insulin-signaling pathway, while TNF-α antagonists have been shown to improve insulin resistance in some models.

Leptin is a peptide derived from adipose tissue that acts through a cytokine receptor. It is expressed and secreted in direct proportion to fat mass. Leptin exerts its effect predominantly through receptors in the hypothalamus, but it may also have peripheral actions. Leptin serves as a marker of energy sufficiency by rapidly decreasing during starvation and weight loss. With the development of increased visceral fat during aging, leptin levels are increased in proportion to fat mass, but its activity to decrease appetite seems reduced. This failure of leptin action may be partially due to human eating behavior where meals are eaten regularly regardless of plasma leptin levels, degree of appetite, or degree of obesity.

IL-6 is a cytokine derived from adipose tissue. Its expression and circulating levels correlate directly with obesity, and weight loss will lower circulating levels. Elevation of circulating IL-6 is a predictor of the development of cardiovascular disease and diabetes. In experimental models, infusion of IL-6 results in hyperlipidemia, hyperglycemia, and insulin resistance. Additionally, IL-6 decreases the expression of *adiponectin*, an antidiabetic cytokine.

Adiponectin is highly expressed in adipose tissue, and is one noncytokine fat-derived peptide that is thought to be protective. Unlike most fat-derived peptides, circulating levels are inversely proportional to obesity: levels tend to be low in obesity and to increase with weight loss. Animal models have shown that low adiponectin levels increase smooth muscle proliferation in response to injury, increase free fatty acid levels, and cause insulin resistance, while adiponectin administration improves insulin sensitivity. The prodiabetic and pro-atherogenic effects of low adiponectin levels seen in the metabolic syndrome provide another link between inflammation and obesity.

Plasminogen activator inhibitor-1 (PAI-1) is the primary inhibitor of *fibrinolysis* and is highly expressed in adipose tissue, and may have a significant role in thrombosis. PAI-1 levels are correlated with adiposity and are significantly overexpressed in the adipose tissue of obese compared to lean animals. Levels are decreased by weight loss. The relationship of PAI-1 to obesity provides a link between obesity and acute coronary events.

Angiotensinogen, as along with all of the other peptides in the renin-angiotensin system, are produced in adipose tissue. The strong correlation between obesity and hypertension implies that adipose tissue may play a role in blood pressure regulation, and in fact there is a correlation between circulating angiotensinogen levels and obesity/hypertension. Animal studies have shown that overexpression of angiotensinogen results in hypertension, while underexpression results in decreased blood pressure.

Other inflammatory cytokines, such as *interleukin-1*, *interleukin-8*, *interleukin-18*, and *serum amyloid A*, have been shown to increase with obesity and may have a role in the development of obesity-related disease.

Deleterious Effects of Visceral Adiposity in Aging

There is increasing evidence of visceral fats' deleterious effects in aging. Waist-to-hip ratio is an epidemiological tool that demonstrates a correlation between visceral fat and development of type II diabetes, stroke, coronary artery disease, and mortality. Experimental data from rodent models further supports the relationship of visceral fat to obesity-related illness. For example, *caloric restriction* reversed aging-related increases in plasma insulin, glucose, and glycosylated hemoglobin and restored liver and muscle insulin sensitivity to youthful levels independent of age. Furthermore, *surgical extraction of visceral fat* in rats has dramatically reversed defects in insulin action. A recent human study showed that removal of subcutaneous fat did not provide the same improvement in insulin sensitivity seen with removal of visceral fat, emphasizing that visceral fat may be more active biologically.

Conclusion

A typical older person may have normal body mass index. However, within this normal range, the ratio between fat mass and lean-body mass is usually increased. In addition, fat infiltrates other tissue, such as muscle and liver, and accumulates substantially at the visceral region. Aging-related processes may be due to the interplay of the different fat-derived peptides originating from different fat depots. Thus, prevention of adiposity/visceral adiposity may be key in preventing aging-related diseases, such as type II diabetes, dyslipidemia, coronary artery disease, and hypertension. Moreover, understanding *fat tissue biology* may be helpful in finding therapy to prevent these aging-related processes.

Nir Barzilai
Eric Rudin

See also
Body Composition
Diabetes

BIOMARKER OF AGING

Although the term "biomarker of aging" has been applied widely in gerontological research, no consensus has emerged regarding a clear definition of the concept and the standards for its application to research questions. In its simplest application, the term refers to any biological parameter that is correlated with the chronological age of an organism, but this has little use other than being descriptive. In a more complex application, a biomarker of aging is a biological parameter intended as a quantitative measure of the rate of aging in an organism that represents a more accurate index than can be provided by the organism's chronological age. In this latter form, the standards and procedures for defining and validating a biomarker of aging have generated considerable debate within gerontology.

The more complex application of a biomarker of aging emerged from the research demand to assess the effectiveness of interventions that purport to alter the rate of aging. If 2 individuals are of the same chronological age but have experienced an intervention that might affect the rate of aging, how can this difference be detected? In 1982 Reff and Schneider published a monograph entitled *Biological Markers of Aging* that initiated a discussion of how interventions might be assessed using biomarkers of aging representing a variety of physiological systems. This issue was considered further in a report by Regelson and Sinex published in 1983, referenced as *Intervention in the Aging Process*. A special issue of the journal *Experimental Aging Research* titled "The *Measurement of Biological Age*," edited by Ludwig and Masoro, was also published in 1983 and offered additional views on this topic. In 1984, Chebortarev, Tokar, and Voitenko published a monograph in Russian entitled *Biological Age, Heredity and Aging,* also addressing the issue of biomarkers of aging.

It was not until 1988, however, that a formal definition of biomarker of aging was offered by Baker and Sprott in a special edition of *Experimental Gerontology* emerging from a 1987 workshop that considered current strategies of *biomarker research* (Sprott & Baker, 1988). The definition offered was as follows: "A biological parameter of an organism that either alone or in some multivariate composite will, in the absence of disease, better predict functional capacity at some later age than will chronological age" (Baker & Sprott, 1988; p. 223). Although the concept had not been formally defined previously, specific criteria of a biomarker of aging had been offered by Reff and Schneider as follows: (1) nonlethal, (2) highly reproducible, (3) displays significant alterations during relatively short time periods, and (4) critical to effective maintenance of health and prevention of disease. To this set of criteria, Baker and Sprott offered the following additions: (5) reflects a measurable parameter that can be predicted at a later age, (6) reflects some basic biological process of aging and metabolism, and (7) should have high reproducibility in cross-species comparisons.

Ingram (1983, 1988) and McClearn (1988) attempted to clarify the criteria offered above and offer a strategy for developing a biomarker of aging in its more complex application. The structure of this strategy had been used for developing psychological tests. The major challenge is how to determine the *reliability* and *validity* of a biomarker of aging. Reliability relates to criterion 2 above: are the data obtained in an assay reproducible? Reliability refers to how much of the variability in a parameter can be attributed to genuine *individual differences* versus measurement error. Several statistical procedures exist for addressing this question, such as estimation of test-retest correlations. Over a longer period of time, the term *stability* of individual differences emerges in considering reliability issues, but this concept also addresses the ability of the biomarker to be predictive and thus also begins to relate to validity. Validity refers to demonstrating the utility of a biomarker. Predictive validity relates to criterion 5 above: can a measure at one age predict future performance in this measure or represent future status in some other measure or set of measures? Inherent in Baker and Sprott's definition is an emphasis on functional capacity at a later age. Several criteria related to this predictive ability can be considered, such as life span or the age of onset of specific age-related diseases. If functional capacity is the primary predictive criterion, then the ability to withstand a specific stressor could be considered. Construct validity relates to criteria 4, 6, and particularly 7. How well does a biomarker of aging reflect the underlying construct or definition of aging? Strong support for construct validity of a biomarker of aging would be provided if the biomarker could differentiate between groups with established differences in the rate of aging and/or life span.

This latter approach was central to efforts initiated by the National Institute on Aging (NIA) to identify biomarkers of aging in rodent models (Baker & Sprott, 1988; Sprott, 1999). The validation process involved comparing a candidate biomarker in rodent populations on control and experimental diets. Specifically, on the experimental diet rodents underwent *calorie restriction* (CR) compared to ad libitum feeding for the controls. This is a well-established intervention that produces marked differences in the rate of aging evidenced as reduced mortality rates and incidence of age-related pathology. Thus, if the candidate biomarker of aging showed a slower rate of change in the CR group compared to controls, such demonstration would support the construct validity of the biomarker. Clearly the parameter would reflect "effective maintenance of health and prevention of disease (criterion 4)" as well as "reflects some basic biological process of aging and metabolism (criterion 6)."

Miller (2001) provided further consideration and clarification regarding criteria for a biomarker of aging as follows: (1) it should predict the outcome of a wide range of age-sensitive tests in multiple physiological domains, in an age-coherent way, and do so better than chronological age, (2) it should predict remaining longevity at an age at which 90% of the population is still alive, and (3) its measurement should not alter either life expectancy or the outcome of subsequent tests of other age-sensitive traits. As an example of this strategy for *biomarker development* that used defined populations of mice with varied life spans, Miller (1997) examined age-related changes in subsets of T-cells of mice to identify immunological biomarkers of aging. The proportion of cells known as *CD-4 memory T-cells* increased with age as measured cross-sectionally and longitudinally, and the change in this parameter was slowed in mice undergoing CR. As an additional demonstration of the validity of this biomarker of aging, Miller, Chrisp, and Galecki (1997) also demonstrated that this parameter measured at 18 months of age was predictive of individual life span in these mice.

While this strategy would apply to validating biomarkers of aging in short-lived species, it is difficult to apply to longer-lived species, such as humans, in which populations that differ in the rate of aging are much more difficult to discern and life span data requires decades to accumulate. To this end, research has addressed the issues of reliability and validity that can be applied to studies of long-lived species, such as nonhuman primates (Nakamura, Lane, Roth, Cutler, & Ingram, 1994; Nakamura, Lane, Roth, & Ingram, 1998; Ingram, Nakamura, Smucny, Roth, & Lane, 2001). They offered the following criteria of a biomarker of aging that are more statistically oriented than those proposed by Baker and Sprott (1988): (1) significant cross-sectional correlation with age, (2) significant longitudinal change with age consistent with the cross-sectional correlation, (3) significant stability of individual differences, and (4) rate of age-related change proportional to differences in life span among related species. Criterion 3 relates to reliability in the short term and predictive validity in the long term. Criterion 4 is an extension of Criterion 7 offered by Baker and Sprott. Examples of this approach are represented in papers by Lane, Ingram, Ball, and Roth (1997) and Sell and colleagues (1996). In the former, the age-related change in serum *dihydroepiandosterone*, an adrenal steroid, was examined across different species, while the latter looked at age-related change in *pentosidine*, an *advanced glycation endproduct* measurable in skin samples. The logic here is that if a biomarker of aging is a valid reflection of the rate of aging, then the rate of change across different species should be proportional to differences in species' life spans. Thus, for example, the rate of change in a candidate biomarker of aging in chimpanzees should be twice that of humans (60 vs. 120 years maximum life span); in rhesus monkeys, 3 times that of humans (40 vs. 120 years maximum life span). Although this strategy of cross-species comparison has been applied in efforts to identify genetic determinants of longevity (Cutler, 1982), this method of validation for identifying biomarkers of aging has been used sparingly, but it clearly applies to a demonstration of construct validity.

The ability to conduct cross-species comparisons of biomarkers of aging is hindered by a lack of data. To address this issue, the NIA has supported the construction of the *Primate Aging Database* (PAD). A recent report by Smucny and colleagues (2004) demonstrated the power of combining data from different sources to assess the rate of aging in candidate biomarkers of aging in rhesus monkeys.

As the number of interventions that purport to retard the rate of aging increases, the demand for identifying biomarkers of aging will also increase. In this regard progress will emerge as a consensus is built to determine the definition and methods for establishing the reliability and validity of biomarkers of aging, and with the further growth of databases, such as the PAD, that will permit comparisons across species as a means of validation.

DONALD K. INGRAM

References

Baker, III, G. T., & Sprott, R. L. (1988). Biomarkers of aging. *Experimental Gerontology, 23*, 223–239.

Chbortarev, F., Tokar, A. V., & Voitenko, V. P. (1984). Geriatrics and gerontology yearbook (USSR): *Biological age, heredity and aging*. Kiev: Institute for Gerontology.

Cutler, R. G. (1982). Longevity is determined by specific genes: Testing the hypothesis. In R. Adelman & G. S. Roth (Eds.), *Testing the theories of aging* (pp. 25–114). Boca Raton: CRC Press.

Ingram, D. K. (1983). Toward the behavioral assessment of biological aging in the laboratory mouse: Concepts, terminology, and objects. *Experimental Aging Research, 9*, 225–238.

Ingram, D. K. (1988). Key questions in developing biomarkers of aging. *Experimental Gerontology, 23*, 429–434.

Ingram, D. K., Nakamura, E., Smucny, D., Roth, G. S., & Lane, M. A. (2001). Strategy for identifying biomarkers of aging in long-lived species. *Experimental Gerontology, 36*, 1025–1034.

Lane, M. A., Ingram, D. K., Ball, S. S., & Roth, G. S. (1997). Dehydroepiandrosterone sulfate: A biomarker of primate aging slowed by caloric restriction. *Journal of Clinical Endocrinology and Metabolism 82*, 2093–2096.

Ludwig, F. C., & Masoro, E. J. (1983). The measurement of biological age. *Experimental Aging Research, 9*, 219–255.

McClearn, G. E. (1988). Strategies for biomarker research: Experimental and methodological design. *Experimental Gerontology, 23*, 245–255.

Miller, R. A. (1997). Age-related changes in T cell surface markers: A longitudinal analysis in genetically heterogeneous mice. *Mechanisms of Ageing and Development, 96*, 181–196.

Miller, R. A. (2001). Biomarkers of aging. SAGE KE. Available: http://sageke.sciencemag.org/cgi/content/full/sageke;2001/1/pe2

Miller, R. A., Chrisp, C., & Galecki, A. (1997). CD4 memory T-cell levels predict life span in genetically heterogeneous mice. *FASEB Journal, 11*, 775–783.

Nakamura, E., Lane, M. A., Roth, G. S., Cutler, R. G., & Ingram, D. K. (1994). Evaluating measures of hematology and blood chemistry in male rhesus monkeys as biomarkers of aging. *Experimental Gerontology, 29*, 151–177.

Nakamura, E., Lane, M. A., Roth, G. S., & Ingram, D. K. (1998). A strategy for identifying biomarkers of aging: Further evaluation of hematology and blood chemistry data from a caloric restriction study in rhesus monkeys. *Experimental Gerontology, 35*, 421–443.

Reff, M. E., & Schneider, E. L. (1982). *Biological markers of aging*. (NIH Publication No. 82-2221). Washington, DC: U.S. Government Printing Office.

Regelson, W., & Sinex, F. M. (1983). *Intervention in the aging process*. New York: Alan R. Liss.

Sell, D. R., Lane, M. A., Johnson, W. A., Masoro, E. J., Mock, O. B., Reiser, K. M., Fozarty, J. F., Cutler, R. G., Ingram, D. K., Roth, G. S., et al. (1996). Longevity and the genetic determination of glycooxidation kinetics in mammalian senescence. *Proceedings of the National Academy of Sciences of the U.S.A. 93*, 485–490.

Smucny, D. A., Allison, D. A., Ingram, D. K., Roth, G. S., Kemnitz, J. W., Kohama, S. G., Lane, M. A., & Black, A. (2004). Update to: Changes in blood chemistry and hematology variables during aging in captive rhesus macaques (*Macaca mulatta*). *Journal of Medical Primatology, 33*, 48–54.

Sprott, R. L. (1999). Biomarkers of aging. *Journal of Gerontology: Biological Sciences, 54A*, B464–B465.

Sprott, R. L., & Baker, III, G. T. (1988). Biomarkers of aging. *Experimental Gerontology, 23*, 223–438.

BLOOD

Blood is composed of 2 major components: formed elements (cells) that constitute 45% of the volume; and the fluid phase (plasma) comprising 55% of the total volume, in which the former are suspended. The cells include 99% red blood cells (erythrocytes), 1% white blood cells (leukocytes), and platelets (thrombocytes) (Beutler, Lichtman, Coller, & Kipps, 2001). Plasma is an aqueous solution that is 90% to 92% water and is made up of electrolytes, nutrients, and lipids plus a large variety of proteins. These components transport substances that are of vital importance to the maintenance of normal homeostasis to the body's tissues and cells, and transport waste substances away from these tissues and cells to points of excretion. The blood is an extremely complex structure, and the array of functions it performs equally so.

Functions

Respiration. This vital function involves the transport of oxygen from the lungs to all living cells. Of equal importance is the removal of the waste product of cellular metabolism, carbon dioxide, from the cells to the lungs where it is expired. This function is performed mainly by hemoglobin contained within the red blood cells.

Nutrition. All nutrients required by cells are transported by the blood, including minerals, salts, amino acids (the building blocks for proteins), carbohydrates (glucose), fats, and vitamins. These are mainly transported in the plasma, frequently bound to specific transport proteins.

Excretion. Waste products and some toxic substances are carried by the blood to the major excretory organs—the liver, kidneys, and lungs. These products include water, electrolytes, nitrogen-containing compounds, certain drugs, and the breakdown products of hemoglobin (bilirubin).

Defense. A major function of the blood involves the body's defense against foreign substances (bacteria, viruses, etc.). Both cells and plasma contribute to defense, with *neutrophils* being the first leukocyte to respond to bacterial invasion of the body. The *monocytes* respond later, and both types of cells kill the bacteria by releasing certain enzymes and by *phagocytosis*. *Lymphocytes* also act directly, as well as participating in the production of antibodies that circulate as part of the plasma protein component, and assist in the destruction of such invading organisms.

Vascular Integrity. The blood helps maintain the vascular tree and protects it against destruction from trauma. This function, called *hemostasis*, is accomplished by an interaction of the platelets and protein clotting factors to form a blood clot to seal such destructions.

Components of the Blood and Changes with Age

Plasma. This consists predominantly of water (more than 90%) and the major soluble substances are the proteins. Salts, glucose, amino acids, vitamins, hormones, and waste products are the other constituents. Most proteins (including albumin, the one with the highest concentration) are produced in the liver. *Immunoglobulins* (*antibodies*) are produced by lymphocyte-derived cells in many organs, including the bone marrow, lymph nodes, and spleen. The general composition of plasma does not change dramatically with age. There are small decreases in the serum albumin concentration, perhaps related to chronic disease, and subtle alterations in the concentration of the types of antibody molecules. The most striking of these is the emergence of an aberrant immunoglobulin protein, in up to tenfold normal concentration, in as many as 10% to 15% of people over the age of 70 (Cohen, 1999). These proteins are known as *monoclonal immunoglobulins* because of their derivation from a single clone of lymphocyte-derived cells, the plasma cells.

Another age-related change occurring in the blood, in part related to the plasma, is a change in the *erythrocyte sedimentation rate* (ESR). This phenomenon, which measures the rate of sedimentation of red blood cells in the plasma, is an indirect measure of the viscosity of the plasma. Both the ESR and *plasma viscosity* increase somewhat with age. This is brought about by a number of different plasma proteins but appears to be related more to an increase in the number of infectious and inflammatory diseases with age, rather than the aging process itself.

Cell Changes and Disease

The more prominent changes in the blood with age and disease involve the cells (Gautier, Crawford, & Cohen, 1998). All blood cells are produced in the bone marrow from a common stem cell. With advancing age, the cell production in bone marrow decreases by approximately one-third; however, renewal of peripheral blood cells remains normal except in circumstances of excess stress. There appears to be some reduction in bone marrow stem cell reserve for both red and white blood cells, with the decrease in the latter perhaps the partial cause of the somewhat decreased response to infection in older adults. With normal aging, there appears to be only a very slight decrease in the number of red blood cells and the level of the main red blood cell protein, hemoglobin, which is the major oxygen-carrying molecule. The leukocyte count in peripheral blood in older persons tends to decrease only slightly but may be less readily mobilized under stress. The ability of the phagocytic leukocytes (*granulocytes* and *monocytes*) to kill bacteria appears unchanged. The platelet count appears to remain normal throughout the life span in normal aging individuals.

Most of the changes seen in the blood cells with age are related to the increased prevalence of a number of age-related diseases. *Anemia*, or a decrease in red cells and hemoglobin, is the most frequently encountered hematologic problem in older adults (Gautier, Crawford, & Cohen, 1998). Patients may present with pale skin, fatigue, and weakness, and this usually is a sign of potential underlying primary diseases. Older patients with anemia have been known to have decreased physical performance and muscle strength (Pennix, Guralnik, Onder, Ferrucci, Wallace, & Pahor, 2003). These patients also have significantly lower survival rates (Ania, Suman, Fairbanks, Rademacher, & Melton, 1997). In general, anemia can result from either an underproduction of red blood cells or their overdestruction. Anemia frequently results in characteristic changes in the appearance of the red blood cells; one type, in which the cells become much smaller than normal (microcytic), includes the common anemia produced by iron deficiency. *Iron deficiency* is generally the result of blood loss, often from the gastrointestinal tract, and much more rarely from dietary deficiency. Treatment of this condition with iron replacement may be easily accomplished, but the initial cause of the deficiency must be actively sought. Another microcytic form of anemia is the anemia of chronic disease. This is a secondary form of anemia in which iron appears to be trapped in storage sites within the body and not made available to the developing erythrocytes. In this case, treatment with iron is not indicated but rather, when possible, resolution of the illness in question—e.g., infection, or inflammation—is necessary.

A second major group of anemias is those in which the red blood cells are larger than normal, or macrocytic. These are most frequently produced by deficiency of either vitamin B12 or of folic acid. *Folic acid deficiency* is common in the elderly and is usually a result of dietary insufficiency. *Vitamin B12 insufficiency* is frequently caused by an intrinsic failure to absorb the vitamin because of the lack of certain transport proteins in the stomach, which leads to pernicious anemia; dietary deficiency of vitamin B12 is relatively infrequent. However, a somewhat decreased blood level of vitamin B12 appears to occur with advancing age. Both of these vitamins are critical in the formation of the DNA (basic genetic material) of the cell, which is necessary for cell proliferation. Once diagnosed, these anemias can be easily treated by replacement of the appropriate vitamin. Less frequently, increased destruction of red blood cells occurs and is referred to as *hemolytic anemia*. Most often this is due to the production of an antibody directed against certain membrane components of the red blood cell, which then induces destruction of these cells; this is called *autoimmune hemolytic anemia*. The process of *autoantibody production* appears to increase rather strikingly with age, although red blood cell destruction still remains relatively infrequent.

Overproduction of red blood cells may occur, but this is usually accompanied by overproduction of the white blood cells and/or platelets as well. Such disorders constitute the *myeloproliferative disorders*, which also occur with increasing frequency in the elderly (Gautier, Crawford, & Cohen, 2004). In *Polycythemia rubra vera*, all 3 cell lines proliferate, resulting in high red blood cell counts (and hemoglobin levels), high white blood cell counts, and high platelet counts. In *chronic granulocytic leukemia*, there is dramatic overproduction of granulocytes and platelets due to an uncontrolled hyperactivity of the bone marrow. This disease requires treatment with chemotherapeutic agents. After a period of a few years of relatively easy control, it frequently becomes uncontrollable and changes into a more acute form of the disease similar to acute granulocytic leukemia, and usually results in death. *Acute granulocytic (or myeloblastic) leukemia* is a dramatic disease with a rapid clinical course and short survival; more than half of all patients with acute granulocytic leukemia are over the age of 65. In this disorder, there is an overproduction and accumulation of the most primitive form of the granulocyte, called the *myeloblast*. These cells invade and occupy the major portion of the bone marrow and, by overcrowding and failing to differentiate to more mature forms, prevent the production of the normal cellular elements. Thus, marked reductions in granulocytes, platelets, and red blood cells result. These primitive myeloblasts may also break loose from the bone marrow and circulate in the blood peripherally in large numbers, although in older adults they are frequently confined to the bone marrow, making the diagnosis somewhat more difficult. Treatment for this condition involves chemotherapy along with careful monitoring of patients for any side effects and toxicities. More recently, new drugs have been approved by the Food and Drug Administration to treat patients over 60 years of age. Chronic *lymphocytic leukemia* is the most common leukemia in older adults and is characterized by the accumulation of large numbers of lymphocytes in the bone marrow, blood, and other organs. Patients in the early stage of this disease do well even without therapy and have a good quality of life and life expectancy. Patients who are in the later stages need to be treated with chemotherapy. Several new drugs have been approved recently for the treatment of this condition, and most older patients respond well to these agents.

Specific disorders of the thrombocyte also occur in older persons, with *thrombocytopenia* (decreased platelets) being the most common. This may be due to a myeloproliferative disorder, as described above, or may be caused by antibodies to the thrombocytes, in a manner similar to that described above for red blood cells. A frequent problem in older adults is thrombocytopenia produced by drugs, which may result from immune reactions or from suppression of the bone marrow. Drugs in general may play an important role in causing blood disorders in the elderly, as many drugs have side effects that produce either immunologic reactions or direct suppression of the bone marrow, resulting in decreases in all the cellular elements, as in *pancytopenia*, or decreases in individual components, as in *aplastic anemia* (decreased red blood cells), *granulocytopenia*, and thrombocytopenia. With the generally increased numbers of drugs used by older individuals, this etiology must be strongly considered when these phenomena are noted.

HARVEY JAY COHEN
ARATI V. RAO

References

Ania, B. J., Suman, V. J., Fairbanks, V. F., Rademacher, D. M., & Melton, L. J., III. (1997). Incidence of anemia in older people: An epidemiologic study in a well defined population. *Journal of the American Geriatrics Society*, *45*, 825–831.

Beutler, E., Lichtman, M. A., Coller, B. S., & Kipps, T. J. (Eds.). (2001.) *Williams hematology* (6th ed.). New York: McGraw Hill.

Cohen, H. J. (1999). Disorders of the blood. In J. G. Evans & T. F. Williams (Eds.). *Oxford textbook of geriatric medicine* (2nd ed.). Oxford: Oxford University Press.

Gautier, M., Crawford, J., & Cohen, H. J. (1998). Hematologic disorders. In E. H. Duthie & P. R. Katz (Eds.), *Practice of geriatrics* (3rd ed., pp. 397–409). Philadelphia: WB Saunders.

Gautier, M., & Cohen, H. J. Hematologic malignancies. (2004). In C. K. Cassel, R. M. Leipzig, H. J. Cohen, E. B. Larson, & D. E. Meier (Eds.). *Geriatric medicine*, (4th ed., pp. 487–506). New York: Springer-Verlag.

Pennix, B. W., Guralnik, J. M., Onder, G., Ferrucci, L., Wallace, R. B., & Pahor, M. (2003). Anemia and decline in physical performance among older persons. *American Journal of Medicine*, *115*, 104–110.

BLOOD PRESSURE

See
Hypertension

BODY COMPOSITION

One might expect that studies of body composition would include the volume and chemical composition of body fluids and the size and composition of organs. However, although many of these subjects have been studied individually, body composition as a whole has not been assessed in such a detailed fashion. Rather, when investigating body composition, physiologists have concentrated on measuring height and weight (body mass), as well as components of *body mass*. The model most used to determine components of body mass has been the classic *2-compartment model*, in which body mass is divided into fat mass and fat-free mass (often called *lean body mass*). To estimate the size of these 2 compartments, measurements of body density or total body water or total body potassium are most commonly used (Holloszy & Kohrt, 1995). Because each of these yields data on fat mass and fat-free mass that are based on different assumptions, each yields somewhat different numerical values. In recent years, improvements in the technology of *neutron activation analysis* and *dual-energy x-ray* radiography have led to the development of *multicompartment models*. The components of a *6-compartment model* (Heymsfield & Waki, 1991) are fat, water, protein, osseous mineral (mineral content of bone), extraosseous mineral, and carbohydrate. The first component is the same as the fat component of the 2-compartment model; the combined last 5 components are similar to the fat-free mass, or lean body mass, of the 2-compartment model.

Height and Weight

Height decreases with age, starting at age 20 in women and age 25 in men (Spirduso, 1995). Over an 11-year period, the height of men in the 55–64 age range decreased on average one-half inch; that of women in the same age range decreased by one inch. The loss in height is primarily due to compression of the cartilaginous disks between the vertebrae and to vertebral bone loss.

Based on both cross-sectional and longitudinal studies, body weight increases in men and women up to age 55. In cross-sectional studies, body weight was found to decrease after age 55. However, longitudinal studies show that it continues to increase until age 65, after which it decreases, probably accelerating with advancing age (Carmelli, McElroy, & Rosenman, 1991). The difference between the cross-sectional and longitudinal studies is probably due to a birth-cohort effect.

Fat-Free Mass and Its Components

Based on cross-sectional studies, it appears that fat-free mass (lean body mass) is relatively stable in men and women until about age 40 (Holloszy & Kohrt, 1995). Between ages 40 and 60, fat-free mass declines with age, a decrease of about 3% per decade in men and 4% per decade in women; the decline between ages 60 and 80 is about 6% per decade for men and 10% per decade for women. However, these values are based on cross-sectional studies and thus may be an overestimate due to birth-cohort effects.

In a cross-sectional study on nonhuman primates, fat-free mass was also found to decrease with advancing age (Hudson, Baum, Frye, Roecker, & Kemnitz, 1996). However, in a longitudinal study on rats, there was no decrease in fat-free mass until just before death (Yu, Masoro, Murata, Bertrand, & Lynd, 1982).

Whereas total body water decreases in humans with increasing adult age, there is debate as to whether this decrease relates primarily to a change in intracellular or extracellular water (Steen, 1988). The decrease in total body water is proportional to the decrease in fat-free mass.

Osseous mineral decreases with age in both men and women (Snead, Birge, & Kohrt, 1993). In men the decrease is proportional to the decrease in fat-free mass, but in postmenopausal women the decrease is greater than the decrease in fat-free mass.

Fat Mass

In humans, body fat content increases until late middle age (Kohrt, Malley, Dolsky, & Holloszy, 1992). For example, sedentary men in their 20s have a fat content of about 17%, compared to 29% for sedentary men in their 60s. Although endurance-trained men have a lower fat content than do sedentary men, they also show an age-associated increase in body fat; endurance-trained men in their 20s have a fat content of about 10%, compared to 17% for comparably trained men in their 60s. A similar pattern has been shown in women. Sedentary women in their 20s have a fat content of about 24%, compared to 38% for sedentary women in their 60s. Endurance-trained women in their 20s have a fat content of about 17%, compared to 25% for endurance-trained women in their 50s. However, at ages older than the 60s, the body fat content *of* both men and women decreases (Kannel, Gordon, & Castelli, 1979).

Rhesus monkeys also exhibit an increasing fat content through middle age, followed by a decrease in old age (Hudson, Baum, Frye, Roecker, & Kemnitz, 1996). In rats, too, body fat increases until middle age and declines in late life (Bertrand, Lynd, Masora, & Yu, 1980). It seems likely that this pattern of change in fat content with age is common to most mammals.

The increase in *body fat with age* occurs preferentially in the abdominal region in humans (Shimokata, Tobin, Muller, Elahi, Coon, & Andres, 1989). Men have a progressive *increase in abdominal fat* with increasing adult age, but such an increase does not occur in women until they are postmenopausal. (Young women have a preferential distribution of fat in the buttocks and thighs.) Studies using magnetic resonance imaging or dual-energy absorptiometry indicate that the *age-associated increase in abdominal fat* is primarily visceral rather than subcutaneous (Ley, Lees, & Stevenson, 1992). Habitual exercise decreases the age-associated redistribution of body fat (Kohrt, Malley, Dolsky, & Holloszy, 1992). Increased levels of abdominal visceral fat heighten the risk of coronary heart disease (Williams, Jones, Bell, Davies, & Bourne, 1997), stroke (Walker, Rimm, Ascherio, Kawachi, Stampfer, & Willett, 1996), hypertension (Selby, Friedman, & Quesenberry, 1989), and diabetes mellitus (Ohlson, Larsson, Svardsudd, Welin, Eriksson, Wilhelmsen, et al., 1985).

EDWARD J. MASORO

See also
Biology of *FAT*
Sodium Balance and Osmolality Regulation

References

Bertrand, H. A., Lynd, F. T., Masora, E. J., & Yu, B. P. (1980). Changes in adipose mass and cellularity through the adult life of rats fed ad libitum or life-prolonging restricted diet. *Journal of Gerontology*, *35*, 827–835.

Carmelli, D., McElroy, M. R., & Rosenman, R. H. (1991). Longitudinal changes in fat distribution in the Western Collaborative Group Study: A 23-year follow-up. *International Journal of Obesity*, *15*, 67–74.

Heymsfield, S. B., & Waki, M. (1991). Body composition in humans: Advances in the development of multi-compartmental chemical models. *Nutrition Reviews*, *49*, 97–108.

Holloszy, J. O., & Kohrt, W. M. (1995). Exercise. In E. J. Masoro (Ed.) *Handbook of physiology: Aging* (sect. 11, pp. 633–666). New York: Oxford University Press.

Hudson, J. C., Baum, S. T., Frye, D. M. D., Roecker, E. B., & Kemnitz, J. W. (1996). Age and sex differences in body size and composition during Rhesus monkey adulthood. *Aging Clinical and Experimental Research*, *8*, 197–204.

Kohrt, W. M., Malley, M. J., Dolsky, G. P., & Holloszy, J. O. (1992). Body composition of healthy sedentary and trained, young and older men and women. *Medicine and Science in Sports and Exercise*, *24*, 832–837.

Kannel, W. B., Gordon, T., & Castelli, W. P. (1979). Obesity, lipids and glucose tolerance: The Framingham study. *American Journal of Clinical Nutrition*, *32*, 1238–1245.

Ley, C. J., Lees, B., & Stevenson, J. C. (1992). Sex- and menopause-associated changes in body fat distribution. *American Journal of Clinical Nutrition*, *55*, 950–954.

Ohlson, L. O., Larsson, B., Svardsudd, K., Welin, L., Eriksson, H., Wilhelmsen, L., Bjorntorp, P., & Tibbin, G. (1985). The influence of body fat distribution on the incidence of diabetes mellitus: 13.5 years of follow-up of the participants in the study of men born in 1913. *Diabetes*, *34*, 1055–1058.

Selby, J. V., Friedman, G. D., & Quesenberry, C. P. (1989). Precursors of essential hypertension. *American Journal of Epidemiology*, *129*, 43–53.

Shimokata, H., Tobin, J. D., Muller, D. C., Elahi, D., Coon, P. J., & Andres, R. (1989). Studies in the distribution of body fat: I. Effects of age, sex and obesity. *Journal of Gerontology*, *44*, M66–M73.

Snead, D. B., Birge, S. J., & Kohrt, W. M. (1993). Age-related differences in body composition by hydrodensitometry and dual-energy x-ray absorptiometry. *Journal of Applied Physiology*, *74*, 770–775.

Spirduso, W. W. (1995). *Physical dimensions of aging*. Champaign, IL: Human Kinetics.

Steen, B. (1988). Body composition and aging. *Nutrition Reviews*, *46*, 45–61.

Williams, S. R. P., Jones, E., Bell, W., Davies, B., & Bourne, M. W. (1997). Body habitus and coronary heart disease in men. A review with reference to methods of body habitus assessment. *European Heart Journal*, *18*, 376–393.

Walker, S. P., Rimm, E. B., Ascherio, A., Kawachi, L., Stampfer, M. J., & Willett, W. C. (1996). Body size and fat distribution predictors of stroke among U.S. men. *American Journal of Epidemiology*, *144*, 1143–1150.

Yu, B. P., Masoro, E. J., Murata, I., Bertrand, H. A., & Lynd, F. T. (1982). Life span study of Fischer 344 male rats fed *ad libitum* or restricted diets: Longevity, growth, lean body mass and disease. *Journal of Gerontology*, *37*, 130–141.

BOOMERS

See
Baby Boom Generation

C

CALCIUM METABOLISM

Calcium and Life

Calcium is the fifth most abundant element in the earth's crust, where life evolved. A unique relationship exists between this key mineral and the molecules of life. Proteins, which constitute both the structural elements and the catalytic machinery of all cells, are essentially limp, floppy molecules. Their three-dimensional structure and functional activities depend upon binding metal ions that effectively stabilize and activate them. While several metals serve this role for specific proteins, the ionic radius of the calcium atom is just right for binding to the folds of the peptide backbone of proteins, and hence calcium functions as a principal activator of most *cell functions* (Heaney, 1999).

To regulate that activation, resting cells must maintain low levels of calcium in their internal water (the cytosol), typically less than one one-thousandth the concentration outside the cell. Then, when a cell action is called for (e.g., a muscle fiber is signaled to contract), *calcium channels* in the cell membrane open, calcium pours into the *cytosol* from the extracellular fluid and intracellular stores, the contractile machinery is activated, and the cell contracts. The calcium is then promptly pumped back out, and the cell rests again. This description oversimplifies a much more complex process, but it captures its essential elements: (1) the role of calcium in activating virtually every cell function, and (2) the way cells regulate this activation.

Multicellular organisms use calcium in 2 additional ways. Calcium is maintained at relatively high concentrations in the blood and extracellular fluids, where it is needed to facilitate such functions as blood coagulation and intercellular communication. Calcium is also the principal cation of the mineral of bones and teeth, tissues which serve mechanical functions essential to higher organisms.

Integration of the Calcium Control System

These 3 roles of calcium in animals—the intracellular, the extracellular, and the skeletal—are beautifully integrated in ways that are still being explored. The best understood aspect of the control system involves the regulation of ionized calcium level in the blood and extracellular fluid (ECF [Ca^{++}]), which in all vertebrates is maintained at about 1.25 mmol/L. This is accomplished in mammals by the concerted action of 3 hormones, *parathyroid hormone* (PTH), *calcitonin*, and *calcitriol* (the most active form of vitamin D). PTH prevents ECF [Ca^{++}] from falling by: (1) activating *bone resorption*, thus releasing calcium into the circulation, (2) raising the calcium excretory threshold at the kidney, and (3) stimulating conversion of *vitamin D* to calcitriol, thereby increasing extraction of calcium from ingested food. Calcitonin, working in the other direction, prevents ECF [Ca^{++}] from rising by suppressing bone resorption. In all these interactions, the skeleton serves as a large, portable reserve of calcium, a reservoir to be drawn upon in time of need, and, within limits, a place to store a calcium surplus in times of plenty.

Calcium Metabolism and Calcium-Related Disease

Calcium-related disease falls into 3 broad categories, which reflect the basic mechanisms by which calcium influences health. These are: (1) disorders of the regulation of [Ca^{++}] in the blood and extracellular fluid, (2) deficient intestinal luminal activity of calcium, and (3) cell functional disorders developing as a consequence of the body's own adaptive response to inadequate calcium intake.

Disorders of ECF Calcium Regulation. The principal disorders involving the regulation of ECF [Ca^{++}], particularly prominent at the end of life, are over- or underactivity of the *parathyroid glands* and depletion of the skeletal calcium reserves. These result in *hyperparathyroidism*, *hypoparathyroidism*, and *osteoporosis*, respectively. Hypoparathyroidism is quite uncommon except as a consequence of thyroid surgery, and is otherwise not preventable. Hyperparathyroidism occurs relatively often in postmenopausal women, probably because of long-standing calcium and vitamin D deficiency.

Depletion of the Reserve. Osteoporosis is the most common of all bone diseases in the industrialized nations, and contributes to virtually all late-life fractures. Osteoporosis has many causes (Heaney, 1997), but one is low calcium intake, particularly later in life when the ability to use dietary calcium generally wanes. Calcium deficiency osteoporosis can be prevented by insuring a high calcium intake, lifelong but particularly at 2 critical life stages—adolescence when most bone is being amassed under the impetus of growth, and after menopause, when the body's capacity to adapt to a low calcium intake decreases (thereby unmasking preexisting dietary inadequacies). More than 150 studies have been reported on this topic in the past 15 years (Heaney, 2000). Essentially all the investigator-controlled studies of augmented calcium intake showed greater bone gain during growth or reduced bone loss and fractures in older adults. Additionally, more than 80% of the observational studies relating calcium intake to bone status have found higher bone mass and/or reduced bone loss with age in those consuming high-calcium diets. These findings have led to substantial upward revisions in recommended calcium intakes for most ages, but especially for older adults (Food and Nutrition Board, 1997).

These revised recommendations move closer to, but are still substantially below, the calcium intakes of hunter-gatherer humans and high primates. The abundance of calcium in the biosphere and the essential link of calcium with life are reflected in the high calcium contents of many plant tissues (which, of course, constitute the ultimate food of animals). The diets of all agriculture-based societies, by contrast, exhibit low calcium densities, mainly because they are based on seed foods (cereal grains and legumes), which today provide more than 60% of the caloric intake of the world's population but were virtually absent from the *paleolithic diet* to which our physiologies adapted over the millennia of evolution.

The Luminal Function of Diet Calcium. A second group of disorders is based on the functionality of unabsorbed calcium in the gut lumen. Our bodies are adapted to prevent calcium intoxication rather than to deal with chronic scarcity, and hence gut absorption of calcium is very poor, with net absorption averaging about 10% to 15% at recommended intakes. The unabsorbed calcium forms complexes with (and hence detoxifies) certain other food residues, mainly *oxalic acid* and unabsorbed bile acids and fatty acids. *Oxalate* is an important contributor to *kidney stone* risk and, by preventing its absorption from the intestinal lumen, high-calcium diets reduce the risk of developing kidney stones (Curhan, Willett, Rimm, & Stampfer, 1993; Borghi, Schianchi, Meschi, Guerra, Allegri, Maggiore, et al., 2002). Similarly, by forming salts with unabsorbed fatty acids and bile acids, calcium neutralizes their irritant effect on the colon mucosa. In individuals with a propensity for *colon cancer*, high-calcium diets effectively remove these substances from the colon contents and stop their calcium-promoting action (Holt, Atillasoy, Gillman, Guss, Moss, Newmark, et al., 1998; Baron, Beach, Mandel, van Stolk, Haile, Sandler, et al., 1999).

Dietary Calcium and Cellular Calcium Dysregulation. A final group of disorders arises because of sensitivity to the body's normal adaptive response to low calcium intakes. When absorbed dietary calcium is insufficient to sustain ECF [Ca^{++}], PTH secretion rises and, as already noted, stimulates synthesis of *calcitriol* from vitamin D, which thereby directly improves intestinal calcium absorption. In addition to this action, calcitriol also opens slightly the calcium channels in cells throughout the body, allowing calcium to move more readily into their cytosol. The cells work to pump it back out, but in certain individuals with limited capacity, cytosolic [Ca^{++}] rises, leading to partial cellular activation. This appears to be the mechanism by which low calcium intakes contribute to *hypertension* (Appel, Moore, Obarzanek, Vollmer, Svetkey, Sacks, et al., 1997). In this case it is the arteriolar smooth muscle cell which is activated, maintaining a higher than appropriate level of arteriolar contractile tension. Recently, similar effects have been observed in human fat cells which, when exposed to high levels of calcitriol, exhibit elevated cytosolic [Ca^{++}] and switch cell activity from lipolysis to *lipogenesis* (Zemel, Shi, Greer, DiRienzo, & Zemel, 2000). This latter effect, for which there is now an impressive array of ancillary evidence, is probably behind the otherwise puzzling observation that risk of obesity is inversely related to dietary calcium intake. Other disorders linked to low calcium intake and possibly explained by the same basic mechanism, include 2 problems of the reproductive years, *premenstrual syndrome* (Thys-Jacobs, Starkey, Bernstein, & Tian, 1998) and *polycystic ovary syndrome* (Thys-Jacobs, Donovan, Papadopoulus, Sarrel, & Bilezikian, 1999), and the *insulin resistance syndrome* (Pereira, Jacobs, Van Horn, Slattery, Kartashov, & Ludwig, 2002).

In this third group of disorders, tissues with limited ability to counter the tendency of calcium ions to enter the cell express 1 or more of their characteristic actions, but in this case inappropriately. Such disorders may be likened to *favism*, a *hemolytic anemia* occurring in individuals of Mediterranean ancestry who have a defective gene for a key energy-producing enzyme (*glucose-6-phosphate dehydrogenase*). When such individuals consume fava beans (or are given certain drugs such as antimalarials), which interfere with energy metabolism in red blood cells, cell access to energy drops and the cells die, releasing their hemoglobin into the blood stream. It takes an inherent susceptibility (G-6-PD deficiency) plus a trigger (fava beans) for the anemia to manifest itself. Similarly, in these calcium-related disorders, it takes a combination of at least 2 (and perhaps 3) factors for the disease to express itself (e.g., an inherent sensitivity, triggered by low calcium intake). Thus, not all persons with low calcium intakes will be obese, or develop hypertension, or suffer PMS. All these disorders are, of course, multifactorial, and low calcium intakes explain only a part of each problem. Nevertheless, removing the trigger prevents the expression of the disorder in the subsets of the population with the requisite susceptibilities.

Race and the Calcium Requirement. There are important racial differences in how these interactions express themselves. Thus, blacks have a bony apparatus relatively resistant to PTH (Aloia, Mikhail, Pagan, Arunachalan, Yeh, & Flaster, 1998; Cosman, Morgan, Nieves, Shen, Luckey, Dempster, et al., 1997). Hence they are able to build and maintain a skeleton on lower calcium intakes than whites or Asians. But, for the same low calcium intakes, they necessarily have higher PTH and calcitriol levels than whites. This may well be the explanation for both the low risk of osteoporosis and the high risk of *hypertension in blacks*, as well as for the blood pressure reduction that milk produces when consumed by blacks. Currently the functional indicator for determination of the human calcium requirement is skeletal health. This is probably the wrong indicator for blacks, in whom the calcium requirement for cardiovascular health appears to be higher than for skeletal health.

The primitive human diet, for persons of contemporary body size, would have provided 2,000 to 3,000 mg/day of calcium. Intakes today of 1,200 to 1,800 mg/day probably provide most or all of the benefits of the aboriginal diet. Intakes lower than 1,200 mg will almost certainly increase individual risk of a bewildering variety of seemingly unrelated diseases, as well as the population burden and cost of those disorders.

ROBERT P. HEANEY

References

Aloia, J. F., Mikhail, M., Pagan, C. D., Arunachalan, A., Yeh, J. K., & Flaster, E. (1998). Biochemical and hormonal variables in black and white women matched for age and weight. *Journal of Laboratory and Clinical Medicine, 132*, 383–389.

Appel, L. J., Moore, T. J., Obarzanek, E., Vollmer, W. M., Svetkey, L. P., Sacks, F. M., Bray, G. A., Vogt, T. M., Cutler, J. A., Windhauser, M. M., Lin, P.-H., & Karanja, N. (1997). A clinical trial of the effects of dietary patterns on blood pressure. *New England Journal of Medicine, 336*, 1117–1124.

Baron, J. A., Beach, M., Mandel, J. S., van Stolk, R. U., Haile, R. W., Sandler, R. S., Rothstein, R., Summers, R. W., Snover, D. C., Beck, G. J., Bond, J. H., & Greenberg, E. R. (1999). Calcium supplements for the prevention of colorectal adenomas. *New England Journal of Medicine, 340*, 101–107.

Borghi, L., Schianchi, T., Meschi, T., Guerra, A., Allegri, F., Maggiore, U., & Novarini, A. (2002). Comparison of two diets for the prevention of recurrent stones in idiopathic hypercalciuria. *New England Journal of Medicine, 346*, 77–84.

Cosman, F., Morgan, D. C., Nieves, J. W., Shen, V., Luckey, M. M., Dempster, D. W., Lindsay, R., & Parisien, M. (1997). Resistance to bone resorbing effects of PTH in black women. *Journal of Bone and Mineral Research, 12*, 958–966.

Curhan, G. C., Willett, W. C., Rimm, E. B., & Stampfer, M. J. (1993). A prospective study of dietary calcium and other nutrients and the risk of symptomatic kidney stones. *New England Journal of Medicine, 328*, 833–838.

Food and Nutrition Board, Institute of Medicine. (1997). Dietary reference intakes for calcium, magnesium, phosphorus, vitamin D, and fluoride. Washington, DC: National Academies Press.

Heaney, R. P. (1997). Pathogenesis of postmenopausal osteoporosis. In M. Favus (Ed.), *Osteoporosis, fundamentals of clinical practice* (pp. 74–76). Philadelphia: Lippincott-Raven.

Heaney, R. P. (1999). Bone biology in health and disease. In M. E. Shils, J. A. Olson, M. Shike, & A. C. Ross (Eds.), *Modern nutrition in health and disease* (9th ed., pp. 1327–1337). Baltimore: Williams & Wilkins.

Heaney, R. P. (2000). Calcium, dairy products, and osteoporosis. *Journal of the American College of Nutrition, 19*(2), 83S–99S.

Holt, P. R., Atillasoy, E. O., Gilman, J., Guss, J., Moss, S. F., Newmark, H., Fan, K., Yang, K., & Lipkin, M. (1998). Modulation of abnormal colonic epithelial cell proliferation and differentiation by low-fat dairy foods. *Journal of the American Medical Association, 280*, 1074–1079.

Pereira, M. A., Jacobs D. R., Jr., Van Horn, L., Slattery, M. L., Kartashov, A. I., & Ludwig, D. S. (2002). Dairy consumption, obesity, and the insulin resistance syndrome in young adults. *Journal of the American Medical Association, 287*, 2081–2089.

Thys-Jacobs, S., Starkey, P., Bernstein, D., & Tian, J. (1998). Calcium carbonate and the premenstrual syndrome: Effects on premenstrual and menstrual symptomatology. *American Journal of Obstetrics and Gynecology, 179*, 444–452.

Thys-Jacobs, S., Donovan, D., Papadopoulos, A., Sarrel, P., & Bilezikian, J. P. (1999). Vitamin D and calcium dysregulation in the polycystic ovarian syndrome. *Steroids, 64*, 430–435.

Zemel, M. B., Shi, H., Greer, B., DiRienzo, D., & Zemel, P. C. (2000). Regulation of adiposity by dietary calcium. *FASEB Journal, 14*, 1132–1138.

CANADIAN RESEARCH ON AGING

This overview briefly situates Canadian aging research in terms of funding and focus, and highlights several of the major multicenter and multidisciplinary research programs currently underway in Canada. It identifies numerous Web sites and resources with information on a diversity of Canadian research on aging and later life. The full scope and depth of research on aging in Canada cannot be captured in a single entry, and additional insights are provided through other entries in this volume.

Among the developed countries, Canada, along with Japan, has the most rapidly aging population with an increase not only in the relative and absolute number of people over age 65 years, but particularly of the *oldest old*. Between 1991 and 2001, the population aged 80 and over increased by 41%, and is projected to increase an additional 43% from 2001 to 2011 (McPherson, 2004).

Canada has had a national association on gerontology (www.cagacg.ca) since 1971 and a national geriatrics society since 1981. Both organizations serve to improve the lives of aging and older Canadians through the creation and dissemination of knowledge in gerontological policy, practice, research, and education. As Maddox (2001) has noted, the "intellectual reach" of Canadian research is well beyond Canada, with much Canadian research on aging published in journals of the Gerontological Society of America, the *Journal of the American Geriatrics Society*, and other journals worldwide. However, *Canadian Journal on Aging/La revue canadienne du vieillissement* (*CJA*) is a primary vehicle for dissemination of research on aging in Canada. *CJA* publishes, in both English and French, papers from the biological sciences, health research, psychology, social sciences, social policy and practice, and educational gerontology. The journal of the *Canadian Geriatrics Society* also publishes original research on the health and care of older Canadians.

Federal and provincial research funding has influenced the nature and types of strategic research initiatives in aging, and the infrastructure required to support substantial initiatives. The creation in 2000 of a national *Institute of Aging* as 1 of 13 virtual institutes of the *Canadian Institutes of Health Research* (CIHR, www.cihr.ca) has also had a substantial impact on the climate of funding and activity across the full spectrum of research on health and aging, from cells to society. The CIHR, which replaced the Medical Research Council of Canada, takes a problem-based and multidisciplinary approach to biomedical, clinical, health systems, and services research, as well as research on the social, cultural, and environmental factors that affect the health of populations.

The creation of the Institute of Aging has provided a focal point for Canadian aging research, both in its identification of nationally relevant strategic initiatives in aging and in activities designed to synthesize research results and promote their translation into policy and practice. Over a short period the institute's mandate to partner with other funding agencies (such as the *Quebec Research Network in Aging*, national health charities, and private sector funders) has led to a substantial leveraging of research funding in the field of aging in Canada. One significant outcome of these early initiatives has been the development of a *Canadian Longitudinal Study of Aging*, described below.

Other sources of infrastructure support for research in aging are the federal *Networks of Centers of Excellence Program* (which funded *CARNET*: The *Canadian Aging Research Network* in the 1990s), and the *Canadian Foundation for Innovation*, which recently has provided substantial research infrastructure related to aging—one on innovative rehabilitation therapies involving technology (*IDAPT*, led by Geoff Fernie, University of Toronto), and the other on technologies related to falls and hip fracture prevention and therapies in older adults (led by Tom Oxland, University of British Columbia).

Canadian researchers have been particularly innovative in their forging of broad, multidisciplinary and multicenter alliances in aging. Among these is the *Canadian Study of Health and Aging* (CSHA), one of the largest epidemiologic studies of dementia, involving a population-based cohort study of dementia with a sample of 10,263 participants aged 65 years and over, studied 3 times over a 10-year period (www.csha.ca). The CSHA has provided estimates of prevalence, incidence, and risk factors for dementia, and associated burdens on family caregivers; presented patterns of disability, frailty, and healthy aging; and has recorded use of health services for different diagnostic groups. Canadian research "on the difficult notion of '*pre-dementia*'" has been described as pioneering (Clarfield, 2001). With more than 100 publications, the CSHA "is increasingly recognized as contributing to understanding the epidemiology of dementia, to studies of frailty, and also to a range of methodological aspects of research on aging" (Rockwood, McDowell & Wolfson, 2001).

Another prominent area of clinical research on older adults in Canada involves the study of frailty. The *Canadian Initiative on Frailty and Aging* (www.frail-fragile.ca) conducts research designed to improve understanding of the causes and trajectory of frailty, promote wellness, and improve the quality of health care and life for older Canadians (Hogan, MacKnight, & Bergman, 2003). The initiative involves a consortium of researchers, partner research groups, and organizations across Canada and Europe, and links with the developing National Institute on Aging/American Geriatrics Society frailty initiative.

However, multicenter research initiatives in Canada are by no means restricted to issues of health and aging. For example, one research program, *Social and Economic Dimensions of an Aging Population* examines social and economic aspects of population aging across 4 themes: population aging and the economy, aging and health, aging and family life, and retirement and financial security. A special supplement of *CJA* in fall 2004 reports on the findings of this 5-year research program. Similarly, an interdisciplinary research program at the University of Alberta, scheduled to run until 2008, examines the hidden costs of care and often invisible contributions of older adults and adults with chronic illness/disabilities, as well as the nature of these costs and contributions in social, political, historic, and cultural contexts (www.hecol.ualberta.ca/RAPP/).

Most Canadian provinces still have mandatory retirement policies at age 65, and thus the issue of the appropriate age for retirement is the focus of considerable policy debates in Canada. Research on the *aging of the Canadian workforce* is important to these debates. One project recently launched by the federal Policy Research Initiative focuses on issues of population aging and life-course flexibility (www.policyresearch.gc.ca).

However, *Workforce Aging in the New Economy*—one of the largest social science research initiatives ever funded in Canada—also examines the aging of the workforce in a global economic context, particularly in relation to growth in information technology employment (www.wane.ca). This project, headed by *Julie McMullin* of the University of Western Ontario, involves an international research consortium from Canada, the United States, the European Union, and Australia. In a recent examination of the relationship between skills shortages and labor force aging, McMullin and colleagues conclude that "workforce aging is not the only, nor necessarily the most significant determinant of skill shortages" (www.cprn.org/en/doc.cfm?doc=1088). This consortium is currently examining the responses of employers to issues of aging workforces, the barriers in the information technology industry that restrict access to employment for older workers and women, and how work in this industry influences the timing and sequencing of key life course events and transitions.

In addition to these cutting-edge multicenter and internationally relevant research initiatives and research programs, there are several longitudinal studies on aging. The *Aging in Manitoba (AIM) Longitudinal Study* is the longest continuous study of aging in Canada and between 1971 and 2001 has involved almost 9,000 older Manitobans in personal interviews. AIM focuses on socio-demographic, social psychological, physical and mental health status and functioning, economics, leisure activities, care and support networks, and consumption of services. Recent publications of this research program examine issues of healthy and successful aging, diabetes, and the challenges of conducting longitudinal research on aging populations (www.umanitoba.ca/faculties/medicine/community_health_sciences/AIM/). The *Manitoba Follow-up Study* (www.mfus.ca), now in its 56th year, is Canada's largest and longest-running investigation of cardiovascular disease. The recently funded Quebec longitudinal study, *NuAge*, is Canada's first longitudinal study on nutrition as a determinant of successful aging. This study, led by *Helene Payette* of the Université de Sherbrooke, examines relationships between multiple factors associated with lifestyle and nutrition, and their long-term consequences for health in later life.

Building on the experiences learned from conducting these and other longitudinal studies in Canada, as well as the CSHA multicenter initiative described earlier, an ambitious Canadian Longitudinal Study of Aging (CLSA) is currently under development. The CLSA proposes to follow a group of approximately 50,000 Canadian men and women aged 40 and older for a period of at least 20 years. The study will collect information on the changing biological, medical, psychological, social, and economic aspects of their lives. This proposal emerged as one of the early initiatives of the *Institute of Aging*, and to date has involved over 200 researchers from across Canada, led by principal investigators *Christina Wolfson*, *Parminder Raina*, and *Susan Kirkland*. While the research protocol is still under development, the CLSA is scheduled for pilot testing in 2006 and launch in 2008 (www.cihr-irsc.gc.ca/e/22982.html or www.fhs.mcmaster.ca/clsa).

Guided by a "determinants of health" framework, the CLSA will examine ways in which the social and physical environment, genetic, biological, clinical, lifestyle and behavioral factors, economic prosperity, and the health care system are interrelated, and how they influence disease, health, and well-being. One of its key aims is to distinguish aging from the effects of disease processes and cohort effects.

Two strengths of the Canadian research environment in aging have contributed to the success of many of the initiatives noted above (and others not described here). The first is the aging research community's link with *Statistics Canada*, generally considered to be one of the foremost national data collection agencies in the world. The research products of this collaboration and cooperation are manifest in the 1991 *Study of Ageing and Independence*, as well as the 20 years of *General Social Surveys (GSS) of Canada*, which includes national data on, and frequently oversampling of, the population aged 65 and over for such topics as social support and aging, family, time use, social engagement, and education, work, and retirement.

The GSS program, originating in 1985, conducts telephone surveys on 10,000 to 25,000 people; each survey has a core topic, focus, or exploratory questions and a standard set of socio-demographic questions used for classification. Recent cycles also have included some qualitative questions, which explore opinions and perceptions. The 2 primary objectives of the GSS are to gather data on social trends in order to monitor temporal changes in the living conditions and well-being of Canadians, and to provide immediate information on specific social policy issues of current or emerging interest. The recent creation of *Statistics Canada Research Data Centers* across the country, enabling researchers to access the linked files of major national databases in a master file format, also stands to enhance national research on aging.

A second strength of the Canadian research environment in aging is the link between research and policy. These collaborations are reflected in the now-completed *Seniors' Independence Research program of Health Canada*; it funded research on the concepts of independence and autonomy for seniors, focusing on the health, social, and economic aspects of seniors' independence. Research results have been reported in various publications, including a joint issue of the *Canadian Journal on Aging* and *Canadian Public Policy* titled "Bridging Research and Policy on Aging" (1997), and a *CJA* special issue on "Setting an evidence-based policy agenda for seniors' independence" (2000). Related national initiatives include the research findings of the *Trends project* (Cheal, 2000). In addition, the *Health Transition Fund* was a $150 million fund that from 1997–2001 supported 140 projects across Canada to test and evaluate innovative ways to deliver health care services, including those to older persons.

One question that emerges from time to time in overviews of Canadian research on aging involves the uniqueness of the research conducted within the shadow of the United States. In a review of 20 years of Canadian social research on aging, Lesemann states that "the preoccupation to build a Canadian social gerontology, distinct from the American, is ever present" (2001). He cites Marshall (1980) in noting that Canadian scholarship on aging is "generally more structured, collectivist, and anchored in history than... [U.S. research which is]... more individualistic, consensual and centered around attitudes and behavior." Chappell and Penning (2001) have similarly described Canadian social science research consistent with principles of a political economy perspective: that aging is inextricably tied to larger socio-political and economic realities. This approach has certainly been reflected in Canadian research on the health care system and structural biases in that system, especially as services shift from acute care to community-based care, with a perception of "down-loading onto the community" (Keating & Cook, 2001).

This overview has identified some of the unique characteristics and contributions of Canadian research on aging. These have been considered elsewhere in editorials and reviews (Béland, 1997; Keating & Cook, 2001; Martin-Matthews, 2001), and most fully in a special issue of the *Canadian Journal on Aging* (Martin-Matthews & Béland, 2001), prepared on the occasion of the 17th World Congress of the International Association of Gerontology, held in Canada. In that volume, Canadian researchers and international commentators considered both the national relevance and international contributions of Canadian research on aging. In addition to some of the distinct approaches to Canadian research on aging (as noted above), research reported in that issue made clear that Canada's national health insurance program, often defined as a hallmark of national identity, creates a context for service delivery to *elderly Canadians*, and for their lives in old age, that is quite different from that of other countries. As Clarfield (2001) has noted, "... even if research results fit within the international literature and reflect clinical problems of people everywhere, work... in a particularly Canadian context... is of interest to others because it highlights what is possible, and what yet remains difficult, in a system that provides universal access to health care." Clearly, Canada's structural and cultural distinctiveness has much to contribute to our understanding of aging and old age; as Maddox (2001) has exhorted us to do, probing the consequences of that distinctiveness presents both challenges and opportunities for Canadian research on aging.

ANNE MARTIN-MATTHEWS

References

Béland, F. (1997). Building Canadian gerontology: A springboard for international recognition? *Canadian Journal on Aging*, *16*(1), 6–10.

Chappell, N. L., & Penning, M. (2001). Sociology of aging in Canada: Issues for the Millennium. *Canadian Journal on Aging*, *20*(Suppl. 1), 82–110.

Cheal, D. (2000). Aging and demographic change. *Canadian Public Policy* (Special Supplement on the Trends Project), *26*, S109–S122.

Clarfield, A. M. (2001). Commentary: Canadian geriatrics. A view from Israel. *Canadian Journal on Aging*, *20*(Suppl. 1), 21–24.

Hogan, D. B., MacKnight, C., & Bergman, H. (Eds.) (2003). The Canadian initiative on frailty and aging. *Aging Clinical and Experimental Research* [supplement], *15*(3).

Keating, N., & Hopper Cook, L. (2001). "Current thinking in gerontology in Canada. *Ageing and Society*, *21*(1), 131–138.

Lesemann, F. (2001). Twenty years of Canadian social research on aging: An attempted understanding. *Canadian Journal on Aging*, *20*(Suppl. 1), 58–66.

Maddox, G. (2001). Commentary: Sociological issues for the millennium. *Canadian Journal on Aging*, *20*(Suppl. 1), 111–117.

Martin-Matthews, A. (2001). A decade of gerontological research in Canada. *Contemporary Gerontology*, *7*(2), 2–5.

Martin-Matthews, A., & Béland, F. (Eds.). (2001). Northern lights: Reflections on Canadian gerontological research. *Canadian Journal on Aging*, *20*(Suppl. 1).

McPherson, B. (2004). *Aging as a social process* (4th ed.). Toronto: Thompson Educational Publishing.

Rockwood, K. McDowell, I., & C. Wolfson (Eds.). (2001). *International Psychogeriatrics* [Special issue on the Canadian Study of Health and Aging], *13*(Suppl. 1).

CANCER

Cancer occurs when malignant cells proliferate uncontrollably and inappropriately. Although even young children can have cancer, cancer is chiefly a disease of aging, in cells of the epithelial type (i.e., cells of the skin, or those that line the stomach or colon). Such cells normally undergo a rapid turnover and thus proliferate throughout life. In this way, cancer can be thought of as a disorder of cell proliferation. As the cells grow, they disrupt the normal surrounding tissue and can invade adjacent tissues or spread to more distant sites in a process called *metastasis*.

Exactly why some cells that proliferate begin to proliferate abnormally, why they are not locally controlled, and how and why they spread are each the subject of intensive investigation. Despite tantalizing insights (e.g., in the way that certain tumors are able to develop their own blood supplies, or how certain types of mutations, including viruses can induce mutations to give rise to cancer) much of the biology remains unknown. Clearly, an interplay between genetics and environmental factors is involved in the development of cancer. A large body of evidence indicates that stable mutations of the cellular DNA must occur before a cell becomes malignant. These mutations can arise from exposure to chemical carcinogens in the environment, endogenous or exogenous oxidants, ionizing radiation, or UV light. In the absence of a perfectly efficient DNA repair system, such *DNA lesions* or mutations become fixed in the cellular genome and accumulate with time (Skinner & Turker, 2005).

There are many links between *cancer and aging*, which relate not just to the duration of exposure but also the importance of interaction factors. For example, the pattern of increase in the cumulative cancer risk strongly suggests that multiple events are required for the development of cancer. In addition, cancer and aging are linked intrinsically; there is a considerable amount of evidence that the induction and accumulation of somatic mutations caused by excessive stress, combined with age-related faulty repair mechanisms, is of particular importance (Skinner & Turker, 2005). As with other aspects of the so-called *theory of antagonistic pleiotropy*, (Campisi, 2005) there appear to be some factors that operate favorably in early life (such as *prostasomes*, which protect spermatozoa during reproduction) but which are cancer conducive in later life (Ronquist & Nilsson, 2004).

The incidence of many human cancers rises exponentially with age. Cumulative cancer risk increases with the fourth power of age in both short-lived species such as rats and mice (30% have cancer by the end of the 2- to 3-year life span) and long-lived species such as humans (30% have cancer by the end of an 85-year life span) (Denduluri & Ershler, 2004) across a range of cancers (Lichtman & Rowe, 2004). This data strongly suggests that multiple cumulative events are required for the development of cancer. In fact, cancers that occur more often in older adults, such as lung, colon, breast, and prostate cancer, have been shown to require multiple mutagenic events. This multistep process of carcinogenesis begins with preneoplastic changes that may, under certain conditions, progress to malignant cancers. Studies of *colorectal cancer* have demonstrated this multistep process at the molecular level (Kinzler & Vogelstein, 1996). The development of colorectal tumors requires the progression from normal mucosa to late-stage adenomas, and finally to carcinoma. During neoplastic *progression of colon cancer*, colonic mucosal cells accumulate a series of genetic alterations/oncogenes, as well as the inactivation of the p53 tumor suppressor gene.

Other evidence that cancer and age are linked in ways that go beyond duration of exposure comes from studies of *calorie reduction*, which inhibits the expression of biological age and increases longevity. Reduction of total calories consumed per day (30% to 40% reduction) has been shown to have dramatic effects on aging and cancer in several experimental animal models. *Caloric restriction* (CR) retards the rate of aging, delays the appearance of age-related pathologies including cancer, and extends the life span of several animal species (Hursting, Lavigne, Berrigan, Perkins, & Barrett, 2003). Considerable evidence indicates that CR markedly retards spontaneous tumor formation in rodents (Nicolas, Lanzmann-Petithory, & Vellas, 1999). However, the mechanism(s) of tumor suppression by CR are poorly understood: it is not known if a single common mechanism or multiple mechanisms are involved in tumor suppression and life span extension, although aspects of metabolic pathways particularly are implicated, for example involving insulin-like growth factor-1 (Longo & Finch, 2003). Studies are underway in nonhuman primates to determine if CR has similar effects on aging, age-related diseases, and life span (Roth, Mattison, Ottinger, Chachich, Lane, & Ingram, 2004). The effects of CR on human aging processes and age-related disease are not known.

Usually, cells that develop abnormalities are detected and removed from tissues by the process of *apoptosis*. In contrast with the process of necrosis (the form of *cell death* that follows, for example, lack of oxygen), apoptosis does not provoke inflammatory responses from the surrounding tissue. Normal cells are already primed to undergo apoptosis but are inhibited from doing so by messages exchanged with other cells. If some abnormality in a cell disrupts its capacity to participate properly in this exchange of messages, the apoptotic mechanism will be triggered. It is possible that the ability to evade this complex process of "mutual policing" in tissues is an important element in the survival of potentially cancerous cells.

It has been known for many years that normal cells in culture can undergo only a limited number of cell divisions, the so-called *Hayflick limit* (Hayflick, 1965). Human fetal cells can divide about 50 times, but cells from older persons have a capacity for fewer divisions than cells from younger ones. Cancer cells can continue to divide indefinitely. The means by which normal cells can "count" how many divisions they have undergone has been obscure, but is thought to rest with the telomere.

Telomeres are specialized structures at the ends of chromosomes that function in chromosome protection and replication (Chan & Blackburn, 2004; Ahmed & Tollefsbol, 2003). In vertebrates, telomeres consist of hundreds to thousands of tandem repeats of the DNA sequence TTAGGG and associated proteins (Chan & Blackburn, 2004). Such sequences can also be found not just at the ends of chromosomes, but also at other interstitial sites, where they appear to have a role in protein and ribonucleoprotein binding (Wells, Germino, Krishna, Buckle, & Reeders, 1990). In normal somatic cells examined to date, chromosomes lose about 50 to 200 nucleotides of telomeric sequence per cell division (Ahmed & Tollefsbol, 2003). This telomere shortening and other markers of *telomere dysfunction* are important causes of genomic instability, itself a hallmark of cancer (Rodier, Kim, Nijjar, Yaswen, & Campisi, 2005). While the response to telomere dysfunction includes apoptosis and permanent cell cycle arrest, these means of tumor suppression have also been linked to *phenotypic aging*. (Rodier, et al., 2005). Telomeres are believed to shorten because most normal somatic cells lack the enzyme *telomerase*, a specialized enzyme needed to synthesize new telomeric repeats (Chan & Blackburn, 2004). In cancer, cellular production of the telomerase enzyme appears somehow to be reactivated, an event that may contribute to the cells' ability to divide continuously or become "immortal" (Yaswen & Stampfer, 2002). A survey of telomerase activity in a wide variety of human cells and tissues revealed the presence of telomerase in 98 of 100 cultured immortal cell lines, 90 of 101 primary tumors, and adult germ line tissues. Telomerase was undetectable in 22 normal somatic cells cultures and in 50 normal or benign tissue samples. It has now been shown that introducing telomerase into human cells will, as predicted, extend their capacity to divide (Bodnar, Ouellette, Frolkis, et al., 1998).

It has been suggested that in long-lived species such as humans, lack of telomerase in somatic cells evolved as a means of reducing the probability of cancer. This seems unlikely since the Hayflick limit is set at a level more than sufficient to support fatal malignancies. Furthermore, because cancer is, in general, a disease of later life, selection pressure against it would have been weak during our evolution (Medawar, 1952). It is more likely that the lack of infinite capacity for replications of somatic cells, as distinct from germ cells, evolved simply as a means of not wasting energy and resources in attempts to prolong the existence of bodies that inevitably have limited life spans (Kirkwood & Rose, 1991). Still, interest in telomerase interventions in cancer is strong, with potential for applications in diagnosis and prognosis (Kelland, 2001).

A new heuristic for cancer biology has recently been developed, based upon the concept of the *cancer stem cell*. When primary cancer cells are cultured in the laboratory, only a tiny fraction of them are capable of extensive cell division, while the vast majority fail to proliferate. The cancer *stem cell* model accounts for this heterogeneity by postulating that each cancer consists of a small population of cells capable of unlimited growth and self-renewal, known as cancer stem cells, and a much larger population of cells, descendants of the cancer stem cells, that have lost self-renewal capacity. Experimental evidence for the existence of cancer stem cells has been described in several malignancies including acute leukemia, breast cancer, and brain cancer. The cancer stem cell model has important implications for cancer therapy—eradication of cancer stem cells, the cells responsible for maintenance of the neoplasm, would be necessary and sufficient to achieve cure. Even more fundamentally, the cancer stem cell model suggests that cancer arises not from "de-differentiation" of a terminally differentiated epithelial cell, but rather from accumulation of mutations in a long-lived normal stem cell. Cancer may therefore be considered a disease of the *aging stem cell* (Reya, Morrison, Clarke, & Weissman, 2001).

Molecular biology continues to make enormous contributions to our understanding of the regulation of normal cell proliferation and the genetic and molecular bases of cancer and aging. The idea of genome maintenance, the role that telomeres play in it, and the molecular basis of cell immortalization join earlier discoveries in *oncogene sequencing*, human *DNA proto-oncogene activation*, and *tumor suppressor genes* (and their mutation as *anti-oncogenes*) in helping us understand the critical balance between positive and negative regulators of cell division. That aspects of *phenotypic aging* might occur as a result of means to prevent uncontrolled cell proliferation is both a humbling and exciting prospect, one that is bound to inspire further research on the fundamentals of cell division and its regulation.

ANNA M. MCCORMICK
HUBER R. WARNER
DAVID B. FINKELSTEIN
Updated by KENNETH ROCKWOOD

See also
Cancer Control

References

Ahmed, A., & Tollefsbol, T. (2003). Telomeres, telomerase, and telomerase inhibition: Clinical implications for cancer. *Journal of the American Geriatrics Society*, *51*, 116–122.

Bodnar, A. G., Ouellette, M., Frolkis, M., et al. (1998). Extension of life span by introduction of telomerase into normal human cells. *Science*, *279*, 349–352.

Campisi, J. (2005). Aging, tumor suppression and cancer: High wire-act! *Mechanisms of Ageing and Development*, *126*, 51–58.

Chan, S. R., & Blackburn, E. H. Telomeres and telomerase. (2004). *Philosophical Transactions of the Royal Society of London Series B Biological Sciences*, *359*, 109–121.

Denduluri, N., & Ershler, W. B. (2004). Aging biology and cancer. *Seminars in Oncology*, *31*, 137–148.

Hayflick, L. (1965). The limited in vitro lifetime of human diploid cell strains. *Experimental Cell Research*, *37*, 614–636.

Hursting, S. D., Lavigne, J. A., Berrigan, D., Perkins, S. N., & Barrett, J. C. (2003). Calorie restriction, aging, and cancer prevention: Mechanisms of action and applicability to humans. *Annual Review of Medicine*, *54*, 131–152.

Kelland, L. R. (2001). Telomerase: Biology and phase I trials. *Lancet Oncology*, *2*, 95–102.

Kinzler, K. W., & Vogelstein, B. (1996). Lessons from hereditary colorectal cancer. *Cell*, *87*, 159–170.

Kirkwood, T. B., & Rose, M. R. (1991). Evolution of senescence: late life survival sacrifices for reproduction. *Philosophical Transactions of the Royal Society of London, B Biological Science, 332*, 15–24.

Lichtman, M. A., & Rowe, J. M. (2004). The relationship of patient age to the pathobiology of the clonal myeloid diseases. *Seminars in Oncology*, *31*, 185–197.

Longo, V. D., & Finch, C. E. (2003). Evolutionary medicine: From dwarf model systems to healthy centenarians? *Science*, *299*, 1342–1346.

Medawar, P. B. (1952). *An Unsolved Problem of Biology*. London: H.K. Lewis.

Nicolas, A. S., Lanzmann-Petithory, D., & Vellas, B. (1999). Caloric restriction and aging. *Journal of Nutrition, Health and Aging*, *3*, 77–83.

Reya, T., Morrison, S. J., Clarke, M. F., & Weissman, I. L. (2001). Stem cells, cancer, and cancer stem cells. *Nature*, *414*(6859), 105–111.

Rodier, F., Kim, S. H., Nijjar, T., Yaswen, P., & Campisi, J. (2005). Cancer and aging: The importance of telomeres in genome maintenance. *International Journal of Biochemistry and Cell Biology*, *37*, 977–990.

Ronquist, G., & Nilsson, B. O. (2004). The Janus-faced nature of prostasomes: Their pluripotency favors the normal reproductive process and malignant prostate growth. *Prostate Cancer and Prostatic Diseases*, *7*, 21–31.

Roth, G. S., Mattison, J. A., Ottinger, M. A., Chachich, M. E., Lane, M. A., & Ingram, D. K. (2004). Aging in rhesus monkeys: Relevance to human health interventions. *Science*, *305*, 1423–1426.

Wells, R. A., Germino, G. G., Krishna, S., Buckle, V. J., & Reeders, S. T. (1990). Telomere-related sequences at interstitial sites in the human genome. *Genomics*, *8*, 699–704.

Yaswen, P., & Stampfer, M. R. (2002). Molecular changes accompanying senescence and immortalization of cultured human mammary epithelial cells. *International Journal of Biochemistry and Cell Biology*, *34*, 1382–1394.

CANCER CONTROL

Cancer control involves primary and secondary cancer prevention, with the goal of reducing cancer-related morbidity and mortality. Primary prevention includes elimination of environmental carcinogens and arrest or *reversal of carcinogenesis* with drugs (*chemoprevention*). Secondary prevention includes early detection of cancer by screening individuals at risk (Beghe & Balducci, 2005).

Age is the major risk factors for all common cancers, and cancer is the major cause of mortality for the American population under age 86 (Jemal, Murray, & Ward, et al., 2005). Cancer prevention would be particularly beneficial for individuals aged 65 to 85, who account for 50% of all malignancies (Yancik & Ries, 2004). However, reduced life expectancy (Carey, Walter, & Lindquist, et al., 2004), higher prevalence of more indolent tumors, and increased susceptibility to the complications of surgery may lessen the benefits of cancer prevention. Thus, cancer control strategies should be individualized and focused on older individuals who are more likely to benefit from them according to life expectancy and treatment tolerance (Beghe & Balducci, 2005).

Epidemiology highlights the importance of cancer prevention in older individuals:

- Common cancers, especially *breast cancer*, affect preferentially healthy older individuals who would live even longer if they had not developed cancer (Beghe & Balducci, 2005)
- Though breast cancer is more indolent in older patients, the stage at diagnosis is more advanced in the aged, suggesting underutilization of preventative measures (Beghe & Balducci, 2005)
- The complications of advanced cancer treatment, especially of cytotoxic chemotherapy, are more common and more severe at age 65 years and older, making cancer prevention all the more desirable (Cova & Balducci, 2004).
- New epidemiologic trends indicate promising areas of research in cancer control. For example, the median age of persons with lung cancer has progressively risen since 1950, and currently is 71 (Wingo, Cardinez, & Landis, et al., 2003). It appears that most lung cancer in older individuals occurs in ex-smokers, is more indolent than in younger persons, and may be cured by early diagnosis and local treatment.

Primary Prevention

Carcinogenesis is a step-wise process that transforms a normal cell into a neoplastic one through a number of genetic changes effected by different substances called carcinogens (Anisimov, 2005). *Aging and carcinogenesis* share a number of molecular events: one reason that the incidence and prevalence of cancer increase with age is that older tissues are more susceptible to environmental carcinogens than younger tissues. These data suggest that primary cancer prevention may be most effective in elderly people.

Elimination of environmental carcinogens. The most common environmental carcinogen in the Western world is tobacco smoke; the recent drop in cancer-related mortality in the United States (Jemal, et al., 2005) may be ascribed in part to *smoking cessation*. Importantly, one is never too old to quit smoking. Smoking cessation leads to reduced risk of cancer of the lung, the upper airways, the pancreas, and the urothelium, and to improvement in atherosclerosis and chronic respiratory diseases. Exercise and limited intake of alcohol and calories, especially fat-related calories, may also be beneficial, though the effects of these lifestyle changes on the incidence and prevalence of cancer are more difficult to quantify.

Chemoprevention. Clinical studies have demonstrated that 4 groups of substances reduce the risk of common cancers (Beghe & Balducci, 2005). The clinical indications of chemoprevention are not well defined however, due to the risk of treatment complications and a lack of evidence that chemoprevention improves survival.

Selective Estrogen Receptor Modulators (SERMs), such as *tamoxifen* and *raloxifene*, reduce the incidence of breast cancer by almost 50%, but they have not reduced breast cancer-related mortality and cause severe side effects, the risk of which increases for those age 70 and older. The complications of both drugs include hot flashes, vaginal secretions, dysuria, deep vein thrombosis, and arterial thrombo-embolisms. Tamoxifen has been associated with a two- to threefold increased risk of endometrial cancer. In a decision analysis, a 70-year-old woman may benefit from SERMs chemoprevention only if her risk of breast cancer over the following 5 years is 7% or higher.

Finsteride inhibits the enzyme *5-α reductase* and reduces by approximately 30% the risk of *prostate cancer* in an older man. As in the case of SERMs, it has not reduced the mortality from prostate cancer. In addition, there is some concern that finsteride might enhance the risk of poorly differentiated and more aggressive prostate cancer. Side effects of finsteride include gynecomastia, hot flushes, and loss of libido.

Retinoic acid has reduced the risk of smoking-related cancer in the upper airways, but the toxicity of this substance makes its use prohibitive, especially in older individuals.

Both *COX1 and COX2 inhibitors* have caused a reduction in mortality from *colon cancer*, and in the size and the number of precancerous polyps. However, concerns about the cardiovascular safety of these drugs may prevent future studies of chemoprevention. In addition, the same doses of aspirin associated with a reduction in coronary death appear effective in reducing the incidence of colorectal cancer, but it is not clear whether these doses are optimal.

While at present chemoprevention does not appear to be viable for older individuals, it may have a role in the near future. Promising agents of chemoprevention include the lipid-lowering *statins* for cancer of the large bowel and of the breast, the *aromatase inhibitors* for breast cancer, and the new and more powerful 5-α reductase inhibitor *dusteride* for prostate cancer.

Secondary Prevention

Three assumptions support the benefits of *early cancer detection*: (1) cancer undergoes a prolonged preclinical phase, (2) it is diagnosable during the preclinical phase by screening individuals at risk, and (3) early diagnosis of cancer leads to improved curability (Beghe & Balducci, 2005). We will review common screening strategies and their relevance to older individuals.

Breast Cancer. Serial *mammography* has reduced by 20% to 30% the breast cancer mortality for women aged 50 to 70 years. Of 8 randomized controlled studies only 2 involved women aged 70 to 75 years, and none involved women over age 75. The benefits of screening mammography in women over 70 were inferred by 2 reviews of the Medicare-linked Surveillance, Epidemiology and End Results (SEER) data, which showed that women who had undergone at least 2 screening mammographies between ages 70 to 79 years experienced a reduction in breast cancer mortality (Beghe & Balducci, 2005). Though circumstantial, this is the best level of evidence achievable. Imaging technology is changing rapidly, and the results of randomized controlled studies with current technology would be obsolete by the time the studies are concluded. Based on current information, it appears reasonable to recommend screening mammography for all women with a life expectancy of 5 more years or greater, as the first benefits of breast cancer screening are seen after 5 years.

The main objections to screening older women for breast cancer include cost and inconvenience. These may be addressed with various approaches:

- Biennial mammography may be sufficient. It has never been proven that annual examinations yield better results than biennial ones, and this may be particularly true for older women, whose breast cancer experiences a slower growth.
- Examinations may be limited to women at a higher risk of breast cancer, including those with a previous history of cancer or those with the highest bone density. At present, this approach is only theoretical and needs to be validated by clinical trials.

- The value of *clinical breast examination* by a physician or a nurse should be explored. In previous studies clinical breast examination appeared as sensitive as mammography in detecting invasive breast cancer.
- New imaging techniques, such as *breast MRI* or *digital mammography*, may prove more sensitive than standard mammography and may be required less frequently.

Cancer of the Large Bowel. Randomized and controlled studies demonstrated that serial examinations of stool for *fecal occult blood* decreased the mortality of *colorectal cancer* for persons aged 50 to 80 years. Though less effective than annual examinations, biennial examinations are also acceptable. Retrospective studies suggest that endoscopic screening also improves the mortality of patients with cancer of the large bowel. Of the various options, a full *colonoscopy* every 10 years for individuals aged 50 years and older appears to be the most cost effective. As in the case of breast cancer, it appears reasonable to institute some form of screening for colorectal cancers for all individuals with a 5-year or more life expectancy, irrespective of chronologic age.

Prostate Cancer. Though serial determinations of circulating levels of *prostate-specific antigen* lead to early diagnosis of prostate cancer, it has never been conclusively demonstrated that early diagnosis reduces cancer-related mortality. For this reason, the value of screening asymptomatic men for prostate cancer is controversial. Screening definitely appears unnecessary in individuals with a life expectancy shorter than 10 or 15 years, as the benefits of treatment in these men have not been demonstrated.

Lung Cancer. In the 1970s, 3 studies comparing a yearly chest radiograph with a chest radiograph and sputum cytology in smokers failed to reduce the mortality of this disease. This issue needs to be revisited given the changing epidemiology of lung cancer, which currently occurs preferentially in otherwise healthy former smokers and is more indolent. In addition, computerized tomography technology is more sensitive than plain radiographs to small lung lesions and more likely to detect curable disease. Until ongoing clinical trials are completed, however, screening of former smokers for lung cancer should be limited to the research setting.

Cervical Cancer. Although the incidence of cervical cancer decreases with age, the mortality for *metastatic cervical cancer* has been increasing among older women. It is difficult to establish whether increased mortality is due to inadequate screening or to a completely different biology of the disease in older and younger individuals. It appears reasonable to recommend serial *Papanicolaou screening* for women aged 60 years and older who had not undergone regular screening, especially those who are sexually active.

Special Issues for Prevention in Older Adults

Endpoints of clinical trials. It is customary to judge the effectiveness of a preventative technique by its ability to reduce the mortality of a specific cancer in randomized controlled trials (Beghe & Balducci, 2005). Other endpoints, such as more prolonged survival for individuals undergoing screening, or diagnosis of cancer at an earlier stage in the screened population, are fraught with biases of lead time, length time, and overdetection. In addition, only a reduction of cancer-specific mortality may justify the risks and the economic and time investments of cancer prevention. It should be emphasized that the risks are not trivial and include the complications of agents used for chemoprevention, unnecessary surgery, and anguish from the results of screening. These complications are more common and more severe for older individuals, who also gain less from prevention due to more limited life expectancy. Yet a decline in *cancer-related mortality* may not be a realistic endpoint of prevention studies in older individuals; other endpoints should be explored, not to risk missing some real benefit of prevention. As preservation of function is essential to independence and quality of life, and is an important component of survival of older individuals, functional preservation may represent a more realistic endpoint for clinical trials.

Barriers to cancer prevention: A number of barriers have been identified to cancer prevention in the older person that are both patient- and provider-related (Beghe & Balducci, 2005). Ageism—that is, the misconception that older individuals do not benefit from preventative interventions—is pervasive and concerns the patients, their families, and their providers. In the case of the provider, ageism is translated as a lack of support for cancer prevention, which confirms patients and families in their prejudice. An intensive operation of public and professional education may overcome this impasse. New ways to assess life expectancy and cancer risks may help focus prevention on patients who need it most, and favor an individualized, more cost- and time-effective approach.

Conclusion

From this review, it may be concluded:

1. Nobody who is still functional is too old to benefit from cancer-preventative lifestyle changes.
2. Chemoprevention of some cancer in older individuals may become a reality in the next decade or so. There is evidence that commonly used drugs, such as statins and aspirin, to some extent may prevent cancers of the large bowel and the breast.
3. Individuals with a life expectancy of at least 5 years may benefit from regular screening for breast and colorectal cancer. The benefit of screening older ex-smokers for lung cancer remains to be confirmed. Screening may be made more user-friendly and time- and cost-effective.
4. To optimize the benefits of prevention, functional preservation should be considered as an endpoint of clinical trials. In addition, effective means should be found to overcome ageism among both patients and providers.

LODOVICO BALDUCCI

See also
Cancer

References

Anisimov, M. (2005). Biologic interactions of aging and carcinogenesis. In L. Balducci, & M. Extermann, *Biological basis of geriatric oncology* (pp. 17–50). New York: Springer Publishing.

Beghe, C., & Balducci, L. (2005). Biological basis of cancer in the older person. In L. Balducci, & M. Extermann, *Biological basis of geriatric oncology* (pp. 189–221). New York: Springer Publishing.

Carey, E. C., Walter, L. C., & Lindquist, K., et al. (2004). Development and validation of a functional morbidity index to predict mortality in community-dwelling elderly. *Journal of General Internal Medicine, 19*, 1027–1033.

Cova, D., & Balducci, L. (2004). Cancer chemotherapy in the older patient. In L. Balducci, G. H. Lyman, W. B. Ershler, & M. Extermann, *Comprehensive geriatric oncology* (pp. 463–488). London: Taylor & Francis.

Jemal, A., Murray, T., & Ward, E., et al. (2005). Cancer statistics, *2005CA Cancer Journal for Clinicians, 55*(1), 10–30.

Wingo, P. A., Cardinez, C. J., & Landis, S. H., et al. (2003). Long-term trends in cancer mortality in the United States, 1930–1998. *Cancer, 97*(S21), 3133–3275.

Yancik, R., & Ries, L. A. (2004). Cancer in older patients: An international issue in an aging world. *Seminars in Oncology, 31*, 128–136.

CANCER PREVENTION

See
Cancer Control

CARBOHYDRATE METABOLISM

Aging is associated with altered regulation of carbohydrate metabolism. The most significant clinical manifestation of altered carbohydrate metabolism, the syndrome of diabetes mellitus, is a growing health problem among the elderly. Diabetes in the elderly is most commonly associated with a stable elevation of blood glucose levels both after an overnight fast and following ingestion of a meal. This condition is often termed noninsulin dependent diabetes mellitus (NIDDM), but the American Diabetes Association has recently recommended that this terminology be replaced with type 2 diabetes (American Diabetes Association, 1999). The elevation of blood glucose levels with type 2 diabetes is not immediately life-threatening and does not usually require insulin therapy. However, type 2 diabetes is associated with a number of long-term complications, including accelerated atherosclerosis, kidney failure, nerve damage, and disturbances in vision.

The problem of overt diabetes represents only the tip of the iceberg of the abnormality of glucose and insulin dynamics in the elderly. Many studies have demonstrated that aging is associated with a more subtle abnormality characterized by a delay in the return of blood glucose to basal values following glucose ingestion (Davidson, 1979). Insulin resistance refers to a condition in which a given amount of insulin elicits a subnormal biological effect. Most older people with type 2 diabetes are insulin resistant, and even many older people who are not diabetic are insulin resistant. Independent of glucose tolerance status (i.e., the ability to lower glycemia after an oral glucose load), insulin resistance has been implicated as a risk factor in the development of atherosclerosis (Howard, O'Leary, Zaccaro, Haffner, Rewers, Hamman, et al., 1996).

Pathophysiology of Glucose Regulation in Aging

Skeletal muscle, liver, and adipose tissue are important insulin-sensitive tissues for regulating blood glucose concentration. Even in the absence of diabetes, each of these tissues may become insulin resistant in older people (Muller, Elahi, Tobin, & Andrew, 1996). Skeletal muscle is quantitatively the most important tissue for insulin-stimulated glucose disposal. The rate of glucose transport into the muscle cell is a critical, rate-controlling step for skeletal muscle glucose metabolism (Holman & Kasuga, 1997).

At the cellular level, insulin's binding to the insulin receptor leads to activation of the receptor's tyrosine kinase, which in turn phosphorylates several intracellular proteins, including the insulin receptor substrate (IRS) proteins (Holman & Kasuga, 1997). The tyrosine phosphorylated IRS proteins (in skeletal muscle, IRS-1 and IRS-2 are expressed) bind to downstream signaling proteins, including phosphatidylinositol-3-kinase (PI3-kinase). This enzyme is crucial for insulin-stimulated translocation of intracellular GLUT4 glucose transporter proteins to the cell surface and thereby increasing the glucose transport rate.

Skeletal muscle levels of GLUT4 are not greatly influenced by advancing age during adulthood (Houmard, Weidner, Dolan, Leggett-Frazier, Gavigan, Hickey, et al., 1995). This finding suggests that, rather than low GLUT4 abundance, the insulin resistance is attributable to a reduced ability of insulin to cause the GLUT4 glucose transporter to move from the cell interior to the cell surface, where it can facilitate glucose uptake. The precise molecular reason for the putative reduction in GLUT4 translocation is unknown.

Studies with experimental animals have clearly demonstrated an age-related impairment of function of the pancreatic B cells that secrete insulin (Reaven & Reaven, 1981). In elderly humans insulin levels during oral glucose tolerance tests tend to be relatively normal (Davidson, 1979), although interpretation of such responses is difficult because of the higher glucose levels during the test in the elderly. When this is taken into account, it appears that impaired B-cell adaptation to insulin resistance also plays a role in the age-related deterioration of glucose tolerance (Chen, Bergman, Pacini, & Porte, 1985). Circulating insulin concentration is determined by both insulin secretion and insulin clearance. Some, but not all, studies have indicated that, in addition to abnormal insulin secretion, insulin clearance rate is attenuated in older people (Muller, Elahi, Tobin, & Andres, 1996).

A number of potential mechanisms could be contributing to the age-related impairment of B-cell function or tissue insensitivity to insulin. Morphological studies of pancreatic islets suggest the presence of age-related B-cell damage (Reaven & Reaven, 1981). Reduced carbohydrate in the diet, which has been reported in some studies of dietary patterns of the elderly, also can result in diminished insulin secretion or carbohydrate intolerance.

Role of Lifestyle in Age-Related Changes in Glucoregulation and Insulin Action

Lifestyle plays a pivotal role in age-related insulin resistance. Increased adiposity in elderly subjects appears to be a critical factor, because there is a close association between adiposity and insulin resistance. Chronic physical inactivity is associated with elevated abdominal fat stores and insulin resistance (Holloszy & Kohrt, 1995). In young and old people, regular exercise training can improve insulin sensitivity. This benefit is the result of several adaptations, including reduced fat mass and increased skeletal muscle GLUT4 protein levels. Independent of these chronic adaptations, a single bout of vigorous exercise can lead to enhanced insulin sensitivity for as long as a day after the activity (Holloszy & Kohrt, 1995). Many insulin-resistant older people can benefit from physical activity–induced improvements in insulin action. However, exercise is not usually effective in restoring glucose tolerance when there is a profound deficit in pancreatic B-cell function.

Reduced calorie intake can lead to improved insulin sensitivity and glucose homeostasis. Calorie restriction leads to weight loss, especially visceral fat loss, and this effect is likely important for improved insulin action (Holloszy & Kohrt, 1995). Studies with rats indicate that the diet-induced improvement in insulin action is attributable, at least in large part, to enhanced glucose transport in skeletal muscle because of greater translocation of GLUT4 in response to insulin (Dean, Brozinick, Cushman, & Cartee, 1998).

Despite the known benefits of altered lifestyle on body composition and insulin sensitivity, the recent trend for increased prevalence of obesity in many societies suggests that age-related glucose intolerance and insulin resistance will continue to be important health problems.

GREGORY D. CARTEE

See also
Diabetes

References

American Diabetes Association. (1999). Report of the expert committee on the diagnosis and classification of diabetes mellitus. *Diabetes Care*, *22*(Supplement 1), S5–S19.

Chen, M., Bergman, R. N., Pacini, G., & Porte Jr., D. (1985). Pathogenesis of age-related glucose intolerance in man: Insulin resistance and decreased beta-cell function. *Journal of Clinical Endocrinology and Metabolism*, *60*(1), 13–20.

Davidson, M. B. (1979). The effect of aging on carbohydrate metabolism: A review of the English literature and a practical approach to the diagnosis of diabetes mellitus in the elderly. *Metabolism*, *28*(6), 688–705.

Dean, D. J., Brozinick, J. T., Jr., Cushman, S. W., & Cartee, G. D. (1998). Calorie restriction increases cell surface GLUT4 in insulin-stimulated skeletal muscle. *American Journal of Physiology*, *275*, E957–E964.

Holloszy, J. O., & Kohrt, W. M. (1995). Exercise. In E. J. Masoro (Ed.), *Handbook of physiology: Aging* (sect. 11, pp. 633–666). New York: Oxford University Press.

Holman, G. D., & Kasuga, M. (1997). From receptor to transporter: Insulin signalling to glucose transport. *Diabetologia*, *40*, 991–1003.

Houmard, J. A., Weidner, M. D., Dolan, P. L., Leggett-Frazier, N., Gavigan, K. E., Hickey, M. S., Tyndall, G. L., Zheng, D., & Alshami, A. (1995). Skeletal muscle GLUT4 protein concentration and aging in humans. *Diabetes*, *44*, 555–560.

Howard, G., O'Leary, D. H., Zaccaro, D., Haffner, S., Rewers, M., Hamman, R., Selby, J. V., Saad, M. F., Savage, P., & Bergman, R. (1996). Insulin sensitivity and atherosclerosis. *Circulation*, *93*, 1809–1817.

Muller, D. C., Elahi, D., Tobin, J. D., & Andres, R. (1996). The effect of age on insulin resistance and secretion: A review. *Seminars in Nephrology*, *16*(4), 289–298.

Reaven, E. P., & Reaven, G. M. (1981). Structure and function changes in the endocrine pancreas of aging rats with reference to the modulating effects of exercise and caloric restriction. *Journal of Clinical Investigation*, *68*, 75–84.

CARDIOVASCULAR SYSTEM: HEART

A number of important changes in the structure and function of the human heart are thought to occur with aging. Whether these changes are the result of an adaptive process or whether they represent preclinical disease is a matter of debate. However, age-related changes in the structure and function of human hearts do occur in the absence of clinical signs of heart disease.

Cardiac Structure in the *Aging Heart*

The gross morphological structure of the heart changes with advancing age. One prominent modification in heart structure that occurs in aging is increased deposition of fat on the outer, epicardial surface of the heart. Calcium deposition (calcification) of specific regions of the heart also is common in aging. The atria increase in size, a process called hypertrophy; furthermore, the atria dilate and their volume increases with aging. While some studies have reported that the size and weight of the left ventricle increases with age, others have concluded that ventricular size does not increase with age if subjects with underlying heart disease are excluded. It does seem clear, however, that the thickness of the wall of the left ventricle increases progressively with age.

Alterations in *heart structure in aging* are apparent at the level of the individual heart cell. Beginning at age 60 there is a marked decline in the number of pacemaker cells in the sinoatrial node, which is the *pacemaker of the heart*. The actual number of cardiac muscle cells (myocytes) in the heart declines with age; indeed, the total population of myocytes in the heart declines by approximately 35% between the ages of 30 and 70 years. Interestingly, the remaining cardiac myocytes enlarge, or hypertrophy, as a function of advancing age. This cellular hypertrophy may compensate, at least in part, for *cell loss in aging*. In addition to the myocytes, the heart also contains large numbers of fibroblasts, which are cells that produce connective tissues such as collagen and elastin. As the number of myocytes declines with aging, the relative number of fibroblasts increases. Some studies also suggest that not only does the amount of collagen (a fibrous protein that holds heart cells together) increase with advancing age, but also that its properties may change in aging. The amount and/or properties of elastin, a connective tissue protein responsible for the elasticity of body tissues, also may be altered in aging. Alterations in connective tissues in the aging heart would be expected to affect cardiac function in aging, resulting, for example, in decreased elastic recoil in the heart. These changes largely combine to increase the work of the heart, although their effects are chiefly manifest not at rest but with exercise.

Cardiac Function in the *Aging Heart at Rest*

Significant age-associated changes in cardiac function occur in the hearts of older adults at rest. When individuals are reclining, heart rate is similar in younger and older subjects. However, when older individuals move from a supine to a seated position, heart rate increases less in older adults than in younger adults. This reduction in the ability to augment heart rate in response to positional change may be linked to age-related changes in the sympathetic nervous system. In contrast, left ventricular systolic function, which is a measure of the ability of the heart to contract, is well preserved at rest in older adults. Other measures of cardiac contractile function at rest also are unchanged with age. The volume of blood ejected from the ventricle per beat (stroke volume) is generally comparable or slightly elevated in older adults when compared to their younger counterparts. Similarly, the left ventricular ejection fraction, which is the ratio of the stroke volume to the volume of blood left in the ventricle at the end of diastole, is unchanged in aging. Thus, systolic function is relatively well preserved in healthy older adults at rest.

Unlike systolic function, diastolic function is altered in the hearts of older adults at rest. Indeed aging is associated with an increase in left ventricular diastolic stiffness, which causes reduced left ventricular compliance in aging. Furthermore, the rate of left ventricular filling in early diastole declines by up to 50% between the ages of 20 and 80 years. The mechanisms responsible for left ventricular filling are changed in aging. In the hearts of young adults, left ventricular filling occurs rapidly and is due primarily to ventricular relaxation, with only a small amount due to atrial contraction. In contrast, the rate of left ventricular filling slows in early diastole in the hearts of older adults, because left ventricular relaxation is slowed in aging and most of the filling is attributable to atrial contraction. Interestingly, although there is less filling in early diastole in the aging heart, there is more filling in late diastole. This is likely a consequence of the more forceful atrial contraction observed in the aging heart, which compensates for the reduced filling in early diastole.

Several mechanisms likely contribute to the reduction in left ventricular early diastolic filling rate in the aging heart. Age-associated structural changes in the left ventricle, such as an increase in the amount of connective tissue or a change its properties, may reduce early diastolic filling. Furthermore, residual calcium from the previous systole may cause persistent activation of contraction and delay relaxation in the aging heart. Despite this evidence for diastolic dysfunction, left ventricular end diastolic pressure does not decline with age in older healthy adults at rest. Indeed, aging is actually associated with a small increase in left ventricular end diastolic pressure, in particular in older males.

Thus, although the filling pattern in diastole is altered in aging, this does not lead to marked changes in end diastolic pressure in older hearts at rest.

Response of the *Aging Heart to Exercise*

Although cardiac function is relatively well preserved in aging hearts at rest, aging has major effects on cardiovascular performance during exercise. The VO_2 max, which is the greatest amount of oxygen that a person can use during exercise, declines progressively with age starting in early adulthood. The *age-related changes in maximum heart rate*, cardiac output, and stroke volume described below compromise delivery of blood to the muscles during exercise and contribute to this decline in VO_2 max in aging.

The maximum heart rate attained during exercise decreases gradually with age in humans. Interestingly, this decrease is not affected by physical conditioning, as it is present in both sedentary and fit individuals. Several mechanisms have been implicated in the reduction in maximum heart rate during exercise in aging. Normally, the sympathetic nervous system becomes activated during exercise and releases catecholamines (norepinephrine and epinephrine) to act on beta-adrenergic receptors in the heart. This beta-adrenergic stimulation leads to an increase in heart rate and in the strength of heart contraction. However, it is well established that the responsiveness of the heart to sympathetic stimulation declines in aging, and this limits maximum heart rate during exercise. In addition, the age-associated decline in the number of sinoatrial *pacemaker cells* and the increase in elastin and collagen in the conducting system of the heart may impair the response of the heart to sympathetic stimulation during exercise.

The decrease in maximal heart rate during *exercise in aging* has an impact on the response of the cardiovascular system to exercise. A number of studies have shown that cardiac output during exercise is lower in older adults compared to their younger counterparts. As cardiac output is determined by both heart rate and stroke volume, the decrease in maximum heart rate during exercise would be expected to lead to a reduction in cardiac output during exercise in older adults. There also is some evidence that stroke volume during peak exercise is reduced in aging, although this is controversial. The decrease in *stroke volume in aging* is thought to arise as a result of the reduction in the ability of catecholamines to increase the strength of contraction in the aging heart. As stroke volume is a major determinant of cardiac output, a reduction in stroke volume during exercise also would contribute to the age-related reduction in cardiac output in exercise. These changes in cardiovascular function are thought to be mitigated, at least in part, by an age-associated increase in end-diastolic volume during exercise, which increases the amount of blood in the ventricle at the end of diastole and the stretch on the heart. It is well established that an increase in the amount of blood in the ventricle at the end of diastole results in an increase in the strength of heart contraction, a property known as the Frank Starling mechanism. Thus, an increase in the reliance on the *Frank Starling mechanism in aging* may compensate in part for the decrease in heart rate and stroke volume during exercise.

Summary

The structure and function of the human heart changes as a result of aging, even in the absence of clinical signs of heart disease. Whether these alterations result from adaptation or whether they represent preclinical disease is not yet clear. Although the impact of these changes on cardiovascular function at rest is minimal, they impair cardiovascular performance during exercise. Additional information on this topic can be found in a number of excellent recent reviews: Lakatta & Sollott, 2002; Lakatta & Levy, 2003; Oxenham & Sharpe, 2003.

SUSAN E. HOWLETT

See also
Cardiovascular System: Overview

References

Lakatta, E. G., & Sollott, S. J. (2002). Perspectives on mammalian cardiovascular aging: Humans to molecules. *Comparative Biochemistry and Physiology. Part A. Molecular and Integrative Physiology*, *132*, 699–721.

Lakatta, E. G., & Levy, D. (2003). Arterial and cardiac aging: Major shareholders in cardiovascular disease enterprises. Part II: The aging heart in health: Links to heart disease. *Circulation*, *107*, 346–354.

Oxenham, H., & Sharpe, N. (2003). Cardiovascular aging and heart failure. *European Journal of Heart Failure*, *5*, 427–434.

CARDIOVASCULAR SYSTEM: OVERVIEW

The cardiovascular system includes all of the blood vessels throughout the body and the heart, which provides the force necessary to move blood through the system. The effects of aging on this system are often confused with diseases and the effects of inactivity or *deconditioning*. Diseases of the cardiovascular system are the leading cause of death throughout the nation: it is estimated that 40% of individuals over the age of 65 die of heart disease, and 15% of deaths in the aged are attributed to strokes. Both represent malfunctions within the cardiovascular system. Intense effort is focused on understanding cardiovascular diseases in an attempt to control illness and to preserve functioning of individuals until late in life.

Components of the Cardiovascular System

Arteries are relatively thick-walled tubes that carry blood away from the heart. A branching network of vessels carries blood to tissues throughout the body where the arteries terminate in extremely small vessels called capillaries. The *capillaries* are microscopic in size, barely large enough for the passage of one blood cell at a time. Their walls are extremely thin, permitting transfer of nutrients and waste products between the blood within the capillary and surrounding tissues. The capillaries eventually join together and terminate in larger vessels called veins, which collect the blood and return it to the heart. *Veins* are relatively thin-walled when compared with arteries but still contain muscle cells within their walls that permit contraction and expansion of the vessel size. As will be seen later, this contributes to the body's ability to adjust the system capacity as needed. The purpose of the *circulation system* is to permit the collection of nutrients from ingested food and body stores and transport them to tissues in need of sustenance. By-products of the energy production process are carried away by the blood and discarded through the lungs and kidneys. *Body temperature* is preserved through heat retention or radiation, by diverting blood to surface areas of extremities where heat is lost or by retaining blood circulation within the body core, thus preserving heat.

The heart provides *blood movement*. This organ represents 2 pumps in a single package. Each pump has 2 chambers: an atrium and a ventricle, each of which contributes to pump performance. The right side of the heart receives blood returning from body tissues and forwards it to the lungs at a low pressure. In the lungs, oxygen is received and carbon dioxide eliminated. Blood returns from the lungs to the left side of the heart where it is sent throughout the body at a relatively high pressure. Hormones secreted into the blood stream are moved to target organs where they induce various reactions. Nutrients from the intestine are transported to the liver for processing and then to body stores or tissues for metabolism. Wastes are moved to the kidneys and discarded in urine. Heat generated in this process is dissipated through the passage of warm blood through skin in the extremities where radiation or sweat evaporation provides needed cooling. All this is accomplished involuntarily.

The regulation of this remarkable system is exceedingly complex. Constant adjustments are being made to compensate for changes in workload, alterations in position, changing thermal demands, shifts in emotions, dietary intake, or trauma. The result of regulation is a precisely metered flow to vital organs in response to their need. Sensors detect changes in flow, pressure, temperature, metabolic components, and fluid composition, which are then balanced through system adjustments. Variations in heart rate and muscle tone in artery and vein walls and variable fluid reabsorption and excretion of blood components permit a careful balance of the system in the face of repeated environmental challenges. Even in the face of extreme conditions, a remarkable degree of balance is achieved.

Normal Aging

With the passage of time, elastin within the arterial walls changes somewhat. It becomes less resilient and somewhat elongated. Calcium deposition may occur where none was previously evident. The result is a loss of elasticity and slight elongation of arteries resulting in tortuosity. Heart valves become less flexible. Some circulation shifts occur in blood flow as tissues decline in function. Kidney flow is substantially reduced. However, flow to the head and heart remains virtually constant throughout life. A rise in blood pressure occurs in part due to loss of arterial elasticity with resultant failure to absorb the peak pressure generated by each heartbeat. Instead, the pulse is transmitted throughout the system as a rapid high pressure wave.

Heart changes with age are modest. A slight increase in the size of the heart muscle is attributed partly to higher arterial pressures. Loss of valve flexibility causes blood turbulence with subsequent creation of murmurs. The maximum *heart rate declines with age*, yielding loss of some reserve. This is compensated in part by a dilation of the heart with exercise, allowing more blood to enter the heart and a higher percentage of blood ejection per beat, resulting in little loss of performance throughout life. In the absence of disease, cardiovascular performance is capable of remaining excellent throughout life.

Cardiovascular Diseases

Atherosclerosis is the major problem affecting the cardiovascular system. Atheromatous plaques, which progressively restrict flow, develop within the interior lining of arteries. The plaques are composed of inflammatory cells, muscle cells, fat, and calcium. Initially evident as small streaks of yellow discoloration within arterial walls seen in early life, the problem progresses until large areas of arterial wall are covered with thickened plaques in later years.

The cause of atherosclerosis is not fully understood. Age and genetic background are important. Males are more prone to the disease than females. Smoking substantially escalates atheromatous change, as does uncontrolled hypertension. Persons suffering from blood lipid abnormalities, diabetes, and obesity are known to suffer increased disease frequency. *Personality factors* (*Type A*) also have been thought to be associated with accelerated atheromatous degeneration.

Vessel narrowing effectively reduces flow capacity. Initially, no effect is evident because the flow rate may still equal peak demand. Later, in stress situations, flow will be inadequate and symptoms develop. Late in the disease, symptoms will be evident at rest. Common clinical syndromes associated with atherosclerosis include leg pain when walking, the result of inadequate nutrient flow to leg muscles. Surgery can sometimes reopen narrowed vessels. On occasion, vessel replacement with grafts taken from elsewhere in the body or the use of synthetic materials may be necessary. When heart vessels are narrowed, chest pain (angina pectoris) may occur on exertion. Brief episodes of thinking problems, paralysis, or sensory disorders may be evident when *brain circulation* is compromised. When blood clots form at the site of narrowing, complete block of the artery can occur. Occasionally, small clots will form on the surface of plaques and break free to drift downstream (emboli). As the arterial system narrows, these clots will lodge and block circulation. A toe may suddenly turn blue. Occasionally, a foot or leg may be deprived of circulation by such events. When blockage occurs in arteries supplying the heart, a *heart attack* (*myocardial infarction*) will occur. *Blockage in brain circulation* results in a *stroke* (cerebral infarction). Medications can sometimes reestablish flow. Often there is no alternative but to await spontaneous recovery or development of alternative circulation routes around the blocked artery.

Aneurysms represent a weakness within arterial walls with subsequent bulging. Aging, hypertension, and a small number of inherited diseases have been associated with this condition. As a result of such events, the artery wall becomes stretched beyond its usual dimensions and is subject to rupture, commonly resulting in death. In its mildest form, no treatment is necessary. If life-threatening enlargement occurs, surgical replacement of the vessel using a synthetic graft is possible.

Venous diseases are fairly common among elderly persons. *Varicosities* (dilated and tortuous veins) are caused by nonfunctioning valves that normally direct blood flow back toward the heart. Genetic causes are usually suspected as the underlying problem. In many situations, varicose veins present purely cosmetic difficulties, and no treatment is required. If moderate or severely tortuous veins are present, skin deterioration and ulcer formation can occur. *Elastic support stockings* are extremely helpful in promoting normal blood return to the heart. Sometimes surgical removal of veins is helpful.

Phlebitis or *thrombophlebitis* is a term used to describe the formation of clots within veins, which subsequently become inflamed. Causes include *coagulation disorders* within the circulating blood system, local trauma, or inactivity. Failure to move extremities for prolonged periods results in sluggish blood flow and can promote clotting. Veins involved in clotting may become tender and firm to the touch, making diagnosis easy. Sometimes veins deep within the legs, arms, or pelvis will become clotted. Symptoms tend to be nonspecific, such as swelling of an extremity or mild fever. The diagnosis can be established with contrast *venography* or color *doppler sonography*. Prevention involves regular physical activity to promote normal circulation, and avoiding long episodes of sitting in a chair or lying without motion. Elastic support hose will improve venous return and minimize chances of coagulation. Individuals placed at bed rest may require anticoagulants to reduce the chance of phlebitis formation.

Pulmonary emboli can occur when *deep venous thrombosis* (DVT) subsequently breaks free and drifts back to the lung (embolization) after passing through the right side of the heart. Small clots cause little problem, as ample reserve circulation exists to bypass blocked lung vessels. If large numbers of clots break free or a single large clot enters the lung circulation, life-threatening blockage can result. The body is capable of dissolving clots and reestablishing circulation, provided serious flow disruption does not occur. Diagnosis of this condition can be exceedingly difficult because symptoms are vague and nonspecific. Anticoagulants are sometimes effective in reducing clot formation and subsequent *embolization* during the healing process.

Heart valves can be damaged by a variety of mechanisms resulting in *heart murmurs*, which are due to turbulent blood flow across a valve. Flow can be blocked by failure of the valve to properly open. Valve leakage with blood backflow is possible when leaflets fail to properly seal. *Valve replacement* may be required to reestablish normal flow patterns through the heart. Valve damage can also occur when bacteria lodge on their surface, resulting in local destruction and valve dysfunction (*bacterial endocarditis*). Bacteria cast into the bloodstream from valve infections can spread throughout the body and present a host of confusing symptoms for the diagnostician. This condition requires intensive antibiotic therapy, and often replacement with a synthetic valve is necessary. For this reason anyone with a heart murmur should be considered for antibiotic therapy during diagnostic and surgical procedures associated with transient bacteria in the bloodstream, such as dental procedures and colonoscopy. Individuals with synthetic valves are at particular risk for developing bacterial endocarditis.

Angina pectoris occurs when arterial narrowing prevents satisfactory flow to heart muscle. The patient experiences chest pain or pressure, which spreads to the arms or jaw, commonly on the left side. Symptoms may be more vague in older adults, such as extreme fatigue or shortness of breath. Exercise aggravates the pain, and rest relieves it. Medications that limit cardiac response to exercise or alter blood circulation flow throughout the body can relieve symptoms. No heart muscle damage occurs, and each symptom episode is usually short-lived.

Myocardial infarction, commonly know as heart attack, is a more serious manifestation of arterial narrowing that results in heart muscle death, when an atherosclerotic plaque ruptures and a clot forms. At the time of muscle injury, some individuals may be totally unaware that a problem exists. Diabetics are particularly susceptible to such silent events owing to changes in their nervous system. Some individuals may suspect they are suffering "heartburn." Many elderly persons will manifest confusion, stomach upset, or weakness as their only symptoms. When severe, crushing, and prolonged chest pain occurs associated with nausea, myocardial infarction is extremely likely. An *electrocardiogram* and measurement of enzymes within the bloodstream can provide definitive evidence of muscle damage. Treatment may involve *thrombolytic agents* to dissolve the clot or emergent revascularization with *balloon angioplasty* and stent placement or *coronary artery bypass graph surgery*. Early mobilization rather than bed rest is now advocated following myocardial infarction. This does not interfere with healing and helps to prevent orthostatic symptoms, thromboembolic complications, and musculoskeletal deconditioning. An outpatient *cardiac rehabilitation program* is generally recommended. Repeated infarction results in replacement of heart muscle with fibrous tissue and subsequent severe performance limitations.

Congestive heart failure is a syndrome characterized by cough, shortness of breath, and poor exercise tolerance. Sluggish flow through the lungs leads to fluid accumulation, with a characteristic cough and change in breath sounds heard through a stethoscope. Fluid may accumulate in feet and legs, giving a swollen, bloated appearance. Occasionally fluid accumulation can progress to include the torso and body organs. Poor exercise tolerance is an inevitable result of decreased pumping ability of heart muscle. There are many causes of congestive heart failure. Atherosclerotic heart disease and myocardial infarction can damage the heart muscle, leading to dilation of the heart and decreased pumping ability. Untreated hypertension can lead to a thickening of the heart muscle, which compromises the ability of the heart to fill with blood, again limiting the pumping ability. It is estimated that 30% of individuals aged 90 have suffered deposits of a material called *amyloid* within heart muscle, which reduces performance substantially; these deposits are especially common in the presence of chronic diseases such as *rheumatoid arthritis*. Viral illness can also sometimes seriously deteriorate heart muscle performance. *Heart muscle disease* of all types reduces pump performance, causing symptoms of congestive heart failure. Another common cause of congestive heart failure is a particular arrhythmia called *atrial fibrillation*, in which the pumping ability of the atria is lost and the heart functions with contraction of only the ventricles. Treatment of congestive heart failure includes fluid elimination by means of *diuretics*. Blood pressure and arterial resistance may be altered with a variety of new medications that have yielded outstanding symptom control. In the most serious cases of congestive heart failure, *heart transplantation* may be necessary.

Arrhythmia (*irregular heartbeat*) is an exceedingly common problem in older persons. The normal smooth sequential spread of electric activity throughout the heart chambers activating muscle contraction is interrupted. Absence of initiation of the beat, blockage of normal spread, and premature initiation in remote heart areas represent the most common malfunctions encountered. Failure to initiate the heartbeat within the normal sites found in the atrium can be compensated by initiation of the heartbeat elsewhere within the system, albeit at a reduced rate. Insertion of artificial pacemakers can often return the heart to its former level of performance. Blockage of normal beats as electric transmission through the muscle can likewise be offset by artificial pacemakers activating muscle beyond the block. Of much greater concern is initiation of rapid, uncoordinated beats or sudden absence of heart beat, which commonly occur at the moment of myocardial infarction. For this reason, persons are placed on electronic monitoring equipment in coronary care units for a period of 2 or 3 days following a heart attack. Stability of heart rate over a period of 48 hours is associated with relatively few complications and monitoring can be discontinued.

Orthostasis represents a loss of ability to quickly adjust blood pressure to changes in position. Most individuals have experienced episodes of lightheadedness when quickly arising from a reclining or sitting position. Older adults are particularly affected by this condition as arterial flexibility and changes in the nervous system reduce their ability to quickly raise blood pressure in response to position changes. Avoiding diuretics and use of support hose can reduce symptoms in some individuals. Others are obliged to change position extremely slowly to avoid losing consciousness.

Syncope (*fainting*) is the result of a transient *blood pressure loss*. A frightening appearance is presented to the onlooker when an individual suddenly falls to the ground unconscious: the countenance is extremely pale, and blood pressure and pulse may be unobtainable. Usually spontaneous recovery begins immediately upon falling to the ground, and within a short period the person regains consciousness and improves in appearance. An evaluation is usually necessary to determine the cause, such as cardiac arrhythmia, blood loss, acute illness, stroke, or seizure. Frequently, no specific cause can be found, and it is attributed to orthostasis or nervous system dysfunction of unknown origin. At the first sign of *dizziness*, one should sit or recline to avoid total loss of consciousness. Regular meals and frequent position changes are thought to reduce the occurrence of this relatively common problem.

Shock is a term used to describe *loss of blood pressure* due to serious vessel damage. Unlike syncope, which is transient and benign, shock is life threatening. *Blood loss* is a common cause of this condition. In older persons, bleeding from an intestinal ulcer, diverticulitis, or angiodysplasia within the gait may be contributing factors. *Anticoagulation* can contribute to blood loss that may initially be hidden within body cavities, making diagnosis difficult. Immediate blood replacement is essential to bring blood pressure back to normal. Serious infections can cause loss of blood pressure due to the effects of bacterial toxin on capillary walls. Fluid loss correlates with a dramatic drop in circulating blood volume and subsequent pressure reduction. Intensive antibiotic therapy coupled with fluid replacement is essential. Shock invariably requires intensive care, which is often delivered in specialized hospital units with automated monitoring equipment.

Hypertension is a particularly widespread problem in older persons. Although diastolic blood pressure levels off after age 60, the *degeneration of elastin* results in gradually increasing systolic blood pressure throughout later life. Elevated pressures increase the risk for stroke, atherosclerotic heart disease, heart failure, kidney disease, aortic dissection, aortic aneurysm rupture, and retinal damage with loss of vision. Thus, maintenance of pressures below a level of 140-160/90 is desirable, with avoidance of orthostatic hypotension and maintenance of renal function. Weight loss, reduction of dietary salt intake, and modest exercise may lower blood pressure and avoid the need for medication. Diuretics are commonly employed to reduce vascular volume. Numerous agents are available to alter arterial and venous muscle tone with subsequent pressure reduction. Flexibility and caution are required when approaching hypertension therapy in older adults, due to the potential side effects of the medications.

Deconditioning of the cardiovascular system is thought to be a prevalent condition among older adults. Loss of heart muscle strength and vessel responsiveness to central nervous system control is thought to result from inactivity. Data to support such a theory has begun to emerge from studies of astronauts experiencing prolonged weightlessness in space. Exercise protocols are now routine for space flights and have reversed the terrible debilitation documented in early exploration efforts. Exercise programs tailored to the needs of older adults may prevent deterioration in muscle strength and cardiovascular performance as well. This is currently an area of intense research.

Diagnosis

Numerous diagnostic methods are involved in determining cardiovascular diseases. Most important among them are a careful history and physical examination with measurement of blood pressure and heart rate, and with auscultation of cardiac sounds using the stethoscope. Electric activity of the heart can be documented by means of the *electrocardiogram*. Additional information is obtained when electric activity is checked during an *exercise stress test*, such as a *treadmill* or *bicycle ergometer* evaluation. X-rays can determine abnormal cardiac configuration, and sound waves can be bounced from interior chambers to assess architectural variations (*echocardiogram*). Radioactive material injected within the bloodstream permits painless assessment of heart performance at rest and exercise. Dye injected within the heart by means of a catheter passed through the arterial system can determine valve damage, cardiac chamber abnormalities, and cardiac circulation difficulties (*cardiac catheterization, cardiac angiogram*). Additional cardiac assessment tools are under development, which will further our understanding of performance of this critical system.

Health Promotion and Disease Prevention

A number of steps are possible to encourage optimal performance of the cardiovascular system. Smoking should be avoided because it promotes atherosclerosis and is associated with myocardial infarction. Blood pressure regulation in hypertension will also retard atheroma formation and reduce the occurrence of strokes. Careful regulation of sugar levels in diabetes is also valuable in retarding cardiovascular problems. For those with elevated blood cholesterol level and in particular elevated LDL cholesterol level, a diet low in fat can help reduce the risk of cardiovascular disease. Medication may be necessary to meet recommended levels of LDL cholesterol. *Regular exercise*, even of moderate intensity such as walking, performed 5 to 6 times per week has been proposed as important for maintenance of cardiovascular system performance. Maintenance of an ideal weight by control of sugar and fat intake may promote health through its effects on blood pressure and cholesterol blood level. Taken together, such elements comprise a "*healthy lifestyle*" promoting *cardiovascular health*.

For additional research and its clinical implications, see the following references: Cassel, Cohen, Larson, Meir, & Capello, 1997; Friesinger, 1999; Hazzard, Blass, Ettinger, Halter, & Ouslander, 1999.

HEIDI K. WHITE
ROBERT J. SULLIVAN JR.

See also
Cardiovascular System: Heart
Cardiovascular System: Vasculature

References

Cassel, C. K., Leipzig R. M., Cohen, H. J., Larson, E. B., Meier, D. E., & Capello, C. F. (Eds.) (2003). *Geriatric medicine* (4th ed.). New York: Springer Publishing.

Friesinger, G. C. (Ed.) (1999). *Cardiology clinics: Cardiovascular disease in the elderly*. Philadelphia: W. B. Saunders.

Hazzard, W. R., Blass, J. P., Ettinger, W. H., Halter, J. B., & Ouslander J. G. (Eds.) (2003). *Principles of geriatric medicine and gerontology* (5th ed.). New York: McGraw-Hill.

CARDIOVASCULAR SYSTEM: VASCULATURE

The major risk factor for the development of *vascular disease* is advancing age. Why age so greatly increases the risk of vascular disease is much debated. According to some views, the increased risk arises simply because there is more time to be exposed to risk factors such as hypertension, smoking, and dyslipidemia—i.e., there is nothing specific about age itself. Others have proposed that with time, there is an accumulation of age-related changes in blood vessels (themselves reflecting an accumulation of subcellular and cellular deficits) that render the vasculature susceptible to the effects of cardiovascular diseases. While increased exposure to risk factors likely contributes to the development of *vascular disease in aging*, there is considerable evidence that the structure and function of the vasculature change markedly with age, even in the absence other vascular risk factors and overt disease.

Changes in *Vascular Structure in Aging*

In humans, the structure of the arterial wall changes with age. The arterial wall is composed of 3 different layers, or tunics. The outermost layer is the tunica adventitia, which consists of collagen fibers and elastic tissue. The middle layer, which is the thickest layer, is known as the tunica media. It is composed of connective tissue, smooth muscle cells, and elastic tissue, although the precise composition varies between small and large arteries. The mechanical properties of the arterial wall are determined primarily by these variations in the composition of the media. The innermost layer of the arterial wall is the tunica intima. The intima consists of a connective tissue layer and an inner layer of endothelial cells. Endothelial cells are squamous epithelial cells that line the lumen of all blood vessels. The endothelium plays a major role in the regulation of normal vascular function, and endothelial dysfunction is thought to contribute to vascular disease.

The process by which the structure of the arterial wall changes as a function of increasing age is known as *arterial remodelling*. Some of these structural changes are apparent even in early adulthood. Structural changes are more pronounced in large, elastic arteries such as the carotid artery, rather than smaller, muscular arteries such as the brachial artery. One of the most prominent age-related changes in arterial structure in humans is an increase in the size of the lumen of large elastic arteries. In addition, the walls of large elastic arteries thicken as a function of aging. Studies of carotid wall intima plus media (IM) thickness in adult arteries have shown that IM thickness increases between two- and threefold by the age of 90 years. Although there is some evidence that thickening of the media occurs in aging (vascular smooth muscle cells decrease in number, but the remaining ones increase in size), thickening of the arterial wall in aging is due mainly to thickening of the intima.

Thickening of the intima in aging is due in part to alterations in connective tissues in *aging arteries*. The collagen content of the intima has been shown to increase in arteries from aging humans;

the elastin content of the intima, however, declines, and elastin fraying and fragmentation have been reported. In addition to changes in intima connective tissues in aging, there also is evidence of endothelial cell structure changes in arteries from aging humans. Endothelial cells increase in size in aging, and they become irregular. In addition, endothelial cell permeability is thought to increase with aging, and vascular smooth muscle cells may infiltrate the subendothelial space in aging arteries. Finally, numerous substances that are released by the endothelium are altered in the intima of aging arteries. This is discussed in more detail below.

Alterations in *Endothelial Cell Function in Aging* Vasculature

A number of studies have shown both that aging is a major risk factor for *endothelial dysfunction*, and that endothelial dysfunction is an important cause of cardiovascular disease. Thus, *age-related endothelial dysfunction* is thought to make a major contribution to the increased risk of vascular disease in older adults.

The normal vascular endothelium synthesizes and releases a wide variety of regulatory substances in response to various chemical and mechanical stimuli. For example, endothelial cells release substances such as nitric oxide, prostacyclin, endothelins, interleukins, endothelial growth factors, adhesion molecules, plasminogen inhibitors, and von Willebrand factor. These substances are involved in the regulation of vascular tone, angiogenesis, thrombosis, thrombolysis, and many other functions. Together, the effect is to make blood vessels stiffer, and more likely to collect atheromatous deposits with age.

Endothelial dysfunction may reflect disruption of any of the normal functions of endothelial cells, but it is most often measured as a disruption in *endothelium-dependent relaxation*. Endothelium-dependent relaxation is mediated by *nitric oxide*, which is released from the endothelium by a wide range of stimuli such as increased blood flow (shear stress), acetylcholine, serotonin, bradykinin, and thrombin. Released nitric oxide causes vascular smooth muscle relaxation by increasing levels of cyclic guanosine 3,5-monophosphate, which prevents the interaction of actin and myosin. Studies have shown that the levels of nitric oxide are greatly reduced in aging human blood vessels. Interestingly, blood vessels from older adults also show a reduced nitric-oxide dependent vasodilator response to acetylcholine. The mechanism by which the nitric oxide activity is reduced in aging is controversial. Nitric oxide is synthesized in endothelial cells by a constitutive enzyme called *endothelial nitric oxide synthase* (eNOS, or NOS III). Some evidence suggests that the levels of eNOS may be reduced in aging, which could account for the decrease in nitric oxide activity in aging vasculature. However, other studies suggest that factors such as the production of oxygen free radicals in aging endothelial cells may impair nitric oxide production in aging. Further studies will be necessary to fully elucidate the mechanism or mechanisms responsible for endothelial dysfunction in aging vasculature.

Alterations in *Arterial Stiffness in Aging* Arteries

Age-associated remodelling of the large elastic arteries has important functional consequences for the *aging cardiovascular system*. One of the best-characterized functional changes in aging arteries is a reduction in the compliance or distensibility of aging arteries. This reduction in compliance is known as an increase in arterial stiffness in aging. This stiffness impairs the ability of the aorta, and its major branches, to expand and contract with changes in pressure, leading to an increase in the velocity at which the pulse wave travels within large arteries in older adults. *Pulse wave velocity* is related to, but can be measured separately from, hypertension. The increase in pulse wave velocity in aging is a risk factor for future adverse cardiovascular events.

Structural changes in the arterial wall make an important contribution to the age-related increase in arterial stiffness. Factors such as increased collagen content and increased *collagen cross-linking* have been implicated in greater arterial stiffness in aging. Other factors such as reduced elastin content, elastin fragmentation, and increased elastase activity also may increase stiffness in aging arteries. In addition, changes in the endothelial regulation of vascular smooth muscle tone, and changes in other aspects of the arterial wall and vascular function may contribute to the age-associated increase in arterial stiffness.

Arterial stiffness is thought to be the major determinant of blood pressure in the elderly. This is in contrast to young adults, where peripheral vascular resistance is the primary determinant of blood pressure. The increase in stiffness of large arterial walls in aging causes an increase in central systolic arterial pressure and a decrease in diastolic arterial pressure. These factors lead to an increase in *pulse pressure in aging*. As systolic pressure increases in aging and diastolic pressure declines, isolated systolic hypertension is the most common form of *hypertension in older adults*, and studies have shown that isolated *systolic hypertension* is associated with an increased risk of cardiovascular disease. Thus, age-related changes in stiffness of large elastic arteries make a major contribution to the changes in blood pressure observed in aging, and may contribute to the increased risk of cardiovascular disease in older adults.

Summary

There are prominent changes in the structure and function of aging human vasculature. These changes are apparent even in the absence of other vascular risk factors and overt cardiovascular disease. Many of the age-associated changes in vascular structure and function are known risk factors for cardiovascular diseases. Thus, age-related alterations in the vasculature may render the cardiovascular system more susceptible to the detrimental effects of cardiovascular disease. Additional information on this topic can be found in a number of excellent recent reviews (Ferrari, Radaelli, & Centrola, 2003; Lakatta & Levy, 2003; Lakatta, 2003).

SUSAN E. HOWLETT

See also
Cardiovascular System: Heart

References

Ferrari, A. U., Radaelli, A., & Centrola, M. (2003). Physiology of aging invited review: Aging and the cardiovascular system. *Journal of Applied Physiology, 95*, 2591–2597.

Lakatta, E. G., & Levy, D. (2003). Arterial and cardiac aging: Major shareholders in cardiovascular disease enterprises: Part I: Aging arteries: A "set up" for vascular disease. *Circulation, 107*, 139–146.

Lakatta, E. G. (2003). Arterial and cardiac aging: Major shareholders in cardiovascular disease enterprises: Part III: Cellular and molecular clues to heart and arterial aging. *Circulation, 107*, 490–497.

CAREGIVER BURDEN

See
Caregiving (Informal)

CAREGIVING (INFORMAL)

The provision of care by a family member or other individual for a person who has become dependent due to the effects of chronic illness is not a new phenomenon. In fact, families in the United States, as well as in other parts of the world, have always provided care to dependent family members. However, there is growing recognition among service providers and researchers that family caregiving in the United States and in other countries has become a salient service delivery and policy issue because of a number of recent (and anticipated) demographic, economic, and social changes (Olson, 2003).

A number of key trends are shaping the future of informal caregiving in the United States and other countries. Life expectancy and the aging of the population have increased dramatically during this century, with the world's *population aging* at a fast rate, especially in developing countries. A shift in the epidemiology of disease from acute to chronic diseases and a decrease in accidental deaths in developed countries have resulted in a rise in the number of persons in the population with functional activity and mobility limitations. The number of *multigenerational families* has increased, resulting in a growing number of *elderly caregivers* as well as increased numbers in the "*sandwich generation*" (middle-aged women simultaneously caring for their parents and children). Greater numbers of women, the traditional caregivers, have entered the labor force in the United States and in developed countries, and the combination of working outside the home and providing care for dependent family members has become increasingly more difficult. The search for alternatives to institutional care due to financial considerations and efforts to reduce unnecessary institutionalization have led to more community-based treatment options, and therefore have placed more demands on family caregivers. In developed countries, changes in health care reimbursement and medical technology have shifted the burden of post-acute care to family caregivers. Meanwhile, increased geographic mobility in the United States and the movement of youth from rural to urban areas in developing countries has distanced *adult children* from chronically ill siblings and/or parents (Barusch, 1995; Levkoff, Macarthur, & Bucknall, 1995; Olson, 2003). In addition, increases in the divorce rate have weakened caregiving ties.

The Extent of *Informal Caregiving*

The prevalence of caregiving in the United States and in other countries is high. As social welfare costs rise in many nations, increasing obligations are placed on family members—primarily women—to undertake caregiving responsibilities (Barusch, 1995; Olson, 1994). A recent study by the National Alliance for Caregiving and the AARP (2004) estimates that there are over 44 million caregivers aged 18 years and older in the United States; of this number, almost 34 million (16% of the U.S. adult population) provide unpaid care to adults aged 50 years and older. Thus, almost one-fifth of all U.S. households are providing care to someone aged 50 years or older. Over three-fifths (61%) of all caregivers are female, and over two-fifths (43%) are aged 50 years and older. One-quarter (25%) of all caregivers provide care for 20 or more hours per week. Most of the care provided to older adults (86%) is to other family members. The findings of this study indicate that the types of care provided by caregivers and the stresses of caregiving are similar across ethnic groups.

Nature of *Family Caregiving*

The provision of assistance and support by one family member to another is a regular and usual part of family interactions, and is a normative and pervasive activity. Thus, caregiving due to chronic illness and disability represents something that, in principle, is not very different from traditional tasks and activities rendered to family members. This is especially true for women, who across cultures have traditionally shouldered a disproportionate amount of family caregiving responsibility. The difference, however, is that caregiving in chronic illness often represents an increment in care that goes beyond the bounds of normal or usual care.

Caregiving in chronic illness requires a significant expenditure of time and energy over extended periods of time, involves tasks that may be unpleasant and uncomfortable, is likely to be nonsymmetrical, and is a role that might not have been anticipated by the caregiver. When these unanticipated roles are incongruent with stereotypical gender expectations (e.g., when a male caregiver must attend to a disabled relative's bathing or laundry), the stress can be exacerbated.

Although much of the empirical research on caregiving limits the definition of family caregivers to blood relatives, factors such as families' nationality and race/ethnicity and the sexual orientation of the ill relative may dictate broader conceptualizations. These may include more extended kin and non-kin relationships. The roles and functions of family caregivers vary by type and stage of illness and include both direct and indirect activities. Direct activities can include provision of *personal care tasks*, such as helping with bathing, grooming, dressing, or toileting; health *care tasks* such as catheter care, giving injections, or monitoring medications; and *checking and monitoring tasks*, such as continuous supervision, regular checking, and telephone monitoring. Indirect tasks include *care management*, such as locating services, coordinating service use, monitoring services, or advocacy; and *households tasks*, such as cooking, cleaning, shopping, money management, and transportation of family members to medical appointments and daycare programs (Noelker & Bass, 1994). The intensity with which some or all of these caregiving activities are performed varies widely; some caregivers have only limited types of involvement for a few hours per week, while others might provide more than 40 hours a week of care and be on call 24 hours per day.

Caregiver Burden and Gratifications of Caregiving

Significant problems of family caregivers identified by researchers include: coping with increased needs of the dependent family member caused by physical and/or mental illnesses; coping with disruptive behaviors, especially those associated with cognitive disorders such as dementia; restrictions on social and leisure activities; infringement of privacy; disruption of household and work routines; conflicting, multiple role demands; lack of support and assistance from other family members; disruption of family roles and relationships; and lack of sufficient assistance from human service agencies and agency professionals (Coen, Swanwick, O'Boyle, & Coakley, 1997).

Many families report that caregiving is an emotional, physical, and at times financial burden that can impact caregivers' physical health as well as increase the risk of caregiver mortality (Alspaugh, Stephens, Townsend, Zarit, & Greene, 1999; Pinquart & Sorensen, 2003; Schulz & Beach, 1999; Shaw, Patterson, & Semple, 1997; Vitaliano, Young, & Zhang, 2004; Vitaliano, Zhang, & Scanlan, 2003). Care recipient behavioral problems and caregiver burden may be a major factor in the decision to institutionalize an elderly parent (McFall & Miller, 1992; Thomas, Ingrand, Lalloue, Hazif-Thomas, Billon, Vieban, et al., 2004; Townsend, 1990). *Caregiver distress* may not end with the placement of a relative into a long-term care facility; there is some evidence that levels of caregiver anxiety and depression remain as high after placement as before placement (Schulz, Belle, Czaja, McGinnis, Stevens, & Zhang, 2004).

When one examines the relationship between a range of caregiver and care-recipient demographic, socioeconomic, and illness characteristics to caregiver burden, the results across studies are consistent for some variables and inconsistent for others. Generally, findings concerning the role of objective stressors and illness-related variables are more consistent than findings concerning contextual variables such as caregiver demographic and socioeconomic characteristics, and social support.

Concerning objective stressors, one consistent finding across illnesses that vary considerably in terms of symptomatology, pattern of onset, and trajectory is that the more severe the illness, the greater the burden on caregivers (Biegel, Sales, & Schulz, 1991). Additionally, in illnesses with a sudden onset or sudden diagnosis, such as stroke, cancer, or heart attacks, caregiver stress is highest at the acute stage of the illness. There is also a strong relationship between care-recipient behaviors and caregiver burden. Care-recipient behaviors that are known to be especially burdensome include: incontinence, severe functional impairments, hallucinations, suspiciousness, agitation, wandering, catastrophic emotional reactions, disruptiveness at night, behaviors dangerous to the patient, and the need for constant supervision (Pearlin, Mullan, Semple, & Skaff, 1990). Because many of these characteristics are common among dementia patients, it is believed that caregiving for an elderly person with dementia is more difficult than providing care to an older person with physical (rather than mental) limitations (Ory, Hoffman III, Yee, Tennstedt, & Schulz, 1999).

Although the literature shows a moderate relationship between the level of patient disability and the psychological distress of the caregiver, there is considerable variability in caregiver outcomes. Such outcomes are thought to be mediated and/or moderated by a variety of factors, including economic and social support resources available to the caregiver, the quality of the relationship between caregiver and care recipient, and a host of individual differences such as gender, personality attributes (optimism, self-esteem, self-mastery), and coping strategies used (Bookwala & Schulz, 2000; Kendig & Brooke, 1997; Lawrence, Tennstedt, & Assman, 1998; Schulz, O'Brien, Bookwala, & Fleissner, 1995; Townsend & Franks, 1997; Williamson, Shaffer, & Schulz, 1998; Yates, Tennstedt, & Chang, 1999). Researchers have further extended basic stress-coping models to include examination of secondary stressors, such as the number and variety of the caregivers' other roles and role conflict engendered by caregiving demands (Pearlin, Aneshensel, & LeBlanc, 1997), and have applied additional theoretical perspectives borrowed from social and clinical psychology, sociology, and the health and biological sciences to help understand specific aspects of the caregiving situation.

A number of studies indicate that *female caregivers* show higher levels of caregiver burden than males (Bookwala & Schulz, 2000; Miller & Cafasso, 1992; Raschick & Ingersoll-Dayton, 2004). Raschick and Ingersoll-Dayton (2004) believe that these differences are due to differences in types of caregiving roles, in which men have more involvement in managing care while women provide more hands-on care that tends to be both more time consuming and less within the caregiver's control.

Studies show that *spouse caregivers* have higher burden levels than nonspouse caregivers, but this finding may be confounded with age. Malone and colleagues (1991) believe that some of the inconsistencies in the effects of caregiver characteristics on caregiver burden are due to a failure to disentangle caregiver gender, age, and relationship, which can interact to cause confounding effects.

It has also been noted, however, that caregiving can have positive aspects for the caregiver as well, although this research has been far more limited than examinations of the costs of caregiving (Beach, Schulz, Yee, & Jackson, 2000; Picot, 1995; Mausbach, Coon, Depp, Rabinowitz, Wilson-Arias, & Kraemer, et al., 2004; Raschick, & Ingersoll-Dayton, 2004; Tarlow, Wisniewski, Belle, Rubert, Ory, & Gallagher-Thompson, 2004; Walker, Pratt, & Eddy, 1995). Caregivers report satisfaction, enjoyment, and benefits and rewards from caregiving. Adult children who are caregivers to elderly parents report that they find caregiving gratifying because they can "pay back" the care which the parent provided to them when they were young. Similarly, spouses who view caregiving as a reciprocation of past affection report caregiving to be more gratifying. In addition, caregivers report that being a caregiver helps them gain inner strength or learn new skills (Archer & MacLean, 1993). Raschick & Ingersoll-Dayton (2004) found that adult-child caregivers experienced greater rewards than did spouse caregivers. The author surmises that spousal caregiving may be viewed by caregivers as an expected role, while parental caregiving might be seen by caregivers as exceeding normal expectations and thus more rewarding.

Research on the role of race and ethnicity, which in the past has received relatively little attention in caregiving literature, is increasing. It has been the subject of a number of recent empirical studies as well as literature reviews (Coon, Rubert, Solano, Mausbach, Kraemer, Arguelles, et al., 2004; Daker-White, Beattie, & Means, 2002; Dilworth-Anderson, Goodwin, & Williams, 2004; Dilworth-Anderson, Williams, & Gibson, 2002; Gupta & Pillai, 2002; Haley, Gitlin, Wisniewski, Mahoney, Coon, Winter, et al., 2004; Li, Edwards, & Morrow-Howell, 2004). Dilworth-Anderson and colleagues' (2002) comprehensive review of race, ethnicity, and culture in caregiving research over the past 20 years provides support for the differences in the constellation of caregivers between minority and nonminority caregivers, with *minority caregivers* consisting of a more diverse group. However, they found no support for the previously held belief that minority caregivers receive more help from their family and friends than do non-Hispanic Caucasian caregivers. In addition, Dilworth-Anderson and colleagues found that the impact of race and ethnicity on the negative effects of caregiving, as measured by burden and depression, was somewhat mixed. For example, while some studies found that burden and depression were higher among Caucasian than African-American caregivers, other studies found no differences. Recent reports from analyses of combined sites of the REACH study of dementia caregivers find no significant differences in levels of depression between Caucasian and African-American caregivers, or between Caucasian and Latina caregivers (Coon, et al., 2004; Haley, et al., 2004).

There is some evidence that race and ethnicity affect appraisal of the difficulties of the caregiving process and the benefits of caregiving (Coon, et al., 2004; Dilworth-Anderson, Williams, & Gibson, 2002; Haley, et al., 2004). Dilworth-Anderson and colleagues (2002) found that African-American caregivers, as compared to Caucasian caregivers, used more positive reappraisal in addressing the difficulties of caregiving. Similarly, findings in the REACH study by Haley and colleagues (2004) that *African-American caregivers* appraised behavioral problems of their family members with dementia as less stressful and caregiving to be a more positive experience than Caucasian caregivers is consistent with previous research (Lawton, Rajagopal, Brody, & Kleban, 1992; Macera, Eaker, Goslar, Deandrade, Williamson, Cornman, et al., 1992). Other findings from the *REACH study* (Coon, et al., 2004) indicate similar results for *Latina caregivers* as compared to Caucasian female caregivers. Dilworth-Anderson and colleagues (2002) point out, however, that more research is needed to better understand the mechanisms and pathways through which culture impacts the degree to which client behavioral problems are seen as stressful by caregivers.

Overall, as Dilworth-Anderson and colleagues and others (Aranda & Knight, 1997; Connell & Gibson, 1997; Dilworth-Anderson, Goodwin, & Williams, 2002; Li, Edwards, & Morrow-Howell, 2004) point out, there are a number of significant weaknesses in the extant caregiving literature on the role of race and ethnicity. These weaknesses include: the lack of clear conceptual frameworks that are culturally relevant and that include measures of culture/racial identity in the models to be tested; use of small samples that do not allow full testing of conceptual models for each race or ethnic group examined, nor the examination of diversity within racial and ethnic groups; lack of culturally sensitive measurement instruments; failure to examine differences in contextual factors of caregiving, such as the role of multiple family caregivers in various racial and ethnic groups; and, the lack of multimethod studies that include qualitative as well as quantitative methodologies.

Interventions to Support Caregivers

A variety of interventions for caregivers have been developed that are designed to reduce the negative impacts of caregiving for caregivers and to provide supportive assistance to enable families to continue in their caregiving roles. However, there is no agreed upon system for classifying these interventions (Schulz, 2001). Intervention types examined in research studies have included: education, psychoeducation, peer support, counseling/psychotherapy, respite/adult daycare, and training of care recipients. Some interventions are offered in a group format to multiple caregivers, while others are offered to caregivers individually. There is a trend for interventions to be multicomponent in recognition of the multiple needs of caregivers. Recently interventions have also incorporated the use of technology, such as automated telecommunications systems, to provide information and social support. Interventions for caregivers also differ in the degree to which they are professionally or peer-led, as well as in the duration of the intervention.

Anecdotal reports of early intervention efforts were generally positive. However, as Biegel and Schulz (1999) noted, the first critical reviews of the literature were considerably more sobering (Bourgeois, Schulz, & Burgio, 1996; Knight, Luszky, & Macofsky-Urban, 1993; Toseland & Rossiter, 1989; Zarit & Teri, 1992). The growing number of studies of *interventions for family caregivers* and their increasing sophistication in design and implementation have led to a number of additional recent reviews of caregiver intervention literature. Some of these reviews are restricted to caregiving interventions in dementia (Acton & Kang, 2001; Brodaty, Green, & Koschera, 2003; Schulz, O'Brien, Czaja, Ory, Norris, & Martire, et al., 2002), while others focused on non-dementia caregiving (Sorensen, Pinquart, & Duberstein, 2002; Yin, Zhou, & Bashford, 2002).

Overall, despite some differences such as the lack of statistically significant reductions of caregiver burden in some reviews (Acton & Kang, 2001; Brodaty, Green, & Koschera, 2003), findings are fairly consistent and show that many intervention studies report small to moderate statistically significant effects on a variety of outcomes, albeit not always consistently. The recent report that the REACH study found only a modest overall intervention effect (Gitlin, Belle, Burgio, Czaja, Mahoney, Gallagher-Thompson, et al., 2003) is consistent with these reviews.

The comprehensive review by Sorensen and colleagues (2002) of 6 types of interventions and 6 outcome variables in 78 caregiver interventions studies found that overall the interventions had statistically significant effect sizes that ranged from 0.14 to 0.41 standard deviation units for caregiver burden, depression, subjective well-being, perceived caregiver satisfaction, ability/knowledge, and care-receiver symptoms. This review found that effect sizes varied by outcomes measured and type of intervention. In addition, a number of moderator variables—pertaining to characteristics of the intervention, the caregiving situation, and study characteristics—also impacted effect sizes. For example, group interventions were less effective in reducing burden and improving well being than individual or mixed interventions but were more effective at reducing care-receiver symptoms than nongroup interventions were. Interventions for caregivers of persons with dementia, as compared to those for caregivers of persons without dementia or when the sample was mixed, were less effective in improving most outcomes. Finally, most outcomes showed less improvement in studies that used randomized designs.

Schulz and colleagues (2002) remind us of the limitations of statistical significance, and that findings of intervention studies should also be measured by their clinical significance, or the "practical value" of an intervention's effects to make an actual difference in people's lives (Kazdin, 1999). In reviewing the clinical significance of caregiver intervention outcomes in dementia, the review of Schulz and colleagues finds that only a small proportion of studies achieved clinically significant outcomes, at the same time cautioning that there is no widely accepted definition of clinical significance. Nonetheless, the authors indicate that caregiver interventions show promise of achieving clinically significant outcomes in reducing depressive symptoms and to a lesser degree in reducing anxiety, anger, and hostility. Other findings indicate that clinically significant effects have been found in delaying institutionalization of the care recipient.

Despite improvements in the quality of interventions for caregivers over time and in the quality of the research studies that have examined these interventions, a number of recommendations have been raised for improving caregiver interventions and for strengthening future caregiving intervention research studies (Belle, Czaja, Schulz, Zhang, Burgio, Gitlin, et al., 2003; Brodaty, Green, & Koschera, 2003; Gitlin, Belle, Burgio, Czaja, Mahoney, Gallagher-Thompson et al., 2003; Mittleman, Roth, Haley, & Zarit, 2004; Schulz, 2001; Schulz, O'Brien, Czaja, Ory, Norris, Matire, et al., 2002; Schulz, Burgio, Burns, Eisdorfer, Gallagher-Thompson, Gitlin et al., 2003; Sorensen, Pinquart, & Duberstein, 2002). Reviews of intervention studies make it clear that no single type of intervention can achieve clinically significant outcomes across all caregivers. Rather, it has been suggested that interventions should be multicomponent and tailored to the needs of specific target populations, and should be of longer rather than shorter duration. Interventions should focus both on the caregiver and the dependent elderly family member. While continued use of standardized treatments is desired, dosages and depths of treatment should vary according to the specific needs of the study subjects. In addition, studies should pay more attention to matching the intervention subjects with the problems to be addressed by the intervention. Finally, attention needs to be paid to barriers to obtaining and using services, especially by racial and ethnic minorities.

Future research studies need to identify and measure the impact of discrete components of multicomponent interventions. Studies should include better descriptions of the intervention, with more specific information about the target population, the domain being targeted, delivery method, etc. In so doing, the linkage between an intervention and its hypothesized outcomes should be specified. Building upon the stronger designs of a number of recent caregiver intervention studies, future studies should make greater use of randomized clinical trials with a large number of subjects, should follow up with subjects for at least 6 to 12 months after the intervention ends, and should measure both proximal and distal outcomes using well-validated and reliable outcome measures. Finally, attention should be paid to issues of clinical significance, in addition to statistical significance.

David E. Biegel

See also
Stress and Coping

References

Acton, G. J., & Kang, J. (2001). Interventions to reduce the burden of caregiving for an adult with dementia: A meta-analysis. *Research in Nursing and Health, 24*, 349–360.

Alspaugh, M. E. L., Stephens, M. A. P., Townsend, A. L., Zarit, S. H., & Greene, R. (1999). Longitudinal patterns of risk for depression in dementia caregivers: Objective and subjective primary stress as predictors. *Psychology and Aging, 14*(1), 34–43.

Aranda, M. P., & Knight, B. G. (1997). The influence of ethnicity and culture on the caregiver stress and coping process: A sociocultural review and analysis. *Gerontologist, 37*(3), 342–354.

Archer, C. K., & MacLean, M. J. (1993). Husbands and sons as caregivers of chronically ill elderly women. *Journal of Gerontological Social Work, 21*(1-2), 5–23.

Barusch, A. S. (1995). Programming for family care of elderly dependents: Mandates, incentives, and service rationing, *Social Work, 40*(3), 315–322.

Beach, S. R., Schulz, R., Yee, J. L., & Jackson, S. (2000). Negative and positive health effects of caring for a disabled spouse: Longitudinal findings from the

Caregiver Health Effects Study. *Psychology and Aging*, *15*(2), 259–271.

Belle, S. H., Czaja, S. J., Schulz, R., Zhang, S., Burgio, L. D., Gitlin, L. N., et al. (2003). Using a new taxonomy to combine the uncombinable: Integrating results across diverse interventions. *Psychology and Aging*, *18*(3), 396–405.

Biegel, D. E., Sales, E., & Schulz, R. (1991). *Family caregiving in chronic illness: Alzheimer's disease, cancer, heart disease, mental illness and stroke*. Family Caregiver Applications Series (Vol. 1). Newbury Park, CA: Sage Publications.

Biegel, D. E., & Schulz, R. (1999). Caregiving and caregiver interventions in aging and mental illness. *Family Relations*, *48*(4), 345–354.

Bookwala, J., & Schulz, R. (2000). A comparison of primary stressors, secondary stressors, and depressive symptoms between elderly caregiving husbands and wives: The Caregiver Health Effects Study. *Psychology and Aging*, *15*, 607–616.

Bourgeois, M. S., Schulz, R., & Burgio, L. (1996). Interventions for caregivers of patients with Alzheimer's disease: A review and analysis of content, process, and outcomes. *International Journal of Aging and Human Development*, *43*, 35–92.

Brodaty, H., Green, A., & Koschera, A. (2003). Meta-analysis of psychosocial interventions for caregivers of people with dementia. *Journal of the American Geriatrics Society*, *51*(5), 657–664.

Coen, R. F., Swanwick, G. R. J., O'Boyle, C. A., & Coakley, D. (1997). Behavior disturbance and other predictors of carer burden in Alzheimer's disease. *International Journal of Geriatric Psychiatry*, *12*, 331–336.

Connell, C. M., & Gibson, G. D. (1997). Racial, ethnic, and cultural differences in dementia caregiving: Review and analysis. *Gerontologist*, *37*(3), 355–364.

Coon, D. W., Rubert, M., Solano, N., Mausbach, B., Kraemer, H., Arguelles, T., et al. (2004). Well-being, appraisal, and coping in Latina and Caucasian female dementia caregivers: Findings from the REACH study. *Aging and Mental Health*, *8*(4), 330–345.

Daker-White, G., Beattie, A. M., Gilliard, J., & Means, R. (2002). Minority ethnic groups in dementia: A review of service needs, service provision and models of good practice. *Aging and Mental Health*, *6*(2), 101–108.

Dilworth-Anderson, P., Goodwin, P. Y., & Williams, S. W. (2004). Can culture help explain the physical health effects of caregiving over time among African-American caregivers? *Journal of Gerontology*, *59B*(3), S138–S145.

Dilworth-Anderson, P., Williams, I. C., & Gibson, B. E. (2002). Issues of race, ethnicity and culture in caregiving research: A 20-year review (1980–2000). *Gerontologist*, *42*(2), 237–272.

Gitlin, L. N., Belle, S. H., Burgio, L. D., Czaja, S. J., Mahoney, D., Gallagher-Thompson, D., et al. (2003). Effect of multicomponent interventions on caregiver burden and depression: The REACH multisite initiative at 6-month follow-up. *Psychology and Aging*, *18*(3), 361–374.

Gupta, R., & Pillai, V. K. (2002). Elder caregiving in South Asian families: Implications for social service. *Journal of Comparative Family Studies*, *33*(4), 565–576.

Haley, W. E., Gitlin, L. N., Wisniewski, S. R., Mahoney, D. F., Coon, D. W., Winter, L., et al. (2004). Well-being, appraisal, and coping in African-American and Caucasian dementia caregivers: Findings from the REACH study. *Aging and Mental Health*, *8*(4), 316–329.

Kazdin, A. E. (1999). The meanings and measurement of clinical significance. *Journal of Consulting and Clinical Psychology*, *67*, 332–339.

Kendig, H., & Brooke, L. (1997). Australian research on ageing and social support. *Australian Journal on Ageing and Social Support*, *16*(3), 127–130.

Knight, B. G., Lutzky, S. M., Macofsky-Urban, F. (1993). A meta-analytic review of interventions for caregiver distress: Recommendations for future research. *Gerontologist*, *33*(2), 240–248.

Lawrence, R. H., Tennstedt, S. L., & Assman, S. F. (1998). Quality of the caregiver-recipient relationship: Does it offset negative consequences of caregiving for family caregivers. *Psychology and Aging*, *13*(1), 150–158.

Lawton, M. P., Rajagopal, D., Brody, E., & Kleban, M. H. (1992). The dynamics of caregiving for a demented elder among black and white families. *Journal of Gerontology: Social Sciences*, *47*(4), S156–S164.

Levkoff, S. E., Macarthur, I. W., & Bucknall, J. (1995). Elderly mental health in the developing world. *Social Science and Medicine*, *41*(7), 983–1003.

Li, H., Edwards, D., & Morrow-Howell, N. (2004). Informal caregiving networks and use of formal services by inner-city African American elderly with dementia. *Families in Society*, *85*(1), 55–62.

Macera, C., Eaker, E., Goslar, P., Deandrade, S., Williamson, J., Cornman, C., et al. (1992). Ethnic differences in the burden of caregiving. *American Journal of Alzheimer's Care and Related Disorders*, *7*(5), 4–7.

Malone, Beach, E. E., & Zarit, S. H. (1991). *International Journal of Aging and Human Development*, *32*(2) 103–114.

Mausbach, B. T., Coon, D. W., Depp, C., Rabinowitz, Y. G., Wilson-Arias, E., Kraemer, H. C., et al. (2004). Ethnicity and time to institutionalization of dementia patients: A comparison of Latina and Caucasian female family caregivers. *Journal of the American Geriatrics Society*, *52*, 1077–1084.

McFall, S., & Miller, B. (1992). The effect of caregiver burden on nursing home admissions of frail older persons. *Journal of Gerontology: Social Sciences, 47*, S73–S79.

Miller, B., & Cafasso, L. (1992). Gender differences in caregiving: Fact or artifact? *Gerontologist, 32*, 498–507.

Mittleman, M. S., Roth, D. L., Haley, W. E., & Zarit, S. H. (2004). Effects of a caregiver intervention on negative caregiver appraisals of behavior problems in patients with Alzheimer's disease: Results of a randomized trial. *Journal of Gerontology: Psychological Sciences, 59B*(1), P27–P34.

National Alliance for Caregiving and AARP. (2004). *Caregiving in the U.S.* Washington, DC: AARP.

Noelker, L. S., & Bass, D. M. (1994). Relationships between the frail elderly's informal and formal helpers. In E. Kahana, D. E. Biegel, & M. L. Wykle (Eds.), *Family caregiving across the lifespan. Volume 4, Family Caregiver Applications Series*. Newbury Park, CA: Sage Publications.

Olson, L. K. (2003). *The not so golden years: Caregiving, the frail elderly and the long-term care establishment.* Lanham, MD: Rowman & Littlefield Publishers.

Ory, M. G., Hoffman III, R. R., Yee, J. L., Tennstedt, S., & Schulz, R. (1999). Prevalence and impact of caregiving: A detailed comparison between dementia and nondementia caregivers. *Gerontologist, 39*, 177–185.

Pearlin, L. I., Mullan, J. T., Semple, S. J., & Skaff, T. (1990). Caregiving and the stress process: An overview of concepts and their measures. *Gerontologist, 30*, 583–591.

Pearlin, L. I., Aneshensel, C. S., & LeBlanc, A. I. (1997). The forms and mechanisms of stress proliferation: The case of AIDS caregivers. *Journal of Health and Social Behavior, 38*, 223–236.

Picot, S. J. (1995). Rewards, costs, and coping of African-American caregivers. *Nursing Research, 44*, 147–152.

Pinquart, M., & Sorensen, S. (2003). Differences between caregivers and non-caregivers in psychological health and physical health: A meta-analysis. *Psychology and Aging, 18*(2), 250–267.

Raschick, M., & Ingersoll-Dayton, B. (2004). The costs and rewards of caregiving among aging spouses and adult children. *Family Relations, 53*(3), 317–325.

Schulz, R. (2001). Some critical issues in caregiver intervention research. *Aging and Mental Health, 5*(Suppl. 1), S112–S115.

Schulz, R., & Beach, S. (1999). Caregiving as a risk factor for mortality: The Caregiver Health Effects Study. *Journal of the American Medical Association, 282*, 2215–2219.

Schulz, R., Belle, S. H., Czaja, S. J., McGinnis, K. A., Stevens, A., & Zhang, S. (2004). Long-term care placement of dementia patients and caregiver health and well-being. *Journal of the American Medical Association, 292*(8), 961–967.

Schulz, R., Burgio, L., Burns, R., Eisdorfer, C., Gallagher-Thompson, D., Gitlin, L. N., et al. (2003). Resources for enhancing Alzheimer's caregiver health (REACH): Overview, site-specific outcomes and future directions. *Gerontologist, 43*(4), 514–520.

Schulz, R., O'Brien, A. T., Bookwala, J., & Fleissner, K. (1995). Psychiatric and physical morbidity effects of dementia caregiving: Prevalence, correlates, and causes. *Gerontologist, 35*, 771–791.

Schulz, R., O'Brien, A., Czaja, S., Ory, M., Norris, R., Martire, L. M., et al. (2002). Dementia caregiver intervention research: In search of clinical significance. *Gerontologist, 42*(5), 589–602.

Shaw, W. S., Patterson, T. L., & Semple, S. J. (1997). Longitudinal analysis of multiple indicators of health decline among spousal caregivers. *Annals of Behavioral Medicine, 19*, 101–109.

Sorensen, S., Pinquart, M., & Duberstein, P. (2002). How effective are interventions with caregivers: An updated meta-analysis. *Gerontologist, 42*(3), 356–372.

Tarlow, B. J., Wisniewski, S. R., Belle, S. H., Rubert, M., Ory, M. G., & Gallagher-Thompson, D. (2004). Positive aspects of caregiving: Contributions of the REACH project to the development of new measures for Alzheimer's caregiving. *Research on Aging, 26*(4), 429–453.

Thomas, P., Ingrand, P., Lalloue, F., Hazif-Thomas, C., Billon, R., Vieban, F., et al. (2004). Reasons of informal caregivers for institutionalizing dementia patients previously living at home: The Pixel study. *International Journal of Geriatric Psychiatry, 19*, 127–135.

Toseland, R. W., & Rossiter, C. M. (1989). Group interventions to support family caregivers: A review and analysis. *Gerontologist, 29*(4), 438–448.

Townsend, A. (1990). Nursing home care and family caregivers' stress). In M. A. P. Stephens, J. H. Crowther, S. E. Hobfoll, & D. L. Tennenbaum (Eds.), *Stress and coping in later-life families* (pp. 267–285). New York: Hemisphere Publishing Corporation.

Townsend, A. L., & Franks, M. M. (1997). Quality of the relationship between elderly spouses: Influence on spouse caregivers' subjective effectiveness. *Family Relations, 46*, 33–39.

Vitaliano, P. P., Young, H. M., & Zhang, J. (2004). Is caregiving a risk factor for illness? *Current Directions in Psychological Science, 13*(1) 13–16.

Vitaliano, P. P., Zhang, J., & Scanlan, J. M. (2003). Is caregiving hazardous to one's physical health? A meta-analysis. *Psychological Bulletin, 129*(6), 946–972.

Walker, A. J., Pratt, C. C., & Eddy, L. (1995). Informal caregiving to aging family members: A critical review. *Family Relations*, *44*(4), 402–411.

Williamson, G. M., Shaffer, D. R. & Schulz, R. (1998). Activity restriction and prior relationship history as contributors to mental health outcomes among middle-aged and older spousal caregivers. *Health Psychology*, *17*(2), 152–162.

Yates, M. E., Tennstedt, S., & Chang, B. H. (1999). Contributors to and mediators of psychological well-being for informal caregivers. *Journals of Gerontology: Series B, Psychological and Social Sciences*, *54B*(1), P12–P22.

Yin, T., Zhou, Q., & Bashford, C. (2002). Burden on family members. Caring for frail elderly: A meta-analysis of interventions. *Nursing Research*, *51*(3), 199–208.

Zarit, S. H., & Teri, L. (1992). Interventions and services for caregivers (pp. 287–310). In K. W. Schaie & M. P. Lawton (Eds.), *Annual Review of Gerontology and Geriatrics, Volume 11*. New York: Springer Publishing Company.

CARE MANAGEMENT

See
Case Management

CASE MANAGEMENT

Case management (often called "*care management*") is typically a combination of clinical, coordinative, and administrative functions. It is directed at locating, arranging, and monitoring care from a variety of resources in response to a client's identified need. Goals include maximizing independence, providing choices, and enhancing functioning in the client's living setting. The case manager assumes responsibility for identifying needs, planning and arranging service delivery, and monitoring service provision and outcomes. Primarily a process that links individuals and families with needed services, case management has some specific characteristics.

- It is individualized to the unique needs of each client.
- It is based on a holistic orientation that views all aspects of the individual, situation, and environment.
- It seeks to enhance client *self-care* and *self-determination* by involving the client in problem solving and decision making and focusing on client values and preferences.
- It is aimed at providing continuity of appropriate care.
- It utilizes a wide range of services from a variety of sources.
- It is implemented through coordinating an existing set of services and resources from both formal and informal systems.
- It seeks to assure quality care and cost effective use of resources.

Evolution of Case Management

The principal function of case management—that of obtaining essential resources on behalf of clients in collaboration with both formal and informal sources—is rooted in social casework, public health and community nursing, child and family services, and related services. Every discipline can, and does, lay claim to contributing toward what is now case management (White, 2005). Although aspects of these disciplines remain an integral part of case management, the dimension of managing and monitoring many types of care, systems, service delivery, interagency agreements, cost containment, provider efficiency, and quality add complexity and a greater level of formalization to more traditional methods.

The emergence of *community-based, long-term care research* and *demonstration projects* under *Medicaid waivers* in the early 1970s and 1980s stimulated case management development, particularly in community-based and in-home programs serving dependent populations such as the *frail elderly*. Over time, the case management function has become more systematic. This is most apparent in client-related tasks, relationships with providers, the development of professional training for case managers, more clearly defined target groups, and stated requirements for case management in funded research, demonstration, and on-going programs. Increasingly present in service delivery systems, it "plays a key role in efforts to integrate long-term care services into a seamless continuum of care" (Scharlach, Giunta, & Mills-Dick, 2001).

The popularity and success of case management are evidenced by its proliferation in all types of settings, where it is performed by professionals from most human service disciplines not only in the United States, but in other parts of the world including Europe, Canada, Israel, Japan, and China. Another growth indicator is its use in a broad range of service arenas for many functions and activities including:

- Telephone screening, assessment, and consultation;
- Information and referral services;
- Eldercare services for corporations and businesses;
- Long-term care insurance assessments and care management;
- Private practice care management;
- Acute care facility and medical case management, and managed care;
- Home health and custodial management;
- Physician office linkages to community services;
- Guardianship/conservatorship and fiscal management;
- Community-based programs and senior center services; and,
- State, local, and national referral and insurance service networks.

Case Management Process

The case management process generally includes the set of tasks and activities shown in Figure 1.

After intake, client status is assessed to determine needs, and a plan of care is developed to address them. Assessment instruments vary from program to program but most commonly include health, functional, cognitive, and psychosocial elements that assist in determining the appropriate level of care

Case Identification (outreach, eligibility determination intake)
→ **Assessment** (current status, problem identification)
→ **Care Planning** (develop plan addressing needs)
→ **Coordination** (locate, arrange services)
→ **Follow Up** (monitor client status, service delivery)
→ **Reassessment** (periodic re-evaluation)
→ **Case Closure** (discharge)

FIGURE 1 Case Management Process

needed and the supports available for the individual client. A social work, health care, or other professional with good interviewing skills usually conducts the assessment. In some settings, members of a multidisciplinary team, including population (e.g., elderly) or service (e.g., physical therapy) specialists do the assessment. Family members, other informal sources, physicians, attorneys, and current or past service providers may be contacted for verification or additional information.

The *care plan* is implemented by locating, arranging, or coordinating the delivery of services from available sources. In a community setting, for example, the case manager may obtain such services as home chores, bathing and personal care, laundry, shopping, day care, and transportation. In cases where a family is a caregiver for a homebound person, arrangements may be made for periodic respite services. Often case managers assist families who are making placement or relocation decisions.

Service provision is monitored to assure continuity, quality, and appropriateness; clients are monitored for response to care and for changes in status. Regular contact with the client, the clients' national support sources, and providers establishes a channel of communication to ensure early intervention if problems arise. In addition to this ongoing interaction, a periodic reassessment is conducted to evaluate whether the clients' situation is better or worse and whether the client needs more, fewer, or different services. Follow-up activities provide the opportunity to monitor client status and service delivery and respond to changes or problems. This is essential for continuity and to assist clients to maintain or improve their situation. Finally, discharge from case management takes place under a variety of circumstances: the client's situation stabilizes, the client no longer requires the service, or the client no longer wishes to receive the service. Clients can also fall out of eligibility by virtue of changes in income, place of residence, or condition.

Although the process is depicted as linear, it is not unusual for clients to avail themselves of only a part of it. For instance, there may be a request for just an assessment and suggestions for services or, a family may ask for monitoring of services already in place. This is particularly true for private practice and fee-for-services case management, where clients are not required to meet eligibility criteria or follow a prescribed schedule.

The conduct of the specific tasks varies considerably among programs. For example, some programs provide only short-term case management (normally defined as 3 months or less), whereas others continue service as long as needed. Some acquire clients from a host agency or an affiliate organization that may perform the case finding or assessment tasks. Some programs limit coordination to those services that can be delivered directly, whereas others develop contractual relationships and agreements with a variety of providers. Regardless of how, by whom, or where the activities are actually carried out, the case management process itself remains relatively intact.

Case Management Program Models

Case management models are usually described by a variety of program elements, which distinguish case management programs from one another. Among them are the level of responsibility for client care and the degree of authority to purchase and allocate resources. The complexity of case management functions is directly related to the presence or absence of these characteristics. Examples of other variables that affect case management models are shown in Table 1.

The purpose of a case management program is related to its goals and, most commonly, to its funding source, which typically defines the target population. For example, if the purpose of a program is to provide alternatives to nursing home placement, the focus will be on individuals eligible for nursing home care. In such programs the goals would likely be to maintain the individuals in the community at a lower cost than that of the nursing home. Eligibility for case management can be based on age, income, geographic location, and functional, cognitive, or physical status as in publicly funded programs, or simply on an ability to pay for services as in the fee-for-service model.

TABLE 1 Selected Case Management Program Variables

Variable	Examples
Purpose	Nursing home alternative, service access
Target	Frail, high cost, ability to pay
Funding	Grants, contracts, fees
Function	Broker, provider
Staffing	Social worker, nurse, gerontologist
Caseload	Mandated, mix/intensity
Duration	Short term, long term
Setting	Community, acute care, managed care
Authority	Admission, planning, purchase
Outcomes	Cost savings, client satisfaction
Tools	Information systems, care pathways

Staffing depends largely upon funding, the type of intervention needed or offered, the function that the case manager performs, and the type of client served. Case managers with psychosocial skills usually staff community-based and mental health programs, whereas nurses or other health care case managers work with those who need skilled care. In some programs, *case management teams* offer both health and psychosocial perspectives. Programs also differ by the size of their caseloads and the duration of case management services variables, which are often mandated by their funders. Other variations include the level of authority to admit clients into programs; care planning and how services are acquired; the anticipated outcomes to be achieved, ranging from dollar savings to client satisfaction; and the type of tools used to facilitate information flow and tracking of cases and costs. To date, no one case management program or model has emerged to suit all situations.

Continuing Challenges in Case Management

In spite of increasing numbers and types of case management programs and practices, several issues remain unresolved. One is the ongoing practice of payers to reimburse solely for medically related case management services. Another is the proliferation of case management credentialing organizations with little consensus between them on content, purpose, or even terminology (Rosen, Bodie-Gross, Young, Smolenski, & Howe, 2000). The continuing effort to "professionalize" case management through credentialing activities and formulation of standards (Geron & Chassler, 1994; Golden & White, in press) has significant implications for future education and training needs. A related and important issue is the ability of case managers to identify and resolve ethical issues, whether such conflicts are associated with client values and preferences, finances, or care (Cress, 2001).

Diversity—whether it is ethnic, cultural, language, or sexual orientation—is growing in the aging population and presents several challenges for case managers. Personal biases, societal misconceptions, and stereotypes all require knowledge and sensitivity (Woodside & McClam, 2003). Other issues requiring continuing clarification and resolution include:

- Strengthening service systems to counter resource limitations;
- Improving targeting methods to assure appropriate client populations;
- Clarifying the goals of case management vis-à-vis/ the host agency or payer;
- Determining the best staffing qualifications and mix;
- Determining the most appropriate and feasible caseload size and mix;
- Strategizing cooperative agreements with service providers;
- Integrating medical and nonmedical services and care;
- Determining intake, service provision, and monitoring and reporting methods among multiple providers;
- Defining case management outcome measures;
- Improving information systems to facilitate communication, management, and clinical tasks;
- Determining pricing and reimbursement mechanisms for direct case management services; and
- Resolving authority issues where multiple case managers are involved.

Conclusion

Case management has proved to be particularly successful with vulnerable and dependent populations such as the frail elderly and the disabled. It has provided a means for assisting clients to maintain an optimal level of independence in the midst of a fragmented, duplicative, and confusing "nonsystem." It has also facilitated inter-organizational linkages, collaborative planning, and community-wide awareness of system gaps for needy populations.

There is both public and private support for the basic concepts underlying case management. Increasing numbers of autonomous agencies are participating in developing a continuum of care through networking and systems-building activities. Technological advances are being used to assist case managers in tracking the most effective and efficient services and enhancing productive decision making. The future of case management programs may rest on their ability to fit into existing structures, to mold their function to suit current policies and programs, to operate at varying levels of complexity, and to further refine their purpose. As care increasingly moves from acute and institutional facilities to home and community settings, the principles of collaboration and coordination inherent to case management are essential to the success of future service systems. Yet, we must be careful not to use case management as a substitute for change and to continue to improve policies, systems, and practice. As noted by Dill (2001):

- The hardest symbolic work on case management has yet to be done. We must dare to reconceptualize and reinvent it as a fully human enterprise, not a neutral tool; as a way of fulfilling not just the ends, but the potential of our service programs and professions. We must confront the values that deter us from accepting responsibility for our service systems, in principle and in practice. We have ample opportunity to make case management all that it promises to be.

Monika White

See also

Cash Payments for Care

References

Cress, C. (2001). *Handbook of geriatric care management.* Gaithersburg, MD: Aspen Publishers.

Dill, A. E. P. (2001). *Managing to care: Case management and service system reform.* Hawthorne, NY: Walter de Gruyter.

Geron, S. M., & Chassler, D. (1994). *Guidelines for case management practice across the long-term continuum.* Report of the National Advisory Committee on Long-Term Care Case Management [Monograph prepared under a grant from the Robert Wood Johnson Foundation.] Bristol, CT: Connecticut Community Care, Inc.

Golden, R., & White, M. (2005, in press). Credentialing opportunities. In B. Berkman & S. D'Ambruoso (Eds.), *The Oxford handbook of social work in aging*. New York: Oxford University Press.

Rosen, A. L., Bodie-Gross, E., Young, E., Smolenski, M., & Howe, D. (2000). To be or not to be? Case/care management credentialing. In R. Applebaum & M. White (Eds.), *Key issues in case management around the globe*. San Francisco: American Society on Aging.

Scharlach, A. E., Giunta, N., & Mills-Dick, K. (2001). *Case management in long-term care integration: An overview of current programs and evaluations*. Berkeley: University of California, Berkeley, Center for the Advanced Study of Aging Services.

White, M. (2005). Case management. In C. Evashwick (Ed.), *The continuum of long-term care* (3rd ed.). Clifton Park, NY: Thomson Delmar Learning.

Woodside, M., & McClam, T. (2003). *Generalist case management: A method for human service delivery* (2nd ed.). Pacific Grove, CA: Brooks/Cole Thomson Learning.

CASH AND COUNSELING

See
Cash Payments for Care

CASH PAYMENTS FOR CARE

Cash payments for care refers to various financing mechanisms that provide a cash benefit to consumers or their representatives, thus allowing them to address their particular needs and preferences for *personal assistance services* (PAS). Depending on program rules, consumers may have complete latitude on how the cash is spent, or they may have to use cash allowances only for PAS and other types of services (i.e., assistive devices, home modifications, transportation) needed to maintain their independence. Personal assistance services encompass a range of human and technological assistance provided to persons with disabilities who need help with certain types of activities, such as *activities of daily living* (ADLs), including bathing, dressing, toileting, transferring, and eating, and *instrumental activities of daily living* (IADLs), including housekeeping, cooking, shopping, laundry, and managing money and medication. In recent years, the idea of cash payments has been extended to additional areas, including employment supports and vocational rehabilitation.

Although *cash payment programs* are not new, there has been growing interest in them as policy makers seek new ways to control long-term service costs while maintaining or increasing consumer satisfaction. When a program design emphasizes minimal restrictions on uses of a cash benefit, cash payments may be considered an ultimate form of consumer direction.

Consumer-directed services, which emanated from the disability rights and independent living movements more than 3 decades ago, promote maximum consumer choice and control (DeJong, Batavia, & McKnew, 1992). The language of the *disability movement*—referring to "consumers" rather than "patients"—reflects its *empowerment goals*. The aging community began to adopt *consumer-direction principles* in the late 1980s, with the development of a coalition between the communities of the aging and of younger persons with disabilities (Ansello & Eustis, 1992; Kapp, 1996; Simon-Rusinowitz & Hofland, 1993).

Traditional Home Care Payment Methods

To understand cash payments for care, it is helpful to describe basic methods for financing PAS in the United States. Public or private third-party payers can use any of 3 PAS financing methods: (1) *cash benefits* (payments to qualified clients or their representatives), (2) *vendor payments* (a case-manager determines the types or amounts of covered services, and arranges for and pays authorized PAS providers to deliver these services), and (3) *vouchers* (clients use funds for authorized purchases).

Most existing public programs that finance PAS in the United States follow a *vendor-payment model*, in which the program purchases services for consumers from authorized vendors (i.e., service providers or equipment suppliers). In some programs, the list of covered services and authorized vendors is restricted. Others may have a broader range of covered services, adding adult day care, transportation, home modifications, and assistive devices. Sometimes clients may hire independent providers not employed by home health agencies to be in-home aides.

In recent years, many state program officials have heeded the concerns of disability rights advocates, who want PAS programs that promote consumer choice and avoid program rules that may foster dependency in the name of consumer protection. In addition, most Medicaid PAS programs require case managers (registered nurses or social workers) to assess clients and monitor care plans. *Case management* can be expensive, and researchers and administrators question whether it is always necessary.

Although the primary focus here is on programs in the United States, cash payment programs are available in many other countries (Tilly, 1999). Cameron and Firman (1995) reported that most Western industrialized countries provide some sort of long-term care allowance for persons with disabilities. Freedman and Kemper (1996) studied home- and community-based service programs in 9 foreign countries and identified disability allowances in Austria and Germany, as well as an individualized cash benefit in the Netherlands.

In the United States, there has been increased interest in "*cash and counseling*," a consumer-directed cash payment demonstration that offers a cash allowance and information services to persons with disabilities. This program is currently under study in a national demonstration and evaluation conducted in 3 state Medicaid programs (Arkansas, New Jersey, and Florida). The cash-and-counseling design can be considered a modified pure cash benefit. The accountability required by publicly funded programs imposes some restrictions on uses of the cash; the cash option, which is basically the cash equivalent of the care plan the consumer would have been receiving under the traditional agency delivery system, can *only* be used to meet PAS needs. Consumers develop "*cash plans*," but they can be creative in proposing how they intend to meet their individual needs. For the most up-to-date results from the *Cash and Counseling Demonstration and Evaluation*, see www.cashandcounseling.org.

Cash and Counseling Demonstration and Evaluation: An Overview

The Cash and Counseling Demonstration and Evaluation (CCDE), a policy-driven study funded by the U.S. Department of Health and Human Services and the Robert Wood Johnson Foundation, has been evaluating the impact of cash payments for services. The University of Maryland Center on Aging (UMCA) served as the national program office. The evaluation compares the cash option with traditional agency-delivered services. The 3 demonstration states are offering the cash option to elders (over 65 years old) and adults with disabilities (ages 18 to 64). Children with developmental disabilities are also included in Florida.

The method for administering the cash option varies somewhat across the demonstration states. However, in general, persons eligible for participation include those who are currently receiving Medicaid personal care (or in Florida, Home and Community-Based Services waiver services), are age 18 or older, require assistance with ADLs, and are interested and willing to participate. Using the cash benefit, consumers choose who provides their services as well as when and how the services are provided. For example, consumers may hire a friend or relative who knows their preferences to help them on evenings or weekends when agency services may be unavailable. Counseling and bookkeeping services are offered to help consumers manage the cash allowance and required fiscal tasks. Persons who need help making decisions about their daily personal assistance may have a representative.

Background work for this national demonstration began in October 1995, and implementation began in December 1998, when Arkansas enrolled the first cash-option consumers. New Jersey began enrollment in November 1999, and Florida began enrolling consumers in early 2000. The evaluation, conducted by Mathematica Policy Research, randomly assigned consumers interested in the cash option to treatment and control groups. This comprehensive evaluation focuses on consumers' service use and preferences, quality of care, and service costs, as well as issues related to paid and informal workers. A companion ethnographic study has been conducted by researchers at the University of Maryland, Baltimore County. Results from Arkansas, the first state to implement cash and counseling, show that compared to clients receiving care from traditional home care agencies, consumers managing a cash allowance were more satisfied, had less unmet need, experienced similar or better health outcomes, and enjoyed an enhanced quality of life (Foster, et al., 2003). Furthermore, access to care was greatly improved and, although personal care costs were higher, overall public costs were not statistically different due to reductions in nursing facility usage by those managing their own budget (Dale, et al., 2003). Results from all 3 states are due out in 2005.

Issues to Consider

When implementing cash payment programs, policy makers and program managers need to consider numerous issues. Several key decisions they must make in designing cash payment programs include: defining policy objectives, choosing whether to offer a cash payment as the only option versus one option among others, deciding whether to offer support services, and addressing fraud and abuse concerns. For more detailed information on these topics, see "Lessons from the Implementation of Cash and Counseling in Arkansas, Florida and New Jersey" available at www.cashandcounseling.org.

Defining Policy Goals. Policy makers should be clear about the policy objectives they want to achieve with a cash payment program. At times, policy makers may be interested in many, possibly conflicting, policy goals. For example, they may see cash payment programs as a vehicle to enhance the quality of life for persons with disabilities (and their families) by offering more consumer choice. However, policy makers may be primarily concerned about controlling public spending. This latter priority could result in a program that restricts program eligibility (to avoid a "*woodwork effect*") and uses of the cash payment.

Key Cash Payment Program Design Choices. When considering types of cash payment programs to offer, program designers will need to consider 2 key program choices: (1) will they offer only a cash payment program, without giving consumers the choice of traditional services, as in Austria, or provide a choice of a cash payment program and traditional services, as in the CCDE; (2) will they offer a cash benefit alone, without support services for those consumers needing help in managing the cash benefit, as is typical in the German program, or will they make available support services, such as those in the CCDE, to teach consumers how to manage their services and possibly conduct the fiscal tasks for those consumers who choose not to do so. Each program choice reflects a philosophy and program goal.

When considering whether to offer a cash payment as the only option, it is important to consider consumers' preferences for traditional versus consumer-directed services. Background research conducted for the CCDE by the UMCA indicated strong interest in a consumer-directed cash option; however, a sizable number of consumers would want to maintain their traditional services. Across the demonstration states, interest in a cash option among consumers answering for themselves ranged from 29% to 59%; interest among representatives answering for consumers ranged from 39% to 49% (Simon-Rusinowitz, Mahoney, Desmond, Shoop, Squillace, & Fay, 1998). In addition, survey respondents also thought it was important to be able to back out of the cash option and return to traditional services if they so desired. This information provides support for offering a cash option as one choice among others.

Offering Support Services. When considering whether to offer support services along with a cash option, several design choices must be addressed: what type of support services should be offered, and should these services be offered on a voluntary or a mandatory basis? The decision whether to offer support services also has implications for program costs. Background research for the CCDE and initial program experience indicate a strong desire for support services and can provide guidance regarding some choices for types of services. For instance, nearly all the participants in the CCDE chose to utilize a "*fiscal management service*" to issue checks, pay taxes, and handle the paperwork, rather than serve as their own fiscal agents. Consumers seemed more interested in managing an individualized budget than in handling the cash itself (although substantial numbers in all 3 states chose to receive 10% to 20% of their allowance in cash for miscellaneous incidental purchases.

Fraud and Abuse Concerns. Finally, especially in programs that restrict the use of funds, concern about potential *fraud and abuse in cash payment programs* receives much attention from policy makers and program administrators. Experience from the CCDE may be instructive, as this project has needed to address such concerns in each demonstration state's program design, including the possibility that consumers and/or their families might abuse the cash benefit or be exploited by others (Doty, 1997). Misuse of the cash benefit also includes the possibility that consumers might not pay taxes on their workers. In summary, there have been no major cases of consumer fraud and abuse during the first 6 years of operation.

To prevent consumer exploitation by others (and their subsequent suffering of the ill effects), the CCDE allows and encourages the use of surrogate decision makers to represent consumers who are unable to make all decisions independently. The use of representatives may be especially comforting for those concerned about frail elders and consumers with intellectual disabilities who may not be able to conduct all employer tasks independently.

Conclusion

Cash payments for care, a financing mechanism that provides a cash benefit to consumers and/or their representatives, is not new in the United States or abroad. However, policy makers have become increasingly interested in this payment method, as it has the potential to contain program costs and maintain or increase consumer satisfaction by enhancing consumer autonomy. There is much to learn about the impact of a cash payment program's design on outcomes (such as enhanced consumer choice) and cost. A national trial of one type of cash payment program, Cash and Counseling Demonstration and Evaluation, is nearly complete in 3 state Medicaid programs. This research sheds light on design issues, as well as consumer interest in and satisfaction with this cash option. Initial results have proven so positive the Centers for Medicare and Medicaid Services have issued model waiver templates (called *Independence Plus waiver templates*) making it easier for states to develop consumer-directed program options. In October 2004, the *Robert Wood Johnson Foundation*, in collaboration with the Office of the Assistant Secretary for Planning and Evaluation and the Administration on Aging in the U.S. Department of Health and Human Services, funded an additional 11 states to replicate the cash and counseling model and help bring this promising practice to scale, with hope that in the near future every state might offer such a consumer-directed option.

KEVIN J. MAHONEY
LORI SIMON-RUSINOWITZ
LORI N. MARKS

See also
Case Management

References

Ansello, E. F., & Eustis, N. N. (1992). A common stake? Investigating the emerging intersection of aging disabilities. *Generations, 16*, 5–8.

Cameron, K., & Firman, J. (1995). International and domestic programs using "cash and counseling" strategies to pay for long-term care. Washington, DC: National Council on Aging.

Dale, S., Brown, R., Phillips, B., Schore, J., & Carlson, B. (2003). The Effects of Cash and Counseling on Personal Care Services and Medicaid Costs In Arkansas, 19 November 2003. http://content.healthaffairs.org/cgi/content/full/hlthaff.w3.566v1/DC1

DeJong, G., Batavia, A. I., & McKnew, L. (1992). The independent living model of personal assistance in national long-term care policy. *Generations, 16*, 89–95.

Doty, P. (1997). *Internal briefing paper addressing the possible fraud and abuse issues in the cash option.* Unpublished report. Office of the Assistant Secretary for Planning and Evaluation, U.S. Department of Health and Human Services.

Freedman, V. A., & Kemper, P. (1996). Designing home care benefits: The range of options and experience. In M. E. Cowan & J. Quadagno (Eds.), *From nursing homes to home care* (pp. 129–148). Binghamton, NY: Haworth Press.

Foster, L., Brown, R., Phillips, B., Schore, J., & Carlson, B. (2003). Improving the Quality of Medicaid Personal Assistance through Consumer Direction, 26 March 2003. http://content.healthaffairs.org/cgi/content/full/hlthaff.w3.162v1/DC1

Kapp, M. (1996). Enhancing autonomy and choice in selecting and directing long-term care services. *Elder Law Journal, 4*(1), 55–97.

Simon-Rusinowitz, L., & Hofland, B. F. (1993). Adopting a disability approach to home care services for older adults. *Gerontologist, 33*, 159–167.

Simon-Rusinowitz, L., Mahoney, K. J., Desmond, S. M., Shoop, D. M., Squillace, M. R., & Fay, R. A. (1998). *Determining consumer preferences for a cash option: Background research to support the cash and counseling demonstration and evaluation (synthesis of key telephone survey findings: Arkansas, New York, New Jersey, and Florida elders and adults with physical disabilities.)* Presentation at the 51st annual scientific meeting of the Gerontological Society of America, Philadelphia.

Tilly, J. (1999). *Consumer-directed long-term care: Participants' experiences in five countries.* Washington, DC: AARP.

CELL AGING: RELATIONSHIP BETWEEN IN VITRO AND IN VIVO MODELS

Interactive Components of Organism Aging

Senescent changes in the organism involve different types of cells and tissues and thus may have multiple mechanisms for their occurrence. For example, aging in fixed post mitotic cells, such as neurons, may proceed by different mechanisms than those driving aging in proliferating tissues such as skin, the lining of the gut, or the blood-forming elements. Matrix macromolecules, such as *collagen* and *elastin*, are also altered by aging, but with their own unique parameters of senescent degeneration since these molecules are directly affected by both environmental factors and by changes in the cells that produce them. The interactions of different types of cells and biological components also may change with time, potentially exerting profound effects at the level of the organism.

Decline of Replicative Capacity In Vivo

In general, *proliferating cells in vivo* exhibit an initially high rate of cell doubling (during developmental phases), followed by a gradual but sustained decline in proliferation rate. With the notable exception of cells of the stomach lining, there is an age-associated decline in mitotic activity and proliferation rates in a wide variety of human and rodent tissues in vivo. However, many studies of cell proliferation in vivo fall short of elucidating the relative contribution of intrinsic versus extrinsic factors (such as alterations in the extracellular matrix) to this decline. Thus, evaluation of various biochemical and morphological parameters of functional capacity that accompany the decline in proliferative capacity in vitro may be of considerable importance to our understanding of the mechanisms of senescence and of the control of cell proliferation in vivo. A group of studies bearing on this point involves the serial transplantation of normal somatic tissues to new, young, inbred hosts each time the recipient approaches old age. In general, normal cells serially transplanted to inbred hosts seem to show a decline in proliferative capacity and probably cannot survive indefinitely (for review, see Cristofalo & Pignolo, 1993). Also, mouse epidermis from old donors retains an increased susceptibility to carcinogens, whether transplanted into young or old recipients.

Decreased antibody production by spleen cells (but not bone marrow cells) from old mice transplanted into young irradiated recipients suggests that senescence of immune-reactive cells in mice may be related to a change undergone by these cells when they migrate from bone marrow to spleen. The proliferative capacity of spleen cells derived from old animals and transplanted into young irradiated hosts is reported to be reduced; however, the trauma of transplantation can not be ruled out as a contributing factor to this *proliferative decline*.

Cell Culture as a Model for Aging In Vivo

The suggestion that aging changes in vivo are reflected in various properties of tissue cultures has a long history. For example; it has been known since the early 1900s that age-associated changes that occur in plasma can inhibit cell growth in vitro. In addition, the time elapsing prior to cell migration from explanted tissue fragments increases with increasing age. Both are examples of the expression in vitro of aging in vivo.

In vitro studies on aging have used two kinds of cell culture models. The predominant one has been fetal- or neonatal-derived cultures that show aging changes when serially subcultured; some of these alterations parallel aging changes in vivo. The other is that of cells derived from donors of different ages and studied after only one or a few subcultivations. Both these models have been used in attempts to relate changes that occur in individual cells to changes occurring in organisms as they age.

There is little doubt that organismic failures in aging have a cellular basis. *Replicative senescence* in culture fits the description and definition of cell senescence; with subcultivation there is a gradual loss of proliferative capacity in the population until the culture can no longer be subcultivated. In vivo there is a gradual attenuation of proliferation rates of some cell types with age, suggesting parallel changes in proliferative regulation in vivo and in vitro (Cristofalo and Pignolo, 1995; Cristofalo et al., 2003). Thus the study of replicative senescence in vitro as a model for cellular changes in vivo is attractive since it brings the experimental advantage of cells that exhibit some features of senescence that are maintained in an environment that is under the control of the investigator.

Despite numerous published studies on replicative senescence over the last 40 years, the relevance of in vitro studies to aging in vivo has been controversial. The question of major interest is whether, and to what extent, the changes observed in replicative senescence duplicate the pathways and mechanisms of cell senescence in situ. One of the major sources of support for the direct relationship of replicative senescence to cell senescence in situ has been the putative decline in the replicative lifespan of skin fibroblasts (and other cell types) in culture as a function of donor age, (Martin et al., 1970; Schneider and Mitsui, 1976). Such a relationship would suggest that aging in situ, which is a function of donor age, modulates proliferative life span and that the physiological effect of aging in vivo are reflected by the life span of cells maintained in vitro. However, failure to consistently show this inverse relationship of donor age to proliferative lifespan has been problematic for defining the relevance of the cell culture model to organismic aging. In fact, several studies (Goldstein et al., 1978a; Cristofalo et al., 1998a; Smith et al., 2002), using healthy donors of different ages, have demonstrated that there is large variability and no statistically significant age association with replicative lifespan for human fibroblast cultures (Goldstein et al., 1978a; Cristofalo et al., 1998a).

Existing evidence indicates that the replicative lifespan of a culture reflects the maximum replicative capacity of the longest-lived clone in the population (Smith and Hayflick, 1974). Thus, the procedure of comparing donor age to replicative lifespan is confounded by selection pressures against slower growing cells that take place from the first outgrowth, through serial subcultivation, to senescence. To avoid variability due to selection, some investigators have used the *colony size distribution (CSD) assay* to measure proliferative potential as a function of donor age. CSD evaluates the capacity of cell populations to form colonies of a certain minimal size within a defined period of time, and while populations examined by the CSD method are not free of selection effects, the cells have experienced "less selection" than populations subcultivated multiple times over long periods in culture. However, even by this approach there are discrepancies among studies; some investigators reported that the colony-forming capacity of individual cells declines as a function of donor age while others found no significant correlation. Furthermore, experimental evidenced suggests that CSD is also affected by selection pressures and in general is not useful as a method for estimating total replicative lifespan [reviewed by (Cristofalo et al., 2003)]. For example, Balin, et al. (Balin et al., 2002) have shown that no matter how soon cells are examined after their initial outgrowth from biopsy pieces, there may still be artifacts that complicate the interpretation of results. They found, that the way tissue cultures are typically established, the initial outgrowth population does not accurately reflect the total population of viable cells in a tissue biopsy. Thus, with regard to human aging, methods that determine either total cumulative lifespan or colony size distribution may be misleading when interpreted to reflect the proliferative capacity of the tissue from which the culture was derived.

An additional problem in evaluating the relevance of replicative senescence arises from the fact that several authors have shown that modulation of the expression of certain genes (Serrano et al., 1997; Uhrbom et al., 1997; McConnell et al., 1998) as well as some changes in the culture environment (von Zglinicki et al., 1995; Chen et al., 2000; Severino et al., 2000b) can produce a phenotype that is apparently indistinguishable from replicative senescence. Thus, the senescent phenotype can be achieved irrespective of proliferation. The fact that many different stimuli can produce the so-called senescent phenotype suggests that this phenotype may be a final, common pathway for replicating cells in which signaling or metabolic imbalances occur. When placed in culture, cells may be unable to achieve their "true" differentiated fate (identical to the one in vivo) either because of signals missing from the culture medium or failure to process these signals. Despite reports to the contrary (Dimri et al., 1995), the fact that the senescent phenotype has never been confirmed in healthy tissues in vivo is consistent with this view (Robbins et al., 1970; Severino et al., 2000b).

Another confounding issue relates to the "*telomere hypothesis of aging*" that proposes that replicative aging may be regulated by telomere shortening. Since replication-driven telomere shortening is a general phenomenon during senescence in culture, alterations of telomere length and/or integrity in vivo would provide strong evidence that replicative senescence does occur during aging in vivo. To date, only small decreases in telomere length in proliferating and non proliferating tissues have been reported (Allsopp et al., 1992a; Frenck et al., 1998; Kveiborg et al., 1999; Aikata et al., 2000). Allshopp et al (Allsopp et al., 1992b) reported that, although telomere length was marginally correlated to donor age, a much stronger correlation was observed between the proliferative capacity of clones and telomere length. Interestingly, telomere length was found to be highly variable in multiple clones established from a single individual (Allsopp and Harley, 1995). Kang et al. reported a small but significant decrease in telomere length of oral keratinocytes with increasing donor age but no decrease in oral fibroblasts (Kang et al., 2003). Thus, the large number of variations and exceptions to the original formulation of the Telomere Hypothesis, as well as the evidence for selection in serial subcultivations, demonstrate that the data fail to support clearly a relationship between donor age and average telomere length in vitro [for reviews see (Rubin, 2002; Cristofalo et al., 2003; Cristofalo et al., 2004)].

In summary, it appears that no method of determining or estimating the replicative lifespan of fibroblasts in culture supports the direct relationship between replicative capacity in vitro and adult donor age. Hence, the generally accepted relationship between replicative lifespan in vitro and donor age as evidence for the direct applicability of studies in fibroblast culture to organismic aging is fundamentally flawed. The fact that this relationship cannot be demonstrated reproducibly will undoubtedly lead some to conclude that the cell culture senescence model is not relevant for studies on aging. However, while the putative inverse relationship between donor age and proliferative lifespan has been widely used to support the utility of the cell culture model, it is not a requirement for using cell culture as a model of aging. In fact, the original speculation by Hayflick and Moorhead of cell culture senescence as a model of aging was proposed before any relationship between donor age and proliferative capacity had been published or suggested.

Human *fibroblasts in culture* express human genetic, metabolic and regulatory behavior. The use of cell cultures permits study of the mechanisms of changes that occur while the cells undergo a predictable and reproducible deterioration in a constant environment. Fibroblast cultures are valuable for examining a variety of questions and hypotheses relevant to the biology of aging. In fact, the human fibroblast model has already been valuable for explaining the cellular basis of some mechanisms underlying cellular aging changes observed in situ; also for testing hypotheses that address what may be common mechanisms underlying cell deterioration and loss of integrative function such as the effects of reactive oxygen species, overexpression and underexpression of signaling molecules, and other modulations particularly important to the mechanisms underlying aging.

Genetic Disorders and Cellular Aging In Vivo

Goldstein et al (Goldstein et al., 1978b) and Martin (Martin, 1978) showed that cells from patients with Hutchinson-Gilford syndrome or Werner's syndrome, both diseases associated with *progeroid syndromes*, have a reduced proliferative capacity, compared with control cells from normal donors of the same ages. Interestingly, fibroblast cultures established from individuals with Hutchinson-Gilford progeria syndrome exhibit shorter telomeres and a lower proliferative capacity than do cells from normal individuals; however, the rate of telomere shortening per cell division appears to be similar in progeria fibroblasts and normal cells (Allsopp et al., 1992a). Progeroid syndromes are generally defined by the premature appearance of characteristics of senescence. None of them can be considered an exact phenocopy of normal human aging. Thus, Martin (Martin, 1978) has suggested that they be referred to as "segmental" progeroid syndromes that approximate certain aspects of the aging process. Other workers have reported decreased mitotic activity, DNA synthesis, and cloning efficiency for cells from these persons. In addition, cells derived from diabetic individuals have a reduced ability to grow and survive in culture, as reflected in a reduced plating efficiency, although these studies are complicated by other factors. Cultures established from patients with Werner's syndrome and from individuals with Down's syndrome also have been reported to exhibit decreased proliferative potential, albeit, results with the replication of Down's syndrome cells are more variable and remain controversial.

Biomarkers of Cellular Aging In Vitro and In Vivo

In addition to the loss of division potential associated with aging in vitro and in vivo, as described above, many other significant alterations that occur with senescence in vitro also occur with cellular senescence in vivo. These changes include but are not limited to increased chromosome number (ploidy), increased cell size, decreased response to growth signals, the decreased expression of genes potentially involved in growth control, the increased expression of genes that help shape the extracellular matrix, and various changes in cell morphology (for review, see (Cristofalo and Pignolo, 1993; Cristofalo et al., 1998b; Cristofalo et al., 2004). In addition, numerous studies have shown that cellular processes affected by age in vitro are also altered with age of the organism. For example transduction of mitogenic signals, response to environmental stress and proteolysis are impaired in both senescent cultures and various tissues of old animals.

One potentially universal marker of aging was reported by Dimri et al (Dimri et al., 1995), who observed increases in cytochemically detectable β-galactosidase activity (SA β-gal) at pH 6.0, both in cell cultures and in tissue sections obtained from old donors. They also observed that immortal cells exhibited no SA β-gal staining under identical culture conditions (Dimri et al., 1995). Additionally, they interpreted their results as providing a link between replicative senescence and aging in vivo. Their observation appeared to be supported by Pendergrass et al (Pendergrass et al., 1999) who reported that SA β-gal positive staining increased as a function of age in rhesus monkeys. However, these observations remain controversial. SA β-gal positive cells have been observed in quiescent cultures of Swiss 3T3 as well as some types of human cancer cells that were chemically stimulated to differentiate, neither of which can be classified as senescent. Furthermore, biochemical analysis has been used to demonstrate SA β-gal activity in a number of different tumor lines at both pH 6.0 and pH 4.5. We also examined this phenomenon recently and observed that SA β-gal positive staining was present in subconfluent senescent WI-38 fibroblasts but was essentially absent from subconfluent early-passage cells, which supported the conclusion of Dimri and colleagues (Dimri et al., 1995). Conversely, we were unable to detect any correlation with donor age, either in tissue sections or in skin fibroblast cultures established from donors of different ages (Severino et al., 2000a). The source of these discrepancies cannot be entirely elucidated; however, it is clear that this type of staining cannot be used as a marker for all types of aging under all conditions.

The possibility exists that these relationships are indirect and that the cell culture system is simply a model to study the regulation of cell proliferation, which, in turn, shows age-associated changes. Even then, however, it remains an important model for aging in vivo because the two principal age-associated diseases, cancer and atherosclerosis, represent failures in the regulation of cell proliferation. Overall, it is clear that characteristic aging changes in vivo are expressed in cell culture. Detailed analysis of these changes in vivo shows that they have the same apparent trajectory as aging in vitro and appear tightly coupled to the capacity for cell proliferation. For a comprehensive review of cell aging in vivo, including reference material prior to 1980, see (Cristofalo and Pignolo, 1993; Cristofalo et al., 1998b; Cristofalo et al., 2003; Cristofalo et al., 2004).

Maria Tresini
Robert J. Pignolo
Robert G. Allen
Vincent J. Cristofalo

See also
Cytogerontology
Telomere Senescence Theory

References

Aikata, H., Takaishi, H., Kawakami, Y., Takahashi, S., Kitamoto, M., Nakanishi, T., Nakamura, Y., Shimamoto, F., Kajiyama, G., and Ide, T. (2000). Telomere reduction in human liver tissues with age and chronic inflammation. *Experimental Cell Research, 256*, 578–582.

Allsopp, R. C., and Harley, C. B. (1995). Evidence for a critical telomere length in senescent human fibroblasts. *Experimental Cell Research*, *219*, 130–136.

Allsopp, R. C., Vaziri, H., Patterson, C., Goldstein, S., Younglai, E. V., Futcher, A. B., Greider, C. W., and Harley, C. B. (1992a). Telomere length predicts replicative capacity of human fibroblasts. *Proceedings of the National Academy of Science USA*, *89*, 10114–10118.

Allsopp, R. C., Vaziri, H., Patterson, C., Goldstein, S., Younglai, E. V., Futcher, A. B., Greider, C. W., and Harley, C. B. (1992b). Telomere length predicts replicative capacity of human fibroblasts. *Proceedings of the National Academy of Science USA*, *89*, 10114–10118.

Balin, A. K., Fisher, A. J., Anzelone, M., Leong, I., and Allen, R. G. (2002). Effects of establishing cell cultures and cell culture conditions on the proliferative life span of human fibroblasts isolated from different tissues and donors of different ages. *Experimental Cell Research*, *274*, 275–287.

Chen, Q. M., Tu, V. C., and Liu, J. (2000). Measurements of hydrogen peroxide induced premature senescence: Senescence-associated β-galactosidase and DNA synthesis index in human diploid fibroblasts with down-regulated p53 or Rb. *Biogerontology*, *1*, 335–339.

Cristofalo, V. J., Allen, R. G., Pignolo, R. P., Martin, B. M., and Beck, J. C. (1998a). Relationship between donor age and the replicative life spans of human cells in culture: A re-evaluation. *Proceedings of the National Academy of Science USA*, *95*, 10614–10619.

Cristofalo, V. J., Beck, J., and Allen, R. G. (2003). Cell senescence: An evaluation of replicative senescence in culture as a model for cell aging in situ. *Journal of Gerontolology, A*, *58*, B776–779; discussion 779–781.

Cristofalo, V. J., Lorenzini, A., Allen, R. G., Torres, C., and Tresini, M. (2004). Replicative senescence: A critical review. *Mechanisms of Aging and Development*, *125*, 827–848.

Cristofalo, V. J., and Pignolo, R. J. (1993). Replicative senescence of human fibroblast-like cells in culture. *Physiology Review*, *73*, 617–638.

Cristofalo, V. J., and Pignolo, R. J. (1995). Cell culture as a model. In: *Handbook of physiology—aging*, vol. 4, ed. E. J. Masoro, New York: Oxford University Press, 53–82.

Cristofalo, V. J., Volker, C., Francis, M. K., and Tresini, M. (1998b). Age-dependent modifications of gene expression in human fibroblasts. *Critical Reviews in Eukaryotic Gene Expression*, *8*, 43–80.

Dimri, G. P., Lee, X., Basile, G., Acosta, M., Scott, G., Roskelley, C., Medrano, E. E., Linskens, M., Rubelj, I., Pereira-Smith, O., and et al. (1995). A biomarker that identifies senescent human cells in culture and in aging skin in vivo. *Proceedings of the National Academy of Science USA*, *92*, 9363–9367.

Frenck, R. W., H., B.E., and Shannon, K. M. (1998). The rate of telomere sequence loss in human leukocytes varies with age. *Proceedings of the National Academy of Science USA*, *95*, 5607–5610.

Goldstein, S., Moerman, E. J., Soeldner, J. S., Gleason, R. E., and Barnett, D. M. (1978a). Chronologic and physiologic age affect replicative life-span of fibroblasts from diabetic, prediabetic, and normal donors. *Science*, *199*, 781–782.

Goldstein, S., Moerman, E. J., Soeldner, J. S., Gleason, R. E., and Barnett, D. M. (1978b). Chronologic and physiologic age affect replicative life-span of fibroblasts from diabetic, prediabetic, and normal donors. *Science*, *199*, 781–782.

Kang, M. K., Kameta, A., Shin, K. H., Baluda, M. A., Kim, H. R., and Park, N. H. (2003). Senescence-associated genes in normal human oral keratinocytes. *Experimental Cell Research*, *287*, 272–281.

Kveiborg, M., Kassem, M., Langdahl, B., Eriksen, E. F., Clark, B. F., and Rattan, S. I. (1999). Telomere shortening during aging of human osteoblasts in vitro and leukocytes in vivo: Lack of excessive telomere loss in osteoporotic patients. *Mechanisms of Aging and Development*, *106*, 261–271.

Martin, G. M. (1978). Genetic syndromes in man with potential relevance to the pathobiology of aging. *Birth Defects Original Article Series*, *14*, 5–39.

Martin, G. M., Sprague, C. A., and Epstein, C. J. (1970). Replicative life-span of cultivated human cells. *Laboratory Investigations*, *23*, 86–92.

McConnell, B. B., Starborg, M., Brookes, S., and Peters, G. (1998). Inhibitors of cyclin-dependent kinases induce features of replicative senescence in early passage human diploid fibroblasts. *Current Biology*, *8*, 351–354.

Pendergrass, W. R., Lane, M. A., Bodkin, N. L., Hansen, B. C., Ingram, D. K., Roth, G. S., Yi, L., Bin, H., and Wolf, N. S. (1999). Cellular proliferation potential during aging and caloric restriction in rhesus monkeys (Macaca mulatta). *Journal of Cell Physiology*, *180*, 123–130.

Robbins, E., Levine, E. M., and Eagle, H. (1970). Morphologic changes accompanying senescence of cultured human diploid cells. *Journal of Experimental Medicine*, *131*, 1211–1222.

Rubin, H. (2002). The disparity between human cell senescence in vitro and lifelong replication in vivo. *National Biotechnology*, *20*, 675–681.

Schneider, E. L., and Mitsui, Y. (1976). The relationship between in vitro cellular aging and in vivo human age. *Proceedings of the National Academy of Science USA*, *73*, 3584–3588.

Serrano, M., Lin, A. W., McCurrach, M. E., Beach, D., and Lowe, S. W. (1997). Oncogenic ras provokes premature cell senescence associated with accumulation of p53 and p16^{ink4a}. *Cell, 88*, 593–602.

Severino, J., Allen, R. G., Balin, S., Balin, A., and Cristofalo, V. J. (2000a). Is beta-galactosidase staining a marker of senescence in vitro and in vivo? *Experimental Cell Research, 257*, 162–171.

Severino, J., Allen, R. G., Balin, S., Balin, A., and Cristofalo, V. J. (2000b). Is β-galactosidase staining a marker of senescence *in vitro* and *in vivo*? *Experimental Cell Research, 257*, 162–171.

Smith, J. R., and Hayflick, L. (1974). Variation in the lifespan of clones derived from human diploid cell strains. *Journal of Cell Biology, 62*, 48–53.

Smith, J. R., Venable, S., Roberts, T. W., Metter, E. J., Monticone, R., and Schneider, E. L. (2002). Relationship between in vivo age and in vitro aging: Assessment of 669 cell cultures derived from members of the Baltimore Longitudinal Study of Aging. *Journal of Gerontology: A, 57*, B239–246.

Uhrbom, L., Nist, R. M., and Westermark, B. (1997). Induction of senescence in human malignant glioma cells by p16^{ink4A}. *Oncogene 15*, 505–514.

von Zglinicki, T., Saretzki, G., Döcke, W., and Lotze, C. (1995). Mild hyperoxia shortens telomeres and inhibits proliferation of fibroblasts: A model for senescence? *Experimental Cell Research, 220*, 186–192.

CELL AGING IN VITRO

Limited Proliferative Capacity of Normal Human Cells

Early studies by Carrel and coworkers suggested that individual cells, when separated from the organism, were potentially immortal, in the same way that bacteria and most protozoa are considered immortal. However, subsequent studies conducted in a number of laboratories, especially those of Hayflick at the Wistar Institute in Philadelphia, established that normal human diploid cells replicate only a finite number of times (Hayflick & Moorhead, 1961).

After explantation from the tissue, during the proliferative life span of fibroblast cultures, there is an initial phase of rapid proliferation followed by a period of declining replicative frequency; ultimately, cultures become senescent and are incapable of further proliferation. During this later phase, the cells change in size and morphology, become granular, and accumulate debris. Early studies showed that the inability of cell cultures to proliferate indefinitely could not be ascribed to various technical difficulties, such as inadequate nutrition, pH variation, toxic metabolic products, and microcontaminants, or to depletion by serial dilution of some essential metabolite. It was also shown that the loss of proliferation potential is not affected significantly by chronological time; rather, the total number of division events is what determines *life span in vitro* (Cristofalo & Pignolo, 1993). Hayflick and Moorhead concluded that the *limited life span phenomenon* could be programmed and/or that genetic damage may accumulate, and they interpreted their observation as a *cellular expression of aging* (Hayflick & Moorhead, 1961).

Replicative senescence is not specific to human fibroblasts; it has been described in cultures from chickens as well as cell lines derived from numerous mammalian species. Senescence also occurs in a variety of cell types other than fibroblasts, including glial cells (Ponten, 1973), keratinocytes (Rheinwald, 1975), vascular smooth muscle cells (Bierman, 1978), lens cells (Tassin, Malaise, & Courtois, 1979), endothelial cells (Mueller, Rose, & Levine, 1980), and lymphocytes (Tice, Schneider, Kram, & Thorne, 1979). Interestingly, although the proliferative capacity differs among various types of cells, for any given cell type the proliferative capacity tends to be relatively constant.

In general, *loss of proliferative capacity* in human diploid cell populations appears to be a well-regulated phenomenon, during which substantial heterogeneity develops in the population. Cristofalo (1972) suggested that *cellular aging* may follow a differentiation lineage model while Martin and colleagues (1974) postulated that the finite life span may represent differentiation of cell types and that the process of diploid cell growth may have an in vivo counterpart in hyperplastic processes.

Changes in Cell Morphology and Contact

Although the hallmark of replicative senescence is the loss of responsiveness to mitogens, the "*senescent phenotype*" is also characterized by altered growth properties, morphology, and a general dysregulation of coordinated processes. The morphology of fibroblasts near the end of their replicative life span is mainly evidenced by cellular enlargement and flattening with a concomitant increase in the size of the nucleus and nucleoli, an increase in the number of lysosomes and Golgi (Cristofalo & Kritchevsky, 1969; Mitsui & Schneider, 1976; Greenberg, Grove, & Cristofalo 1977), the appearance of vacuoles in the cytoplasm and endoplasmic reticulum, and an increase in the number of cytoplasmic microfilaments (Comings & Okada, 1970; Brandes, Murphy, Anton, & Barnard, 1972; Lipetz & Cristofalo, 1972). In addition to the morphological changes, populations of senescent cells exhibit an increase in the number of multinucleated cells (Yanishevsky & Carrano, 1975; Galloway & Buckton, 1978; Matsumura, Pfendt, & Hayflick, 1979; Matsumura, 1980).

The gradual loss of replicative potential that senescent cells exhibit results in reduced harvest densities and saturation densities (Macieira-Coelho, 1966; Cristofalo, 1988). At the end of their life span in vitro, substantial *cell death* occurs; however, a stable population emerges that can exist in a viable, nonproliferative state for many months (Pignolo, Rotenberg, & Cristofalo 1994). This stable population is capable of maintaining only an extremely low saturation density, equivalent to less than 5% of that reached by early-passage cultures; this likely reflects an increased sensitivity to intercellular contact, rather than increased numbers of larger cells (Pignolo, Rotenberg, & Cristofalo 1994). Changes at the level of extracellular matrix (ECM), specific secretory proteins not connected with the ECM, and membrane-associated molecules occur in late-passage cells, but it is unclear whether they account for alterations in the nature of contact among these cells (Cristofalo, Volker, Francis, & Tresini, 1998; Cristofalo, Lorenzini, Allen, Torres, & Tresini, 2004).

Changes in Macromolecular Content, Synthesis, and Cell Cycle Progression

As cells approach the end of their proliferative life span in vitro, the *synthesis rate of macromolecules* decreases, whereas the cellular content of macromolecules, except DNA, increases. These observations are reminiscent of the phenomenon of unbalanced growth in bacteria described more than 40 years ago by Cohen and Bamer. It appears that in late passage cultures, DNA synthesis becomes uncoupled from other macromolecular syntheses, and there is a general dysregulation of coordinated processes [(Cristofalo, Lorenzini, Allen, Torres, & Tresini, 2004). Cells tend to remain essentially diploid until the very near the end of their life span in vitro, when they exhibit structural chromosomal changes and increasing levels of tetraploidy and polyploidy. DNA, RNA, and protein synthetic rates decrease in late population-doubling level cultures and may be related to the altered chromatin template activity in senescent cells.

Extensive studies in cell cycle timing and regulation show that rapidly proliferating populations of early passage cells evolve gradually into more slowly cycling populations with successive subcultivations. Ultimately, cultures maintained under conditions that do not allow cessation of growth exhaust their proliferative capacity and can no longer double in number. Cell cycle time becomes progressively protracted principally as a result of prolongation of G1. Although the cells within a senescing population reach a state in which they can no longer initiate replication, this happens asynchronously, so that at any given moment in actively mitotic cultures, the population is a heterogeneous mixture of senescent and nonsenescent cells that are at various stages in their proliferative life. Early passage cultures consist primarily of cells that exhibit short cell cycle periods. With successive subcultivations, there is an increase in the percentage of cells in the population that exhibit longer generation times and those unable to proliferate.

Senescent cells reach an irreversibly arrested condition that is distinct from either the G0 phase that young cells achieve or any other definable state within the cell cycle. When cultured under conditions that would define the quiescent state in early passage cells, the pattern of gene expression exhibited by senescent cells is different from that of a functional G0 state. Furthermore, experiments that examined the expression of cell cycle regulated genes, chromatin fluorescence, and nucleoli number have shown that senescent cells are arrested prior to entering the S phase of the cell cycle, with many characteristics resembling late G1 (Gorman & Cristofalo, 1986; Pignolo Martin, Horton, Kalbach, & Cristofalo, 1997). This state however appears to be distinct from the G1/S interface of early passage cells: while both young and senescent cultures appear to respond to mitogenic growth factors by carrying out some of the same cell cycle processes in roughly the same time frame, expression of several genes normally expressed early in G1 (*c-fos*, *erg-1*, *id-1H*, *id-2H*) is impaired in senescent cultures (Cristofalo, Volker, Francis, & Tresini, 1998; Cristofalo, Lorenzini, Allen, Torres, & Tresini, 2004).

There are numerous studies on the expression and possible contributing role of *cell-cycle regulators* in replicative senescence. Some examples include the overexpression of CDK inhibitors p16 and p21 (Nakanishi Robetorye, Pereira-Smith, & Smith, 1995; Alcorta, Xiong, Phelps, Hannon, Beach, & Barrett, 1996), and the increased activity of the checkpoint inhibitors, p53 and Rb (Futreal & Barrett, 1991; Hara, Tsurui, Shinozaki, Nakada, & Oda, 1991; Shay, Pereira-Smith, & Wright, 1991; Atadja, Wong, Garkavtsev, Veillette, & Riabowol, 1995). Most of these proteins are associated with inhibition of cell cycle progression, but it is still unclear whether overexpression of these proteins plays a causative role in replicative senescence or is the result of the arrest of senescent cells prior to S phase.

Response of Senescent Cells to Growth Signals

Since the hallmark of senescence in culture is the inability of cells to replicate their DNA, the possibility that replicative enzymes themselves and/or replication-associated processes are reduced or altered was addressed extensively in early studies. The lack of confirming evidence together with the observation that simian virus 40 (SV40) can initiate an additional round of semiconservative DNA synthesis in old cells provided strong evidence that this machinery is still capable of functioning (Gorman & Cristofalo, 1985). Furthermore, this observation led to the hypothesis that the impaired responsiveness of senescent fibroblast to mitogenic growth factors is the result of inappropriate transmission of mitogenic signals.

Cellular responses to environmental cues are mediated via activation of complex signaling cascades that invariably induce changes in gene expression. For example, the first event in a cascade initiated by growth factors is the activation of their cognate receptors, followed by formation of multiprotein complexes, phospholipid turnover, calcium mobilization and activation of protein kinases, phosphatases, and transcription factors. In response to mitogenic signals, the machinery of nuclear proteins that regulate progression through the cell cycle is also activated, together with proteins that ensure proper DNA replication, timing, and coordination of processes. Successful completion of these events leads ultimately to cell proliferation. Human diploid cells, at or near the beginning of their in vitro replicative life span, vigorously respond to serum or a defined combination of growth factors (mitogens) by initiating DNA synthesis and mitosis. As these cells approach the end of their proliferative potential in culture, they become increasingly refractory to mitogenic signals. The basis for this loss of responsiveness cannot be attributed to any dramatic reductions in the number of cell surface growth-factor receptors, or to the affinities with which these receptors bind ligands. Intrinsic changes at the level of the growth-factor receptors, however, have been delineated (Cristofalo, Volker, Francis, & Tresini, 1998; Cristofalo, Lorenzini, Allen, Torres, & Tresini, 2004).

Senescence-associated alterations in postreceptor transduction pathways have been documented and involve many of the processes that occur in response to receptor ligation, such as, phospholipid turnover, calcium mobilization, association of multiprotein complexes, and activation of protein kinases. Furthermore, proper activation of the 2 major signal transduction pathways, the PI3/Akt and the MAPK pathway, is impaired during replicative senescence (Cristofalo, Lorenzini, Allen, Torres, & Tresini, 2004).

Arrest of Senescent Cells: The *Telomere Hypothesis*

An important biomarker that is linked to the cessation of mitotic activity associated with cellular senescence is the progressive loss of chromosomal telomeric repeats (Levy, Allsopp, Futcher, Greider, & Harley, 1992). Telomeres are nucleoprotein complexes at the ends of the chromosomes that protect chromosomes from degradation, rearrangements, end-to-end fusions, and chromosome loss (Feng, Funk, Wang, Weinrich, Avilion, Chiu, et al., 1995). The telomeres of human chromosomes are composed of several kilobases of simple repeats (TTAGGG)n. During replication, DNA polymerases synthesize DNA in a 5′ to 3′ direction; they also require an RNA primer for initiation. The terminal RNA primer required for DNA replication cannot be replaced with DNA, which results in a loss of telomeric sequences with each mitotic cycle of normal cells (Levy, Allsopp, Futcher, Greider, & Harley, 1992; Feng, Funk, Wang, Weinrich, Avilion, Chiu, et al., 1995). The observation that telomere shortening correlates with senescence leads to the hypothesis that, with the shortening of telomeres, there is an associated loss of genetic information at or near the ends of chromosomes that is responsible for replicative decline. It also provides an attractive model for the way in which cells might "count" divisions.

This hypothesis further suggests there is a loss of telomerase activity in normal human fibroblasts that is preserved or restored in cells that have obtained an immortalized phenotype. Wright and Shay (1992) have proposed that senescence could be regulated by essential genes near the ends of chromosomes, not as the result of a physical loss of genetic material at these regions (although this also would occur) but by the activation or inactivation of telomeric sequences by changes in adjacent local chromatin condensation. Alternatively, loss of telomeric DNA could trigger stress response pathways that, when they reach a critical level, could result in cell cycle arrest. Despite its attractiveness, the telomere hypothesis is not always supported by experimental evidence. Conflicting results led some investigators to suggest that the limited replicative potential of diploid cells is the result of "*2 barriers to immortality*": the progressive alteration in the maintenance of telomeres, and the gradual accumulation of damage due to the stressful nature of cell culture (Stewart & Weinberg, 2002; Wright & Shay, 2002).

Genetic Basis for Cellular Aging

Skin fibroblasts from pairs of monozygotic twins show no significant difference in replicative life span within each pair, but did show differences among pairs. This observation would support the existence of a genetically regulated mechanism that, at least partially, controls the *rate of aging*. It is also noteworthy that in heterokaryons formed by the fusion of early- and late-passage cells, the nonproliferative senescent phenotype is dominant over the early-passage, proliferative phenotype and over immortalization. Exceptions to this dominant effect were found in immortalized variants having high levels of DNA polymerase alpha (DNA pol α) or those transformed by DNA tumor viruses. Numerous reports document the presence of inhibitor(s) of DNA synthesis in senescent cells, although the nature of these inhibitor(s) is poorly understood, and whether any of them plays a causal role in senescence is unclear (Cristofalo, Volker, Francis, & Tresini, 1998; Cristofalo, Lorenzini, Allen, Torres, & Tresini, 2004). The idea that senescent cells actively make an inhibitor of DNA synthesis, however, is supported further by the observation that poly A+ RNA derived from senescent fibroblasts, when microinjected into proliferation-competent cells, can inhibit their entry into DNA synthesis (Lumpkin McClung, Pereira-Smith, & Smith, 1986). Some of the most compelling evidence in support of a *genetic component for cellular senescence* has been the finding that introduction of particular chromosomes into immortalized cells causes them to acquire a senescent, or at least a nongrowing, phenotype. Evidence that the cessation of proliferation may be a programmed phenomenon has been provided by studies that characterized the apparently reversible escape from cellular senescence using SV40 large T antigen as a mediator of this transition; this suggests that senescence confers at least 2 distinct mortality states. The search for chromosomes carrying senescence-inducing genes has relied on the cytogenetic comparison of hybrids between immortal and normal human diploid fibroblasts for the loss of specific chromosomes and the concomitant potential for unlimited division. These studies have implicated human chromosomes 1, 4, and 7 (Ning, Weber, Killary, Ledbetter, Smith, & Pereira-Smith, 1991; Ogata, Ayusawa, Namba, Takahashi, Oshimura, & Oishi, 1993; Hensler Annab, L. A., Barrett, J. C., & Pereira-Smith, 1994) as putative sites for senescence-related genes. It is not clear, however, if genes located in these chromosomes encode inhibitors of cell cycle progression or proteins that can actually induce a state of growth arrest identical to senescence. Genetic influences over the process of cellular senescence would necessarily be reflected in reproducible changes in gene expression. The list of molecular markers of senescence in culture has dramatically increased as the result of examining genes isolated from selective libraries and monoclonal antibody pools. The number of genes isolated by these methods remarkably includes those involved with the extracellular matrix (ECM), secretory proteins involved in growth factor-mediated function, differentiation and shock proteins, inhibitors of DNA synthesis, and genes of unknown function (Cristofalo, Volker, Francis, & Tresini, 1998). Currently, it is not known whether differentially expressed genes are regulators of the process of senescence or downstream effects of a higher-order change which then results in a new but dysfunctional phenotype.

Maria Tresini
Robert J. Pignolo
Vincent J. Cristofalo

See also
Senescence and Transformation
Telomeres and Cellular Senescence

References

Alcorta, D. A., Xiong, Y., Phelps, D., Hannon, G., Beach, D., & Barrett, J. C. (1996). Involvement of the cyclin-dependent kinase inhibitor p16 (INK4a) in replicative senescence of normal human fibroblasts. *Proceedings of the National Academy of Sciences of the U.S.A., 93*, 13742–13747.

Atadja, P., Wong, H., Garkavtsev, I., Veillette, C., & Riabowol, K. (1995). Increased activity of p53 in senescing fibroblasts. *Proceedings of the National Academy of Sciences of the U.S.A., 92*, 8348–8352.

Bierman, E. L. (1978). The effects of donor age on the *in vitro* life span of cultured human arterial smooth-muscle cells. *In Vitro Cellular and Developmental Biology, 14*, 951–955.

Brandes, D., Murphy, D. G., Anton, E. B., & Barnard, S. (1972). Ultrastructural and cytochemical changes in cultured human lung cells. *Journal of Ultrastructural Research, 39*, 465–483.

Comings, D. E., & Okada, T. A. (1970). Electron microscopy of human fibroblasts in tissue culture during logarithmic and confluent stages of growth. *Experimental Cell Research, 61*, 295–301.

Cristofalo, V. J. (1972). Animal cell cultures as a model for the study of aging. In B. L. Strehler (ed.), *Advances in gerontological research* (pp. 45–79). New York: Academic Press.

Cristofalo, V. J. (1988). Cellular biomarkers of aging. *Experimental Gerontology, 23*, 297–307.

Cristofalo, V. J., & Kritchevsky, D. (1969). Cell size and nucleic acid content in the human diploid cell line WI-38 during aging. *Med. Exp. Int. J. Exp. Med. 19*, 313–320.

Cristofalo, V. J., Lorenzini, A., Allen, R. G., Torres, C., & Tresini, M. (2004). Replicative senescence: A critical review. *Mechanisms of Ageing and Development, 125*, 827–848.

Cristofalo, V. J., & Pignolo, R. J. (1993). Replicative senescence of human fibroblast-like cells in culture. *Physiological Reviews, 73*, 617–638.

Cristofalo, V. J., Volker, C., Francis, M. K., & Tresini, M. (1998). Age-dependent modifications of gene expression in human fibroblasts. *Critical Reviews in Eukaryotic Gene Expression, 8*, 43–80.

Feng, J., Funk, W. D., Wang, S. S., Weinrich, S. L., Avilion, A. A., Chiu, C. P., Adams, R. R., Chang, E., Allsopp, R. C., Yu, J., & et al. (1995). The RNA component of human telomerase. *Science, 269*, 1236–1241.

Futreal, P. A., & Barrett, J. C. (1991). Failure of senescent cells to phosphorylate the RB protein. *Oncogene, 6*, 1109–1113.

Galloway, S. M., & Buckton, K. E. (1978). Aneuploidy and ageing: Chromosome studies on a random sample of the population using G-banding. *Cytogenetics and Cell Genetics, 20*, 78–95.

Gorman, S. D., & Cristofalo, V. J. (1985). Reinitiation of cellular DNA synthesis in BrdU-selected nondividing senescent WI-38 cells by simian virus 40 infection. *Journal of Cellular Physiology, 125*, 122–126.

Gorman, S. D., & Cristofalo, V. J. (1986). Analysis of the G1 arrest position of senescent WI38 cells by quinacrine dihydrochloride nuclear fluorescence. Evidence for a late G1 arrest. *Experimental Cell Research, 167*, 87–94.

Greenberg, S. B., Grove, G. L., & Cristofalo, V. J. (1977). Cell size in aging monolayer cultures. *In Vitro, 13*, 297–300.

Hara, E., Tsurui, H., Shinozaki, A., Nakada, S., & Oda, K. (1991). Cooperative effect of antisense-Rb and antisense-p53 oligomers on the extension of life span in human diploid fibroblasts, TIG-1. *Biochemical and Biophysical Research Communications, 179*, 528–534.

Hayflick, L., & Moorhead, P. S. (1961). The serial cultivation of human diploid cell strains. *Experimental Cell Research, 25*, 585–621.

Hensler, P. J., Annab, L. A., Barrett, J. C., & Pereira-Smith, O. M. (1994). A gene involved in control of human cellular senescence on human chromosome 1q. *Molecular and Cellular Biology, 14*, 2291–2297.

Levy, M. Z., Allsopp, R. C., Futcher, A. B., Greider, C. W., & Harley, C. B. (1992). Telomere end-replication problem and cell aging. *Journal of Molecular Biology*, *225*, 951–960.

Lipetz, J., & Cristofalo, V. J. (1972). Ultrastructural changes accompanying the aging of human diploid cells in culture. *Journal of Ultrastructural Research, 39*, 43–56.

Lumpkin, C. K., Jr., McClung, J. K., Pereira-Smith, O. M., & Smith, J. R. (1986). Existence of high abundance antiproliferative mRNAs in senescent human diploid fibroblasts. *Science*, *232*, 393–395.

Macieira-Coelho, A. (1966). Action of cortisone on human fibroblasts *in vitro*. *Experientia*, *22*, 390–391.

Martin, G. M., Sprague, C. A., Norwood, T. H., & Pendergrass, W. R. (1974). Clonal selection, attenuation and differentiation in an in vitro model of hyperplasia. *American Journal of Pathology*, *74*, 137–154.

Matsumura, T. (1980). Multinucleation and polyploidization of aging human cells in culture. *Advances in Experimental Medicine and Biology*, *129*, 31–38.

Matsumura, T., Pfendt, E. A., & Hayflick, L. (1979). DNA synthesis in the human diploid cell strain WI-38 during in vitro aging: An autoradiography study. *Journal of Gerontology*, *34*, 323–327.

Mitsui, Y., & Schneider, E. L. (1976). Relationship between cell replication and volume in senescent human diploid fibroblasts. *Mechanisms of Ageing and Development*, *5*, 45–56.

Mueller, S. N., Rose, E. M., & Levine, E. M. (1980). Cellular senescence in a cloned strain of bovine fetal aortic endothelial cells. *Science*, *207*, 889–891.

Nakanishi, M., Robetorye, R. S., Pereira-Smith, O. M., & Smith, J. R. (1995). The C-terminal region of p21SDI1/WAF1/CIP1 is involved in proliferating cell nuclear antigen binding but does not appear to be required for growth inhibition. *Journal of Biological Chemistry*, *270*, 17060–17063.

Ning, Y., Weber, J. L., Killary, A. M., Ledbetter, D. H., Smith, J. R., & Pereira-Smith, O. M. (1991). Genetic analysis of indefinite division in human cells: Evidence for a cell senescence-related gene(s) on human chromosome 4. *Proceedings of the National Academy of Sciences of the U.S.A.*, *88*, 5635–5639.

Ogata, T., Ayusawa, D., Namba, M., Takahashi, E., Oshimura, M., & Oishi, M. (1993). Chromosome 7 suppresses indefinite division of nontumorigenic immortalized human fibroblast cell lines KMST-6 and SUSM-1. *Molecular and Cellular Biology*, *13*, 6036–6043.

Pignolo, R. J., Martin, B. G., Horton, J. H., Kalbach, A. N., & Cristofalo, V. J. (1997). The pathway of cell senescence: WI-38 cells arrest in late G1 and are unable to traverse the cell cycle from a true G0 state [In process citation]. *Experimental Gerontology*, *33*, 67–80.

Pignolo, R. J., Rotenberg, M. O., & Cristofalo, V. J. (1994). Alterations in contact and density-dependent arrest state in senescent WI-38 cells. *In Vitro Cellular and Developmental Biology Animal*, *30A*, 471–476.

Ponten, J. (1973). Aging properties of glia. In Y. C. F. Bourliere, A. Maciera-Coelho, & L. Robert (Eds.), INSERM (vol. 27, pp. 53–64). Paris: INSERM.

Rheinwald, J. H. (1975). Serial cultivation of strains of human epidermal keratinocytes: The formation of keratinizing colonies from single cells. *Cell*, *6*, 331–334.

Shay, J. W., Pereira-Smith, O. M., & Wright, W. E. (1991). A role for both RB and p53 in the regulation of human cellular senescence. *Experimental Cell Research*, *196*, 33–39.

Stewart, S. A., & Weinberg, R. A. (2002). Senescence: Does it all happen at the ends? *Oncogene*, *21*, 627–630.

Tassin, J., Malaise, E., & Courtois, Y. (1979). Human lens cells have an in vitro proliferative capacity inversely proportional to the donor age. *Experimental Cell Research*, *123*, 388–392.

Tice, R. R., Schneider, E. L., Kram, D., & Thorne, P. (1979). Cytokinetic analysis of impaired proliferative response of peripheral lymphocytes from aged humans to phytohemagglutinin. *Experimental Medicine*, *149*, 1029–1041.

Wright, W. E., & Shay, J. W. (1992). Telomere positional effects and the regulation of cellular senescence. *Trends in Genetics*, *8*, 193–197.

Wright, W. E., & Shay, J. W. (2002). Historical claims and current interpretations of replicative aging. *Nature Biotechnology*, *20*, 682–688.

Yanishevsky, R., & Carrano, A. V. (1975). Prematurely condensed chromosomes of dividing and non-dividing cells in aging human cell cultures. *Experimental Cell Research*, *90*, 169–174.

CENTENARIANS

Centenarians are, of course, people who have lived to the age of 100 or beyond. Centenarians are becoming more common, with some 100,000 estimated to have been living in 2000 (Coles, 2004), and about 40,000 of these in the United States. Death rates are decreasing exponentially among the *oldest-old*, suggesting that the numbers of centenarians will continue to increase rapidly. Some researchers believe that half of all girls born in the developed world today and a good part of the boys will live to the age of 100 or beyond (Vaupel, 2000). *Supercentenarians* (those aged 110 years and older) are also appearing

(Coles, 2004): there are now approximately 40 proven supercentenarians alive at any one time. The oldest age ever attained is 122, by *Jeanne Calment* of France, who died in 1997. The oldest proven age for a male is 115 years, by *Christian Mortensen*, a Danish-born American who died in 1998.

There appear to be clusters of centenarians. In most of the developed world, there is a ratio of 1 centenarian per 10,000 population. In Sardinia, this ratio is about 1.5/10,000. On the Japanese island of *Okinawa*, it is closer to 3.5/10,000. The reasons for clusters are not known. These populations may have genes which promote longevity or good health, or it could be a combination of lifestyle and luck.

Death rates among centenarians do not increase as rapidly as death rates for people in their 90s—in other words, there is a deceleration in the rate of mortality increase. This is believed to be due to *heterogeneity of frailty*, or the fact that some people have a low probability of death all their life, and in extreme old age only they are left (as those with higher probabilities of death are no longer alive), thus giving the appearance of a drop in death rates (Vaupel, Carey, Christensen, Johnson, Yashin, Holm, et al., 1998).

Popular beliefs hold that old age is a difficult time, with profound disability and many losses, but detailed studies of centenarians show that this is not true. These studies carefully prove the ages of the centenarians; reports of communities with many people living to 150 years or beyond have been shown to be false, which is why recent studies put a great deal of effort into validating the ages. Although most centenarians worldwide are women (in a ratio of 5:1), on the island of *Sardinia* the ratio is only 2 women for every 1 man (Koenig, 2001); the reason for this is not known, but it may be genetic.

Regarding health, one area where most centenarians do have a great deal of trouble is with sensation: most have significant impairment in sight and hearing. Not all centenarians have been healthy all their lives. Researchers from the *New England Centenarian Study* classified centenarians into 3 groups: those who had escaped most major illnesses, those who had delayed major illnesses, and those who had survived major illnesses (Evert, Lawler, Bogan, & Perls, 2003). There was a difference between men and women, with more men in the group of having escaped illnesses (32% vs 15%). Few centenarians had experienced heart disease, cancer, or stroke. *Children of centenarians* have similar health profiles, with many not having the common risk factors predisposing them to heart disease or stroke.

Many centenarians share a characteristic *"serene" personality*: they generally accept what they cannot change, and enjoy the life they have been given. Although long studies would be required to prove this, it is likely that this attitude is lifelong for many centenarians.

Not all centenarians are cognitively impaired; after detailed testing in population-based studies 20% to 40% were shown to have no cognitive impairment (Silver, Jilinskaia, & Perls, 2001). Pure Alzheimer's disease may be less common in this age group, and a susceptibility gene for late onset Alzheimer's, the *E4 allele* of the *apolipoprotein E gene*, may not exert any negative affect among centenarians. The work of Perls and colleagues suggests that a substantial number of centenarians are relatively independent in their level of function (37%).

Supercentenarians are overwhelmingly (90%) female (Coles, 2004). As with younger centenarians, most have significant hearing, vision, and mobility problems, as well as difficulty with memory. Most also come from long-lived families, and have been in good health all their lives.

Centenarians are of interest to the general public because of their accomplishment, but their interest to science is more than just novelty. The study of centenarians can provide insight into the *biology of aging*, as well as the mechanisms and prevention of frailty. For example, *calorie restriction* has been shown to delay signs of aging in laboratory animals. Both observational and population level studies suggest that calorie restriction may be beneficial in humans, too. Studies of *centenarians and their diets* may shed some light on this possibility.

There is a great deal of interest in using centenarians to study the *genetics of aging*. Laboratory research with simple organisms suggests that there actually may be genes which control aging (Hekimi & Guarente, 2003). Researchers in New England have found *long-lived families* and identified chromosomes that may carry genes related to their longevity (Perls & Terry, 2003). Other researchers have found that centenarians carry forms of genes that lower the risk for common health problems, like high cholesterol, leading to the question of whether the absence of disease might explain centenarians' longevity (Barzilai, Atzmon, Schechter, Schaefer, Cupples, Lipton, et al., 2003). However, it may also be that centenarians do not carry genes which increase the risk of common diseases, or that they are somehow resistant to the effects of detrimental genes. This last possibility fits with the theory of *Inflamm-Aging*, developed by researchers with the *Italian Centenarian Studies*. They have found evidence that centenarians are relatively resistant to the negative effects that the inflammatory response usually has on the human organism (Franceschi & Bonafe, 2003). A new European study, the *Genetics of Healthy Ageing*, will provide a large amount of valuable data over the coming decades, and hopefully answer many questions about centenarians and aging. Nevertheless, some scientists believe that aging is random process and that an aging gene will never be found (Hayflick, 2004).

We have much to learn from centenarians, but probably the most valuable lesson is that it is possible to live a long, healthy, happy life. Although part of a centenarian's success may be genetic, genes are not everything. It is important to remember that lifestyle does affect how we age, and it is never too late to make a change for the better.

CHRIS MACKNIGHT

See also
Life Span
Longevity: Societal Impact
Long-Lived Human Populations

References

Barzilai, N., Atzmon, G., Schechter, C., Schaefer, E. J., Cupples, A. L., Lipton, R., Cheng, S., & Shuldiner, A. R. (2003). Unique lipoprotein phenotype and genotype associated with exceptional longevity. *Journal of the American Medical Association*, *290*(15), 2030–2040.

Coles, L. S. (2004). Demography of human supercentenarians. *Journal of Gerontology: Biological Sciences*, *59A*(6), 579–586.

Evert, J., Lawler, E., Bogan, H., & Perls, T. (2003). Morbidity profiles of centenarians: Survivors, delayers, and escapers. *Journal of Gerontology: Biological Sciences and Medical Sciences*, *58*(3), 232–237.

Franceschi, C. & Bonafè, M. (2003). Centenarians as a model for healthy aging. *Biochemical Society Transactions*, *31*, 457–461.

Hayflick, L. (2004). "Anti-aging" is an oxymoron. *Journal of Gerontology: Biological Sciences*, *59A*(6), 573–578.

Hekimi, S., & Guarente, L. (2003). Genetics and the specificity of the aging process. *Science*, *299*, 1351–1354.

Koenig, R. (2001). Sardinia's mysterious male methuselahs. *Science*, *291*, 2074–2076.

Perls, T., & Terry, D. (2003). Determinants of exceptional longevity. *Annals of Internal Medicine*, *139*(5 Pt 2), 445–449.

Silver, M. H., Jilinskaia, E., & Perls, T. T. (2001). Cognitive functional status of age-confirmed centenarians in a population-based study. *Journal of Gerontology: Psychological Sciences*, *56B*(3), P134–P140.

Vaupel, J. (2000). Setting the stage: A generation of centenarians? *Washington Quarterly*, *23*(3), 197–200.

Vaupel, J. W., Carey, J. R., Christensen, K., Johnson, T. E., Yashin, A. I., Holm, N. V., Iachine, I. A., Kannisto, V., Khazaeli, A. A., Liedo, P., Longo, V. D., Zeng, Y., Manton, K. G., & Curtsinger, J. W. (1998). Biodemographic trajectories of longevity. *Science*, *280*(8), 855–860.

CENTRAL AND PERIPHERAL NERVOUS SYSTEMS MORPHOLOGY

The nervous system may be divided into the central nervous system (CNS)—the brain and spinal cord—and the peripheral nervous system (PNS), the receptors and effectors of the body, the peripheral ganglia, and the nerve processes connecting these structures with the CNS. Given the complexity of the human nervous system, an appreciation of normal structure and function is necessary so that the reader may understand the changes that may occur with increasing age. The first section of this review will, therefore, concentrate on the anatomical parts of the brain (brain stem, cerebellum, and cerebral hemispheres) before continuing with changes that describe the relationship with aging.

The CNS occupies the cavity of the skull lying above the foramen magnum, where it continues caudally into the vertebral canal as the spinal cord. The brain may be subdivided into the brain stem, the cerebellum, and the telencephalon. The brain stem is most caudal, extending from the spinal cord to the anterior end of the third ventricle at the lamina terminalis. It makes up about 4.5% of total brain weight and is subdivided into four main subdivisions: medulla oblongata, pons, midbrain, and diencephalon. Dorsal to and overriding the medulla and pons is the cerebellum, about 10.5% of total brain weight, and the remaining telencephalon forms about 85% of total brain weight. It is composed of the cerebral cortex and cortical white matter, the basal ganglia with its component major nuclear groups, the caudate nucleus, the lentiform nucleus, the amygdaloid complex and claustrum, and the basal forebrain, which, although poorly demarcated and understood, contains nuclei and fiber connections that associate it with the limbic and olfactory systems.

Brain Stem

The most caudal portion of the brain, which is continuous with the spinal cord at the foramen magnum, is the medulla oblongata. This also constitutes the lowest part of the brain stem, a name applied to the central area of the brain appearing identical to a stalk from which two structures grow: the cerebral hemispheres, and the cerebellum. Fiber systems that originate from the spinal cord, the cerebral hemisphere, or the cerebellum may ascend or descend the CNS by passing through the brain stem. The brain stem is the location of groups of cells related to the cranial nerves, which receive and project information between structures in the head (eye and ear) and the CNS. It also plays a major role in the control of automatic activity in thoracic and abdominal viscera.

Diencephalon

The diencephalon is the most rostral portion of the brain stem, and the structures contained within it have an appearance and organization different from the remainder of the brain stem. In part, it is composed of several collections of neurons with intervening white matter, including the thalamus and hypothalamus. The thalamus is a major relay and processing center concerned with communicating sensory information to and from the cerebral cortex. Although the hypothalamus occupies about only 0.5% of the volume of the human brain, "it plays a major role in the regulation of the release of hormones from the pituitary gland, maintenance of body temperature, and the organization of goal seeking behaviors such as feeding, drinking, mating and aggression, and behavioral adjustments to changes in the internal and external environment" (Carpenter & Sutin, 1983, p. 552). The basal ganglia, also located in the diencephalon, include groups of cells whose normal activity is involved in the initiation and control of motor activity. Among these groups of cells are those that form the substantia nigra, a structure that is implicated in Parkinson's disease and is more specifically located in the midbrain.

Cerebellum

On the dorsal surface of the brain stem positioned over the surface of the medulla and pons is the cerebellum. This structure is related anatomically and physiologically to the brain stem by bundles of fibers that are the means by which information may be communicated with the spinal cord and the more rostral levels of the brain stem and secondarily with the cerebral cortex. The cerebellum is involved in the control of posture, eye movements, and auditory and vestibular functions; patients with cerebellar dysfunction experience unsteadiness of gait and inability to estimate the range of voluntary movement, resulting in overshooting the mark, as in attempting to grasp an object. Such an individual may also exhibit difficulty in performing rapid movements and may have slurred speech and a tremor that is exaggerated as the target is approached. *Dizziness* in the elderly may have its focus in the brain stem or the cerebellum but equally at fault may be diseases of the cerebral cortex or the influence of systemic disease on function in the inner ear or the CNS. Whatever the source, dizziness occurs in many elderly persons. Although 30% of the elderly have experienced dizziness, Luxon (1984) indicates that by 80 years of age, 66% of women and 33% of men have had episodes of dizziness, and Koch and Smith (1985) report dizziness as the most common complaint in patients older than 75 years. Faced with secondary factors affecting normal age changes, dizziness is paramount among the complaints from the older age group. Parker (1994) has reported that the syndrome of multiple sensory deficits seen more frequently but not exclusively among the elderly is a common cause of dizziness and impairment of balance.

Cerebral Hemispheres

Situated over the diencephalon are the cerebral hemispheres, each of which may be divided into lobes: the frontal, parietal, temporal, and occipital.

The surface of each lobe is folded into convolutions, or gyri, separated from each other by grooves or sulci. If one were to cut across a gyrus with a knife, one would find that the surface is composed of nerve cells arranged in layers parallel to the surface of the gyrus. Thus, the cerebral cortex may be 1.5 mm to 4.5 mm in thickness and for the entire cortex comprises an area of approximately 2.5 sq ft, most of it hidden within the sulci. It has been estimated that the cerebral cortex contains between 10 and 12 billion nerve cells. The center of each gyrus (the white matter) is composed of nerve processes either entering or leaving that particular gyrus. Although the functions of each lobe may be distinct, a most remarkable aspect of the central nervous system is the degree of integration occurring between these areas.

Frontal Lobe. This is the most anterior lobe of the hemisphere. It extends posteriorly for approximately one half the length of the brain. A large portion of the frontal lobe is concerned with the control of movement of the limbs and trunk of the body, head, and eyes. A region of the left inferior frontal gyrus is known as Broca's area and (in most individuals) is associated with expression or motor mechanisms of speech. The most anterior (frontal) part of the frontal lobe (the prefrontal cortex) controls certain aspects of personality, judgment, and foresight and is involved in permitting an evaluation of the consequences of one's actions.

Parietal Lobe. This lobe is located between the frontal and occipital lobes. Within it is Wernicke's area, a region associated with receptive or comprehensive speech, and in the most anterior position in this lobe is the primary somesthetic area, which receives somesthetic information from the opposite half of the body (Burt, 1993).

Temporal Lobe. Hearing and olfaction are two major systems whose conscious level is related to the temporal lobe, which lies laterally in the skull, deep in the temple region of the head. In addition to these activities, the temporal lobe contains within its deeper region structures that are prominent in the limbic system. These are the amygdaloid nucleus and the hippocampus, intimately related to learning and memory.

Occipital Lobe. This lobe is located most posteriorly in the brain and occupies an area in the back of the skull. Its primary function is to serve as the conscious level for the visual system.

General Considerations of Aging in the Brain

Brain. Consideration of aging and its relationship to the brain requires recognition, if not acceptance, of the concept that the aging process is best understood as a stage in development, albeit an end stage. In the normal aging process, therefore, it should be expected that time and use may alter the functioning of the organism. It is a concern with these changes and their effect on behavior and the physiology of the nervous system that directs attention to this area. The prospect that alterations in behavior and cognitive function may interfere with a person's ability to carry out what have been normal life processes has been emphasized in recent years in relation to the increase in human life expectancy. A better appreciation of this process may have an impact on medical care and social relationships in the elderly population. Humans age in different ways. Examination of a randomly selected group of elderly persons will reveal that although some individuals may show very slight deterioration in motor, sensory, or cognitive ability, others will have a marked loss in memory and in the ability to relate to others and to the environment. This latter group has increased in step with the increase in life expectancy, resulting in increased costs for care and a concern as to whether this is an ultimate problem that most older persons will face in the future.

The CNS consists of a complex series of structures containing numerous types of cells, with basic functions of communication and elaboration of information brought to it by stimuli in the environment, in addition to the maintenance of a normal metabolism and milieu. The basic cell types are neurons, or nerve cells and neuroglia cells. These will be considered in relation to aging. Other factors that may have an influence on aging in the CNS relate to brain weight and the size of the ventricular system.

Brain Weight. The brain at birth weighs approximately 375 g, whereas in the adult the weight of the brain is about 1,400 g in the male and 1,250 g in the adult female.

Age-related changes in brain weight have been investigated well back into the 19th century. This was probably related to the practice of weighing the brain as a normal part of the standard autopsy. These studies showed a decrease in brain weight, that peaked in the third decade (20–30 years of age). An article by Dekaban and Sadowsky (1978) reviewed their own as well as six other large series of brain studies and found that a peak occurred in male subjects at about 20 years of age and at 17 in female subjects. These continue to be generally acceptable as a period when maximum brain weight is achieved. Brain weight then decreases at a rough average of 100 g per brain or 2 g per decade for both sexes and 7%–11% by the 10th decade (Miller, Alston, & Corsellis, 1980). These authors also reported an increasing ratio between gray and white matter, suggesting that the predominant loss was in the white matter, a fact that has been supported by careful imaging studies. This confirms the fact that gyral atrophy affecting both gray and white matter occurs in aging rather than in cortical atrophy alone. This usually affects the convexities of the frontal lobes, the parasagittal region, and the temporal and parietal lobes. It should be noted that these same regions are involved in Alzheimer's disease. The base of the brain and the occipital lobe are generally spared.

Because specimens are examined at one point (cross-sectional series) rather than in a longitudinal fashion, differences between younger and older individuals may relate more to overall larger body size (and consequently larger brain size) in the younger generation than to an actual loss in brain weight in the elderly. Although a great deal of attention has been given to the question of brain weight changes, the results may not be true changes unless the subject's body size is also considered. This has not been done up to this time. Other considerations are the time elapsed between death and weighing of the brain, as well as the cause of death. Both factors may result in brain shrinkage and a consequent lower weight, especially in the older person. Conversely, the number of studies performed on diverse populations (and even under different conditions) indicates that a decrease in brain weight is a true concomitant of aging in the human.

Ventricular System

Within the substance of each hemisphere, a system of spaces or ventricles exists. These are continuous with each other, finally communicating with the subarachnoid space that surrounds the brain and spinal cord. The ventricles and subarachnoid spaces contain a colorless fluid (cerebrospinal fluid) that is produced by the filtration and secretory actions of blood vessels contained within the ventricles. The largest of the ventricles are found within each hemisphere. When enlargement of the ventricles occurs, it does so at the expense of neighboring white and gray matter, interfering with the normal activity of nerve cells and their processes.

Although there have been conflicting statements in the literature regarding changes in ventricular size, the bulk of the studies support the concept that ventricular enlargement does occur and is related to increasing age. This has been confirmed by imaging studies, most recently in 79 healthy male subjects below the age of 87 years, in which the fluid volume remained stable until age 60 and then increased dramatically, a finding in agreement with five other studies (Stafford, Albert, Naeser, Sandor, & Garvey, 1988). It has also been stated by Massman, Bigler, Cullum, and Naugle (1986) that although ventricular enlargement and gyral atrophy often appear in the same specimen, the processes are independent of each other. It should be possible to examine this question of ventricular change in a series of living subjects, correlating imaging findings with behavioral and other functional examinations in the living person, which may provide a final answer to this question.

Spinal Cord

Relatively little is known about age changes in the spinal cord. This may be related to the difficulty in obtaining suitable specimens. The anterior horn cells provide motor fibers to peripheral nerves, and these large-sized nerve cells demonstrate age-related degenerative changes during the fifth decade of life. Lipofuscin deposition begins at about 40 years of age and, as indicated in the "Lipofuscin" entry, the entire cytoplasm is often filled with this material by age 60. A loss of Nissl material, which leads to reduced protein synthesis, is also observed; however, as occurs in brain stem nuclei, the relation between Nissl loss and cell death is not clear. Tomlinson and Irving (1977), however, counted anterior horn cells in lumbosacral spinal cord segments of subjects 13–95 years old and found no changes in neuronal number until age 60, after which there was a continuing decrease of one third until the 91–95 age.

Cells of the CNS

The two major groups of cells in the CNS are the neuroglia and neurons, or nerve cells. The neuroglia are found in gray and white matter, whereas neurons are present in only gray matter.

Neuroglia. Little attention has been given to changes of neuroglia with age. These cells are difficult to identify in a tissue section, and their functional relationships have not been completely understood. There are several neuroglial (glial) types.

Oligodendrocytes are responsible for the production of the myelin covering of nerve fibers in the CNS. These cells show no change with increasing age.

Astrocytes have traditionally been considered to provide the basic support or matrix for the CNS. More important, they are involved in providing an ionic homeostatic environment in the CNS, and they aid in the metabolism of several neurotransmitters. Although lipofuscin is found in astrocytes with increasing age, it appears in different parts of the brain at different ages.

To determine changes in the number of astrocytes in aging human cerebral cortex, Hansen, Armstrong, and Terry (1987) examined the cortices of 25 dementia-free persons, using immunolabeling of fibrous astrocytes. They found that although changes in cell numbers could not be correlated with increasing age, there was a significant linear increase in the older specimens when they were divided into those younger than age 70 and those older.

Microglia are the smallest of the neuroglial cells. They appear to have developed from blood cells (monocytes). Functionally, they are considered to be the phagocytes of the CNS. Microglia have been examined more thoroughly than any other glial cell. With increasing age, large amounts of lipofuscin are found in these cells, lending support to a concept that the microglial cell ingests the material from neighboring abnormal brain tissue. The lipofuscin may, conversely, be a product of microglial metabolism, just as it may have a similar relationship in the neuron (see "Lipofuscin").

Sturrock (1983) emphasizes the few studies of changes in glial numbers with increasing age. A finding similar to that in neurons indicates a regional difference in changes in glial numbers. Microglia increase to the largest extent among neuroglial cells, but this may be related to a response to neuronal loss or other pathology. An increase in the number of astrocytes appears to be related to neuronal death or metabolic changes that occur in aging brain. The question of changes in the number of astrocytes, however, is unsettled, although proliferation of processes of existing astrocytes has been noted in animals and humans. In this way, changes in glial cell activity or in numbers may be a mechanism adopted by the nervous system to compensate for the loss of neurons. Although previously ignored, the relationship of neuroglial cells to CNS metabolism and activity should encourage further aging studies.

The Neuron. The neuron is the major functional unit of the CNS. It is composed of a cell body containing the nucleus and a number of processes or nerve fibers, including the dendrites, which bring information from other cells to the cell body, and a single axon that communicates this information to other neurons in the specific pathway. The point of contact for transmission of information between neurons occurs at the synapse.

Neuron population studies in the aging CNS emphasize the unique character of the nervous system. It is clear that there is a specificity for cell loss in certain brain areas and not in others (e.g., between 13 and 85 years in the human, there is a neuronal loss of 52% in the subiculum of the hippocampal area and 31% in the hilus of the dentate gyrus, whereas none of the remaining hippocampal structures shows significant change in cell numbers [West, 1993]), that certain species demonstrate cell loss whereas others do not, and that the age at which cell loss occurs varies from one brain region to another. In the human cerebral cortex, significant decreases in the numbers of neurons have been reported in the superior frontal gyrus, superior temporal gyrus, precentral gyrus (most posterior portion of the frontal lobe), and occipital cortex, whereas no changes were evident in the inferior temporal gyrus or the postcentral gyrus (most anterior part of the parietal lobe). Decreases are of a linear nature, continuing from 20 years of age. The cell types involved also appear to have a specificity in that smaller size neurons (Golgi type II neurons)—the association cells that play a role in the integration of nervous system activity—are affected to a greater degree than those of large size. Because smaller cells are considered to develop later than larger cells, there may be a time sequence resulting in the greater loss of younger cortical cells.

In contrast to earlier changes in cell numbers, which have been reported since the 1950s, the use of newer technology has made possible more specific and repeatable examination of the cerebral cortex. A series of nonbiased cell counts by Pakkenberg, Evans, Møller, Braendgaard, and Gundersen in 1989 did not demonstrate a cell loss with increasing age; therefore, it appears from these studies that with a changing technology, the argument regarding age-related neuronal losses is still unsettled.

In the cerebellar cortex, the decrease in Purkinje cells in the vermis was statistically significant (Sjobeck, Dahlen, & Englund, 1999).

There is a distinct difference between aging effects in brain stem nuclei and those in the cerebral cortex. Of the many brain stem structures that have been examined, only two demonstrate a significant reduction in cell number. The cells in these structures (locus ceruleus and substantia nigra) are characterized by their content of melanin and their elaboration of two major neurotransmitters, norepinephrine and dopamine, respectively.

In addition to the decrease in the number of neurons, another significant change occurs in the dendrites of neurons in the normal aging process. The axon of a neuron communicates with the next order of neurons in a particular pathway (sensory or motor) through synaptic endings or spines on the dendrites. If the dendritic branches or spines should decrease in number, though the cell body is relatively normal, the effect could be disastrous for the continuing ability of that neuron to maintain its normal communication with other nerve cells. There is abundant evidence that this is precisely what occurs, at least when one considers the morphological integrity of the nerve cell (Scheibel & Scheibel, 1975). Whether the physiological activity is altered is not presently known, although this would be a natural conclusion. Evidence indicates that although the dendritic changes occur in some cells in normal aging, there is a simultaneous increase and thickening of these branches in other cortical neurons, suggesting an attempt to compensate for the degenerative neuronal changes (Buell & Coleman, 1981; Coleman & Buell, 1985: Coleman & Flood, 1987). Of significance is the absence of such growth in the cortical neurons of Alzheimer's disease subjects, suggesting a differing potential for neuronal repair between normal aging individuals and those with this form of dementia. Increased longevity is unfortunately associated with increasing illness and susceptibility to deterioration in several of the body's systems. None is more challenging and provocative for study than the effect on the structure and function of the CNS. Neuronal loss and dendritic change may have the ultimate effect of interfering with normal activity. It is this fear that is uppermost in the minds of older individuals. The changes that occur must be understood if we are to be able to deal with the effect of normal changes in the CNS and with its disease states.

The Peripheral Nerves. Sensory stimulation, such as stroking of the skin, is transmitted from a receptor (nerve ending in skin) to the CNS by way of a peripheral nerve. This nerve also carries the response to the stimulus from the CNS to an effector organ, which in this case may be a muscle. Nerve fibers that communicate between the CNS and the body are collected in bundles, forming spinal nerves when related to the spinal cord and cranial nerves when connected with the brain. The connection between the spinal nerve and the spinal cord is by roots or nerve fibers oriented to the dorsal and ventral aspects of the cord. The dorsal root contains sensory fibers from somatic and visceral structures and is a means by which sensory information passes from the spinal nerve into the CNS. The ventral root contains motor fibers that transmit information from the CNS into the peripheral nerve to be distributed to muscles and visceral organs. The peripheral nerve, therefore, contains a mixture of sensory and motor fibers that are difficult to distinguish from each other.

Although the presence or amount of myelin around nerve fibers may vary, each nerve fiber is enclosed by a neurilemmal sheath, from which myelin may develop and which itself originates as the plasma membrane of a neurilemmal cell. Surrounding the nerve fiber and its neurilemmal sheath are a series of connective tissue coverings. The first of these is the endoneurium, which is a delicate membrane surrounding each nerve fiber. A group of nerve fibers are collected together into bundles, or fascicles, by connective tissue (perineurium), and groups of fascicles are combined into the peripheral nerve by an encircling thick layer of connective tissue called the epineurium.

In animal studies of aging, some features are recognized as being related to increasing age. Whether quantitative changes occur in peripheral nerves is controversial and may depend on the specific nerve studied. Although in the rat a decrease in the number of fibers has been reported (Krinke, 1983), a stability in the population of myelinated fibers (Sharma, Bajada, & Thomas, 1980) has also been maintained. A prominent feature of changes in the peripheral nervous system in the aging rat is the development of spontaneous, demyelinating changes in the roots, manifested by myelin balloon formation, infoldings and reduplication, and axonal atrophy. The ventral root is frequently more affected than the dorsal root, and lesions may extend distally into spinal nerves or centrally into the spinal cord (Braund, McGuire, & Lincoln, 1982). Among the common changes occurring in human nerve fibers are a progressive reduction in the number and density of myelinated fibers directly related to fiber size. This is accompanied by thickening of the perineurial, epineurial, and endoneurial sheaths. As a reflection of generalized atherosclerotic change, blood vessels of peripheral nerves may be involved. A complex relationship between Wallerian degeneration and axonal regeneration also occurs after 60 years of age, although these changes are not as common as are the demyelinating lesions (Vital, Vital, Rigal, Decamps, Emeriau, & Galley, 1990).

Among age changes seen in the spinal roots are mild fibrosis, endothelial hyperplasia, and vascular thickening. With these degenerative changes affecting ventral roots to a greater extent than dorsal roots, the elderly patient will have difficulty in motor activity to a greater extent than sensory impairment and a greater involvement of the lower extremities, because the lumbosacral roots are more involved than the cervicothoracic roots. Atrophy of root myelinated fibers also may be found, with a significant reduction occurring by 50–60 years of age (Mittal & Logmani, 1987). Still, in the interests of developmental anatomy, it should be emphasized that the most dramatic reduction in myelinated fiber density occurs between birth and 2 years of life (from 20,000 to 4,000–7,000 myelinated fibers per mm^2) (Jacobs & Love, 1985).

There are conflicting findings regarding changes in anterior horn cells that contribute motor fibers in peripheral nerves. Lipofuscin deposition begins at about 40 years of age and, as is the case in the brain stem nucleus of the inferior olive, 75%–95% of the cell volume may be occupied by this pigment by the age of 80 years. This accumulation of lipofuscin pigment probably does not have a relation to cell death (see "Lipofuscin"). Nevertheless, computer-assisted analysis of anterior horn cells in the L3, L4, and L5 segments of the spinal cord have demonstrated a loss of 175 to 260 cells per decade (Kawamura, O'Brien, Okazaki, & Dyck, 1977), a fact that may relate to the decline in myelinated fibers in peripheral nerves.

Just as changes have been reported in anterior horn cells, spinal roots, and peripheral nerves, age-related changes also have been noted at the neuro-muscular junction beginning during the third decade. Meissner's tactile corpuscles, which are related to reception of light touch stimuli, are reduced by 80% in the elderly. Pacinian pressure corpuscles also become smaller in size. Sensory nerve conduction studies illustrate abnormalities, becoming obvious between 30 and 50 years of age, with a decrease in the amplitude of the action potential. Sensory and motor nerve velocities also are decreased, indicating in the latter case a loss of motor units after 60 years of age.

Indications of peripheral neuropathy in older persons have been reported in otherwise intact individuals. Complaints of tingling, numbness, diffuse weakness, decreased deep tendon reflexes, the loss of ankle reflexes, and poor balance, together with increased sensory thresholds to the usual sensory stimuli, are commonly reported by patients without other neurological complaints. These may be related to some of the factors discussed in this section. For a general discussion of degenerative disorders of the peripheral nerve see Aisen (1994).

Autonomic Nervous System

The reader is advised to obtain a basic understanding of the anatomy, physiology, and chemical importance of the autonomic nervous system by referring to chapters on the subject in a standard neuroanatomy textbook by authors such as de Groot and Chusid, 1988, and Afifi and Bergman, 1986.

Basically, the response to stress is under the control of the autonomic nervous system. This may influence activities of internal organ systems such as the heart, kidney, endocrine glands, gastrointestinal system, and urinary system, which receive information from the brain or spinal cord, and transmit these signals to end organs in the body. The end structure that receives input from the central nervous system may then be stimulated to either increase or decrease its activity, resulting in an increase or decrease in its output, so the organ (e.g., the heart) may show slowing or quickening of its action.

The response to stress is the critical difference or hallmark of aging; in comparison with the younger individual, it is not the resting level of performance but how the organ (or organism) adapts to external stress that determines the effect of aging (Kane, Ouslander, & Abrass, 1999). This decreased response to stress can be seen in the performance of other endocrine systems or the cardiovascular system. The older person may have a normal resting pulse and cardiac output but not be able to achieve an adequate increase in either with exercise. It is essential, therefore, that the examiner be aware of the range of responses, or lack thereof, of a specific organ when stressed in order to understand the image of responses that are possible.

HAROLD BRODY

See also

Neuroplasticity
Neurotransmitters in the Aging Brain
Neutrophic Factors in Aging

References

Afifi, A. K., & Bergman, R. A. (1986). *Basic neuroscience*. Baltimore: Urban & Schwarzenberg.

Aisen, M. (1994). Spinal and peripheral nerve syndrome: Weakness: Peripheral nerve disease. In W. Hazzard, E. Bierman, J. Blass, W. Ettinger, & J. Halter (Eds.), *Principles of geriatric medicine and gerontology* (3rd ed., pp. 1291–1292). New York: McGraw-Hill.

Braund, K. G., McGuire, J. A., & Lincoln, C. E. (1982). Age-related changes in peripheral nerves of the dog: 2. A morphologic and morphometric study of cross-sectional nerve. *Veterinary Pathology*, *19*, 379–398.

Burt, A. M. (1993). *Textbook of neuroanatomy*. Philadelphia: W.B. Saunders.

Carpenter, M. B., & Sutin, J. (1983). *Human neuroanatomy*. Baltimore, MD: Williams & Williams.

Coleman, P. D., & Buell, S. J. (1985). Regulation of dendritic extent in developing and aging brain. In C. W. Cotman (Ed.), *Synoptic plasticity* (pp. 331–333). New York: Guilford Press.

Coleman, P. D., & Flood, D. G. (1987). Neuron numbers and dendritic extension in normal aging and Alzheimer's disease. *Neurobiology of Aging*, *8*, 521–545.

de Groot, J., & Chusid, J. G. (1988). *Current correlative neuroanatomy*. East Norwalk, CT: Appleton & Lange.

Dekaban, A. S., & Sadowski, B. S. (1978). Changes in brain weights during the span of human life: Relation of brain to body heights and body weights. *Annals of Neurology*, *4*, 345–356.

Hansen, L. A., Armstrong, D. M., & Terry, R. D. (1987). An immunolustochemical quantification of fibrous astrocytes in the aging human cerebral cortex. *Neurobiology of Aging*, *8*, 1–6.

Jacobs, J. M., & Love, S. (1985). Qualitative and quantitative morphology of human sural nerve at different ages. *Brain*, *108*, 897–924.

Kane, R. L., Ouslander, J. G., & Abrass, I. B. (1999). *Essentials of clinical geriatrics*. New York: McGraw-Hill.

Kawamura, Y., O'Brien, P., Okazaki, H., & Dyck, P. J. (1977). Lumbar motoneurones of man: 2. The number and diameter distribution of large- and intermediatediameter cytons in motoneuron columns of spinal cord of man. *Journal of Neuropathology and Experimental Neurology*, *36*, 861–870.

Koch, H., & Smith, M. C. (1985). *Office based ambulatory care for patients 75 years old and over: National Ambulatory Medical Care Survey, 1980, 1981*. Hyattsville, MD: U.S. Government Printing Office, National Center for Health Statistics, Public Health Service.

Krinke, G. (1983). Spinal radiculoncuropathy in aging rats: Demyelination secondary to neuronal dwindling. *Acta Neuropathologica (Berlin)*, *59*, 63–69.

Luxon, L. M. (1984). A bit dizzy. *British Journal of Hospital Medicine*, *32*, 315.

Massman, P. J., Bigler, E. D., Cullum, C. M., & Naugle, R. I. (1986). The relationship between cortical atrophy and ventricular volume. *International Journal of Neuroscience*, *30*, 87–99.

Miller, A. K. H., Alston, R. L., & Corsellis, J. A. N. (1980). Variations with ages in the volumes of gray and white matter in the cerebral hemisphere of man: Measurements with an image analyser. *Neuropathalogy and Applied Neurobiology*, *6*, 119–132.

Mittal, K. R., & Logmani, F. H. (1987). Age related reduction in 8th cervical ventral root myelinated fiber diameters and numbers in man. *Journal of Gerontology*, *42*, 8–10.

Pakkenberg, B., Evans, S. M., Møller, A., Braendgaard, H., & Gündersen, H. J. G. (1989). Total number of neurons in human neocortex related to age and sex estimated by way of optical dissectors. *Acta Stereologica*, *8*, 251–256.

Parker, S. W. (1994). Dizziness in the elderly. In M. L. Albert & J. E. Knoefel (Eds.), *Clinical neurology of aging* (2nd ed.). New York: Oxford University Press.

Scheibel, M. E., & Scheibel, A. B. (1975). Structural changes in the aging brain. In H. Brody, D. Harman, & J. M. Ordy (Eds.), *Aging: Vol. 1. Clinical, morphological and neurochemical aspects in the aging central nervous system* (pp. 11–37). New York: Raven Press.

Sharma, A. K., Bajada, S., & Thomas, P. K. (1980). Age changes in the tibial and plantar nerves of the rat. *Journal of the Anatomy*, *130*, 417–428.

Sjöbeck, M., Dahlen, S., & Englund, E, (1999). Neuronal loss in the brain stem and cerebellum: Part of the normal aging process? A morphometric study of the vermis cerebelli and inferior olivary nucleus. *Journal of Gerontology*, *54A*, B363-B368.

Stafford, J. L., Albert, M. S., Naeser, M. A., Sandor T., & Garvey, A. J. (1988). Age-related differences in computed tomographic scan measurements. *Archives of Neurology*, *45*, 409–415.

Sturrock, R. R. (1983). Problems of glial identification and quantification in the aging central nervous system. In J. Cervor-Navarro & H. I. Sarkinder (Eds.), *Brain aging: Neuropathology and neuropharmacology: Vol. 32. Aging*. New York: Raven Press.

Tomlinson, B. E., & Irving, D. (1977). The numbers of limb motor neurons in the human lumbosacral cord throughout life. *Journal of the Neurological Sciences*, *34*, 213–219.

Vital, A., Vital, C., Rigal, B., Decamps, A., Emeriau, J. P., & Galley, P. (1990). Morphological study of the aging human peripheral nerve. *Clinical Neuropathology*, *9*, 10–15.

West, M. J. (1993). Regionally specific loss of neurons in the aging human hippocampus. *Neurobiology of Aging*, *14*, 287–293.

CEREBROVASCULAR DISEASE: STROKE AND TRANSIENT ISCHEMIC ATTACK

Definitions

Stroke refers to the clinical syndrome of sudden onset of focal or global disturbance of the central nervous system function, with no apparent cause other than a vascular one (Warlow, Dennis, van Gijn, et al., 2001). Ischemic stroke is responsible for about 80% of all strokes, *intracerebral hemorrhage* for 15%, and *subarachnoid hemorrhage* for 5%. A *transient ischemic attack* (TIA) has the same symptom complex as a stroke, but with a resolution of these symptoms within 24 hours (National Institute of Neurological Disorders and Stroke, 1990). Most *TIAs* resolve within 1 hour. It is increasingly understood that TIAs and minor strokes represent a continuum of disease; some now suggest that the time-based definition of TIA yield to a tissue-based definition, as approximately one-third of people with clinically diagnosed TIAs will actually have structural changes visible on neuroimaging, such as *diffusion-weighted MRI scanning* (DWI) (Albers, Caplan, Easton, et al., 2002; Warach, & Kidwell, 2004). Other terms used in the past to describe stroke and TIA, such as *cerebrovascular accident* (CVA) and *reversible ischemic neurological deficit* (RIND), lack specificity and have generally fallen out of common use.

Epidemiology

Each year, about 15 million people worldwide will experience a stroke; of these, 5 million die, and 5 million are left permanently disabled (MacKay & Mensah). In developed countries stroke is a leading cause of death and dementia, and is the number 1 cause of adult disability (MacKay & Mensah). In general, stroke is a disease of the older adult, and so these trends will increase over the next several decades as the result of an aging population combined with the disturbing persistence of many well understood "modifiable" risk factors, including hypertension, dyslipidemia, smoking, diabetes, obesity, physical inactivity, excessive alcohol intake, and diets high in saturated fats and low in fruits and vegetables.

Anticipated Trends and Economic Implications

With advances made in early diagnosis and treatment of stroke, more people are surviving their acute stroke and thereafter live with the effects of stroke. Thus, stroke is expected to remain a significant and increasing economic burden. The American Heart Association has estimated the direct and indirect cost of stroke in the United States in 2004 to be $54 billion (MacKay & Mensah). The Dutch government estimates that *costs related to stroke care* will increase by up to 40% by 2015 (MacKay & Mensah). Similar burdens are also anticipated in the developing world, where resources for *stroke care* and prevention are often not well established. The emotional costs of stroke for patients and families cannot be calculated.

Mechanism and Pathophysiology

Strokes and TIAs occur when the blood supply to the brain is disrupted, usually for one of the following reasons:

1. *Occlusion of the lumen* of an artery by a blood clot that develops as a local thrombus, often in relation to atherosclerotic plaque rupture and endothelial injury, with activation of the local coagulation cascade.
2. Distal occlusion of the lumen of an artery by a blood clot that has embolized from the heart (atrial fibrillation), aortic arch, or arterial system.
3. Local or embolic blood clots related to *hypercoagulable states* (hereditary or, secondary to systemic disease or malignancy).
4. Occlusion of the arterial lumen following the *dissection of an arterial wall.*
5. Narrowing of smaller arteries due to *arteriosclerosis.*
6. Rupture of a blood vessel wall (artery or vein), leading to hemorrhage.
7. Hypotension secondary to cardiac arrest or decreased circulating blood volume.

During stroke or TIA, normal cellular function is lost in the affected area of the brain, leading to the presenting symptoms. If normal blood flow is not restored quickly, an *infarct core* of dead cells will form; these cells do not recover. In many cases of stroke, there also exists an area of tissue around the infarct core (the *ischemic penumbra*) that is metabolically threatened but theoretically viable (Lassen, 1990). If blood flow can be restored quickly, this penumbral tissue may be salvagable, hopefully resulting in a better clinical outcome for the patient.

Clinical Approach

A focused clinical history is needed to determine the specific time of symptom onset, the course of events, vascular risk factors and co-morbidities, and medications. A physical examination is essential to evaluate vital signs, localize the lesion by brain region and vascular territory, determine cause and severity of the stroke, and assess other conditions that could affect treatment and prognosis. Stat laboratory tests include routine bloodwork (CBC and INR, and blood glucose to rule out hypoglycemia as a stroke mimic), an electrocardiogram (to rule out atrial fibrillation, myocardial infarction, and left ventricular hypertrophy), and urgent brain imaging (computed tomographic or magnetic resonance imaging) to rule out intracerebral hemorrhage and *stroke mimics*, such as tumor. In many cases, urgent vascular imaging (*duplex carotid ultrasonography*, *computed tomographic angiography*, or *magnetic resonance angiography*) is needed to determine the degree of carotid stenosis in patients with TIAs or nondisabling carotid territory strokes who may be suitable for *carotid endarterectomy*.

Goals of *Acute Stroke Management*

1. **Minimize brain damage and restore perfusion.** *Thrombolytic therapy* with *recombinant tissue plasminogen activator* (rt-PA) administered intravenously within 3 hours of stroke onset for highly selected patients who meet strict eligibility criteria has been shown to save lives and reduce disability despite an early risk of intracerebral hemorrhage (Wardlaw, del Zoppo, Yamaguchi, & Berge, 2003). An individual patient data meta-analysis has suggested that the time window for intravenous rt-PA may extend beyond 3 hours (Hacke, Donnan, Fieschi, et al., 2004); eligibility criteria and the time window for thrombolysis may be redefined as more data from randomized trials becomes available (ECASS-3, 2003; IST-3). Intra-arterial administration of thrombolytic agents is presently of limited clinical application, except in highly specialized centers, where research continues. Nonpharmacologic methods of achieving recanalization are under investigation. A policy of administering *aspirin* (75 to 150 mg per day) within the first few days after stroke will reduce the relative risk of stroke (and other adverse vascular events) by about 20% (Antithrombotic Trialists' Collaboration, 2002). The use of anticoagulants in acute stroke has not been proven to be of net benefit (Gubitz, Sandercock, & Counsell, 2004). Neuroprotective agents to salvage the ischemic

penumbra have been developed, but none have been proven to be effective in randomized trials. *Craniectomy* is sometimes performed on patients with massive infarcts whose level of consciousness is declining, but this is not generally supported by the literature (Mendelow, Gregson, Fernandes, et al., 2005). In practice, patients with *cerebellar strokes* may benefit from surgical intervention in this situation. New research is being conducted evaluating *recombinant activated factor VI* I (a *pro-coagulant drug*) in patients with acute intracerebral hemorrhage (Mayer, Brun, Begtrup, et al., 2005).

2. **Restore functional independence**. Reliable evidence from systematic reviews of randomized trials strongly supports a policy of caring for *all* patients with acute stroke on a geographically defined stroke unit with a coordinated multidisciplinary team (Stroke Unit Trialists' Collaboration, 2001). On a population basis, such an approach will result in less death and dependency than thrombolytic therapy because far more patients are eligible for stroke unit care.
3. **Prevent complications**. People with acute stroke are at higher risk of complications, such as infection, pneumonia, skin breakdown, and deep venous thrombosis. All of these are preventable with excellent nursing care (**Langhorne, Pollock, & Stroke Unit Trialists Collaboration, 2002**). In addition, there is at least some evidence supporting the maintenance adequate oxygenation, treating fevers with antipyretics, and maintaining a normal blood glucose level (**Langhorne, Pollock, & Stroke Unit Trialists Collaboration, 2002**). Blood pressure alteration in acute stroke has not been shown to be beneficial, and may be harmful (**Blood pressure in Acute Stroke Collaboration (BASC), 2001**). Further research is ongoing (**Stroke trials directory**).
4. **Reduce the risk of stroke recurrence**. Secondary prevention is accomplished by careful attention to risk factor modification. Hypertension must be treated aggressively, and blood pressure maintained at acceptable standards (Canadian Hypertension Society, 2005; PROGRESS Collaborative Group, 2001). There is now convincing evidence for the use of *statins* in people with stroke and TIA, even if their LDL cholesterol level is not significantly elevated (PROGRESS Collaborative Group, 2001). Regular monitoring of blood glucose levels in diabetics is essential, and smoking cessation strategies should be employed wherever possible. Patients in atrial fibrillation with no contradictions to anticoagulation should be treated with *warfarin* at a dose to maintain the INR in the range 2.0 to 3.0 (Heart Protection Study Collaborative Group, 2002; Hart, Benavente, McBride, & Pearce, 1999). Pooled data from the randomized trials of *endarterectomy* for symptomatic *carotid stenosis* indicates that the benefits of surgery are greatest in men, for patients aged 75 years or older, and for patients operated on soonest after their symptoms took place (Albers, Dalen, Laupacis, Manning, Petersen, & Singer, 2001). The benefit of surgery is lost after 4 weeks for patients with 50% to 69% stenosis, and after 12 weeks for patients with stenosis greater than 70%. Delaying carotid endarterectomy therefore exposes these patients to an unnecessary risk of recurrent stroke.

Gord Gubitz

References

Albers, G., Caplan, L., Easton, D., et al. (2002). Transient ischemic attack: Proposal for a new definition. *New England Journal of Medicine*, *347*, 1713–1716.

Albers, G., Dalen, J., Laupacis, A., Manning, W., Petersen, P., & Singer, D. (2001). Antithrombotic therapy in atrial fibrillation. *Chest*, *119*(1 Suppl), 194S–206S.

Antithrombotic Trialists' Collaboration. (2002). Collaborative meta-analysis of randomized trials of antiplatelet therapy for the prevention of death, myocardial infarction, and stroke in high-risk patients. *British Medical Journal*, *324*, 71–86.

Blood pressure in Acute Stroke Collaboration (BASC) (2001). Interventions for deliberately altering blood pressure in acute stroke. *Cochrane Database of Systematic Reviews*, *2*, CD000039.

Canadian Hypertension Society. (2005). Canadian Hypertension Education Program (CHEP) 2005 guidelines. Available: http://www.hypertension.ca/

ECASS-3. (2003). A placebo controlled trial of alteplase (rt-PA) in acute ischemic hemispheric stroke where thrombolysis is initiated between 3 and 4 hours after stroke onset. American Stroke Association. Available: http://www.strokeconference.org/sc_includes/pdfs/CTP34.pdf

Gubitz, G., Sandercock, P., & Counsell, C. (2004). Anticoagulants for acute ischemic stroke. *Cochrane Database of Systematic Reviews*, *2*, CD000024.

Hacke, W., Donnan, G., Fieschi, C., et al. (2004). Association of outcome with early stroke treatment: Pooled analysis of ATLANTIS, ECASS, and NINDS rt-PA stroke trials. ATLANTIS Trials Investigators; ECASS Trials Investigators; NINDS rt-PA Study Group Investigators. *Lancet, 363*, 768–774.

Hart, R., Benavente, O., McBride, R., & Pearce, L. (1999). Antithrombotic therapy to prevent stroke in patients with atrial fibrillation: A meta-analysis. *Annals of Internal Medicine, 131*, 492–501.

Heart Protection Study Collaborative Group. (2002). MRC/BHF Heart Protection Study of cholesterol lowering with simvastatin in 20,536 high-risk individuals: A randomized placebo-controlled trial. *Lancet, 360*, 7–22.

IST-3. The Third International Stroke Trial (thrombolysis). Available: http://www.dcn.ed.ac.ukist3/.

Langhorne, P., Pollock, A., & Stroke Unit Trialists Collaboration. (2002). What are the components of effective stroke unit care? *Age and Ageing, 31*, 365–371.

Lassen, N. A. (1990). Pathophysiology of brain ischemia as it relates to the therapy of acute ischemic stroke [Review]. *Clinical Neuropharmacology, 13*(Suppl. 3), S1–S8.

MacKay, J., & Mensah, G. The atlas of heart disease and stroke. World Health Organization. Available: http://www.who.int/cardiovascular_diseases/resources/atlas/en/

Mayer, S., Brun, N., Begtrup, M., et al. (2005). Recombinant activated factor vii for acute intracerebral hemorrhage. *New England Journal of Medicine, 352*, 777–785.

Mendelow, A., Gregson, B., Fernandes, H., et al. (2005). Early surgery versus initial conservative treatment in patients with spontaneous supratentorial intracerebral hematomas in the International Surgical Trial in Intracerebral Haemorrhage (STICH): A randomized trial. *Lancet, 365*, 387–397.

National Institute of Neurological Disorders and Stroke. (1990). Classification of cerebrovascular diseases III. *Stroke, 21*, 637–676.

PROGRESS Collaborative Group. (2001). Randomized trial of a perindopril-based blood-pressure-lowering regimen among 6105 individuals with previous stroke or transient ischemic attack. *Lancet, 358*, 1033–1041.

Rothwell, P., Eliasziw, M., Gutnikov, S., (2004). Endarterectomy for symptomatic carotid stenosis in relation to clinical subgroups and timing of surgery. *Lancet, 363*, 915–924.

Stroke trials directory. Internet Stroke Center, Washington University School of Medicine. Available: http://www.strokecenter.org/trials/

Stroke Unit Trialists' Collaboration. (2001). Organized inpatient (stroke unit) care for stroke. *Cochrane Database of Systematic Reviews, 3*, CD000197.

Warach, S., & Kidwell, C. (2004). The redefinition of TIA: The uses and limitations of DWI in acute ischemic cerebrovascular syndromes. *Neurology, 62*, 359–360.

Wardlaw, J. M., del Zoppo, G., Yamaguchi, T., & Berge, E. (2003). Thrombolysis for acute ischemic stroke. *Cochrane Database of Systematic Reviews* 3CD000213.

Warlow, C. P., Dennis, M. S., van Gijn, J., et al. (2001). What caused this transient or persisting ischemic event? In *Stroke: A practical guide to management* (pp. 223–300). Oxford: Blackwell Science.

CHRONOBIOLOGY: RHYTHMS, CLOCKS, CHAOS, AGING, AND OTHER TRENDS

Chronobiology (n): a computer-aided science, particularly important for the elderly, quantifying, mapping, and investigating mechanisms of biological time structure(s), chronome(s), consisting of rhythms, organizing chaos, and underlying trends, with age and/or with any other manifestation of life, such as change in disease risk and/or actual injury and illness (Cornelissen & Halberg, 1994; Halberg, Cornelissen, Halberg, Fink, Chen, Otsuka, et al., 1998; Halberg, 1969).

Rhythm means a "measure," denoting a recurring quantitatively or qualitatively patterned change of a biological or natural physical variable. Often, not invariably, the rhythm can be seen with the naked eye, wherever it occurs. The site of a rhythm may be biological (e.g., sleep/wake behavioral rhythm, with the alternation of closed vs. open eyes), or it may be geographic, such as the alternation of snow and rain and other features of summer and winter or other hot/cold and/or light/dark rhythms (e.g., of day and night). There are other, more subtle rhythms in natural environmental and/or organismic factors, related perhaps to some nonphotic as well as photic solar and galactic drivers, with about 10-yearly and about 21-yearly rhythms. The heartbeat shows different ways to define any rhythm in us or around us: it is seen with the unaided eye once the chest is opened; it is palpated and plotted as the radial pulse; it can also be visualized in a plot as a function of time of the heart's action potentials, such as R-R intervals, all time-macroscopically in an electrocardiogram. When resampled (e.g., at 4 Hz), the action potentials can be coded for a time-microscopic computer analysis in order to quantify the characteristics of a chaotic and/or rhythmic time structure or chronome.

The prefix *circa-*, meaning about, here used as an uncertainty to be measured in inferential statistical terms, is applied to biological rhythms in several ways, which are best validated as mathematical endpoints. "About," then, stands for the fact that we are dealing, in the case of biological rhythms, with approximations that invariably have some margin of error. The rhythms of life, like those of physical nature such as the weather or the broader climate, all involve recurrences of about the same phenomena, but they are not the recurrence of identical events at identical intervals in identical sequences. In the similarity as opposed to identity lies a world of inferential statistics. The intervals between the recurrence of similar events differ greatly in the spectrum of rhythms encountered in any one variable. The intervals may stem from the firing of brain cells, being contributed by action potentials, such as those recorded in an electroencephalogram in fractions of a second; they may be in the region of a second or so in the electrocardiogram. They may also involve 10.5- and 21-year cycles in the human heart rate or the urinary excretion of hormonal metabolites (17-ketosteroids). Certain intervals or the periods they represent, such as a day, a week, a month, a year, or a decade, correspond to about (the fifth circa) but not precisely to the length of (nearly) matching environmental cycles. These circa-periodicities persist when organisms (1) are kept under ordinary conditions but deprived by surgery or genetics of the major transducer of the dominant synchronizing environmental cycle, such as the eyes, (2) are isolated under conditions rendered as constant as possible on earth with respect to environmental light, temperature, and the absence of societal interactions, and/or (3) are able to self-select the given regimen (e.g., of lighting and/or eating) or (4) are constrained to periodic rest-activity regimens exceeding the range of synchronizability of the circadian system, whether these are, for example, 21- or 28-hour days of activity and rest in bright or dim light or whether one administers (as treatment for schizophrenia) regressive electric shocks at 12-hour intervals until the subject is disoriented in space and time. Under all these conditions, the organism can show about 24-hour or circadian or other circa-periods, described as free-running when they differ with statistical significance from those found under synchronization with their environmental near (circa) match, such as a day, a half-week, a week, a month, a half-year, a year, or even a decade.

The foregoing fifth use of *circa* includes the indirect demonstration of desynchronized, if not free-running, periods as the genetic basis of rhythms that characterize and constitute the mechanisms of life, such as the heartbeat, respiration, and practically every biological variable examined thus far. Operationally, in an original study of 18 sham-operated mice, the period synchronized by a regimen of 12 hours of light alternating with 12 hours of darkness was estimated as 23.99 hours with a standard deviation of 0.0175 hours, standard error of 0.004 hours, and a coefficient of variation of 0.073%. The corresponding slightly, yet clearly, different nonoverlapping values for 14 blindedmice were 23.49 hours, 0.1231 hours (*SD*), 0.033 (*SE*), and CV of 0.524% (Halberg, 1969). Behind these superficially tight summary statistics lies a great deal of variability from one fraction of a second to the next in the brain and from hour to hour and day to day in metabolism, once we turn to the study of everyday physiology. Hence, the first four circas qualify rhythms as inferential statistical phenomena and render methods of biometry indispensable for a complete quantification of rhythms (Halberg, 1969).

When beat-to-beat electrocardiographic records are analyzed, an entire spectrum of rhythms with widely differing periods (τ) may be found, including an about 1-second and an about 10-year period, among others. In any given variable one or the other component may be missing: an about-yearly component, prominent in the blood pressure, may not be found in the heart rate of the same person. Time series can also be made of indices of variability, such as standard deviations, or of intermediate computations (imputations), such as endpoints of rhythms or deterministic chaos, for variables such as heart rate and blood pressure. For instance, an endpoint of chaos is the correlation dimension that in its turn undergoes rhythms and underlies trends, as do characteristics of rhythms such as the amplitude, acrophase, and mean.

Rhythms—parts of time structures, chronomes—complement cells in spatial structures. Like genes in genomes, some biological rhythms in chronomes may not be seen by the unaided eye in an original record such as that of telemetered body core temperature, in mice with bilateral suprachiasmatic nuclear (SCN) lesions. The circadian (about 24-hour) temperature rhythm, however, becomes apparent by stacking data, a method for time macroscopy (i.e., they are seen even without quantification by computer analyses). Circadian rhythms—not only in core temperature but also in alcohol drinking, cell division in the cornea, and DNA labeling throughout the gastrointestinal tract, as well as in serum corticosterone sampled every 4 hours for 24 hours—persist, usually with a reduced amplitude and advanced phase, quantified by time microscopy, with cosine fitting, while the about 24-hour rhythms of motor activity and water drinking cannot be detected. Likewise, the loss of the outer part of the adrenal gland, its cortex, entails the loss of the circadian rhythm in the count of blood eosinophils and in pinnal epidermal cell division but not of the circadian rhythm in serum iron. Different rhythms behave differently when tested by a remove-and-replace approach. A master clock illusion could have been laid to rest when a rhythm persisted after removal of the brain above the pons, a need that became even more obvious when "clocks galore" were found not only in peripheral parts of fruit flies but in single cells. Doubts about the merits of replacing the concept of a cell by that of a clock led to the formulation of time structures, chronomes, an empirical approach analyzing the components of variation in time series. In essence, the concept of a "clock" has to be broadened to incorporate the important "circas," conveying much variability and also a critical integration feature for within-organism and external "adaptation"—summarized as "coordination" of the dynamics of life itself in the everyday range of chronomes in and around us.

Too much "regularity" can be a warning of an elevated disease risk. For instance, once a reduced heart rate variability sinks below a threshold, so that the heartbeat approaches the regularity of a metronome's beat, the risk of coronary artery disease, stroke, and nephropathy is high. Such a disease risk syndrome also occurs when blood pressure swings too much each day along the scale of 24 hours (Halberg, Cornelissen, Halberg, Fink, Chen, Otsuka, et al., 1998). Recognizing such conditions requires inferential statistical tools for the objective quantification of rhythms, chaos, and trends. Thereby, one acquires a time-microscopic test of a hypothesis about the presence of a rhythm or of deterministic chaos or of a trend. Whether or not the null hypothesis (e.g., no-rhythm or zero-amplitude) is rejected, one can proceed to estimate parameters with their confidence intervals. One can use the endpoints thus obtained as an intermediate result for further summaries (e.g., by quality-control procedures, such as cumulative sums).

The midline-estimating statistic of rhythm (MESOR) is usually more accurate and/or more precise than the arithmetic mean; the derivation of added parameters, the amplitude and acrophase, as a measure of the extent and timing of change, can be informative when the best mean value is not, for example, when the circadian amplitudes of circulating aldosterone and melatonin decrease with aging from adulthood to senescence without a change in average concentration. An elevated circadian amplitude of urinary melatonin can give a warning of a high risk of breast cancer. The assessment of endpoints from both rhythms and deterministic chaos differentiates coronary artery disease from health, for example, by the assessment of a 24-hour and a 12-hour component in a series of 4-hourly correlation dimensions covering 24 hours. A multifrequency patterning is critical in immuno(chrono)therapy. When equal daily doses of an intended immunomodulator, lentinan, are given "as usual," the tumor is made to grow faster and the life span is shortened. An administration of the same total weekly dose with an about 7-day pattern, gradually increasing and then decreasing doses, contributes to reversing the stimulation of a malignancy into an inhibition and the shortening into a prolongation of the life span (Cornelissen & Halberg, 1994).

Curve-fitting also helps recognize, by an unduly elevated circadian amplitude of blood pressure, the highest risk of stroke among those tested, higher than the risk of a high blood pressure or advanced age, although the overall average pressure may be acceptable (Halberg, Cornelissen, Halberg, Fink, Chen, Otsuka, et al., 1998). The study of biological rhythms developed into the topic of a discipline in its own right, chronobiology, over the documentation of biological clocks and calendars, still specialized areas of research, on biological time measurement per se. These areas should but as yet mostly do not focus with inferential statistical approaches on periods and phases, but even when they eventually do, it will be useful also to consider amplitudes and MESORs, which can be computed concurrently.

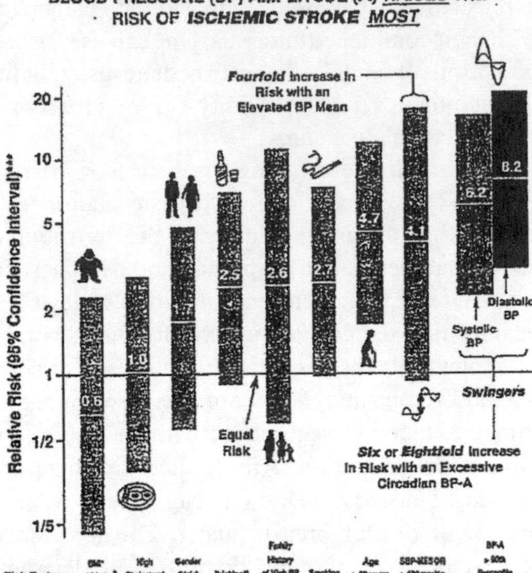

FIGURE 1 In a 6-year prospective study involving 297 patients, the incidence of cerebral ischemic events (top) and nephropathy (bottom) was statistically significantly larger in those patients who had an excessive vs. those who had an acceptable circadian amplitude of blood pressure, i.e., blood pressure overswinging or CHAT (*c*ircadian *h*yper-*a*mplitude-*t*ension) (20–25% vs. <5%). This result was extended by a meta-analysis of data using the proxy outcome of a left ventricular mass index (LVMI) on over 1,000 patients. With either index, event or LVMI, the relation of the circadian blood pressure amplitude to disease risk was nonlinear (not shown). A threshold had to be exceeded before the relative risk increased (not shown).

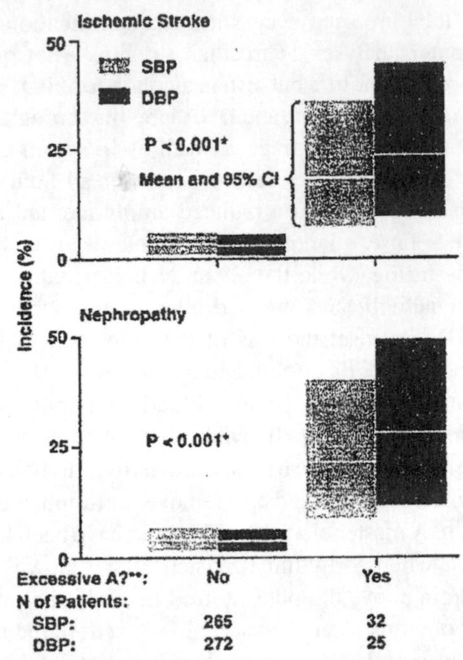

FIGURE 2 In the 6-year study summarized in Figure 1, the relative risk of ischemic stroke associated with blood pressure overswinging, CHAT, was higher than that of any other condition investigated. Diastolic CHAT had a risk of 720%, blood pressure elevation a risk of 310%, old age a risk of 370%, alcohol or tobacco use a risk of 150%, and positive family history of vascular disease a risk of 160%.

As prominent circadian rhythmicity was found at different levels of organization, several series of experiments were carried out under rigorous standardized laboratory conditions that investigated the effect of a single physical stimulus, such as the exposure to noise. Outcomes were as different as no response, convulsion, and even death, as a function of the circadian stage at which the organism was exposed to noise. Whether the stimulus was audiogenic or consisted of the exposure to an endotoxin, to drugs such as ouabain, or to whole-body irradiation, predictable changes were found as a function of the circadian stage at which the stimulus was applied, albeit with differences in timing (Halberg, 1969). Remove-and-replace experiments established the roles of the adrenal cortex and the central nervous system, each for the maintenance of some but not all rhythms yet both contributing to circadian amplitude and phase relations.

Chronomes and Aging

Time structure or chronome characteristics (i.e., those of rhythm, chaos, and trend at different levels of organization) provide scholars of aging with opportunities for both a better basic science of aging and progress in disease prevention, diagnosis, and treatment, based on the combination of several new technologies. These are:

- the availability of portable, personal, long-term ambulatory monitors of biological variables. Blood pressure, the electrocardiogram and electroencephalogram, motor activity, core temperature, and gastric acidity are cases in point. These and other variables undergo changes that recur spontaneously and as responses;
- the availability of database systems to acquire, edit, and archive volumes of data obtained from personal monitors;
- the availability of statistical procedures to analyze and model the biological dynamics and from them to devise optimal dosage time patterns for specific individuals;
- the availability of portable, programmed devices to administer therapy (e.g., by physiological rate-adjusted cardiac pacemakers, defibrillators, or drug pumps that respond in a closed loop to the diagnostic information analyzed as one goes);
- a chronobiological understanding of the health effect of time structures that quantify aging and health positively, inside the range of usual variation.

Thus, effects of aging on the circadian and extracircadian amplitudes are detected that otherwise go unrecognized, such as a change from circadian to extracircadian variance with age in heart rate and blood pressure. Rhythms and their broader discipline, chronobiology, constitute an objective, useful, and often indispensable way of approaching any problem in biology broadly and particularly in aging. Rhythmic changes in many variables (e.g., those recurring each day) can be greater in extent than those occurring over many decades and are thus powerful confounders of aging research if ignored. Alternatively, changes in chronome characteristics, if evaluated, are sometimes extremely useful sources of information occurring in the absence of changes in mean values, indicating, by a decrease in circadian amplitude of circulating melatonin and aldosterone, a participation in aging of potentially important critical central pineal and peripheral adrenocortical mechanisms. Temperature telemetry on the rodent demonstrates an advance in circadian acrophase and/or a decrease in circadian amplitude with aging that corresponds to the effect of SCN. The detection by 7-day monitoring of disease risk syndromes, such as an excessive blood pressure variability (circadian hyper-amplitude-tension, CHAT) or a decrease below a threshold of circadian heart rate variability are disease risk syndromes that detect a risk elevation greater than an increase in the average of blood pressure and/or old age, the use of alcohol or tobacco, or a positive family history of vascular disease. Other changes within the currently neglected normal range can also be anticipated to be diagnostically useful and to prompt timed treatment that has already doubled 2-year disease-free survival time from the historically and methodologically interesting treatment of large perioral cancers by treating at the time of peak tumor temperature rather than at other times or as usual.

For the supplementary text, consult *Introduction to Chronobiology* and the *New SIRMCE Confederation Resolution* (Brussels, March 17–18, 1995) on our website: *http://revilla.mac.cie.uva.es/chrono*.

FRANZ HALBERG
GERMAINE CORNÉLISSEN

See also
Melatonin

CIRCULATORY SYSTEM

See
Cardiovascular System: Heart
Cardiovascular System: Overview
Cardiovascular System: Vasculature

COGNITIVE BEHAVIORAL THERAPY

See
Cognitive Therapy

COGNITIVE DYSFUNCTION: DRUG TREATMENT

Cognitive disorders in older individuals can be attributed to a wide variety of causes (e.g., infections, exposure to toxic substances, medications, avitaminosis, head trauma, cerebrovascular disease, and tumors). *Neurodegenerative disorders* are by far the most frequent cause of cognitive decline, and *Alzheimer's disease* (AD) is the most frequent cause of dementia. AD has been reported in up to 10% of the population age 65 or older (Jorm & Jolley, 1998), and it is estimated that by the year 2040, 14 million Americans will have AD. Not surprisingly, there is a significant effort to develop medications that can treat or ameliorate AD symptoms. All suspected known etiological mechanisms of AD have been explored with specific and non-specific treatments. The second most frequent form of dementia is that caused by vascular disease (Lopez, Kuller, Fitzpatrick, Ives, Becker, & Beauchamp, 2003), and consequently, multiple lines of treatment have also been tested for this condition. In the following, we review the experience of the treatment of dementia, with particular emphasis on the treatment of AD.

Neuropathological Basis of *Dementia Treatment*

The neuropathological and biochemical changes in AD can be divided into 2 general areas: structural changes, and alterations in neurotransmitters systems. The structural changes involve amyloid metabolism alterations, *neurofibrillary tangles* (NFT), *neuritic plaques* (NP), synapse loss, and neuronal death, especially in the cortical association regions and portions of the limbic system. It is important to note that deposits of NP can trigger an inflammatory response that leads to additional neuropil destruction and stimulates additional neuritic plaque formation (Joachim, Morris, & Selkoe, 1989). Recent studies with amyloid ligands have shown that *amyloid deposits* are present in frontal and parietal areas with less involvement of the medial temporal lobe in mildly demented subjects (Klunk, Engler, Nordberg, Wang, Blomqvist, Holt, et al., 2004).

One of the most consistent findings in the brain of AD patients is the loss of cholinergic neurons in the *nucleus basalis of Meynert* (nbM) (Whitehouse, Price, Clark, Coyle, & DeLong, 1981). The nbM sends cholinergic projections to all areas of the neocortex, especially the temporal lobes and frontal and parietal association areas, and the integrity of this system is essential for normal cognitive functioning. Other neurotransmitters are affected in AD, such as *serotonin* and *norepinephrine*, which can also contribute to the global cognitive deficits, although they appear to be associated with the behavioral symptoms of AD (Lopez, Kaufer, Reiter, Carra, DeKosky, & Palmer, 1996; Zubenko & Moossy, 1988).

Biochemical studies have found that there is a significant loss of cortical *choline acetyltransferase* (ChAT) (Baskin, Browning, Pirozzolo, Korporaal, Baskin, & Appel, 1999) and *acetylcholinesterase* (AChE) activity in AD patients. ChAT is found only in presynaptic cholinergic neurons, while AChE is found in presynaptic and postsynaptic cholinergic pathways (Davies & Maloney, 1976) . Interestingly, while there is a significant reduction of *nicotinic receptor* density (Schroder, Zilles, Luiten, Strosberg, & Aghchi, 1989; Schroder, Zilles, Maelicke, & Hajos, 1989), the overall *muscarinic receptor* density remains relatively stable. However, the muscarinic (M) receptor M2 appeared to be depleted in AD (Flynn, Ferrari-Di Leo, Levey, & Mash, 1995). This receptor is believed to be on the presynaptic bouton and may serve an autoregulatory function. By contrast, the M1 receptors are predominantly on the postsynaptic side, and their density remains stable in AD. Thus, function may be abnormal, even though structure remains normal. M3 receptors are normal or up-regulated (Rodriguez-Puertas, Pascual, Vilaro, & Pazos, 1997).

Compounds That Can Modify Structural Changes

Neuritic Plaques and Neurofibrillary Tangles. Several compounds have been proposed for the treatment of AD that can modulate *beta amyloid processing* through inhibition of *secretases* activity (NP) (Xu, Sweeney, Greengard, & Gandy, 1994), preventing amyloid aggregation (e.g., *homotaurine* or *Alzhemed*), or that can inhibit kinases/phosphatases that participate in the hyperphosphorylation of *tau proteins* (NFT) (e.g., *Glycogen synthetase kinase [GSK] 3 inhibitors*) (Aoki, Yokota, Sugiura, Sasaki, Hasegawa,

Okumura, et al., 2004; Imahori & Uchida, 1997; Lee, 1996; Nuydens, De Jong, Nuyens, Cornelissen, & Geerts, 1995). An interesting new approach is the peripherally administered antibodies against beta amyloid proteins in the central nervous system (Bard, Cannon, Barbour, Burke, Games, Grajeda, et al., 2000; Chen, Chen, Knox, Inglis, Bernard, Martin, et al., 2000; Pericak-Vance , Grubber, Bailey, Hedges, West, Santoro, et al., 2000). Unfortunately, the first trial resulted in an unacceptable number of adverse events (i.e., *meningoencephalitis*) (Orgogozo, Gilman, Dartigues, & Laurent, 2003). Nevertheless, new antibodies have been developed, and it seems that this line of treatment will continued to be investigated.

Inflammation. There are many lines of evidence that point to *inflammatory mechanisms* contributing to the pathology of AD: (1) population studies have shown that the use of steroids and *non-steroidal anti-inflammatory drugs* (NSAIDs) reduces the risk of developing AD (Anthony, Breitner, Zandi, Meyer, Jurasova, Norton, et al., 2000; McHeer, Schulzer, & McGeer, 1996); (2) inflammatory cytokines, complement proteins, a1-antichymotrypsin, and activated microglial cells are associated with the presence of NP (McGeer & McGeer, 1995; Mrak, Sheng, & Griffin, 1995), and it has been suggested that an inflammatory process is necessary in the formation of NP (Aisen & Davis, 1994); (3) *inflammation markers*, such as *protein-C reactive* and *tumor necrosis factor a* are elevated in the serum of demented subjects (Collins, Perry, Watson, Harrell, Acton, Blacker, et al., 2000; Kuller, Tracy, Shaten, & Meilahn, 1996). However, the majority of the studies that investigated whether anti-inflammatory medications can delay progression of AD have not shown positive results. Although a small double-blind placebo-controlled study showed that *indomethacin* improved cognition in AD patients (Rogers, et al., 1993), more recent clinical trials showed that neither prednisone (Aisen, Davis, Berg, Schafer, Campbell, Thomas, et al., 2000), diclofenac/misoprosol (Scharf, Mander, Ugoni, Vajda, & Christophidis, 1999), nor naproxen (Aisen, Schafer, Grundman, Pfeiffer, Sano, Davis, et al., 2003) improved cognition in AD patients. Recent studies conducted with *cyclooxygenase 2 (COX2) inhibitors*, which have fewer side effects than traditional NSAIDs and steroids, have not shown positive results (e.g., *nimesulide, rofecoxib*) (Aisen, Schafer, Grundman, Pfeiffer, Sano, Davis, et al., 2003; Aisen, Schmeidler, & Pasinetti, 2002; Reines, Block, Morris, Liu, Nessly, Lines, et al., 2004).

Other drugs that modulate inflammatory processes that have been proposed for the treatment of AD, and include *antimalarial drugs* (Aisen, 1997) and *colchicine* (Aisen, Marin, Fusco, Baruch, Ryan, & Davis, 1996). The latter also has anti-amyloid activity (Kisilevsky, 1996), and it appears to have a γ-aminobutyric acid receptor blocker activity (Weiner, Buhler, Whatley, Harris, & Dunwiddie, 1998). *Astrocyte-derived cytokines (S100beta) inhibitors* are also promising treatments for AD. The astrocyte-derived S100B protein is encoded in chromosome 21, and it appears to be increased in AD, resulting in the formation of amyloid plaques (NP) (Mrak & Griffin, 2001).

Estrogens and Neurosteroids. There were several lines of evidence that suggest that ovarian steroids play a critical role in the memory process of normal individuals and AD. Experimental studies have found that *estrogens* and *progestins* stimulate *synaptogenesis* in the hippocampus of animal models (McEwen, Alves, Bulloch, & Weiland, 1997) and modulate the cholinergic system (Urani, Privat, & Maurice, 1998). Ovariectomy and 17β-estradiol levels modulate levels of β amyloid in the human brain (Petanceska, Nagy, Frail, & Gandy, 2000). Estrogens increase activation of the superior parietal lobes, and decrease activation in inferior parietal lobes and right frontal lobe during specific memory tasks in functional neuroimaging studies (Shaywitz, Shaywitz, Pugh, Fulbright, Skudlarski, Mencl, et al., 1999). Further, population studies have found that postmenopausal women who have received estrogen replacement therapy have a lower risk of developing AD (Tang, Jacobs, Stern, Marder, Schofield, Gurland, et al., 1996; Waring, Rocca, Petersen, O'Brien, Tangalos, & Kokmen, 1999). *Estrogen replacement therapy* may improve response to *acetylcholinesterase inhibitors* treatment (Schneider, Farlow, Henderson, & Pogoda, 1996). However, 2 placebo-controlled studies showed that estrogen replacement therapy did not modify the course and progression of AD (Henderson, Paganini-Hill, Miller, Elble, Reyes, Shoupe, et al., 2000; Wang, Liao, Liu, Liu, Chao, Lu, et al., 2000), and the results of a recent prevention study

(*Women Health Initiative Memory Study*) showed that women who received progestagins and estrogens had increased risk of developing dementia (Shumaker, Legault, Rapp, Thal, Wallace, Ockene, et al., 2003), and strokes (Wassertheil-Smoller, Hendrix, Limacher, Heiss, Kooperberg, Baird, et al., 2003). Similarly, studies using male hormones (dehydroepiandrosterone) have not shown any benefits (Wolkowitz, Kramer, Reus, Costa, Yaffe, Walton, et al., 2003).

Nerve Growth Factors. Several studies have shown that *nerve growth factors* (NGFs) are reduced in cholinergic neurons of the nbM (Murer, Boissiere, Yan, Hunot, Villares, Faucheux, et al., 1999; Scott, Mufson, Weingartner, Skau, & Crutcher, 1995), which suggests a lack of trophic support for this specific neuronal population (Hock, Heese, Hulette, Rosenberg, & Otten, 2000). In addition, experimental studies in animal models have shown that NGF compounds had a neuroprotective effect (Fournier, Steinberg, Gauthier, Keane, Guzzi, Coude, et al., 1993), and intraventricular administration of NGF in AD patients can improve cognition (Eriksdotter, Nordberg, Amberla, Backman, Ebendal, Meyerson, et al., 1998; Jonhagen, 2000). However, the major problem with the use of NGF compounds is that they cannot cross the brain-blood barrier. Therefore, the use of NGF in AD remains in the experimental field until new forms of administration can be found (Nabeshima & Yamada, 2000). Other neurotropic compounds, such as *monosialoganglioside* GM-1 (Ala, Romero, Knight, Feldt, & Frey, 1990) and *Neotrofin* (Grundman, Capparelli, Kim, Morris, Farlow, Rubin, et al., 2003) have shown no efficacy in AD patients.

Statins. Cholesterol is essential for the formation of cell membrane fluidity and permeability. Consequently, it has been hypothesized that cholesterol levels can influence the formation and distribution of beta amyloid within the cholesterol-rich membranes. In addition, clinical studies have found that the prevalence of AD is lower in patients taking *statins* (e.g., *simvastatin*, *lovastatin*, *pravastatin*) than in those who were never exposed to these medications (Rockwood, Kirkland, Hogan, MacKnight, Merry, Verreault, et al., 2002; Wolozin, Kellman, Ruosseau, Celesia, & Siegel, 2000). However, the results of these cross-sectional studies require further confirmation. This should be done in longitudinal studies, where the association between statins use and incident dementia cases can be better determined. There are several clinical trials underway using statins in combination with CEIs.

Cerebrospinal Fluid Drainage. It has been shown that subjects with AD have low beta amyloid levels in the cerebrospinal fluid (CSF) (Galasko, Chang, Motter, Clark, Kaye, Knopman, et al., 1998). This has been attributed to decreased clearance and increased deposition of amyloid in the form of NP. Therefore, the hypothesis that restoring CSF turnover and clearance will ameliorate NP deposition and consequently slow down AD progression was tested using a ventriculoperitoneal shunt (Silverberg, Levinthal, Sullivan, Bloch, Chang, Leverenz, et al., 2002). The results of this study were modest, and they did not justify the risk of undergoing a surgical procedure to slow progression of AD. The long-term use of *ventriculoperitoneal shunts* has a significant number of complications (e.g., infections).

Modulation of Neurotransmitter Systems

Cholinesterase Inhibitors and Cholinergic Compounds. For several decades researchers have been able to modulate the cholinergic system activity, especially using CEIs. Experimental studies have shown that *physostigmine* (a cholinergic agonist and acetycholinesterase inhibitor) can increase *memory performance* (Smith, Coogan, & Hart, 1986), and the CNS effects of *scopolamine* (a cholinergic antagonist) can be reverted by *physostigmine* (Crowell & Ketchum, 1967; Duvosin & Katz, 1968) in nondemented individuals. This, coupled with the fact that ACh is the most affected neurotransmitter in AD, has made it possible to develop CEIs as the main line of treatment of AD. In 1986, it was demonstrated that the long term (12 months) use of *tacrine* can improve cognition in AD patients (Summers, Majoviski, Marsh, Tachiki, & Kling, 1986); and in 1993, this drug was approved by the Food and Drug Administration as the first palliative treatment for AD (Farlow, Gracon, Hershey, Lewis, Sadowsky, & Dolan-Ureno, 1992) . Within a decade, 3 other CEIs have been approved: *donepezil* (Rogers & Friedhoff, 1996), *rivastigmine* (Rosler, Anand, Cicin-Sain, Gauthier, Agid, Dal-Bianco, et al., 1999), and *galanthamine* (Tariot, Solomon, Morris, Kershaw, Lilienfield, & Ding, 2000). Other CEIs (e.g., *epastigmine*, *metrifonate*) have proven efficacy in AD, but the potential for adverse events limited their clinical utility (Farlow, Cyrus, Nadel, Lahiri, Brashear, & Gulanski, 1999; Imbimbo, Martelli, Troetel, Lucchelli, Lucca, & Thal, 1999). Interestingly, although one of the first approaches to the treatment of AD was the administration of *intraventricular bethanechol* (a cholinergic agonist), the results of these studies showed only minimal cognitive improvement, and it came at the expense of increased depressive symptomatology (Harbaugh, 1988; Penn, Martin, Wilson, Fox, & Savoy, 1988).

CEIs have been useful in improving cognition in subjects with *mild cognitive impairment*, a clinical syndrome that precedes the onset of AD (Salloway, Ferris, Kluger, Goldman, Griesing, Kumar, et al., 2004). CEIs have also been found to be effective in subjects with *vascular dementia* (Black, Roman, Geldmacher, Salloway, Hecker, Burns, et al., 2003; Erkinjuntti, Kurz, Gauthier, Bullock, Lilienfeld, & Damarju, 2002). However, one of the major problems in the assessment of efficacy of treatment in vascular dementia is that it is difficult to know whether these subjects have concomitant AD pathology. Recent studies have found that *donepezil* was efficacious in the treatment of the cognitive deficits associated with *multiple sclerosis* (Krupp, Christodoulou, Melville, Scherl, MacAllister, & Elkins, 2004) .

Experimental studies in animal models (DeLapp, Wu, Belagaje, Johnstone, Little, Shannon, et al., 1998) and humans (Farde, Suhara, Halldin, Nyback, Nakashima, Swahn, et al., 1996) have shown that selective M1 *muscarinic agonists* can improve cognition (e.g., *xanomeline*, *oxotremorine*, *milameline*, *arecoline*) (Bymaster, Carter, Peters, Zhang, Ward, Mitch, et al., 1998; Raffaele, Berardi, Asthana, Morris, Haxby, & Soncrant, 1991; Wettstein & Spiegel, 1984). Double-blind, placebo-controlled studies have shown that xanomeline improves cognition in AD patients (Bodick, Offen, Levey, et al., 1997; Bodick, Offen, Shannon, et al., 1997; Veroff, Bodick, Offen, Sramek, & Cutler, 1998). However, this compound appears to have a better effect on psychiatric symptoms than on cognition (Bodick, Offen, Levey, et al., 1997). By contrast, other muscarinic (Thal, Forrest, Loft, & Mengel, 2000) and nicotine (*dermal plaster*) (Snaedal, Johannesson, Jonsson, & Gylfadottir, 1996) agonists have shown no efficacy in AD patients.

Other Compounds that may Improve Acetylcholine Synthesis. *Citicoline* or *CDP-choline*, which dissociates to choline and citidine on entering the human body, appears to promote ACh biosynthesis, stimulates synaptic transmission by facilitating membrane formation, and attenuates *arachidonic acid* release, which limits its oxidative metabolism (neuroprotective effect) (Baskaya, Dogan, Rao, & Dempsey, 2000; Calvani & Carta, 1991; Rao, Hatcher, & Dempsey, 2000). There are some studies that have shown that citicoline or CDP-choline improve cognition in non-demented individuals (Spiers, Myers, Hochanadel, Lieberman, & Wurtman, 1996), in AD (Alvarez, Mouzo, Pichel, Perez, Laredo, Fernandez-Novoa, et al., 1999), and in cerebrovascular disease (Warach, Lettigrew, Dashe, Pullicinto, Lefkowitz, Sabounjian, et al., 2000). However, current data is limited to small studies, and it seems that this compound has a better efficacy in cerebrovascular disease than in AD (Fioravanti & Yanagi, 2000). Another drug that stimulates the release of ACh, *4-aminopyridine*, showed no improvement of cognition in AD patients (Davidson, Zemishlany, & Mohs, 1988).

Cathecholamine Agonists. Because clinical studies have found that the noradrenergic system is involved in learning processes (Stein, Belluzzi, & Wise, 1975), and neuropathological studies have found a loss of adrenergic neurons in the brains of AD patients (Chan-Palay & Asan, 1989; Zubenko & Moossy, 1988), it was thought that adrenergic agonists may improve cognition in AD patients. However, studies conducted with a2 receptor agonists (*clonidine*) have shown negative results (Mohr Schlegel, Fabbrini, Williams, Mouradian, Mann, et al., 1989). Similarly, early studies investigating psychostimulant use among cognitive impaired elderly subjects have shown no improvements (Crook, Ferris, & Sathananthan, 1977).

Compounds That Modulate *Oxidative Stress*

There are a number of mechanisms that protect the human body from free-radical damage, including enzymes such as *superoxide dismutase* and *catalases* and reduced *gluthatione*; tissue damage occurs when the balance among these mechanisms is lost. Because free radical damage increases with age and there is some evidence of increased *lipid peroxidation* in AD cases (Friedlich & Butcher, 1994), the use of medication that can modulate oxidative stress has been a logical approach to the treatment of AD. Most importantly, the majority of the compounds that can modulate oxidative stress can also have effects in other metabolic pathways that lead to neuronal loss.

Acetyl-L-Carnitine (ALC). *ALC* is structurally similar to ACh, plays a key role in the carbohydrate, lipid, and amino acid metabolism, and stimulates natural scavenger functions to reduce oxidized radicals (Calvani & Carta, 1991). Studies conducted in small groups of AD patients showed that ALC improves cognition (Sano, Bell, Cote, Dooneief, Lawton, Legler, Marder, et al., 1992; Spagnoli, Lucca, Menasce, Bandera, Cizza, Forloni, et al., 1991). However, a 1-year multicenter placebo-controlled study of ALC in AD patients showed that those patients on ALC progressed at the same rate as those on placebo. Nevertheless, a subanalysis by age that compared early onset (younger than 65 years) versus late onset (older than 66 years) patients showed that those patients with early onset AD on ALC tended to progress slower than late onset patients, or placebo (Thal et al., 1996).

Vitamin E. A study conducted by the Alzheimer's Disease Cooperative with 2 antioxidants, tocopherol (vitamin E) and *selegiline*, showed a possible beneficial effect of vitamin E on AD (Sano, Ernesto, Thomas, Klauber, Schafer, Grundman, et al., 1997). The authors found neither vitamin E nor selegiline improved cognition. However, the time to reach the secondary outcomes (death, institutionalization, or loss of the ability to perform 2 of the 3 activities of daily living from the Blessed Dementia Rating Scale) was longer in patients taking vitamin E than in those taking selegiline, both drugs, or placebo. These 2 drugs were selected for the study because vitamin E is a *free radical scavenger* that limits lipid peroxidation in membranes (Yoshida, Busto, Watson, Santiso, & Ginsberg, 1985), and selegiline inhibits oxidative deamination. Interestingly, prevention studies have shown that the combination of vitamin E and C can lower the risk of developing vascular dementia, but not AD (Masaki, Losonczy, Izmirlian, Foley, Ross, Petrovitch, et al., 2000).

Monoamine Oxidase B (MAO-B) Inhibitors. *Selegiline* (*L-deprenyl*), a selective *MAO-B inhibitor* with antioxidant activity, has been found to improve cognition (Burke et al., 1993; Tariot, Sunderland, & Weingartner, 1987), and behavior in AD patients (Lawlor, Aisen, Green, Fine, & Schmeidler, 1997). However, this has not been confirmed by others (Freedman, Rewilak, Xerri, Cohen, Gordon, Shandling, et al., 1998). *Milacemide*, another MAO-B inhibitor and glycine pro-drug, has shown no efficacy in the treatment of AD (Dysken, Mendels, & LeWitt, 1992).

Idebenome. This is a benzoquinona derivative, which is currently marketed in Europe, Asia, and South America (Bergamasco, Scarzella, & LaCommare, 1994). Experimental studies have shown that idebenone increases cerebral glucose metabolism (Nagai, Toshida, Narumi, Tauayama, & Nagaoaka, 1989), improves neurological deficits following cerebral insult (Otomo, Abe, Araki, Ito, Omae, Nishimura, et al., 1985; Otomo, Nanja, Saso, Narikawa, Terao, Yoshino, et al., 1985), probably through an antioxidant mechanism (Bruno, Battaglia, Copani, Sortino, Canonico, & Nicoletti, 1994; Weiland, Schutz, Armstrong, Kuthe, Heller, & Oellerich, 1995) , and increases NGF levels in the brain (Yamada, Nitta, Hasegawa, Fuji, Hiramatsu, Kameyama, et al., 1997). Placebo-controlled studies have shown that idebenone improves cognition in AD patients, even after 1-year follow-up (Senin, Parnetti, Barbagallo-Sangiorgi, Bartorelli, Bocola, Capurso, et al., 1992). However, there is a need to further examine this medication with additional large, multi-center placebo-controlled studies and determine its possible effects on cognition when combined with cholinesterase inhibitors.

Propentophylline and Pentoxifylline. These are *xanthine derivatives* and *adenosin re-uptake/phosphodiesterase inhibitors* that modulate microglial activation and restore microglial cells (Mcrae, Ling, Schubert, & Rudolphi, 1998; Ringheim, 2000; Schubert et al., 1998). In addition, experimental studies have shown that propentophylline increases NGF synthesis (Wirtz-Brugger

& Giovanni, 2000). Placebo-controlled studies have shown that both pentoxifylline and propentophylline improved cognition in AD, and in vascular dementia (Black, Barclay, Nolan, Thaler, Hardiman, & Blass, 1992; Marcusson, Rother, Kittner, Rossner, Smith, Babic, et al., 1997; Rother, Erkinjuntti, Roessner, Kittner, Marcusson, & Karlssor, 1998).

Neuroprotective Agents. There are several lines of research that suggest there is a common pathway for neuronal damage in neurological disorders (Lipton & Rosenberg, 1994). A noxious stimulus can activate the *n-methyl-d-aspartate (NMDA) receptor-operated channels*, resulting in an excessive influx of calcium leading to neuronal damage. This results in glutamate release, and the cycle continues causing more irreversible neuronal damage. Therefore, *NMDA receptor blockers* have been recommended to treat several pathological processes that lead to neuronal damage, including vascular dementia and stroke (Mobius, 1999), human inmunodeficiency virus cognitive deficits (Lipton, 1992), and other neurological disorder (Parsons, Danysz, & Quack, 1999).

Because it is believed that amyloid deposits can activate the NMDA receptor, it has been proposed that NMDA receptor blockers can prevent neuronal death in AD. *Memantine* is a noncompetitive NMDA receptor blocker and modulator of the *glutamatergic system* (Gortelmeyer, Pantev, Parsons, & Quack, 1993; Muller, Mutschler, & Riederer, 1995). However, at this time clinical trials have shown that memantine is effective only in late stages of AD (Winblad & Poritis, 1999). In 2003, the Food and Drug Administration approved memantine for moderate/severe AD (Tariot, Farlow, Grossberg, Graham, McDonald, & Gergel, 2004). Placebo-controlled studies are underway to test *neramexine*, a compound similar to memantine. Another NMDA receptor blocker is *d-cycloserine* (an antibiotic) (Riekkinen, Ikonen, & Riekkinen, 1998), and some experimental studies have shown that it may improve cognition in AD (Tsai, Falk, Gunther, & Coyle, 1999), while others did not (Fakouhi, Jhee, Sramek, Benes, Schwartz, Hantsburger, et al., 1995).

Because calcium influx is a critical step for neuronal damage, it has been proposed that *calcium channel blockers* may be useful in the treatment of AD (Brorson, Bindokas, Iwama, Marcuccilli, Chisholm, & Miller, 1995). A few studies with a small number of subjects have found that *nimodipine* can improve cognition in AD (Tollefson, 1990), and it has limited efficacy in vascular dementia (Pantoni, Bianchi, Beneke, Inzitari, Wallin, & Erkinjuntti, 2000; Pantoni, Rossi, Inzitari, Bianchi, Beneke, Erkinjuntti, et al., 2000).

Nootropic Agents. Cyclic derivatives of the γ-aminobutiric acid have been considered potential treatments for dementia (e.g., *piracetam, pramiracetam, aniracetam, oxiracetam*). The mechanism of action is not clear, although experimental studies in animals suggested that they stimulate synthesis and release of ACh (Bartus, Dean, & Sherman, 1981; Ferris, Reisberg, & Crook, 1982; Friedman, Sherman, Ferris, & Schneck, 1981; Wurtman, Magil, & Reinstein, 1981). The prototype for the entire group of nootropic agents is piracetam, and some studies have shown both a short- and long-term benefit of this treatment in AD patients (Chouinard, Annable, & Ross-Chouinard, 1981; Croisile Trillet, Fondarai, Laurent, Mauguiere, & Billardon, 1993), especially in attention and memory functions (Growdon, Corkin, Huff, & Rosen, 1986). Oxiracetam, a hydroxylated analogue of piracetam, can improve cognition in AD and vascular dementia (Baumel, Eisner, & Karukin, 1989; Falsaperla, Pret, & Oliani, 1990), although this has not been confirmed by others (Green, Goldstein, Auchus, Presley, Clark, Van Tuyl, et al., 1992). There are no known multi-center placebo-controlled studies with nootropic agents.

Herbal Alternative Medicine

There is a considerable increase in the use of *herbal medicines* in neuropsychiatry (LaFrance Lauterbach, Coffey, Salloway, Kaufer, Reeve, Royall, et al., 2000), and the most well-known herbal medicine for the treatment of AD is *gingko biloba* (Oken, Storzbach, & Kaye, 1998). It is important to note that in the U.S. gingko biloba is considered an herbal preparation and is regulated as a dietary supplement. Therefore, manufacturers are not obligated to complete the strict approval process that the Food and Drug Administration require for drugs. In addition, there is no control over the content of active ingredients in each preparation.

Experimental studies in animals have shown that the active compounds of gingko biloba act as scavengers, are antagonists of platelet-activating factor, provide membrane protection, increase γ-aminobutiric acid and glutamic decarboxilase levels, and increase muscarinic receptor population (Klein, Charrerlee, & Loffeholz, 1997; Sasaki, Hatta, & Haga, 1999; Taylor, 1986). There are multiple publications that have found that gingko biloba improves cognition in AD patients (Ditzler, 1991; Hofferberth, 1989; Kanoeski, Hermann, Stephan, Wierich, & Horr, 1996; LeBars et al., 1997; Vorberg, Schenk, & Schmidt, 1989; Wesnes, Simmons, Rook, & Simpson, 1987), and a few reported lack of efficacy (van Dongen, van Rossum, Kessels, Sielhorst, & Knipschild, 2000). The majority of these studies did not use current standardized measures to determine cognitive improvement, and have been conducted in mixed populations. A recent review of 50 studies on gingko biloba concluded that current data are limited and inconsistent, and additional studies are recommended (Oken et al., 1998). Currently, there are 2 studies (one in the United States and another in Europe) investigating the prevention of AD using gingko biloba.

Huperazine, an alkaloid from the Chinese herb *Huperzia serrata*, has proven to have acetylcholinesterase activity. Experimental studies in animal models have shown that Huperazine was able to cross the blood brain barrier, and had similar acetylcholinesterase inhibition to rivastigmine and donepezil (Liang & Tang, 2004).

Other Treatments

Early approaches to the treatment of dementia were based on the concept that dementia was a form of avascular disease, and several cerebral *avasodilators* were proposed for the treatment of AD (e.g., *papaverine*, *cyclandelate*, *nafronyl*, *isoxsuprime*, *vincamine*, *hydergine*). This avascular approach to the treatment of AD is no longer valid, and none of these compounds showed efficacy (Waters, 1988). Similarly, *hyperbaric oxygen* treatments have shown no evidence of cognitive improvement (Raskin, Gershon, Crook, Sathananthan, & Ferris, 1978).

Because *neuropeptides* (e.g., *vasopressin*, *adrenocorticotrophic hormone*) and thiamine-dependent enzymes are diminished in the brains of AD patients (Bissette, Reynolds, Kilts, Widerlov, & Nemeroff, 1985; Mazurek, Beal, Bird, & Martin, 1986; Nolan, Black, Sheu, Langberg, & Blass, 1991), it was proposed to use these compounds in the treatment of AD (Desouza, Whitehouse, Kuhar, & Price, 1986; Peabody, Thiemann, & Pigache, 1985; Tinklenberg, Pfefferbaum, & Berger, 1981; Tinklenberg, Pigache, Berger, & Kopell, 1982). An *opiate antagonist*, *naloxone*, which has a facilitatory effect on memory tasks, has also been tested in the treatment of AD (Reisberg, Ferris, & Anand, 1983). All of these approaches had negative results.

Early observations suggested that *aluminum exposure* could increase the risk of AD (McLachlan, Bergeron, Smith, Boomer, & Rifat, 1996) due to possibly increasing neurofibrillary tangle formation (Savory, Exley, Forbes, Huang, Joshi, Kruck, et al., 1996), and facilitating neuronal and astrocyte toxicity (Levesque, Mizzen, McLachlan, & Fraser, 2000). There was one study that used intramuscular *desferrioxamine*, a chelating agent, in a single-blind, placebo controlled, parallel trial of AD subjects treated for 2 years (McLachlan, Dalton, Kruck, Bell, Smith, Kalow, et. al, 1991) .

Conclusion

The goal of the treatment of AD is to prevent, slow, or revert the neurodegenerative process. Although there have been significant advances in the treatment of AD over the past 20 years, at this time all available medications slow down the disease process for an unknown period of time. Nevertheless, as discussed here, there is considerable effort by the medical community and industry to develop compounds that will either prevent the onset or halt the neurodegenerative process. Research using NGF, anti-inflammatory, antioxidant agents, and drugs that may affect the production of NP and NFT brings hope for the treatment of AD.

Oscar L. Lopez
Judith Saxton

See also

Dementia
Memory: Neurochemical Correlates
Memory Assessment: Clinical

References

Aisen, P. S. (1997). Inflammation and Alzheimer's disease: Mechanisms and therapeutic strategies. *Gerontology, 43*(1-2), 143–149.

Aisen, P. S., & Davis, K. L. (1994). Inflammatory mechanisms in Alzheimer's disease: Implications for therapy. *American Journal of Psychiatry, 151*, 1105–1113.

Aisen, P. S., Davis, K. L., Berg, J. D., Schafer, K., Campbell, K., Thomas, R. G., Weiner, M. F., Farlow, M. R., Sano, M., Grundman, M., & Thal, L. J. (2000). A randomized controlled trial of prednisone in Alzheimer's disease. *Neurology, 54*, 588–593.

Aisen, P. S., Marin, D., Fusco, M., Baruch, B., Ryan, T., & Davis, K. L. (1996). A pilot study of colchicine in Alzheimer's disease. *Alzheimer's Research, 2*, 153–156.

Aisen, P. S., Schafer, K. A., Grundman, M., Pfeiffer, E., Sano, M., Davis, K. L., Farlow, M. R., Jin, S., Thomas, R. G., & Thal, L. J. (2003). Effects of rofecoxib or naproxen vs placebo on Alzheimer disease progression. *Journal of the American Medical Association, 289*(21), 2819–2826.

Aisen, P. S., Schmeidler, J., & Pasinetti, G. M. (2002). Randomized pilot study of nimesulide treatment in Alzheimer's disease. *Neurology, 58*, 1050–1054.

Ala, T., Romero, S., Knight, F., Feldt, K., & Frey, W. H. (1990). GM-1 treatment of Alzheimer's disease: A pilot study of safety and efficacy. *Archives of Neurology, 47*(10), 1126–1130.

Alvarez, X. A., Mouzo, R., Pichel, V., Perez, P., Laredo, M., Fernandez-Novoa, L., Corzo, L., Zas, R., Alcaraz, M., Secades, J. J., Lozano, R., & Cacabelos, R. (1999). Double-blind placebo-controlled study with citicoline in APOE-genotyped Alzheimer's disease patients. Effects on cognitive performance, brain bioelectrical activity and cerebral perfusion. *Methods and Findings in Experimental and Clinical Pharmacology, 21*(9), 633–644.

Anthony, J. C., Breitner, J. C. S., Zandi, P. P., Meyer, M. R., Jurasova, I., Norton, M. C., & Stone, S. V. (2000). Reduced prevalence of AD in users of NSAIDs and H2 receptor antagonists: The Cache Count Study. *Neurology, 54*, 2066–2071.

Aoki, M., Yokota, T., Sugiura, I., Sasaki, C., Hasegawa, T., Okumura, T., Okumura, C., Ishig, K., Kohno, T., Sugio, S., & Matsuzaki, T. (2004). Structural insight into nucleotide recognition in tau-protein kin: I/glycogen synthase kinase 3 beta. *Acta Crystallographica D Biological Crystallography, 60*(Pt 3), 439–446.

Bard, F., Cannon, C., Barbour, R., Burke, R. L., Games, D., Grajeda, H., Guido, T., Hu, K., Huang, J., Johnson-Wood, K., Khan, K., Kholodenko, D., Lee, M., Lieberburg, I., Motter, R., Nguyen, M., Soriano, F., Vasquez, N., Weiss, K., Welch, B., Seubert, P., Schenk, D., & Yednock, T. (2000). Peripherally administered antibodies against amyloid beta-peptide enter the central nervous system and reduce pathology in a mouse model of Alzheimer's disease. *Nature Medicine, 6*(8), 916–919.

Bartus, R. T., Dean, R. L., & Sherman, K. A. (1981). Profound effects of combining choline and piracetam on memory enhancement and cholinergic function in aged rats. *Neurobiology of Aging, 2*, 105–111.

Baskaya, M. K., Dogan, A., Rao, A. M., & Dempsey, R. J. (2000). Neuroprotective effects of citicoline on brain edema and blood-brain barrier breakdown after traumatic brain injury. *2000, 92*(3), 448–452.

Baskin, D. S., Browning, J. L., Pirozzolo, F. J., Korporaal, S., Baskin, J. A., & Appel, S. H. (1999). Brain choline acetyltransferase and mental function in Alzheimer disease. *Archives of Neurology, 56*, 1121–1123.

Baumel, B., Eisner, L., & Karukin, M. (1989). Oxiracetam in the treatment of multi-infarct dementia. *Progress in Neuropsychopharmacology and Biological Psychiatry, 13*, 673–682.

Bergamasco, B., Scarzella, L., & LaCommare, P. (1994). Idebenone: A new drug for the treatment of cognitive impairment in patients with dementia of the Alzheimer type. *Functional Neurology, 9*, 161–168.

Bissette, G., Reynolds, G., Kilts, C. D., Widerlov, E., & Nemeroff, C. B. (1985). Corticotropin-releasing factor-like immunoreactivity in senile dementia of the Alzheimer type. *Journal of the American Medical Association, 254*, 3067–3069.

Black, R. S., Barclay, L. L., Nolan, K. A., Thaler, H. T., Hardiman, S. T., & Blass, J. P. (1992). Pentoxifylline in cerebrovascular dementia. *Journal of the American Geriatrics Society, 40*, 237–244.

Black, S., Roman, G. C., Geldmacher, D. S., Salloway, S., Hecker, J., Burns, A., Perdomo, C., Kumar, D., & Pratt, R. (2003). Efficacy and tolerability of Donepezil in vascular dementia: Positive results of a 24-week, multi-center, international, randomized, placebo-controlled clinical trial. *Stroke, 34*(10), 2323–2330.

Bodick, N. C., Offen, W. W., Levey, A. L., Cutler, N. R., Gauthier, S. G., Satlin, A., Shannon, H. E., Tollefson, G. D., Rasmussen, K., Bymaster, F. P., Hurley, D. J., Potter, W. Z., & Paul, S. M. (1997). Effects of xanomeline, a selective muscarinic receptor agonist, on cognitive function and behavioral symptoms in Alzheimer disease. *Archives Neurology, 54*(4), 465–473.

Bodick, N. C., Offen, W. W., Shannon, H. E., Satterwhite, J., Lucas, R., van Lier, R., & Paul, S. M. (1997). The selective muscarinic agonist xanomeline improves both the cognitive deficits and behavioral symptoms of

Alzheimer disease. *Alzheimer Diseases and Associated Disorders*, *11*(Suppl. 4), S16–S22.

Brorson, J. R., Bindokas, V. P., Iwama, T., Marcuccilli, C. J., Chisholm, J. C., & Miller, R. J. (1995). The Ca2+ influx induced by beta-amyloid peptide 25-35 in cultured hippocampal neurons results from network excitation. *Journal of Neurobiology*, *26*(3), 325–338.

Bruno, V., Battaglia, G., Copani, A., Sortino, M. A., Canonico, P. L., & Nicoletti, F. (1994). Protective action of idebenone against excitotoxic degeneration in cultured cortical neurons. *Neuroscience Letters*, *178*, 193–196.

Burke, W. J., Roccaforte, V. H., Wengel, S. P., Bayer, B. L., Ranno, A. E., & Willcockson, N. K. (1993). L-deprenyl in the treatment of mild dementia of the Alzheimer type: Results of a 15-month trial. *Journal of the American Geriatrics Society*, *41*, 1219–1225.

Bymaster, F. P., Carter, P. A., Peters, S. C., Zhang, W., Ward, J. S., Mitch, C. H., Calligaro, D. O., Whitesitt, C. A., DeLapp, N., Shannon, H. E., Rimvall, K., Jeppesen, L., Sheardown, M. J., Fink-Jensen, A., & Sauerberg, P. (1998). Xanomeline compared to other muscarinic agents on stimulation of phosphoinositide hydolysis *in vivo* and other cholinomimetic effects. *Brain Research*, *795*(1-2), 179–190.

Calvani, M., & Carta, A. (1991). Clues to mechanism of action of acetyl-L-carnitine in the central nervous system. *Dementia*, *2*, 1–6.

Chan-Palay, V., & Asan, E. (1989). Alterations in catecholamine neurons of the locus coeruleus in senile dementia of the Alzheimer type and in Parkinson's disease with and without dementia and depression. *Journal of Comparative Neurology*, *287*(3), 373–392.

Chen, G., Chen, K. S., Knox, J., Inglis, J., Bernard, A., Martin, S. J., Justice, A., McConlogue, L., Games, D., Freedman, S. B., & Morris, R. G. (2000). A learning deficit related to age and beta-amyloid plaques in a mouse model of Alzheimer's disease. *Nature*, *408*(6815), 975–979.

Chouinard, G., Annable, L., & Ross-Chouinard, A. (1981). A doubleblind placebo-controlled study of piracetam in elderly psychiatric patients. *Psychopharmacology Bulletin*, *17*, 129.

Collins, J. S., Perry, R. T., Watson, B., Harrell, L. E., Acton, R. T., Blacker, D., Albert, M. S., Yanzi, R. E., Bassett, S. S., McInnis, M. G., Campbell, R. D., & Go, R. C.P. (2000). Association of a haplotype for tumor necrosis factor in siblings with late-onset Alzheimer disease genetics initiative: The NIMH Alzheimer disease genetics initiative. *American Journal of Medical Genetics*, *96*, 823–830.

Croisile, B., Trillet, M., Fondarai, J., Laurent, B., Mauguiere, F., & Billardon, M. (1993). Long-term and high-dose piracetam treatment of Alzheimer's disease. *Neurology*, *43*(2), 301–305.

Crook, T., Ferris, S., & Sathananthan, G. (1977). The effect of methylphenidate on test performance in the cognitively impaired aged. *Psychopharmacology Bulletin*, *13*(3), 46–48.

Crowell, E. B., & Ketchum, J. S. (1967). The treatment of scopolamine-induced delirium with physostigmine. *Clinical Pharmacology and Therapeutics*, *8*(3), 409–414.

Davidson, M., Zemishlany, Z., & Mohs, R. C. (1988). 4-Aminopyridine in the treatment of Alzheimer's disease. *Biological Psychiatry*, *23*, 485–490.

Davies, P., & Maloney, A. J. F. (1976). Selective loss of central cholinergic neurons in Alzheimer's disease. *Lancet*, *2*, 1403.

DeLapp, N., Wu, S., Belagaje, R., Johnstone, E., Little, S., Shannon, H., Bymaster, F., Calligaro, D., Mitch, C., Whitesitt, C., Ward, J., Sheardown, M., Fink-Jensen, A., Jeppesen, L., Thomsen, C., & Sauerberg, P. (1998). Effects of the M1 agonist xanomeline on processing of human beta-amyloid precursor protein (FAD, Swedish mutant), transfected into Chinese hamster ovary-m1 cells. *Biochemical and Biophysical Research Communications*, *244*(1), 156–160.

Desouza, E. G., Whitehouse, P. J., Kuhar, M. J., & Price, D. L. (1986). Reciprocal changes in corticotropin-releasing factor (CRF)-like immunoreactivity and CRF receptors in cerebral cortex of Alzheimer's disease. *Nature*, *319*, 593–595.

Ditzler, K. (1991). Efficacy and tolerability of memantine in patients with dementia syndrome. *Arzneimittel-Forschung/Drug Research*, *41*(8), 773–780.

Duvosin, R. C., & Katz, R. (1968). Reversal of central anticholinergic syndrome in man by physostigmine. *Journal of the American Medical Association*, *206*(9), 1963–1965.

Dysken, M., Mendels, J., & LeWitt, P. (1992). Milacemide: A placebo-controlled study in senile dementia of the Alzheimer type. *Journal of the American Geriatrics Society*, *40*, 503–506.

Eriksdotter, J. M., Nordberg, A., Amberla, K., Backman, L., Ebendal, T., Meyerson, B., Olson, L., Shigeta, M., Theodorsson, E., Viitanen, M., Winblad, B., & Wahlund, L. O. (1998). Intracerebroventricular infusion of nerve growth factor in three patients with Alzheimer's disease. *Dementia and Geriatric Cognitive Disorders*, *9*(5), 246–257.

Erkinjuntti, T., Kurz, A., Gauthier, S., Bullock, R., Lilienfeld, S., & Damarju, C. V. (2002). Efficacy of galantamine in probable vascular dementia and Alzheimer's disease combined with cerebrovascular disease: A randomized trial. *Lancet*, *359*(9314), 1283–1290.

Fakouhi, T. D., Jhee, S. S., Sramek, J. J., Benes, C., Schwartz, P., Hantsburger, G., Herting, R., Swabb, E. A., & Cutler, N. R. (1995). Evaluation of cycloserine in the treatment of Alzheimer's disease. *Journal of Geriatric Psychiatry and Neurology*, *8*(4), 226–230.

Falsaperla, A., Pret, P., & Oliani, C. (1990). Selegiline versus oxiracetam in patients with Alzheimer-type dementia. *Clinical Therapeutics*, *12*, 376–384.

Farde, L., Suhara, T., Halldin, C., Nyback, H., Nakashima, Y., Swahn, C. G., Karlsson, P., Ginovart, N., Bymaster, F. P., Shannon, H. E., Foged, C., Suzdak, P. D., & Sauerberg, P. (1996). PET study of the M1-agonists (11C) xanomeline and (11C) butylthio-TZTP in monkey and man. *Dementia*, *7*(4), 187–195.

Farlow, M., Gracon, S. I., Hershey, L. A., Lewis, K. W., Sadowsky, C. H., & Dolan-Ureno, J. (1992). A controlled trial of tacrine in Alzheimer's disease. The Tacrine Study Group. *Journal of the American Medical Association*, *268*(18), 2523–2529.

Farlow, M. R., Cyrus, P. A., Nadel, A., Lahiri, D. K., Brashear, A., & Gulanski, B. (1999). Metrifonate treatment of AD: influence of APOE genotype. *Neurology*, *53*(9), 2010–2016.

Ferris, S. H., Reisberg, B., & Crook, T. (1982). Pharmacologic treatment of senile dementia choline: L-DOPA, piracetam and choline plus piracetam. In S. Corkin (Ed.), *Alzheimer's disease: A report of progress* (Aging, Vol.19, pp. 475–481). New York: Raven Press.

Fioravanti, M., & Yanagi, M. (2000). Cytidinediphosphocholine (CDP choline) for cognitive and behavioral disturbances associated with chronic cerebral disorders in the elderly. *Cochrane Database of Systematic Reviews*, *4*, CD000269.

Flynn, D. D., Ferrari-Di Leo, G., Levey, A. I., & Mash, D. C. (1995). Differential alterations in muscarinic receptor subtypes in Alzheimer's disease: Implications for cholinergic-based therapies. *Life Sciences*, *56*(11-12), 869–876.

Fournier, J., Steinberg, R., Gauthier, T., Keane, P. E., Guzzi, U., Coude, F. X., Bougault, I., Maffrand, J. P., Soubrie, P., & Le Fur, G. (1993). Protective effects of SR 57746A in central and peripheral models of neurodegenerative disorders in rodents and primates. *Neuroscience*, *55*(3), 629–641.

Freedman, M., Rewilak, D., Xerri, T., Cohen, S., Gordon, A. S., Shandling, M., & Logan, A. G. (1998). L-deprenyl in Alzheimer's disease: Cognitive and behavioral effects. *Neurology*, *50*, 660–668.

Friedlich, A. L., & Butcher, L. L. (1994). Involvement of free oxygen radicals in beta-amyloidosis: An hypothesis. *Neurobiology and Aging*, *15*, 443–455.

Friedman, E., Sherman, K. A., Ferris, S., & Schneck, M. K. (1981). Clinical response to choline plus piracetam in senile dementia: Relation to red-cell choline levels. *New England Journal of Medicine*, *304*, 1490–1491.

Galasko, D., Chang, L., Motter, R., Clark, C. M., Kaye, J., Knopman, D., Thomas, R., Kholodenko, D., Schenk, D., Lieberburg, I., Miller, B., Green, R., Basherad, R., Kertiles, L., Boss, M. A., & Seubert, P. (1998). High cerebrospinal fluid tau and low amyloid B42 levels in the clinical diagnosis of Alzheimer disease and relation to apolipoprotein E genotype. *Archives of Neurology*, *55*, 937–945.

Gortelmeyer, R., Pantev, M., Parsons, C. G., & Quack, G. (1993). The treatment of dementia syndrome with akatinol memantine, a modulator of the glutamatergic system: Preclinical and clinical results. In K. von Wild (Ed.), *Spektrum der Meurorehabilitation* (pp. 50–56). Munich: W. Zuckschwerdt Verlag.

Green, R. C., Goldstein, F. C., Auchus, A. P., Presley, R., Clark, S., Van Tuyl, L., Green, J., Hersch, S. M., & Karp, H. R. (1992). Treatment trial of oxiracetam in Alzheimer's disease. *Archives of Neurology*, *49*, 1135–1136.

Growdon, J. H., Corkin, S., Huff, F. J., & Rosen, T. J. (1986). Piracetam combined with lecithin in the treatment of Alzheimer's disease. *Neurobiology of Aging*, *7*(4), 269–276.

Grundman, M., Capparelli, E., Kim, H. T., Morris, J. C., Farlow, M., Rubin, E. H., Heidebrink, J., Hake, A., Ho, G., Schultz, A. N., Schafer, K., Houston, W., Thomas, R., & Thal, L. J. (2003). A multicenter, randomized, placebo-controlled, multiple-dose, safety and pharmacological study of AIT-082 (Neotrofin) in mild Alzheimer's disease patients. *Life Sciences*, *73*, 539–553.

Harbaugh, R. E. (1988). Intracerebroventricular bethanechol chloride administration in Alzheimer's disease. *Annals of the New York Academy of Sciences*, *531*, 174–179.

Henderson, V. W., Paganini-Hill, A., Miller, B. L., Elble, R. J., Reyes, P. F., Shoupe, D., McLeary, C. A., Klein, R. A., Hake, A. M., & Farlow, M. R. (2000). Estrogen for Alzheimer's disease in women: Randomized, double-blind, placebo-controlled trial. *Neurology*, *54*, 295–301.

Hock, C., Heese, K., Hulette, C., Rosenberg, C., & Otten, U. (2000). Region-specific neurotrophin imbalances in Alzheimer disease: Decreased levels of brain-derived neurotrophic factor and increased levels of nerve growth factor in hippocampus and cortical areas. *Archives of Neurology*, *57*(6), 846–851.

Hofferberth, B. (1989). Einfluss von Ginkgo biloba Extract auf neurophysiologische und psychometrische Messergeonisse bei Patienten mit hirnorganischen. Psychosyndrom ein Doppelbindstudie gegen Placebo. *Drug Research*, *39*, 918–922.

Imahori, K., & Uchida, T. (1997). Physiology and pathology of tau protein kinases in relation to Alzheimer's disease. *Journal of Biochemisty (Tokyo), 121*(2), 179–188.

Imbimbo, B. P., Martelli, P., Troetel, W. M., Lucchelli, F., Lucca, U., & Thal, L. J. (1999). Efficacy and safety of eptastigmine for the treatment of patients with Alzheimer's disease. *Neurology, 52*, 700–708.

Joachim, C. L., Morris, J. H., & Selkoe, D. J. (1989). Diffuse senile plaques occur commonly in the cerebellum in Alzheimer's disease. *American Journal of Pathology, 135*, 309–319.

Jonhagen, M. E. (2000). Nerve growth factor treatment in dementia. *Alzheimer Diseases and Associated Disorders, 14*(Suppl. 1), S31–S38.

Jorm, A. F., & Jolley, D. (1998). The incidence of dementia: A meta-analysis. *Neurology, 51*(3), 728–733.

Kanoeski, S., Hermann, W. M., Stephan, K., Wierich, W., & Horr, R. (1996). Proof of efficacy of the ginkgo biloba special extract EGb 761 in outpatients suffering from mild to moderate primary degenerative dementia of the Alzheimer type or multi-infarct dementia. *Pharmacopsychiatry, 29*, 47–56.

Kisilevsky, R. (1996). Anti-amyloid drugs: Potential in the treatment of diseases associated with aging. *Drugs and Aging, 8*(2), 75–83.

Klein, J., Charrerlee, S. S., & Loffeholz, K. (1997). Phospholipid breakdown and choline release under hypoxic conditions: Inhibition by bilobalide, a constituent of Ginkgo biloba. *Brain Research, 755*, 347–350.

Klunk, W. E., Engler, H., Nordberg, A., Wang, Y., Blomqvist, G., Holt, D. P., M., B., Savitcheva, I., Huang, G., & Estrada, S. (2004). Imaging brain amyloid in Alzheimer's disease with Pittsburgh Compound-B. *Annals of Neurology, 55*, 306–319.

Krupp, L. B., Christodoulou, C., Melville, P., Scherl, W. F., MacAllister, W. S., & Elkins, L. E. (2004). Donepezil improved memory in multiple sclerosis in a randomized clinical trial. *Neurology, 63*, 1579–1585.

Kuller, L. H., Tracy, R. P., Shaten, J., & Meilahn, E. N. (1996). Relation of C-reactive protein and coronary heart disease in the MRFIT nested case-control study. *American Journal of Epidemiology, 144*, 537–547.

LaFrance, W. C., Lauterbach, E. C., Coffey, C. E., Salloway, S. P., Kaufer, D. I., Reeve, A., Royall, D. R., Aylward, E., Rummans, T. A., & Lovell, M. R. (2000). The use of herbal alternative medicines in neuropsychiatry. *Journal of Neuropsychiatry and Clinical Neurosciences, 12*, 177–192.

Lawlor, B. A., Aisen, P. S., Green, C., Fine, E., & Schmeidler, J. (1997). Selegiline in the treatment of behavioral disturbance in Alzheimer's disease. *International Journal of Geriatric Psychiatry, 12*(3), 319–322.

LeBars, P. L., Katz, M. M., Berman, N., Itil, T. M., Freedman, A. M., & Schatzberg, A. F. (1997). A placebo-controlled, double-blind, randomized trial of an extract of Gingko biloba for dementia. North American EGb Study Group. *Journal of the American Medical Association, 278*(16), 1327–1332.

Lee, V. M.Y. (1996). Regulation of tau phosphorylation in Alzheimer's disease. *Annals of the New York Academy of Sciences, 777*, 107–113.

Levesque, L., Mizzen, C. A., McLachlan, D. R., & Fraser, P. E. (2000). Ligand-specific effects on aluminum incorporation and toxicity in neurons and astrocytes. *Brain Research, 877*(2), 191–202.

Liang, Y. Q., & Tang, X. C. (2004). Comparative effects of huperzine A, donepezil, and rivastigmine on cortical acetylcholine level and acetylcholinesterase activity in rats. *Neuroscience Letters, 361*, 56–59.

Lipton, S. A. (1992). Memantine prevents HIV coat protein-induced neuronal injury in vitro. *Neurology, 42*, 1403–1405.

Lipton, S. A., & Rosenberg, P. A. (1994). Excitatory amino acids as a final common pathway for neurologic disorders. *New England Journal of Medicine, 330*, 613–622.

Lopez, O. L., Kaufer, D., Reiter, C. T., Carra, J., DeKosky, S. T., & Palmer, A. M. (1996). Relationship between CSF neurotransmitter metabolites and aggressive behavior in Alzheimer's disease. *European Journal of Neurology, 3*, 153–155.

Lopez, O. L., Kuller, L. H., Fitzpatrick, A., Ives, D., Becker, J. T., & Beauchamp, N. (2003). Evaluations of dementia in the cardiovascular health cognition study. *Neuroepidemiology, 22*(1), 1–12.

Marcusson, J., Rother, M., Kittner, B., Rossner, M., Smith, R. J., Babic, T., Folnegovic-Smalc, V., Moller, H. J., & Labs, K. H. (1997). A 12-month, randomized, placebo-controlled trial of popentofylline (HWA 285) in patients with dementia according to DSM III-R. The European Propentofylline Study Group. *Dementia and Geriatric Cognitive Disorders, 8*(5), 320–328.

Masaki, K. H., Losonczy, K. G., Izmirlian, G., Foley, D. J., Ross, G. W., Petrovitch, H., Havlik, R., & White, L. R. (2000). Association of vitamin E and C supplement use with cognitive function and dementia in elderly men. *Neurology, 54*, 1265–1272.

Mazurek, M. F., Beal, F., Bird, E. D., & Martin, J. B. (1986). Vasopressin in Alzheimer's disease: A study of postmortem brain concentrations. *Annals of Neurology, 20*, 665–670.

McEwen, B. S., Alves, S. E., Bulloch, K., & Weiland, N. G. (1997). Ovarian steroids and the brain: Implications for cognition and aging. *Neurology, 48*(Suppl. 7), S8–S15.

McGeer, P. L., & McGeer, E. G. (1995). The inflammatory response system of the brain: implications for therapy of Alzheimer's and other neurodegenerative disease. *Brain Research Reviews*, *21*, 195–196.

McHeer, P. L., Schulzer, M., & McGeer, E. G. (1996). Arthritis and anti-inflammatory agents as possible protective factors for Alzheimer's disease: A review of 17 epidemiologic studies. *Neurology*, *47*, 425–432.

McLachlan, D. R., Bergeron, C., Smith, J. E., Boomer, D., & Rifat, S. L. (1996). Risk for neuropathologically confirmed Alzheimer's disease and residual aluminum in municipal drinking water employing weighted residential histories. *Neurology*, *46*(2), 401–405.

McLachlan, D. R. C., Dalton, A. J., Kruck, T. P. A., Bell, N. Y., Smith, W. L., Kalow, W., & Andrews, D. F. (1991). Intramuscular desferioxamine in patients with Alzheimer's disease. *Lancet*, *337*, 1304–1308.

McRae, A., Ling, E. A., Schubert, P., & Rudolphi, K. (1998). Properties of activated microglia and pharmacologic interference by propentofylline. *Alzheimer Diseases and Associated Disorders*, *12*(Suppl. 2), S15–S20.

Mobius, H. J. (1999). Pharmacologic rationale for memantine in chronic cerebral hypoperfusion, especially vascular dementia. *Alzheimer Diseases and Associated Disorders*, *13*(Suppl. 3), S172–S178.

Mohr, E., Schlegel, J., Fabbrini, G., Williams, J., Mouradian, M. M., Mann, U. M., Claus, J. J., Fedio, P., & Chase, T. N. (1989). Clonidine treatment of Alzheimer's disease. *Archives of Neurology*, *46*, 376–378.

Mrak, R. E., & Griffin, W. S.T. (2001). The role of activated astrocytes and of the neurotrophic cytokine S100B in the pathogenesis of Alzheimer's disease. *Neurobiology of Aging*, *22*, 915–922.

Mrak, R. E., Sheng, J. G., & Griffin, W. S.T. (1995). Glial cytokines in Alzheimer's disease: Review and pathogenic implications. *Human Pathology*, *26*, 816–823.

Muller, W. E., Mutschler, E., & Riederer, P. (1995). Noncompetitive NMDA receptor antagonists with fast open-channel blocking kinetics and strong voltage-dependency as potential therapeutic agents for Alzheimer's disease. *Pharmacopsychiatry*, *28*, 113–124.

Murer, M. G., Boissiere, F., Yan, Q., Hunot, S., Villares, J., Faucheux, B., Agid, Y., Hirsch, E., & Raisman-Vozari, R. (1999). An immunohistochemical study of the distribution of brain-derived neurotrophic factor in the adult human brain, with particular reference to Alzheimer's disease. *Neuroscience*, *88*(4), 1015–1032.

Nabeshima, T., & Yamada, K. (2000). Neurotrophic factor strategies for the treatment of Alzheimer disease. *Alzheimer Diseases and Associated Disorders*, *14*(Suppl. 1), S39–S46.

Nagai, Y., Toshida, T., Narumi, S., Tauayama, S., & Nagaoaka, A. (1989). Brain distribution of Idebenone and its effect on local cerebral glucose utilization in rats. *Archives of Gerontology and Geriatrics*, *8*, 257–272.

Nolan, K. A., Black, R. S., Sheu, K. F. R., Langberg, J., & Blass, J. P. (1991). A trial of thiamine in Alzheimer's disease. *Archives of Neurology*, *48*, 81–83.

Nuydens, R., De Jong, M., Nuyens, R., Cornelissen, F., & Geerts, H. (1995). Neuronal kinase stimulation leads to aberrant tau phosphorylation and neurotoxicity. *Neurobiology of Aging*, *16*, 465–475.

Oken, B. S., Storzbach, D. M., & Kaye, J. A. (1998). The efficacy of Gingko biloba on cognitive function in Alzheimer disease. *Archives of Neurology*, *55*, 1409–1415.

Orgogozo, J. M., Gilman, S., Dartigues, J. F., & Laurent, B. (2003). Subacute meningoencephalitis in a subset of patients with AD after Abeta42 immunization. *Neurology*, *61*(1), 46–54.

Otomo, E., Abe, H., Araki, G., Ito, E., Omae, T., Nishimura, T., & Hasegawa, K. (1985). Usefulness of CV-2619 tablets in patients with cerebrovascular disorders, etc. Non-blind controlled trial in comparison with calcium hopatenate. *Therapeutic Research*, *3*(1), 117–136.

Otomo, E., Nanja, E., Saso, S., Narikawa, H., Terao, T., Yoshino, Y., Sakuma, T., Tsuchiya, M., Nozaka, M., Haynski, M., Asada, T., & Merugo, M. (1985). Clinical evaluation of Idebenone in patients with cerebrovascular disease. *Therapeutic Research*, *2*(4), 703–715.

Pantoni, L., Bianchi, C., Beneke, M., Inzitari, D., Wallin, A., & Erkinjuntti, T. (2000). The Scandinavian Multi-Infarct Dementia Trial: a double-blind, placebo-controlled trial on nimodipine in multi-infarct dementia. *Journal of Neurological Sciences*, *175*, 116–123.

Pantoni, L., Rossi, R., Inzitari, D., Bianchi, C., Beneke, M., Erkinjuntti, T., & Wallin, A. (2000). Efficacy and safety of nimodipine in subcortical vascular dementia: A subgroup analysis of the Scandinavian multi-infarct dementia trial. *Journal of Neurological Sciences*, *175*(2), 124–134.

Parsons, C. G., Danysz, W., & Quack, G. (1999). Memantine is a clinically well-tolerated N-methyl-D-aspartate (NMDA) receptor antagonist-A review of preclinical data. *Neuropharmacology*, *38*(6), 735–767.

Peabody, C., Thiemann, S., & Pigache, R. (1985). Desglycinamide-9-arginine-8 vasopressin (DGAVP, Organon 5667) in patients with dementia. *Neurobiology of Aging*, *6*, 95–100.

Penn, R. D., Martin, E. M., Wilson, R. S., Fox, J. H., & Savoy, S. M. (1988). Intraventricular bethanechol infusion for Alzheimer's disease: Results of double-blind and escalating-dose trials. *Neurology, 38*, 219–222.

Pericak-Vance, M. A., Grubber, J., Bailey, L. R., Hedges, D., West, S., Santoro, L., Kemmerer, B., Hall, J. L., Saunders, A. M., Roses, A. D., Small, G. W., Scott, W. K., Conneally, P. M., Vance, J. M., & Haines, J. L. (2000). Identification of novel genes in late-onset Alzheimer's disease. *Experimental Gerontology, 35*(9-10), 1343–1352.

Petanceska, S. S., Nagy, V., Frail, D., & Gandy, S. (2000). Ovariectomy and 17 beta-estradiol modulate the levels of Alzheimer's amyloid beta peptides in brain. *Neurology, 54*, 2212–2217.

Raffaele, K. C., Berardi, A., Asthana, S., Morris, P., Haxby, J. V., & Soncrant, T. T. (1991). Effects of long-term continuous infusion of the muscarinic cholinergic agonist arecoline on verbal memory in dementia of the Alzheimer type. *Psychopharmacology Bulletin, 27*(3), 315–319.

Rao, A. M., Hatcher, J. F., & Dempsey, R. J. (2000). Lipid alterations in transient forebrain ischemia: Possible new mechanisms of CDP-choline neuroprotection. *Journal of Neurochemistry, 75*(6), 2528–2535.

Raskin, A., Gershon, S., Crook, T. H., Sathananthan, G., & Ferris, S. (1978). The effects of hyperbaric and normobaric oxygen on cognitive impairment in the elderly. *Archives of General Psychiatry, 35*(1), 50–56.

Reines, S. A., Block, G. A., Morris, J. C., Liu, G., Nessly, M. L., Lines, C. R., Norman, B. A., & Baranak, C. C. (2004). No effect on Alzheimer's disease in a 1-year, randomized blinded controlled study. *Neurology, 62*, 66–71.

Reisberg, B., Ferris, S. H., & Anand, R. (1983). Effects of naloxone in senile dementia: A double-blind trial. *New England Journal Medicine, 308*, 721–722.

Riekkinen, P., Ikonen, S., & Riekkinen, M. (1998). D-cycloserine, a partial NMDA receptor-associated glycine-B site agonist, enhances reversal learning, but a cholinesterase inhibitor and nicotine has no effect. *Neuroreport, 9*(16), 3647–3651.

Ringheim, G. E. (2000). Glial modulating and neurotrophic properties of propentofylline and its application to Alzheimer's disease and vascular dementia. *Annals of the New York Academy of Sciences, 903*, 529–534.

Rockwood, K., Kirkland, S., Hogan, D. B., MacKnight, C., Merry, H., Verreault, R., Wolfson, C., & McDowell, I. (2002). Use of lipid-lowering agents, indication bias, and the risk of dementia in community-dwelling elderly people. *Archives of Neurology, 59*, 223–227.

Rodriguez-Puertas, R., Pascual, J., Vilaro, T., & Pazos, A. (1997). Autoradiographic distribution of M1, M2, M3, and M4 muscarinic receptor subtypes in Alzheimer's disease. *Synapse, 26*(4), 341–350.

Rogers, J., Kirby, L. C., Hempelman, S. R., Berry, D. L., McGeer, P. L., Kaszniak, A. W., Zalinski, J., Cofield, M., Mansukhani, L., & Willson, P. (1993). Clinical trial of indomethacin in Alzheimer's disease. *Neurology, 43*(8), 1609–1611.

Rogers, S. L., & Friedhoff, L. T. (1996). The efficacy and safety of donepezil in patients with Alzheimer's disease: Results of a US multicenter, randomized, double-blind, placebo-controlled trial. *The Donepezil Study Group. Dementia, 7*(6), 293–303.

Rosler, M., Anand, R., Cicin-Sain, A., Gauthier, S., Agid, Y., Dal-Bianco, P., Stahelin, H. B., & Gharabawi, M. (1999). Efficacy and safety of rivastigmine in patients with Alzheimer's disease: International randomized controlled trial. *British Medical Journal, 318*(7184), 633–638.

Rother, M., Erkinjuntti, T., Roessner, M., Kittner, B., Marcusson, J., & Karlssor, I. (1998). Propentofylline in the treatment of Alzheimer's disease and vascular dementia: A review of phase III trials. *Dementia and Geriatris. Cognitive Disorders, 9*(Suppl. 1), 36–43.

Salloway, S., Ferris, S., Kluger, A., Goldman, R., Griesing, T., Kumar, D., & Richardson, S. (2004). Efficacy of donepezil in mild cognitive impairment. A randomized placebo-controlled trial. *Neurology, 63*, 651–657.

Sano, M., Bell, K., Cote, L., Dooneief, G., Lawton, A., Legler, L., Marder, K., Naini, A., Stern, Y., & Mayeux, R. (1992). Double-blind parallel design pilot study of acetyl levocarnitine in patients with Alzheimer's disease. *Archives of Neurology, 49*, 1137–1141.

Sano, M., Ernesto, C., Thomas, R. G., Klauber, M. R., Schafer, K., Grundman, M., Woodbury, P., Growdon, J., Cotman, C. W., Pfeiffer, E., & Schneider, L. S. (1997). A controlled trial of selegiline, alphotocopherol, or both as treatment for Alzheimer disease. *New England Journal of Medicine, 336*, 1216–1222.

Sasaki, K., Hatta, S., & Haga, M. (1999). Effects of bilobalide on gamma-aminobutyric acid levels and glutamic acid decarboxylase in mouse brain. *European Journal of Pharmacology, 367*(2-3), 173–173.

Savory, J., Exley, C., Forbes, W. F., Huang, Y., Joshi, J. G., Kruck, T., McLachlan, D. R., & Wakayama, I. (1996). Can the controversy of the role of aluminum in Alzheimer's disease be resolved? What are the suggested approaches to this controversy and methodological issues to be considered? *Journal of Toxicology and Environmental Health, 48*(6), 615–635.

Scharf, S., Mander, A., Ugoni, A., Vajda, F., & Christophidis, N. (1999). A double-blind, placebo-controlled trial of diclofenac/misoprostol in Alzheimer's disease. *Neurology, 53*, 197–201.

Schneider, L. S., Farlow, M. R., Henderson, V. W., & Pogoda, J. M. (1996). Effects of estrogen replacement therapy on response to tacrine in patients with Alzheimer's disease. *Neurology, 46*, 1580–1584.

Schroder, H., Zilles, K., Luiten, P. G. M., Strosberg, A. D., & Aghchi, A. (1989). Human cortical neurons contain both nicotinic and muscarinic acetylcholine receptors: An immunocytochemical double-labeling study. *Synapse, 4*, 319–326.

Schroder, H., Zilles, K., Maelicke, A., & Hajos, F. (1989). Immunohisto- and cytochemical localization of cortical nicotinic cholinoceptors in rat and man. *Brain Research, 502*, 287–295.

Schubert, P., Ogata, T., Miyazaki, H., Marchini, C., Ferroni, S., & Rudolphi, K. (1998). Pathological immuno-reactions of glial cells in Alzheimer's disease and possible sites of interference. *Journal of Neural Transmission Supplementum, 54*, 167–174.

Scott, S. A., Mufson, E. J., Weingartner, J. A., Skau, K. A., & Crutcher, K. A. (1995). Nerve growth factor in Alzheimer's disease: Increased levels throughout the brain coupled with declines in nucleus basalis. *Journal of Neuroscience, 15*(9), 6213–6221.

Senin, U., Parnetti, L., Barbagallo-Sangiorgi, G., Bartorelli, L., Bocola, V., Capurso, A., Cuzzupoli, M., Denario, M., Marigliano, V., Tammaro, A. E., & Fioravanti, M. (1992). Idebenone in senile dementia of the Alzheimer type: A multicenter study. *Archives of Gerontology, 15*, 249–260.

Shaywitz, S., Shaywitz, B. A., Pugh, K. R., Fulbright, R. K., Skudlarski, P., Mencl, W. E., Constable, R. T., Naftolin, F., Palter, S. F., Marchione, K. E., Katz, L., Shankweiler, D. P., Fletcher, J. M., Lacadie, C., Keltz, M., & Gore, J. C. (1999). Effect of estrogen on brain activation patterns in postmenopausal women during working memory tasks. *Journal of the American Medical Association, 281*(13), 1197–1202.

Shumaker, S. A., Legault, C., Rapp, S. R., Thal, L., Wallace, R. B., Ockene, J. K., Hendrix, S. L., Jones, B. N., & Assaf, A. R. (2003). Estrogen plus progestin and the incidence of dementia and mild cognitive impairment in postmenopausal women. The Women's Health Initiative Memory Study: A Randomized Controlled Trial. *Journal of the American Medical Association, 289*, 2651–2662.

Silverberg, G. D., Levinthal, E., Sullivan, E. V., Bloch, D. A., Chang, S. D., Leverenz, J., Flitman, S., Winn, R., Marciano, F., Saul, T., Huhn, S., Mayo, M., Pharm, D., & McGuire, D. (2002). Assessment of low-flow CSF drainage as a treatment for AD: Results of a randomized pilot study. *Neurology, 59*, 1139–1145.

Smith, C. M., Coogan, J. S., & Hart, S. (1986). Effects of physostigmine on memory test performance in normal volunteers. *Psychopharmacology (Berl), 90*(3), 364–366.

Snaedal, J., Johannesson, T., Jonsson, J. E., & Gylfadottir, G. (1996). The effects of nicotine in dermal plaster on cognitive functions in patients with Alzheimer's disease. *Dementia, 7*, 47–52.

Spagnoli, A., Lucca, U., Menasce, G., Bandera, L., Cizza, G., Forloni, G., Tettamanti, M., Frattura, L., Tiraboschi, P., & Comelli, M. (1991). Long-term acetyl-L-carnitine treatment in Alzheimer's disease. *Neurology, 41*(11), 1726–1732.

Spiers, P. A., Myers, D., Hochanadel, G. S., Lieberman, H. R., & Wurtman, R. J. (1996). Citicoline improves verbal memory in aging. *Archives of Neurology, 53*, 441–448.

Stein, L., Belluzzi, J. D., & Wise, C. D. (1975). Memory enhancement by central administration of norepinephrine. *Brain Research, 84*, 329–335.

Summers, W. K., Majoviski, L. V., Marsh, G. M., Tachiki, K., & Kling, A. (1986). Oral tetrahydroaminoacridine in long-term treatment of senile dementia, Alzheimer type. *New England Journal of Medicine, 315*(20), 1241–1245.

Tang, M. X., Jacobs, D., Stern, Y., Marder, K., Schofield, P., Gurland, B., Andrews, H., & Mayeux, R. (1996). Effect of oestrogen during menopause on risk and age at onset of Alzheimer's disease. *Lancet, 348*(9025), 429–432.

Tariot, P. N., Farlow, M. R., Grossberg, G. T., Graham, S. M., McDonald, S., & Gergel, I. (2004). Memantine treatment in patients with moderate to severe Alzheimer's disease already receiving donepezil. *Journal of the American Medical Association, 291*(3), 317–324.

Tariot, P. N., Solomon, P. R., Morris, J. C., Kershaw, P., Lilienfield, S., & Ding, C. (2000). A five-month, randomized, placebo-controlled trial of galantamine in AD. *Neurology, 54*, 2269–2276.

Tariot, P. N., Sunderland, T., & Weingartner, H. (1987). Cognitive effects of selegeline in Alzheimer's disease. *Psychopharmacology (Berl), 91*, 489–495.

Taylor, J. E. (1986). Neuromediator binding to receptors in the rat brain: The effect of chronic administration of Ginkgo biloba extract. *Presse Medicale, 15*, 1491–1493.

Thal, L. J., Carta, A., Clarke, W. R., Ferris, S. H., Friedland, R. P., Petersen, R. C., Pettegrew, J. W., Pfeiffer, E., Raskind, M. A., Sano, M., Tuszynski, M. H., & Woolson, R. F. (1996). A 1-year multicenter placebo-controlled study of acetyl-L-carnitine in patients with Alzheimer's disease. *Neurology, 47*, 705–711.

Thal, L. J., Forrest, M., Loft, H., & Mengel, H. (2000). Lu 25-109, a muscarinic agonist, fails to improve cognition in Alzheimer's disease. *Neurology*, *54*, 421–426.

Tinklenberg, J., Pfefferbaum, A., & Berger, P. (1981). 1-Desamino-D-arginine vasopressin (DDAVP) in cognitively impaired patients. *Psychopharmacology Bulletin*, *17*, 206–207.

Tinklenberg, J., Pigache, R., Berger, P., & Kopell, B. (1982). Desglycinamide-9-arginine-8-vasopressin (DGAVP, Organon 5667) in cognitively impaired patients. *Psychopharmacology Bulletin*, *18*, 202–204.

Tollefson, G. D. (1990). Short-term effects of the calcium channel blocker nimodipine (Bay-e-9736) in the management of primary degenerative dementia. *Biological Psychiatry*, *27*(10), 1133–1142.

Tsai, G. E., Falk, W. E., Gunther, J., & Coyle, J. T. (1999). Improved cognition in Alzheimer's disease with short-term D-cycloserine treatment. *American Journal of Psychiatry*, *156*(3), 467–469.

Urani, A., Privat, A., & Maurice, T. (1998). The modulation by neurosteroids of the scopolamine-induced learning impairment in mice involves an interaction with sigma1 (sigma1) receptors. *Brain Research*, *799*(1), 64–77.

van Dongen, M. C. J. M., van Rossum, E., Kessels, A. G. H., Sielhorst, H. J. G., & Knipschild, P. G. (2000). The efficacy of ginkgo for elderly people with dementia and age-associated memory impairment: New results of a randomized clinical trial. *Journal of the American Geriatrics Society*, *48*, 1183–1194.

Veroff, A. E., Bodick, N. C., Offen, W. W., Sramek, J. J., & Cutler, N. R. (1998). Efficacy of xanomeline in Alzheimer disease: Cognitive improvement measured using the Computerized Neuropsychological Test Battery (CNTB). *Alzheimer Diseases and Associated Disorders*, *12*(4), 304–312.

Vorberg, G., Schenk, N., & Schmidt, U. (1989). Wirksamkelt eines neuen Ginkgo-biloba Extraktes bei 100 Patienten mit zerebraler insuffizienz. *Herz Gefasse*, *9*, 936–941.

Wang, P. N., Liao, S. Q., Liu, R. S., Liu, C. Y., Chao, H. T., Lu, S. R., Yu, H. Y., Wang, S. J., & Liu, H. C. (2000). Effects of estrogen on cognition, mood, and cerebral blood flow in AD: A controlled study. *Neurology*, *54*, 2061–2066.

Warach, S., Lettigrew, L. C., Dashe, J. F., Pullicinto, P., Lefkowitz, D. M., Sabounjian, L., Harnett, K., Schwiderski, U., & Gammans, R. (2000). Effect of citicoline on ischemic lesions as measured by diffusion-weighted magnetic resonance imaging. Citicoline 010 investigators. *Annals of Neurology*, *48*(5), 713–722.

Waring, S. C., Rocca, W. A., Petersen, R. C., O'Brien, P. C., Tangalos, E. G., & Kokmen, E. (1999). Postmenopausal estrogen replacement therapy and risk of AD: A population-based study. *Neurology*, *52*, 965–970.

Wassertheil-Smoller, S., Hendrix, S. J., Limacher, M., Heiss, G., Kooperberg, C., Baird, A., Kotchen, T., Curb, J. D., Black, H., & Rossouw, J. E. (2003). Effect of estrogen plus progestin on stroke in postmenopausal women. The Women's Health Initiative: A randomized trial. *Journal of the American Medical Association*, *289*, 2673–2684.

Waters, C., (1988). Cognitive enhancing agents: Current status in the treatment of Alzheimer disease. *Canadian Journal of Neurological Sciences*, *15*(249-256).

Weiland, E., Schutz, E., Armstrong, V. W., Kuthe, F., Heller, C., & Oellerich, M. (1995). Idebenone protects hepatic microsomes against oxygen radical-mediated damage in organ preservation solution. *Transplantation*, *60*, 444–451.

Weiner, J. L., Buhler, A. V., Whatley, V. J., Harris, R. A., & Dunwiddie, T. V. (1998). Colchicine in a competitive antagonist at human recombinant gamma-aminobutyric acidA receptors. *Journal of Pharmacology and Experimental Therapeutics*, *284*(1), 95–102.

Wesnes, K., Simmons, D., Rook, M., & Simpson, P. (1987). A double-blind placebo-controlled trial of tanakan in the treatment of idiopathic cognitive impairment on the elderly. *Human Psychopharmacology*, *2*, 159–169.

Wettstein, A., & Spiegel, R. (1984). Clinical trials with the cholinergic drug RS 86 in Alzheimer's disease (AD) and senile dementia of the Alzheimer type (SDAT). *Psychopharmacology*, *84*, 572–573.

Whitehouse, P., Price, D. L., Clark, A. W., Coyle, J. T., & DeLong, M. R. (1981). Alzheimer's disease: Evidence from selective loss of cholinergic neurons in the Nucleus Basalis. *Annals of Neurology*, *10*, 122–126.

Winblad, B., & Poritis, N. (1999). Memantine in severe dementia: Results of the 9M-Best Study (Benefit and efficacy in severely demented patients during treatment with memantine). *International Journalof Geriatric Psychiatry*, *14*(2), 135–146.

Wirtz-Brugger, F., & Giovanni, A. (2000). Guanosine 3′, 5′-cyclic monophosphate mediated inhibition of cell death induced by nerve growth factor withdrawal and beta-amyloid: protective effects of propentofylline. *Neuroscience*, *99*(4), 737–750.

Wolkowitz, O. M., Kramer, J. H., Reus, V. L., Costa, M. M., Yaffe, K., Walton, P., Raskind, M., Peskind, E., Newhouse, P., Sack, D., DeSouza, E., Sadowski, C., & Roberts, E. (2003). DHEA treatment of Alzheimer's disease: A randomized, double-blind, placebo-controlled study. *Neurology*, *60*, 1071–1076.

Wolozin, B., Kellman, W., Ruosseau, P., Celesia, G. C., & Siegel, G. (2000). Decreased prevalence of Alzheimer disease associated with 3-hydroxy-3-methyglutaryl

Coenzyme A reductase inhibitors. *Archives of Neurology, 57,* 1439–1443.

Wurtman, R. J., Magil, S. G., & Reinstein, D. K. (1981). Piracetam diminishes hippocampal acetylcholine levels in rats. *Life Sciences, 28,* 1091–1093.

Xu, H. X., Sweeney, D., Greengard, P., & Gandy, S. (1994). Metabolism of Alzheimer beta-amyloid precursor protein: Regulation by protein kinase A in intact cells and in a cell-free system. *Proceedings of the National Academy of Sciences of the USA, 93,* 4081–4084.

Yamada, K., Nitta, A., Hasegawa, T., Fuji, K., Hiramatsu, M., Kameyama, T., Hayashi, K., & Nabeshima, T. (1997). Orally active NGF synthesis stimulators: Potential therapeutic agents in Alzheimer's disease. *Behavioral Brain Research, 83*(1-2), 122–122.

Yoshida, S., Busto, R., Watson, B. D., Santiso, M., & Ginsberg, M. D. (1985). Postischemic cerebral lipid peroxidation in vitro: Modification by vitamin E. *Journal of Neurochemistry, 44,* 1593–1601.

Zubenko, G., & Moossy, J. (1988). Major depression in primary dementia: Clinical and neuropathological correlates. *Archives of Neurology, 45,* 1182–1186.

COGNITIVE IMPAIRMENT

See
Memory Assessment: Clinical
Cognitive Dysfunction: Drug Treatment

COGNITIVE PROCESSES

Internal mental processes control behavior. Although mental, or cognitive, processes cannot be observed directly, they are necessary components of an adequate description of behavior. *Cognitive processes* are intervening variables that come between the array of stimuli in the environment and the responses or behaviors that can be directly observed. Cognitive processes are inferred through a careful analysis of human behavior observations. However, with functional imaging, recently cognitive neuroscientists have been able to correlate behaviors and brain activities, validating many of the cognitive constructs developed through behavioral observation (Cabeza, 2004).

Cognitive psychologists studying aging have devoted a great deal of effort to understanding the *cognitive processes of older adults* and how they may be different from those of younger adults. In fact, a majority of the psychological research published in the *Journal of Gerontology* over the past 30 years has dealt with cognitive aging. The interest in *cognitive aging* has generated several good integrated research reference books (Blanchard-Fields & Hess, 1996; Craik & Salthouse, 2000; Park & Schwarz, 1999). These sources provide good summaries of the research findings in cognitive aging.

There are several approaches to the study of cognitive processes. The *information-processing paradigm* has been adopted by many psychologists to organize the complex array of mental abilities assumed to comprise cognition. We perceive, remember, reason, make decisions, solve problems, and form complex mental representations of world knowledge. We have developed elaborate symbolic systems to represent the knowledge we gain from our experiences, and these natural language and imagery systems provide the format for cognitive representations.

In addition to the *information-processing approach to cognition*, there are 2 other approaches: the psychometric approach, and the contextual approach. Some psychologists are more interested in individual differences than in normative principles of cognition and have pursued the psychometric approach. *Psychological tests* are developed to measure differences in cognitive processes among individuals. In early psychometric research, the definition of cognition using this approach was empirical. Subtests that measure some particular cognitive ability are assumed to be important measures only if they contribute empirically to detecting individual differences among people. If variance among individuals is not accounted for by a particular subtest, the subtest is not included in a battery used to measure individual differences in cognition.

A third approach attempts to combine the individual difference (psychometric) and the normative (information-processing) approaches. This contextual view of cognition assumes that individual differences, information-processing abilities, and the context of the cognitive performance are all important in understanding cognition. Because cognitive processes are used in a specific context, the everyday social context and the individual traits of the person interact in dynamic ways. Therefore, both are important in understanding complex behavior.

Psychometric Approach

The *psychometric approach to cognition* has concentrated primarily on measuring intelligence, i.e., the cognitive abilities and capacities contributing to intelligent behavior. Early research using intelligence tests found large "deficits" as a function of aging (Wechsler, 1958). Cross-sectional studies comparing cognitive measures across different age groups often found dramatic declines in performance across the life span. These declines, however, were found by Schaie and his colleagues to be overestimated (1996). Using *cross-sequential designs* (a combination of longitudinal and cross-sectional strategies), Schaie found that much of the decline was due to the different birth cohorts and not due to age per se. Even with these sequential designs, however, substantial declines in cognitive measures were found after age 60. Another result of more careful analysis of psychometric measures of cognitive functioning is that different subtests in intelligence batteries show differential age effects. Vocabulary, for example, declines only in very old age, whereas the ability to substitute digits for symbols declines across the adult life span. It is difficult to compare cross-sectional and longitudinal studies, however, because of confounds between type of cognition often being measured in the 2 types of studies, the fact that repeated measurement in longitudinal studies provides practice on the tests, and because the intervals between ages are often much shorter in longitudinal studies (often 5 to 7 years). When age-related changes in cognition are described as change per year, longitudinal and cross-sectional estimates are very similar (.02 –.04 standard deviations per year) (Schulz & Salthouse, 1999).

To account for the differential declines of different abilities, Horn (1982) distinguishes between crystallized and fluid intelligence. *Fluid intelligence* declines across the adult age span because it represents the efficiency of cognitive functioning. *Crystallized intelligence* is assumed to remain relatively stable or even increase through the adult age span because it represents the accumulation of world knowledge (e.g., the products of past fluid activities) (Salthouse, 1999).

While cognition measured by psychometric intelligence tests shows age effects, measures of *practical intelligence* or *tacit knowledge* are not correlated with age (Colonia-Willner, 1998). Practical intelligence correlates with performance evaluations and salaries of managers, but not with age; psychometric intelligence measures of the same managers did not correlate.

Information-Processing Approach

Rather than designing tests to account for individual variation, *information-processing tests* typically measure some hypothesized component of the information-processing system (e.g., working memory, encoding into semantic memory). There has been a concentration on memory as the focus of cognitive operations. For this reason, much of the information-processing research on cognitive processes has examined memory functioning. In general, the research has demonstrated that *age-related memory differences* are selective and that not all memory changes with age (Smith, 1996; Bäckman, Small, & Wahlin, 2001). In general, laboratory *information-processing research on aging and memory* shows that adult age differences are small or nonexistent when the tasks are designed to provide support of learning and remembering with little self-initiated processing required to perform the task. Age differences emerge, however, when the processing requirements of the task increase. In fact, recent modeling studies have shown that much of the age-related variance in cognitive performance (such as on memory tasks) can be accounted for by simple cognitive mechanisms such as *perceptual speed* (Salthouse, 1997) or *working memory* (Park, Lautenschlager, Hedden, Davidson, Smith, & Smith, 2002). These mechanisms are assumed to represent measures of cognitive resources. In a sense, these modeling studies showing the moderating effects of cognitive mechanisms on cognitive processes represent a blending of individual difference research (psychometric) and theory-driven information-processing research.

Contextual Approach

The contextual approach assumes that 4 classes of variables must be considered simultaneously to understand the cognitive processing of different aged adults (Smith, 1980). These classes are: the tasks used in the evaluation or measurement of cognition (e.g., criterial tasks), the individual characteristics of the subjects (e.g., age, cognitive ability, and health), the cognitive strategies and *self-efficacy beliefs* of the subjects (e.g., expectations and mode of processing), and the materials used in the task (e.g., familiarity and meaningfulness of the stimuli). In other words, there are many influences that determine cognitive performance, and all of these must be considered. Another characteristic of the contextual approach is an emphasis on functional or practical behavior. Because cognition is seen as adaptive to different contexts, there is a greater emphasis studying the context in which cognition takes place (Hess & Pullen, 1996).

When using a *contextual approach to cognitive processes*, some psychologists have attempted to identify qualitative differences between the cognitive processes of different adult age groups. It is assumed that these qualitative differences in cognitive processes among adult age groups reflect adaptive responses of the different groups to changing contexts and the cognitive requirements necessary to deal with those contexts. For example, Labouvie-Vief (1992) reviews research on changes in the ways in which adults of different ages interpret narrative text passages. In general, the research shows that older adults' interpretations are more interpretive and subjective, suggesting a unique mature adult style of symbolic processing, which is qualitatively different from that of younger adults.

Often the goal of contextual research—especially that dealing with everyday cognition—is to show that the deficits in older adults, so characteristic of psychometric and experimental approaches to cognition, do not reflect the true underlying relationship between aging and cognitive processes. Early researchers viewed the poorer performance of older adults on cognitive tasks as contrived and not reflective of the everyday memory requirements of older adults. The tasks used to measure cognition in older adults were not seen as ecologically valid (Poon, Rubin, & Wilson, 1989). More recently, however, it has become clear that age differences are found on ecologically valid, everyday cognitive tasks (Smith, 1996). So rather than assuming that age deficits are artifacts of the tasks used, most contextually oriented cognitive aging researchers now concentrate on individual differences in how these deficits become manifest in everyday life. For example, Baltes and Baltes (1990) view "successful" cognitive aging not as the absence of cognitive deficits, but rather as adaptation to these changes through the processes of selection (emphasizing those cognitive abilities that show minimum change), optimization (continued improvement through practice and training), and compensation (accomplishing the cognitive task in different ways). Clearly, such an approach emphasizes the adaptive nature of cognition. To achieve a better understanding of the cognitive processes of older adults, we need better research procedures, ones that are sensitive to the everyday cognitive operations required for daily living and are able to separate cognitive performance from cognitive competence, and theories of adult cognition that are sensitive to these issues.

ANDERSON D. SMITH

See also

Intelligence
Learning
Memory and Memory Theory

References

Bäckman, L., Small, B. J., & Wahlin, Å. (2001). Aging and memory: Cognitive and biological perspectives. In J. E. Birren & K. W. Schaie (Eds.), *Handbook of the psychology of aging* (5th Ed.). San Diego: Academic Press.

Baltes, P. B., & Baltes, M. M. (1990). Psychological perspectives on successful aging: The model of selective optimization with compensation. In P. B. Baltes & M. M. Baltes (Eds.), *Successful aging*. New York: Cambridge University Press.

Blanchard-Fields, F., & Hess, T. M. (1996). *Perspectives on cognitive change in adulthood and aging*. New York: McGraw-Hill.

Cabeza, R. (2004). Neuroscience frontiers of cognitive aging: Approaches to cognitive neuroscience of aging. In R. A. Dixon, L. Bäckman, & L.-G. Nilsson (Eds.), *New frontiers in cognitive aging*. New York: Oxford University Press.

Colonia-Willner, R. (1998). Practical intelligence at work: Relationship between aging and cognitive efficiency among managers in a bank environment. *Psychology and Aging*, *13*, 45–57.

Craik, F. I. M., & Salthouse, T. A. (2000). *Handbook of aging and cognition* (2nd Ed.). Hillsdale, NJ: Lawrence Erlbaum.

Hess, T. M., & Pullen, S. M. (1996). Memory in context. In F. Blanchard-Fields & T. M. Hess (Eds.), *Perspectives on cognitive change in adulthood and aging*. New York: McGraw-Hill.

Horn, J. L. (1982). The theory of fluid and crystallized intelligence in relation to concepts of cognitive psychology and aging in adulthood. In F. I. M. Craik & S. Trehub (Eds.), *Aging and cognitive processes*. New York: Plenum Press.

Labouvie-Vief, G. (1992). A neo-Piagetian perspective on adult cognitive development. In R. J. Sternberg & C. A. Berg (Eds.), *Intellectual development*. New York: Cambridge University Press.

Park, D. C., & Schwarz, N. (2000). *Aging and cognition: A student primer*. New York: Taylor and Francis.

Park, D. C., Lautenschlager, G., Hedden, T., Davidson, N., Smith, A. D., & Smith, P. K. (2002). Models of visuospatial and verbal memory across the adult lifespan. *Psychology and Aging, 17*, 299–320.

Poon, L. W., Rubin, D. C., & Wilson, B. A. (Eds.) (1989). *Everyday cognition in adulthood and late life*. New York: Cambridge University Press.

Salthouse, T. A. (1997). The processing speed theory of adult age differences in cognition. *Psychological Review, 103*, 403–429.

Salthouse, T. A. (1999). Cognitive and information-processing perspectives on aging. In I. H. Nordhus, G. R. Vanden Bos, G. R., & S. Berg (Eds.), *Clinical Geropsychology*. Washington, DC: American Psychological Association.

Schaie, K. W. (1996). *Intellectual development in adulthood: The Seattle Longitudinal Study*. New York: Cambridge University Press.

Schulz, R., & Salthouse, T. (1999). *Adult development and aging: Myths and emerging realities* (2nd ed.). Upper Saddle River, NJ: Prentice-Hall.

Smith, A. D. (1980). Cognitive processes. In L. W. Poon (Ed.), *Aging in the 1980s*. Washington, DC: American Psychological Association.

Smith, A. D. (1996). Memory. In J. E. Birren, & K. W. Schaie (Eds.), *Handbook of the psychology of aging* (4th ed.). San Diego: Academic Press.

Wechsler, D. (1958). *The measurement and appraisal of adult intelligence* (4th ed.). Baltimore: Williams & Wilkins.

COGNITIVE THERAPY

Cognitive therapy refers to a highly influential school of psychotherapy originated by *Aaron Beck* and colleagues in the 1960s at the Presbyterian Medical Center of Philadelphia. Beck posited that cognitive errors (e.g., overgeneralizing from a single incident) were the main cause of depression and anxiety. For example, Beck and colleagues (Beck, Rush, Shaw, & Emery, 1979) observed that *depression* is almost universally characterized by a triad of *negative cognitions*: a negative view of the self, the world, and the future. Cognitive therapy can also be viewed as an extension and refinement of *Albert Ellis' rational-emotive therapy* (Ellis & Harper, 1961), developed in the late 1950s. His approach is predicated on the idea that common irrational beliefs (e.g., "It is absolutely necessary to have love and approval from peers, family, and friends") were at the root of *mood disorders*. In both instances, *cognitions* (i.e., thoughts) are viewed as the driving force behind mood and mood disorders.

The *cognitive school of psychotherapy*, in tandem with behavioral therapy, has led to a paradigm shift in the field of clinical psychology away from the Freudian view that understanding the underlying causes of dysfunctional thoughts and behaviors (i.e., *unconscious conflicts* or early traumas) is essential for meaningful clinical change. Similarly, the role of the therapist has shifted away from being an "analyst" who makes expert interpretations to that of a "coach" who collaborates with the patient to help him or her develop more positive patterns of thinking. In addition, cognitive therapy, in contrast to neo-Freudian therapies, is designed to be a short-term treatment. As a result of these factors, psychotherapy has become more rational and acceptable to the general public, contributing to a large-scale increase in the utilization of mental health services during the past 2 decades in the United States and other Western countries.

To treat mood disorders, such as anxiety and depression, psychotherapists coach patients to recognize their dysfunctional thoughts and beliefs, often described as "*automatic thoughts*," and replace them with ones that are more mood and ego enhancing. To challenge these negative thoughts, patients are asked to do such things as weigh the evidence for and against a belief, do experiments to test the accuracy of their beliefs, and evaluate the pros and cons for holding a particular belief. In addition, patients are trained to identify the most common types of cognitive errors, defined as systematic biases in thinking. These include *black-and-white thinking* (i.e., not seeing a middle ground), *negative filtering* (i.e., dwelling exclusively on a single negative aspect of a situation), *jumping to conclusions*, *catastrophic thinking* ("I will never be happy again if I get divorced") and *emotional reasoning* (e.g., "I feel useless, therefore I am useless"). To increase awareness of *negative self-talk*, cognitive therapy emphasizes the importance of keeping track of thoughts outside of the therapy session. This homework usually takes the form of completing a daily log that records dysfunctional thinking as it occurs in situations, noting the immediate effects of these thoughts on mood, and recording an alternative thought that would have been more adaptive.

Cognitive therapy has several distinct advantages for older adult patients. For one, the practical emphasis on dealing with problems that are in the present counteracts the common belief among older adults that it is too late to deal with issues from earlier in life. Similarly, the underlying assumption that anyone can change their mood by simply changing their thinking is likely to have more appeal than models that imply that substantial changes in personality or relationships are required. Finally, compared to other models where the therapist is viewed as the all-knowing expert, the collaborative aspect of cognitive therapy affords a greater opportunity for typically younger psychotherapists to give credit to older patients for their experiences and knowledge acquired with age. Conversely, cognitive therapy may not be ideal for older patients who have some age-related cognitive deficits, due to the heavy emphasis on learning new concepts and homework assignments.

Cognitive therapy is the most rigorously tested method of psychotherapy, with numerous studies showing equal or greater efficacy relative to medication treatment for anxiety disorders and depression. Rates of improvement have been shown to be equivalent in younger and older adult samples (Scogin & McElreath, 1994). In more recent research and practice, cognitive therapy is often combined with behavioral therapy. This cognitive-behavioral combination has also been shown to be an effective treatment for older adults both with depression (Thompson, Coon, Gallagher-Thompson, Sommer, & Koin, 2001) and anxiety (Barrowclough, King, Colville, Russell, Burns, & Tarrier, 2001).

The cognitive and behavioral models of therapy are highly compatible and complimentary, due to the reciprocal nature of cognition and behavior. Negative cognitions lead to a downward spiral of depressed mood and ineffective behaviors, which then leads to more negative cognitions. The behavioral treatment portion of *cognitive-behavioral therapy* usually includes instruction in methods for increasing everyday pleasant events, problem solving, effective communication, and relaxation. With late-life depression, these complimentary cognitive and behavioral approaches are particularly important. For example, depressed older adults often get locked into a belief they are too old to develop new interests, hobbies, or social connections, and they need to both relinquish this belief and learn practical strategies for developing such activities.

With late-life depression most common in older adults with chronic medical diseases, it is essential for cognitive psychotherapists to target the depressive cognitions that are common in this group (Rybarczyk, Gallagher-Thompson, Rodman, Zeiss, Gantz, & Yesavage, 1992). For instance, a frequently expressed belief that contributes to depression in this population is that misery is inevitable if one has a serious medical condition (e.g., "Anyone would be depressed if they had to live with my condition."). With cognitive therapy, this belief can be challenged with information about how the majority of individuals with a chronic disease are not depressed and enjoy a reasonable quality of life. Similar cognitive errors that are often identified in *depressed, chronically ill older adults* include: *all-or-nothing thinking* ("If I cannot play golf the way I used to, I might as well not do it at all, because it won't be satisfying"); *negative filtering* ("I'm nothing but a burden to my family"); *negative forecasting* ("Soon nobody will want to be around me anymore"); and *mind reading* ("My kids are fed up with my medical problems.")

In addition to effectively treating depression and anxiety disorders, cognitive-behavioral therapy also has been extended to effectively address a broad spectrum of issues commonly faced by older adults. Research indicates that cognitive-behavioral techniques are effective for the *treatment of insomnia* (Murtagh & Greenwood, 1995) and *chronic pain* (Yonan & Wegener, 2003), as well as for *coping with chronic illness* (Rybarczyk, DeMarco, DeLaCruz, Lapidos, & Fortner, 2001) and being a caregiver (Gallagher-Thompson, Lovett, Rose, McKibbin, Coon, Futterman, & Thompson, 2000). The tenets and methods of the cognitive model are also straightforward enough to be easily presented in a *psycho-educational format*, resulting in a proliferation of self-help books, videos, audiotapes, and Web sites. Controlled studies have demonstrated that *self-help cognitive-behavioral treatments* for such problems as coping with chronic disease (Rybarczyk, DeMarco, DeLaCruz, & Lapidos, 1999) and insomnia (Mimeault & Morin, 1999) can be both cost-effective and efficacious.

Finally, the cognitive model has arguably had an even broader cultural effect on everything from schools and businesses to sports organizations. Many of these organizations have adopted the basic cognitive therapy tenet that *self-talk* has a large influence on performance and, more importantly, can be modified to be more positive and optimistic. Cognitive therapy will more than likely continue to be the most widely used method of psychotherapy, but recent research has suggested that changing negative cognitions may not be as important as learning how to detach from and not respond to one's negative thoughts. Newer versions of cognitive therapy (Hayes, Strosahl, & Wilson, 1999), which integrate approaches such as *mindfulness meditation*, show promise in making cognitive treatment more effective with difficult-to-treat mental health problems (e.g., addictions, personality disorders).

BRUCE RYBARCZYK

See also
Psychotherapy

References

Barrowclough, C., King, P., Colville, J., Russell, E., Burns, A., & Tarrier, N. (2001). A randomized trial of the effectiveness of cognitive-behavioral therapy and supportive counseling for anxiety symptoms in older adults. *Journal of Consulting and Clinical Psychology, 69*, 756–762.

Beck, A. T., Rush, A. J., Shaw, B. F., & Emery, G. (1979). *Cognitive therapy of depression*. New York: Guilford Press.

Ellis, A., & Harper, R. A. (1961) *A Guide to rational living*. Englewood Cliffs, NJ: Prentice-Hall.

Gallagher-Thompson, D., Lovett, S., Rose, J., McKibbin, C., Coon, D., Futterman, A., & Thompson, L. W. (2000). Impact of psychoeducational interventions on distressed family caregivers. *Journal of Clinical Geropsychology, 6*, 91–110.

Hayes, S. C., Strosahl, K. D., & Wilson, K. G. (1999). *Acceptance and commitment therapy: An experiential approach to behavior change*. New York: Guilford.

Mimeault, V., & Morin, C. M. (1999). Self-help treatment for insomnia: Bibliotherapy with and without professional guidance. *Journal of Consulting and Clinical Psychology, 67*, 511–519.

Murtagh, D. R., & Greenwood, K. M. (1995). Identifying effective psychological treatments for insomnia: A meta-analysis. *Journal of Consulting and Clinical Psychology, 63*, 79–89.

Rybarczyk, B., DeMarco, G., DeLaCruz, M., & Lapidos, S. (1999). Comparing two types of mind-body wellness programs for older adults with chronic illness: Classroom vs. home instruction. *Behavioral Medicine, 24*, 181–190.

Rybarczyk, B., DeMarco, G., DeLaCruz, M., Lapidos, S., & Fortner, B. (2001). A classroom mind-body wellness intervention for older adults with chronic illness: Comparing immediate and one-year benefits. *Behavioral Medicine, 27*, 15–27.

Rybarczyk, B., Gallagher-Thompson, D., Rodman, J., Zeiss, A., Gantz, F., & Yesavage, J. (1992). Applying cognitive-behavioral psychotherapy to the chronically ill elderly: Treatment issues and case illustration. *International Psychogeriatrics, 4*, 127–140.

Scogin, F., & McElreath, L. (1994). Efficacy of psychosocial treatments for geriatric depression: A quantitative review. *Journal of Consulting and Clinical Psychology, 62*, 69–74.

Thompson, L., Coon, D. W., Gallagher-Thompson, D., Sommer, B. R., & Koin, D. (2001). Comparison of desipramine and cognitive/behavioral therapy in the treatment of elderly outpatients with mild-to-moderate depression. *American Journal of Geriatric Psychiatry, 9*, 225–240.

Yonan, C. A., & Wegener, S. T. (2003). Assessment and management of pain in the older adult. *Rehabilitation Psychology, 48*, 4–13.

COMMUNICATION DISORDERS

Communication disorders comprise impairments of voice, speech, language and hearing. Age-cohort-specific incidence and prevalence data are limited, but approximately 1 in 6 people in the United States is living with a communication disorder (Castrogiovanni, 2004). Race-linked conditions like hypertension, diabetes, and sickle cell anemia are responsible for the disproportionate number of *African American elderly who have communication disorders* (www.asha.ucf.edu/harris.html).

The biomedical entities that cause most communication disorders in older age are diagnosed by a variety of specialists, including neurologists, otolaryngologists, and geriatricians. Behavioral assessment and management of communication disorders is the purview of *speech-language pathologists* (SLPs) and *audiologists*. SLPs also evaluate and manage *disorders of eating and swallowing* that compromise nutrition and hydration, and *disorders of cognition* that cause or contribute to communication disorders.

Information for professionals and consumers is available from sources such as the *American Speech-Language-Hearing Association* (www.asha.org), the *National Institute of Deafness and Other Communication Disorders* (NIDCD, www.nidcd.nih.gov), and the *National Institute of Neurological Disorders and Stroke* (www.ninds.nih.gov). Some international informational sites include those of the United Kingdom's *Royal College of Speech and Language Therapists* (www.rcslt.org); the *Canadian Association of Speech-Language Pathologists and Audiologists* (www.caslpa.ca); and *Speech Pathology Australia* (www.speechpathologyaustralia.org.au).

Disorders of Voice, Speech, and Swallowing

Voice depends on a complex interplay of biomechanical and aerodynamic events that enables modulations of the respiratory air stream by vibrations of the vocal folds in the larynx. Voice is most commonly used for speaking, but it also occurs without speech, as in laughing or humming. The primary acoustic parameters of voice production are fundamental frequency (perceived as pitch), intensity (perceived as loudness), and quality (with many dimensions, such as hoarseness).

It has long been documented that naïve listeners can identify elderly voices (Linville, 2001; Ramig, 2001). Linville (2001) provides an excellent summary of the broad variety of normal age-associated physical, physiologic, acoustic, aerodynamic, and endocrine-related changes in pulmonary and laryngeal systems that can affect vocal parameters, although without affecting the voice-user's intelligibility. Among these are weaker and less efficient *laryngeal closure* (Baker, Ramig, Sapir, Luschei, & Smith 2001) leading to perceptions of hoarseness, breathiness, and decreased loudness; and thickening or *atrophy of the vocal folds* in women and men, respectively, generating lower or higher voice fundamental frequency, respectively (Linville, 2001). In addition, gender differences are numerous in *vocal aging*, with many decrements affecting men (Linville, 2001). Ramig and colleagues (2001) notes that vocal aging is different in individuals of the same chronological age, and that physiologic indices of age are likely to be more important determinants of vocal function.

These normal voice changes may or may not be considered "disorders," depending on their impact on an individual in question. Most *voice disorders in elderly* adults stem from an age-related pathology, such as Parkinson disease or other neurologic conditions, or head and neck cancer (Linville, 2004). Some of these conditions have quite specific and predictable effects on voice; i.e., low vocal volume is a defining feature in Parkinson's disease. Nonspecific laryngitis can result from poor hydration, smoking, medication side effects, and gastroesophageal reflux disease and other inflammatory conditions (Linville, 2004). The biology of *vocal fold inflammation* is among the current topics of great interest in voice disorders (Verdolini, Branski, Rosen, & Hebda, 2003).

Speech involves coordination of respiratory, laryngeal, resonatory, and articulatory systems to communicate planned utterances verbally. It is the fastest of all discrete human motor performances (Kent, 2000). As with voice production, chronologic age is a poor marker of speech function (see NIDCD, www.nidcd.nih.gov/health/statistics/vsl.asp). There are a variety of physiologic and anatomical changes that occur in the speech mechanism as individuals age. Among these are diminished accuracy of the lower lip and jaw when performing rapid movements (Ballard, Robin, Woodworth, & Zimba, 2001), *decreased lip strength* and reduced tactile acuity for a series of repeated movements (Wohlert & Smith, 1998), and decreased vital capacity (Seikel, King, & Drumright, 2000). But despite some marked changes of this sort, and a slower overall speaking rate, speech intelligibility and general communicative function are unimpaired in the older adult population (Wohlert & Smith, 1998).

Again, most *speech disorders* of advancing age result from age-related medical conditions. Primary among these are cerebrovascular accidents and other neurologic pathologies such as Parkinson's or Alzheimer's disease. There are 2 main classes of *speech disorders in the elderly*: *dysarthrias* and *apraxia of speech* (AOS). The dyarthrias are a group of related speech disorders in which deficits of muscle tone and/or movement strength, speed, range, steadiness, timing, or accuracy compromise motor control of respiration, phonation, resonance, and articulation (Duffy, 2004). The site of damage in the central and/or peripheral nervous system(s) generally predicts the nature of the dysarthria; for example, a brainstem stroke yields lower motor neuron damage and a flaccid dysarthria. Specific perceptual correlates in this case would depend on which cranial nerves are affected, but might include imprecise consonants, breathiness, and hypernasal voice quality along with preserved timing of repetitive and sequential speech movements. As another example, Parkinson's disease generates a *hypokinetic dysarthria*, characterized by consonant imprecision, rapid speech rate, significantly reduced vocal intensity, reduced pitch and loudness variation, and muscular rigidity. Dysarthria is estimated to occur in 50% to 90% of people with Parkinson's disease (Duffy, 2004). Severity of dysarthria, and effects on speech intelligibility, can vary substantially within categories of dysarthria. One important focus of current research is to determine the nature and extent of relationships among perceptually based dysarthria types, intelligibility ratings, and precise speech acoustic, physiologic, and neural control mechanisms (Duffy, 2004).

AOS is a disorder of programming the synergistic movements for speech production (e.g., jaw opening, lip rounding, tongue-tip raising) that cannot be attributed to neuromuscular or sensory deficits, or to language impairment (McNeil & Doyle, 2004). AOS is quite rare in isolation, and nearly always co-occurs with *aphasia* (see Aphasia entry, this volume), dysarthria, or other forms of apraxia. There are a number of competing accounts for AOS (McNeil & Doyle, 2004), but theory development has been hampered by difficulties in defining and diagnosing this condition, and because many neuropsychologists and neurolinguists do not recognize AOS as an entity distinct from aphasia. The lesion site for AOS is a matter of some controversy, although it most often occurs in the language-dominant hemisphere of the brain (the left hemisphere, for most people).

Dysphagia, or *swallowing disorder*, results from a disturbance of any of a number of neuroanatomical and/or neurophysiological aspects of the swallowing mechanism. The specific neurobiological causes of dysphagia in the elderly remain largely unknown, and it is controversial whether dysphagia is a consequence of adult aging in the absence of disease. Most pertinent studies rely on self-report to select disease-free subjects, and latent disease processes cannot be ruled out (Caruso & Max, 1997). There is consensus, however, that some aerodynamic, mechanical, and sensory components of swallowing change with age. For example, aging is associated with delayed oral and pharyngeal swallowing movements (Gleeson, 1999), prolonged positive pharyngeal air pressures (Yokoyama, Mitomi, Tetsuka, Tayama, & Niimi, 2000), and decreased oral and pharyngeal sensitivity (Caruso & Max, 1997). Some qualitative differences have been reported as well: younger adults never, but older adults at times, exhibited multiple tongue-pumping movements and inefficient formation of the bolus to be swallowed (Dejaeger, Pelemans, Ponette, & Vantrappen, 1994). Laryngeal contributions to swallowing are relatively preserved in older age, but are not completely spared. For instance, Yokoyama and colleagues (2000) report a delay in anterior laryngeal movements that, in concert with ill-timed air pressure changes, decrease airway protection and increase *aspiration risk during swallowing*. Despite the accumulation of descriptive data and emerging norms, more evidence is needed to determine when changes in the swallowing mechanism become pathological.

Dysphagia is a common consequence of diseases that accompany aging, including dementing conditions, cerebrovascular accident, and carcinoma. It is associated with either upper or lower motor neuron damage, and linked with malnutrition risk and respiratory difficulties (Perlman, 2004). Chewing and swallowing problems account for unintended weight loss in a large proportion of elderly residents of nursing homes (Gilmore, Robinson, Posthauer & Raymond, 1995). Dysphagia can also be a side effect of medical intervention, including medications, surgery, and radiation.

Disorders of Language and Cognition

Language, a symbol system used to convey and interpret knowledge, thoughts, beliefs, and emotions, is the primary means of human communication, interaction, and learning. The comprehension and production of language depend on mental representations and processes related to syntax (grammar), morphology and semantics (meaning), lexical retrieval (vocabulary), phonology (speech sound system), and pragmatics (language use appropriate to context). Language is intricately linked with perceptual and nonlanguage cognitive systems. For example, to interpret a conversation a listener at minimum engages sensory, perceptual, attentional, and working memory functions and accesses representations in semantic memory. Age changes in these perceptual and cognitive domains are detailed in other sections of this volume.

Normal age-related changes in language processing are rather minor. Comprehension accuracy is retained in all but the most demanding conditions, as when speech rate is very rapid (Wingfield, Peelle, & Grossman, 2003). Some differences are notable, though, such as age-related lengthening of response times in syntactic comprehension tasks (e.g. Wingfield, Peelle, & Grossman, 2003) and changes in brain regions involved in grammatical processing (Kemmer, Coulson, De Ochoa, & Kutas, 2004). Older language users experience more difficulties on the language production side. For instance, longitudinal investigation shows age-related reductions in grammatical complexity and propositional content of language (Kemper, Thompson, & Marquis, 2001). Additionally, the *retrieval of specific words*, particularly proper names, declines in accuracy with increases in *tip-of-the-tongue* states and response latency (Burke, MacKay, & James, 2004). Older adult language users perform better than younger adults in a number of domains, though, such as pragmatically adjusting their storytelling to the age of a listener (Adams, Smith, Pasupathi, & Vitolo, 2002). *Vocabulary test scores* also increase with age.

Language function in older age typically has been explained with reference to accounts of cognitive aging in general. Currently, among the most influential of these accounts is the frontal lobe/executive function hypothesis (e.g., West, 1996; Dywan, Segalowitz, & Arsenault, 2002; Souchay & Isingrini, 2004). This hypothesis links age-related cognitive changes, particularly in episodic memory, to evidence of various biological changes in the frontal lobe (Raz, 1999). This popular account is problematic for several reasons. One is that altered biology does not necessitate behavioral change (Band, Ridderinkhof, & Segalowitz, 2002); another is that the large and multifunctional frontal lobes are treated in an undifferentiated way; a third is that age effects on tasks classically used to engage the frontal lobes are small or nonexistent when factors like processing speed (Shilling, Chetwynd, & Rabbitt, 2002) and practice (Rabbitt, Diggle, Smith, Holland, & McInnes, 2001) are taken into consideration. Burke and colleagues (2004) recently reviewed the application of their *transmission deficit hypothesis* to language function in older age, instantiated in an interactive activation model that attempts to account for the overall comprehension/production asymmetry as well as specific problems like proper name retrieval and tip-of-the-tongue experiences. Other recent work is examining subcortical white matter abnormalities (Van Petten, Plante, Davidson, Kuo, Bajuscak, Glisky, 2004). Band and colleagues (2002) argue that neurocognitive aging cannot be explained by any single factor, and any account of cognitive aging will have to address large individual differences in longitudinal patterns of behavioral performance.

The most common language disorders of aging are aphasia, *right hemisphere language disorders* (RHLD), and language of generalized intellectual impairment in dementing conditions. Aphasia, including primary progressive forms, is covered elsewhere in this volume.

RHLD, like aphasia, is primarily due to cerebrovascular accident that causes relatively focal brain damage, but unlike aphasia the damage is to the so-called "minor" or nonlanguage-dominant hemisphere. In most individuals, this is the right hemisphere. The disorder has an anatomical label because this is a relatively new area of investigation and psycholinguistic, cognitive, and neuropathological features are still being delineated. Definitional vagueness has impeded scientific progress in this area (Myers, 1999; Blake, Duffy, Myers, & Tompkins, 2002). However, estimates are that RHLD occurs in about 50% of adults with right hemisphere stroke (Joanette, Goulet, Hannequin, 1990), and that more than 90% of such adults have cognitive deficits that can disrupt their communication and social interaction (Blake, Duffy, Tompkins, & Myers, 2003).

Again unlike aphasia, RHLD is primarily pragmatic in nature: syntax, morphology, phonology, and most aspects of semantics are well preserved

(Tompkins & Fassbinder, 2004). Adults with RHLD thus may appear to comprehend fully and speak without error, but their social interactions may be perceived as somehow "off." Among their difficulties may be compromised production and use of prosody (the melodic and emphatic elements of speech); vague referents or lack of other markers that enhance conversational coherence; impaired understanding of irony, jokes, and other nonliteral or ambiguous forms; and uninhibited peripheral associations in both production and comprehension that take them away from main points and core interpretations (Baum, 2004; Myers, 2004; Tompkins & Fassbinder, 2004). The signs and symptoms of RHLD likely have a basis in attentional and/or working memory disruptions (Tompkins, Fassbinder, Lehman-Blake, & Baumgaertner, 2002), and also perhaps in deficits of social cognition (Brownell, 2004; Tompkins & Fassbinder, 2004). Communication impairments can be complicated by other cognitive deficits like hemispatial neglect and *anosognosia*. Behavioral heterogeneity is the watchword for those diagnosed with RHLD, due to factors such as the inherent variability in pragmatic communication abilities in nonbrain-damaged individuals, the as-yet undifferentiated nature of potential subsets of the RHLD population, and the undetermined nature and consequences of interactions of deficits in communication and nonlanguage cognition.

Language of generalized intellectual impairment (LGII; Wertz, 1985) is a diagnostic label that refers to language disorders resulting from neurologically degenerative conditions such as presumed Alzheimer's disease (AD). The term is used primarily in the clinical aphasiology community; for other professionals the medical diagnostic label (e.g., AD) suffices. Unlike aphasia and RHLD, LGII is associated with bilateral, diffuse brain damage. Language deficits are proportional to and predicted by those in nonlanguage cognition, and language impairments worsen progressively. The NIDCD estimates that about 2 million people with progressive dementing conditions have a significant impairment in language.

Most of what is known about LGII is based on studies of patients with presumed AD. Bayles (2004) outlines generalizations about communication function at various stages of AD. Early on, deficits of short-term memory consolidation are reflected in communication. Syntax and phonology remain largely intact until late in the disease progression. With the onset of disorientation and semantic memory impairment, language content suffers more and meaningful communication decreases. Pragmatic appropriateness may begin to decline as well. In late stages, if adults with AD speak at all, they speak little other than nonsense, and they comprehend only simple input with strong cuing. Procedural memory is retained until fairly late, and procedural skills—like turning the pages of a book or dealing cards—are the basis of some behavioral treatment approaches. In early to mid stages, *communication aids* such as memory books and index cards, paired with the patient's well preserved oral reading skills, can provide a means for enhancing direct interaction with the patient (Bourgeois, Burgio, Schulz, Beach, & Palmer, 1997). Later, such aids can be used to redirect patients and help address difficult problems like *sundowning*. *Errorless learning*—a process to minimize errors in new learning trials—is another treatment approach used with some success in the early stages of AD (Clare, Wilson, Carter, Breen, Gosses, & Hodges, 2000).

In multi-infarct dementias, language profiles will depend on the sites and extent of associated brain lesions (Bayles, 2004). The course is fluctuating, with periods of improvement possible after each infarct. Little is known about the language profiles of dementing conditions other than AD, such as Huntington's or Parkinson's diseases (Murray & Stout, 1999). There is also little evidence about language in a newer diagnostic category, "*mild cognitive impairment*," that describes a group of individuals with memory function disproportionately lower than age- and education-based expectations, in the context of preserved general cognitive functions and basic activities of daily living (Joanette, Goulet, Hannequin, 2002; Peterson, Doody, Kurz, Mohs, Morris, Rabins, et al., 2001). Individuals with this diagnosis are at high risk for developing AD or other dementing conditions. It is possible that subtle language testing would help determine who does and who does not so evolve.

Disorders of Hearing

Presbycusis is an age-associated high frequency hearing loss. Higher frequencies are crucial for identifying consonants, especially in noisy backgrounds and in women's and children's speech, which are inherently higher in frequency than men's. Thus, this pattern of loss contributes to the most frequent complaint of adults with presbycusis: while they hear speech, they have trouble understanding it, particularly in noise. *Audiologic testing* indicates presbycusis prevalence rates of up to 83% for adults age 55 and older in the United States (Moscicki, Elkins, Baum, & McNamara, 1985). A more recent longitudinal investigation in the United Kingdom and Denmark found 97% of adults experience decreased hearing over time (Davis, Ostri, & Parving, 1991). Presbycusis is more common in urban areas, suggesting a likely link to noise exposure (Hain, 2003). It also has a clear genetic component and may be compounded by the use of *ototoxic drugs* (Dubno & Mills, 2004). Despite its prevalence, there are large individual differences in the daily life impact of presbycusis that cannot be predicted directly from an audiogram (Dubno & Mills, 2004).

Presbycusis occurs gradually and is typically bilateral and sensorineural; that is, due to cochlear or auditory nerve damage. Cochlear alterations include inner and outer hair cell loss (Jennings & Jones, 2001) and disrupted potassium metabolism in the stria vascularis, the endolymph-producing tissue in the lateral cochlear wall (Frisina, 2004). There are also age-related changes in the brain, such as decreases in the inhibitory neurotransmitter gamma-aminobutyric acid (GABA), that may be related to presbycusis (Dubno & Mills, 2004; Frisina, 2004). Changes in gene expression with aging are of current interest for determining the underlying nature of presbycusis. Frisina (2004) indicates that aging mice with hearing losses similar to presbycusis have alterations in genes related to the immune system, glucose metabolism, and cochlear neurotransmitters, among others. Other current hypotheses focus on age-related reductions in neural asymmetries in temporal lobe representations of speech sounds (Bellis, Nicol, & Kraus, 2000), increases in auditory neural refractory periods (Tremblay, Billings, & Rohila, 2004), and increases in mitochondrial DNA mutations (Hain, 2003) that are potentially associated with apoptosis, or programmed cell death (Hain, 2003; Jennings & Jones, 2001). Relevant to the DNA mutation evidence, treatment with L-carnitine, a compound essential to cell metabolism, has reduced age-associated changes in the auditory pathways of mice (Derin, Agirdir, Derin, Dinc, Guney, Ozcaglar, et al., 2004).

Hearing loss plays a major role in functional health status and life satisfaction in the elderly (Bess, Lichtenstein, Logan, & Burger, 1989), and when left untreated its impact far exceeds that of decreased communication alone (Mulrow, Aguilar, Endicott, Tuley, Velez, Charlip, 1990). Currently, hearing aids and other assistive listening devices are the primary treatment options for presbycusis, although satisfaction with them is low, as they cannot fix the problem (Dubno & Mills, 2004). Investigation is ongoing to improve hearing aid fitting and technology (Dubno & Mills, 2004). A potential breakthrough in the quest to develop new treatments for hearing loss was recently reported by Izumikawa and colleagues (2005). In the first demonstration of its kind, mature guinea pigs whose hair cells had been destroyed by exposure to ototoxic drugs grew new hair cells, and displayed improved hearing thresholds, after therapy with Atoh1, a gene that regulates the development of inner hair cells.

Connie A. Tompkins
Victoria L. Scharp
Kimberly M. Meigh

See also
Aphasia
Language Comprehension
Language Production

References

Adams, C., Smith, M. C., Pasupathi, M., & Vitolo, L. (2002). Social context effects on story recall in older and younger women: Does the listener make a difference? *Journal of Gerontology: Psychological Sciences*, *57B*(1), P28–P40.

Baker, K. K., Ramig, L. O., Sapir, S., Luschei, E. S., & Smith, M. E. (2001). Control of vocal loudness in young and old adults. *Journal of Speech, Language, and Hearing Research*, *44*, 297–305.

Ballard, K., Robin, D., Woodworth, G., & Zimba, L. (2001). Age-related changes in motor control during articulator visuomotor tracking. *Journal of Speech, Language, and Hearing Research*, *44*, 763–777.

Band, G. P. H., Ridderinkhof, K. R., & Segalowitz, S. (2002). Explaining neurocognitive aging: Is one factor enough? *Brain and Cognition*, *49*, 259–267.

Baum, S. R. (2004). Prosodic deficits. In R. D. Kent (Ed.), *The MIT encyclopedia of communication disorders* (pp. 381–383). Cambridge, MA: The MIT Press.

Bayles, A. D. (2004). Dementia. In R. D. Kent (Ed.), *The MIT encyclopedia of communication disorders* (pp. 291–294). Cambridge, MA: The MIT Press.

Bellis, T. J., Nicol, T., & Kraus, N. (2000). Aging affects hemispheric asymmetry in the neural representation of speech sounds. *Journal of Neuroscience*, *20*(2), 791–797.

Bess, F. H., Lichtenstein, M. J., Logan, S. A., & Burger, M. C. (1989). Comparing criteria of hearing impairment in the elderly: A functional approach. *Journal of Speech and Hearing Research*, *32*, 795–802.

Blake, M. L., Duffy, J. R., Myers, P. S., & Tompkins, C. A. (2002). Prevalence and patterns of right hemisphere cognitive/communicative deficits: Retrospective data from an inpatient rehabilitation unit. *Aphasiology*, *16*, 537–547.

Blake, M. L., Duffy, J. R., Tompkins, C. A., & Myers, P. S. (2003). Right hemisphere syndrome is in the eye of the beholder. *Aphasiology*, *17*, 423–432.

Bourgeois, M., Burgio, L., Schulz, R., Beach, S., & Palmer B. (1997). Modifying repetitive verbalization of community-dwelling patients with AD. *Gerontologist*, *37*, 30–39.

Brownell, H. (2004). Right hemisphere language and communication functions in adults. In R. D. Kent (Ed.), *The MIT encyclopedia of communication disorders* (pp. 291–294). Cambridge, MA: The MIT Press.

Burke, D. M., MacKay, D. G., & James, L. E. (2004). Theoretical approaches to language and aging. In T. J. Perfect & E. A. Maylor (Eds.), *Models of cognitive aging* (pp. 204–237). Oxford: Oxford University Press.

Caruso, A. J., & Max, L. (1997). Effects of aging on neuromotor processes of swallowing. *Seminars in Speech and Language*, *18*(2), 181–192.

Castrogiovanni, A. (2004). *Incidence and prevalence of speech, voice, and language disorders in adults in the United States—2004 Edition.* Available: http://www.asha.org/members/research/reports/speech_voice_language.htm

Clare, L., Wilson, B. A., Carter, G., Breen, K., Gosses, A., & Hodges, J. R. (2000). Intervening with everyday memory problems in dementia of Alzheimer's type: An errorless learning approach. *Journal of Clinical and Experimental Neuropsychology*, *22*(1), 132–146.

Davis, O. C., Ostri, B., & Parving, A. (1991). Longitudinal study of hearing. *Acta Oto-laryngologica Supplement*, *476*, 12–22.

Dejaeger, E., Pelemans W., Ponette E., & Vantrappen, G. (1994). Effect of body position on deglutition. *Digestive Diseases and Sciences*, *39*(4), 762–765.

Derin, A., Agirdir, B., Derin, N., Dinc, O., Guney, K., Ozcaglar, H., et al. (2004). The effects of L-carnitine on presbyacusis in the rat model. *Clinical Otolaryngology*, *29*, 238–241.

Dubno, J. R. & Mills, J. H. (2004). Presbyacusis. In R. D. Kent (Ed.), *The MIT encyclopedia of communication disorders* (pp. 527–531). Cambridge, MA: The MIT Press.

Duffy, J. R. (2004). Dysarthrias: Characteristics and classification. In R. D. Kent (Ed.), *The MIT encyclopedia of communication disorders* (pp. 126–129). Cambridge, MA: The MIT Press.

Dywan, J., Segalowitz, S. & Arsenault, A. (2002). Electrophysiological responses during source memory decisions in older and younger adults. *Brain and Cognition*, *49*, 322–340.

Frisina, R. D. (2004). Molecular and neural perspectives on age-related hearing loss. *The ASHA Leader*, 16.

Gilmore, S. A., Robinson, G., Posthauer, M. E., & Raymond, J. (1995). Clinical indicators associated with unintentional weight loss and pressure ulcers in elderly residents of nursing facilities. *Journal of the American Dietetic Association*, *95*(9), 984–992.

Gleeson, D. (1999). Oropharyngeal swallowing and aging: A review. *Journal of Communication Disorders*, *32*, 373–396.

Hain, T. C. (2003). Presbycusis. Available: http://www.dizziness-and-balance.com/disorders/hearing/presby.html

Harris, J. L. (n.d.) *Aging and ethnicity: Communication services for older African Americans.* The University of Memphis School of Audiology and Speech-Language Pathology. Available: http://www.asha.ucf.edu/harris.html

Izumikawa, M., Minodal, R., Kawamoto, K., Abrashkin, K. A., Swiderski, D. L., Dolan, D. F., Brough, D. E, & Raphael, Y. (2005). Auditory hair cell replacement and hearing improvement by Atoh1 gene therapy in deaf mammals. *Nature Medicine*, *11*, 271–276.

Jennings, C. R., & Jones, N. S. (2001). Presbyacusis. *Journal of Laryngology and Otology*, *115*, 171–178.

Joanette, Y. (2002). The elderly cognitive profile. Available: http://upload.mcgill.ca/management/cognitive.pdf

Joanette, Y., Goulet, P., Hannequin, D. (1990). *Right hemisphere and verbal communication.* New York: Springer-Verlag Publishing.

Kemmer, L., Coulson, S., De Ochoa, E., & Kutas, M. (2004). Syntactic processing with aging: An event-related potential study. *Psychophysiology*, *41*(3), 372–384.

Kemper, S., Thompson, M., & Marquis, J. (2001). Longitudinal change in language production: Effects of aging and dementia on grammatical complexity and propositional content. *Psychology and Aging, 16*(4), 600–614.

Kent, R. D. (2000). Research on speech motor control and its disorders: A review and prospective. *Journal of Communication Disorders, 33*, 391–428.

Linville, S. E. (2001). *Vocal aging*. San Diego: Singular Publishing Group.

Linville, S. E. (2004). Voice disorders of aging. In R. D. Kent (Ed.). *The MIT encyclopedia of communication disorders* (pp. 72–75). Cambridge, MA: MIT Press.

McNeil, M. R. & Doyle, P. J. (2004). Apraxia of speech: Nature and phenomenology. In R. D. Kent (Ed.). *The MIT encyclopedia of communication disorders* (pp. 101–104). Cambridge, MA: MIT Press.

Moscicki, E. K., Elkins, E. F., Baum, H. M., & McNamara, P. M. (1985). Hearing loss in the elderly: An epidemiologic study of the Framingham Heart Study Cohort. *Ear and Hearing, 6*(4), 184–190.

Mulrow, C. D., Aguilar, C., Endicott, J. E., Tuley, M. R., Velez, R., Charlip, W. S. et al. (1990). Quality of life changes and hearing impairment. Results of a randomized trial. *Annals of Internal Medicine, 113*(3), 188–94.

Murray, L. L., & Stout, J. C. (1999). Discourse comprehension in Huntington's and Parkinson's diseases. *American Journal of Speech-Language Pathology, 8*, 137–148.

Myers, P. S. (1999). *Right hemisphere damage: Disorders of communication and cognition*. San Diego: Singular Publishing Group.

Myers, P. S. (2004). Aprosodia. In R. D. Kent (Ed.), *The MIT encyclopedia of communication disorders* (pp. 107–110). Cambridge, MA: The MIT Press.

National Institute on Deafness and Other Communication Disorders. (2004). *Statistics on voice, speech and language*. Available: http://www.nidcd.nih.gov/health/statistics/vsl.asp

Perlman, A. L. (2004). Dysphagia, oral and pharyngeal. In R. D. Kent (Ed.), *The MIT encyclopedia of communication disorders* (pp. 132–135). Cambridge, MA: The MIT Press.

Peterson, R. C., Doody, R., Kurz, A., Mohs, R. C., Morris, J. C., Rabins, P. V. et al. (2001). Current concepts in mild cognitive impairment. *Archives of Neurology, 58*, 1985–1992.

Rabbitt, P., Diggle, P., Smith, D., Holland, F., & McInnes, L. (2001). Identifying and separating the effects of practice and of cognitive ageing during a large longitudinal study of elderly community residents. *Neuropsychologia, 39*(5), 532–543.

Ramig L. O., Gray S., Baker K., Corbin-Lewis K., Buder E., Luschei E., et al. (2001). The aging voice: A review, treatment data and familial and genetic perspectives. *Folia Phoniatrica et Logopaedica, 53*(5), 252–265.

Raz, N. (1999). Aging of the brain and its impact on cognitive performance: Integration of structural and functional findings. In F. I. M. Craik & T. A. Salthouse (Eds.), *Handbook of aging and cognition* (Vol. 2). Mahwah, NJ: Lawrence Erlbaum.

Seikel, J. King, D., & Drumright, D. (2000). *Anatomy and physiology for speech, language, and hearing* (2nd ed.). San Diego: Singular Publishing Group.

Shilling, V. M., Chetwynd, A., & Rabbitt, P. M. (2002). Individual inconsistency across measures of inhibition: An investigation of the construct validity of inhibition in older adults. *Neuropsychologia, 40*(6), 605–619.

Souchay, C., & Isingrini, M. (2004). Age related differences in metacognitive control: Role of executive functioning. *Brain and Cognition, 56*, 89–99.

Tompkins, C. A., Fassbinder, W., Lehman-Blake, M. T., & Baumgaertner, A. (2002). The nature and implications of right hemisphere language disorders: Issues in search of answers. In A. Hillis (Ed.), *Handbook of adult language disorders: Integrating cognitive neuropsychology, neurology, and rehabilitation* (pp. 429–448). Psychology Press.

Tremblay, K. L., Billings, C., & Rohila, N. (2004). Speech-evoked potentials: Effects of age and stimulus presentation rate. *Journal of the American Academy of Audiology, 15*, 226–237.

Van Petten, C., Plante, E., Davidson, P. S. R., Kuo, T. Y., Bajuscak, L., Glisky, E. L. (2004). Memory and executive function in older adults: Relationships with temporal and prefrontal gray matter volumes and white matter hyperintensities. *Neuropsychologia, 42*, 1313–1335.

Verdolini, K., Branski, R. C., Rosen, C. A., & Hebda, P. A. (2003). Shifts in biochemical markers associated with wound healing in laryngeal secretions following phonotrauma: A preliminary study. *Annals of Otology, Rhinology, and Laryngology, 112*(12), 1021–1025.

Wertz, R. T. (1985). Neuropathologies of speech and language: An introduction to patient management. In D. F. Johns (Ed.), *Clinical management of neurogenic communication disorders* (2nd ed., pp. 1–96). Boston: Little, Brown.

West, R. L. (1996). An application of prefrontal cortex function theory to cognitive aging. *Psychological Bulletin, 120*, 272–292.

Wingfield, A., Peelle, J. E., & Grossman, M. (2003). Speech rate and syntactic complexity as multiplicative factors in speech comprehension by young and older adults. *Aging, Neuropsychology, and Cognition, 10*(4), 310–322.

Wohlert, A., & Smith, A. (1998). Spatiotemporal stability of lip movement in older adult speakers. *Journal of Speech, Language, and Hearing Research, 41*, 41–50.

Yokoyama, M., Mitomi, N., Tetsuka, K., Tayama, N., & Niimi, S. (2000). Role of laryngeal movement and effect of aging on swallowing pressure in the pharynx and upper esophageal sphincter. *Laryngoscope, 110*(3), 434–439.

COMMUNICATION TECHNOLOGIES AND OLDER ADULTS

While there has been a limited awareness of the potential of communication technology to enhance the lives of older adults for decades, it has only blossomed in the last decade, and still faces considerable barriers. Communication technologies offer a promising future for older adults. We tend to overlook the possibility that new communication technologies can help us avoid isolation and helplessness (Mundorf & Laird, 2002). In the dawn of the 21st century, personal computers, the Internet, smart house and mobile devices, as well as digital imaging and video, can be used by older adults as valuable supplements to face-to-face encounters (Coughlin, 2001). Older adults use them to overcome environmental and physical barriers while fulfilling interpersonal needs, but many are deterred by numerous real or perceived obstacles.

Attitude and Experience. The over-60 population tends to be more comfortable with technology than previous generations, since some were introduced to technology in the workplace, or through friends and family. However, elderly returning to employment are often ill equipped to deal with new technologies. The over-80 generation has little or no experience with new communication technologies. Consequently, they are reluctant to learn about new media and take advantage of available services and information.

Health. Poor health, such as hearing and vision loss, and fine and large motor skills affected by illness, are deterrents to technology usage. This is especially acute with the over-85 population. On the other hand, with appropriate modifications and financial backing, existing technology can also serve as a remedy to such age-related shortcomings (Pew & Van Hemel, 2004).

The Promise of Digital Technologies. Technological progress generated a number of communication tools for older adults. Some communication networks, such as SeniorNet, were designed early on specifically with older adults in mind. During the past decade, numerous Web sites, discussion lists, and the like have emerged which focus on the needs of older adults. They have been successful among those adults with the appropriate skills and motivation. Some hospitals now install Internet service for long-term patients to make their stay more tolerable and keep them connected with the outside world (Lee, 2004). Older adults who learn to use computers are developing practical and conversational skills with which the younger generations are familiar, enhancing possibilities for intergenerational relationships.

Digital technologies have become widely available, with considerable decrease in price and increase in performance. These technologies were primarily designed for and marketed to teenage and college age adopters or to baby boomers. Hardware and software developments have made computer-based technologies more user-friendly and suitable for the needs of older individuals. Voice recognition and touch-screen technologies are particularly suited to facilitate appropriate interactions. We have witnessed a widespread introduction of multimedia to the home, as well as adoption of high-speed Internet delivered through cable and phone systems (Mundorf & Laird, 2002). Although younger demographics were the driving force originally, home access to all age groups is increasing.

Families and Internet. Independent living, safety, and communication with family and friends determine priorities. Schools and libraries nationwide have expanded the use of computer technologies, and the Internet has become an important tool in education and information access; more families have gone online. Grandchildren have stimulated intergenerational use of the Internet to coordinate reunions, vacations, weddings, graduations, and other family-oriented occasions.

The Internet has offered many grandparents an almost immediate look at a new grandchild via a photograph on a Web site or in an email, and regular, efficient, and low-cost access to family dialogues. Individuals, who might have felt isolated from a generation that may not write even thank-you notes, can now interact frequently and even instant message family members for more immediacy. Others forward messages or Internet links to their family members and friends, thus sharing news, amusing stories, and issues of concern. Some use electronic greeting cards complete with sound effects, songs, and colorful graphics. There is, of course, the downside that some family members without computer technology may become isolated. Many consult the Internet for extensive information on medications and various health products and services; this information access empowers older adults to play more significant and more informed roles in their own health care.

Practical Applications. Individuals with serious mobility problems, people isolated by bad weather conditions, and individuals unable to drive or use local transportation can find what they need through the Internet and purchase it on-line or via the phone. Various search engines and Web sites make location of products and services easier and faster. Specialty items that might never have been carried by a local retailer are readily available at affordable prices via the Internet. Some older adults have enjoyed bidding for collectible items through auctions, purchasing stock, managing their money and investments, and submitting their tax returns all via the Internet.

Barriers to Adoption. Older adults are not a homogeneous group. Certain types of technologies have considerable appeal to particular segments. Despite positive examples, older adults have exhibited some reluctance to accept change, and new communication technologies typically generate dramatic changes in how we interact with other people. Technology adoption tends to be inversely related to age and positively related to income and education. In particular, the aging of the baby boom generation is expected to contribute to greater technology acceptance among older demographics. There is still some reluctance among many older adults to bank or make purchases online. While online banking and shopping may be more convenient, such transactions may provide welcome opportunities for personal contact when conducted face to face. Also, in light of recent publicity surrounding identity and credit card theft via the Internet, older persons may lack trust in the system and feel particularly vulnerable.

A key issue is the concern about the added complexity that the invasion of the home by the computer will bring for older persons. Some authors call for a small, self-sufficient "information appliance" which can interface with other household appliances without the need for central programming or computer expertise.

Communication needs are addressed by the Internet, even though keyboard skills can be a problem for those who are inexperienced, have had a stroke or health problem that limits mobility, or those who suffer from arthritis. In addition, video conferencing technology is becoming more affordable. Several field trials during the 1990s successfully installed ISDN-based videophones in older-adult households. This technology avoids the keyboard as a bottleneck; but cost and especially little penetration of video conferencing technology in private households currently makes it limited. Internet-based videoconferencing is feasible and should become widely available within a few years. Nevertheless, low-tech solutions can have considerable utility at lower cost and complexity, and may provide lower barriers to adoption until more comprehensive, affordable solutions become widely available.

Smart House. The "smart house" uses technology to increase comfort, health, and safety in a living environment by integrating communication and control systems to maximize independence and functioning of older adults (Willems, 2003). Such intelligent homes can reduce the risk of injury from falls, burns, poison gases, crime, and fires. If connected with telephone or cable networks, added security features can be available when an older person is outside the home. Affordable security systems are now available for visually impaired individuals that feature voice warnings when specific doors to the residence are opened. Given the needs and concerns of older adults, types of technology that enhance feelings of security would be more likely to gain acceptance. Future scenarios project comprehensive home automation with interconnected kitchen appliances, audio and video electronics, and other systems like heating or laundry. One area of need identified in the literature is lighting (Boyce, 2003); individualized smart home technology can be utilized to improve lighting and to adapt it to the changing needs of an aging user.

Smart house technology typically is developed for high-end or special needs homes and some of these technologies filter down into existing and mid-level homes. Smart house features are often built into stand-alone appliances. A key problem is rewiring and networking of existing homes, which can be prohibitively expensive. Wireless alternatives can create considerable cost savings. Many smart house features still lend themselves better to newly constructed or remodeled independent living facilities. Another key issue is that for older persons many smart home applications are only useful when technology is combined with meaningful service arrangement (Dewsbury, 2003).

Mobile Computing and Communication. During the past few years, both mobile technologies and handheld devices (PDAs) have seen tremendous technical improvements along with widespread adoption. Following the convergence of computers and communication, PDAs increasingly incorporate mobile communication functionalities, such that ultimately mobile phones and PDAs may become indistinguishable. Like most other communication technologies, they were designed with younger adults or even teenagers as the primary target audience. However, they have tremendous potential to improve the lives of older adults, who are discovering the communication, security, and convenience benefits of mobile devices (Pew & Van Hemel, 2004).

While mobile phones have gained moderate popularity among some older adults, PDAs in their current usage are difficult to use for this group due to the miniaturization of input and display devices. However, with appropriate design and content development they would have great potential to address a number of age-related disadvantages. Notably, diabetes patients could track their insulin levels and medication needs. PDAs can also serve as reminders for a person's medication schedule. They can also record vital signs and transmit them in real time. Medical records and information contained on a PDA could facilitate emergency access if such information is needed. Mobile communication functionality can connect a person with an emergency service.

If modified to be more user friendly for older adults, PDAs could also serve many non-medical needs. For instance, they could help keep track of financial information (bill paying, banking, insurance) and serve as appointment reminders. Also, the Contacts function in a PDA could be used to jog a person's memory for names and other information.

Telemedicine and Aging-in-Place. A particularly promising development for older adults is telemedicine. Remote access to health care is particularly critical in cases of limited mobility. Other benefits of telemedicine include access to specialists and quality care for patients in remote rural areas. The Internet again helps the older user obtain information and access to people and health professionals in a way that has never been possible before. Interactive computer-based education appears to have a beneficial effect on mental stimulation, competencies, skills, and feelings of autonomy in long-term-care residents.

Telemedicine is also critical for the trend toward aging-in-place. Instead of the physician- and clinic-centered approach, the focus is on using technology to enable older persons to remain in their familiar social and physical surroundings. A range of technologies, from the "low-tech" telephone to "high-tech" video conferencing and data transmittal, facilitate attention to the needs of an older person in the home. Although the focus of discussion has been on these high-tech aspects such as remote surgery, even low-tech interventions have great potential especially in medication compliance and prevention. For instance, transmission of glucose levels from patients to physicians leads to significant decreases in risk for diabetics thanks to better monitoring and management of care; similar findings are reported for diet education programs and treatment compliance (Pew & Van Hemel, 2004). Incentives for the use of telemedicine are greater in areas where access to physicians and specialists are limited, and in cases of routine transactions which do not necessarily require the physical presence of the patient.

Adoption of telemedicine has tremendous potential, but realizing it requires considerable training and a shift in attitudes by providers and users of these services. Telemedicine has the potential to improve health services to the home, enhance consumer knowledge, and significantly improve the effectiveness and reach of health promotion campaigns.

Health Promotion. A number of researchers have been developing Internet-based health promotion programs. One lead example is a stage-based smoking cessation system using Prochaska's Transtheoretical Model (Velicer, Prochaska, Fava, Rossi, Redding, Laforge, et al., 2000). This model permits targeting of people at different stages of readiness to change risky behaviors. An expert system collects data including the stage of change, temptations for risky behavior, and suitable processes of change. The system then produces an individualized report, which gives the subject appropriate feedback and recommendations. The model combines the public health approach, which is designed to reach a large number of people at low per-person cost, and the individualized clinical approach, in which small numbers of individuals are treated at fairly high cost. Linking this system to a Web site will permit thousands of users to access it at low incremental cost. Such an approach has the potential to improve health behavior independent of user location. In the future, such a system may be connected with virtual support groups that might give elderly users support from their peers.

Aging and the Digital Divide

The ability to access and manipulate technology has become a requirement for living in the 21st century (McCormack, 2002). Currently, a gap exists between those within the United States and internationally who have the resources to use this technology and those who do not. This gap, known as the "digital divide," is largely determined by age, gender, race, education, and income.

A large percentage of the population, especially the elderly, women, and minorities, is not in a position to fully take advantage of this information. Globally, developing countries are struggling to keep pace or catch up to technologically advanced countries; age-related disadvantages are amplified in these developing countries.

Aging and the Technology Gap in the United States. Older populations do not have the access and the education needed to bridge the technology gap. Access for the aged is determined by income, experience, attitude, health, and infrastructure. Gender, culture, and race also affect the type and level of use. America's elderly are characterized by growth and diversity. The projected growth in the older (60+) population is expected to increase steadily. After 2010 the population of the oldest old (75+) will increase exponentially, according to the U.S. Census Bureau. As baby boomers reach retirement age, they are potentially the fastest-growing segment of technology users. This group is diverse in terms of age, gender, race, and ethnicity.

Income. For a major part of the older adult population, retirement reduces the level of disposable income. With limited resources available, technology purchases may seem superfluous to many. Unlike the younger generation, they are unfamiliar with what the new technologies have to offer, and are often driven by fear of learning a new system.

Gender. Until recently, white, educated, upper-income men in their 30s represented the typical Internet user, while women were reluctant to use computer technology. Traditionally most of the hardware and software was designed by and for men. Although women now have an equal presence on the Web to men (according to www.digitaldivide.gov), and Web sites targeting women are increasing, most older women are still on the "other side" of the digital divide. Some Web sites such as the National Center on Woman & Aging, AARP, and the Center for Aging Services Technologies, focus on the needs of older women.

Culture: Immigrants and Minorities. Among minority groups within the United States, the digital divide can be attributed to a lack of education (knowledge about how to use technology and what it has to offer), design (most Web sites are designed by whites), and access (Davis, 2001). Access is a significant barrier to equal integration of computer use; home access of school-age children is 41% among Blacks and Hispanics compared with 77% among whites, according to the U.S. Department of Education. These figures illustrate the inequality of the "techno haves and have-nots" (Davis, 2001).

These issues are magnified for older minority populations. Economic, political, and social ramifications for minorities who are not on the information superhighway are significant. They are cut off from information, entertainment, and employment possibilities. If recent immigrants lack English language skills, they are even more disconnected from online information on health, economics, and entertainment.

International Digital Divide. The biggest percentage of aging population growth during the next 50 years will be in developing countries. Older females will outnumber males almost 2 to 1 internationally. The female advantage of life expectancy is a global phenomenon, according to the U.S. Census Bureau.

Access to information varies widely across the globe. Most developed countries have a reasonable level of Internet penetration. Some, such as Scandinavia and the Netherlands, may be further along than the United States in terms of creating equitable access, while others, particularly in Southern Europe, have low adoption levels in private homes. Within these countries, demographic differences in access and use are similar to the United States, although the impact of those differences may be more pronounced.

For developing countries, the gap between the information haves and have-nots is far wider. Although literacy among children is widespread today, most elderly received little or no education. This is especially true of older women and the elderly in rural areas in many countries. Major problems arise from cultural factors and lack of education, financial resources, and technology infrastructure.

Access to technology in developing countries is sparse, mainly limited to the corporate and academic sector. For most of the population, the cost of access is prohibitive. Currently, the gulf between countries equipped with state-of-the-art high-bandwidth technology and nations with a minimal capacity for any kind of access is growing or languid at best. However, creative solutions utilizing limited resources have the potential to alleviate some of the existing deficiencies.

Solutions. Even though utilizing the Internet will not take care of the basic needs of the elderly, it can help meet them. Improved communication and information can help in areas such as communication, economics, safety, and health care. For instance, telemedicine can make medical information quickly available to remote regions. Often experts live hundreds or thousands of miles away and getting information quickly is essential. Interventions that require a low level of technology have great potential, e.g. in medication compliance and prevention (Pew & Van Hemel, 2004).

The benefits for the older generation of users are numerous. To older adults who are physically and socially isolated, e-mail offers an opportunity for continuous interaction with friends and loved ones. Socioemotional selectivity theory (Nussbaum, Pecchioni, Robinson, & Thompson, 2000) supports the importance of frequent contact with those closest to us. Online chatrooms available through Web sites specifically designed for seniors (such as www.seniornet.org,) offer the opportunity to develop new friendships and sometimes even romantic relationships. Internet classes and information on health, travel, and culture help stimulate mental processes and encourage independence (see for example AARP at www.aarp.com, ElderWeb at www.elderweb.com, or Center for Aging Services Technologies at www.agingtech.org). Familiarity with the Internet also enhances intergenerational relationships as older users learn the (technology) language of the younger computer-literate generation (Mundorf, Brownell, & Bryant, 1997).

Convergence. As information technologies converge, Internet access through other appliances, especially television, will become more feasible. In Europe and Asia, satellite-based technologies are available, and digital cable is designed for interactive applications. Digital convergence will include access to the Internet from a number of inexpensive, easy-to-use devices, notably the television.

Assessing and tailoring the technology for the older population is the key. Today, more people in the world own a television than even a telephone. TV offers a viable solution since it is an essential component in the lives of many elderly. Interactive television is now being looked at as the new wave of future technology (Schmidt, 2001), since TV is user friendly, inexpensive, and requires little maintenance or expertise.

Inexpensive wireless Web access devices are being developed and are already widely used in Japan, which will also have greater appeal to diverse populations. Wireless technology will enable older people in developing countries without telephone infrastructure to connect to family and friends who live in geographically varied locations.

Older adults will adopt technologies when advantages are offered and communicated. Older consumers tend to be more reluctant to use emerging technologies than are their younger counterparts. This tendency is somewhat confounded by gender effects, as men across age groups tend to feel more comfortable with most technologies than do women. Many age differences appear to be the result of perceptions about challenges which older adults face rather being insurmountable hurdles in the use of communication technologies. Developing attractive, user-friendly applications and inexpensive technological solutions will help bring about change for the better. Older adults who are most likely to adopt new communication technologies include those with higher income, those living in multi-unit dwellings, and those who use print media.

Communication technologies offer important advantages for older adults. Although familiarity, acceptance, and adoption of new communication technologies may not be as high among older as in younger adults today, they will increase as older adults have a chance to learn more about the potential for these technologies to improve the quality of their lives. Efforts should be directed toward providing training and access for older adults to communication technologies so that discretionary income and education do not limit their opportunities.

NORBERT MUNDORF
JOANNE MUNDORF
WINIFRED BROWNELL

See also
Health Information Through Telecommunication

References

Boyce, P. R. (2003). Lighting for the elderly. *Technology and Disability, 15*, 165–181.

Coughlin, J. F. (2001). Technology and the future of aging. *Journal of Rehabilitation Research and Development, 38*, S40–S42.

Dewsbury, G., Clarke, K., Rouncefield, M., Sommerville, I., Taylor, B., & Edge, M. (2003). Designing acceptable 'smart' home technology to support people in the home. *Technology and Disability, 15*, 191–199.

Davis, A. (2001). Bridging the digital divide: Leading the disenfranchised into the information age. In T. Silvia (Ed.), *Global news: Perspectives on the information age* (2nd ed.). Iowa State University Press.

Pew, R. W., & Van Hemel, S. B. (2004). *Technology for adaptive aging*. Board on Behavioral, Cognitive, and Sensory Sciences and Education (BCSSE).

Huffman, G. B. (1998). Long-distance medicine by way of telecommunications. *American Family Physician, (February)*, 537–538.

Lee, W. (2004). Web helps make hospital stay more tolerable. *The Boston Globe, July 26, 2004*, E6.

McCormack, D. (2002). *Web 2.0: The future of the internet and technology economy*. Aspatore.

Mundorf, N., Brownell, W., & Bryant, J. (1997). Information technology and the elderly. In N. Al-Deen, *Cross-cultural communication and aging in the United States* (pp. 43–62). Hillsdale, NJ: Erlbaum.

Mundorf, N., & Laird, K. (2002). Social and psychological effects of information technologies and other interactive media. In J. Bryant & D. Zillmann (Eds.), *Media effects: Advances in theory and research* (pp. 583–602). Mahwah, NJ: Lawrence Erlbaum Associates.

Nussbaum, J. F., Pecchioni, L. L., Robinson, J. D., & Thompson, T. L. (2000). *Communication and aging* (2nd ed.). Mahwah, NJ: Lawrence Erlbaum.

Schmidt, R. (2001). Murdoch reaches for the sky. *Brill's Content*, 74–79.

Velicer, W. F., Prochaska, J. O., Fava, J. L., Rossi, J. S., Redding, C. S., Laforge, R. G., & Robbins, M. L. (2000). Using the transtheoretical model for population based approaches to health promotion and disease prevention. *Homeostasis in Health and Disease, 40*(5), 174–195.

Willems, C. G. (2003). Smart homes. *Technology and Disability, 15*, 163–164.

COMMUNITY NEEDS ASSESSMENT

Assessing the individual needs of older persons and developing community resource profiles was an important activity during the 1970s and early 1980s. These activities became much less influential, as witnessed by the decreased number of relevant citations in *AgeLine*, during the 1980s. However, they enjoyed a relative rediscovery in the early 1990s because of their use in resource allocation decisions (Lagergren, 1994; Young, 1993); an increased number of AgeLine citations documented this reestablished importance. During the latter half of the 1990s, the devolution of resource allocation decisions to smaller, more local geographic units, generally tied to health reforms, has firmly entrenched both *individual needs assessments* and *community resource profiles* among administrative planners in these new planning units. This has had the effect of seeing community needs assessments used more broadly, in terms of age groups, rather than being dominated by the needs of older persons. At the same time, however, the number of AgeLine citations has markedly increased, and the studies cited tend to be either based on the smaller geographic units or on more specialized subpopulations, such as hospital dischargees, and those entering residential long-term care or suffering from dementia (McWalter, Toner, McWalter, Eastwood, Marshal, Turvey, et al., 1998; Reynolds, Thornicroft, Abas, Woods, Hoe, Leese, & Orrell, 2000). Within a health reform context, one relatively recent title sums up the former group: *Introduction of Needs-Based Allocation of Resources to Saskatchewan District Health Boards for 1994–95* (Saskatchewan Health, 1994). It is particularly notable that the increased use of needs assessments in the United Kingdom has far out-stripped that in other countries. In part, this is the result of needs assessments being mandated by the NHS and *Community Care Act* of 1990.

Issues in Community Needs Assessment

Like the field of gerontology, the technology of individual assessment has become multidimensional and multidisciplinary. However, several major issues continue to plague designers and users of this technology. These issues include lack of unanimity about the definition of needs—or perhaps more importantly of unmet needs—and lack of specificity about the difference between individual needs assessments and community resource profiles. There is a continuing lack of agreement on the dimensions and, hence, the disciplines to be involved in these assessments. Finally, lack of clarity about the appropriate uses for, or applications of, assessments and profiles continues, despite the increased use of these techniques. A recent literature review by Billings and Cowley (1995) ably summarizes these issues. The authors indicate that much of the history of community needs assessments derive from epidemiology, sociology, and more recently from health economics. This is certainly true of community profiles; however, they have neglected the importance of developmental psychology in individual needs assessments. They have made an important contribution to this literature by calling particular attention to the reliability and validity of the data and data sources used in community needs assessments.

One of the difficulties encountered in searching for consensus on the *definition of needs* is that "needs" means different things to different people. Dill (1993) and Calsyn and colleagues place the definitional issue in a systems context. However, much of the work on individual needs assessment within gerontology has been derived from the tradition of developmental psychology. Tobin (1965) synthesized the major elements of this approach. Within this tradition, the tautology of equating needs with service use is avoided; that is, if the services of community resources are used, then one can argue that need no longer exists. Simultaneously, this approach recognizes explicitly that use can occur only within the context of community resources.

The conceptualization of community resource profiles is less well developed. The unit of analysis for community resource profiles must be the community or similar geographic area or cultural group. It is inappropriate to infer the needs of a community from either the characteristics of its resources or the use of resources within the community. It is equally inappropriate to infer the community resource profile as the aggregation of the individual needs of older residents in that community. Resources exist at the aggregate community level, whereas needs exist at an individual level. Use is, at best, a proxy for the relationship between these 2 concepts. However, to substitute measures of use for either individual needs assessments or community resource profiles means ignoring both individual and structural dimensions of use.

Typically, the dimensions of individual needs assessment include: physical health status or functioning, mental health status or functioning, and the basic and instrumental activities of daily living (ADLs and IADLs). Also generally included are *psychosocial functioning* (e.g., general well-being, morale, social networks, loneliness), cultural needs (e.g., racial, ethnic, or religious), housing (or shelter) needs, household maintenance capability, and economic functioning or status. To complete the dimensions of individual needs, one should include the *availability* of and *accessibility* to services from both *formal resources* and *informal support* networks. Although community resource profiles include these same dimensions, they are structured to indicate the degree to which community resources are capable of responding to the needs of individuals. Given the range of dimensions, it is difficult to identify any human service-related profession or discipline that would not be involved appropriately in a comprehensive needs assessment or community resource profile.

A final area of confusion stems from incomplete specification of the goals of needs assessments and resource profiles. For example, assessments may be used to expand our knowledge about the aging process, to determine whether needs are hierarchical, to form the basis of planning processes, or to allocate or redistribute human and fiscal resources. It is, therefore, essential to specify adequately the goals of each needs assessment and community resource profile activity to determine the most appropriate methodology, measurement technique, and data collection. It is not only possible but desirable for any given needs assessment or community profile to use more than 1 methodology in order to be comprehensive and satisfy all the goals specified. The steps in the iterative process of needs analysis, according to McKillip (1987), include: identifying users and uses, describing both the target population and the service environment, identifying needs through describing both problems and solutions, evaluating the primacy of needs, and communicating the results.

Methodological Approaches

Within the field of gerontology, individual needs assessments and *community resource profiles* have typically employed 7 different methodologies or approaches. Warheit, Bell, and Schwab (1974) have provided the most concise summary of these methods, to date. The 7 approaches are based on: epidemiology, social statistics or social indicators, surveys, community forums, key informants, economics, and consumer polls. All of the current assessment, screening, and data collection tools and techniques have been derived from 1 or some combination of these methods or approaches.

All of these methods have been employed to measure or assess the needs of older individuals and to construct community resource profiles. Each method has its own strengths and weaknesses, and no single method is appropriate in all situations. A review of research instruments available to gerontologists in assessing needs and developing community profiles has been reported by this author elsewhere (Havens, 1984).

BETTY HAVENS

References

Billings, J. R., & Cowley, S. (1995). Approaches to community needs assessment: A literature review. *Journal of Advanced Nursing, 22*(4), 721–730.

Dill, A. (1993). Defining needs, defining systems: A critical analysis. *Gerontologist, 33*, 453–460.

Havens, B. (1984). Individual needs and community resources. In D. J. Mangen & W. A. Peterson (Eds.), *Research instruments in social gerontology, volume 3: Health, program evaluation and demography* (pp. 137–174). Minneapolis: University of Minnesota Press.

Lagergren, M. (1994). Allocation of care and services in an area-based system for long-term care of elderly and disabled people. *Ageing and Society, 14*, 357–381.

McKillip, J. (1987). *Needs analysis: Tools for the human services and education*. Newbury Park, CA: Sage Publications.

NHS and Community Care Act 1990. (1990). Chapter 19. London: HMSO.

Reynolds, T., Thornicroft, G., Abas, M., Woods, B., Hoe, J., Leese, M., & Orrell, M. (2000). Camberwell Assessment of Need for the Elderly (CANE). *British Journal of Psychiatry*, 176, 444–452.

Saskatchewan Health. (1994). *Introduction of needs-based allocation of resources to Saskatchewan District Health Boards for 1994–95*. Regina, SK: Saskatchewan Health.

Tobin, S. S. (1965). Basic needs of all older people. *Planning welfare services for older people* (pp. 47–52). Washington, DC: U.S. Department of Health, Education, and Welfare.

Warheit, G. J., Bell, R. A., & Schwab, J. J. (1974). *Planning for change: Needs assessment approaches*. Gainesville, FL: University of Florida.

Young, J. J. (1993). Resource allocation to the aged according to greatest social need. *Journal of Aging and Social Policy, 5*, 7–29.

COMPETENCE

Behavioral competence in adulthood has been studied from multiple perspectives, including functional competence, everyday competence, socio-emotional competence, and legal competence. *Functional competence* has received the most attention, given that the study of competence originated in the health and clinical domains. Functional competence is concerned with the individual's ability to care for himself or herself and to engage in activities required for independent living (Fillenbaum, 1987; Morris, Fries, Steel, et al., 1997). The study of everyday *cognitive competence* is concerned with the application of cognitive abilities and skills to the solution of problems experienced in daily life (Allaire & Marsiske, 2002; Diehl & Willis, 2003; Schaie & Willis, 1999; Sternberg & Grigorenko, 2000). *Socio-emotional competence* focuses on the role of the context, examining cognitive, socio-emotional, and cultural factors that influence adaptation to specific contexts (Berg & Klaczynski, 2002; Blanchard-Fields & Chen, 1996; Labouvie-Vief, 2003). Recently both everyday and socio-emotional approaches to competence have studied collaborative cognition in which competency represents the joint decision making of more than one individual, such as a couple (Meegan & Berg, 2002; Strough & Margrett, 2002). In addition, both approaches have studied domain-specific areas of competence, such as *financial competence* (Chen & Sun, 2003), health decision making (Johnson & Drungle, 2000; Meyer, Russo & Talbot, 1995; Willis, Dolan, & Bertrand, 1998; Zwahr, Park, & Shifren, 1999), and driving competence (Willis, 2000). *Legal competence* has focused largely on judgment regarding the adult's capacity or incapacity to care for himself or to manage his/her property, and the assignment of guardian or conservator responsibilities (Grisso, 1994; Marson, Chatterjee, Ingram, & Harrell, 1996).

Since competence has been studied by diverse disciplines, methods of *assessment of competence* have varied, as have the definitions of competence (Schaie, Willis, & Boron, in press). Assessment of functional competence has typically relied on self- or proxy ratings of performance (Bertrand & Willis, 1999; Lawton & Brody, 1969). Several "objective" measures of competence have been developed within the everyday competence approach (Allaire & Marsiske, 2002; Diehl, Marsiske, Horgas, Rosenbert, Saczynski, & Willis, 2005; Marsiske & Willis, 1995; Willis, 1996). Within the socio-emotional or adaptation perspective, the dominant approach to assessment has been for adults to rate the efficacy of different coping strategies for hypothetical or personal problems in daily life (Berg, Strough, Calderone, Sansone, & Weir, 1998). In the legal domain, which relies solely on professional judgment to assess competence, competence is not considered an "all-or-nothing" proposition but domain-specific areas of competence are considered (Sabatino, 1996).

The various approaches to the study of competence share important commonalities in the conception of the phenomena, which contribute to a more complete understanding of competence in adulthood (Baltes, Maas, Wilms, Borchelt, & Little, 1999; Berg, et al., 1998; Schaie & Willis, 1999). First, *competence as defined* in each perspective represents the potential or capacity of the individual to perform a task, not the actual daily behavior of the individual. It is important to differentiate between competence and the behaviors that the adult regularly performs in daily life. For example, functional assessment has traditionally addressed the question "Can the individual perform an activity?", rather than "Does the individual perform the activity on a regular basis?" Similarly, in legal judgments the focus recently has been on whether the individual is capable of making sound financial decisions, not whether the individual behaves in a manner considered financially astute by others (Grisso, 1994; Sabatino, 1996).

Second, each approach is concerned with the capacity to carry out significant real-world activities involved in daily living. The question arises, then: what are considered the critical activities for functioning in the real world? Capacity to live independently within one's society has been the criterion used most frequently in functional and legal approaches (Fillenbaum, 1987). Both of these approaches have emphasized 2 broad activity domains associated with independent living: the ability to care for oneself (e.g., bathing, toileting), and the ability to manage one's affairs. Within the study of functional competence, care of oneself is represented by the *activities of daily living* (ADLs) (Morris, et al., 1997) and management of one's affairs by *instrumental activities of daily living* (IADLs)

(Lawton & Brody, 1969). The legal perspective distinguishes between legal proceedings regarding care of the person (guardianship), and those related to property (conservatorship) (Smyer, Schaie, & Kapp, 1996). From a socio-emotional approach to competence, a broader range of real-world tasks would be included, since the focus is on adaptation or fit between the individual and that person's environment (Berg & Klaczynski, 2002).

Given the emphasis on real-world activities and the context, the specific activities representing competence will vary both culturally and developmentally. Different activities are considered necessary for independent living or adaptation within various cultures or within subgroups in a given society (Berg & Klaczynski, 1996; Blanchard-Fields & Chen, 1996; Diehl & Willis, 2003). Likewise, strategies that are effective in one context may be less effective in another context (Berg, et al., 1998). Although a contextual perspective is central to most approaches in the study of competence, there has been relatively little research on cultural or ethnic differences in activities representative of competence (Whitfield & Wiggins, 2003). From a developmental perspective, the specific activities associated with competence will vary with age and level of development (Labouvie-Vief, 2003; Schaie & Willis, 2000; Thornton & Dumke, 2005). Developmental changes in competence may be related to shifts in cognitive ability (Schaie & Willis, 1999; Walsh & Hershey, 1993) or to socio-emotional maturity (Watson & Blanchard-Fields, 1998).

Third, each approach to competence acknowledges that there are multiple factors associated with competence, including cognitive ability, emotions, social-cultural perspective, and motivation (Klaczynski, 2000; Labouvie-Vief, 2003). In research on functional competence, cognition has been viewed as one of the major contributors to adequate functioning, along with physical health and social support (Allaire & Willis, in press). The cognitive demands of everyday activities are a major focus of applied cognitive aging research. Solving problems related to IADL-type activities (e.g., comprehending a prescription drug label, managing finances) involves multiple mental abilities including abstract reasoning, verbal ability, and memory (Allaire & Marsiske, 2002; Willis, 1996). A socio-emotional perspective to competence has found that individuals draw on their abilities to regulate emotions, utilize the social context to facilitate problem solving, and draw on broader styles of coping with life stressors (Blanchard-Fields, Chen, & Norris, 1997).

Finally, each perspective recognizes that competence and perception of competence does not reside solely in the individual (Staudinger & Baltes, 1996). A person's level of competence represents the congruence between that individual's knowledge and skills and the demands of the environment (Diehl & Willis, 2003). Recent research on *collaborative cognition* indicates that problem solving with other individuals may enhance or reduce the level of competence demonstrated (Margrett & Willis, in press; Meegan & Berg, 2002; Saczynski, Margrett, & Willis, 2004). In an environment that is both physically and socially supportive, even an individual with some deficiencies may function adequately. Conversely, a well-functioning individual may have difficulty in a resource-deprived environment.

SHERRY L. WILLIS

References

Allaire, J. C., & Marsiske, M. (2002). Well- and ill-defined measures of everyday cognition: Relationship to older adults' intellectual ability and functional status. *Psychology and Aging*, *17(1)*, 101–115.

Allaire, J., & Willis, S. L. Everyday activities as a predictor of cognitive and mortality. *Aging, Neuropsychology and Cognition* (in press).

Baltes, M. M., Maas, I., Wilms, H.-U., Borchelt, M., & Little, T. D. (1999). Everyday competence in old and very old age: Theoretical considerations and empirical findings. In P. B. Baltes & K. U. Mayer (Eds.), *The Berlin Aging Study: Aging from 70 to 100* (pp. 384–402). New York: Cambridge University Press.

Berg, C. A., & Klaczynksi, P. (1996). Practical intelligence and problem solving: Searching for perspectives. In F. Blanchard-Fields & T. M. Hess (Eds.), *Perspectives on cognition in adulthood and aging* (pp. 323–357). New York: McGraw-Hill.

Berg, C. A., Strough, J., Calderone, K. S., Sansone, C., & Weir, C. (1998). The role of problem definitions in understanding age and context effects on strategies for solving everyday problems. *Psychology and Aging*, *13*, 29–44.

Bertrand, R. M., & Willis, S. L. (1999). Everyday problem solving in Alzheimer's patients: A comparison of subjective and objective assessments. *Aging and Mental Health*, *3*, 281–293.

Blanchard-Fields, F., & Chen, Y. (1996). Adaptive cognition and aging. *American Behavioral Scientist*, *39*(3), 231–248.

Blanchard-Fields, F., Chen, Y., & Norris, L. (1997). Everyday problem solving across the life span: Influence of domain specificity and cognitive appraisal. *Psychology and Aging*, *12*, 684–693.

Chen, Y., & Sun, Y. (2003). Age differences in financial decision-making: Using simple heuristics. *Educational Gerontology*, *29*, 627–635.

Diehl, M., Marsiske, M., Horgas, A. L., Rosenbert, A., Saczynski, J., Willis, S. L. (2005). The revised observed tasks of daily living: A performance-based assessment of everyday problem solving in older adults. *Journal of Applied Gerontology*, *24*, 211–230.

Diehl, M., & Willis, S. L. (2003). Everyday competence and everyday problem solving in aging adults: The role of physical and social context. In H. W. Wahl, R. Scheidt, & P. Windley (Eds.), *Annual review of gerontology and geriatrics* (Vol. 23, pp. 130–166). New York: Springer Publishing.

Fillenbaum, G. G. (1987). Multidimensional functional assessment. In G. L. Maddox (Ed.), *The encyclopedia of aging* (pp. 460–464). New York: Springer Publishing.

Grisso, T. (1994). Clinical assessment for legal competency of older adults. In M. Storandt & G. R. Vanden Bos (Eds.), *Neuropsychological assessment of dementia and depression in older adults: A clinician's guide* (pp. 119–139). Washington, DC: American Psychological Association.

Johnson, M. M. S., & Drungle, S. C. (2000). Purchasing over-the-counter medications: The influence of age and familiarity. *Experimental Aging Research*, *26*, 245–261.

Klaczynski, P. A. (2000). Motivated scientific reasoning biases, epistemological beliefs, and theory polarization: A two-process approach to adolescent cognition. *Child Development*, *71*, 1347–1366.

Labouvie-Vief, G. (2003). Dynamic Integration: Affect, cognition, and the self in adulthood. *Current Directions in Psychological Science*, *12*, 201–206.

Lawton, M. P., & Brody, E. M. (1969). Assessment of older people: Self-maintaining and instrumental activities of daily living. *Gerontologist*, *9*, 179–185.

Margrett, J. A., & Willis, S. L. (in press). In-home cognitive training with older married couples: Individual versus Collaborative Learning. *Aging, Neuropsychology and Cognition.*

Marsiske, M., & Willis, S. L. (1995). Dimensionality of everyday problem solving in older adults. *Psychology and Aging*, *10*, 269–283.

Marson, D., Chatterjee A., Ingram K., & Harrell, L. (1996). Toward a neurologic model of competency: Cognitive predictors of capacity to consent in Alzheimer's disease using three different legal standards. *Neurology*, *46*, 666–672.

Meegan, S. P., & Berg, C. A. (2002). Contexts, functions, forms, and processes of collaborative everyday problem solving in older adulthood. *International Journal of Behavioral Development*, *26*, 6–15.

Meyer, B. J. F., Russo, C., & Talbot, A. (1995). Discourse comprehension and problem solving: Decisions about the treatment of breast cancer by women across the life span. *Psychology and Aging*, *10*, 84–103.

Morris, J. N., Fries, B. E., Steel, K., et al. (1997). Comprehensive clinical assessment in community setting: Applicability of the MDS-HC. *Journal of the American Geriatrics Society*, *45*, 1017–1024.

Sabatino, C. P. (1996). Competency: Refining our legal fictions. In M. Smyer, K. W. Schaie, & M. Kapp (Eds.), *Older adults' decision-making and the law* (pp. 1–28). New York: Springer Publishing.

Saczynski, J. S., Margrett, J. M., & Willis, S. L. (2004). Older adults' strategic behavior: Effects of individual versus collaborative cognitive training. *Educational Gerontology*, *30*, 587–610.

Schaie, K. W., & Willis, S. L. (1999). Theories of everyday competence and aging. In V. L. Bengtson & K. W. Schaie (Eds.), *Handbook of theories of aging* (pp. 174–195). New York: Springer Publishing.

Schaie, K. W., & Willis, S. L. (2000). A stage theory model of adult cognitive development revisited. In B. Rubinstein, M. Moss, & M. Kleban (Eds.), *The many dimensions of aging: Essays in honor of M. Powell Lawton* (pp. 173–191). New York: Springer Publishing.

Schaie, K. W., Willis, S. L., & Boron, J. (2005). Everyday competence. In M. Johnson (Ed), *The Cambridge handbook of age and ageing*. London: Cambridge University Press.

Smyer, M., Schaie, K. W., & Kapp, M. (Eds.). (1996). *Older adults' decision-making and the law*. New York: Springer Publishing.

Staudinger, U. M., & Baltes, P. B. (1996). Interactive minds: A facilitative setting for wisdom-related performance? *Journal of Personality and Social Psychology*, *71*(4), 746–762.

Sternberg, R. J., & Grigorenko, E. L. (2000). Practical intelligence and its development. In R. Bar-Oh, & J. D. A. Parker (Eds.), *The handbook of emotional intelligence: Theory, development, assessment, and application at home, school, and in the workplace* (pp. 215–243). San Francisco: Jossey-Bass/Pfeiffer.

Strough, J., & Margrett, J. (2002). Overview of the special section on collaborative cognition in later adulthood. *International Journal of Behavioral Development*, *26*, 2–5.

Thornton, W. J. L., & Dumke, H. A. (2005). Age differences in everyday problem-solving and decision-making effectiveness: A meta-analytic review. *Psychology and Aging*, *20*, 85–99.

Walsh, D. A., & Hershey, D. A. (1993). Mental models and the maintenance of complex problem solving skills into old age. In J. Cerella & W. Hoyer (Eds.), *Adult information processing: Limits on loss* (pp. 553–584). New York: Academic Press.

Watson, T. L., & Blanchard-Fields, F. (1998). Thinking with your head and your heart: Age differences in everyday problem-solving strategy preferences. *Aging, Neuropsychology, and Cognition*, *5*, 225–240.

Whitfield, K. E., & Wiggins, S. (2003). The influence of social support and health on everyday problem solving in adult African Americans. *Experimental Aging Research*, *29*, 1–13.

Willis, S. L. (1996). Everyday problem solving. In J. E. Birren & K. W. Schaie (Eds.), *Handbook of the psychology of aging* (4th ed., pp. 287–307). San Diego: Academic Press.

Willis, S. L. (2000). Driving competence: The Person x Environment Fit. In K. W. Schaie & M. Pietrucha (Eds.), *Mobility and transportation in the elderly* (pp. 269–278). New York: Springer Publishing.

Willis, S. W., Dolan, M. M., & Bertrand, R. M. (1998). Problem solving on health-related tasks of daily living. In D. C. Park, R. W. Morrell, & K. Shifren (Eds.), *Processing of medical information in aging patients: Cognitive and human factors perspective* (pp. 199–218). New York: Lawrence Erlbaum.

Zwahr, M. D., Park, D. C., & Shifren, K. (1999). Judgments about estrogen replacement therapy: The role of age, cognitive abilities, and beliefs. *Psychology and Aging*, *14*, 179–191.

COMPLEMENTARY AND ALTERNATIVE MEDICINE

There are several ways to define complementary and alternative medicine (CAM). The term itself implies that any practice that complements or is seen as an alternative to "typical" medicine would be considered CAM. Although in some countries or cultures certain CAM therapies are considered mainstream (for example in China, where traditional *Chinese medicine* is commonly used in the same hospitals where Western medicine is also practiced), use of descriptive terms such as "unconventional," "traditional," and "Oriental or Eastern" is one way to define CAM because it broadens instead of restricts knowledge. In the United Kingdom and Europe, the term complementary was combined with the term alternative in an attempt to show acceptance of these types of therapies (British Medical Association, 1993).1 In the United States, the most often-used definition of CAM is "those practices neither taught widely in U.S. medical schools nor generally available in U.S. hospitals" (Eisenberg, Kessler, Foster, Norlock, Calkins, & Delbanco, 1993). Whichever definition one uses, the most important step in understanding how to define CAM is that the more it can be done in a nonjudgmental manner, the more it will help those unfamiliar with CAM understand why patients are attracted to and find effectiveness in these therapies, learn how to deal with the increasing use of these therapies by patients, and decide if CAM has anything to offer patients.

There are several reasons why it is necessary to gain knowledge about CAM.

- In most parts of the world, whether East or West, the use of CAM is prevalent (Flaherty, Takahashi, Teoh, Habib, Ito, & Matsushita, 2001), and its use is increasing (Eisenberg, Davis, Ettner, Appel, Wilkey, Van Rompay, et al., 1998).
- The majority of patients who use CAM believe that CAM therapies are effective, and they often do not tell their Western-trained physicians that they are using CAM (Eisenberg, Kessler, Foster, Norlock, Calkins, & Delbanco, 1993; Flaherty, Takahashi, Teoh, Habib, Ito, & Matsushita, 2001; Astin, Pelletier, Marie, & Haskell, 2000; Astin, 1998).
- The majority of physicians do not ask about these therapies (Eisenberg, Kessler, Foster, Norlock, Calkins, & Delbanco, 1993; Flaherty, Takahashi, Teoh, Habib, Ito, & Matsushita, 2001; Astin, Pelletier, Marie, & Haskell, 2000; Astin, 1998).
- Only 30% of U.S. medical schools have required CAM courses, and 21% of schools offer electives in CAM (American Association of Medical Colleges). However, one survey showed that approximately 80% of medical students and 70% of family physicians want training in CAM (National Center for *Homeopathy*, 2000).

It seems counterintuitive that knowledge about CAM pertains to aging, since one would think that as more people live longer, with more illnesses, there would be an increased reliance on Western medicine. However, the treatment of chronic illnesses is one of the compelling reasons patients turn to CAM (Friedrich, 2001). As infectious causes of mortality around the world decline, and as people survive events such as myocardial infarction, stroke, and cancer, chronic illnesses will increase. Furthermore, there have been several reports that use of CAM may be higher in older persons (Flaherty, Takahashi, Teoh, Habib, Ito, & Matsushita, 2001; Astin, Pelletier, Marie, & Haskell, 2000).

Although whole books on specific CAM therapies could be and have been written, the following are some of the most commonly used CAM therapies by older persons. Some have limited Western medicine type evidence and are safe. Others have risks associated with their use.

Herbal therapies have been used for thousands of years in countries around the world. In some countries, such as Germany and Japan, herbs are a part of drug formularies, and they are prescribed and even covered under some insurance plans. In other countries, such as the United States, herbs are available to the public under names such as "natural foods" or "supplements."

As an example of the Western type evidence that exists for herbs, one meta-analysis found the following. "Potentially safe herbs include feverfew, garlic, ginkgo, Asian ginseng, saw palmetto, St. John's wort, and valerian. Clinical trials have been used to evaluate *feverfew* for migraine prevention and rheumatoid arthritis; *garlic* for hypertension, hyperlipidemia, and infections; *ginkgo* for circulatory disturbances and dementia; *ginseng* for fatigue and cancer prevention; and *saw palmetto* for benign prostatic hyperplasia. Also studied in formal trials have been *St. John's wort* for depression, and *valerian* for insomnia. The clinical trial results are suggestive of efficacy of some herbal therapies for some conditions." It was also noted in this meta-analysis that some herbs "have been identified as unsafe, including borage, calamus, coltsfoot, comfrey, life root, sassafras, chaparral, germander, licorice, and *ma huang*" (Klepser & Klepser, 1999). Safety issues for herbs also means being aware that some herbs may have unsafe amounts of ingredients such as heavy metals. One study of *ayurvedic herbal medicine* products (HMPs) available in South Asian grocery stores in Boston revealed that 14 of 70 HMPs contained the heavy metals lead, mercury, and/or arsenic, each of which could result in heavy metal intakes above published regulatory standards (Saper, Kales, Paquin, Burns, Eisenberg, Davis, & Phillips, 2004).

Since so many herbs exists, it is recommended that practitioners use a source such as the *German Commission E*, a regulatory body that evaluates the safety and efficacy of herbs on the basis of clinical trials, cases, and other scientific literature, and has established indications and dosage recommendations for many herbal therapies (Blumenthal, Busse, Goldberg, et al., 1998). Another useful tool is the Physician Desk Reference (PDR) for herbal medicines (Gruenwald, Brendler, Jaenicke, et al., 2000).

Massage comes in many forms and styles, but is intended to induce relaxation and reduce stress by stimulating the skin, muscles, and nervous system. Some data exist for certain populations among older persons. For example, several studies have found favorable results in institutionalized persons and persons with dementia in reducing anxiety, agitation, and behavioral problems (Fraser & Kerr, 1993; Simington & Laing, 1993; Remington, 2002; Kilstoff & Chenoweth, 1998). One caution is that not all people are comfortable with touch or massage as a form of therapy. More evidence will be needed to clearly define the role of this CAM therapy.

Acupuncture has been used for millennia. It is the technique of using needles (or pressure in *acupressure*) to manipulate energy pathways (called meridians) in the body in order to maintain or regain balance of a person's "qi" (pronounced "chee"). *Qi* has 2 essential qualities: *yin and yang* (a basic Chinese concept of interdependence and relationship of opposites). Qi has been translated to mean "living force" or "vital energy," and the proper flow of qi along energy channels is essential for health. When flow is out of balance, deficient, blocked, excessive, or does not flow smoothly, illness occurs. Although most randomized trials evaluating the effectiveness of acupuncture on various medical conditions and illnesses have not shown the accepted "statistical significant difference," enough favorable studies exist that these techniques warrant further scientific inquiry. For example, although in recent years 2 meta-analyses and 2 Cochrane Database reviews have failed to support that acupuncture is better than control treatments for chronic pain, recurrent headache, acute and chronic back pain, and smoking cessation (Ezzo, Berman, Hadhazy, Jadad, Lao, & Singh,

2000; Melchart, Linde, Fischer, White, Allais, Vickers, et al., 1999; van Tulder, Cherkin, Berman, Lao, & Koes, 1999; White & Rampes, 2003) 1 meta-analysis of 9 studies found clinical improvement for back pain (Ernst & White, 1998).

The term *chiropractic* means "hands-on healing" and the practice focuses on the relationship between structure (primarily the spine) and function (as coordinated by the nervous system), and how that relationship affects the preservation and restoration of health. This discipline, through the use of the chiropractic adjustment (also referred to as "*spinal manipulative therapy*") emphasizes the inherent recuperative powers of the body to heal itself without the use of drugs and surgery (Killinger, 2004). More than 30% of patients seeking care for low-back pain use chiropractic services. Two large randomized trials of spinal manipulation for low-back pain have shown it to have similar results to typical medical care (Hurwitz, Morgenstern, Harber, Kominski, Belin, Yu, & Adams; University of California-Los Angeles, 2002) and physical therapy (Cherkin, Deyo, Battie, Street, & Barlow, 1998).

Spirituality, religion, and prayer in all it forms can be considered a form of CAM. Health care practitioners need to be aware of the interplay these "forces" have in a patient's care, because according to one study 77% of patients felt that their doctors should consider their spiritual needs, and 68% said they would like their doctors to pray with them (King & Bushwick, 1994). Although one cannot prove "cause and effect," evidence exists that religious persons have better outcomes than nonreligious (Koenig, Hays, Larson, George, Cohen, McCullough, et al., 1999; Helm, Hays, Flint, Koenig, & Blazer, 2000).

Tai-chi is a technique that employs controlled breathing with purposeful movements to regulate body physiology and induce a state of equilibrium. The benefits of tai-chi in community-dwelling older adults include enhanced balance and reduced risk of falls (Wolf, Barnhart, Kutner, McNeely, Coogler, & Xu, 1996), but these benefits were not seen in a frail congregate-living population (Wolf, Sattin, Kutner, O'Grady, Greenspan, & Gregor, 2003).

Health care practitioners may need to caution patients about the risks of certain CAM therapies. Cellular therapy attempts to regenerate human tissue and revitalize the body by injecting mammalian cells or cell extracts into human recipients.

Apitherapy is a treatment using *bee venom injections*. *Chelation therapy* is intended to bind lead, iron, copper, and calcium to stabilize and induce regression of atherosclerotic plaque; it has not been supported by the medical literature, and may be harmful by inducing anemia, nausea, and renal dysfunction. (Gammack & Morley, 2004).

The list and descriptions of CAM therapies goes on and on. This text does not have room to discuss areas such as aromatherapy, homeopathy, hypnosis, imagery, music therapy, pet therapy, magnet therapy, light therapy, Snoezelen therapy, hormonal therapy, and reflexology. However, the following recommendations can be made (Flaherty & Takahashi, 2004). Inquiry into use of any type of CAM needs to be a part of the patient interview. Use of CAM is prevalent, and predictors of use among older persons are not that predictable (Flaherty, Takahashi, Teoh, Habib, Ito, & Matsushita, 2001; Astin, Pelletier, Marie, & Haskell, 2000), so that all older patients, of all backgrounds, in all countries, need to be asked about CAM. At the same time, patients need to tell their practitioners, whether the practitioners are CAM practitioners or practitioners of conventional medicine, about the use of therapies. Finally, all practitioners have a responsibility to their patients, more so for practitioners of CAM, to critically assess the effectiveness, safety, and cost-benefit of CAM therapies (Fisher & Hill, 2004).

JOSEPH H. FLAHERTY

See also
Anti-Aging Medicine

References

American Association of Medical Colleges. LCME annual medical school questionnaire 2001–2002. Available: http://services.aamc.org/currdir/section2/LCME_Hot.xls.

Astin, J. A. (1998). Why patients use alternative medicine: Results of a national study. *Journal of the American Medical Association, 279*(19), 1548–1553.

Astin, J. A., Pelletier, K. R., Marie, A., & Haskell, W. L. (2000). Complementary and alternative medicine use among elderly persons: One-year analysis of a Blue Shield Medicare supplement. *Journal of Gerontology Medical Sciences, 55A,* M4–M9,

Blumenthal, M., Busse, W. R., Goldberg, A., et al., (Eds.). (1998). The complete German Commission E monographs: Therapeutic guide to herbal medicines. Boston: Integrative Medicine Communications.

British Medical Association. (1993). *Complementary medicine: New approaches to good practice.* Oxford: Oxford University Press

Cherkin, D. C., Deyo, R. A., Battie, M., Street, J., & Barlow, W. (1998). A comparison of physical therapy, chiropractic manipulation, and provision of an educational booklet for the treatment of patients with low back pain. *New England Journal of Medicine, 339*(15), 1021–1029.

Eisenberg, D. M., Davis, R. B., Ettner, S. L., Appel, S., Wilkey, S., Van Rompay, M., et al. (1998). Trends in alternative medicine use in the United States, 1990–1997: Results of a follow-up national survey. *Journal of the American Medical Association, 280*(18), 1569–1575.

Eisenberg, D. M., Kessler, R. C., Foster, C., Norlock, F. E., Calkins, D. R., & Delbanco, T. L. (1993). Unconventional medicine in the United States: Prevalence, costs, and patterns of use. *New England Journal of Medicine, 328,* 246–252.

Ernst, E., & White, A. R. (1998). Acupuncture for back pain: A meta-analysis of randomized controlled trials. *Archives of Internal Medicine, 158*(20), 2235–2241.

Ezzo, J., Berman, B., Hadhazy, V. A., Jadad, A. R., Lao., L., & Singh, B. B. (2000). Is acupuncture effective for the treatment of chronic pain? A systematic review. *Pain, 86*(3), 217–225.

Fisher, A. L., & Hill, R. (2004). Ethical and legal issues in antiaging medicine. *Clinics in Geriatric Medicine, 20*(2), 361–82.

Flaherty, J. H., & Takahashi, R. (2004). The use of complementary and alternative medical therapies among older persons around the world. *Clinics in Geriatric Medicine, 20*(2), 179–200.

Flaherty, J. H., Takahashi, R., Teoh, J., Habib, S., Ito, M., & Matsushita, S. (2001). Use of alternative therapies in older outpatients in the United States and Japan: Prevalence, reporting patterns, and perceived effectiveness. *Journals of Gerontology Medical Sciences, 56A,* M650–M655.

Fraser, J., & Kerr, J. R. (1993). Psychophysiological effects of back massage on elderly institutionalized patients. *Journal of Advanced Nursing, 18*(2), 238–245.

Friedrich, M. J. (2001). Chinese and US health care leaders discuss challenges of the 21st century. *Journal of the American Medical Association, 286*(10), 659–661.

Gammack, J. K., & Morley, J. E. (2004). Anti-aging medicine—the good, the bad, and the ugly. *Clinics in Geriatric Medicine, 20*(2), 157–177.

Gruenwald, J., Brendler, T., Jaenicke, C., et al. (Eds.). (2000). *PDR for herbal medicines* (2nd ed.). Montvale, NJ: Medical Economics Co.

Helm, H. M., Hays, J. C., Flint, E. P., Koenig, H. G., & Blazer, D. G. (2000). Does private religious activity prolong survival? A six-year follow-up study of 3,851 older adults. *Journals of Gerontology Series A-Biological Sciences and Medical Sciences, 55*(7), M400–M405.

Hurwitz, E. L., Morgenstern, H., Harber, P., Kominski, G. F., Belin, T. R., Yu, F., & Adams, A. H.; University of California-Los Angeles. (2002). A randomized trial of medical care with and without physical therapy and chiropractic care with and without physical modalities for patients with low back pain: 6-month follow-up outcomes from the UCLA low back pain study. *Spine, 27*(20), 2193–2204.

Klepser, T. B., & Klepser, M. E. (1999). Unsafe and potentially safe herbal therapies. *American Journal of Health-System Pharmacy, 56*(2), 125-138; quiz 139–141.

Killinger, L. Z. (2004). Chiropractic and geriatrics: A review of the training, role and scope of chiropractic in caring for aging patients. *Clinics in Geriatric Medicine. 20*(2), 223–235.

Kilstoff, K., & Chenoweth, L. (1998). New approaches to health and well-being for dementia day-care clients, family carers, and day-care staff. *International Journal of Nursing Practice, 4*(2), 70–83.

King, D. E., & Bushwick, B. (1994). Beliefs and attitudes of hospital inpatients about faith healing and prayer. *Journal of Family Practice, 39*(4), 349–352.

Koenig, H. G., Hays, J. C., Larson, D. B., George, L. K., Cohen, H. J., McCullough, M. E., Meador, K. G., & Blazer, D. G. (1999). Does religious attendance prolong survival? A six-year follow-up study of 3,968 older adults. *Journals of Gerontology Series A-Biological Sciences and Medical Sciences, 54*(7), M370–M376.

Melchart, D., Linde, K., Fischer, P., White, A., Allais, G., Vickers, A., & Berman, B. (1999). Acupuncture for recurrent headaches: A systematic review of randomized controlled trials. *Cephalalgia, 19*(9), 779–786 (discussion 765).

National Center for Homeopathy. (2000). CAM FactsM: Complementary and Alternative Medicine in the United States. Available: http://www.healthlobby.com/camfacts.html

Remington, R. (2002). Calming music and hand massage with agitated elderly. *Nursing Research, 51*(5), 317–323.

Saper, R. B., Kales, S. N., Paquin, J., Burns, M. J., Eisenberg, D. M., Davis, R. B., & Phillips, R. S. (2004). Heavy metal content of ayurvedic herbal medicine products. *Journal of the American Medical Association, 292*(23), 2868–2873.

Simington, J. A., & Laing, G. P. (1993). Effects of therapeutic touch on anxiety in the institutionalized elderly. *Clinical Nursing Research, 2*(4), 438–450.

van Tulder, M. W., Cherkin, D. C., Berman, B., Lao, L., & Koes, B. W. (1999). The effectiveness of acupuncture in the management of acute and chronic low back pain. A systematic review within the framework of the Cochrane Collaboration Back Review Group. *Spine, 24*(11), 1113–1123.

White, A. R., Rampes, H. (2003). *Cochrane Database of Systematic Reviews.*

Wolf, S. L., Barnhart, H. X., Kutner, N. G., McNeely, E., Coogler, C., & Xu, T. (1996). Reducing frailty and falls in older persons: An investigation of tai chi and computerized balance training. Atlanta FICSIT Group. Frailty and injuries: Cooperative studies of intervention techniques. *Journal of the American Geriatrics Society, 44*(5), 489–97.

Wolf, S. L., Sattin, R. W., Kutner, M., O'Grady, M., Greenspan, A. I., & Gregor, R. J. (2003). Intense tai chi exercise training and fall occurrences in older, transitionally frail adults: A randomized, controlled trial. *Journal of the American Geriatrics Society, 51*(12), 1693–1701.

COMPLIANCE

See
Adherence

COMPREHENSIVE GERIATRIC ASSESSMENT

See
Geriatric Assessment Programs

COMPRESSION OF MORBIDITY

The health of seniors is both the largest health challenge and the largest economic challenge for our age, since this is the age group in which the great majority of the illness burden and of medical costs resides. *Prevention of illness* should play a major role in meeting these challenges. Yet *health education, disease prevention*, and health promotion have been in great need of an underlying theoretical paradigm. Lacking such a paradigm the *health promotion* community had been subject to the criticisms of confusing association with causality on the one hand and of promoting a future world of long-lived but disabled and demented individuals on the other. Now, with proof in hand (Fries, 2003) and general acceptance, the compression of morbidity paradigm (Fries, 1980) informs strategies to improve senior health.

The *compression of morbidity* paradigm envisions a reduction in overall morbidity and of health care costs, now heavily concentrated in the senior years, by squeezing the period of morbidity and high costs between an increasing average age of onset of disability and the age of death, increasing perhaps more slowly. The healthy life is seen as potentially a vigorous and vital life until shortly before its natural close. Intuitively, the concept of *postponing the onset of disability* through reduction in health risks and prevention of diseases seems natural enough. However, in the early and middle years of the 20th century most observers believed that there was a steady increase in the amount of life spent in ill health. The prevalent acute illnesses of 1900 had given way to chronic diseases such as cancer, heart disease, lung disease, and stroke, with longer periods of disability and morbidity. Medical success equated with social failure.

If people took better care of themselves and thus lived even longer, the pessimists suggested, they would live into those years in which disability is greatest and would experience an increase in lifetime disability. Morbidity would be extended. They assumed that life could be prolonged, but that aging and chronic disease could not be postponed (Vita, 1998). Such critics predicted that better health would lead to a huge population of enfeebled, demented elders who would place an immense strain on medical resources. The direct test of compression (or *extension) of morbidity* depends on the effects, studied prospectively and longitudinally, of reduced health risks on cumulative lifetime disability and mortality. Another test would be to see if age-specific disability declines more rapidly than age-specific mortality, or vice versa.

Trends in Longevity

Emerging data document that these fears were unfounded. First, life expectancy *from advanced ages* has not increased as rapidly as predicted. In the

United States, *life expectancy of women* from age 65 increased only 0.7 years over the past 20 years. From age 85, *female life expectancy* in the United States has been nearly constant at 6.4 years since 1980. There will be a large increase in senior populations in the future, but this will be because of larger birth cohorts and increased survival to age 65, rather than from large longevity increases after age 65 or 85.

The Epidemiology of Postponement of Disability

Recent longitudinal studies document the ability to greatly postpone the onset of disability with age. For the past 21 years, our research group at Stanford has studied the effects of vigorous *exercise* on patient outcomes in 537 members of a runners club, with participants at least age 50 years old in 1984, compared with 423 age-matched community controls. The study was designed as a test of the compression of morbidity hypothesis. Appropriate controls for self-selection bias included: longitudinal study; x-rays of hands, knees, and hips; intention-to-treat analysis; exclusion of those with pre-existing disability; and statistical adjustment for possibly confounding variables. Disability levels were assessed yearly, allowing the area under the disability curve to be assessed. The exercise group, exercising vigorously for an average of 280 minutes per week, delayed the onset of disability *by over 12 years* compared with controls, far more than any associated differences in longevity. Both male and female exercisers increased disability at a rate only one-third that of controls. As these subjects moved from age 58 toward age 74, the differences in physical functional abilities between the exercising and the control population continued to increase. Lifetime *disability in exercisers* is only one-third to one-half that of sedentary individuals (Wang, 2002).

In a University of Pennsylvania study, 1,741 university attendees were studied in 1939 and 1940, surveyed again in 1962 at an average age of 43, and then annually since 1986. Health risk strata were developed for persons at high, moderate, and low risk, based on the 3 risk factors of smoking, body mass index, and lack of exercise. Cumulative disability from 1986 (at an average age of 67) to 1994 (at an average age of 75) or at death served as a surrogate for lifetime disability. Persons with high health risks in 1962 or in 1986 had approximately twice the cumulative disability of those with low health risks. Results were consistent across survivors, deceased, males, females, those without disability in 1986, and over the last 1 and 2 years of observation. Deceased low-risk subjects had only one-half the disability of high-risk subjects in their last 1 and 2 years of life. Onset of disability was postponed by approximately 7.75 years in the low-risk stratum as compared with the high-risk stratum. The 50% reduction in disability rates was balanced against only a 25% reduction in mortality rates, documenting compression of morbidity.

Recent major studies by at least 4 other groups confirm these findings. Studies of favored populations such as these provide an excellent perspective on the potential for *healthy aging*, because confounding effects of education, poverty, and lack of access to medical care are avoided and benefit at the margin can be examined. Compression of morbidity is readily demonstrable in those who exercise vigorously, those with few behavioral health risks, and those with high educational attainment, providing proof of concept. Health risk behaviors, as determined in midlife and late adulthood, strongly predict subsequent lifetime disability. Both cumulative morbidity and morbidity at the end of life are decreased in those with good health habits. Morbidity is postponed and compressed into fewer years in those with fewer health risks.

Randomized Clinical Trials of *Health Improvement in Seniors*

Randomized controlled trials have now proved that health improvement and risk-reduction programs can reduce health risks, improve health status, and reduce the need and demand for medical services in seniors. A Bank of America study of 4,700 retirees reduced costs by 20% and improved health indices by 10% to 20%. The California Public Employees Retirement System study of 57,000 seniors yielded closely similar results. Chronic disease self-management programs in arthritis and in Parkinson's disease documented the effectiveness of similar interventions in persons with chronic illness. *Self-management programs in seniors* have improved health and reduced costs (Fries, 2003).

Declining Disability Rates at the Population Level

Finally, proof of compression of morbidity has come from major population surveys in several countries, the most important of which are the *National Long-Term Care Survey* (NLTCS) (Manton, 2001) and the *National Health Interview Survey*. These and 12 other studies examined by meta-analysis (Freedman, 2002) were consistent in documenting declines in disability of over 2% per year, increasing in more recent years, and with broadening of the phenomenon to minority populations. Mortality rates over the same period declined by only 1% per year, documenting compression of morbidity at the population level (Fries, 2003).

Health Policy Mandates

There are 4 stages in developing documentary evidence to support a national health policy to improve senior health. First, the conceptual base, represented by the compression of morbidity paradigm, provides the theoretical structure. Second, the epidemiological data associating health risk behaviors with cumulative lifetime health outcomes provide proof of concept. Third, the multiple large surveys provide documentation of trends at the population level. Fourth, the randomized controlled trials, now available (Fries, 2003) prove that effective behavioral interventions can decrease senior morbidity and reduce medical care costs.

The paradigm of a long, healthy life with a relatively rapid terminal decline represents an attainable ideal. Health policies must be directed specifically at modifying those health risks that precede and cause morbidity if this ideal is to be approached for a population. *Medicare demonstration projects*, now planned, can document the effectiveness of tailored interventions to improve senior health and reduce medical care costs, setting the stage for prevention benefits under Medicare. Reduction of disability by 1% or more will result in economic stabilization of the Medicare program. The presently increasing epidemic of obesity and the health losses in formerly Soviet countries remind us that continued compression of morbidity in the United States, although attainable, is not inevitable.

Further information can be obtained on the Internet at the Web site for the Health Project: healthproject.stanford.edu. Policy issues are described at: healthpromotionadvocates.org.

JAMES F. FRIES

See also
Anti-Aging Medicine
Longevity: Societal Impact

References

Freedman, V. A., Martin, L. G., & Schoeni, R. F. (2002). Recent trends in disability and functioning among older adults in the United States: a systematic review. *Journal of the American Medical Association, 288*, 3137–3146.

Fries, J. F. (1980). Aging, natural death, and the compression of morbidity. *New England Journal of Medicine, 303*, 130–135.

Fries, J. F. (2003). Measuring and monitoring success in compressing morbidity. *Annals of Internal Medicine, 139*(5), 455–459.

Manton, K. G., & Gu, X. (2001). Changes in the prevalence of chronic disability in the United States black and nonblack population above age 65 from 1982 to 1999. *Proceedings of the National Academy of Sciences of the United States of America, 98*, 6354–6359.

Vita, A. J., Terry, R. B., Hubert, H. B., & Fries, J. F. (1998). Aging, health risks, and cumulative disability. *New England Journal of Medicine, 338*(15), 1035–1041.

Wang, B. W. E., Ramey, D., Schettler, J. D., Hubert, H. B., & Fries, J. F. (2002). Postponed development of disability in elderly runners: A 13-year longitudinal study. *Archives of Internal Medicine, 162*, 2285–2294.

CONNECTIVE TISSUES

With increasing biologic age, human and animal connective tissues undergo a variety of changes—for example, skin becomes thin, rigid, and less elastic, and in blood vessels the walls thicken and the lumen widens (Hall, 1976). In rats, tendon from the tail loses elasticity and tensile strength (Vogel, 1978). Although the biochemical events leading to such changes are not completely understood, studies of *age-related changes in collagen* and elastic fibers have furnished some clues. For a review of mechanisms of the age-associated connective tissue alterations in the dermis, see Uitto and colleagues (1989) or Tzaphlidou (2004).

Collagen

Collagen is the major structural protein of the body. It makes up approximately 70% of the dry weight of the skin, and it gives the dermis its mechanical and structural integrity. It is not a single molecule, but consists of at least 20 types, each present in different tissues in different amounts. The basic *collagen molecule* is long and narrow, measuring 3,000 Å by 15 Å, with an approximate molecular weight of 285,000 daltons. Each molecule consists of 3 chains, known as alpha chains, which are held together by hydrogen bonds and wound like the strands of a rope. Except for short segments at each end of the alpha chain, every third amino acid is *glycine*. At least 19 different (genetically distinct) types of collagen have been recognized. Many of them, but not all, have been found in the skin. In the body, the most abundant collagen is collagen type I, and in the skin types I and III are most prevalent (Tzaphlidou, 2004). Collagen is synthesized in a precursor form called *procollagen*, which undergoes further modifications that result in stabilizing cross-links between individual chains by the formation of interchain disulfide bonds near the carboxyl termini of the component pro-α chains.

Aging collagen undergoes a variety of structural alterations. Collagen fibrils from skin, tendon, cornea, sclera, and meninges thicken with age. Wide-angle x-ray diffraction studies of chorda tendinae and Achilles tendon have shown an age-related increase in the degree of order within the collagen fibril (Gross, 1961). Changes in various physical properties also occur with aging collagen. For example, old tendon fibers show enhanced thermal shrinkage and are able to contract with greater strength upon being heated (Gross, 1961). Collagen from lung (Kohn, 1959), tendon (Kohn & Rollerson, 1958), and myocardium (Kohn & Rollerson, 1959) show an age-dependent decrease in osmotic swelling. In addition, aging collagen becomes stiffer, less soluble in salt solution, more difficult to extract with acetic acid, and more resistant to proteolytic attack by bacterial collagenase (Balazs, 1977).

The resistance of aging collagen to external influences is believed to be a result of the formation of cross-links between collagen molecules. Cerami (1985) has shown that these cross-links result from interaction between glucose and proteins. In a series of reversible, nonenzymatic reactions, the amino group of a protein interacts with the aldehyde function of glucose, forming a Schiff base that undergoes Amadori rearrangement. The *Amadori product* then undergoes further irreversible rearrangements to result in cross-linking of the involved proteins. One example of such an advanced glycosylation end product is 2-furoyl-4(5)-(2-furanyl)-1H-imidazole, a condensation product of 2 glucose molecules and 2 lysine-derived amino groups (Cerami, 1985). Such protein cross-links can also explain the *fluorescent properties of aging collagen*. Collagen obtained from human Achilles tendon shows an age-dependent increase in a substance that fluoresces at 406 nm (Labella & Paul, 1965). This is believed to result from progressive cross-linking of peptide chains (Balazs, 1977).

Recently, considerable progress has been made in our understanding of nonenzymatic glycation of collagen (Odetti, Aragno, Garibaldi, Valentini, Pronzato, & Rolandi, 1998; Chen, Brodsky, Goligorsky, Hampel, Li, Gross, et al., 2002) and the relationship between glycation and oxidation during collagen aging in vitro and in vivo. It has also been established that during aging the synthesis of collagen gradually declines, which is a major cause of the skin becoming thinner in sun-protected skin, especially after age 70 (Oikarinen, 1999). *Photoaged skin* is characterized by a substantial collagen loss. Early studies suggested that total collagen content in sun-exposed skin is approximately half that of sun-protected skin; however, Kligman's group showed that quantitatively, collagen loss on per mg protein basis is much less (Kligman, Schwartz, Sapadin, & Kligman, 2000).

Elastic Fibers

In contrast to collagen, elastic fibers make up only a small proportion of human skin (0.6% of dry weight). They are abundant in ligamentum nuchae, aorta, lung, Achilles tendon, and the cardiovascular system. Electron microscopy has shown that elastic fibers consist of an amorphous component called *elastin*, which is surrounded by microfibrillar protein. Elastin consists of linear polypeptides with a molecular weight of approximately 72,000 daltons. Its content is high in alanine and valine, but it is devoid of hydroxylysine, tryptophan, histidine, and methionine. As in collagen, glycine accounts for one-third of the amino acids but is unevenly distributed along the polypeptide chain. A unique feature is the presence of *desmosine*, a compound formed by covalent linkage of 4 lysine residues, which serves to connect individual elastin polypeptides. Microfibrillar proteins are thin fibers that surround elastin. Their contents are high in cysteine, methionine, and histidine, but low in alanine, glycine, and valine (Ryhänen & Uitto, 1983). Microfibrillar component proteins consist of fibrillins, TGF-beta binding proteins, fibulins, and other microfibril associated proteins.

Although less is known about aging of elastic tissues than about aging of collagen, a variety of age-related changes are well recognized. In the skin, wrinkling and laxity with advancing age are believed to result from loss of the vertical, subepidermal fine skeins of elastic fibers (Kligman, Grove, & Balin, 1985). In contrast, elastic material located deeper in the dermis shows the opposite change. Here, elastic fibers become thicker, more numerous, and more branched and disarrayed (Kligman, Grove, & Balin, 1985). Studies have demonstrated that elastin gene expression is markedly activated in sun-damaged dermis, or in cells exposed to reactive oxygen species (ROS) generated by a xanthine/xanthine oxidase system (Uitto, Fazio, & Olsen., 1989; Bernstein, 2002). In *sun-damaged skin*, there is massive accumulation in the dermis of an amorphous material that takes up elastic stains; this substance has been shown by electron microscopic studies to represent degenerating elastic fibers (Lavker, 1979). Although it has been shown that the concentration of desmosine in sun-exposed skin is 4 times that of sun-protected skin, this increase is felt to be insufficient to account for the massive deposition of elastotic material in the dermis (Kornberg, Matsouka, & Uitto, 1985).

The composition of elastic fibers changes with age. During embryologic development, newly developed fibers contain microfibrillar protein almost exclusively. With increasing age, an amorphous component (elastin) appears (Ryhänen & Uitto, 1983). The mature elastic fiber consists mainly of elastin surrounded by microfibrillar protein (Ryhänen & Uitto, 1983). Like collagen, elastin exhibits increasing fluorescence with age. In addition, elastin becomes yellow and increasingly calcified (Balazs, 1977). It is possible that like collagen, elastin also undergoes progressive cross-linking with age (Kohn, 1977).

In several hereditary diseases elastin is deficient, leading to the appearance of accelerated aging. For example, elastin fibers are deficient or completely lacking in cutis laxa associated with sagging of the skin (Oikarinen, 1994.)

Ground Substance

Although ground substance makes up less than 0.2% of dermal dry weight, it is important in determining rheologic properties of the skin. Because of its extraordinary capacity to hold water, hyaluronic acid is responsible for the normal turgor of the dermis (Kligman, Grove, & Balin, 1985). In addition, the ground substance provides a pathway for diffusion of nutrients through the interstices of the dermis and probably functions as a lubricant by allowing collagen fibers to slide past each other (Kligman, Grove, & Balin, 1985.)

Between newborn and infancy, a significant reduction in soluble fraction of dermal glycosaminoglycan (GAG) has been noted. Dermal GAG level remains stable through middle age and drops further during old age (Fleischmajer, Perlish, & Bashey, 1972), probably as a result of decreased synthesis (Fleischmajer, Perlish, & Bashey, 1973). It has also been suggested that age-related collagen changes may result from the interaction of GAG and collagen (Jackson & Bentley, 1968). For further study, see Kefalides and Alper (1988).

Matrix Metalloproteinases

The degradation of the matrix components of a tissue is controlled by the protein family of *matrix metalloproteinases* (MMP) that maintain the equilibrium between the synthesis and degradation of connective tissue under physiological conditions (Herouy 2001). Matrix metalloproteinases consist of interstitial collagenases, gelatinases, stromelysins, matrilysin, metalloelastase, and membrane-type matrix metalloproteinases. These enzymes are involved in the turnover of extracellular matrix macromolecules, including collagen, elastin, glucosaminoglycans, and glycoproteins (Seltzer & Eisen, 1999). They are important for wound healing, morphogenesis, angiogenesis, and photoaging and other skin pathology, including that which is associated with skin aging (Herouy, 2001; Brennan, Bhatti, Nerusu, Bhagavathula, Kang, Fisher, et al., 2003).

Arthur K. Balin
Michael M. Vilenchik

References

Balazs, E. E. (1977). Intercellular matrix of connective tissue. In C. E. Finch & L. Hayflick (Eds.), *Handbook of biology of aging* (pp. 222–240). New York: Van Nostrand Reinhold.

Bernstein, E. F. (2002). Reactive oxygen species activate the human elastin promoter in a transgenic model of cutaneous photoaging. *Dermatologic Surgery, 28*, 132–135.

Brennan, M., Bhatti, H., Nerusu, K. C., Bhagavathula, N., Kang, S., Fisher, G., Varani, J., & Voorhees, J. J. (2003). Matrix metalloproteinase-1 is the major collagenolytic enzyme responsible for collagen damage in UV-irradiated human skin. *Photochemistry and Photobiology, 78*, 43–48.

Chen, J., Brodsky, S. V., Goligorsky, D. M., Hampel, D. J., Li, H., Gross, S. S., & Goligorsky, M. S. (2002). Glycated collagen I induces premature senescence-like phenotypic changes in endothelial cells. *Circulation Research, 90*, 1290–1298.

Cerami, A. (1985). Hypothesis: Glucose as a mediator of aging. *Journal of the American Geriatrics Society, 33*, 626–634.

Fleischmajer, R., Perlish, J. S., & Bashey, R. I. (1972). Human dermal glycosaminoglycin and aging. *Biochemica et Biophysica Acta, 279*, 265–275.

Fleischmajer, R., Perlish, J. S., & Bashey, R. I. (1973). Aging of human dermis. In C. L. Robert (Ed.), *Frontiers of matrix biology* (Vol. 1, pp. 90–106). Basel: S. Karger.

Gross, J. (1961). Aging of connective tissue: The extracellular components. In G. G. Bourne (Ed.), *Structural aspects of aging* (pp. 179–195). New York: Hafner.

Hall, D. D. (1976). *The aging of connective tissue*. New York: Academic Press.

Herouy, Y. (2001). Matrix metalloproteinases in skin pathology. *International Journal of Medicine, 7*, 3–12.

Jackson, D. S., & Bentley, J. P. (1968). Collagen-glycosaminoglycan interactions. In B. S. Gould (Ed.), *Treatise on collagen* (Vol. 2, pp. 189–214). London: Academic Press.

Kefalides, N. A., & Alper, R. (1988). Structure and organization of macromolecules in basement membranes. In M. E. Nimni (Ed.), *Chemistry, biology, and biotechnology* (Vol. 2, pp. 73). Boca Raton: CRC Press.

Kligman, A. M., Grove, G. L., & Balin, A. K. (1985). Aging of human skin. In C. E. Finch & E. L. Schneider (Eds.), *Handbook of the biology of aging* (pp. 820–841). New York: Van Nostrand Reinhold.

Kligman, L. H., Schwartz, E., Sapadin, A. N., & Kligman, A. M. (2000). Collagen loss in photoaged human skin is overestimated by histochemistry. *Photodermatology, Photoimmunology, and Photomedicine, 16*, 224–228.

Kohn, R. R., & Rollerson, E. R. (1958). Relationship of age to swelling properties of human diaphragm tendon in acid and alkaline solution. *Journal of Gerontology, 13*, 241–247.

Kohn, R. R., & Rollerson, J. (1959). Studies on the effect of heat and age in decreasing ability of human collagen to swell in acid. *Journal of Gerontology, 14*, 11–15.

Kohn, R. R. (1977). Heart and cardiovascular system. In C. E. Finch & L. Hayflick (Eds.), *Handbook of the biology of aging* (pp. 281–371). New York: Van Nostrand Reinhold.

Kornberg, R. L., Matsouka, L. Y., & Uitto, J. (1985). Actinic elastosis-histopathologic, ultrastructural and biochemical studies of the dermis (abstract). 23rd Annual Meeting, American Society of Dermatopathology, 86.

Labella, F. S., & Paul, G. J. (1965). Structure of collagen from human tendon as influenced by age and sex. *Journal of Gerontology, 20*, 54–59.

Lavker, R. M. (1979). Structural alterations in exposed and unexposed aged skin. *Journal of Investigative Dermatology, 73*, 59–66.

Odetti, P., Aragno, I., Garibaldi, S., Valentini, S., Pronzato, M. A., & Rolandi, R. (1998). Role of advanced glycation end products in aging collagen. A scanning force microscope study. *Gerontology, 44*, 187–191.

Oikarinen, A. (1994). Aging of the skin connective tissue: How to measure the biochemical and mechanical properties of aging dermis. *Photodermatology, Photoimmunology, and Photomedicine*; *10*, 47–52.

Ryhänen, L., & Uitto, J. (1983). Elastic fibers of the connective tissue. In L. A. Goldsmith (Ed.), *Biochemistry and physiology of the skin* (pp. 433–447). New York: Oxford University Press.

Seltzer, J. L., & Eisen, E. Z. (1999). Native type I collagen is not a substrate for MMP2 (Gelatinase A). *Journal of Investigative Dermatology, 112*, 993–994.

Tzaphlidou, M. (2004). The role of collagen and elastin in aged skin: An image-processing approach. *Micron, 35*, 173–177.

Uitto, J., Fazio, M. J., & Olsen, D. R. (1989). Molecular mechanisms of cutaneous aging: Age-associated connective tissue alterations in the dermis. *Journal of American Academy of Dermatology, 21*, 614–622.

Vogel, H. G. (1978). Influence of maturation and age on mechanical and biochemical parameters of connective tissue of various organs in the rat. *Connective Tissue Research, 6*, 161–166.

CONSUMER EDUCATION

See
Consumer Issues

CONSUMER FRAUD

See
Consumer Issues

CONSUMER ISSUES

Market Definition

The mature market is defined as all products and services purchased by or for consumers over the age of 50. The term "mature market" also may refer to the older adults and others who buy and/or consume such products and services. For the purposes of the following discussion, it must be noted that segmentation strategies such as demographics have limitations. Segmentation strategies need to be tied to a specific product, issue, or service. The measures need to be carefully considered, and multiple psychographic segmentation approaches need to be evaluated. A multidimensional perspective, one that emphasizes the complexity and individual differences of mature consumers, needs to be used (Morgan & Levy, 2002; Wolfe & Snyder, 2003).

There are more than 79 million Americans over the age of 50—about 28% of all adults in the United States. This group includes leading-edge *baby boomers* born between 1946 and 1955, with over 37.3 million people. The over-50 age group has a total annual income of more than $2 trillion. Mature Americans control about three-quarters of the total net worth of all U.S. households—more than $7 trillion of wealth. (Dychtwald, 1999; Green, 2003; U.S. Census, 2004).

Spending Habits

Mature market consumers are the most affluent group in the United States, and those aged 50 to 64 are the most affluent of all. Americans over age 50 hold 77% of the nation's financial assets and 50% of all discretionary income. Per capita spending is about 2 times that of the general population; mature householders account for 50% of all discretionary spending in the United States.

Mature consumers tend to spend more money than younger consumers on financial services, health, travel, and entertainment. Mature householders aged 55 to –64 years spend more than average on their homes, household furnishings, women's and girls' apparel, vehicle purchases, and entertainment. They also have over $2,000 left annually after major spending to invest, save, or contribute to charitable organizations.

Those aged 55 and older spend more than average on health insurance, medical services, prescription and over-the-counter drugs, and personal care supplies. Thirty-two percent of all health care dollars are spent by or on the behalf of older consumers. Health care products and services will become a $75-billion industry by the time the baby boomers retire. Americans aged 50 and older spend more in drugstores than do any other age group. They purchase 37% of all over-the-counter medicines, and those aged 65 and over consume 30% of all prescription drugs (Morgan & Levy, 2002; Senior Citizens Marketing Group, 1991).

Older consumers buy 43% of all new domestic cars, 48% of all luxury cars, and 51% of all recreational vehicles, and more of them join auto clubs than do those in any other age group. They spend more per capita in grocery stores than any other age group, and buy 67% of all dining out and cultural events and 40% of all live-theater tickets.

Housing and *home furnishing purchases* are also strong among older consumers. Condos appeal most to older homebuyers. Between 20% to 30% of new homebuyers aged 50 and older buy condos, compared to 15% of new homebuyers in younger age groups. Of course, this age group is the largest purchaser of retirement housing. Mature adults purchase 37% of all curtains and draperies, 54% of all color television sets, and 36% of all new furniture.

The age group 50 and older spends more money on travel, recreation, and other leisure activities than any other age group. Mature consumers spend 30% more on travel than do younger travelers. Eighty percent of all commercial *vacation travel*, especially first-class air travel and luxury sea cruises, is purchased by mature consumers.

One-third of adults aged 45 to –64 and 25% of those over 65 years exercise regularly and have been doing so for at least 5 years; 52% regularly engage in *sports and exercise*. *Walking* is the favorite sport among those aged 55 and older. Older consumers buy 32% of all walking shoes, 45% of treadmills, and 37% of all spa memberships. Fifty-seven percent of older Americans engage in *gardening*; this group buys one-third of the garden tools purchased annually and represents 75% of the National Gardening Association membership.

Sixty-six percent of mature consumers read regularly. Seventy-four percent of the 55- to 64-year-olds and 69% of those 66 and older read a daily newspaper. Over 50% of all book and magazine subscriptions are sold to people over age 65. The circulation of *Modern Maturity* is bigger than that of *Time, Newsweek, and U.S. News and World Report* combined. Seventy-six percent watch television, and this age group constitutes about half of all heavy viewers in prime time, early, and fringe viewing. Seventy-seven percent visit friends, spending money on home entertainment.

When purchasing products and service, older consumers shop for convenience, comfort, quality, service, luxury items, and brand-name products. Older consumers know what good service is and are willing to pay for it. A positive purchase and ownership experience is valued.

Mature Market Segmentation

Mature consumers display greater heterogeneity and diversity than in any other age group. Following Neugarten's categories of young-old and old-old, the mature market is often divided into 4 major segments, based on age and life-cycle events.

The young-old are aged 55 to –64 years, and are generally active and healthy. Consisting of about 24.3 million consumers, often these individuals are preparing for retirement. They are "working to live—not living to work." Also called the "*sandwich generation*," the *young-old* are prime targets for products and services related to exercise equipment, health programs, and maintaining a youthful appearance. Consumers in this category are increasingly taking early retirement, changing careers (not all willingly), or working part-time.

The *middle-old* are aged 65 to 74 years. Most of the 18.4 million consumers in this category are generally retired. They are prime targets for health and nutrition products/services, leisure products and activities (eating out, travel), and condos and retirement housing.

The *old-old* are aged 75 to 84 years. Consisting of about 12.4 million consumers, this group is increasingly frail and displays greater health limitations with increasing age. Individuals in this category more often fit the "senior citizen" stereotype. Most are still healthy, although health may be increasingly problematic. For this reason, financial security is a major concern among the old-old. The most important asset for consumers in this category is their fully paid home.

The *oldest old* are 85 And older. This age group is growing in numbers more rapidly than any other age group. With about 4.2 million members, this group is less independent, less mobile, and more in need of support services to accomplish tasks of daily living; they may require acute and chronic medical and hospital care. These consumers are prime targets for home health care products and services, in-home chore services, and assisted living (U.S. Census, 2000).

Age per se is a poor segmentation device (Morgan & Levy, 2002). A better way to segment older consumers is through milestone events, use of time, money, and health. Health segments mature Americans into 3 basic categories: healthy individuals who improve or maintain physical well-being with a wholly independent lifestyle, those need to make some lifestyle accommodations due to limitations posed by health status, and those with major limitations, requiring significant product and service purchases.

Health is a unique segmentation device because it affects who makes the ultimate purchase decision and the purchase itself. Healthy people generally make their own purchase decisions; less-active individuals may send someone else to the store, leaving the purchase decision to a caregiver or other person. Those with major limitations often do not make their own decisions; the product or service is recommended by a professional, and the caregiver makes the purchase.

Time is another segmentation device, categorizing mature consumers into those who are still working versus those who are retired. Purchases of products and services often depend of the activity of work or leisure. Money and attitude toward money are still another means of segmenting the mature market. Only 13% of older adults fall below the poverty level; about 25% struggle financially.

Segmentation of the mature market as a means to predict purchase behavior is perhaps more difficult than with younger age groups, because of the heterogeneity and range of individual differences among older consumers. Psychographic approaches offer important insights and need to be carefully considered (Morgan & Levy 2002; Wolfe & Snyder, 2003).

Shopping Attitudes and Behaviors

Older consumers tend to be loyal, willing to spend, and extremely quality-conscious, and they demand a hassle-free shopping experience. Older consumers respond to many of the same purchase influences as do younger consumers. However, older consumers are significantly more likely than younger consumers to be influenced by quality, an unconditional guarantee, and a respected spokesperson.

Mature adults prefer to shop in stores that offer: convenience and comfort, everyday discounts (vs. frequent sales), a rest area, proximity to a variety of other stores, convenient parking, a variety of sizes and styles of apparel suited to their age, knowledgeable salespeople, phone-in ordering, and a policy allowing return of unsatisfactory products. Such shopping environment preferences mirror similar desires among younger consumers for convenient parking, a good return policy, and apparel that is right for them.

The Better Business Bureau reports that the number-1 complaint against business is unsatisfactory service—38% of complaints among those aged 61 and older, compared to 25% of all age groups. The primary shopping barrier for mature consumers is customer service, followed by complaints related to shopping in general, dissatisfaction with store amenities, and difficulties in finding merchandise.

Perhaps because of these difficulties in shopping and some physiological changes that make shopping harder, mature consumers tend to shop in department and specialty shops more often than in discount stores. According to Management Horizons in Columbus, Ohio, mature consumers are more likely than those in other age groups to shop in department or specialty stores for apparel, domestics, gifts, appliances, home furnishings, and jewelry. These environments, as opposed to discount stores, tend to afford helpful salespeople who can provide the convenience of one-to-one service.

The U.S. Department of Commerce reports that 85% of people over the age of 50 make mail order purchases. Individuals aged 50 and over are among the highest purchasing group for Internet sales. In 2002, Internet shopping among 55- to 70-year-olds increased by 50%.

Ronni S. Sterns
Harvey L. Sterns

References

Dychtwald, K. (1999). *Age power*. New York: Tarcher, Putnam.

Green, B. (2003). *Marketing to leading-edge baby boomers*. New York: Writers Advantage.

Morgan, C. M., & Levy, D. J. (2002). *Marketing to the mindset of boomers and their elders*. St. Paul, Minnesota: Attitude Base.

Senior Citizens Marketing Group. (1991). *America ages: Did you know? Report*.

Wolfe, D. B., & Snyder, R. E. (2003). *Ageless marketing: Strategies for reaching the hearts and minds of the new customer majority*. Chicago: Dearborn Financial Publishing.

U.S. Census Bureau. (2000).

U.S. Census Bureau. (2004).

CONSUMER PROTECTION

See
Consumer Issues

CONTINUITY THEORY

Continuity theory originated from the observation that despite widespread changes in health, functioning and social circumstances, a large proportion of older adults showed considerable consistency over time in their patterns of thinking, activity profiles, and social relationships. But the long-term consistency that became the foundation of continuity theory was not the homeostatic stability predicted by activity theory. Instead, continuity was conceived of more flexibly, as strong probabilistic relationships between past, present and anticipated patterns of thought, behavior, and social arrangements. Since the late 1960s, the concept of continuity has gone through several stages: empirical description (Maddox, 1968), concept development (Atchley, 1971), theory building (Atchley, 1989), and empirical testing (Atchley, 1999).

Because continuity can mean either an absence of change or evolution linked to the individual's past, its use in gerontology has been ambiguous. In some studies, continuity has been equated with absolute stability or lack of change and in others it has been defined as gradual development and relatedness over time. Perhaps a better word for the evolutionary, developmental concept of continuity would have been consistency, which does not imply an absence of change, but it is doubtful that the field will switch labels at this point.

In its most elaborated form, continuity theory is a social psychological theory of continuous adult development (Atchley, 1989, 1999). It uses *feedback systems theory imagery* to create a view of adults as dynamic, self-aware entities who use patterns of thought created over their lifetimes to describe, analyze, evaluate, decide, act, pursue goals, and interpret input and feedback. Although social processes such as socialization and social control have input to the person's internal system, the conscious being who interprets the input also creates the resulting personal constructs, including personal constructions of the life course, life events, life stages, age norms, and age grading.

Continuity theory makes a number of theoretical assumptions: Individuals invest themselves in the internal and external frameworks of their lives and these relatively robust frameworks allow individuals to accommodate a considerable amount of evolutionary change without experiencing crisis. Change is assessed in relation to themes of continuity. People are motivated to use continuity of past patterns as their first choice in pursuing goals and adapting to change because the personal systems they have spent their lifetimes developing seem to offer the highest probability for successfully constructing their future. To the extent that a continuity strategy for making plans and coping with change is reinforced by experience, continuity becomes an increasingly strong first choice. Choice of a continuity strategy may be conscious, but it may also be an unconscious path of least resistence.

Elements of Continuity Theory

Continuity theory involves four major constructs: internal structure, external structure, goal setting, and maintaining adaptive capacity. The following sections define these constructs and elaborate their operation in the context of continuity theory.

Internal Structure. The ideas, mental skills, and information stored in the mind are organized into loose structures such as self-concept, personal goals, world-view, philosophy of life, moral framework, attitudes, values, beliefs, knowledge, skills, temperament, preferences, and coping strategies. Note that each of these constructs is a general label under which a large number of specific thoughts and feelings could be subsumed. These general structures represent different dimensions that, when combined, form a unique whole that distinguishes one person from another. In making life choices and in adapting to change, people are motivated to maintain the inner structures that represent a lifetime of selective investment. Ongoing consistency of psychological structures is viewed by individuals as an important prerequisite for psychological security.

External Structure. Social roles, activities, relationships, living environments, and geographic locations are also organized in a person's mind. As a result of priority setting and selective investment throughout adulthood, by middle age most adults have unique and well-mapped external life structures or lifestyles that differentiate each person from others. Most people attempt to set priorities and make selective investments that will produce the greatest possible satisfaction for them given their constraints. As a result, they see their evolving life structure as an important source of social security. Also, continuity of activities and environments concentrates people's energies in familiar domains where practice can often prevent or minimize the social, psychological, and physical losses that cultural concepts of aging might lead us to expect. Continuity of relationships preserves the network of social support that is important for creating and maintaining solid concepts of self and lifestyle.

Goal Setting. Continuity theory assumes that adults have goals for developmental direction: ideals about themselves, their activities, their relationships, and their environments toward which they want to evolve. Specific *developmental goals*, even whether people have such goals, are influenced by both socialization and location in the social structure—family ties, gender, social class, organizational environment, and so forth, but these goals can also be profoundly affected by life experience. Adults use life experiences to make decisions about selective investments: which aspects of themselves to focus their attention on, which activities to engage in, which careers to pursue, which groups to join, what community to be part of, and so on.

Maintaining Adaptive Capacity. As they continue to evolve, adults also have increasingly clear ideas about what gives them satisfaction in life, and they fashion and refine an external life structure that complements their internal structures and delivers the maximum life satisfaction possible given their circumstances. The ideas aging adults have about adaptation to life are results of a lifetime of learning, adapting, personal evolution, and selective investment, all in interaction or negotiation with their external social and physical environments. It should not be surprising, then, that in adapting to change, including changes in life stage, adults are motivated to continue to use the internal and external patterns they have spent so much time and energy developing.

Continuity Theory, Positive Outcomes, and *Determinism*

Continuity theory does not assume that the results of continuity are necessarily positive. The evidence indicates that even those with low self-esteem, abusive relationships, and poor social adaptation resist the idea of abandoning their internal and external frameworks. Apparently, firm ground to stand on, even if it predicts a miserable future, is for some people preferable to an unknown future. Similarly, positive feedback loops may produce positive change, but negative feedback loops can produce disorder.

Continuity theory is not deterministic. It does not predict the content of psychological or social development at any given life stage, during any specific life course transition, or in any particular period of history. Instead, it points to the common social psychological structures and processes that underlie the setting and seeking of goals as well as response to change. It provides a conceptual way of organizing the search for coherence in life stories and of understanding the dynamics that produce basic story lines, but continuity theory has no ideology concerning which stories are 'right' or 'successful.' Through its diagnostic concepts, continuity theory can help us understand why particular people have developed in the way they have. However, similar *types* of social psychological structures and processes are presumed to be at work even though they produce widely varying individual results. The heart of continuity theory is the presumption that people are motivated to continue to use the adaptive resources they have developed throughout adulthood to diagnose situations, chart future courses and to adapt to change.

Studying Continuity and Change

How can continuity theory be tested? First, continuity is most likely to occur in generalized social psychological constructs such as the hierarchy of personal goals, general activity preferences or networks of social relationships rather than in perceptions and memories of very specific ideas, behaviors, or relationships. This conception deals effectively with the apparent paradox that continuity and change usually coexist within individual lives. Continuity is seen by individuals in terms of general themes running through their lives (Kaufman, 1986; Fiske and Chiriboga, 1990), even though there may be substantial changes in the specifics surrounding those themes.

How much relatedness is needed over time in order to qualify as continuity? By tracing measured individual patterns in attitudes, behavior and relationships over multiple points in time, researchers usually can easily distinguish consistency from sudden change from chaos. Such objective measures are useful for determining the prevalence of continuity. Here it is important to emphasize substantively meaningful similarities and differences over time rather than simply statistically significant differences, which are often quite small in practical terms. *Testing continuity theory requires longitudinal data.*

Ultimately, how much change can occur without triggering perceptions of discontinuity is a judgment that can be made only by the individual experiencing change. Researchers often use definitions of continuity that require more stability than do the definitions used by the research participants. As a result, the findings tend to underestimate the prevalence of perceived continuity.

The difference between objective and subjective assessments of continuity has important implications for research. When it occurs, *objective continuity* in ideas, behavior, or relationships can be assumed to result from choices on the individual's part. However, it is also important to study *subjective continuity*, the individual's perceptions of the relative amount of continuity and change over time. Subjective continuity also includes the extent to which individuals express a preference for continuity as a strategy for planning, making decisions, or adapting to change. Research results generally suggest that subjective continuity is indeed both a goal and an outcome for most aging individuals and that objective continuity of ideas, behavior and relationships is the most prevalent outcome among aging individuals over time. In a 20-year longitudinal study of adults who were age 70 or older at the conclusion, Atchley (1999) found that two-thirds or more of study participants showed objective continuity in psychological factors such as self-confidence or personal goals and in social factors such as frequency of interaction with family or friends.

Continuity theory seeks to explain why most adults show considerable consistency in their patterns of thought, behavior and relationship as they move through the later stages of life, often even in the face of substantial external changes such as widowhood or physical disability. Humans create and constantly revise and refine robust patterns of thought and action that become their front-line strategies for planning, making life decisions and adapting to life changes. By preferring these strategies, adults produce consistencies over time that can provide a sense of security, ease life transitions and cushion the effects of sudden life changes.

The essence of continuity theory is very straightforward and intuitively appealing. However, to test and refine the theory requires moving from its abstract form toward operational forms that can guide the research process. Continuity theory is currently in this stage of development (Atchley, 1999). Since the late 1990s, continuity theory has been used to structure research on a wide variety of topics: adjustment to retirement, sports participation in later life, stability of identity and self, adaptation to disability, mental health, social support systems, reminiscence, and leisure activities. This wide-ranging list of topics suggests that continuity theory is serving as a general framework for research on adaptation, which was its initial intent.

ROBERT C. ATCHLEY

See also

Activity Theory
Disengagement Theory
Personality
Social Gerontology: Theories

References

Atchley, R. C. (1971). Retirement and leisure participation: Continuity or crisis? *The Gerontologist, 11,* 13–17.

Atchley, R. C. (1989). A continuity theory of normal aging. *The Gerontologist, 29,* 183–90.

Atchley, R. C. (1999). *Continuity and adaptation in aging: Creating positive experiences*. Baltimore, MD: Johns Hopkins University Press.

Fiske, M., & Chiriboga, D. A. (1990). *Change and continuity in adult life*. San Francisco: Jossey-Bass.

Kaufman, S. R. (1986). *The ageless self: Sources of meaning in late life*. Madison, WI: University of Wisconsin Press.

Maddox, G. L. (1968). Persistence of life style among the elderly: A longitudinal study of patterns of social activity in relation to life satisfaction. In B. L. Neugarten (Ed.), *Middle age and aging*. Chicago: University of Chicago Press, pp. 181–83.

CREATIVITY

In investigating the relationship between *creativity and aging*, most researchers adopt 1 of 2 available strategies (Adams-Price, 1998; Lindauer, 2003). First, some investigators assume that creativity represents a cognitive skill that can be recorded by a suitable psychometric instrument. Under this assumption, the main task is to show how scores on these tests change over the life span. Second, other researchers focus on creativity as an overt behavior that results in the production of concrete works. From this viewpoint, the aim of research is to show how the output of creative products—whether paintings, poems, compositions, patents, books, or journal articles—changes as a function of a creator's age.

Divergent Thinking Across the Life Span

A large number of psychometric instruments exist that purport to assess creativity. However, most investigators have relied on those *creativity tests* that evaluate a person's capacity for "*divergent thinking*." Measures of divergent thinking examine whether a person can produce a large number of alternative and novel responses to test stimuli. There actually exist several such instruments, each concentrating on a particular process (fluency, flexibility, originality, etc.) or medium (verbal versus visual). Whatever the details, studies using these divergent-thinking tests have often found that creativity tends to exhibit a roughly inverted-U function of age, with a consistent tendency for performance to decline in the latter half of life (Levy & Langer, 1999).

Nevertheless, we cannot infer from these psychometric findings that creativity necessarily declines after an individual reaches middle age. First, many of these studies rely exclusively on cross-sectional data, an approach that confounds age and cohort effects. Thus, we must take special care to estimate the magnitude of the aging effects from genuinely longitudinal data. Second, the form of the age curve depends greatly on the specific tests used. Indeed, divergent-thinking measures represent only 1 possible psychometric assessment of creativity, and consequently, rather different longitudinal trends can be obtained when alternative measures are used. For example, tests that evaluate problem-solving skills in more everyday situations can actually produce scores that increase with age (Simonton, 1990). Third, many experts in the area of creativity research seriously question the validity of all so-called creativity tests. Validation studies usually show that such tests display rather modest correlations with direct measures of creative behavior. This suggests that a more optimal strategy might be to use behavioral indicators in the first place.

Creative Productivity as a Function of Age

The scientific study of the relation between age and creative productivity began over 150 years ago, and thus represents one of the oldest topics in life-span developmental psychology (Simonton, 1988). The classic investigations are those conducted by *Harvey C. Lehman*, especially as summarized in his 1953 book *Age and Achievement*. Although Lehman's work suffered from many methodological deficiencies, research employing more sophisticated techniques has verified the central conclusion: the output of creative products tends to increase with age until a peak is reached, after which productivity declines. In fact, the point of maximum output corresponds fairly closely to the age peak where scores on divergent-thinking tests tend to be highest.

Nonetheless, this same research also suggests that the prospects for creativity in the later years are not so dismal as might first appear (see also Lindauer, 2004). There are 7 relevant findings:

1. The specific shape of the age curve, including the location of the peak and the magnitude of the post-peak drop, varies according to the domain of creative activities (Simonton, 1997). In some disciplines the peak will appear much later in life, and the decline will be very gradual, even imperceptible.
2. The predicted level of creative productivity rarely drops to zero (Simonton, 1997). In most domains of creative activity, individuals in their 70s will be more productive than they were in their 20s, and they will be producing ideas at a rate only 50% below what they accomplished during their career peaks.

3. Individual differences in *creative productivity* are so substantial that this cross-sectional variation explains more variance than do the longitudinal fluctuations (Simonton, 1997). Hence, highly prolific contributors in their 70s and 80s can still display more creative productivity than much less prolific contributors who are active at their career peaks.
4. Changes in creative output across the life span are not strictly a function of chronological age but rather of career age (Simonton, 1997). This means that "*late bloomers*" who launch their careers much later in life will not reach their career optima until much later in life as well.
5. A large proportion of the decline in output in the last half of life is by no means inevitable, but rather much of it can be attributed to extraneous factors (Simonton, 1990). In contrast, certain environments can operate to sustain creativity well into old age. In the sciences, for example, those individuals who are embedded in a rich disciplinary network of colleagues and students tend to display much longer creative careers.
6. If one calculates the "quality ratio" of successful works to total works produced in consecutive age periods, that ratio stays more or less constant across the life span (Simonton, 1997). Thus, the success rate does not decline with age. Creative elders may be generating fewer masterpieces in their last years, but they are also producing fewer neglected pieces besides.
7. Creative output across the life span undergoes qualitative changes that can compensate for quantitative declines. For example, mature creators will more often concentrate on more ambitious works, such as epics, operas, novels, and monographs. More importantly, creators entering their last years often dramatically alter the approach they take to their creative activities (Lindauer, 1999). In the visual arts this sudden shift has been called the "*old-age style*," while in music this change is known as the "*swan-song* phenomenon." The result is frequently a masterwork that serves as a capstone for a creative career.

In combination, these 7 considerations indicate that research using psychometric measures may underestimate the creativity of older individuals. The decline may be neither drastic nor inexorable.

DEAN KEITH SIMONTON

See also
Intelligence

References

Adams-Price, C. (Ed.). (1998). Creativity and successful aging: Theoretical and empirical approaches. New York: Springer Publishing.

Levy, B., & Langer, E. (1999). Aging. In M. A. Runco & S. Pritzker (Eds.), *Encyclopedia of creativity* (Vol. 1, pp. 45–52). San Diego: Academic Press.

Lindauer, M. S. (1999). Old age style. In M. A. Runco & S. Pritzker (Eds.), *Encyclopedia of creativity* (Vol. 2, pp. 311–318). San Diego: Academic Press.

Lindauer, M. S. (2003). Aging, creativity, and art: A positive perspective on late-life development. New York: Kluwer Academic/Plenum Publishers.

Simonton, D. K. (1988). Age and outstanding achievement: What do we know after a century of research? *Psychological Bulletin, 104,* 251–267.

Simonton, D. K. (1990). Creativity and wisdom in aging. In J. E. Birren & K. W. Schaie (Eds.), *Handbook of the psychology of aging* (3rd ed., pp. 320–329). New York: Academic Press.

Simonton, D. K. (1997). Creative productivity: A predictive and explanatory model of career trajectories and landmarks. *Psychological Review, 104,* 66–89.

CRIME: VICTIMS AND PERPETRATORS

Crimes Against the Elderly

Victimization Rates. Attention in the media to crimes committed against older persons may leave the impression that the aged are a major target of violent crime in the United States. However, annual data from the *National Crime Victimization Surveys* over the period 1976–2000 consistently indicated that the composite violent crime victimization rate (i.e., homicide, rape, robbery, aggravated assault, simple assault) for persons aged 65 years and older was the lowest of any age group (Bureau of Justice Statistics, 2002). The most recent data available (for 2002) showed that this statistic holds true for each category of violent crime; only for the crime of personal theft did those 65 and older have a slightly higher rate of victimization (Bureau of Justice Statistics, 2002). Detailed data from 2002 that examine differences in victimization rates across even more detailed categories showed that no age group had lower rates than persons aged 65 and older for 11 out of 12 types of personal crimes; the only personal crime for which their rates were equal to or slightly higher than other age groups occurred in the purse snatching/pickpocketing category (Bureau of Justice Statistics, 2003). Furthermore, the violent crime rate for older persons generally decreased from 1973 to 2002 (Bureau of Justice Statistics, 2003).

Also, those 65 and older had lower rates of violent crime than younger cohorts in all gender and racial categories, but differences existed among groups with the cohort. Older white men and women had crime rates close to 3 per thousand, while the rates were 7.3 per thousand for older black women and 12.1 per thousand for older black men (Bureau of Justice Statistics, 2003).

Consequences of Victimization. Elderly persons are clearly less likely to be victimized by personal crimes. For those who experience *victimization*, there are conflicting findings on whether outcomes are more serious for them than for younger victims. Data from the 1992, 1993, and 1994 National Crime Victimization Surveys analyzed by Bachman, Dillaway, and Lachs (1998) indicated that injuries and the need for medical care resulting from victimization may be more prevalent among older persons than among younger persons. In terms of financial outcomes of crime victimization, detailed analysis of the consequences of victimization (Cook, Skogan, Cook, & Antunes, 1978) indicated that absolute financial losses incurred by older persons were no greater than those incurred by other adults, but relative losses (percentage of monthly income) were the same or higher. The costs of medical care associated with injuries constituted a larger proportion of their income. In contrast, 1992–1997 data from the U.S. Department of Justice (1999) suggest that the likelihood and level of injury inflicted on elderly victims of crime do not differ from victims in other age groups; all adults over the age of 25 had a similar likelihood of sustaining severe injuries from nonlethal violence. Of persons age 65 and older who reported being a victim of violence, 22% were injured, 11% required medical care, and 1% were hospitalized overnight—rates typical of other age groups.

Fear of Crime

Actual victimization is only one of the ways that crime can touch the lives of older persons. In the 2000 Harris American Perceptions of Aging in the 21st Century Study, 35% of persons aged 65 and older reported that fear of crime was a "serious" problem for them personally (Louis Harris and Associates, 2000). Of 7 problem areas about which respondents were asked, fear of crime was the third most frequently cited concern (after poor health and not having enough money to live on) for persons aged 65 and older. Data from the 2002 National Opinion Research Center's General Social Survey showed that 44% of older Americans lived near an area where they would be afraid to walk alone at night (Davis & Smith, 2003). The fear of crime reported among older adults far exceeds their actual criminal victimization rates.

Whether fear of crime is more prevalent among older persons has been the subject of some debate. For example, data collected for Are We Safe? The 2000 National Crime Prevention Survey indicated that persons aged 55 years and older were significantly more likely than younger adults to take a variety of precautions against crime, including locking the car, rolling up windows, parking in well-lighted areas, avoiding carrying valuables, and avoiding deserted shortcuts (National Crime Prevention, 2001). Although many studies have noted a positive relationship between age and fear of criminal victimization, analyses using a multiple-indicators approach to measure fear of crime and risk of criminal victimization have not found such a relationship (Ferraro & LaGrange, 1992).

While it has also been alleged that fear confines the elderly to their homes, most research has failed to support this assumption. One large study of public housing tenants (Lawton & Yaffe, 1980) concluded that there was no evidence to indicate that "elderly tenants respond to victimization, high crime risk, or even fear of crime, by becoming housebound." On the other hand, a study by Ragland and colleagues (2004) found that 16% of women aged 65 and older and 5% of older men cited concern about crime as a reason for limiting or giving up *driving*.

Crimes by the Elderly

Few published studies on criminal acts committed by the elderly exist, perhaps because criminal behavior is relatively infrequent in this age group. Though they accounted for 12% of the population of the United States in 2002, persons aged 65 and older made up considerably less than 1% of persons arrested, a smaller percentage than any other age group and about a fourth of the rate for persons aged 15 years and younger (U.S. Department of Justice, 2003). This low rate prevailed for specific types of crimes as well; for no category of crime did the percentage of older persons arrested approximate their distribution in the population. Older persons made up less than 1% of those arrested in 22 of 27 categories of offenses, and accounted for as high as 2.3% of those arrested in only 1 category (gambling). It is important to note that the vast majority of crimes—over 86%—for which *older persons are arrested* are minor offenses (i.e., crimes that are not included in the FBI's Crime Index) (U.S. Department of Justice, 2003). Not only are arrest rates for older adults low, but they are decreasing; from 1995 to 2002 those over 65 had a 22% decline in their arrest rates even though this age group's number increased. When arrested, older offenders are treated more leniently than their younger counterparts; they are less likely to receive prison sentences and if imprisoned, they receive somewhat shorter prison terms (Steffensmeier & Motivans, 2000).

STEPHEN J. CUTLER
MEGAN M. JOHNSON

References

Bachman, R., Dillaway, H., & Lachs, M. S. (1998). Violence against the elderly: A comparative analysis of robbery and assault across age and gender groups. *Research on Aging*, *20*, 183–198.

Cook, F. L., Skogan, W. G., Cook, T. D., & Antunes, G. E. (1978). Criminal victimization of the elderly: The physical and economic consequences. *Gerontologist*, *18*, 338–349.

Davis, J. A., & Smith, T. W. (2003). *General social surveys, 1972–2002: Cumulative codebook*. Storrs, CT: Roper Center for Public Opinion Research, University of Connecticut.

Ferraro, K. F., & LaGrange, R. L. (1992). Are older people most afraid of crime? Reconsidering age differences in fear of victimization. *Journal of Gerontology: Social Sciences*, *47*, S233–S244.

Lawton, M. P., & Yaffe, S. (1980). Victimization and fear of crime in elderly public housing tenants. *Journal of Gerontology*, *35*, 768–779.

Louis Harris and Associates. (2000). *American perceptions of aging in the 21st century*. Washington, DC: National Council on the Aging.

National Crime Prevention Council. (2001). *The 2000 National Crime Prevention Survey*. http://www.ncpc.org

Ragland, D., Satariano, W., & Macleod, K. (2004). Reasons given by older people for limitation or avoidance of driving. *Gerontologist*, *44*, 237–244.

Steffensmeier, D., & Motivans, M. (2000). Sentencing the older offender: Is there an age bias. In M. Rothman, B. Dunlop, & P. Entzel (Eds.), *Elders, crime, and the criminal justice system* (pp. 185–205). New York: Springer Publishing.

U.S. Department of Justice. (1999). *Crimes against persons age 65 or older, 1992–97*. Washington, DC: U.S. Government Printing Office.

U.S. Department of Justice. (2003). *Crime in the United States, 2002*. Washington, DC: U.S. Government Printing Office.

U.S. Department of Justice, Bureau of Justice Statistics. (2002). *Age patterns in violent victimization, 1976–2000*. Washington, DC: U.S. Department of Justice.

U.S. Department of Justice, Bureau of Justice Statistics. (2003). *Criminal victimization in the United States, 2002*. Washington, DC: U.S. Department of Justice. Statistical tables available: http://www.ojp.usdoj.gov/bjs/pub/pdf/cvus0201.pdf

CRITICAL THEORY AND CRITICAL GERONTOLOGY

The term "critical gerontology" has served to denote a wide range of ideas that seek to challenge or oppose prevailing theories, methods, and orientation of contemporary gerontology. This oppositional stance embodies a feeling that something is wrong with dominant approaches in the study of aging. However, the label "critical gerontology" can mean several distinct things:

- An application of perspectives drawn from the humanities (philosophy, history, literature) in opposition to prevailing scientific approaches to aging (Moody, 1988);
- A version of cultural studies applied to human aging (Laborsky & Sankar, 1993), an outlook increasingly visible in fields such as anthropology, literary theory, ethnic studies, and women's studies;
- A critique of the positivist paradigm (Tornstam, 1992) and, more broadly, a critique of objectivity in favor of interpretation or social construction (Baars, 1991) closely allied with phenomenology and hermeneutics;
- A broader movement of insurgent voices impatient with all forms of hegemony (Cole, Achenbaum, Jakobi, & Kastenbaum, 1993). In this respect, critical gerontology shows an affinity with the left-wing political economy perspective that has its own body of literature in gerontology (Minkler & Estes, 1991).

Background of Critical Theory

Critical theory in the proper sense refers to a group of thinkers originally associated with the Frankfurt School, above all figures such as T. Adorno, M. Horkheimer, and H. Marcuse, who were inspired by some aspects of Marxism to develop a far-reaching intellectual critique of contemporary society. They took issue with the idea of a "value-free" science or technology and instead sought to expose the dominant ideology behind all forms of cultural organization. More recently, the German philosopher Jurgen Habermas has continued the tradition of critical theory (Turner, 1991). While rejecting any clear demarcation between facts and values, Habermas (1984) favors an approach based on the patterns of communication and social interaction. Habermas calls attention to a variety of human interests, ranging from the instrumental logic of the sciences to the "emancipatory interest" in freedom and equality.

As applied to gerontology, Habermas's (1984) version of critical theory is provocative because he is eager for philosophy and social criticism to incorporate findings from and also influence empirical social science. At the same time, he emphasizes that human beings remain free subjects capable of critical thinking and political action. This openness to both science and human values is congenial to the historical spirit of gerontology, which has elements of both science and advocacy. However, Habermas's writings are abstract and programmatic, containing relatively few examples of how critical theory would actually redirect policy, research, or clinical practice in the field of aging.

Critical Theory and Current Issues in Gerontology

Critical theory has much to offer in stimulating research, education, and social criticism in an aging society. A few topics suggest the possible heuristic impact of critical gerontology in years to come.

Theory and Practice. Today there is a growing sense of the gap between theory and practice, between social norms and actual behavior at both the policy level and for clinical practice. In the field of geriatric health care, for example, critical theory can help elucidate the reasons for this failure (Moody, 1992). Bridging the gap between theory and practice has far-reaching applications for more realistic education for service providers in health and social welfare systems.

Gerontology and Ideology Critique. Critical theory can be understood as a form of ideology critique applied to knowledge and professional practice in aging. Ideology critique demands that gerontologists recognize covert interests that shape intellectual traditions and that have influenced the rise of gerontology as a field (Atchley, 1994). Self-reflectiveness and self-criticism are indispensable if gerontology is to contribute to the well-being of older people in the future.

Methodology and Philosophy of Science. Critical gerontology responds to ongoing methodological problems in the scientific study of aging; for example, consider the causes and meaning of retirement, one of the widespread features of later life (Atchley, 1993). Instead of simply measuring labor force participation or examining measures of subjective well-being, a critical perspective would ask deeper questions about the phenomenon of retirement and the social purposes it serves as an institution.

Qualitative Methods in Research. The ongoing dialogue between Habermas and Gadamer about hermeneutics finds its echo in the recent call for qualitative methods and interpretive social science applied to aging studies (Thomas, 1989). By recovering the human voice, the lived experience of old age, qualitative gerontology can help chart an emancipatory perspective on what it means to grow old.

At bottom, critical gerontology urges us to question and reject what might be called the social engineering approach to gerontology whereby "the elderly" appear as clients, that is, essentially as objects susceptible to instrumental control through social policy or professional practice. Instead, critical gerontology invites us to appreciate the last stage of life as an opportunity for freedom and then to reshape our institutional practices in pursuit of this ideal.

HARRY R. MOODY

See also
Social Gerontology: Theories

References

Atchley, R. C., (1993). Critical perspectives on retirement. In T. R. Cole, W. A. Achenbaum, P. L. Jakobi, & R. Kastenbaum (Eds.). *Voices and visions of aging: Toward a critical gerontology* (pp. 3–19). New York: Springer Publishing.

Baars, J. (1991). The challenge of critical gerontology: The problem of social constitution. *Journal of Aging Studies, 5*, 219–243.

Cole, T. R., Achenbaum, A. W., Jacobi, P., & Kastenbaum, R. (Eds.). (1993). *Voices and visions of aging: Toward a critical gerontology*. New York: Springer Publishing.

Habermas, J. (1984). *Theory of communicative action*. Boston: Beacon Press.

Laborsky, M. R., & Sankar, A. (1993). Extending the critical gerontology perspective: Cultural dimensions. *The Gerontologist, 33*, 440–454.

Minkler, M., & Estes, C. L. (1991). *Critical perspectives on aging: The political and moral economy of growing old*. Amityville, NY: Baywood Publishing.

Moody, H. R. (1988). *Abundance of life*. New York: Columbia University Press.

Moody, H. R. (1992). *Ethics in an aging society*. Baltimore: Johns Hopkins University Press.

Thomas, E. (1989). *Aging and the human sciences*. Albany: State University of New York Press.

Tornstam, L. (1992). The quo vadis of terontology: On the scientific paradigm of gerontology. *The Gerontologist, 32*, 318–326.

Turner, J. H. (1991). Critical theorizing: Jurgen Habermas. In *The structure of sociological theory* (pp. 254–281). Belmont, CA: Wadsworth.

CROSS-CULTURAL RESEARCH

Cross-cultural research designs are among the most powerful available to researchers. Gerontology has always had a healthy respect for comparative research since the early contribution of *Leo Simmons* (1945). Elders from one context have been compared with their counterparts elsewhere, and our understanding of aging and the experiences of aging can only be enhanced by cross-cultural research. By using the comparative method, it is possible to increase the range of variation and allow for a full evaluation of theoretical models and potential universality. Intracultural research investigates the variance within a defined context such as a nation, region, city or other unit. Here, the cultural context is presumed to be a near constant. Only selected characteristics of individuals and their differing situational circumstances are the study variables. Cross-cultural research, on the other hand, investigates variance across defined contexts such as cultures, nations, or ethnic and minority groups. Hence, the cultural context becomes an important part of the variation.

Cross-cultural research is expensive, especially if it involves a research design calling for the collection of primary data and a staff to collect it. Thus the reason for undertaking cross-cultural research must be more than curiosity. *Comparative research* calls for the examination of an issue in markedly different cultural contexts. The rational is twofold. First, the effort is to examine the effects of cultural context on the phenomena under investigation. Secondly, by disentangling the effects of cultural context, it is possible to discover if some aspects of the research question are universal to humans. If we find effects from context, then our investigations turn to an examination of what it is about that cultural context that shapes the relationships among variables. With a comparative design, we also have the potential to determine if the intracultural variation is a spurious product of the culture itself. Cross-cultural research not only increases the generalizability of findings, but also clarifies the relationships between variables.

Aging is an area in need of cross-cultural research. Aging is a process that is universal to humankind. At the same time, it is a process that is only experienced and interpreted in diverse cultural contexts of the world. In the past 5 decades, we have revealed much about the aging process in 1 cultural type—the industrialized nations. We know precious little about the rest of the world and have yet to evaluate our accumulated knowledge using the comparative perspective.

Cross-Cultural Research Strategies

Research projects of a comparative design have used 1 of 2 major strategies. The first is collecting primary data with a particular problem in mind. The second involves employing a re-examination of existing data and analysis of this secondary data.

Primary Research. Projects calling for the collection of new data from multiple research sites are differentiated by the units selected. This includes projects that are:

1. *Cross-ethnic:* The research design calls for administration of parallel instruments or data collection techniques within different ethnic groups in order to examine the effects of ethnic identification or membership on the study variables. This is exemplified by Groger & Kunkel's (1995) study of black and white older adults, as well as Henderson's (1996) study of dementia in Cuban-American and Puerto Rican Americans.
2. *Cross-national:* These comparative research designs call for parallel data collection techniques and collaboration between teams of researchers in different nations. The nation state is the unit selected and national probability samples are used within that unit to examine the differences and similarities across nations and the cultural and structural differences. Shanas and colleagues (1968) used this research design in their pioneering study of old people in 3 industrial societies. Other examples of *cross-national research* included Bengtson and colleagues' (1975) study of modernization and perceptions of aging, and Heikkinen and colleagues' (1983) survey of health and social factors in 11 countries.
3. *Cross-cultural:* A cross-cultural project takes as its unit a culture, which provides the most heterogeneous of comparative research designs. This may range from a team of investigators systematically investigating the same question in diverse cultures, to a single investigator sequentially examining the same question in different cultures. The team project is represented by *Project AGE*, which studied the effects of community and cultural differences on the well being of older people (Keith, Fry, Glascock, Ikels, Dickerson-Putman, Harpending, & Draper, 1994) and by Myerhoff and Simic's (1978) study of life histories in 5 cultures. Guttman (1987) has investigated personality changes in late life in several cultures to evaluate the potential universality of those shifts. Comparative studies also have focused on aging issues in a geographic area such as the Pacific (Counts & Counts, 1985).
4. *Case Study of Another Culture:* Although technically not comparative, these studies are implicitly comparative in that the researcher is reporting on a setting different that his/her own and that of the intended audience. Generally these studies take the form of an ethnographic description of another culture. Implicit in this type of study is a comparison of the culture under investigation with one's own culture. Because *ethnographic studies* of another culture usually involve a single researcher and possibly their family, the costs of the research are much less. Consequently this type of study is the most common. Examples of this type of comparative study is the Hennessys' study of caregiver burden among Native Americans (1995) and studies of aging in India (Lamb, 2000; Cohen, 1998).

Secondary Data. Some projects call for the reanalysis or *secondary analysis* of existing data. The research strategies involved differentiate these projects. This can range from a re-analysis of primary data collected by experienced fieldworkers to the secondary analysis of a worldwide sample of ethnographic accounts of specific cultures, such as the *Human Relations Area Files*.

1. *Re-examination of Fieldnotes:* Cowgill and Holmes (1972) used this strategy in their study of aging and modernization. They invited a team of experienced investigators to re-examine data they had collected for other purposes for its relevance to problems of aging and the treatment of the aged. Later Cowgill (1986) expanded this earlier study with more secondary data from a wide variety of sources.
2. *Analysis of Existing Reports:* Existing case studies and data are selected on either a regional basis or using some other criterion such as societal type. Press and McKool's (1972) study of the status of the aged used data from Mesoamerica. Foner and Kertzer (1978) investigated age transitions within 1 type of society, that having age sets. Foner (1984) used ethnographic resources in her comparative analysis of age conflict.
3. *Holocultural Analysis:* This is a distinctive kind of cross-cultural research which is based on the Human Relations Area Files. *Holocultural research* involves a statistical evaluation of the relationship between 2 or more variables in a world sample of human societies derived from the Human Relations Area Files (HRAF) (Rohner, Naroll, Barry, Divale, Erickson, Schaeffer, et al., 1978; Naroll, 1976). Simmons' (1945) pioneering work on the *aged in primitive societies* was among the first to use this research design. Contemporary research using this design is represented by Silverman and Maxwell's (1987) study of information and prestige, and in Glascock's (1997) study of the treatment of older people and death-hastening behavior.

The Questions Asked. Gerontological research was stimulated by an emergent crisis within industrialized nations, which by the middle of the 20th century were showing signs of a majority of people living longer while at the same time having fewer children. Old age was increasingly seen as a problematic state for individuals and their societies. Comparative research on aging began with the work of Simmons (1945), who used the HRAF files to investigate the status of older people in over 100 nonindustrial societies. From the beginning, researchers have used cross-cultural research to investigate successful aging, health, economic security, aging and families, the meaning of age and the life course, and the impact of societal transformations.

Successful Aging. Initial speculation that older adults were much better off in smaller, less technological societies where they do not retire has not received much empirical support. Each culture has both strengths and weaknesses. In smaller-scaled cultures, older people continue to work with kin and often increase in importance because of accumulated knowledge or control of resources. On the other hand, the lack of amenities such as indoor plumbing and medical technology can make daily living more demanding and illness far more problematic. By comparison, older adults in industrialized contexts take the laborsaving devices made possible by electricity for granted along with medical technology. However, they must have enough accumulated wealth with which to purchase these goods and services on the market. What makes for a good old age? Good and bad are culturally defined, and hence there is much variation. One issue is quite clear: a way to have a bad old age is to have poor health and limited functionality (Fry, Keith, Glascock, Ikels, Dickerson-Putnam, Harpending, et. al., 1997).

Health and Functionality. Human bodies are quite variable (Crews & Garruto, 1994). Human bodies begin to experience difficulties around age 60, some earlier and some later; physical problems increase with age, but not equally in all cultures. For instance, blood pressure remains stable across adulthood in non-industrial societies (James & Baker, 1995), unlike the lamented increases with age in industrial societies. Also loss of bone mass does not appear to be universal (Silverman & Madison, 1988).

The body is also subject to cultural interpretation. For instance, the age-related changes associated with menopause are universal for older women, but the specific symptoms are not (Lock, 1993; 1998). Questions of what one must be able to do to function as an adult (activities of daily living) are defined by specific context. What may be problematic in one place may not be in another—such as lifting water from a well—versus having access to indoor plumbing. Even difficulties in the ability to see may not hinder people where literacy is not a feature and recreation does not involve watching television or the computer screen.

Economic Security and Political Economies. Wealth is another factor that promotes successful aging. Where material accumulation is possible, this seems to hold true. However, there are economies where wealth is impossible to accumulate, such as foraging societies or those that base their livelihood on herding animals. Here work must be continuous, and with physical decline survival becomes increasingly problematic for an older person. The economic basis for social life is quite variable (Halpern, 1987). One point of variation for industrial societies is a *political economy of aging*, which in spite of inequities has worked to the benefit of older people in these nations through pensions and social security.

Aging and Families. With the advent of industry and rising prosperity, the family has been seen as a declining institution. The landmark work of Shanas and colleagues (1968) decidedly demonstrated that regardless of change, families were still involved with and supporting their older members. With an expanded comparative view, we know that families are universal but highly variable in size, definition of genealogical connections, and political and economic involvement in people's lives. In this diversity kinship is quite variable in providing a supportive environment for aging (Fry, 2003). For older adults, grand parenting is an important relationship, but it, too, is quite variable (Ikels, 1998; Schweitzer, 1999).

Age and the Life Course. Aging is a temporal phenomena, and age is the time of human lives. On a comparative basis, time is probably experienced much the same, but it certainly is not measured the same way and does not figure into people's lives in identical fashions (Kertzer & Schaie, 1989; Fry, 2002). For people in smaller-scaled societies, age is reckoned relatively. One is older than or younger than someone else, and this is calculated through the temporal aspects of kinship, generations, and birth orders. Only in state-level societies and especially industrialized nations is age measured absolutely through chronology. Here certificates document birth dates, and age is measured in terms of years lapsed and compared to a timeline starting with a fixed point, the year one. Age is important the world around, but in industrialized contexts it takes on heightened importance. Age defines thresholds of privilege, e.g. drinking, driving, marriage, voting, and entitlements to Social Security and Medicare. Here, the life course is seen as punctuated by age thresholds and is divisible into stages reflecting responsibilities and involvement. Otherwise, adulthood is seen as a long period of work that is gradually marked by physical decline.

Societal Transformations. One of the most well developed generalizations using cross-cultural analysis is aging and modernization theory, developed by Cowgill and Holmes (1972; Cowgill, 1986). This theory predicts that older people lose status as a nation becomes modernized because of health and economic technology, urbanization, and education. Although explicitly formulated, this theory has not received much empirical substantiation. Modernization has largely been abandoned in favor of *globalization*, which is affecting life all over the world in ways we are just beginning to understand. Comparative research is greatly needed to comprehend what aging in the present has become around the world in all of its diversity.

Although it is clear that gerontology has benefited from cross-cultural research, it is also apparent that global changes have significantly altered this type of research (Ikels & Beall, 2001). Most obvious are the political transformations of the last half of the 20th century, notably the Cold War and the decolonization of the pre World War II colonies (Chomsky, Katznelson, Lewentin, Montgomery, Nader, Ohmann, et al., 1997). Access to foreign field sites became increasingly restricted. In addition, local people can become resentful of politically advantaged foreign researchers speaking authoritatively on indigenous issues. Further complications rest in the postmodern response to the changing world. Comparative research is seen as being of little value, since science is of little value. Comparative research invites a scientific evaluation of hypothesis; postmodernism and discourse theory go on to argue that ethnographic reports describing a single reality are problematic, since realities are multivocal. Likewise, globalization has altered variation, since many people around the world participate in a common economic system. At present, it is unclear if the world is becoming increasingly homogenized or if the variation is simply changing as peoples participate in globalization in different ways. The net effect is that younger researchers are increasingly turning their attention to their own societies and are responding to the priorities of funding sources. Instead of questions about the consequences of differences in social organization and culture, the emphasis turns to issues defined as problematic, such as medical concerns, caregiving, social support, and well being and successful aging.

Comparative research has enriched the development of theory in gerontology. One of its most important benefits is that it places our understanding and interpretation of experience in a much broader perspective and range of variation. We can look at what we consider every day through comparative research to see the ordinary as alien. Our ideas are sharpened and possibly redefined. Of the most recent resources on comparative research in gerontology, the reader is referred to The *Journal of Cross-Cultural Gerontology*; Albert and Cattell's volume (1994), which synthesizes the comparative; and to a reader by Sokolovsky (1997), which presents original comparative work.

CHRISTINE L. FRY

References

Albert, S. M., & Cattell, M. G., (1994). *Old age in global perspective*. New York: G. K. Hall and Co..

Bengtson, V. L., Dowd, J. J., & Smith, J. H., (1975). Modernization, modernity and perceptions of aging: A cross-cultural study. *Journal of Gerontology, 30,* pp. 688–695.

Chomsky, N., Katznelson, I., Lewentin, R. C., Montgomery, D., Nader, L., Ohmann, R., Siever, R., Wallerstein, I., & Zinn, H. (1997). *The Cold War and the university; Toward an intellectual history of the postwar years*. New York: New Press.

Cohen, L. (1998). *No aging in India: Alzheimer's, the bad family and other modern things*. Berkeley: University of California Press.

Counts, D. A., & Counts, D. R., (Eds.) (1985). *Aging and its transformations: Moving toward death in pacific societies*. Lanham: University Press of America.

Cowgill, D. O., (1986). *Aging around the world*. Belmont: Wadsworth.

Cowgill, D. O., & Holmes, L. D., (Eds.) (1972). *Aging and modernization*. New York: Appleton-Century-Crofts.

Crews, D. E., & Garruto, R. M., (1994). *Biological anthropology and aging: Perspectives on human variation over the life span*. New York: Oxford University Press.

Foner, A., & Kertzer, D. I., (1978). Transitions over the life course: Lessons from age-set societies. *American Journal of Sociology, 83,* 1081–1104.

Foner, N. (1984). *Ages in conflict: A cross-cultural perspective on inequality between old and young*. New York: Columbia University Press.

Fry, C. L., (2002). The life course as a cultural construct. In R. Settersen (Ed.), *Invitation to the life course* (pp. 269–294). Amityville, NY: Baywood Publishing.

Fry, C. L., (2003). Kinship and supportive environments of aging. In H.-W. Wahl, R. J. Scheidt, & P. G. Windley (Eds.), *Annual review of gerontology and geriatrics. Aging in context: socio-physical environments*. (Vol. *23*, pp. 313–333). New York: Springer Publishing.

Fry, C., Keith, J., Glascock, A. P., Ikels, C., Dickerson-Putnam, J., Harpending, H. C., & Draper, P. (1997). Culture and the meaning of a good old age. In J. Sokolovsky (Ed.), *The cultural context of aging: Worldwide perspectives* (2nd ed., pp. 99–124). Westport, CT: Bergin and Garvey.

Glascock, A. P., (1997). When is killing acceptable: The moral dilemma surrounding assisted suicide in America and other societies. In J. Sokolovsky (Ed.), *The cultural context of aging: Worldwide perspectives* (2nd ed., pp. 56–70). Westport, CT: Bergin and Garvey.

Groger, L., & Kunkel, S. (1995). Aging and exchange: Differences between black and white elders. *Journal of Cross-Cultural Gerontology, 10,* 269–287.

Guttman, D. (1987). *Reclaimed powers: Toward a new psychology of men and women in later life*. New York: Basic Books.

Halpern, R. H., (1987). Age in cross-cultural perspective: an evolutionary approach. In P. Silverman (Ed.), *The elderly as modern pioneers* (pp. 283–311). Bloomington: Indiana University Press.

Heikkinen, E., Waters, W. E., & Brzezinski, Z. J., (1983). *The elderly in eleven countries: A socio-medical study*. Copenhagen: World Health Organization.

Henderson, J. N., (1996). Cultural dynamics of dementia in a Cuban and Puerto Rican population in the United States. In G. Ueo & D. Gallagher-Thompson (Eds.), *Ethnicity and the dementias* (pp. 153–166). Washington, DC: Taylor & Francis.

Hennessy, C. H., & Hennessy, J. R., (1995). The interpretation of burden among Pueblo Indian caregivers. *Journal of Aging Studies, 9,* 215–229.

Ikels, C. (1998). Grandparenthood in cross-cultural perspective. In M. Szinovacz (Ed.), *Handbook of grandparenthood* (pp. 40–52). New York: Plenum.

Ikels, C., & Beall, C. M., (2001). Age, aging, and anthropology. In R. H. Binstock & L. K. George (Eds.), *Handbook of aging and the social sciences* (5th ed., pp.125–140). San Diego: Academic Press.

James, G. D., & Baker, P. T., (1995). Human population biology and blood pressure: Evolutionary and ecological considerations and interpretations of population studies. In J. H. Laragh & B. M. Brenner (Eds.), *Hypertension, pathophysiology, diagnosis, and management* (pp. 115–126). New York: Raven Press.

Keith, J., Fry, C., Glascock, A. P., Ikels, C., Dickerson-Putnam, J., Harpending, H. C., & Draper, P. (1994). *The aging experience: Diversity and commonality across cultures*. Thousand Oaks: Sage Publications.

Kertzer, D. I., & Schaie, K. W., (Eds.) (1989). *Age structuring in comparative perspective*. Hillsdale, NJ: Lawrence Erlbaum.

Lamb, S. (2000). *White saris and sweet mangoes: Aging, gender and body in North India*. Berkeley: University of California Press.

Lock, M. (1993). *Encounters with aging: mythologies of menopause in Japan and North America*. Berkeley: University of California Press.

Lock, M. (1998). Menopause: Lessons from anthropology. *Psychomatic Medicine, 60,* 410–419.

Myerhoff, B., & Simic, A. (Eds.) (1978). *Life's career: Aging*. Beverly Hills: Sage Publications.

Press, I., & McKool, M. Jr. (1972). Social structure and status of the aged: Toward some valid cross-cultural generalizations. *Aging and Human Development, 3,* 297–306.

Rohner, R. P., Naroll, R., Barry, H., Divale, W. T., Erickson, E., Schaeffer, J. M. & Sipes, R. G. (1978). Guidelines of holocultural research. *Current Anthropology, 19,* 128–129.

Schweitzer, M. M., (Ed.) (1999). *American Indian grandmothers; Traditions and transitions*. Albuquerque: University of New Mexico Press.

Shanas, E., Townsend, P., Wedderburn, D., Friis, H., Milhoj, P. & Stehouwer, J. (1968). *Old people in three industrial societies*. New York: Atherton Press.

Silverman, S. L., & Madison, R. E., (1988). Decreased incidence of hip fracture in Hispanics, Asians and Blacks. *American Journal of Public Health, 78*(11), 1482–1483.

Silverman, P., & Maxwell, R. J., (1987). The significance of information and power in the comparative study of the aged. In J. Sokolovsky (Ed.), *Growing old in different societies: Cross-cultural perspectives* (pp. 43–55). Acton, MA: Copley.

Simmons, L. W., (1945). *The role of the aged in primitive society*. New Haven, CT: Yale University Press.

Sokolovsky, J. (Ed.). (1997). *The cultural context of aging: Worldwide perspectives* (2nd ed.). Westport, CT: Bergin and Garvey.

D

DAILY ACTIVITIES

See
Activities of Daily Living

DEATH AND DYING

Dying and death are major categories of human experience that are culturally determined. Social science research documents the fact that defining someone as dying is a social process. Although critical medical conditions certainly have a physiological basis, disease states are given significance through interpretation (Muller & Koenig, 1988). Perceptions that dying has begun and the meanings associated with those perceptions are contingent on a range of social and cultural factors, such as: the state of biological knowledge; the value of prolonging life or accepting finitude; the relative roles of religion, science, and medicine in creating meaning in everyday life; and personal familiarity with the dying transition. Dying today is shaped by particular notions of therapeutic possibility as well as ideals about approaching the end of life. The distinguishing feature about the process of dying today is that it can be negotiated and controlled depending on the preferences of the dying person, the goals of particular medical specialties, the organizational features of technology-intensive medical settings, and the presence and wishes of family members. It is impossible to think about death today except in language informed by institutionalized medicine.

A century ago, the leading causes of death in the United States were communicable diseases, especially influenza, tuberculosis, and diphtheria, and more than half of deaths occurred among individuals age 14 or younger. Over the century, average *life expectancy* increased and the chance of dying in childhood was greatly diminished (Quadagno, 1999). Since the post-World War II era, heart disease, cancer, and stroke have become the leading causes of death. In 1995 they accounted for 67% of deaths for persons aged 65 years and older. The fact that more people than ever before are dying in advanced age of chronic conditions creates unprecedented challenges—for individuals as they confront the dying process of relatives and friends, for the health care delivery system, and for U.S. society as its members struggle to define and implement the idea of a *good death*.

The *Medicalization of Dying*

In 1900, most Americans died at home, frequently surrounded by multiple generations of family members. By 1950, approximately half of all deaths occurred in hospitals, nursing homes, or other institutions. By the mid-1990s, 80% of Americans died in medical institutions, attended by paid staff. Persons over age 65 comprised less than 13% of the population, yet they represented 73% of all deaths in the United States in the mid-1990s. At the beginning of the 21st century, 55% to 60% of persons over the age of 65 die in the acute-care hospital, though patterns vary considerably across the nation (Institute of Medicine, 1997). Those persons fall into 2 distinct groups. The first includes elderly who were functioning independently until they were struck by a serious illness, for example heart attack, stroke, or fractured hip. Most of those patients receive relatively intensive care. The second group includes people who are older, frail, and debilitated, and have multiple degenerative and chronic conditions but are not clearly dying. The second group comprises 70% to 80% of elderly patients in the hospital; they may require repeated hospitalizations for supportive or intensive care, to stabilize conditions, and treat acute problems (Scitovsky & Capron, 1986).

As the location of death has shifted from the home to the hospital, as a system of knowledge medicine has become the dominant cultural framework for understanding death, the process of dying, and how to act when death approaches. Health professionals have the assumed responsibility, once held by family and community, for the care of persons at the end of life, and they now widely influence how that care is understood and delivered. Physicians have become the gatekeepers of the dying transition in the United States. They, rather than the dying person or family, define when the dying process has begun. This is most obvious in the hospital intensive care unit (ICU), where the inevitability of death frequently is not acknowledged until the end is very near, and the discontinuation of life-sustaining treatments often signifies the beginning of the dying process. Moreover, in the intensive care unit, medical staff are able to orchestrate and control the timing of death (Slomka, 1992).

A growing older population, cultural ambivalence about the social worth of the frail and very old, medical uncertainty about whether or not to prolong frail lives, and rising health care costs contribute to controversy both among health professionals and the wider public about decision-making and responsibility at the end of life. The costs of medical care—and especially the costs of intensive care—are high in the last months of life. Those rising costs have been the source of debate about rationing health care to older persons to reduce costs. For many people both within and outside of medicine, the value of prolonging life by technological means competes with the value of allowing death to occur without medical intervention. This cultural tension has given rise to a vast array of seemingly insoluble dilemmas about the management of dying. Literature in *bioethics* illustrates dilemmas in treatment and care for dying older persons, for which there are competing claims and no clear solutions. Common dilemmas about technologically prolonging life include: whether or not to artificially feed (through a feeding tube) a person who can no longer feed him- or herself; whether or not to place a person who has difficulty breathing on a mechanical ventilator; and whether or not to admit a dying person to an intensive care unit.

As more technological and clinical innovations become available, there is more that can be done to postpone death. The technological imperative in medicine—to order ever more diagnostic tests, to perform procedures, to intervene with ventilators, medications, and surgery in order to prolong life or stave off death whenever there is an opportunity to do so—is the most important variable in contemporary medical practice, influencing much decision-making at the end of life. There are no formulas that health professionals, patients, or families can use to decide between life-extending treatments and care that is not aimed at prolonging life. It is common for patients, family members, and health professionals to feel obligated to continue aggressive medical treatment even though they do not wish to prolong the dying process.

The conflict between comfort only and life-extending treatment as death approaches has never been more poignant or demanding. The largest study ever conducted on the process of dying in the hospital was carried out in 5 university hospitals across the United States over a 4-year period beginning in 1989 (*SUPPORT Principal Investigators*, 1995). In the first 2-year phase of the project, 4,300 patients with a median age of 65 years and diagnosed with life-threatening illnesses were enrolled in order to understand the character and quality of dying in the hospital. The SUPPORT investigators concluded that the dying process in the hospital was not satisfactory. For example, only 47% of physicians knew when their patients wanted to avoid cardiopulmonary resuscitation (CPR); 38% of patients who died spent 10 or more days in an intensive care unit preceding death; 46% of *do-not-resuscitate* (*DNR*) orders were written within 2 days of death, even though 79% of the patients had an existing DNR order and for 50% of the conscious patients, families reported moderate to severe pain at least half the time in the 3 days preceding death. The second 2-year intervention phase, involving approximately 5,000 different patients, was intended to affect positively the perceived quality of hospital deaths by enhancing the flow of information between doctors and patients. The startling results were that interventions aimed at improving physician-patient communication and physician knowledge of patients' end-of-life wishes did not change the practice of medicine regarding the use of intensive care unit treatments, timing of DNR orders, avoidance of CPR, or provision of pain relief, nor did those interventions alter the quality of patient and family experience. Even when a focused effort was made to reduce pain and to respect patient wishes regarding end-of-life care, no overall improvement in care or outcomes was made.

The technological imperative shapes activities and choices in the hospital, even though death without high-technology intervention is valued by many in principle. One survey of nurses and physicians revealed that health professionals would not want aggressive life-prolonging treatments for themselves, and many would decline aggressive care on the basis of age alone (Gillick, Hesse, & Mazzapica, 1993). In another study of end-of-life preferences conducted at 5 hospitals, approximately half of physicians and nurses interviewed stated they had acted contrary to their own values by providing overly aggressive treatment (Solomon, et al., 1993).

Philosopher Daniel Callahan has noted that U.S. society, including the institution of medicine, has lost a sense of the *normal* or *natural* life span, including the inevitability of decline and death. He, along with many other critics, has observed that death is now considered an option, one of several available to practitioners and consumers of health care (Callahan, 1993). Medicine pays little credence to the biological certainty of death; the tendency instead is to believe that dying results from disease or injury that may yield to advances in technology (McCue, 1995). The lack of clarity about what constitutes normal aging and decline and distinguishes them from disease, and the disregard for the fact that the human organism will eventually die, are important sources of the problem of technology use—considered by many to be inappropriate—at the end of life.

Family members are sometimes confronted with the choice of prolonging the life of a person who they consider to have died already as the result of a stroke, coma, or other serious condition that destroys or masks the individual's personality. In those instances, *social death*, in which the person no longer can express the same identity as before the health crisis, occurs days, weeks, months, or years before biological death, in which the physical organism dies. The discrepancy between social and biological death is one of the most difficult features of contemporary medical decision-making.

The use of *hospice* programs in which clinical, social, and spiritual support are given to dying persons and their families without the intention of prolonging life began in the United States in 1974. The hospice embodies a philosophy, originating with *Cicely Saunders* in Great Britain, that pain control, dignity, and the reduction of spiritual and psychological suffering are the most important goals of patient care as death approaches. Hospice care, delivered both in the home and institutional setting, has been growing steadily since the 1980s. Yet in 1995 only about 17% of all deaths (all ages) took place in a hospice setting. The notion of *palliative care*—medical care that seeks to reduce and relieve symptoms of disease during the dying process without attempting to effect a cure or extend life—is gaining support and acceptance among health care practitioners and the public, but the desire to control and conquer end-stage disease still strongly influences most medical thought and action (Institute of Medicine, 1997).

Cultural Diversity

There is not just 1 attitude or approach toward dying and death among Americans. Studies in the social science and health literatures on how cultural diversity influences patient, family, and provider responses to end-of-life treatments and decision-making have been appearing slowly but steadily since the mid-1980s. Two themes emerge from this research. First, health workers are trained in particular professional cultures and bring their own experiences to bear on the dying process. Physicians, nurses, social workers, chaplains, and other professionals hold different assumptions about how death should be approached as a result of their different types of training, and those sets of assumptions differ from the experiences of patients and families (Koenig, 1997). Second, the relationships among ethnic identification, religious practices, ways of dying, and beliefs and priorities about care, autonomy, and communication are complex and cannot be neatly organized along ethnic, class, or professional lines. In assessing cultural variation in patient populations for example, cultural background is only meaningful when it is interpreted in the context of a particular patient's unique history, family constellation, and socioeconomic status. It cannot be assumed that patients' ethnic origins or religious background will lead them to approach decisions about their death in a culturally specified manner (Koenig & Gates-Williams, 1995).

In an increasingly pluralistic society, there is growing diversity among health care workers as well as among patient populations. Especially in urban areas, the cultural background of a health professional is often different from that of a dying patient to whom care is being given. It is impossible and inappropriate to use racial or ethnic background as straightforward predictors of behavior among health professionals or patients. In their study of ethnic difference, dying, and bereavement, Kalish and Reynolds found that although *ethnic variation* is an important factor in attitudes and expectations about death, "individual differences within ethnic groups are at least as great as, and often much greater than, differences between ethnic groups" (1976). The impact of cultural difference on attitudes and practices surrounding death in the United States cannot be denied. The challenge for society is to respect cultural pluralism in the context of an actively interventionist medical system.

SHARON R. KAUFMAN

See also
Death Anxiety
End-of-Life Care

References

Callahan, D. (1993). *The troubled dream of life: Living with mortality*. New York: Simon and Schuster.

Gillick, M., Hesse, K., & Mazzapica, N. (1993). Medical technology at the end of life: What would physicians and nurses want for themselves? *Archives of Internal Medicine, 153*, 2542–2547.

Institute of Medicine. (1997). *Approaching death: Improving care at the end of life*. Washington, DC: National Academies Press.

Kalish, R. A., & Reynolds, D. K. (1976). *Death and ethnicity: A psychocultural study*. New York: Baywood.

Koenig, B. (1997). Cultural diversity in decision making about care at the end of life. In M. Field & C. K. Cassel (Eds.), *Approaching death: Improving care at the end of life* (Appendix E. pp. 363–382). Washington, DC: National Academies Press.

Koenig, B., & Gates-Williams, J. (1995). Understanding cultural difference in caring for dying patients. *Western Journal of Medicine, 163*, 244–249.

Muller, J., & Koenig, B. (1988). On the boundary of life and death: The definition of dying by medical residents. In M. Lock & D. Gordon (Eds.), *Biomedicine Examined* (pp. 351–374). Boston: Kluwer.

McCue, J. D. (1995). The naturalness of dying. *Journal of the American Medical Association, 273*, 1039–1043.

Quadagno, J. (1999). *Aging and the life course: An introduction to social gerontology*. Boston: McGraw-Hill.

Scitovsky, A. A., & Capron, A. (1986). Medical care at the end of life. *American Review of Public Health, 7*, 59–75.

Slomka, J. (1992). The negotiation of death: Clinical decision making at the end of life. *Social Science and Medicine, 35*, 251–259.

Solomon, M., et al. (1993). Decisions near the end of life: Professional views on life-sustaining treatments. *Journal of Public Health, 83*, 14–23.

SUPPORT Principal Investigators. (1995). A controlled trial to improve care for seriously ill hospitalized patients. *Journal of the American Medical Association, 274*, 1591–1634.

DEATH ANXIETY

Philosophers in the modern era have almost unanimously assumed that the human encounter with death is one marked by angst, dread, uncertainty, and fear—in a word, anxiety. At the same time, advances in life-extending technology, diet, and general lifestyle (at least in industrialized countries) have improved the longevity of the majority of people, effectively associating death with old age in the popular imagination. As a result of these 2 converging trends, one might assume that older adults, who are statistically "closest" to death, would experience considerable death anxiety. This article summarizes the principal findings in the growing literature on the *death attitudes of elderly* persons, focusing on those factors associated with elevated death concerns among older respondents.

Perhaps paradoxically, the general trend across studies points to a decrease, rather than an increase, in death anxiety with advancing age, at least through the adult years. Moreover, well-designed survey studies have demonstrated that age is a relatively good predictor of *fear of death*, accounting for more of the variation in death anxiety than other important demographic and social strata variables such as education, income, and ethnicity. However, in later adulthood, death anxiety tends to stabilize. This does not mean that all older people have uniformly low levels of death anxiety, but that as a group they have lower levels of death anxiety than middle-aged people, and that death anxiety does not appear to continue decreasing with age in later life. Future researchers need to pay closer attention to factors specific to older adults, such as perceived nearness of death, quality of life, subjective passing of time, and achievement of the developmental tasks of late adulthood, to gain a clearer picture of the psychological transitions in late life that may affect attitudes toward death.

Research has shown that the *gender difference in death anxiety* evident in younger adults—with women reporting more death fears than men—is not present in older adults. This finding is consistent with research showing that older adults are less differentiated by gender and exhibit a more androgynous gender identity. Ethnicity has been associated with greater death awareness, with African Americans and Hispanics reporting greater familiarity with death and greater exposure to violence than Caucasians. However, results of studies have been mixed regarding whether these ethnic differences are associated with greater anxieties about death among various subgroups.

Because deteriorating health and diminished income necessitates changes in residence for many elderly people, researchers have become interested in whether living arrangements (e.g., in the community vs. in an institution) have an impact on the death attitudes of the elderly. Some evidence suggests that nursing home residents report greater death fears than do those who live more independently, although this may be confounded with the association between death anxiety on the one hand and poor health and diminished life satisfaction on the other. Nonetheless, the findings that the institutionalized elderly are more likely to encounter death, think of it often, experience reduced control over their lives, and suffer deterioration in quality of life make further study of the death concerns of this vulnerable group a continued priority in future research (Fortner & Neimeyer, 1999).

Many studies in this area correlate death anxiety with another single variable, such as physical health, psychological status, and *religiosity*. A systematic review of this literature indicates that greater physical and emotional problems predict higher levels of death anxiety in older adults, although much work is needed to clarify the specific medical and psychological characteristics that are responsible for these general trends. In younger age cohorts, people who are more religious generally report lower levels of death anxiety. This relationship is less evident in older adults, although some studies suggest that religious orthodoxy and belief are associated with greater death acceptance, whereas simple church attendance and involvement in religious activities are unrelated to death attitudes.

Perhaps a more enlightened approach in future studies would be to focus on individual personality traits, *coping styles*, and competencies among older persons and how these interact with environmental conditions to accentuate or ameliorate their specific fears about death and dying. For example, *ego integrity* or *life satisfaction* of elderly respondents has been found to interact with their place of residence; institutionalized elderly with low ego integrity are especially vulnerable to heightened concerns about their mortality. Other work has concentrated on the particular coping skills used by older persons (e.g., prayer and reminiscence) to deal with the specific aspects of death anxiety of greatest relevance to them (e.g., helplessness, questions about the afterlife, and the pain of dying). Sophisticated studies that examine discrete death fears as a function of styles of coping with developmental transitions would clearly contribute to the information yield of future research.

Unfortunately, our understanding of the nature and predictors of heightened death fear among older individuals has been hampered by several factors, both theoretical and methodological. Theoretically, researchers have concentrated on easily measured demographic characteristics and measures of physical and mental illness, rather than on the potential resources of older adults (e.g., coping and family support) that could yield a more optimistic view of their ability to face death with equanimity, acceptance, or even affirmation. The recent theoretical formulations of Pyszczynski, Greenberg and Solomon (1999) show promise by focusing on systems that are activated to defend against thoughts of ones' mortality. Methodologically, investigators have also relied too heavily on unvalidated, idiosyncratic *death anxiety scales* that treat death attitudes as a single, uni-dimensional trait, rather than a complex construct with many aspects (e.g., fear of pain associated with dying, anxieties about loss of control, and apprehension about punishment in the afterlife). However, valid and reliable multidimensional measures of death anxiety and acceptance are now available that are beginning to add clarity and richness to current studies. Likewise, investigators have only recently begun to ground their studies in more comprehensive psychological, sociological, and developmental theories that could give coherence and direction to future research. As we continue to clarify the environmental and personal determinants of death anxiety, we will be in a better position to design educational, counseling, and policy interventions to promote a more humane encounter with death and loss at all points in the life span.

ROBERT A. NIEMEYER
BARRY FORTNER
Updated by RICHARD SCHULZ

See also
Anxiety
Death and Dying

References

Fortner, B. V., & Neimeyer, R. A. (1999). Death anxiety in older adults: A quantitative review. *Death Studies, 23,* 387–411.

Pyszczynski, T., Greenberg, J., & Solomon, S. (1999). A dual-process model of defense against conscious and unconscious death-related thoughts: An extension of Terror Management Theory. *Psychological Review, 106,* 835–845.

DELIRIUM

Delirium is a common and challenging disorder of cognition. It is characterized by an acute onset or worsening of confusion, generally in association with physical illness. It is most common in older people, in particular those who are frail. Delirium has been described in medical literature for centuries, and both the terminology and definition have evolved. The core features of delirium include a disturbance of consciousness and cognition, rapid onset and fluctuating course, and evidence of an external cause.

Prevalence and Prognosis

Delirium is a common problem in hospitalized older patients, occurring in between 5% and 60%, depending on the population studied and specific methodology used. Approximately one-half of these are delirious on admission, and the other half develop delirium while in the hospital. Having an episode of delirium is associated with an increased risk of adverse outcome, including high mortality rates of 25% to 35% and greater hospital costs (McCusker, Cole, Abrahamowicz, Primeau, & Belzile, 2002). Even after adjusting for baseline age, illness severity, and cognitive and functional impairment, delirium is independently associated with an increased length of hospital stay, iatrogenic complications, functional decline, and increased rates of nursing home placement.

Although delirium is generally considered to be transient and reversible, cognitive deficits can persist for 12 or more months. The hypoactive form of delirium and residence in a nursing home are both risk factors for persistent delirium. Patients who have an episode of delirium are at an increased risk of subsequently developing dementia over the ensuing few years (Rockwood, Cosway, Carver, Jarrett, Tadnyk, & Fisk, 1999). Possible explanations include that underlying, subclinical, cognitive impairment predisposes them to developing delirium, or that metabolic abnormalities during the delirium episode causes persistent cerebral damage in vulnerable people. The association with mortality and poor functional recovery persists long after hospital discharge as well.

Diagnosis and Differential Diagnosis

Several screening tools can detect delirium. The *Confusion Assessment Method* (CAM) is a rapid and easily administered screening instrument, although nonphysicians may require training in its use (Inouye, van Dyck, Alessi, Balkin, Siegal, & Horwitz, 1990). It is based on the diagnostic criteria of the DSM-III-R. Four cardinal features of delirium—acute onset and fluctuating course, inattention, disorganized thinking, and altered level of consciousness—constitute the CAM algorithm (Table 1). The presence of the first and the second criteria plus that of either the third or fourth criterion are required for a diagnosis of delirium.

Delirium is commonly under-recognized by nurses and physicians. This is in part due to the misconception that all delirious patients are agitated, when in fact the purely hyperactive form of delirium represents a minority of cases. Delirious patients who are hypoactive or somnolent often remain undiagnosed, or are misdiagnosed as demented. The likelihood that nurses will detect delirium during routine clinical care is lowest in the presence of dementia, high baseline delirium risk, and the hypoactive form of delirium (Andersson, Gustafson, & Hallberg, 2001). Patients with pre-existing dementia are at greatest risk of developing superimposed delirium, having it go unrecognized and thus untreated, and of accelerated and long-term cognitive and functional decline. Detection could be improved by documentation of baseline cognitive status, incorporating cognitive screening into routine clinical practice, educational programs, and clinical pathways (Meagher, 2001).

In some studies, the hypoactive form of delirium was associated with poorer outcomes, including

TABLE 1 The Confusion Assessment Method

The diagnosis of delirium requires the presence of features 1 and 2 and either 3 or 4.

1. **Acute change in mental status and fluctuating course**.
   - Is there evidence of an acute change in cognition from the patient's baseline?
   - Does the abnormal behavior fluctuate during the day, i.e., tend to come and go, or increase and decrease in severity?
2. **Inattention**
   - Does the patient have difficulty focusing attention, e.g. being easily distractible, or having difficulty keeping track of what was being said?
3. **Disorganized thinking**
   - Is the patient's thinking disorganized or incoherent, e.g., rambling or irrelevant conversation, unclear or illogical flow of ideas, or unpredictable switching from subject to subject?
4. **Altered level of consciousness**
   - Is the patient's mental status anything besides alert, i.e., vigilant (hyperalert), lethargic (drowsy, easily aroused), stuporous (difficult to arouse), or comatose (unarousable).

longer length of stay, hospital related complications, and functional decline. Severe delirium is associated with worse outcomes than mild delirium, and patients who do not meet the full criteria but have some symptoms of delirium—so-called subsyndromal delirium—have worse outcomes than if they had no or few symptoms.

The differential diagnosis of delirium includes dementia, depression, and other psychiatric conditions including mania or psychosis. Depression can be confused with hypoactive delirium. Mania and psychosis might resemble hyperactive delirium. Dementia is itself a risk factor for delirium. To determine if a newly presenting patient with confusion has delirium, dementia, or both, it is essential to collect information on the patient's baseline cognitive and functional status. This information can be obtained from family members, caregivers, neighbors, friends, or the family physician. An acute change is not compatible with most dementias and is suggestive of delirium.

Risk Factors and Precipitants

The risk factors for delirium are fairly well studied and include advanced age, pre-existing cognitive and functional impairment, sensory impairment, and a myriad of medical and social comorbidities. The concept of frailty captures this state of susceptibility. *Frailty* is a syndrome that arises from dysregulation across multiple systems, and people who are frail have multiple, interacting medical and social problems. Their reserve is compromised, and they are more susceptible to stressors (Rockwood, 2005).

Delirium involves a disruption of consciousness. Maintenance of consciousness can be considered a complex function maintained by the human organism. When the complex system fails, its highest order functions fail first. In this view, delirium represents a failure of the whole organism, and explains why delirium is a sensitive but nonspecific sign of illness. One can think of delirium as a balance between the fitness/frailty of the individual in whom

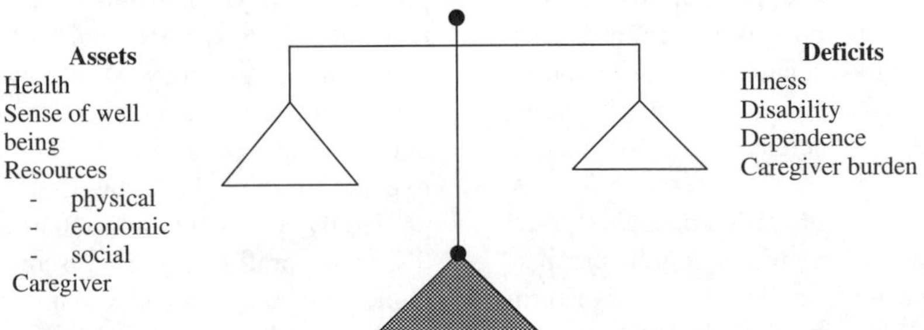

FIGURE 1 Fitness and frailty can be conceived of as a dynamic interaction between multiple medical and social problems.

TABLE 2 ***Causes of Delirium* in Frail Elderly Patients Admitted to a Medical Service***

- Medications
  - Prescribed
  - Over-the-counter
  - Alcohol, illicit, withdrawal
- Infection
  - Pneumonia
  - Urinary tract infection
  - Any
- Congestive heart failure
- Metabolic problems
- Some combination or something else

*Most common causes of delirium in 150 consecutive cases, in patients admitted to a Geriatric Assessment Unit.

it occurs, and the degree of the insult. This can be portrayed as a balance beam (Figure 1). Seen in this way, a large insult (or a brain-specific one) is needed to cause delirium in a very fit person, whereas a much smaller insult can cause delirium in a very frail person.

As such, delirium in older individuals represents not a specific brain disease as much as a nonspecific sign of an acute medical illness. Thus, while brain disorders such as stroke and meningitis need to be excluded as causes, this can usually be accomplished quickly. What is left is the inventory of illnesses that commonly befall older people. While in theory the list is long, in practice it amounts to comparatively few causes, readily grouped as medications, infections, heart problems, and metabolic abnormalities (Table 2). Not infrequently, these problems will occur in combination. These common disorders should be screened for in a cost-effective way before embarking on more exotic causes.

Post-Operative Delirium

Delirium is quite common in surgical patients, with incidence estimates between 10% to 50%, depending on the type of surgery, with cardiovascular, orthopaedic, neurosurgery, and emergency surgery having the highest rates. Postoperative delirium is associated with adverse outcomes, including failure to regain preoperative cognitive or functional status. Risk factors for postoperative delirium include older age, pre-existing cognitive or functional impairment, sensory impairment, alcohol abuse, the use of certain medications (benzodiazepines, those with anticholinergic effects), and laboratory abnormalities. It is possible to preoperatively identify patients at high risk of developing postoperative delirium by using baseline risk factor information. Unfortunately, information on delirium risk factors is not usually systematically collected during routine clinical care. In particular, cognitive screening is not generally included as a part of usual preoperative assessment. A great challenge in delirium research is to translate known principles of delirium prediction and prevention to routine perioperative care (Bekker & Weeks, 2003).

Whereas the route of intraoperative anesthesia does not greatly impact the risk of developing delirium, perioperative medication management is implicated. The use of benzodiazepines, medications with anticholinergic effects, and opioid analgesics are associated with an increased risk of developing delirium. Careful attention to fluid balance, postoperative hemoglobin level, bowel and bladder management, and early mobilization are hallmarks of good "delirium-friendly" care. Recognition of delirium, a targeted search for underlying causes, and avoidance of sedating medications which may perpetuate the confusion are essential.

Delirium Prevention

A number of studies have evaluated the effectiveness of delirium prevention strategies. A nurse-led intervention, involving systematic cognitive screening, regularly scheduled pain medications, and education of nursing staff resulted in decreased severity and shorter duration of delirium in hip fracture patients (Marcantonio, Flacker, Wright, & Resnick, 2001). Proactive geriatric medicine consultation, with attention to environmental issues, medications, and metabolic abnormalities reduced postoperative delirium by over one-third in orthopaedic patients. A combined *geriatric-anesthesiologic intervention* program focusing on intra- and postoperative medical complications in hip fracture patients resulted in a lower incidence and shorter duration of delirium, fewer postoperative complications, and a shorter length of hospital stay. A multifactorial intervention team consisting of specially trained nurses, therapists, and volunteers targeted known delirium risk factors, including cognitive impairment, sleep deprivation, immobility, sensory impairment, and dehydration in medical inpatients that were at increased risk of developing delirium (Inouye, Bogardus, Charpentier, Leo-Summers, Acampora, et al., 1999). This intervention was successful in preventing delirium, but had no impact on delirium once it had developed. Delirium prevention appears to be achievable, and the principles of delirium management are likely similar to those of prevention.

Management of Delirium

Management begins with recognition, and this may be facilitated by routine cognitive assessment as a part of standard care for older patients. Once delirium has been identified, appropriate investigations must be carried out to detect underlying causes, including careful review of medications. Laboratory testing should include, at the minimum, a complete blood count, electrolyte and renal function tests, oxygen saturation, electrocardiogram, urinalysis, and chest x-ray. Correction of *electrolyte imbalance* is associated with significant shortening in the duration of delirium. Supportive measures include maintaining a consistent, comfortable, and familiar environment. Restraints, both physical and chemical, are not only inhumane, but are associated with increased severity of delirium, morbidity, and mortality. Identifying sensory impairment and ensuring that glasses and hearing aids are in place need to be part of routine care. Whenever possible, medication schedules should allow uninterrupted sleep overnight. Involving the family, if possible, may foster a sense of security. Family members benefit from education and reassurance as well. Unfortunately, such environmental strategies are frequently overlooked.

In some cases of hyperactive delirium, agitation, aggression, or psychotic symptoms are so disruptive as to pose a danger to the patient or others, and thus merit pharmacological treatment. As the medications used to alleviate these symptoms can worsen confusion on their own, it is important to use caution in dosing. Haloperidol has generally been considered the drug of choice because of its minimal anticholinergic effects, and should be prescribed in low doses, regularly, for a limited time period (e.g. Haloperidol 0.5-mg q6h for 3 days). However, low doses of the atypical antipsychotic risperidone may be equally effective.

Challenges

Delirium is a challenging problem, which is better prevented than treated (Cole, McCusker, Bellavance, Primeau, Bailey, Bonnycastle, & Laplante, 2002). A high prevalence of delirium often points to widespread problems in health care delivery (Inouye, Schlesinger, & Lydon, 2001). Coming to grips with delirium prevention and optimizing management will be essential as the population ages.

SUSAN FRETER

References

Andersson, E. M., Gustafson, L., & Hallberg, I. R. (2001). Acute confusional state in elderly orthopedic patients: Factors of importance for detection in nursing care. *International Journal of Geriatric Psychiatry, 16,* 7–17.

Bekker, A. Y., & Weeks, E. J. (2003). Cognitive function after anesthesia in the elderly. *Best Practice and Research, Clinician Anaesthesiology, 17,* 259–272.

Cole, M. G., McCusker, J., Bellavance, F., Primeau, F. J., Bailey, R. F., Bonnycastle, M. J., & Laplante, J. (2002). Systematic detection and multidisciplinary care of delirium in older medical inpatients: A randomized trial. *Canadian Medical Association Journal, 167,* 753–759.

Inouye, S. K., Bogardus, S. T., Charpentier, P. A., Leo-Summers, L., Acampora, D., et al. (1999). A multicomponent intervention to prevent delirium in hospitalized older patients. *New England Journal of Medicine, 340,* 669–676.

Inouye, S. K., Schlesinger, M. J., & Lydon, T. J. (1999). Delirium: A symptom of how hospital care is failing older persons and a window to improve quality of hospital care. *American Journal of Medicine, 106,* 565–573.

Inouye, S. K., van Dyck, C. H., Alessi, C. A., Balkin, S., Siegal, A. P., & Horwitz, R. I. (1990). Clarifying confusion: The confusion assessment method. A new method for detection of delirium. *Annals of Internal Medicine, 113,* 941–948.

Marcantonio, E. R., Flacker, J. M., Wright, J., & Resnick, N. M. (2001). Reducing delirium after hip fracture: A randomized trial. *Journal of the American Geriatrics Society, 49,* 516–522.

McCusker, J., Cole, M., Abrahamowicz, M., Primeau, F., & Belzile, E. (2002). Delirium predicts 12 month mortality. *Archives of Internal Medicine, 162,* 457–463.

Meagher, D. J. (2001). Delirium: Optimizing management. *British Medical Journal, 322,* 144–149.

Rockwood, K. (2005). The causes of delirium. *Psychiatry, 4,* 66–69.

Rockwood, K., Cosway, S., Carver, D., Jarrett, P., Tadnyk, K., & Fisk, J. (1999). The risk of dementia and death after delirium. *Age and Ageing, 28,* 551–556.

DEMENTIA

Dementia is a term of medieval origin from the Latin *demens* meaning out of one's mind. In contemporary usage, it is a syndrome of progressive and persistent decline in (multiple) cognitive domains with associated changes in behavior, personality, and/or social functioning, produced by brain impairment. From the 1960s, operational criteria for the *diagnosis of dementia* (initially termed *chronic brain syndrome*) were developed for research, as well as for clinical management and service provision (e.g. DSM II and ICD-8). *Senile* (or late-life) dementia is clearly the commonest cause of the dementia syndrome in a rapidly aging world, with its incidence doubling every 5 years from around 2% at age 65 years to around 60% at age 90 years (Jorm & Jolley, 1998). In the 1970s, senile dementia (previously considered largely vascular in origin) was relabelled as *senile dementia* of the *Alzheimer type*, following the work of Blessed and colleagues at Newcastle on Tyne and the Albert Einstein Group in New York (Katzman, 2004). With the new emphasis on Alzheimer's disease, research criteria for dementia (e.g. DSM III and DSM III R) have made memory impairment the key cognitive domain, followed by frontal executive, language, and spatial dysfunctions. More recent research criteria (e.g. DSM IV, ICD-1) have emphasized specific types of dementia, rather than *dementia as a syndrome*. The most common dementia type associated with aging remains *Alzheimer's disease*, followed by dementia with *Lewy bodies* and *vascular* dementia. *Frontotemporal dementia* is usually considered a rare *presenile disorder*, but it is not uncommon and frequently is missed in older persons when the symptoms are muted by coexistent brain disorders, and at autopsy because frontotemporal (non-Pick) pathology is often nonspecific and coincident with Alzheimer's, Lewy body, and vascular pathologies. A clinical phenotype (or pattern of decline in cognitive, motor, and behavioral domains) has been identified for the common types of dementia. Alzheimer's disease generally presents with a specific memory impairment, characterized by rapid forgetting or loss of episodic memory (Graham, Emery, & Hodges, 2004) followed by semantic, language, and spatial impairments (characteristically temporoparietal in type) with retention of basic personality structure but early loss of personal insight. Clinical features suggesting dementia with Lewy bodies include visual hallucinations, deficits in attention with fluctuations in cognition, mild *Parkinsonism* with progressive gait disorder and falls, and early visuospatial deficits; memory complaint or impairment is common but less severe and more frontal in type (Ballard, 2004). Vascular dementia is more variable clinically, dependent on the site, size, number, and nature of vascular brain lesions; clinical features are mild memory impairment and mild behavioral changes, both of a frontal type with semantic, language, and visuospatial deficits less common (Graham, Emery, & Hodges, 2004). There may be characteristic progression of gait and motor deficits. The diagnosis of vascular dementia is assisted by the presence of (multiple) vascular risk factors and clinical and/or imaging evidence of (multiple) strokes. However, clinical and pathological studies have shown that senile (late-life) dementia is often a mix of these common dementia types (Neuropathology Group of the Medical Research Council Cognitive Function and Ageing Study; Ince, 2001; Waite, Broe, Grayson, & Creasey, 2001a). The *dementia syndrome* may also be caused by external insults (such as vasculitis, toxins, drugs, infectious agents, brain trauma, and systemic organ failure) and caused (or exacerbated) by other systemic disorders including disturbances in thyroid, vitamin, and calcium metabolism, albeit rarely.

Historical Development

The contemporary term dementia arises from, and retains, some of the concepts prevalent in the 17th to 19th centuries when it was synonymous with insanity; but even then dementia had the meaning of permanent and final loss of mental faculties, as opposed to "mania" in which the mental faculties were considered to still exist "though exercised in a confused and disordered manner," with at least potential for recovery (Roberts, 1981). Dementia was also differentiated from "idiocy" in which the mental faculties were never developed. In this early usage dementia was thought to arise both from longstanding (chronic and protracted) "mania" (modern mental illness) and also as a primary form of mental derangement in old age (modern senile dementia). In contemporary usage dementia has retained the concept of progression, to differentiate it from mental retardation, developmental delay, lack of education, or other static conditions. It also retains the concept of persistence or irreversibility of symptoms, primarily to differentiate it from the reversible cognitive decline of delirium, but also from potentially reversible syndromes of mental illness, such as depression or psychosis. Around the turn of the 19th century Pick (in 1892) and Alzheimer (in 1907) demonstrated the organic basis and pathology of 2 important presenile dementias. The leader of the Munich School, *Kraepelin*, named the clinical syndrome described by Alzheimer, with its distinctive plaque and tangle pathology, Alzheimer's disease; however he separated the more common senile dementia (considered arteriosclerotic) from that disorder. In 1893 Kraepelin had coined the term "*dementia praecox*" for contemporary schizophrenia (the latter term introduced by Bleuler in 1908), but subsequent confirmation of its organic basis eluded Kraepelin. The early 20th century influence of Freud, Bleuler, and Jung then produced the concept of "*functional psychoses*" as psychological disorders of the mind, emotions, and social environment, while eventually freeing the term dementia for the "*organic psychoses*." Freud's influence in particular led to the separation of psychiatry and neurology and to the relative neglect of dementia by both disciplines for around 50 years (Martin, 2002).

Aging, Risk Factors, and Neurodegenerative Diseases

The strongest risk factor for dementia is age. In the 1970s the close identification of senile dementia with Alzheimer's disease created an instant epidemic, assisted the separation of dementia as a concept from the aging process, and advanced dementia research (Katzman, 2004). Alzheimer's disease became the paradigm for age-related *neurodegenerative disorders*, which typically present with a more severe but rare early-onset familial form and a common later-onset sporadic form. This group of disorders is distinguished by the following common features: "primary" neuronal loss (i.e. not due to known metabolic, toxic, inflammatory, vascular, or other cause); a relatively specific neuropathology (neuritic plaques and neurofibrillary tangles in the case of Alzheimer's disease); abnormal protein accumulation (*B Amyloid*, *tau* and *synuclein* in Alzheimer's disease); and spread through a specific neuronal system (the cortical connections of the hippocampal and posterior cingulate networks in Alzheimer's disease). Other neurodegenerative diseases, which have their own pathological and protein markers, progress to age-related dementia with involvement of fronto-subcortical circuits and motor systems. These include dementia with Lewy bodies and Parkinson disease dementia (the *synucleinopathies*); less common frontotemporal dementias, cortico-basal degeneration and progressive supranuclear palsy (the *tauopathies*); and motor neuron disease and other rarer types of dementia. These clinico-pathological findings led to the concept of selective neuronal vulnerability producing the dementia subtypes, and to the search for genetic and environmental risk factors and interactions causal for Alzheimer's disease and the other neurodegenerative syndromes (Morrison, 2000). Potentially modifiable risk or protective factors suggested, but unproven, for Alzheimer's disease include anti-inflammatory drugs, statins, red wine, metal binding agents, oestrogens, education and mental and physical activity, and the role of antioxidants in age-related neurodegeneration more broadly (Haan & Wallace, 2004). Mid-life vascular risk factors, causing later-life small vessel vascular brain disease, have also come to be regarded more as risk factors for mixed pathology senile dementia than as common predictors of vascular dementia.

Pre-Dementia Syndromes and *Mild Cognitive Impairment*

The operational criteria (DSM, ICD) for the diagnosis of dementia have been criticized as providing dichotomous definitions, using an arbitrary cut-off for what is clinically a continuum of decline from "normal aging." Widespread neuronal loss is no longer considered inevitable in normal aging and, where selective neuronal loss occurs it is considered syndromal or "disease" related (Morrison, 2000). The search for prevention and therapy has led to attempts to identify early clinical states or pre-dementia syndromes, with operational criteria that predict subsequent development of dementia. Much of the recent focus has been on the entity of memory-defined mild cognitive impairment, predicting progression to Alzheimer's disease (Davis & Rockwood, 2004). However pre-dementia syndromes are likely to be heterogeneous in older people, and other clinical markers (e.g. gait and extrapyramidal slowing, mild executive dysfunction) may predict progression to other dementias or to mixed senile dementia, such as with Alzheimer, Lewy body, vascular, and other components. (Waite, Broe, Grayson, & Creasey, 2001b; Broe & Waite, 2005).

It is becoming more accepted that the course of the dementia syndrome, while still usually progressive, may be static or remittent. This follows the (limited) success of cholinergic therapy in Alzheimer's disease and in dementia with Lewy bodies, and advances in management of potentially treatable or reversible factors, both of which may modify the progression of symptoms in some patients with dementia. The concept of dementia, as a syndrome, remains important for management, therapy, carer support, and service provision, as well as for etiological research and prevention. This is particularly true for older age groups where mixed dementia is common. It requires redefinition of the clinical syndrome of late onset Alzheimer's disease (with and without extrapyramidal features) and separation of the relative contributions of Alzheimer's disease, Lewy body diseases, vascular disease, and other dementia types to senile (late-onset) dementia, as our knowledge of specific dementia types progresses.

G. A. Broe

See also

Alzheimer's Disease: Clinical
Cognitive Dysfunction: Drug Treatment
Dementia: Frontotemporal
Dementia: Lewy Body
Mild Cognitive Impairment

References

Ballard, C. G. (2004). Definition and diagnosis of dementia with Lewy bodies. *Dementia and Geriatric Cognitive Disorders, 17*(Suppl. 1), 15–24.

Broe, G. A., & Waite, L. M. (2005). Gait slowing as a predictor of dementia: The Sydney Older Persons Study. *Research and Practice in Alzheimer's Disease and Cognitive Decline, 8.* (Accepted for publication.)

Davis, H. S., & Rockwood, K. (2004). Conceptualization of mild cognitive impairment: A review. *International Journal of Geriatric Psychiatry, 19*, 313–319.

Graham, N. L., Emery, T., & Hodges, J. R. (2004). Distinctive cognitive profiles in Alzheimer's disease and subcortical vascular dementia. *Journal of Neurology, Neurosurgery and Psychiatry, 75*, 61–71.

Haan, N. H., & Wallace, R. (2004). Can dementia be prevented? Brain ageing in a population-based context. *Annual Review of Public Health, 25*, 13.1–13.24.

Jorm, A. F., & Jolley, D. (1998). The incidence of dementia: A meta-analysis. *Neurology, 51*, 728–733.

Katzman, R. (2004). A neurologist's view of Alzheimer's disease and dementia. *International Psychogeriatrics, 16*, 259–273.

Martin, J. B. (2002). The integration of neurology, psychiatry and neuroscience in the 21st century. *American Journal of Psychiatry, 159*, 695–704.

Morrison, J. H. (2000). Age-related shifts in neural circuit characteristics and their impact on age-related cognitive impairment. In P. C. Stern & L. L. Carstensen (Eds.), *The ageing mind: Opportunities in cognitive research. Committee on future directions for cognitive research on ageing* (pp. 83–113). Commission on Behavioral and Social Sciences and Education, National Research Council. Washington, DC: National Academies Press.

Neuropathology Group of the Medical Research Council Cognitive Function and Ageing Study; Ince, P. (2001). Pathological correlates of late-onset dementia in a multicenter, community-based population in England and Wales. *Lancet, 357*, 169–175.

Roberts, A. (1981). Forms of disease, in *The lunacy commission.* Available: http://www.mdx.ac.uk/www/study/01.htm

Waite, L. M., Broe, G. A., Grayson, D. A., & Creasey, H. (2001a). The incidence of dementia in an Australian community population: The Sydney Older Persons Study. *International Journal of Geriatric Psychiatry, 16*, 680–690.

Waite, L. M., Broe, G. A., Grayson, D. A., & Creasey, H. (2001b). Preclinical syndromes predict dementia: The Sydney Older Persons Study. *Journal of Neurology, Neurosurgery and Psychiatry, 71*, 296–302.

DEMENTIA: FRONTOTEMPORAL

Frontotemporal dementia (FTD) is a progressive neurodegenerative condition with a mean onset at about 60 years of age (Brun & Gustafson, 1993; Haase, 1977; Harvey, Rossor, Skelton-Robinson, & Garralda, 1998; Knopman, Petersen, Edland, Cha, & Rocca, 2004; Ratnavalli, Brayne, Dawson, & Hodges, 2002; Rosso, Kaat, Baks, Joosse, de Koning, Pijnenburg, et al., 2003a; Snowden, Neary, & Mann, 1996). The estimated prevalence of *FTD* is 9.4 to 53.4 cases per 100,000 (Harvey, 2001; Knopman et al., 2004; Ratnavalli et al., 2002; Rosso, Kaat, Baks, Joosse, de Koning, Pijnenburg, et al., 2003b; Rossor, 1999; Snowden, Neary, & Mann, 1996). FTD thus is as common as Alzheimer's disease (AD) in those younger than age 65 years (Harvey, 2001; Knopman, et al., 2004; Ratnavalli, et al., 2002).

Analysis of a large series of patients indicates that about 7% of FTD patients have a mutation on the q21-22 portion of chromosome 17 where the microtubule-associated protein *tau* (*MAPT*) is coded (Poorkaj, Grossman, Steinhart, Payami, Sadovnick, Nochlin, et al., 2001). Another 15% to 25% of FTD patients have a highly significant family history despite no abnormality on *chromosome 17* (Chow, Miller, Hayashi, & Geschwind, 1999; Rosso, et al., 2003a). *Chromosome 3* also is implicated in FTD (Ashworth, Lloyd, Brown, Gydesen, Sorensen, Brun, et al., 1999), although the precise locus remains to be defined. Most cases of FTD appear to be sporadic.

Clinical features. The major clinical features of FTD are: (1) a progressive form of *aphasia*, and (2) a disorder of social comportment and personality (Grossman, 2002; Grossman & Ash, 2004; Neary, Snowden, Gustafson, Passant, Stuss, Black, 1998; Snowden et al., 1996). Each of these phenotypes represents about half of the patients with FTD.

One form of progressive aphasia is known as *semantic dementia* (Hodges, Patterson, Oxbury, & Funnell, 1992; Snowden, Goulding, & Neary, 1989). These patients have significant *naming difficulty* associated with *impaired knowledge of word meaning*. Over time, all knowledge associated with the concept underlying a word is compromised, including poor recognition of the object associated with a word, and difficulty knowing how to use an object (Lambon, Ralph, McClelland, Patterson, Galton, & Hodges, 2001). Imaging studies associate semantic dementia with disease in the ventral and inferior temporal cortex of the left hemisphere, and disease in this region appears to correlate with a semantic memory impairment (Gorno-Tempini, Dronkers, Rankin, Ogar, Phengrasamy, Rosen, et al., 2004; Grossman, et al., 2004; Mummery, Patterson, Price, & Hodges, 2000).

Another form of progressive aphasia is known as *progressive nonfluent aphasia* (Grossman, et al., 1996; Hodges & Patterson, 1996). These individuals have slow, effortful speech with many phonemic paraphasic errors that may become quite distorted. Their speech also appears to be agrammatic, and this grammatical difficulty extends to comprehension of sentences. Imaging studies relate this phenotype to disease in the left inferior frontal cortex (Gorno-Tempini, et al., 2004; Grossman et al., 1996; Grossman, et al., 2004), and this appears to correlate with sentence comprehension difficulty (Grossman, Work, Gee, McMillan, & Moore, 2004).

The *disorder of social comportment* and personality is associated with apathy, disinhibition, loss of empathy, hyperorality, ritualistic behavior, and poor insight into these difficulties (Miller, Darby, Swartz, Yener, & Mena, 1995; Miller, Darby, Benson, Cummings, & Miller, 1997; Rankin, Kramer, Mychack, & Miller, 2003). Imaging studies associate these manifestations of FTD with right frontal and right temporal disease (Miller, Chang, Mena, Boone, & Lesser, 1993; Mychack, Kramer, Boone, & Miller, 2001; Rosen, et al., 2002). FTD also can be associated with *motor neuron disease* (MND), and a surprisingly large number of patients with MND have mild cognitive features consistent with FTD (Bak, O'Donovan, Xuereb, Boniface, & Hodges, 2001; Lomen-Hoerth, Anderson, & Miller, 2002; Lomen-Hoerth, Murphy, Langmore, Kramer, Olney, & Miller, 2003).

Diagnosis and Biomarkers. Diagnosis depends on recognizing these clinical phenotypes, and excluding other causes of progressive dementia. Clinical criteria have been published that help guide identification of FTD patients (McKhann, Trojanowski, Grossman, Miller, Dickson, & Albert, 2001; Neary, et al., 1998). In addition to the characteristic imaging features associated with each of the clinical phenotypes, *biomarkers* in the cerebrospinal fluid such as the level of the protein tau also may be helpful in diagnosing FTD and distinguishing it from other more common conditions such as Alzheimer's disease (Grossman et al., 2005).

Treatment. Although there is no known cure for FTD, symptomatic treatment may be helpful in managing some of the clinical features that can be disruptive to the quality of life of patients and their caregivers. *Antidepressants* such as serotonin-specific reuptake inhibitors and other serotonin-containing medications have been shown to be helpful in a small series of patients, for example. Atypical *neuroleptic* agents and some *anticonvulsants* also can help moderate disturbing behaviors. While *acetylcholinesterase inhibitors* may improve naming in progressive aphasics, it is important to avoid this class of medications in patients with a behavioral disturbance, since disturbing behaviors can be exacerbated.

Recent advances suggest new therapeutic approaches that may treat the underlying disorder of *tau metabolism*. This work is based on animal models of FTD that may be responsive to low doses of taxol-like substances that help stabilize microtubules and possibly reverse the neurodegenerative process (Zhang, Maiti, Shively, Lakhani, McDonald-Jones, Bruce, et al., 2005).

Behavioral interventions also may be helpful. A structured environment appears to assist in the management of patients with a social disorder. Communication support for progressive aphasics may include speaking slowly and redundantly, using multiple modalities (gesture as well as speech) and a rich, supportive context.

Pathology. Despite currently available interventions, FTD typically progresses relentlessly over a course of about 5 to 7 years until death (Hodges, Davies, Xuereb, Kril, & Halliday, 2003). A wide range of pathologies appears to be implicated in FTD (Lee, Goedert, & Trojanowski, 2001). Perhaps the most common cause is dementia lacking distinctive histopathology (Knopman, Mastri, Frey, Sung, & Rustan, 1990), or *frontotemporal lobar degeneration* (Brun, 1987). These conditions are associated with neuronal dropout, vacuolar degeneration, and gliosis that is most prominent in the frontal and anterior temporal regions. The hallmark of this condition is the virtual absence of *soluble tau* (Zhukareva, et al., 2001; 2003). Recently, the brains of some of these patients have been shown to have *ubiquitin-positive inclusions*. These appear to be identical to the ubiquitin-positive inclusions seen in patients with motor neuron disease, although the clinical features of motor neuron disease frequently were not present in these FTD patients during life. Another common cause of FTD is *Pick's disease* (Constantinidis, Richard, & Tissot, 1974; Delacourte, Sergeant, Wattez, Gauvreau, & Robitaille, 1998; Lieberman, Trojanowski, Lee, Balin, Ding, Greenberg, et al., 1998). This condition shows dense, globular cytoplasmic inclusions known as *Pick bodies* that are most prominent in a frontal and anterior temporal distribution, associated with *hyperphosphorylated tau* that is predominated by a particular allelic form. Other disorders of tau metabolism also can result in FTD, collectively known as *tauopathies* (Lee et al., 2001).

MURRAY GROSSMAN

See also

Alzheimer's Disease: Clinical
Dementia
Dementia: Lewy Body

References

Ashworth, A., Lloyd, S., Brown, J., Gydesen, S., Sorensen, S. A., Brun, A. et al. (1999). Molecular genetic characterization of frontotemporal dementia on chromosome 3. *Dementia and Geriatric Cognitive Disorders, 10*, 93–101.

Bak, T., O'Donovan, D. G., Xuereb, J., Boniface, S., & Hodges, J. R. (2001). Selective impairment of verb processing associated with pathological changes in Brodmann areas 44 and 45 in the motor neurone disease-dementia-aphasia syndrome. *Brain, 124*, 103–120.

Brun, A. (1987). Frontal lobe degeneration of the non-Alzheimer type: I. Neuropathology. *Archives of Gerontology and Geriatrics, 6*, 193–208.

Brun, A., & Gustafson, L. (1993). The Lund longitudinal dementia study. A 25-year perspective on neuropathology, differential diagnosis, and treatment. In B. Corain, K. Iqbal, M. Nicolini, B. Winblad, H. Wisniewski, & P. Zatta (Eds.), *Alzheimer's disease: Advances in clinical and basic research* (pp. 3–18). London: John Wiley and Sons.

Chow, T. W., Miller, B. L., Hayashi, V. N., & Geschwind, D. H. (1999). Inheritance of frontotemporal dementia. *Archives of Neurology*, *56*, 817–822.

Constantinidis, J., Richard, J., & Tissot, R. (1974). Pick's disease: Histological and clinical correlations. *European Neurology*, *11*, 208–217.

Delacourte, A., Sergeant, N., Wattez, A., Gauvreau, D., & Robitaille, Y. (1998). Vulnerable neuronal subsets in Alzheimer's disease and Pick's disease are distinguished by their tau isoform distribution and phosphorylation. *Annals of Neurology*, *43*, 193–204.

Gorno-Tempini, M., Dronkers, N. F., Rankin, K. P., Ogar, J. M., Phengrasamy, L., Rosen, H. J. et al. (2004). Cognition and anatomy in three variants of primary progressive aphasia. *Annals of Neurology*, *55*, 335–346.

Grossman, M. (2002). Frontotemporal dementia: A review. *Journal of the International Neuropsychological Society*, *8*, 564–583.

Grossman, M., & Ash, S. (2004). Primary progressive aphasia: A review. *Neurocase*, *10*, 3–18.

Grossman, M., Farmer, J., Leight, S., Work, M., Moore, P., Van Deerlin, V. M. D. et al. (2005). Cerebrospinal fluid profile distinguishes frontotemporal dementia from Alzheimer's disease. *Annals of Neurology*, submitted for publication.

Grossman, M., McMillan, C., Moore, P., Ding, L., Glosser, G., Work, M. et al. (2004). What's in a name: Voxel-based morphometric analyses of MRI and naming difficulty in Alzheimer's disease, frontotemporal dementia, and corticobasal degeneration. *Brain*, *127*, 628–649.

Grossman, M., Mickanin, J., Onishi, K., Hughes, E., D'Esposito, M., Ding, X.-S. et al. (1996). Progressive non-fluent aphasia: Language, cognitive, and PET measures contrasted with probable Alzheimer's disease. *Journal of Cognitive Neuroscience*, *8*, 135–154.

Grossman, M., Work, M., Gee, J. C., McMillan, C., & Moore, P. (2004). Sentence comprehension difficulty in progressive non-fluent aphasia: A voxel-based morphometric analysis. Submitted for publication.

Haase, G. R. (1977). Diseases presenting as dementia. In C. E. Wells (Ed.), *Dementia* (2nd ed., pp. 27–67). Philadelphia: F. A. Davis.

Harvey, R. J. (2001). Epidemiology of presenile dementia. In J. R. Hodges (Ed.), *Early-onset dementia: A multidisciplinary approach* (pp. 1–23). Oxford: Oxford University Press.

Harvey, R. J., Rossor, M. N., Skelton-Robinson, M., & Garralda, E. (1998). Young onset dementia: Epidemiology, clinical symptoms, family burden, support, and outcome. Available: http://www.dementia.ion.ac.uk.

Hodges, J. R., Davies, R., Xuereb, J., Kril, J. J., & Halliday, G. M. (2003). Survival in frontotemporal dementia. *Neurology*, *61*, 349–354.

Hodges, J. R., & Patterson, K. (1996). Nonfluent progressive aphasia and semantic dementia: A comparative neuropsychological study. *Journal of the International Neuropsychological Society*, *2*, 511–524.

Hodges, J. R., Patterson, K., Oxbury, S., & Funnell, E. (1992). Semantic dementia: Progressive fluent aphasia with temporal lobe atrophy. *Brain*, *115*, 1783–1806.

Knopman, D. S., Mastri, A. R., Frey, W. H., Sung, J. H., & Rustan, T. (1990). Dementia lacking distinctive histologic features: A common non- Alzheimer degenerative dementia. *Neurology*, *40*, 251–256.

Knopman, D. S., Petersen, R. C., Edland, S. D., Cha, R. H., & Rocca, W. A. (2004). The incidence of frontotemporal lobar degeneration in Rochester, Minnesota, 1990 through 1994. *Neurology*, *62*, 506–508.

Lambon Ralph, M. A., McClelland, J. L., Patterson, K., Galton, C. J., & Hodges, J. R. (2001). No right to speak? The relationship between object naming and semantic impairment: Neuropsychological evidence and a computational model. *Journal of Cognitive Neuroscience*, *13*, 341–356.

Lee, V. M. Y., Goedert, M., & Trojanowski, J. Q. (2001). Neurodegenerative tauopathies. *Annual Review of Neuroscience*, *24*, 1121–1159.

Lieberman, A. P., Trojanowski, J. Q., Lee, V. M. Y., Balin, B., Ding, X.-S., Greenberg, J. et al. (1998). Cognitive, neuroimaging, and pathologic studies in a patient with Pick's disease. *Annals of Neurology*, *43*, 259–264.

Lomen-Hoerth, C., Murphy, J., Langmore, S., Kramer, J. H., Olney, R. K., & Miller, B. (2003). Are amyotrophic lateral sclerosis patients cognitively normal? *Neurology*, *60*, 1094–1097.

Lomen-Hoerth, C., Anderson, T., & Miller, B. (2002). The overlap of amyotrophic lateral sclerosis and frontotemporal dementia. *Neurology*, *59*, 1077–1079.

McKhann, G., Trojanowski, J. Q., Grossman, M., Miller, B. L., Dickson, D., & Albert, M. (2001). Clinical and pathological diagnosis of frontotemporal dementia: Report of a work group on frontotemporal dementia and Pick's disease. *Archives of Neurology*, *58*, 1803–1809.

Miller, B. L., Chang, L., Mena, I., Boone, K., & Lesser, I. M. (1993). Clinical and imaging features of right focal frontal lobe degenerations. *Dementia*, *4*, 204–213.

Miller, B. L., Darby, A., Benson, D. F., Cummings, J. L., & Miller, M. H. (1997). Aggressive, socially disruptive and anti-social behavior associated with frontotemporal dementia. *British Journal of Psychiatry*, *170*, 150–154.

Miller, B. L., Darby, A., Swartz, J. R., Yener, G. G., & Mena, I. (1995). Dietary changes, compulsions, and sexual behavior in frontotemporal degeneration. *Dementia*, *6*, 195–199.

Mummery, C. J., Patterson, K., Price, C. J., & Hodges, J. R. (2000). A voxel-based morphometry study of semantic dementia: Relationship between temporal lobe atrophy and semantic memory. *Annals of Neurology, 47*, 36–45.

Mychack, P., Kramer, J. H., Boone, K. B., & Miller, B. L. (2001). The influence of right frontotemporal dysfunction on social behavior in frontotemporal dementia. *Neurology, 56*, 11–15.

Neary, D., Snowden, J. S., Gustafson, L., Passant, U., Stuss, D., Black, S. et al. (1998). Frontotemporal lobar degeneration: A consensus on clinical diagnostic criteria. *Neurology, 51*, 1546–1554.

Poorkaj, P., Grossman, M., Steinhart, E., Payami, H., Sadovnick, A., Nochlin, D. et al. (2001). Frequency of tau gene mutations in familial and sporadic cases of non-Alzheimer dementia. *Archives of Neurology*, 383–387.

Rankin, K. P., Kramer, J. H., Mychack, P., & Miller, B. L. (2003). Double dissociation of social functioning in frontotemporal dementia. *Neurology, 60*, 266–271.

Ratnavalli, E., Brayne, C., Dawson, K., & Hodges, J. R. (2002). The prevalence of frontotemporal dementia. *Neurology, 58*, 1615–1621.

Rosen, H. J., Gorno-Tempini, M. L., Goldman, W. P., Perry, R. J., Schuff, N., Weiner, M. et al. (2002). Patterns of brain atrophy in frontotemporal dementia and semantic dementia. *Neurology, 58*, 198–208.

Rosso, S. M., Kaat, L. D., Baks, T., Joosse, M., de Koning, I., Pijnenburg, Y. A. L. et al. (2003a). Frontotemporal dementia in The Netherlands: Patient characteristics and prevalence estimates from a population-based study. *Brain, 126*, 2016–2022.

Rosso, S. M., Kaat, L. D., Baks, T., Joosse, M., de Koning, I., Pijnenburg, Y. et al. (2003b). Frontotemporal dementia in The Netherlands: Patient characteristics and prevalence estimates from a population-based study. *Brain, 126*, 2016–2022.

Rossor, M. N. (1999). Early diagnosis of dementia. *Journal of Neurology, 246*, 4–5.

Snowden, J. S., Goulding, P. J., & Neary, D. (1989). Semantic dementia: A form of circumscribed cerebral atrophy. *Behavioral Neurology, 2*, 167–182.

Snowden, J. S., Neary, D., & Mann, D. M. (1996). *Frontotemporal lobar degeneration: Fronto-temporal dementia, progressive aphasia, semantic dementia.* (1st ed.). New York: Churchill Livingstone.

Zhang, B., Maiti, A., Shively, S., Lakhani, F., McDonald-Jones, G., Bruce, J. et al. (2005). Microtubule-binding drugs offset tau sequestration by stabilizing microtubules and reversing fast axonal transport deficits in a tauopathy model. *Proceedings of the National Academy of Sciences, 102*, 227–231.

Zhukareva, V., Sundarraj, S., Mann, D. M., Sjogren, M., Blenow, K., Clark, C. M. et al. (2003). Selective reduction of soluble tau proteins in sporadic and familial frontotemporal dementias: An international follow-up study. *Acta Neuropathologica, 105*, 469–476.

Zhukareva, V., Vogelsberg-Ragaglia, V., Van Deerlin, V. M. D., Bruce, J., Shuck, T., Grossman, M. et al. (2001). Loss of brain tau defines novel sporadic and familial tauopathies with frontotemporal dementia. *Annals of Neurology, 49*, 165–175.

DEMENTIA: LEWY BODY

Frederick Lewy first described *Lewy bodies*, in 1914, as *cytoplasmic inclusions* found in cells of the substantia nigra in patients with idiopathic Parkinson's disease (PD). Lewy body pathology is pathognomic for a spectrum of disorders, the most familiar of which is PD. PD is the prototypic *Lewy body disease*, characterised by extrapyramidal symptoms and the presence of Lewy bodies in the brainstem. Widespread Lewy bodies in the cerebral cortex of patients with dementia was first noted with significant frequency by Kosaka (Kosaka, Yoshimura, Ikeda, & Budka, 1984). Since then, this condition has emerged as the second most common form of *degenerative dementia* in older persons after Alzheimer's disease (AD), accounting for 15% to 20% of demented patients. Unlike AD, the cognitive impairments of DLB can fluctuate markedly.

Immunohistochemical visualization of ubiquitin-positive and, more recently, α-synuclein-positive Lewy bodies has played an important part in revealing the prevalence of this condition. "Dementia with Lewy bodies" was the recommended term for a syndrome that has been ascribed numerous other names (Perry, McKeith, & Perry, 1996). Pathologically, it is defined by the formation of both brainstem and cortical Lewy bodies in the presence of sparse or absent neurofibrillary pathology. Although there is some overlap between DLB and both AD and PD, a fairly coherent picture of the clinical features of DLB is starting to emerge, and this has been fostered by international workshops held in 1995, 1998, and 2003.

Clinical Symptoms, Diagnosis, and Management

DLB is a progressive dementia, often accompanied by psychiatric symptoms and occasionally with mild extrapyramidal symptoms. The prevalence increases with advancing age. Most patients are characterized by a syndrome in which there is a fluctuating confusional state, behavioral disturbance, visual or auditory hallucinations, and progressive dementia (McKeith, Galasko, Kosaka, Perry, Dickson, Hansen, et al., 1996; Perry, McKeith, & Perry, 1996). Motor symptoms, characteristic of idiopathic PD, tend to be rare as a presenting feature in DLB. The fluctuating *confusional states* can lead to a misdiagnosis of vascular dementia. Patients often suffer transient episodes of loss of consciousness, and severe or fatal *neuroleptic sensitivity* is common. Cognitive decline and mortality tend to be accelerated in DLB when compared with AD.

Consensus criteria for the diagnosis of DLB continue to be refined (McKeith, et al., 1996; 1999). The key presenting symptom of DLB is a progressive cognitive decline leading to a global dementia over a period that can vary from months to years. There are 3 core features of DLB and a number of further symptoms that are supportive of the diagnosis. The core triad consists of: (1) fluctuating cognition with pronounced variation in attention and alertness, (2) recurrent visual hallucinations, and (3) spontaneous motor features of parkinsonism. Two of these features must be present for a diagnosis of probable DLB, and 1 for a diagnosis of possible DLB. Symptoms supporting a diagnosis are: (1) repeated falls, (2) syncope, (3) transient loss of consciousness, (4) neuroleptic sensitivity, (5) systematized delusions, (6) nonvisual hallucinations, and (7) rapid eye movement (REM) sleep behavioral disorders.

Although specificity of diagnosis remains high, the sensitivity can be as low as 20% to 30% in some studies (McKeith, et al., 1999b). This appears to reflect the extent of concurrent Alzheimer-type pathology that may co-exist (Merdes, et al., 2003). The classic clinical triad becomes less prominent as tangle pathology increases.

There are no consensus pathologic criteria for diagnosis of DLB. Attempts to validate the guidelines have had mixed success. The progression of Lewy pathology through stages would appear to exist, but it is not clear how predominant amygdala pathology fits into these stages. A further problem lies with the concurrent Alzheimer-type pathology that exists in many cases (Duda, et al., 2004). *Parkinson's disease with dementia* (PDD) appears to be a form of dementia that is indistinguishable from DLB pathologically. Thus, cortical Lewy bodies are the predominant pathology in both of these disorders; whether the 2 constitute the same disease is uncertain.

DLB causes many problems for disease management largely because of the conflicting requirements of the neuropsychiatric symptoms and parkinsonism (Perry, et al., 1996). In general, treatments for hallucinations and behavioral disturbance tend to aggravate movement disorder and vice versa. Accurate diagnosis is important to avoid potential neuroleptic sensitivity. *Cholinergic drugs* (e.g. *rivastigmine*, *donepezil*, and *galantamine*) may have benefits on the cognitive impairment of DLB, but prospective trials are still required to establish both safety and efficacy. The greater cholinergic deficit in DLB, as compared with AD, suggests that *cholinesterase inhibitor* treatment is warranted for DLB. Patient management, however, is still required and atypical antipsychotics are frequently indicated for the behavioral disorders in DLB.

There is no noninvasive diagnostic test for DLB. Although the clinical criteria for diagnosis are useful in confirming suspected cases of DLB, they do not make a good screening tool. Attempts at overcoming this by neuroimaging methods are still in development but progress has been made with the detection of reduced dopamine transporter activity of the basal ganglia using the cocaine analogue, ^{123}I-2-β-carbomethoxy-3β-[4-iodophenyl]-N-[3-fluoropropyl]nortropane, that enables a distinction between DLB and AD to be made (Walker et al., 2004).

Establishing valid diagnostic criteria for DLB is crucial for the future design and conduct of clinical trials. The drug regulatory authorities view the treatment of disorders that are not yet classified in DSM-IV differently than that of operationally defined diagnostic categories, such as AD. It is likely that a broad indication for a therapy such as "dementia" will not be acceptable to the regulators and so the development of validated criteria for diagnosis of DLB is urgently needed.

Support and advice for people with DLB is available from various organisations, including the following: The Parkinson's Disease Society (www.parkinsons.org.uk), Alzheimer's Disease Education and Referral Center (www.alzheimer's.org), and National Institute of Neurological Disorders and Stroke (www.ninds.nih.gov).

Etiopathogenesis

The etiology of DLB is not understood. Nevertheless, changes at neuropathological, neurochemical, genetic, and molecular levels have all been observed in DLB. The Lewy body is an intraneuronal, eosinophilic inclusion body, 5–25 μm in diameter. DLB is characterized by the presence of a moderate number of neocortical Lewy bodies, and sparse or absent neurofibrillary lesions (Dickson, et al., 1989; Perry, Irving, Blessed, Fairbairn, & Perry, 1990). Although lacking the tau pathology characteristic of AD, DLB shares with AD the increased risk that is associated with possession of the apolipoprotein E ϵ4 allele (Harrington et al., 1994). Lewy bodies in limbic and neocortical regions are smaller than those found in the brainstem and rarely have the electron-dense cores of the latter. The Lewy body is composed of amorphous material and filaments, 10–20 nm in diameter, consisting of α-synuclein that has been identified recently as the major component of this inclusion body (Spillantini, et al., 1997). Truncated fragments of α-synuclein have been found in isolated Lewy bodies (Baba, et al., 1998). Neurofilament subunits and *ubiquity* and other related, cell-stress response proteins are also present (Perry, et al., 1996).

Although the quantity of *amyloid β-protein* deposits is similar to that found in AD, the relative proportion of plaques containing Aβ terminating at residues 40 or 42 distinguish DLB from that in AD. While Aβ42 plaque numbers are similar in both conditions, the Aβ40 plaques are more frequent in AD than DLB (Lippa, et al., 1999). In addition, Lewy-related neurites are found in the CA2/CA3 region of the hippocampus in DLB that are absent in AD (Dickson, et al., 1991), and these *neurites* also contain both α-synuclein and ubiquitin.

Neurochemically, DLB shows features of both PD and AD (Perry, et al., 1996). Dopamine levels in DLB are decreased in the caudate and patients are particularly susceptible to typical *neuroleptic drugs* (dopaminergic D2-receptor antagonists). The cholinergic deficit in DLB is generally more severe than that found in AD, except for the hippocampus, which is usually spared. A correlation, however, between choline acetyltransferase depletion and the prevalence of cortical Lewy bodies in DLB has not been found. This would support the notion that Lewy bodies themselves are not responsible for the clinical phenotype.

Lewy bodies may represent pathological end-products that simply serve as a biomarkers for PD and DLB. Almost certainly cortical Lewy bodies themselves do not account for the clinical symptoms of DLB, since the number of affected neurons is approximately 1000th of the number affected by neurofibrillary pathology in AD. Nevertheless, the process that leads to the formation of Lewy bodies may be central to the pathogenesis of DLB and other *"synucleinopathy" disorders.*

α-Synuclein is a small (140 amino acids), soluble protein that is predominantly expressed in central nervous system neurons, where it is concentrated at presynaptic terminals. It is found within intracellular lesions that are characteristic of several neurodegenerative diseases (Goedert, 1999). Insoluble aggregates of α-synuclein in Lewy bodies are found not only in DLB, but also in familial AD patients with mutations in presenilin or amyloid precursor protein genes (Lippa, et al., 1998) and in patients with multiple system atrophy. Mutations in α-synuclein have been reported in a few families with PD (Polymeropoulos, et al., 1997) and such mutations accelerate α-synuclein aggregation *in vitro* (Conway, Harper, & Lansbury, 1998) to form filaments that are distinct from those formed from normal α-synuclein (Giasson, Uryu, Trojanowski, & Lee, 1999). Furthermore, the fibrillization of mutant α-synuclein promotes the formation of filamentous tau inclusions *in vitro* and in transgenic mouse models (Lee, et al., 2004). This may account for the frequent co-existence of AD pathology with DLB.

Although rare cases of familial DLB have been reported, mutations have not been found in sporadic PD or in DLB and, in PD, such mutations exhibit incomplete penetrance. The identification of a protein, synphilin-1, which interacts with α-synuclein and which produces cytoplasmic eosinophilic inclusions when the 2 proteins are introduced into mammalian cells, provides another aspect of the pathogenesis of α-synuclein aggregation (Engelender, et al., 1999).

The possibility that α-synuclein is not necessary for Lewy body formation but is still involved in the neurodegenerative process is supported by the finding of α-synuclein-negative Lewy bodies in the cortex of a patient lacking the clinical signs of parkinsonism and/or dementia (van Duinen, Lammers, Maat-Schieman, & Roos, 1999). Studies with transgenic *Drosophila* flies expressing normal and mutant forms of α-synuclein have demonstrated an increased loss of dopaminergic neurons and locomotor dysfunction associated with the neuronal inclusions containing of α-synuclein (Feany & Bender, 2000). This further indicates that the presence of α-synuclein deposits in DLB may not simply be a marker for the disease, but may play a more important role.

It is still necessary to determine whether or not the accumulation of filamentous inclusions is a key pathogenic event in DLB. If not, then is synaptic dysfunction a consequence of abnormal α-synuclein processing in these patients. It has been suggested that Lewy bodies may even play a protective role, perhaps by sequestering toxic species of α-synuclein (Goldberg & Lansbury, 2000). Further clinical and biological research is still required to address this and other outstanding questions.

CHARLES R. HARRINGTON

See also

Alzheimer's Disease: Clinical
Dementia
Dementia: Frontotemporal
Parkinson's Disease
Vascular Cognitive Impairment

References

Baba, M., Nakajo, S., Tu, P.-H., Tomita, T., Nakaya, K., Lee, V. M.-Y., Trojanowski, J. Q., & Iwatsubo, T. (1998). Aggregation of α-synuclein in Lewy bodies of sporadic Parkinson's disease and dementia with Lewy bodies. *American Journal of Pathology*, *152*, 879–884.

Conway, K. A., Harper, J. D., & Lansbury, P. T. (1998). Accelerated in vitro fibril formation by a mutant α-synuclein linked to early-onset Parkinson disease. *Nature Medicine*, *4*, 1318–1320.

Dickson, D. W., Crystal, H., Mattiace, L. A., Kress, Y., Schwagerl, A., Ksiezak-Reding, H., Davies, P., & Yen, S.-H. C. (1989). Diffuse Lewy body disease: Light and electron microscopic immunohistochemistry of senile plaques. *Acta Neuropathologica*, *78*, 572–584.

Dickson, D. W., Ruan, D., Crystal, H., Mark, M. H., Davies, P., Kress, Y., & Yen, S.-H. (1991). Hippocampal degeneration differentiates diffuse Lewy body disease (DLBD) from Alzheimer's disease: Light and electron microscopic immunocytochemistry of CA2-3 neurites specific to DLBD. *Neurology*, *41*, 1402–1409.

Duda, J. E. (2004). Pathology and neurotransmitter abnormalities in dementia with Lewy bodies. *Dementia and Geriatric Cognitive Disorders*, *17* (Suppl. 1), 3–14.

Engelender, S., Kaminsky, Z., Guo, X., Sharp, A. H., Amaravi, R. K., Kleiderlein, J. J., Margolis, R. L., Troncoso, J. C., Lanahan, A. A., Worley, P. F., Dawson, V. L., Dawson, T. M., & Ross, C. A. (1999). Synphilin-1 associates with α-synuclein and promotes the formation of cytosolic inclusions. *Nature Genetics*, *22*, 110–114.

Feany, M. B., & Bender, W. W. (2000). A *Drosophila* model of Parkinson's disease. *Nature*, *404*, 394–398.

Giasson, B. I., Uryu, K., Trojanowski, J. Q., & Lee, V. M. Y. (1999). Mutant and wild type human α-synucleins assemble into elongated filaments with distinct morphologies *in vitro*. *Journal of Biological Chemistry*, *274*, 7619–7622.

Goedert, M. (1999). Filamentous nerve cell inclusions in neurodegenerative diseases: Tauopathies and alpha-synucleinopathies. *Philosophical Transactions of the Royal Society of London Series B, Biological Sciences*, *354*, 1101–1118.

Goldberg, M. S., & Lansbury, Jr., P. T. (2000). Is there a cause-and-effect relationship between alpha-synuclein fibrillization and Parkinson's disease? *Nature Cell Biology*, 2, E115–E119.

Harrington, C. R., Louwagie, J., Rossau, R., Vanmechelen, E., Perry, R. H., Perry, E. K., Xuereb, J. H., Roth, M., & Wischik, C. M. (1994). Influence of apolipoprotein E genotype on senile dementia of the Alzheimer and Lewy body types. Significance for etiological theories of Alzheimer's disease. *American Journal of Pathology*, *145*, 1472–1484.

Kosaka, K., Yoshimura, M., Ikeda, K., & Budka, H. (1984). Diffuse type of Lewy body disease: Progressive dementia with abundant cortical Lewy bodies and senile changes of various degree—a new disease? *Clinical Neuropathology*, *3*, 185–192.

Lee, V. M.-Y., Giasson, B. I., & Trojanowski, J. Q. (2004). More than just two peas in a pod: Common amyloidogenic properties of tau and α-synuclein in neurodegenerative diseases. *Trends in Neurosciences*, *27*, 129–134.

Lippa, C. F., Fujiwara, H., Mann, D. M. A., Giasson, B., Baba, M., Schmidt, M. L., Nee, L. E., O'Connell, B., Pollen, D. A., St George-Hyslop, P., Ghetti, B., Nochlin, D., Bird, T. D., Cairns, N. J., Lee, V. M. Y., Iwatsubo, T., & Trojanowski, J. Q. (1998). Lewy bodies contain altered α-synuclein in brains of many familial Alzheimer's disease patients with mutations in presenilin and amyloid precursor protein genes. *American Journal of Pathology*, *153*(5), 1365–1370.

Lippa, C. F., Ozawa, K., Mann, D. M. A., Ishii, K., Smith, T. W., Arawaka, S., & Mori, H. (1999). Deposition of β-amyloid subtypes 40 and 42 differentiates dementia with Lewy bodies from Alzheimer disease. *Archives of Neurology*, *56*, 1111–1118.

McKeith, I. G., Galasko, D., Kosaka, K., Perry, E. K., Dickson, D. W., Hansen, L. A., Salmon, D. P., Lowe, J., Mirra, S. S., Byrne, E. J., Lennox, G., Quinn, N. P., Edwardson, J. A., Ince, P. G., Bergeron, C., Burns, A., Miller, B. L., Lovestone, S., Collerton, D., Jansen, E. N.H., Ballard, C., De Vos, R. A. I., Wilcock, G. K., Jellinger, K., & Perry, R. H. (1996). Consensus guidelines for the clinical and pathologic diagnosis of dementia with Lewy bodies (DLB): Report of the consortium on DLB international workshop. *Neurology*, *47*, 1113–1124.

McKeith, I. G., Perry, E. K., Perry, R. H., & The Consortium on Dementia with Lewy Bodies. (1999). Report of the second dementia with Lewy body international workshop. Diagnosis and treatment. *Neurology*, *53*, 902–905.

McKeith, I. G., O'Brien, J. T., & Ballard, C. (1999). Diagnosing dementia with Lewy bodies. *Lancet*, *354*, 1227–1228.

Merdes, A. R., Hansen, L. A., Jeste, D. V., Galasko, D., Hofstetter, C. R., Ho, G. J., Thal, L. J., & Corey-Bloom, J. (2003). Influence of Alzheimer pathology on clinical diagnostic accuracy in dementia with Lewy bodies. *Neurology*, *60*, 1586–1590.

Perry, R., McKeith, I., & Perry, E. (Eds.). (1996). *Dementia with Lewy bodies. Clinical, pathological, and treatment issues*. Cambridge: Cambridge University Press.

Perry, R. H., Irving, D., Blessed, G., Fairbairn, A., & Perry, E. K. (1990). Senile dementia of the Lewy body type. A clinically and neuropathologically distinct form of Lewy body dementia in the elderly. *Journal of Neurological Sciences*, *95*, 119–139.

Polymeropoulos, M. H., Lavedan, C., Leroy, E., Ide, S. E., Dehejia, A., Dutra, A., Pike, B., Root, H., Rubenstein, J., Boyer, R., Stenroos, E. S., Chandrasekharappa, S., Athanassiadou, A., Papaetropoulos, T., Johnson, W. G., Lazzarini, A. M., Duvoisin, R. C., Di Iorio, G., Golbe, L. I., & Nussbaum, R. L. (1997). Mutation in the α-synuclein gene identified in families with Parkinson's disease. *Science*, *276*, 2045–2047.

Spillantini, M. G., Schmidt, M. L., Lee, V. M.-Y., Trojanowski, J. Q., Jakes, R., & Goedert, M. (1997). α-Synuclein in Lewy bodies. *Nature*, *388*, 839–840.

van Duinen, S. G., Lammers, G.-J., Maat-Schieman, M. L. C., & Roos, R. A. C. (1999). Numerous and widespread α-synuclein-negative Lewy bodies in an asymptomatic patient. *Acta Neuropathologica*, *97*, 533–539.

Walker, Z., Costa, D. C., Walker, R. W. H., Lee, L., Livingstone, G., Jaros, E., Perry, R., McKeith, I., & Katona, C. L. E. (2004). Striatal dopamine transporter in dementia with Lewy bodies and Parkinson disease: A comparison. *Neurology*, *62*, 1568–1572.

DEMOGRAPHY

Social scientists in a variety of disciplines consider it important to understand the process of *population aging* and its impact on society. Scholars in disciplines such as sociology, economics, psychology, and geography now devote considerable time to studying the aspects of population aging. Increasingly, interdisciplinary research teams and perspectives are involved in the *demography of aging*, whether it is the aging of whole populations or that of a single cohort.

The process of population aging transforms the total population structure and its distribution in a variety of ways over time. For example, the population's composition according to marital status tends to change during a prolonged period of population aging. This change will in turn affect the population's distribution among different kinds of living arrangements.

The *aging of birth cohorts* throughout their life courses is becoming a major focus of the demography of aging. The process of aging of a major set of birth cohorts—such as the *baby boom* generation in North America, which comprises primarily those persons born between 1946 and 1966—has an important impact upon society. When aging cohorts enter the ranks of the older population, they may change its characteristics because they differ in behavior and composition from the cohorts departing the older population via deaths.

For example, in demography as well as other disciplines, the aging of the baby boom generation has been the subject of a growing body of literature. Because of its size and its distinctive behavior patterns, this generation has had a major effect upon social institutions and government policies at every stage of its maturation. There is great concern about correctly forecasting how it will alter institutions and policies that target the older population when its large numbers invade the main ages for retirement, starting in the second decade of this century.

The pace of population aging depends upon the aging processes and relative sizes of sequences of cohorts passing from birth to extinction. In turn, the impact of population aging upon society depends upon the pattern of succession among cohorts possessing different characteristics and passing through the older ages (Stone, 1999; Gauthier, Jean, Langis, Nobert, & Rochon, 2004).

The demography of aging also deals with the current demographic profile of the older population, as well as the changes in its numbers, proportionate size, composition, and territorial distribution. Moreover, this disciplinary field addresses the determinants and consequences of changes in attributes of the older population.

The Growing Controversy over What Constitutes Old

The emergence of population aging as a prominent concept in demography has rested partly on the notion that there is a meaningful and commonly accepted basis upon which to classify a person as being "old" or "elderly," or a member of the "older population." Over 2 decades ago, Siegel (1980) wrote that: "The demography of aging brings demographers to focus holistically on a population group, the elderly, and a demographic process, aging." The most common definition of population aging refers to an increase in the relative weight (percentage) of the older population. (Usually, this is accompanied by an increase in the average age of the population.)

For decades, it was commonly thought that a person could be considered old after age 65; more recently it is acknowledged that such a fixed age is a socially constructed age threshold that was set by governments primarily to demarcate an age beyond which people could gain access to certain classes of government benefits or work-related pension income. Just who is considered old, elderly, or a member of the older population has become a subject of important controversy.

In future years, the notion of *oldness* may be defined most usefully by 1 of 2 approaches: (1) survival for a certain number of years beyond the expected length of life of one's cohort, or (2) entry into an age group where the risk of frailty rises to unusually high levels (Robine & Michel, 2004). If approach 2 is used to establish the age threshold beyond which a person is said to be old, that threshold would probably be agreed upon as a fixed chronological age (probably the mid-80s or higher). However, if approach 1 is used, there would be a changing threshold depending upon the cohort in question.

Even the second approach may lead to a variable age threshold, if advances in the biology of aging and related lifestyle interventions were to permit the average age of onset of frailty to rise in future decades. That this is a prospect to be taken seriously is suggested in the 2002 work of Vaupel and his colleagues at the Max Planck Institute.

The rising challenge to the idea that a person is old simply because he or she has reached age 65 helps to shift the focus of the demography of aging away from a subpopulation of "the elderly" and toward aging as a dynamic, lifelong process for cohorts and historically for whole populations.

A recent feature of this shift has been an implicit broadening of the concept of population aging to take into account not only an increasing percentage of persons beyond a certain chronological age but also the proportions of such persons without moderate or severe disability (Robine & Michel, 2004). If it becomes widely accepted among demographers this idea will probably lead to an increased focus on the notion that "oldness" should be defined in terms of entry to chronological ages where the probability of frailty is much higher than average for the adult population. Even today, these are ages well above 65 years.

Despite the doubt now being cast upon 65 as a threshold beyond which a person is reasonably said to be old, this age remains an important marker in societies for reasons that deserve to be elaborated. In the social construction of opportunities to obtain or keep jobs, as well as that of access to certain kinds of government benefits, age 65 remains an important marker. Secondly, people beyond this age, but below ages where the probability of frailty becomes unusually high, are often considered to be in the Third Age. In several developed countries, this population is predominantly in good health, and there is pressure upon government leaders and organizations to find ways of making more effective use of the economic potential of groups of healthy older persons who have passed the age of 65. Moreover, as new cohorts enter the Third Age, this population will be increasingly better educated and well prepared to carry on vigorous activity in the economy and in civil society. They thus represent an enormous resource in such countries.

Measurement and Analysis of Population Aging

Measurement and analysis of population aging received a key stimulus from the formal modeling of *Alfred Lotka*, who developed a mathematical model of demographic changes and related aspects of population aging. His model enabled demographers to examine the long-term effects of different levels and age patterns of fertility and mortality on population aging when they are held constant over time in a closed population. Many articles on this topic now exist among the literature.

Lotka's model was later extended by relaxing the assumption of a closed population to include assumptions about the existence of certain age-specific rates of net migration. It has been shown that if an age-adjusted fertility rate and the schedules of age-specific mortality and migration rates were held constant for a long period, the population would assume a stable age structure even in the presence of the migration.

As regards analysis of the causes of population aging, for decades demographers have presented population aging as a byproduct of the demographic transition. In this transition, fertility decline follows an earlier mortality decline, thus promoting aging from the base of the age pyramid. A *declining birth rate* contributes to population aging by depressing the growth rate at the youngest ages, thus creating a faster growth rate among older persons than among youth.

Later on in the demographic transition, declines in mortality rates at the older ages contribute to "aging at the apex" of the *age pyramid*. Aging at the apex also develops when relatively large birth cohorts from the past (such as the baby boom generation) reach older ages. *Aging at the apex* has been particularly important in accounting for more recent increases in both the numbers and proportions of the elderly in developed countries.

In most national settings, net international migration has not been large enough to have a substantial impact on population aging (this may not apply to certain regions within countries that undergo large migratory movements). However, recent literature includes analyses of the extent to which migration might be a source of relief from pressures attributed to population aging (Meyerson, 2001). The pertinent analyses find that "replacement migration can only temporarily relieve population aging" (Meyerson, 2001).

As noted above, the move to bring the consideration of disability into discussions of population aging could eventually lead to a challenge to the traditional definition of population aging, relying as it does only on chronological age. One way to sense the importance of this development is to reflect that in this broadened approach to the meaning of "aging," one asks not only how many years a person has lived (or can be expected to live starting now) but what portions of those future years can be expected to be free of disability, especially severe disability (Robine & Michel, 2004). Thus a group with chronological average age of 70 could, in certain circumstances associated with their functional capacities, be effectively younger than another group with chronological average age at 55.

The potential consequences of this new line of thinking for the demography of aging include major revision of the estimated proportion of elderly in a population, since demographers would have to take into account the distribution of certain functional capacities. Also, analyses of the causes of demographic aging would have to be broadened to take into account factors that affect the retention of functional capacities in a population.

A most important development in recent decades has been the spread of demographic aging to a wide spectrum of countries around the world. Formerly, this phenomenon was thought to be an attribute of the more developed countries. This aging on the world scale will become a topic of major concern in the future demography of aging (Kinsella & Velkoff, 2001).

Changing Characteristics Among the Older Population

The continuing *aging of the population* produced by the momentum of growth from previous levels of high fertility, the fall in the birth rate since the early 1960s, and recent marked declines in mortality at older ages, has been accompanied by changes in the characteristics of the older population.

A notable aspect of these changes is the growing proportion of the older population that is aged 85 or more in developed countries (Perls, 2004). This trend will continue until the influx of large numbers of persons from the post-World War II baby-boom cohorts reach age 65 or more, beginning in the second decade of the 21st century. Then some 20 years later, the baby boomers will provide an enormous boost to the size of the population aged 85 or more.

Another important attribute of the older populations of most countries can be characterized as sex disparity. There is a much greater *number of older women* than older men, which results from differential mortality risks that favor women. Along a wide range of social and economic variables, gender disparity is a characteristic feature of the older population.

Conclusion

The demography of aging provides theoretical and methodological perspectives on various aspects of population aging. The field has been enriched not only by the contributions from general demography, but by recent developments arising from gerontological research issues and modeling work done by scholars concerned with economic issues. Especially notable among these developments is a new focus upon population aging in developing countries, proposals to broaden the concept of demographic aging to take into account functional capacity as well as chronological measurement of age, and research in *biodemography* that suggests future increases in human life span (maximum length of life). These developments are likely to lead to major revisions of existing statistical series about population aging and to new lines of analysis that explicitly deal with issues related to retention of functional capacity in the older population and to extension of the human life span.

Also notable is the priority accorded to aging-related issues in many countries' social and economic policy making. This is a result of the shared perception that population aging is or will soon generate major financing pressures upon national pension systems.

The aging of major sets of cohorts, such as those that comprise the baby boom generation, is gaining increased attention. With hindsight on the extent to which the baby boom generation has disrupted institutions and culture at each stage of its maturation, it is likely to upset expectations concerning attributes of the older population, since those expectations are based on the study of earlier cohorts.

Leroy O. Stone

See also
Population Aging

References

Gauthier, H., Jean, S., Langis, G., Nobert, Y., & Rochon, M. (2004). *Vie des générations et personnes âgées: aujourd'hui et demain*. Québec: Gouvernement du Québec.

Kinsella, K., & Velkoff, V. A. (2001). *An aging world*. Washington, DC: U.S. Department of Commerce, Economics and Statistics Administration, U.S. Census Bureau.

Martin, L. G., & Preston, S. H. (Eds.). (1994). *Demography of aging*. Washington, DC: National Academies Press.

Meyerson, F. A. B. (2001). Replacement migration: A questionable tactic for delaying the inevitable effects of fertility transition. *Population and Environment*, *22*(4), 401–409.

Perls, T. T. (2004). The oldest old. *Scientific American*, *14*(3), 6–11.

Robine, J. M., & Michel, J. P. (2004). Looking forward to a general theory on population aging. *Journals of Gerontology*, *59*(6), 560–597.

Siegel, J. S. (1980). On the demography of aging. *Demography*, *17*, 345–364.

Stone, L. O. (Ed.). (1999). *Cohort flow and the consequences of population aging, an international analysis and review*. Ottawa: Minister of Industry.

Vaupel, J. (2000). Setting the stage: A generation of centenarians? *Washington Quarterly*, *23*(3), 197–200.

DENTISTY, GERIATRIC

See
Oral Health

DEPRESSION

Depression is among the most common complaints of older adults and the leading cause of *suicide in late life*. Depressive disorders therefore should be considered disorders of major concern to all persons caring for older adults. For an overview of research and experience in the management of *late-life depression*, see Blazer (2003).

Depression, by definition, is so varied in its manifestations and so easily confused with other conditions, such as dementia and hypochondriasis, that clinically depressed older adults are often unidentified. As the term depression is ambiguous, many clinicians have reverted to the use of a somewhat archaic term, *dysphoria*, to describe those everyday normal experiences of feeling low, blue, or down in the dumps. Given the inevitable illnesses experienced by older persons, not to mention other stressful life events, symptoms of depression are frequently encountered by those who serve or observe older adults (Beekman, Copeland, & Prince, 1999; Blazer, 1994). Nevertheless, these dysphoric episodes in late life are usually transient, and recovery is spontaneous (Hughes, DeMallie, & Blazer, 1993).

Of greater importance are those *major depressive disorders* that may occur for the first time after the age of 60 or that recur in later life after first occurring earlier. Such "*clinical depressions*" are characterized by severe symptoms and a prolonged duration of a profound depressed mood. Clinicians and other health care providers must learn to recognize these depressive disorders, for they can potentially precipitate a suicide attempt or even a successful suicide (Conwell, Duberstein, & Caine, 2002). Suicide remains one of the 10 most frequent causes of death in late life and may be preventable if the symptoms of major depression are recognized (National Center for Health Statistics, 2000). Severe depression is also associated with nonsuicidal mortality, though the association of less severe depression and mortality may be confounded by factors associated with both *depression and aging*, such as functional impairment. (Blazer, Hybels, & Pieper, 2001; Schulz, Drayer, & Rollman, 2002) Unfortunately, severe depressive episodes often remain undetected, and older adults suffer unnecessarily from the burden of depressive illness. Clinical depression is not easily diagnosed in late life because many symptoms are expectations of changes commonly associated with normal aging. For example, older persons have more *difficulty sleeping* and often complain of broken sleep patterns and early morning awakening—cardinal symptoms of major depression at any stage of the life cycle. *Lethargy*, a frequent physical symptom that accompanies depression, can also be overlooked in older individuals for physical illness, and even aging may lead to decreased energy and activity. Late-life depression is frequently associated with physical illness, usually chronic but not life threatening. (Black, Goodwin, & Markides, 1998; Frasure-Smith, Lesperance, & Talajic, 1993) Other older adults with depressive symptoms complain that they cannot concentrate and notice problems with memory. Such persons may be diagnosed as suffering from an irreversible dementing process and be denied appropriate treatment, yet most cases of *depression and memory loss* in older adults reflect a comorbid process of *dementia* (even mild forms) and depression (Rubin, Veiel, Kinscherf, Morris, & Storandt, 2001). The depression may be treatable even though the cognitive impairment does not improve (Reifler, Teri, Raskind, Veith, & Barnes, 1989). The unfortunate circumstance of not treating a depression associated with memory loss may lead to long-term institutionalization for an individual who is suffering from a treatable illness. However, persons experiencing depression with cognitive impairment, even if the cognitive impairment improves with remission of the depression, are at greater risk in the future for a permanent dementing disorder (Alexopoulos, Meyers, Young, Mattis, & Kakuma, 1993).

The *biopsychosocial model* fits the etiology of depression (Engel, 1980). Two putative biological causes have received much attention in recent years. First, vascular disease may lead to *microinfarcts in the brain* that in turn disrupt critical pathways which are associated with late-onset depression as well as *executive function* (Alexopoulos Meyers, Young, Campbell, Silbersweig, & Charlson, 1997). Second, *stress* over many years may lead to chronic increased levels of steroids that in turn damage the brain, especially the hippocampus. (Sheline, 2003) Psychological origins of depression have focused upon cognitive distortions that result from unrealistic appraisals of adverse events in the older person's life (Devenand, Kim, Paykina, & Sackeim, 2002). Potential social origins include stressful life events (Fiske,

Gatz, & Pedersen, 2003) and impaired social support (Chi & Chou, 2001). *Depression in caregivers* (where stressful events as well as impaired social support may be operative) is of especial importance (Livingston, Manela, & Katona, 1996).

Diagnosis

Recent advances in understanding the psychobiology of depression has assisted clinicians in distinguishing older adults experiencing clinical depression from those who report the symptoms of normal aging or other age-related physical and psychiatric disorders. Many depressed elders exhibit *subcortical hyperintensities* on magnetic resonance imaging (MRI). These hyperintensities probably reflect decreased blood flow to the areas of the brain that have been associated with mood (i.e., the hypothalamic region), resulting in vascular depression (Krishnan, Hays, & Blazer, 1997). In addition, approximately one-half of those who, throughout the life cycle, develop a major depression with melancholia exhibit an abnormal response to the administration of a synthetic corticosteroid, *dexamethasone* (Davis, David, Mathe, Mohs, & Rothpearl, 1984). The inability of dexamethasone to "turn down" the *hypothalamic-pituitary-adrenal (HPA) axis*, which regulates the *secretion of cortisol*, produces an abnormally elevated blood level of cortisol 18 to 24 hours following the dexamethasone challenge. This *dexamethasone suppression challenge*, although not a diagnostic test, can provide valuable data regarding the behavior of the HPA axis during a late-life depression. Advances in the evaluation of *sleep patterns of depressed older adults* have enabled researchers to distinguish the depressed elderly from those suffering from dementia and those who are aging normally (Reynolds, Busse, Kupfer, Hoch, & Houch, 1990). The depressed, throughout the life cycle, have a shortened rapid eye movement (REM) latency (i.e., it takes less time to enter first-stage REM, or "dream" sleep, once the individual falls asleep).

Treatment

Severe depression is a treatable illness. When late-life clinical depression is identified, the use of appropriate medications, such as *selective serotonin reuptake inhibitors* (SSRIs) and *tricyclic antidepressants* (TCAs), can reverse symptomology in over 70% of persons so diagnosed. However, the physician who prescribes medications to the older adult must always be aware of the potential for adverse side effects from these medications. The SSRIs, such as *paroxetine*, *citalopram*, *escitalopram*, *fluoxetine*, and *sertraline*, are the first-line treatments of choice because side effects are much less frequent; *venlafaxine* is often the second-line therapy (Alexopoulos, Katz, Reynolds, Carpenter, & Docherty, 2001). Patients who exhibit significant anxiety along with the depression symptoms may be treated with anxiolytic agents such as *benzodiazepines* without use of an antidepressant. By adjusting the medications carefully, therapists can assist most depressed older adults to tolerate medications without difficulty.

When medications fail or when the depression is accompanied by psychotic features, *electroconvulsive therapy* (ECT) often produces dramatic improvement (Flint & Rifat, 1998). The negative public image of this therapeutic modality ensures that it is selected only in the most resistant, severe cases of major depression. Its use must be prescribed with special care for older adults, as health problems and difficulties with memory may complicate the therapeutic course. In addition, older adults with recent severe cardiovascular problems must be treated judiciously with ECT because transient increases in blood pressure frequently accompany the treatment process.

The effectiveness of biologic treatments for severe depression in late life has overshadowed the use of psychotherapy in the elderly. Nevertheless, investigators have reported that individuals suffering from major depression with fewer "biological signs" (e.g., sleep problems) can be treated effectively with *short-term psychotherapy* (Gallagher & Thompson, 1982). These psychotherapies generally have been cognitive and behaviorally oriented and may serve, at the least, as useful adjuncts to biological treatments. Recent studies of the *young-old* have documented that treatment with a combination of interpersonal therapy (a variant of *cognitive behavioral therapy*) and *antidepressant medications* is more effective than either alone both in producing a remission and in preventing a recurrence of an episode of major depression (Reynolds, Frank, Perel, Imber, Cornes, Miller, et al., 1999). When psychotherapeutic medication and/or ECT are not effective, the clinician must rely exclusively on psychotherapy. For severe depression, there is always the hope that remission will occur spontaneously, because depression, by definition, is a self-limiting illness.

DAN G. BLAZER

See also
Anxiety

References

Alexopoulos, G., Katz, I., Reynolds, C., Carpenter, D., & Docherty, J. (2001). The Expert Consensus Guideline Series: Pharmacotherapy of depressive disorders in older patients. *Postgraduate Medicine*, Special Issue October, 1–86.

Alexopoulos, G., Meyers, B., Young, R., Campbell, S., Silbersweig, D., & Charlson, M. (1997). 'Vascular depression' hypothesis. *Archives of General Psychiatry, 54*, 915–922.

Alexopoulos, G., Meyers, B., Young, R., Mattis, S., & Kakuma, T. (1993). The course of geriatric depression with "reversible dementia": A controlled study. *American Journal of Psychiatry, 150*, 1693–1699.

Beekman, A., Copeland, J., & Prince, M. (1999). Review of community prevalence of depression in later life. *British Journal of Psychiatry, 174*, 307–311.

Black, S., Goodwin, J., & Markides, K. (1998). The association between chronic diseases and depressive symptomology in older Mexican Americans. *Journal of Gerontology: Medical Sciences, 53*, M118–M194.

Blazer, D. (1994). Is depression more frequent in late life? An honest look at the evidence. *American Journal of Geriatric Psychiatry, 2*, 193–199.

Blazer, D. (2003). Depression in late life: Review and commentary. *Journal of Gerontology: Medical Science, 58A*, 249–265.

Blazer, D., Hybels, C., & Pieper, C. (2001). The association of depression and mortality in elderly persons: A case for multiple independent pathways. *Journal of Gerontology: Medical Science, 56A*, M505–M509.

Chi, I., & Chou, K. (2001). Social support and depression among elderly Chinese people in Hong Kong. *International Journal of Aging and Human Development, 52*, 231–252.

Conwell, Y., Duberstein, P., & Caine, E. (2002). Risk factors for suicide in later life. *Biological Psychiatry, 52*, 193–204.

Davis, K., David, B., Mathe, A., Mohs, R., & Rothpearl, A. (1984). Age and the dexamethasone suppression test in depression. *American Journal of Psychiatry, 141*, 872–874.

Devenand, D., Kim, M., Paykina, N., & Sackeim, H. (2002). Adverse life events in elderly patients with major depression or dysthymia and in healthy control subjects. *American Journal of Geriatric Psychiatry, 10*, 265–274.

Engel, G. (1980). The clinical application of the biopsychosocial model. *American Journal of Psychiatry, 137*, 535–544.

Fiske, A., Gatz, M., & Pedersen, N. (2003). Depressive symptoms and aging: The effects of illness and non-health-related events. *Journal of Gerontology: Psychological Sciences, 58B*, P320–P328.

Flint, A., & Rifat, S. (1998). The treatment of psychotic depression in later life: A comparison of pharmacotherapy and ECT. *Journal of Geriatric Psychiatry, 13*, 23–28.

Frasure-Smith, N., Lesperance, F., & Talajic, M. (1993). Depression following myocardial infarction. Impact on 6-month survival. *Journal of the American Medical Association, 270*, 1819–1825.

Gallagher, D., & Thompson, L. (1982). Treatment of major depressive disorder in older outpatients with brief psychotherapies. *Psychotherapy: Theory Research and Practice, 19*, 482–490.

Hughes, D., DeMallie, D., & Blazer, D. (1993). Does age make a difference in the effects of physical health and social support on the outcome of a major depressive episode? *American Journal of Psychiatry, 150*, 728–733.

Krishnan, K., Hays, J., & Blazer, D. (1997). MRI-defined vascular depression. *American Journal of Psychiatry, 154*, 497–501.

Livingston, G., Manela, M., & Katona, C. (1996). Depression and other psychiatric morbidity in carers of elderly people living at home. *British Medical Journal, 312*, 153–156.

National Center for Health Statistics, C. f. D. C. a. P. (2000). *Death Rates for Suicide, 1950–1998.*

Reifler, B., Teri, L., Raskind, M., Veith, R., & Barnes, R. (1989). Double-blind trial of imipramine in Alzheimer's disease patients with and without depression. *American Journal of Psychiatry, 146*, 45–49.

Reynolds, C., Busse, D., Kupfer, D., Hoch, C., & Houch, P. (1990). Rapid eye movements, and sleep-deprivation as a probe in elderly subjects. *Archives of General Psychiatry, 47*, 1128–1136.

Reynolds, C., Frank, E., Perel, J., Imber, S., Cornes, C., Miller, M., et al. (1999). Nortriptyline and interpersonal psychotherapy as maintenance therapies for recurrent major depression: A randomized controlled trial in patients older than 59 years. *Journal of the American Medical Association, 281*, 39–45.

Rubin, E., Veiel, L., Kinscherf, D., Morris, J., & Storandt, M. (2001). Clinically significant depressive symptoms and very mild to mild dementia of the Alzheimer type. *International Journal of Geriatric Psychiatry, 16*, 694–701.

Schulz, R., Drayer, R., & Rollman, B. (2002). Depression as a risk factor for non-suicide mortality in the elderly. *Biological Psychiatry, 52*, 205–225.

Sheline, Y. (2003). Neuroimaging studies of mood disorder effects on the brain. *Biological Psychiatry, 54*, 338–352.

DEVELOPING NATIONS

See
Population Aging: Developing Countries

DEVELOPMENTAL PSYCHOLOGY

Developmental psychology deals with the description, explanation, and modification of the ontogenesis (intraindividual, age-related change) of mind and behavior, from conception to death. Two central goals underlie developmental research: to obtain information about interindividual similarities and differences in ontogenetic development, and to understand the range and conditions of individual plasticity or modifiability of development. The antecedents or causes of development are located in 2 interacting systems of influences (biological and environmental factors), each associated with specific mechanisms (such as maturation and learning). When basic knowledge about psychological development is used for corrective or therapeutic purposes, one speaks of applied developmental science. Historically and conceptually, the field of developmental psychology has roots both in psychology and medicine, as well as social and life sciences (Baltes, Lindenberger, & Staudinger, 1998; Cairns, 1998; Lerner, 2002; Valsiner, 1998).

Developmental psychology is not a single coherent field. There are numerous specialties that concentrate on either age-graded periods (infancy, childhood, adolescence, adulthood, midlife, old age) or domains of functioning (e.g., cognition, personality, social and emotional development). Many of the subspecialties of psychological development have their own institutional base, peer community, and journals (e.g., American Psychological Association Divisions 7 and 20, Society for Research in Child Development, Society for Research in Adolescence, gerontological societies). One international organization, the *Society for the Study of Behavioral Development*, founded in 1969, is devoted to attracting scholars interested in the entire life course.

Theoretical Frameworks

There is no unified theoretical framework of developmental psychology. Scholars generally work within one of the major approaches, such as social learning theory, cognitive neuroscience, dynamic systems theory, biogenetic or ecological models, life-span models, or psychoanalysis. Most handbooks are age- or topic-specific. For infancy, childhood, and adolescence, summaries of theoretical and empirical work are contained in the Handbook of Child Development series of 4 volumes (Damon, 1998) and the Handbook of Adolescent Psychology (Lerner & Steinberg, 2004). For adulthood and old age, the handbooks edited by Birren and Schaie (e.g., 1996), Lachman (2001), and Craik and Salthouse (e.g., 2000) are standard references.

In the present context, it is not possible to review specific substantive theories of development. Instead, 3 themes are highlighted: the definition of "development," metatheoretical frameworks about *ontogeny*, and *life-span scripts* about development.

Concept of Development. Not all behavioral change is considered developmental in nature. Rather, the longstanding historical influences of developmental biology and gestalt psychology (reflected, for example, in cognitive structuralism of *Piaget* or genetic structuralism of *Heinz Werner*) have resulted in a family of criteria that are often used as indicators of development. Among these criteria are: (1) direction toward a state of maturity, (2) quantitative and qualitative (stage-like) change, (3) relative robustness or irreversibility of change, and (4) a movement toward greater complexity and differentiation. An extreme view proposes that all of these criteria need to be fulfilled in order to categorize behavioral change as a reflection of development.

Applying the entire family of criteria to the definition of development results in a precise but possibly too restricted concept. The disadvantages of such a restricted definition are most conspicuous when applied to later periods of the life span. Indeed, there is continued discussion about whether processes associated with development differ from those associated with aging (Baltes & Smith, 2004; Bengtson & Schaie, 1999). Beginning with adolescence, the causes and forms of development are more diverse and open than a universalistic and stage-like definition of development would suggest. The greater regularity of development observed in infancy and childhood compared to later age periods may be attributed to the fact that the biological and cultural forces which shape childhood are more programmed (genetically and culturally) than is true for later periods of the life span. In old age, the conjoint dynamics of biological and cultural forces are less well-orchestrated because the architectural plan of human ontogeny is incomplete (Baltes, 1997).

Metatheoretical Perspectives. Major metatheoretical positions on the descriptive and causal nature of psychological ontogenesis emphasize action-theoretical, transactional, contextualist, dialectical, and dynamic systems perspectives. These models highlight 2 types of interactions between organisms and their environment. The first is the dynamic interaction in ontogenesis between individuals and their microenvironment. The second is the interactive relationship between individual development and societal change at the level of macrostructure and populations. Organisms do not only develop and age from within, nor do they develop in a stable ecology. Individuals develop and age in a changing society from which they receive and to which they give. Endogenous and exogenous factors interact as static and dynamic elements: they are closely intertwined and themselves undergo change (Bronfenbrenner & Morris, 1998; Elder, 1998; Lerner, 2002).

Lifespan Scripts. Traditionally, developmental psychology focused primarily on forms of development that represented positive change in the structure and function of behavior (adaptive capacity or growth). As the study of development was extended to the entire life span, it was recognized that ontogenesis is more complex than the concept of growth suggests. The life span approach is characterized by a number of general scripts (or proposals) about the complex nature of development and aging: for example, proposals about *multidirectionality*, a *gain-loss dynamic*, and processes of *selection, optimization, and compensation* (Baltes, Lindenberger, & Staudinger, 1998).

Embedded in the notion of *multidirectionality* is the idea that categories of behavior show different trajectories of positive and negative change or stability across the life span. A classic example of this script is research on the trajectories of fluid versus crystallized intelligence during adulthood and into old age. Phenomema of differential aging and subgroup differences in systemic profiles of functioning also illustrate the concept. Expanding the concept of development from a growth model to a multidirectional model led to the insight that development is likely always a combination of *gains and losses:* any developmental change entails a dynamic tradeoff between features of growth and decline. A gain in one direction, for example, may exclude alternative pathways of development. The search for gains and losses across the life span has been paralleled by the rapid growth of investigations into the range and limits of plasticity of mind and behavior. Research into age-related changes in *plasticity* (intraindividual variability) is motivated, firstly, by a search for the latent potential of structure and function, and secondly by questions about fundamental component processes of "*developmental reserve*" or competence. At a more general level, research into the gain-loss dynamic has stimulated various questions about the fundamental role of processes of *selection, optimization*, and *compensation* in development (Baltes, 1997). Selection defines the direction, goals, and outcomes of development. Optimization involves the acquisition or application of means to achieve selected goals. Compensation occurs in response to a loss or blockage of previously available goal-relevant means (resources) and involves the acquisition or application of alternative means designed to maintain functioning or re-enable goal attainment.

Influences on Development

The methodological requirements of developmental psychologists are complex. In essence, research designs have to take into account both that development is determined by multiple factors and mechanisms, and that it is a *time-related process* that occurs within specific sociocultural and historical contexts. Consensus has been reached about the importance of investigating 3 systems of influence: *age-graded*, *history-graded*, and *nonnormative* (Baltes & Smith, 2004). Each of the 3 influences involves biological and environmental conditions. Age-graded influences include, for example, biological and physical changes (e.g., puberty, menopause) as well as exposure to age-related social factors (e.g., schooling, family life cycle, retirement). History-graded influences imply changes in societal structure and function (e.g., economic depression, medical and technical modernization, periods of war or political oppression). Nonnormative influences are conditions that show little correlation with chronological age or historical time, but affect an individual's development in important ways. Most developmental theories can be located with regard to a focus on 1 or more of these influences.

The age-graded and history-graded influences produce not only similarities in development but also conditions for individual differentiation during development and aging. On the one hand, there are biogenetic differences that operate throughout life and produce differentiation. On the other hand there are social-structural differences, like social class, that are relevant in differentiating individuals in terms of level and directionality of ontogenesis.

The dynamic of influences in development illustrates the multidisciplinary connections of developmental psychology. To fully understand age-graded influences, for example, requires research in which biologists, psychologists, and sociologists collaborate. Similarly, the analysis of history-graded influences cannot be accomplished by psychologists alone. In addition to cultural anthropologists and sociologists, social historians have much to offer when the task is one of charting constancy and change in the societal context of human development (Elder, 1998). For developmental psychology to be a fertile speciality, it needs solid ties to its parent discipline. At the same time, it cannot neglect its conceptual and empirical linkages to other specialties forming the larger umbrella of the developmental sciences.

JACQUI SMITH

References

Baltes, P. B. (1997). On the incomplete architecture of human ontogeny: Selection, optimization, and compensation as foundation of developmental theory. *American Psychologist*, *52*, 366–380.

Baltes, P. B., Lindenberger, U., & Staudinger, U. M. (1998). Life-span theory in developmental psychology. In R. M. Lerner (Ed.), *Handbook of child psychology: Vol. 1. Theoretical models of human development* (5th ed., pp. 1029–1143). New York: Wiley.

Baltes, P. B., & Smith, J. (2004). Life-span psychology: From developmental contextualism to developmental biocultural co-constructivism. *Research on Human Development*, *1*, 123–144.

Bengtson, V. L., & Schaie, K. W. (Eds.). (1999). *Handbook of theories of aging*. New York: Springer Publishing.

Birren, J. E., & Schaie, K. W. (Eds.). (1996). *Handbook of the psychology of aging* (3rd ed.). San Diego: Academic Press.

Bronfenbrenner, U., & Morris, P. A. (1998). The ecology of developmental processes. In W. Damon & R. M. Lerner (Eds.) *Handbook of child psychology: Vol. 1. Theoretical Models of Human Development* (5th ed.). New York: Wiley.

Cairns, R. B. (1998). The making of developmental psychology. In R. M. Lerner (Ed.), *Handbook of child psychology: Vol. 1. Theoretical models of human development* (5th ed., pp. 25–106). New York: Wiley.

Craik, F. I. M., & Salthouse, T. A. (Eds.). (2000). *The handbook of aging and cognition*. Mahwah, NJ: Erlbaum Lawrence.

Damon, W. (Ed.) (1998). *Handbook of child psychology* (4 volumes). New York: Wiley.

Elder, G. H. (1998). The life course and human development. In R. M. Lerner (Ed.), *Handbook of child psychology: Vol. 1. Theoretical models of human development* (5th ed., pp. 939–991). New York: Wiley.

Lachman, M. E. (2001). *Handbook of midlife development*. New York: Wiley.

Lerner, R. M. (2002). *Concepts and theories of development* (3rd ed.). Mahwah, NJ: Lawrence Erlbaum.

Lerner, R. M., & Steinberg, L. (Eds.) (2004). *Handbook of adolescent psychology*. New York: Wiley.

Valsiner, J. (1998). The development of the concept of development: Historical and epistemological perspectives. In R. M. Lerner (Ed.), *Handbook of child psychology: Vol. 1. Theoretical models of human development* (5th ed., pp. 189–232). New York: Wiley.

DEVELOPMENTAL TASKS

A developmental task is one that arises at or about a certain period in the life of an individual (Havighurst, 1948, 1953). The concept of developmental tasks assumes that human development in modern societies is characterized by a series of tasks that individuals have to learn throughout their lives. Some of these tasks are part of childhood and adolescence, whereas others arise during adulthood and old age. Successful achievement of a certain task is expected to lead to happiness and to success with later tasks, while failure might result in unhappiness for the individual, disapproval from society, and difficulty with later tasks.

Developmental tasks develop from 3 different sources (Havighurst, 1948, 1953). First, some are based on *physical maturation* (e.g., learning to walk). Other developmental tasks are related to *sociostructural and cultural forces*. For example such influences may be based on laws (e.g., minimum age for marriage) and culturally shared expectations of development (e.g., age norms; Neugarten, Moore, & Lowe, 1965), which determine the age when specific developmental tasks have to be solved. The third source of developmental tasks involves *personal values and aspirations*. These personal factors result from the interaction between ontogenetic and environmental factors and play an active role in the emergence of specific developmental tasks (e.g., choosing a certain occupational path).

Childhood and Adolescence

Early childhood is characterized by basic tasks, such as learning to walk, to take solid food, or to control the elimination of body waste. In addition, young children have to achieve complex cognitive and social tasks, such as learning to talk, to form simple concepts of reality, and to relate emotionally to other people. In middle childhood, developmental tasks relate to the expansion of the individual's world outside of the home (e.g., getting along with others their age, learning skills for culturally valued games) and to the mental thrust into the world of adult concepts and communication (e.g., skills in writing, reading, and calculating). Achieving adolescent developmental tasks requires the individual to develop personal independence and a philosophy of life: for example, learning new forms of intimate relationships, preparing for an occupation, gaining emotional independence from parents, and developing a mature set of values and ethical principals. The peer group plays a major role in facilitating the achievement of adolescents' developmental tasks by providing a context in which some of these tasks can be accomplished.

Adulthood and Old Age

The concept of developmental tasks describes development as a lifelong process. Thus, it is also an early and significant contributor to the emerging field of *lifelong human development* (e.g., *life-span psychology* and life-course sociology).

In young adulthood, developmental tasks are concentrated in 3 different areas: family, work, and social life. Family-related developmental tasks are described as finding a mate, learning to live with the marriage partner, having and rearing children, and managing the family home. One task that requires young adults to invest an enormous amount of time and energy relates to the achievement of an occupational career. Family- and work-related tasks represent a potential conflict, given that a person's internal resources are limited; thus, young adults might postpone one task to secure the achievement of another. With respect to social life, young adults are also confronted with assuming responsibility in the larger community and establishing new friendships.

During midlife, people reach the peak of their control upon society and their personal development. In addition, social responsibilities are maximized. Midlife is also an age period during which people confront the onset of physical health changes. Examples of *developmental tasks during midlife* include achieving adult responsibilities, maintaining a standard of living, assisting children with the transition into adulthood, and adjusting to the physiological changes of middle age (e.g., menopause).

Old age has often been characterized as a period of loss and decline. However, development in any period of life consists of both gains and losses, although the gain-loss ratio becomes increasingly negative with advancing age (Heckhausen, Dixon, & Baltes, 1989; Baltes, 1987). A central developmental task that characterizes the transition into old age is adjustment to *retirement*. The period after retirement has to be filled with new projects and is characterized by few valid cultural guidelines. Adaptation to retirement involves both potential gains (e.g., *self-actualization*) and losses (e.g., loss of self-esteem). The achievement of this task might also be obstructed by the management of another task—that is, living with a reduced income after retirement.

In addition, older adults are generally challenged to create a positive sense of their lives as a whole. The feeling that life has had order and meaning is expected to result in happiness (ego-integrity, Erikson, 1986). Older adults also have to adjust to decreasing physical strength and health. The prevalence of chronic and acute diseases increases in old age. Thus, older adults might be confronted with life situations that are characterized by not being in perfect health, serious illness, and dependency on other people's help. Moreover, older adults themselves might become caregivers for their spouses (Schulz & Beach, 1999). Some older adults also have to adjust to the death of their spouses; this task arises more frequently for women than for men. After having lived with their spouses for many decades, widowhood might force older individuals to adjust to emotional states of loneliness, moving to smaller places, and learning about business matters.

There also are other potential gains in old age that relate to the task of meeting social and civic obligations. For example, older people might accumulate knowledge about life (e.g., wisdom) and thus contribute to the development of other (younger) people and to society. It should be considered that the proportion of older people in society is increasing, which is a historically recent phenomenon. Thus, advancements in understanding the aging process might lead to identifying further developmental tasks associated with gains for and purposeful lives among older adults.

CARSTEN WROSCH

See also

Adult Development
Life-Span Theory of Control
Successful Aging

References

Baltes, P. B. (1987). Theoretical propositions of life-span developmental psychology: On the dynamics between growth and decline. *Developmental Psychology*, *23*, 611–626.

Erikson, E. H. (1986). *Identity: Youth and crisis*. New York: Norton.

Havighurst, R. J. (1948). *Developmental tasks and education*. Chicago: University of Chicago Press.

Havighurst, R. J. (1953). *Human development and education*. New York: Longmans, Green and Co.

Heckhausen, J., Dixon, R. A., & Baltes, P. P. (1989). Gains and losses in development throughout adulthood as perceived by different adult age groups. *Developmental Psychology*, *25*, 109–121.

Neugarten, B. L., Moore, J. W., & Lowe, J. C. (1965). Age norms, age constraints, and adult socialization. *American Journal of Sociology*, *70*, 710–717.

Schulz, R., & Beach, S. (1999). Caregiving as a risk factor for mortality: The Caregiver Health Effects Study. *Journal of the American Medical Association*, *282*, 2215–2219.

DHEA

Dehydroepiandrosterone (*DHEA*) and dehydroepiandrosterone-sulfate (*DHEA-S*) are the most abundant steroids produced by the human adrenal gland (Ebeling & Koivisto, 1994; Herbert, 1995). DHEA-S, sometimes considered as a plasma "reservoir" for the hormone, appears in the circulation at about 1,000 times the concentration of DHEA, is water soluble and is capable being bound to albumin (Watson, 1996). Although it is the DHEA that has been identified as having biological activity, the cellular receptor for and molecular mode of action of DHEA/DHEA-S remains uncertain. Depending upon the species and tissue, the possibilities for the former seem to include the NMDA sigma receptor (Monnet, 1995), the GABAA receptor (Majewska, 1992), the estrogen receptor (Bruder, et al., 1997), and the PPAR alpha receptor (Yen & Laughlin, 1998). In addition, and further complicating the situation, is the possibility that DHEA/S works indirectly rather than directly on target tissues, either following conversion into more potent steroids including estrogen and testosterone (Baulieu, et al., 1995), through another mediator, or as an antagonist to still another potent steroid, cortisol (Yen & Laughlin, 1998).

DHEA and DHEA-S are synthesized in large amounts by the fetal adrenal gland, with the levels dropping dramatically in the newborn and in children (Parker, 1999). Beginning in about mid-adolescence, and coincident with the development of the zona reticularis in the adrenal cortex, the levels begin to rise sharply again. This onset of heightened activity of the *adrenal gland* is referred to as "*adrenarche*" (Hinson & Raven, 1999). At about puberty, the blood hormone levels in boys and girls are similar; thereafter the serum concentration in males begins to exceed that of females (Watson, 1996). In both sexes, the levels of circulating DHEA/DHEA-S reach their peak during young adult life. Subsequently, in humans and other higher primates (Sapolsky et al., 1993), the levels of DHEA and DHEA-S undergo on average a steady decline with advancing age (Orentriech et al., 1984; 1992). In humans, this decline in circulating hormone reaches ~30% of young adult levels by ages 60 to 65 years and ~10% by ages 85 years and older. The reduction in DHEA/DHEA-S is thought to result, at least in part, from an involution of the *zona reticularis* (Yen & Laughlin, 1998; Parker, 1999). The latter, age-associated change in adrenal gland structure and DHEA production is referred to as "*adrenopause*."

In spite of the substantial individual variation in the hormone levels, their progressive decline with age on average has led to consideration of DHEA and DHEA-S as *biomarkers of the aging process*, i.e., as chemical indicators useful in tracking age-related senescent change, morbidity, and mortality (Lane et al., 1997). More importantly, the decline in levels of the 2 closely related steroids has also been implicated as being responsible, at least in part, for many of the senescent changes seen in advanced aged individuals and in individuals with chronic illness. These changes include but are not limited to body composition, some forms of cancer, type 2 diabetes, atherosclerosis, and ischemic heart disease (Herbert, 1995; Hinson & Raven, 1999; Shealy, 1995). At least some of these associations are sex specific but not always in a readily understood manner. For example, DHEA-S appears to be related to body composition (fat and lean body mass) in men but not women (Abbasi, et al., 1998). On the other hand, a similar association of DHEA to *body composition* may be present in women (De Pergola, et al., 1996). Whatever the limitations and contradictions in the existing literature, it is the notion that diminished hormone levels in older persons are causally linked to age-related functional decline and structural change that provides the rationale for the currently, well-promoted use of DHEA as an "*anti-aging*" intervention. In the United States, DHEA is readily available without prescription. However, data documenting that DHEA supplementation is clinically useful in humans is limited to very few examples. Indeed, to date most of the impressive findings reported on the effects of DHEA treatment have come from studies in rodent models of aging and senescent change, not from human subjects (Svec & Porter, 1998).

Serum lupus erythematosus (SLE) appears to be one circumstance where taking DHEA benefits the patient. Using the steroid has been reported to reduce the symptoms of the SLE and to permit lowering the dose of corticosteroid used to treat the disease (Barry, et al., 1998; van Vollenhaven, et al., 1998). The latter is important because of the potential negative side effects associated with the chronic use of corticosteroids. DHEA may also useful in the treatment of major *depression*. Barrett-Conner and colleagues (1999) found endogenous DHEA-S levels to be significantly and inversely associated with depressed mood. This finding complements an earlier report that in patients with major depression and low plasma DHEA-S values, modest doses of DHEA over 4 weeks improves depression ratings (Wolkowitz et al., 1997).

Although the hormone replacement seems a rational approach for ameliorating the possible negative consequences of naturally occurring, age-related declines in hormone levels, at present the only circumstance in which there is clear documentation supporting such a strategy is *estrogen replacement* in postmenopausal women. Even here, however, the approach remains controversial because of the risk of increasing the incidence of cancer in estrogen sensitive tissues. The justification for using DHEA in hormone replacement is, for now at least, much weaker, with the prevailing view that more long-term, carefully controlled, and larger clinical trials are needed before such action can be justified (Wolkowitz et al., 1997; Nippoldt & Nair, 1998). In particular, more work is needed to confirm those special circumstances where initial findings are promising, as for example in treating major depression. In addition, there appears to be growing support for the idea of using DHEA to help mitigate the negative side effects of corticosteroids (e.g., prednisone) in patients where the latter are an essential part of therapy, e.g., chronic inflammatory disease and SLE (Barry, et al., 1998; van Vollenhaven, et al., 1998; Steel, 1999). Thus, while no compelling reasons can be found for recommending *DHEA supplementation* to the healthy elderly, there may well be clinical circumstances where such supplementation will ultimately prove of significant value.

ARNOLD KAHN

References

Abbasi, et al. (1998). Association of dehydroepiandrosterone sulfate, body composition, and physical fitness in independent community-dwelling older men and women. *Journal of the American Geriatrics Society, 46*, 263–273.

Barrett-Connor, E., et al. (1999). Endogenous levels of dehydroepiandrosterone sulfate, but not other sex hormones, are associated with depressed mood in older women: the Rancho Bernardo Study. *Journal of the American Geriatrics Society, 47*, 685–691.

Barry, N. N., et al. (1998). Dehydroepiandrosterone in systemic lupus erythematosus: relationship between dosage, serum levels, and clinical response. *Journal of Rheumatology, 25*, 2352–2356.

Baulieu, Robel P., et al. (1995). Dehydroepiandrosterone (DHEA) is a neuroactive neurosteroid. *Annals of the New York Academy of Sciences, 774*, 16–18.

Bruder, et al. (1997). Dehydroepiandrosterone stimulates the estrogen response element. *Journal of Steroid Biochemistry and Molecular Biology, 65*, 461–466.

De Pergola, et al. (1996). Body fat accumulation is possibly responsible for lower dehydroepiandrosterone circulating levels in premenopausal obese women. *International Journal of Obesity and Related Metabolic Disorders, 20*, 1105–1110.

Ebeling, P., & Koivisto, V. A. (1994). Physiological importance of dehydroepiandrosterone. *Lancet, 343*, 1479–1481.

Herbert, J. (1995). The age of dehydroepiandrosterone. *Lancet, 345*, 1193–1194.

Hinson, J. P., & Raven, P. W. (1999). DHEA deficiency syndrome: a new term for old age? *Journal of Endocrinology, 163*, 1–5.

Lane, et al. (1997). Dehydroepiandrosterone sulfate: a biomarker of primate aging slowed by calorie restriction. *Journal of Clinical Endocrinology and Metabolism, 82*, 2093–2097.

Majewska, M. D. (1992). Neurosteroids: endogenous bimodal modulators of the GABAA receptor. Mechanism of action and physiological significance. *Progress in Neurobiology, 38*, 379–395.

Monnet, F. P., et al. (1995). Neurosteroids, via sigma receptors, modulate the [3H]norepinephrine release evoked by N-methyl-D-aspartate in the rat hippocampus. *Proceedings of the National Academy of Sciences U.S.A., 82*, 3774–3778.

Nippoldt, T. B., & Nair, K. S. (1998). Is there a case for DHEA replacement? *Baillière's Clinical Endocrinology and Metabolism, 12*, 507–520.

Orentreich, et al. (1984). Age changes and sex differences in serum dehydroepiandrosterone sulfate concentrations throughout adulthood. *Journal of Clinical Endocrinology and Metabolism, 59*, 551–555.

Orentreich, et al. (1992). Long-term longitudinal measurements of plasma dehydroepiandrosterone sulfate in normal men. *Journal of Clinical Endocrinology and Metabolism, 75*, 1002–1004.

Parker, C. R. Jr. (1999). Dehydroepiandrosterone and dehydroepiandrosterone sulfate production in the human adrenal during development and aging. *Steroids, 64*, 640–647.

Sapolsky, et al. (1993). Senescent decline in serum dehydroepiandrosterone sulfate concentrations in a population of wild baboons. *Journal of Gerontology, 48*, B196–B200.

Shealy, C. N. (1995). A review of dehydroepiandrosterone (DHEA). *Integrative Physiological and Behavioral Science, 30*, 308–313.

Steel, N. (1999). Dehydro-epiandrosterone and ageing. *Age and Ageing, 28*, 89–91.

Straub, R. H., et al. (2000). Replacement therapy with DHEA plus corticosteroids in patients with chronic inflammatory diseases—substitutes of adrenal and sex hormones. *Rheumatology, 59*(suppl. 2), 108–118.

Svec & Porter, (1998). The actions of exogenous dehydroepiandrosterone in experimental animals and humans. *Proc. Soc. Exp. Biol. Med, 218*, 174–191.

van Vollenhoven, et al., (1998). Treatment of systemic lupus erythematosus with dehydroepiandrosterone: 50 patients treated up to 12 months. *Journal of Rheumatology, 25*, 285–289.

Watson, R. R. et al. (1996). Dehydroepiandrosterone and diseases of aging. *Drugs and Aging, 9*, 274–291.

Wolkowitz, et al. (1997). Dehydroepiandrosterone (DHEA) treatment of depression. *Biological Psychiatry, 41*, 311–318.

Yen, & Laughlin, (1998). Aging and the adrenal cortex. *Experimental Gerontology, 33*, 897–910.

DIABETES

Diabetes mellitus is one of the most common chronic illnesses of older adults. More than 18 million Americans have diabetes, and by 2030 the World Health Organization predicts this number will double. By 2050, there will be 29 million Americans with diabetes (Boyle, Centers for Disease Control, 2001), 13% of whom will be older than age 70 years (Harris, Flegal, Cowie, et al., 1998). The personal and financial *costs of diabetes* are considerable.

Diabetes is a metabolic disorder characterized by the presence of *hyperglycemia* due to defective insulin secretion, insulin action, or both. It is divided into 3 classifications: type 1 (beta cell destruction of unknown etiology), type 2 (a dual defect of insulin production and insulin resistance exists, which is the most common form of diabetes) and gestational diabetes. This third type refers to *glucose intolerance* that is first recognized during pregnancy. Other causes of diabetes can be seen in the presence of diseases of the pancreas (pancreatitis, trauma, surgery), diseases such as Cushing or schizophrenia, and with medications (glucocorticoids, thiazide diuretics, nicotinic acid, opiates, phenytoin, etc.).

Type 1 diabetes usually affects a younger population (younger than 30 years of age), with a rapid progression due to autoimmune beta cell destruction. This population develops *ketoacidosis* with hyperglycemia and requires insulin to maintain normal glucose levels. Ninety percent of diabetes diagnoses are type 2, and it results from a combination of *insulin resistance* and *insulin deficiency* usually affecting people older than age 30. However, in the last 2 decades it has also grown to be a problem in obese children (Alexandrai, 2004). These patients are often overweight, with a slow onset of mild symptoms and complications at the time of diagnosis. Ketoacidosis is rare in *type 2 diabetes*. Blood glucose control does not necessarily require insulin, and more often requires a combination of diet and oral medications (Canadian Diabetes Association Clinical Practice Guidelines Expert Committee, 2003).

While diabetes is a common disease in older people, it can be difficult to diagnose because they are often asymptomatic. Between the ages of 64 and 70 years, a cohort of 11% of older people is unaware that they have diabetes (Harris, Flegal, & Cowie, 1998). Hyperglycemia in older adults rarely results in ketoacidosis or the other symptoms of the disease discussed below. Many older people can go years being unaware that they have type 2 diabetes; however, hyperglycemia can still take its toll and once diagnosed there may be complications such as atherosclerosis, or microangiopathy may be present already. Older persons are at higher risk of falls, have less social interactions, and a decrease in their quality of life when affected by diabetes (Brown, Mangione, Saliba, & Sakinsain, 2003).

Metabolic Syndrome

Diagnosis of diabetes may be just one piece of a bigger picture, the so-called "metabolic syndrome." The components of this syndrome include impaired fasting glucose, hypertension, hyperlipidemia (elevated triglycerides and low HDL), and *abdominal obesity*. This syndrome leads to diabetes and cardiac disease and is a serious condition in older adults, and of late is on the rise in overweight children. The importance of recognizing and treating this syndrome aggressively by treating insulin resistance, hyperglycemia, and cardiac risk factors is key in reducing the cardiac mortality and morbidity that these patients will face (Alexandrai, 2004; Isomaa, Almgren, & Tuomi, 2001).

Clinical Presentation and Diagnosis

Diabetes in older adults often presents itself atypically in the form of falls, urinary incontinence, cognitive impairment, or functional decline. Late-stage presentations are also seen with such complications as visual problems, myocardial infarction, and infections such as gangrene. These presentations may not always trigger investigations such as an immediate fasting glucose level, but it should be considered. Many people are unaware that they have the disease until they have routine blood work for dementia screening or are admitted to the hospital for other illnesses. Older people tend not to manifest the classic symptoms of fatigue, nocturia, blurred vision, polyuria, weight loss, infections, polydipsia, and hunger. Elderly individuals have a high renal threshold and therefore polyuria is less frequent. Polydipsia is often absent due to no renal water loss and impaired thirst mechanism. Weight loss is often attributed to other illness.

According to 2003 clinical guidelines, all individuals over the age of 40 years should be assessed annually for risk factors for diabetes and *fasting plasma glucose* should be done every 3 years. Screening should be performed earlier and more often if symptoms or risk factors, such as diabetes in a first-degree relative, are present. Similarly, people who are members of a high-risk ethnic group, have any manifestation of metabolic syndrome, macrovascular, and/or microvascular complications, should be tested. Twenty percent of people older than age 65 have diabetes, but only half are accurately diagnosed in a timely fashion. Diagnosing these individuals may prevent complications of renal failure, cardiovascular disease, and blindness.

The diagnosis of diabetes is accomplished by measuring fasting plasma glucose with a laboratory venous blood result of 7.0 mmol/L or higher on 2 separate occasions. It can also be established with a 2-hour PG (plasma glucose) and a 75-g glucose load with a blood result of greater than 11.1 mmol/L. Delaying the diagnosis or telling patients that they have a "touch of sugar" or are "borderline" is no longer acceptable and delays early intervention.

Complications

Hyperglycemia as a result of inadequate glucose control in older people can affect quality of life. The older adult may exhibit *nocturia*, nocturnal incontinence leading to poor sleep patterns, decreased energy, or even depression. Cognitive function may be impaired in areas of concentration and attention, conceptual thinking, and memory. In the elderly, infections can present atypically and be potentially life threatening. With hyperglycemia, the older person is more at risk for multiple infections as well as a higher frequency of hyperglycemic coma.

Older persons also run the risk of developing long-term difficulties such as microvascular insults like nephropathy and retinopathy, macrovascular complications related to heart disease, amputation, and stroke. Diabetes continues to be the leading cause of blindness, kidney failure, and amputations in the elderly population. These serious issues have a huge impact on quality of life, altered living situations resulting in nursing home placement, and even death. This reinforces the need for optimal glucose control in diabetes among older adults. The United Kingdom Perspective Diabetes Study and other trials have demonstrated a reduction in complications with best possible control.

Treatment

According to the 2003 Clinical Practice Guidelines, the goals for therapy in older individuals are no different than for others with diabetes. For many elderly people with diabetes, there is lack of adequate control. Target glucose levels for healthy older patients should range from 4.0–7.0 mmol/L for fasting plasma glucose. The 2-hour postprandial should range from 5.0–10.0 mmol/L, and the target AIC should be under 7.0 mmol/L. The aim is to prevent acute symptoms and complications, avoid hypoglycemia, and prevent or delay chronic complications. In the older adult it is important to consider coexisting illness such as dementia, life expectancy, and quality of life. Individualized approaches may be necessary. Treatments range from diet and physical activity to oral hypoglycemic agents and insulin. Proper treatment can be challenging because of other comorbidities, social situations, or limited finances, each of which can impair the ability to adhere to the treatment.

Lifestyle Modifications. Changes in diet and physical activity are key to optimal *glucose control*. To endorse this, an interdisciplinary team approach is necessary, including a dietician/nutritionist to teach healthy eating and develop meal plans for individual patients. This is difficult for many who are on the "tea and toast" regimen; a diet with adequate protein, soluble fiber, and adequate fluid intake can pose a challenge. Often with type 2 diabetes, a weight management program is necessary to attain acceptable glucose levels.

An *exercise prescription* of *resistance training* and aerobic activity is recommended for improved glucose control, improved lipid levels, and improved blood pressure. Together these decrease the risk of cardiovascular disease. Even the frail elderly will benefit from a modified, low-intensity exercise program that includes *strength training*, even if it is from a sitting position. Overall, exercise in the elderly has been shown to improve balance and strength and benefit overall health.

Self-Monitoring of Blood Glucose

All people with diabetes will benefit from being educated to monitor their glucose and, in turn, self-manage their disease. There are a variety of self-monitoring machines available that take into account the elderly population (e.g. *glucometers* with larger font or alternate-site testing). The frequency of testing is individualized by the diabetes team based on stability of lifestyle and glucose control.

Pharmacological intervention. After starting with lifestyle modifications, an oral agent may be added for improved control. There are a variety of options. There is a subgroup of lean older patients who respond to *insulin secretagogues* that potentiate insulin secretion; these medications include the *sulfonylureas* and *meglitinides*. This class should be used with caution in older patients because of the risk of hypoglycemia, which increases exponentially with age. The rule of thumb for starting any medication in older adults applies: "start low and go slow." The medication should be started at half the adult dosage, as is often done in elderly patients. *Gliclazide* and *glimepiride* are the preferred sulfonylureas, as they are associated with a reduced frequency of hypoglycemia (Tessier, Dawson, Tetrault, Bravo, & Meneilly, 1994). The nonsulfonylurea insulin secretagogues such as *repaglinide* and *nateglinide* may be associated with a lower frequency of hypoglycemia in the elderly.

Biguanides such as *metformin* act by reducing insulin resistance. This is widely used in older patients and has been shown to improve blood sugar levels in this population. The United Kingdom Prospective Diabetes Study (1998) suggests that this family of medication may reduce the risk of morbid events. This drug is contraindicated with renal impairment (creatinine clearance less than 60 ml/min) or hepatic dysfunction because it can increase the risk of lactic acidosis. *Thiazolinediones* (*rosigitazone*, *pioglitazone*) also reduce insulin resistance and do not cause hypoglycemia when used alone but cannot be used in the presence of heart failure. These medications are useful and should be reserved for treatment in obese older patients. Liver enzymes need to be monitored every 2 months for the first 12 months with this medication.

Decreasing or delaying gut absorptions is another aid in glucose control. Medications such as *alpha-glucosidase inhibitors* (*acarbose*) or *lipase inhibitors* (*orlistat*) have proven to be modestly effective; however, these drugs are not well tolerated due to potential gastrointestinal side effects. *Insulin therapy* is the next line of treatment for older adults when oral medications do not suffice. It can substantially improve blood sugar control and quality of life. Mixing insulin in syringes is not the safest method for the elderly. Pens or other devices to facilitate administration of insulin are helpful to avoid mixing errors and are useful when there is vision impairment or manual dexterity problems. There are a variety of regimens available, including using premixed insulin, multiple daily injections, and split mixed regimens. Initially with type 2 diabetics, a daily dose is initiated, with the oral medications continuing. Eventually the insulin injections increase and the oral medications are stopped altogether.

Management of Hypertension and Dyslipidemia

Controlling risk factors for cardiovascular disease is essential in patients who have diabetes. Smoking cessation is necessary to delay complications that can increase morbidity and mortality. Research suggests that optimal *blood pressure control* can reduce cardiovascular events, which are the leading cause of death for people with diabetes according to the Systolic Hypertension in the Elderly Study (Perry, Davis, & Price, 2000). Treatment of isolated systolic hypertension can also improve renal function in elderly patients (Heart Outcomes Prevention Evaluation Study Investigators, 2000). There are a variety of treatments available, such as *thiazide diuretics* for those older than age 60 with diabetes and systolic hypertension (Perry, Davis, & Price, 2000). *Ace inhibitors* have been shown to reduce hypertension and prevent the progression of renal disease in those patients with type 2 diabetes (Diabetes Control and Complications Trial Research Group, 1993).

Data is limited regarding *dyslipidemia* in the elderly but it is reasonable to treat elevated cholesterol levels in older adults who have diabetes. The targets would be to reduce the LDL below 2.5 mol/L and to reduce total cholesterol below 4 mmol/L in most patients who have diabetes. In diabetes, the triglyceride level and total plasma cholesterol are largely influenced by blood glucose control, and therefore optimal control will improve lipid abnormalities.

In summary, optimal glucose control is the goal of improving overall health with diabetes. It gives patients a feeling of control over their health along with giving them more energy, less anxiety, fewer symptoms, and fewer sick days, improving overall quality of life. The economic impact of this disease will continue to grow, but with a team approach to improve the health of these patients both the health care system and patients will benefit.

CHRISTINA MCNAMARA

See also
Biology of *FAT*

References

Alexandrai, V. (2004). Metabolic syndrome on the rise among children and adults. *Diabetes Care*.

Boyle, J. P., et al. Projection of diabetes burden through 2050: impact of changing demography and disease prevalence in the U. S. (2001). Centers for Disease Control and Prevention. *Diabetes Care, 24*, 1963–1940.

Brown, A. F., Mangione, C. M., Saliba, D., & Sakinsain, C. (2003). Foundation/American Geriatrics Society panel on improving care for elders with diabetes. Guidelines for improving the care of the older person with diabetes mellitus. *Journal of the American Geriatrics Society*, *51*(suppl. 5), S265–S280.

Diabetes Control and Complications Trial Research Group. (1995). The effect of intensive treatments of diabetes on the development and progression of long-term complications in insulin-dependent diabetes mellitus. *New England Journal of Medicine*, *329*(4), 977–986.

Canadian Diabetes Association Clinical Practice Guidelines Expert Committee. (2003). Clinical practice guidelines for the prevention and management of diabetes in Canada. *Canadian Journal of Diabetes*, *27*, S21–S23.

Harris, M. J., Flegal, K. M., Cowie, C. C. et al. Prevalence of diabetes, impaired fasting glucose, and impaired glucose tolerance in U.S. adults. The Third National Health and Nutrition Examination Survey, 1988-94. *Diabetes Care*, *21*, 518–524.

Heart Outcomes Prevention Evaluation (HOPE) Study Investigators. (2000). Effects of ramipril on cardiovascular and microvascular outcomes in people with diabetes mellitus: Results of the HOPE study and MICRO-HOPE substudy. *Lancet*, *355*, 253–259.

Isomaa, B., Almgren, P., & Tuomi, T. (2001). Cardiovascular morbidity and mortality associated with the metabolic syndrome. *Diabetes Care*, *24*, 683–689.

Perry, H. M., Davis, B. R., & Price, T. R. (2000). Effect of treating isolated systolic hypertension on the risk of developing various types and subtypes of stroke: The Systolic Hypertension in the Elderly Program (SHEP). *Journal of the American Medical Association*, *284*(4), 465–741.

Tessier, D., Dawson, K., Tetrault, J. P., Bravo, G., & Meneilly, G. S. (1994). Glibenclamide vs gliclazide in type 2 diabetes of the elderly. *Diabetic Medicine*, *11*(10), 974–980.

United Kingdom Prospective Diabetes Study Group. (1998). Tight blood pressure control and risk of macrovascular and microvascular complications in type 2 diabetes. *British Medical Journal*, *317*, 703–713.

DIET RESTRICTION

Diet restriction is also commonly referred to as dietary restriction, *caloric restriction*, calorie restriction, *food restriction*, or *energy restriction*. Diet restriction basically refers to any regimen of feeding or eating less nutrients than normal (typically defined as *ad libitum food intake*) without causing malnutrition, usually for the purpose of extending life span and retarding aging (senescence). A frequently used and catchy shorthand definition is "*undernutrition without malnutrition*." It should be noted, however, that to nutritionists the term "*undernutrition*" automatically refers to a form of malnutrition, and it is quite possible that some diet-restricted animals may become malnourished in old age, just as animals eating *ad libitum* frequently become malnourished in old age (for further information on nutrition and malnutrition, see Infoaging.org at www.infoaging.org/l-nutr-2-what.html#under).

The most commonly used methods of imposing diet restriction are every-other-day *ad libitum* feeding or feeding rations weighed out in direct proportion (e.g. 60%) to the intake of *ad libitum* fed controls (Pugh, Klopp, & Weindruch, 1999). Some studies include supplemental vitamins and minerals to minimize the risk of malnutrition. Diet restriction can also be achieved by severely restricting a single dietary component, such as protein, that limits the utilization of other nutrients. It is also frequently overlooked that feeding or overfeeding a bad-tasting, bad-smelling, or slightly toxic compound also can decrease food intake, which could potentially confound studies testing for a life extension effect by that compound.

Usually use of terms like caloric restriction or energy restriction imply that the physiological and biochemical changes produced by diet restriction are due to the restriction of calories per se, rather than any single component of the diet. Although there are controlled studies showing that life extension by diet restriction in rodents is most likely due to the restriction of calories (Weindruch & Walford, 1988), it should be noted that the vast majority of "caloric restriction" studies do not actually run controls to demonstrate that the particular response being investigated is also specific to the calorie restriction. Readers should thus be wary whenever such terms are used, and authors would do well to avoid them in the absence of a controlled study (Weindruch & Walford, 1988).

Because diet restriction studies are often conducted using *ad libitum*-fed animals as controls, there has been an amazingly persistent and widely circulated portrayal of diet restriction-induced life extension as a possible artifact due to returning short-lived, overeating animals to their natural or normal levels of food intake (Austad, 2001; Olshansky, Hayflick, & Carnes, 2002; Morley, 2002). Although there have been cases in which the control animals were likely overeating, studies have shown that life extension continues to increase with increasing levels of restriction and that life extension is still obtained relative to lean, food-restricted controls (Weindruch & Walford, 1988). Furthermore, studies of laboratory mice in particular have shown that maximal life extension under diet restriction occurs at levels in which females stop estrus cycling (Nelson, Gosden, & Felicio, 1985)—clearly not a natural or normal level of food intake.

At the severest levels of restriction, diet restriction has been shown to remarkably extend life span by as much as 50% in rodents. It is often inferred from such studies that severe levels of restriction are necessary for life extension. As noted above, however, diet restriction appears to have efficacy at all levels of restriction, and thus even moderate levels of restriction—such as 15%—can still produce a significant life-extension benefit (Weindruch & Sohal, 1997). Although a small cadre of people are severely restricting themselves voluntarily in hopes of extending their life span, such diets put one at considerable risk for malnutrition, particularly at older ages. In addition, there is no proof as yet that diet restriction retards aging in every individual (or even that it does not do life-shortening harm to some individuals), or that diet restriction will significantly retard the aging process in species such as humans that are already remarkably long-lived. In the United States, the National Institutes of Health is currently sponsoring several diet restriction studies in monkeys to test for life extension (so far with promising results), and short-term studies are being conducted in humans to test for beneficial effects on mortality risk factors.

Other active areas of diet restriction research include using large-scale protein- or gene-expression arrays to define a diet restriction-like physiological state (Weindruch, Kayo, Lee, & Prolla, 2002; Dhahbi, Kim, Mote, Beaver, & Spindler, 2004), developing *diet restriction mimetics* (Ingram, Anson, de Cabo, Mamczarz, Zhu, Mattison, Lane, & Roth, 2004), defining how quickly responses to diet restriction are turned on and off (Mair, Goymer, Pletcher, & Partridge, 2003; Dhahbi, Kim, Mote, Beaver, & Spindler, 2004), selectively testing various induced mutations (transgenics, knockouts, RNAi knockdowns) for the effects of specific genes on diet restriction-induced *life extension* (Lakowski & Hekimi, 1998; Rogina & Helfand, 2004), and genetically dissecting responses to diet restriction using strain variation (Forster, Morris, & Sohal, 2003; Rikke, Yerg, Battaglia, Nagy, Allison, & Johnson, 2004). Current model systems include yeast, nematodes, fruit flies, zebra fish, mice, rats, monkeys, and even in vitro cell cultures bathed in serum from diet-restricted animals (de Cabo, Furer-Galban, Anson, Gilman, Gorospe, & Lane, 2003). Prior to the current, most of the diet restriction research (Weindruch & Walford, 1988; Masoro, 2003) focused on describing numerous aging-related changes and diseases retarded by diet restriction, showing that it extends life span across a broad variety of taxa and that the life extension is not simply due to retarding development, reducing adiposity, reducing dietary fat, or reducing specific metabolic rate (i.e. metabolic rate normalized to body mass).

Diet restriction has been an important tool for studying aging for many years, often being cited as the most robust and reproducible method of retarding aging in mammals. However, the mechanism by which diet restriction extends life span is still an enigma, largely because its anti-aging benefits are consistent with nearly all theories of aging. A dominant, overarching theory is that diet restriction's benefits are the byproduct of a survival strategy to shift metabolic resources from growth and reproduction to repair and maintenance. However, in recent studies in mice, we have found that many of the physiological hallmarks of diet restriction—such as the responses of body temperature, body weight, growth, and fertility—are surprisingly variable among strains and show almost no correlation with each other (Rikke & Johnson, 2004). These results suggest that there is not a single, coordinated response to diet restriction, which implies that the vast majority of hallmark responses to diet restriction are actually unrelated to life extension or that multiple mechanisms contribute to life extension (or both).

Given the current level of research and funding support, and especially the progress in testing induced mutations in nematodes and fruit flies, the prospects for identifying some of the molecular players by which diet restriction extends mammalian life span appears to be quite promising within the next decade. With this knowledge, it should then be feasible to begin rationally designing interventions that provide the same anti-aging benefits as diet restriction but without the need for severely restricting food intake.

For additional information, see the *American Federation for Aging Research* at www.infoaging.org/; the *Calorie Restriction Society* at calorierestriction.org/; *Science of Aging Knowledge Environment* at sageke.sciencemag.org/ (requires subscription); and *Telemakus* at www.telemakus.net/CR-aging/.

BRAD A. RIKKE

See also
Anti-Aging Medicine
Life Extension
Nutrition

References

Austad, S. N. (2001). Does caloric restriction in the laboratory simply prevent overfeeding and return house mice to their natural level of food intake? *Science of Aging Knowledge Environment*, *2001*(6), pe3.

de Cabo, R., Furer-Galban, S., Anson, R. M., Gilman, C., Gorospe, M., & Lane, M. A. (2003). An in vitro model of caloric restriction. *Experimental Gerontology*, *38*, 631–639.

Dhahbi, J. M., Kim, H. J., Mote, P. L., Beaver, R. J., & Spindler, S. R. (2004). Temporal linkage between the phenotypic and genomic responses to caloric restriction. *Proceedings of the National Academy of Sciences U.S.A.*, *101*, 5524–5529.

Forster, M. J., Morris, P., Sohal, R. S. (2003). Genotype and age influence the effect of caloric intake on mortality in mice. *FASEB Journal*, *17*, 690–692.

Ingram, D. K., Anson, R. M., de Cabo, R., Mamczarz, J., Zhu, M., Mattison, J., Lane, M. A., & Roth, G. S. (2004). Development of calorie restriction mimetics as a prolongevity strategy. *Annals of the New York Academy of Sciences*, *1019*, 412–423.

Lakowski, B., & Hekimi, S. (1998). The genetics of caloric restriction in *Caenorhabditis elegans*. *Proceedings of the National Academy of Sciences U.S.A.*, *95*, 13091–13096.

Mair, W., Goymer, P., Pletcher, S. D., & Partridge, L. (2003). Demography of dietary restriction and death in *Drosophila*. *Science*, *301*, 1731–1733.

Masoro, E. J. (2003). Subfield history: Caloric restriction, slowing aging, and extending life. *Science of Aging Knowledge Environment*, *2003*, RE2.

Morley, J. E. (2002). Editorial: Citations, impact factor, and the *Journal*. *The Journals of Gerontology Series A: Biological Sciences and Medical Sciences*, *57*, M765–M769.

Nelson, J. F., Gosden, R. G., & Felicio L. S. (1985). Effect of dietary restriction on estrous cyclicity and follicular reserves in aging C57BL/6J mice. *Biology of Reproduction*, *32*, 515–522.

Olshansky, S. J., Hayflick, L., & Carnes, B. A. (2002). Position statement on human aging. *Journals of Gerontology Series A: Biological Sciences and Medical Sciences*, *57*, B292–B297.

Pugh T. D., Klopp, R. G., & Weindruch, R. (1999). Controlling caloric consumption: Protocols for rodents and rhesus monkeys. *Neurobiology of Aging*, *20*, 157–165.

Rikke, B. A., Yerg, J. E. III, Battaglia, M. E., Nagy, T. R., Allison, D. B., & Johnson, T. E. (2004). Quantitative trait loci specifying the response of body temperature to dietary restriction. *Journals of Gerontology Series A: Biological Sciences and Medical Sciences*, *59*, 118–125.

Rikke, B. A., & Johnson, T. E. (2004). Genetic dissection of dietary restriction. *Journal of the American Aging Association, Abstract 78*. Available: http://www.americanaging.org/acceptedabs.html.

Rogina, B., & Helfand, S. L. (2004). Sir2 mediates longevity in the fly through a pathway related to calorie restriction. *Proceedings of the National Academy of Sciences, U.S.A. 101*, 1598–6003.

Weindruch, R., Kayo, T., Lee, C. K., & Prolla, T. A. (2002). Gene expression profiling of aging using DNA microarrays. *Mechanisms of Ageing and Development*, *123*, 177–193.

Weindruch, R., & Sohal, R. S. (1997). Caloric intake and aging. *New England Journal of Medicine 337*, 986–994.

Weindruch, R., & Walford, R. L. (1988). *The retardation of aging and disease by dietary restriction*. Springfield, IL: Charles C. Thomas.

DISABILITY

For some years, a profound change has been occurring in the way we think about disability. Among the many definitions, that of the World Health Organization's International Classification of Impairment, Disability, and Handicap (ICIDH) forms a convenient starting-point (World Health Organization, 1980). According to this definition, disability refers to "any restriction or lack (resulting from an impairment) of ability to perform an activity in a manner or within the range considered normal for a human being. The term disability reflects the consequences of impairment in terms of functional performance and activity by the individuals; disabilities thus represent disturbance at the level of the person." The World Health Organization took impairments to refer to a reduction in physical or mental capacities, generally at the organ level. These need not have adverse consequences for the individual, as when impaired vision is corrected by wearing glasses, but where the effects of an impairment are not corrected, a disability may result. In turn, disability can (but need not) limit the individual's ability to function and fulfil a normal social role, depending on the severity of disability and on what the person wishes to do. *Handicap* refers to the social disadvantage (e.g., loss of earnings) that can result from a disability. This varies from person to person: a minor injury can handicap an athlete but may not restrict someone else. Although medical care generally concentrates on treating impairments, the patient's complaint is usually expressed in terms of functional difficulties, disability, or handicap, so the outcomes of care are commonly assessed using disability or handicap indicators rather than measures of impairment. The *impairment*-disability-handicap triad served well for 20 years, but the need to develop clear operational definitions and measurements of disability has led to pressures toward a reconceptualization.

Most definitions of disability refer to "normal" activities, but what is normal will vary by personal preference, age, gender, and place. The notion of function is central in assessing disability (Long & Pavalko, 2004), but the choice of functions to include in an operational definition is largely arbitrary. The result is that prevalence estimates of disability vary widely according to the definition used (Kind, Dolan, Gudex, & Williams, 1998). But there is pressure to agree on a set definition, if only because in a welfare state, decisions have to be made on whom to include in compensation for disability. Most traditional measures of disability focused on physical function, and conceptual foundations were described by Nagi (1979), Verbrugge (Verbrugge & Jette, 1994; Verbrugge, 1990) and others. The notion of basic activities of daily life (ADL) played a central role: capacities such as self-care and mobility that a person in any society requires on a daily basis. But as a basis for defining disability, ADLs set the bar relatively low, and few people in general population samples of older adults report ADL disabilities (Canadian Study of Health and Aging Working Group, 2001), while many experience activity limitations that are missed by ADL measures. Furthermore, the ADL problems most commonly reported include tasks (such as preparing a meal) that reflect gender roles as much as physical or mental capacity. As a result, the scope of operational definitions of functional disability was expanded to include instrumental activities of daily living, which cover supplementary activities (such as managing money, using a telephone) that are important but not central to survival. This approach serves to classify more people as disabled, but still encounters problems of age and gender bias and continues to rely on an inherently arbitrary selection of activities.

An alternative approach would be to define disability in terms of people's own judgment and most surveys include summary self-rating questions that hold remarkably good predictive validity (Idler & Benyami, 1997; Ho, 1991; Idler, Russell, & Davis, 2000). For example, Gold and colleagues analyzed the *National Health and Examination Survey* and showed that self-ratings predicted a range of subsequent health outcomes better than did the Health Utilities Index (Gold, Franks, & Erickson, 1996). But reliance on self-ratings can conflict with more objective judgments: subjectively a person may not report a problem, but objectively may be disabled.

The change in an older person's perception has been called "*response shift*," whereby a chronic patient's perception shifts as the disease progresses—typically they lower expectations and thereby score better on disability measures despite physical deterioration (Sprangers & Schwartz, 1999). Need and demand may not correspond: an elderly person might benefit from glasses or a hearing aid even though he or she is not asking for them.

The cumulative effect of these definitional difficulties has been to shift recent thinking on functioning away from the consequences of disease toward viewing it as a component of health (Üstün, Chatterji, Kostansjek, & Bickenbach, 2003). In 2001, the ICIDH was revised and renamed the *International Classification of Functioning, Disability, and Health* (*ICF*) (World Health Organization, 2001; Üstün, 2002). This represented a shift in thinking about disability away from a categorical model toward a dimensional view: instead of the population containing some people with disabilities, it recognizes that we all have areas of greater and lesser functional ability. The ICF considers contextual factors that can influence activity levels, so function is viewed as a dynamic interaction between health conditions (a disease or injury) and the context in which the person lives (including physical environment and cultural norms relevant to the disease). It aims to bring the experience of disability into the mainstream, to reflect a universal human experience. But the language is positive, and from labeling people as disabled, it emphasizes the level of health and functional capacity of all people (Üstün, Chatterji, Kostansjek, & Bickenbach, 2003). This also has the advantage of broadening the blame for loss of function from exclusively health issues toward interactions between the person's inherent ability and the features of the physical and social environment. Evidence shows that function can be improved by environmental manipulations and that disability arising from chronic disease is preventable (Clauser & Bierman, 2003). The wide range of factors that predict disability for a given impairment are brought into focus by this approach, and responsibility for function comes to involve not only the individual and his or her physician, but family and friends, employers, and also architects, engineers, and urban planners.

In addition, this population health perspective on disability has incorporated complexity thinking: there need not be a linear link between the extent of impairment and resulting disability. Minor changes in circumstance can profoundly modify the connections. From a population health perspective, disability will increasingly be viewed as a continuum rather than a state, and as resulting from the complex interaction between a person and all aspects of his or her environment. The coming years will reveal how this thinking translates into formal measures of disability, but agencies such as the World Health Organization have been working on developing internationally applicable measurement instruments (Skevington, Sartorius, Amir, & WHOQOL Group, 2004).

IAN MCDOWELL

See also

Activities of Daily Living
Mobility
Self-Care Activities

References

Canadian Study of Health and Aging Working Group. (2001). Disability and frailty among elderly Canadians: A comparison of six surveys. *International Psychogeriatrics, 13*(Suppl. 1), 159–167.

Clauser, S. B., & Bierman, A. S. (2003). Significance of functional status data for payment and quality. *Health Care Financing Review*, *24*(3), 1–12.

Gold, M., Franks, P., & Erickson, P. (1996). Assessing the health of the nation. The predictive validity of a preference-based measure and self-rated health. *Medical Care*, *34*, 163–177.

Ho, S. C. (1991). Health and social predictors of mortality in an elderly Chinese cohort. *American Journal of Epidemiology*, *133*, 907–921.

Idler, E. L., & Benyami, Y. (1997). Self-rated health and mortality: A review of twenty-seven community studies. *Journal of Health and Social Behavior*, *38*, 21–37.

Idler, E. L., Russell, L. B., & Davis, D. (2000). Survival, functional limitations, and self-rated health in the NHANES I Epidemiologic Follow-up Study, 1992. First National Health and Nutrition Examination Survey. *American Journal of Epidemiology*, *152*, 874–883.

Kind, P., Dolan, P., Gudex, C., & Williams, A. (1998). Variations in population health status: Results from a United Kingdom national questionnaire survey. *British Medical Journal*, *316*, 736–741.

Long, J. S., & Pavalko, E. (2004). Comparing alternative measures of functional limitation. *Medical Care*, *42*, 19–27.

Nagi, S. Z. (1979). The concept and measurement of disability. In E. D. Berkowitz (Ed.), *Disability policies and government programs* (pp. 1–15.). New York: Praeger.

Skevington, S. M., Sartorius, N., Amir, M., & WHO-QOL Group. (2004). Developing methods for assessing quality of life in different cultural settings. *Social Psychiatry and Psychiatric Epidemiology, 39*, 1–8.

Sprangers, M. A. G., & Schwartz, C. E. (1999). Integrating response shift into health-related quality of life research: A theoretical model. *Social Science and Medicine, 48*, 1507–1515.

Üstün, B. (2002). The international classification of functioning, disability and health—a common framework for describing health states. In C. J. L. Murray, J. A. Salomon, C. D. Mathers, & A. D. Lopez (Eds.), *Summary measures of population health: Concepts, ethics, measurement, and applications* (pp. 343–348.). Geneva: World Health Organization.

Üstün, T. B., Chatterji, S., Kostansjek, N., & Bickenbach, J. (2003). WHO's ICF and functional status information in health records. *Health Care Financing Review, 24*(3), 77–88.

Verbrugge, L. M. (1990). Disability. *Rheumatic Disease Clinics of North America, 16*, 741–761.

Verbrugge, L. M., & Jette, A. M. (1994). The disablement process. *Social Science and Medicine, 38*, 1–14.

World Health Organization. (1980). *International classification of impairments, disabilities, and handicaps. A manual of classification relating to the consequences of disease.* Geneva: World Health Organization.

World Health Organization. (2001). *International classification of functioning, disability and health* (Rep. No. A54/18). Geneva: World Health Organization. Available: http://www.who.int/gb/ebwha/pdf_files/WHA54/ea5418.pdf

DISCRIMINATION

See

Age Stereotype
Ageism
Americans with Disabilities Act

DISENGAGEMENT THEORY

Disengagement, often said to be the first formalized *theory of aging*, was developed by Cumming and Henry (1961) using data from the *Kansas City Study of Adult Life*. The theory describes the relationship between chronological age and the individual's level of involvement in social life, and suggests that aging is universally characterized by the gradual separation of aging individuals from the society in which they live. Morale does not lessen as the individual withdraws from society, and society from the individual; however, lessened involvement may occur from losses of opportunities, of others, and of vigor. This process is described as inevitable and irreversible, and can be seen as a desocialization that reverses the socialization processes of youth.

Disengagement theory is often contrasted with *activity theory*, and researchers such as Tobin and Neugarten (1961) have tested empirically the validity of the 2 theories. Maddox pointed out the distinction between social and psychological disengagement, and later criticized disengagement for lacking empirical justification (Maddox, 1969). Disengagement theory also has been contrasted with *continuity theory*, which posits that older adults who maintain mid-life habits, lifestyles, and relationships will have more success in aging (Atchley, 1972).

Hochschild (1975) claims that aging is a biological process, while disengagement is primarily a social process. Building on work by Streib (1968), he describes disengagement as a historical artifact of 1950s sociocultural norms, when older adults were more likely to feel discarded or abandoned by a society full of negative public attitudes and lacking in social policy for older adults. In this framework the meaning of disengagement is determined by social structures that vary across places, times, and cohorts. Further empirical work has confirmed this variation, and the consensus is that disengagement is neither natural nor inevitable. Johnson and Barer (1992) found that the shrinking of personal networks and a decrease in vitality after age 85 can cause older adults to withdraw from social activity. However, sense of self and locus of control persist through disengagement. Tornstram (1997) and Oberg (2003) describes this as *gerotranscendence*: older adults experience some *social withdrawal*, but this happens concurrently with a shift in life perspective from a materialistic and rational worldview to a more metaphysical one that transcends common norms. Quinnan's (1997) analysis of life history narratives found that older adults feel a greater sense of connection in old age. Feeling connected while nevertheless being withdrawn supports gerotranscendence over disengagement.

For more information, visit the following Web sites:

The development of theories of aging, at www.ln.edu.hk/apias/ageing/html/CA/DRT.htm
The Theory of Gerotranscendence, at www.soc.uu.se/research/gerontology/gerotrans.html
Gerotranscendence from Young Old Age to Old Old Age, at www.soc.uu.se/publications/fulltext/gtransoldold.pdf
Successful Aging, at www.ces.ncsu.edu/depts/fcs/pub/aging.html

Adam T. Perzynski

See also
Activity Theory
Continuity Theory
Social Gerontology: Theories

References

Atchley, R. C. (1972). The social forces in later life: An introduction to social gerontology. Belmont, CA: Wadsworth.

Cumming, E. (1975). Engagement with an old theory. *International Journal of Aging and Human Development*, *6*(3), 187–191.

Cumming, E. & Henry, W. (1961). *Growing old*. New York: Basic Books.

Hochschild, A. R. (1975). Disengagement theory: A critique and proposal. *American Sociological Review*, *40*, 553–569.

Johnson, C. & Barer, B. (1992). Patterns of engagement and disengagement among the oldest old. *Journal of Aging Studies*, *6*, 351–364.

Maddox, G. (1969). Disengagement theory: A critical evaluation. *Gerontologist*, *4*, 80–83.

Oberg, P., Tornstam, L. (2003). Attitudes toward embodied old age among Swedes. *Int J Aging Hum Dev*, *56*, 133–153.

Quinnan, E. J. (1997). Connection and autonomy in the lives of elderly male celibates: Degrees of disengagement. *Journal of Aging Studies*, *11*(2), 115–130.

Streib, G. F. (1968). Disengagement theory in sociocultural perspective. *International Journal of Psychiatry*, *6*, 69–76.

Tobin, S. S., & Neugarten, B. L. (1961). Life satisfaction and social interaction in the aging. *Journal of Gerontology*, *16*, 344–346.

Tornstam, L. (1997). Gerotranscendence: The contemplative dimension of aging. *Journal of Aging Studies*, *11*(2), 143–154.

DISPOSABLE SOMA THEORY

Disposable soma theory explains aging by simultaneously addressing the questions of why aging occurs, as a problem in evolutionary biology, and how aging is caused, as a problem in physiology (Kirkwood, 1977, 1981; Kirkwood & Holliday, 1979). It explains aging by asking how best an organism should allocate its metabolic resources (primarily energy) between keeping itself going from one day to the next (maintenance) and producing progeny to secure the continuance of its genes after it has died (reproduction).

No species is immune to hazards of the environment, such as predation, starvation, and disease. These hazards limit the average survival time, even if senescence does not occur. It follows that maintenance is only needed to an extent which ensures that the body (soma) remains in sound condition until an age when most individuals will have died from accidental causes. In fact, a greater investment in maintenance is a disadvantage, because it eats into resources that in terms of natural selection are better used for reproduction. The theory concludes that the optimum course is to invest fewer resources in the maintenance of somatic tissues than would be necessary for indefinite somatic survival.

The disposable soma theory is named for its analogy with disposable goods, which are manufactured with limited investment in durability, on the principle that they have a short expected duration of use. The theory, as outlined above, applies to any species that exhibits an *iteroparous (repeatedly reproducing) life-history plan* and that has a clear distinction between soma and germ line (sensu Weismann; see Kirkwood & Cremer, 1982). The principle of optimizing the tradeoff between maintenance and reproduction can be extended, however, to other life-history patterns (Kirkwood, 1981).

Central to the disposable soma theory is the idea that maintenance involves energy costs. Although it is not yet possible to quantify all of the costs of maintenance in detail, there is evidence that the overall maintenance cost is substantial. Basal metabolism accounts for the major part of the energy budget of a typical organism and is largely concerned with maintenance of one type or another. In particular, there is an extensive network of intracellular processes (DNA repair, antioxidant defenses, proofreading macromolecule synthesis, etc.) whose operation is essential for maintaining cellular homeostasis. Each of these processes requires energy.

In addition to explaining why aging occurs, the disposable soma theory also suggests how the genetic control of life span is arranged, and how different species have evolved different life spans. *Natural selection* operates on the genes that regulate key aspects of somatic cell maintenance in such a way as to secure the optimum balance between surviving long enough and spending too much on survival. The "*set point*" of a maintenance function determines the average period of longevity assured. As a specific example, consider DNA repair. If it is supposed that the exposure of DNA to damaging agents is constant but the level of DNA repair is increased, then the rate at which *DNA damage* accumulates is reduced while the energy cost associated with DNA repair rises. The rate of DNA damage accumulation determines the average length of time taken before DNA defects reach harmful levels and, hence, longevity.

Recalling that it is the presence of extrinsic mortality that makes it not worthwhile to invest in better maintenance than is needed to preserve somatic functions through the normal expectation of life in the wild, we can see that it is the level of environmental risk that provides the basis of selection for a longer or shorter intrinsic life span. A species subject to high environmental risk will do better to invest in rapid and profile reproduction at the expense of somatic maintenance, whereas a species that has a low level of environmental risk will tend to do the reverse.

A number of predictions about the *biology of aging* follow from the disposable soma theory:

1. Aging is caused by the lifelong accumulation of unrepaired somatic damage, and so the genetic control of longevity is effected primarily through genes that affect levels of repair and resistance to damage-inducing stresses.
2. Multiple maintenance mechanisms contribute to aging and longevity. This is because the evolutionary logic of the theory applies with equal force to each of the different processes that form a part of the somatic maintenance network.
3. The *mechanisms of aging* are inherently stochastic, which may explain the marked intrinsic variation in individual life span and in how the aging process contributes within individuals to age-related frailty, disability, and disease (Finch & Kirkwood, 2000).
4. Immortality of the germ line may be secured by enhanced maintenance and repair processes. Examples matching this prediction include the actions of the enzyme *telomerase*, which maintains telomere length in germ cells but which is switched off in most somatic cells, and the enhanced levels of antioxidant stress resistance recently reported in embryonic stem cells (Saretzki, Armstrong, Leake, Lako, & von Zglinicki, 2004).
5. Tradeoffs should exist between longevity (secured through investing in somatic maintenance) and traits such as fertility and growth rate. The existence of such tradeoffs at the genetic level is an essential prediction of the theory. Tradeoffs may also be seen at the physiological level, but only when reducing the level of one activity, e.g., reproduction, makes extra resources directly available for another, e.g., maintenance.

A further implication of the theory is the possibility of an evolved capacity to respond to short-term changes in environmental factors, such as the level of the food supply, by adjusting the optimal balance between somatic maintenance and growth or reproduction. This *adaptive plasticity* might, for example, explain the response of rodents to calorie restriction if during a period of famine the animal shuts down its reproduction and invests extra effort into maintenance (Shanley & Kirkwood, 2000).

The disposable soma theory is complementary to other theories on the evolution of aging, notably the mutation accumulation and *antagonistic pleiotropy* theories (Kirkwood & Rose, 1991). Antagonistic pleiotropy, in particular, also predicts tradeoffs, while all 3 theories predict the same general relationship between *longevity* and extrinsic mortality. Predictions 1-4 above, however, are distinctive elements of the disposable soma theory, with its emphasis on the roles of damage and repair (Kirkwood, 2005).

THOMAS B. L. KIRKWOOD

See also
Evolutionary Theory

References

Finch, C. E., & Kirkwood, T. B. L. (2000). *Chance, development and aging*. New York: Oxford University Press.

Kirkwood, T. B. L. (1977). Evolution of aging. *Nature, 270*, 301–304.

Kirkwood, T. B. L. (1981). Repair and its evolution: Survival versus reproduction. In C. R. Townsend & P. Calow (Eds.), *Physiological ecology: An evolutionary approach to resource use* (pp. 165–189.). Oxford: Blackwell Scientific Publications.

Kirkwood, T. B. L., & Cremer, T. (1982). Cytogerontology since 1881: A reappraisal of August Weismann and a review of modern progress. *Human Genetics, 60*, 101–121.

Kirkwood, T. B. L., & Holliday, R. (1979). The evolution of aging and longevity. *Proceedings of the Royal Society of London, Series B, 205*, 531–546.

Kirkwood, T. B. L., & Rose, M. R. (1991). Evolution of senescence: Late survival sacrificed for reproduction. *Philosophical Transactions of the Royal Society of London, Series B, 332*, 15–24.

Kirkwood, T. B. L. (2005). Understanding the odd science of aging. *Cell, 120*, 437–447.

Saretzki, G., Armstrong, L., Leake, A., Lako, M., & von Zglinicki, T. (2004). Stress defense in murine embryonic stem cells is superior to that of various differentiated murine cells. *Stem Cells, 22*, 962–971.

Shanley, D. P., & Kirkwood, T. B. L. (2000). Calorie restriction and aging: A life history analysis. *Evolution, 54*, 740–750.

DISRUPTIVE BEHAVIORS

Disruptive behaviors are observable actions that have the potential for or are perceived by caregivers as (1) endangering the person or others, (2) stressing, frightening, or frustrating the person, the caregiver, or others, and (3) socially unacceptable or isolating (Mace, 1990). Disruptive behaviors represent a broad range of actions including *aggression* (i.e., indicating some specific verbal or physical action) or *agitation* (i.e., an interpretation of some behavioral actions).

Disruptive behaviors exhibited by older adults in both long-term care and community settings present a significant problem for both nursing staff and family and informal caregivers (Burgio, Scilley, Hardin, Janosky, Bonino, & Slater, 1994; Chrisman, Tabar, Whall, & Booth, 1991; Cohen-Mansfield, Marx, & Werner, 1992; Everitt, Fields, Soumerai, & Avorn, 1991). Some of the consequences of these behaviors include (1) stress experienced by both residents and staff (Cohn, Horgas, & Marsiske, 1994); (2) decreased quality of resident care because of the use of physical or pharmacological restraints (Frengley & Mior, 1986; Robbins, Boyko, Land, Cooper, & Jahnigen, 1987); (3) economic consequences, including injuries, property damage, staff burnout, absenteeism, and turnover (Semala, Palla, Poddig, & Brauner, 1994; Spector & Jackson, 1994); (4) emotional costs to the disruptive person through social isolation (Ryden, 1988); and (5) increased incidence of falls (Cohen-Mansfield, Weiner, Marx, & Freedman, 1991; Gilley, Wilson, Bennett, Bernard, & Fox, 1991).

Estimates suggest approximately 60% to 80% of all nursing home residents are cognitively impaired, and the incidence of disruptive behavior is higher in these residents (Aronson, Post, & Guastadisegni, 1993; Cohen-Mansfield, Billing, Lipson, Rosenthal, & Pawlson, 1990; National Center for Health Statistics, 1985; Reichel, 1989; Teri, Larson, & Reifler, 1988). Consistently, research studies have demonstrated an association between the degree of disruptive behavior and the level of *cognitive impairment in older adults* with dementia. Mace (1990) and others (Cariaga, Burgio, Flynn, & Martin, 1991; V. K. Lee, 1991; Richter, Bottenberg, & Roberto, 1993) provide clinical support for these findings by observing that nursing home residents with behavior problems lose insight and self-control but often retain the language and/or motor skills to carry out the behaviors.

The body of research on physical, psychological, and/or social correlates of disruptive behaviors continues to grow. Although some investigators have found no significant relationship between *aggression and cognitive status* (Bridges-Parlet, Knopman, & Thompson, 1994), most studies have demonstrated that cognitive impairment is associated with some behavior problems (Burns, Jacoby, & Levy, 1990; Cooper, Mungas, & Weiler, 1990; Jackson, Drugovich, Fretwell, Spector, Sternberg, et al., 1989). Several studies have linked decreased cognitive status to specific behaviors, such as wandering (Algase, 1992), pacing (Cohen-Mansfield, Werner, Marx, & Freedman, 1991), screaming (Cohen-Mansfield, Billing, Lipson, Rosenthal, & Pawlson, 1990), and assaultiveness (Swearer, Drachman, O'Donnell, & Mitchell, 1988). Cohen-Mansfield and colleagues (1990) reported that cognitive impairment was associated with both physically aggressive and nonaggressive behaviors but to a lesser extent with verbally aggressive behaviors. Another investigator found that those who engaged in disruptive vocalizations (including screaming and *verbal aggression*) were more likely to be diagnosed with dementia than were those who did not but were not significantly more impaired on cognitive testing (Cariaga, Burgio, Flynn, & Martin, 1991). A more recent study revealed that the frequency and duration of disruptive vocalizations was significantly negatively correlated with cognitive deterioration (Burgio, Scilley, Hardin, Janosky, Bonino, & Slater, 1994). Gilley, Wilson, Bennett, Bernard, and Fox (1991) determined that age at onset and *extrapyramidal symptoms* modified the relationship between cognitive impairment and behavioral disturbance.

An early 1980s study found that psychoactive drugs were used on a regular basis to treat 58% of the subjects with serious behavior problems in a nursing home, although only 14.8% had received a psychiatric consultation (Zimmer, Watson, & Treat, 1984). Ryden, Bossenmaier, and McLachlan (1991) reported that psychotropic drugs were given to 68.5% of the observed residents and that those residents had significantly higher aggression scores. Cohen-Mansfield, Billing, Lipson, Rosenthal, and Pawlson (1990) observed that residents who received more major tranquilizers screamed more often than those who did not. Cariago and colleagues (Cariago, Burgio, Flynn, & Martin, 1991) noted that nursing home residents who engaged in disruptive vocalizations received significantly more neuroleptics than did those who did not, and Kolanowski and colleagues (Kolanowski, Hurwitz, Taylor, Evans, & Strumpf, 1994) reported a significant correlation between *psychotropic drug use and agitated psychomotor behavior*.

Kolanowski and colleagues (1994) operationalized communication difficulty as disruptive behavior itself. Other studies have considered communication as a correlate of disruptive behavior, and they have been increasingly linked. Cohen-Mansfield and Marx (1988) used communication as an indicator of social functioning, a dimension of depression. Poor ability to communicate was significantly related to general aggressive behavior and physically nonaggressive behavior. Ability to communicate effectively was positively correlated with verbally agitated behaviors such as complaining and negativism. Meddaugh (1990) found that the aggressive group in her study was generally nonverbal, compared with the nonaggressive group, who retained some verbal skills.

Inconsistent findings on the relationship between the time of day and occurrence of disruptive behaviors point out the need for further research in this area. Cohen-Mansfield and colleagues (1990) observed that screaming occurred significantly more often on the evening shift. Burgio and colleagues (1994) found an upward trend in the occurrence of disruptive vocalizations across the day shift, but Cariaga and colleagues (1991) noted that disruptive vocalizations occurred most often upon awakening in the morning, before meals, and before bathing. Malone, Thompson, and Goodwin (1993) concluded that the majority of *aggressive behaviors in nursing home residents* occurred mainly during the evening and day shifts. These findings were confirmed by Beck, Baldwin, Modlin, and Lewis (1990).

Although disruptive behaviors in older adults, regardless of etiology, have received increasing attention in the past decade from both researchers and clinicians, many contradictory findings remain among the significant correlates, such as the relationship between disruptive behaviors and functional ability, social support, gender, age, sleep patterns, premorbid personality traits, and depression. Greater emphasis is being placed on nonpharmacological approaches to disruptive behavior patterns in the elderly, including positive interaction responses from the caregivers (Burgener & Barton, 1991), the use of touch (Beck & Shue, 1994; Cariaga, Burgio, Flynn, & Martin, 1991), positive reinforcement schedules (Brink, 1980; Vaccaro, 1988), exercise (McGrowder-Lin & Bhatt, 1988), environmental changes (Negley & Manley, 1990), and staff training

(Mentes & Ferrario, 1989). The impact of these and other behavioral, social, and environmental interventions on the disruptive behaviors of the elderly is still unclear. Further studies of specific behaviors and the individualization of interventions for older adults in a variety of settings are still needed. The impact on the caregiver, although receiving some research and clinical attention, has not been fully explored.

BEVERLY A. BALDWIN

See also

Alzheimer's Disease: Clinical
Delirium
Restraints: Physical/Chemical
Wandering

References

Aronson, M. K., Post, D. C., & Guastadisegni, P. (1993). Dementia, agitation, and care in the nursing home. *Journal of the American Geriatrics Society, 41*, 507–512.

Algase, D. (1992). Cognitive discriminants of wandering among nursing home residents. *Nursing Research, 41*, 78–81.

Burns, A., Jacoby, R., & Levy, R. (1990). Psychiatric phenomena in Alzheimer's disease: 4. Disorders of behavior. *Journal of Psychiatry, 157*, 86–94.

Beck, C., Baldwin, B., Modlin, T., & Lewis, S. (1990). Management of aggressive behaviors in cognitively impaired nursing home residents. *Journal of Neuroscience Nursing*.

Beck, C., & Schue, V. (1994). Interventions for treating disruptive behavior in demented elderly people. *Nursing Clinics of North America, 29*, 143–155.

Bridges-Parlet, S., Knopman, D., & Thompson, T. (1994). A descriptive study of physically aggressive behavior in dementia by direct observation. *Journal of the American Geriatrics Society, 42*, 192–197.

Burgio, K. L., Scilley, K., Hardin, J. M., Janosky, J., Bonino, P., & Slater, S. C. (1994). Studying disruptive vocalization and contextual factors in the nursing home using computer-assisted real-time observation. *Journal of Gerontology: Psychological Sciences, 49*, 230–239.

Burgener, S. C., & Barton, D. (1991). Nursing care of cognitively impaired, institutionalized elderly. *Journal of Gerontological Nursing, 17*, 37–43.

Brink, T. L. (1980). Geriatric paranoia: Case report illustrating behavioral management. *Journal of the American Geriatrics Society, 28*, 519–522.

Cohen-Mansfield, J., Billing, N., Lipson, S., Rosenthal, A. S., & Paulson, L. G. (1990). Medical correlates of agitation in nursing home residents. *Comprehensive Gerontology B, 2*, 141–146.

Cariaga, J., Burgio, L., Flynn, W., & Martin, D. (1991). Disruptive vocalizations in institutionalized geriatric patients. *Journal of the American Geriatrics Society, 39*, 501–507.

Chrisman, M., Tabar, D., Whall, A. L., & Booth, D. E. (1991). Agitated behavior in the cognitively impaired elderly. *Journal of Gerontological Nursing, 17*, 9–13.

Cohen-Mansfield, J., & Marx, M. S. (1988). Relationship between depression and agitation in nursing home residents. *Comprehensive Gerontology B, 2*, 141–146.

Cooper, Mungas, & Weiler, (1990). Relation of cognitive status and abnormal behaviors in Alzheimer's disease. *Journal of the American Geriatrics Society, 38*, 867–870.

Cohen-Mansfield, J., Weiner, P., Marx, M. S., & Freedman, L. (1991). Two studies of pacing in the nursing home. *Journal of Gerontology: Medical Sciences, 46*, M77–M83.

Cohen-Mansfield, J., Marx, M. S., & Werner, P. (1992). Agitation in elderly persons: An integrative report of findings in a nursing home. *International Psychogeriatrics, 4*, 221–240.

Everitt, D. E., Fields, D. R., Soumerai, S. S., & Avorn, J. (1991). Resident behavior and staff distress in the nursing home. *Journal of the American Geriatrics Society, 39*, 792–798.

Cohn, M. D., Horgas, A. L., & Marsiske, M. A. (1994). Behavior management training for nurses aides: Is it effective? *Journal of Gerontological Nursing, 16*, 21–25.

Frengley, J. D., & Mior, L. C. (1986). Incidence of physical restraints on general medical wards. *Journal of the American Geriatrics Society, 34*, 565–568.

Gilley, D. W., Wilson, R. S., Bennett, D. A., Bernard, B. A., & Fox, J. H. (1991). Predictors of behavioral disturbances in Alzheimer's disease. *Journal of Gerontology: Psychological Sciences, 46*, 362–371.

Kolanowski, A., Hurwitz, S., Taylor, L. A., Evans, L., & Strumpf, N. (1994). Contextual factors associated with disturbing behaviors in institutionalized elders. *Nursing Research, 43*, 73–79.

Jackson, M., Drugovich, M., Fretwell, M., Spector, W., Sternberg, J., et al. (1989). Prevalence and correlates of disruptive behavior in the nursing home. *Journal of Aging and Health, 7*, 27–34.

McGrowder-Lin, R., & Bhatt, A. (1988). A wanderer's lounge program for nursing home residents with Alzheimer's disease. *Gerontologist, 28*, 607–609.

Mentes, J., & Ferrario, J. (1989). Calming aggressive reactions: A preventive program. *Journal of Gerontological Nursing, 15*, 22–27.

Mace, N. L. (1990). The management of problem behavior in dementia. In N. L. Mace (Ed.), *Dementia care: Patient, family and community*. Baltimore: Johns Hopkins University Press.

Meddaugh, D. (1990). Reactance understanding aggressive behavior in long-term care. *Journal of Psychosocial Nursing, 28*, 28–32.

Malone, M. L., Thompson, L., & Goodwin, J. S. (1993). Aggressive behaviors among the institutionalized elderly. *Journal of the American Geriatrics Society, 41*, 853–856.

National Center for Health Statistics. (1985). *National Nursing Home Survey micro-data tape* (NTIS Order No. PB89-159503). Springfield, VA: National Technical Information Service.

Negley, E. N., & Manley, J. T. (1990). Environmental interventions in assaultive behavior. *Journal of Gerontological Nursing, 16*, 29–33.

Lee, V. K. (1991). Language changes and Alzheimer's disease: A literature review. *Journal of Gerontological Nursing, 17*, 16–19.

Richter, J. M., Bottenberg, D., & Roberto, K. A. (1993). Communication between formal caregivers and individuals with Alzheimer's disease. *American Journal of Alzheimer's Care and Related Disorders and Research*, 20–26.

Reichel, W. (1989). *Clinical aspects of aging* (3rd ed.). Baltimore: Williams and Wilkins.

Robbins, L. J., Boyko, E., Land, J., Cooper, D., & Jahnigen, D. W. (1987). Binding the elderly: A prospective study of the use of mechanical retrains in acute care hospital. *Journal of the American Geriatrics Society, 35*, 290–291.

Ryden, M. (1988). Aggressive behavior in persons with dementia who live in the community. *Alzheimer's Disease and Associated Disorders, 2*, 342–355.

Ryden, M. B., Bossenmaier, M., & McLachlan, C. (1991). Aggressive behavior in cognitively impaired nursing home residents. *Research in Nursing and Health, 14*, 87–95.

Semala, T. P., Palla, K., Poddig, B., & Brauner, D. J. (1994). Effect of the Omnibus Reconciliation Act of 1987 on antipsychotic prescribing in nursing home residents. *Journal of the American Geriatrics Society, 42*, 648–652.

Swearer, J. M., Drachman, D. A., O'Donnell, B. F., & Mitchell, A. L. (1988). Troublesome and disruptive behaviors in dementia: Relationships to diagnosis and disease severity. *Journal of the American Geriatrics Society, 36*, 784–790.

Teri, L., Larson, E., & Reifler, B. (1988). Behavioral disturbance in dementia of the Alzheimer's type. *Journal of the American Geriatrics Society, 36*, 1–6.

Vaccaro, F. J. (1988). Application of operant procedures in a group of institutionalized aggressive geriatric patients. *Psychology and Aging, 3*, 22–28.

Spector, W. D., & Jackson, M. E. (1994). Correlated of disruptive behaviors in nursing homes. *Journal of Health and Aging, 6*, 173–184.

Zimmer, G., Watson, N., & Treat, A. (1984). Behavioral problems among patients in skilled nursing facilities. *American Journal of Public Health, 74*, 1118–1121.

DIVORCE

Increasingly middle-aged and older persons are being touched by the experience of divorce, although it continues to be primarily an event that occurs among younger adults. U.S. census data indicate that the median age of the termination of first marriages is age 30 years and 29 years for men and women, respectively. For second marriages, the median age of divorce is still under age 40 years. Twenty-seven percent of men and 18% of women who divorce during a given year are between the ages of 45 and 64 years, and only 2% of the men and women are older than 65. For men, the probability of future divorce is 23% among 40-year-olds, 8% among 50-year-olds, and 2% among 60-year-olds. For women, the probability decreases from 18% at age 40 to 6% at age 50 and 2% at age 60 (Kreider & Fields, 2002).

Although the actual event of divorce is still relatively uncommon in midlife and rare among older persons, its prevalence is increasing (Cooney & Dunne, 2001). Among the Canadian population, the divorce rate among 45- to 49-year-olds has doubled since 1971, and it has tripled among those aged 50 to 54 years (Wu & Penning, 1997). Predictors of mid- and *later-life divorce* include higher education, discrepancy in spouses' marital history, the marriage being a second marriage, older ages among children, and a small number of siblings (Wu & Penning, 1997). A recent national study of people who divorced after age 40 found that the majority of the time women initiate the divorce. Females reported that the most frequent reasons for the divorce were, in order: verbal, physical, and emotional abuse, different values and lifestyles, infidelity, and alcohol or drug abuse. Men reported that the most common reasons were: falling out of love, different values and lifestyles, verbal, physical, and emotional abuse, and infidelity (Montenegro, 2004).

An increasing proportion of people are entering old age already divorced. As the divorce rate in midlife has increased substantially in recent decades, coupled with a decrease in *remarriage rates* (Shapiro, 2003), cohorts entering later life include a greater proportion of divorced people. In the 2000 U.S. census, 8% and 10% of men and women, respectively, between the ages of 65 and 74 were currently divorced. Five percent of men and 6% of women aged 75 through 84 were divorced, and 3% of men and women older than age 85 were divorced (Kreider & Simmons, 2003). This reflects a substantial increase of divorce among the older population, compared to earlier years: the proportion of the older population who are divorced is double that of 1970, and triple that of 1950 (Kreider & Simmons, 2003). Moreover, the proportion of divorced persons in later life is expected to increase in the future, as more middle-aged cohorts with relatively high percentages of divorced people enter old age.

Marital dissolution generally has negative economic and psychological consequences for those who experience divorce. One study found that divorced men between the ages of 50 and 73 who had been married at least 15 years experienced a 61% decline in income, while women suffered a 66% decline (Gander, 1991). Divorce also disrupts savings and asset accumulation, as couples must divide assets such as home equity and pensions (Cooney & Dunne, 2001). In addition, older people who are divorced are at higher risk for depression, health problems, and death (Wu & Penning, 1997). Thirty-five percent of the women and 21% of the men in a national study reported suffering significant symptoms of depression following the divorce, with 31% of the women and 18% of the men having been diagnosed by a physician with depression (Montenegro, 2004). The negative feelings that follow divorce, such as loneliness, are mediated by the frequency of contact with children, the quality of contact with children, and the frequency of contact with friends (Pinquart, 2003).

Despite these negative consequences, there is evidence that people divorcing in mid- and later-life have an easier adjustment than those who divorce earlier in adulthood. Women divorcing after age 40 are less likely than younger women to suffer from depression and feelings of hostility (Marks & Lambert, 1998). Among those who have been divorced at least twice, 53% of the men and 42% of the women in one study reported that their first divorce, when they were younger, was more difficult, usually because of the emotional and legal complexities of having younger children. Twenty-eight percent of the men and 35% of the women felt that their divorce later in life was more difficult, with the others perceiving that the 2 divorces were about the same (Montenegro, 2004).

Divorce in mid- and later-life affects *intergenerational relationships*. Research has consistently found that divorced older men experience deteriorated relationships with their adult children. They are less likely than married older men to live with an adult child, and they have substantially less contact with their children (Shapiro, 2003). In addition, adult children report significantly worse relationships with their fathers after their parents divorce in later life (Kaufman & Uhlenberg, 1998). Silverstein and Bengtson (1997) found that adult children whose parents are divorced are 33% more likely than children of married parents to have a detached relationship with their father.

The research on intergenerational relationships of divorced older women is less consistent. Although older mothers' transition to divorce is associated with an increase in at least weekly contact with an adult child, they are at greater risk than married mothers of having at least 1 child with whom they have little contact (Shapiro, 2003). Kaufman and Uhlenberg (1998) found that parents' divorce was not associated with the quality of the relationship between adult children and their mothers. However, Silverstein and Bengtson (1997) reported that divorce was modestly associated with an increased likelihood that adult children would have an obligatory or detached relationship with their mother, although the magnitude of the effect was much less than it was for fathers. The research is consistent that the *divorce status of older women* is not associated with the probability of them co-residing with an adult child (Pezzin & Schone, 1999; Shapiro, 2003).

The effects of divorce on relationships between parents and adult children are reflected in the help and support that is exchanged between generations.

Compared to married counterparts, divorced older persons have fewer exchanges with their adult children, especially for the fathers (White, 1992). Among the elderly who live alone, divorced fathers are significantly less likely than widowed fathers to provide cash transfers to their adult children, and they received substantially less informal care from their children (Pezzin & Schone, 1999). Divorced women, on the other hand, experience similar exchanges of cash and informal care relative to widowed women.

Although parental divorce generally has a strong impact on relationships between grandchildren and grandparents when the children are young, divorce among parents in mid- and later-life has little effect on the grandchild-grandparent relationship. Grandchildren who are in late adolescence or adulthood when their parents divorce are able to establish relationships with their grandparents that are independent of their parents, and the custodial arrangements in divorced families that have such a dramatic effect on grandparents and grandchildren when the children are young are less relevant when the grandchildren are older. As a result, *adult grandchildren* whose parents divorce in mid- and later-life have relationships with their grandparents that are similar to adult grandchildren whose parents are still married (Cooney & Smith, 1996).

RICHARD B. MILLER

See also
Family Relationships

References

Cooney, T. M., & Dunne, K. (2001). Intimate relationships in later life: Current realities, future prospects. *Journal of Family Issues*, *22*, 838–858.

Cooney, T. M., & Smith, L. A. (1996). Young adults' relations with grandparents following recent parental separation. *Journal of Gerontology: Social Sciences*, *51*, S91–S95.

Gander, A. M. (1991). Economics and well being of older divorced persons. *Journal of Women and Aging*, *3*, 37–57.

Kaufman, G., & Uhlenberg, P. (1998). Effects of life course transitions on the quality of relationships between adult children and their parents. *Journal of Marriage and the Family*, *60*, 924–938.

Kreider, R. M., & Fields, J. M. (2002). *Number, Timing, and Duration of Marriages and Divorces: 1996*. Current Population Reports, P70-80. Washington, DC: U.S. Census Bureau.

Kreider, R. M., & Simmons, T. (2003). *Marital Status: 2000*. Current Population Reports, C2KBR-30. Washington, DC: U.S. Census Bureau.

Marks, N. F., & Lambert, J. D. (1998). Marital status continuity and change among young and midlife adults. *Journal of Family Issues*, *19*, 652–686.

Montenegro, X. P. (2004). *The divorce experience: A study of divorce in midlife and beyond*. Washington, DC: AARP.

Pezzin, L. E., & Schone, B. S. (1999). Parental marital disruption and intergenerational transfers: An analysis of lone elderly parents and their children. *Demography*, *36*, 287–297.

Pinquart, M. (2003). Loneliness in married, widowed, divorced, and never-married older adults. *Journal of Social and Personal Relationships*, *20*, 31–53.

Shapiro, A. (2003). Later-life divorce and parent-adult child contact and proximity. *Journal of Family Issues*, *24*, 264–285.

Silverstein, M., & Bengtson, V. L. (1997). Intergenerational solidarity and the structure of adult child-parent relationships in American families. *American Journal of Sociology*, *103*, 429–460.

White, L. K. (1992). The effect of parental divorce and remarriage on parental support for adult children. *Journal of Family Issues*, *13*, 234–250.

Wu, Z., & Penning, M. J. (1997). Marital instability after midlife. *Journal of Family Issues*, *18*, 459–478.

DNA (DEOXYRIBONUCLEIC ACID): REPAIR PROCESS

DNA in cells is constantly exposed to insults from both endogenous and exogenous factors that may cause a variety of lesions to DNA. In response to DNA damage, multiple repair pathways have evolved in cells (for a review, see Carr & Hoekstra, 1995). In general, these pathways include direct reversal, mismatch, recombinational, base excision, and nucleotide excision repair. The simplest DNA repair pathways involve only single enzymes that catalyze a direct reversal of specific damage (e.g., alkyltransferase, which removes the methyl group from O^6-methylguanine). Mismatch repair corrects mispaired bases, which often occur as a consequence of an error in replication. The importance of this system in mammals is illustrated by the defects in the human homologues of bacterial MutS and MutL, which may be the primary cause of hereditary nonpolyposis colorectal cancer in humans. Recombinational repair occurs when both strands of the DNA helix are damaged and there is no intact template for the DNA polymerase to copy (e.g., double-strand breaks and interstrand cross-links). This pathway has been relatively well characterized in bacteria; however, it is poorly understood in mammalian cells. Base excision and nucleotide excision are involved in repair of much of the DNA damage that occurs in cells. Through base excision repair, simple base modifications (e.g., oxidation and monofunctional alkylation) are repaired. This pathway is characterized by a series of glycosylases that specifically cleave the glycosylic bond between the damaged bases and the de-oxyribose. The resulting apurinic/apyrimidinic site is removed by AP endonuclease and deoxyribophosphodiesterase, and the gap is filled by DNA polymerase β and sealed by DNA ligase. Through nucleotide excision repair, bulky helix-distorting lesions such as cyclobutane primidine dimers and large alkylating adducts are repaired. In addition, some oxidative DNA lesions are corrected by nucleotide excision repair. In mammalian cells, nucleotide excision repair is a complex process involving at least 25 proteins for damage recognition, dual incision, repair synthesis, and ligation. More recently, it has been demonstrated that there are two nucleotide excision repair subpathways, that is, transcription-coupled repair, which preferentially repairs lesions in the transcribed strand of expressed genes, and bulk genome repair, which repairs lesions in the nontranscribed DNA at a relatively slow rate.

The DNA repair theory of aging proposes that DNA repair declines with age and eventually falls below a threshold level necessary to maintain the integrity of the genome. When this occurs, unrepaired damage and mutations accumulate in the genome of cells, resulting in a decrease in cellular function. This theory is supported by the four lines of evidence described below:

1. DNA repair decreases with age (for a review, see Guo & Richardson, 1999). Over the past two decades, a large number of studies have compared the DNA repair capacity of cells/ tissues from young and old organisms to determine if DNA repair declines with age. In most of these studies, DNA repair was measured as unscheduled DNA synthesis (UDS) after the cells were exposed to DNA damaging agents, such as ultraviolet (UV) radiation or methyl methanesulfonate; therefore, these studies were measuring primarily nucleotide and base excision repair. UDS has been observed to decrease approximately 30% to 50% in cells from mice, hamsters, rats, rabbits, and humans. However, there are also studies with cells from these animal models that show no change in UDS with age. It has been proposed that this controversy could be the result of the assay. UDS is a relatively crude assay, which neither directly nor selectively measures the removal of a specific type of damage; it measures the induction of non-replicative DNA synthesis by a damaging agent. Thus, changes in the specific activity of the thymidine precursor pool or replicative DNA synthesis could affect the level of DNA repair measured in the UDS assay. Recently, other techniques have been used to study the effect of age on DNA repair. For example, using a ^{32}P-postlabeling assay, studies have shown a significant decrease in removal of benzo(a)pyrene-DNA adducts from the genome of old mice. Using UV-irradiated plasmids transfected into human lymphocytes, it has been found that the repair of the plasmid declines with age at a rate of 0.6% per year from the first to the tenth decade of life. T4 endonuclease V, which specifically cleaves UV-induced cyclobutane pyrimidine dimers (CPDs), has been used to measure the removal of CPDs from specific genes/DNA regions. An age-related decrease in removal of CPDs has been observed for telomeres of human fibroblasts, as well as transcribed and nontranscribed genes in rat hepatocytes (Guo & Richardson, 1999). However, the age-related decrease in repair appears to be greater in nontranscribed genes/regions of the genome.
2. DNA damage/mutations accumulate with age (for a review, see Walter, Grabowski, Street, Conrad, & Richardson, 1997). For example, one of the most common DNA lesions, DNA strand

breaks, has been found to increase with age. In addition, a number of studies have shown an age-related accumulation of oxidative damage (8-hydroxydeoxyquanosine) in nuclear and mitochondrial DNA from cells from humans and animals. An age-related increase in mutations has also been demonstrated. For example, lymphocytes from old individuals have been shown to have higher levels of mutations in the hypoxanthine phosphoribosyl transferase (*hprt*) gene than those from young individuals. Using the recently developed bacterial *LacZ* and *LacI* transgenic systems, several investigators have shown an increased mutation frequency in the transgene in various tissues of mice.

3. Dietary restriction attenuates age-related changes in DNA repair and DNA damage/mutations (for a review, see Haley-Zitlin & Richardson, 1993). The age-related decrease in DNA repair observed may be physiologically important in aging because studies have shown that the age-related increase in DNA damage/mutations and the age-related decrease in DNA repair can be attenuated by dietary restriction, which has been shown to retard aging and result in increased life span in rodents. For example, studies have shown that the frequency of spontaneous and chemically induced mutations in the *hprt* gene is significantly reduced in lymphocytes of rats and mice fed a calorie-restricted diet compared with the animals fed ad libitum. In addition, studies have shown that rats and mice fed a calorie-restricted diet exhibited lower levels of oxidative damage in DNA isolated from a variety of tissues than DNA isolated from tissues of rodents fed ad libitum. Studies have also shown that dietary restriction significantly increases the ability of cells from rats and mice to repair DNA damage. For example, the levels of unscheduled DNA synthesis after UV irradiation is higher in the cells obtained from rats and mice fed a calorie-restricted diet than in the cells from animals fed ad libitum. Recent results also show that dietary restriction attenuated the age-related decrease in gene-specific repair in transcriptionally active genes and nontranscribed genes/region in rat hepatocytes.
4. Animal species with a long life span have a higher level of DNA repair. Another approach that has been used to study the relationship of aging and DNA repair is to measure the ability of cells from animals of various life spans to repair DNA damage. The original study by Hart and Setlow showed that UV-induced UDS in fibroblasts from several mammalian species was positively correlated with species life span. Although subsequent studies with additional classes of organisms have shown some limitation in this correlation, there is reasonable evidence to support the view that cells from a mammalian species with a long life span have a higher level of DNA repair as measured by UDS (Cortopassi & Wang, 1996).

In summary, there are several lines of evidence that support the DNA repair theory of aging; however, it is not clear if there is a causal relationship between DNA repair and aging. In addition, because almost all studies that have measured DNA repair with age have focused on nucleotide excision repair, very little is known on how aging affects the other DNA repair pathways.

ZhongMao Guo
Arlan Richardson

See also
Somatic Mutations and Genome Instability

References

Carr, A. M., & Hoekstra, M. F. (1995). The cellular responses to DNA damage. *Trends in Cell Biology*, *5*, 32–40.

Cortopassi, G. A., & Wang, E. (1996). There is substantial agreement among interspecies estimates of DNA repair activity. *Mechanisms of Ageing and Development*, *91*, 211–218.

Guo, A., & Richardson, A. (1999). Effects of aging and dietary restriction on DNA repair. *Molecular Biology of Aging*, *44*, 362–372.

Haley-Zitlin, V. & Richardson, A. (1993). Effect of dietary restriction on DNA repair and DNA damage. *Mutation Research*, *295*, 237–245.

Walter, C. A., Grabowski, D. T., Street, K. A., Conrad, C. C., & Richardson, A. (1997). Analysis and modulation of DNA repair in aging. *Mechanisms of Ageing and Development*, *98*, 203–222.

DOCTOR–PATIENT RELATIONSHIPS

The growth of the older adult population presents the physician and society with significant challenges. The rapid increase in the number of frail elderly, with multiple pathologies, functional decline, and the resultant increase in the need for services, requires that caregivers and physicians in almost all specialties develop the necessary skills to care for these patients (Rockwood, Howlett, MacKnight, Beattie, Bergman, & Hebert, et al., 2004). On the more positive side of the therapeutic spectrum, there is an expanding population of healthy older people who are both physically and mentally active (Jacobzone, 2000). The medical needs of these older individuals demand an organized approach to health promotion, as well as the prevention of those conditions that may lead to frailty. The doctor—most often the *primary care physician*—stands at the helm of medical services providing for the needs of the older population. It is thus essential that the relationship between the doctor and patient be structured on mutual respect and understanding, and that the physician acquire those unique communication and clinical skills needed in caring for older patients.

An almost inevitable consequence of aging is the acquisition of multiple medical conditions. The presence of heart disease, diabetes mellitus, stroke, and dementia can understandably lead to these problems becoming the central focus of attention between the doctor and the older patient. However, a strictly disease-orientated approach is frequently not appropriate in this population. Rather, emphasis should be placed on the assessment and maintenance of functional abilities and the diagnosis of syndromes common to the frail elderly. Termed the "*giants of geriatrics*" by Isaacs (1992), the most significant functional syndromes affecting older adults include the four Is: incontinence, immobility, instability, and intellectual impairment.

The Problems

The essential aspect of a successful doctor-patient relationship is communication. Unfortunately, what is often taken for granted in younger people may become an almost impossible task when interacting with older adults. Both visual and hearing impairments are common in older persons, and the physician often finds acquiring an accurate history to be both difficult and frustrating, and within the constraints of office practice, unacceptably prolonged.

History-taking is further complicated by the frequent presence of multiple conditions, many of which may not be immediately relevant to the patient's presenting problem. The physician is often faced with the formidable task of dealing with a seemingly unending list of previous surgical interventions and traumatic events, hospital admissions, and medical conditions. Some older patients will insist on providing the doctor with a comprehensive report as to all aspects of their past medical history, enjoying the opportunity to share their life experiences with the physician. Doctors, on the other hand, may be hesitant to interject and focus the discussion on the immediate problem so as not to create the impression that they have no interest in what patients are reporting. This difference in perceived aims of the interview can lead to tension in the therapeutic relationship.

An equally common, and possibly even more problematic, situation occurs when the patient is unable to provide the doctor with reasonably accurate information. The passage of years may result in some dulling of the memory: events are forgotten, dates become vague, and medical summaries and test reports are mislaid or untraceable. In many jurisdictions older patients often will have migrated from another city or even country, and medical notes from the precomputerization era are increasingly unavailable. In addition, cognitive impairment and dementia are prevalent, to the extent that the patient may not even recall the reason for the visit. Add to this the almost impossible task of recalling the names and dosages of a rather long list of medications that the older patient may be taking.

The clinical presentation of many conditions, particularly in the frail elderly, is frequently atypical. For example, patients with severe infections can be afebrile, or urinary infection may present with incontinence, and myocardial infarction may present as confusion. The final pathway of many separate clinical conditions may include delirium, drowsiness, dyspnea, weight loss or anorexia, among others (Dwolatzky, Clarfield, & Bergman, 2004). The physician will thus need to develop adroitness in deciphering such nonspecific symptoms, particularly since older patients with these symptoms may be severely ill and rapid diagnosis by an alert physician may be life saving.

Possible Solutions

One of the main dividends of a proper clinical relationship is the demonstration that the physician has a genuine interest in the patient's health and well-being. The first step is a warm introduction, a smile, and a handshake. As Isaacs (1992) put it so well, "A handshake between doctor and patient is a courtesy and an investigation." *Empathic communication* is the cornerstone of a successful relationship between the older patient and the doctor. Even when both physician and patient share the same mother tongue—an increasingly rare event in our globalizing world—attention must be paid to both language and the sophistication of terminology. This is especially the case when doctor and patient come from a different social class. In the case where language per se is a problem, it is absolutely essential to have a competent translator. While family members are often not ideal for this task, given the emotional ties between patient and relative, it may often be the only recourse (Clarfield, 1998).

Ideally the interview should be conducted in a quiet, well-lit room, with the patient facing the physician; sensory limitations such as impaired vision and hearing loss can be compensated for by the physician speaking slowly and clearly, allowing the patient to lip-read and comprehend through body language as well. Once the necessary demographic details have been obtained, the patient should be asked as to the specific complaint that has brought him or her to see the doctor. This having been determined, the relevant past medical history is obtained. If the patient begins to describe aspects of the medical history that have limited relevance to the current condition, the physician should interject gently yet firmly, stating that although this information is certainly important it will be discussed in greater detail later in the visit or at a subsequent one.

When faced with a patient who is unaware of aspects of the medical history, or where cognitive impairment affects a patient's ability to describe the condition, sufficient effort must be made to acquire the relevant information from other sources (the concomitant history). Family members and caregivers are often the most valuable source of such data and should be interviewed, ideally in the clinic or at least by telephone. Medical records from primary care physicians, specialists, hospital admissions, and laboratory and other investigations may provide valuable information.

The list of medications that appears in the medical records should be regarded with some suspicion, since older patients often knowingly limit the medications that they actually take and may be reticent to reveal this, so as not to anger or upset the physician. Other patients may take medications that were prescribed by another physician and are hesitant to inform their doctor of this, so as not to imply a lack of confidence and trust. Still others may obtain medications from acquaintances without the physician's knowledge, and finally many older patients freely use over-the-counter medications, homeopathic preparations, and vitamins. It is thus essential that the doctor be aware of all substances that the patient is receiving.

Essential features of the life circumstances of an older person include living conditions, social and family support system, the financial situation, affect and mood, and attitude. A thorough knowledge of these aspects of the patient's life not only provides invaluable clinical data, but is essential in promoting a better understanding and relationship between patient and doctor.

The Impact of the Internet

The Internet, where available, has irreversibly changed the relationship between the physician and the patient, especially for the younger generation. However, older people are becoming increasingly computer literate and the upcoming cohorts of older adults will no doubt be completely familiar with the Internet. Constantly updated information (such as the *WebMD* health site at www.webmd.com) regarding medical conditions, diagnostic methods, and novel treatments can be acquired at the click of a mouse, and the previous paternalistic model where the physician decides for the patient is rapidly being replaced by a more mutual decision-making process (Ballas, 2001). However, much of the information available on the Web is at best not evidence-based and at worst inaccurate, a situation which can lead to conflict between the patient and doctor.

Conclusion

Although care of the older patient often demands more time and special skills from the physician, the doctor-patient relationship is of critical importance to the provision of appropriate clinical care for older individuals. Lack of attention to this relationship not only may cause mental anguish to the older patient but can directly affect the quality of care provided.

TZVI DWOLATZKY
A. MARK CLARFIELD

References

Ballas, M. S. (2001). The impact of the Internet on the health care industry: A close look at the doctor-patient relationship, the electronic medical record, and the medical billing process. *Einstein Quarterly Journal of Biology and Medicine*, *18*, 79–83.

Clarfield, A. M. (1998). Your older patients also need respect. *Annals Long-Term Care 6*(5), 197–198.

Dwolatzky, T., Clarfield, A. M., & Bergman, H. (2004). Non-specific presentations of illness in the elderly. In R. Jones, N. Britten, L. Culpepper, R. Gral, D. A. Gass, D. Mant, C. Silagy, (Eds.), *Oxford textbook of primary medical care* (pp. 1247–1250.). Oxford: Oxford University Press.

Isaacs, B. (1992). *The challenge of geriatric medicine*. New York: Oxford University Press.

Jacobzone, S. (2000). International challenges: What are the implications of greater longevity and declining disability levels? *Health Affairs*, *19*(3), 213–225.

Rockwood, K., Howlett, S. E., MacKnight, C., Beattie, B. L., Bergman, H., Hebert, R., Hogan, D. B., Wolfson, C., & McDowell, I. (2004). Prevalence, attributes, and outcomes of fitness and frailty in community-dwelling older adults: Report from the Canadian Study of Health and Aging. *Journals of Gerontology: Medical Sciences*, *59*, 1310–1317.

DRIVING

The *senior driver* is the most rapidly growing segment of the active driving population. Younger and older drivers have the highest *motor vehicle crash (MVC) rates* per mile driven (Reuban, Silliman, & Traines, 1998; Cerrelli, 1989). Older drivers crash due to the functional decline experienced as a result of the accumulation and progression of age-associated medical conditions (e.g., Alzheimer's disease and other dementias, strokes, Parkinson's disease, diabetes, cataracts, glaucoma, macular degeneration) and the side effects of medications used to treat such illnesses (Parker, McDonald, Rabbitt, & Sutcliffe, 2000). When involved in an MVC, older persons are more likely to suffer long-term disability and mortality than younger persons (Williams & Carsten, 1989; Evans, 1988; Distiller & Kramer, 1996). This combination of increasing numbers of older drivers on the road, increased risk of MVC in this population, and the increased susceptibility to serious injury when an older person is involved in an MVC represents a rapidly escalating problem with huge impacts of both personal suffering and health care costs.

Clearly, permitting unfit drivers to remain on the road has substantial personal and societal costs. On the other hand, there are negative aspects of reporting patients as being unfit to drive, including *social isolation*, an increase in depressive symptoms, and increased caregiver stress (Marottoli, Mendes de Leon, & Glass, et al., 1997; Marottoli, Mendes de Leon, Glass, et al., 2000; Azad, Byszewski, Amos, & Molnar, 2002). The physician-patient relationship can be negatively affected, resulting in a diminished ability to help those with other important clinical problems (Marshall & Gilbert, 1999). The key to optimally balancing these opposing costs is to accurately and fairly assess fitness to drive, thereby preventing premature licence revocation for those who are still safe while removing unfit drivers from the road before they cause an MVC. Ideally this process should be coupled with the provision of realistic transportation alternatives for those who are no longer safe to drive. The following is a review of the resources available to assist the assessment of fitness to drive.

Front-line Clinical Assessment

Physicians have an unmatched knowledge of their patients' medical problems. In some jurisdictions, physicians are legally mandated to report a person to their respective licensing authority if they feel a patient is no longer fit to drive. Whether or not such a legal mandate exists, all physicians have an ethical responsibility to report unfit drivers in order to prevent avoidable injury and death of drivers, passengers, and pedestrians.

To assist front-line clinicians in the challenging task of assessing fitness to drive, a number of guidelines and consensus-based approaches have been developed. In 2000, the Canadian Medical Association (CMA) published "Determining Medical Fitness to Drive; A Guide for Physicians" (Sixth Edition, 2000), which is available online at www.cma.ca/index.cfm/ci_id/18223/la_id/1.htm. These guidelines are primarily disease-based; they do not provide detailed information regarding the specific functional impairments that preclude driving. Perhaps the most detailed guidelines are the American Medical Association's "*Physician's Guide to Assessing and Counseling Older Drivers*" (www.ama-assn.org/ama/pub/category/10791.html) (Wang, Kosinski, Schwartzberg, & Shanklin, 2003). These guidelines provide extensive information on the health-related aspects of driving, including medications to review, medical problems that may affect driving, physical examinations to be performed, and questionnaires for patients that screen for potential risk for MVC. Regrettably, these guidelines are primarily consensus-based rather than evidence-based and are overly inclusive (i.e. they would likely select the majority of patients in a clinical practice for further assessment).

The above guidelines are too complex to employ in day-to-day practice but rather represent resources to refer to in selected cases. Consensus-based algorithms have also been published that provide a streamlined breakdown of issues to consider when assessing fitness to drive. While these lack the detail of the guidelines, they do have the merit of ease of recall. These include the *SAFEDRIVE algorithm* (Wiseman & Souder, 1996) and the more recently published *CANDRIVE algorithm* (Molnar, Byszewski, Marshall, & Man-Son-Hing, in press, 2005).

The assessment of fitness to drive in persons with dementia is the most challenging and pressing driving issue. Guidelines have been developed that focus on *dementia and driving*, including the European and American Academy of Neurology consensus statements (Johansson & Lundberg, 1997; Dubinsky, Stein, & Lyons, 2000). Their conclusions are similar: some persons with early dementia remain safe to drive albeit for a limited period of time, and periodic retesting of those who continue to drive is recommended (with 6 months being most often cited as the time period recommended). Regrettably, such recommendations are too general to employ at the individual driver level.

Specialized Testing

Several levels of specialized testing exist but, unfortunately, are of limited availability and could not replace physicians in the screening and assessment of the millions of older drivers who pass through physicians' offices annually. Consequently, these services should be employed selectively when an individual patient's fitness to drive remains unclear despite best efforts in the front-line clinical setting. Such specialized assessment includes office-based assessments (e.g., occupational therapy, neuropsychology, neurology, psychiatry, and geriatric medicine), driving simulators, and on-road driving assessments.

Regrettably, *driving simulators* have not yet reached the point of widespread clinical applicability. There is a great deal of variability in the use of simulators in terms of hardware, software, testing protocols and pass/fail thresholds. There is no consensus regarding how the findings on a simulator assessment should be interpreted and acted upon.

On-road testing remains the clinical gold standard for specialized driver evaluation. Variability still exists between testing sites in terms of skills tested, scoring, and pass/fail criteria. Efforts are currently underway to standardize on-road assessment.

Research

To date, the bulk of the information provided by the above-mentioned guidelines and acronyms has been consensus-based. The next step in the evolution of this field is the move from opinion to evidence.

Groups leading the research in this area include the Canadian Institutes of Health Research (CIHR) *CanDRIVE* research program (www.candrive.ca) (Man-Son-Hing, Marshall, Molnar, Wilson, Crowder, & Chambers, 2004), the European *AGILE project* (www.agile.iao.fraunhofer.de/indexi.html), and the U.S. National Highway Traffic Safety Administration (www.nhtsa.dot.gov/people/injury/olddrive/index.html).

Recommended Clinical Approach

The above programs of research will require years to complete. In the interim strategies must be adopted to most effectively use existing resources. An approach that recognizes the limited availability of specialized assessors would be to organize the front-line screening and assessment of older drivers using one of the published algorithms (e.g. SAFEDRIVE or CANDRIVE) while selectively referring to the consensus-based guidelines (e.g. CMA or AMA guidelines) to answer specific clinical questions. Cases that remain unclear would be referred to specialist physicians (e.g. neurology, psychiatry, and geriatric medicine) or specialized testers (e.g. occupational therapy, neuropsychology) for in-office assessment. Those cases that still remain unclear would then be sent for on-road testing for a final determination of fitness to drive.

FRANK J. MOLNAR

See also
Cognitive Dysfunction: Drug Treatment
Dementia

References

Azad, N., Byszewski, A., Amos, S., & Molnar, F. J. (2002). A survey of the impact of driving cessation on older drivers. *Geriatrics Today; Journal of the Canadian Geriatrics Society*, *5*, 170–174.

Canadian Medical Association. (2000). *Determining medical fitness to drive—A guide for physicians* (6th ed). Ottawa: Canadian Medical Association.

Cerrelli, E. (1989). Older drivers, the age factor in traffic safety. Springfield, VA: National Technical Information Service.

Distiller, L. A., & Kramer, B. D. (1996). Driving and diabetics on insulin therapy. *South African Medical Journal*, *86*(8 Suppl.), 1018–1020.

Dubinsky, R. M., Stein, A. C., & Lyons, K. (2000). Practice parameter: Risk of driving and Alzheimer's disease (an evidence-based review). Report of the Quality Standards Subcommittee of the American Academy of Neurology. *Neurology*, *54*, 2205–2211.

Evans, L. (1988). Older driver involvement in fatal and severe traffic crashes. *Journal of Gerontology*, *43*(6), S186–S193.

Johansson, K., & Lundberg, C. (1997). The 1994 International Consensus Conference on Dementia and Driving: A brief report. *Alzheimer Disease and Associated Disorders*, *11*(1), 62–69.

Man-Son-Hing, M., Marshall, S. C., Molnar, F. J., Wilson, K. G., Crowder, C., & Chambers L. W. (2004). A Canadian research strategy for older drivers: The CanDRIVE program. *Geriatrics Today*, *7*, 86–92.

Marottoli, R. A., Mendes de Leon, C. F., & Glass, T. A. et al. (1997). Driving cessation and increased depressive symptoms: Prospective evidence from the New Haven EPESE. *Journal of the American Geriatrics Society*, *45*, 202–207.

Marottoli, R. A., Mendes de Leon, C. F., Glass, T. A. et al. (2000) Consequences of driving cessation: Decreased out-of-home activity levels. *Journals of Gerontology Series B Psychological Sciences and Social Sciences*, *55B*, S334–340.

Marshall, S. C., & Gilbert, N. (1999). Saskatchewan physicians' attitudes and knowledge regarding assessment of medical fitness to drive. *Canadian Medical Association Journal*, *160*(12), 1701–1704.

Molnar, F. J., Byszewski, A. M., Marshall, S. C., & Man-Son-Hing, M. (2005). In-office evaluation of medical fitness to drive: practical approaches for assessing older people. *Canadian Family Physician, 51*, 372–379.

Parker, D., McDonald, L., Rabbitt, P., & Sutcliffe, P. (2000). Elderly drivers and their accidents: The aging driver questionnaire. *Accident Analysis and Prevention*, *32*(6), 751–759.

Reuban, D. B., Silliman, R. A., & Traines, M. (1998). The aging driver. Medicine, policy, and ethics. *Journal of the American Geriatrics Society*, *36*(12), 1135–1142.

Wang, C. C., Kosinski, C. J., Schwartzberg, J. G., & Shanklin, A. V. (2003). *Physician's guide to assessing and counseling older drivers*. Washington, DC: National Highway Traffic Safety Administration.

Williams, A. F., & Carsten, O. (1989). Driver age and crash involvement. *American Journal of Public Health*, *79*(3), 326–327.

Wiseman, E. J., & Souder, E. (1996). The older driver: A handy tool to assess competence behind the wheel. *Geriatrics*, *51*, 36–45.

DRUG INTERACTIONS

A drug interaction occurs when the combination of one agent with another (*drug-drug interaction*), a food or nutrient (*drug-nutrient interaction*), or a disease (*drug-disease interaction*) results in a change in the pharmacologic effect or toxicology of a drug (Hansten & Horn, 2005). One of the most important risk factors for drug interactions is the number of medications taken (Hajjar, Hanlon, Artz, Lindblad, Pieper, Sloane, Ruby, & Schmader, 2003). As many older adults take multiple medications, they are at increased risk of experiencing drug interactions. Of particular concern is the potential for drug interactions to result in negative outcomes in this population (Gray, Mahoney, & Blough, 1999).

Drug interactions can be either pharmacokinetic or pharmacodynamic in nature. Pharmacokinetic interactions occur through changes in absorption, distribution, or elimination of the drug in question (Hansten & Horn, 2005). Pharmacodynamic interactions result from one medication directly magnifying or inhibiting the action of another agent, usually in the same physiologic system (Hansten & Horn, 2005). Many drug interactions occur that are of little clinical relevance. However, negative consequences are most likely when the affected drug has a narrow therapeutic range.

Patients are at the greatest risk of experiencing a drug interaction when the interacting drug is started or stopped. While often clinicians are aware of the potential for interactions when initiating new therapy, adjusting the dose of the drug affected, the impact of discontinuing an interacting medication is frequently overlooked. Thus, if an interacting drug is stopped without adjusting the dose of the affected agent, toxicity or therapeutic failure can result.

Pharmacokinetic Interactions

Absorption Interactions. There are several mechanisms by which *absorption interactions* occur. These include the following (Hansten & Horn, 2005):

- Drug binding in the gut
- Changes in gastric motility
- Changes in gastric pH
- Changes to drug metabolism in the intestinal wall

Drug binding interactions occur when one agent binds to another, forming complexes that cannot be absorbed across the intestinal wall. Examples of such interactions include the concurrent use of medications or foods containing *cationic compounds* (aluminum, calcium, iron, or magnesium) with *bisphosphonates*, *levothyroxine*, *quinolone* antibiotics, and some *tetracyclines* (Neuvonen, 1976; Porras, Holland, & Gertz, 1999; Singh, 1999; Singh, Singh, & Hershman, 2000; Aminimanizani, Beringer, & Jelliffe, 2001). Patients taking these agents do not need to avoid antacids, vitamins, or specific foods, however, as the interaction can generally be avoided by separating the administration of the interacting drug or food by 1 to 2 hours. This strategy also works well for avoiding drug absorption interactions with resins, such as *cholestyramine*, which has been reported to impair the absorption of both *levothyroxine* and *warfarin* (Harmon, & Seifert, 1991; Bays & Dujovne, 1998).

Agents that change gastric motility can influence absorption by delaying the delivery of some drugs to their absorption sites in the intestine. For the most part, these interactions are not clinically important, but there are some notable exceptions. One is the concurrent use of *levodopa* and agents with anticholinergic properties. Because the absorption of levodopa is delayed, the onset of its therapeutic effect is postponed (Pfeiffer, 1996), leading to worsening symptom control. Conversely, *prokinetic agents* increase levodopa absorption (Bedford & Rowbotham, 1996), potentially increasing levodopa-related dyskinesias.

The pH of the gut may affect absorption either by enhancing or interfering with drug dissolution. Most drugs are weak acids or bases, and dissolve more readily in more alkaline or acidic environments, respectively (Hansten & Horn, 2005). As with drug interaction involving gastric motility, most interactions involving changes in pH of the gut are not clinically relevant, but there are some important exceptions. This includes *ketoconazole*, with drugs that raise gastric pH (H2 antagonists, proton pump inhibitors, sucralfate, antacids), resulting in poor absorption and treatment failure (Piscitelli, Goss, Wilton, D'Andrea, Goldstein, & Schentag, 1991; Sadowski, 1994; Lew, 1999). Similarly, drugs that induce *achlorhydria* can impair the absorption of calcium carbonate, but not calcium citrate (Shangraw, 1989).

Of the numerous mechanisms by which drug interactions can occur via absorption, perhaps the most clinically important is that involving changes to drug metabolism in the intestinal wall, which can significantly increase the pharmacologic effect of some drugs, leading to serious adverse effects. Several types of metabolism have been identified in the intestinal wall, including glucuronidation, sulfation, monoamine oxidation, and oxidation by isozymes of cytochrome P450 (CYP450) (Hansten & Horn, 2005). The most well-documented interaction is that of *grapefruit juice*, which was discovered quite serendipitously during a study of the bioavailability of the calcium-channel blocker *felodipine* (Bailey, Spence, Edgar, Bayliff, & Arnold, 1989). When administered with grapefruit juice, used to mask the taste of ethanol, serum concentrations were observed to be significantly higher, accompanied by symptomatic hypotension. Since then, numerous interactions have been identified, including *amiodarone*, the *dihydropyridine calcium-channel blockers*, *HMG CoA reductase inhibitors*, *carbamazepine*, and the *immunosuppressants cyclosporin* and *tacrolimus* (Garg, Kumar, Bhargava, & Prabhakar, 1998; Libersa, Brique, Motte, Caron, Guedon-Moreau, Humbert, et al., 2000; Kane & Lipsky, 2000; Fujita, 2004). As many other potential interactions remain to be identified, it is generally recommended that most oral medications not be taken with grapefruit juice (Spence, 1999).

Distribution Interactions. Most distribution interactions involve *protein binding*. These can be drug-drug interactions, where one drug displaces another from its binding site on albumin. However, such interactions are clinically important only infrequently, unless they occur in conjunction with other mechanisms, such as reduced elimination (Sands, Chan, & Welty, 2002; Benet & Hoener, 2002).

Drug-disease interactions involving decreased albumin concentrations are more clinically relevant. For example, *hypoalbunemia* secondary to poor nutrition can significantly affect *phenytoin*, a commonly used agent in the older adult population. Phenytoin is highly protein bound, and when serum albumin concentrations are decreased, there will be more unbound (and therapeutically active) drug available. Phenytoin levels are typically measured using total levels (bound plus unbound). With low albumin concentrations, the total level may fall within the therapeutic range while the free level (representing only unbound drug) will be supratherapeutic. Thus, patients may exhibit signs of toxicity within the therapeutic range because the free level is high, warranting a reduction in dose (Bourdet, Gidal, & Alldredge, 2001; Bergey, 2004).

Elimination Interactions Interactions affecting drug elimination usually involve either renal excretion or drug metabolism. Renal interactions involve competition between 2 agents at sites of active secretion. One such example is between *digoxin* and *quinidine*, where competition for renal excretion results in toxic digoxin concentrations (Hanratty, McGlinchey, Johnston, & Passmore, 2000).

Drug metabolism interactions occur when one agent increases or decreases the metabolism of the other medication. Induction of metabolism results in lower concentrations of the drug reaching the site of action, potentially causing failure of therapy. Inhibition of metabolism results in higher concentrations of the drug reaching the site of action, increasing the risk of an adverse reaction occurring.

Most clinically important drug interactions involve *oxidation reactions* of the *cytochrome P450 system*. Numerous interactions have been identified and reported in the literature. While it is impossible to be aware of all potential metabolic interactions, it is important to consider their potential when prescribing new medications for older patients. A metabolic drug interaction should be considered when the patient experiences an unexplained exaggerated pharmacologic response, or failure of therapy when a drug is discontinued or when a new medication is added to the therapeutic regimen.

Some common metabolic interactions involve medications that induce CYP450 metabolism, such as *carbamazepine*, *rifampin*, or *phenobarbital* (Niemi, Backman, Fromm, Neuvonen, & Kivisto, 2003; Patsalos, Froscher, Pisani, & van Rijn, 2002). Commonly used drugs with high potential to inhibit specific isozymes of CYP450 include *amiodarone*, *clarithromycin*, *co-trimoxazole*, *erythromycin*, *fluovoxamine*, *metronidazole*, some of the *quinolone* antibiotics, *omeprazole, paroxetine*, and *sertraline* (Gillum, Israel, & Polk, 1993; Petersen, 1995; Wells, Holbrook, Crowther, & Hirsh, 1994; Westphal, 2000; Spina & Scordo, 2002; Yamreudeewong, DeBisschop, Martin, & Lower, 2003).

The use of natural health products is growing among older populations, so the potential for these compounds to cause metabolic drug interactions should also be considered. *St. John's wort* is reported to be widely used in the senior population (Barnes, Powell-Griner, McFann, & Nahin, 2004; Foster, Phillips, Hamel, & Eisenberg, 2000; Williamson, Fletcher, & Dawson, 2003; Gold, Laxer, Dergal, Lanctot, & Rochon, 2001) and is known to interact with numerous medications through metabolic

TABLE 1 Common Drug Interactions in Older Adults

Affected Drug	Interacting Drug	Mechanism	Management
Bisphosphonates, quinolone antibiotics, tetracyclines	Antacids, vitamins with minerals	Cations bind with the drug forming an insoluble complex that cannot be absorbed	Separate administration of the affected drugs with the interacting drugs by 1 to 2 hours
Agents with anticholinergic properties (diphenhydramine, dimenhydrinate, opioids, oxybutynin, tricyclic antidepressants, tolterodine)	Other agents with anticholinergic properties	Additive anticholinergic properties add to total anticholinergic load	Avoid some agents (diphenhydramine, dimenhydrinate, some tricyclic antidepressants) and minimize total anticholinergic load
Benzodiazepines	Other agents with sedative properties (alcohol, opioids, neuroleptics, tricyclic antidepressants)	Additive sedative properties	Avoid agents with sedative properties when possible Reduce concurrent use of agents with sedative properties
Potassium-sparing diuretics	Potassium supplements Angiotensin-converting enzyme inhibitors	Decreased excretion of potassium results in hyperkalemia	Avoid use of potassium supplements in combination with potassium-sparing diuretics Monitor potassium when potassium-sparing diuretics and ACEIs taken concurrently
Phenytoin	Erythromycin, some quinolone antibiotics	Inhibit phenytoin metabolism resulting in elevated serum concentrations	Monitor phenytoin levels and adjust phenytoin dose accordingly
	Carbamazepine, rifampin, phenobarbital	Induce phenytoin metabolism resulting in decreased serum concentrations	Monitor phenytoin levels and adjust phenytoin dose accordingly
Warfarin	Amiodarone, clarithromycin, co-trimoxazole, erythromycin, metronidazole, omeprazole	Inhibit warfarin metabolism resulting in elevated INR	Monitor INR and adjust warfarin dose accordingly
	Rifampin, phenobarbital	Induce warfarin metabolism resulting in decreased INR	Monitor INR and adjust dose accordingly
	Levothyroxine	Increases catabolism of vitamin K-dependent clotting factors resulting in elevated INR	Monitor INR and adjust dose accordingly

NOTE: This table is not meant to be a complete list of drug interactions.

induction (Zhou, Chan, Pan, Huang, & Lee, 2004). Interactions that are particularly relevant to older individuals include the *HMG CoA reductase inhibitors* (except pravastatin) and *warfarin* (Zhou, Chan, Pan, Huang, & Lee, 2004).

Pharmacodynamic Interactions

Pharmacodynamic interactions are not as well studied, and consequently are poorly understood relative to pharmacokinetic interactions. The majority of documented pharmacodynamic interactions involve medications with similar pharmacologic activity being used at the same time, resulting in an exaggerated therapeutic response. For example, the degree of sedation will worsen as the number of drugs causing sedation increases. One important consideration for pharmacodynamic interactions in the older population is the concept of total *anticholinergic load* (Gray, Lai, & Larson, 1999; Moore & O'Keeffe, 1999). The use of multiple agents with anticholinergic activity increases the risk of *anticholinergic-related delirium*.

A number of pharmacodynamic interactions have been documented with natural health products. *Serotonin syndrome* has been reported when *SSRI*s and St. John's wort are taken concurrently, as both have activity on serotonin in the central nervous system (Izzo & Ernst, 2001). *Ginkgo biloba* affects platelet function and is associated with bleeding when taken concurrently with warfarin, ASA, and other NSAIDs (Izzo & Ernst, 2001; Fugh-Berman, 2000).

There also are some circumstances in which pharmacodynamic drug-nutrient interactions can occur. For example, if dietary *vitamin K* increases significantly from food sources, nutritional supplements or enteral feeds, it can interfere with the anticoagulant effect of warfarin. Conversely, if nutritional intake of vitamin K decreases significantly, an increased anticoagulant effect will be observed. When difficulties occur stabilizing patients on warfarin, the history should not only include medication changes but also a review of alteration to diet (Franco, Polanczyk, Clausell, & Rohde, 2004).

Another pharmacodynamic interaction involving warfarin is both drug- and disease-related. In the hypothyroid state, catabolism of vitamin K-dependent clotting factors are decreased, resulting in higher warfarin dosing requirements to achieve a therapeutic international normalized ratio. When the hypothyroid state is reversed with treatment, then warfarin dosing requirements decline (Stephens, Self, Lancaster, & Nash, 1989). The opposite occurs in the setting of *hyperthyroidism*, where warfarin dosing requirements are decreased (Woeber & Warner, 1999). Upon correction of the hyperthyroid state, warfarin dosing requirements will increase.

SUSAN K. BOWLES

See also
Drug Reactions

References

Aminimanizani, A., Beringer, P., & Jelliffe, R. (2001). Comparative pharmacokinetics and pharmacodynamics of the newer fluoroquinolone antibacterials. *Clinical Pharmacokinetics*, *40*, 169–187.

Bailey, D. G., Spence, J. D., Edgar, B., Bayliff, C. D., & Arnold, J. M. (1989). Ethanol enhances the hemodynamic effects of felodipine. *Clinical Investigative Medicine*, *12*, 357–362.

Barnes, P. M., Powell-Griner, E., McFann, K., & Nahin, R. L. (2004). Complementary and alternative medicine use among adults: United States, 2002. *Advance Data*, *27*, 1–19.

Bays, H. E., & Dujovne, C. A. (1998). Drug interactions of lipid-altering drugs. *Drug Safety*, *19*, 355–371.

Bedford, T. A., & Rowbotham, D. J. (1996). Cisapride. Drug interactions of clinical significance. *Drug Safety*, *15*, 167–175.

Benet, L. Z., & Hoener, B. A. (2002). Changes in plasma protein binding have little clinical relevance. *Clinical Pharmacology and Therapeutics*, *71*, 115–121.

Bergey, G. K. (2004). Initial treatment of epilepsy: Special issues in treating the elderly. *Neurology*, *63*(Suppl. 4), S40–S48.

Bourdet, S. V., Gidal, B. E., & Alldredge, B. K. (2001). Pharmacologic management of epilepsy in the elderly. *Journal of the American Pharmacists Association*, *41*, 421–436.

Foster, D. F., Phillips, R. S., Hamel, M. B., & Eisenberg, D. M. (2000). Alternative medicine use in older Americans. *Journal of the American Geriatrics Society*, *48*, 1560–1565.

Franco, V., Polanczyk, C. A., Clausell, N., & Rohde, L. E. (2004). Role of dietary vitamin K intake in chronic oral anticoagulation: Prospective evidence from observational and randomized protocols. *American Journal of Medicine*, *116*, 651–656.

Fugh-Berman, A. (2000). Herb-drug interactions. *Lancet*, *355*, 134–138.

Fujita, K. (2004). Food-drug interactions via human cytochrome P450 3A (CYP3A). *Drug Metabolism and Drug Interactions*, *20*, 195–217.

Garg, S. K., Kumar, N., Bhargava, V. K., & Prabhakar, S. K. (1998). Effect of grapefruit juice on carbamazepine bioavailability in patients with epilepsy. *Clinical Pharmacology and Therapeutics*, *64*, 286–288.

Gillum, J. G., Israel, D. S., & Polk, R. E. (1993). Pharmacokinetic drug interactions with antimicrobial agents. *Clinical Pharmacokinetics*, *25*, 450–482.

Gold, J. L., Laxer, D. A., Dergal, J. M., Lanctot, K. L., & Rochon, P. A. (2001). Herbal-drug therapy interactions: A focus on dementia. *Current Opinion in Clinical Nutrition and Metabolic Care*, *4*, 29–34.

Gray, S. L., Lai, K. V., & Larson, E. B. (1999). Drug-induced cognition disorders in the elderly: Incidence, prevention and management. *Drug Safety*, *21*, 101–122.

Gray, S. L., Mahoney, J. E., & Blough, D. K. (1999). Adverse drug events in elderly patients receiving home health services following hospital discharge. *Annals of Pharmacotherapy*, *33*, 1147–1153.

Hajjar, E. R., Hanlon, J. T., Artz, M. B., Lindblad, C. I., Pieper, C. F., Sloane, R. J., Ruby, C. M., & Schmader, K. E. (2003). Adverse drug reaction risk factors in older outpatients. *American Journal of Geriatric Pharmacotherapy*, *1*, 82–89.

Hanratty, C. G., McGlinchey, P., Johnston, G. D., & Passmore, A. P. (2000). Differential pharmacokinetics of digoxin in elderly patients. *Drugs and Aging*, *17*, 353–362.

Hansten, P. D., & Horn, J. (2005). *Drug interactions. Analysis and management. Facts and comparisons*. St. Louis: Wolters Kluwer Healt.

Harmon, S. M., & Seifert, C. F. (1991). Levothyroxine-cholestyramine interaction reemphasized. *Annals of Internal Medicine*, *115*, 658–659.

Izzo, A. A., & Ernst, E. (2001). Interactions between herbal medicines and prescribed drugs: A systematic review. *Drugs*, *61*, 2163–2175.

Kane, G. C., & Lipsky, J. J. (2000). Drug-grapefruit juice interactions. *Mayo Clinic Proceedings*, *75*, 933–942.

Lew, E. A. (1999). Review article: Pharmacokinetic concerns in the selection of anti-ulcer therapy. *Alimentary Pharmacology and Therapeutics*, *13*(Suppl. 5), 11–16.

Libersa, C. C., Brique, S. A., Motte, K. B., Caron, J. F., Guedon-Moreau, L. M., Humbert, L., Vincent, A., Devos, P., & Lhermitte, M. A. (2000). Dramatic inhibition of amiodarone metabolism induced by grapefruit juice. *British Journal of Clinical Pharmacology*, *49*, 373–378.

Moore, A. R., & O'Keeffe, S. T. (1999). Drug-induced cognitive impairment in the elderly. *Drugs and Aging*, *15*, 15–28.

Neuvonen, P. J. (1976). Interactions with the absorption of tetracyclines. *Drugs*, *11*, 45–54.

Niemi, M., Backman, J. T., Fromm, M. F., Neuvonen, P. J., & Kivisto, K. T. (2003). Pharmacokinetic interactions with rifampicin: Clinical relevance. *Clinical Pharmacokinetics*, *42*, 819–850.

Patsalos, P. N., Froscher, W., Pisani, F., & van Rijn, C. M. (2002). The importance of drug interactions in epilepsy therapy. *Epilepsia*, *43*, 365–385.

Petersen, K. U. (1995). Review article: Omeprazole and the cytochrome P450 system. *Alimentary Pharmacology and Therapeutics*, *9*, 1–9.

Pfeiffer, R. F. (1996). Antiparkinsonian agents. Drug interactions of clinical significance. *Drug Safety*, *14*, 343–354.

Piscitelli, S. C., Goss, T. F., Wilton, J. H., D'Andrea, D. T., Goldstein, H., & Schentag, J. J. (1991). Effects of ranitidine and sucralfate on ketoconazole bioavailability. *Antimicrobial Agents and Chemotherapy*, *35*, 1765–1771.

Porras, A. G., Holland, S. D., & Gertz, B. J. (1999). Pharmacokinetics of alendronate. *Clinical Pharmacokinetics*, *36*, 315–328.

Sadowski, D. C. (1994). Drug interactions with antacids. Mechanisms and clinical significance. *Drug Safety*, *11*, 395–407.

Sands, C. D., Chan, E. S., & Welty, T. E. (2002). Revisiting the significance of warfarin protein-binding displacement interactions. *Annals of Pharmacotherapy*, *36*, 1642–1644.

Shangraw, R. F. (1989). Factors to consider in the selection of a calcium supplement. *Public Health Reports*, *104*(Suppl.), 46–50.

Singh, B. N. (1999). Effects of food on clinical pharmacokinetics. *Clinical Pharmacokinetics*, *37*, 213–255.

Singh, N., Singh, P. N., & Hershman, J. M. (2000). Effect of calcium carbonate on the absorption of levothyroxine. *Journal of the American Medical Association*, *283*, 2822–2825.

Spence, J. D. (1999). Fruitful discussions about drug interactions. *Canadian Medical Association Journal*, *161*, 946.

Spina, E., & Scordo, M. G. (2002). Clinically significant drug interactions with antidepressants in the elderly. *Drugs and Aging*, *19*, 299–320.

Stephens, M. A., Self, T. H., Lancaster, D., & Nash, T. (1989). Hypothyroidism: Effect on warfarin anticoagulation. *Southern Medical Journal*, *82*, 1585–1586.

Wells, P. S., Holbrook, A. M., Crowther, N. R., & Hirsh, J. (1994). Interactions of warfarin with drugs and food. *Annals of Internal Medicine*, *121*, 676–683.

Westphal, J. F. (2000). Macrolide-induced clinically relevant drug interactions with cytochrome P-450A (CYP) 3A4: An update focused on clarithromycin, azithromycin and dirithromycin. *British Journal of Clinical Pharmacology*, *50*, 285–295.

Williamson, A. T., Fletcher, P. C., & Dawson, K. A. (2003). Complementary and alternative medicine. Use in an older population. *Journal of Gerontological Nursing*, *39*, 20–28.

Woeber, K. A., & Warner, I. (1999). Potentiation of warfarin sodium by amiodarone-induced thyrotoxicosis. *Western Journal of Medicine*, *170*, 49–51.

Yamreudeewong, W., DeBisschop, M., Martin, L. G., & Lower, D. L. (2003). Potentially significant drug interactions of class III antiarrhythmic drugs. *Drug Safety*, *26*, 421–438.

Zhou, S., Chan, E., Pan, S. Q., Huang, M., & Lee, E. J. (2004). Pharmacokinetic interactions of drugs with St John's wort. *Journal of Psychopharmacology*, *18*, 262–276.

DRUG REACTIONS

The term "*adverse drug reaction*" is defined by the World Health Organization as an effect that is "noxious and unintended" and that "occurs at doses normally used by humans" (World Health Organization, 2002). Adverse reactions can be unexpected or idiosyncratic, "one that is not expected based on the characteristics of the drug," or they can be a side effect resulting from the pharmacologic activity of the medication (World Health Organization, 2002). Both type of adverse reactions can result in an "*adverse event*," which is considered any untoward medical occurance during treatment with a medicine, although causality is not implied (World Health Organization, 2002). While idosyncratic reactons, such as an *allergic reaction* to a particular drug, do occur in older persons, the majority of adverse events are related to the expected pharmacologic action of medications. Indeed, it has been suggested that in the senior population, many adverse drug events, and their associated morbidities, can be prevented (Gurwitz, Field, Harrold, Rothschild, Debellis, Seger, et al., 2003).

A number of risk factors for adverse drug reactions among older individuals have been identified and include both patient characteristics and medication-related factors. Important risk factors appear to be *polypharmacy*, multiple prescribers, and inappropriate drug use (Gurwitz, Field, Harrold, Rothschild, Debellis, Seger, et al., 2003; Hajjar, Hanlon, Artz, Lindblad, Pieper, Sloane, et al., 2003; Tamblyn, McLeod, Abrahamowicz, & Laprise, 1996; Schmader, Hanlon, Pieper, Sloane, Ruby, Twersky, et al., 2004; Perri, Menon, Deshpande, Shinde, Jiang, Cooper, et al., 2005; Klarin, Wimo, & Fastbom, 2005; Lau, Kasper, Potter, Lyles, & Bennett, 2005). Specific medications associated with a high incidence of adverse drug effects include agents with *anticholinergic effects*, *benzodiazepines*, other *psychotropic agents*, *nonsteroidal anti-inflammatory drugs*, *opioid analgesics*, and *warfarin* (Gurwitz, Field, Harrold, Rothschild, Debellis, Seger, et al., 2003; Fick, Cooper, Wade, Waller, Maclean, & Beers, 2003; Zhan, Correa-de-Araujo, Bierman, Sangl, Miller, Wickizer, et al., 2005; Pirmohamed, James, Meakin, Green, Scott, Walley, et al., 2004; Edwards & Aronson, 2000).

Just as there are multiple risk factors for *adverse drug reactions in the older population*, there are multiple mechanisms by which adverse events can occur. These have been classified as follows (Edwards & Aronson, 2000):

- Non-dose related
- Dose related
- Time-related
- Dose- and time-related
- Withdrawal
- *Unexpected failure of therapy*

The non-dose related classification is the same as an "*idiosyncratic" drug reaction*, one that is generally unpredictable, uncommon, and not related to the expected pharmacological activity of the drug. Examples of this type of adverse drug reaction would include *penicillin* or *sulfa allergies*, or the *neuroleptic malignant syndrome*. The managment of these types of reactions generally involves witholding the suspected agent, treating any symptoms, and avoiding future use of the offending drug.

Whereas non-dose-related adverse reactions are predominately unpredictable and uncommon, dose-related effects are quite the opposite. They are among the most frequent causes of adverse reactions experienced by older people and can be predicted on either a pharmacokinetic or pharmacodynamic basis, (Papaioannou, Clarke, Campbell, & Bedard, 2000; Misiaszek, Heckman, Merali, Turpie, Patterson, Flett, et al., 2005). Many of these adverse reactions are linked to age-related decline in renal function. Any drug that is primarlily eliminated unchanged by the kidney will require a decrease in dose. Examples include *digoxin* and *amantadine*. In addition, some drugs have active or toxic metabolites that are renally eliminated. As dosing adjustments of these agents results in a less predictable outcome, some of these medications are best avoided in the senior population. *Meperidine* is one such example, although it is used very often in older people (Adunsky, Levy, Heim, Mizrahi, & Arad, 2002). The active metabolite of meperidine, *normeperidine*, undergoes renal elimination and accumulates quickly as a result of age-related decline in renal function. As normeperidine is CNS toxic, its accumulation can result in drug-related delirum or even seizure activity.

Dose-related adverse events can also occur by a pharmacodynamic mechansim. One example that is of particular relevance to older persons is accumulating effects of multiple drugs with anticholinergic activity. This is known as *total anticholinergic load*, where the anticholinergic activity of multiple drugs are additive, potentially causing *drug-related delirium*, other cognitive changes, or acute urinary retention. To avoid these adverse reactions, anticholinergic agents are best avoided in the frail senior population. When anticholinergic-related adverse effects do occur, they are generally reversible upon discontinuation or lowering the doses of the offending agent or agents.

Time-related adverse effects occur after the drug has been used for a period of time and are often related to dose. A common example of a time-dependent reaction is that of *tardive dyskinesia*, a neurological disorder caused by the long-term use of neuroleptic agents. Unfortunately, time-dependent adverse reactions such as tardive dyskinesia are often irreversible, even when the offending agent or agents are discontinued (Trosch, 2004). Likewise, for the most part treatment with other drugs has not shown clinically significant benefits to date (Grath & Soares, 2000). While there is some suggestion that the risk of tardive dyskinesia is less with the newer atypical neuroleptics than with the traditional agents, this remains to be confirmed. Certainly cases of tardive dyskinesia have been reported in those taking atypical agents over the long-term. The example of neuroleptic-associated tardive dyskinesia as a time-related adverse effect is particularly noteworthy, as inappropriate use and duration of use of neuroleptic agents is common (Bronskill, Anderson, Sykora, Wodchis, Gill, Shulman, et al., 2004). Perhaps the best way to avoid this particular adverse reaction is to ensure that psychotropic agents are not used for inappropriate indications.

Dose- and time-related adverse reactions are thought to be fairly uncommon and generally related to cummulative dose. *Supression of the hypothalamic-pituitary adrenal* (HPA) gland or development of osteoporosis related to prolonged corticosteroid use are examples that apply to older populations. Seniors may require *long-term corticosteroids* for a variety of conditions, such as temporal arteritis or polymyalgia rheumatica. Corticosteroid-related osteoporosis can be prevented by treating individuals with *bisphosphonates* (Sambrook, 2005). Suppression of the HPA axis can be managed by a slow and tapered withdrawal period.

Just as initiation of medications can be associated with adverse reactions, so can the withdrawal of some agents in certain circumstances. Typically, *withdrawal reactions*, although dependent somewhat on the half-life of the drug in question, occur relatively soon after discontinuation of the medication, such as with the *selective serotonin reuptake inhibitor* (*SSRI*) antidepressants. Symptoms of *SSRI discontinuation syndrome* have been reported with all the SSRIs, although there is some suggestion that they occur less frequently with the longer half-life agents such as *fluoxetine* (Black, Shea, Dursun, & Kutcher, 2000). This syndrome has also been reported with *venlafaxine* and *mirtazapine*, both of which also exhibit some serotoninergic activity. Upon abrupt cessation of an SSRI, individuals may complain of dizziness, nausea/vomiting, headache, fatigue/lethargy, insomnia, and an unstable gait. *Parathesia* occurs less commonly, but has been reported. Suggested criteria for identifying *withdrawal syndromes* have been suggested and include the following (Black, Shea, Dursun, & Kutcher, 2000):

- Characteristic symptoms as described above
- Onset shortly after discontinuation of the medication (usually within 1 to 3 days but has been

reported up to 7 days). Although less common, may also occur with a reduction in dose. There is also some relationship with duration of treatment, with the likelihood of occurance being more frequent with a longer duration of therapy.
- Of short duration
- Rapid reversal upon restarting the medication
- Distinct from the symptomatology of the underlying disorder
- Cannot be attributed to another cause

Tapering regimens have been reported to prevent symptoms associated with SSRI discontinuation syndrome, especially with the shorter half-life agents such as paroxetine and venlafaxine. There is some suggestion that fluoxetine, which has a very long half-life and an active metabolite, does not require tapering. However, this is controversial, and many clinicians will taper fluoxetine when discontinuing it.

A particularly difficult situation may arise with tapering regimens when the SSRI is being discontinued to initiate another antidepressant and there is potential for a drug interaction. In such cases, a washout period for the SSRI may be indicated, and the risks of a rapid tapering schedule must be weighed against the risks of an adverse reaction occuring secondary to the drug interaction. However, in most cases this can be done safely when consideration is given to the pharmacokinetic and pharmacodynamic properties of both antidepressants.

Considerations should also be given to tapering regimens for the benzodiazepines to avoid potential withdrawal reactions (Grymonpre, Mitenko, Sitar, Aoki, & Montgomery, 1988). This includes individuals who have been receiving low-dose benzodiazepines for insomnia over a prolonged period. While fulminent withdrawal will not appear with regular, low-dose benzodiazepine use, the incidence of rebound reactions is high. Symptoms include worsening insomnia, anxiety, and agitation. There is also some evidence that the use of cognitive-behavioral therapies for insomnia, in conjunction with appropriate tapering regimens, will increase the success of discontinuing benzodiazepines in the older population.

Finally, *failure of therapy* is a common cause of adverse reactions in older individuals. This can be related to numerous factors including nonadherence, prescribing low doses that are ineffective in treating a particular condition, or drug interactions. It has been estimated that up to 27% of hospital admissions for older adults are related to intentional noncompliance and 19% associated with failure of therapy (Grymonpre, Mitenko, Sitar, Aoki, & Montgomery, 1988). The issue of ineffective dosing regimens in older persons has been identified as a cause of treatment failure in the management of depression, stroke prophylaxis secondary to atrial fibrillation, the use of ACE inihibitors to treat congestive heart failure, and the use of beta-blockers post-myocardial infarction.

One particularly disturbing aspect of adverse drug reactions in the older adult population is that often not only do they go undetected, but they are sometimes interpreted as the onset of a new medical condition, for which another agent is prescribed. The addition of new medication further increases the risk of more adverse effects occuring. This is known as the *prescribing cascade* (Rochon & Gurwitz, 1997). Some examples include the onset or exacerbation of hypertension with the use of nonsteroidal anti-inflammatory agents or anti-Parkinson's medications prescribed for extrapyramidal symptoms with the use of *metoclopramide*.

Identifying adverse reactions in older persons is challenging due to the often-atypical presentation. Frequently, adverse events first present as functional change with decline in cognition or mobility observed (Owens, Fretwell, Willey, & Murphy, 1994). In general, clinicians should consider any symptom or change in function as a potential adverse drug reaction until proven otherwise. A review of medications should be performed to determine if there is a temporal relationship to the onset of the symptom with the initation of the medication or any dosage change. Consideration should also be given as to whether there is a biologically plausible explanation for the medication to cause the particular symptom or symptoms observed. Improvement or resolution of symptoms upon discontinuation of the medication or a decrease in dosage should be viewed as evidence supporting an adverse drug reaction.

SUSAN K. BOWLES

See also

Drug Interactions

References

Adunsky, A., Levy, R., Heim, M., Mizrahi, E., & Arad, M. (2002). Meperidine analgesia and delirium in aged hip fracture patients. *Archives of Gerontology and Geriatrics, 35,* 253–259.

Black, K., Shea, C., Dursun, S., & Kutcher, S. (2000). Selective serotonin reuptake inhibitor discontinuation syndrome: Proposed diagnostic criteria. *Journal of Psychiatry and Neuroscience, 25,* 255–261.

Bronskill, S. E., Anderson, G. M., Sykora, K., Wodchis, W. P., Gill, S., Shulman, K. I., & Rochon, P. A. (2004). Neuroleptic drug therapy in older adults newly admitted to nursing homes: Incidence, dose, and specialist contact. *Journal of the American Geriatrics Society, 52,* 749–755.

Edwards, I. R., & Aronson, J. K. (2000). Adverse drug reactions: Definitions, diagnosis, and management. *Lancet, 356,* 1255–1259.

Fick, D. M., Cooper, J. W., Wade, W. E., Waller, J. L., Maclean, J. R., & Beers, M. H. (2003). Updating the Beers criteria for potentially inappropriate medication use in older adults: Results of a U.S. consensus panel of experts. *Archives of Internal Medicine, 163,* 2716–2724.

Grymonpre, R. E., Mitenko, P. A., Sitar, D. S., Aoki, F. Y., & Montgomery, P. R. (1988). Drug-associated hospital admissions in older medical patients. *Journal of the American Geriatrics Society, 36,* 1092–1098.

Gurwitz, J. H., Field, T. S., Harrold, L. R., Rothschild, J., Debellis, K., Seger, A. C., et al. (2003). Incidence and preventability of adverse drug events among older persons in the ambulatory setting. *Journal of the American Medical Association, 289,* 1107–1116.

Hajjar, E. R., Hanlon, J. T., Artz, M. B., Lindblad, C. I., Pieper, C. F., Sloane, R. J., Ruby, C. M., & Schmader, K. E. (2003). Adverse drug reaction risk factors in older outpatients. *American Journal of Geriatric Pharmacotherapy, 1,* 82–89.

Klarin, I., Wimo, A., & Fastbom, J. (2005). The association of inappropriate drug use with hospitalization and mortality: A population-based study of the very old. *Drugs and Aging, 22,* 68–82.

Lau, D. T., Kasper, J. D., Potter, D. E., Lyles, A., & Bennett, R. G. (2005). Hospitalization and death associated with potentially inappropriate medication prescriptions among elderly nursing home residents. *Archives of Internal Medicine, 165,* 68–74.

McGrath, J. J., & Soares, K. V. (2000). Neuroleptic reduction and/or cessation and neuroleptics as specific treatments for tardive dyskinesia. *Cochrane Database of Systematic Reviews, 2,* CD000459.

Misiaszek, B., Heckman, G. A., Merali, F., Turpie, I. D., Patterson, C. J., Flett, N., & McKelvie, R. S. (2005). Digoxin prescribing for heart failure in elderly residents of long-term care facilities. *Canadian Journal of Cardiology, 21,* 281–286.

Owens, N. J., Fretwell, M. D., Willey, C., & Murphy, S. S. (1994). Distinguishing between the fit and frail elderly, and optimizing pharmacotherapy. *Drugs and Aging, 4,* 47–55.

Papaioannou, A., Clarke, J. A., Campbell, G., & Bedard, M. (2000). Assessment of adherence to renal dosing guidelines in long-term care facilities. *Journal of the American Geriatrics Society, 48,* 1470–1473.

Perri, M. III, Menon, A. M., Deshpande, A. D., Shinde, S. B., Jiang, R., Cooper, J. W., Cook, C. L., Griffin, S. C., & Lorys, R. A. (2005). Adverse outcomes associated with inappropriate drug use in nursing homes. *Annals of Pharmacotherapy, 39,* 405–411.

Pirmohamed, M., James, S., Meakin, S., Green, C., Scott, A. K., Walley, T. J., Farrar, K., Park, B. K., & Breckenridge, A. M. (2004). Adverse drug reactions as cause of admission to hospital: Prospective analysis of 18 820 patients. *BMJ, 329,* 15–19.

Rochon, P. A., & Gurwitz, J. H. (1997). Optimizing drug treatment for elderly people: The prescribing cascade. *BMJ, 315,* 1096–1099.

Sambrook, P. N. (2005). How to prevent steroid-induced osteoporosis. *Annals of the Rheumatic Diseases, 64,* 176–178.

Schmader, K. E., Hanlon, J. T., Pieper, C. F., Sloane, R., Ruby, C. M., Twersky, J., Francis, S. D., Branch, L. G., Lindblad, C. I., Artz, M., Weinberger, M., Feussner, J. R., & Cohen, H. J. (2004). Effects of geriatric evaluation and management on adverse drug reactions and suboptimal prescribing in the frail elderly. *American Journal of Medicine, 116,* 394–401.

Tamblyn, R. M., McLeod, P. J., Abrahamowicz, M., & Laprise, R. (1996). Do too many cooks spoil the broth? Multiple physician involvement in medical management of elderly patients and potentially inappropriate drug combinations. *Canadian Medical Association Journal, 154,* 1177–1184.

Trosch, R. M. (2004). Neuroleptic-induced movement disorders: Deconstructing extrapyramidal symptoms. *Journal of the American Geriatrics Society, 52* (12 Suppl.), S266–S271.

World Health Organization. (2002). Safety of medicines. A guide to detecting and reporting adverse drug reactions. Why health professionals need to take action. Geneva: World Health Organization. Available: http://www.who.int/medicines/library/qsm/who-edm-qsm-2002-2/esd_safety.pdf.

Zhan, C., Correa-de-Araujo, R., Bierman, A. S., Sangl, J., Miller, M. R., Wickizer, S. W., & Stryer, D. (2005). Suboptimal prescribing in elderly outpatients: Potentially harmful drug-drug and drug-disease combinations. *Journal of the American Geriatrics Society, 53,* 262–267.

DRUG SIDE EFFECTS

See
Drug Reactions

DUKE LONGITUDINAL STUDIES

The Duke Longitudinal Studies of Aging, initiated in 1955 (Busse & Maddox, 1985), consist of 3 separate studies:

The First Longitudinal Study began in 1955 with 271 persons aged 60 to 90 years. The individuals were not a probability sample but were selected from a pool of volunteers who lived in Durham, North Carolina. Each panelist came to the Duke Medical Center for a 2-day series of medical, psychiatric, psychological, and social examinations. The examinations were repeated periodically until 1976 (Palmore, 1970, 1974, 1981).

The Second Longitudinal Study, also know as the "*Adaptation Study*," began in 1968 with 502 persons aged 46 to 70 years. These panelists were a probability sample of the members of the local health insurance association, stratified by age and sex. The study was designed so that at the end of 5 years approximately 40 persons would remain in each of 10 5-year, age-sex cohorts. This design makes possible various kinds of cross-sequential analyses to separate the effects of age, period, and cohort (Palmore, 1978). Each person was brought in for a 1-day series of examinations and was reexamined at 2-year intervals until 1976.

The Third Longitudinal Study, also known as the "*Old-Old Study*," began in 1972 with the *Older American Resources and Services* (OARS) community survey of 1,000 Durham residents aged 65 years and older. During 1980 to 1983, 300 of the individuals (then aged 75 or older) were brought to the Center for 6 hours of comprehensive physical, mental, and social examinations; each was given 1 or 2 annual follow-up examinations (Palmore, Nowlin, & Wang, 1985).

Purposes

The studies focused on "normal aging" in 2 senses: healthy aging and typical aging. The individuals were relatively healthy in that most were noninstitutionalized, ambulatory, community residents who were willing and able to come to the Duke Medical Center for tests and examination. The more common or typical patterns and problems of aging were on the focus, rather than the abnormalities. The goal was to help distinguish between normal processes of aging and those that may accompany aging because of accident, stress, maladjustment, or disuse.

A second purpose was to use the longitudinal method of repeated observations over time, which is the best way to accurately measure changes. Longitudinal studies have several unique advantages over cross-sectional studies: each member can be used as his or her own control; consistent trends can be distinguished from temporary fluctuations; errors due to retrospective distortion are minimized; early warning signs of disease or death can be studied; cohort differences can be distinguished from age changes; and the effect of 1 kind of change on another kind of later change can be studied.

The third purpose was to do as much interdisciplinary analysis as possible. Representatives from the major disciplines dealing with aging were on the staff, and insofar as possible the analyses attempted to take into account all relevant factors.

Themes

The 5 volumes reporting the results of these studies contain more than 100 specific findings. However, 4 general themes tie together findings from several substantive areas:

1. *Declining health and physical function.* The typical pattern of normal aging is one of declining health and physical functions in most of the areas studied.
2. *Exceptions to physical decline.* Despite the declines as measured by averages or group percentages, substantial minorities show no decline and may even have improvement in sexual activity, cardiovascular function, hypertension, depression, hypochondriasis, vibratory thresholds, serum antigens, skin condition, vision, hearing, and health ratings. Thus, health and function can and do improve for some older persons, just as they do for some younger persons.
3. *Little or no decline in social and psychological function.* The studies found little or no decline in activities, attitudes, cautiousness, recall, general adjustment, intelligence scores, reaction

times, correct signal detection, most measures of mental health, coping, personality, internal orientation, self-concept, life satisfaction, voluntary association, activity, and religious attitudes. This evidence tends to refute the disengagement theory that social and psychological decline are typical and normal.

4. *Wide variations in aging patterns*. Individual variation tends to persist or increase with aging. There are wide individual and group differences in the aging processes, which document both how multifaceted aging processes are and how much variety there is in the patterns of normal aging.

ERDMAN B. PALMORE

See also
Longitudinal Data Sets
Longitudinal Research

References

Busse, E. W., & Maddox, G. L. (1985). *The Duke Longitudinal Studies of Normal Aging 1955–1980*. New York: Springer Publishing.

Palmore, E. (Ed.) (1970). *Normal aging*. Durham, NC: Duke University Press.

Palmore, E. (Ed.) (1974). *Normal aging II*. Durham, NC: Duke University Press.

Palmore, E. (1978). When can age, period, and cohort be separated? *Social Forces*, *57*, 282–295.

Palmore, E. (1981). *Social patterns in normal aging*. Durham, NC: Duke University Press.

Palmore, E., Nowlin, J., & Wang, H. (1985). Predictors of function among the old-old. *Journal of Gerontology*, *40*, 244–250.

E

EARLY ONSET DEMENTIA

See
Dementia: Frontotemporal

ECONOMICS

The *economics of aging* concerns the *economic well-being* of older persons; life cycle decisions concerning work, retirement, and savings; national retirement programs, including Social Security and Medicare; and national policies such as regulation of employer pensions and age discrimination; and the macroeconomic implications of aging populations, especially the impact of population aging on the cost of retirement programs.

Economic Well-Being of Older Adults

Economic well-being is determined by an individual's ability to consume goods and services. Household wealth and current income limit consumption possibilities and require individuals to make choices. Households of older persons face the same choices as that of other families; however, they may differ in their consumption needs as well as their wealth accumulation, income level, and income source. These differences are attributable, among other things, to changes in health status, life cycle patterns of work, and age-based government transfer programs.

Real and Relative Economic Status. The *economic status of older Americans* has improved significantly over the past 4 decades, as illustrated by a reduction in the *elderly poverty rate* from 35.2% in 1959 to 10.2% in 2003. Today, the poverty rate among households aged 65 and older is below that of the entire U.S. population and, more specifically, below that of 2 other subsets of the population—children under 18 years and individuals between 18 and 64 years (U.S. Census Bureau, 2004a). From 1969 to 2002, the median real income (in 2002 dollars) of householders 65 years and older increased from $13,995 to $23,152, a gain of 65%. This increase was much larger than that recorded by younger households (McNeil, 1998; U.S. Census Bureau, 2004b).

Older persons also receive considerable *in-kind transfers* from the government. The most prominent in-kind transfer is access to medical services through *Medicare*. An alternative measure of economic status is based on cash income plus non-cash benefits received, capital gains, and imputed return on home equity minus taxes paid. When this measure is used, the median *income of elderly households* increases by more than 40%, while there is relatively little change for all households (Clark, Burkhauser, Moon, Quinn, & Smeeding, 2004).

Despite the impressive reduction in elderly poverty rates and improvements in median income, certain groups among older adults, such as widows, minorities, and the very old, remain particularly vulnerable. Median household net worth for individuals aged 51 and older in 1998 was about $105,000 (Kapteyn & Panis, 2003), and older households in the bottom 10% of the wealth distribution had little or no wealth accumulations (Smith, 1997).

Sources of Income. The traditional three-legged stool of *retirement income* consists of Social Security, private pensions, and savings. *Social Security* is the primary source of income among households aged 65 and older, as about 90% of older households receive some income from Social Security. Social Security accounts for about 38% of retirement income among older households, and its importance increases dramatically as income declines and as people age. Social Security accounts for more than 80% of income among individuals in the bottom 40 percent of the income distribution, and for about 57% of income among individuals age 85 and older. Pensions and assets each account for about 17% of income among older households. Both sources become more important as income rises (U.S. Social Security Administration, 2002; Clark Burkhauser, Moon, Quinn, & Smeeding, 2004).

Recent changes to the retirement income landscape affect each of the traditional retirement income sources. Social Security replacement rates are expected to decline in the future due to fiscal pressures and already-legislated changes. Private pensions have been shifting away from traditional defined benefit plans toward defined contribution plans, such as *401Ks*, and *hybrid plans*, such as *cash-balance plans*. At the same time, private savings rates have declined dramatically. These changes have made work later in life more attractive. Today, earnings account for 23% of income among older households (U.S. Social Security Administration, 2002). As the three-legged retirement income stool becomes wobbly, earnings will be an important stabilizing fourth leg.

Work and Retirement

"Retirement" can mean different things to different people. Some people base retirement on Social Security benefit receipt or current work status. For research purposes, retirement is commonly viewed as complete labor force withdrawal. Around age 55, older persons begin to permanently leave the labor force. Their *retirement decisions* are influenced by health status, income, wealth, pension status, Social Security benefit receipt, and family characteristics.

For much of the last century, the *average retirement age* for men, or the youngest age at which half of men exited the labor force, declined from age 74 in 1910 to age 63 in the early 1980s (Burtless & Quinn, 2002). The decline is predominantly a result of increasing prosperity over the past century. As per capita gross domestic product (GDP) increased, workers spent a portion of their wealth on leisure, including earlier retirements. Since the mid-1980s, however, the average retirement age among men has remained relatively unchanged. Older women have also experienced a change in trend, although the break since the mid-1980s is somewhat different. Labor force participation rates for older women were basically flat from the mid-1960s to the mid-1980s, reflecting both the trend toward earlier retirement seen among men and a trend of increasing *labor force participation among women* overall in the post-WWII era. As the former trend stopped, the latter dominated, and labor force participation among older women began to rise (Quinn, 1999).

While there is some debate over the cyclical or permanent nature of this break, changes to financial incentives have altered the retirement landscape. For many, retirement is no longer a one-time permanent event. Older workers who retire from career jobs today do not necessarily move directly into complete retirement. Many individuals—estimated at between one-half and one-third of older Americans,—now choose to enter new jobs and work for several additional years either full- or part-time. These jobs bridge the gap between full-time career employment and complete labor force withdrawal and are often referred to as "*bridge jobs*."

National Programs and Policies

The 2 major age-based national retirement programs in the United States are Social Security and Medicare. Social Security provides monthly retirement benefits based on payroll tax contributions over an individual's work history. Medicare provides health insurance to all individuals aged 65 and older, and has been expanded recently to include some prescription drug coverage. Both programs have played an important role in the economic well being of the elderly, and both programs are a large and growing component of the federal budget. Today, Social Security and Medicare make up 4.3% and 2.6% of GDP, respectively. In the next 30 years, these percentages are projected to increase to about 6.3% and 7.7%, respectively (U.S. Social Security Administration, 2004; U.S. Centers for Medicare and Medicaid Services, 2004).

The *aging of the population* has sharply increased the tax rates necessary to finance these national retirement benefits. Social Security reform is thus one of the most import policy debates of the 21st century. Restoring the financial integrity of the Social Security system will require higher taxes, lower benefits, or higher retirement ages. Alternatively more fundamental changes, such as providing individual retirement accounts for workers, could be introduced. Like Social Security, the aging of the population will strain the Medicare program.

Economic issues are at the heart of the reform debate for Social Security and Medicare. Important concerns include the effect of higher tax rates, the impact of lower benefits, the effect on national saving, and specific to Social Security, the result of investing national retirement funds in private equity markets (Advisory Council on Social Security, 1997).

The economics of aging also concerns national policies related to the employment of older workers, such as the elimination of mandatory retirement for most workers in 1986 and laws aimed at preventing age discrimination. As the population ages, prime-age workers will become scarce and older workers may become a valuable resource for employers, since other alternatives, such as relocation or immigration, are unlikely to fill the void entirely. On the one hand, older workers are well educated and healthier than in the past, they have a lifetime of experience, and many jobs are no longer physically demanding. On the other, older workers are expensive and may need training, and many existing employment policies encourage early retirement. Policies could be implemented to address these concerns and help facilitate a match between employers' needs and older workers' desires to remain in the labor force (Munnell, Cahill, Eschtruth, & Sass, 2004).

Macroeconomic Implications of Aging Populations

Population aging refers to an increase in the relative number of older persons in a population and is associated with an increase in the median age of the population. According to both of these measures, the United States is growing older. Today, about 12.2% of the population is aged 65 to 84 years, and about 2.1% of the population is aged 85 years and older. By 2030, these percentages will swell to 18.3% and 3.4%, respectively (U.S. Census Bureau, 2004c). Over the same period, the median age of the population is expected to increase from about 35.7 years to 38.7 years (U.S. Census Bureau, 1996). This change in the population age structure can influence aggregate economic activity due to age-specific differences in employment, productivity, savings, and consumption.

Dependency Ratios. *Dependency ratios* are used to measure the relative productive potential of a population. The old-age dependency ratio generally measures the number of elderly persons at or above a certain age divided by the number of persons of working age. The ratio rises with population aging. For example, today there are 3.3 workers for every Social Security beneficiary. By 2030, there will only be slightly more than 2. (U.S. Social Security Administration, 2003).

The economic interpretation of the *old-age dependency ratio*, however, remains clouded. First, if population aging follows from reduced fertility, the relative number of youths falls. As a result, the total dependency ratio (youths plus elderly) may fall even as the old-age ratio is rising. Second, age-based dependency ratios are not perfect proxies for the ratio of inactive to active persons. To address this problem, labor force participation rates can be used to determine the dependency ratio. Finally, significant compositional changes may occur within the elderly, youth, and working age populations. These changes have economic effects that may be as important as the effects of changes in the dependency ratio itself.

Economic Responses to Population Aging. The changing age structure of a population can alter the level of economic activity and productivity. Layoff and quit rates, for example, are a decreasing function of age. Because employment stability increases with age, national *unemployment rates* tend to decline with population aging. Considerable attention also has been given to the change in individual productivity with age. As an individual ages, productive capacity generally rises upward to a peak, levels off, and eventually begins to decline. This movement reflects age-specific investment in human capital, changes in physical and mental abilities, and worker expectations concerning future events. The importance of any decrements in job performance in later working years depends on the job requirements, and whether the worker or the employer attempts to maintain skills through continued training. The life cycle pattern of job performance differs substantially across workers and jobs.

Any decline in productivity will also be influenced by the extent to which older workers adapt their existing human capital to fit the needs of an economy marked by technological change. Given the diversity of individuals and job requirements, it is not surprising that research studies have found significant overlap in the age-specific productivity distributions. Older workers may be able to offset productivity declines by having lower absence rates, reduced likelihood of job turnover, and increased accuracy or quality of performance. The *macroeconomic significance of population aging* on national productivity depends on individual age-specific productivity, and any ensuing changes in investment, consumption, and savings behavior. The net effect of these factors is unclear.

The effect of population aging on national savings and the rate of economic growth depend on age-specific savings rates, consumption, and the age structure of the population. The net effect of aging on growth also will depend on the cause of population aging. If population aging results from slowing population growth, then the economic response to population size and the rate of population growth will be observed simultaneously with the aging effect. In general, the independent effect of population aging will only be one factor influencing future economic growth and development.

ROBERT L. CLARK
Updated by KEVIN E. CAHILL

See also
Employment
Older Workers
Pensions: Policies and Plans
Poverty
Productivity
Retirement
Social Security

References

Advisory Council on Social Security. (1997). Report of the 1994–1996 Advisory Council on Social Security. Washington, DC: U.S. Government Printing Office. Available: http://www.ssa.gov/history/reports/adcouncil/report/toc.htm

Burtless, G., & Quinn, J. (2002). *Is working longer the answer for an aging workforce*? (Issue in brief 11 December). Chestnut Hill, MA: Center for Retirement Research at Boston College.

Clark, R. L., Burkhauser, R. V., Moon, M., Quinn, J. F., & Smeeding, T. M. (2004). *The economics of an aging society*. Malden, MA: Blackwell Publishing.

Kapteyn, A., & Panis, C. (2003). *The size and composition of wealth holdings in the United States, Italy, and the Netherlands*. Santa Monica, CA: RAND Labor and Population Program Working Paper 03–05, DRU-3002.

McNeil, J. (1998). Changes in median household income: 1969 to 1996 (Current Population Reports Special Studies, P23–196). Washington, DC: U.S. Government Printing Office. Available: http://www.census.gov/prod/3/98pubs/p23-196.pdf

Munnell, A. H., Cahill, K. E., Eschtruth, A. D., & Sass, S. A. (2004). *The graying of Massachusetts: Aging, the new rules of retirement, and the changing workforce.* Boston, MA: Massachusetts Institute for a New Commonwealth.

Quinn, J. F. (1999). Retirement patterns and bridge jobs in the 1990s. *EBRI Issue Brief, No. 206*. Washington, DC: Employment Benefit Research Institute.

Smith, J. P. (1997). The changing economic circumstances of the elderly: Income, wealth, and social security. *Maxwell School of Citizenship and Public Affairs/ Center for Policy Research Policy Brief, no. 8*. Syracuse, NY: Syracuse University.

U.S. Census Bureau. (1996). Population projections of the United States by age, sex, race, and Hispanic origin: 1995 to 2050. *Current Population Reports (P25–1130)*. Washington, DC: U.S. Government Printing Office. Available: http://www.census.gov/prod/1/pop/p25-1130/p251130.pdf

U.S. Census Bureau. (2004a). Income, poverty, and health insurance coverage in the United States: 2003. *Current Population Reports* (P60–226). Washington, DC: U.S. Government Printing Office. Available: http://www.census.gov/prod/2004pubs/p60-226.pdf

U.S. Census Bureau. (2004b). Historical income tables–households (Table H-10). *Current Population Survey, Annual Social and Economic Supplements.* Washington, DC: U.S. Government Printing Office. Available: http://www.census.gov/hhes/income/histinc/h1001.html

U.S. Census Bureau. (2004c). U.S. interim projections by age, sex, race, and Hispanic origin. Washington, DC: U.S. Government Printing Office. Available: http://www.census.gov/ipc/www/usinterimproj/

U.S. Centers for Medicare and Medicaid Services. (2004). The 2004 Annual Report of the Board of Trustees of the Federal Hospital Insurance and Federal Supplementary Medical Insurance Trust Funds. Washington, DC: U.S. Government Printing Office. Available: http://www.cms.hhs.gov/publications/trusteesreport/2004/tr.pdf

U.S. Social Security Administration. (2002). *Income of the population 55 and older, 2000.* Washington, DC. Available: http://www.ssa.gov/policy/docs/statcomps/inc_pop55/2000/incpop00.pdf

U.S. Social Security Administration. (2003). *Fast facts and figures about Social Security.* Washington, DC: U.S. Government Printing Office. Available: http://www.ssa.gov/policy/docs/chartbooks/fast_facts/2003/ff2003.pdf

U.S. Social Security Administration. (2004). *The 2004 annual report of the Board of Trustees of the Federal Old-Age and Survivors Insurance and Disability Insurance Trust Funds.* (Table V1.F11). Washington, DC: U.S. Government Printing Office. Available: http://www.ssa.gov/OACT/TR/TR04/tr04.pdf

ECONOMIC SECURITY

See
Savings

ELDER ABUSE AND NEGLECT

Abuse of any person is difficult to understand, but the mistreatment, exploitation, and intentional harm of the elderly is particularly disturbing. Older adults are vulnerable to abuse of all kinds, and these violations of the basic human rights of senior citizens should concern us all. The increasing needs of older adults for assistance and dependence on caregivers, social isolation, and frailty, combined with a reluctance to complain about their abusers, make *elder abuse* an extremely underreported crime (Mosqueda, Burnight, Liao, & Kemp, 2004).

Mistreatment of the older adult includes the infliction of physical, emotional, or psychological harm, *sexual abuse*, financial exploitation, and *neglect by caregivers*. *Self-neglect* by older adults who require assistance may be a form of abuse if no attempts are made to offer or provide needed services. Abuse places an older adult in danger, and typically isolates the person from contact with those who can provide help. Abuse of the elderly is associated with significant morbidity and mortality. Older adults who have suffered abuse or neglect have 3 times the mortality rate of those who have no history of mistreatment (Lachs & Pillemer, 2004).

Elder abuse occurs among all racial, ethnic, and socioeconomic groups. It involves the rich, the poor, and the middle class, and requires that professionals who come in contact with older adults be vigilant in identifying warning signs that may indicate elder abuse. Many screening instruments are available for the *identification of elder abuse* and neglect, collectively referred to as *elder mistreatment screening* (Fulmer, Guadagno, Bitondo Dyer, & Connolly, 2004). Many of these rating scales are lengthy and impractical for routine clinical use. Several, such as the *Brief Abuse Screen for the Elderly*, the *Elder Assessment Instrument*, and the *Conflict Tactics Scale*, are brief and reliable but require formal training (Fulmer, Guadagno, Bitondo Dyer, & Connolly, 2004). It is strongly recommended that all clinicians include a basic level of screening for abuse and neglect when evaluating older adults, and interview the patient and caregiver individually (Shugarman, Fries, Wolf, & Morris, 2003).

Older adults who are victims of abuse and neglect often visit emergency rooms, and present with a variety of physical and emotional complaints (Clarke & Pierson, 1999). *Denial of the abuse* is common, as many elderly live in fear of their abusers and suffer from shame and embarrassment. Assessment of the older adult should include careful physical evaluation of injuries and bruises, as well as gentle questions regarding living arrangements, financial and social supports and emotional stressors (Table 1). Observing the interaction between the patient and family members or caregivers may offer important information (Shugarman, Fries, Wolf, & Morris, 2003).

Culture and ethnicity affect how behavior may be considered acceptable in some families, yet abusive in others (Takeshita & Ahmed, 2004). For example, in some cultures sharing of all family finances is the norm and use of the older person's funds for multiple purposes is common. In other cultures, this practice could easily be interpreted as financial exploitation. Among some cultures, there is an expectation that younger family members will care for their elders at home. This may lead to conflicts when family members are faced with economic, child-care, and job pressures, creating an environment of *caregiver burden and stress* (Takeshita & Ahmed, 2004). Other care options may not be used due to cultural barriers, leading to situations of neglect and even abuse.

Family members are the most common persons involved in elder abuse. In almost 90% of cases in the community setting, the *abuser is a family member*. In two-thirds of cases, it is a spouse or adult child. *Financial exploitation* and abuse of the older adult's funds is a frequent occurrence, found in up to 90% of cases (Tueth, 2000). The abuser frequently depends on the older adult for housing, financial support, or assistance. Those who commit abuse and neglect toward the elderly are often troubled family members who are overburdened and have multiple responsibilities. Typically they do not feel that their behavior is abusive (Jogerst, Dawson, Hartz, Ely, & Schweitzer, 2000). Emotional problems, substance abuse disorders, and psychosocial stressors are factors that increase the risk of abusive behavior and

TABLE 1 Warning *Signs and Symptoms of Elder Abuse* and Neglect

Physical Abuse
- Bruises or grip marks around the arms, neck, or legs
- Puncture wounds, burns, or welts
- Repeated unexplained injuries
- Pain or wincing when touched
- Inappropriate use of physical restraints

Emotional Abuse
- Symptoms of fear, anxiety, agitation
- Depression and withdrawal
- Hesitation to talk openly, evasiveness, and ambivalence
- Contradictory statements about condition or well-being
- Fear of leaving room or home due to intimidation

Neglect
- Malnutrition or dehydration with no explainable cause
- Lack of follow-up with medical care, medications, or treatments
- Soiled clothing and unkempt appearance
- Forced isolation due to lack of assistance

Financial Abuse or Exploitation
- Large or frequent withdrawals from bank accounts
- No longer paying bills or accumulating new, unexplainable debt
- Caregiver's name added to bank accounts, credit cards, checks
- Caregiver refusal to spend money for older adult's needs
- Large or expensive "gifts" from older adult to caregiver

Sexual Abuse
- Unexplained vaginal or anal injuries
- Bruises on the breasts or genitals
- Sexually transmitted diseases

neglect. Sometimes the abuse is a continuation of a pattern of violence and exploitation within the family. The most common types of elder abuse, in order of prevalence are: financial exploitation, neglect, *emotional abuse*, *physical abuse*, and sexual assault (Lachs & Pillemer, 2004). Sexual abuse is the least reported form of elder abuse, but unfortunately still occurs.

The incidence of elder abuse has been difficult to identify, in part due to the fearfulness and isolation that prevents may older adults from seeking help. The *National Elder Abuse Incidence Study*, conducted in 1996 by the National Center on Elder Abuse (NCEA), estimated that nearly 450,000 adults older than age 60 years were the victims of abuse or neglect in community settings (National Center on Elder Abuse, 1997). This is consistent with additional data collected by the Administration on Aging in 1998 that identified more than 550,000 elderly persons who experienced abuse or neglect in community or institutional settings (Administration on Aging, 1999). As these numbers reflect only those cases that were reported to agencies, the actual incidence is believed to be significantly higher.

The NCEA concluded that less than 20% of elder abuse is reported to local *Adult Protective Service* agencies, leading many researchers to suggest that the actual number of elder abuse victims may be as high as 2.5 million per year (Lachs & Pillemer, 2004). At greatest risk for elder abuse are women, those over age 80, and elderly who suffer from frailty, confusion, and depression (Jogerst, Dawson, Hartz, Ely, & Schweitzer, 2000). Older adults who die as a result of abuse or neglect typically are *female victims of a male caregiver*, particularly a spouse, son, or other relative (Shields, Hunsaker, & Hunsaker, 2004).

Abuse of the elderly also occurs in institutional settings, including hospitals, nursing homes, assisted living facilities, and board and care homes. Potential warning signs of *abuse in a nursing home* or other institutional setting include disinterested or untrained staff, lack of activities, use of restraints, and residents isolated in their rooms or sitting in hallways for extended periods of time (U.S. Preventative Services Task Force, 2004). Older adults who require nursing home care are particularly vulnerable, as they are often incapable of reporting abuse or become easily frightened. Nursing homes have *ombudsman programs* with representatives able to take confidential reports of abuse and provide ongoing surveillance. In addition, each facility is required to post a toll-free number for reporting suspected abuse to the state Department of Health. The increase in the number of assisted living facilities for older adults raises concern that this group is vulnerable to abuse yet often unaware of the means to seek help (Woods & Stephens, 2003).

The most valuable intervention that a clinician or caregiver may provide in cases of suspected elder abuse or neglect is making an initial report to an appropriate agency (Lachs & Pillemer, 2004). Currently, 47 states have laws requiring licensed health care professionals to report the suspected abuse of an older person who is incapacitated or unable to report for themselves. All 50 states encourage the voluntary reporting of elder abuse (Clarke & Pierson, 1999).

Every state has an agency designated to receive and investigate allegations of elder abuse and neglect. In most regions, this is an Adult Protective Services agency. The *Eldercare Locator* (800-677-1116), a nationwide assistance directory provided by the *National Association of Area Agencies on Aging*, will provide referral to the local agency that will investigate a report of elder abuse or neglect. The outcome of each case will depend upon the results of an investigation, the nature of the abuse, and the social and legal options available.

Often several agencies are involved in investigating cases of elder abuse, and coordination of services is vital. The most common problems involve older persons who are evaluated and require services, but are unable to arrange follow-up. An interdisciplinary team approach has been found to be useful both in providing needed services and coordinating care (Mosqueda, Burnight, Liao, & Kemp, 2004). If an older adult has the capacity to make decisions, her or his wishes must be respected even when a choice is made to return to an abusive relationship. It is frustrating when an older adult refuses to press charges if a crime has been committed, or refuses to leave an abusive relationship. Offers of assistance should always be made, and periodic attempts to intervene may eventually result in improvement in the situation. When an elderly person is cognitively impaired, assessment of decision-making capacity and legal options of guardianship or conservatorship may be needed (Mosqueda, Burnight, Liao, & Kemp, 2004).

Elder abuse assistance resources can be obtained from the following organizations:

- *National Center on Elder Abuse* (www.elderabusecenter.org)
- *National Committee for the Prevention of Elder Abuse* (www.elderabusecenter.org)
- Eldercare Locator (www.eldercare.gov/Eldercare/Public/Home.asp)
- *National Citizens' Coalition for Nursing Home Reform* (www.nursinghomeaction.com)

MELINDA S. LANTZ

References

Clarke, M. E., & Pierson, W. (1999). Management of elder abuse in the emergency department. *Emergency Medical Clinics of North America, 17*(3), 631–644.

Fulmer, T., Guadagno, L., Bitondo Dyer, C., & Connolly, M. T. (2004). Progress in elder abuse screening and assessment instruments. *Journal of the American Geriatrics Society, 52*(2), 297–304.

Jogerst, G. J., Dawson, J. D., Hartz, A. J., Ely, J. W., & Schweitzer, L. A. (2000). Community characteristics associated with elder abuse. *Journal of the American Geriatrics Society, 48*(5), 513–518.

Lachs, M. S., & Pillemer, K. (2004). Elder abuse. *Lancet, 364*(9441), 1263–1272.

Mosqueda, L., Burnight, K., Liao, S., & Kemp, B. (2004). Advancing the field of elder mistreatment: A new model for integration of social and medical services. *Gerontologist, 44*(5), 703–708.

National Center on Elder Abuse. (1997). *Elder abuse in domestic settings: Information Series*. Washington, DC: American Public Human Services Administration.

Shields, L. B., Hunsaker, D. M., & Hunsaker, J. C. III. (2004). Abuse and neglect: A ten-year review of mortality and morbidity in our elders in a large metropolitan area. *Journal of Forensic Science, 49*(1), 122–127.

Shugarman, L. R., Fries, B. E., Wolf, R. S., & Morris, J. N. (2003). Identifying older people at risk of abuse during routine screening practices. *Journal of the American Geriatrics Society, 51*(1), 24–31.

Takeshita, J., & Ahmed, I. (2004). Culture and geriatric psychiatry. In W.-S. Tseng & J. Streltzer (Eds.), *Cultural competence in clinical psychiatry*. Washington, DC: American Psychiatric Publishing.

Tueth, M. J. (2000). Exposing financial exploitation of impaired elderly persons. *American Journal of Geriatric Psychiatry, 8*(2), 104–111.

U.S. Department of Health and Human Services, Administration on Aging. (1999). The National Elder Abuse Incidence Study. Available: http://www.aoa.dhhs.gov/abuse/report/default/htm

U.S. Preventative Services Task Force. (2004). Screening for family and intimate partner violence: Recommendation statement. *Annals of Family Medicine, 2*(2), 156–160.

Woods, S., & Stephens, M. (2003). Vulnerability to elder abuse and neglect in assisted living facilities. *Gerontologist, 43*(5), 753–757.

ELECTRONIC PATIENT RECORDS

See
Health Informatics

EMOTION

Although virtually absent prior to the last 2 decades, the study of human aging has seen a groundswell of research documenting changes in emotions and *emotion regulation*. In part, the increasing momentum that adult emotions research is garnering echoes the continuing relevance of *emotions to an aging population*, but it also reflects the centrality of emotions and emotion regulation to social relationships, health outcomes, and health behavior.

Research examining emotions in later life has focused primarily on developmental differences in physiology, physiognomy, and the subjective experience of emotion and, more recently, on the ability to regulate emotional states. Although most studies have been cross-sectional rather than longitudinal, are primarily based on self-reported data, and are in need of replication and extension, some important discoveries have emerged. Perhaps most importantly, while early perspectives depicted the *emotional lives of older adults* as comparatively rigid and unsatisfying, recent data suggests a more complex and balanced picture. Although later life is typified by numerous physical, financial, cognitive, and interpersonal losses, some aspects of emotional functioning appear differentially preserved in later life, and some may improve.

To begin, it is important to briefly consider the nature of emotions—what they are, where they come from, and what their uses are. Discarding earlier views of emotions as turbulent, disruptive, and something to be controlled, contemporary theory largely views emotions as response and social communication systems that emerged across our development as a species in response to recurring environmental challenges and opportunities; emotions are adaptive. According to this view, core emotional responses such as fear, anger, sadness, happiness, and pride emerge when historically recurrent patterns of events (external or internal) are detected. Once activated, the emotions comprise a coordinated pattern of physiological, experiential, expressive, cognitive, and behavioral changes that together motivate and prepare the organism to engage in the appropriate class of adaptive action.

Importantly, while the basic building blocks of emotions are provided by genetic inheritance, the final form of emotions depends substantially on culture, learning, and the organism's developing capacities. Of particular note are the modifications in emotion expression and experience that occur as a result of our acquiring "display" and "feeling" rules. This emotion regulation—defined as the processes by which individuals influence their emotions, when they have them, and how they experience and express them—occurs at multiple points in the emotion process, from choosing situations based on their emotional affordances to enhancing or suppressing *emotion expressions* once an emotion is felt. Predominantly determined by culture and family, rules regarding emotion regulation represent a set of prescriptions and proscriptions concerning which emotions should be felt, how (or if) they should be expressed, to whom, under what circumstances, and in what form.

Five major areas have been examined by researchers interested in how emotions change in later life: experience, expression, physiology, cognitive processing of emotions, and emotion regulation.

Emotion Experience

Current data is mixed on differences in global emotion experience. Several studies have shown increasing positive emotions (Mroczek & Spiro, 2003) and decreasing negative emotions (Mroczek & Kolarz, 1998) in later life. One 23-year longitudinal study, for example, assessed positive and negative emotion for 3 cohorts of adults at 5 points in time using growth curve analysis. The authors found that positive emotion remained constant across 20 years for all cohorts, and only decreased slightly among the very oldest individuals (mid-60s to mid-80s). Negative affect declined in frequency across groups, and there was a noteworthy absence of cohort effects (Charles, Reynolds, & Gatz, 2001). Other studies have found reductions in *positive emotion* in later life (Smith, Fleeson, Geiselmann, Settersten, & Kunzmann, 1999), have reported few differences (Carstensen, Mayr, Pasupathi, & Nesselroade, 2000), or have suggested that both positive and negative affect may decline (Diener & Suh, 1997). Thus, in general changes in emotions at this global level appear small, although there are indications of a "turning point" as people approach very late life. What may be a generally more positive emotional balance seems to taper off in the mid-70s (Gross, Carstensen, Pasupathi, Tsai, Goetestam-Skorpen, & Hsu, 1997; Mroczek, 2001), while *negative affect* begins to increase (Kunzmann, Little, & Smith, 2000) and is most strongly evident in persons older than 85 years (Smith, et al., 1999).

As an alternative to more global changes, several recent theories have suggested that discrete emotions such as anger, sadness, fear, and shame may change both *quantitatively and qualitatively* in later life. Carstensen's *socioemotional selectivity theory* suggests that a perception of time as finite leads older adults to prioritize emotional goals and adjust emotion regulation and social interactions to maximize positive experiences (Carstensen, Fung, & Charles, 2003; Carstensen & Löckenhoff, 2003). Consedine and colleagues argue that later life changes in emotion stem from differences in the primary life tasks people of different ages confront, as well as from changes in the physiological, social, cognitive, and behavioral capabilities they possess (Consedine & Magai, in press; Consedine, Magai, & King, 2004). Finally, Labouvie-Vief and colleagues suggest that changes in emotion occur across the adult life span as cognition and emotion become more tightly interwoven and the individual develops the ability to experience multiple and conflicting emotions simultaneously (Labouvie-Vief & Diehl, 2000; Labouvie-Vief & Medler, 2002).

Despite such rich theory, however, descriptive data regarding discrete emotions is uncommon, and results seem to vary whether "online" versus retrospective reports are used. One study of nuns aged 24 to 101 years found that anger, sadness, and fear (but not disgust) were lower in older adults (Gross, et al., 1997). Older adults have been shown to refer less frequently to *anger* when describing interpersonal problems than adolescents and younger adults, although there were no differences in sadness (Birditt & Fingerman, 2003). Interestingly, it has been found that older adults did not differ from younger cohorts in their "online" emotional reactions when watching emotionally stimulating video clips, but were retrospectively less positive when rating their feelings regarding sad and amusing film clips (Tsai, Carstensen, & Levenson, 2000). Overall, it has been suggested that of the discrete emotions, only anger becomes less frequent in later life, a finding that holds even when a host of background variables are controlled (Schieman, 1999).

Other changes in emotion experience may include age differences in intensity and/or differences in the complexity of emotion experiences. There are few studies of emotional intensity and, again, the presence of developmental differences seems to vary depending on the method. Retrospective ratings sometimes suggest diminished intensity, although there may be cross-cultural variation (Gross, et al., 1997). Online ratings, however, suggest few differences in the intensity of emotion (Carstensen, et al., 2000), as do laboratory studies (Malatesta-Magai, Jonas, Shepard, & Culver, 1992).

The complexity of emotional experience also seems to change across the adult life span. Studies in which narrative descriptions of emotional experiences are coded have suggested that older adults more frequently refer to *inner feelings*, are less likely to describe their experiences in terms of norms and conventions, and are more capable of discussing complex feelings and enduring states of conflict and ambivalence. Some research suggests that complexity peaks in middle age and is lower in both younger and older adults (Labouvie-Vief, Chiodo, Goguen, Diehl, & Orwoll, 1995); however other studies imply that complexity may continue to develop in later years (Carstensen, et al., 2000) and may predict greater resilience (Ong & Bergman, 2004).

Emotion Expression

Although common wisdom has tended to suggest dampened *emotional expressivity in later life*, the data depicts a far more complex pattern. Some studies have shown no age differences (Tsai, Carstensen,

& Levenson, 2000), others that older adults are less "accurate" when posing emotion expressions (Borod, Yecker, Brickman, Moreno, Sliwinski, Foldi, et al., 2004), and still others implying that reduced expressivity may occur in situations where the expression of negative emotions would be unhelpful (Carstensen, Gottman, & Levenson, 1995). In the latter case, this now classic study of marital interaction, showed that older adults expressed less anger, belligerence, humor, disgust, and interest, but more affection during discussions of problem areas in the marriage. Other research has suggested that expressivity may be greater and more "on target" in later life (Malatesta-Magai, Jonas, Shepard, & Culve, 1992; Moreno, Borod, Welkowitz, & Alpert, 1990), and that it may be retained even during cognitive decline (Magai, Cohen, Gomberg, Malatesta, & Culver, 1996). Finally, there may be additional changes in expression other than total expressivity. One early study found fewer, but greater numbers of, component muscle movements in the facial expressions of middle-aged and older versus younger women (Malatesta & Izard, 1984). Overall, however, conclusive evidence in this area remains elusive. Although later-life expressions of emotion appear more complex and more difficult for naive raters, especially younger raters, to interpret, the available literature does not suggest that older adults are any less expressive, at least once aroused.

Emotion Physiology

Given that the emotion system is grounded in basic neurophysiologic processes that, in general, decline in later life (Cacioppo, Berntson, Klein, & Poehlmann, 1998; Kupperbusch, Kunzmann, & Levenson, 2001), examination of possible developmental changes in emotion physiology has increased in recent years. In general, findings across a variety of study methods have suggested that the arousal associated with emotion declines in later life. Reduced *cardiovascular arousal* among older adults has been shown in response to directed facial tasks where participants voluntarily generate emotional faces (Levenson, Carstensen, Friesen, & Ekman, 1991; Levenson, Ekman, & Friesen, 1990), during marital interactions (Levenson, Carstensen, & Gottman, 1994), during sad and amusing video clips (Tsai, Carstensen, & Levenson, 2000) and during relived experiences (Labouvie-Vief, Lumley, Jain, & Heinze, 2003). The recent study by Labouvie-Vief and colleagues, for example, found lower heart rate reactivity among older adults for anger, fear, sadness, and happiness. However, this study also found that gender interacted with age, such that while younger women had higher heart rate reactivity for anger and fear inductions, there were no gender differences in the older group. There is some suggestion that later-life changes in emotion physiology may vary depending on the emotion being considered, the physiological index employed, and the means by which the emotion is induced.

Emotions and Cognitive Processing

The notion that emotions are somehow more salient or are differentially preserved in later life has found considerable support in data describing emotion recognition, cognitive processing, and neurology. Despite likely declines in global cognitive ability in later life, there appear few global differences in emotion recognition (Moreno, Borod, Welkowitz, & Alpert, 1993). Intriguingly, however, recent data seem to suggest differences at the level of discrete emotions (Mather & Johnson, 2000), with studies suggesting that older adults may be less accurate in recognizing negative emotions including sadness, anger, and fear (Mather & Johnson, 2000; McDowell, Harrison, & Demaree, 1994; Phillips, MacPherson, & Sala, 2002), but either more accurate (Mather & Johnson, 2000) or no different for happiness (McDowell, Harrison, & Demaree, 1994); a similar pattern of accuracy/error is evident in studies of body movements and gestures (Montepare, Koff, Zaitchik, & Albert, 1999).

This data is consistent with neurological data suggesting that the brain regions responsible for emotions and social judgment are differentially preserved. More specifically, functions associated with dorsolateral regions (executive functioning and working memory) appear the most impaired with age, while orbitoventral functions (processing of emotions and regulation of social behavior) are differentially preserved (Phillips, MacLean, & Allen, 2002; Phillips, MacPherson, & Sala, 2002). One recent study examined age differences in the brain regions that were active during the processing of emotional faces (Gunning-Dixon, Gur, Perkins, Schroeder, Turner, Turetsky, et al., 2003). These authors found that visual, frontal, and limbic regions were differentially active in younger participants, while parietal, temporal, and frontal regions were more active in older participants. It is not yet clear what implications such differences may hold for our understanding of emotions and aging.

However, the cognitive processing of older adults seems to preferentially rely on, and be more permeable or sensitive to, emotional information. Adults in later life endorse more emotion-based, rather than problem-focused, coping styles when dealing with emotionally salient problems (Blanchard-Fields, Camp, & Jahnke, 1995). They show superior incidental memory for emotional content in narratives (Carstensen & Charles, 1994), preferentially reconstruct verbal information to "match" conflicting nonverbal (emotional) cues (Thompson, Aidinejad, & Ponte, 2001), and weight emotional information more heavily in representations of social partners (Carstensen & Fredrickson, 1998). Later life adults are also more strongly influenced by induced moods when problem-solving (Knight, Maines, & Robinson, 2002). Finally, there has been some suggestion that the importance of emotion in later life may be particularly evident in studies of positive emotion. It has been shown that older adults have an attentional bias in favor of positive versus sad or angry faces (Mather & Carstensen, 2003), and that the amygdala is differentially active in response to positive stimuli in older adults (Mather, Canli, English, Whitfield, Wais, Ochsner, et al., 2004). It is however, currently unclear whether this pattern represents developmental/cohort differences in cognitive abilities or alterations in motivation.

Emotion Regulation

Taken collectively, the above literature directly challenges, if not contradicts, the notion of decline in emotional functioning in later life, and the small body of available evidence also suggests that emotion regulation may be differentially preserved. Adults in later life report greater ability to control the internal experience of emotion (Gross, Carstensen, Pasupathi, Tsai, Goetestam-Skorpen, Hsu, et al., 1997). Studies have shown that aggressive, impulsive, and inhibition control increases with age (McConatha & Huba, 1999), as does the preference for, and ability to, *avoid conflict* and delay expression (Diehl, Coyle, & Labouvie-Vief, 1996). Adults in later life seem to use a wider range of coping and defense strategies and are more likely to positively reappraise or re-evaluate situations (Gross, 2001).

Improvements in emotion regulation appear particularly salient in 2 areas. First, it seems as if changes are primarily "aimed" at preventing the negative social effects of unrestrained expressions of negative emotion. The studies of marital interaction described earlier showed that older married couples were less likely to engage in "negative start-up" (an interaction sequence in which neutral affect on the part of one spouse was followed by negativity in the other) and more likely to de-escalate interactions by following negative expressions with neutral ones (Carstensen, Gottman, & Levenson 1995; Levenson, Carstensen, & Gottman, 1994). According to these authors, older couples appear to have learned to exert a degree of control over negative sequences in their interactions. More globally, Carstensen has suggested that the well-documented narrowing of social networks in later life is an adaptive development that later life adults use to regulate emotions. Indeed, older people indicate that they restrict their social contacts to those that are the most emotionally rewarding. Second, older adults seem to differentially employ regulatory strategies that prevent *negative emotions* from arising in the first place. Although more data are needed, later-life adults appear to seek out the kinds of environments and persons that allow them to avoid negative affect and conflict (Carstensen, Fung, & Charles, 2003), an emotion regulatory strategy referred to as situational selection.

Summary

Although later life has historically been viewed as a time in which individuals managed a series of losses and degradations in functioning, a growing body of empirical research suggests that the domain of emotion functioning is differentially preserved. Although our ability to infer generalized developmental trends from the extant literature is hampered by a preponderance of cross-sectional and non-experimental studies, they certainly offer grounds for encouragement. Indeed, most facets of emotion functioning—including experience, expression, and recognition—appear well-preserved into later life, and some aspects appear to undergo improvement. Although longitudinal designs are needed to eliminate the possibility of cohort effects and the reasons for change remain unclear at present, emotions remain central to the lives of individuals across the life span.

CAROL MAGAI
NATHAN S. CONSEDINE

See also
Depression

References

Birditt, K., & Fingerman, K. L. (2003). Age and gender differences in adults' descriptions of emotional reactions to interpersonal problems. *Journal of Gerontology Series B: Psychological Sciences, 58B,* 237–245.

Blanchard-Fields, F., Camp, C., & Jahnke, H. C. (1995). Age differences in problem-solving style: The role of emotional salience. *Psychology and Aging, 10,* 173–180.

Borod, J., Yecker, S., Brickman, A., Moreno, C., Sliwinski, M., Foldi, N., et al. (2004). Changes in posed facial expression of emotion across the adult life span. *Experimental Aging Research, 30,* 305–331.

Cacioppo, J. T., Berntson, G. G., Klein, D., & Poehlmann, K. M. (1998). Psychophysiology of emotion across the life span. In K. W. Schaie & M. P. Lawton (Eds.), *Annual review of gerontology and geriatrics: Vol. 17. Focus on emotion and adult development* (pp. 27–74). New York: Springer Publishing.

Carstensen, L. L., & Charles, S. T. (1994). The salience of emotion across the adult life span. *Psychology and Aging, 9,* 259–264.

Carstensen, L. L., & Fredrickson, B. L. (1998). Influence of HIV status and age on cognitive representations of others. *Health Psychology, 17,* 494–503.

Carstensen, L. L., Fung, H., & Charles, S. T. (2003). Socioemotional selectivity theory and the regulation of emotion in the second half of life. *Motivation and Emotion, 27,* 103–123.

Carstensen, L. L., Gottman, J. M., & Levenson, R. W. (1995). Emotional behavior in long-term marriage. *Psychology and Aging, 10,* 140–149.

Carstensen, L. L., & Löckenhoff, C. E. (2003). Aging, emotion, and evolution: The bigger picture. *Proceedings of the National Academy of Sciences, 1000,* 152–179.

Carstensen, L. L., Mayr, U., Pasupathi, M., & Nesselroade, J. R. (2000). Emotional experience in everyday life across the adult life span. *Journal of Personality and Social Psychology, 79,* 644–655.

Charles, S. T., Reynolds, C., & Gatz, M. (2001). Age-related differences and change in positive and negative affect over 23 years. *Journal of Personality and Social Psychology, 80,* 136–151.

Consedine, N. S., & Magai, C. (in press). Emotion development in adulthood: A developmental functionalist review and critique. In C. Hoare (Ed.), *The Oxford handbook of adult development and learning*. Oxford: Oxford University Press.

Consedine, N. S, Magai, C., & King, (2004). Deconstructing positive affect in later life: A differential functionalist analysis of joy and interest. *International Journal of Aging and Human Development, 58,* 49–68.

Diehl, M., Coyle, N., & Labouvie-Vief, G. (1996). Age and sex differences in strategies of coping and defense across the life span. *Psychology and Aging, 11,* 127–139.

Diener, E., & Suh, E. (1997). Measuring quality of life: Economic, social, and subjective indicators. *Social Indicators Research, 40,* 189–216.

Gross, J. J. (2001). Emotion regulation in adulthood: Timing is everything. *Current Directions in Psychological Science, 10,* 214–219.

Gross, J. J., Carstensen, L. L., Pasupathi, M., Tsai, J., Goetestam-Skorpen, C. G., & Hsu, Y. C. (1997). Emotion and aging: Experience, expression, and control. *Psychology and Aging, 12,* 590–599.

Gunning-Dixon, F. M., Gur, R. C., Perkins, C., Schroeder, L., Turner, T., Turetsky, B., et al. (2003). Aged-related differences in brain activation during emotional face processing. *Neurobiology of Aging, 24,* 285–295.

Knight, B. G., Maines, M. L., & Robinson, G. S. (2002). The effects of sad mood on memory in older adults: A test of the mood congruence effect. *Psychology and Aging, 17,* 653–661.

Kunzmann, U., Little, T. D., & Smith, J. (2000). Is age-related stability of subjective well-being a paradox? Cross-sectional and longitudinal evidence from the Berlin Aging Study. *Psychology and Aging, 15,* 511–526.

Kupperbusch, C., Kunzmann, U., & Levenson, R. W. (2001). *The diminution of autonomic activation with age: General or specific to emotion?* Paper presented at the 41st Annual Meeting of the Society for Psychophysiological Research, Quebec.

Labouvie-Vief, G., Chiodo, L. M., Goguen, L., Diehl, M., & Orwoll, L. (1995). Representations of self across the life span. *Psychology and Aging, 10,* 404–415.

Labouvie-Vief, G., & Diehl, M. (2000). Cognitive complexity and cognitive-affective integration: Related or separate domains of adult development? *Psychology and Aging, 15,* 490–504.

Labouvie-Vief, G., Lumley, M., Jain, E., & Heinze, H. (2003). Age and gender differences in cardiac reactivity and subjective emotion responses to emotional autobiographical memories. *Emotion, 3,* 115–126.

Labouvie-Vief, G., & Medler, M. (2002). Affect optimization and affect complexity: Modes and styles of regulation in adulthood. *Psychology and Aging, 17,* 571–588.

Levenson, R. W., Carstensen, L. L., Friesen, W. V., & Ekman, P. (1991). Emotion, physiology, and expression in old age. *Psychology and Aging, 6,* 28–35.

Levenson, R. W., Carstensen, L. L., & Gottman, J. M. (1994). The influence of age and gender on affect, physiology, and their interrelations: A study of long-term marriages. *Journal of Personality and Social Psychology, 67,* 56–68.

Levenson, R. W., Ekman, P., & Friesen, W. V. (1990). Voluntary facial action generates emotion specific autonomic nervous system activity. *Psychophysiology, 27,* 397–405.

Magai, C., Cohen, C., Gomberg, D., Malatesta, C., & Culver, C. (1996). Emotional expression during mid- to late-stage dementia. *International Psychogeriatrics, 8,* 383–395.

Malatesta, C. Z., & Izard, C. E. (1984). Facial expression of emotion in young, middle-aged, and older adults. In C. Malatesta & C. E. Izard (Eds.), Emotion and adult development. *Beverly Hills: Sage Publications.*

Malatesta-Magai, C., Jonas, R., Shepard, B., & Culver, C. (1992). Type A personality and emotional expressivity in younger and older adults. *Psychology and Aging, 7,* 551–561.

Mather, M., Canli, T., English, T., Whitfield, S., Wais, P., Ochsner, K., et al. (2004). Amygdala responses to emotionally valenced stimuli in older and younger adults. *Psychological Science, 15,* 259–263.

Mather, M., & Carstensen, L. L. (2003). Aging and attentional biases for emotional faces. *Psychological Science, 14,* 409–415.

Mather, M., & Johnson, M. K. (2000). Choice-supportive source monitoring: Do our decisions seem better to us as we age? *Psychology and Aging, 15,* 596–606.

McConatha, J. T., & Huba, H. M. (1999). Primary, secondary, and emotional control across adulthood. *Current Psychology: Developmental, Learning, Personality, Social, 18,* 164–170.

McDowell, C. L., Harrison, D. W., & Demaree, H. (1994). Is the right hemisphere decline in the perception of emotion a function of aging? *International Journal of Neuroscience, 79,* 1–11.

Montepare, J., Koff, E., Zaitchik, D., & Albert, M. (1999). The use of body movements and gestures as cues to emotions in younger and older adults. *Journal of Nonverbal Behavior, 23,* 133–152.

Moreno, C., Borod, J. C., Welkowitz, J., & Alpert, M. (1990). Lateralization for the expression and perception of facial emotion as a function of age. *Neuropsychologia, 28,* 199–209.

Moreno, C., Borod, J. C., Welkowitz, J., & Alpert, M. (1993). The perception of facial emotion across the adult life span. *Developmental Neuropsychology, 9,* 305–314.

Mroczek, D. K. (2001). Age and emotion in adulthood. *Current Directions in Psychological Science, 10,* 87–90.

Mroczek, D. K., & Kolarz, C. (1998). The effect of age on positive and negative affect: A developmental perspective on happiness. *Journal of Personality and Social Psychology, 75,* 1333–1349.

Mroczek, D. K., & Spiro, A. (2003). Modeling intra-individual change in personality traits: Findings from the Normative Aging Study. *Journal of Gerontology: Psychological Sciences, 58B,* 153–165.

Ong, A., & Bergman, C. (2004). The complexity of emotions in later life. *Journals of Gerontology: Psychological Sciences, 59B,* P117–P122.

Phillips, L. H., MacLean, R. D. J., & Allen, R. (2002). Age and the understanding of emotions: Neuropsychological and sociocognitive perspectives. *Journal of Gerontology: Psychological Sciences, 57B,* 526–530.

Phillips, L., MacPherson, S., & Sala, S. (2002). Age, cognition, and emotion: The role of anatomical segregation in the frontal lobes. In J. Grafman (Ed.), *Handbook of neuropsychology, 2nd ed.* (Vol. 7, pp. 73–97): Elsevier Science B.V.

Schieman, S. (1999). Age and anger. *Journal of Health and Social Behavior, 40,* 273–289.

Smith, J., Fleeson, W., Geiselmann, B., Settersten, R., & Kunzmann, U. (1999). Sources of well-being in very old age. In P. B. Baltes & K. U. Mayer (Eds.), *The Berlin Aging Study: Aging from 80–100* (pp. 450–471): Cambridge: Cambridge University Press.

Thompson, L., Aidinejad, M. R., & Ponte, J. (2001). Aging and the effects of facial and prosodic cues on emotional intensity ratings and memory reconstructions. *Journal of Nonverbal Behavior, 25,* 101–125.

Tsai, J., Carstensen, L. L., & Levenson, R. W. (2000). Automatic, subjective, and expressive responses to emotional films in older and younger Chinese Americans and European Americans. *Psychology and Aging, 15,* 684–693.

EMPLOYEE RETIREMENT INCOME SECURITY ACT

The Employee Retirement Income Security Act (*ERISA*), signed by President Gerald Ford on Labor Day in 1974, was acclaimed as the most important *pension legislation* since the Social Security Act of 1935. ERISA was enacted to standardize participation and eligibility criteria to all nongovernmental pensions and to secure adequate funding of pension plans by redefining them as corporate liabilities. At its enactment, it covered all plans in existence provided by companies engaged in interstate commerce and set minimum standards for all future plans. It does not apply to government pensions.

The private pension system in the United States had been in existence, and steadily growing, for approximately 100 years by 1974. However, the system was not regulated. Consequently, participation and eligibility standards varied considerably from plan to plan, and corporate fiduciary responsibility for adequate and competent management was not mandated. ERISA and its subsequent amendments have been relatively successful in correcting many earlier abuses.

Major Provisions of ERISA

The major provisions of ERISA, also known as *Public Law 93-406*, fall under 4 titles. Title I lays down both general and regulatory provisions for the protection of employee benefit rights. These provisions cover reporting and disclosure, participation and vesting, funding, fiduciary responsibility, and administration and enforcement. Title II amends the Internal Revenue Code of 1954 relating to pension plans to regulate payroll accounting. Title III addresses general jurisdiction, administration, and enforcement of the law by explicitly coordinating the secretary of the treasury and the Department of Labor through the Joint Pension Task Force. *Title IV* provides for plan termination insurance with the establishment of the *Pension Benefit Guaranty Corporation* (PBGC) and with the definition of liability criteria in the case of plan termination.

Important among the most recent laws enacting or amending the 1974 provisions of ERISA are the *Retirement Equity Act* of 1984, the *Pension Protection Act* of 1987, and the 1990 amendment of Title I of ERISA to require qualifying employer securities to include interest in publicly traded partnerships. Several revisions of Title II have followed tax reform, revenue, and omnibus budget enactments.

PBGC, established by *Title IV of ERISA*, is a self-financing, government-owned corporation whose purpose is to guarantee basic pension benefits in covered private plans if they terminate with insufficient funds. Two benefit insurance programs are administered for single-employer and multi-employer plans, respectively. All defined benefit plans (i.e., pensions plans with fixed benefits established in advance of retirement) must pay prescribed premiums to PBGC per plan participation. Multi-employer plans can be insured for insolvency instead of termination to assist them when they are unable to pay basic benefits; however, these plans are obligated to repay. Workers whose pensions are guaranteed by the PBGC are protected up to a limit of under $3,000 per month (adjusted annually for inflation). By the mid-1980s, debates had developed over the growing deficit of the PBGC. Part of the *Consolidated Omnibus Budget Reconciliation Act* of 1987 (*COBRA*) amended ERISA by requiring tougher minimum funding standards and establishing stricter upper limits on tax-deductible contributions to defined benefit plans.

However, in the last decade the PBGC has faced a steadily worsening situation as an unsteady economy, low stock market returns, and low interest rates have persisted. Due to these trends and to PBGC premiums that did not reflect market risks, underfunded and unfunded plans have become widespread, particularly in certain industries (e.g., airlines) (Boyce & Ippolito, 2002).

Other retirement savings strategies, such as *individual retirement accounts* (*IRAs*), defined contribution plans (including *401K*), and *employment stock ownership plans* (*ESOPs*), are not covered by the PBGC. These alternative savings strategies have grown steadily since the passage of ERISA, and especially since the early 1980s. Investments in defined contribution plans have exceeded those in defined benefit plans covered by ERISA; by 2000, 7 of every 10 participants and more than 80% of pension contributions were to defined contribution or 401K plans (Munnell & Sunden, 2004). An important implication of these trends is the increased vulnerability of women workers in achieving pension savings, since women participate disproportionately in retirement savings strategies not protected by ERISA. The cash-out and portability features of these new pensions make them attractive and useful in the short-term for managing expected and unexpected financial needs (home-buying, college tuition, hospitalization costs, etc.).

Finally, a number of amendments to ERISA have been directed to expanding health benefit protections. COBRA provides for some workers (and their families) to continue health coverage for a limited period following job loss. Another amendment, the *Health Insurance Portability and Accountability Act* (*HIPAA*), added protection for workers and their families with preexisting medical conditions that might otherwise disqualify them from *health insurance* coverage (see the U.S. Department of Labor Web site at www.dol.gov/dol/topic/health-plans/erisa.htm for more information).

ANGELA M. O'RAND

See also
Pensions: History
Retirement Income and Pensions

References

Boyce, S., & Ippolito, R. A. (2002). The cost of pension insurance. *Journal of Risk and Insurance*, *69*, 121–170.

Munnell, A. H., & Sunden, A. (2004). Coming up short: *The challenge of 401k plans*. Washington, DC: Brookings Institution.

EMPLOYMENT

The *Older Labor Force*

Employment in what has conventionally been regarded as old age remains the exception among both men and women in the United States. As of 2004, only 5 million of the more than 34.6 million noninstitutionalized persons aged 65 and older, or 14.4% of the total, were working or looking for work (U.S. Bureau of Labor Statistics, 2005). Not surprisingly, older men are more likely than older women to be in the labor force—19% and 11.1%, respectively, among those aged 65 and older in 2004. Somewhat higher proportions have some paid work experience over the course of a year, but for the majority of older men and women, participation in the formal labor force is an activity of the past. However, this may be changing.

Few labor force developments of the postwar era have been as pronounced as the labor force withdrawal of men aged 65 and older, 45.8% of whom were in the labor force in 1950 (Table 1). Eligibility for Social Security retired worker benefits as early as age 62 and the availability of private pension benefits at even younger ages have contributed to a decline in labor force participation rates among younger workers as well. Men between the ages of 55 and 64, for example, had a labor force participation rate of 68.7% in 2004, down from 86.9% in 1950.

The picture is demonstrably different for middle-aged women, millions of whom have accompanied their younger counterparts into the labor force over the past 5 decades. In 2004, the labor force participation rate of 55- to 64-year-old women stood at 56.3%, up sharply from 27% in 1950. Far less change has occurred among women aged 65 or older, whose attachment to the labor force has historically been weak; their 2004 labor force participation rate of 11.1% was not much above the 9.7% of 1950.

The steady march of middle-aged women into the labor force has not been enough to offset the withdrawal of men, with the result that there are relatively fewer middle-aged and older labor force participants today than in 1950. For example, nearly 43% of the 55-plus population were working or looking for work in 1950; by 2004, that was the case for only 36.2%. The divergent trends for men and women have markedly altered the gender composition of the older workforce (persons aged 55 or older). Women currently comprise just over 46% of that older labor force, in contrast to about 23% in 1950.

The trends of the past half-century appear to be changing, at least for men. By the mid-1980s, the decline in their labor force participation had begun to taper off; for some age groups within the 55-plus population, attachment to the labor force has increased, in some cases quite sharply. Among men aged 65 to 69 years, for instance, the labor force participation rate rose by almost 6 percentage points between 1994 and 2004. While it is still premature

TABLE 1 Labor Force Participation Rates for Older Men and Women, 1950–2004 (in percentages)

Year	Ages 55–64 Men	Ages 55–64 Women	Ages 65+ Men	Ages 65+ Women
1950	86.9	27.0	45.8	9.7
1955	87.9	32.5	39.6	10.6
1960	86.8	37.2	33.1	10.8
1965	84.6	41.1	27.9	10.0
1970	83.0	43.0	26.8	9.7
1975	75.6	40.9	21.6	8.2
1980	72.1	41.3	19.0	8.1
1985	67.9	42.0	15.8	7.3
1990	67.7	45.3	16.4	8.7
1995	66.0	49.2	16.8	8.8
2000	67.3	51.8	17.5	9.4
2001	68.1	53.0	17.7	9.7
2002	69.2	55.1	17.8	9.9
2003	68.7	56.6	18.6	10.6
2004	68.7	56.3	19.0	11.1

Source: U.S. Bureau of Labor Statistics, *Handbook of Labor Statistics*, June 1985; U.S. Bureau of Labor Statistics, *Employment and Earnings*, January 1986, 1991, 1996, 2001, 2002, 2003, 2004, 2005.

to conclude that these increases herald a reversal of early retirement trends—most people continue to retire before the age of eligibility for full *Social Security* retired worker benefits—a shift toward more work at upper ages appears to be underway.

Official Projections and Worker Expectations

Recent projections from the U.S. Bureau of Labor Statistics point to continued increases in the *labor force participation of older persons* in the United States (Toossi, 2004). Nearly 40% of persons aged 55 and older are expected to be in the labor force in 2012, an increase of 3.5 percentage points over the rate for 2004. Within the 55-plus population, the annual growth rate in participation is projected to be somewhat greater for those aged 65 to 74 than for other age groups. It is also projected to be substantially greater among older women than among older men. Should these projections prove close to the mark, the ratio of male to female participation rates in the 55-plus population will stand at 75% in 2012, up from just under 28% in 1950 and 66% as recently as 2000.

Official projections may underestimate the number of older persons who will remain at work in their later years for several reasons, including: the meager savings on the part of many workers nearing retirement age; little or no anticipated income from private pensions for a sizable percentage of workers; the shift from defined benefit pension plan coverage to age-neutral defined contribution plans, under which workers rather than employers bear the investment risk; employer cutbacks in retiree health benefits, which may mean a lack of health care coverage for workers not yet eligible for Medicare; and the gradual increase from 65 to 67 in the age of eligibility for full Social Security benefits, often referred to as the full or normal retirement age. Workers will still be able to collect benefits at age 62 as the age of eligibility for full benefits rises, but the early benefits will be lower than they were when the full retirement age was 65. A growing proportion of workers may find themselves financially unprepared for retirement at the young ages many in their parents' generation retired. Staying at work longer can significantly enhance ultimate retirement security (U.S. Congressional Budget Office, 2004a).

In addition, increased life expectancy, improved health status, higher educational attainment on the part of older workers, and a decline in the share of jobs that are physically demanding may encourage more older workers to postpone retirement, make older workers more attractive to employers, and make work itself more appealing to older workers. The annual growth rate of the 55-and-older population will be substantially greater than that of younger age groups. This development, along with the impending retirement of the *baby boomers* (born from 1946–1964), may result in labor and skill shortages that further encourage employers to expand employment opportunities for older workers.

Expectations of Work and Retirement

The majority of workers plan to work in retirement. For example, in a 2002 national survey 69% of workers aged 45 to 74 years reported that they expect to work in some capacity in retirement (AARP, 2002). A year later, 68% of workers aged 50 to 70 contended that working or never retiring best represented what they expect to do in retirement (AARP, 2003). Almost 80% of baby boomers surveyed the same year said they expect to work at least part-time in retirement, virtually the same percentage as 5 years earlier (AARP, 2004).

Pre-retirees expect to work in retirement for a variety of reasons: they are interested in or enjoy what they are doing, want to do something productive, wish to remain active, or need the income (AARP, 2002; 2003). Yet when asked for the 1 major factor in their decision to work in retirement, the need for money tops the list, followed by the need for health benefits (AARP, 2003). Retirees who continue to work also cite a variety of nonfinancial reasons as factors, but money again eclipses all other reasons as the major factor in the decision to work (AARP, 2003).

Financial need, coupled with a desire to remain active and productive, may indeed keep older workers on the job longer, but remaining at work may not be as easy as it sounds. Today's workers plan on remaining at work considerably longer than today's retirees actually worked. The 14th Annual *Retirement Confidence Survey* found that the average non-retiree plans on retiring at age 65; the average retiree retired at 62 (Helman, Greenwald & Associates, & Paladino, 2004). Baby boomers say they expect to retire at 65.5, on average, later than they did in 1998 (AARP, 2004). Nonetheless, while over one-third of baby boomers declare that they will never want to retire, more than two-fifths cannot wait to do so (AARP, 2004).

Health problems, job loss, and family caregiving responsibilities may propel workers out of the labor force before they would like, or might be ready, to leave. In 2004, the Congressional Budget Office reported that many baby boomers are not waiting until age 65, or even 62, to stop working; more than 4 million of them (the oldest of whom was only 58 in 2004) have already left the labor force, most frequently because they are disabled. The Congressional Budget Office report observes that if the baby boomers "follow in the footsteps of workers now in their early 60s, perhaps one-third of the men and nearly half of the women will be out of the labor force before their 62nd birthday."

Once workers begin collecting pension benefits, they are unlikely to remain at work. Among recipients of employer pensions or retirement savings plans, only about 11% to 12% of men and 6% to 8% of women aged 65 and older were employed from 1994 to 2003 (Purcell, 2004). Employment rates were higher for pension recipients aged 55 to 64, but even in this age group, the majority of pension recipients were no longer working—61% of men and 67% of women in 2003, percentages that fluctuated slightly between 1994 and 2003 (Purcell, 2004).

Once out of the labor force, older workers express little interest in paid employment. Barely more than 2% of 40.5 million persons aged 55 and older who were not in the labor force in 2004 said that they wanted to work, and few of them officially qualify as discouraged workers, i.e., they are not looking for work because they fear employers would find them too old, or they lack the necessary training or schooling (U.S. Bureau of Labor Statistics, 2005). If attractive employment options were available, or if older workers did not face barriers such as age discrimination in their search for employment, more nonworking men and women might convey interest in employment. If more appealing options to continue working but at reduced work hours were also available, greater numbers of older workers might be inclined to push back the date of full retirement.

Patterns and Type of Employment

Most older workers—more than 7 out of 10—work full-time, although *part-time employment* rises with age. About 1 in 6 workers between the ages 55 to 64, but 1 in 2 aged 65 and older, work part-time (U.S. Bureau of Labor Statistics, unpublished data). The large majority of older part-time workers are employed part-time by choice; few part-time workers prefer but have been unable to find full-time employment. Whether more workers would remain at work if they could reduce their work hours is not known for certain, but the data suggest they would. About half of older workers with retirement plans express a desire to scale back their work hours or otherwise change the type of work they do before or instead of fully retiring; however, those who actually manage to do this are in the minority (Abraham & Houseman, 2004). Few older workers plan on working full-time in retirement (AARP, 2003; 2004).

Apparently older workers would like to phase into retirement by cutting back the hours they work at their current jobs. Nearly two-thirds of workers aged 50 to 70 hope for reduced work hours or more flexible schedules prior to full retirement, and one-third say they would work longer than planned if a phased retirement arrangement were available (Watson Wyatt Worldwide, 2004). Many workers transition into retirement via full- or part-time bridge jobs following long-term or career employment (Quinn, 1999), and many cushion the retirement shock as rehired retirees or temporary workers; nonetheless, formal phased retirement programs are rare (Hutchens & Papps, 2004).

Bridge work and *phased retirement* may also come in the form of *self-employment*. Although the large majority of older workers, like their younger counterparts, are wage and salary workers, self-employment rates rise with age. This is partly because the self-employed typically work later in life than wage and salary workers (Quinn, 1998) and partly because some older workers move into self-employment after retiring from wage and salary jobs. About 1 in 3 self-employed workers between the ages of 51 and 69 years became self-employed at or after age 50, often as part of the transition to retirement (Karoly & Zissimopoulos, 2004).

Middle-aged and older workers can be found in virtually every industry, although *agriculture* is the only one in which older workers stand out: workers aged 65 and older are 2 to 3 times as likely as workers in other age groups to be in agriculture. Even so, only about 1 in 14 is an agricultural worker. Four out of every 10 middle-aged and older workers are employed in the *services industry*. Two industries—services and trade—claim about 6 in 10 workers in all age groups older than 20. Compared to middle-aged and prime-aged workers, workers aged 65 and older are somewhat more likely to be in the *retail trade*, perhaps because of the availability of part-time work in this industry.

When it comes to industry, gender differences are more apparent than age differences. Service industries employ more than half of middle-aged and older women, for example, but only about one-third of their male counterparts. Middle-aged and older men, in contrast, are considerably more likely to be in manufacturing, construction, transportation, communication, and public utilities.

Occupational differences by age also are relatively minor, at least after the mid-20s. Workers aged 65 and older are somewhat more likely than all but the youngest to be in sales or farming, forestry, and fishing. Few older workers are in technical support occupations, but that is the case for workers of all ages.

Gender differences in occupational distribution are again more striking than age differences: women, including those who are middle-aged and older, are about 4 to 5 times as likely as older men to have administrative support jobs.

Unemployment

The labor force consists of persons who are employed or who are without a job but are available and have recently looked for work. If they are in the labor force, almost all older persons have jobs. *Unemployment rates* tend to fall with age, in part because access to retirement benefits gives many older workers the option of leaving the labor force if they do lose their jobs. Workers who withdraw from the labor force are not counted among the unemployed, even if they would prefer to be working. Persons aged 55 and older had an average unemployment rate of 3.7 in 2004 versus 5.9% for those under age 55.

Of all workers who were displaced from their jobs between January 2001 and December 2003, older workers were far less likely than their younger counterparts to be reemployed by January 2004, and far more likely to be out of the labor force. Among displaced workers aged 55 to 64, for example, 57% were reemployed and 20% were no longer in the labor force; this compares to a reemployment rate of 69% for displaced workers aged 25 to 54, just 11% of whom were out of the labor force. Among displaced workers aged 65 or older, only 25% were reemployed and over 60% had left the labor force (U.S. Bureau of Labor Statistics, 2004).

Lower unemployment rates obscure the formidable barriers that older persons face if they decide to undertake a job search. A number of factors, not the least of which is *age discrimination*, contribute to the difficulties older jobseekers experience when looking for work. As a result, average duration of unemployment remains substantially longer for older unemployed job seekers, and older jobseekers are more likely than younger ones to find themselves among the long-term unemployed (U.S. Bureau of Labor Statistics, 2005).

Public Policy and Older Workers

Older workers and the *aging workforce* do not yet feature prominently on the nation's public policy agenda. Some of the most significant policy initiatives designed to foster longer work lives, in large part to alleviate projected public costs of supporting an aging population, were enacted in 1983. These amendments to the *Social Security Act* gradually increased the age of eligibility for full Social Security benefits from 65 to 67, beginning with workers turning age 62 in 2000. They also increased the Social Security retired worker benefit for each year that workers delay collecting benefits after the full retirement age but before age 70.

Since reduced Social Security benefits first became available (in 1956 for women, and in 1961 for men), workers have availed themselves of the opportunity to collect those benefits before the full retirement age. In recent years, about half of workers have been awarded retired worker benefits at age 62 (Social Security Administration, 2004). Until 2000, employed Social Security beneficiaries under age 70 were subject to a retirement earnings test that many viewed as a work disincentive. The *Senior Citizens' Freedom to Work Act of 2000* eliminated this test for beneficiaries who remain at work at or after the full retirement age up to age 70. (The test remains in effect for workers between the ages of 62 and the full retirement age; these workers lose $1 in benefits for every $2 in earnings above the limit, set at $12,000 for 2005.) While elimination of this test for workers above the full retirement age appears to have resulted in substantial earnings increases among higher earners, it does not yet seem to have had much impact on the employment of older persons (Song, 2003/2004).

Age-based discrimination against older workers and jobseekers aged 40 years and older has been illegal under the provisions of the *Age Discrimination in Employment Act* (ADEA) of 1967 and its subsequent amendments. Most occupations saw the end of mandatory retirement with the ADEA amendments of 1986.

Discrimination against older workers remains a problem, although its incidence cannot be ascertained with any precision. About two-thirds of older workers report that they have "personally witnessed or experienced *age discrimination on the job*;" still, over three-fourths believe that their age causes their employers to treat them no differently than other workers (AARP, 2002).

There are few public sector employment or training programs aimed specifically at older workers. The major public vehicle for job training in the United States is the *Workforce Investment Act* (WIA) of 1998, the successor to the *Job Training Partnership Act* (JTPA). While WIA provides a variety of services at one-stop employment centers to youth, adults, and dislocated workers, it eliminated a requirement in the JTPA to reserve monies specifically for older workers, and most states no longer fund programs targeted at older age groups.

Funded under *Title V* of the *Older Americans Act*, the *Senior Community Service Employment Program* (SCSEP) provides subsidized *minimum-wage employment* to *low-income elderly*, many of whom are women and/or minorities. This relatively small program ($439 million in fiscal year 2004) is designed to assist a group of disadvantaged jobseekers.

The future is likely to see renewed interest in public policies for older workers. Given workers' stated enthusiasm for phased retirement, efforts will likely be made to eliminate some of the legal impediments to formal phased retirement. These include, for example, the fact that employers have been barred under the *Employee Retirement Income Security Act* (*ERISA*) from making in-service distributions from a defined benefit pension plan to workers who have not reached the plan's normal retirement age (typically age 65). Workers who might want to reduce their work hours prior to that age have been unable to supplement their reduced wages with partial pension benefits. If made final, proposed regulations on phased retirement (distributed for comment by the Internal Revenue Service in late 2004) would eliminate some of the restrictions on phased retirement programs.

Given the increases in life expectancy, proposals to further raise the Social Security retirement age or to index it to life expectancy can be expected.

Private-Sector Policies and the Older Worker

There remains scant evidence that private-sector employers are actively responding to the aging of the workforce with programs or policies that might keep older workers employed or employable. Most employers are cognizant of the aging workforce but have done little about it, in part because according to the U.S. Government Accountability Office (formerly known as the General Accounting Office), they "simply [have] not considered" doing so (U.S. General Accounting Office, 2001). The real labor crunch will not materialize until baby boomers begin reaching conventional retirement age, and not everyone is convinced that the United States will experience *labor shortages* (Cappelli, 2003). Without such shortages, employers have few incentives to develop and/or implement older worker policies and programs.

Furthermore, employers are concerned about the cost of older workers—their performance, technological competence, and ability to learn new technology. Some employer concerns, as the National Research Council and Institute on Medicine observe, "are better grounded in evidence" than others and do "pose substantial challenges" for employers as well as for older workers and the nation (Wegman & McGee, 2004). Additional research is needed to better understand the public and private sector policies and investments that would best promote the healthy, safe, and productive employment of older workers.

Although private-sector programs and policies specifically designed to hire, retain, train, or retrain older workers tend to be few and far between, isolated good company practices can be found and may be on the increase. If employers face labor and skills shortages, they are likely to offer the types of work incentives—such as flexible work schedules and phased retirement—that older workers say they want.

Sara E. Rix

The views expressed in this article are those of the author and do not necessarily represent the official policy of AARP.

See also
Economics

References

AARP. (2002). *Staying ahead of the curve: The AARP Work and Career Study*. Washington, DC: AARP.

AARP. (2003). *Staying ahead of the curve 2003: The AARP working in retirement study*. Washington, DC: AARP.

AARP. (2004). *Baby boomers envision retirement II*. Washington, DC: AARP.

Abraham, K. G., & Houseman, S. N. (2004). *Work and retirement plans among older Americans*. Upjohn Institute Staff, Working Paper No. 04-105. Available: http://www.upjohninstitute.org/publications/wp/04-105.pdf.

Cappelli, P. (2003). Will there really be a labor shortage? *Organizational Dynamics*. Available: http://www.nga.org/cda/files/wf03Cappelli.pdf.

Helman, R., Greenwald & Associates, & Paladino, V. (2004). Will Americans ever become savers? The 14th Retirement Confidence Survey, 2004. Issue Brief No. 268. Washington, DC: Employee Benefit Research Institute.

Hutchens, R., & Papps, K. L. (2004). Developments in phased retirement. PRC WP 2004-14. Philadelphia: University of Pennsylvania, The Wharton School, Pension Research Council. Available: http://rider.wharton.upenn.edu/~prc/PRC/WP/WP2004-14.pdf.

Karoly, L. A., & Zissimopoulos, J. (2004). *Self-Employment and the 50+ Population*. Washington, DC: AARP.

Purcell, P. J. (2004). *Older workers: Employment and retirement trends*. Washington, DC: Congressional Research Service.

Quinn, J. F. (1998). New paths to retirement. Paper presented at the Pension Research Council Conference, "Forecasting Retirement Needs and Retirement Wealth." Philadelphia: Wharton School, University of Pennsylvania.

Quinn, J. F. (1999). Retirement patterns and bridge jobs in the 1990s. EBRI Issue Brief No. 206. Washington, DC: Employee Benefit Research Institute.

Song, J. G. (2003/2004). Evaluating the initial impact of eliminating the retirement earnings test. *Social Security Bulletin, 65*(1), 1–15.

Toossi, M. (2004). Labor force projections to 2012: The graying of the U.S. workforce. *Monthly Labor Review, 127*(2), 37–57.

U.S. Bureau of Labor Statistics. (2004). Worker displacement, 2001–03. *(News USDL 04-1381.)*

U.S. Bureau of Labor Statistics. (2005). *Employment and earnings*. Washington, DC: U.S. Government Printing Office.

U.S. Congressional Budget Office. (2004a). *Retirement age and the need for saving*. Washington, DC: U.S. Congressional Budget Office. Available: http://www.cbo.gov/showdoc.cfm?index=5419&sequence=0.

U.S. Congressional Budget Office. (2004b). *Disability and retirement: The early exit of baby boomers from the labor force*. Washington, DC: U.S. Congressional Budget Office.

U.S. General Accounting Office. (2001). *Older workers: demographic trends pose challenges for employers and workers* (GAO-02-85). Washington, DC: U.S. General Accounting Office.

U.S. Social Security Administration. (2004). *Annual Statistical Supplement to the Social Security Bulletin 2003*. Washington, DC: U.S. Government Printing Office.

Watson Wyatt Worldwide. (2004). *Phased retirement: Aligning employer programs with worker preferences*. Washington, DC: Watson Wyatt Worldwide.

Wegman, D. H., & McGee, J. P. (Eds.). (2004). *Health and safety needs of older workers*. Washington, DC: National Academy of Sciences.

END-OF-LIFE CARE

Palliative care is comprehensive, interdisciplinary care focused primarily on improving the quality of life for people with terminal illness and for their families. Palliative care attempts to address the unmet needs of individuals facing the end of life. Patients want relief from pain and symptoms, to maintain a sense of control, and to avoid burdening their family. Unfortunately, their care is often characterized by undertreatment of symptoms, interpersonal conflicts, impairment of caregivers' health, and depletion of family resources (Emanuel, Fairclough, et al., 2000).

Hospice and *palliative care programs* developed in response to these limitations. The first modern hospices appeared in the late 1960s and 1970s and were patterned after *St. Christopher's Hospice* in London, a facility dedicated to the physical, emotional, and spiritual care of the dying. In recognition of the comprehensive nature of end-of-life care, hospices are staffed by medical professionals, social workers, therapists, and clergy. Recently, the number of hospices in the United States has more than doubled in little more than 5 years to over 2,400 (National Association for Home Care and Hospice, 2004). In addition, roughly 15% of U.S. hospitals have a hospital-based palliative care program, most commonly an inpatient consultation service, and many more are planning to implement these services (Pan, Morrison, et al., 2001).

Core Components of End-of-Life Care

Palliative care aims to improve the quality of life for patients and their families by managing a patient's pain and symptoms, maintaining communication, providing psychosocial, spiritual, and bereavement support, and coordinating a variety of medical and social services (Morrison & Meier, 2004).

Pain and Symptoms. Good end-of-life care requires familiarity with the management of symptoms resulting from many different illness processes. Successful approaches to the assessment and management of pain and other symptoms have been established in controlled trials. Between 85% to 95% of terminally ill patients' pain can be relieved with oral regimens that do not produce troublesome side effects (Doyle, Hanks, & Cherny, 2004).

Depression, delirium, or anxiety are present in 25% to 80% of the terminally ill. Although effective treatments exist, these conditions are typically underdiagnosed, thereby contributing to patient and family distress (Abrahm, 2003). Adequate symptom control is associated with improved patient and family satisfaction and quality of life.

Communication. How clinicians *communicate a terminal diagnosis* has a significant impact on the patient's remaining quality of life. Breaking bad news is a complicated task that requires the involvement of patients and families, responding to the emotional reactions of the involved parties, and projecting support even when the situation is bleak. This complex task can be considered as a series of manageable steps (Buckman, 2001).

- *Getting started:* The goals of the discussion cannot be met unless interruptions are minimized. Family members should be involved if possible.
- *Finding out what the patient knows:* It is necessary for clinicians to explore the patient's knowledge, expectations, and hopes before discussing medical findings. This information allows clinicians to correct misinformation and tailor the bad news to what the patient can understand.
- *Finding out how much the patient wants to know:* While over 80% of patients typically express a desire for full information, others do not. If the patient does not want to know all the details, clinicians should offer to answer questions in future discussions or to talk to a family member.
- *Sharing the information:* Clinicians should start the discussion at the level of the patient's comprehension, giving information in small pieces while periodically assessing the patient's understanding.
- *Responding to the patient's and family's feelings:* Responding to these emotions is one of the most difficult challenges of breaking bad news. Common reactions include silence, disbelief, crying, and anger. Recognizing these emotions and responding to them validates the feelings and is necessary prior to continuing the discussion.
- *Planning and follow-up:* Breaking bad news is not a one-time event. Patients and families need time to process information. Plans should be made to continue the discussion and answer questions at a later date.

Communication is also the key to *advance care planning*. Because life-prolonging treatments may be more burdensome than beneficial, outlining realistic and attainable goals assumes increased importance in the setting of advanced disease. The process includes discussions of a patient's preferences, values, goals, and fears, as well as preparing advance directives and naming a health care proxy. The result, however, should not be a static document or list of instructions, but should be an ongoing process that reflects changing clinical circumstances. In particular, advance care planning at end of life should shift from discussing specific treatments to defining an acceptable quality of life and setting goals of care.

Psychosocial, Spiritual, and Bereavement Support. It is necessary for clinicians to pay attention to patients' and families' psychosocial and spiritual distress. Patients who experience spiritual and psychological distress are more likely to express a desire for death (McClain, Rosenfeld, & Breitbart, 2003). Their family members are also at higher risk for *bereavement morbidity*. Attention to these needs is necessary for ameliorating patients' and families' distress.

Rather than ending with the patient's death, comprehensive palliative care includes providing comfort to the bereaved family. Not only does this contact demonstrate caring, it allows for health care professionals to assess for bereavement related morbidity and may improve bereavement outcomes.

Coordination of Care. The personal and practical care needs of patients at end of life and their families are not adequately addressed by routine office visits or hospital stays, resulting in patient and caregiver burden. The ability of clinicians to coordinate an array of social and medical services on behalf of patients and families assumes increased importance at end of life.

Hastening Death

The ethics of *physician-assisted suicide* for the terminally ill, or the prescribing of lethal medications for patients to self-administer, has been the subject of increased debate. In the Netherlands, physician-assisted suicide and *euthanasia* (physician-administered lethal injection) have been practiced openly for approximately 20 years. These practices have been recently codified into law (New York Times, 2002).

Oregon is the only state in the United States to have legalized physician-assisted suicide. The *Oregon Death with Dignity Act* legalized physician-assisted suicide only under certain circumstances and specifically prohibits euthanasia. (Information about Oregon's Death with Dignity Act can be found at http://egov.oregon.gov/DHS/ph/pas/index.shtml.) Data from Oregon has shown that half of terminally ill patients would like the option of physician-assisted suicide to be available. However, 10% of patients seriously consider physician-assisted suicide, but only 1% request it, and 10% of those patients actually receive and take a lethal prescription (Bascom & Tolle, 2002).

Most patients' desire for physician-assisted suicide diminishes as their underlying concerns are identified and addressed. In general, physical symptoms rarely serve as the primary motivation. The strongest predictors of the desire for hastened death are depression and hopelessness (Breitbart, Rosenfeld, 2000). To help address patients' motivations for physician-assisted suicide, physicians should talk with patients about their expectations and fears, provide options for end-of-life care, discuss family concerns and burdens, and screen for depression. It is important for patients to know that they will not be abandoned.

A broad introduction to palliative care can be found in Doyle and colleagues (2004). Web site sources on palliative care include www.lastacts.org and the *National Consensus Project for Quality Palliative Care* at www.nationalconsensusproject.org.

Randy S. Hebert

See also
Death and Dying
Palliative Care

References

Abrahm, J. L. (2003). Update in palliative medicine and end-of-life care. *Annual Review of Medicine, 54,* 53–72.

Bascom, P. B.,& Tolle, S. W. (2002). Responding to requests for physician-assisted suicide: "These are uncharted waters for both of us . . . " *Journal of the American Medical Association, 288*(1), 91–98.

Breitbart, W., et al. (2000). Depression, hopelessness, and desire for hastened death in terminally ill patients with cancer. *Journal of the American Medical Association, 284*(22), 2907–2911.

Buckman, R. (2001). Communication skills in palliative care: A practical guide. *Neurologic Clinics, 19*(4), 989–1004.

Doyle D., Hanks G., & Cherny N. (2004). *Oxford textbook of palliative medicine* (3rd ed.). Oxford: Oxford University Press.

Dutch legalize euthanasia, the first such national law. (April 1, 2002.) *New York Times,* p. A9.

Emanuel, E. J., et al. (2000). Understanding economic and other burdens of terminal illness: The experience of patients and their caregivers. *Annals of Internal Medicine, 132*(6), 451–459.

McClain C. S., Rosenfeld B., & Breitbart W. (2003). Effect of spiritual well-being on end-of-life despair in terminally-ill cancer patients. *Lancet, 361*(9369), 1603–1607.

Morrison, R. S., & Meier, D. E. (2004). Clinical practice. Palliative care. *New England Journal of Medicine, 350*(25), 2582–2590.

National Association for Home Care and Hospice. (2004). *Hospice Facts and Statistics 2002.* Available: http://www.nahc.org/Consumer/hpcstats.html.

Pan, C. X., et al. (2001). How prevalent are hospital-based palliative care programs? Status report and future directions. *Journal of Palliative Medicine, 4*(3), 315–324.

ENERGY AND BIOENERGETICS

Limited life span and the occurrence of age-related disease may be viewed as consequences of decreased availability of the energy required for maintenance of cellular integrity. The concept is supported by studies of DNA mutation in the mitochondria of mammalian tissues, yeast, and other fungi (Linnane, 1992). These studies suggest accumulation with time of random mutations of mitochondrial DNA (mtDNA) leading to decreased ability of the organelles to supply energy for maintenance of cellular function. Research linking bioenergetics and aging also suggests that the constant presence of highly reactive metabolic fuels and damaging by-products of oxidative metabolism may be deleterious in the long term (B. Ames, 1992; Masoro & McCarter, 1991).

Metabolic Rate and Body Composition

Twenty-four-hour whole body energy expenditure (24EE) can be measured under free-living conditions in humans, using the "doubly labeled water" (D2180) method, but insufficient data are currently available for definite conclusions (Young, 1992). Studies by McGandy, Barrows, Spania, Meredith, Stone, and Norris (1966) of caloric intake indicate total daily energy expenditure decreases with age in healthy adult men 20 to 99 years of age. Vaughan, Zurlo, and Ravussin (1991) used indirect calorimetry to estimate 24EE in men and women 18 to 85 years old under conditions of restricted physical activity. Their results show significantly lower total energy expenditure in the older versus younger age groups.

These and other studies suggest decreased rates of cellular metabolism or decreased intensity of metabolism with advancing age. Such a conclusion cannot be drawn, however, because of the confounding effects of age-related changes in body mass and composition. A key factor is the almost 100-fold range in metabolic rate (MR) per unit mass of different tissues: Adipose tissue, skeletal muscle, intestines, and bone represent a different class of metabolic activity (30 to 100 times lower activity) in comparison with that of heart, liver, kidney, and brain (Elia, 1991). Current methods of normalizing 24EE to fat-free mass (FFM), lean mass, or an exponential function of body mass ("metabolic mass") assume scaled proportions of vital organs, as well as constancy of tissue composition with age. Both of these are questionable assumptions, indicating the need for more information in this area (Elia, 1991). There is, therefore, no precise basis at present for comparing MRs of individuals of different ages. Strong correlations have been demonstrated between MR and FFM in individuals of different ages (Vaughan, Zurlo, & Ravussin, 1991), possibly because much of the variability of mass with age is due to loss of muscle mass, the major component of FFM (Tzankoff & Norris, 1977). Decreased 24EE with age may be a consequence either of decreased rate of cellular metabolism or of increased proportions of tissues of lower MRs. Major components of 24EE are basal MR (BMR), 60% to 75% of total metabolism; physical activity, 15% to 30%; and diet-induced thermogenesis (DIT) (energy required for processing of ingested nutrients), plus or minus 10% of total metabolism. There is evidence that BMR decreases with age independent of changes in FFM (Fukagawa, Bandani, & Young, 1990) and that physical activity declines with age. The latter effect also has a positive feedback because decreased activity would lead to loss of FFM and altered body composition. There is little evidence indicating change in DIT with age (Young, 1992). Current information therefore suggests FFM and physical activity, rather than aging processes, are important factors regulating 24EE in humans. Data obtained in rodents by indirect calorimetry do not show decreased 24EE or resting MR with age (McCarter & Palmer, 1992).

Modulators of MR

Many factors influence MR. In the context of aging, those of current interest are mitochondrial content and activity, neuroendocrine systems, and nutrition. A. J. Hulbert, Mantaj, and Janssens (1991) demonstrated differences in rates of energy metabolism of vital organs associated with differences in mean mitochondrial membrane surface area (MMSA). It might be expected, therefore, that during senescence there is loss of capacity for energy metabolism associated with loss of MMSA. The few morphological studies available demonstrate such an effect in liver and heart of aging rodents (Herbener, 1976). In contrast, functional measurements of oxidative capacity in liver of 10- to 30-month-old Fischer 344 rats indicate no loss of capacity with age (Rumsey, Kendrick, & Starnes, 1987). Extensive literature documents age-related changes in mitochondrial structure and function (Gafni, 1987). However, conflicting results have been obtained when studies were conducted in vitro, using homogenates and tissue slices (Peng, Peng, & Chen, 1977). It is not clear how these data relate to MRs in vivo because such results depend greatly on conditions of incubation (Elia, 1991).

Regulation of MR by the nervous and hormonal systems occurs via control of skeletal muscle and fuel mobilization. Activation by the central nervous system of skeletal muscles during physical activity can produce a 10-fold increase in whole-body MR. With advancing age in humans there is decreased intensity and duration of physical activity (Cunningham, Montoye, Metzner, & Keller, 1968). Similarly, with age, laboratory rodents exhibit decreased voluntary wheel running and decreased spontaneous movement in cages (Holloszy, Smith, Vining, & Adams, 1985; Yu, Masoro, & McMahan, 1985). The sympathetic nervous system (SNS) regulates MR directly and also indirectly via effects on DIT. There is evidence of increased sympathetic tone with advancing age, as seen in increased levels of plasma norepinephrine and blunted responsiveness of the SNS in response to a meal (R. S. Schwartz, Jaeger, & Veith, 1990). A direct effect of SNS activity on MR occurs via activation of brown adipose tissue (BAT) in small animals and via skeletal muscle and vital organ metabolism in humans. The extensive studies of Scarpace and colleagues (Scarpace, Mooradian, & Morley, 1988) indicate less capacity for thermogenesis with age in rats, a consequence of decreased mitochondrial content and diminished activation of BAT in older animals. In humans there is little evidence of significant involvement of BAT in facultative thermogenesis. Rather, skeletal muscle metabolism may be modulated by SNS activity (Astrup, Simonsen, Bullow, Madsen, & Christensen, 1989), but variation with age has not been established.

Thyroid hormones (T3 and T4) are known to play a role in regulating MR. There are no consistent data regarding changing levels of plasma T3 and T4 with age, but there is evidence of decreased turnover of T4 with advancing age in humans (Gregerman, 1964). Available literature suggests decreased influence of thyroid hormone on MR, possibly a consequence of peripheral factors rather than decreased output of the thyroid gland with age (Perlmutter & Riggs, 1949).

Nutrition as MR Modulator. There is overwhelming evidence that restriction of food intake leads to decreased MR per unit mass (Garrow, 1978). The metabolic response appears to vary with age, however. In weanling rats the decrease in MR is transient: Within 6 weeks lean mass adjusts so that MR per unit of lean mass is the same as that of ad libitum–fed rats. When restriction is initiated in older animals (6 months of age), the decrease in MR persists beyond 6 weeks (Gonzales-Pacheco, Buss, Koehler, Woodside, & Alpert, 1993). Indeed, food consumption studies (Yu, Masoro, & McMahan, 1985) suggest that restriction in adulthood would lead to decreased metabolism over several months in rats or several years in the case of longer-lived species such as nonhuman primates (Ramsey, Roecker, Weindruch, & Kemnitz, 1997). The results are of conceptual importance for aging because the life-prolonging action of dietary restriction has been ascribed to decreased MR, in accordance with the "rate of living" theory of aging (Sacher, 1977). Measurements of 24EE following long-term restriction of food intake (initiated at weaning) show that MR per unit of mass is the same in rats fed ad libitum and those fed the restricted diet (P. H. Duffy, Fevers, Leakey, Nakamura, Turturro, & Hart, 1989; McCarter & Palmer, 1992). These measurements demonstrate that decreased MR is not essential for the retardation of aging processes by dietary restriction.

Current Status

The foregoing discussion suggests that age is not a major determinant of MR. It is not clear if the MR of cells of individual tissues declines with age. Altered body and tissue composition with age will change MR via the relative contributions of different tissues to total metabolism. The direct involvement of MR in aging processes is not clear, despite long-standing acceptance of the "rate of living theory" of aging. Support for this theory has come from experiments using poikilotherms, but interpretation of these results has been questioned (Lints, 1989). In addition, Austad and Fischer (1991) reviewed data on lifetime energy expenditures of 164 mammalian species. They concluded that increased body size and behavioral characteristics were more important determinants of life span than MR. Other studies involving increased MR in the absence of decreased survival (Holloszy, 1993) also suggest that aging processes are not directly linked to rate of metabolism. Rather, evidence implicates components of the metabolic system as contributors to aging processes. Components identified by current research include oxidative modification of proteins and nucleic acids (Ames, 1992; Stadtman, 1992), reactive by-products of oxidative metabolism such as free radicals (Sohal, 1993), and metabolic fuels, such as glucose, that undergo nonenzymatic reactions and modify macromolecular structures (Cerami, 1985). It seems likely that the gradual accumulation of modified cellular structures arising from oxidation, glycation, free-radical, and other reactions will in time compromise function and limit survival. This involvement of energy metabolism in aging processes may depend not on the rate of metabolism but rather on the passage of time.

Roger J. M. McCarter

See also

Mitochondrial DNA Mutations
Musculoskeletal System
Oxidative Stress Theory

References

Ames, B. (1992). Oxidants are a major contributor to aging. *Annals of the New York Academy of Science, 663*, 85–96.

Astrup, A. L., Simonsen, L., Bullow, J., Madsen, J., & Christensen, N. J. (1989). Epinephrine mediates facultative, carbohydrate-induced thermogenesis in human skeletal muscle. *American Journal of Physiology, 257*, E340–E345.

Austad, S. N., & Fischer, K. E. (1991). Mammalian aging, metabolism and ecology: Evidence from the bats and marsupials. *Journal of Gerontology, 46*, B47–B53.

Cerami, A. (1985). Hypothesis: Glucose as a mediator of aging. *Journal of the American Geriatrics Society, 33*, 626–634.

Cunningham, D., Montoye, H., Metzner, H., & Keller, J. (1968). Active leisure time activities as related to age among males in a total population. *Journal of Gerontology, 23*, 55–559.

Duffy, P. H., Fevers, R. J., Leakey, J. A., Nakamura, K., Turturro, A., & Hart, R. W. (1989). Effect of chronic caloric restriction on physiological variables related to energy metabolism in the male Fischer 344 rat. *Mechanisms of Ageing and Development, 48*, 117–133.

Elia, M. (1991). Organ and tissue contribution to metabolic rate. In J. M. Kinney & H. N. Tucker (Eds.), *Energy metabolism* (pp. 61–79), New York: Raven Press.

Fukagawa, N. K., Bandani, L. G., & Young, J. B. (1990). Effect of age on body composition and resting metabolic rate. *American Journal of Physiology, 259*, E233–E238.

Gafni, A. (1987). Energy and bioenergetics. In G. L. Maddox (Ed.), *Encyclopedia of aging* (pp. 211–212). New York: Springer Publishing.

Garrow, J. S. (1978). *Energy balance and obesity in man*. Oxford, UK: Elsevier/North Holland.

Gonzales-Pacheco, D. M., Buss, W. C., Koehler, K. M., Woodside, W. F., & Alpert, S. S. (1993). Energy restriction reduces metabolic rate in adult male Fischer-344 rats. *Journal of Nutrition, 123*, 90–97.

Gregerman, R. I. (1964). The age-related alteration of thyroid function and thyroid hormone metabolism in man. In L. Gitman (Ed.), *Endocrines and aging* (pp. 161–173). Springfield, IL: Charles C. Thomas.

Herbener, G. H. (1976). A morphometric study of age-dependent changes in the mitochondrial populations of mouse liver and heart. *Journal of Gerontology, 31*, 8–16.

Holloszy, J. O. (1993). Exercise increases average longevity in female rats despite increased food intake and no growth retardation. *Journal of Gerontology, 48*, B97–B100.

Holloszy, J. O., Smith, E. K., Vining, M., & Adams, S. (1985). Effect of voluntary exercise on longevity of rats. *Journal of Applied Physiology, 59*, 826–831.

Hulbert, A. J., Mantaj, W., & Janssens, P. A. (1991). Development of mammalian endothermic metabolism: Quantitative changes in tissue mitochondria. *American Journal of Physiology, 261*, R561–R568.

Linnane, A. W. (1992). Mitochondria and aging: The universality of bioenergetic disease. *Aging, 4*, 267–271.

Lints, F. A. (1989). The rate of living theory revisited. *Gerontology, 35*, 36–57.

Masoro, E. J., & McCarter, R. (1991). Aging as a consequence of fuel utilization. *Aging, 3*, 117–128.

McCarter, R. J. M., & Palmer, J. (1992). Energy metabolism and aging: A lifelong study of Fischer 344 rats. *American Journal of Physiology, 263*, E448–E452.

McGandy, R. B., Barrows, C. H., Jr., Spania, A., Meredith, A., Stone, J. L., & Norris, A. H. (1966). Nutrient intake and energy expenditure in men of different ages. *Journal of Gerontology, 21*, 581–587.

Peng, M., Peng, Y., & Chen, F. (1977). Age-dependent changes in the oxygen consumption of the cerebral cortex, hypothalamus, hippocampus and amygdaloid in rats. *Journal of Gerontology, 32*, 517–522.

Perlmutter, M., & Riggs, D. S. (1949). Thyroid collection of radioactive iodide and serum protein-bound iodine concentration in senescence, in hypothyroidism and in hypopituitarism. *Journal of Clinical Endocrinology, 9*, 430–439.

Ramsey, J. J., Roecker, E. B., Weindruch, R., & Kemnitz, J. W. (1997). Energy expenditures of adult male rhesus monkeys during the first 30 months of dietary restriction. *American Journal of Physiology: Endocrinology and Metabolism, 272*, E901–E907.

Rumsey, W. L., Kendrick, Z. V., & Starnes, J. W. (1987). Bioenergetics in the aging Fischer 344 rat: Effects of exercise and food restriction. *Experimental Gerontology, 22*, 271–287.

Sacher, G. A. (1977). Life table modification and life prolongation. In C. Finch & L. Hayflick (Eds.), *Handbook of the biology of aging* (pp. 582–638). New York: Van Nostrand Reinhold.

Scarpace, P. J., Mooradian, A. D., & Morley, J. E. (1988). Age-associated decrease in beta-adrenergic receptors and adenylate cyclase activity in rat brown adipose tissue. *Journal of Gerontology, 43*, B65–B70.

Schwartz, R. S., Jaeger, L. F., & Veith, R. (1990). The thermic effect of feeding in older men: The importance of the sympathetic nervous system. *Metabolism, 39*, 733–737.

Sohal, R. S. (1993). The free radical hypothesis of aging: An appraisal of the current status. *Aging, Clinical Experimental Research, 5*, 3–17.

Stadtman, E. R. (1992). Protein oxidation and aging. *Science, 257*, 1220–1224.

Tzankoff, S. P., & Norris, A. H. (1977). Effect of muscle mass decrease on age-related BMR changes. *Journal of Applied Physiology, 43*, 1001–1006.

Vaughan, L., Zurlo, F., & Ravussin, E. (1991). Aging and energy expenditure. *American Journal of Clinical Nutrition, 53*, 821–825.

Young, V. R. (1992). Energy requirements in the elderly. *Nutrition Reviews, 50*, 95–101.

Yu, B. P., Masoro, E. J., & McMahan, C. A. (1985). Nutritional influences on aging of Fischer 344 rats: 1. Physical, metabolic, and longevity characteristics. *Journal of Gerontology, 40*, 657–670.

ENVIRONMENTAL ASSESSMENT

Measuring the *quality of living environments* is important for research and the provision of long-term care services that are designed to optimize the functioning of older adults. Environments vary in their degree and type of impact on behavior based on a person's competence, personal appraisals, and the type of transactions between the person and the environment (Wahl, 2001). Environmental assessment is particularly important for older adults with physical disability or cognitive impairment. These groups are especially vulnerable to their living environments, which place them at increased risk of diminished life quality, maladaptive behaviors, falls, and functional decline (Gitlin, in press).

Environmental assessments have been developed to evaluate dimensions of specific settings, such as the private home, nursing home, or special care unit, and specific populations, such as residents with dementia or the physically frail. Although there is growing recognition of its importance, the conceptualization and measurement of living environments remains complex; there is no agreed-upon, uniform approach, and it is not incorporated into geriatric assessments.

Theoretical Conceptions

Defining the environment and specifying and operationalizing the dimensions to measure are challenging. A core debate is whether an environmental assessment should be transactional, accounting for the interplay of *person and environmental* characteristics, or fractional, measuring environmental attributes that are subsequently related to person outcomes (Lawton, 1999; Wahl & Weisman, 2003). Most environmental assessments assume the latter and assess specific attributes as independent variables that are then linked to behavioral outcomes.

One conceptualization offered by Lawton (1990) and based in an ecology of aging framework suggests that *environment is multicomponent*, comprising 5 dimensions: physical, personal (the presence of others), group, suprapersonal (geographic proximity to transportation, shopping, etc.), and social. Each dimension has objective, measurable attributes and subjective "personal meanings or functional significance for the individual" (Lawton, 1999). Although the dimensions have not been adequately operationalized, the framework offers an integrated perspective, emphasizes objective conditions and how they are subjectively experienced, and considers proximal, physical attributes, and distal, social structural and cultural features that may impact persons. Nevertheless, most environmental assessments are not well-grounded in theory or well-developed conceptualizations of the environment, and attributes tend to be selected for measurement based principally on their clinical relevance.

Approaches to Assessment

Environmental assessments differ as to their measured characteristics, the response formats, and the source from which ratings are derived. Assessments are either descriptive, in which specific features are identified and described, or evaluative, in which measured dimensions represent desirable attributes, or a combination of these. Examples of measured characteristics are: physical characteristics (lighting, distances, and space), safety, affordance of daily activities (accessibility, prosthetic aids), support of orientation (way-finding), social interaction (privacy and socialization), and support of novelty, stimulation, and challenge. Response formats tend to be nominal (presence or absence of a condition), although ordinal and interval ratings have been developed to reflect the extent to which a desirable attribute is present. Ratings can be obtained through self-report, observation, or both. Evidence suggests, however, that older adults do not accurately report environmental conditions and that professional observation yields more reliable information, particularly regarding *home safety and environmental modification* needs (Carter, Campbell, Sanson-Fisher, Redman, & Gillespie, 1997; Ramsdell, Swart, Jackson, & Renvall, 1989).

Existing Measures

Although environmental assessments tend to be undeveloped, there are measures with theoretical underpinnings and adequate psychometric properties (Carp, 1994; Lawton, Weisman, Sloane, & Calkins, 1997; Letts, Law, Rigby, Cooper, Stewart, & Strong, 1994). The *Multiphasic Environmental Assessment Procedure* (*MEAP*; Moos & Lemke, 1988) is the most well developed measure for residential, planned settings and provides descriptive and evaluative assessments along multiple dimensions. The 131-item *Therapeutic Environment Screening Scale* (*TESS 3*; Sloane, Schatzberg, Weisman, & Zimmerman, 1997) is an observational tool that includes descriptive and qualitative indicators of special care units for people with dementia. Likewise, the well-tested *Professional Environmental Assessment Protocol* (*PEAP*; Norris-Baker, Weisman, Lawton, & Sloane, 1999) provides a global evaluative approach of special care units that consists of 5-point ratings of 9 dimensions (e.g., maximizing awareness and orientation).

Environmental assessments of private residences date back to Carp's early work on objective and subjective neighborhood and dwelling unit features (Carp & Carp, 1982). More recent measures have focused on home safety (Johnson, Cusick, & Chang, 2001) for physically frail older adults (Oliver, Blathwayt, Brackley, & Tamaki, 1993; Westmead *Home Safety Assessment*; Clemson, 1997) and are designed and used primarily by health professionals. The *Home Environmental Assessment Protocol* (*HEAP*; Gitlin, Schinfeld, Winter, Corcoran, & Hauck, 2002) is an observational tool designed for use in homes of persons with dementia to assess safety and suggest home modifications in support of function and orientation. At present only 1 assessment, the *Housing Enabler*, attempts a transactional approach in which a *person-environment fit* index is derived by rating physical features of homes based on a person's capabilities (Iwarsson, & Isacsson, 1996).

LAURA N. GITLIN

See also
Disability
Home Modifications
Housing

References

Carp, F., & Carp, A. (1982). Perceived environmental quality of neighborhoods. *Journal of Environmental Psychology, 2,* 4–22.

Carp, F. M. (1994). Assessing the environment. In M. P. Lawton & J. S. Teresi (Eds.), *Annual review of gerontology and geriatrics, 14,* (pp. 302–323). New York: Springer Publishing.

Carter, S. E., Campbell, E. M., Sanson-Fisher, R. W., Redman, S. , & Gillespie, W. J. (1997). Environmental hazards in the homes of older people. *Age and Aging, 26,* 195–202.

Clemson, L. (1997). *Home fall hazards: A guide to identifying fall hazards in the homes of elderly people and an accompaniment to the assessment tool the Westmead Home Safety Assessment (WeHSA).* West Brunswick, Victoria: Co-ordinates Publications.

Gitlin, L. N. (in press). The impact of housing on quality of life: Does the home environment matter now and into the future? In H.-W. Wahl & C. Tesch-Romer (Eds.), *Emergence of new person-environment dynamics in old age: A multidisciplinary exploration.* Amityville, NY: Baywood Publishing.

Gitlin, L. N., Schinfeld, S., Winter, L., Corcoran, M., & Hauck, W. (2002). Evaluating home environments of persons with dementia: Interrater reliability and validity of the home environmental assessment protocol (HEAP). *Disability and Rehabilitation, 24,* 59–71.

Iwarsson, S., & Isacsson, A. (1996). Development of a novel instrument for occupational therapy assessment of the physical environment in the home—A methodological study on "The Enabler." *Occupational Therapy Journal of Research, 16,* 227–244.

Johnson, M., Cusick, A., & Chang, S. (2001). Homescreen: A short scale to measure fall risk in the home. *Public Health Nursing, 18,* 169–177.

Lawton, M. P. (1990). Residential environment and self-directedness among older people. *American Psychologist, 45*(5), 638–640.

Lawton, M. P. (1999). Environmental taxonomy: Generalizations from research with older adults. In S. L.

Friedman & T. D. Wachs (Eds.), *Measuring environment across the life span: Emerging methods and concepts* (pp. 91–124). Washington, DC: American Psychological Association.

Lawton, M. P., Weisman, G. D., Sloane, P., & Calkins, M. (1997). Assessing environments for older people with chronic illness. *Journal of Mental Health and Aging, 3,* 83–100.

Letts, L., Law, M., Rigby, P., Cooper, B., Stewart, D., & Strong, S. (1994). Person-environmental competence amongst independent elderly households. *American Journal of Occupational Therapy, 48,* 608–618.

Moos, R., & Lemke, S. (1988). *Multiphasic Environmental Assessment Procedure (MEAP) manual*. Palo Alto, CA: Stanford University and VA Medical Center, Social Ecology Laboratory.

Norris-Baker, L., Weisman, G., Lawton, M. P., & Sloane, P. (1999). Assessing special care units for dementia: The Professional Environmental Assessment Protocol. In E. A. Steinfeld, & G. S. Danford (Eds.), *Enabling environments: Measuring the impact of environment on disability and rehabilitation* (pp. 165–182). New York: Plenum Publishers.

Oliver, R., Blathwayt, J., Brackley, C., Tamaki, T. Development of the Safety Assessment of Function and the Environment for Rehabilitation (SAFER) tool. *Canadian Journal of Occupational Therapy, 60,* 78–82.

Ramsdell, J. W., Swart, J., Jackson, E., & Renvall, M. (1989). The yield of a home visit in the assessment of geriatric patients. *Journal of the American Geriatrics Society, 13,* 17–24.

Sloane, P. D., Schatzberg, K., Weisman, G., & Zimmerman, S. (1997). *The revised Therapeutic Environment Screening Scale (TESS-3)*. Chapel Hill, NC: University of North Carolina, Department of Family Medicine.

Wahl, H.-W. (2001). Environmental influences on aging and behavior. In J. E. Birren & K. W. Schaie (Eds.), *Handbook of the psychology of aging* (5th ed., pp. 215–237). San Diego: Academic Press.

Wahl, H.-W., & Weisman, G. (2003). Environmental gerontology at the beginning of the new millennium: Reflections on its historical, empirical, and theoretical development. *Gerontologist, 43*(5), 616–627.

EPESE

See

Established Populations for Epidemiological Studies of the Elderly (EPESE)

EPILEPSY

A seizure is a paroxysmal event caused by the sudden onset of abnormal, excessive, and hypersynchronous output from a group of neurons in the cortex of the brain. Epilepsy is defined as the chronic unprovoked recurrence of *seizures*.

Epidemiology

Seizures occur more commonly in older people than in any other age group. The incidence of epilepsy has been estimated at 134 per 100,000 persons, per year, among those age 60 and older, and the likelihood of a first presentation *seizure increases steadily with age* after 45 years (Hauser, Annegers, & Kurland, 1984).

Etiology

Seizures can result from virtually any pathologic process that affects the cortex. Seizures can be categorized as acute symptomatic (AS) and chronic unprovoked. Sudden insults to the cerebral cortex produce AS seizures. Examples of causes of *AS seizures include*: acute ischemia (stroke or *transient ischemic attack*), intracranial hemorrhage, metabolic derangements (e.g. low blood glucose, low blood sodium, uremia), medications, and ethanol withdrawal.

Chronic unprovoked seizures can result from structural lesions such as tumors (primary or metastatic), and the sequelae of cerebral infarction or hemorrhage. The role of *neurodegenerative diseases* is important, with seizure rates as high as 17% in autopsy-proven cases of Alzheimer's disease (generally occurring in later stages) (Mendez, Catanzaro, Doss, Arguello, & Frey, 1994). Approximately 25% of cases of chronic seizures in older persons (older than 60 years) yield no cause despite optimal investigation (Hauser, 1992).

Clinical Features and Diagnosis

The clinical features of a seizure correspond to the area of cortex involved, including the site of seizure onset and subsequent spread (propagation).

The term *"aura"* is used for a subjective *ictal phenomenon* that, in a given patient, may precede an observable seizure; if alone, it constitutes a *sensory seizure* (Blume, Luders, Mizrahi, Goldensohn, Hufnagel, King, et al., 2001). Other clinical features, including impaired consciousness and motor phenomenon, may occur if the seizure spreads through the cortex. Propagation of a focally originating seizure may be rapid and prevents the patient from experiencing an aura. The seizure is followed by a post-ictal phase of depressed neuronal function that varies from focal weakness to a confusional state to a deep sleep.

Seizures are classified as partial or generalized (Commission on Classification and Terminology, 1981). *Partial seizures* start in restricted ("focal") areas of the cortex, in contrast to *generalized seizures* that involve both cerebral hemispheres diffusely from the outset. Partial seizures are subdivided to those with retained consciousness (simple partial seizures) and those that alter consciousness (complex partial seizures). Partial seizures can further evolve to secondarily generalized *tonic-clonic seizures*. Primary generalized epilepsy begins in children and young adults; new onset "generalized" tonic-clonic seizures in the older population virtually always have a focal onset.

Seizures are usually self-limited. However, occasionally the innate suppressive mechanisms of cortex fail and result in a state of continuous or reiterative seizures known as *status epilepticus*. Status epilepticus is defined as a single seizure lasting longer than 30 minutes, or frequent seizures without interictal return to baseline. Partial complex status epilepticus may be the cause of an abrupt-onset "confusional" state with altered consciousness in the elderly.

Seizures in older people can be difficult to diagnose. In one cohort of patients, for example, the mean time to diagnosis it was 1.7 years from the first seizure (Spitz, Bainbridge, Winzenburg, Ramsey, Pryor, Uthman, et al., 2003). Many reasons account for delays in diagnosis. The diagnosis of a seizure is made with the history obtained from the patient and a witness, and the common seizure types presenting in old age tend to be more difficult to recognize and describe. In addition, other medical conditions capable of producing episodic symptoms, such as *cardiogenic syncope* and transient ischemic attacks, increase in prevalence with age.

Electroencephalography (EEG) can be diagnostically helpful if specific interictal epileptiform abnormalities (spikes, sharp waves) are found. Importantly, a normal *EEG* or a recording demonstrating only nonspecific abnormalities does not exclude seizures. Patients with frequent "spells" of an unknown nature may benefit from simultaneous *video-EEG telemetry* in an attempt to capture one of the patient's habitual attacks. Focal neurological signs on physical exam, laboratory abnormalities, and cerebral imaging are most useful in identification of the underlying cause of an established seizure disorder.

Treatment

Seizures can be devastating for older people. Generalized tonic-clonic seizures in people who have arthritis and osteoporosis can result in dislocations and fractures. Seizures may cause falls as a source of trauma. The *anticoagulated patient with seizures* is at a particularly high risk of additional injury from trauma. Seizures can also cause social isolation and loss of independence by damaging self-confidence and forcing restriction of driving privileges.

The goals of treatment are to minimize seizure frequency and adverse effects of *anti-epileptic drugs* (AEDs). AED treatment is indicated unless a reversible underlying cause can be identified and corrected. Drug tolerance can be a limiting factor to *seizure control*; 20% of patients are intolerant of the initial AED (Ramsey, Rowan, & Pryor, 2004). Common adverse effects of AEDs include drowsiness, imbalance, osteoporosis, and negative effects on cognition. Pharmacodynamic differences in older adults further complicate medical management. Age and comorbidity alter hepatic metabolism, renal clearance, volume of distribution, and rates of protein binding. Drug interactions are common, especially with older AEDs. High rates of *polypharmacy in the elderly* increase this risk further.

Relatively few trials exist that examine AED treatment in the elderly. In contrast to the newer AEDs, the older drugs (e.g. phenytoin, carbamazepine, phenobarbital, valproic acid) produce more adverse effects, require monitoring of drug concentrations in the blood, have more potential drug interactions, and have pharmacokinetic properties that complicate their use. Newer AEDs are substantially more expensive, but have similar or better efficacy and generally much better safety profiles. In one prospective, randomized controlled trial, more patients were seizure-free at 4 months using *lamotrigine* (39%) than *carbamazepine* (21%). Patients were also twice as likely to experience adverse effects requiring discontinuation of therapy with carbamazepine than lamotrigine (Brodie, Overstall, & Giorgi, 1999). The final result of a large prospective study comparing carbamazepine, lamotrigine, and *gabapentin* in older American veterans is forthcoming (Ramsay, Rowan, & Pryor, 2003). These advantages of newer AEDs are well documented in younger populations (French, Kanner, Bautista, Abou-Khalil, Browne, Harden, et al., 2004).

Prognosis

Uncontrolled epilepsy in older adults is associated with detrimental effects on cognitive, social, and physical function. Fortunately, medical therapy is often successful. Once a tolerated AED is found, 60% of patients remain seizure-free after 12 months (Ramsey, Rowan, & Pryor, 2004). Poor control should raise suspicions of problems with medication adherence. (Maa, Spitz, & Bainbridge, 2004). Epilepsy in general carries a small decreased life expectancy, and underlying causes carry prognoses of their own. The specific applicability of this measurement to the elderly population is uncertain at present.

MARK SADLER
PATRICK J. G. FELTMATE

References

Blume, W. T., Luders, H. O., Mizrahi, E., Goldensohn, E., Hufnagel, A., King, D., et al. (2001). ILAE Commission Report. Glossary of descriptive terminology for ictal semiology: Report of the ILAE task force on classification and terminology. *Epilepsia, 42,* 1212–1218.

Brodie, M. J., Overstall, P. W., & Giorgi, L. (1999). Multicenter, double-blind, randomized comparison between lamotrigine and carbamazepine in elderly patients with newly diagnosed epilepsy. The UK Lamotrigine Elderly Study Group. *Epilepsy Research, 37,* 81–87.

Commission on Classification and Terminology of the International League Against Epilepsy. (1981). Proposal for revised clinical and electroencephalographic classification of epileptic seizures. *Epilepsia, 22,* 489–501.

French, J. A., Kanner, A. M., Bautista, J., Abou-Khalil, B., Browne, T., Harden, C. L., et al. (2004). Efficacy and tolerability of the new anti-epileptic drugs I: Treatment of new onset epilepsy. *Neurology, 62,* 1252–1260.

Hauser, W. A. (1992). Seizure disorders: The changes with age. *Epilepsia, 33*(Suppl. 4), 6–14.

Hauser, W. A., Annegers, J. F., & Kurland, L. T. (1993). Incidence of epilepsy and unprovoked seizures in Rochester, Minnesota: 1935–1984. *Epilepsia, 34,* 453–468.

Maa, E., Spitz, M. C., & Bainbridge, J. L. (2004). Intractability that occurs in elderly-onset epilepsy. *Epilepsia, 45*(Suppl. 7), 263.

Mendez, M. F., Catanzaro, P., Doss, R. C., Arguello, R., & Frey, W. H., II. (1994). Seizures in Alzheimer's disease: Clinicopathologic study. *Journal of Geriatric Psychiatry and Neurology, 7,* 230–233.

Ramsay, R. E., Rowan, A. J., & Pryor, F. M. (2004). Special considerations in treating the elderly patient with epilepsy. *Neurology, 62*(Suppl. 2), S24–S29.

Spitz, M. C., Bainbridge, J. L., Winzenburg, K. V., Ramsey, R. E., Pryor, F., Uthman, B. M., et al. (2003). Observations on the delay in the diagnosis of seizures in the elderly: Update 3. *Epilepsia, 44*(Suppl. 9), 18.

EPISODIC MEMORY

See
Memory: Autobiographical

ESTABLISHED POPULATIONS FOR EPIDEMIOLOGICAL STUDIES OF THE ELDERLY (EPESE)

Epidemiological studies completed before 1970 rarely provided age-specific descriptive statistics for persons older than 65 years of age. Usually data for the older age groups were summarized into a single statistic to represent the average or cumulative rate for the entire age span. With the increase in the number of persons surviving for more than 65 years, it became necessary to know the age-specific rates and the patterns of change in these rates. The increase in mortality and morbidity rates could not be assumed to increase linearly. In fact, many rates increased geometrically. The lack of specific descriptive statistics led to the creation of the surveys entitled the *Established Populations for Epidemiological Studies of the Elderly* (EPESE) (Cornoni-Huntley, Ostfeld, Taylor, Wallace, Blazer, Berkman, et al., 1993).

The *Epidemiology, Demography, and Biometry Program of the National Institute on Aging* (NIA) initiated studies of representative community populations to provide information on the identification of the leading health problems and the magnitude of these problems for elderly people. Specifically, the goals were to:

- estimate the prevalence of diseases, health problems, impairments, and disabilities for elderly persons living in communities;
- estimate the incidence of diseases, health problems, impairments, and disabilities for elderly persons living in communities;
- identify and investigate risk factors that may be associated with or predictive of mortality, morbidity, hospitalization, and use of long-term care facilities;
- quantify changes in the physical and social functioning of elderly persons and evaluate how these changes are associated with changes in related health conditions;
- explore in population context diseases and conditions for which little population data were available, such as sleep disorders, bereavement, and pain syndromes.

Sample Populations

In 1980, the NIA initiated contracts to fund 3 population studies. Five years later, in 1985, a fourth population sample was established to provide the descriptive and comparative data for black elderly persons. All 4 locations were selected by the competitive process. The first 3 locations of the studies were in East Boston, Massachusetts, 2 rural counties in Iowa, and New Haven, Connecticut. The fourth study location was segments of 5 counties in the north-central Piedmont area of North Carolina. Each location adopted a personalized study name: in East Boston, the *Senior Health Project*; in Iowa, Iowa 65+ *Rural Health Study*; in New Haven, *Yale Health and Aging Project*; and in North Carolina, *Piedmont Health Survey of the Elderly*. The sampling methods were different in each location.

The study population of East Boston, Massachusetts, consisted of all persons within the community who were 65 years of age and older. Middle- and low-income working-class persons, many of Italian-American background, lived in this urban area. Of the 4,562 people eligible to be included, 3,813 (84%) participated in the study.

The Iowa study population consists of all residents of 2 rural counties in east-central Iowa, namely, Iowa and Washington counties, who were 65 years of age and older. Most of this population is classified as rural. Of approximately 4,600 people eligible to be included, 3,673, or 80%, participated.

The study population of New Haven, Connecticut, is a stratified, representative sample of persons 65 years of age and older living in the area. The sample was stratified to include representative public housing and ethnic minorities. Of the 3,337 people in the sample, 82%, or 2,811 people, participated. New Haven is primarily a middle- and low-income urban residential area.

The North Carolina study population was a stratified representative sample of persons residing in 5 geographically contiguous counties of the north-central part of the state. Franklin, Granville, Vance, and Warren counties are predominantly rural, and Durham is predominantly urban. The area has a wide range of socioeconomic status, but residents are primarily middle- and low-income residents. Of the 5,224 persons sampled, 4,165 participated, for a response rate of 80%. The study population was 51% African American.

Methods

Study Design. The basic EPESE design was a *longitudinal study* consisting of a baseline survey and 6 follow-up interviews. During the first years the initial (baseline) survey (1982–1983 for East Boston, Iowa, and New Haven, and 1986–1987 for North Carolina) was a personal interview completed in the residence of the participant to provide estimates of specific health problems and related factors. The second through the seventh years (1983–1989 for east Boston, Iowa, and New Haven, and 1987–1993 for North Carolina) were devoted to continuing surveillance of the population using annual follow-up contacts, either by a personal or telephone interview, and acquiring data on mortality, hospitalization, and admission to nursing homes. Follow-up data provided estimates of incidence or onset of health problems and change in physical and social functioning.

The schedule for annual interviews by year and type was the same at all locations, but, chronologically, the interviews for the North Carolina location were completed 5 years after the original 3 locations. The design included 3 personal, face-to-face interviews, at baseline, and at the third and sixth follow-up or re-contact. The first, second, fourth, and fifth re-contacts (follow-up interviews) were by telephone. Attempts were made to complete annual re-contacts for both noninstitutionalized and institutionalized participants.

During the course of the study, the investigators developed substudies of problems frequently experienced by older persons. The areas of substudies encompassed health and psychosocial problems, such as incontinence, dementia, sleep problems, depression, bereavement, and adjustment to retirement. Some studies required the collection of additional data, whereas others involved an in-depth analysis of the existing data.

Data Collection. The health problems and related conditions investigated in EPESE reflected the recognition of a need for community estimates of the extent of the problems, and that data concerning these problems could be collected by a survey instrument. Published research results and clinical impressions were used in generating the questionnaires. An attempt was made to use standardized items that were contained in ongoing national surveys for comparative purposes.

For all EPESE locations the baseline questionnaire consisted of identical, core questions on chronic conditions; related health problems and behavior; and physical, social, and cognitive functioning (see Table 1). The baseline questionnaire included additional questions that were not common to all sites and reflected the interest of investigators at different locations.

Identical questions that were common to all EPESE locations were included on personal, face-to-face follow-up interviews (third and sixth re-contact). Lifetime history was not repeated, and only current status was obtained. The follow-up

TABLE 1 Items Included on Baseline Questionnaire or *EPESE Project*

Demographic factors[a]	Ethnic origin, education, occupation and work status, income, residential mobility, marital status, housing type, and recent death of close relatives or friends
Social functioning	Household composition, religion, group membership, and contacts with friends and relatives
Physical functioning	Functional disability,[b] vision,[c] and hearing[c]
Chronic conditions	Cardiac, exertional chest pain, intermittent claudication,[d] stroke, cancer, diabetes, factures, chronic respiratory symptoms, and hypertension
Related health problems	Cognitive function,[e] depression,[f] bowel habits, weight and weight history, sleep, and self perceived health status
Health-related behavior	Alcohol, prescription and nonprescription drug use in past 2 weeks, digitalis, and smoking
Use of services	Hospitalizations, nursing home episodes, and dental

[a] All centers obtained Social Security number, Medicare number, name, address, and telephone number of related persons who do not live with them but know where they are for future contacts.
[b] Questions included (1) 7 activities of daily living (Katz, Ford, Moskowitz, Jackson, & Jaffe, 1963); (2) an abbreviated measure of functional health (3 of the 6 items reported by Rosow & Breslau, 1969); and (3) 4 physical activity items (adapted from Nagi, 1976).
[c] Questions from National Health and Nutrition Examination Survey (NHANES) I (National Center for Health Statistics, 1978).
[d] The London School of Hygiene Cardiovascular Questionnaire (NCHS, 1978).
[e] Nine-Item Mental Statics Questionnaire (MSQ) (Pfeiffer, 1975).
[f] Modification of Center for Epidemiology-Depression Modification (CES-D) scale (Berkman, Berkmen, Kasl, Freeman, Leo, Ostfeld, et al., 1986).
Note: Adapted from "Established populations for epidemiologic studies of the elderly" by J. Cornoni-Huntley et al., 1993, *Aging/Clinical and Experimental Research, 5,* 27–37. Copyright 1993, Editrice Kuttis s.r.l. Adapted by permission.

TABLE 2 Major Outcomes of EPESE Report

Outcomes	Obtained by
Mortality	Continual surveillance, including local sources, state record, and the National Death Index (death certificates reviewed by single nosologist)
Morbidity	
Chronic conditions and impairments	Annual follow-up interview
Hospitalizations	Annual follow-up interview, continual surveillance, and Medicare Part A files
Nursing home admissions	Annual follow-up interview
Disability in physical functioning	Annual follow-up interview

Reprinted from "Established populations for epidemiologic studies of the elderly" by J. Cornoni-Huntley et al., 1993, *Aging/Clinical and Experimental Research, 5,* 27–37. Copyright 1993, Editrice Kurtis, s.r.l. Reprinted by permission.

telephone interviews were abbreviated. Identical data on the evaluation of outcome (mortality, morbidity, hospitalizations, and admissions to nursing homes) were included on each of the annual recontacts (see Table 2).

During the baseline and third and sixth follow-up interviews the participant's blood pressure was measured. At the time of the sixth follow-up interview, a blood sample was obtained for analysis of a complete blood count (including hemoglobin, hematocrit, white cell count, differential count, and platelet count), as well as automated chemistry measures of 24 biochemical determinations, low-density lipoprotein cholesterol, and high-density lipoprotein cholesterol. Also, the sixth follow-up included several physical performance measures.

Continual surveillance of the study populations occurred during the follow-up period. Data were obtained on the major outcomes, mortality, morbidity (chronic conditions and impairments, mainly through the annual surveys), hospitalization (in some populations) and admission to nursing homes. A computer match with the Health Care Financing Administration (now CMS) Medicare records (Medicare Provider and Analysis Review files) was implemented, although it was not until 1986 that suitable records were available.

Further details of the methodology can be obtained in previous publications (Cornoni-Huntley, Ostfeld, Taylor, Wallace, Blazer, Berkman, et al., 1993). Baseline questionnaires and survey tabulations are available in 2 federal publications (Established Populations for Epidemiologic Study of the Elderly. Resource Data Book. U.S. Department of Health and Human Services, National Institutes of Health, NIH Publication nos. 86-2443 and 90-495.)

Results

Approximately 350 reports have been published based on the EPESE data. Incidence and prevalence rates for hypertension, heart disease, cancer, depression, and loss in physical and cognitive functioning, plus factors related to these conditions among elderly persons, have been published (Berkman, Berkman, Kasl, Freeman, Leo, Ostfeld, et al., 1986; Scherr, Albert, Funkenstein, Cook, Hennekens, Branch, et al., 1988; Seeman, Mendes de Leon, Berkman, & Ostfeld, 1993; Taylor, Cornoni-Huntley, Curb, Manton, Ostfeld, Scherr, et al., 1991). The positive aspect of regular physical activity also has been reported (Mendes de Leon, Beckett, Fillenbaum, Brock, Branch, Evans, et al., 1997). Descriptive and analytical articles have been published from the extensive data on use of medication obtained from the participants (Chrischilles, Foley, Wallace, Lemke, Semla, Hanlon, et al., 1992). Reports on the relationship of social factors, such as social networks and social support, also have been published (Seeman & Berkman, 1988).

Investigators have generated in-depth studies of specific diseases, with independent methodology but using the EPESE populations. For example, reports have been published on a study of Alzheimer's disease in east Boston presenting the prevalence for a community-living population (Hebert, Scherr, Beckett, Albert, Pilgrim, Chown, et al., 1995). Reports on periodontal and other oral health problems have been published from dental studies completed for the Iowa and North Carolina populations (Beck, Koch, Rozier, & Tudor, 1990).

Although a significant number of studies have been published, there exists a large amount of data that has not been analyzed. New scientific reports from EPESE continue to appear. Public-use tapes are available for the surveys through the *National Archive for Computerized Data on Aging* (www.icpsr.umich.edu/NACDA/archive.html) or possibly through the *National Institute on Aging*. The linkage with hospitalization data from the Medicare Provider Analysis and Review files broadens the opportunity for identifying factors that are related to, or are predictive of, the occurrence of health problems for older adults.

ROBERT B. WALLACE

See also
Longitudinal Data Sets
Longitudinal Research

References

Beck, J. D., Koch, G., Rozier, R. G., & Tudor, G. E. (1990). Prevalence and risk indicators for periodontal attachment loss in a population of older community-dwelling blacks and whites. *Journal of Periodontology, 61*, 521–528.

Berkman, L., Berkman, C., Kasl, S., Freeman, D., Leo, L., Ostfeld, A., Cornoni-Huntley, J., & Brody, J. (1986). Depressive symptoms in relation to physical health and functioning in the elderly. *American Journal of Epidemiology, 124*, 372–399.

Chrischilles, E. A., Foley, D., Wallace, R. B., Lemke, J. H., Semla, T. P., Hanlon, J. T., Glynn, R. J., Ostfeld, A. M., & Guralnik, J. M. (1992). Use of medications by persons 65 and older: Data from the Established Populations for Epidemiologic Studies of the Elderly. *Journal of Gerontology in Medical Science, 45*(5), M137–M144.

Cornoni-Huntley, J. C., Ostfeld, A. M., Taylor, J. O., Wallace, R. B., Blazer, D., Berkman, L. F., Evans, D. A., Kohout, F. J., Lemke, J. H., Scherr, P. A., & Korper S. P. (1993). Established populations for epidemiologic studies of the elderly: Study design and methodology. *Aging and Clinical Experimental Research, 5*, 27–37.

Hebert, L. E., Scherr, P. A., Beckett, L. A., Albert, M., Pilgrim, D. M., Chown, M. J., Funkenstein, H. H., & Evans, D. A. (1995). Age-specific incidence of Alzheimer's disease in a community population. *Journal of the American Medical Association, 273*(17), 1354–1359.

Katz, S., Ford, A. B., Moskowitz, R. W., Jackson, B. A., & Jaffe, M. W. (1963). Studies of illness in the aged. Index of ADL: A standardized measure of biological and psychological function. *Journal of the American Medical Association, 185*, 914–919.

Mendes de Leon, C. F., Beckett, L. A., Fillenbaum, G. G., Brock, D. B., Branch, L. G., Evans, D. A., & Berkman, L. F. (1997). Black-white differences in risk of becoming disabled and recovering from disability in old age: A longitudinal analysis of two EPESE populations. *American Journal of Epidemiology, 145*, 488–497.

Nagi, S. Z. (1976). An epidemiology of disability among adults in the United States. *Milbank Memorial Fund Quarterly, 6*, 493–508.

National Center for Health Statistics. (1978). Plan and operation of the Hanes I augmentation survey of adults 25–74 years. *Vital and Health Statistics: Series I. Programs and collections procedure:* No. 14. Hyattsville, MD: Public Health Service.

Pfeiffer, E. (1975). A short portable mental status questionnaire for the assessment of organic brain deficit in elderly patients. *Journal of the American Geriatrics Society, 23*(10), 433–441.

Rosow, I., & Breslau, N. (1969). A Guttman health scale for the aged. *Journal of Gerontology, 21*, 556–559.

Scherr, P. A., Albert, M. S., Funkenstein, H. H., Cook, N. R., Hennekens, C. H., Branch, L. G., White, L., Taylor, J. O., & Evans, D. A. (1988). Correlated of cognitive functions in an elderly community population. *American Journal of Epidemiology, 128*, 1084–1101.

Seeman, T., & Berkman, L. F. (1988). Structural characteristics of social networks and their relationship with social support in the elderly: Who provides support? *Social Science and Medicine, 26*, 737–749.

Seeman, T., Mendes de Leon, C., Berkman, L., & Ostfeld, A. (1993). Risk factors for coronary heart disease among older men and women: A prospective study of community-dwelling elderly. *American Journal of Epidemiology, 138*, 1037–1049.

Taylor, J. O., Cornoni-Huntley, J., Curb, J., Manton, J., Ostfeld, A. M., Scherr, P., & Wallace, R. B. (1991). Blood pressure and mortality risk in the elderly. *American Journal of Epidemiology, 134*, 489–501.

ESTROGEN REPLACEMENT THERAPY

See
Hormone Replacement Therapy (HRT)

ETHICS

In recent years there has been expanding interest in questions of *ethics in the field of aging*. This interest has been stimulated by 2 broad trends: (1) advances in medical technology that have led to dilemmas of clinical *bioethics* (e.g., decisions surrounding death and dying), and (2) the coming of an aging society with rising numbers of dependent elderly whose care raises far-reaching questions of social policy. The dilemmas of bioethics have principally been of concern to physicians, nurses, social workers, and other professionals; questions of social policy and social ethics in an aging society have become more broadly intertwined with debates about allocation of resources and the role of government. In this article both the clinical and policy issues are examined. For more detailed discussions, see Agich (1993); Collopy, Boyle, and Jennings (1991); Collopy, Dubler, and Zuckerman (1990); Jecker (1991); Moody (1992); and Sachs and Cassel (1994).

Bioethics and Aging

Since the 1960s there has been a revival of analytical work in normative ethics with clear implications for policy and practice. A landmark was *John Rawls's* (1971) theoretical treatise, *A Theory of Justice*, but major stimulus also came from controversies about war and peace, biomedical technology, and similar public issues. By the early 1980s, ethicists, as well as others, were giving serious attention to ethics and aging. A major achievement of early work in bioethics was a strong emphasis on *patients' rights* and *informed consent*. The ideal of autonomy and individual *self-determination*—so fundamental in American ideology—was readily extended to the elderly. But implementation of the idea in practice quickly encountered obstacles. With advancing age, chronic illness and physical dependency are often accompanied by diminished capacity for decision making. Particularly among the *old-old* and those in nursing homes, there are growing numbers who are unable to make their own decisions. Along with the clinical problem of competency, there is a widespread tendency for both families and professionals to treat older people in the style of *paternalism*: acting for a person's "best interest," rather than respecting autonomy.

This conflict between paternalism and self-determination is apparent in many arenas of gerontological practice: in the design of social services for individuals and families, in elder abuser and adult protective services, in decisions about involuntary nursing home placement, and, most acutely, in life-and-death decisions involving termination of treatment or *withdrawal of life-support* systems. In 1975, the *Karen Ann Quinlin* case brought these questions to wide public attention, and the courts have repeatedly been involved since. In these cases there have been those with strong opinions, for example favoring sanctity of life on one side and beneficent euthanasia on the other. But gradually there has grown a strong public consensus in support of the right of a severely ill patient to refuse treatment in order to "*die with dignity*." To this extent, both law and ethics have worked in favor of expanded autonomy for the severely ill.

But in considering the ethical dilemmas of care for the elderly, other troubling questions remain unanswered. Proponents of patient autonomy have endorsed the concept of *advance directives*: instruments such as the *living will* or *durable power of attorney* that could be invoked when an individual no longer has the capacity to make medical decisions. Yet determination of mental competency is often a matter of drawing borderlines. What about those elderly suffering from dementia or those with fluctuating mental competency? Similar problems arise for diseases that create physical incapacity but are not immediately fatal. What about withholding food and water from those not terminally ill? Far less social consensus has been reached on these controversial matters. Through a series of court decisions, the legal system has moved in contradictory directions: sometime setting clear limits, more often reflecting societal ambivalence about bioethical dilemmas in the last stage of life. For health care professionals and hospitals, another complicating factor has been the fear of malpractice liability, which has promoted a tendency to overtreat patients (Kapp, 1991). Will these practices change under the pressure of cost containment? In the future it seems likely that clinicians will continue to be troubled by decision making for elderly patients of questionable mental competency.

In hospitals and long-term care settings, these familiar dilemmas of clinical practice have been exacerbated by new demands. Placement and discharge planning are becoming major practice problems with unavoidable ethical difficulties. Although ethicists have closely examined problems in hospital settings, until recently, ethical dilemmas in long-term care were relatively neglected. In nursing home settings, for example, many dilemmas are not dramatic life-and-death choices but are likely to involve constraints of institutional living (Kane & Caplan, 1990). Sometimes limits are imposed either for the patient's individual welfare or for the sake of other residents: for example, what to do about residents at risk of falling or wandering and how to secure the tranquility of the healthier residents in an institutional environment where growing numbers of severely demented, sometimes disruptive people are living.

For professionals who are employees of institutions, there can be distinctive dilemmas that arise from the dual roles of professional and employee. For example, when client or patient advocacy is in conflict with the rules or policies of an institution, practitioners are caught in the middle. Clearly, new approaches to conflict resolution are needed. In hospitals, one promising innovation has been the introduction of *institutional ethics committees*, now virtually required by standards of the Joint Commission on Accreditation of Healthcare Organizations, and a number of nursing homes are introducing similar forums to address the ethical issues that arise in practice.

Comparable ethical problems arise outside institutions and within private family life. There are serious ethical dilemmas in cases of elder abuse: for example, when a social service provider has no recourse except to place an abused elder in a nursing home and this outcome is often precisely what the abused elder does not want. Despite the reluctance of some older persons to enter long-term care facilities, there are serious problems that families face in maintaining an elderly relative at home. Often these "tragic choices" involve issues of distributive justice: for example, which family members are to bear the burden of extraordinary day-to-day care for Alzheimer's disease sufferers living at home. Traditional appeals to filial responsibility are sometimes invoked, but distributive justice issues remain unresolved. As ethicists examine the problem of family caregiving in advanced industrialized societies, it becomes evident that traditional forms of filial responsibility were never intended to take into account developments in longevity, family structure, and the changing roles of women. Thus, the balance between family and formal caregiving, a topic of considerable attention among gerontologists, turns out to involve far-reaching ethical questions (Cantor, 1994).

Social Ethics in the Aging Society

This conclusion about *family caregiving* points to a broader conclusion, namely, that individual ethical dilemmas are fully intelligible only in a wider social and cultural context. Indeed, ethicists have been quick to identify how political and economic policy decisions—for example, reimbursement systems under Medicare and Medicaid—serve to generate many of the dilemmas and contradictions faced in practice (Mehlman & Visocan, 1992). As all public expenditures come under increasing pressure, a major dilemma of social ethics stands out: Will society make use of all of its available, yet expensive, medical technology to prolong life for those at advanced ages (Binstock & Post, 1991; Callahan, 1987)? At the other end of the life cycle, among newborns, decisions are increasingly being made with consideration for a quality-of-life standard. This concept remains controversial, yet many would urge that the same standard be applied to life-and-death decisions in old age. Extension of this idea, for example, could lead to approval of so-called *rational suicide* on quality-of-life grounds—a concept originally endorsed by the ancient Stoic philosophers.

It is one thing for a person to make an individual judgment about his or her own life, but it becomes a different matter when we make those decisions on a collective basis. The danger is that quality of life becomes equal to worth of life. In an era of cost containment, the dangers of such an ethic are clear. Policy makers in fields such as transportation and occupational health and safety are tempted by the clear economic rationality of cost-benefit calculations. But all such calculations suffer from a classic problem of utilitarianism: above all, the failure of utilitarian ethics to provide a place for ordinary ethical convictions about the value of individual life. In the case of the aged, utilitarian calculations could easily underwrite the prejudices of ageism and negative attitudes toward old age.

This is precisely the line of argument offered by those who warn against the dangers of the quality-of-life standard and who reject utilitarian cost-benefit calculations for allocating scarce health care resources to the aged ("Caring for an aging world," 1994; ter Meulen, Topinkova, & Callahan, 1994).

The problem is that if the utilitarian argument is rejected, how are difficult allocation decisions to be made? American public policy for the aging supports a 3-level allocation system: an age-based public provision (Medicare), a means-tested public provision (Medicaid), and the option of provision through private payment or health insurance. This arrangement is open to challenge on grounds of distributive justice. But alternatives suffer from serious drawbacks. For example, advocates for the aging are likely to be dismayed by the practice—widespread in the industrialized nations of Europe—of denying some expensive health care on grounds of age alone. In England, older people are routinely denied kidney dialysis.

The current policy debates in health care have a certain parallel in other arenas, such as work and retirement and Social Security. For example, advocates for the aging generally reject mandatory retirement or other limitations based on chronological age, but at the same time they favor other age-based entitlements such as Social Security and Medicare. These contradictions raise interacting questions: Are there principles of distributive justice that could provide a uniform framework for appraising the claims of older people, particularly in a period when governments are faced with difficult allocation decisions? Is there a basis in social ethics for appraising the claims of future generations of older people, an argument on behalf of "*intergenerational equity*" (Laslett & Fishkin, 1992)? The answers to these questions are not clear. What is clear, however, is that the terms of the new debate on ethics and aging are now very different from what they were as recently as the 1970s. Instead of access, social policy today is dominated by cost containment, and at the clinical level the stubborn problems of autonomy and paternalism, death and life prolongation, the family and social welfare remain vexing for practitioners.

Contemporary debates on clinical and *social ethics* tend to concentrate on debates about rights and distributive justice. Rarely have they examined deeper issues, such as the nature of the good life, the meaning of the last stage of life, or the ways in which rights and obligations toward the aged might be grounded in some concept of the common good. Yet the meaning of choice in old age is, to some degree, intertwined with the meaning of death. Does death make life meaningful, or does it signify the end of meaning? With biomedical technology and life prolongation, the question no longer remains speculative. The timing of death becomes increasingly a matter of explicit decision. Therefore, clinical bioethics cannot take either individual or collective meaning for granted in trying to weight competing values such as welfare, justice, and autonomy.

Contemporary ethics has developed a powerful style of conceptual analysis, likely to prove fruitful for gerontologists in the years ahead. Yet the limits of contemporary philosophical ethics should also be noted because those limits are tied to our current cultural environment. By contrast, other cultures have cultivated very different views about the rightness of specific actions, for example, filial responsibility, self-determined death, and the entitlements of different age groups to common resources. Where modern Western culture prizes individualism, rationality, and law, traditional cultures have favored collective decision making, family piety, and religious virtues tied to distinctive life stages. These cultural and historical variations suggest that contemporary debates in bioethics and social policy could benefit from being placed in a wider philosophical context. As current industrial societies seek to cope with the aging of populations and advances in medical technology, concern for ethics and aging is likely to grow in the future.

HARRY R. MOODY
MARSHALL B. KAPP

See also

Ageism
Elder Abuse and Neglect
Euthanasia
Elder Law
Living Wills and Durable Powers of Attorney
Physician-Assisted Suicide

References

Agich, G. (1993). *Autonomy and long-term care*. New York: Oxford University Press.

Binstock, R. H., & Post, S. G. (Eds.) (1991). *Too old for health care? Controversies in medicine, law, economics, and ethics*. Baltimore: Johns Hopkins University Press.

Callahan, D. (1987). *Setting limits: Medical goals in an aging society*. New York: Simon & Schuster.

Caring for an aging world: Allocating scarce resources. (1994). *Hastings Center Report, 24*(5), 3–41.

Cantor, M. H. (Ed.) (1994). *Family caregiving: Agenda for the future*. San Francisco: American Society on Aging.

Collopy, B., Boyle, P., & Jennings, B. (1991). New directions in nursing home ethics. *Hastings Center Report, 21*(2) (Special Suppl.), 71–103.

Collopy, B., Dubler, N., & Zuckerman, C. (1990). The ethics of home care: Autonomy and accommodation [Special issue]. *Hastings Center Report, 20*(2).

Jecker, N. S. (Ed.) (1991). *Aging and ethics*. Clifton, NJ: Humana Press.

Kapp, M. B. (1991). Our hands are tied: Legally induced moral tensions in health care delivery. *Journal of General Internal Medicine, 6,* 345–348.

Kane, R. A., & Caplan, A. L. (Eds.) (1990). *Everyday ethics: Resolving dilemmas in nursing home life*. New York: Springer Publishing.

Laslett, P., & Fishkin, J. S. (Eds.) (1992). *Justice between age groups and generations*. New Haven, CT: Yale University Press.

Mehlman, M. J., & Visocan, K. A. (1992). Medicare and Medicaid: Are they just health care systems? *Houston Law Review, 29,* 835–865.

Moody, H. R. (1992). *Ethics in an aging society*. Baltimore: Johns Hopkins University Press.

Rawls, J. (1971). *A theory of justice*. Cambridge, MA: Belknap Press.

Sachs, G. A., & Cassel, C. K. (Eds.) (1994). Clinical ethics. *Clinics in Geriatric Medicine, 10,* 403–556.

ter Meulen, R., Topinkova, E., & Callahan, D. (1994). What do we owe the elderly? Allocating social and health care sources [Special issue]. *Hastings Center Report. 24*(2).

ETHNICITY

The process of *defining ethnicity* involves the designation of a group of people who emphasize common origins and language, shared history, and selected aspects of cultural difference (Ember & Ember, 2004). In the United States, immigration trends include both voluntary and involuntary immigrants. In addition to the *voluntary immigration* of the Irish and the Germans in the 1840s and the late-19th and early-20th centuries, there existed the *forced immigration* of enslaved *African* peoples, a large cohort of *involuntary immigrants*. There also were large numbers of *Native Americans* here long before the influx of Europeans. While today the older population in the United States is predominately Caucasian, *ethnically diverse older persons* are projected to represent 25.5% of the aged in 2030, up from 16.1% in 1999 (Yoon & Lee, 2004). In 2003, non-Hispanic whites represented nearly 83% of the *aged population of the United States*; by the year 2050 it is predicted that the composition of the aged population will be 61% non-Hispanic white, 18% Hispanic, 12% African American, and 8% Asian (Federal Interagency Forum on Aging-Related Statistics, 2004). In contrast to the "*melting pot*" *theory*, in which all ethnic groups are fully assimilated into American life, many groups have retained cultural boundaries. This is especially true among those groups who are more recent immigrants to the United States.

Ethnicity may be defined variously from a categorical perspective, in which cultural content and uniformity within a group is emphasized, and from a transactional perspective, which emphasizes heterogeneity of ethnic group boundaries in the expression of social and behavioral cultural features (Coreil, Bryant, & Henderson, 2001; Green, 1999). The *ethnic aged* exist in a complex world in which their unique cultural values and obligations co-exist with those of a larger society. Consequently, within each individual's life there exists a spectrum of experiences that vary in the extent to which their ethnically derived values may be validated or expressed. This phenomenon is known as "*situational ethnicity*." *Assimilation* into a dominant society through *intermarriage*, as well as other factors, may cause second- and third-generation immigrants to depart from earlier cultural values and norms. This may adversely affect family caregiving structures, as well as how the aging person perceives the prospect of growing older. Societal and economic factors may be such that patterns of respect and support for elders that are linked to cultural traditions may or may not be operable (Sokolovsky, 1997).

The concept of "*ethnic compensation*" has that ethnic elderly may benefit from positive cultural emphases on respect and care for the aged as defined by the ethnic group, and that this may operate to ensure quality of life for the older person in later years (Sokolovsky, 1997; Markides, Liang, & Jackson, 1990). For example, the ethnic older person incorporated into the family home as a valued grandparent and keeper of traditions constitutes ethnic compensation. However, there is substantial ethnic-based variation across and within culture groups. The benefits of ethnic compensation may be compromised due to second- and third-generation adult children assuming a transient lifestyle to seek employment. They may be unavailable for eldercare, and in some instances cultural values act against the seeking of outside services when *family care* is not available. For example, an increasingly large number of grandparents from diverse groups are assuming the role of primary caregiver for grandchildren. In Latino communities, cultural norms that condemn seeking help from outside of the family may add additional stressors to already burdened older persons (Kropf & Kolomer, 2004; Baird, John, & Hayslip, 2000; Caputo, 1999).

Another perspective on ethnic aging is the concept of "*multiple jeopardy*," which suggests that minority aged may experience life within the context of deprivation and hardship, thus exacerbating the problems of old age. For example, it can be said that *American Indian and Alaska Native* (AI/AN) older people experience multiple jeopardy: they are members of a minority group, are impoverished, and are in poor health when compared to the general population (Henderson & Henderson, 2004). Indeed, *American Indian older persons* are cited as being the most disadvantaged aged population in the United States (Matcha, 1997). Approximately 76% of urban elders and 86% of rural elders live below the poverty level (U.S. Department of Health and Human Services, Indian Health Service, 1997). Thirty-three percent of *African American elderly* live in poverty, with 50% living at or below that level in rural areas (Yoon & Lee, 2004). In 2002, 21% of older Hispanics were more likely to be living in poverty, as compared to 8% of their white counterparts (Federal Interagency Forum on Aging-Related Statistics, 2004). As the number of minority aged increases, so do their health care needs. Early in life, many minority elders had labor-intensive jobs, inadequate health care access, and substandard nutrition. Because of these experiences, ethnic elders may experience greater burdens of morbidity than their counterparts in the mainstream population (Haber, 1994).

"Minority" status may be accorded to persons from ethnic populations who are "singled out for differential and inferior treatment on the basis of such characteristics as their race, sex, nationality, or language" (Jackson, 1980). While many of the immigrant populations from the distant past have been assimilated into the mainstream, more recent immigrants have not, and some may be considered to have minority status.

For the American Indian/Alaska Native (AI/AN), African American, and Hispanic communities, health disparities continue to exist. Over half of the African American elderly experience higher morbidity rates than the majority population (Yoon & Lee, 2004). There is excess mortality in the elder AI/AN population associated with cardiovascular disease, respiratory disease, diabetes, alcoholism, and injuries (Indian Health Service, 1997). Regarding self-perceived health status, more elderly from Hispanic/Latino (13.1%), African American (14.1%), and AI/AN (13.1%) populations rank their health status as "fair" or "poor," as compared to the respondent assessed health status of the white population (8.6%). In contrast, 6.7% of Asian elderly assessed their health status as "fair" or "poor" (Centers for Disease Control and Prevention, 2004).

During the 21st century, there will continue to be new immigrants to the United States. These persons will someday become the society's ethnic aged. The consideration of ethnicity as a factor affecting the quality of old age will continue to be a topic of interest to gerontologists, as well as other researchers in diverse fields.

L. CARSON HENDERSON

References

Baird, A., John, R., & Hayslip, B. (2000). Custodial grandparents among African Americans: A focus group perspective. In B. Hayslip, Jr. & R. Goldberg-Glen (Eds.), *Grandparents raising grandchildren: Theoretical, empirical, and clinical perspectives* (pp. 125–144). New York: Springer Publishing.

Caputo, R. K. (1999). Grandmothers and co-resident grandchildren. *Families in Society, 80,* 120–126.

Centers for Disease Control and Prevention, (2004). *National Health Interview Survey*. National Center for Health Statistics, USA.

Coreil, J., Bryant, C., & Henderson, J. (2001). *Social and behavioral foundations of public health* (pp. 127–145). Thousand Oaks: Sage Publications.

Ember, C., & Ember, M. (2004). *Encyclopedia of medical anthropology: Health and illness in the world's cultures*, (Vol. 1, p. xxix). New York: Kluwer Academic/ Plenum Publishers.

Federal Interagency Forum on Aging-Related Statistics. (2004). *Older Americans 2004: Key indicators of well-being.* Washington, DC: U.S. Government Printing Office.

Green, J. W. (1999). *Cultural awareness in the human services* (3rd ed., pp. 3–47). Boston: Allyn and Bacon.

Haber, D. (1994). *Health promotion and aging* (pp. 233–254). New York: Springer Publishing.

Henderson, J. N., & Henderson, L. C. (2004). Oklahoma Choctaw. In C. R. Ember & M. Ember (Eds.), *Encyclopedia of medical anthropology: Health and illness in the world's cultures* (Vol. 2., pp. 915–922). New York: Kluwer Academic/Plenum Publishers.

U.S. Department of Health and Human Services, Indian Health Service (1997). *Indian health focus: Elders (data report).* Rockville, MD: Indian Health Service.

Jackson, J. J. (1980). *Minorities and aging.* Belmont, CA: Wadsworth.

Kropf, N. P., & Kolomer, S. (2004). Grandparents raising grandchildren: A diverse population. In S. M. Cummings & C. Galambos, (Eds.), *Diversity & aging in the social environment* (pp. 65–83). New York: Haworth Social Work Practice Press.

Markides, K., Liang, J., & Jackson, J. S. (1990). Race, ethnicity, and aging: Conceptual and methodological issues. In R. Binstock & L. K. George (Eds.), *Handbook of aging and the social sciences.* San Diego: Academic Press.

Matcha, D. A. (1997). *The sociology of aging: A social problems perspective.* Boston: Allyn and Bacon.

Sokolovsky, J. (1997). Starting points: A global, cross-cultural view of aging. In J. Sokolovsky (Ed.), *The cultural context of aging: Worldwide perspectives* (2nd ed., p. xv). Westport, CT: Bergin and Garvey.

Sokolovsky, J. (1997). Aging, ethnicity, and family support. Race and ethnicity are related to poverty among the older population. In J. Sokolovsky (Ed.), *The cultural context of aging: Worldwide perspectives* (2nd ed., pp. 263–275). Westport, CT: Bergin & Garvey.

Yoon, D. P., & Lee, E. O. (2004). Religiousness/ spirituality and subjective well-being among rural elderly Whites, African Americans, and Native Americans. In S. M. Cummings & C. Galambos (Eds.), *Diversity and aging in the social environment* (pp. 191–211). New York: Haworth Social Work Practice Press.

ETHNOGRAPHIC RESEARCH

Ethnographic research is the primary methodological tool anthropologists have used for exploring the cultural framework and dynamics of contemporary societies. This kind of investigation explores the fabric of values, perceptions, human relationships, and socially engineered behavior that guides people as they pass through the life cycle (Ikels & Beall, 2000). Such varied patterns of created ideology, social organization, and the ways people produce and distribute valued objects constitute the cultural systems into which all humans grow. Ethnographic research has been centered on the community context of how culture dynamically shapes the world people live in. This usually involves long-term residence or extensive contact within a community or in locales where people carry out their everyday lives. The prolonged, very personal encounter with the community under study can provide a special insight into how people experience aging in varied social settings. For example, one of the earliest applications of the ethnographic methods to a specific gerontological issue was the work of medical anthropologist *Otto von Mering* (1957). In the mid-1950s he conducted fieldwork in the geriatric wards of psychiatric hospitals, illustrating how the cultural devaluing of old age in the United States led to a withdrawal of psychosocial care for older patients.

The "Native" View of Aging

The essential aim of ethnographic research is to understand, as comprehensively as possible, the world through the eyes of the people being studied. This holistic construction of cultural systems is learned through direct observation, participating in daily life, and recording in the native language the meanings of things, persons, and actions. This generalized process of "*participant observation*" enables researchers to gather data about a culture by living with, or having direct and frequent contact for a prolonged period with, the people they are trying to comprehend (Keith, 1988). The broad connection of ethnographic research techniques to the field of gerontology has been delineated in the volume *New Methods for Old Age Research* (Fry & Keith, 1986). This approach applies as much to studying aging in small villages in the South Pacific as it does to research in nursing homes, in ethnic communities in North America, or among urban Japanese households (Sokolovsky, 1997). For example, anthropologists Dorothy and David Counts (1985, 1996) followed up their long-term *ethnographic work on aging* in Papua New Guinea with a 2-year study of the communities formed by seniors who travel North America in recreational vehicles (RVs). They undertook this latest project by buying an RV and becoming very active participant observers in the nomadic lifestyle of older adults who travel throughout Canada and the United States.

Global Comparison

To date, the most comprehensive and sophisticated *cross-cultural study of aging* has been *Project AGE* (Age, Generation, Experience), codirected by *Christine Fry* and *Jennie Keith*. Using a common methodology, complex ethnographies of age and aging were conducted at 6 sites around the world between 1982 and 1990. The research shows how both "system-wide" community features (e.g., social inequality) and "internal mechanisms" (e.g., values) create distinct contexts for conceptualizing the life cycle, establishing age norms, and influencing the perception of well-being in old age. Key results of this project can be found in *The Aging Experience: Diversity and Commonality Across Cultures* (Keith, Fry, Glascock, Ikels, Dickerson-Putnam, Harpending, et al., 1994).

Over the past 25 years the ethnographic study of aging has produced a large body of work covering most regions of the world. Ethnographic approaches to aging not only have looked at the general influence of cultural differences on aging but also have begun to focus on specific gerontological issues, such as the cultural response to late-life frailty, long-term care environments, senior centers, the impact of community redevelopment, minority/ethnic aging, and gender. Access to this rapidly expanding literature can be found in several texts: *The Cultural Context of Aging* (Sokolovsky, 1997); *Other Cultures, Elder Years* (Rhodes & Holmes, 1995) and *Old Age in Global Perspective* (Albert & Cattell, 1994). Information about new and ongoing ethnographic aging research and related publications can be followed through the Cultural Context of Aging Web site at: www.stpt.usf.edu/~jsokolov.

Ethnographic research in aging studies overlaps with a multidisciplinary movement sometimes referred to as "*qualitative gerontology*" (Gubrium & Sankar, 1994; Rowles & Schoenberg, 2000). This embraces a wide range of disciplinary practitioners, from qualitative sociologists, cultural geographers, and clinical psychologists who rely on case study materials to humanists who use literature, art, and other expressive media to enhance our understanding of aging. It should be emphasized that the ethnographic variant of this qualitative approach to studying aging does not just involve long, complex personal interviews. Rather, it situates culture within a community framework and requires witnessing how meaning is expressed in everyday life.

JAY H. SOKOLOVSKY

See also
Longitudinal Research

References

Albert, S. M., Cattell, M. G., & Cattell, A. (1994). *Old age in global perspective*. New York: G. K. Hall.

Counts, D. A., & Counts, D. R. (Eds.) (1985). *Aging and its transformations: Moving toward death in Pacific societies*. Lanham, MD: University Press of America.

Counts, D. A., & Counts, D. R. (Eds.) (1996). *Over the next hill: An ethnography of RVing seniors in North America*. Petersborough, Ontario: Broadview Press.

Fry, C. L., & Keith, J. (Eds.). (1986). *New methods for old age research: Anthropological alternatives*. South Hadley, MA: Bergin and Garvey.

Keith, J., Fry, C. L., Glascock, A. P., Ikels, C., Dickerson-Putnam, J., Harpending, H. C., & Draper, P. (1994). *The aging experience: Diversity and commonality across cultures*. Thousand Oaks, CA: Sage Publications.

Gubrium, J., & Sankar, A. (Eds.) (1994). *Qualitative methods in aging research*. Newbury Park, CA: Sage Publications.

Ikels, C., & Beall, C. (2000). Age, aging and anthropology. In R. Binstock & L. George (Eds.), *Handbook of aging and the social sciences* (5th ed.). San Diego: Academic Press.

Keith, J. (1988). Participant observation: A modest little method whose presumption may amuse you. In K. W. Schaie, R. T. Campbell, W. Meredith, & S. C. Rawlings (Eds.), *Methodological issues in aging research* (pp. 211–230). New York: Springer Publishing.

von Mering, O. (1957). A family of elders. In O. von Mering & S. King (Eds.), *Remotivating the mental patient* (pp. 96–114). New York: Russel Sage Foundation.

Rhodes, E., & Holmes, L. D. (1995). *Other cultures, elder years* (2nd ed.). Thousand Oaks, CA: Sage Publications.

Rowles, G., & Schoenberg, N. (Eds.) (2000). *Qualitative gerontology* (2nd ed.). New York: Springer Publishing.

Sokolovsky, J. (Ed.). (1997). *The cultural context of aging: Worldwide perspectives* (2nd ed.). Westport, CT: Bergin and Garvey.

ETHNOGRAPHY

See
Ethnographic Research

EUROPEAN ACADEMY FOR MEDICINE OF AGEING (EAMA)

In the 1990s, an informal group of European professors of medical gerontology concerned about the greater need for geriatric training created the European Academy for Medicine of Ageing (EAMA). A survey of existing *geriatric teaching programs* was conducted to better define the training needs in geriatrics in Europe for the 21st century. The group noted a lack of structured geriatric core curriculum and the need of an "advanced postgraduate geriatric course for junior geriatricians in the European universities." The first 1-week residential session of what was called the "*European Academy for Medicine of Ageing*" course took place in January 1995 in the University Institute Kurt Boesch in Sion (Switzerland). Ten years later during the celebration of the EAMA anniversary, a group of former students and excecutive board members identified the main reasons for the outstanding success of EAMA, as outlined here (Bonin-Guillaume et al., 2005; Sieber et al., 2002; Swine, 2004).

First, a group of extremely motivated academic geriatricians (S. *Duursma*, J. *Grimley* Evans, J.-P. *Michel*, and H. *Staehelin*) anticipated the future care needs of the oldest old European population. EAMA's exclusive goal "to teach the future *teachers in geriatrics*," including enhancing, updating, and improving use of scientific knowledge and educational and managerial competences in geriatrics. EAMA also contributes to harmonizing the attitudes and goals of future opinion leaders in *geriatric medicine* throughout Europe. Most importantly, EAMA initiates an excellent and invaluable international network among young geriatricians.

The *University Institute Kurt Boesch*, an outstanding teaching facility, is located in Sion, ideally situated in the Wallis canton of Switzerland, easy to reach by plane or train. Furthermore, Sion is close to facilities but far enough from bigger towns, such as Geneva or Lausanne, to encourage students to associate together there in the evenings. The 2-year residential course consists of 4 intense, 1-week sessions (twice a year, in January and June). This course is characterized by the most up-to-date teaching curriculum and innovative, interactive education with strong participation of the EAMA scientific board members. A networking meeting with former EAMA students is organized during the session's final days. These meetings draw high attendance and allow integration of the new members into the growing community of EAMA members.

EAMA comprises a multicultural melting pot of young and promising geriatricians from 24 different European countries as well as Argentina, China, Costa Rica, Cuba, Estonia, Israel, Lebanon, Mexico, Senegal, South Africa, Tunisia, Ukraine and the United States) who constitute the academic geriatric relief of tomorrow. Furthermore, the best geriatrics teachers specialists and, experts from all over the world play an important role during the sessions, as they update the scientific knowledge and stimulate research ideas in various and promising fields. Well-known colleagues interact with the students and strongly contribute to EAMA's success.

The academy has defined learning objectives. Attending an EAMA course, students are expected to acquire skills in identifying learning deficiencies and setting priorities within different geriatric topics, as well as in formulating important messages, leading discussions, and presenting lectures with the most up-to-date and appropriate teaching technology. Students are asked to generate new research ideas and develop their abilities to collect and critically interpret data. This intensive training allows students on one hand to become more familiar with and confident of their use of the English language, and on the other hand to improve their abilities in oral presentations or writing of scientific articles.

Variety of teaching methods are used: in "*state-of-the-art lectures*" (45 minutes), international leaders in the field present the most recent information in their specialty, followed by a 30-minute debate during which students can ask questions and express opinions. These plenary sessions complete the scientific knowledge and stimulate research ideas. In a similar way, each student is asked to give a lecture on a topic determined and communicated by the scientific board a few weeks before the session. Usually, the topic is not within the student's field of research or competence. Prior to the session, the student prepares and submits an abstract to a designated member of the scientific committee. The student then presents a 15-minute lecture on the most recent information on the topic, using the most appropriate educational techniques, and then answers questions from peers and the instructor. An expert final comment and judgment closes the student's presentation. In addition, small group discussions (7 to 9 members) on clinical, managerial, or ethical topics represent another aspect of the course. In each group, 1 student is designated as the chairperson to lead the discussion (10 minutes) and then help the designated reporter summarize and present the important ideas to the other groups. All of the students as well as experts in the field discuss this report in a plenary session. The composition of the discussion groups is changed from one session to the next, to improve intercultural communication and networking. The chairperson and reporter are designated shortly before the discussion takes place, and they differ for each group discussion.

Since the very first EAMA session, both teachers' and students' activities have been evaluated. Students assess the performance of teachers and experts as well as the skills of their peers. The EAMA scientific board members not only interact with the students as tutors but also realize a formal evaluation of each student's performance. A comparison of the evaluation results among students and teachers has shown that students are more strict and severe with their peers than the instructors. Each student gets a written report as to his/her skills, as evaluated by the student colleagues, and is apprised of his/her personal improvement within the group. For example, students' scores from the first to the last session of the third EAMA course showed significant improvement in each training goal. The scientific content of lectures, the formulation of take-home messages, and oral presentation techniques improved between 23% to 33%. The group's peer evaluation from the first to the fourth sessions increased by 31%. A self-evaluation of the students' specific skills as related to EAMA goals shows that each session is important. During the first sessions students improved in general geriatric knowledge, data gathering, priority identification, and better use of methodology; during the last sessions, they felt more confident in the formulation of important communications, the generation of new research ideas, and establishing an international academic network. Ninety-one percent of former EAMA students received a geriatric professional promotion, and 20% of those working in academic facilities were nominated to professor of geriatric medicine.

EAMA's concept has received confirmation and validation with its recent accreditation (2001) by the European Community and the *European Union Geriatric Medicine Society*. Numerous international bodies include EAMA sessions within their scientific programs, such as the *Austrian Geriatric Society*, the European Union Geriatric Medicine Society, the *Swiss Geriatric Society*, and the World Congress of the International Association.

Former students, who constitute a strong international network, have launched similar courses in different parts of the world, including the Middle East European Academy for Medicine of Ageing, the *Latin America Academy for Medicine of Ageing*, the *Saint Louis University Geriatric Academy*, and the *European Nursing Academy for the Care of Olders*.

JEAN-PIERRE MICHEL

Acknowledgments

We would like to thank the entire executive board committee, the heads of nongovernmental organizations, the Novartis

Foundation for Aging Research, and the Merck Institute on Health and Aging, as well as the teachers, experts, and students who have supported and promoted EAMA to its high level of international recognition and interest.

References

Bonin-Guillaume, S., Kressig R. W., Gavazzi, G. et al. (2005 in press). Teaching the future teachers in geriatrics: The ten years success story of the European Academy for Medicine of Ageing (EAMA). *Journal of Gerontology and Geriatrics.*

Sieber, C., Zekry, D., Swine, C., & Michel, J. P. (2002). Back to the future: The European Academy for Medicine of Ageing revisited. *Gerontology. 48*, 56–58.

Swine, C., Michel, J. P., Duursma, S., Grimley Evans, J., & Staehelin, H. B. (2004). Evaluation of the European Academy for Medicine of Ageing "Teaching the Teachers" program (EAMA course II 1997–1998). *Journal of Nutrition, Health and Aging, 8*, 181–186.

EUTHANASIA

"Euthanasia" comes from Greek words meaning "a gentle and easy death" or "the means of bringing about a gentle and easy death." Most ancient Greek and Roman practitioners—Socrates, Plato, and Stoic philosophers from Zeno to Seneca—supported physician-induced death of the sick and suffering to bring about a gentle and easy death (Vanderpool, 1995). In contrast to these dominant Graeco-Roman traditions, the *Hippocratic oath* required physicians to swear "neither to give a deadly drug to anybody if asked for it, nor . . . [to] make a suggestion to this effect" (Temkin & Temkin, 1976). The oath, which continues to exert a towering influence in Western medicine, reflects the *Pythagorean* conviction that human beings are owned by *God* or *gods* and should abide by a divine determination of life's completion (Carrick, 1985). Indeed, its influence extends even to those people who have no such notion of their life being owned by others than themselves.

Contemporary discussions of euthanasia have increasingly dealt with "the action of inducing a gentle and easy death." Although the action could be undertaken by anyone, the question has particular resonance for physicians, who commonly are involved with patients who are dying. Ethical debates about the permissibility of *physician involvement in euthanasia* concern the question: are physicians ethically permitted to act to end a patient's life? This question should be distinguished from other ethical questions that may arise at the end of life. For example, the term "euthanasia" as commonly used today does not concern questions related to refraining from using or continuing life-sustaining treatments (passive euthanasia), nor those related to providing patients with the means necessary to end their own lives (assisted suicide). Many who defend the permissibility of *physician-assisted suicide* do not support *physician-assisted euthanasia.* Advocates of physician-assisted suicide approve of letting physicians prescribe medications that patients may use to end their lives; they do not necessarily approve of letting physicians actually administer, for example, *lethal injections* for the purpose of terminating patients' lives.

Ethical Perspectives

Contemporary *ethical arguments supporting euthanasia* often appeal to compassion for the suffering of a *terminally ill* and imminently dying patient. These arguments purport to show that to aid another person in dying is ethically permissible under circumstances where that person's condition is associated with severe and unrelenting suffering that is not the result of inadequate pain control or comfort care.

Other arguments defending the permissibility of euthanasia make reference to the ethical principle of *autonomy.* The principle of autonomy requires respecting the informed choices of competent patients. In this approach, euthanasia is ethically limited to situations in which competent people make informed repeated requests for aid in dying, in the face of terminal illness.

Critics of euthanasia charge that both compassion-based and autonomy-based ethical arguments are inadequate. Arguments invoking compassion are faulted on the ground that there is no principled basis for limiting euthanasia to competent people who choose it. After all, many suffering people are not competent. Therefore, if the ethical basis for providing aid in dying is compassion, then aid in dying should logically be extended to incompetent persons.

Arguments relying on the ethical principle of autonomy are also criticized for failing to offer a principled basis for appropriately limiting euthanasia. The autonomy-based arguments do not require limiting euthanasia to those experiencing severe and unrelenting suffering, but presumably would allow applying euthanasia to healthy people who wished to die. Critics of these arguments also doubt that patients' requests to die reflect autonomous choices, since such requests may occur due to inadequate palliative and comfort care, continued use of invasive and futile interventions, and failure to diagnose and treat other underlying causes of the request, such as depression (Emanuel, 1999). In such cases, meeting a person's request for assistance in dying is not supported by a principle of respect for the individual's autonomy.

Both autonomy-based and compassion-based arguments are vulnerable to the further objection that there is no principled basis for restricting euthanasia to persons who are imminently dying. After all, the prospect of suffering for a long period of time is arguably worse than the prospect of suffering briefly. Likewise, the principle of respect for autonomy presumably applies to all competent individuals, irrespective of whether they are about to die.

Legal Perspectives

Just as the ethical status of euthanasia is controversial, the legal status of both euthanasia and assisted suicide has been the subject of intense debate in the United States. At present, legislative statutes make *assisted suicide a criminal act* in 29 states; however, the constitutionality of these statutes has been challenged in the states of Michigan and Washington. Defenders of physician-assisted death have placed citizen initiatives on the ballots of several Western states to decriminalize euthanasia and/or assisted suicide. In 1997, Oregon passed the *Oregon Death With Dignity Act*, which allows terminally ill Oregon residents to obtain from their physicians prescriptions for self-administered, lethal medications. However, the act specifically prohibits euthanasia by barring physicians (and others) from directly administering a medication to end a patient's life.

Although euthanasia is illegal in the United States and in most other nations, it is no longer against the law in the *Netherlands*. In 2002, the Dutch parliament passed an act formally exempting physicians from criminal liability for euthanasia and assisted suicide provided certain conditions are met. These conditions include that: (1) the patient's request is voluntary and well considered; (2) the patient experiences lasting and unbearable suffering; (3) the physician has informed the patient about their situation and prospects; (4) the physician and patient believe there is no other reasonable solution; (5) the physician consults with one other independent physician regarding 1 through 4 above; and (6) the physician exercises due care in terminating the life or assisting with suicide.

Euthanasia and Older Adults

Although debates about euthanasia apply to persons of all ages, they may bear special relevance to elderly persons. This is because death is nearer in old age, and therefore aging individuals may be more likely than younger persons to think about death and the dying process. Perhaps the aging of the population that is occurring in most developed nations will lead societies to focus greater attention on how to assure humane care at the end of life. The question of whether or not euthanasia represents humane medical care for dying patients will continue to be discussed.

NANCY S. JECKER

See also

End-of-Life Care
Physician-Assisted Suicide

References

Carrick, P. (1985). *Medical ethics in antiquity: Philosophical perspectives on abortion and euthanasia.* Dordrecht, Netherlands: D. Reidel.

Emanuel, L. L. (1999). Facing requests for physician-assisted suicide. *Journal of the American Medical Association, 280*(7), 643–647.

Temkin, O., & Temkin, C. L. (Eds.). (1967). Ancient medicine: Selected papers of Ludwig Edelstein. Baltimore: Johns Hopkins University Press.

Vanderpool, H. Y. (1995). Death and dying: Euthanasia and sustaining life. In W. T. Reich (Ed.), *Encyclopedia of bioethics* (revised ed., pp. 554–561). New York: Simon and Schuster, MacMillan.

EVOLUTIONARY THEORY

What is the cause of *biological aging*? This is a question that can be addressed at 2 different levels, the proximate and the ultimate. The proximate level of explanation addresses mechanistic questions, such as those of physiology, biochemistry, and pathology. It considers the question above as, *how* do organisms age. The ultimate level of explanation approaches a question from the perspective of evolutionary theory. It considers the initial question as, *why* do organisms age. Because the 2 levels of explanation give such different answers to the same question, it might seem that they have little or nothing to offer each other. In tackling the proximate question, researchers have proposed myriad theories involving the immune system, the neuroendocrine system, the reproductive system, free radical accumulation, somatic mutations, and collagen cross-linkage. Each theory can be based on empirical observation, but as the proverbial group of blind men discovered when each described a different part of an elephant, these proximate theories can fall short of offering a complete answer. The ultimate explanation provided by evolutionary theory of the causes of biological aging has turned out to be an indispensable tool guiding the formulation and interpretation of proximate explanations.

The answer to the proximate question of how we age is complex and far from being known. The answer to the ultimate question, conversely, likely resides in the "*evolutionary theory of aging*," which considers the inevitability of aging as a simple consequence of the fact that the force of natural selection is lessened at later ages (Rose, 1991).

According to Darwin's mechanism of evolutionary change via *natural selection*, when there is heritable variation for a trait within a population, and when certain variants lead their carriers to produce relatively greater numbers of offspring, those beneficial variants of the trait will be present in an increasing proportion of the population over time. Conversely, alleles that reduce the reproductive success of individuals carrying them occur in fewer and fewer individuals with each successive generation. The variation that natural selection acts on is the result of a constant, albeit low, rate of mutation occurring in the germ cells of all individuals. *Mutations* usually have a relatively specific age-of-action, and generally their effects are slight, but negative (Simmons & Crow, 1977), although their effects occasionally can produce an increase in fitness. Mutations, although making possible all the adaptations we see, also are responsible for many of the decrements in physiological processes that are phenotypically observable as "aging."

Medawar (1946, 1952) first suggested that the declining force of natural selection with advancing age had important ramifications for the problem of human aging. Deleterious alleles for genes with late ages-of-action, he proposed, would accumulate to higher frequencies than deleterious alleles for genes with early ages-of-action. Imagine, to use a simplistic example, 2 mutations in humans, each of which causes a fatal breakdown in some key biochemical pathway. In one individual the mutation's age-of-action is 13 years. In another, the same deleterious effect is specified, but it does not have this effect until 100 years of age. One generation hence, the mutation with the early age-of-action will not be present because the individual carrying the fatal trait dies before she can pass it on to offspring. The mutation with the late age-of-action, conversely, will be present in all of the offspring of the original carrier because they will be born long before the mutation has its fatal effect. Additionally, environmental sources of mortality, such as predation, starvation, and infectious diseases, will also have greater opportunity to limit the number of individuals in the population whose fitness is reduced by the harmful allele. The later a deleterious trait is expressed, the less likely that it will reduce its carrier's fitness (the less a mutation will have *any* effect on its carrier's fitness). Consequently, harmful alleles with later ages-of-action will accumulate in the genome of each species. This is often referred to as the *mutation-accumulation mechanism*.

A variation of this mechanism, mentioned by Medawar (1946, 1952) and discussed in detail by Williams (1957), is referred to as the *antagonistic pleiotropy mechanism* for the evolution of senescence. G. C. Williams (1957) proposed and Charlesworth (1980) gave a formal mathematical demonstration of the possibility that alleles having favorable early effects on fitness but negative later effects may be selected for and thus increase in frequency in a population. As a possible example of an *antagonistic pleiotropy*, consider estrogen production in human females. Although estrogen is critical for reproduction, cumulative exposure is linked to increased mortality risk from breast cancer (McManus & Welsch, 1984) and endometrial cancer (Henderson, Ross, Pike, & Casagrande, 1982). Additional interesting examples of the antagonistic pleiotropy mechanism include the many semelparous or "big-bang" reproducers, such as several species of Pacific salmon (see Finch, 1990, for review). In these fish, dramatic rapid senescence and death occur as a specific result of reproduction, yet if the fish are prevented from spawning via castration or some other means, senescence is delayed long past the usual age, and life span may be more than doubled (Robertson, 1961). Analogously, it has been suggested that diet restriction's extending of life span may be brought about in part by delaying maturation and reproduction (Phelan & Austad, 1989).

Together, these two mechanisms, mutation-accumulation and antagonistic pleiotropy, comprise the evolutionary theory of aging. They are not mutually exclusive, and empirical evidence suggests they both are responsible for the evolution of aging, although the relative importance of each is a matter of debate (Rose, 1991; Rose & Charlesworth, 1980). However, each suggests a slightly different role for natural selection in the process. The mutation accumulation mechanism posits a more passive natural selection unable to weed out the deleterious alleles responsible for aging. The antagonistic pleiotropy mechanism suggests active selection for aging when those deleterious alleles responsible for it are simultaneously responsible for positive early traits.

A notable, but often overlooked, aspect of the evolutionary theory of aging is that it defines aging demographically, or as a population process. Different late-acting harmful alleles will accumulate in different lineages of individuals within a population. Consequently, the more closely related any 2 individuals are, the more likely they will share any of these alleles, and in an entire population of organisms, there will be a variety of deleterious late-acting alleles present. This view of the aging process has important ramifications for the experimental designs used by researchers asking both proximate and ultimate questions. Although it is true that individuals age, the specific aging process can differ from individual to individual. Thus, the aging process as a whole must be described as the collective sum of mechanisms of aging in a population, including the full range of different causes that can occur along with the probabilities that each will occur within any individual. In other words, an accurate and complete understanding of aging in a population is only possible by examining many genotypes to observe a representative sampling of the deleterious alleles in the population. Just as close observation of a single human would provide a portrait of aging that is woefully incomplete at best and seriously misleading at worst, observations made on a few inbred strains of animals are inadequate. For example, Phelan (1992) noted the significant differences—including little overlap—in rates of occurrence of common pathological lesions among strains of mice and rats. Animals of different strains seem to experience different patterns of disease and mortality.

Empirical support for the evolutionary theory of aging is found both in the laboratory and the wild. Perhaps the strongest evidence comes from comparisons of populations evolving under conditions of *high versus low environmental mortality*. Populations living in relatively *safe habitats*, also known as habitats with a low "hazard factor" (Edney & Gill, 1968), are predicted to have slower rates of senescence than those evolving in habitats with high hazard factors. A high hazard factor quickly reduces the power of natural selection to weed out harmful late-acting alleles, whereas individuals living in an environment with a low hazard factor are more likely to reach the age at which their reproduction will be curtailed by a late-acting harmful allele's expression.

Two examples that support this prediction include comparison between island and mainland populations of opossum, and studies of artificial selection for delayed reproduction in fruit flies. Austad (1993) found that in a genetically isolated, island opossum population with a low hazard factor, senescence (measured as the acceleration of age-specific mortality) was significantly reduced when compared with a nearby mainland opossum population with a high hazard factor. Consistent with the predictions of Edney and Gill (1968), the island opossums, evolving in an environment free from the major opossum predators, exhibited smaller litter sizes and increased longevity relative to opossums from the mainland. In addition, in laboratory selection experiments, the force of natural selection in later ages can be varied. Rose (1984), for example, found that as long as there is sufficient genetic variability present, stocks of fruit flies perpetuated by only permitting individuals to reproduce at later ages showed a postponement of senescent changes when compared with stocks of early reproducing flies. In essence, these late reproducing lines have an experimentally reduced hazard factor: The only flies contributing to the gene pool are those with a genome sufficiently devoid of deleterious alleles to allow the individual to survive to advanced ages.

The evolutionary theory of aging has given us an answer to the question, why do organisms age. This answer, valuable in its own right, is increasingly put to productive use in helping to address the more pragmatic questions, how do we age, and can we postpone it.

John P. Phelan

See also
Disposable Soma Theory

References

Austad, S. N. (1993). Retarded senescence in an insular population of Virginia opossums (*Didelphis virginiana*). *Journal of Zoology* (London), *229,* 695–708.

Charlesworth, B. (1980). *Evolution in age-structured populations*. Cambridge, UK: Cambridge University Press.

Edney, E. B., & Gill, R. W. (1968). Evolution of senescence and specific longevity. *Nature, 220,* 281–282.

Finch, C. E. (1990). *Longevity, senescence, and the genome*. Chicago: University of Chicago Press.

Henderson, B. E., Ross, R. K., Pike, M. C., & Casagrande, J. T. (1982). Endogenous hormones as a major factor in human cancer. *Cancer Research, 42,* 3232–3239.

Medawar, P. B. (1946). Old age and natural death. *Modern Quarterly, I,* 30–56.

Medawar, P. B. (1952). *An unsolved problem of biology*. London: H. K. Lewis.

McManus, M. J., & Welsch, C. W. (1984). The effect of oestrogen, progesterone, thyroxine and human placental lactogen on DNA synthesis of human breast ductal epithelium maintained in athymic nude mice. *Cancer, 54,* 1920–1927.

Phelan, J. P., & Austad, S. N. (1989). Natural selection, dietary restriction, and extended longevity. *Growth Development and Aging, 53,* 4–6.

Phelan, J. P. (1992). Genetic variability and rodent models of human aging. *Experimental Gerontology, 27,* 147–159.

Rose, M. R. (1991). *The evolutionary biology of aging*. New York: Oxford University Press.

Rose, M. R. (1984). Laboratory evolution of postponed senescence in *Drosophila melanogaster*. *Evolution, 38,* 1004–1010.

Rose, M. R., & Charlesworth, B. (1980). A test of evolutionary theories of senescence. *Nature, 287,* 141–142.

Robertson, O. H. (1961). Prolongation of the lifespan of kokanee salmon (*O. nerka kennerlyi*) by castration before beginning development. *Proceedings of the National Academy of Sciences of the U.S.A., 47,* 609–621.

Simmons, M. J., & Crow, J. F. (1977). Mutations affecting fitness in *Drosophila* populations. *Annual Review of Genetics, 11,* 49–78.

Williams, G. C. (1957). Pleiotropy, natural selection and the evolution of senescence. *Evolution, 11,* 398–411.

EXCHANGE THEORY

Predicated on an assumption that actors seek returns on personal investments in social interaction, exchange theory utilizes a derivative neo-economic model to explain interpersonal relations. Exchange theorists have generated a considerable corpus of literature identifying positive and negative consequences of interaction in laboratory experiments and field investigations attuned to the ebb and flow of personal relations as a function of recompense or expenditure. In the course of successive iterations, the focus has shifted from neo-economic origins of exchange theory and its contention that people approach all interaction with an eye to maximizing rewards and minimizing costs, to a broader concern with extracting value, questions of diminishing returns in sustained interaction, or exerting power over interaction partners. As Cook (2000) points out, definitions of returns, diminished takings, and marginal costs are dependent on actors' determinations. In gerontology, exchange theory has aided the analysis of the dynamic quality of *interpersonal relations* and their centrality to successful aging. Here, too, conceptualization has evolved from a circumscribed focus on exchange theory to an interest in socioemotional selectivity, selective optimization, social resources, and parallel explanations of differential association, whether those be inclusive or exclusionary. Variations of exchange theory underpin much *caregiving research*, examination of intergenerational relations, as well as the experience of perturbations (Raschick & Ingersoll-Dayton, 2004).

Gerontologists commonly assert that supportive bonding provides salutary effects, satisfaction, and sustenance even as they recognize that such ties can also be stressful and discomforting. Recognizing the importance of interaction, it is widely held that interpersonal relations are salubrious throughout life, emergent issues notwithstanding. *Social support* and *interpersonal networks* mediate stress and facilitate accommodation even as they encompass differential power and resource distributions and influence among interaction partners, or provide fixed or variable avenues to equivalent ends (Cook, 2000; Cook & Yamagishi, 1992; Rook, 2003; Willer, Lovaglia, & Markovsky, 1997; Willer, 1999). In gerontology, analysis of social exchanges looks at the way older people are perceived, at various facets of interaction and reciprocity, whether negotiations yield positive or negative results, and whether being embedded in supportive relationships buffers sundry ill effects (Allen & Ciambrone, 2000; Liang, Krause, & Bennett, 2001; Cohen, Colantonio, & Vernich, 2002; Krause, 2004; Rook, 2001; 2003). Patterns of support, assistance, intergenerational interaction, and historical changes in opportunity or network structures, as well as the ostensible value of the elderly, are frequently explored from an exchange theory perspective (Clarke, 1997; Davey & Eggebeen, 1998; Davey & Norris, 1998; Silverstein, Conroy, Wang, Giarrusso, & Bengtson, 2002).

Exchange theory was foreshadowed in classical economics (Adam Smith, Ricardo, Mill, Bentham), sociology (Weber, Simmel, Durkheim), and anthropology (Frazer, Levi-Straus, Maus, Malinowski), as well as in operant principles of behavioral psychology. The seminal contributions of Homans, Blau, and Emerson in sociology, or Thibaut and Kelley in psychology, provided archetypal formulations that laid the groundwork for subsequent modifications. Iterations include game theory, rational choice theory, and other efforts to highlight how choices are structured by incentives. In another variant, following from Emerson's early emphasis on structural aspects of social relations, an inventive offshoot addresses formalized structural considerations of power in exchange networks. Exchange theorists have focused extensively on what have been termed power and resource differentials within networks, on the emergent structural basis for positional power within networks and on coercive or potentially castigatory control in social networks (Cook, 2000). Despite varying assumptions and predictions, there is an emerging consensus among exchange proponents that structural placement is as important for manifestations of power within networks as are individual attributes. Continuation or termination of social relationships is predicated at least in part on maintaining an endurable balance of power.

According to some research, successful negotiations and inclusion in social processes raise expectations and demands for valued resources while unsuccessful exchanges or exclusion lowers demands and prompts conciliatory behavior, including more modest calls for comparable resources. Furthermore, less powerful actors find themselves competing for inclusion, and as a consequence, more powerful actors gain relatively greater advantage from exchanges and greater benefits still when there is an absence of substitutable alternatives (Thye, Lovaglia, & Markovsky, 1997; Willer, 1999). Notwithstanding many definitional and operational disparities, the problem of open versus closed exchange networks, structural power and status, or a conflation of power and influence, exchange theory offers enticing leads applicable to gerontology. The attention focused on development of inequalities arising out of structural factors implicit in social relations may be particularly helpful for investigating changes that accompany age.

Despite considerable variation, most exchange-based explanations found in the gerontological literature are predicated on 2 assumptions. First, the quest for individual gain is deeply rooted in all behavior; we all seek rewards. Second, activity that is positively reinforced will endure, that which is not will cease. A corollary of the latter is that actions of others are a primary source of emotional well-being and morale. A more general principle is that insofar as situations appear similar to situations in which rewards had previously accrued, they will be reacted to favorably. Another proposition is that the more consequential the result of an action, the more likely it is that action will recur until satiation occurs. Generally no single transaction is sufficient to affect behavior, because interaction occurs as a part of a complex series of interactions. Therefore patterns of success must be considered along with examining indirect or displaced satisfactions in open and closed networks of exchange. Clearly the primary theoretical thrust has major implications for ameliorative as well as disruptive social interaction and the creation of dependencies in the absence of alternative means to an end.

Buttressing these assumptions are propositions that actors bring an array of personal resources with them to any exchange, that resources are not distributed equally, and that all interaction involves an interchange of value, material or nonmaterial. Continued participation is predicated on actors obtaining rewards from interaction while minimizing costs. People will persevere in personal exchanges so long as benefits outweigh costs, depending on availability of alternatives. However, no single interaction occurs in isolation and therefore need not bear the entire calculation of *cost-benefit* reckoning (Cook, 2000). Still, should rewards, tangible or intangible, be devalued relative to opportunity costs to obtain them, social contact becomes unstable and eventually ceases absent qualifying factors. An assessment of costs also entails appraisal of the status of potential partners and availability of alternatives for reaching the same goal or a viable substitute. According to the logic of the exchange model, relationships involving a unidirectional flow of goods, services, or emotions are intrinsically imbalanced and may become increasingly precarious, even brittle (Morgan, Schuster, & Butler, 1991), and potentially exploitative or abusive. Furthermore, to understand the effect diverse types of exchanges have on an actor, the complex of life events characterizing an actor's biography must be part of the estimation (Akiyama, Antonucci, Takahashi, & Langfahl, 2003).

Criticisms of exchange theory have concentrated on issues of inference, empirical referents, the meaning of rewards, their temporal dimensions plus subjectivity of cost assessments. Another theme revolves around the question of the relational nature of statuses, role expectations and benefits derived. Some critics maintain exchange theory has failed to move beyond methodological individualism, simplistic notions of reinforcement, a tendency to rely on reductionist logic and problematic assessment of effects. Although the symbiotic nature of roles, identity, and sense of self is potentially one of the major contributions of exchange theory, few researchers have sought to examine how components of interaction become validating or affirming factors for actors involved or what kinds of timeframes are involved (Davey & Eggebeen, 1998). Nor has sufficient attention yet been paid to how normative expectations define roles—their parity and boundaries—or determine behavior. Network characteristics per se have not yet received close attention.

In response to these and comparable criticisms, a number of reformulations have appeared. Emphasis has shifted from unilateral maximization of investments to maintaining an optimal balance of costs and benefits to greater specification of the influence of the norms of distributive justice, relating these to moral economies, and the determination of normative expectations, especially those of reciprocity. In light of contentions of too heavy an emphasis on psychologistic explanations, variations known as social-environmental, personal resource, and equity theories have addressed issues of transactional definitions of the situation, normative pluralism, and the structural basis of power and influence in decision making. Besides positive effect and reinforcement, negative consequences may also adhere to exchange-based relationships (Cook, 2000; Davey & Norris, 1998; Rook, 2003).

Exchange Theory and Aging

Those who adopt an exchange perspective in social gerontology presume there is a rebalancing of exchange relations as a consequence of aging processes. Changes in the social world of the elderly have been analyzed in terms of realignments of personal relationships brought on by a redefinition of older people's roles, skills, contributions, interpersonal values, or ability to wield power and influence. Since its introduction into gerontology in the 1970s, exchange theory has provided a valuable heuristic tool to analyze changes in primary relationships, strengths and weaknesses of social support networks, family interaction, status decline, and those aspects of interaction predicated on the ability of older persons to impose their will upon their environments. Exchange theory has also been utilized for analyzing fluid dimensions of *self-concepts* and a range of other subjective factors crucial to an individual's sense of personal worth. More recently it has been used as a template for making sense of negative consequences or in the identification of "weak power" as a way to channel interaction. Discussions of human, social, and *cultural capital* also have linkages to exchange theory (Bourdieu, 1986; Lin, Cook, & Burt, 2001).

Particularly important contributions have derived from analyses of the seeming docility, compliance, and deference apparent among some elderly as a mediating strategy for bartering with younger interaction partners or bureaucracies. Recent research has concentrated on the structure of opportunity as a key factor in the accrual or power in intergenerational interaction (Akiyama, Antonucci, Takahashi, & Langfahl, 2003). Becker and colleagues (2003) utilized an exchange model in a 5-year longitudinal investigation of *intergenerational reciprocity* and mutual assistance in 4 ethnic populations and found explanatory value in exchange theory, cultural overlays notwithstanding. Investigations in other cultures (Chou & Chi, 2001; Cornman, Goldman, Glei, Weinstein, & Chang, 2003) buttress the potential explanatory impact of exchange theory. In the past decade, exchange models have expanded their focus to examine differential buffering effects of network size and the effect on various outcomes (Allen & Ciambrone, 2000; Keyes, 2002; Liang, Krause, & Bennett, 2001; Newsom, Nishishiba, Morgan & Rook, 2003; Rook 2003; Unger, McAvay, Bruce, Berkman, & Seeman, 1999).

An innovative variation of exchange theory can be found in *socioemotional selectivity theory*. One of the most intriguing aspects of socioemotional theory is the contention that older people exercise agency in deciding on interaction partners and are not merely passive partners in social relations. As formulated by Carstensen (1995; Fung, Carstensen, & Lang, 2001) and colleagues, socioemotional selectivity theory contends that volitional social relations reflect preferences whenever feasible. As people age, it is hypothesized that they select social relationships based on criteria meaningful to them, jettisoning peripheral involvements as not worth their effort. What is particularly interesting is the implicit notion that power does not reside, ex parte, in other parties to the relationship but that older persons also exercise agency, selecting relationships in terms of relevancy for one or another agenda. In a series of empirical investigations, including contrasting ethnic and cultural differences, proponents of socioemotional selectivity theory have identified credible evidence of a process in which judicious interaction choices are reflected in social exchanges (Fung & Carstensen, 2004; Fung, Carstensen, & Lang, 2001; Fung, Lai, & Ng, 2001; Hendricks & Cutler, 2004).

Social exchange theory has given rise to a number of avenues of research examining how social interaction is structured and how aging is involved. Aldwin and Gilmer (2004) have pointed out the need to be more creative in characterizing social relations and that greater attention must be paid to the emotional significance of interaction partners, not merely their density. Considerable research examines whether social relationships are a factor in the experience of stress, ill–health, and other forms of distress. Investigators are also beginning to consider exogenous determinants of interaction patterns within networks. Cross-linkages with political and moral economics and social capital are shifting away from the early formulation and leading to macro levels of analysis that may portend even greater contributions (Hendricks, 2003; Lin, Cook, & Burt, 2001).

JON HENDRICKS

See also
Social Gerontology: Theories

References

Akiyama, H., Antonucci, T., Takahashi, K., & Langfahl, E. (2003). Negative interactions in close relationships across the life span. *Journal of Gerontology: Psychological Sciences, 58,* P70–79.

Allen, S. M., & Ciambrone, D. (2000). Stage of life course and social support as a mediator of mood state among persons with disabilities. *Journal of Aging and Health, 12,* 318–341.

Aldwin, C., & Gilmer, D. (2004). *Health, illness, and optimal aging*. Thousand Oaks, CA: Sage Publications.

Becker, G., Beyene, Y., Newson, E., & Mayen, N. (2003). Creating continuity through mutual assistance: Intergenerational reciprocity in four ethnic groups. *Journal of Gerontology: Social Science, 58B,* S151–S159.

Bourdieu, P. (1986). The forms of capital. In J. Richardson

(Ed.), *Handbook of theory and research for the sociology of education* (pp. 241–258). Westwood, CT: Greenwood Publishing.

Carstensen, L. (1995). Evidence for a life-span theory of socioemotional selectivity. *Current Directions in Psychological Science, 4,* 151–156.

Chou, K-L., & Chi, I. (2001). Social support exchange among elderly Chinese people and their family members in Hong Kong: A longitudinal study. *International Journal of Aging and Human Development, 53,* 329–346.

Clarke, E. (1997). Social exchange and symbolic interaction perspectives: Exploring points of convergence in research on family and aging. *International Journal of Comparative Sociology, 38,* 296–304.

Cohen, C., Colantonio, A., & Vernich, L. (2002). Positive aspects of caregiving: Rounding out the caregiver experience. *International Journal of Geriatric Psychiatry, 17,* 184–188.

Cook, K. (2000). Social exchange theory. In E. F. Borgatta & R. J. V. Montgomery (Eds.), *Encyclopedia of Sociology* (vol. 4, pp. 2669–2676). New York: Macmillan.

Cook, K., & Yamagishi, T. (1992). Power in exchange networks: A power-dependence formulation. *Social Networks, 14,* 245–265.

Cornman, J., Goldman, N., Glei, D., Weinstein, M., & Chang, M-C. (2003). Social ties and perceived support: Two dimensions of social relationships and health among the elderly in Taiwan. *Journal of Aging and Health, 15,* 616–644.

Davey, A., & Eggebeen, D. (1998). Patterns of intergenerational exchange and mental health. *Journal of Gerontology: Psychological Sciences, 53B,* P86–P95.

Davey, A., & Norris, J. (1998). Social networks and norms across the adult life span. *Canadian Journal on Aging, 17,* 212–233.

Fung, H., & Carstensen, L. (2004). Motivational changes in response to blocked goals and foreshortened time: Testing alternatives to socioemotional selectivity theory. *Psychology and Aging, 19,* 68–78.

Fung, H., Carstensen, L., & Lang, F. (2001). Age-related patterns in social networks among European Americans and African Americans: Implications for socioemotional selectivity across the life span. *International Journal of Aging and Human Development, 52,* 185–206.

Fung, H., Lai, P., & Ng, R. (2001). Age differences in social preferences among Taiwanese and mainland Chinese: The role of perceived time. *Psychology and Aging, 16,* 351–356.

Hendricks, J. (2003). Structure and identity—mind the gap: Toward a personal resource model of successful aging. In S. Biggs, A. Lowenstein, & J. Hendricks (Eds.), *The need for theory* (pp. 63–87). Amityville, NY: Baywood Publications.

Hendricks, J., & Cutler, S. (2004). Volunteerism and socioemotional selectivity in later life. *Journal of Gerontology, 59B,* S251–S257.

Keyes, C. (2002). The exchange of emotional support with age and its relationship with emotional well-being by age. *Journal of Gerontology: Psychological Sciences, 57B,* P518–P525.

Krause, N. (2004). Stressors in highly valued roles, meaning in life, and the physical health status of older adults. *Journal of Gerontology: Social Sciences, 59B,* S287–S297.

Liang, J., Krause, N., & Bennett, J. (2001). Social exchange and well-being: Is giving better than receiving? *Psychology and Aging, 16,* 511–523.

Lin, N., Cook, K., & Burt, R. (2001). *Social capital.* The Netherlands: Aldine de Gruyter.

Morgan, D., Schuster, T. & Butler, E. (1991). Role reversals in the exchange of social support. *Journal of Gerontology: Social Sciences, 46,* S278–S287.

Newsom, J., Nishishiba, M., Morgan, D., & Rook, K. (2003). The relative importance of three domains of positive and negative social exchanges: A longitudinal model with comparable measures. *Psychology and Aging, 18,* 746–754.

Raschick, M., & Ingersoll-Dayton, B. (2004). The costs and rewards of caregiving among aging spouses and adult children. *Family Relations, 53,* 317–326.

Rook, K. (2003). Exposure and reactivity to negative social exchanges: A preliminary investigation using daily diary data. *Journal of Gerontology: Psychological Sciences, 58B,* P100–P111.

Rook, K. (2001). Emotional health and positive versus negative social exchanges: A daily diary analysis. *Applied Developmental Science, 5,* 86–97.

Silverstein, M., Conroy, S., Wang, H., Giarrusso, R., & Bengtson, V. (2002). Reciprocity in parent-child relations over the adult life course. *Journal of Gerontology: Social Science, 57B,* S3–13.

Thye, S., Lovaglia, J., & Markovsky, B. (1997). Responses to social exchange and social exclusion in networks. *Social Forces, 75,* 1031–1047.

Unger, J., McAvay, G., Bruce, M., Berkman, L., & Seeman, T. (1999). Variation in the impact of social network characteristics on physical functioning in elderly persons: MacArthur studies of successful aging. *Journal of Gerontology: Social Sciences, 54B,* S245–S251.

Willer, D. (1999). *Network exchange theory.* Westport, CT: Praeger.

Willer, D., Lovaglia, M., & Markovsky, B. (1997). Power and influence: A theoretical bridge. *Social Forces, 76,* 571–603.

EXECUTIVE FUNCTION

See
Dementia: Frontotemporal

EXERCISE

More than 80% of the U.S. population does not achieve minimal standards for physical activity. Lack of physical activity is associated with considerable impairments and limitations in function, promoting disability and chronic illness. *Physical inactivity* is recognized as an independent risk factor for coronary artery disease and cardiovascular mortality (Fletcher, Balady, Blair, Blumenthal, Caspersen, Chaitman, et al., 1996). *Exercise* confers the greatest benefit for mortality reduction for sedentary individuals who become moderately active. *Physical activity* is defined as "any bodily movement produced by skeletal muscles that results in energy expenditure beyond resting expenditure." Exercise represents the "subset of physical activity that is planned, structured, repetitive, and purposeful in the sense that improvement or maintenance of physical fitness is the objective" (Thompson, 2003). Recommendations to achieve this goal have been well delineated: "At least 30 minutes of moderate-intensity physical activity on most or preferably all days of the week" (National Institutes of Health, 1996). There is a dose-dependent relationship between exercise in the range of 700 to 2000 kcal of energy expenditure per week and both all-cause and cardiovascular mortality in middle-aged and in older adults (Fletcher, et al., 1996).

The most recent recommendations from the American College of Sports Medicine (ACSM) outline a regimen including *cardiovascular activity* (any of several rhythmic exercises involving the large muscle groups such as walking, swimming, biking, and jogging); *resistance training*; *flexibility training*; and appropriate warm-up and cool-down periods (ACSM, 1998). For maintenance of *weight loss* in people who were previously obese or overweight, current recommendations are 80 to 90 minutes of moderate intensity, or 35 minutes of high-intensity activity such as jogging (Klein, Burke, Bray, Blair, Allison, Pi-Sunyer, et al., 2004).

Cardiovascular Responses to Exercise in Older Adults

Participation in an exercise regimen is an effective means to avert or prevent age-related functional decline. Maximum ventilatory oxygen uptake (VO_2 max), a measure of peak cardiovascular function, declines 5% to 15% each decade after age 25. This age-associated change in VO_2 max is a consequence of decreases in both cardiac output and maximal arteriovenous O_2 difference. Maximum *heart rate* declines by 6 to 10 beats per minute per decade, and this reduction accounts for the majority of decline in cardiac output seen with aging. Older adults have smaller stroke volumes and are more dependent on the *Frank-Starling mechanism* to augment stroke volume during exercise. They also experience reduced early diastolic filling and consequently are more dependent on late atrial diastolic filling. With peak exercise, end-systolic volumes are typically higher in older adults, with resultant lower ejection fractions. Older persons also tend to have diminished left ventricular contractility, higher blood pressure, and higher systemic vascular resistance during maximal exercise. However, a lifetime of exercise maintains VO_2 at a level higher than expected for age. The rate of decline in oxygen uptake correlates directly with level of physical inactivity (ACSM, 1998).

Cardiovascular Benefits of Exercise

Exercise can reduce morbidity, physiologic impairments, and functional decline. In addition, physical activity is integral to primary and secondary prevention of chronic diseases. Exercise increases VO_2 max by 2 means: increasing maximum cardiac output, and increasing the capacity of muscles to extract and utilize oxygen from the bloodstream (Fletcher, et al., 1996). Compared to younger counterparts, older adults experience 10% to 30% increases in VO_2 max with prolonged endurance training proportional to *training intensity*. Light intensity training produces minimal changes at most, while higher intensity training yields more substantial results. Increased exercise capacity leads to myriad benefits, including improvements in pulmonary, hormonal, metabolic, hemodynamic, and neurological functions (ACSM, 1998).

Impact on *Metabolic Syndrome*

Physiologic changes related to aging, such as loss of lean body mass, are associated with declines in resting energy expenditure, whole body fat oxidation, physical activity, and activity-related energy expenditure. These changes in lean body mass and metabolism can lead to increased adiposity and visceral fat distribution with a subsequent development of metabolic syndrome and its spectrum of disorders, including *insulin resistance*, *dyslipidemia*, and *hypertension* (Hunter, McCarthy, & Bamman, 2004). Exercise training increases high density lipoprotein and produces favorable effects on insulin sensitivity and adipose tissue distribution (Fletcher, et al., 1996). Prior to changes in body composition or weight, *endurance training* is associated with reductions in both fasting and glucose-stimulated plasma insulin levels as well as improved glucose tolerance and insulin sensitivity. There is some suggestion that older adults do not experience the same magnitude of improvement in insulin level and insulin sensitivity as young adults. The disparity may be attributable to diminished exercise capacity in the elderly and consequently less energy expenditure (ACSM, 1998). Patients with hypertension experience an 8 to 10 mm Hg decrease in systolic and diastolic blood pressure with aerobic exercise (Fletcher, et al., 1996). Both younger and older adults enjoy similar *reductions in blood pressure* with light to moderate exercise (40% to 50% and 50% to 60% of VO_2 max, respectively). Improvements in lipids due to exercise are possibly the consequence of a reduction in fat mass, which leads to increases in HDL and HDL2 levels and reductions in triglyceride and cholesterol:HDL ratio (ACSM, 1998). Exercise reduces the risk of depression, obesity, diabetes, and certain malignancies, including colon and breast. Older adults demonstrate improvements in exercise training comparable to younger adults, and are highly adherent to exercise regimens (Fletcher, et al., 1996).

Improving Body Composition

Seniors who participate in regular exercise experience *improvement in body composition* with 1% to 4% reduction in their percentage of body fat without a decrease in weight (ACSM, 1998). *Sarcopenia* and loss of strength are essentially universal in aging (Hunter, McCarthy, & Bamman, 2004). The etiology of sarcopenia is not yet elucidated, but its consequences are well defined. *Bone density* is linked to strength and muscle mass in the elderly. Thus, sarcopenia could contribute to the development of *osteopenia* and *osteoporosis* (Hunter, McCarthy, & Bamman, 2004). Sarcopenia is associated with loss of muscle strength primarily due to atrophy of Type II muscle fibers (ACSM, 1998). Excretion of urinary creatinine, as a surrogate marker of total muscle mass, decreases almost 50% between ages 20 and 90 years. *Muscle strength decreases* by 15% per decade for the sixth and seventh decade, and 30% per decade after the age of 70 (ACSM, 1998). Reductions in strength are most notable in the lower extremities. Loss of strength in the elderly can contribute to development of impaired ability to perform activities of daily living. By the age of 80, 57% of men and 70% of women are no longer able to perform heavy housework. Physical inactivity in the elderly contributes to decline in muscle function and strength. The main goal of a resistance exercise in older persons is to induce hypertrophy and thus offset the effects of sarcopenia (Hunter, McCarthy, & Bamman, 2004). Older adults who participate in high intensity strength training experience a two- to threefold increase in muscle strength in 3 to 4 months, compared to results for younger individuals. Higher intensity resistance training improves nitrogen balance and is important for weight loss in older adults. *Strength training* is associated with increased resting metabolic rate and decreased body fat mass, and is a requirement for increased energy intake to maintain weight in older adults (ACSM, 1998). A key functional impairment associated with sarcopenia is loss of muscle power output. Multiple studies indicate that resistance training for older adults can result in increased power production; a resistance exercise prescription including a component of low-resistance, high-velocity contractions is recommended to achieve this goal (Hunter, McCarthy, & Bamman, 2004).

Bone loss accelerates with advancing age, leading to markedly decreased bone mineral density and increased risk for osteoporotic fractures. Because physical activity provides the mechanical stimulus for bone health, low bone mineral density in old adults is in part due to disuse atrophy. Both vigorous endurance exercise and resistance training can prevent or *reverse bone loss* in the hip and lumbar spine of older persons. In addition, resistance training decreases the risk for fractures in older persons by improving muscle mass, strength, and balance.

Psychological Well-Being

Regular participation in physical activity is associated with lower incidence and prevalence of depressive symptoms and a more positive psychological profile. These benefits are more prominent in individuals with concurrent medical illness, such as major depressive disorder, cardiovascular disease, or pulmonary disease (Singh, 2002). Thus, increased physical activity may make a significant contribution to the overall quality of life, especially for older adults.

MONIQUE M. WILLIAMS
DENNIS T. VILLAREAL

See also
Exercise Promotion

References

American College of Sports Medicine. (1998). ACSM position stand on exercise and physical activity for older adults. *Medicine and Science in Sports and Exercise, 30*(6), 992–1008.

Fletcher, G. F., Balady, G., Blair, S. N., Blumenthal, J., Caspersen, C., Chaitman, B., et al. (1996). Statement on exercise: Benefits and recommendations for physical activity programs for all Americans. A statement for health professionals by the Committee on Exercise and Cardiac Rehabilitation of the Council on Clinical Cardiology, American Heart Association. *Circulation, 94*(4), 857–862.

Hunter, G. R., McCarthy, J. P., & Bamman, M. M. (2004). Effects of resistance training on older adults. *Sports Medicine, 34*(5), 329–348.

Klein, S., Burke, L. E., Bray, G. A., Blair, S., Allison, D. B., Pi-Sunyer, X., et al. (2004). Clinical implications of obesity with specific focus on cardiovascular disease: A statement for professionals from the American Heart Association Council on Nutrition, Physical Activity, and Metabolism, endorsed by the American College of Cardiology Foundation. *Circulation, 110*(18), 2952–2967.

National Institutes of Health, Consensus Development Panel on Physical Activity and Cardiovascular Health. (1996). Physical activity and cardiovascular health. *Journal of the American Medical Association, 276*(3), 241–246.

Singh, M. A. (2002). Exercise comes of age: Rationale and recommendations for a geriatric exercise prescription. *Journals of Gerontology Series A, Biological Sciences and Medical Sciences, 57*(5), M262–M282.

Thompson, P. D. (2003). Exercise and physical activity in the prevention and treatment of atherosclerotic cardiovascular disease. *Arteriosclerosis, Thrombosis, and Vascular Biology, 23*(8), 1319–1321.

EXERCISE PROMOTION

Regular exercise is beneficial to physical and mental health at any age (Paffenbarger, 2004), but how best to encourage people to make healthy lifestyle choices is less clear. The following basic series of recommendations can feasibly be adopted by generally healthy people at any age, although the degree of vigor is usually modified as one gets older.

Although popular media contains a great deal of advice about *what* changes to make—in exercise, weight-loss, and so forth—Western populations, and in particular in the United States, continue to engage in unhealthy behaviors. This likely reflects the inadequate attention that has been paid to *the mental process* of getting ready to make any personal *health-promoting behavior change*, which is the key to success (Kolt, Driver, & Giles, 2004; Phillips, Schneider, & Mercer, 2004).

Most people who succeed in health-promoting behavior change have first gone through this mental process, which has also been called the "*Wellness Process for Healthy Living*" (Jonas, 2000). The 5 steps of this process focus on an individual's thinking through it to develop an individualized action plan. The first step is self-assessment, and if indicated (age 40 or older is an indicator), assessment by a health professional. The next step is to define success for oneself in realistic terms. Third is to set goals, as determined by the definition of success, and fourth is to establish priorities among those goals. The final step is to mobilize motivation by going through steps 1–4 and then taking control of the process. Since for most people this process is the key to long-term success, it would appear that this is the most important element for clinicians to focus on.

As far as professional assessment is concerned, for persons older than age 40, a thorough medical evaluation is in order. This is especially true if the individual has a history of: previous heart attack; chest pain or severe shortness of breath on exertion; lung disease; any bone, joint, or musculoskeletal disorder; obesity; high serum cholesterol or blood pressure; cigarette smoking or abuse of other drugs or alcohol; prescribed medication used on a regular basis; or any other chronic illness. The use of *exercise stress testing* in asymptomatic individuals with cardiac risk factors has been proposed (Aktas, Ozduran, Pothier, Lang, & Lauer, 2004).

Exercising Regularly: The First Steps

How Much Is Enough. Any amount of exercise is better than nothing. The U.S. Department of Health and Human Services *2005 Dietary Guidelines* contain their most recent recommendation: "Engage in at least 30 minutes of moderate-intensity *physical activity*, above usual activity, at work or at home most days of the week. For most people, greater health benefits can be obtained by engaging in physical activity of more vigorous intensity or longer duration." This can be either of the leisure-time/sports variety or the "lifestyle" variety (e.g., extra household physical activity, walking to work). In any case, it has to be scheduled—even if in "lifestyle bytes" throughout the day—and it has to be regular.

Regularity does not mean every day, however. Many people cannot do that, whether the interfering factor is the weather, job, family responsibilities, or motivation. In general, 5 days rather than 7 are advisable (Cleroux, Feldman, & Petrella, 1999). This approach gives the body a chance to recover from the extra physical activity twice a week, something many regular exercisers find beneficial both for sticking with it and for reducing the risk of injury, and it reduces the mental pressure.

The Need for Regularity. For most people, the most difficult element in becoming and being a regular exerciser is the "regular" part, not the "exercise." However, only regular exercise is beneficial for health, for 3 reasons. First, none of the exercise-related mental or physical health benefits can be derived from irregular exercise. Second, irregular exercise often leads to undue musculoskeletal pain and increases the risk of *exercise-related injury*. Third, because pain and injury lead to a failure to feel good and to feel good about oneself, and interfere with the achievement of other exercise-related goals, if one exercises irregularly the chances of quitting altogether increase significantly.

Establishing a Schedule. For most people starting from scratch, or getting back into it after a long layoff, the first step should be to focus on the "regular," not the exercise. People can safely be advised to just get out there and walk at their regular pace—not fast, with no sweating or hard–breathing—at a convenient time of day, *on a regular schedule*, for 10 minutes or so, 3 times a week for 2 weeks. For the next 2 weeks, 20 minutes 3 times per week is enough, and for a third set do 20 minutes of regular walking, 4 times per week. From there, it is usually a straightforward matter to continue to gradually proceed to 2.5 to 3 hours per week, spread over 5 days. If at this point the person is looking for a sport to do, a useful guide for making that choice is: "The right activity/sport for you is the activity/sport that is right for you." *Pace Walking* (Jonas, 1995), a form of *power walking*, is a popular one to start with, but of course there are many other choices (for examples see Aging and Physical Activity/Personal Resources at www.humankinetics.com,).

Protecting Against Illness and Injury. Pain or strange feelings in the chest or arms that do not seem to be related to the specific muscles used while exercising should be taken seriously, as should feeling faint, weak, short of breath for any extended period of time, pounding or fluttering in the chest, loss of feeling in a limb, or similar sensations. There are 2 groups of exercise-related injury: intrinsic and extrinsic. Intrinsic injury—"*overuse injury*," such as *shin splints*, *swimmer's shoulder*, *tennis elbow*, *stress fracture* of the leg—results from overdoing it, poor technique, or improper equipment. Extrinsic injury results from a collision, be it with an automobile, a pothole, a bump in the road, or another exerciser. The key to avoiding the first is not to overdo it, to learn good technique, and to have proper equipment. The key to avoiding the second is to be safe—"heads-up" at all times.

Advice from Health Professionals. Health professionals who are advising patients/clients should avoid using words like "should," ought," "must," and "have to." Guilt is a poor motivator, often leading to anger, frustration, injury, and quitting. Avoid the term "exercise prescription" unless it is for disease rehabilitation. Unlike most other health-promoting personal behavior changes, regular exercise takes time in one's life for as long as one does it—a significant commitment to personal health. Thus, the clinician best "recommends" rather than "prescribes."

Exercise Is Never Too Late

In 1998, a 101-year-old shot-putter at the World Masters Games in Eugene, Oregon set a world record of 10 feet for his age group. He began training for the event at age 98. Then there was the 65-year-old woman, about 5'2" tall and weighing 180 pounds, who was brought on a ski trip by her daughter to baby-sit the grandchildren. With everyone on the slopes she got tired of waiting around and decided to take her first ski lesson. At the end of that first day, stopping and turning in full control, her smile lit up the mountain. Then there was the former non-athlete who did his first triathlon at age 46; 23 years and 150-plus multisport races later he was still having the time of his life. No, sports are not for everybody. However, if while recognizing personal limitations as to skill and speed, one becomes a regular exerciser and then explores the limits as to activities and time, you never know what one might discover.

STEVEN JONAS

See also
Exercise

References

Aktas, M. K., Ozduran, V., Pothier, C. E., Lang, R., & Lauer, M. S. (2004). Global risk scores and exercise testing for predicting all-cause mortality in a preventive medicine program. *Journal of the American Medical Association, 292*, 1462–1468.

Cleroux, J., Feldman, R. D., & Petrella, R. J. (1999). Lifestyle modifications to prevent and control hypertension. 4. Recommendations on physical exercise training. Canadian Hypertension Society, Canadian Coalition for High Blood Pressure Prevention and Control, Laboratory Centre for Disease Control at Health Canada, Heart and Stroke Foundation of Canada. *Canadian Medical Association Journal, 160*(9 Suppl.), S21–S28.

Jonas, S. (1995). *Regular exercise: A handbook for clinical practice.* New York: Springer Publishing.

Jonas, S. (2000). *Talking about health and wellness with patients: Integrating health promotion and disease prevention into your practice.* New York: Springer Publishing.

Kolt, G. S., Driver, R. P., & Giles, L. C. (2004). Why older Australians participate in exercise and sport. *Journal of Aging and Physical Activity, 12*, 185–198.

Paffenbarger, R. S. Jr., Morris, J. N., Haskell, W. L., Thompson, P. D., & Lee, I-M. (2004). An introduction to the *Journal of Physical Activity and Health. Journal of Physical Activity and Health, 1*, 1–3.

Phillips, E. M., Schneider, J. C., & Mercer, G. R. (2004). Motivating elders to initiate and maintain exercise. *Archives of Physical Medicine and Rehabilitation, 85*(7 Suppl. 3), S52–S57.

U.S. Department of Health and Human Services, & U.S. Department of Agriculture. (2005). *Dietary guidelines for Americans, 2005, executive summary.* Washington, DC: U.S. Government Printing Office. Available: http://www.healthierus.gov/dietaryguidelines/.

EYE: CLINICAL ISSUES

Normally, *aging of the eye* is expressed as a bilateral degeneration of tissues within the eye and its adnexa. Longstanding systemic diseases such as diabetes mark their effects in the eye after time, as do a few notable heritable diseases that only express themselves late in life. Examples of the latter are *corneal dystrophies* and *glaucoma*. The symptoms of *ocular aging* can be experienced by a reduction in vision, centrally, peripherally, and globally. Other age-related visual symptoms include *changes in color vision*, *glare* from bright lights, and the *entoptic phenomena* of *flashes* and *floaters*. Discomfort and redness can indicate changes to the external eye and cornea. The following reviews the effects of aging for the different structures of the eye and its surrounding tissues, beginning with those most anterior and concluding with the optic nerve.

Lids, Lashes and Lacrimals

Nowhere is the passage of time more apparent than around the eyes. *Wrinkles* appear first in the thin, loose *skin of the eyelids* and adjacent facial areas. Redundancy of the skin over the upper lids can lead to overhanging tissue termed *dermatochalasis* and its removal, *blepharoplasty*, is one of the most common *cosmetic oculoplastic procedures* performed worldwide. Age-related thinning of the orbital septum causes *prolapse of orbital fat* resulting in the familiar "*bags under the eyes*." A huge cosmetic medical and surgical industry has developed for the "correction" of these aging changes. Aside from excisional surgery, *injection of collagen* and other substances, such as small doses of *botulinum toxin* (Botox®), that improve the appearance of facial lines by relaxation of muscles (Lowe & Yamauchi, 2004) are becoming increasingly popular.

Later in life, the edges of the eyelids show the changes of a lifetime of *blepharitis* or inflammation of the eyelids. Chronic inspissation of the oil-producing *Meibomian glands* and focal ischemia leads to tissue necrosis and ultimately notching of the lid margin. *Lash loss*, or *madarosis*, is typical, and generally the eyelid margins become somewhat thickened and inflamed in appearance. Regular lid hygiene with warm water compresses applied morning and night encourage Meibomian glands to function properly and may improve lid margin blood flow.

Some common symptoms that older people experience are burning, stinging, and the feeling that there is a *foreign body in the eyes*. These are symptoms of *dry eye* and, paradoxically, they are often accompanied by excessive *reflex tearing*. Normal tear production diminishes with aging, and the outermost oily layer of the tear film becomes deficient because of the aforementioned blepharitis. Occasionally, the dryness goes beyond irritative symptoms and can lead to structural damage to the corneal epithelium, inviting *infectious keratitis*, ulceration, and permanent vision loss. Treatment of age-related *keratitis sicca* involves frequent application of preservative-free artificial tears, temporary or permanent obstruction of the lacrimal drainage system, and warm face cloth compresses to stimulate the Meibomian glands into producing more oil, which stabilizes the tear film and retards its evaporation.

Cornea

The *cornea* is the dome-shaped window that makes up the anterior wall of the eye. It has a steeper radius of curvature than the sclera, and as such provides most of the refractive power of the eye's optical system to focus light on the retina. The precise transmission and bending of the light depends on the maintenance of a smooth, wet anterior surface, as well as keeping the stroma and cornea in a dehydrated state. There is a single layer of endothelial cells lining the posterior surface, which actively pumps water out of the corneal stroma into the anterior chamber. In childhood, the number of endothelial cells per millimeter square is in the vicinity of 4,000; by the age of 80 years, counts as low as 1,000 cells per millimeter square are not uncommon (Faragher, Mulholland, Tuft, Sandeman, & Khaw, 1997). Despite this loss of endothelial cells, the cornea can maintain a relatively youthful clarity and thickness.

One of the most common heritable corneal dystrophies, known as *Fuchs endothelial dystrophy*, expresses itself only later in life. In Fuchs dystrophy, there is an accelerated loss of endothelial cells with thickening of the underlying basement membrane (Descemet's) and formation of nodular excrescences of the membrane termed *guttata*. Treatment of Fuchs starts with efforts to chemically and mechanically dehydrate the cornea, with the application of hypertonic saline solutions topically and directing a hair dryer on the eyes for a period of time each morning. Ultimately, the progressive and irreversible thickening and opacification of the cornea may necessitate a *corneal transplant*.

One of the more common signs of *corneal aging* is the development of a whitish ring around the peripheral cornea near the limbus where the cornea joins the sclera. This *arcus senilis*, as it is called, represents deposition of lipid. It is universal in all races but can be most noticeable cosmetically in eyes with dark irides. A corneal arcus in youth could signify a hyperlipidemia requiring investigation. The age-related corneal arcus is asymptomatic and requires no treatment.

The Lens

The earliest age-related symptom of vision is the progressive inability to read at near, experienced by people in their early- to mid-forties. While the cornea provides most of the refractive power of the eye's optical system, the lens allows the fine adjustments for focusing at near and distant. The accommodative ability of the eye is gradually lost as the lens becomes stiffer and loses the elasticity, enabling it to change shape (Krag & Andreassen, 2003). For many healthy people, the requirement for *reading glasses* or *bifocals* is the first definitive indication that they are getting older.

Another *refractive disturbance* that occurs in the aging lens reflects its continued growth over time. Embryologically, the lens is a pinched off piece of surface ectoderm, and epithelial cells are continuously being produced by the basement membrane or lens capsule. The lens capsule is on the outside of the lens, and therefore a new epithelium is laid down internally in the subcapsular space. This results in gradual *enlargement of the lens*, which at the very least can cause a myopic shift in refractive error due to the increased convexity and plus power in the lens. A very large lens can occupy so much space in the anterior portion of the eye that *phacomorphic angle closure glaucoma* can develop, resulting in a sudden painful loss of vision. This latter catastrophic event is more likely in very old people who have small hyperopic eyes to start with.

Aside from the lens becoming larger over time, it also loses its clarity. In youth the crystalline lens, as it is correctly termed, is truly as clear as crystal. Metabolic changes within the lens nucleus cause *clouding of the lens* material leading to nuclear sclerosis or *age-related cataract*. Other secondarily acquired cataracts are more noticeable and symptomatic with aging as well. *Cortical cataracts* are likely caused—or at least aggravated—by exposure to ultraviolet light (Truscott, 2003), and small *congenital cataracts* that would have been visually insignificant early in life progress to the point of true disability.

Nuclear sclerosis causes a generalized clouding of central vision at distance more so than near. Cortical cataracts are characterized by glare with bright lights such as car headlights at night, and focal opacification centrally in the posterior subcapsular portion of the lens reduces near vision more so than the distance. Posterior subcapsular cataracts are more common in diabetics and people receiving long-term corticosteroid treatments. The surgical removal of a visually significant cataract is one of the great success stories in medicine and surgery. Primitive procedures to dislocate an opacified lens, a procedure termed *couching*, have been practiced for more than a thousand years and continue to this day in some parts of the world. The safest and most predictable way to remove a cataract today uses a technology termed *phacoemulsification* in which the phakos (Greek work for lens) is emulsified using high-frequency ultrasound. The capsular envelope is left intact to receive a *lens implant*. This latter refinement has obviated the requirement for thick plus power spectacles or aphakic contact lenses. Phacoemulsification with posterior chamber lens implantation has become the most commonly performed major surgical procedure in the Western world and is performed on people whose vision has merely dropped to the level which threatens their driver's license (20/40 to 20/50). Provided that the remainder of the eye is healthy, it is not unusual to have acuities of 20/20 restored with this procedure. Unfortunately, accuses to this technology is uneven geographically, and cataract remains the number one cause of reversible blindness and low vision worldwide (Resnikoff, Pascolini, Etya'ale, Kocur, Pararajasegaram, Pokharel, et al., 2004).

The Vitreous and Peripheral Retina

One of the more dramatic symptoms older people experience is the sudden development of bright flashes of light, usually followed by the appearance of a dense floating object. This age-related phenomenon, known as a *posterior vitreous detachment*, occurs because of natural aging changes of the vitreous body. The largest cavity in the eye is filled with a formed vitreous gel that does not circulate. The passage of years leads to the gradual liquefaction of the gel, known as *syneresis*. The central portion of the vitreous body liquefies first, and eventually the cortical portions peel off the retina. The mechanical traction caused by this separation stimulates the photoreceptors in the retina to create artificial light. *Light flashes* are typically noted in the periphery, but a floater becomes apparent when the vitreous body finally separates from its point of most firm attachment to the wall of the eye, the optic nerve head. The cortical vitreous that attaches to the optic nerve head has some glial and connective tissue in it, which makes it more opaque that the rest of the vitreous cortex. This relative opacity casts a focal shadow on the retina, producing the image of a floater. Over the ensuing weeks to months, the floater becomes less noticeable and can disappear as the vitreous opacity moves more anteriorly in the eye, thus projecting less of a shadow on the retina. Also, natural syneresis of the vitreous results in clumping of collagen fibrils, which in themselves can induce multiple threadlike floaters that swirl around a person's visual field with normal eye or head movement.

The management of a posterior vitreous detachment involves a careful examination of the peripheral retina using an indirect ophthalmoscope or mirrored contact lens system to rule out retinal tears. Sometimes a small retinal vessel will be avulsed with a vitreous detachment, causing a *vitreous hemorrhage*. Most of these hemorrhages will resolve on their own, but should a retinal tear be discovered, it may require *laser treatment* or cryotherapy to prevent development of a *retinal detachment*. The vast majority of symptomatic posterior vitreous detachments do not result in a retinal tear or detachment, but patients need to be advised that the development of a curtain-like defect in their visual field is the principal symptom of a retinal detachment and requires immediate attention. A variety of surgical methods are used to reattach retinas in these circumstances. *Rhegmatogenous retinal detachments*, or *detached retinas* in the presence of a hole, are rare events. The incidence is 1 in 10,000 per year with high myopia, a positive family history or a history of previous intraocular surgery or trauma being the principle risk factors (Lewis, 2003).

The Central Retina (Macula)

A person's fine vision is served by only a small area of the central retina. This *macula* (Greek for spot) is where the cones—the photoreceptors involved in color vision—reside and the highest density of interconnections between the retinal neurons occur. The neurosensory retina has approximately 10 relatively well-defined layers, the outer most layer being that of the photoreceptors themselves. The outer segments of the photoreceptors interdigitate with the processes of the *retinal pigment epithelium* (RPE). The RPE serves many roles in the physiology of vision, not least of which are nutritional and metabolic support to the neurosensory retina. The most common age-related degeneration of the retina involves a deterioration of the RPE under the macula. This *age-related macular degeneration* (AMD) is the most common cause of *legal blindness* in the developed world (Resnikoff, Pascolini, Etya'ale, Kocur, Pararajasegaram, Pokharel, et al., 2004; Congdon, Friedman, & Lietman, 2003; Eye Diseases Prevalence Research Group, 2004a). It is much more common in whites than other races. Typical symptoms include a gradual difficulty discerning letters and words during reading due to an ill-defined central haze or distortion (*metamorphopsia*).

Age-related *macular degeneration* broadly occurs as 2 types: dry and wet. The dry type is much more common and is characterized by geographic atrophy of the RPE with loss and clumping of pigment and the formation of *drusen*, which appear as yellow granular deposits. Drusen are excrescences of *Bruch's membrane*, which is a composite structure consisting of both the basement membranes of the RPE and the underlying *choroid*. The choroid is a vascular structure that has at its innermost level a fine capillary network (choriocapillaris) adjacent to Bruch's membrane. When the degeneration of the RPE and its basement membrane are focal, resulting in a break in Bruch's membrane, the vessels of the choroid grow through the break into the subretinal space. The vessels leak blood and serum and are responsible for the (wet) form of AMD (Gottlieb, 2002; Zarbin, 2004).

Active *treatment of macular degeneration* has proven to be one of the most challenging aspects of ophthalmology. Recent evidence provided by the *Age-Related Eye Diseases Study* (AREDS) showed that vitamin supplements containing high doses of *beta-carotenes* and *zinc* slowed the progression of moderate and severe macular degeneration (Age-Related Eye Diseases Study Research Group, 2001). Focal neovascularization situated away from the center of the macula or fovea can be obliterated with *focal argon laser*. More recently, some hope has emerged for sufferers of subfoveal wet lesions with the use of *photodynamic therapy*. This treatment modality involves intravenous injection of a photosensitive chemical that when irradiated on passage through the eye causes thrombosis of the aberrant vessels in the subretinal space. While improvement of vision with this treatment is relatively rare, the size of the *scotoma*, or *blind spot*, caused by the neovascular process of wet AMD is reduced in size. The mainstay of managing both dry and wet macular degeneration involves the training of the individual to use *low vision aids*. Both optical (magnifiers, telescopes) and nonoptical aids (large print or audio books, expanded computer text) are helpful in preserving a sufferer's independence.

A lifetime of diabetes mellitus inevitably leads to some *retinopathy* or *maculopathy*. In the United States, a recent study reported that 1 in 12 persons with diabetes mellitus will have *diabetic retinopathy* (Eye Diseases Prevalence Research Group, 2004b). The earliest retinopathy of diabetes can be asymptomatic and includes such signs as *microaneurysms* and small dot/blot-shaped hemorrhages in the plexiform layers of the retina. The basic pathology of diabetic retinopathy involves incompetence of the endothelium, leakage of serum into the surrounding retina, and loss of capillaries resulting in ischemia and a focal infarction. If the *infarcted retina* is widespread enough, a *vascular endothelial growth factor* (VEGF) is elaborated to stimulate the growth of new vessels or *neovascularization*. These new vessels are typically misdirected, growing away from the retina into the vitreous where they leak, causing a *vitreous hemorrhage*. Extensive and repeated vitreous hemorrhages cause membrane formation over the retina leading to tractional detachment and permanent loss of vision.

The treatment of diabetic retinopathy is to prevent this chain of events from occurring. Once neovascularization has been detected, the ischemic VEGF-producing retina is ablated with laser treatment known as *panretinal photocoagulation*. This treatment has been successful in preventing permanent vision loss. Should vitreous hemorrhages and tractional retinal detachments develop, there are a multitude of surgical procedures that can be undertaken to salvage some navigational vision. Tight blood pressure and blood sugar control as well as avoidance of smoking have been shown to be critical in the management of diabetic retinopathy. Some diabetics specifically have incompetence of the macular vessels. Leakage of serum into the macula causes edema and exudate formation. If specific criteria are met, focal laser treatment has been shown to be effective in drying up this interstitial fluid. A *fluorescein angiogram* is used to guide this treatment.

The Optic Nerve and Glaucoma

A young optic nerve contains approximately 1.2 million ganglion cell axons in addition to glial cells, blood vessels, and connective tissue. There is a slow age-related loss of ganglion cells and their axons over time, but this is markedly accelerated later in life in glaucoma. This disease is characterized by a pathognomonic appearance of the optic nerve head as visualized by ophthalmoscopy. The central portion of the nerve head becomes evaginated, or "cupped," as neural and supportive tissue is lost. Glaucomatous cupping or *glaucomatous optic neuropathy* (GON) causes loss of peripheral vision before the central acuity is affected. Ultimately, untreated glaucoma can lead to complete blindness. Worldwide, glaucoma is felt to be the number 2 cause of preventable blindness after cataract (Resnikoff, Pascolini, Etya'ale, Kocur, Pararajasegaram, Pokharel, et al., 2004; Congdon, Friedman, & Lietman, 2003).

The pathophysiology of glaucomatous optic neuropathy likely involves many factors, which may be mechanical, vascular, and neurochemical (Coleman, 1999). Most, if not all, chronic glaucomas are heritable with incomplete penetrance. Advanced age, black race, positive family history, and elevated intraocular pressure are the best recognized constitutional risk factors for the idiopathic chronic varieties. Elevated *intraocular pressure* is presently the only modifiable risk factor for glaucoma, and all of the treatments, both medical and surgical, involve lowering intraocular pressure.

Elevated intraocular pressure results from obstruction of aqueous outflow at its usual pathways in the iridocorneal angle. Glaucoma is broadly classified as either open or closed angle. In *open-angle glaucoma*, there is an intrinsic problem with the porosity of the trabecular meshwork in the iridocorneal angle of the eye. In *angle closure glaucoma*, the iris root physically covers the drainage structures including the trabecular meshwork.

Primary open-angle glaucoma affects approximately 1% of the population in the Western world and is much more common among blacks than whites. Asians are more likely to suffer from chronic angle closure glaucoma, and because of the size of the Asian population, chronic angle closure glaucoma is felt to be the most common glaucoma globally (Foster & Johnson, 2001; Quigley, 1996). While the causes of the idiopathic varieties of chronic glaucomas, both open- and closed-angle, are unknown, the most common identifiable cause of glaucoma is *exfoliation syndrome*. In this condition exfoliated basement membrane-like material is elaborated from a variety of structures within the eye. When it is deposited in the trabecular meshwork, the clogging effect results in elevated intraocular pressure.

The treatment of glaucoma involves medical and surgical modalities to lower intraocular pressure. It is felt that the mechanical and vascular stresses to the optic nerve head are reduced and there is now good evidence from controlled clinical trials to show that lowering intraocular pressure, at least surgically, preserves vision (Goldberg, 2003). The most effective pressure lowering drugs are *beta blockers*, *prostaglandin (PGF 2 Alpha) analogues*, *Alpha 2 agonists*, *carbonic anhydrase inhibitors*, and *parasympathomimetic agents*. Most of these drugs are delivered topically as an *eye drop*. Laser modalities are useful for both open- and *closed-angle glaucomas*. Glaucomatous eyes with normal open iridocorneal angles can be treated with *laser trabeculoplasty* using a variety of wavelengths, and some closed-angle glaucomas can be successfully treated with a *YAG laser iridotomy*. When medical and laser methods are ineffective or unavailable, surgical intervention becomes the mainstay of therapy. There are a variety of filtering procedures available, which involve the creation of a fistula, or vent, between the anterior chamber and the subconjunctival space. Occasionally drainage tubes made of silicone rubber are used to shunt the fluid from the anterior chamber into the orbital cavity.

Summary

Some common vision-threatening conditions of older adults, such as *dermatochalasis*, are considered cosmetic blemishes, while others such as glaucoma can lead to total blindness if neglected. Most conditions are treatable, and patients can maintain sufficient vision to provide a good quality of life and extend their independence. Many people can continue to drive their cars at ages where previously cataracts would have stopped them. The greatest frustration remains for the sufferer of macular degeneration. While this condition does not cause complete blindness, and most people can maintain a high degree of self-sufficiency (albeit without driving cars), the pleasure of reading and recognizing faces is often lost. Great strides have been made in the diagnosis and treatment of glaucoma in the developed world. While it is still considered to be a number two cause of *preventable blindness* worldwide, it has dropped behind macular degeneration and diabetic retinopathy in the West. Regardless of the condition, access to eye care and the development of new diagnostic and treatment modalities remain the biggest issues in preserving vision in the older individual.

For further information, see also:

- American Academy of Ophthalmology at www.aao.org
- Association for Research in Vision and Ophthalmology at www.arvo.org
- Aging Eye Times at www.agingeye.net
- National Eye Institute at www.nei.nih.gov
- Prevent Blindness America at www. preventblindness.org

Paul E. Rafuse
Melanie E. M. Kelly

See also
Vision: System, Function, and Loss

References

Age-Related Eye Diseases Study Research Group. (2001). A randomized, placebo-controlled clinical trial of high-dose supplementation with vitamins C and E, beta-carotene, and zinc for age-related macular degeneration and vision loss (AREDS report no 8). *Archives of Ophthalmology, 119,* 1417–1436.

Coleman, A. L. (1999). Glaucoma. *Lancet, 354,* 1803–1810.

Congdon, N., Friedman, D., & Lietman, T. (2003). Important causes of visual impairment in the world today. *Journal of the American Medical Association, 290,* 2057–2060.

Faragher, R. G. A., Mulholland, B., Tuft, S. J., Sandeman, S., & Khaw, P. T. (1997). Aging and the cornea. *British Journal of Ophthalmology, 81,* 814–817.

Foster, P. J., & Johnson, G. J. (2001). Glaucoma in China: How Big Is the Problem? *British Journal of Opthalmology, 85,* 1271–1272.

Goldberg, I. (2003). Relationship between intraocular pressure and the preservation of visual field in glaucoma. *Survey of Ophthalmology, 48*(Suppl. 1), S3–S7.

Gottlieb, J. (2002). Age-related macular degeneration. *Journal of the American Medical Association, 288,* 2233–2236.

Krag, S., & Andreassen, T. T. (2003). Mechanical properties of the human lens capsule. *Progress in Retinal and Eye Research, 22,* 749–767.

Lewis, H. (2003). Peripheral retinal degenerations and the risk of retinal detachment. *Am J Ophthalmology, 136,* 155–160.

Lowe, N. J., & Yamauchi, P. (2004). Cosmetic uses of botulinum toxins for lower aspects of the face and neck. *Clinics in Dermatology, 22,* 18–22.

Quigley, H. A. (1996). Number of people with glaucoma worldwide. *British Journal of Ophthalmology, 80,* 389–393.

Truscott, R. J. W. (2003). Human cataract: The mechanisms responsible; light and butterfly eyes. *International Journal of Biochemistry and Cell Biology, 35,* 1500–1504.

Eye Diseases Prevalence Research Group. (2004a). Causes and prevalence of visual impairment among adults in the United States. *Archives of Ophthalmology, 122,* 477–485.

Eye Diseases Prevalence Research Group. (2004b). The prevalence of diabetic retinopathy among adults in the United States. *Archives of Ophthalmology, 122,* 552–563.

Zarbin, M. A. (2004). Current concepts in the pathogenesis of age-related macular degeneration. *Archives of Ophthalmology, 122,* 598–614.

F

FAMILY AND MEDICAL LEAVE ACT

On February 5, 1993, President Bill Clinton signed into law the Family and Medical Leave Act (FMLA) (U.S. *Public Law 130-3*), the first law passed by the 103rd Congress. The FMLA was enacted after a long political campaign. Family and medical leave legislation had been debated in the U.S. Congress since the mid-1980s. The private sector generally opposed the passage of the FMLA, perceiving it as costly and not beneficial to their organizations. The National Federation of Independent Business, for example, argued vigorously that the law would reduce business efficiency and damage the global competitiveness of American businesses. In contrast, women's organizations, such as the Women's Legal Defense and the National Organization for Women, stressed the necessity of a federally mandated leave policy by underscoring the difficulties experienced by American workers in their efforts to strike a balance between the competing demands of the workplace and home. They buttressed their argument by citing the dramatic demographic changes that were impacting workers' ability to achieve a healthy balance, including: the increasing numbers of working women, particularly those with young children; the rise in single-parent households, many of which are headed by single working parents; and the growth of the older adult population, who often rely on the support of working adult children.

Under this act, which became effective on August 5, 1993, businesses with 50 or more employees are required to grant up to 12 weeks of unpaid leave annually when a child is born or adopted, when an immediate family member with a serious health condition needs care, or when the employee is unable to work because of a serious health condition. The FMLA defines a serious health condition as an illness, injury, impairment, or physical or mental condition that requires inpatient care in a hospital, hospice, or residential medical facility or continuing treatment by a health care worker. The employee has the right to take the leave intermittently or on a reduced schedule basis. The employer must maintain any preexisting health coverage during the leave period, and once the leave is completed, reinstate the employee to the same or an equivalent job. For retirement or pension plans, the FMLA leave is counted as continued service for purposes of vesting and eligibility to participate.

To receive an *FMLA leave*, the employee must fulfill certain responsibilities. First, the employer may require the employee to provide certification from a health care provider confirming the serious health condition. Second, if practical and the employer so requires, the employee should provide 30 days' notice for the leave. If due to circumstances such as a *medical emergency* such notification is not possible, the employee must provide notice "as soon as practical." Third, if the employer has a policy requiring all workers taking a medical leave to provide certification of fitness to return to work, the employee may be required to produce this documentation. Finally, if the health insurance premium normally requires an employee co-payment, the employee will be required to continue to pay this portion while on leave (Gowan & Zimmerman, 1996).

The United States was among the last industrialized countries to offer a *leave policy*. By the time of the FMLA's passage, 32 states already had some form of *family leave policy*, and many were stronger than the federal version. Indeed, until the passage of the FMLA the United States was the only country out of 118 nations surveyed by the International Labor Organization that had no mandated parental leave policy. A comparison of the American legislation with the leave policies of other countries further reveals the limitations of the FMLA. Most other countries' parental leave policies affect all employers, offer a longer leave period, and mandate paid leave. For example, Canada mandates 15 weeks of leave at 60% of normal pay, France has established 16 weeks of leave at 90% of normal pay, and Germany mandates 14 to 19 weeks of leave at 100% of normal pay.

Based on its recent systematic study of 168 countries' policies supporting workers' ability to care for children and family members, the Project on Global Working Families at Harvard University concludes that the United States continues to lag far behind most other nations. Its 2004 report, *Work, Family, and Equity Index:* Where Does the United States Stand Globally? revealed that although 163 countries offer guaranteed *paid leave to women* in conjunction with childbirth, the United States still does not. Moreover, Australia, the only other industrialized country that does not mandate paid *maternity or parental leave* to mothers, guarantees a full year of unpaid leave versus the United States' 12 weeks of leave. The survey also found that whereas 139 countries provide paid leave for short- and long-term illnesses, with 117 providing a week or more annually, the United States provides only unpaid leave for serious illness (Heymann, Earle, Simmons, Breslow, & Kuehnhoff, 2004).

To date, the impact of the FMLA has generally been described as modest. This limited impact can be attributed largely to the process of policy minimalization or compromises that were necessary to ensure the act's passage. Since the FMLA only applies to employers who have 50 or more employees, it is estimated that only slightly more than 10% of private sector worksites are covered under the FMLA. This relatively small percentage of U.S. businesses, however, employs almost 60% of American workers. Yet not all workers of covered employers are eligible for benefits under the act. The FMLA only provides benefits to employees who have worked for their employer for at least 12 months (although these need not have been consecutive months) and who, during the 12-month period prior to the leave, worked for the employer for at least 1,250 hours (which reflects an average of 25 hours per week). Because of these criteria, it is estimated that only 47% of employees working in the private sector are eligible for a leave under the FMLA (Commission on Family and Medical Leave, 1996).

The Institute for Social Research (ISR) at the University of Michigan conducted one of the large-scale studies of the FMLA as mandated by the legislation under the auspices of the *Commission on the Family and Medical Leave Act.* The institute's 1995 national random sample survey of employees found that while almost 17% of workers reported taking a leave for reasons covered under the FMLA and another 3% stated they needed but did not take leaves, only 7% of this group actually took a leave under the FMLA. The ratio of leave taking under the FMLA at covered private sector worksites was 3.6 for every 100 workers. Moreover, the ISR survey found few differences in leave-taking patterns among employees in covered and exempted worksites. Among covered workers in 1995, 60% took leave for the employee's own health reasons (other than maternity disability), 23% took leave to care for an ill relative, and 13% took leave for a newborn or adopted child. For workers in exempt worksites, however, the corresponding figures were quite comparable—56%, 22% and 15% respectively (Commission on Family and Medical Leave, 1996).

One of the key compromises in the FMLA, the failure to require paid leave, has also contributed greatly to the restrained use. The 1995 ISR survey found that of those who were eligible for leave but did not take it, the most frequently cited reason (64%) was financial constraints. The failure to mandate paid leave suggests that, using Lowi's 1964 framework, the FMLA can be understood as invoking a regulatory versus a redistributive approach to a broad-scale social issue. The act followed the regulatory approach of mandating a noncompensated leave policy on large employers on behalf of only noncontingent workers rather than using public tax dollars to pay for an employee's family leave, especially needed by low-income workers.

A more recent survey commissioned by the Department of Labor, *Balancing the Needs of Families and Employers: Family and Medical Leave Surveys, 2000 Update,* revealed that since its enactment approximately 35 million employees have taken a leave under the FMLA. Of workers taking a leave, 52% did so for their own serious illness, 26% for care of a newborn, adoption, or maternity disability, 13% for care of a seriously ill parent, 12% for care of a seriously ill child, and 6% for care of a seriously ill spouse. (The sum is greater than 100% as some took more than one leave.) The median length of the leave was 10 days. Almost all (98%) who took an FMLA leave returned to work for the same employer (Cantor, Waldfogel, Kerwin, Wright, Levin, Rauch, et al., 2001).

The 2000 Update Survey found significant differences in use of the FMLA leave by gender; 58% of leave-takers were women and 42% of leave-takers were men. The survey also revealed significant gender differences in the reason for use. Approximately 58% of men, as compared to 49% of women, took an FMLA leave because of their own serious illness. There was also a significant difference in use by income: 27% of leave-takers earned less than $30,000, 51% of leave-takers earned between $30,000 and

$74,999, and 22% of leave-takers earned $75,000 or more. Consistent with the earlier 1995 survey, one of the primary barriers to use of FMLA leave is the lack of paid leave. In the 2000 survey, approximately 78% of those who desired to take a leave stated they could not do so because of financial reasons. Those individuals who were unable to take leave because they could not afford the associated loss of wages were more likely to be African American, to be hourly wage earners, and to have low levels of family income. Even among leave-takers, the financial hardship can be great. More than half (58%) of leave-takers who did not receive their full pay or who did not receive any pay while on leave reported that it was somewhat or very difficult to make ends meet (Cantor, Waldfogel, Kerwin, Wright, Leveni, Rauch, et al., 2001).

Given the level of usage, it is not surprising that employers ascribe only modest benefits or costs to the FMLA. Both the 1995 and 2000 surveys found that the vast majority of employers felt that the FMLA had "no noticeable effect" on business productivity, business profitability, or business growth. Given the median length of the FMLA leave is 10 days, almost all companies (97%) indicted that the most common method of covering the work performed by the leave-taker was to assign the tasks to other employees. The second most common method, used by 41% of employers, was to hire temporary replacement workers (Cantor, Waldfogel, Kerwin, Wright, Leveni, Rauch, et al., 2001).

Proposals to *reform the FMLA* continue to be debated in the U.S. Congress. On the right, legislators continue to question the basic premises of the law. Republican members of Congress are pressing for clarifying amendments to restore the definition of "serious medical condition" and "intermittent leave" to the original intent of FMLA. In contrast, Democratic proposals build upon the ideology that government has a legitimate role in addressing employment-related tensions between employer and employee. One Democratic proposal would expand coverage to employers with at least 25 employees. Analysis of this proposed legislation suggests that it would significantly increase the number and percentages of employees covered without affecting a large number of employers. An additional 14% of the private workforce would be covered by FMLA—for a total employee coverage rate of 71%. However, only an additional 6% of private employers would be newly covered. Other Democratic proposals include: extending coverage beyond "immediate family members" to include a parent-in-law, adult child, sibling, grandchild, grandparent, and domestic partner with a serious health condition; increasing flexibility in use by allowing parents to take up to 4 hours in any 30-day period to go with children to school or extracurricular activities or accompany ill relatives to routine medical appointments; and allowing victims of domestic violence to take an FMLA leave to get shelter, medical help, and legal protection.

Perhaps the most important *Democratic proposal* focuses on the importance of *wage-replacement* to leave-taking and the fundamental need for the FMLA to mandate paid leave. Although there has been little progress on the federal level to expand the FMLA, there has been considerable activity at the state level to make family leave more accessible. Twenty-four states now have laws allowing public employees to use their sick leave to care for certain sick family members, and 3 states (California, Minnesota, and Washington) require private employers to allow workers to use sick leave to care for certain sick family members. Five states (New York, New Jersey, Rhode Island, California, and Hawaii) and Puerto Rico allow the use of *Temporary Disability Insurance* (TDI) to provide partial wage replacement to employees who are temporarily disabled for medical reasons, including pregnancy and childbirth.

In 2002, California became the first state in the country to enact a comprehensive paid family leave program. Effective as of January 1, 2003, and administered through the State Disability Insurance (SDI) system, the legislation mandates that workers will receive up to 6 weeks of paid leave per year to care for a new child (birth, adoption, or foster care) or a seriously ill family member (parent, child, spouse or domestic partner). The benefit will replace up to 55% of wages, up to a maximum of $728 per week in 2004. The program is 100% employee funded with an estimated average cost of $27 per worker per year.

California may be just the beginning; the National Partnership for Women and Families notes that bills to explore paid leave have been introduced in 27 states. Although in the Democratic and Republican proposals we see a division in fundamental beliefs about personal, private, and public responsibilities for the care of dependent members, both political parties are aware that work-family balance is an important issue to American families. A 1998 national survey funded by the National Partnership for Women & Families, for example, revealed that two-thirds of Americans say that *time pressures on working families* are getting worse, not better, and that most want both employers (90%) and government (72%) to do more to help working families. Moreover, 82% of the women and 75% of the men surveyed favored the idea of developing an insurance program that would provide families with partial wage replacement when a worker takes a family or medical leave (Lake Snell Perry and Associates, 1998).

JUDITH G. GONYEA

References

Cantor, D., Waldfogel, J., Kerwin, J., Wright, M. M., Leveni, K., Rauch, J., Hagerty, T., Kudela, M. S. (2001). *Balancing the needs of families and employers: The family and medical leave surveys, 2000 update*. Washington, DC: U.S. Department of Labor. Available: http://www.dol.gov/dpl/asp/public/fmla/main2000.htm.

Commission on Family and Medical Leave. (1996). *A workable balance: Report to Congress on Family and Medical Leave Policies*. Washington, DC: U.S. Department of Labor.

Gowan, M. A., & Zimmerman, R. A. (1996). The Family and Medical Leave Act of 1993: Employee rights and responsibilities, employer rights and responsibilities. *Employee Responsibilities and Rights Journal, 9*, 57–71.

Heymann, J., Earle, A., Simmons, S., Breslow, S. M., & Kuehnhoff, A. (2004). *The work, family and equity index: Where does the United States stand globally?* Cambridge, MA: Harvard University Project on Global Working Families; Available: http://www.harvard.edu/globalworkingfamilies/images/report.pdf.

Lake Snell Perry and Associates. (1998, February). *Family matters: A national survey of women and men*, conducted for the National Partnership for Women and Families, Washington, DC.

Lowi, T. J. (1964). American business, public policy, case studies, and political theory. *World Politics, 16*, 677–715.

FAMILY RELATIONSHIPS

In the past 100 years, *world demographics* have changed radically, with an ever-increasing life expectancy (years a person is expected to live) coupled with a significantly decreasing number of births. Similarly, marital customs have changed, with many people marrying later and others never marrying at all. Divorce is more common, as are multiple, serial marriages. Individuals more often live in nuclear rather than extended multigenerational residential units. People in the United States and many other parts of the developed world are having fewer children, more children are living in nontraditional family units, including single-parent families, combined families consisting of biological and adopted children, and blended families. Although there have been both historical and cohort changes in the structure of the family, people clearly still prefer to live in families. The family, as the fundamental unit for human development, serves a critical function for the psychological, social, and even biological needs of the individual.

To grasp the function and influence of the family on the individual, it is useful to think of the family as a convoy that surrounds the individual over the life course, one that is a source of positive support as well as stress. The individual experiences life span development and socialization within the family. The quality and quantity of family relations, whether these relationships are positive or negative, gender, and the role occupied in the familial unit influence an individual. This text briefly addresses each of these influences in turn.

The quantity and quality of family relations influence physical health, psychological well-being, and the manifestation of genetic propensities. Life span developmental science emphasizes the cumulative effect of life experiences on the maturing individual. From conception to death, there is a continuity of development wherein each experience builds on and derives from prior experiences. It is well known that the "child is father to the man," but what *life span developmental science* increasingly recognizes is the enormity of this influence. For example, prenatal conditions influence physical health from infancy to old age (Jackson, Antonucci, & Gibson, 1990; Rossi & Rossi, 1990). Similarly, *early life experiences* influence psychological and sociological characteristics, such as emotion regulation and relationships (Thompson, 1998). While our knowledge of individual development is increasing at an exponential rate, this has not led to a simplification of our understanding. For example, the identification of the human genome led many to expect that the genetic basis of individual characteristics or diseases would be identified. Instead, what we have learned is that human characteristics are rarely determined by singular genetic factors (Singer & Antonucci, 2004. One might have a genetic predisposition which is only manifest under certain environmental conditions. Many diseases thought to be genetically based are now known to develop only if other genetic characteristics and environmental circumstances are present. It is understood that the principles of multifinality and equifinality apply to life-span development. Adulthood can be achieved through many paths, and the same paths can produce different results. A life-span developmental perspective proposes that the individual evolves based on inherited characteristics as well as *biopsychosocial experiences* (Jackson, Antonucci, & Brown, 2004. While the child is still father to the man, an updated version of this phrase might claim that the child (infant, embryo, cellular/chromosomal structure) provides a basis for but does not predetermine the adult.

Family relations are experienced as positive or negative, improving and enhancing development and/or contributing to vulnerability and decline. Indeed, most individuals belong to a family—in fact, 2 families—during the course of their lifetime: a *family of origin* (as a child, with parents and perhaps siblings) and a *nuclear family* (as a parent with a partner and children). These families exert considerable influence on the developing individual across the life span. The nuclear family represents the first world to which the young child is exposed—usually their first exposure to adults, older people, and the aging process. In addition to providing physical care and shelter, it is also a critical source of socialization. The attachment and early socialization literature has extended the adult-infancy *attachment* to demonstrate the cumulative effects of these early relationships on *later relationships* in adulthood. Infant attachment categories are related to adolescent and adult attachment styles in sibling, peer, romantic and later relationships with one's own children (Antonucci, Akiyama, & Takahashi, 2004). Family relations are both experienced and observed. Thus, in addition to one's own experiences, people also have the opportunity to observe how others are treated, including family expectations and responsibilities toward one another.

Also interesting is that these "social" or interpersonal aspects of the family are related to both physical and intellectual growth. Children with qualitatively better relationships with their parents are more likely to be assessed as more competent by their peers and teachers (Thompson, 1999). Interestingly, they are also more likely to make better romantic and partner choices as they themselves reach adulthood and form their own nuclear family. In the gerontological literature, it is now being demonstrated that people with good active, positive social relations often live healthy longer lives (Antonucci & Akiyama, 1997).

It is normative in U.S. society for children to leave their family of origin and form their own nuclear family. While many alternatives to this norm have been identified, e.g. same-sex partnerships, heterosexual partnerships with children, single-parent families, at some level the experiences are similar. Each member of this new family unit brings to it their own individual characteristics and experiences. Some families have overwhelmingly positive relationships that are mutually supportive and helpful, but other families are characterized by negativity and conflict in their relationships. Unfortunately, this too affects the individual, making him or her more susceptible to suboptimal outcomes including increased stress, poor health, and generally lower levels of well-being.

Attention has recently been given to the impact of the quality of relationships. Positive relationships are often assumed within families, but unfortunately conflict and avoidance are also common. *Interpersonal problems* are the most detrimental source of stress for well-being (Bolger, Delongis, Kessler, & Shilling, 1989). In addition, how people respond to these problems appears to lead to variations in well-being, with more negative strategies associated with poorer physical health and psychological well-being (Kiecolt-Glaser & Newton, 2001. Interestingly, while there tends to be continuity within families concerning the quality of relationships, older people report fewer problems in their relationships than younger people (Fingerman & Birditt, 2003). Further, older people report using fewer destructive strategies and more avoidance when they experience problems in their relationships as compared to younger people (Birditt, Fingerman, & Almeida, in press).

Gender and social roles similarly influence how the family is experienced. Although men and women have similar relationships, e.g. parent, child, sibling, they experience them differently. Women, as daughters, wives, and mothers are benefited by those relationships, i.e. deriving comfort from them but are also burdened by them, often feeling personally responsible to solve the problems and meet the needs of their family members. While men also care deeply about their families, as sons, husbands, and fathers they seem to experience these relationships differently. Some research suggests that compared to women, men benefit less from these relationships but paradoxically are also disadvantaged more by both poor quality relationships and/or the lack of such close personal connections (Antonucci, 2001.

In sum, the family, while undergoing significant and often radical structural changes, continues to be a critical source of support as well as stress. The family often fundamentally influences every aspect of the individual's life including well-being, as well as the nurture and care provided to others.

Toni C. Antonucci
Kira S. Birditt

See also
Caregiving (Informal)
Divorce

References

Antonucci, T. C. (2001). Social relations. In J. E. Birren & K. W. Schaie (Eds.), *Handbook of the psychology of aging* (pp. 53–77). San Diego, CA: Academic Press.

Antonucci, T. C., & Akiyama, H. (1997). Social support and the maintenance of competence. In S. Willis & K. W. Schaie (Eds.), *Societal mechanisms for maintaining competence in old age*. New York: Springer Publishing.

Antonucci, T. C., Akiyama, H. A., & Takahashi, K. (2004). Attachment and close relationships across the lifespan. *Attachment and Human Development, 6*, 353–370.

Birditt, K. S., Fingerman, K. L., & Almeida, D. (2005). Age differences in exposure and reactions to interpersonal tensions:A daily diary study. *Psychology and Aging, 20*, 330–340.

Bolger, N., Delongis, A., Kessler, R. C., & Shilling, E. A. (1989). Effects of daily stress on negative mood. *Journal of Personality and Social Psychology, 57*(5), 808–818.

Fingerman, K. L., & Birditt, K. S. (2003). Does variation in close and problematic family ties reflect the pool of living relatives? *Journals of Gerontology: Psychological Sciences, 58,* P80–P87.

Jackson, J. S., Antonucci, T. C., & Brown, E. (2004). A cultural lens on biopsychosocial models of aging. *Advances in Cell Aging and Gerontology, 15*, 221–241.

Jackson, J. S., Antonucci, T. C., & Gibson, R. C. (1990). Cultural, racial, and ethnic minority influences on aging. In J. E. Birren & K. W. Schaie (Eds.), *Handbook of the psychology of aging*. New York: Academic Press.

Kiecolt–Glaser, J. K., & Newton, T. L. (2001). Marriage and health: His and hers. *Psychological Bulletin, 127*(4), 472–503.

Rossi, A., & Rossi, P. (1990). *Of human bonding: Parent-child relations across the life course*. New York: Aldine de Gruyter.

Singer, E., & Antonucci, T. C. (2004). *Genetics and health disparities*. Ann Arbor, MI: Institute for Social Research.

Thompson, R. A. (1998). Early sociopersonality development. In W. Damon & N. Eisenberg (Eds.), *Handbook of child psychology: Social, emotional, and personality development*. New York: Wiley.

Thompson, R. A. (1999). Early attachment and later development. In J. Cassidy & P. R. Shaver (Eds.), *Handbook of attachment: Theory, research, and clinical applications*. Guilford Press: 2002.

FEAR OF DEATH

See
Death Anxiety

FECAL AND URINARY INCONTINENCE

Fecal incontinence is defined as defecation in socially inappropriate situations, occurring at least once a month after the age of 4 years. *Urinary incontinence* is defined as a condition in which involuntary loss of urine is a social or hygienic problem. Incontinence in an older person is a major clinical problem with significant medical and social consequences. It has been estimated that 7.5 per 1,000 community-dwelling persons 65 to 74 years old have problems associated with the control of urination or defecation, and that among persons over the age of 75 the prevalence is 46.7 per 1,000

(Feller, 1983). In a community-based survey of 541 healthy, middle-aged women, 42 to 50 years old, 58% reported urine loss at some time, and 30.7% reported incontinence at least once a month (Burgio, Matthews, & Engel, 1991). Although bladder incontinence is more prevalent than bowel incontinence, the latter is much more disruptive socially and is more likely to lead to institutionalization. The prevalence of incontinence in nursing home residents is much higher than among community-dwelling persons and is frequently associated with increased dependency, such as cognitive impairment or mobility limitation.

Among the elderly, fecal incontinence often is progressive, with an indefinite onset but a worsening course. Incontinence can occur because the patient is unable to retain stool, or it can occur in conjunction with chronic, severe constipation or diarrhea (Whitehead, 1996). The most common mediating conditions for failure to retain stool are post-surgical trauma, neuromuscular deficits associated with progressive diseases such as diabetes mellitus and multiple sclerosis, mobility deficits that prevent the person from toileting appropriately, and cognitive deficits that disrupt usual social inhibitions. Constipation leads to incontinence when there is severe rectal distension (megacolon), followed by loss of stool when the internal anal sphincter is no longer able to provide an adequate barrier against the passage of stool. Treatment for fecal incontinence varies depending on the existence of concomitant disorders; however, many studies have shown that biofeedback can be a highly effective behavioral intervention for reducing the frequency of incontinent episodes (Farrugia, Camilleri, & Whitehead, 1996).

Urinary incontinence can occur as a result of malfunctions in the urethral sphincter or pelvic floor muscles, in the detrusor muscle of the urinary bladder, or in the nervous control of any of these muscles. Among the elderly there are many forms and causes of incontinence; however, there are four distinct kinds of incontinence that probably account for most of the clinically significant instances of the disorder:

1. Stress incontinence, which can be a sign or a symptom reflecting loss of urine during physical activity. It is most common in women, is usually associated with small-volume loss during an activity, and is usually a long-standing problem that may have worsened with age.
2. Urge incontinence, which is loss of urine as sociated with a strong desire to void. The sense of urgency may be a pure sensory phenomenon, or it may include uncontrollable detrusor contractions. Urge incontinence typically is associated with large-volume losses and can affect men or women.
3. Overflow incontinence, which is an involuntary loss of urine that occurs when pressure in a chronically full bladder exceeds urethral pressure. The rise in bladder pressure is associated with excessive bladder distension attributable to inadequate bladder emptying. Overflow incontinence also can occur in persons of either sex.
4. "Inappropriate" urination, which can occur in cognitively impaired persons or in persons who have severe motor disabilities that prevent them from toileting themselves. Clearly, in this case the inappropriateness of the urination is defined socially and not physiologically.

The so-called graying of America has caused clinicians and public health officials to recognize the seriousness of incontinence. With this recognition has come the realization that most incontinent patients can be treated successfully, and that proper clinical management of incontinence in an older person calls on the skills of a number of professionals, not only physicians but also nurses, psychologists, and other social service agents. Depending on the underlying disorder, it is possible that proper treatment of an incontinent patient can come from traditional medical procedures, such as drug therapy and surgery; from improved medical management, such as careful supervision of drug regimens (Agency for Health Care Policy and Research, 1996); from improved staff management of the institutionalized patient (Schnelle, Traughber, Morgan, Embry, Binion, & Coleman, 1983); or from a variety of training methods (Burgio, Locher, Goode, & Hardin, 1998; Burgio, Stutzman, & Engel, 1989; Burgio, Whitehead, & Engel, 1985; Whitehead, Burgio, & Engel, 1985). Recently, the United States Public Health Service, Agency for Health Care Policy and Research of the U.S. Department of Health and Human Services, published guidelines for the management of urinary incontinence. The panel of experts responsible for these guidelines concluded that incontinent patients should always have a basic diagnostic evaluation and that behavioral and pharmacological therapies usually are reasonable first steps in management (Agency for Health Care Policy and Research, 1996).

BERNARD T. ENGEL

See also
Behavior Management
Chronobiology: Rhythms, Clocks, Chaos, Aging, and Other Terms
Gastrointestinal Functions and Disorders
Kidney and Urinary System

References

Agency for Health Care Policy and Research (1996). *Urinary incontinence in adults: Acute and chronic management* (AHCPR Publication No. 96-0682). Washington, DC: U.S. Department of Health and Human Services, Public Health Service.

Burgio, K. L., Matthews, K. A., & Engel B. T. (1991). Prevalence, incidence, and correlates of urinary incontinence in healthy, middle-aged women. *Journal of Urology*, *146*, 1255–1259.

Burgio, K. L., Locher, J. L., Goode, P. S., & Hardin J. M. (1998). Behavioral vs. drug treatment for urge urinary incontinence in older women: A randomized controlled trial. *Journal of the American Medical Association*, *280*, 1995–2000.

Burgio, K. L., Stutzman, R. E., & Engel, B. T. (1989). Behavioral training for post-prostatectomy urinary incontinence. *Journal of Urology*, *141*, 303–306.

Burgio, K. L., Whitehead, W. E., & Engel B. T. (1985). Behavioral treatment of urinary incontinence in the elderly: Bladder-sphincter biofeedback and toileting skills training. *Annals of Internal Medicine*, *103*, 507–515.

Farrugia, G., Camilleri, M., & Whitehead, W. E. (1996). Therapeutic strategies for motility disorders: Medications, nutrition, biofeedback and hypnotherapy. *Gastroenterology Clinics of North America*, *25*, 225–246.

Feller, B. (1983). Americans needing help to function at home. *Vital and Health Statistics of the National Center for Health Statistics*, *92*, 1–12.

Schnelle, J. F., Traughber, B., Morgan, D. B., Embry, J. E., Binion, A. F., & Coleman A. (1983). Management of geriatric incontinence in nursing homes. *Journal of Applied Behavioral Analysis*, *16*, 235–241.

Whitehead, W. E. (1996). Functional anecdotal disorders. *Seminars in Gastrointestinal Disease*, *7*, 230–236.

Whitehead, W. E., Burgio, K. L., & Engel, B. T. (1985). Biofeedback treatment of fecal incontinence in geratric patients. *Journal of the American Geriatrics Society*, *33*, 320–324.

FEMALE REPRODUCTIVE SYSTEM

The *menopause* signals the permanent end of fertility and occurs in women at approximately 51 years of age. Ovarian follicles are depleted in postmenopausal women, resulting in a permanent decrease in ovarian secretion of steroid and peptide hormones. Thus, one consequence of the menopause is a permanent and dramatic decrease in circulating estrogen levels. Until about 1900, most women died before they were 50 years old and therefore never experienced the postmenopausal period of their lives. However, during this century, the average life span of women has increased dramatically, to over 80 years of age. Since the age of the menopause has remained essentially fixed, an increasing number of women will spend a larger fraction of their lives in the postmenopausal state than ever before. Thus, until recently this profound change in the physiology of females never presented the challenge to clinicians, basic scientists, and social and behavioral scientists that it does today.

We are beginning to appreciate that the postmenopausal chronic hypoestrogenic state not only has an impact on the hypothalamic-pituitary-ovarian axis, but also has major effects on bone and mineral metabolism, cardiovascular function, memory and cognition, and the progression of age-related diseases. Thus, it becomes ever more important to understand the mechanisms that regulate this change and the biological, medical, societal, and economic implications of the transition women make from a reproductive to a nonreproductive status. Much progress has been made; however, much needs to be learned before we fully understand the physiology of the menopause or reproductive decline.

It is important to note that only female primates undergo a true menstrual cycle. Therefore, only these species undergo a true menopause (i.e., cessation of the menstrual cycle). Other species exhibit reproductive cycles that are not punctuated by a menstrual bleed, but are nevertheless characterized by a cyclic pattern of hormone release. Many of these species undergo reproductive senescence that is similar in some aspects to menopausal changes. It is important to develop animal models in which we can study the mechanisms of reproductive senescence since humans cannot be used to investigate many of the mechanisms that underlie the menopause.

Maintenance of regular menstrual cyclicity requires a complex interplay of neurochemical and endocrine signals that are precisely timed, occur in a specific order, and are released in the proper amounts (Yen, 1999). The synthesis and release of gonadotropin releasing hormone (GnRH) from neurons in the hypothalamus is regulated by a repertoire of neurotransmitters and neuromodulators. In turn, GnRH stimulates the synthesis and secretion of the gonadotropins, luteinizing hormone (LH) and follicle-stimulating hormone (FSH) from the anterior pituitary gland. These hormones, which are secreted in a pulsatile manner, determine the rate and number of follicles that undergo the final stages of development and differentiation. In addition, they govern the synthesis and secretory patterns of the major ovarian steroids, estradiol and progesterone, and the peptides inhibin and activin. Feedback of ovarian steroids to the level of the anterior pituitary and brain are essential for the menstrual cycle to recur every month. This constellation of endocrine hormones and others that have not been discussed results in a regular and repetitive menstrual cycle of predictable length.

The ovaries play a critical role in the menopause. Females are born with a finite, nonrenewable, postmitotic reserve of follicles. In humans, at birth, this pool consists of approximately 500,000 to 1,000,000 primordial follicles that are made up of a germ cell and surrounding granulosa cells. When mitosis ceases during fetal development, no new germ cells will ever be added to the reserve. Throughout life, germ cells reawaken from a dormant state and begin to grow. The vast majority of follicles die as they grow and develop through a process of programmed cell death. Thus, only a minuscule portion of this pool undergoes full growth, final differentiation, and ovulation. The vast majority of follicles die because they do not receive the trophic and hormonal support required for the final stages of growth and differentiation: They reach a juncture when critical hormonal support is not in synchrony with the stage of follicular development. By the time women are postmenopausal, the ovary no longer contains any follicles and no longer synthesizes ovarian steroids or peptides. The absence of ovarian estrogen and the consequent lack of negative feedback results in hypersecretion of both FSH and LH. For many years, scientists believed that the menopause resulted simply from the exhaustion of ovarian follicles (vom Saal, Finch, & Nelson, 1994). It has been hypothesized that the vast pool of follicles is required to maintain a stream of follicles in the developmental pipeline, and when the number of follicles falls below a critical number, the number that enter the growing pool becomes less well regulated. Subsequently, the patterns of hormone secretion by the larger follicles becomes less dependable, the length of time between cycles becomes more variable, and, consequently, fertility declines.

Changes in the hypothalamus and central nervous system play critical roles during the initial stages of the perimenopausal transition because neuroendocrine changes are already apparent before the final exhaustion of ovarian follicles. As mentioned earlier, the hypothalamus provides precise neurochemical and neuroendocrine signals that determine the patterns of secretion of the gonadotropins, which, in turn, govern the development of follicles and the ovulatory surge of LH. Hypothalamic changes, as measured by several indices, become evident during middle age, at the same time as the diminishing ovary follicular pool reaches the critical size that may no longer be able to support regular reproductive cycles. Therefore, follicular loss may not reflect the need to maintain a threshold number of follicles in the reserve but may be a direct consequence of a change in the pattern of neuroendocrine messages that govern the dynamics of follicular reawakening, recruitment, growth, and differentiation.

Recently, investigators have focused on the period prior to the establishment of permanent acyclicity (the perimenopausal period), that is, the events that occur in women during their early 40s or the equivalent stage in experimental animal models. We now realize that before ovarian follicles are exhausted, fertility and fecundity decrease markedly, reproductive cycles become increasingly irregular in length, and patterns of gonadotropin secretion are altered. One of the first signs that heralds this menopausal transition is an elevation in levels of FSH. Investigators have thought that these alterations indicate simply changes in ovarian estradiol and inhibin feedback. However, alterations in gonadotropin secretion have been reported recently in middle-aged, regularly menstruating women prior to any change in plasma estradiol. Data from several laboratories suggest that during middle age the precise, synchronized, and interactive patterns of hypothalamic neurotransmitter and neuropeptide activity, which are critical to maintain a specific pattern of GnRH secretion, become less ordered (Wise, Kashon, Krajnak, Rosewell, Cai, Scarbrough, et al., 1999). First, hot flushes, a hallmark of deterioration of the hypothalamic thermoregulatory centers, have been reported in normally cycling women when ovarian follicles may not be limiting. Second, using animal models of the menopause, changes have been observed in several aspects of neurotransmitter activity in middle-aged animals still exhibiting regular reproductive cyclicity. Some researchers propose that this deterioration in the coupling of neurotransmitter signals that regulate GnRH secretion or an uncoupling of the composite of neurochemical signals from GnRH neurons brings about the initial changes in patterns of gonadotropin secretion.

A common feature of these neurochemical changes is that their daily rhythmicity is affected far more frequently than their overall average level of activity or expression, suggesting that deterioration of the "biological clock" underpins the desynchronization of multiple rhythms that may be critical to cyclic GnRH secretion. In mammals, there is a group of neurons in the ventral part of the hypothalamus, which constitutes the suprachiasmatic nucleus, that have the unique property of exhibiting inherent 24-hour rhythmicity in several properties. Even more important, this small region of the brain is considered the master circadian pacemaker because these nuclei not only exhibit 24-hour rhythmicity themselves, but they communicate extensively with many regions of the brain and drive the timing of multiple outputs. The impact of this is so great that virtually all physiological functions show a pervasive daily rhythm. The menstrual cycle is fundamentally grounded upon a circadian foundation. Thus, a fundamental deterioration in this neural pacemaker or the coupling to its outputs may be a component of the gradual disintegration of the temporal organization of neurotransmitter rhythms that are critical for stable, precise, and regular cyclic LH secretion. This may initiate a cascade that leads to the transition to irregular cycles and ultimately contributes to acyclicity.

In summary, the evidence that both the ovary and the brain are key pacemakers in the menopause is compelling. Many more studies will be necessary to understand the precise orchestration of physiological, cellular, and molecular events that weave together and ultimately, lead to reproductive acyclicity. Ultimately, we hope to be able to treat post-menopausal women more effectively during this period in their lives.

PHYLLIS M. WISE
MATTHEW J. SMITH

See also
Hormone Replacement Therapy (HRT)

References

Vom Saal, F. S., Finch, C. E., & Nelson, J. F. (1994). Natural history and mechanisms of reproductive aging in humans, laboratory rodents and other selected vertebrates. In E. Knobil & J. D. Neill (Eds.), *The physiology of reproduction* (Vol. 2, pp. 1213–1314). New York: Raven Press.

Wise, P. M., Kashon, M. L., Krajnak, K. M., Rosewell, K. L., Cai, A., Scarborough, K., Harney, J. P., McShane. T. M., Lloyd, J. M. & Weiland, N. G. (1997). Aging of the female reproductive system: A window into *brain* aging. In P. M. Conn (Ed.), *Recent progress in hormone research* (pp. 279–305). New York: Academic Press.

Yen, S. S. C. (1999). The human menstrual cycle: Neuroendocrine regulation. In S. S. C. Yen, R. B. Jaffe, & R. L. Barbieri (Eds.), *Reproductive endocrinology. Physiology, pathophysiology and clinical management* (pp. 191–217). Philadelphia: W.B. Saunders.

FILIAL RESPONSIBILITY

Family members confronted with the long–term care needs of an ill or disabled relative are faced with the question of whether they have any legally enforceable responsibility to provide *caregiving* assistance to the dependent individual. This issue is especially critical when active family involvement is necessary to implement the individual's desired *care plan* (for instance, when the individual prefers to remain in his or her own home, rather than entering a nursing home). Although strong arguments may support a moral obligation in this situation (Hirschfeld & Wikler, 2003–04), no secular law requires family members to personally provide direct, hands–on care to dependent relatives.

Once a family member has volunteered to undertake the caregiver role, however, every state has a statute that makes it illegal (as a form of *elder mistreatment*) for the caregiver to willfully ignore the basic needs of or otherwise actively or passively endanger the dependent person. Elder mistreatment laws are triggered only once a caregiving relationship has been established, and they do not compel any family member to enter into such a relationship in the first place. Even when such a relationship has been established, the family may fulfill its obligation to refrain from neglect by arranging for professional caregiving—institutional or community-based—for the dependent person, rather than provide the needed services itself.

While society does not impose direct caregiving responsibilities on families, around 30 states (in addition to several other countries, including Italy, Israel, Japan, and Singapore) (Moskowitz, 2002) have filial responsibility (also called *family responsibility*) statutes, enacted more than a half-century ago. These statutes impose a duty on adult children, if they are able, to provide financial assistance to indigent parents. A few states impose a financial duty only on children who were themselves reasonably supported as minors by their parents; the duty in those jurisdictions is limited to reciprocation for what the children's parents did for them. The courts generally have upheld the validity of *filial responsibility statutes* against the claims (among others) that they violate the U.S. Constitution's 14th Amendment mandate of equal protection of the law and the 5th Amendment prohibition against the government taking property from individuals without just compensation. As a practical matter, though, these statutes are rarely vigorously enforced; almost a dozen states' filial responsibility statutes have never been invoked against any nonsupporting adult child (Wise, 2002).

Moreover, federal Medicaid law blocks the use of *state filial responsibility laws* as a direct means to compel families to pay for nursing home care (Pearson, 2004). The 42 Code of Federal Regulations Section 435.602(a)(1) prohibits states from considering "income and resources of any [applicant's] relative as available to an [applicant]" in determining a person's eligibility for Medicaid. According to Pearson (2004):

> This provision is one of a number of provisions tying Medicaid eligibility to the prospective resident's inability to pay, without consideration of the resources of adult children or grandchildren. These provisions are representative of a national public policy against forcing an individual's extended family to bear the costs of that individual's long-term care.

The financial status of *adult children* concerning the formal care of disabled parents needs to be distinguished from the duties of spouses of people receiving paid *long-term care services*. Under the historic legal doctrine of "*necessaries*," each spouse has been held equally (jointly and severally) liable for debts incurred by the other spouse for "necessary" goods and services. A number of states recently have modified the apportionment of financial responsibility for necessaries between the 2 spouses by holding the spouse who incurred the necessary expense primarily liable for payment, with the other spouse becoming secondarily liable when the spouse who incurred the expense does not have sufficient assets or income to satisfy the debt (Simons, 1998).

MARSHALL B. KAPP

See also

Caregiving (Informal)
Elder Abuse and Neglect

References

Hirschfeld, M. J., & Wikler, D. (2003-04). An ethics perspective on family caregiving worldwide: Justice and society's obligations. *Generations, 27,* 56–60.

Moskowitz, S. (2002). Adult children and indigent parents: Intergenerational responsibilities in international perspective. *Marquette Law Review, 86,* 401–455.

Pearson, K. C. (2004). The responsible thing to do about "responsible party" provisions in nursing home agreements: A proposal for change on three fronts. *University of Michigan Journal of Law Reform, 37,* 757–790.

Simons, J. S. (1998). Is the doctrine of necessaries necessary in Florida? *Florida Law Review, 50,* 934–954.
Wise, K. (2002). Caring for our parents in an aging world: Sharing public and private responsibility for the elderly. *New York University Journal of Legislation and Public Policy, 2,* 563–598.

FOSTER HOMES

See
Adult Foster Care Homes

FRAILTY

Mrs. P. is a 71-year-old widow with 4 adult children. Her medical history includes diabetes and osteoarthritis. She lives alone, tends to be *socially isolated,* and has mild depressive symptoms. Her nutritional intake is poor. She walks without aids but seems to have slowed down lately. Her cognition is normal, and she is independent for activities of daily living.

Is she frail? What is frailty, and how can it be identified? Is frailty inevitable if we all live long enough? What are the risk factors for its development? Are there interventions that effectively delay the onset of frailty and/or prevent adverse outcomes?

Frailty: An Emerging and Enigmatic Concept

Frailty has emerged as an increasingly important concept from both the standpoint of the clinical care of older individuals and research on aging. Since the 1980s, there has been an exponential increase in the number of publications that refer to frailty, from 36 between 1986 and 1990 to over 1,100 between 2000 and mid-2004. Frailty has also received increasing interest in the lay press, including a full-page article in the *New York Times* (Kolata, 2002).

In the 1980s, frailty was equated with disability, the presence of chronic disease, extreme old age, or the need for geriatric services (Hogan, MacKnight, & Bergman, 2003). Recently frailty has been separated from these other concepts, but the concept of frailty remains enigmatic. In clinical settings, the term frailty is often used to describe *older persons "at risk"* (or vulnerable) for all types of negative outcomes. Unlike their "nonfrail" contemporaries, these individuals are seemingly unable to withstand insults like environmental stresses (e.g., heat, cold), injuries, and acute illness. These insults either provoke a downward spiral, or the frail, older individual cannot recover and return to their baseline state. Clinicians often say, "I know frailty when I see it, but I can't define it." This is not surprising, given that in spite of a growing body of knowledge, there is no widely accepted definition. The literature abounds with different models, criteria, and definitions (Hogan, MacKnight, & Bergman, 2003).

A Complex Syndrome of Increased Vulnerability

Among those studying frailty, there is a growing consensus that frailty is a syndrome that can be identified and measured in both the clinical and community setting. It represents a state of reduced homeostasis and resistance to stress that leads to increased vulnerability and risk for adverse outcomes such as the progression of disease, falls, disability, and premature death. Frail individuals have higher rates of health care use with a greater need for continuing and long-term care. There is growing agreement that frailty lies on a continuum, is age-related (although not uniformly present with aging), and at a biological level is the result of the impact of *multiple system impairment* (or multiple system reduction in reserve capacity). Some currently undefined threshold of impairments in the endocrine-metabolic, cardiovascular, musculoskeletal, immunologic, and neurological systems is seemingly crossed. Frailty might well represent a dynamic, complex interaction of biological, psychological, cognitive, and social factors. There is an interplay of assets and deficits in a given individual within a given context (Lebel, Leduc, Kergoat, Latour, Leclerc, Beland, et al., 1999).

Frailty and disability are distinct but overlapping concepts (Fried, Ferrucci, Darer, Williamson, & Anderson, 2004). *Disability* often refers to the inability to independently carry out instrumental and basic activities of daily living. This may be on the basis of single or multiple impairments. Not all older persons with disabilities are frail, and not all frail elders have disabilities (Fried, Tangen, Walston, Newman, Hirsch, Gottdiener, et al., 2001). Disability, though, can be an adverse outcome of frailty, and if frailty is the pathway to disability for an individual, they do not cease to be frail with the onset of disability.

Fried and colleagues (2001) have developed the most coherent and clearly articulated approach to frailty to date. Central to their concept are neuromuscular changes (e.g., sarcopenia), neuroendocrine dysregulation, and immunologic dysfunction. Five characteristics of their "*frailty phenotype*" have been defined: weakness, poor endurance, reduced physical activity, slow gait speed, and unintentional weight loss over the prior year. Individuals with 3 or more of these characteristics are classified as "frail" while those with 1 or 2 are labelled "*pre-frail*." Using data from the Cardiovascular Health Study, Fried and colleagues (2001) showed that those meeting their frailty criteria were at significantly higher risk for *falls*, mobility and functional decline, hospitalization, and death within 3 years.

There are other approaches that attempt to capture the complexity of frailty and are also predictive of adverse outcomes. For example, Mitnitski and colleagues (2004) developed a *frailty index* comprised of 40 self-reported variables representing symptoms, attitudes, illnesses, and function. Applied to a sample of 9,008 community-dwelling people aged 65 years and older in the Canadian Study of Health and Aging, the index showed an exponential increase with age and was strongly correlated with survival.

Researchers and clinicians in the *Canadian Initiative on Frailty and Aging* have proposed a working framework for studying frailty (www.frail-fragile.ca). This holds that biological, psychological, social, and environmental factors that interact across the life course are the *determinants of frailty*. The candidate components of frailty include those identified by Fried (weakness, poor endurance, reduced physical activity, slow gait, and unintentional weight loss) with the addition of cognitive, psychological, and perhaps social factors. The pathway from frailty to its adverse outcomes is affected by various biological, psychological, social, and societal modifiers (Bergman, Wolfson, Hogan, Béland, & Karunananthan, 2004).

Determinants and Risk Factors

A complex entity such as frailty is likely to have a complex etiology. The life course approach to chronic disease (Ben Shlomo & Kuh, 2002) provides an attractive framework for understanding frailty and its determinants. As applied to frailty, it is an integrative approach that considers biological, social, clinical, cognitive, psychological, and environmental factors interacting across a person's life span that may either promote healthy aging or the emergence of frailty. Both early- and late-life factors are important to consider in identifying risk/protective factors for the development and progression of frailty.

Studies of *risk factors for frailty* or characteristics associated with frailty support the use of this approach. For example, data from the 1946 British birth cohort study showed that low birth weight was associated with decreased grip strength and increased risk of diabetes and cardiovascular disease some 50 years later (Kuh, Bassey, Hardy, Aihie, Wadsworth, & Cooper, 2002; Aboderin, Kalache, Ben-Shlomo, Lynch, Yajnik, Kuh, et al., 2001). Other studies have examined risk factors in mid- and late-life. In a systematic review, Stuck and colleagues (1999) identified several biological, psychological, and social factors (cognitive impairment, depression, disease burden, increased/decreased body-mass index, lower extremity function limitation, decreased social contacts, low physical activity, none compared to moderate alcohol consumption, poor self-perceived health, smoking, vision impairment) that were predictive of later-life functional decline.

Opportunities for Effective Interventions

Even before achieving a full understanding of frailty, it might still be possible to identify effective forms of prevention and management. Observational studies on aging suggest associations between several lifestyle factors (e.g., exercise, nutrition, education, socioeconomic status, social/intellectual activity) and the onset of frailty. These findings provide opportunities for the development of interventions to promote *healthy aging*, reduce the incidence of frailty, delay its onset, and/or reduce the number of years of dependency (Fries, 2002). Secondary prevention with early detection and treatment of certain chronic conditions such as hypertension, diabetes, heart disease, and osteoporosis could play an important role.

Effective programs for the care of frail individuals can minimize the impact on the individual, their families, and society. Evidence suggests that comprehensive, integrated health and social service interventions for frail older adults may have an important impact on health, quality of life, satisfaction, caregiver burden, pattern of health care use and cost (Bergman, Béland, & Perreault, 2002). Continuing functional decline is not inevitable in frail older people. *Exercise* and rehabilitation have the potential to improve their functional state (Gill, Baker, Gottschalk, Peduzzi, Allore, & Byers, 2002). The introduction of *assistive technologies* for physically or cognitively impaired people could have an important impact on the quality of life of both caregivers and care-receivers.

Conclusion

Although there continues to be active debate on the exact nature of frailty, there is no disagreement of its impact on the older individual, their family (particularly those involved in caregiving), and society as a whole. It is clear that further study is necessary to advance the quality and strength of the evidence on frailty across the biological, clinical, population, and social domains. Certain key issues need to be addressed including the difference between frailty and aging, its determinants and pathophysiology, the identification of its core components, modifiers of its progression, and the relationship between the biological, cognitive, psychological, and social factors.

Frailty represents the essence of clinical care for older persons. It moves away from an organ-by-organ to an integrative approach. Ultimately, work on frailty will be relevant to clinicians, older individuals, and society by identifying effective health promotion, prevention, treatment, rehabilitation, and care interventions.

Howard Bergman
David Hogan
Sathya Karunananthan
François Béland
Christina Wolfson

See also
Disability

References

Aboderin, I., Kalache, A., Ben–Shlomo, Y., Lynch, J. W., Yajnik, C. S., Kuh, D., Yach, D. (2002). *Life course perspectives on coronary heart disease, stroke and diabetes: Key issues and implications for policy and research.* Geneva: World Health Organization.

Ben Shlomo, Y., & Kuh, D. (2002). A life course approach to chronic disease epidemiology: Conceptual models, empirical challenges and interdisciplinary perspectives. *International Journal of Epidemiology, 31,* 285–293.

Bergman, H., Béland, F., & Perreault, A. (2002). The global challenge of understanding and meeting the needs of the frail older population. *Aging Clinical and Experimental Research, 14*(4), 223–225.

Bergman, H., Wolfson, C., Hogan, D. B., Béland , F., & Karunananthan, S. (2004). Developing a working framework for understanding frailty. Canadian Initiative on Frailty and Aging. Available: http://www.frail-fragile.ca/e/documentation.htm.

Fried, L. P., Ferrucci, L., Darer, J., Williamson, J. D., & Anderson, G. (2004). Untangling the concepts of disability, frailty, and comorbidity: Implications for improved targeting and care. *Journals of Gerontology: Biological Sciences and Medical Sciences, 59*(3), M255–M263.

Fried, L. P., Tangen, C. M., Walston, J., Newman, A. B., Hirsch, C., Gottdiener, J., et al. (2001). Frailty in older adults: Evidence for a phenotype. *Journals of Gerontology: Biological Sciences and Medical Sciences, 56A*(3), M146–M156.

Fries, J. F. (2002). Reducing disability in older age. *Journal of the American Medical Association, 288,* 3164–3166.

Gill, T. M., Baker, D. I., Gottschalk, M., Peduzzi, P. N., Allore, H., & Byers, A. (2002). A program to prevent functional decline in physically frail, elderly persons who live at home. *New England Journal of Medicine, 347,* 1068–1074.

Hogan, D. B., MacKnight, C., Bergman, H.; Steering Committee, Canadian Initiative on Frailty and Aging. (2003). Models, definitions, and criteria of frailty. *Aging Clinical and Experimental Research,* 15(Suppl. 3), 3–29.

Kolata, G. (2002, November 19). Is frailty inevitable? Some experts say no. *New York Times, 5.*

Kuh, D., Bassey, J., Hardy, R., Aihie, S. A., Wadsworth, M., & Cooper, C. (2002). Birth weight, childhood size, and muscle strength in adult life: Evidence from a birth cohort study. *American Journal of Epidemiology, 156*(7), 627–633.

Lebel, P., Leduc, N., Kergoat, M. J., Latour, J., Leclerc, C., Beland, F., et al. (1999). Un modèle dynamique de la fragilité. *L'Année Gérontologique 1999,* 84–94.

Mitnitski, A. B., Song, X., Rockwood, K. (2004). The estimation of relative fitness and frailty in community-dwelling older adults using self-report data. *Journals of Gerontology: Biological Sciences and Medical Sciences, 59A*(6), 627–632.

Stuck, A. E., Walthert, J. M., Nikolaus, T., Bula, C. J., Hohmann, C., & Beck, J. C. (1999). Risk factors for functional status decline in community-living elderly people: A systematic literature review. *Social Science and Medicine, 48*(4), 445–469.

FRIENDSHIP

Friends are important during adulthood in many ways, by serving as companions, sources of affection, and emotional and instrumental supporters. They contribute to psychological well being, physical health, and longevity (Sabin, 1993). Being a friend may be as important as seeing others as *friends among older adults* (Siebert, Mutran, & Reitzes, 1999). Research in friendship has increased over the past 3 decades, marked by the appearance of monographs synthesizing and reviewing extant research, edited collections focused on the friendships of specific adult populations, and volumes reporting primary research results.

In Western societies, friendship is not institutionalized and thus varies considerably in terms of what is expected from a friend. Basic perceptions of what friendship is differ by age, gender, and culture (Adams, Blieszner, & De Vries, 2000). Compared to other relationships, friendship is considered voluntary, although it is influenced by such factors as proximity (who one meets, physical location) and situation (sharing a specific medical disorder) (Dykstra, 1990). Friends tend to be similar to one another in terms of gender, race, class, and marital status (Dykstra, 1990).

Researchers who view friendship as voluntary pay special attention to psychological factors in *friendship initiation and maintenance*. In contrast, those who have a sociological perspective emphasize the effects of social structure and influences mainly beyond individual control. These 2 traditions differ in another way as well. Psychological theorists tend to focus on the interactive processes that take place in *friendship dyads*, whereas structuralists tend to study the form of individuals' entire *friendship networks* (Blieszner & Adams, 1992).

Gerontologists have focused more attention on friendship than other researchers in the recent literature. This is related to the role of friendship as a factor affecting the psychological and physical *well-being* of older adults and as a source of *social support*. In contrast to early studies of friendship among older adults, recent ones have focused more on the internal structures and processes of friendship and on predictors of friendship patterns, rather than exclusively on the effects of quantity of social contact (Adams & Torr, 1998; Dugan & Kivett, 1998). Rather than focusing exclusively on the positive aspects of friendships, contemporary researchers also examine their negative qualities (Blieszner & Adams, 1998). More recently, the focus has turned to using the quality and extent of friendship as factors in mental and physical health (Horowitz, Reinhardt, & Travis, 2003).

Researchers now more commonly compare the friendships of adults of various ages and sometimes examine changes in friendship patterns longitudinally (Holmen & Furakawa, 2002; Morgan, Carder, & Neal, 1997; Roberto, 1997). Knowledge of why friendship patterns change over time is still limited, however, because researchers often use the variable age as a proxy measure for both stage of life course and stage of development, without distinguishing between these 2 aspects of aging (Blieszner & Adams, 1992).

For many years researchers accepted the common perception that as people age, their friendship circles gradually become smaller. More recent research suggests, however, that the relationship between aging and number of friends varies across types of people and contexts. Rather than viewing the aging process as synonymous with *social losses* and constraints on friendship activity, researchers now examine the role changes accompanying old age as liberating as well (Johnson & Troll, 1994; Riggs, 1997). Holmen and Furakawa (2002) found that older adults continued to express high satisfaction with their friendships despite the decrease in the number of friends available to them over time. They found that a loss of satisfaction with contacts, rather than the number of contacts, was associated with feelings of *loneliness*.

Research has focused in recent years on the role of friendship in maintaining psychological and physical health. Perception of friendship as an important part of one's life leads to increased positive affect (Siu & Phillips, 2002). Satisfaction with social support and friendship is related to better ability to take care of the basic activities of daily living (ADL) as well as fewer hospitalizations (Ostir, Simonsick, Kasper, & Guralnik, 2002), less cognitive decline (Zunzunegui, Alvarado, Del Ser, & Otero, 2003), and a better response to rehabilitation (Horowitz, Reinhardt, Boerner, & Travis, 2003; Reinhardt, Boerner, & Benn, 2003). This research has suggested that the improvement of friendships and social support can be a major factor in improving overall quality of life (Stevens, 2001).

While earlier research on friendship focused almost exclusively on populations of Caucasian residents of the United States, research has become increasingly cross-cultural in nature (deVries, Jacoby, & Davis, 1996; Zunzunegui, Alvarado, Del Ser, & Otero, 2003). However, this research almost never directly compares findings across cultural and economic variables. Researchers need to consider the implications for friendship patterns of the characteristics of this period of history, such as the culture of individualism, an emphasis on personal freedom, the privatization of social life, and the development of emerging communication media (such as the Internet and cellular phones) and transportation technologies (Adams & Allan, 1998).

CHARLES J. GOLDEN

References

Adams; R. G., Blieszner, R., & De Vries, B. (2000). Definitions of friendship in the third age: Age, gender, and study location effects. *Journal of Aging Studies, 14,* 117–133.

Holmen, K., & Furukawa, H. (2002). Loneliness, health and social network among elderly people—a follow-up study. *Archives of Gerontology and Geriatrics, 35,* 261–274.

Horowitz, A., Reinhardt, J. P., Boerner, K., & Travis, L. A. (2003). The influence of health, social support quality and rehabilitation on depression among disabled elders. *Aging and Mental Health, 7,* 342–350.

Ostir, G. V., Simonsick, E., Kasper, J. D., & Guralnik, J. M. (2002). Satisfaction with support given and its association with subsequent health status. *Journal of Aging and Health, 14,* 355–369.

Reinhardt, J. P., Boerner, K., & Benn, D. (2003). Predicting individual change in support over time among chronically impaired older adults. *Psychology and Aging, 18,* 770–779.

Siebert, D. C., Mutran, E. J., & Reitzes, D. (1999). Friendship and social support: The importance of role identity to aging adults. *Social Work, 44,* 522–533.

Siu, O., & Phillips, D. R. (2002). A study of family support, friendship and psychological well-being among older women in Hong Kong. *International Journal of Aging and Human Development, 55,* 299–319.

Stevens, N. (2001). Combating loneliness: A friendship enrichment program for older women. *Ageing and Society, 21,* 183–202.

Zunzunegui, M., Alvarado, B. E., Del Ser, T., & Otero, A. (2003,). Social networks, social integration, and social engagement determine cognitive decline in community-dwelling Spanish older adults. *Journals of Gerontology: Series B: Psychological Sciences and Social Sciences, 58,* S93–S100.

FRONTAL LOBE DYSFUNCTION

Situated just behind the forehead are the frontal lobes of the brain. Although the frontal lobes are sensitive to the effects of aging, deficits in this area are difficult to measure and report, as well as understand. In the posterior portion lies the motor cortex, mostly responsible for motor functioning. However, impairments to the anterior portion of the frontal lobes (the prefrontal cortex) reflect the executive cognitive deficits, which are most, often referred to as "frontal lobe deficits."

Adults have the capacity to engage in higher order cognitive functioning as a result of the development of the prefrontal area of the brain during late childhood and adolescence. These functions include the ability to plan, to possess judgment over one's actions, to think in terms of abstract concepts, to be cognitively flexible, to inhibit inappropriate responses, to delay gratification for extended periods of time, to generate new approaches and ideas to familiar and unfamiliar situations, to control and regulate emotions, and to search memory efficiently and accurately, as well as regulation over internal states of the body. Additionally, the prefrontal lobes are responsible for allowing an individual to monitor his or her own actions, including the development of an internal set of ethics. The prefrontal lobes consists of those abilities that allow one to engage successfully in independent, purposive, self-serving behavior characteristic of adulthood.

Frontal lobe dysfunction reflects deficits in one or more of these skills. These frontal lobe syndromes (groups of symptoms) are not characterized by symptoms such as aphasia, motor deficit, intellectual loss, or other more easily recognized problems. As a result, the individual may appear outwardly to be perfectly normal. However, when frontal lobe functions are impaired, the person may no longer be capable of satisfactory self-care, of performing work independently, or of maintaining normal social relationships. Cases can range from mild (subtle deficits) to severe (more obvious). Milder cases are characterized by patients who are rigid and inflexible in their thinking but otherwise seem normal. Although memory problems exists, they are usually mild and are often dismissed as the effects of normal aging. Change in personality can also occur, with no apparent cognitive problems (intellect, motor).

Moderate cases typically are characterized by difficulty in decision making and poor judgment. Slower thoughts, labile emotions, a deterioration of daily independent living skills, some denial and defensiveness regarding one's problems, impulsivity, and an inability to see the nature of one's problems exist. Noticeable memory changes begin to occur. However, this does not pertain to the actual event, but rather to remembering it at the appropriate time. For example, a patient may be unable to tell you when his or her birthday is when asked but may spontaneously be able to provide such information in the midst of a conversation. The individual begins to have more difficulty taking care of himself or herself. During this stage, financial and personal decisions may become seriously impaired. During this stage and later, it is crucial to monitor such decisions.

In severe cases, patients often become disoriented to time and place. For example, they may not be able to tell you the city and state they live in or what year it is. These are often hallmark signs of severe dysfunction. Symptoms become very exaggerated when they forget personal and family responsibilities. At this stage, it is clear that they are incompetent to handle their own as well as others' affairs and that constant supervision must be employed.

Degenerative diseases, such as dementia of the Alzheimer's type and multi-infarct dementia, are the most common causes of frontal lobe dysfunction. Pick's disease results primarily in atrophy of the frontal and temporal areas of the brain, resulting in marked personality and behavioral changes along with language problems. Other frontal lobe dementias may show symptoms similar to Pick's disease but without the pathological changes seen in that disease. Other causes include head trauma, stroke, demyelinating diseases, tumor, hydrocephalus, and metabolic disorders secondary to problems elsewhere in the body. In almost all cases where brain damage is being considered, an assessment of the frontal lobe dysfunction should be considered mandatory because of the sensitivity of the frontal lobes to many disorders associated with aging.

A variety of measures have been used to assess frontal lobe dysfunction (or the numerous symptoms that accompany it). For example, there are a number of tests that have been devised to assess abstraction capacities and mental flexibility, including tests of concept formation. Such tests include the Similarities subtest of the Wechsler Adult Intelligence Scale (WAIS) (Wecshler, 1981), the Proverb Interpretation Test, the Reasoning subtest of the Primary Mental Abilities Battery (PMA; Thurstone, 1938), and the Category Test of the Halstead-Reitan Battery (Halstead, 1947). Additionally, the Similarities subtest of the WAIS shows the greatest decline with age. Other tests used to assess mental flexibility are the Wisconsin Card Sorting Test (Berg, 1948) and the Visual-Verbal Test (Feldman & Drasgow, 1951), which are tests of sorting and set shifting. In many cases, however, norms for the elderly (especially the very old) are inadequate, and caution should be taken in test interpretation.

Series completion tests also show significant declines with age. These tasks require the patient to examine a series of letters or numbers and determine the rule that governed the sequencing of the items in the series. Such measures that assess this ability include the Abstraction subtest of the Shipley–Hartford Scale and the Reasoning subtests of the PMA (Cornelius, 1984). The Gorham's Proverbs Test is also a measure that can be used to assess abstract formation (Albert, Duffy, & Naeser, 1987). Abstraction tasks that make attentional and memory demands on patients have also produced declines with age. A study by Mack and Carlson (1978) showed that subjects over the age of 60 have been shown to commit significantly more errors on the Halstead–Reitan Category Test than young subjects, even in the absence of obvious pathology. The elderly subjects were most impaired on the subtest that contained the greatest tasks of complexity.

Other measures that have been used to assess frontal lobe dysfunction and executive functions (higher order cognitive processing) include the Trail Making Test (Reitan, 1958); the Modified Card Sorting Test (Nelson, 1976); the Stroop Color and Word Interference Test (Golden, 1978); tests of verbal fluency, such as the Controlled Oral Word Association Test; and tests of visual-motor integration and planning, such as the Rey–Osterrieth Complex Figure Test (Grodzinsky & Diamond, 1992).

CHARLES J. GOLDEN
SAMANTHA DEVARAJU-BACKHAUS

See also

Alzheimer's Disease: Clinical
Alzheimer's Disease: Genetic Factors
Central and Peripheral Nervous Systems Morphology
Cognitive Processes
Dementia: Frontotemporal
Memory: Neurochemical Correlates

References

Albert, M. S., Duffy, F. H., & Naeser, M. A. (1987). Nonlinear changes in cognition and their neurophysiologic correlates. *Canadian Journal of Psychology*, *41*, 141–157.

Berg, E. A. (1948). A simple objective test for measuring flexibility in thinking. *Journal of General Psychology*, *39*, 15–22.

Cornelius, S. W. (1984). Classic pattern of intellectual aging: Test familiarity, difficulty and performance. *Journal of Gerontology*, *39*, 201–206.

Feldman, J. J., & Drasgow, J. A. (1951). A visual-verbal test for schizophrenia. *Psychiatric Quarterly Supplement*, *25*, 55–64.

Golden, C. J. (1978). *Stroop Color and Word Test Manual*. Chicago: Stoelting.

Grodzinsky, G. M., & Diamond, R. (1992). Frontal lobe functioning in boys with attention deficit hyperactivity disorder. *Developmental Neuropsychology*, *8(4)*, 427–445.

Halstead, W. C. (1947). *Brain and intelligence*. Chicago: University of Chicago Press.

Mack, J. L., & Carlson, J. J. (1978). Conceptual deficits and aging: The category test. *Perceptual and Motor Skills*, *46*, 123–128.

Nelson, H. E. (1976). A modified card sorting test sensitive to frontal lobe defects. *Cortex*, *12*, 313–324.

Reitan, R. M. (1958). Validity of Trail Making Test as an indication of organic brain damage. *Perceptual and Motor Skills*, *8*, 271–276.

Thurstone, L. L. (1938). *Primary mental abilities*. Chicago: University of Chicago Press.

Wechsler, D. (1981). *WAIS-R Manual*. New York: Psychological Corporation.

FUNCTIONING

See

Activities of Daily Living

G

GASTROINTESTINAL FUNCTIONS AND DISORDERS

Introduction

The main functions of the *gastrointestinal system* consist of digestion and absorption. Both clinical and basic investigations have demonstrated that there are age-related changes in gastrointestinal functions and that these physiological changes may contribute to the development of various gastrointestinal disorders that are more prevalent among older persons. Moreover, clinical manifestations of certain *gastrointestinal diseases* may be different in older individuals.

Oropharyngeal Structures and the *Esophagus*

Age-related changes in oropharyngeal and esophageal structures include subtle structural changes (such as thinning of the tongue and weaker oropharyngeal muscles) and functional changes (such as altered pharyngeal sensation and taste acuity, prolonged swallowing, altered peristaltic response after deglutition, and minor changes in esophageal motility). Salivary output and flow remain unchanged in older adults. *Corkscrew esophagus* (or *presbyesophagus*), which describes tertiary contractions of the esophagus commonly detected by radiographic evaluation in older adults, has no known pathophysiologic consequence (Holt, 1995; Tack & Vantrappen, 1997).

Available data suggests that most *swallowing problems* in older individuals are due to other medical problems (such as neuromuscular disorders) and the intake of numerous drugs. Among frail elderly individuals, transient swallowing difficulties are common when they become acutely ill, because various systemic diseases may cause esophageal neuromuscular dysfunction. Clinically, *esophageal diverticular disease* (such as *Zenker diverticulum*), *achalasia* (a motility disorder), and *esophageal cancer* occur more frequently in the elderly. Although *hiatus hernias* are more prevalent among older individuals, most epidemiological studies report that there are no significant differences by age for symptomatic *gastroesophageal reflux* disease (Curless, 2000; Holt, 1995).

The *Stomach*

Gastric acid secretion changes little with aging, unless there is concomitant gastric pathology (such as *atrophic gastritis*). Notable age-related physiological changes in the stomach include modest reduction in *pepsin* output and significantly reduced mucosal prostaglandin biosynthesis. While the *gastric emptying rate* for solids in healthy persons does not change with age, gastric emptying of liquids may be impaired (Holt, 1995; Lee & Feldman, 1997).

Epidemiological studies have demonstrated that peptic ulcer disease and its complications are more common among older adults. Potential explanations for this include a significantly higher prevalence of *Helicobacter pylori* infection and increased use of nonsteroidal anti-inflammatory drugs among older adults; both are known causes of *peptic ulcer disease*. Data from animal and human studies also suggest that age-related declines in gastric mucosal protective factors (such as prostaglandin biosynthesis, bicarbonate secretion, and expression of mucosal protective growth factors) may predispose the elderly to the development of peptic ulcer disease (Lee, 2000; Lee, 2004).

While gastric acid secretion remains unchanged in the majority of older, healthy individuals, 25% of the older subjects may develop *acid hyposecretion* (or *hypochlorhydria*) secondary to *atrophic gastritis*. *Gastric hypochlorhydria* may predispose these older individuals to various enteric infections (such as typhoid, salmonella, cholera, and Giardia), since a low intragastric pH is a known defense mechanism against bacterial infections of the gut. Gastric hypochlorhydria may also contribute to the development of *malabsorption* of iron, folic acid, vitamin B_6, vitamin B_{12}, calcium carbonate, and various trace minerals in the aged. Furthermore, chronic gastritis and associated hypochlorhydria from

Helicobacter pylori infection have been implicated by epidemiological studies in the progressive development of atrophic gastritis, *gastric metaplasia*, and *adenocarcinomas of the stomach*, which occur more commonly in older persons (Holt, 1995; Lee, 2000).

The Intestines

While overall intestinal absorption does not change with age, subtle reduction in carbohydrate absorptive capacity and altered calcium absorption can be detected in older adults. Although there are no significant changes in intestinal functions with increasing age, clinically significant malabsorption occurs more frequently in the elderly and is the consequence of various age-related disorders, such as *celiac sprue* and other mucosal diseases, *mesenteric ischemia*, bacterial overgrowth associated with small bowel *diverticulosis* and strictures, and *postgastrectomy states* (Holt, 1995).

Although there are no significant differences in bowel transit time between healthy younger and older individuals, various *anorectal dysfunctions* (such as reduced rectal wall elasticity and sensation, and delays in rectal evacuation) are frequently detected in elderly patients with *constipation*. Clinically, aging is associated with an increased incidence of diverticular disease, constipation, *fecal incontinence*, *volvulus*, *pseudo-obstruction*, *microscopic colitis*, *ischemic bowel disease*, and *colorectal cancer*. Acute *appendicitis* and inflammatory bowel diseases (such as *Crohn disease* and *ulcerative colitis*) are less common in older persons, but they can present with atypical findings, which may lead to a delay in diagnosis and higher frequency of complications. Moreover, several epidemiological studies have shown that there is a significant increase in the incidence of inflammatory bowel diseases at about age 70 years, leading to a second peak or bimodal distribution in inflammatory bowel diseases (Chey & Chey, 2000; Holt, 1995).

The *Liver*

Age-related changes in liver functions are not physiologically significant. Modest reductions in liver size, blood flow and perfusion, and dynamic liver functions can be detected with aging. Animal studies have shown that while the rate and time course of hepatic regeneration are delayed in senescent animals, complete regeneration of the liver occurs as in young animals. These observations have led to the increased use of livers from older donors for *hepatic transplantation*. While most *liver diseases* in older adults do not differ from those in the young, *autoimmune liver diseases* (such as *primary biliary cirrhosis*) and *hepatocellular carcinoma* occur primarily in older individuals (James, 1997).

The *Gallbladder* and *Biliary Tract*

Age-related physiological changes in the biliary tree include gradual narrowing of the distal *common bile duct*, increased incidence of *periampullary diverticula*, less responsive gallbladder contractions, and more *lithogenic bile* (due to increased secretion of cholesterol and reduced bile acid synthesis). Consequently, aging is associated with an increased incidence of *gallstones* and related complications (such as *cholecystitis* and *cholangitis*), *biliary tract disease*, *cholangiocarcinoma*, and *cancer of the gallbladder* (Siegel & Kasmin, 1997).

The *Pancreas*

Age-related physiological changes in the pancreas include gradual reduction in pancreatic weight (accompanied by atrophy of the gland and symmetrical ductal dilatation), and an increased frequency of *pancreatic duct stones*. Subtle declines in exocrine functions with aging are not clinically significant. There is no evidence that these modest changes in pancreatic functions predispose older persons to the development of malabsorption. Clinically, aging is associated with an increased incidence of *pancreatic malignancies* (Cohen, 1996).

The Gastrointestinal Epithelium and Carcinogenesis

The gastrointestinal tract is an epithelial organ with rapid cell turnover and proliferation. Data from animal and human studies have shown increased *gastrointestinal mucosal proliferation* as well as impaired proliferative response (to injury or feeding) with aging. In experimental models, *dietary (or caloric) restriction*, which is a widely used *anti-aging intervention*, has been shown to retard the development of *gastrointestinal hyperproliferation* and reduce experimentally induced *gastrointestinal tumors* in aged animals. These observations suggest that age-associated hyperproliferation in the gastrointestinal tract may contribute to an increase in the risk of tumor formation, as the incidence of various *malignancies of the digestive tract* increases with age (Holt, 1995; Lee, 2004).

Conclusion

Aging is associated with various physiological and structural changes in the digestive system. Due to the enormous reserve capacity of the gastrointestinal tract, digestion and absorption are well preserved in older individuals. Certain gastrointestinal disorders, particularly malignancies, are more common among older adults.

Makau Lee

References

Chey, W. D., & Chey, W. Y. (2000). Colonic diseases. In J. G. Evans, T. F. Williams, B. L. Beattie, J-P. Michel, & G. K. Wilcock (Eds.), *Oxford textbook of geriatric medicine* (2nd ed., pp. 300–311). New York: Oxford University Press.

Cohen, S. (1996). Pancreatic disease in the elderly. In A. M. Gelb (Ed.), *Clinical gastroenterology in the elderly* (pp. 213–226). New York: Marcel Dekker.

Curless, R. (2000). Disorders of the esophagus. In J. G. Evans, T. F. Williams, B. L. Beattie, J-P. Michel, & G. K. Wilcock (Eds.), *Textbook of geriatric medicine* (2nd ed., pp. 250–270). New York: Oxford University Press.

Holt, P. R. (1995). Approach to gastrointestinal problems in the elderly. In T. Yamada (Ed.), *Textbook of gastroenterology* (2nd ed., pp. 968–988). Philadelphia: Lippincott.

James, O. F. W. (1997). Parenchymal liver disease in the elderly. *Gut, 41,* 430–432.

Lee, M. (2004). Aging. In L. R. Johnson (Ed.), *Encyclopedia of gastroenterology* (pp. 5–7). San Diego: Academic Press/Elsevier.

Lee, M. (2000). Disease of the stomach. In J. G. Evans, T. F. Williams, B. L. Beattie, J-P. Michel, & G. K. Wilcock (Eds.), *Oxford textbook of geriatric medicine* (2nd ed., pp. 270–278). New York: Oxford University Press.

Lee, M., & Feldman, M. (1997). The aging stomach: Implications for NSAID gastropathy. *Gut, 41,* 425–426.

Siegel, J. H., & Kasmin, F. E. (1997). Biliary tract diseases in the elderly: Management and outcomes. *Gut, 41,* 433–435.

Tack, J., & Vantrappen, G. (1997). The aging esophagus. *Gut, 41,* 422–424.

GENDER

Gender is one of the most basic elements of human identity. In combination with race, ethnicity, and age, gender fundamentally defines who we are. In contrast to *sex*, which denotes the biologically based categorization of male or female, *gender* refers more broadly to the socially defined rules of behavior. *Gender roles* are contextual and define what it means to live as a man or woman in a specific culture at a particular historical time. Gender roles are taught and reinforced via social institutions such as the family, school, media, and community.

Cultures differ in how strictly they define and enforce gender roles, and in all cultures it is possible for gender roles to be modified in response to a change in circumstances. For example, American expectations about the participation of women in the labor force were modified during World War II because the social circumstances required it. As men left their place of employment, joined the armed services, and were deployed overseas, women flooded into the manufacturing employment sector, which had been predominantly a male domain. After the war ended and men returned to the United States, many of these women exited the labor force and resumed more traditional gender roles. Similarly, in the Middle East dramatic changes may occur with a change in government or religious leadership. Societal expectations for *women's behavior* may change from allowing women to work or study or dress as they wish to the imposition of strict limitations (e.g., not being allowed to leave one's home at all, or without a spouse's permission).

A person's location in a society's social structure is influenced by gender, because gender influences access to essential *social opportunities*, such as education, employment, or promotion. *Feminist theory* notes that gender is relational, and that the roles, responsibilities, and lives of men and women must be viewed in relation to one another (Calasanti,

2004). Yet heated debate continues to rage about whether environmental influences or innate biological differences explain *gender differences* in science and math achievement (Summers, 2005a; Lawler, 2005; *Nature*, 2005). However, even Harvard University President Lawrence Summers admitted that his provocative remarks hypothesizing that the dearth of women obtaining tenured positions in science and engineering at top universities was due to innate factors substantially understated "the impact of socialization and discrimination, including implicit attitudes—patterns of thought to which all of us are unconsciously subject" (Summers, 2005b). Feminist theory argues against this explanation for the disparity and notes that all *gender relations* are dynamic, constructed *power relations* embedded in social processes and institutionalized in social arenas with important consequences for life opportunities (Calasanti & Zajicek, 1993).

The extent to which the observed differences in major geriatric health indicators (such as morbidity, mortality, and disability) are due to socially constructed, and thus potentially modifiable, factors or to biological differences is not clear. Except for mortality, women have poorer health than men. Older women report more disease; however, as compared to men, those illnesses are generally less serious or catastrophic (Institute of Medicine, 2003). Women show higher prevalence of functional impairment than men, but there are no gender differences in incidence (Institute of Medicine, 2003). Self-reported perceptions of health are lower for women than men. Of interest to gerontologists has been the effort to understand to what extent categories of *gender intersect with those of race, ethnicity, class, and sexuality*. However, progress in the area is slow because research to identify the social determinants of health is both methodologically and conceptually challenging.

For further reading on gender, see: National Women's Studies Association at www.nwsa.org;/ the women's studies section of the Association of College and Research Libraries/American Library Association at www.libr.org/wss/wsslinks/; the University of Maryland women's studies database at www.mith2.umd.edu/WomensStudies/ and women's studies at Smith College at www.smith.edu/wst/home.html.

Elizabeth Dugan

References

Calasanti, T. (2004). Feminist gerontology and old men. *Journals of Gerontology Series B Psychological Sciences and Social Sciences*, *59*(6), S305–S314.

Calasanti, T., & Zajicek, A. M. (1993). A socialist-feminist approach to aging: Embracing diversity. *Journal of Aging Studies*, *7*, 117–131.

Institute of Medicine of the National Academies. (1998). Institute of Medicine Report. Gender differences in susceptibility to environmental factors: A priority assessment. Available: http://www.iom.edu/reports.asp?id=5672.

Institute of Medicine of the National Academies. (2001). Institute of Medicine Report. Exploring the biological contributions to human health: Does sex matter? Available: http://www.iom.edu/reports.asp?id=5437.

Lawler, A. (2005). Diversity: Summers's comments draw attention to gender, racial gaps. *Science*, *307*(5709), 492–493.

Summers, L. H. (2005). Remarks at NBER conference on diversifying the science and engineering workforce. Office of the President, Harvard University. Available: http://www.president.harvard.edu/speeches/2005/nber.html.

Summers' winter of discontent [Editorial]. (2005). *Nature*, *433*(7024), 339.

GENE EXPRESSION

Proteins catalyze and regulate virtually all of the chemical reactions in a cell, and the ability of cells to function and grow depends on their capacity to make a large number of different proteins. Each protein is a linear chain of amino acids, and its properties are dictated by its *amino acid sequence*. The information needed to make proteins is stored in *DNA* (*deoxyribonucleic acid*), the cell's genetic material. DNA is made up of 4 bases: adenine, thymine, guanine, and cytosine (A, T, G, and C) linked together in a linear chain. The cell must extract the information coded in the chain of DNA nucleotides to produce a chain of amino acids with a specific amino acid sequence. The flow of information by which information in DNA is used to produce proteins has been described as the central dogma of molecular biology. This dogma states that the information in DNA is first copied into *RNA*, and the RNA then is used to make protein. Thus, the information flow is unidirectional—from nucleotide sequence to amino acid sequence, and never the reverse.

Genetic information in genes is extracted through a multistep process involving a series of different enzymes. It is almost entirely dedicated to direct the synthesis of proteins. Proteins constitute more than half the dry mass of a cell and their actions as catalysts carry out and regulate virtually all of the chemical reactions in a cell. *Protein synthesis* depends upon the collaboration of a complex set of RNA (ribonucleic acid) molecules and proteins. In the nucleus, a molecule of *messenger RNA* (*mRNA*) is copied from a gene in the DNA in a process called *transcription*. In the cytoplasm, the mRNA is used to synthesize protein in a process called *translation*. During translation, mature mRNAs combine with *ribosomes* (complex assemblies of *ribosomal RNA*s, known as *rRNA*s, and ribosomal proteins) and transfer RNAs (tRNAs; small RNA molecules that carry activated amino acids to the ribosome). As a single molecule of mRNA moves through a cavity in the ribosome, the sequence of nucleotides in the mRNA molecule is translated into a corresponding sequence of amino acids. The information in the mRNA is decoded in units of 3 RNA bases to specify the sequence of amino acids that are linked together into *polypeptide chains*. The protein thereby produced has a sequence that has been specified by the DNA sequence of the gene.

mRNAs are extensively modified prior to their use as templates in translation. Perhaps the most remarkable modification is a sequence of reactions called *splicing*, which removes sequences from the RNA transcript. The sequences that are removed are called *introns* and the sequences that are retained are called *exons*. The initial transcript is a faithful copy of the gene and contains both introns and exons, while the mature transcript has been stitched together after the intron sequences have been cut out.

The process of gene expression is regulated at many levels, including mRNA half-life, translation efficiency, maturation, transport and synthesis. Regulation of RNA synthesis involves DNA sequences to which protein transcription factors bind. These proteins can have a variety of activities that either enhance or depress transcription; most act by regulating transcription initiation, and they recognize the sequences of gene control regions without exposing the interior of the DNA double helix. Other regulatory proteins act by controlling the elongation of transcripts. A second level of regulation involves *chromatin* structure. DNA in eukaryotes is compacted by wrapping around a histone core to form *nucleosomes*. Higher-order compaction of nucleosomes is likely to be negatively correlated with gene expression, and it is thought that highly condensed chromatin can prevent gene expression. The mechanisms that regulate the interconversion between active and inactive chromatin are thought to involve covalent modifications of the *histones*, since different modifications are associated with these chromatin states.

Developments in genetic technology have produced *DNA chips* that allow for the simultaneous analysis of the level of gene expression for thousands of genes (Gerhold, Rushmore, & Caskey, 1999). These chips hold the promise of being able to analyze gene expression changes during aging for the first time at the whole genome level. For example, a preliminary comparison of the levels of mRNA expression for some 6,000 known genes in actively dividing fibroblast cells from young, middle-aged, old, and progeric individuals revealed that approximately 1% of genes, primarily those involved with mitotic regulation and with extracellular matrix remodeling, show dramatic changes in their levels of expression with aging (Ly, Lockhart, Lerner, & Schultz, 2000). Such investigation should be able to help to elucidate age-related changes in gene regulatory functions of the whole organism.

Different cell types in multicellular organisms differ both in structure and function, their unique features and attributes a consequence of the selective and partial expression of their genomes. Current estimates are that less than 10% of the encoded information is expressed in any cell, and recently developed technologies for quantifying transcripts using DNA chips allow for direct comparisons of expression profiles for different cell types. Understanding the mechanisms that regulate gene expression and the improving ability to define the constellation of genes that are expressed in different cells hold great promise for elucidating the changes that underlie normal developmental processes and aging.

THOMAS KORNBERG

See also

DNA (Deoxyribonucleic Acid): Repair Process
Gene Therapy
Genetic Programming Theories

References

Gerhold, D., Rushmore T., & Caskey, C. T. (1999). DNA chips: Promising toys have become powerful tools. *Trends in Biological Sciences*, *24*, 168–173.

Ly, D. H., Lockhart, D. J., Lerner, R. A., & Schultz, P. G. (2000). Mitotic misregulation and human aging. *Science*, *287*, 2486–2491.

GENERALIZED ANXIETY DISORDER

See
Anxiety

GENERATIVITY, THEORY OF

In his *psychosocial theory* of development over the life course, Erikson (1963) described a series of 8 crisis stages in personality growth, of which *generativity versus stagnation* was the seventh. Although issues pertaining to this stage can arise at any point in the life course, this *psychosocial stage* most typically arises in the middle-adult years and beyond. The polarity implied in this, and all other, stage descriptions reflects Erikson's definition of psychosocial crisis stages in terms of pairs of opposites. Each pair describes the most favorable and the least favorable resolution of a crisis that can occur after the individual passes through the stage. The individual's ability to achieve a favorable resolution of a stage depends in part on the particular combination of biological, psychological, and social forces that operate at the time of the stage's ascendancy, and in part on how well prior crisis stages have been resolved. The assumption that each *psychosocial crisis* is associated with a particular point in the life course is based on the likelihood that individuals experience heightened vulnerability to the issues represented by that psychosocial stage due to their maturational levels.

As the favorable end of *Erikson's continuum* for the seventh psychosocial stage, generativity represents the component of the individual's personality that develops to incorporate concern beyond the self to the needs, interests, and well-being of future generations. The unfavorable resolution represented by stagnation involves a selfish interest in oneself to the exclusion of others who may follow. Although generativity is most commonly thought of in terms of commitment to parenting and providing for one's own children, there are many ways in which generativity may be expressed in the middle and later years of adulthood. Involvement in occupation is one form of generativity, particularly when this involvement is intended to help future generations through mentoring activities. Efforts to improve the quality of the physical environment, the political climate, or social welfare may also be seen as expressions of generativity, as are creative endeavors in which the individual leaves something behind for the benefit of future generations.

Erikson regarded the stage of generativity versus stagnation (along with the other adult stages of intimacy versus isolation and ego integrity versus despair) as resulting in the development of new qualities of the ego. In the case of generativity, this quality is care. This view has been challenged in the proposal that it is the self or identity that remains at the core of psychosocial development throughout adulthood. The stage of generativity versus stagnation would be seen, according to this view, as a "*developmental task*" (Havighurst, 1972). It is theoretically more appropriate to view the adult *Eriksonian stages* as demands that must be confronted as individuals grow older, rather than as stages that present the possibility of fundamental alterations in the ego (Whitbourne & Connolly, 1999).

Apart from this issue, Eriksonian theorists regard the major theoretical components of generativity to be procreation, productivity, and *creativity*. Although generativity reaches its ascendancy in a socially oriented phase of life, Erikson believed that like the other psychosocial qualities, this quality is biologically based. Initially, Erikson wrote that generativity could only be achieved through conceiving and parenting children. He later came to revise his views toward a more inclusive definition of generativity based on a drive to provide for society in ways that could include new products and ideas.

Along these lines, Kotre (1984) outlined 4 types of generativity. The first is *biological generativity*, which relates to conceiving, bearing, and raising an infant, the generative object. The feelings toward the child fall into the category of *parental generativity*, which includes feeding, clothing, housing, and raising a child over time. Biological and parental generativity are oriented toward helping children navigate their own initial psychosocial crises and thereby building the strengths within them of hope, will, purpose, competence, and fidelity. Parental generativity also socializes children into the family structure and society. *Technical generativity*, the third type of generativity, involves teaching skills to the next generation that are beyond mere parenting. The generative objects are both the skill and the pupil learning the skill. Individuals who are technically generative are transmitting the symbol systems of a culture. The final type of generativity, *cultural generativity*, teaches what it means to engage in a particular activity. Cultural generativity is the essence of *mentorship* in which the individual passes to the next generation an element of the culture's identity. The generative objects in this phase are the culture itself and the disciple. As with technical creativity, cultural generativity is not age-specific and can manifest at any time, although it is most likely to emerge following becoming a parent. Likewise, according to Kotre, the creative aspect of cultural generativity is likely to emerge in early adulthood.

Expanding on the view of generativity as a multidimensional construct and individual difference, McAdams and de St. Aubin (1992) conceptualize the construct as having 7 interrelated features: cultural demand, inner desire, generative concern, belief in the species, commitment, generative action, and personal narration. According to these authors, cultural demand and inner desire provide motivation for generative attitudes and commitments that may lead to generative behaviors, and finally to an integration of both personal and cultural significance.

The extent to which the concept of generativity has been subjected to empirical testing is limited when considered narrowly within the context of *Erikson's theory*. In part, lack of specific data on generativity is due to the vagueness of Erikson's definition—he gave few operationalizable criteria that could be used to develop methodologically sound indices or scales (Erikson & Erikson, 1981). One generativity scale devised using an extension of a questionnaire format designed to measure the first 6 Eriksonian stages (Constantinople, 1969) has proven to have a positive relationship to well-being and adjustment in older adults (Walasky, Whitbourne, & Nehrke, 1983). A large longitudinal sequences study using this measure on a sample ranging from college age to middle adulthood yielded age differences favoring the adult samples (Whitbourne, Zuschlag, Elliot, & Waterman, 1992). Moreover, changes in psychosocial development in related areas of identity and intimacy were found to be related in predicted ways to life events in adulthood in the areas of marital and career involvement (Van Manen & Whitbourne, 1997). More recent investigations using data from the follow-up conducted when the oldest participants were in their mid-50s indicated that individuals most likely to show increases in generativity throughout the midlife period were those who had settled into stable family patterns early in adulthood but had experienced patterns of job changes throughout their middle years (Whitbourne, 2002).

Further support based on empirical measures of generativity comes from a series of longitudinal studies conducted by Vaillant (1993). Based on this research, Vaillant concluded that the stage of generativity versus stagnation is composed of 2 substages: one concerned with the individual's own career, labeled "career consolidation vs. self-absorption," and one concerned with caring and commitment to the individual's entire community or culture.

Another line of investigation is based on longitudinal studies of several samples of college-educated women in midlife, including those in Helson's investigation of personality from college through middle adulthood (Helson & Moane, 1987; Helson & Wink, 1992). Although in both studies there was evidence for considerable personality stability, there were longitudinal increases for variables that might be theorized to show increases in adulthood based on Erikson's concept of generativity. These include personality attributes such as assurance, independence, and self-control, which can be regarded as indicative of an overall growth of the ego's ability to control and regulate behavior. Furthermore, certain variables measured in college such as "psychological mindedness," were predictive of higher ego development at age 43 (Helson & Roberts, 1994). Identity also seems to play a role in influencing personality change in *women in midlife*. Women measuring higher in identity at age 43 were more likely to have achieved higher levels of generativity at age 48, in part through the influence of identity on involvement in multiple social roles (Vandewater, Ostrove, & Stewart, 1997). Moreover, women who score high on generativity were more likely to be interested in political activities and social movements (Peterson & Stewart, 1996), indicating, in Vaillant's terms, that they were in some ways carrying out the role of "keepers of the meaning."

If generativity is more broadly conceived in terms of the involvement of adults in occupational pursuits and parenting, the amount of evidence bearing on the concept is far more extensive. *Work involvement* forms an important route for the expression of generativity in middle-aged adults up through the time of retirement (Parnes & Sommers, 1994). Although not all older workers retain a sense of intrinsic or inner satisfaction with their jobs, they do maintain a high level of commitment to the organization (Mathieu & Dennis, 1990). On the negative side, older workers may begin to disengage mentally when they feel that they are subject to age stereotypes, pressured to retire, and the message that their skills are becoming obsolete (Lease, 1998; Warr, 1992).

In the area of family life, it is well-established that by the time individuals reach middle age and beyond, involvement in the parental role is associated with overall feelings of life satisfaction and well-being (Brubaker, 1991). Mothers are especially likely to remain involved with their adult children, but parents of both genders maintain interest and involvement, even after children have left the home. According to the concept of *developmental stake*, parents maintain a psychological investment in their children, more so than children do in their parents (Bengtson & Kuypers, 1971). However, the existence of these strong feelings directed toward children may have unintended negative consequences. A developmental schism may occur, in which an emotional gap is created between parents and their children, due to a discontinuity between generations that reflects their differing emotional concerns (Fingerman, 1996). Tension or divisions between parents and children may also arise from a related phenomenon, the tendency of parents to see their grown children as reflections of the quality of their parenting.

According to Ryff and colleagues (Ryff, Lee, Essex, & Schmutte, 1994), parents regard the accomplishments of their children as an indication of the *quality of parenting* they provided. On the positive side, the ability to have produced a successful child may enhance the parent's feeling of being competent in this very crucial life role, and hence it may become a step toward building a sense of generativity. One study on college students' parents found that parents with high levels of generativity were more likely to parent using an *authoritative parenting style* (Peterson, Smirles, & Wentworth, 1997). Another study found a relationship between authoritative parenting and mother's generativity but not father's generativity (Pratt, Danso, Arnold, Norris, & Filyer, 2001). Beyond parenting, Peterson (2002) found that generativity levels in women at age 43 predicted family involvement up to 10 years later. Women with higher levels of generativity were more likely to be invested in the roles of mother and caretaker, which emphasizes the intergenerational nature of generativity.

As the concept of generativity continues to be refined from theoretical and empirical perspectives, it is becoming clear that rather than viewing generativity as a stage of development, it is more accurate to regard it as a set of attitudes and skills that are a crucial feature of normative changes throughout the life span. Specifically, generativity is conceptualized as generative concern, generative goals, and generative action (McAdams & Logan, 2004). As a feature of normative development, generativity is subject to social pressures and expectations (McAdams, Diamond, de St. Aubin, & Mansfield, 1997).

The relationship between generativity and a wide range of other psychosocial variables has been investigated. As theorized by Erikson, generativity is related to a sense of *well-being*, whether defined as life satisfaction, happiness, or *self esteem*. For instance, Hart et al. reported that high levels of generativity were related to both higher levels of social support and greater satisfaction with *social support*. Ackerman and colleagues (2000) showed that generativity predicted *positive affectivity*, as well as satisfaction with life and work. Conversely, generativity is negatively related to depression (McAdams, Hart, & Maruna, 1998). More broadly, in a sample of African American women and Caucasian women, generativity at midlife was correlated with community involvement and political efficacy (Cole & Stewart, 1996).

When he originally conceived the notion though, Erikson could not have envisioned the widespread interest in generativity that would follow among subsequent theorists and researchers. As is evident, however, the concept remains a useful one for heuristic purposes and as a stimulus to further inquiry regarding the notion of change during the middle and later years of adulthood.

SUSAN KRAUSS WHITBOURNE
JOSHUA R. BRINGLE

See also
Adult Development
Personality
Social Gerontology: Theories

References

Ackerman, S., Zuroff, D., & Muscowitz, D. S. (2000). Generativity in midlife and young adults: Links to agency, communion and well-being. *International Journal of Aging and Human Development*, *50*, 17–41.

Bengtson, V. L., & Kuypers, J. A. (1971). Generational difference and the developmental stake. *Aging and Human Development*, *2*, 249–260.

Brubaker, T. H. (1991). Families in later life: A burgeoning research area. In A. Booth (Ed.), *Contemporary families: Looking forward, looking back*. Minneapolis, MN: National Council on Family Relations.

Cole, E. R., & Stewart, A. J. (1996). Meanings of political participation among Black and White women: Political identity and social responsibility. *Journal of Personality and Social Psychology*, *71*, 130–140.

Constantinople, A. (1969). An Eriksonian measure of personality development in college students. *Developmental Psychology*, *1*(4), 357–372.

Erikson, E., & Erikson, J. (1981). On generativity and identity: From a conversation with Erik and Joan Erikson. *Harvard Educational Review*, *51*, 249–269.

Erikson, E. H. (1963). *Childhood and society* (2nd ed.). New York: Norton.

Fingerman, K. L. (1996). Sources of tension in the aging mother and adult daughter relationship. *Psychology and Aging*, *11*, 591–606.

Havighurst, R. J. (1972). *Developmental tasks and education*. New York: McKay.

Helson, R., & Moane, G. (1987). Personality change in women from college to midlife. *Journal of Personality and Social Psychology*, *53*(1), 176–186.

Helson, R., & Roberts, B. W. (1994). Ego development and personality change in adulthood. *Journal of Personality and Social Psychology*, *66*(5), 911–920.

Helson, R., & Wink, P. (1992). Personality change in women from the early 40s to the early 50s. *Psychology and Aging*, *7*(1), 46–55.

Kotre, J. (1984). *Outliving the self*, Baltimore: Johns Hopkins Press.

Lease, S. H. (1998). Annual review, 1993–1997: Work attitudes and outcomes. *Journal of Vocational Behavior*, *53*(2), 154–183.

Mathieu, J. E. Z., & Dennis M. (1990). A review and meta-analysis of the antecedents, correlates, and consequences of organizational commitment. *Psychological Bulletin*, *108*, 171–194.

McAdams, D. P., & de St. Aubin, E. (1992). A theory of generativity and its assessment through self-report, behavioral acts, and narrative themes in autobiography. *Journal of Personality and Social Psychology*, *62*, 1003–1015.

McAdams, D. P., & Logan, R. L. (2004). What is generativity? In E. de St. Aubin, D. P. McAdams, & T. Kim (Eds.), *The Generative Society: Caring for future generations* (pp. 15–32). Washington, DC: American Psychological Association.

McAdams, D. P., Diamond, A., de St. Aubin, E., & Mansfield, E. (1997). Stories of commitment: The psychosocial construction of generative lives. *Journal of Personality and Social Psychology*, *72*(3), 678–694.

McAdams, D. P., Hart, H. M., & Maruna, S. (1998). The anatomy of generativity. In D. P. McAdams & E. D. S. Aubin (Eds.), *Generativity and adult development: How and why we care for the next generation* (pp. 7–43). Washington, DC: American Psychological Association.

Parnes, H. S., & Sommers, D. G. (1994). Shunning retirement: Work experience of men in their seventies and early eighties. *Journal of Gerontology*, *49*, S117–S124.

Peterson, B. E. (2002). Longitudinal analysis of midlife generativity, intergenerational roles and caregiving. *Psychology and Aging*, *17*(1), 161–168.

Peterson, B. E., Smirles, K. A., & Wentworth, P. A. (1997). Generativity and authoritarianism: Implications for personality, political involvement and parenting. *Journal of Personality and Social Psychology*, *72*, 1202–1216.

Peterson, B. E., & Stewart, A. J. (1996). Antecedents and contexts of generativity motivation at midlife. *Psychology and Aging*, *11*, 21–33.

Pratt, M. W., Danso, H. A., Arnold, M. L., Norris, J. E., & Filyer, R. (2001). Adult generativity and the socialization of adolescents: Relations to mothers' and fathers' parenting beliefs, styles, and practices. *Journal of Personality*, *69*, 89–120.

Ryff, C. D., Lee, Y. H., Essex, M. J., & Schmutte, P. S. (1994). My children and me: Midlife evaluations of grown children and self. *Psychology and Aging*, *9*, 195–205.

Vaillant, G. E. (1993). *The wisdom of the ego*. Cambridge, MA: Harvard University Press.

Van Manen, K.-J., & Whitbourne, S. K. (1997). Psychosocial development and life experiences in adulthood: A 22-year sequential study. *Psychology and Aging*, *12*(2), 239–246.

Vandewater, E. A., Ostrove, J. M., & Stewart, A. J. (1997). Predicting women's well-being in midlife: The importance of personality development and social role involvements. *Journal of Personality and Social Psychology*, *72*(5), 1147–1160.

Walasky, M., Whitbourne, S. K., & Nehrke, M. F. (1983). Construction and validation of an ego integrity status interview. *International Journal of Aging and Human Development*, *18*(1), 61–72.

Warr, P. (1992). Age and occupational well-being. *Psychology and Aging*, *7*, 37–45.

Whitbourne, S. K. (2002). *Personality at midlife in the baby boomers: Individual patterns of change*. Paper presented at the 110th Annual Meeting of the American Psychological Association, San Francisco.

Whitbourne, S. K., & Connolly, L. A. (1999). The developing self in midlife. In J. D. Reid & S. L. Willis (Eds.), *Life in the middle: Psychological and social development in middle age* (pp. 25–45). San Diego: Academic Press.

Whitbourne, S. K., Zuschlag, M. K., Elliot, L. B., & Waterman, A. S. (1992). Psychosocial development in adulthood: A 22-year sequential study. *Journal of Personality and Social Psychology*, *63*, 260–271.

GENE THERAPY

The most effective way yet found to delay age-related physiological and cognitive decline in model organisms is to *limit their caloric intake* or sensing. Unfortunately, both data and evolutionary theory suggest that this will work only modestly in humans (de Grey, 2005a). Thus, effective postponement of human aging may require a piecemeal, "engineering" approach, comprising multiple interventions to repair the many molecular and cellular alterations that accumulate throughout life as side effects of metabolism and are eventually pathogenic (de Grey, Ames, Andersen, Bartke, Campisi, Heward et al., 2002; de Grey, 2003; de Grey, website). A successful approach must be comprehensive, substantially (though not necessarily totally) repairing all types of such "damage" in all tissues. It will thus almost certainly require powerful gene therapy technology.

Altering Our *Proteome*: The Options

There are 4 fundamentally distinct ways to introduce a protein (or RNA—for brevity we will hereafter mention only proteins) into an individual's cells and/or extracellular milieu. Gene therapy will play a critical role in *future medicine*, because it potentially avoids major limitations of the other 3 approaches.

The simplest of the 4 is transplantation: introduce cells or organs from someone who already expresses the protein. This is clearly limited to proteins that some humans express (a relevant limitation, as discussed below), and generally also carries the side effect of an immune response which must be suppressed by lifelong drug administration, impairing the recipient's resistance to infections and possibly to cancer (Krieger & Emre, 2004).

Another approach is to synthesize the protein *in vitro* and inject it. This method is used to treat *lysosomal storage diseases*, such as *Gaucher* and *Fabry diseases*, that result from the congenital absence of enzymes or transporters involved in lysosomal catabolism, and has given thousands of sufferers an essentially normal life when they would otherwise have died in childhood (Brady & Schiffmann, 2004). However, its scope is limited by the impermeability of the blood-brain barrier to circulating proteins and the limited cell-type specificity of uptake and intracellular targeting that can be achieved by altering the protein (such as by glycosylation) before injection.

The third option is *ex vivo* genetic modification of cells followed by their introduction into the recipient (Keating, 2004). This has many advantages over the first 2—e.g., genes expressing nonhuman proteins can be added, *autologous cells* (ones taken from the patient) can be used and an immune response thereby avoided, and expression can be long-term without repeated treatment. However, this approach (generically termed "*cell therapy*") still has limitations: the cells that the *engineered cells* are designed to replace must be eliminated. Sometimes they are already gone and that is precisely the problem to be rectified, but sometimes they are present but failing (or being actively toxic (Campisi, 1998; Duplomb, Takaishi, Park, Visser, & Unger, 2004; de Grey, 2002). They can theoretically be eliminated in conjunction with introducing new cells, but there are profound technical difficulties in doing this smoothly enough to maintain tissue function throughout the procedure.

Thus, a comprehensive "*rejuvenation therapy*" will almost certainly require the fourth approach to altering the proteome: gene therapy. Gene therapy entails introduction of *DNA into cells in situ*, where proteins that it encodes can be expressed. The term "gene therapy" is sometimes used to encompass cell therapy, with "*somatic gene therapy*" describing the *in situ* modification of cells' genes, but this tends to be confusing, so the narrower definition is recommended. *Ex vivo genetic modification* of gametes or pre-implantation embryos is termed "*germline gene therapy*;" some have argued that it may play a major role in medical treatment in the future (Stock, 2002), but it seems unlikely that what germline gene therapy can do in year N will ever compare with what somatic gene therapy can do in year N+50, so germline gene therapy will probably never be relevant to postponing aging and will not be discussed further here.

Methods for Delivering DNA to Cells *In Situ*

Most current delivery methods exploit the ability of viruses to enter cells and express their genes using the host's transcription and translation machinery. Viruses can be stripped of their pathogenic genes but not those mediating infectivity, and genes of interest can be added. Viruses vary greatly in terms of maximum cargo size, target cell type, and other key characteristics; none presently suits all purposes. Those enjoying widespread interest include adenovirus, adeno-associated virus, lentivirus, HIV, Sindbis, and herpes simplex virus (Machida, 2002).

The major nonviral approach to *gene delivery* is in *liposomes* (Miller, 2004). The DNA is packaged in droplets of positively charged (cationic) lipids; these are taken up readily by many cell types, so a particular organ can be targeted by choosing an appropriate site of injection. Once inside the cell the DNA is liberated from its casing.

Intracellular Destination of Exogenous DNA

Random Integration. Most viral vectors integrate into the host genome at a random location. The level and pattern of expression of therapeutic genes can be made relatively independent of its site of insertion by standard molecular tools. A major problem, however, is disruption of an endogenous gene, especially because this can be oncogenic. Therefore, and especially for anti-aging treatments where the desired effect is extremely long-term, viruses that insert randomly are not ideal.

Extrachromosomal. Circular, *extrachromosomal DNA* molecules (*plasmids*) generally are inefficiently replicated during cell division, so they are diluted out over time in continuously dividing cell types. They can support long-term expression in cells that do not divide, however, and because they remain extrachromosomal (with rare spontaneous integration) they are relatively unlikely to disrupt endogenous genes. The tendency of plasmids to lose gene expression over time can be abrogated by silent substitutions depleting their sequences of CpG dinucleotides (Hodges, Taylor, Joseph, Bourgeois, & Scheule, 2004).

For extrachromosomal expression in dividing cells, an alternative is to use constructs that are efficiently replicated and segregated. It has proven possible to engineer *linear DNA* containing a functioning *centromere*, which is handled by the mitotic machinery just like normal chromosomes and is thus termed a *human artificial chromosome* or (HAC). HACs have been successfully introduced into mammalian cells; their delivery into tissues *in situ*, however, remains to be perfected (Larin & Mejia, 2004).

Mitochondrial. Mitochondrial mutations have been long touted as a contributor to aging. Replacement of mutant mitochondrial DNA can theoretically reverse their accumulation (although another approach, described below, is further advanced). A variant on the cationic liposome, termed the *DQAsome*, has shown some promise in delivering exogenous DNA to mitochondria (D'Souza, Rammohan, Cheng, Torchilin, & Weissig, 2003). An alternative is to attach the DNA to a polypeptide that is recognized by the mitochondrial protein import machinery (Kahn & Bennett, 2004).

Targeted Replacement. The homologous recombination machinery of mammalian cells affords several options for introducing exogenous DNA preferentially at specific genomic locations. This is generally accompanied by the removal of a segment of endogenous DNA: it is targeted replacement. Promising results have been reported involving linear double-stranded DNA, but the transfection efficiency is extremely low (Yanez & Porter, 1998). Much higher levels have been reported using *DNA-RNA hybrids* (Kmiec, 2003) and triplex-forming *oligonucleotides* (Kuan & Glazer, 2004), but these results have often proven hard to reproduce elsewhere, and in any case can only introduce small changes such as single base-pair substitutions.

Targeted Integration. One much-used viral vector, the *adeno-associated virus* (AAV), inserts preferentially into a specific site on human *chromosome 19*. This makes it potentially much less risky than viruses that integrate randomly. Unfortunately, it has a small maximum cargo size, severely limiting its applicability. Efforts to circumvent this limitation have advanced recently; an example is the development of *hybrid adenovirus/AAV vectors* (Recchia, Perani, Sartori, Olgiati, & Mavilio, 2004).

AAV, however, is a single-stranded DNA vector and thus inevitably is prone to integrate at (or otherwise to mutate) random sites, despite its aforementioned preference for one site. Since plasmids seldom integrate spontaneously, a safer vector would be a plasmid that integrated into a defined location on demand, for example upon administration of a drug. In model systems whose genome can be manipulated in the germ line to include the target sequence for such a vector, this approach is relatively straightforward and has become a major tool in genetics; the *Cre/loxP* system is especially popular. However, since the human genome does not naturally contain a *loxP* site, this is unavailable for gene therapy. Also, even if such a site existed, the reversibility of the integration reaction catalyzed by Cre means that successive administrations of the vector would not necessarily raise the proportion of cells transfected.

Both these shortcomings may be avoided by the recent development of the *bacteriophage phiC31* as an integration system (Olivares, Hollis, Chalberg, Meuse, Kay, & Calos, 2002). Unlike Cre, phiC31 integrase recombines 2 nonidentical sequences, thereby destroying them both; excision of the integrated DNA is performed only by another enzyme. Further, the *phiC31* target site specificity is just relaxed enough that a few sites in the human and mouse genomes function as integration sites. Better yet, the preferred target sequence can be somewhat altered by directed evolution (Sclimenti Thyagarajan, & Calos, 2001).

Anti-aging Applications of Gene Therapy

Innumerable human diseases are amenable to treatment and cure by gene therapy once it becomes safe and efficient, and aging is no exception. Space constraints permit brief discussion of just 3; see (de Grey, website) for further analysis.

Allotopic Expression of mtDNA

Thirteen proteins, all components of the respiratory chain, are encoded in the *mitochondrial DNA* (mtDNA). *mtDNA mutations* clonally expand in nondividing cells, causing respiration-incompetence; however, such cells survive and may be systemically toxic (de Grey, 2002) or cause sarcopenia (McKenzie, Bua, McKiernan, Cao, Aiken, & Wanagat, 2002), thus contributing significantly to aging even though few cells are affected. Around 1,000 other proteins are nuclear-coded and cytosolically synthesized but then imported into mitochondria. Theoretically, mtDNA mutations could thus be obviated by introducing copies of the 13 relevant genes into the nucleus with modifications, causing them to be targeted by the same pathway. This approach, termed "*allotopic expression*," initially showed promise in yeast (Nagley, Farrell, Gearing, Nero, Meltzer, & Devenish, 1988) and has recently progressed further (Zullo, Parks, Chloupkova, Wei, Weiner, Fenton, et al., 2005). Sequences from other species will surely be useful in perfecting this approach (Gonzalez-Halphen, Funes, Perez-Martinez, Reyes-Prieto, Claros, et al., 2004; Daley, Clifton, & Whelan, 2002); these proteins' extreme hydrophobicity is probably the only major obstacle to be overcome (de Grey, 2005b).

Lysosomal Enhancement

Numerous age-related diseases, notably atherosclerosis (Jerome & Yancey, 2003), age-related macular degeneration (Sparrow, Fishkin, Zhou, Cai, Jang, Kranem, et al., 2003) and probably all forms of neurodegeneration (Nixon, 2004) are wholly or partly caused by the inability of certain cell types to degrade certain substances; these substances therefore accumulate, typically in the *lysosome*, whose function consequently declines. (Extralysosomal aggregates in neurodegeneration are probably protective responses to *lysosomal failure* [Ravikumar, Vacher, Berger, Davies, Luo, Oroz, et al., 2004]). Thus it should be beneficial to introduce enzymes capable of degrading these substances. Some microbes in environments containing human remains, such as graveyards, should carry genes for such enzymes, according to the principles of bioremediation, and preliminary studies support this (de Grey, Alvarez, Brady, Cuervo, Jerome, McCarty, et al., 2005). If these genes can be isolated, engineered for *lysosomal targeting*, and proven nontoxic, the benefits could be enormous. The many ostensible obstacles to developing such a therapy are less formidable on closer inspection, and it is rapidly gaining support (de Grey, Alvarez, Brady, Cuervo, Jerome, McCarty, et al., 2005).

Whole-Body Interdiction of Lengthening of Telomeres

Cancer is the hardest aspect of aging to postpone, because it exploits its genomic instability to evade endogenous or exogenous attempts to destroy it. A *cancer therapy* much more powerful than today's may be possible only if it cannot be escaped by any gene expression changes (for example of telomerase or multi-drug transporters). *Whole-body interdiction of lengthening of telomeres* (WILT) is a highly ambitious (some might say futuristic) proposal of the author for deleting the genes for telomerase and (if possible, when they are identified) the ALT telomere-elongation pathway pre-emptively, from as many cells as possible in all tissues, and maintaining tissues whose stem cells need telomerase by periodically replenishing them with autologous stem cells expanded *ex vivo* and given full-length telomeres using exogenous telomerase (de Grey, Campbell, Dokal, Fairbairn, Graham, Jahoda, et al., 2004). *WILT* is highly complex, involving ancillary manipulations of chemoresistance and the immune system as well as sophisticated stem cell therapy and *ex vivo* gene targeting (targeted disruption of stem cell genes). It involves gene therapy because mitotically competent but generally quiescent cells, such as glia or myoblasts, must be targeted *in situ*.

Aubrey de Grey

See also
DNA (Deoxyribonucleic Acid): Repair Process
Gene Expression

References

Brady, R. O., & Schiffmann, R. (2004). Enzyme-replacement therapy for metabolic storage disorders. *Lancet Neurology*, *3*, 752–756.

Campisi, J. (1998). The role of cellular senescence in skin aging. *Journal of Investigative Dermatology Symposium Proceedings*, *3*, 1–5.

Daley, D. O., Clifton, R., & Whelan, J. (2002). Intracellular gene transfer: Reduced hydrophobicity facilitates gene transfer for subunit 2 of cytochrome c oxidase. *Proceedings of the National Academy of Sciences U.S.A.*, *99*, 10510–10515.

de Grey, A. D. N. J., Alvarez, P. J. J., Brady, R. O., Cuervo, A. M., Jerome, W. G., McCarty, P. M., Nixon, R. A., Rittmann, B. E., & Sparrow, J. R. (2005). Medical bioremediation: Prospects for the application of microbial catabolic diversity to aging and several major age-related diseases. *Ageing Research Reviews, 4*, 315–338.

de Grey, A. D. N. J., Ames, B. N., Andersen, J. K., Bartke, A., Campisi, J., Heward, C. B., McCarter, R. J. M., & Stock, G. (2002). Time to talk SENS: Critiquing the immutability of human aging. *Annals of the New York Academy of Sciences*, *959*, 452–462.

de Grey, A. D. N. J., Campbell, F. C., Dokal, I., Fairbairn, L. J., Graham, G. J., Jahoda, C. A. B., & Porter, A. C. G. (2004). Total deletion of *in vivo* telomere elongation capacity: An ambitious but possibly ultimate cure for all age-related human cancers. *Annals of the New York Academy of Sciences*, *1019*, 147–170.

de Grey, A. D. N. J. (2002). The reductive hotspot hypothesis of mammalian aging: Membrane metabolism magnifies mutant mitochondrial mischief. *European Journal of Biochemistry*, *269*, 2003–2009.

de Grey, A. D. N. J. (2003). An engineer's approach to the development of real anti-aging medicine. *Science's SAGE KE*, vp1.

de Grey, A. D. N. J. (2005a). The unfortunate influence of the weather on the rate of aging: Why human caloric restriction or its emulation may only extend life expectancy by 2–3 years. *Gerontology, 51*, 73–82.

de Grey, A. D. N. J. (2005b). Forces maintaining organellar genomes: Is any as strong as genetic code disparity or hydrophobicity? *BioEssays, 27*, 436–446.

de Grey, A. D. N. J. (website). Strategies for engineered negligible senescence. http://www.gen.cam.ac.uk/sens/.

D'Souza, G. G., Rammohan, R., Cheng, S. M., Torchilin, V. P., & Weissig, V. (2003). DQAsome-mediated delivery of plasmid DNA toward mitochondria in living cells. *Journal of Controlled Release*, *92*, 189–197.

Duplomb, L., Takaishi, K., Park, B. H., Visser, T. J., & Unger, R. H. (2004). Independence of hyperleptinemia-induced fat disappearance from thyroid hormone. *Biochemical and Biophysical Research Communications*, *323*, 49–51.

Gonzalez-Halphen, D., Funes, S., Perez-Martinez, X., Reyes-Prieto, A., Claros, M. G., Davidson, E., & King, M. P. (2004). Genetic correction of mitochondrial diseases: Using the natural migration of mitochondrial genes to the nucleus in chlorophyte algae as a model system. *Annals of the New York Academy of Sciences*, *1019*, 232–239.

Hodges, B. L., Taylor, K. M., Joseph, M. F., Bourgeois, S. A., & Scheule, R. K. (2004). Long-term transgene expression from plasmid DNA gene therapy vectors is negatively affected by CpG dinucleotides. *Molecular Therapy*, *10*, 269–278.

Jerome, W. G., & Yancey, P. G. (2003). The role of microscopy in understanding atherosclerotic lysosomal lipid metabolism. *Microscopy and Microanalysis*, *9*, 54–67.

Keating, A. (2004). *Regenerative and cell therapy: Clinical advances (Ernst Schering Research Foundation Workshop)*. Berlin: Springer Verlag.

Khan, S. M., & Bennett, J. P. (2004). Development of mitochondrial gene replacement therapy. *Journal of Bioenergetics and Biomembranes*, *36*, 387–393.

Kmiec, E. B. (2003). Targeted gene repair—in the arena. *Journal of Clinical Investigation*, *112*, 632–636.

Krieger, N. R., & Emre, S. (2004). Novel immunosuppressants. *Pediatric Transplantation*, *8*, 594–599.

Kuan, J. Y., & Glazer, P. M. (2004). Targeted gene modification using triplex-forming oligonucleotides. *Methods in Molecular Biology*, *262*, 173–194.

Larin, Z., & Mejia, J. E. (2002). Advances in human artificial chromosome technology. *Trends in Genetics*, *18*, 313–319.

Machida, C. A. (2002). *Viral vectors for gene therapy: Methods and protocols (methods in molecular medicine, 76)*. Totowa, NJ: Humana.

McKenzie, D., Bua, E., McKiernan, S., Cao, Z., Aiken, J. M., & Wanagat, J. (2002). Mitochondrial DNA deletion mutations: A causal role in sarcopenia. *European Journal of Biochemistry*, *269*, 2010–2015.

Miller, A. D. (2004). Nonviral liposomes. *Methods in Molecular Medicine*, *90*, 107–137.

Nagley, P., Farrell, L. B., Gearing, D. P., Nero, D., Meltzer, S., & Devenish, R. J. (1988). Assembly of functional proton-translocating ATPase complex in yeast mitochondria with cytoplasmically synthesized subunit 8, a polypeptide normally encoded within the organelle. *Proceedings of the National Academy of Sciences U.S.A.*, *85*, 2091–2095.

Nixon, R. A. (2004). Niemann-Pick Type C disease and Alzheimer's disease: The APP-endosome connection fattens up. *American Journal of Pathology*, *164*, 757–761.

Olivares, E. C., Hollis, R. P., Chalberg, T. W., Meuse, L., Kay, M. A., & Calos, M. P. (2002). Site-specific genomic integration produces therapeutic Factor IX levels in mice. *Nature Biotechnology*, *20*, 1124–1128.

Ravikumar, B., Vacher, C., Berger, Z., Davies, J. E., Luo, S., Oroz, L. G., Scaravilli, F., Easton, D. F., Duden, R., O'Kane, C. J., & Rubinsztein, D. C. (2004). Inhibition of mTOR induces autophagy and reduces toxicity of polyglutamine expansions in fly and mouse models of Huntington disease. *Nature Genetics*, *36*, 585–595.

Recchia, A., Perani, L., Sartori, D., Olgiati, C., & Mavilio, F. (2004). Site-specific integration of functional transgenes into the human genome by adeno/AAV hybrid vectors. *Molecular Therapy*, *10*, 660–670.

Sclimenti, C. R., Thyagarajan, B., & Calos, M. P. (2001). Directed evolution of a recombinase for improved genomic integration at a native human sequence. *Nucleic Acids Research*, *29*, 5044–5051.

Sparrow, J. R., Fishkin, N., Zhou, J., Cai, B., Jang, Y. P., Kranem, S., Itagaki, Y., & Nakanishi, K. (2003). A2E, a byproduct of the visual cycle. *Vision Research*, *43*, 2983–2990.

Stock, G. B. (2002). *Redesigning humans*. Boston: Houghton Mifflin.

Yanez, R. J., & Porter, A. C. (1998). Therapeutic gene targeting. *Gene Therapy*, *5*, 149–159.

Zullo, S. J., Parks, W. T., Chloupkova, M., Wei, B., Weiner, H., Fenton, W. A., Eisenstadt, J. M., & Merril, C. R. (2005). Stable transformation of CHO cells and human NARP cybrids confers oligomycin resistance (oli^r) following transfer of a mitochondrial DNA-encoded oli^r ATPase 6 gene to the nuclear genome: A model system for mtDNA gene therapy. *Rejuvenation Research*, *8*, 18–28.

GENETIC HETEROGENEITY

The concept of genetic heterogeneity is of central importance in understanding genetics, genetic differences in aging patterns, and *genetic theories of aging*. Frequently, different genetic mutations, or polymorphisms, underlie similar genetic conditions, a situation known a *genetic heterogeneity*. When a given genetic disease is investigated, it is common to find that what initially looked like a single disease is in fact 2 or more slightly different genetic diseases (McKusick, 1994). These may resemble each other in many or most ways but have basic differences at the gene level. Similar disorders also can be caused by mutations that differ at the same genetic locus. They are termed *alleles* and usually have identical modes of inheritance, i.e., dominant, recessive, or X-linked. They may be caused by mutations that occur at different genetic loci, which may lead to quite different modes of inheritance. The following are a number of methods for demonstrating genetic heterogeneity in humans.

Differing Inheritance Modes. If it can be shown that a disease may be inherited in 2 or 3 different modes, then this is proof that different mutations can cause the same apparent disease. For example, *Ehlers-Danlos syndrome* is a common *connective tissue disorder* in which extremely loose joints are present. This syndrome shows different modes of inheritance in different families, including dominant, recessive, and X-linked, which indicates at least 3 different genetic loci are involved.

Non-allelism of Recessives. In some diseases it is possible to show by mating studies that there are different mutations involved. For example, if 2 persons with *albinism* marry, the expected result is for them to have all albino offspring. However, it is commonly observed that none of the children of 2 albino parents is albino. This implies different genetic mutations underlying the albino locus in both parents.

Linkage Relationships. Another genetic method for demonstrating heterogeneity is with differing *linkage relationships*. For example, familial *Alzheimer's disease* has been linked in different families to locations on more than 3 different chromosomes.

Phenotypic Analysis. The *phenotype* is the physical expression of a gene. Some diseases, such as the *mucopolysaccharidoses*, which were previously lumped together and called *gargoylism*, have now been phenotypically distinguished. Different degrees of corneal cataracts or clouding are found in the different forms.

Biochemical Analysis. Biochemical differences can be used to demonstrate genetic heterogeneity. For example, different types of hereditary *hemolytic anemias* are due to the deficiencies of different enzymes involved in red blood cell metabolism.

Physiological Analysis. Genetic heterogeneity can sometimes be defined by physiological studies. For example, different types of *hemophilia* (A and B) can be shown to correct each other when a cross-transfusion is given, thus indicating that differing clotting deficiencies exist.

Cell Culture Studies. Genetic heterogeneity can sometimes be defined by *cell-culture mixing studies*. For example, genetic diseases in which there is an accumulation of abnormal substances such as the mucopolysaccharidoses can sometimes be corrected by *coculture of cells* from one individual to those of another individual. Thus, each cell supplies a missing enzyme that the other cell is lacking, showing cross-correction and the genetic heterogeneity that exists in this group of conditions.

Somatic Cell Genetics. *Cell hybridization* studies have allowed recognition that distinct forms of *DNA repair* exist in the group of conditions known as *Xeroderma pigmentosum* (XP) and *Cockayne syndrome* (CS). When cells from 2 individuals with different types of XP or CS are fused together, defects in DNA repair disappear if genetic heterogeneity is present. This has allowed 7 DNA repair complementation groups to be defined in XP and 3 in CS.

Molecular Genetic Analysis. Defining different alleles at the molecular level is the most basic way to define genetic heterogeneity. For example, various forms of *beta-thalassemia* can be shown to result from different specific molecular defects by molecular techniques involving restriction-enzyme mapping or direct sequencing of the underlying mutations.

These various analytic methods may be used to elucidate genetic differences in the aging rates of different individuals and species, both at the cellular and the organismic level.

W. Ted Brown

See also
Gene Expression
DNA (Deoxyribonucleic Acid): Repair Process

Reference

McKusick, V. A. (1998). *Mendelian inheritance in man. A catalog of human genes and genetic disorders* (12th ed.). Baltimore, MD: Johns Hopkins University Press.

GENETIC PROGRAMMING THEORIES

Genetic programming theories of aging emphasize that aging is part of a programmed process that is genetically determined. These theories are in contrast to those that emphasize wear-and-tear mechanisms and enivronmentally determined mechanisms.

It is apparent from looking at the wide range of the *maximal potential life spans* (MPLs) of various animals that the species MPL is in large part genetically determined (Brown, 1992). Mice have a *genetically determined life span* of no more than about 3 years, while for humans it is estimated to be about 120 years. These differences are determined by the hereditary blueprint encoded in DNA.

A number of possible genetic mechanisms have been proposed that might contribute to or account for the underlying genetic component to the aging process. The genetic program that encodes the process of aging may regulate the onset of senescence. Program theories of aging often suggest that the features of senescence are the result of a clock mechanism. For example, with age the brain may regulate the production of certain hormones necessary for the maintenance of the youthful vigor of cells and tissues throughout the body. This may be the case in regard to female reproductive aging, which may be under the control of higher brain centers regulating the release of neuroendocrine factors (Finch, 1976). Individual cells within the brain might thus determine the life span of the entire organism. These individual cells may have a finite life span as well. It has been suggested that cells have an internal clock mechanism that may be genetically determined and which regulates their individual life spans. The average life span of cultured cells is on the order of 50 to 100 generations (Hayflick, 1974).

One theory of aging holds that events occur that are genetically programmed to cause the *death of the organism*. For example, a *death hormone* might be released with increasing concentrations during aging and turn off the body's metabolic processes. A decreasing ability to respond to *thyroid hormones* due to the brain's increasing release of an inhibitor has been postulated (Denckla, 1974). Some animal species, such as the Pacific salmon, do undergo a rapid senescence because of a programmed event. The salmon ages rapidly during the period of time it swims upstream to lay eggs because of a massive release of corticosteroid hormones. Aging in human could be a reflection of a less drastic and more gradual imbalance of hormones.

A gradual decrease in the release of growth factors needed to maintain full vigor may be due to an underlying genetic program. Programming does occur with maturation in many body systems. In the immune system there are progressive shifts in the activation of genes from embryonic to more mature forms that occur with maturation. Similar mechanisms occurring at other gene loci could lead to shifts and alterations in gene expression. Genetic expression could also be genetically regulated in part by the composition of the extracellular matrix. The makeup of the matrix could be programmed to change significantly during aging.

Martin (1980) suggested that theories of aging that involve an alteration of the genome (i.e., *genotropic theories of aging*) might be classified into 2 categories: those involving modifications in gene structure, and those emphasizing modifications in gene expression. In the first class are theories that include *intrinsic mutagenesis*, *protein error catastrophe*, *free radical* and *cross-linking*, *autoimmunity*, and slow viruses causing mutation. In the second category are theories that include *neuroendocrine clocks*, progressive transcriptional repression, isoenzyme shifts, allelic exclusion, codon restriction, posttranslational protein modifications, altered protein turnover, terminal differentiation, autoimmunity, and depression.

Rose (1991) has pointed out that there are likely to be 2 different population genetic mechanisms involved with the evolution of aging. The first is *antagonistic pleiotropy*, in which *alleles* (a gene with different genetic varieties) that have beneficial effects at early ages have antagonistic, deleterious effects at later ages. The second is age specificity of gene action, in which alleles with deleterious effects at later ages are essentially neutral at earlier ages and have weak selection at later ages due to the declining force of selection with age.

In summary, genetic programming theories of aging are derived from the observations that species life span appears to be genetically determined. This suggests that development and aging may be under the control of an innate genetic program. A variety of specific mechanisms have been proposed for consideration, but conclusive proof is lacking for any of them.

W. Ted Brown

See also
Gene Expression
DNA (Deoxyribonucleic Acid): Repair Process

References

Brown, W. T. (1992). Longevity and aging. In R. A. King, J. I. Rotter, & A. G. Motulsky (Eds.), *The genetic basis of common diseases* (pp. 915–926). Oxford: Oxford University Press.

Denckla, W. D. (1974). Role of the pituitary and thyroid glands in the decline of minimal O_2 consumption with age. *Journal of Clinical Investigation*, *53*, 572–581.

Finch, C. E. (1976). The regulation of physiological changes during mammalian aging. *Quarterly Review of Biology*, *51*, 49–83.

Hayflick, L. (1974). The longevity of cultured human cells. *Journal of the American Geriatrics Society*, *22*, 1–12.

Martin, G. M. (1980). Genotrophic theories of aging: An overview. *Advances in Pathobiology*, *7*, 5–20.

Roses, M. R. (1991). *Evolutionary biology of aging*. Oxford: Oxford University Press.

GEOGRAPHIC MOBILITY

Geographic mobility in later life is a rapidly growing topic of research. Demography, geography, and gerontology are the primary disciplines from which this literature has arisen. It is of growing interest because of its relationship to the practical concerns for planning and policy, as well as economic development. Most *internal migration* studies use census data and large national surveys; a few use local surveys.

Overall *residential mobility* among older citizens in the United States is gradually slowing. Evidence from the 2000 census indicates that 76% of all persons age 60 and older have not moved in the previous 5 years. Moves within state boundaries have declined, as they have in the general population (Wolf & Longino, 2004). However, since 1980 longer distance moves have held steady among older migrants.

The national redistribution of the population older than age 60 is not due primarily to migration. With a few notable state exceptions the actual geographical distribution of the older population is due more to an uneven aging in place (Bean, Myers, Angel, & Galle, 1994). Areas where concentrations of baby boomers moved to work, for example, will generate a bumper crop of retirees in the future (Frey, 1995) whether or not retirees move there.

The characteristics of local (within the county) movers have become progressively older and more dependent, as a whole, since 1960. Migrants are an advantaged group, by comparison, both economically and socially, and this gap is widening.

Half (54%) of interstate migrants over 60 went to only 10 states between 1995 and 2000, and disproportionately to the top 5: *Florida*, *Arizona*, *California*, *Texas*, and *North Carolina*. The changes since 1980 are patterned. Florida has continued to be the most popular destination state by far, although its proportion has declined from 26% to 19%. California lost its second place to Arizona, a much smaller state. Texas has maintained its fourth place since 1980 and North Carolina its fifth place since 1990. The decline in attractiveness by Florida and California was balanced by a growing attractiveness of some smaller states, particularly *Georgia* and *Nevada* (Longino & Bradley, 2003).

Recent migrants in 2000 composed over a tenth of the total 60+ populations of a few states, indicating a potential impact on the characteristics of those older populations. In Nevada, they are 20%, Arizona, 15%, and Florida, 11%.

Counterstream migration is now clearly documented. Streams from Florida to its major sending states, although small by comparison, contain higher proportions of older, widowed, economically and residentially dependent migrants than the larger streams entering Florida. The reverse is true for California and its exchange partners. Slowly changing cycles of rising and declining attractiveness of particular states may affect the types of older migrants they send and receive (Longino, 1995).

Migration to one's state of birth is not higher among older migrants than others. Such return migrants made up about one-fifth of observed later-life migration in 1980, and 17% in 1990, with the proportion holding steady in 2000. As a national pattern, states seem to be losing some of their pull for their native sons and daughters. An exception is found among older African Americans, who are far more inclined to return to their state of birth than are whites.

The dialogue among researchers concerning whether *seasonal migration* is part of the process leading to permanent migration has concluded that seasonal migration generates its own lifestyle and culture, different from that of permanent migrants but equally valuable in its own right (McHugh & Mings, 1991). Once having adopted the lifestyle, seasonal migration is likely to last for several years, finally interrupted and reluctantly terminated by a fluctuation or decrease in necessary economic or health resources. The small minority who settle down and stay tend to have strong person and place ties to the host community.

The local economic impact of concentrated later-life migrants tends, on balance, to be positive. Their consumption stimulates the economy. There are cases, however, where older migrants have not supported local bond issues for education. Further, they tend to support efforts to conserve the physical beauty of the environment, even if it hinders the development of work opportunities for the nonretired population (Longino, 1995).

Interstate migration is expected to increase through the decade of 2030, because of the socioeconomic upgrading of the older population and the *retirement of baby boomers* (Longino, 1998). The number of retirement-aged persons continues to grow, and their interstate migration rate is stable, so the number of migrants is expected to grow for another 20 years and then decline. The destinations and characteristics of migrants, however, are expected to gradually change over time.

Older people also move geographically from one country to another. Later-life *international migration*, therefore, is also part of the picture. The simplest, and perhaps least nuanced, way of categorizing it is by using the broad categories of *assistance migration*, and *amenity migration*. Among international migrants, assistance migration is most frequently studied in the context of family-motivated migration from Latin American or Asian countries to the United States. Most of older immigrants to the United States come to join children who have become citizens (Treas, 1995) particularly those from Mexico (Angel, Angel, & Markides, 2000). Extended family living, thus, may be a part of a long-term adaptive strategy among older immigrants.

Immigrants arriving in later life may have a particularly difficult time adjusting (Treas & Mazumdar, 2002). It is difficult for these older migrants, due in part to language barriers, to build broad supportive social networks, and to interact with formal institutions in their adopted culture. These factors taken together may lead to family conflict. At issue is a shift in the household balance of power associated with immigration. In less developed countries *filial obligation* is a commonly accepted norm (Treas & Mazumdar, 2002), where old age is accompanied by respect and influence within the family, stemming in part from mastery of traditional knowledge and control of land and wealth. However, uprooted immigrants arriving late in life often are unable to fulfill their traditional roles. In contrast, in industrial and postindustrial societies young adults do not depend upon inheriting land from their parents but command independent income streams. Some return to their country of origin, but they have escaped research scrutiny.

CHARLES F. LONGINO, JR.

References

Angel, J. L., Angel, R. J., & Markides, K. S. (2000). Late-life immigration, changes in living arrangements, and headship status among older Mexican-origin individuals. *Social Science Quarterly*, *81*(1), 389–403.

Bean, F. D., Myers, G. C., Angel J. L., & Galle, O. R. (1994). Geographic concentration, migration and population redistribution among the elderly. In L. G. Martin & S. H. Preston (Eds.), *Demography of aging* (pp. 319–355). Washington, DC: National Academies Press.

Frey, W. H. (1995). Elderly demographic profiles of U.S. states: Impacts of "new elderly births," migration, and immigration. *Gerontologist*, *35*, 761–770.

Longino, C. F., Jr. (1995). *Retirement migration in America.* Houston: Vacation Publications.

Longino, C. F., Jr. (1998). Geographic mobility and the baby boom. *Generations*, *22*, 60–64.

Longino, C. F., Jr., & Bradley, D. E. (2003). Brief report: A first look at retirement migration trends in 2000. *Gerontologist*, *43*, 904–907.

McHugh, K. E., & Mings, R. C. (1991). On the road again: Seasonal migration to a sunbelt metropolis. *Urban Geography, 12*, 1–18.

Treas, J. (1995). Older Americans in the 1990s and beyond. *Population Bulletin, 50*(2), 1–45.

Treas, J., & Mazumdar, S. (2002). Older people in America's immigrant families: Dilemmas of dependence, integration, and isolation. *Journal of Aging Studies, 16*, 243–258.

Wolf, D., & Longino, C. F., Jr. (2004). Our "increasingly mobile society?" The curious persistence of a false belief. *Gerontologist, 45*, 5–11.

GERIATRIC ASSESSMENT PROGRAMS

Over the past 3 decades several types of special geriatric care programs have been developed, centered on the performance of *comprehensive geriatric assessment* (CGA) and associated treatment and follow-up services. *CGA* is a multidimensional, interdisciplinary, diagnostic procedure intended to determine a frail elderly person's medical, psychosocial, and functional capabilities and problems with the objective of developing an overall plan for treatment and long-term follow-up. CGA includes many components of the standard medical diagnostic evaluation, but it goes well beyond the routine examination in its focus on the *frail elderly* individual, emphasis on functional status and quality of life, comprehensiveness, and use of standardized measurement instruments and interdisciplinary teams. The rationale underlying CGA is that frail older people, with their complex clinical presentations and needs, require a special approach to evaluation and care that is not ordinarily supplied by health care providers, and that, given this special approach, geriatric patients will have more accurate and complete diagnosis, receive more appropriate care, have better care outcomes, and ultimately cost less by avoiding unnecessary services.

CGA can be performed in a variety of locations and health care contexts. It is a basic part of care in hospital geriatric units and geriatric consultation teams; it exists in programs within community senior health centers, and it often occurs in primary care settings as a supplement to the standard medical evaluation. Particularly successful model programs perform CGA and follow-up in the home by nurses, health visitors, or individuals from an interdisciplinary home care team. CGA can best be viewed as a continuum, ranging from a limited screening assessment by primary care physicians or community health workers, focused on identifying an older person's functional problems and disabilities, to more thorough evaluation of these problems in specialized geriatric or rehabilitation centers by a geriatrician and/or interdisciplinary team tied to initiation of a therapeutic plan, which often includes long-term case management.

Historical Overview of Geriatric Assessment

The first published reports of programs of *geriatric assessment* came from the British geriatrician *Marjory Warren*, who initiated the concept during the 1930s while she was in charge of a large chronic disease hospital (called a workhouse infirmary). This hospital was filled with bedridden and largely neglected older patients who had not received proper medical diagnosis or rehabilitation and who were thought to be in need of lifelong institutionalization. Skilled nursing care kept the patients alive, but lack of diagnostic assessment and rehabilitation kept them disabled. Warren systematically evaluated these patients, initiated active mobilization and selective rehabilitation, and was able to get most of the patients out of bed and often discharged home. As a result of her experiences, Warren advocated that every older patient receive what we know today as CGA and an attempt at rehabilitation before being admitted to a long-term care hospital or a nursing home.

The concepts of CGA have evolved in different settings around the world. As geriatric care systems have been initiated in multiple locations, CGA concepts and specific programs have generally been assigned central roles, usually as focal points for entry into the geriatric systems. In the United States, programs incorporating CGA principles began to appear in the 1970s. The first major U.S. health care organization to adopt and adapt CGA in a major way was the Department of Veterans Affairs (VA) health care system, which has in recent years served a disproportionately elderly group of patients—by the year 2001, 39% of the veteran population was over age 65 (versus 13%

of the rest of the U.S. population). Anticipating this challenge, in the mid-1970s the VA developed an innovative network of special demonstration programs focused on aging—*Geriatric Research Education and Clinical Centers* (GRECCs)—whose role was to devise creative new clinical care models for the special needs of older veterans, as well as to encourage aging-focused research and education. Several of these GRECCs started inpatient CGA units, typically modeled after U.K. programs. As a result of positive program evaluations, CGA units were mandated system wide, and by 1994, 133 of the 172 VA medical centers had defined CGA programs, usually called *geriatric evaluation and management programs* (GEMs) (Wieland, Rubenstein, Hedrick, Reuben, & Buchner, 1994).

Elsewhere in the world, CGA concepts also have become increasingly a part of standard geriatric care. CGA has not remained restricted to specific geriatric assessment programs, and its concepts can be found in virtually every program providing geriatric care. For example, in many areas, at least a limited geriatric assessment is required by law prior to a person's admission into a rehabilitation program or a nursing home. A 1993 report indicated that 9.7% of hospitals responding to a U.S. national survey (N = 1,639) had a functioning GEM unit (Lavizzo-Mourey, Hillman, Diserens, & Schwartz, 1993). Many managed care organizations have introduced systems of screening older enrollees for geriatric care needs and providing CGA and case management services to high-risk patients. In addition, there are growing numbers of programs that provide limited CGA and case management in the home setting.

Comprehensive Geriatric Assessment Process

The basic components of CGA include evaluation of medical problems and relevant co-morbidity, functional status, psychological status, social support network and activities, economic needs, and environmental safety. Ideally, each component can be assessed by the most appropriate team member(s) and discussed at an interdisciplinary team conference. In more limited settings, CGA involves fewer specialized disciplines, sometimes the physician or nurse alone. This is much less desirable in terms of both expertise and workload efficiency, because a single person alone cannot ordinarily provide sufficient time or expertise to deal optimally with the complex needs of frail older persons.

The process of CGA begins with identifying the patient in need—most commonly, older persons who have experienced deteriorations in health status and level of functioning. This can take place in a screening context outside the usual health care system (e.g., screening and referral programs in senior centers) or in a case-finding context within a physician's practice or other medical care setting. Ordinarily, if health status has worsened but functional level is intact, an elderly person can receive adequate care in the usual primary care setting. However, patients who have new or progressive functional deficits or difficult-to-manage geriatric problems (e.g., incontinence, dementia, frequent falls) should ideally receive CGA in a geriatric care context, because geriatric practitioners are generally better prepared than primary care providers to deal with these kinds of complex problems.

Following review of medical information and performance of a focused physical examination, a typical CGA proceeds to review the major domains of functioning. These are ordinarily captured in measures of basic *activities of daily living* (ADLs) and *instrumental ADLs* (IADLs). These scales are used clinically to detect whether the patient has problems performing activities necessary for independent survival in the community. Basic *ADLs* include *self-care* activities such as eating, dressing, bathing, transferring, and toileting. Patients unable to perform these activities will generally need 12- to 24-hour support by caregivers at home or in an institutional setting. IADLs include heavier housework, going on errands, managing finances, and telephoning—activities required for the individual to remain fully independent in a house or apartment.

After assessment of function, the CGA gathers information about the patient's environment and social situation. For example, the strength of the patient's social network, presence of environmental challenges, the amount and type of caregiver support available, and the level of social activities in which the patient participates will influence the clinical approach taken in managing detected deficits. This information is often best obtained by an experienced nurse or social worker. Two other key items of the CGA are screening evaluations for cognitive impairment and depression.

Sometimes a member of the extended assessment team or an outside specialist will need to evaluate the patient prior to the final formulation. For example, a physical or occupational therapist may need to evaluate a complex patient with difficulty dressing, a condition that could be caused by a number of problems, including cognitive impairment, poor finger mobility, or dysfunction of the shoulders, back, or hips.

Once CGA detects and quantifies medical, psychosocial, and functional problems and disabilities, appropriate treatment and management strategies can be formulated. When a reversible cause is found, a specific treatment may eliminate or ameliorate the disability. When the disability is complex or irreversible, rehabilitative or symptom-relief approaches can often provide substantial relief or improvement in function. Often the involvement and support of community or hospital-based resources are needed to devise an optimal plan for care and long-term follow-up.

Several factors must be considered when deciding where a CGA should take place, including the patient's level of disability and cognition, acuity and complexity of illness, social support strength, and access to transportation. In general, more disabled and complex patients with poorer social supports and transportation access will be more likely to need inpatient CGA services. These patients will be more likely to require prolonged periods of treatment and rehabilitation and less likely to keep outpatient appointments and comply with recommendations. Hospital programs offer greater opportunities for intensive treatment and rehabilitation under the care of interdisciplinary teams. This can occur in designated inpatient geriatric-assessment or special care units or by a careful geriatric team consultation in a nongeriatric hospital service.

Most CGAs do not require the full range of technologic capacity nor the intensity of physician and nurse monitoring found in the acute inpatient setting. A specialized geriatric setting outside an acute hospital ward, such as a day hospital or subacute inpatient geriatric evaluation unit, will provide the easy availability of an interdisciplinary team with the time and expertise to provide needed services efficiently, an adequate level of monitoring, and beds for patients unable to sit or stand for prolonged periods. Inpatient and day hospital assessment programs have the advantage of intensity, speed, and ability to care for particularly frail or acutely ill patients.

Outpatient and *in-home assessment* programs are generally cheaper because the need for inpatient stays and institutional resources is avoided. Although non-hospital programs cannot provide the level of technological care possible in the hospital, most elderly persons who are not acutely ill or severely functionally dependent can obtain adequate CGA outside the hospital. Moreover, in-home CGA and management programs can offer the advantages of observational assessment of the home environment and how well the patient actually functions at home.

Effectiveness of Geriatric Assessment Programs

Substantial literature supports the effectiveness of CGA programs in a variety of settings. The early descriptive studies of CGA described such benefits as improved diagnostic accuracy, reduced discharges to nursing homes, increased functional status, and reduced medications. Yet without concurrent control patients, these studies could not distinguish the effects of the programs from the simple effects of improvement over time, nor was it clear how these apparent benefits—most of which affected process of care—would relate to short- or long-term outcome benefits. Beginning in the 1980s, however, controlled studies began to be published that corroborated some of the earlier studies and documented important additional benefits, such as improved survival, reduced hospital and nursing home use, and in some cases reduced costs. However, these studies were by no means uniform in their results. Some showed a whole series of dramatic and interrelated benefits, whereas others showed few if any benefits (Rubenstein, Josephson, Wieland, English, Sayre, & Kane, 1984; Rubenstein, Stuck, Siu, & Wieland, 1991).

A careful meta-analysis of the controlled trials performed through 1993 provided strong confirmation that these programs can improve survival, decrease use of institutional services, and improve levels of both mental and physical functioning (Stuck, Siu, Wieland, Adams, & Rubenstein, 1993). Although not all studies showed equivalent effects, the meta-analysis was able to indicate a number of variables at both the program and patient levels that tended to distinguish trials with large effects from those with more limited ones. On the program level, hospital CGA units and home-visit assessment teams produced the most dramatic benefits, while benefits in office-based programs could not be confirmed. Programs that provided hands-on clinical care and/or long-term follow-up were generally able to produce greater positive effects than did purely consultative programs or ones that lacked follow-up. Among hospital-based programs, careful *patient targeting* (i.e. selecting patients who were at high risk for deterioration yet who still had "rehabilitation potential") was also associated with larger benefit.

Studies continue to be published testing effectiveness of CGA models. In general, studies have found continuing benefit from CGA, although as care delivered to older persons has improved over time in usual care settings, the added benefit from specialized CGA programs has lessened somewhat. This is clearly a positive trend for eldercare as a whole, and ultimately usual care practice may improve to the point that the need for CGA is eliminated; however, this time is unfortunately still far in the future (Rubenstein, 2004). In the meantime, there is some evidence that even when functional outcomes are equivalent between CGA and usual care, patients and caregivers derive additional benefits (Rockwood, Stadnyk, Carver, MacPherson, Beanlands, Powell, et al., 2000).

We look to further research to define better the most effective and efficient methods for performing CGA, the best program models, and the individuals likely to derive the most benefit. In the meantime, considerable evidence supports the continued growth and expansion of these programs throughout the geriatric care system.

LAURENCE RUBENSTEIN

References

Lavizzo-Mourey, R. J., Hillman, A. L., Diserens, D., & Schwartz, J. S. (1993). Hospitals' motivations tin establishing or closing geriatric evaluation and management units. *Journal of Gerontology: Medical Sciences, 48,* M78–M83.

Rockwood, K., Stadnyk, K., Carver, D., MacPherson, K. M., Beanlands, H. E., Powell, C., Stollee, P., Thoman, V. S., & Tonks, R. S. (2000). A clinimetric evaluation of specialized geriatric care for rural-dwelling, frail older people. *Journal of the American Geriatrics Society, 48,* 1080–1085.

Rubenstein, L. Z., Josephson, K. R., Wieland, G. D., English, P. A., Sayre, J. A., & Kane, R. L. (1984). Effectiveness of a geriatric evaluation unit: A randomized clinical trial. *New England Journal of Medicine, 311,* 1664–1670.

Rubenstein, L. Z., Stuck, A. E., Siu, A. L., & Wieland, G. D. (1991). Impacts of geriatric evaluation and management programs on defined outcomes: Overview of the evidence. *Journal of the American Geriatrics Society, 39*(Suppl.), 8–16.

Rubenstein, L. Z. (2004). Comprehensive geriatric assessment: From miracle to reality. *Journal of Gerontology: Medical Sciences, 59A,* 473–477.

Stuck, A. E., Siu, A. L., Wieland, G. D., Adams, J., & Rubenstein, L. Z. (1993). Comprehensive geriatric assessment: A meta-analysis of controlled trials. *Lancet, 342,* 1032–1036.

Wieland, G. D., Rubenstein, L. Z., Hedrick, S. C., Reuben, D. B., & Buchner, D. M. (1994). Inpatient geriatric evaluation & management units (GEMs) in the VA system: Diamonds in the rough? *Journal of Gerontology: Medical Sciences, 49,* M195–M200.

GERIATRIC EDUCATION CENTERS

Geriatric education centers (GECs) are programs sponsored by the Bureau of Health Professions, U. S. Health Resources and Services Administration to train health professionals in the diagnosis, treatment, and prevention of disease, disability, and other health problems of older adults. Grants to establish or operate GECs are authorized by the U.S. Congress through Title VII of the U.S. Public Health Service Act, as amended. Since the program was established in 1983, approximately 400,000 faculty, students, and practitioners in allopathic medicine, osteopathic medicine, dentistry, pharmacy, nursing, occupational and physical therapy, podiatric medicine, optometry, social work, and related allied and public health disciplines have received training through the *GECs*. As of 2004, there are 47 GECs actively providing comprehensive educational services within their designated geographic regions. Most GECs are consortiums consisting of 3 or more college or university health professions schools, clinical health facilities, or other health-related agencies that provide patient care or health-related services to older people. Although each GEC tailors their educational offerings to the needs of health providers in their region, all GECs: (1) improve the training of health professionals in geriatrics, including geriatric residencies, traineeships or fellowships, (2) develop and disseminate curricula relating to the treatment of the health problems of older individuals, (3) support the training and retraining of faculty to provide instruction in geriatrics, (4) support continuing education of health professionals who provide geriatric care, and (5) provide students with clinical training in geriatrics in nursing homes, chronic and acute disease hospitals, ambulatory care centers, and senior centers. In their educational activities, GECs give special attention to addressing the educational needs of practitioners who care for older minorities, and to prepare practitioners to care for older people who reside in medically underserved areas. The underlying GEC philosophy advocates interdisciplinary and multidisciplinary training in geriatrics and gerontology, and promotes networking, collaborative approaches, and links with other organizations and programs in aging.

In addition to their work as individual programs training health professionals, the GECs as a group form a nationwide network dedicated to advancing *geriatric education* theory and practice. Many GECs participated in establishing the *National Agenda for Geriatric Education* in the 1990s as part of the Bureau of Health Professions' Geriatric Education Futures Project; 11 study groups recommended actions to improve geriatric education in the disciplines of medicine, nursing, dentistry, allied health professions, public health, and social work, and in the areas of managed care, long-term care, case management, ethnogeriatrics, and interdisciplinary education. White papers on these 11 topics formed the basis for subsequent GEC program planning, and new study groups were formed in 2004 to review the current state of education and to make recommendations for future training initiatives in clinical nutrition, palliative care, clinical geriatric pharmacy, and *bioterrorism and aging*.

Other collaborative GEC projects include a National Technical Assistance Center to support GEC data collection and evaluation of the effect of GEC education and training, a national online GEC resource directory to provide a source for curricula, audiovisual products, and other materials produced by the GEC network, and a *Geriatric Resource Information Project* to develop curricula and state-of-the-art learning packages for major topics in geriatrics. The *National Association of Geriatric Education Centers* (NAGEC) provides the forum for helping advance the goals and interests of the GECs. In addition to disseminating information to various organizations and to the general public about priorities in geriatric education, this organization facilitates partnerships, collaborations, and other interactions among GECs and between the GEC network and other organizations with interests in issues related to geriatrics and gerontology education. NAGEC also supports the advancement of geriatric education by sponsoring numerous committees and task forces that address problems and issues of national significance, including the Distance Learning Task Force, the Ethnogeriatrics Task Force, the Evaluation Task Force, and the Bioterrorism and Emergency Preparedness Committee.

For further information, see: the Bureau of Health Professions at bhpr.hrsa.gov, and the National Association of Geriatric Education Centers at www.nagec.org.

John G. Hennon

See also
Organizations in Aging

GERIATRIC MEDICINE

Geriatric medicine is the medical specialty designed to develop and provide care chiefly for older people who are frail (Hazzard, 2004; Rockwood & Hubbard, 2004). This focus on *frailty* has emerged since the early 1990s, after a series of randomized, controlled trials showed that specialized geriatric interventions were effective when delivered not to just anyone who was older, but to those older adults who were frail (Winograd, Gerety, Chung, Goldstein, Dominguez, & Vallone, 1991). Elderly people who are frail have multiple, interacting medical and social problems, so their care requires first assessing these problems, then managing them, and finally, measuring the effectiveness of that management.

Although there were even earlier antecedents, the systematic practice of geriatric medicine as a specialty grew out of the work of pioneering British physicians such as *Marjorie Warren* and *Trevor Howell.* Working with older people who had effectively been abandoned in former workhouses for the poor and other chronic care wards, the first geriatricians focused on properly understanding the medical and social needs of their patients, and setting about treating these needs in a way that maximized function. At the same time, they organized specialty societies that advocated both within and outside the medical profession for better systems of care for older adults (Brocklehurst, 1997).

The discipline began to subject its procedures to controlled trials, particularly during the 1980s. Importantly, many early trials were successful, but the experience with the trials revealed several pragmatic challenges. These included the need for targeting, as noted, isolating which components of multicomponent interventions were most effective, and deciding on which outcomes to be measured. Although early trials showed benefit with respect to function (i.e. improved function in patients who received specialized geriatric care compared with those who received usual care) and mortality, this also meant that some traditional areas of geriatric expertise (e.g. better care for the dying) could not be shown to be beneficial without new methods of outcome measurement. Similar challenges are evident today in the application of disease-specific guidelines to frail older patients (Tinetti, Bogardus, & Agostini, 2004).

Despite these challenges, specialized geriatric medicine was able to establish a sound evidence base. Even with these accomplishments, however, the status of geriatric medicine as a specialty attractive to young physicians is, at best, variable. The reasons for this are complex, but as with many aspects of *physician behavior*, reimbursement is key (Warshaw, Bragg, Shaull, & Lindsell, 2002). Many systems of medical care provide *reimbursement* on a so-called "*fee-for-service*" basis, in which physicians are paid for individual pieces of work. Such reimbursement schemes favor physicians who can perform a large number of well-paid procedures in a comparatively short period of time, with disciplines such as dermatology, radiology, and ophthalmology being well regarded in this way, so that positions for training in these specialties are typically quite competitive. By contrast, many countries find that they have more geriatric training positions available than they have candidates to fill them. This is the case even though *geriatricians* find their work satisfying and report higher work satisfaction and quality of life than do other medical specialists (Leigh, Kravtiz, Schembri, Samuels, & Mobley, 2002).

As a specialty devoted to the care of older people who are frail, geriatric medicine has had to come to grips with the complex needs of its constituents. The complexity of care is reflected in how the specialty proceeds with individual patients. To begin, their needs must be understood. The process by which this occurs is known as *comprehensive geriatric assessment*, which recognizes that although good geriatric medicine is rooted in good medical care, understanding patients' needs must extend beyond medical diagnoses to how disease affects function. Moreover, given that many frail patients are disabled to the extent that they depend on other people, it is important to assess not just the patients but their caregivers, especially their feelings of burden and their views on the viability of the living arrangements. To carry out such multidimensional assessments, and to implement the multifaceted interventions whose need is revealed by the assessment requires a multidisciplinary team. The challenges of implementing interdisciplinary team care are considerable, and require physicians who are willing to take a leadership role, while at the same time recognizing the validity of others points of view (Reuben, Levy-Storms, Yee, et al., 2004). These attitudes are not common among physicians, so those who have them are good candidates to become geriatricians (Cravens, Campbell, & Mehr, et al., 2000).

Geriatric medicine provides care across a spectrum. Acute inpatient hospital care is carried out in specialized wards, such as *geriatric assessment units*, *geriatric evaluation and management (GEM) services*, or *acute care of the elderly* (ACE) units. The acute care hospital is a common setting for specialized geriatric consultation services. After receiving acute care, many patients require some form of inpatient rehabilitation, which typically is offered through geriatric medicine on an inpatient geriatric rehabilitation unit.

As an alternative to inpatient care, which can be dangerous for older adults (who are susceptible to hospital-acquired complications such as *deconditioning*, adverse drug reactions, or pneumonia) many geriatric medicine services provide *day hospitals*. In a day hospital, comprehensive geriatric assessment is carried out and *rehabilitation* is offered in a way that can sort out common diagnoses in a coordinated fashion without exposing patients to the risks of hospitalization. For example, a patient with anemia might need a range of procedures, such as upper and lower gastrointestinal endoscopy or a bone marrow biopsy. The preparation for the former 2 procedures is typically dehydrating, and under the tight deadlines of a typically short inpatient stay, patients can go for a few days without being properly fed, or even maintaining adequate fluid intake. In this state, and confined to bed, they are susceptible to deconditioning. By contrast, the same investigations can be carried out over several day-hospital visits, which can be combined with a *rehabilitation exercise program* as part of a multidisciplinary intervention to improve function and quality of life. Day hospitals are not the only type of ambulatory care provided by specialized geriatric services, which also typically offer outpatient clinics and outreach programs (including house calls). In addition, specialized clinics typically are provided for the evaluation and treatment of memory problems, incontinence, and falls.

The *future of geriatric medicine* depends both on internal and external factors. For the discipline to prosper will require the continued articulation of evidence-based innovations that can be feasibly implemented and that can improve upon usual care. Given the large number of people who will require care and the paucity of geriatricians, the role of the geriatrician as not just a provider of, but also a catalyst for, better care will be ever more crucial. There will be a need for additional collaboration between geriatricians and other specialties, which can be seeded with people able to catalyze better care of the frail elderly within their domains (Rubin, Stieglitz, Vicioso, & Kirk, 2003). External factors will also be important, including recognition by the lay public that the growing number of elderly people who will require specialized care can be expected to translate into increased demand. Part of this is inevitable. Almost every disease society points to the growth in the demand for their constituents, given that the illness is age-associated, and that the population is aging. What is less well appreciated, however, is that many of these diseases will occur in the same people, which will make questionable the provision of services in the usual fashion—"more of the same" is not likely to be effective for patients who are frail.

The influence of external factors is also evident in the differences among countries in the organization of specialized geriatric services. The above description applies broadly within English-speaking countries and select other areas (Sitoh, 2003; Habot & Tsin, 2003), although there are considerable diversities even within this group. Elsewhere, the situation is more variable. Not all countries of the European Union recognize geriatric medicine at the same level, and standards vary widely (Hastie & Duursma, 2003). In this context the European for the disease of the aged.

One organizational tension that was manifest in the United States, and which occurs to varying degrees elsewhere, is that between the geriatrician as a primary care physician or as a consultant. In the United States, such duality of roles is common among other *specialists* (e.g. internists, surgeons) whereas in other countries the distinction is sharper: in many countries, specialists are only accessible through *primary care physicians*. In Holland, the specialty of nursing home medicine has grown from primary care (Schols, Crebolder, & van Weel, 2004), and in Canada a primary care specialty track exists for a diploma in the health care of older people, which is open to family physicians and requires an extra 6 to 12 months of training. Although local circumstances will dictate local solutions, given the magnitude of the work to be done it is likely that, among intelligent people of good will, solutions will emerge rapidly in response to the growing demands.

Geriatric medicine is a specialty with many and important opportunities, as it becomes an instrument whereby societies can make sense of the demands placed upon them by the aging of their populations. As a specialty devoted to complex care for patients with complex needs, it offers intellectually challenging, socially necessary, and personally rewarding careers for physicians everywhere.

KENNETH ROCKWOOD

References

Brocklehurst, J. C. (1997). Geriatric medicine in Britain—the growth of a specialty. *Age and Ageing*, *26*(Suppl. 4), 5–8.

Cravens, D. D., Campbell, J. D., & Mehr, D. R. (2000). Why geriatrics? Academic geriatricians' perceptions of the positive, attractive aspects of geriatrics. *Family Medicine*, *32*, 34–41.

Habot, B., & Tsin, S. (2003). Geriatrics in the new millennium, Israel. *Israeli Medical Association Journal, 5*, 319–321.

Hastie, I. R., & Duursma, S. A. (2003). Geriatric medicine section of the European Union of Medical Specialists. Geriatric medicine in the European Union: Unification of diversity. *Aging Clinical and Experimental Research, 15*, 347–351.

Hazzard, W. R. (2004). I am a geriatrician. *Journal of the American Geriatrics Society, 52*, 161.

Leigh, J. P., Kravtiz, R. L., Schembri, M., Samuels, S. J., & Mobley, S. (2002). Physician career satisfaction across specialties. *Archives of Internal Medicine, 162*, 1577–1584.

Reuben, D. B., Levy-Storms, L., Yee, M. N., et al. (2004). Disciplinary split: A threat to geriatrics interdisciplinary team training. *Journal of the American Geriatrics Society, 52*, 1000–1006.

Rockwood, K. & Hubbard, R. (2004). Frailty and the geriatrician. *Age and Ageing, 33*, 430–432.

Rubin, C. D., Stieglitz, H., Vicioso, B., & Kirk, L. (2003). Development of geriatrics-oriented faculty in general internal medicine. *Annals of Internal Medicine, 139*, 615–620.

Schols, J. M., Crebolder, H. F., & van Weel, C. (2004). Nursing home and nursing home physician: The Dutch experience. *Journal of the American Medical Directors Association, 5*, 207–212.

Sitoh, Y. Y. (2003). Aged care services in Singapore—an overview. *Annals of the Academy of Medicine, Singapore, 32*, 717–722.

Tinetti, M. E., Bogardus, S. T. Jr., & Agostini, J. V. (2004). Potential pitfalls of disease-specific guidelines for patients with multiple conditions. *New England Journal of Medicine, 351*, 2870–2874.

Warshaw, G. A., Bragg, E. J., Shaull, R. W., & Lindsell, C. J. (2002). Academic geriatric programs in U.S. allopathic and osteopathic medical schools. *Journal of the American Medical Association, 288*, 2313–2319.

Winograd, C. H., Gerety, M. B., Chung, M., Goldstein, M. K., Dominguez, F. Jr., & Vallone, R. (1991). Screening for frailty: Criteria and predictors of outcomes. *Journal of the American Geriatrics Society, 39*, 778–784.

GERIATRIC PSYCHIATRY

Geriatric psychiatry is a professional and academic field that addresses *mental disorders* that occur in late life. It focuses both on persons who had experienced the onset of a mental disorder early in life and who are now old (e.g., older patients with schizophrenia or mood disorders) and those whose mental disorder is of late-onset (e.g., dementia, late-onset schizophrenia or mood disorders). It also addresses the differentiation between mental changes (e.g., *cognitive changes*) associated with normal aging and psychopathology emerging in late life (e.g., dementia).

For at least 2 centuries, some psychiatrists have cared for and studied older persons with mental disorders. In the United States, *Benjamin Rush* published the first textbook on geriatric psychiatry in 1805 (*An Account of the State of the Body and the Mind in Old Age; With Observation of Its Diseases and Remedies*). In Europe, German psychiatrist *Alois Alzheimer* was working in a state hospital in Frankfurt in 1906 when he described the neuropathology of the dementia that is now called *Alzheimer's disease*. Still, the mental disorders of old age, lumped under the term "*senility*," remained "a dark corner" of the field of psychiatry until after World War II. At that time, a group of British psychiatrists applied the longitudinal methods earlier developed by *Kraepelin* to systematically differentiate the presentation, course, and neuropathology of the major *mental disorders of old age*: late-life mood disorders, late-life schizophrenia, dementia, and delirium. They also differentiated older patients without dementia who presented with late-onset mental disorders (e.g., late-onset schizophrenia or delusional disorder) from those who had early-onset disorders and had aged. Around the same time, psychiatrists in the United States got involved in the classical Baltimore and Duke longitudinal studies of aging.

In 1965, the first training program in geriatric psychiatry was organized at *Duke University Medical Center* with the financial support of the National Institute of Mental Health (NIMH). It remained the only such program until the mid-1970s. In 1975, less than a year after the *National Institute on Aging* (NIA) was established, the NIMH set up the Center for the Studies of Mental Health of the Aging (the NIMH aging branch). During the following decade, the NIA and the NIMH aging branch played a crucial role in supporting and coordinating research or clinical projects, as well as related training programs, in geriatric psychiatry. The NIA supported programs and projects related to normal aging and diseases associated with aging (including Alzheimer's disease), while the NIMH aging branch focused on the neurobiology, phenomenology, and treatment of late-life mental disorders (including late-life mood or psychotic disorders and behavioral disturbances, psychosis, and agitation associated with Alzheimer's disease).

In 1991, the American Board of Psychiatry and Neurology acknowledged that a sufficient knowledge base and skill set relevant to geriatric psychiatry had been defined; geriatric psychiatry became the first psychiatric subspecialty for which added qualifications were offered. Initially, psychiatrists with substantial clinical experience in geriatric psychiatry were eligible for this certification examination. Now, a year of post-residency specialization in 1 of 60-some accredited geriatric psychiatry fellowships is required. Since 1991, several thousand geriatric psychiatrists have been certified and, more recently, recertified.

The scientific focus and professional interest of geriatric psychiatrists are represented in several professional organizations. The Group for the Advancement of Psychiatry (GAP) first created a Committee on Aging in 1966. In 1979, the American Psychiatric Association established its Council on Aging. In addition, there are now 3 major organizations dedicated specifically to geriatric psychiatry: the *American Association for Geriatric Psychiatry* (AAGP), established in 1978; the *International Psychogeriatric Association* (IPA) established in 1980; and the *International College of Geriatric Psychoneuropharmacology* (ICGP) established in 2000. Several scientific journals are dedicated to geriatric psychiatry, including the *American Journal of Geriatric Psychiatry* (published by the AAGP) and *International Psychogeriatrics* (published by the IPA), the *International Journal of Geriatric Psychiatry*, and the *Journal of Geriatric Psychiatry and Neurology*. While geriatric psychiatry is firmly established as a professional and academic field, the rapid aging of the American population creates both tremendous opportunities and a formidable challenge for geriatric psychiatrists at a time when the number of trainees is barely sufficient to maintain the number of geriatric psychiatrists and research funding has plateaued.

Benoit H. Mulsant

See also
Organizations in Aging

GERIATRIC RESEARCH, EDUCATION, AND CLINICAL CENTERS

Geriatric research, education, and clinical centers (GRECCs) have become leaders in the integrated research education and clinical systems providing care to older veterans (Goodwin & Morley, 1994; Haber & Moravec, 1982). The Veterans Administration (VA) developed out of the "Old Soldiers Homes" at the end of the 19th century. The VA became a separate entity in 1930, and following World War II it began affiliating with medical schools and emphasizing teaching and research as a way to enhance care of the veteran. In 1964 an executive order by President Kennedy and Public Law 88-450 directed the development of long-term care programs within the VA. Recognition of the rapid growth in the aging veteran population, with the prediction that 37% (9 million) of the veteran population would be over 65 years of age by the year 2000, led to increased enthusiasm for the development of expertise in geriatrics within the VA in the early 1970s. At the instigation of Paul Haber, MD, Congress authorized the establishment of five GRECCs. Congress specifically stated that these GRECCs should not only serve the VA but also provide education for health care professionals caring for the aged in the general population. By 1980 eight GRECCs had been established: in Boston (Bedford and Brockton/West Roxbury); Little Rock, Arkansas; Minneapolis, St. Louis, Seattle (Seattle and American Lake), and Palo Alto, Sepulveda and West Los Angeles, California. In 1984, Durham, North Carolina, and Gainesville, Florida, were added. Since 1987 further GRECCs have been opened: Ann Arbor, Michigan; San Antonio, Texas; Madison, Wisconsin; Miami, Salt Lake City, Baltimore, Cleveland, Pittsburgh, Bronx/New York Harbor, and Nashville. Public Law 99-166, passed by Congress in 1985, has authorized an increase in GRECCs to a total of 25. GRECCs are under the direction of the Office of the Assistant Chief Medical Director in the VA central office. Since 1980, GRECCs have also been regularly reviewed by the Geriatrics and Gerontology Advisory Committee (GGAC). All GRECCs are affiliated with a medical school (the Boston GRECC with two schools and Sepulveda and West Los Angeles with UCLA) and have provided a major stimulus in developing geriatric programs at major universities throughout the United States.

The concept behind the GRECCs was that bringing together a cadre of basic and clinical researchers with a focus on aging would stimulate a rapid increase in clinically useful knowledge about older persons. The GRECCs were then required to develop clinical demonstration units to test these concepts. The educational component was responsible for the rapid dissemination of this knowledge throughout the VA and the private sector. Clearly, the most successful example of this strategy was the development of the Geriatric Evaluation and Management Unit (GEMU) at the Sepulveda GRECC, demonstrating its efficacy and its rapid dissemination throughout the VA (133 programs) and the private sector.

GRECCs have proved to be a highly successful research model, with research funding in 1991 averaging over $3 million per GRECC and each GRECC producing over 50 scientific publications in that year. The scientific contributions of the GRECCs have been numerous. They include description of Syndrome X (hypertension, hyperinsulinemia, and hypertriglyceridemia), demonstration (by computer analysis of its receptor structure), that amyloid-beta protein produces amnesia, the finding that 1-alpha-hydroxylase enzyme activity in the kidney is reduced with aging, description of the detrusor hyperactivity and impaired contractility syndrome as a cause of incontinence, pioneering observations on age-related alterations in the immune system, discovery of the key role of protein energy undernutrition in poor outcomes associated with hospitalized older persons, linkage analysis of some familial forms of Alzheimer's disease to chromosome 21, definition of the causes of the anorexia of aging, and the finding that older males develop secondary hypogonadism.

Besides GEMUs, GRECCs have pioneered the development of other clinical demonstration units, including academic nursing home units, special care units, specialized exercise programs, medication reduction clinics, sexual dysfunction clinics, clinics for older persons with spinal cord injuries, a preventive gerontology program for older veterans in the community, and an adapted work therapy program for persons with early dementia. GRECCs, together with other VA sites, have played a leading role in developing interdisciplinary team training.

GRECCs have also played an important role in disseminating geriatric knowledge to health professionals of a variety of disciplines and have played a key part in developing the physician geriatric fellowship. They have developed two novel educational games; Geropady and the Geriatric Challenge Bowl, and were key in introducing the aging game to medical students. GRECCs play a major role in continuing education, with over 5,000 educational activities each year. GRECCs have developed a variety of patient education clinics and a series of videotapes.

GRECCs represent an exciting success story. They have developed key clinical demonstration units and have been leading trainers of health professionals in gerontology. GRECC scientists are among the leaders in geriatric research. The GRECC integration of research, education, and clinical care into "centers of excellence" has played an important role in probing the mysteries of aging and providing insights into the appropriate care of our graying population.

JOHN E. MORLEY

See also

Geriatric Assessment Programs
Organizations in Aging

References

Goodwin, M., & Morley, J. E. (1994). Geriatric research, education, and clinical centers: Their impact in the development of American geriatrics. *Journal of the American Geriatrics Society, 42,* 1012–1019.

Haber, P. A., & Moravec, J. D. (1982). The Veterans Administration's experience with geriatric centers of excellence (geriatric research, education, and clinical centers). *Journal of the American Geriatrics Society, 30,* 206–210.

GERIATRICS

See

Geriatric Medicine
Geriatric Research, Education, and Clinical Centers

GERONTOLOGICAL SOCIETY OF AMERICA

The Gerontological Society of America (GSA) was founded in 1945, an outgrowth of the *Club for Research in Aging*, to promote the scientific *study of aging* and to encourage the exchange of knowledge about aging among scientists, practitioners, and decision makers in the field. As such, it was the first multidisciplinary organization on aging in the United States. These purposes remain the society's primary missions.

From its inception, the GSA embraced the concept that *gerontology* is a multidisciplinary field. Its original incorporation papers spoke of the study of aging in terms of public health, mental hygiene, the science and art of medicine, and the cure of diseases and of understanding the nature and problems of aging.

Although membership in its early years leaned toward researchers in the biological, medical, and behavioral sciences, the GSA has expanded to include social scientists, humanists, administrators, policy analysts, and practitioners particularly interested in encouraging the dissemination of research results beyond the research community. Today the society's 5,700 members belong to 1 of 4 professional sections: biological sciences; clinical medicine; behavioral and social sciences; and social research, policy, and practice. Student and new professional members also belong to the society's Emerging Scholars and Professionals Organization.

In pursuit of its missions, the GSA publishes 5 refereed professional journals: *Journals of Gerontology, Series A: Biological Sciences and Medical Sciences; Journals of Gerontology, Series B: Psychological Sciences and Social Sciences;* and *The Gerontologist*. (These publications are also available online.) The *Journal of Gerontolog*y—the first journal in the field—began in 1946 as one journal. It was revamped in 1988 to 4 separate journals under 1 cover, then further separated to its current format of 4 journals under 2 covers in 1995. *Series A* is now produced monthly; *Series B* is issued bimonthly. *The Gerontologist* was first published in 1961 and focuses on applied research and policy. The GSA also conducts the nation's major annual scientific meeting devoted to the full range of disciplines active in gerontology. The meeting, which attracts an average of 3,500 participants, usually includes more than 2,000 symposia, papers, poster sessions, and special presentations. Each section of the society is responsible for developing its portion of the programs and for multi- and interdisciplinary offerings in cooperation with other sections and committees of the society. In addition, the GSA has more than 30 special interest groups that meet at the annual meeting and present programs. Interest group topics include economics of aging, mental retardation and developmental disabilities, technology and aging, nursing care, religion and aging, oral health, nutrition, grandparents as caregivers, researchers based in long-term care, women's issues, HIV/AIDS, rural aging, transportation, and Alzheimer's disease research.

Over the years, GSA also has promoted the scientific study of aging through the efforts of its individual members and committees. In 1956 and 1957, a special biology and medicine subcommittee developed guidelines that were used to shape federal and private policies supporting research in aging. In 1962, the society's representatives were instrumental in securing support of the *White House Conference on Aging* for 6 major recommendations to encourage development of urgently needed gerontological research and education programs. These recommendations called for graduate scholarships, postdoctoral fellowships, and training programs; long-term stable programs of research in aging; the creation of regional centers of aging research; longitudinal aging studies; the establishment of a national institute of gerontology; and demonstration and evaluation projects on the delivery of services to the elderly. Following the conference, the GSA, working with other organizations, continued to press for these recommendations, all of which have been implemented in some form through various federal, state, and private programs. The society and its members were particularly involved and instrumental in the establishment of the *National Institute on Aging* in 1974, as well as the *Center on Aging* within the National Institute of Mental Health.

The GSA, on its own or in collaboration with other groups, has conducted a number of significant projects over the years—including the development of education and training curricula—identified national training needs, helped design federal research policies, advised key congressional committees and executive branch offices, and published special reports and monographs on key gerontological issues. For example, the society's project from 1971 to 1975 on design and environments for the aged brought together designers, architects, planners, and policy makers and developed some of the baseline data in the area of housing and environments for the elderly. In 1980, with the Association for Gerontology in Higher Education, the Society constructed the first review of components of a basic core of knowledge essential for institutional gerontology programs, as well as for some selected specialties. This was issued in a report titled *Foundations for Gerontological Education*. In response to cutbacks in federal data collection programs, the GSA in 1983 established the Task Force on Data on Aging, which prepared a report on data losses important to aging research and a set of recommendations for the 1990 census. In 1987, it established the Task Force on *Minority Aging*, which has organized special symposia and conferences and issued several publications. The most recent is "Closing the Gap: Improving the Health of Minority Elders in the New Millennium," edited by Keith Whitfield, the fourth in a *series* of publications that examines the information base and policy implications around specific issues of minority aging. The GSA also contributed to the development of key gerontological faculty through its series of summer research and faculty training institutes conducted from 1970 to 1976. Since 1999, GSA has administered the first leadership development program designed specifically for geriatric social work faculty. A program for doctoral fellows was added in 2000.

To help promote the transfer of research results to the media and decision makers, the society initiated its Information Service in 1986, which includes a computerized *database* of experts in the field of aging keyworded by area of expertise.

For 22 years, the GSA conducted a program that placed postdoctoral researchers in 3-month fellowships to work on specific problems of serving the elderly. The program offered academic researchers opportunities to work in practice settings and provided service agencies with high-quality technical assistance.

The GSA has also been instrumental in the development of other aging organizations. The society was a founding member of the International Association of Gerontology (IAG) in 1949 and has hosted or helped organize IAG conferences in the United States in 1951, 1960, 1969, and 1985. The society is also a founding member of the *Leadership Council of Aging Organizations*, a coalition of more than 50 national aging organizations. This organization meets regularly to review the status of aging policies and develop action strategies. The *Association for Gerontology in Higher Education* (AGHE) was conceived by GSA members and established in 1974.

In 1995, GSA celebrated its 50th anniversary and the addition of an independent, nonpartisan public policy institute, the *National Academy on an Aging Society* (NAAS). The academy serves as a national forum for policy analysis and debate on the major issues of concern to the current and future aging society. The NAAS has assisted media and policy makers through its research materials on current policy issues, producing reports and background papers, fact sheets, and special publications on issues including health care, long-term care, and income security in an intergenerational context. In addition, the NAAS has organized special conferences and seminars for experts and community, business, and political leaders. The NAAS also issues *Public Policy and Aging Report*, a quarterly publication that offers a diversity of views on current policy issues. Many of the Academy publications are available at no charge on its Web site.

In January 1999, the Association for Gerontology in Higher Education merged with the GSA. Now a unit of the GSA, the AGHE brings to the society its network of over 300 institutions of higher education and other organizations dedicated to advancing study and scholarship in gerontology. AGHE organizes annual meetings that present the latest information on matters of gerontological education and training, maintains a consultation program to assist in developing new gerontology instruction and expanding or evaluating existing gerontology programs, issues a quarterly newsletter as well as other special publications and reports, and has sponsored several fellowship and scholarship opportunities. Other AGHE resources include a national directory of educational programs in gerontology and geriatrics, a collection of brief bibliographies covering over 30 aging topics, brochures and materials on careers in aging, and special studies and publications on standards and guidelines for gerontology programs.

For more information about GSA, AGHE, and NAAS, go to the GSA Web site at www.geron.org.

ROBERT J. HAVIGHURST
Updated by CAROL A. SCHUTZ

See also
Organizations in Aging

GERONTOLOGY

Gerontology is both the *study of the aging process* and of humans (or other species) who live into later adult years. Although closely related, these 2 missions pursue different questions and often require different research approaches.

Some questions, such as determining the characteristics of aged adults, can be addressed by studying a well-chosen sample at one point in time. This approach is known as a *cross-sectional design* and can be visualized as the taking of a photograph. It is the approach most likely to produce quick results, as well as to be the least expensive. Gerontologists do conduct many cross-sectional studies that provide useful information on a variety of topics.

However, some basic questions require more complex approaches that are extended over many years. For example issues such as what aging is and how it takes place are related questions that cannot be answered by the cross-sectional approach. *Gerontologists* who take on such challenges have several avenues of research to consider, each making significant demands on their ingenuity, stamina, and available resources—as well as the optimism that events beyond their control will not scuttle the study at some point. The simplest approach (not that simple at all, really) involves following participants from youth through age. Known as the *longitudinal method*, this design affords the possibility of observing changes as they occur throughout time—a motion-picture version that captures more of life than a one-time snapshot. Expensive to conduct, longitudinal studies also yield their secrets tantalizingly, slowly over many years—during which time the researchers themselves also age, and some participants die or withdraw before they have "aged enough."

After all that effort on the part of researchers and participants, a successful longitudinal study still leaves the door open for doubt: Have we learned about aging in any pure or universal sense, or have we learned only how one cohort of individuals has moved through their life course? Starting the journey of life (Cole, 1992) in the year 1600, 1800, 1900, 2000 or any other particular sociohistorical moment exposes individuals to different configurations of opportunities, deprivations, stress, cultural values and biases, and environmental influences (Mitchell, 2001; Nelson, 2002; Wahl, Scheidt, & Windley, 2004). People of different cohorts also encounter distinctive and powerful events that can shape the rest of their lives (e.g., death of a family member in a war, financial ruin in the Great Depression). Furthermore, once having reached their later adult years, members of a cohort are likely to experience health, economic, and social integration circumstances that are unique to their generation (Achenbaum, 1995). For example, has an age-related pattern of hearing loss been identified, or have the measures also included "accidents" such as effects of exposure to stressful industrial noise on one generation and of industrial-strength magnification of rock music on another?

Similar questions can be raised regarding other areas of functioning: how much of the loss of vital (respiratory) capacity over time is due to aging, and how much to smoking? In terms of changes in physical activity, how much is due to aging, and how much to society's lesser or greater emphasis on fitness and exercise programs? This also extends to level of cognitive functioning, where depression, grief, overmedication, or a dementing condition of unknown origin play a role, and level of sexual activity, where society's changing attitudes toward sex (and the introduction of Viagra) may exert influence.

Gerontologists have been devising other ways to cope with the challenges of studying complex patterns of change and continuity that occur over extended periods of time. The *cross-sequential design* is one such approach: start a longitudinal study, but then add new waves of people who were born at a later time. This approach helps researchers distinguish between changes that occur over time for all participants and those that are closely related to their cohort. The *experimental approach* can be of great value in gerontology, as it has long been in other fields (Cristofalo & Adelman, 2002). The tightly controlled conditions of *laboratory research* make it possible to manipulate variables and study their effects (e.g., how does early nutrition affect growth, aging, and longevity?) The experimental approach in gerontology lends itself best to the study of animals with life spans short enough to study within a convenient period of time. Experiments with humans raise ethical and other issues that require the most careful attention.

Gerontology, the Individual, and Society

Gerontologists are aware that a total picture of individuals and species aging within their environment requires converging information from a variety of methods and sources. *Metchnikoff* (1903/2003), Pasteur's successor and himself a distinguished life scientist, was the first to propose the new science of gerontology and provide its name. He recognized that improved knowledge of the aging process could have substantial benefits for individuals and society. The ancient quest for eternal youth (Kastenbaum, 1995) was probably beyond reach, but more people would live longer and healthier lives if scientists extended their scope beyond the study of growth and early development. Society would also benefit from the experience and skills of robust older generations.

Metchnikoff would almost certainly approve of the attention given by biomedical gerontologists to the challenge of distinguishing between changes that can be attributed to aging, and those brought about by a combination of disease, genetic flaw, and environmental stress. He would also welcome the varied contributions from the sociobehavioral sciences and the humanities as they examine the ways in which age-related afflictions might be shaped by personal life events, cultural values, and social forces.

The general concept of an aging process is still in play. The movement, however, is toward identifying more specific processes and phenomena on both the biological and sociocultural levels. Advances in the understanding of aging also enhance our comprehension of early development. How and at what point does "development" become "aging?" Is it possible for both *development and aging* to occur at the same time (e.g., the artist with diminishing vision who becomes a more masterful creator)? It is no coincidence that many gerontologists are also students of the total life course. Strange it would be to research aging without attention to youth, and no less strange to isolate youth from its subsequent journey through life.

Therapeutic nihilism—the attitude of "can't do anything about it, so let's not waste resources on aging and the aged"—is gradually yielding to a new foundation of knowledge being established by gerontology, and by demonstrations that such knowledge can be applied effectively in many spheres. Caution is still in order, though, as the public continues to be enticed by claims for anti-aging miracles that are products of commercial zeal rather than competent research. A balanced view of the limitations, potentials, and challenges of a long life will require mature reflection from society as well as continuing contributions from gerontology.

ROBERT J. KASTENBAUM

See also

Geriatric Research, Education, and Clinical Centers

References

Achenbaum, W. A. (1995). *Crossing frontiers: Gerontology emerges as a science*. New York: Cambridge University Press.

Cole, T. (1992). *The journey of life*. New York: Cambridge University Press.

Cristofalo, V. J., & Adelman, A. (Eds.) (2002). *Modern topics in the biology of aging*. New York: Springer Publishing.

Kastenbaum, R. (1995). *Dorian, graying. Is youth the only thing worth having*? New York: Baywood.

Metchnikoff, M. E. (1903/2003). *The nature of man*. New York: Putnam.

Mitchell, S. (2001). *Generation X: Americans aged 18 to 34*. Ithaca, NY: New Strategist Publications.

Nelson, T. (Ed.) (2002). *Ageism*. Cambridge, MA: MIT Press.

Wahl, H-W., Scheidt, R., & Windley, P. (Eds.) (2004). *Aging in context: Socio-physical environments*. New York: Springer Publishing.

GOAL ATTAINMENT SCALING

See

Goal Setting

GOAL SETTING

A distinguishing feature of the problems of older adults, especially those who are *frail*, is their complexity. Problems are complex not just when there are a lot of them, but when they interact. As a consequence of their interaction, it becomes difficult to have a single intervention that produces a discrete effect: as with any complex system, it is impossible to do just one thing at once. Clinically, this means that any intervention will have not just its planned effect, but effects on other variables. For example, an older person who suffers an acute attack of gout might well benefit from the use of an anti-inflammatory drug. On the other hand, people with gout often have hypertension, and people with hypertension often have chronic renal failure or congestive heart failure, each of which is made worse by nonsteroidal anti-inflammatory drugs. But the picture can be more complex still. Acute gout is often disabling; if the patient lives alone but now cannot manage to get to the bathroom or to prepare a meal as a consequence of gout, then that person will require the assistance of someone else. For some individuals, this would be easy—they have family members nearby, or an excellent social network. Others, however, would rather suffer kidney damage than the indignity of being helped to the toilet. The complexity of the problems of frail older adults and the need to intervene judiciously means that priorities must be set, so that goal setting becomes an essential tool. Having outlined the rationale for goal setting, this text will review what constitutes goal setting, how goal setting is done, and experience with its use.

In the care of older people who are frail, goal setting arises in a particular context. Recognizing that *frail older people* have *complex needs*, it is obvious that meeting these needs will require a complex intervention, which begins typically with a *comprehensive geriatric assessment*. The yield of a comprehensive geriatric assessment usually is a problem list, which can identify literally dozens of problems. Goal setting is a way to choose those problems in which interventions can be carried out, and in this way contributes not just to identifying the outcomes of care, but in being part of the process of care (Stolee, Zaza, Pedlar, & Myers, 1999).

The exercise of formal goal setting can help improve care. This might seem obvious, but it often gets lost in moving from the problem list generated by a comprehensive geriatric assessment to the actual intervention carried out in a given patient. Often, while the assessments involve many disciplines, interventions are discipline-specific, and apart from meetings of *multidisciplinary teams*, can occur in relative isolation. Done properly, a formal process of goal setting can promote interdisciplinarity by having the team agree on goals related to a patient's function, comfort, and avoidance of premature death. This can serve to break down barriers in communication. For example, in the rehabilitation of a patient being treated for community-acquired pneumonia, a physician might properly be interested in the patient's breathlessness, fever, increased white cell count, and consolidation on the chest film, the physiotherapist in hip flexor strength and axial stability, the social worker in the resources available when the person returns home, and so on. At a multidisciplinary team meeting, each can report on its own findings in these areas. Goal setting serves as a remedy to these reports otherwise being made in isolation, because it obliges each discipline to discuss a limited range of goals—for example, by discussing the extent to which the patient can get in and out of bed unattended or get dressed. In this way, the interventions carried out in a given discipline are less likely to be carried out to their own end, but rather in aid of the goals of care.

Good goals require that patients and those who care for them have some input into the decision-making about their selection and about determining whether the goals have been met. This does not occur routinely (Bogardus, Bradley, Williams, Maciejewski, van Doorn, & Inouye, 2001), but when it does it can enhance the outcomes of care (Stolee, Zaza, Pedlar, & Myers, 1999; Heisler, Vijan, Anderson, Ubel, Bernstein, & Hofer, 2003; Bogardus, Bradley, Williams, Maciejewski, Gallo, & Inouye, 2004; Needham & Newbury, 2004). In short, requiring input transforms the process of care, by requiring health care professionals to explain how what they are doing will help the patient, in a way that the patient or caregiver can understand (Bradley, Bogardus, Tinetti, & Inouye, 1999). At the same time, it challenges some assumptions about dealing with patient autonomy, especially when disagreements about goals arise (Struhkamp, 2004).

One formal method of setting and monitoring goals, *Goal Attainment Scaling* (GAS), is a means of measuring whether a treatment or intervention meets the goals of patients, caregivers, and treating physicians (Kiresuk & Sherman, 1968). GAS uses a 5-point scale to record the degree of patient attainment in relation to individually defined problem areas (goal areas) between an established baseline (scaled as 0) and a series of follow-up assessments. The scale ranges from +2 (most positive outcome) to −2 (most negative outcome). *GAS* is *individualized*, in that what is measured (the goal area) need not be the same for each patient. However, it has been *standardized* by the use of a summary formula that calculates the extent to which goals have been met; this also allows it to be used as an aggregate measure of the extent to which, in a given group of patients, their goals have been met. GAS was originally developed as a tool for evaluating the effectiveness of therapeutic interventions for mental health patients. Subsequently, the GAS instrument has been adapted to a variety of program evaluation and clinical applications, including inpatient specialized geriatric care (Stolee, Zaza, Pedlar, & Myers, 1999), rural outreach (Rockwood, Howlett, & Stadnyk, 2003), and Alzheimer's disease treatment (Rockwood, Grahame, & Fay, 2002).

In GAS, problem areas are first identified. We can consider that the 2 chief problems of the patient above, from his standpoint, are pain and decreased mobility. Specific inquiry might also reveal whether the decreased mobility, with its dependence on others, is a source of further difficulty, such as worry about being alone, balanced against concern about the burden being placed on his daughter, who is his primary caregiver. Next, the precise nature of these problems is described (e.g. intolerable pain at rest; need for moderate assistance from one person to transfer and walk to the bathroom; worry several times a day about being alone; moderate caregiver burden most days felt by the daughter). In a third step, *goals of care* are set (e.g. pain-free in 5 days; independence in mobility; occasional worry; caregiver moderate burden, only during episodes of increased need). Importantly, both better and worse outcomes are described. Just considering the patient's pain, the goal of freedom from pain in 5 days would be better if it occurred sooner, or if it was reduced enough to lessen dependence sooner. A worse outcome would be if it took longer, or if it was achieved with complications (e.g. worsening heart or kidney problems). Worse still would be if these problems increased dependence. Clinical experience suggests that it is the anticipation of ways to enhance better ones or mitigate worse ones, which often improves clinical care. Note too that this approach evaluates the outcomes of care, and not just the process: it is all too easy to provide an older person who lives alone with emergency telephone contact such as Lifeline, without considering whether it alleviates loneliness and caregiver distress.

As more people become frail, it is important that methods be developed to embrace their complexity and not to treat their many problems in isolation. Formal methods of goal setting appear to better achieve that end, while offering improved patient and caregiver satisfaction.

KENNETH ROCKWOOD

See also
Frailty

References

Bradley, E. H., Bogardus, S. T. Jr., Tinetti, M. E., & Inouye, S. K. (1999). Goal-setting in clinical medicine. *Social Science and Medicine*, *49*(2), 267–278.

Bogardus, S. T., Bradley, E. H., Williams, C. S., Maciejewski, P. K., van Doorn, C., & Inouye, S. K. (2001). Goals for the care of frail older adults: Do caregivers and clinicians agree? *American Journal of Medicine*, *110*, 97–102.

Bogardus, S. T. Jr., Bradley, E. H., Williams, C. S., Maciejewski, P. K., Gallo, W. T., & Inouye, S. K. (2004). Achieving goals in geriatric assessment: Role of caregiver agreement and adherence to recommendations. *Journal of American Geriatrics Society*, *52*, 99–105.

Heisler, M., Vijan, S., Anderson, R. M., Ubel, P. A., Bernstein, S. J., & Hofer, T. P. (2003). When do patients and their physicians agree on diabetes treatment goals and strategies, and what difference does it make? *Journal of General Internal Medicine*, *18*, 893–902.

Kiresuk, T. J., & Sherman, R. E. (1968). Goal Attainment Scaling: A general method for evaluating comprehensive community mental health programs. *Community Mental Health Journal*, *4*, 443–453.

Needham, P. R., & Newbury, J. (2004). Goal setting as a measure of outcome in palliative care. *Palliative Medicine*, *18*, 444–451.

Stolee, P., Zaza, C., Pedlar, A., & Myers, A. M. (1999). Clinical experience with Goal Attainment Scaling in geriatric care. *Journal of Aging and Health, 11*, 96–124.

Struhkamp, R. (2004). Goals in their setting: A normative analysis of goal setting in physical rehabilitation. *Health Care Analysis*, *12*, 131–155.

Rockwood, K., Grahame J. E., & Fay, S. (2002). Goal setting and attainment in Alzheimer's disease patients treated with donepezil. *Journal of Neurology, Neurosurgery, and Psychiatry*, *73*(5), 500–507.

Rockwood, K., Howlett, S., & Stadnyk, K., et al. (2003). Responsiveness of goal attainment scaling in a randomized controlled trial of comprehensive geriatric assessment. *Journal of Clinical Epidemiology*, *56*, 736–743.

GRANDPARENT-GRANDCHILD RELATIONSHIPS

Because of recent sociodemographic changes of greater longevity, decreased fertility, and increased rates of nuclear family disruption through divorce, relationships between *grandparents* and *grandchildren* are becoming increasingly important in today's society. A central issue in research concerning grandparent-grandchild relations is the strength and maintenance of bonds, or the solidarity between them. The lives of grandparents and their grandchildren are linked in a number of ways: through roles, interactions, sentiments, and exchanges of support. It is useful to examine grandparent-grandchild relations in terms of 6 dimensions of *intergenerational solidarity* (Silverstein, Giarrusso, & Bengtson, 1998): affectual, structural, associational, functional, consensual, and normative family solidarity.

Affectual solidarity involves the degree of closeness that is felt between grandparents and grandchildren. Although both grandparents and grandchildren report feeling close to one another, grandparents report a greater degree of closeness than do grandchildren. Further, the relationship between grandparents and grandchildren is often influenced by the middle generation, since they provide the opportunities for grandparents and grandchildren to socialize together when the children reside in the parental household. If parents are emotionally close to grandparents, grandparents and grandchildren are more likely to be close as well. As a result of gender differences in the *kin-keeper role*, there is a tendency for grandchildren to have a closer relationship with their *maternal grandparents* (Chan & Elder, 2000). Whatever the feelings of closeness between grandparents and grandchildren when they are young, these feelings remain relatively consistent as grandchildren grow up and move away geographically from their grandparents. In a study of adult grandparent-grandchild relationships over 23 years, it was found that, after an initial decline, affective relationships tended to improve very late in the lives of grandparents (Silverstein & Long, 1998).

Structural solidarity is the opportunity for association between grandparents and grandchildren, the foremost being the geographic distance between them. In a nationally representative study of the United States, *geographic proximity* was found to be the strongest predictor of association between grandparents and grandchildren (Uhlenberg & Hammill, 1998). However, a variety of other factors also influence opportunities for association including the demographic and personal characteristics of the grandparent and grandchild, such as their age, gender, and health, and the marital, employment, and socioeconomic status of the parents (Cherlin & Furstenberg, 1991; Reitzes & Mutran, 2004). Divorce, single-parenting, and dual-earner marriages have increased drastically in recent years among the parent generation, which in turn has had a dramatic impact on opportunities for grandparents and grandchildren to associate with one another (Drew & Smith, 2002).

Associational solidarity concerns the frequency of contact between the grandparent and grandchild. Most grandparents and grandchildren do stay in regular contact (Uhlenberg & Hammill, 1998). The degree of association is influenced by family consequences particularly in conjunction with adult children's life situations. For instance, parental divorce has 2 consequences for association. It can result in greater interaction and solidarity, as is the case when the daughter returns to the parental home temporarily following divorce, or when a mother is incapable of caring for children. On the other hand, *parental divorce* has a particularly negative effect on the relationship between grandparents and grandchildren whose parents have not been given custody, usually the father. Although all states now have *Grandparents' Rights* legislation, which gives grandparents the power to go to court to secure their right to visit with their grandchildren, associational solidarity will probably become increasingly matrilineal. However, these consequences of divorce do not hold for adult grandchildren whose relationships with grandparents are no longer directly mediated by their parents.

Functional solidarity is the help and assistance that is transferred between grandparents and grandchildren. When grandchildren are young, many if not most American grandparents provide direct help in babysitting them, and an increasing percentage of grandparents assume the role of "*surrogate*" *parent* when the middle generation is unable to provide caregiving as a result of problems such as drug and alcohol addiction, AIDS, divorce, incarceration, or unemployment (Giarrusso, Silverstein, & Feng, 2000). The significant increase in *grandparents raising grandchildren* requires better policies and social services to attend to various needs that are unique to this segment of the population (Fuller-Thompson & Minkler, 2003; Smith, 2003). Development of social support programs (e.g., the *Foster Grandparent Program* and *Kin Care Program*) is one attempt to assist grandparents with tremendous family responsibilities (AARP, 2004). Grandparents typically adhere to the "norm of noninterference," which stipulates that grandparents should not interfere with the activities of the nuclear family (Cherlin & Furstenberg, 1991). In most families, the real value of grandparents lies in their simple *presence,* not their *actions.*

Consensual solidarity indicates the amount of intergenerational similarity in beliefs and values. Grandparents, as well as parents, are the primary *agents of socialization* who transmit to their grandchildren the values and norms of social order. Studies of young adult grandchildren indicate that consensual solidarity between grandparents and grandchildren remains high even after grandchildren reach adulthood. The majority of post-adolescent grandchildren feel their grandparents influence their values and behaviors. Attitudes toward which grandparents have had the greatest influence include adult grandchildren's beliefs about family, morals, and the work ethic (Brussoni & Boon, 1998). However, both maternal and paternal grandmothers seem to have a stronger sway over their grandchildren; grandsons as well as granddaughters indicate that their values are more greatly influenced by their grandmothers than their grandfathers.

Normative solidarity concerns the perceptions of obligations and expectations about intergenerational connections. Research has identified the many *burdens faced by grandparents* who assume direct, full-time caregiving responsibilities for their grandchildren, including: economic difficulties; social isolation; grandchildren who have physical and psychological problems; adult children who are dysfunctional, sick, addicted, or incarcerated; and an overall lack of time. However, normative solidarity tends to mediate the effect of these burdens on the psychological well-being of grandparents. Among *caregiving grandparents*, stronger normative beliefs about the family are negatively associated with the perception of caregiving as stressful and positively associated with the perception of it as rewarding (Giarrusso, Silverstein & Feng, 2000).

The dynamics of grandparent-grandchild relationships entail significant diversity, along with various family sociodemographic and cultural backgrounds (Silverstein, Giarrusso, & Bengtson, 2003). The key to understanding is to evaluate the grandparent-grandchild relationships along multiple dimensions of intergenerational solidarity, and demonstrate substantial variability along those dimensions. As grandparents and grandchildren spend more and more years of adult life together, due to increases in longevity of older people, such information is increasingly important.

ROSEANN GIARRUSSO
MERRIL SILVERSTEIN
EMIKO TAKAGI

See also
Intergenerational Relationships

References

AARP. (2004). AARP life answers: Grandparents. Available: http://www.aarp.org/life/grandparents.

Brussoni, M. J., & Boon, S. D. (1998). Grandparental impact in young adults' relationships with their closest grandparents: The role of relationship strength and emotional closeness. *International Journal of Aging and Human Development, 46,* 267–286.

Chan, C. G., & Elder, G. H., Jr. (2000). Matrilineal advantage in grandchild-grandparent relations. *Gerontologist*, *40*(2), 179–190.

Cherlin, A., & Furstenberg, F. (1991). *The new American*

grandparent: A place in the family, a life apart (2nd ed.). Cambridge, MA: Harvard University Press.

Drew, L. M., & Smith, P. K. (2002). Implications for grandparents when they lose contact with their grandchildren: Divorce, family feuds, and geographical separation. *Journal of Mental Health and Aging, 8,* 95–120.

Fuller-Thompson, E., & Minkler, M. (2003). Housing issues and realities facing grandparent caregivers who are renters. *Gerontologist, 43*(1), 92–98.

Giarrusso, R., Feng, D., Silverstein, M., & Marenco, A. (2000). Primary and secondary stressors of grandparents raising grandchildren: Evidence from a national survey. *Journal of Mental Health and Aging, 6*(4), 291–310.

Giarrusso, R., Silverstein, M., & Feng, D. (2000). Psychological costs and benefits of raising grandchildren: Evidence from a national survey of grandparents. In C. Cox (Ed.), *To grandmother's house we go: The issues, needs, and policies affecting grandparents raising grandchildren.* New York: Springer Publishing.

Reitzes, D. C., & Mutran, E. (2004). Grandparenthood: Factors influencing frequency of grandparent-grandchildren contact and grandparent role satisfaction. *Journal of Gerontology: Social Sciences, 59B*(1), S9–S16.

Silverstein, M., Giarrusso, R., & Bengtson, V. (1998). Intergenerational solidarity and the grandparent role. In M. Szinovacz (Ed.), *Handbook on grandparenthood.* Connecticut: Greenwood Press.

Silverstein, M., Giarrusso, R., & Bengtson, V. (2003). Grandparents and grandchildren in family systems: A social-developmental perspective. In V. L. Bengtson & A. Lowenstein (Eds.), *Global aging and its challenge to families* (pp. 73–102). New York: Aldine De Gruyter.

Silverstein, M., & Long, J. D. (1998). Trajectories of grandparents' perceived solidarity with adult grandchildren: A growth curve analysis over 23 years. *Journal of Marriage and the Family, 60*(4), 912–923.

Smith, C. J. (2003). The role of federal policies in supporting grandparents raising grandchildren: The case of the U.S. *Journal of Intergenerational Relationships, 1*(2), 5–20.

Uhlenberg, P., & Hammill, B. G. (1998). Frequency of grandparent contact with grandchild sets: Six factors that make a difference. *Gerontologist, 38,* 276–285.

GROUP THERAPY

Group therapy may offer advantages for many older adults; it is generally less expensive than individual treatment, and the *social network* provided by group therapy may provide significant therapeutic benefits to those experiencing a loss of interpersonal relationships through the death of friends and spouses. Additionally, a review of the literature reveals empirical support for the effectiveness of group therapy in the *treatment of depression* in older adults.

Controlled clinical trials, which include a comparison group (e. g. placebo, alternative treatment, wait-list condition), provide a significant advantage over uncontrolled trials in that outcomes can be confidently attributed to the intervention. Furthermore, randomized controlled trials (RCTs), in which study participants have an equal likelihood of assignment to each of 2 or more treatment conditions, provide a significant advantage over nonrandomized studies in that they eliminate systematic bias which might interfere with results, allow for the control of trends over time, and significantly reduce the likelihood of finding spurious results. Therefore, while numerous uncontrolled trials have produced results supporting the effectiveness of group therapy in the treatment of older adults with psychological disorders, this review highlights the findings of the RCTs that have been conducted to date.

The majority of controlled trials that have examined the effectiveness of group treatment for older adults have focused upon the treatment of depression. To date, 6 controlled studies of group treatment for noncognitively impaired elderly depression have been published.

- In one of the earliest controlled studies, patients 55 years and older who met diagnostic criteria for depression were treated with 26 weeks of *cognitive-behavioral* or *psychodynamic group therapy* (Jarvik, Mintz, Steuer, & Gerner, 1982). While both groups of patients made significant improvements based upon HAM-D scores, no significant between-groups difference was detected, although this likely results from lack of power due to low sample size. It is important to note, furthermore, that all of these findings are limited by lack of randomization.
- In another nonrandomized study, depressed geriatric patients who completed a 9-month course of weekly cognitive-behavioral or psychodynamic group therapy showed statistically and clinically significant reductions on observer-rated and self-rated measures of depression (Steuer, 1984). Significant between-group differences were found

on self-reports of depressive symptomatology, indicating a statistically significant advantage of cognitive-behavioral group therapy.

- An RCT that examined the effect of group therapy upon depressive symptomatology in older adults showed that cognitive therapy with or without *alprazolam* (an anxiolytic) was more effective than alprazolam alone (Beutler, Scogin, Kirkish, Schretlen, Corbishley, Hamblin, et al., 1987). Results suggest that cognitive group therapy is an effective treatment for depression in older adults.
- Another study examined treatment outcomes for *depressed geriatric inpatients* age 60 and older who participated in 8 sessions of behavioral group therapy plus standard hospital treatment (including pharmacotherapy) and those who only received standard hospital treatment (Brand & Clingempeel, 1992). While investigators failed to find a significant main effect for treatment condition, analyses of clinical significance indicated that individuals who received behavioral group therapy were more likely to be in remission at post-test. It is possible that the absence of a significant main effect of treatment condition was the result of small sample size.
- In another RCT, 34 adults age 60 and older meeting diagnostic criteria for major depression were randomly assigned to a *self-management therapy group*, an *educational therapy group*, or a waiting-list control condition (Rokke, Tomhave, & Jocic, 2000). Participants in both group therapy treatments showed significant decreases in depression over the course of treatment compared to controls, and maintained these gains over a 1-year follow-up period. While no statistically significant differences were found between the 2 treatment groups, 60% to 70% of participants in the treatment groups showed clinically meaningful improvement.
- In a recent RCT, investigators examined the effectiveness of group therapy as an adjunct to *antidepressant medication* for depressed adults age 60 and older (Lynch, Morse, Mendelson, & Robins, 2003). Participants received 28 weeks of antidepressant medication plus clinical management, either alone (MED) or with the addition of a dialectical behavior therapy *skills-training* group and weekly 30-minute scheduled *telephone coaching* sessions (MED+DBT.) At 6-month post-treatment, 73% of MED+DBT patients were in remission compared to only 38% of MED patients, suggesting that participation in a DBT skills training group is an effective adjunct to medication in the treatment of older adults with depression (Lynch, Morse, Mendelson, & Robins, 2003). Furthermore, only those who participated in the DBT skills-training group made significant improvements on dependency and adaptive coping from pre- to post-treatment, improvements that may reduce vulnerability to depression.

Overall these studies provide support for the use of group therapy as a treatment for older adults with depression. Recently, investigators have begun to examine the use of group treatment for other disorders, such as *substance use disorders* (Rathbone-McCuan, & Nelson, 2003; Schonfeld, et al., 2000), *psychotic disorders* (Patterson, et al., 2003), and *personality disorders* (Lynch, Cheavens, Thorp, Bronner, Rosenthal, & Smoski, 2005). For example, one recent RCT examined the relative effectiveness of a *skills-training group therapy* program for older adults with chronic psychotic disorders compared to treatment as usual (Patterson, et al., 2003.) Forty middle-aged and older adults (ranging from 42 to 69 years) residing in long-term board-and-care facilities were randomly assigned to either a 24-session *functional adaptation skills training* (FAST) group therapy program or to a treatment as usual condition (medication only.) Results demonstrated that compared to those in the treatment as usual group, participants in group treatment made significant global improvements on a performance-based measure of daily functioning and reported decreased negative symptoms. These improvements persisted at 3-month follow-up.

Currently, investigators are conducting an RCT focused on treating older adults with depression and comorbid personality disorder (Lynch, Cheavens, Thorp, Bronner, Rosenthal, & Smoski, 2005). Participants were adults aged 55 and older who were not in remission following 8 weeks of antidepressant treatment for depression. Participants received another 24 weeks of antidepressant medication, either alone or in conjunction with a weekly DBT skills-training group. Initial results suggest that following skills-group training, participants in the DBT + medication group showed significant improvement in depressive symptomatology, interpersonal aggression, and interpersonal sensitivity compared to those in the medication-only group, although this advantage did not persist at 24-week follow-up.

In summary, results suggest that group therapy may be a promising mode of treatment for older adults.

THOMAS R. LYNCH
KRISTIN GRACE SCHNEIDER

See also
Psychotherapy

References

Beutler, L. E., Scogin, F., Kirkish, P., Schretlen, D., Corbishley, A., Hamblin, D., Meredith, K., Potter, R., Bamford, C. R., & Levenson, A. I. (1987). Group cognitive therapy and alprazolam in the treatment of depression in older adults. *Journal of Consulting and Clinical Psychology, 55,* 550–556.

Brand, E., & Clingempeel, W. G. (1992). Group behavioral therapy with depressed geriatric inpatients: An assessment of incremental efficacy. *Behavior Therapy, 23,* 475–482.

Jarvik, L. F., Mintz, J., Steuer, J. L., & Gerner, R. (1982). Treating geriatric depression: A 26-week interim analysis. *Journal of the American Geriatric Society, 30,* 713–717.

Lynch, T. R., Cheavens, J., Thorp, S., Bronner, L., Rosenthal, M. Z., & Smoski, M. (2005). *Treatment of older adult depression with personality disorder co-morbidity.* Paper accepted for presentation at the annual meeting of the American Association for Geriatric Psychiatry, San Diego, CA.

Lynch, T. R., Morse J. Q., Mendelson T., & Robins, C. J. (2003). Dialectical behavior therapy for depressed older adults. *American Journal of Geriatric Psychiatry, 11,* 33–45.

Patterson, T. L., et al. (2003). Functional adaptation skills training (FAST): A pilot psychosocial intervention study in middle-aged and older patients with chronic psychotic disorders. *American Journal of Geriatric Psychiatry, 11,* 17–23.

Rathbone-McCuan, E., & Nelson, R. (2002.) Group psychotherapy for elderly substance abusers. In D. W. Brook & H. I. Spitz, (Eds.), *Group therapy of substance abuse* (pp. 309–324). New York: Haworth Press.

Rokke, P. D., Tomhave, J. A., & Jocic, Z. (2000). Self-management therapy and educational group therapy for depressed elders. *Cognitive Therapy and Research, 24,* 99–119.

Schonfeld, L., et al. (2000). Cognitive-behavioral treatment of older veterans with substance abuse problems. *Journal of Geriatric Psychiatry and Neurology, 13,* 124–129.

Steuer, J. L. (1984). Cognitive-behavioral and psychodynamic group psychotherapy in treatment of geriatric depression. *Journal of Consulting and Clinical Psychology, 52,* 180–189.

GROWTH HORMONE AND INSULIN-LIKE GROWTH FACTOR-1

There is abundant empirical and scientific evidence to support the hypothesis that much of the age-related decline in tissue function is closely related to a *decrease in hormone* concentrations and/or hormone action. Growth hormone (GH) and insulin-like growth factor-I (IGF-1) are examples of 2 potent anabolic hormones that have been hypothesized to contribute to the loss of tissue function and the resulting physical disability in older adults. GH is secreted from the anterior *pituitary gland* in discrete pulses that occur throughout the day, with higher amplitude pulses occurring after the onset of sleep. Pulsatile release of GH has been confirmed in every mammalian species examined and is necessary for full biologic actions of the hormone. Activation of the hepatic GH receptor stimulates the synthesis and secretion of *IGF-1* into blood. This latter hormone circulates at high concentrations and mediates the anabolic actions of GH including cellular DNA, RNA, and protein synthesis. Because of the wide distribution of the GH receptor, GH may also have a role in regulating the synthesis and secretion of IGF-1 from many tissues, thereby directly influencing the local or "paracrine" activity of the hormone. Although it was initially proposed that all of the actions of GH were mediated through IGF-1, several studies have provided convincing data that GH has direct effect on specific tissues and/or synergizes with IGF-1 in the regulation of tissue function.

In humans, pulsatile bursts of GH occur at night in association with slow-wave sleep, and the pattern is both species- and gender-specific. For example, high-amplitude secretory pulses occur every 3.5 hours in male and hourly in female rodents. The regulation of these pulses involves at least 2 hormones released by the *hypothalamus*: GH-releasing hormone (GHRH) which increases GH release, and *somatostatin*, which inhibits its release. The dynamic interactions between these hormones regulate high amplitude, pulsatile GH secretion. GH and IGF-1 suppress GH release from the pituitary in a typical feedback relationship, either directly at the level of the pituitary or by stimulating somatostatin and/or inhibiting GHRH release from the hypothalamus.

Early studies in humans reported a substantial decline in GH secretion with age in response to several stimuli, including insulin-induced hypoglycemia and arginine administration. Subsequent studies revealed a loss of the nocturnal surges of GH and a decrease in plasma IGF-1 that paralleled the decline in GH pulses. These results have been confirmed by numerous investigators, and it is now evident that the decline in high-amplitude GH secretion and plasma IGF-I concentrations are one of the most robust and well-characterized events that occur with age (Corpas, Harman, & Blackman, 1993). Similar to humans, decreases in the amplitude of GH pulses are observed in rodent models of aging and, as expected, these changes are closely associated with a decline in plasma IGF-1 (Sonntag, Lynch, Cefalu, Ingram, Bennett, Thornton, et al., 1999; Carter, Ramsey, & Sonntag, 2002). Although the specific etiology for the decline in GH pulse amplitude has not been fully detailed, studies in both humans and animals documented a decline in *in vivo* pituitary response to GHRH with age. However, numerous studies attempting to detail the deficits within the pituitary gland produced controversial results that ultimately were attributed to: (1) differential responses of older animals to the pharmacological agents used to suppress endogenous GH pulses during *in vivo* testing, or (2) technical caveats in culturing anterior pituitary cells from older animals. Research efforts were eventually directed to an analysis of hypothalamic release and inhibiting hormones after studies revealed that: acute administration of somatostatin antiserum *in vivo* increased GH release identically in young and old animals; passive immunization with somatostatin antiserum restored the *in vivo* deficiency in pituitary response to GHRH; and stimulation of hypothalamic slices of old animals in a superfusion system released greater quantities of somatostatin than those of young animals. These results provided compelling evidence that increased somatostatin tone may be the dominant factor in the decline in GH pulses with age. These conclusions were further supported by research in humans, where administration of cholinergic agonists or *arginine*, considered to preferentially inhibit somatostatin release, increased GH secretion in older individuals. Over the past several years, research has supported these conclusions and demonstrated that translational regulatory factors that normally control the association of somatostatin *mRNA* with the polyribosome are altered in aged animals. In addition, decreases in the levels and regulation of GHRH mRNA occur with age. Thus, alterations in both hypothalamic release and inhibiting hormones appear to be a key factor in the decline in GH pulse amplitude with age, although other factors that regulate GH release (including decreases in either levels of, or response to, circulating *ghrelin* from the gastrointestinal tract) may also contribute to the etiology of impaired GH secretion.

Although an attenuation of GH pulse amplitude is an important contributing factor in the decline in plasma IGF-1, response to circulating GH also appears to be diminished in older individuals. In rodents, a two-fold increase in GH receptors has been observed with age that fails to compensate for the reduced levels of GH. More detailed investigations revealed that the K_d and apparent size of the GH receptor were not influenced by age, whereas the capacity of GH to induce IGF-1 gene expression and secretion directly from hepatic slices was 40% to 50% less in old than young animals. Subsequently, deficiencies in the ability of GH to induce JAK, STAT3 and MAP kinases were found, suggesting that an impairment in GH receptor signal transduction contributes to the decline in IGF-1 in both animals and humans (Xu & Sonntag, 1996).

Although GH resistance (e.g. impairment GH signal transduction) is an important component of the decrease in plasma IGF-1 with age, this deficit can be partially overcome by administration of GH. Limited studies in rodents over a decade ago revealed that supplementation of old animals with GH increases IGF-1 and restores cellular protein synthesis demonstrating that the age-related decline in skeletal muscle mass and myocyte function is not solely related to intrinsic deficits within the tissue. Other reports were published that GH or IGF-1 administration could partially reverse the decline in immune function, increase the expression of aortic elastin, and increase life span in rodents. These studies were the first indications that the decrease in the concentration of GH has clinical significance and may be responsible for the generalized catabolic state that accompanies normal aging. It has generally been reported that GH increases IGF-1, lean body mass, muscle mass, and skin thickness, and reduces total body fat content in older adults (Rudman, Feller, Nagraj, Gergans, Lalitha, Goldberg, et al., 1990). In addition, there are some reports of elevations in serum *osteocalcin* (an osteoblast-produced marker of bone formation), urinary *hydroxyproline* (a marker for bone resorption) and *nitrogen retention*, raising the possibility that GH treatment may delay osteoporosis. Interestingly, *aerobic exercise* training for 1 year increases the amount of GH secreted over a 24-hour period, suggesting that the beneficial effects of *exercise* training may be mediated, at least in part, by increasing GH secretion.

Recent studies demonstrate that GH and IGF-1 deficiency contributes to *brain aging*. Administration of GH (sufficient to raise plasma IGF-1 levels) reverses the age-related decline in microvascular density on the surface of the brain. These results led to the concept that the deficiencies in brain levels of IGF-1 that appear with age may be the result of reduced plasma GH and/or IGF-1 levels (Sonntag, Lynch, Cefalu, Ingram, Bennett, Thornton, et al., 1999; Carter, Ramsey, & Sonntag, 2002). In fact, administration of IGF-1 directly to the brains of aged animals has been shown to improve both reference and working memory (Markowska, Mooney, & Sonntag, 1998), glucose utilization, and the function of several neurotransmitter systems. Similar benefits on spatial memory have been noted in rodent studies after twice-daily administration of GHRH to increase plasma levels of GH and IGF-1. Cognitive function in humans also appears to be improved by GH replacement, providing further evidence that decreases in circulating hormones contribute to the genesis of brain aging.

Although a significant number of studies demonstrate that decreases in GH and IGF-1 contribute to functional decline with age, studies in invertebrate models indicate that suppression of IGF-1 signaling increases life span (Kenyon, 2001). In *C. elegans*, disruption of the daf-2 signaling pathway (through which insulin/IGF-1 act in this species) has been shown to extend life span from 30% to 100%. This appears to be the result of the release of the Akt/PKB "brake" on another signaling factor, daf-16, which is the primary target of the daf-2 pathway and is required for extended life span. Daf-16 controls gene expression that regulates environmental stress resistance, development, and dauer formation in this species.

Daf-2 signaling in *C. elegans* shares significant homology with metabolic pathways in flies and yeast, and mutations in genes homologous to the IGF-1 signaling pathway increase life span in these organisms as well. Similarities in insulin/IGF-1-like signaling pathways between invertebrates and mammals raise the possibility that insulin/IGF-1 signaling may influence mammalian longevity. For example, 3 possible homologs of the daf-16 transcription factor, FKHRL1, AFX, and FKHR 9, have recently been discovered in humans but, to date, conclusions relating these proteins, insulin, or IGF-1 signaling to longevity have not been definitively established.

In mammals, the 2 most widely used models of IGF-1 deficiency are the Snell and Ames dwarf mice. These mutant mice are homozygous for mutations at the Pituitary-1 (Pit-1) locus and the prophet of Pit-1 (Prop-1) locus, respectively. These mutations inhibit the development of pituitary cells responsible for producing GH (somatotrophs), prolactin (lactotrophs), and thyroid-stimulating hormone (thyrotrophs). As a result both models are deficient in these hormones, and alterations in the levels of other closely related hormones are evident (e.g. corticosterone and insulin). Both Snell and Ames dwarf mice demonstrate increased longevity (50% in males and 64% in females) relative to their wild-type controls, which has been widely attributed to GH/IGF-1 deficiency. However, the mechanisms that underlie the observed extension in life span are complex and could involve many determinants beyond the simple reduction in GH and IGF-1 secretion. Because the Ames and Snell dwarves exhibit GH, IGF-1, thyroid hormone, and *prolactin* deficiency, and these hormones regulate key aspects of cellular function, the individual contribution of each hormone to the observed increase in life span remains unknown. These issues are compounded further by other phenotypic changes evident in the Ames and Snell dwarf mice including, but not limited to: (1) lower body temperature, (2) decreased body size, (3) increased levels of antioxidant enzymes, (4) decreased insulin sensitivity.

Although it would be reasonable to conclude that the complexities inherent in these models could be reduced or eliminated by using a model with a specific mutation or knockout in the GH/IGF-1 axis, studies of GH receptor/binding protein (GHR/BP) and IGF-1 receptor (IGFR) knockouts indicate that developmental effects of these hormones and interactions with numerous other organ systems produce secondary endocrine abnormalities that limit their use. For instance, the GHR/BP knockout animals exhibit decreases in thyroid hormones, increases in *glucocorticoid* levels, and deficiencies in glucose and insulin levels. Alterations in insulin and glucocorticoid levels indicate abnormalities in the development of the pancreas and hypothalamic-adrenal axis. Similar changes in glucose, insulin, and glucocorticoids have also been found in the Ames and Snell dwarf mice, suggesting that these secondary endocrine alterations are not unique to one model, but are a fundamental consequence of GH/IGF-1 deficiency.

The beneficial and deleterious effects of GH and IGF-1 that are evident in the aforementioned models fit a model of *antagonistic pleiotropy*, a theory on the evolution of aging suggesting that the expression of particular genes, beneficial early in life, become detrimental with age. Evolutionary biologists argue that for antagonistic pleiotropy to be adaptive, GH and IGF-1 must have a direct bearing on reproductive efficacy, a criteria clearly supported by a large volume of published data. Although studies are currently in progress to address the specific role of GH/IGF-1 during aging, high levels of GH and IGF-1 early in life are essential for normal tissue development and function (including optimal reproductive function); however, the long-term presence of these hormones are pathogenic. This latter conclusion is supported by an extensive literature suggesting an important role for GH/IGF-1 in the genesis of neoplastic disease. Thus, the actions of GH/IGF-1 on maturation of tissues early in life and the effects of these hormones on pathology manifest late in life support an important antagonistic pleiotropic role that influences both tissue function and life span.

Invertebrate studies have demonstrated a compelling role for insulin/IGF-1 signaling in the regulation of life span. Our critical analysis of the application of these concepts to mammalian *dwarf models of aging* (e.g. the Ames and Snell dwarfs) is not meant to detract from the importance of these original findings in invertebrate models. Nevertheless, concepts of the nature of *biological aging* across species must be carefully developed and rigorously tested. No matter how intriguing the findings, theoretical constructs related to the effects of the GH/IGF-1 axis on aging cannot be derived from models that produce non-specific alterations in GH and IGF-1 levels. Thus additional, carefully controlled studies will be required to determine the definitive role of GH and IGF-1 in the regulation of biological aging and life span.

William E. Sonntag

See also
Life Extension

References

Carter, C. S., Ramsey, M. M., & Sonntag, W. E. (2002). A critical analysis of the role of growth hormone and IGF-1 in aging and life span. *Trends in Genetics, 18,* 295–301.

Corpas, E., Harman, S. M., & Blackman, M. R. (1993). Human growth hormone and human aging [Review]. *Endocrine Reviews, 14,* 20–39.

Kenyon, C. (2001). A conserved regulatory system for aging. *Cell, 105,* 165–168.

Markowska, A. L., Mooney, M., & Sonntag, W. E. (1998). Insulin-like growth factor-1 (IGF-1) ameliorates age-related behavioral deficits. *Neuroscience, 87,* 559–569.

Rudman, D., Feller, A. G., Nagraj, H. S., Gergans, G. A., Lalitha, P. Y., Goldberg, A. F., Schlenker, R. A., Cohn, L., Rudman, I. W., & Mattson, D. E. (1990). Effects of human growth hormone in men over 60 years old. *New England Journal of Medicine, 323,* 1–6.

Sonntag, W. E., Lynch, C. D., Cefalu, W. T., Ingram, R. L., Bennett, S. A., Thornton, P. L., & Khan, A. S. (1999). Pleiotropic effects of growth hormone and insulin-like growth factor (IGF)-1 on biological aging: Inferences from moderate caloric restricted animals. *Journals of Gerontology Biological Sciences, 54a,* 521–538.

Xu, X., & Sonntag, W. E. (1996). Growth hormone and aging: Regulation, signal transduction and therapeutic intervention. *Trends in Endocrinology and Metabolism, 7,* 145–150.

GUARDIANSHIP/ CONSERVATORSHIP

The question of how to manage the affairs of incapacitated adults has been debated for centuries. *Legal guardianship*, a common remedy in many countries, is said to date back to Roman law. In modern democracies, societal aging and increases in the number of adults with dementing illnesses have made guardianship an increasingly compelling area of research and public policy.

The purpose of legal guardianship is to protect adults who are unable to make reasoned decisions, and, as a result, need help managing their affairs. Adults may be judged to lack capacity to manage if they are unable to provide for their basic necessities such as food, shelter, and clothing, putting them at risk of physical and/or financial harm. Adults, who have been adjudicated by a court of law to lack capacity, generally referred to as "*wards*," may also be called "*conservatees*" "*incapacitated persons*," or "*protected persons*." The ward is relegated to the legal status of a minor child by being placed under "guardianship" (called "conservatorship" in some U.S. states) and appointed a legal "guardian" who is authorized to act on his or her behalf. About 1 million to 1.5 million people in the United States are believed to be under guardianship (Schmidt, 1996; Teaster, 2003). Guardianship disproportionately affects older adults, many of whom suffer from disorders that impair cognitive functioning. Nevertheless, for adults, age per se should not be used as an indicator of need for guardianship (Reynolds, 1997). Consumer-targeted overviews of guardianship and guardianship resources can be found on the National Guardianship Association's Web site at www.guardianship.org/displaycommon.cfm?an=2, and AARP's Web site at www.aarp.org/Articles/a2003-11-07-Guardianship.html.

Legal guardianship is initiated when a petitioner files a formal request for guardianship with the court, setting in motion a court hearing before a judge. The decision to file a petition may be triggered by a specific event, such as a health emergency, acute mental health problem, financial mismanagement, or the need for nursing home placement (Keith & Wacker, 1994). The *petitioner*, who in many cases becomes the guardian, may be a family member or friend, a private agency, a private professional such as an attorney or accountant, or the *public guardian*. The public guardian, available in 42 states, serves people without willing or able friends or family members and without the resources to pay for a *private guardian* (Reynolds, 1997; Siemon, Hurme, & Sabatino, 1993; Schmidt, Miller, Bell, & New, 1981; Teaster, 2003). Filing the petition sets in motion a court hearing before a judge that includes the petitioner and the respondent—the person who is being evaluated for guardianship—and if requested by the respondent, an attorney. In some states a court visitor will assess the person's need prior to the hearing. The judge rules on the need for guardianship based on the state's criteria for incapacity. As a protective intervention, guardianship is intended to serve the "best interests" of the ward. It is also a draconian intervention that restricts *autonomy* and self-determination by legally taking away the civil liberties guaranteed to adults (Rein, 1992; Schmidt, 1996). In addition, guardianship is costly to initiate and maintain, and time-consuming and stressful to the parties involved (Kapp, 1996; Keith & Wacker, 1994).

Authority and Powers

Guardianship authority derives from the state's power of *parens patriae*, which obligates the state to "parent" or protect those who are unable to care for themselves (Sabatino, 1996). In the United States, many state statutes are based on the Uniform Probate Code (UPC), yet there is no national policy and as a result, procedures and terminology vary substantially from state to state (Hurme, 1991; Hommel, 1996; Kapp, 1999).

Guardianship may be plenary or limited. *Plenary guardianship* grants the guardian authority to make virtually all decisions including property and asset management, legal transactions, living arrangements, and medical treatment (Iris, 1988; Schmidt, Miller, Bell, & New, 1981; Hommel, 1996). In limited or "*partial*" *guardianship*, the court delineates the specific areas over which the guardian has authority (Kapp, 1999; Keith & Wacker, 1994; Hommel, 1996). Although many courts appear reluctant to tailor guardianships because of the potential time involved and concern that the intervention will be insufficient, the advantage of *limited guardianship* is that the ward is "protected without over protecting" (Kapp, 2001).

Gove and George (2001) identified efforts in countries in the European Union to make *protective services* such as guardianship more flexible and promote the least restrictive intervention. These include graduated levels of guardianship depending on how much protection is required, as well as more consultation with wards around decision-making and greater consideration of the ward's preferences. In the United States, most states separate guardianship into decisional power of the person (e.g., living arrangements, physical well-being, and medical treatment) and the estate (e.g., managing property, assets, and income). A guardian can be appointed for one or both areas. In states that follow the UPC terminology, *guardian* indicates management of personal decisions and *conservator* denotes management of the *estate* (Hurme, 1991).

Research

Guardianship research falls into 4 broad areas: (1) descriptive characteristics of wards and their guardians, (2) judicial processes and procedures, (3) less restrictive services to avoid or delay guardianship, and (4) ward's experience of guardianship. As reviewed in Reynolds (1997), descriptive studies suggest that wards are likely to be females over age 65 years with relatively low income (Associated Press, 1987; Bulcroft, Kielkopf, & Tripp, 1991; Friedman & Savage, 1988; Keith & Wacker, 1994; Stevenson & Capezuti, 1991). Estimates of the prevalence of dementia among wards ranged from 16% (Associated Press, 1987) to 60% (Stevenson & Capezuti, 1991). In addition to descriptive information, a number of studies have focused on the process and performance of legal guardianship. Identified problems include lack of due process in court proceedings, poor performance and abuse by guardians, lack of sufficient oversight by the courts, and use of guardianship to serve third party interests and social control purposes (Hommel, 1996; Keith & Wacker, 1994; Schmidt, 1990; Zimny, Diamond, Mau, Law, & Chung, 1997). Although a number of reform efforts have been underway during the last decade, implementation has been slow and uneven. For a summary of recent reforms in state guardianship legislation, see a report by the American Bar Association's Commission on Law and Aging at www.abanet.org/aging/guardian1.pdf.

In addition to reform efforts, there has been increasing interest in ensuring that guardianship is used only as a last resort. As a result, a variety of financial and health-related decision-making services have been identified as potential substitutes or preventive interventions for plenary guardianship (Hommel & Wood, 1990; Kapp, 1996; Stiegel, 1992; Wilber, 1991; Wilber & Reynolds, 1995). These include *daily money management* (DMM), *case management*, *durable powers-of-attorney*, *trusts*, and temporary and limited guardianships. Such options hold the promise of safeguarding vulnerable older adults without compromising their rights to make personal and financial decisions. To date, studies of case management and DMM interventions have not demonstrated that these less restrictive services replace or delay guardianship (Center for Social Gerontology, www.tcsg.org/guard.htm; Wilber, 1991; Wilber, 1996; Wilber & Reynolds, 1995). In contrast, a program in which trained volunteers served as *temporary guardians* for hospitalized older persons with no known family or designated decision makers appeared to reduce the need for permanent guardianships (Gibson & Nathanson, 1988). At least 2 studies have looked at guardianship from the ward's perspective. Wilber and colleagues (2001), who examined court documents and interviewed 50 wards, noted that guardians appeared to be doing a reasonable job of managing, and that most wards were either unaware of their guardianship status or did not indicate that it was a problem. Wards did, however, disclose problems of loneliness, personal regrets, and social isolation. Teaster's (2003) study of 13 wards of public guardians found that about half did not realize their status or understand what guardianship was and that *loneliness* and fear were common problems. In both studies, the decision-making roles of wards varied widely. Wilber and colleagues (2001) found that about 40% of the sample exercised no authority, with 25% having responsibility for decisions in 1 or more substantive domains (i.e., health care, spending, living arrangements). These studies support efforts by European Union countries (Gove & Georges, 2001) to encourage consultation with the ward, and, to the extent feasible, support the ward's involvement in both "everyday" and substantive decision-making.

Population aging is likely to result in increases in guardianship and other forms of surrogate decision-making. Despite guardianship's ancient roots in Roman civil law and medieval English common law, the concepts underlying guardianship are still evolving (Schmidt, 1995). Continued efforts to systematically describe the characteristics of guardianship, wards, and guardians, as well as to strike the right balance between civil liberties and the need for protective interventions, present important challenges for the 21st century.

KATHLEEN H. WILBER

See also
Competence

References

American Bar Association's Commission on Law and Aging. (2004). State adult guardianship legislation: Directions of reform. Available: http://www.abanet.org/aging/guardian1.pdf

Associated Press (1987). *A special report: Guardians of the elderly*. New York: Associated Press.

Bulcroft, K. A., Kielkopf, M. R., & Tripp, K. (1991). Elderly wards and their legal guardians: Analysis of county probate records in Ohio and Washington. *Gerontologist, 31,* 156–164.

Center for Social Gerontology. (2004). Guardianship search. Available: http://www.tcsg.org/guard.htm.

Friedman, L., &. Savage, M. (1988). Taking care: The law of conservatorship in California. *Southern California Law Review, 61,* 273–290.

Gibson, J. M., & Nathanson, P. S. (1988). Medical treatment guardian program. *Final Report to the Retirement Research Foundation,* Albuquerque: University of New Mexico School of Law.

Gove, D., & Georges, J. (2001). Perspective on legislation relating to the rights and protection of people with dementia in Europe. *Aging and Mental Health, 5,* 316–321.

Hommel, P. A. (1996). Guardianship reform in the 1980s: A decade of substantive and procedural change. In M. Smyer, K. W. Schaie, & M. B. Kapp (Eds.), *Older adults' decision-making and the law* (pp. 225–253). New York: Springer Publishing.

Hommel, P. A., & Wood, E. F. (1990). Guardianship: There are alternatives. *Aging, 360,* 6–12.

Hurme, S. B. (1991). *Steps to enhancing guardianship monitoring*. Washington, DC: American Bar Association.

Iris, M. A. (1988). Guardianship and the elderly: A multi-perspective view of the decision-making process. *Gerontologist, 28*(Suppl.), 39–45.

Kapp, M. B. (1996). Alternatives to guardianship: Enhanced autonomy for diminished capacity. In M. A. Smyer, K. W. Schaie, & M. B. Kapp (Eds.), *Older adults' decision-making and the law* (pp. 182–201). New York: Springer Publishing.

Kapp, M. B. (1999). *Geriatrics and the law: Patient rights and responsibilities* (3rd ed.). New York: Springer Publishing.

Kapp, M. B. (2001). Legal interventions for persons with dementia in the USA: Ethical, policy, and practical aspects. *Aging and Mental Health, 5,* 312–315.

Keith, P. M., & Wacker, R. R. (1994). *Older wards and their guardians*. Westport, CT: Praeger Publishers.

National Guardianship Association, Inc. (2004). Guardianship search. Available: http://www.guardianship.org/displaycommon.cfm?an=2

Rein, J. E. (1992). Preserving dignity and self-determination of the elderly in the face of competing interests and grim alternatives: A proposal for statutory refocus and reform. *George Washington Law Review, 60,* 1818–1887.

Reynolds, S. L. (1997). Criteria for placing older adults in public conservatorship: Age as proxy for need. *Gerontologist, 37,* 518–526.

Reynolds, S. L., & Wilber, K. H. (1997). Protecting persons with severe cognitive and mental disorders: An analysis of public conservatorship in Los Angeles County, California. *Aging and Mental Health, 1,* 87–97.

Sabatino, C. P. (1996). Competency: Refining our legal fictions. In M. Smyer, K. W. Schaie, & M. B. Kapp (Eds.), *Older adults' decision-making and the law* (pp. 1–28). New York: Springer Publishing.

Schmidt, W. C. (1990). Quantitative information about the quality of the guardianship system: Toward the next generation of guardianship research. *Probate Law Journal, 10,* 61–80.

Schmidt, W. C., Miller, K. S., Bell, W. G., & New, B. E. (1981). *Public guardianship and the elderly*. Cambridge, MA: Ballinger Publishing Company.

Schmidt, W. C. (1996). Revising revisionism in guardianship: An assessment of legal reform of decisional capacity. In M. Smyer, K. W. Schaie, & M. B. Kapp (Eds.), *older adults' decision-making and the law* (pp. 269–282). New York: Springer Publishing.

Siemon, D., Hurme, S. B., & Sabatino, C. P. (1993). Public guardianship: Where is it and what does it need? *Clearinghouse Review,* October, 588–599.

Stevenson, C., & Capezuti, E. (1991). Guardianship: Protection versus peril. *Geriatric Nursing, 12,* 10–13.

Teaster, P. B. (2003). When the state takes over a life: The public guardian as public administrator. *Public Administration Review, 63,* 396–404.

Wilber, K. H. (1991). Alternatives to conservatorship: The role of daily money management services. *Gerontologist, 31*(2), 150–155.

Wilber, K. H. (1996). What's risk got to do with it? Revisiting alternatives to guardianship. In M. A. Smyer, K. W. Schaie, & M. B. Kapp (Eds.), *Older adults' decision-making and the law* (pp: 213–224). New York: Springer Publishing.

Wilber, K. H., & Reynolds, S. L. (1995). Rethinking alternatives to guardianship. *Gerontologist, 35,* 248–257.

Wilber, K. H., Reiser, T., & Harter, K. (2001). New perspectives on conservatorship: Views of older adult conservatees and their conservators, *Aging, Neuropsychology, and Cognition 8,* 225–240.

Zimny, G. H., Diamond, J. A., Mau, M. M., Law, A. C. K., & Chung, C. (1997). Six-year longitudinal study of finances of elderly wards under guardianship. *Journal of Ethics, Law, and Aging, 3,* 91–101.

H

HAIR

Why do some people look older than they are? In an average cross-section of men and women, the answer to this question was their hair color and its distribution in both sexes (Bulpitt, 2001).With such significance, it is important that those who care for older adults understand the simple underlying mechanisms of hair growth, its color, distribution, and common disorders, and to be able to explain these mechanisms in terms tailored for the older individual. This can relieve much anxiety in the elderly.

Race and inheritance, the influence of circulating *androgens* (male hormone) on the hair follicle (root) in different sites, and nutrition should all be considered. The variability of response of the hair bulb to circulating androgens is complex and accounts for the extensive variability in expression (Alonso, 2003). For details of anatomy and physiology, consult earlier editions of this work, the recent review by Paus and colleagues (1999) and papers by Alonso (2003), Hordinsky and colleagues (2002), and Yaar and colleagues (2001).

The approach to a *hair problem* should begin with the scalp, proceed to the hair follicle, and then the shaft. The *scalp* is usually seen easily in the older person due to sparse hair. If the hair is thick, it can be gently moved by pushing it apart with the side of the hand against the direction of growth. *Seborrheic dermatitis* and *psoriasis*, a variety of warty tumors, birthmarks, and, more rarely, malignant tumors can then be seen.

Regarding *hair color*, *aging of the hair* and skin is preordained on a clock-like basis for each species (Yaar & Gilchrest, 2001). *Loss of melanin* pigment is due to decline of the *melanocytes* (pigment producing cells), air being trapped between previously impermeable cell junctions, and possibly nerve supply changes with age. Race and inheritance are important, but there is no evidence that disease or nutrition play an important part in color or normal age-related change.

Heredity plays a large part in the common problem of *hair thinning*. Diffuse, lank hair due to follicular miniaturization is much more pronounced in older persons in the hereditary androgenetic *(male) type of balding*. When the normal anatomical and physiological status of a person's hair is interpreted and explained, there remain the effects of subnutrition and disease to be considered.

Dietary inadequacy with impaired protein intake is a common cause of lusterless hair in those living alone or who are institutionalized. Vitamin and *nutritional deficiencies* are much too common in the older adult population (Schneider & Norman, 2004), and this subject is addressed elsewhere in this publication. It has been estimated that as many as 55% of hospitalized older adults and up to 85% of institutionalized elderly persons are *undernourished.*

Since 1963, a relationship between *iron deficiency* expressed as low serum *ferritin* has been suspected. Evidence for this became much stronger in the preceding decade, when it was realized that iron deficiency expressed as serum ferritin was much more prevalent than previously recognized (Rushton, 2003). There is convincing evidence of the role of iron deficiency in causing impaired oxygen supply and deficiency of iron-containing compounds to the tissues. The optimum range is yet to be established, but the detailed study of Kantor (2003) should be consulted.

Minerals and trace elements have been increasingly recognized as important (McClain, McClain, Barve, & Boosalis, 2002). *Selenium* and *zinc* deficiencies are raised sometimes as possible causes of *hair loss*, but without much supportive evidence (Jacobs & Wood, 2003), and convenient way of detecting poor nutrition and is of prognostic value in older persons.

Once nutrition has been assessed, the possibility of systemic disease should be considered (Sperling, 2001; Hordinsky et al., 2002; Alonso, 2003). *Telogen effluvium* occurs when there is an arrest of normal hair fall and then, after an interval of time, a delayed shedding. This may be physiologic, as after childbirth, or pathologic, such as after a prolonged febrile illness or certain other illnesses.

Medications can cause hair loss. A number (Sperling, 2001) cause telogen effluvium but others, such as *anti-cancer drugs*, target the early growing phase of the hair, primarily causing *anagen loss*.

The patchy, disc-shaped hair loss termed *alopecia areata* is much less common in older adults. It occurs when there is an interruption of the hair growth early in the anagen phase. The hair shaft is then carried to the surface when it falls out after tapering at its scalp end. Sometimes the condition is diffuse, lacking the disc-shaped bald patches. This diagnosis is easily overlooked.

Scarring destruction can cause *baldness*. The causes are varied and include thermal burn, a number of chronic inflammatory disorders, and malignant disease. The malignant disorders are most commonly secondary cancer metastasis, such as from the breast or lung, and malignant lymphoma such as *mycosis fungoides*.

The influence of hormones in older adults, and particularly in males, is a complex issue. Any decision concerning *hormone supplementation* is not undertaken lightly (Vermeulen, 2001). *Hyperthyroidism* may be present with its only sign as fine hair with a friable scalp. Similarly *hypothyroidism* may have as its only sign coarse, brittle hair or diffuse alopecia and thinning of the lateral eyebrows (Schneider & Norman, 2004).

When the assessment of the scalp surface has been done and disorders of the follicle have been considered, there remains the *hair shaft*. Hair shaft abnormalities are rare except for chemical damage from overuse of cosmetic agents such as bleaches. However, if the shaft is not examined, *head lice* with its nits (egg cases) can easily be overlooked, as well as rarer *pubic and body lice* (Huynh & Norman, 2004).

An orderly plan for the investigation of hair disorder in older adults is most important. The recent paper by Barth (2001) provides an excellent summary and should be consulted.

Above all, a patient's concern for hair problems and *self-esteem* must be recognized and respected. Even those suffering from various stages of dementia often remain concerned about their appearance. Good caregivers know of the feeling of well-being after a visit to the hairdresser. A recent paper by Cash (2001) deals with the psychological and emotional aspects relating to hair in detail. It should be read by all who must deal with hair problems in older adults.

J. B. Ross

References

Alonso, L. C. (2003). Molecular genetic and endocrine mechanisms of hair growth. *Hormone Research, 60*(1), 1–13.

Barth, J. H. (2001). Rational investigations in the diagnosis and management of women with hirsutism or androgenetic alopecia. *Clinics in Dermatology, 19*(2), 155–160.

Bulpitt, C. J. (2001). Why do some people look older than they should? *Journal of Postgraduate Medicine, 77*(911), 578–581.

Cash, T. F. (2001). The psychology of hair loss and its implications for patient care. *Clinics in Dermatology, 19*(2), 161–166.

Hordinsky, M., Sawaya, M., & Roberts, J. L. (2002). Hair loss and hirsutism in the elderly. Geriatric dermatology, Part II. *Clinics in Geriatric Medicine, 18*(1), 121–130.

Huynh, T. H., & Norman, R. A. (2004). Scabies and pediculosis. *Dermatology Clinics, 22*(1), 7–11.

Jacobs, P., & Wood, L. (2003). Hematology of malnutrition, part one. *Disease-A-Month, 49*(10), 555–618.

Kantor, J. (2003). Decreased serum ferritin is associated with alopecia in women. *Journal of Investigative Dermatology, 121*(5), 985.

McClain, C. J., McClain, M., Barve, S., & Boosalis, M. G. (2002). Trace metals and the elderly. *Clinics in Geriatric Medicine, 18*(4), 801–818.

Paus, R., & Cotsarelis, G. (1999). The biology of hair follicles. *New England Journal of Medicine, 341,* 491–497.

Rushton, D. H. (2003). Decreased serum ferritin and alopecia in women. *Journal of Investigative Dermatology, 121*(5), xvii .

Schneider, J. B., & Norman, R. A. (2004). Cutaneous manifestations of endocrine-metabolic disease and nutritional deficiency in the elderly. *Dermatologic Clinics, 22,* 23–31.

Sperling, L. C. (2001). Hair and systemic disease. *Dermatologic Clinics, 19*(4), 711–726.

Vermeulen, A. (2001). Androgen replacement therapy in the aging male: A critical evaluation. *Journal of Clinical Endocrinology and Metabolism, 86,* 6.

Yaar, M., & Gilchrest, B. A. (2001). Skin aging: Geriatric dermatology, part I. Postulated mechanisms and consequent changes in structure and function. *Clinics in Geriatric Medicine, 17,* 4.

HEALTH AND RETIREMENT STUDY

The *Health and Retirement Study* (HRS) is a nationally representative, prospective study of persons born in 1953 or earlier, designed to investigate the health, social, and economic implications of the *aging of the U.S. population* (Juster & Suzman, 1995; Soldo, Hurd, Rodgers, & Wallace, 1997). The HRS is funded by the National Institute on Aging and conducted by the Institute for Social Research at the University of Michigan. Detailed information on the study population, survey content, methodology, publications using HRS data, and procedures for obtaining HRS data can be found at the HRS Web site: hrsonline.isr.umich.edu.

The current HRS combines 5 national cohorts of study subjects that were enrolled at different times: (1) the original HRS cohort of individuals born between 1931 and 1941, followed since 1992; (2) the Asset and Health Dynamics Among the Oldest Old (AHEAD) cohort of individuals born between 1890 and 1923, followed since 1993; (3) the Children of the Depression Age cohort of those born between 1924 and 1930, followed since 1998; (4) the War Babies cohort of those born between 1942 and 1947, followed since 1998; and (5) the Early Baby Boomer cohort of those born between 1948 and 1953, enrolled in 2004. (See hrsonline.isr.umich.edu/intro/dataflow.html for more information on the HRS study cohorts.) Spouses of HRS respondents, regardless of their year of birth, are included in the HRS sample. African American and Hispanic individuals are oversampled. With these 5 cohorts the HRS now represents the entire U.S. population over 50 years of age with a national sample of more than 30,000 individuals (including over 5,000 who have died after their entry into the sample).

Interviews are conducted with all HRS respondents every 2 years and current funding supports data collection through the year 2004. Interviews are conducted both by telephone and face-to-face, with the latter mode used preferentially for those age 80 or older. Approximately 10% of the interviews are done with proxy informants for sample members who are unable or unwilling to complete the survey interview themselves, but are willing to have someone else (most often a spouse or daughter) answer for them. Approximately 40% of proxy interviews are performed due to cognitive impairment in the respondent.

HRS Measures

The HRS collects an extensive set of data on the demographics, health, employment, wealth, family structure, and family transfers (both financial and caregiving) of study subjects (Juster & Suzman, 1995). The general categories of HRS questionnaire topics include:

- Health
- Cognitive conditions and status
- Retirement plans and perspectives
- Attitudes, preferences, expectations, and subjective probabilities
- Family structure and transfers
- Employment status and job history
- Job demands and requirements
- Disability
- Demographic background
- Housing
- Income and net worth
- Health insurance and pension plans

Full documentation for all survey measures and variables is available at the HRS web site.

Data Linkages

HRS data is supplemented with administrative data from 4 different sources:

- Pension information from the Employer Pension Study (1993, 1999)
- Medicare claims and summary files from the Centers for Medicare and Medicaid Services (CMS)
- Cause of death from the National Center for Health Statistics (NCHS) National Death Index
- Earnings, benefits, wage and self-employment income, and SSI data derived from Social Security administrative files

HRS Supplemental Studies

Two HRS supplemental studies funded by the National Institute on Aging have allowed the collection of additional and more detailed data on 2 important aging-related health conditions: *dementia* and *diabetes*.

To better understand the impact of dementia on older individuals, their families, and society, the

HRS under took the *Aging, Demographics, and Memory Study* (ADAMS) in 2001. The ADAMS was designed to provide national data on the antecedents, prevalence, outcomes, and costs of dementia and "*cognitive impairment, not demented*" (CIND) using a unique study design building upon the HRS. A sample of 856 individuals aged 70 or older who were HRS participants received an extensive in-home clinical and neuropsychological assessment to determine a diagnosis of normal, CIND, or dementia. Within the CIND and dementia categories, subcategories (e.g., Alzheimer's disease, vascular dementia) were assigned to denote the etiology of cognitive impairment. The ADAMS is the first population-based study of dementia in the United States to include subjects from all regions of the country, while at the same time using a single standardized diagnostic protocol in a community-based sample. Linking the ADAMS clinical assessment data to the wealth of available longitudinal HRS data on health, health care utilization, informal care, and economic resources and behavior will provide a unique opportunity to study the onset of CIND and dementia in a nationally representative population-based sample, as well as the risk factors, prevalence, outcomes, and costs of CIND and dementia. Data from the ADAMS will be available to researchers in 2005.

In 2003, HRS investigators undertook a supplemental mailed survey to provide more detailed information on diabetes management, glycemic control, and its long-term causes and consequences in U.S. adults. About 2,000 HRS respondents who reported having diabetes on the HRS 2002 wave were mailed an additional questionnaire on: diabetes care and self-management (e.g., health care utilization, educational participation, regular monitoring, prescription drug use, exercise); predictors of self-management and use of care (e.g., perceived probabilities of adverse outcomes and complications, and perceived effectiveness of treatments); and the impact of diabetes on their health and well-being (e.g., medical complications and comorbidities, and psychological burden). An innovative feature of the diabetes mail survey was the inclusion of a self-administered kit to collect a blood drop sample from participants. The blood sample was used to determine the level of glycosylated hemoglobin (HgbA1c), a widely used clinical biomarker that measures the average level of blood glucose over the prior 6 to 10 weeks. The availability of HgbA1c in the HRS mail survey will allow researchers to relate self-reported management behaviors and medical treatments directly to a clinical measure of effectiveness. HRS diabetes mail survey data will be available to researchers in 2005.

Two other HRS supplemental mailed surveys have been fielded to provide additional data to the research community. In 2001, the *Human Capital and Educational Expenses Mail Survey* (HUMS) was sent to about 4,000 HRS households who were likely to have had at least 1 child 18 years of age or older. The questions in the HUMS were designed to facilitate research regarding parental investment in the human capital of their children, the allocation of parental resources across their offspring, and the effect of educational expenditures on mid-life savings of parents. Finally, the 2001 *Consumption and Activities Mail Survey* (CAMS) was sent to about 4,000 HRS respondents to gather information on consumption of consumer goods (e.g., cars, household appliances, and computers), activities (e.g., watching TV, exercising, and sleeping), and the use of prescription medications. In 2003, a follow-up CAMS questionnaire was sent to those in the original CAMS cohort to support analyses of change over time in consumption and activities measures.

Results from the HRS

Data from the HRS are available free of charge to the research community. As of April 2004, an estimated 2,500 investigators had either used or were registered to use the HRS data, and over 800 publications and reports had been prepared based on the data. (A searchable bibliography of publications using HRS data is available at the HRS Web site.) The breadth of longitudinal data available in the HRS allows nationally representative studies of a wide range of economic, health, and family issues that critically affect aging in the United States. Selected recent publications include studies of: the causal paths between health and socioeconomic status (Adams, Hurd, McFadden, Merrill, & Ribeiro, 2003); the impact of pension incentives on the decision to retire (Chan & Stevens, 2004); the effect of technological change on older workers (Friedberg, 2003); the impact of marital status on wealth among pre-retirement adults (Wilmoth & Koso, 2002); the influence of cognitive impairment on life expectancy (Suthers, Kim, & Crimmins, 2003); the amount of family care provided to older adults suffering from depression (Langa, Valenstein, Fendrick, Kabeto, & Vijan, 2004); the impact of living arrangements on health (Hughes & Waite, 2002); the effect of gaining Medicare coverage on the health care services received by previously uninsured adults (McWilliams, Zaslavsky, Meara, & Ayanian, 2003); and the impact on health of not taking medicines due to their cost (Heisler, Langa, Eby, Fendrick, Kabeto, & Piette, 2004).

KENNETH M. LANGA

See also
Longitudinal Research

References

Adams, P., Hurd, M. D., McFadden, D., Merrill, A., & Ribeiro, T. (2003). Healthy, wealthy, and wise? Tests for direct causal paths between health and socioeconomic status. *Journal of Econometrics*, *112*(1), 3–56.

Chan, S., & Stevens, A. H. (2004). Do changes in pension incentives affect retirement? A longitudinal study of subjective retirement expectations. *Journal of Public Economics*, *88*(7–8), 1307–1333.

Friedberg, L. (2003). The impact of technological change on older workers: Evidence from data on computer use. *Industrial and Labor Relations Review*, *56*(3), 511–529.

Heisler, M., Langa, K., Eby, E., Fendrick, A., Kabeto, M., & Piette, J. (2004). The health effects of restricting prescription medication use because of cost. *Medical Care*, *42*(7), 626–634.

Hughes, M., & Waite, L. (2002). Health in household context: Living arrangements and health in late middle age. *Journal of Health and Social Behavior*, *43*(1), 1–21.

Juster, F., & Suzman, R. (1995). An overview of the health and retirement study. *Journal of Human Resources*, *30* (Suppl.), S7–S56.

Langa, K. M., Valenstein, M. A., Fendrick, A. M., Kabeto, M. U., & Vijan, S. (2004). Extent and cost of informal caregiving for older Americans with symptoms of depression. *American Journal of Psychiatry*, *161*(5), 857–863.

McWilliams, J. M., Zaslavsky, A. M., Meara, E., & Ayanian, J. Z. (2003). Impact of Medicare coverage on basic clinical services for previously uninsured adults. *Journal of the American Medical Association*, *290*(6), 757–764.

Soldo, B., Hurd, M., Rodgers, W., & Wallace, R. (1997). Asset and health dynamics among the oldest old: An overview of the AHEAD Study. *Journal of Gerontology Series B: Psychological Sciences and Social Sciences*, *52B*(Special Issue), 1–20.

Suthers, K., Kim, J., & Crimmins, E. (2003). Life expectancy with cognitive impairment in the older population of the United States. *Journal of Gerontology: Social Sciences 58B*(3), S179–S186.

Wilmoth, J., & Koso, G. (2002). Does marital history matter? Marital status and wealth outcomes among preretirement adults. *Journal of Marriage and Family*, *64*(1), 254–268.

HEALTH BELIEFS

Reviews of health beliefs typically focus on belief systems underlying behavior for prevention and management of health threats, such as the *health belief model*, *social learning theory*, and the *common-sense model of self-regulation* (CSM). Two other sets of beliefs are included in this brief survey: *self-assessments of health* (SAH) and emotional traits and states. The following text briefly reviews the major themes guiding research in each domain, and points to the relationships among them that warrant their inclusion under a common heading.

More than 50 studies in nations worldwide have related responses to the question of health status to mortality and morbidity (Benyamini & Idler, 1999; Idler & Benyamini, 1997). In response to the question, “Would you rate your health as excellent, very good, good, fair, or poor?”, those in the fair-to-poor range predict elevated risk of mortality over brief (5 months) and extended timeframes (20 years in the NHANES study: Idler, Leventhal, McLaughlin, & Leventhal, 2004), even after controlling for the respondents’ age and medical status at the time of assessment. This provides an excellent measure of health status in *health surveys*. Studies examining the information used for SAH judgments show direct links to studies of *emotion and health*, and beliefs related to self-management. For example, low SAH ratings are associated with increased difficulties in performing activities of daily living, *negative emotional states* (depressed and anxious mood), and greater numbers of physical symptoms and medical diagnoses (Idler, Leventhal,

McLaughlin, & Leventhal, 2004). *Positive emotions* appear to bias reports upward (Benyamini, Idler, Leventhal, & Leventhal, 2000). Although the picture is incomplete, the inability to perform *activities of daily living* appears to be the most important determinant of SAH judgments, and positive affect the weakest determinant of SAH. Surprisingly, there is little evidence that SAH is related to motivation to take preventive or curative action. Finally, although SAH ratings are excellent indicators of future status, there is no evidence that they are *causally* related to health outcomes; prediction is not causation.

Multiple models have guided studies of behavior for prevention and management of chronic diseases such as cancer, diabetes, and hypertension. All identify 2 large sets of behavioral determinants: external factors (e.g., institutional structure and social influences), and internal factors (such as beliefs about and perceptions of health threats and plans for action). A combination of social learning theory (Bandura, 1998) and the CSM (Cameron & Leventhal, 2003) provides the most current and comprehensive approach to the analysis of these behavioral processes. The CSM proposes that both concrete experience with disease and treatment as well as abstract beliefs guide behavior. The abstract representations (e.g., asthma is acute rather than chronic, cancer is an acute lump to be excised by surgery rather than a chronic, systemic condition) are shaped by experience (asthma is experienced as a series of episodic attacks; patients told by their surgeon that he "got it all" communicate this to family and friends). This creates an expanded representation of a potential or existent disease and the framework for formulating and evaluating the efficacy of both preventive and treatment behaviors. These representations have an identity (disease label and associated symptoms), timeline (onset, duration, and time for cure), cause (diet, virus, genes), consequences (death, surgery, physical decline), and control beliefs (breast cancer can be perceived to be incurable). Perceived effectiveness and continued use of specific preventive and treatment behaviors is further influenced by experience with these behaviors (do they control symptoms; enhance positive emotion, etc.) and social observations and direct messages about the behavior's positive and negative effects. Over a half dozen simple questions or heuristics are used to evaluate the meaning of somatic changes (e.g., age vs. illness, stress response vs. illness, location, duration, novelty), and the efficacy of treatment (no effect in expected timeline, did not alter symptoms). The likelihood of performing specific preventive and self-management behaviors is greatly increased by the formation of action plans—that is, the identification of specific cues (places and times) to initiate the first step for a sequence of preventive and/or treatment behaviors (Leventhal, 1970; Ruiter, Abraham, & Kok, 2001). A well structured system will create a sense of control or self-efficacy in threat/disease management. An ongoing increase in the conduct of intervention trials promises major advances in this domain.

Reports of *negative affect* (depressed and anxious moods and cognitions) have been related to mortality over multiple years in epidemiological studies (Herrmann, Brand-Driehorst, Kaminsky, Leibing, Staats, & Rueger, 1998) and over shorter timeframes in clinical populations (e.g., mortality following myocardial infarction: Frasure-Smith, Lesperance, & Talajic, 1995; Lesperance & Frasure-Smith, 2000). Investigators and the participants in these studies share a belief that negative emotions and *stress* predict and cause negative health outcomes. Studies of the direct pathway from stress to susceptibility to infection (Cohen, Frank, Doyle, Skoner, Rabin, & Gwaltney, 1998; Cohen, Tyrrell, & Smith, 1997) and depression as an antecedent to coronary disease mortality are related to studies of health belief, as investigators must control for healthy and risky behaviors to support the hypothesis of a direct pathway. The data for a direct pathway for stress and depression to cancer is negative for both epidemiological studies (Costa & McCrae, 1985) and for studies of social support, positive mood, and survival (Palmer & Coyne, 2004). The connections among emotion, health beliefs, and health outcomes are clear in studies showing that beliefs/perceptions of illness as chronic, unpredictable, and disruptive of daily function (domains of health beliefs) create a pathway to depression, and symptoms of depression are related to poor treatment adherence and poor health outcomes (DiMatteo, Lepper, & Croghan, 2000). Negative emotions however, can encourage health protective behaviors if the emotions are associated with specific beliefs and measured that way. For example, the fear that diabetes can lead to foot amputation is related to better foot care by diabetics, and the fear that HIV/AIDS can lead to death is related to better adherence to antiviral medication.

No studies have examined whether believing that *emotions cause disease* (e.g., the belief that stress is a cause of disease) is responsible for the relationship of emotion either to health behaviors or health outcomes.

The following are the important connections among these 3 domains that are now under study:

(1) Is ability to function in everyday activities the factor that creates the negative association of depression and the positive association of happiness with SAH and mortality?
(2) Do commonsense cultural beliefs about stress and negative moods (i.e., that they have negative effects on health, and happiness has positive effects) encourage respectively the exaggeration and minimization of perceived disease risk, the discouragement of stressful activities that are associated with health benefits, and the encouragement of positive activities that are associated with negative health outcomes?
(3) Are the same or different commonsense beliefs about disease, prevention, treatment and emotion responsible for the initiation and the maintenance of healthy and risky behaviors?
(4) Do sociocultural and institutional structures and professional practices inadvertently create beliefs and perceptions of illness and treatment that have negative effects on adherence to recommended preventive and treatment behaviors?

HOWARD LEVENTHAL
PABLO A. MORA
CRISTINA SHAFER HOWARD

References

Bandura, A. (1998). Health promotion from the perspective of social cognitive theory. *Psychology and Health, 13*(4), 623–649.

Benyamini, Y., & Idler, E. L. (1999). Community studies reporting association between self-rated health and mortality: Additional studies 1995–1998. *Research on Aging, 21*(3), 392–401.

Benyamini, Y., Idler, E., Leventhal, H., & Leventhal, E. A. (2000). Positive affect and function as influences on self-assessments of health: Expanding our view beyond illness and disability. *Journals of Gerontology Series B, Psychological Sciences and Social Sciences, 55B*(2), P107–P116.

Cameron, L. D., & Leventhal, H. (2003). *The self-regulation of health and illness behavior.* London, New York: Routledge.

Cohen, S., Frank, E., Doyle, W. J., Skoner, D. P., Rabin, B. S., & Gwaltney, J. M., Jr. (1998). Types of stressors that increase susceptibility to the common cold in healthy adults. *Health Psychology, 17*(3), 214–223.

Cohen, S., Tyrrell, D. A. J., & Smith, A. P. (1997). Psychological stress in humans and susceptibility to the common cold. In T. W. Miller (Ed.), *Clinical disorders and stressful life events. International Universities Press stress and health series* (pp. 217–235). Madison, CT: International Universities Press.

Costa, P. T., & McCrae, R. R. (1985). Hypochondriasis, neuroticism, and aging: When are somatic complaints unfounded? *American Psychologist, 40*(1), 19–28.

DiMatteo, M. R., Lepper, H. S., & Croghan, T. W. (2000). Depression is a risk factor for noncompliance with medical treatment: Meta-analysis of the effects of anxiety and depression on patient adherence. *Archives of Internal Medicine, 160*(14), 2101–2107.

Frasure-Smith, N., Lesperance, F., & Talajic, M. (1995). The impact of negative emotions on prognosis following myocardial infarction: Is it more than depression? *Health Psychology, 14*(5), 388–398.

Herrmann, C., Brand-Driehorst, S., Kaminsky, B., Leibing, E., Staats, H., & Rueger, U. (1998). Diagnostic groups and depressed mood as predictors of 22-month mortality in medical inpatients. *Psychosomatic Medicine, 60*(5), 570–577.

Idler, E., & Benyamini, Y. (1997). Self-rated health and mortality: A review of twenty-seven community studies. *Journal of Health and Social Behavior, 38*(1), 21–37.

Idler, E., Leventhal, H., McLaughlin, J., & Leventhal, E. A. (2004). In sickness but not in health: Self-ratings, identity, and mortality. *Journal of Health and Social Behavior, 45*(3), 336–356.

Lesperance, F., & Frasure-Smith, N. (2000). Depression in patients with cardiac disease: A practical review. *Journal of Psychosomatic Research, 48*(4-5), 379–391.

Leventhal, H. (1970). Findings and theory in the study of fear communications. In L. Berkowitz (Ed.), *Advances in experimental social psychology* (vol. 5, pp. 120–186). New York: Academic Press.

Palmer, S. C., & Coyne, J. C. (2004). Examining the evidence that psychotherapy improves the survival of cancer patients. *Biological Psychiatry, 56*(1), 61–62.

Ruiter, R. A. C., Abraham, C., & Kok, G. (2001). Scary warnings and rational precautions: A review of the psychology of fear appeals. *Psychology and Health, 16*(6), 613–630.

HEALTH CARE: FINANCING, USE, AND ORGANIZATION

The organization and *financing of health care* in the United States is undergoing continuous and major revisions, leading to constant changes in the patterns of use. Such changes are largely due to attempts by governmental and corporate entities that pay for an overwhelming proportion of American health care to limit their payments in an era when health care prices are inflating at a high rate. Some changes, however, are also due to efforts by reformers to create new mechanisms for providing more effective care on a cost-efficient basis.

Health care of older persons is a central ingredient in these changes, and will remain so for many years. One reason is that persons aged 65 years and older account for about one-third of annual U.S. health care costs. Per capita expenditures on older persons are 4 times greater than on younger persons. In addition, a substantial amount of health care for older persons, especially long-term care, is financed through in-kind services from relatives and friends that are not readily quantifiable as expenditures.

A second reason is that the federal *Medicare program*, which provides a basic package of *health insurance* for 95% of Americans who are aged 65 and older (as well as some 5 million other persons who receive federal *disability insurance*, or who have end-stage renal disease), is the single biggest source of payment for U.S. health care. In 2003, Medicare paid for 17% of all national healthcare expenditures (Centers for Medicare and Medicaid Services, 2005). Its expenditures are projected to increase from $309 billion in 2004 to $561 billion in 2010 (Federal Hospital Insurance and Federal Supplementary Medical Insurance Trust Funds, 2005).

Still another reason is that the economic and political challenges of financing health care for older persons in the first half of the 21st century are substantial. The number of older Americans will grow sharply during this period as the *baby-boom* birth cohort reaches the ranks of old age. Moreover, the number of persons of advanced old age—in their late 70s and older—will increase markedly, and in this older age range the rates of illnesses and disabilities requiring health care are much higher than among the rest of the population. Even if important advances are made in treatments, illness prevention, and health promotion, they are unlikely to have a major impact in eliminating the overall extent of illness and disability in old age in the next several decades. Consequently, the aggregate health care needs of the older population will be even greater in the future than they are now. For example, the proportion of national wealth (gross domestic product) spent on Medicare in 2004 was 2.6%; it is projected to more than double, to 7.5%, in 2035, when most baby boomers will be aged 65 and older (Federal Hospital Insurance and Federal Supplementary Medical Insurance Trust Funds, 2005).

In the current context of rapid change in U.S. health care, in which the challenges of providing care for older people play a central role, the financing, use, and organization of health care are highly interdependent. Because these elements are inextricably linked and dynamic in their relations, the discussion that follows should be interpreted as artificially compartmentalized, to present a brief overview of a highly complex arena.

Sources of Financing

Governments finance nearly two-thirds of health care for older Americans. Medicare accounts for 46% of the total. *Medicare (Part A)* Hospital Insurance is funded by payroll taxes under the Federal Insurance Contributions Act; 25% of *Medicare's Part B* (nonhospital) Supplementary Medical Insurance is financed by voluntary premiums paid by program participants and 75% of U.S. general revenues.

Medicaid insurance for poor persons who qualify through income and asset tests, jointly funded by the federal and state governments, provides another 15.4%, which is principally spent on long-term care. Health care financed through the Department of Veterans Affairs, Department of Defense, Indian Health Services, and a variety of state and local government programs constitutes about 3.5% of the total. An additional 14.5% is funded through private insurance, and less than 1% comes from philanthropy.

Older persons pay 17.4% of the costs of their care out-of-pocket. Much of this outlay is for *skilled nursing*, which has only minimal Medicare coverage. About 25% of national health care expenditures on older people is for *long-term care* in nursing homes, at home, or in other residential settings; nearly half of these costs are paid for *out-of-pocket* by older persons and their families (Wiener & Illston, 1996). Medicaid pays for most of the rest; only about 1% of *nursing home costs* is paid for through private, long-term-care insurance.

About 63% of Medicare beneficiaries have employer-sponsored retiree health insurance and/or "*Medigap*" private insurance that provides coverage for Medicare deductibles, copayments, partial reimbursement for outpatient prescription drugs, and other gaps in Medicare's coverage (Sharma & Lin, 2004). Those who are enrolled in *Medicare health maintenance organizations* (HMOs) also have supplemental coverage. Yet 41% of prescription drug costs are paid for by older persons out-of-pocket (Centers for Medicare and Medicaid Services, 2005). Poor older persons can have their Medicare Part B premiums, deductibles, and copayments paid for by Medicaid through the *Qualified Medicare Beneficiary* program and the *Specified Low-Income Medicare Beneficiary* program, for which they become eligible through low-income "*means tests.*" Nonetheless, out-of-pocket health care spending for a Medicare beneficiary enrolled in the traditional fee-for-service system averages 18.6% of income (Moon, 1999).

In 2003, Congress enacted the *Medicare Prescription Drug, Improvement, and Modernization Act* (MMA) of 2003 (P.L. 108-173). This law created a new prescription drug benefit, known as *Part D*, and a transitional *drug discount card* program. The drug discount card program was intended to enable beneficiaries to save money by signing up for a Medicare-approved discount card; however, relatively few have chosen to do so (Health Policy Alternatives, 2004). The Part D benefit has a $37 monthly premium, a $250 deductible, partial coverage (75% of costs) up to $2,250, and catastrophic coverage (95% of costs) above the $5,100 threshold. There is a $2,850 gap in coverage; the maximum annual out-of-pocket spending is estimated to be $3,600 (Henry J. Kaiser Family Foundation, 2004a). Low-income beneficiaries will receive a subsidy to cover the costs of premiums and deductibles and will face lower cost-sharing. *Medicare managed care plans* will be required to offer a drug benefit, and insurance companies will be able to market stand-alone drug plans to people in traditional fee-for-service Medicare. Employers who offer retiree health insurance with prescription drug benefits comparable to Part D will receive a subsidy to defray some of the cost of continuing to provide drug coverage, but cannot exceed the basic benefit. Medigap plans will only be allowed to offer *catastrophic coverage*, and Medicaid will not be allowed to offer drug coverage to people who are eligible for both Medicare and Medicaid.

Prospective Payment. From the time that it was established in 1965 until very recently, the Medicare program financed medical care in an open–ended fashion, reimbursing physicians, hospitals, and other health care providers on a fee-for-service (FFS) basis. In the mid–1980s, however, the federal government began efforts to control the growth of Medicare expenditures by launching a *prospective payment system* (PPS) through which fixed payments are made to hospitals for a patient's care according to the "*diagnosis-related group*" (DRG) to which the patient is assigned. This measure slowed the growth of payments to hospitals and shortened the average length of *hospital stays.* A related measure, which began to be implemented in the mid-1990s, was Medicare's attempt to contain its spending for physician services without compromising access to or quality of care. The method combines a resource-based relative value schedule of physician fees, with volume performance standards.

Starting July 1, 1998, Medicare adopted a PPS for beneficiaries who need short-term skilled care in a skilled nursing facility following a hospital stay (MedPac, 2004a). Prior to the implementation of PPS, skilled nursing facilities were paid based on their costs. Under the PPS, payments are made based on assignment of patients to 1 of 44 resource utilization groups, which established a *per diem* rate based on the service needs of the patient and incorporate adjustment for labor costs in the local market. The *per diem* rates have been updated several times since 1998.

Medicare covers in-home services by a *home health agency* for beneficiaries who are confined to their homes and require skilled care provided (such as nursing, physical, occupational or speech therapy) on a part-time or intermittent basis. In October 2000, Medicare adopted a new PPS that pays home health agencies a predetermined rate for each 60-day episode of care (MedPac, 2004b). Payment rates are based on assignment of the patient to one of 80 home health resource groups based on diagnosis, functional capacity, and service use, and incorporates an adjustment for local labor market conditions. The base rate is updated annually.

Prepaid Health Plans. Since the early 1990s, the major strategy for containing Medicare costs has been to shift Medicare's financial risk to private-sector organizations by encouraging the proliferation of Medicare HMOs and other forms of *managed care organizations* (MCOs). In contrast to the traditional FFS system, managed care limits the federal government's financial risk, in that the Centers for Medicare and Medicaid Services (CMS; formerly the Health Care Financing Administration) makes a prospective per capita payment to MCOs for each Medicare participant who enrolls. In turn, the MCOs are responsible for providing all needed services that are covered by Medicare. Originally, the amount of the per capita payment was set at 95% of the average fee-for-service reimbursement for Medicare patients in the same county. The Balanced Budget Act of 1997 changed the name of the program to *Medicare + Choice* (M + C) and created new types of MCO plans, such as preferred provider organizations (PPO) and private fee-for-service plans. However, reductions in the way plans were paid led to substantial numbers of plans exiting the market. Under the Medicare Modernization Act of 2003, *prepaid health plans* are now known as *Medicare Advantage* (MA) plans (Henry J. Kaiser Family Foundation, 2004b). To reduce volatility of per capita payments and encourage plans to cover beneficiaries in rural areas, the act also created 26 new regional PPO markets. A regional PPO product must offer the same benefits to everyone living in the region; this is a change from the M + C program which was county-based.

The appeal of MCO plans to some Medicare beneficiaries is twofold. First, many plans provide additional services—such as outpatient prescription drugs, routine physical exams, hearing aids, and eyeglasses—that are not covered under traditional Medicare. Second, enrollment in an MCO obviates much of a patient's need to deal with Medicare and Medigap insurance forms. In 1990, 3% of Medicare beneficiaries were enrolled in MCOs (Medicare Payment Advisory Commission, 1998); by mid-1999, the proportion had climbed to 18% (U.S. General Accounting Office, 1999). However, enrollment fell to 11% in 2004 and is not projected to grow significantly over the next decade (Henry J. Kaiser Family Foundation).

Use of Health Care

Physician Services. Older persons contact physicians far more frequently than the rest of the population for examination, diagnosis, treatment, or advice. In 2002, persons of all ages averaged 3.1 contacts per year; but persons aged 65 to 74 years averaged 6.1 contacts, and persons aged 75 and older averaged 7.2 contacts (Lethbridge-Çejku, Schiller, & Bernadel, 2004). Similarly, the probability of seeing a physician increases by advancing age categories. Among persons 45 to 64 years old, 79.3% see a physician at least once within a 12-month period; 88.3% of persons aged 65 to 74 and 92.4% of people aged 75 and older have such contact in the same time interval.

Hospital Care. Persons aged 65 and older account for 46% of the days of care in short-stay hospitals each year and about 38% of discharged patients (Woodwell & Cherry, 2004). At advanced ages, these dimensions of usage increase in rate. The number of days of care for persons aged 75 to 84 years is 67% higher than for those aged 65 to 74, and the hospital discharge rate is 62% higher.

Nursing Home Care. Nearly 1.5 million older people, or about 4.3% of persons aged 65 and older, live in nursing homes (Gabrel, 2001). The rate of nursing home use increases sharply at older ages within the elderly population. About 1% of Americans aged 65 to 74 years are living in nursing homes; this compares with 4.5% of persons age 75 to 84, and 25% of persons age 85 and older. Older nursing home residents are predominantly white (88%) and female (75% overall), with 82% among residents aged 85 and older. The probability that a person turning age 65 in 200 will spend 1 or more years living in a nursing home over their lifetime is 23% (Spillman & Lubitz, 2002).

Home- and Community-Based Long-Term Care. There are approximately 4.1 million noninstitutionalized people with limitations in activities of daily living or instrumental activities of daily living (Schiller & Bernadel, 2004). Most of them receive some form of long-term care—formal, paid services and/or informal, unpaid assistance—in their own homes or some other residential facility, such as an assisted living facility, a congregate living community, an *adult foster home*, or a *board-and-care facility*. In 1999, 1.3 million persons aged 65 and older received formal home care services (Federal Interagency Forum on Aging Related Statistics, 2004). However, the majority of those with long-term care needs relied solely on unpaid help from family and friends (Health Policy Institute, 2003).

Other Forms of Health Care. In general, older persons tend to use the wide range of available health care goods and services at higher rates than younger population groupings. Persons 65 years and older use medical equipment and supplies at twice the rate of younger persons. They also use prescription drugs and vision and hearing aids at higher rates. On the other hand, older persons visit dentists somewhat less than younger persons (Woodwell & Cherry, 2004).

Organization of Primary and Acute Care

Changes in financing, use, and need for care are reflected in and are giving rise to new forms of organizations for providing health care to older persons. Traditional institutions and modes of care—acute care and rehabilitation hospitals, outpatient clinics, physician's offices, nursing homes, and home health services—are being complemented and linked with a variety of emergent organizational mechanisms, which are briefly described later.

New Methods for Delivering Acute Care. Geriatric emergency medicine is developing as a specialty in recognition of the complex challenges frequently involved in treating older patients beset by multiple clinical disorders. *Multidisciplinary geriatric assessment* teams have been established by hospitals in the belief that they will improve the choice of treatment goals as well as discharge objectives. Special acute care geriatric wards are being developed as environments to facilitate functional recuperation and independence of older patients. The growing need for physicians trained to care for older people has spurred the Hartford Foundation, for example, to invest considerable resources into developing centers of excellence that integrate geriatrics into medical, surgical, and psychiatric residency training programs.

Trends in Delivering Acute Care. There has been a long-term trend toward greater use of ambulatory and outpatient settings to deliver services that were traditionally provided on an inpatient basis. Diagnostic and therapeutic interventions traditionally undertaken on an inpatient basis—such as cataract surgery and coronary angiography—are now being done as outpatient procedures. From 1990 to 2002, the hospitalization rate among the elderly increased from 334 per 1,000 to 358 per 1,000. However, during this time the average length of stay dropped from 8 days to less than 6 (National Center for Health Statistics, 2004). A similar trend was seen in the general population, with average length of stay dropping from 6.5 to 4.9 days. From 1990 to 2000 the proportion of total surgeries conducted on an outpatient basis increased from 51% to 63% (National Center for Health Statistics, 2004). The number of visits to outpatient departments increased 47% from 1992 to 2002 among all age groups (Hing & Middleton, 2004). Among the elderly, visits to outpatient departments increased from 33 per 100 persons in 1995 to 44 per 100 in 2000 (National Center for Health Statistics, 2004).

Hospice Care. Another relatively new development is hospice care for terminally ill patients, provided by a medically directed team of health care professionals, volunteers, and family members. The goals of hospice care are to provide a good quality of life for the *dying* person (rather than curing a patient's disease or extending life) and to help patients and families (or caregivers) deal with approaching death. In addition to palliation of pain, hospice programs provide services based on social, spiritual, and emotional needs during the last stages of illness, during the dying process, and during bereavement. About three-fourths of hospice patients receive services in their own homes (National Hospice and Palliative Care Organization, 2004). From 1986 (when permanent Medicare coverage for hospice care was established) to 2000, Medicare payments for *hospice benefits* increased from $77 million to $2.9 billion. In 2002, about 530,000 Medicare beneficiaries received an average of 49 days of care from 3,300 hospice programs (Hoffman,

Klees, & Curtis, 2002). In addition to hospice, efforts have been made to integrate end-of-life care into geriatric medical training programs. Approximately 70% of geriatric fellows report that they had had a rotation focused on end-of-life care (Pan, Carmody, Lepzig, Granieri, Sullivan, Block, et al., 2005).

Organization of Long-Term Care

The organization of long-term care for chronically ill and disabled older persons has been undergoing rapid change. Prior to the last 2 decades, nursing homes and home care (largely provided by family members) were virtually the only modes of care available. The percentage of frail older persons residing in nursing homes has remained relatively stable over the years. But recently, alternative residential settings, service, and programs have developed rapidly, responding to the varied needs of frail older persons and their caregivers.

Medicaid Waivers for Home and Community-Based Care. Since its inception Medicaid has covered skilled nursing care, whether in nursing homes or at home, for those who are poor or become poor by "*spending down*" their assets on long-term care. But traditionally, it did not cover the nonmedical services that are essential for functionally disabled persons to reside in their own homes or in other community settings. Since the early 1980s, however, the federal government has allowed states (through special waivers) to provide Medicaid reimbursement for nonmedical home care services, if these *home and community-based services* (HCBS) are limited to those patients who otherwise would require Medicaid-financed nursing home care at greater cost. In many states that have HCBS waivers, Medicaid funds for this program are supplemented by state revenues and federal monies obtained through the *Older Americans Act* and *Social Security's (Title XX)* block grant social services funds. As a consequence, home– and community-based care has become a more viable alternative to nursing homes. HCBS spending grew from only $451 million in 1987 to $18.6 billion in 2003; approximately $4.2 billion was spent on programs that target the elderly (Eiken & Burwell, 2004). States vary considerably, however, in their spending on HCBS, with New York spending the most per capita and Mississippi the least (Kane, Kane, & Ladd, 1998).

Medicare-Financed Home Care. Liberalization of Medicare's rules for home health coverage in 1989 (in response to a court order) also made home care a more viable option than in the past. Prior to that time, Medicare only covered skilled nursing care (whether in a nursing home or at home) for short periods of time following an episode of acute illness. The new rules allowed for *skilled nursing* and *home health aide* services up to 35 hours per week and made somewhat easier medical certification of the need for such care on a long-term basis. Subsequently, there was dramatic growth in the volume of *Medicare home care services*, users, and expenditures. From 1988 through 1996, the number of service visits per 1,000 Medicare enrollees increased by 687%, the user rate per 1,000 more than doubled, and payments to home health agencies increased by 861%. Provisions in the *Balanced Budget Act* of 1997, designed to rein in the growth of Medicare home health expenditures, changed this trajectory. From 1996 to 2000, the number of visits per 1,000 dropped 30%, the user rate per 1,000 dropped 65%, and payments to home health agencies dropped 57% (Hoffman, Klees, & Curtis, 2002).

Residential Alternatives. Recent years have also seen the growth of community-based alternatives to home care. State governments have expanded the range of supportive services that it authorizes traditional *"board-and-care" facilities* to provide, either by facility staff or by home health agencies. A relatively recent and rapidly growing variation of board and care is assisted living facilities, which combine residential environments with a variety of supportive services (including nursing care, in some). The average monthly private-pay rates for assisted living nationally was $2,524 in 2004 (MetLife, 2004). By 2002, 32 states had created an assisted living licensure category. In 2002, states reported over 36,000 licensed facilities with nearly 1 million units (Mollica, 2002). In addition, 41 states provided Medicaid services to people living in assisted living or board and care facilities.

Continuing care retirement communities (CCRCs) are a variation on a private insurance approach to financing long-term care, promising their members comprehensive health care services, including long-term care. There are 345 CCRCs accredited by CARF (CARF, 2005). Although about 350,000 persons live in CCRCs, only about one–third of the facilities provide long-term care for their residents under lifetime contracts in which the CCRC assumes financial risks for a resident's long-term care services, including nursing home care (U.S. General Accounting Office, 1997). Residents tend to be middle- and upper-income persons who are relatively healthy when they join the community, and they pay a substantial entrance fee and monthly charge in return for a promise of "*care for life*." It has been estimated that about 10% of older people could afford to join such communities.

Family-Related Care. A number of studies indicate that over 80% of home care services for older persons are provided by their family members on an informal, unpaid basis. In response to this phenomenon, as well as a growing recognition of the stresses experienced by *family caregivers*, new programs emerged in the 1980s and early 1990s that have now spread to most urban communities. *Adult day care* programs enable a caregiver to have time for work, to undertake other activities of daily living, and simply to rest from providing care; at the same time, such programs can provide social interaction, supportive services, and rehabilitation activities for older persons who attend them. In addition, "respite" programs provide caregivers with more extended relief for a fixed period of days by temporarily admitting a disabled older person to an institution or by providing substitute caregivers in a home. Similarly, support groups comprising family caregivers, particularly those caring for persons with dementia, are a vehicle for moderating the *stresses of caregiving* and sharing practical information.

Integrating Acute, Chronic, and Long-Term Care. A long-recognized problem in the financing and organization of health care for older people is the fragmentation of the delivery system. Few units of organization integrate acute, chronic, and long-term care in fashions that are optimal either for patient care or cost-efficiency. Separate sources of financing—especially the separate streams of funding through Medicare and Medicaid, and the incentives associated with them—tend to engender this fragmented and, often, inappropriate care.

Since the early 1980s the federal government has financed innovative managed care demonstration projects, focused on integrating health care services for frail older persons. One of these, the *Program for All-Inclusive Care for the Elderly* (PACE), is aimed at those persons who are sufficiently dependent to be eligible for nursing home placement but still reside in the community; most of them are eligible for Medicaid as well as Medicare. Enrollees are required to attend an adult day health center, where a wide array of medical, supportive, and social services is provided to them by a multidisciplinary team. Although a primary *PACE* objective is to delay or prevent use of hospital and nursing home care, the program pays for these services when they become essential. In 1997, after many years of demonstration and replication, PACE was authorized as a permanent program under Medicare and states were granted the option to offer PACE to their Medicaid enrollees. Currently, 32 PACE sites are operational, and there are 11 pre-PACE sites that serve Medicaid enrollees but do not yet function as Medicare risk contractors. The total number of people served is over 10,000 and the average size of the programs is 328; the largest sites have less than 1,000 participants (National PACE Association, 2005).

Another federal demonstration is the *social/health maintenance organization* (S/HMO). An initial generation of the S/HMO, launched in the 1980s, tested an integrated model of service delivery (including long-term care) and capitated financing in conventional HMO settings, but did not result in effective coordination of chronic and acute medical benefits (Harrington, Lynch, & Newcomer, 1993). A second generation of S/HMO demonstrations was authorized in the 1990s to test the value of incorporating geriatric practices into the plans: comprehensive geriatric assessment, treatment of functional problems, and a team approach combining nurse practitioners, pharmacists, and other health professionals. So far, however, this demonstration is active at only 1 site (Medicare Payment Advisory Commission, 1999). *EverCare*, a demonstration program launched in 1994, enrolls permanent nursing home residents into managed care and endeavors to provide them with more Medicare outpatient services than they would usually receive. The objectives of EverCare are to reduce nursing home residents' use of hospital and emergency room services and to improve the quality of care and health outcomes. An evaluation of 5 EverCare sites found that, compared to a control group, the use of nurse practitioners to provide primary care may have prevented some hospitalizations, but mainly allowed cases to be managed more cost effectively in the nursing home (Kane, Keckhafer, Flood, Bershadsky, & Siadaty, 2003). In addition to these federal demonstrations, a number of state governments are operating Medicaid managed care programs that provide long-term care. For example, the Minnesota Senior Health Options (MSHO) program serves dually eligible elderly. Evidence from an evaluation found that provision of preventive and community-based services reduced hospitalization and emergency department use (Kane, Homyak, Bershadsky, Flood, & Zhang, 2004).

The various organizational mechanisms and experiments outlined above are evolutionary steps toward the development of a reasonably integrated, wide range of health care services needed by America's older population. Yet the effective integration of acute and long-term care services will be inextricably bound up with the broader challenges of financing American health care in an era in which a predominant concern is to slow inflation of health care costs in general, and the costs of health care for the elderly in particular.

Robert H. Binstock
Updated by Howard B. Degenholtz

See also

Health Care Policy for Older Adults: History
Health Maintenance Organizations
Medicaid
Medicare
Nursing Homes
Social Security

References

CARF. (2005). CARF, the Rehabilitation Accreditation Commission. CARF accredited programs. Available: http://www.carf.org/consumer.aspx?content=ConsumerSearch&id=7

Centers for Medicare and Medicaid Services. (2005). *National accounts age tables*. Office of the Actuary, National Statistics Group. Available: http://www.cms.hss.gov/statistics/nhe/age/t1.asp

Federal Hospital Insurance and Federal Supplementary Medical Insurance Trust Funds. (2005). *2005 annual report of the boards of trustees, Federal Hospital Insurance and Federal Supplementary Medical Insurance Trust Funds*. Washington, DC.

Federal Interagency Forum on Aging Related Statistics. (2004). *Older Americans 2004: Key indicators of well-being*. Washington, DC: U.S. Government Printing Office.

Gabrel, C. S. (2000). Characteristics of elderly nursing home current residents and discharges: Data from the 1997 National Nursing Home Survey. *Advance Data from Vital and Health Statistics, 312*.

General Accounting Office. (1997). *Health care services: How continuing care retirement communities manage services for the elderly* (GAO/HEHS-97-36). Washington, DC: U.S. General Accounting Office.

Health Policy Alternatives Inc. (2004). *Medicare drug discount cards: A work in progress* (7136). Menlo Park, CA: Henry J. Kaiser Family Foundation.

Health Policy Institute. (2003). *Who needs long-term care?* (Fact Sheet). Washington, DC: Georgetown University.

Henry J. Kaiser Family Foundation. (2004a). *Medicare: the Medicare prescription drug law* (7044). Menlo Park, CA: Henry J. Kaiser Family Foundation.

Henry J. Kaiser Family Foundation. (2004b). *Medicare Advantage* (2052–07). Menlo Park, CA: Henry J. Kaiser Family Foundation.

Hing, E., & Middleton, K. (2004). National Hospital Ambulatory Medical Care Survey: 2002 outpatient department summary. *Advance Data from Vital and Health Statistics, 345*.

Hoffman, E. D. J., Klees, B. S., & Curtis, C. A. (2002). Overview of the Medicare and Medicaid Programs. *Health Care Financing Review* [statistical supplement].

Kane, R. L., Homyak, P., Bershadsky, B., Flood, S., & Zhang, H. (2004). Patterns of utilization for the Minnesota senior health options program. *Journal of the American Geriatrics Society, 52*(12), 2039–2044.

Kane, R. L., Keckhafer, G., Flood, S., Bershadsky, B., & Siadaty, M. S. (2003). The effect of Evercare on hospital use. *Journal of the American Geriatrics Society, 51*(10), 1427–1434.

Lethbridge-Çejku, M., Schiller, J., & Bernadel, L. (2004). Summary health statistics for U.S. adults: National Health Interview Survey, 2002. *Vital and Health Statistics, 10*(222).

MedPac. (2004a). *Skilled nursing facility payment system*. Washington, DC: Medicare Payment Advisory Commission.

MedPac. (2004b). *Home health care services payment system*. Washington, DC: Medicare Payment Advisory Commission.

Mollica, R. (2002). *State assisted living policy 2002*. Portland, ME: National Academy for State Health Policy.

Moon, M. (1999). Building on Medicare's Strengths. *Issues in Science and Technology, 16*.

National Center for Health Statistics. (2004). *Health, United States, 2004* (DHHS Publication No. 2004-1232). Hyattsville, MD: National Center for Health Statistics.

National Hospice and Palliative Care Organization. (2004). *NHPCO's facts and figures on hospice care*. Alexandria, VA: National Hospice and Palliative Care Organization.

National PACE Association. (2005). PACE programs around the country. Available: http://www.npaonline.org/website/article.asp?id=71

Pan, C. X., Carmody, S., Leipzig, R., Granieri, E., Sullivan, A., Block, S. D., & Arnold, R. M. (2005). There is hope for the future: National survey results reveal that geriatric medicine fellows are well-educated in end-of-life care. *Journal of the American Geriatrics Society*, *53*(4), 705–710.

Schiller, J., & Bernadel, L. (2004). Summary health statistics for U.S. adults: National Health Interview Survey, 2002. *Vital and Health Statistics*, *10*(220).

Sharma, R., & Lin, H. (2004). *Health and health care of the Medicare population: Data from the 2000 Medicare current beneficiary survey*. Rockville, MD: Westat.

Spillman, B. C., & Lubitz, J. (2002). New estimates of lifetime nursing home use: Have patterns of use changed? *Medical Care*, *40*(10), 965–975.

Woodwell, D. A., & Cherry, D. K. (2004). National Ambulatory Medical Care Survey: 2002 summary. *Advance Data from Vital and Health Statistics*, 346.

HEALTH CARE POLICY FOR OLDER ADULTS, HISTORY OF

Health care policy for older persons has developed incrementally throughout U.S. history following the evolution of the rule of government.

History

Health care policies can be divided into roughly 5 periods, characterized by different scopes and interests of the federal government in the health and welfare of the population.

Early Years of the Republic (1776–1860). Government involvement in the health of citizens initially was limited because such activities were seen as the responsibility of individuals and charities. Federal actions were limited to *quarantine* regulations at ports of entry, merchant seamen's health care, and smallpox vaccination. State and local governments were concerned with sanitation and the quarantine of communicable diseases during this time. Health care for the poor was left principally to private charities. Medical care was rudimentary. The few existing hospitals were intended to isolate people with communicable disease or provide care for the indigent. Different health care philosophies, including *allopathy*, *homeopathy*, *herbalism*, *public health*, and lay approaches all competed for legitimacy. The health of the population was poor by current standards: communicable diseases were common, infant and maternal mortality were high, and malnutrition was common among the poor. Life expectancy at birth in Massachusetts in 1798 was estimated to be only 35 years. As such, health care policy for older adults was nonexistent, as a result of limited life expectancy and the government's narrow focus.

Civil War to the Depression (1861–1931). The federal government assumed a limited role in promoting the health and welfare of the population. After 20 years of debate, Congress passed the *Food and Drug Act* in 1906 to regulate the adulteration and misbranding of food and drugs. While intended to protect consumers' pocketbooks, not their health, the act marked new federal involvement in a health-related area previously left to the states. Public health approaches were embraced at the state and local level. By 1915, public health agencies were established in every state and began to expand beyond infectious disease control to include water pollution, sewage disposal, nutrition, housing, and industrial accidents. The resulting improvements, along with improved social and economic conditions, are commonly credited with decreased morbidity and mortality during this period.

Allopathic medicine gained power as the *American Medical Association*'s membership (founded 1847) and influence grew. Organized medicine and private foundations worked to base healing on science and to make medical education requirements uniform and high. Often unable to meet the new requirements, 92 *medical schools* closed their doors or merged between 1902 and 1915, the number of homeopathic and eclectic schools fell by two-thirds, and 5 of the 7 black medical colleges closed. Hospitals became important sites where health care was provided, growing in number from 178 in 1873 to 4,000 by 1909. Payment for these health services remained the responsibility of individuals and charities. The government took interest in medical research and Congress voted to establish the *National Institutes of Health* (NIH) in 1930.

By 1900, *life expectancy* had risen to 47.3 years. Acute diseases accounted for the majority of deaths, led by influenza, pneumonia, and tuberculosis. The elderly comprised 4% of the population, and those who lived to age 65 had a remaining life expectancy of 11.9 years.

The New Deal to New Federalism (1933–1981). This era heralded important political-economic and scientific developments. The *Great Depression* and the *New Deal* brought dramatic new government involvement into the health and welfare of the population, while scientific discoveries furthered progress against infectious disease. This period was characterized by an active federal effort to enact policies to improve access, quality, and distribution of health care. The federal government also greatly expanded its involvement in medical research, beginning with the passage of the *National Cancer Act* in 1937. The National Institutes of Health grew from a small government laboratory to a biomedical research organization with worldwide significance.

Probably the most important piece of social legislation enacted in the history of the United States was the *Social Security Act* of 1935, establishing *social insurance* to assure a degree of financial security in old age. It also established unemployment insurance and federal aid to states for maternal and child health, public health, and public assistance. Other programs important to the elderly that would be established later, including Medicare, follow the principles established in this act.

After World War II, the federal government began to heavily subsidize hospital expansion, providing construction and modernization funds for hospitals, nursing homes, public health clinics, and rehabilitation centers in more than 3,000 communities over a 30-year period. The private, nonprofit institution became the primary type of medical institution because public hospitals, which largely served the poor, were last to receive federal construction funds. New forms of health care financing emerged during this period. *Blue Cross and Blue Shield* medical insurance was established by hospitals and doctors during the Depression to help insure payment of their bills. Federal policies encouraged the spread of private health insurance by defining it as nonwage compensation, allowing workers to bargain for increased health benefits during wartime wage freezes and allowing both employers and employees to avoid taxes on premiums paid. The unemployed, poor, and elderly found private insurance difficult to obtain, leaving them dependent on charity and limited public programs. Blacks and other minorities also suffered from overt discrimination in the provision of care until passage of the Civil Rights Act and Medicare, in the mid-1960s.

Great Society programs in the 1960s continued New Deal trends. Federal medical insurance was established for the elderly and the poor through *Medicare* and *Medicaid*. To overcome organized medical opposition, Medicare incorporated the existing *fee-for-service* payment method and paid hospitals and doctors retrospectively according to what they charged. With guaranteed funding, hospital and nursing home construction and expansion continued, while new and costly technologies were introduced. By 1980, all public and private expenditures for health care equaled 9.4% of the gross national product, with 42% coming from public sources.

Infectious disease reduction slowed in the 1950s, as the major cause of death became chronic illnesses such as cancer and cardiovascular disease. The proportion of older persons in the population rose from 4.0% in 1900 to 11.3% in 1980, as life expectancy rose 50% to 73.7 years, infant mortality fell, and fertility patterns changed. Remaining life expectancy at age 65 increased to 16.4 years by 1980 (National Center for Health Statistics, 1995).

From 1965 to the mid-1970s the primary policy concern was expanding access to health care. As a result, doctor visits per person per year for the poor increased 30% and hospital use (discharges per 100 persons per year) increased between one- and two-thirds for the poor, elderly, and minorities. During this time the debate over national health insurance was seen as key to further health care improvements.

Health Policy under New Federalism and Fiscal Crisis (1981–1993). Federalism and devolution denote the relationships among different levels of government and the transfer of responsibility for programs and services from the federal to the state level. Following President Richard Nixon's lead in initiating policies that increased state and local discretion and responsibilities in the 1970s, President Ronald Reagan vigorously pursued policies in the 1980s to diminish the federal role in health and welfare through block grants, program cuts, and increased state responsibility. A surge of "new" *federalism* initiatives emerged in the mid-1990s, releasing states from the burden of unfunded federal mandates and ushering in *welfare "reform"* that ended entitlement to cash assistance for the poor and imposed restrictions on public benefits for immigrants. A large body of research reveals that these latter policies reduced welfare rolls more than they did poverty itself. Inasmuch as work mandates led most recipients into low-wage service-sector jobs lacking health insurance benefits, we have greater numbers lacking basic preventive and acute-care. Older Americans have also been affected, because more grandparents now are needed to help raise the children of those subject to work mandates.

In its most extreme form, *new federalism* challenges the idea that there is any national responsibility for meeting basic human needs in health, income, housing, or welfare. Historically, it has been argued that because state and local governments do not have the revenue capacity of the federal government, national issues and problems necessitate a strong federal financing role. Moreover, aside from prohibitions against deficit spending, states and localities vary widely in their commitment to health and welfare benefits for the poor, disadvantaged, and the elderly (Estes, 1979; Estes & Gerard, 1983).

Deregulation is a hallmark of new federalism policy and *devolution*. Part of its impact in health care has been the increasing role of for-profit firms in government-financed programs. There is an increased *privatization of health care* with the growth of for-profits and the conversion of non-profits to for-profits in managed care. To promote "market competition" and further deregulation, some recent proposals suggest turning Medicare over to private insurers by permitting (or requiring) older persons to buy private insurance using government-supplied vouchers (called "premium support" proposals). Contentious issues are whether the financing of Medicare is privatized and what the effects of such dramatic policy change might be on older adults. The current administration in Washington D.C. remains committed to attracting Medicare recipients into managed care plans, despite the high failure rate in recent years of those plans catering to older adults. This reflects the strongly ideological nature of health policy.

Two major forces have shaped health care policy for older persons during previous periods of health reform: (1) *austerity* and its political processing, and (2) the aging enterprise and the medical-industrial complex. *Austerity* has been a force of aging politics since the late 1970s as a result of state and local fiscal crises caused by taxpayer revolts, federal budget cuts, economic recession, tax cuts and high defense spending during the Reagan years and afterward. The result was a large federal budget deficit exceeding $3 trillion by the conclusion of President George Bush's term in office in 1993.

Social constructions of reality become a force of their own (Estes, 1979). The concepts of austerity and *deficit reduction* have themselves become the driving ideology behind health and social policy for older adults since the mid-1990s. Austerity policies result from the socially constructed notions that: (1) federal spending on the elderly and poor is a major cause of U.S. economic problems, and (2) federal responsibility for health care is neither appropriate nor feasible. While the U.S. tax burden is lower than virtually all other large industrialized nations, austerity and deficit reduction are represented as the only possible response to declining revenues.

The aging enterprise and the medical-industrial complex consist of the growing concentration of private for-profit hospitals, nursing homes, and other medical care organizations, along with businesses related to medical goods and services (Estes, 1979; Relman, 1980; Wohl, 1984). With health care expenditures in the United States exceeding $1 trillion per year (29% spent for the elderly), there are major incentives for corporate involvement in for-profit markets in medical care for older adults (Estes, Harrington, & Pellow, 2000). The growing role of proprietaries in medicine has intensified a perennial and profound question: should health care be a "market good" that is purchased as a commodity by those who can afford to pay, or should it be provided as a "merit good" available as a right or collective good, regardless of ability to pay (Estes, Gerard, Zones, & Swan, 1984)?

Clinton and Health and Long-Term Care Reform (1993–2000). As a candidate for president, *Bill Clinton* campaigned for *health care reform* that would include cost containment and universal health care coverage. His failed proposal would have provided a core benefit package through private and public plans managed by a *National Health Board.* Through this board the growth in health care costs would have been brought in line with inflation over a 5-year period. Coverage would have been paid for primarily by employers and partially by employees, depending on income level. When he addressed Congress in September 1993 there was general agreement, both in Congress and in the public, about the general principles of his plan.

A unique component of Clinton's plan was specifically addressing the issue of *long-term care.* In the final package brought to Congress in 1993 long-term care was presented as a "merit good" that should be available to all. The long-term care portion of the proposal was an advance over earlier proposals by offering coverage regardless of age or income. In the end, several key decisions reduced its political support; for example, a lack of fiscal relief to states that were given responsibility for long-term care under the plan. There was also no individual federal entitlement, and no defined benefit, with the exception of assessment, case management, and personal assistance services.

Today, more than a decade later, support for universal coverage is still high and as the population ages it is ever more concerned with funding and expanding options in long-term care. By 2004, the number of uninsured had grown to 45 million people (over 15% of the total U.S. population).

Scholars of health policy have analyzed the failure of the Clinton proposal. Central to this interpretation are the 3 incompatible goals of the Clinton plan: to provide universal health insurance, to reduce medical care cost increases, and to reduce the federal deficit (Lee, 2000). Those opposed to him, including new federalist Republicans in control of Congress as well as those opposed to universal coverage, particularly the health insurance industry, recognized this inconsistency and utilized it to mobilize against him (Lee, 2000). Although public support for universal health coverage was high, President Clinton's complicated proposal was manipulated and simplified in the media to create fear among the general public; the technocratic discourse surrounding it undermined the potentially broad-based populist appeal the proposal might have enjoyed. Moreover, the charge of a large federal "takeover" of the health care system resurfaced in the 2004 election, when John Kerry advocated a federal contribution to pay for *catastrophic care.*

Even without passage of Clinton's 1993 health care reform, his administration can claim 2 significant improvements to health care coverage: the *Health Insurance Portability and Accountability Act* (*Kassabaum-Kennedy Act*) of 1996, and the *Child Health Insurance Program* (CHIP) as a part of the *Balanced Budget Act* of 1997. The former protects employees from losing health insurance when they change jobs, and the latter expands the number of poor children eligible for *Medicaid,* increasing the number of insured children by 2 million. (Greenberg, 2000)

Current and Projected Challenges: Prescription Drug Policy Under Medicare and Integrating Acute and Long-Term Care. In the 2000 presidential election health care was a leading topic. Candidates *George Bush* and Al Gore both advocated incremental changes to the health care system, such as the patient's bill of rights, *prescription drug coverage* for the elderly, and *tax credits* to help individuals buy their own health insurance. In the years since, the conciliatory approach of the Clinton plan—which sought to reconcile universal coverage with the interests of private insurers—has given way to a more polarized, ideological climate. More broadly, the backlash against managed care has exposed a lack of public trust in the health care system, low morale among clinicians, and frustration over the failure of *managed care* to translate into expanded access to care (Mechanic, 2001). Furthermore, the pincer effects on the federal budget, imposed by simultaneous tax cuts and military expenditures in Iraq and elsewhere, have intensified the sense of fiscal crisis that has long constrained health policy making. These factors have combined to produce cynicism about the efficacy of health policy reform.

Both in substantive and symbolic terms, the most significant recent event in health policy for the aged is the Bush-sponsored *Medicare Prescription Drug, Improvement, and Modernization Act* (P.L. 108-173), signed in December of 2003. Cost estimates of the plan have ranged from $400 billion to more $500 billion over 10 years. Although promoted as the centerpiece of Bush's "Compassionate

Conservative" domestic policy record during the 2004 election, this policy has been deeply controversial from the outset. According to a comprehensive analysis by Oliver and colleagues (2004), nearly 50% of senior citizens opposed the changes when they were signed into law, twice the percentage voicing support. Lobbying publicly in support of the plan, the AARP had thousands of members resign in protest and was accused of a conflict of interests rooted in the organization's long and close connections with private insurance companies. Beneficiaries face a confusing set of choices, including that of retaining private coverage, enrolling in a new free-standing drug plan, or entering a *Medicare managed care plan*. There are provisions for higher subsidy of low-income seniors, and a "gap" in coverage for many middle-class beneficiaries, who will be liable for out of pocket costs of $3,600 or more.

There are several divisive elements of the plan, including the retreat from universalism (inherent in the tiered, means-tested targeting of benefits), and from the social insurance model of traditional Medicare; the plan's structure of incentives appear intended to draw enrollees out of traditional Medicare and into private health plans. According to Oliver and colleagues (2004), the legacies of earlier policy conflicts are inscribed in the current drug plan; these include its voluntary component, cost-sharing between taxpayers and beneficiaries, and substantial administrative control by private companies, rather than the federal government with its more powerful regulatory power. One must acknowledge the boldness of the Bush plan to address prescription drug coverage. In practical terms, the $12,000 average prescription drug bill is among the "aging shocks" discussed by Knickman and Snell (2002); in political terms, the Bush drug plan allows the Republican Party to claim a major policy victory on an issue that has been a stalwart one for Democrats. The irony is that this step toward drug coverage contains incentives that appear certain to undermine traditional Medicare. When paired with the Bush proposal to partially *privatize Social Security*, one can reasonably detect that the underlying strategy is to dismantle the cornerstones of the federal government's old age welfare state. As Hudson argues (1999), the collective historical gains made by older adults in terms of health and economic security have prompted a counter-reaction; this is based on a more sanguine image of elders (especially against the backdrop of retrenchment in spending on programs directed at children, such as the un-funded schooling mandates of "*No Child Left Behind*"), and also on alarmist warnings about the crushing burden that looms in coming years as the large baby boomer cohort becomes eligible for benefits. Thus, our final task is to scrutinize major myths (Geyman, 2003), claims, and findings bearing on the projected needs of this cohort on health care resources.

Future health care policy for the elderly will depend on at least 2 major conditions: (1) aggregate need, and (2) the political-economic environment. Aggregate need for health and long-term care by older adults in the 21st century will be determined by their numbers and health status, including chronic disease. Demographic projections show the number and proportion of elderly growing in the next century. By 2040, 21% of the population is expected to be aged 65 or older (vs. 11% in 1980) and to number between 70 million and 90 million (vs. 25 million in 1980). Disability rates during the 1990s have been calculated at 38% for men and 42% for women (Kaye, La Plante, Carlson, & Wenger, 1996). Despite evidence of some declines in the disability rates, increases in the number of older adults will exacerbate the call for an adequate long-term care policy. In the future there will be an "increasing number of individuals in quite good health nearly up to the point of death and an increasing number with prolonged severe limitation, with a decline in the duration of infirmity" (Rice & Feldman, 1985). Chronic care services are particularly important for older women and minorities, who are least able to pay out of pocket. Minority elderly, historically small in number, are increasing faster than white elderly and will need expanded, culturally relevant, affordable low-cost health and long-term care.

Knickman and Snell (2002) directly address the alarm surrounding the aging baby boomers, who "in the year 2030 will be aged 66 to 84—the '*young old*'—and will number 61 million people." Their analyses show that total dependency ratios in 2030 will not be appreciably higher than they were during the 1960s, when the youth dependency rate increased with the entry of the baby boomers. Moreover, the authors urge care in the definition of "dependent," inasmuch as this cohort will be better educated, have lower rates of many chronic disabilities, and will thus be even more vital as volunteer and community resources than are current older adults. Clearly, this potential capacity—central to a broader healthy aging/wellness model—will be realized only to the extent that we are successful in channeling the talents of older adults into significant roles and institutions. This integration will require extensive public-private partnerships of a sort that is difficult to envision in the current political environment. Furthermore, given the continued growth in the numbers of the oldest-old, even the most optimistic projections regarding disability will require major changes in the funding and balancing of our long-term care system (to expand and better integrate community care options). Although too rarely discussed in the context of health policy, a fundamental challenge we face is in recruiting and rewarding the tens of thousands of frontline care workers who are central to the quality of life for older adults in assisted living as well as nursing homes (Wellin & Jaffe, 2004).

Finally, we do have models for better integrating acute and long-term care, which are certain to be in greater demand as baby boomers age. (Indeed, providing for the "*least restrictive" care* setting is now legally mandated, after the Supreme Court's 1999 *Olmstead Act* ruled that doing otherwise is in violation of the Americans with Disabilities Act.) For example, in 1997 the *Program of All-Inclusive Care for the Elderly* (*PACE* model) was designated as a permanent program in Medicare; Gross and colleagues explain (2004): "The program's objective is to enable individuals to continue living in the community as long as possible. It achieves this objective by offering a comprehensive set of medical, psychosocial, and long-term care services. At the core of the program is adult day care, augmented by home care and meals at home." There are now some 10,000 elders enrolled in PACE, a considerable number, although a fraction of the estimated 3 million community-dwelling, nursing home-certifiable persons who could potentially benefit (Gross, Temkin-Greener, Kunitz, & Mukamel, 2004). These authors conclude that lack of public knowledge of such programs, competition (from for-profit as well as other state-operated programs), staffing shortages, system fragmentation between acute-care and community providers, and difficulties in penetrating the market of non-Medicaid eligible clients are all implicated in the disappointing rate of growth in PACE programs. Also, they point out that the growth of the nursing home industry, to which PACE seeks to offer an alternative, was fueled by massive federal support that PACE programs have not enjoyed. Finding strategies for expanding and sustaining such integrated care options will be a key to promoting the flexible, integrated care programs we know to be both desired and effective.

If health policy continues to be driven by the devolution of federal responsibility, deregulation, austerity, and an increasingly powerful medical-industrial complex, then privatization, corporatization, fragmentation, and rationing of health care will worsen. Continued federal budget cuts and shifting of responsibility for medical care for the uninsured to states, localities, and individuals could return the nation back to an earlier era of health policy when the federal government took little active interest in the health and welfare of the populace and policies were made at the state and local level. Such an approach leaves the basic health care financing system intact but augments the power and influence of a highly pluralistic and profitable medical industrial complex, while doing little or nothing about the growing urgency to address the need for long-term care.

Among current calls for partial *privatization* of Social Security, Medicare, medical savings accounts and private long-term care insurance, none acknowledge the greater medical needs and out-of-pocket expenses of the poor, the disabled, chronically ill, minorities, and women. A major question concerns who will pay for the costs of these "unprofitable" patients. Relegating health care distribution to the market and to managed care requires that consumers are sufficiently informed so they are able to make the best choice and so that access automatically flows from market decisions. However, from where public knowledge of costs, quality, and optimal treatments will come remains problematic. More importantly, competition is not likely to produce access without universal coverage (Teisberg, Porter & Brown, 1994). As such, the health policy debate and reforms for older persons in the future are indivisible from struggles to achieve universal coverage of health and long-term care in the face of a powerful and well-entrenched, pluralistically financed medical care system (government, private insurance, and out-of-pocket) and a largely private, profit-driven delivery system. The challenge, as stated, is to finance, link, and integrate acute care and community-based long-term care services.

If coalitions were to be formed that transcend age and unite groups with common interests (e.g., the elderly and the disabled), they could change the fundamental conditions that presently affect health policy. In the place of austerity and new federalism, they will have to define the right to health care as part of the Constitution's federal mandate to "promote the general welfare." These groups could become successful advocates for the organization, financing, and delivery of health care for the elderly and disabled as a continuum ranging from respite care to the relief of families who provide most of the care, adequate incomes, and acute medical services. The looming battle over Social Security, affecting millions of beneficiaries who are disabled workers and children as well as older adults, may catalyze such a coalition.

CARROLL L. ESTES
CHRIS WELLIN
DAWN D. OGAWA
TRACY WEITZ

See also
Health Care: Financing, Use, and Organization

References

Estes, C. L. (1979). *The aging enterprise: A critical examination of social policies and services for the aged.* San Francisco: Jossey-Bass.

Estes, C. L., & Gerard, L. E. (1983). Government responsibility: Issues of reform and federalism. In C. L. Estes & R. J. Newcomer and Associates. *Fiscal austerity and aging: Shifting government responsibility for the elderly* (pp. 41–58). Beverly Hills, CA: Sage Publications.

Estes, C. L., Gerard, L. E., Zones, J. S., & Swan, J. H. (1984). *Political economy, health, and aging.* Boston: Little, Brown.

Estes, C. L., Harrington, C., & Pellow, D. (2000). The medical industrial complex. In E. Borgatta & M. Borgatta (Eds.), *The encyclopedia of sociology* (Vol. 2). New York: MacMillan.

Geyman, J. P. (2003). Myths as barriers to health care reform in the United States. *International Journal of Health Services, 33*, 315–329.

Gross, D. L., Temkin-Greener, H., Kunitz, S., & Mukamel, D. B. (2004). The growing pains of integrated health care for the elderly: Lessons from the expansion of PACE. *Millbank Quarterly, 82*, 257–282.

Hudson, R. B. (1999). Conflict in today's aging politics: New population encounters old ideology. *Social Services Review*, (*September*), *73*, 358–379.

Kaye, La Plante, Carlson, & Wenger (1996). Trends in disability rates in the United States, 1970–1994. In *Disability Statistics Abstracts, no. 17.* Washington, DC: National Institute for Disability and Rehabilitation Research.

Knickman, J. R., & Snell, E. K. (2002). The 2030 problem: caring for aging baby boomers. *Health Services Research, 37*(4), 849–884.

Mechanic, D. (2001). The managed care backlash: Perceptions and rhetoric in health care policy and the potential for health care reform. *Millbank Quarterly, 79*, 35–54.

National Center for Health Statistics. (1995). Number and distribution of the population by age group: United States, 1900–2050. *Current Population Reports*, Series P-23, No. 128, and P-25, No. 1018; and *Statistical Abstracts of the United States.* Washington, DC: U. S. Bureau of the Census.

Oliver, T. R., Lee, P. R., & Lipton, H. L. (2004). A political history of Medicare and prescription drug coverage. *Millbank Quarterly, 82*, 283–354.

Relman, A. S. (1980). The new medical industrial complex. *New England Journal of Medicine, 303*, 963–970.

Rice, D. P., & Feldman, J. J. (1983). Living longer in the United States: Demographic changes and health needs of the elderly. *Milbank Memorial Fund Quarterly, 61*, 391.

Teisberg, E., Porter, M., & Brown, G. (1994). The debate on health-care reform continues. *Harvard Business Review, 72*(6), 185–186.

Wellin, C., & Jaffe, D. J. (2004). In search of personal care: Barriers to identity support in residential care for elders with cognitive illness. *Journal of Aging Studies, 18*(3), 275–295.

Wohl, S. (1984). *The medical industrial complex.* New York: Harmony Books.

HEALTH INFORMATICS

Definition

Health informatics uses information technology and techniques to support clinical care, health services administration, health services research, and public and provider education (Shortliffe & Fagan, 2000; Bemmel & Musen, 1997; Wyatt & Liu, 2002; Wyatt & Keen, 2001). The integration of ideas from health care, public health, computer science, and information sciences is key to success in health informatics.

Interdisciplinary collaborations are essential, as experts from different backgrounds work together to deliver information and knowledge to improve the well being of communities and individuals.

Three exciting innovations herald the maturing of health informatics as a discipline:

1. Expansion of *biomedical repositories* and *databases* (hospitals databases, epidemiological national databases, and *registries*) followed by a radical reduction of cost of hardware, including handled devices;
2. Widespread use of the *Internet* and *World Wide Web*, and the availability of effective *search engines*;
3. Development of powerful software to manage information in databases (*data mining*—knowledge discovery in databases, DM-KDD; see Fayyad, Piatetsky-Shapiro, Smyth, & Uthurusamy, 1996; machine-learning algorithms; algorithms for information retrieval).

Advances in data mining and *knowledge discovery* promise the integration of information from different sources (patients' records, literature, hospital and national databases), all contributing to improvements in health and health care. The development of large and sophisticated databases allows communities to collect and use individual and *public health information* to learn about the epidemiology of disease, the meaning of genetic markers, and the benefits and harm of the various diagnostic and treatment tools used to improve individual and population health.

History. Enthusiasm for biomedical applications started as soon as computers became available (first in bioengineering) (Ledley, 1965), and biomedical needs drove progress in computer science. Image processing is crucial to many medical applications. *Artificial intelligence* methods to support diagnostic and treatment decisions (computer programs emulating processes of learning and human reasoning) have the potential to improve the accuracy and pertinence of diagnostic and therapeutic choices.

In the 1960s, the major applications were in *biomedical signal processing* (EKG, EEG, imaging) followed by the development of personal computers. In 1970s, the first attempts to use artificial intelligence in medicine were debated. *Expert systems* that claimed to mimic physician reasoning in diagnostics generated considerable interest, as they promised to help with diagnostic and treatment, (e.g., MYCIN) (Buchanan & Shortliffe, 1984). An application was even developed to deliver Rogerian psychotherapy (ELIZA, http://chayden.net/eliza/Eliza.shtml). Artificial *neural networks* approaches were developing in the 1980s, but the databases were not sufficiently robust. In the 1990s as the cost of information processing and storage decreased, data warehousing and advanced data mining techniques became useful. Digital anatomy and multimedia-based software contributed to education. But while computer science is one driving force for health informatics, there is also a need to develop ways to identify and capture pertinent information, especially regarding the results of care, in order to make health systems (and medicine) more effective.

In the coming years, patient and citizen engagement will become increasingly important. The current decade will see widespread adoption of individual electronic patient records, and an explosion in Internet applications to gather, store, mine, and use information and new knowledge.

Electronic Patients' Records (EPR)

Electronic patient record pilot projects are becoming transformed into widespread local (Alberta Wellnet, http://www.albertawellnet.org/) and national (New Zealand, http://www.hinz.org.nz/) patient record systems. Fully implemented EPR systems promise to change the face of medicine. They will provide timely information to support individual care, and perhaps even more importantly, will support data mining and predictive modeling techniques so that eventually patients, policy makers, and providers will be able to link health care activities and results. EPRs will promote patient self-sufficiency by supporting patient efforts to maintain their information on the web, so that all practitioners who need to will have access. EPRs will also promote patient independence by directing patients to appropriate web sites for information about their particular condition or prescribed drugs.

Widespread adoption of EPRs will happen once the human computer interface challenges are solved. Many physicians find it more convenient to make an illegible scrawl on a piece of paper rather than input information into a computerized record. Developing appropriate policies to support confidentiality of health records represents another challenge. How can developers ensure that people have access when they need it, while also preventing unauthorized disclosure of confidential information? A promising solution is to maintain audit trails, available to patients, with serious penalties for unauthorized access.

Biomedical Imaging and Medical Signal Processing

This is the oldest field of health informatics. New algorithms support image acquisition and data sharing within hospital units and elsewhere. Picture archiving and retrieval systems have made life much better for radiologists and others who are dependent on x-rays or other images. New imaging techniques support more precise definition and measurement of abnormal images.

Medical Information Retrieval

Access to appropriate information has been advanced by the development of algorithms permitting the rapid (almost immediate) search of thousands of documents. The Google *search engine* is a general example, and the Internet-based *Medline* represents a major advance over *Index Medicus*, a paper-based indexing system.

Education

Indexing tools support patient retrieval of pertinent information, and the World Wide Web permits patients and providers almost equal access to the research literature. The *British Journal of Medicine,* for example, is free to everyone. Multimedia tools support professional education.

Clinical Bioinformatics/Computational Biology

Integration molecular and clinical information hold great promise to improve health care. *Computational biology* (CB) deals with managing and organizing molecular information, DNA structures (genomics), and protein structures and functions (proteomics). *Genomics* data, now found only in research databases, will eventually be used in routine clinical care and stored in electronic medical record systems. Medical informatics uses complicated mathematical and statistical models (artificial intelligence, and data mining, artificial neural networks, *Markov models*, etc.). *Bioinformatics* uses these same tools to predict the function of genomic sequences. The integration of this information with the electronic patient record can be expected in several years. Clinical trial and drug discovery information with clinical/molecular databases can also be linked. For a comprehensive summary of the challenges facing clinical applications in the light of growing research results in bioinformatics, see the recent paper by Knaup and colleagues (2004).

Risk Predictions

Medical decision depends on how risks are assessed, and this in turn depends on the available information. In *medical decision making* (as in any decision making) it is essential to assess possible outcomes, and computerized systems enable quantifying the alternatives using predictive models that rely on laboratory data and historical, demographic information. *Risk prediction* (or *risk profiling*) is intensively used in evaluating the risks of adverse outcome following acute cardiac events, such as acute myocardial infarction and congestive heart failure (e.g., Canadian Cardiovascular Outcomes Research Team, http://www.ccort.ca/). Simple *risk scores* are developed for in-hospital use (e.g., Thrombolysis in Myocardial Infarction, http://www.timi.org/home.htm). Different components of the risk score are estimated using *statistical modeling*. Risk profiling may be based on objective information, such as physical signs and lab values; efforts are also being made to use self-rates to assess individual health status (Greenberg & Root, 1995).

In this case, the use of data from patients' self-assessments of physical and mental health substantially improves predictive power. These techniques will help patients and physicians better anticipate an individual's needs.

Intelligent Data Analysis

The goal of *intelligent data analysis* (IDA) in medical applications is to make reasoning about how to analyze data in a human-like fashion. This is particularly important for understanding how to design expert systems and other computer systems that support decision making and diagnostics. Emergence of IDA followed the rapid increase in database use and the relative inefficiency of classical statistical techniques in analyzing large amounts of data. To analyze data, IDA applies artificial intelligence techniques and integrates classical statistical methods with advanced techniques, including data visualization, data mining, machine learning, pattern recognition, classification-clustering, fuzzy logic, Bayesian networks, and rule induction (see the IDA Web site for more information at http://www.ida-society.org/).

Internet Technologies (Web)

Web-based forms (*questionnaires*) allow patients and doctors to use the power of the Internet to collect and instantly process pertinent information. An example of Web-based health risk appraisal can be found at the University of Michigan: http://www.umich.edu/~hmrc/healthasse.html. Other disciplines such as nursing and dentistry are also capitalizing on the power of modern computing, so that eventually patients, policy makers, and providers will have full access to integrated information sets, and will be able to develop predictive models based on a full set of information.

For further reading, see the following:

Selected Web sites related to Health/Medical Informatics:

- *Health Informatics World Wide*, http://www.hiww.org/
- The *American Medical Informatics Association* (AMIA), http://www.amia.org/
- The *International Medical Informatics Association* (IMIA), http://www.imia.org/
- *Society for Medical Decision Making*, http://www.smdm.org/

ARNOLD B. MITNITSKI
DAVID ZITNER

References

Bemmel, J., & Musen, M. A. (1997). *Handbook on medical informatics* (1st ed.). Heidelberg, Gernany: Springer-Verlag.

Buchanan, B. G. & Shortliffe, E. H. (1984). *Rule-based expert systems: The MYCIN experiments of the Stanford heuristic programming project.* Reading, MA: Addison-Wesley.

Fayyad, U. M., Piatetsky-Shapiro, G., Smyth, P., & Uthurusamy, R. (Eds.). (1996). *Advances in knowledge discovery and data mining*. Menlo Park, CA: AAAI/MIT Press.

Greenberg, D. L., & Root, R. K. (1995). Clinical problem-solving. *Decision making by analogy. New England Journal of Medicine, 332*(9), 592–596.

Knaup, P., Ammenwerth, E., Brandner, R., et al. (2004). Towards clinical bioinformatics: Advancing genomic medicine with informatics methods and tools. *Methods of Information in Medicine, 43*, 302–307.

Ledley, R. (1965). *Use of computers in biology and medicine*. New York: McGraw-Hill.

Shortliffe, E. H., & Fagan, L. M. (2000). *Medical informatics: Computer applications in health care and biomedicine (medical informatics)* (2nd ed.). New York: Springer-Verlag.

Wyatt, J. C., & Keen, J. (2001). The new NHS information technology strategy. Technology will change practice. *British Medical Journal, 322*, 1378–1379.

Wyatt, J. C., & Liu, J. L. Y. (2002). Basic concepts in medical informatics. *Journal of Epidemiology and Community Health, 56*, 808–812.

HEALTH INFORMATION THROUGH TELECOMMUNICATION

Health care and health information have always been of great interest to older adults. Many seniors suffer from a chronic disease, often more than one. Managing these diseases can become overwhelming for both the older adult and the caregiver.

Information about the disease, treatment options, drug interactions, prevention, and support groups can make disease management truly manageable. In the past, such information was disseminated through health care professionals, printed materials, and via television and radio. Collecting the information required a concerted effort on the part of the older adult and caregiver; it was rarely at one's fingertips.

Now, however, with the burgeoning of the *Internet* and the *World Wide Web* (*Web*), health information is, literally, at one's fingertips. A plethora of information is just a couple of mouse clicks away from government, commercial, educational, and nonprofit health websites. It is interesting to note that the modern collection, acquisition, and dissemination of health information through the Internet results from a confluence of technologies: electricity, electronics, computers, telephone lines, Internet, imaging, health technologies, and laser and fiber optics. This list represents 8 of the 20 top engineering marvels of the 20th century, according to the National Academy of Engineering (Martindale, 2000). The time is therefore right for the public to take advantage of the wealth of health information that is so easily accessible through the available technology.

The very accessibility of information on the Internet, however, brings its own set of problems. There is too much information, often of dubious origin and reliability, for a lay person to process effectively and efficiently. Interventions such as training programs and vetted Web sites are now being tried to help older adults and their caregivers find reliable health information on the Internet. One such training program is a curriculum for older adults developed by the SPRY Foundation in collaboration with the National Library of Medicine. This curriculum teaches computer-literate older adults how to navigate the Web, find information from reliable sites (such as *MEDLINEplus*), process that information, and put it into printouts from web pages. Thus, the patient has a synthesized version of Web-derived information and a list of specific questions for the doctor.

The provision of health information is equally important to the caregivers and health service providers of older adults as their numbers will almost certainly increase in the future. The rapid expansion of medical knowledge makes it imperative that caregivers and practitioners maintain and improve their competence to provide services and also advise those for whom they care (Patel & Arocha, 1999). Traditional methods of print, video, and individual or group health education may not be enough to meet the demand. Most important, the trend within many governmental agencies is to move away from traditional methods and instead present information in *electronic formats* (i.e., Social Security Administration, Internal Revenue Service). The electronic format allows agencies to update information and reduce printing and distribution costs. Thus, an alternative method of health information delivery must be identified to serve all of those people who will be in need in the future. One of these avenues may be the Web, which is increasingly being used as an invaluable medium for providing information for a global audience. Furthermore, the Web has unlimited potential for supplementing many traditional methods of communication and information exchange.

Health Information on the Web

At present there are several thousand Web sites, with millions of pages devoted to health information (Post, 1997). Information on these health sites ranges from descriptive and diagnostic material concerning specific conditions and support group linkages to available local health services. Some of this information is already targeted to older adults. By mid-2000 there were 2 new consumer-based health information Web sites available that were specifically designed for ease of use by older adults (i.e., *AgePage*, sponsored by the National Institute on Aging and the MEDLINEplus, sponsored by the National Library of Medicine). These efforts are part of an initiative by the federal government to provide health information on the Web that is current, reliable, and easily accessible to the older segment of the population.

This direction in health information dissemination is important because older adults have shown significant interest in the direct application of electronic technology for acquiring health care. Effective electronic interfaces have been provided between older patients and clinicians and adherence to prescribed medication regimens has been increased through computerized voice mail. Moreover, results from a recent survey of middle-aged and older adults indicated that about 60% of the sample reported that they would like to learn how to access health information on the Web (Morrell, Mayhorn, & Bennett,

2002). With this in mind, SPRY Foundation, together with the National Library of Medicine and the National Institutes of Health, has developed a series of innovative research initiatives that have demonstrated the effectiveness of a curriculum to train older adults to search the Web quickly and efficiently to find reliable health information. This curriculum has also taught older adults how to use information to become better informed about their health condition(s), treatment options, and risks and how to use health information in becoming a consumer-partner with their health care providers.

It has also been demonstrated that users without medical training can use the Web to find answers to medical questions as well as to identify potential sources of information. For example, a site established to provide information on the recognition and treatment of cardiac arrhythmias received 10,732 requests for documents in 1 month via commercial Internet providers, commercial firms, educational institutions, and other sites (Widman & Tong, 1997). Therefore, the Web is already becoming a part of many people's daily environment. Newly diagnosed patients are usually eager for information about their illnesses. Information, however, may not always be enough (Mizsur, 1997). The Web also has the potential to provide social contact and encouragement, as well as emotional and informational support through *chatrooms* on specific medical topics (Mallory, 1997).

Health professionals are increasingly using networked, *computer-based technologies* to share information with one another. Furthermore, the Web may serve as a powerful tool for program development and improvement and for health networking between educational institutions for collaborative research. Use of the Web by clinicians may become an integral part of distance medicine technology, or telemedicine (Balas, Jaffrey, Kuperman, Boren, Brown, Pinciroli, et al., 1997). Thus, the Web is an important potential adjunct to cost-effective health care research and delivery (Doyle, Ruskin, & Engel, 1997).

Can Older Adults Use the Web?

Results from several recent surveys indicate that adults over the age of 65 have less experience with *personal computers* and the Web than do younger adults (Rogers, Cabrera, Walker, Gilbert, & Fisk, 1996). They also take more time to acquire computer skills and generally make more mistakes than do younger adults when learning how to use computers (Morrell & Echt, 1997). However, other systematic research has shown that older adults can readily learn how to use computers, and they can retain these skills over time (Echt, Morrell, & Park, 1998). Although only a small portion of older computer users rely on their machines for communication or for information gathering at present, they have shown substantial interest in using the Web. Furthermore, older adults currently constitute the fastest growing number of Web users. One reason, among others, that many older adults are not online may be that most Web sites are complex and difficult to navigate.

The National Institute on Aging has funded a substantial amount of systematic research on the topic of the cognitive aspects of computer use in older adults in the past decade. In March 1999, SPRY Foundation, together with numerous government and private partners, sponsored the first national conference on "Older Adults, Health Information, and the World Wide Web" at the National Institutes of Health in Bethesda, Maryland. This meeting brought together over 300 government and corporate participants and promoted a better understanding of the importance of this topic. A second biennial conference is slated for February 2001.

The findings from basic and applied research on aging and cognition and the use of electronic technology by older adults may well serve as a theoretical framework from which to build a *health information Web site* designed for ease of use and comprehension by older adults. A cornerstone of this research is the demonstration that age-related declines in certain underlying cognitive processes might be mediated by the manner in which instructional materials are constructed and subsequently presented in electronic formats. Age-related declines in vision may be addressed by applying specific design directives when constructing a Web site for use by older adults.

Results have shown that: (1) organizing material in a standard format or small discrete segments, (2) writing the text in simple language, (3) avoiding inferences, and (4) phrasing the text in the active, rather than the passive, voice reduces cognitive demands and can increase comprehension of information presented to older adults in print.

Medical information, in particular, has been shown to be better understood and remembered by both young and old adults when it was clearly structured and organized, or when cognitive demands were reduced. Similarly, when cognitive demands were reduced through careful organization and presentation of instructional materials, procedural tasks were more easily performed by young and old. Finally, it has been demonstrated that older adults can learn how to perform computer tasks with instructions composed of text and animations as well as instructions presented in the traditional format of text and illustrations. When animations portray the material presented in text, the material is better understood.

Other researchers have offered recommendations for building a Web site that takes into consideration age-related *declines in vision*. These include: (1) increasing contrast, especially for detailed stimuli; (2) avoiding subtle discriminations among colors; (3) minimizing the need to discriminate fine detail; (4) omitting the use of distracting visual components such as blinking icons; (5) using at least 14 point type for all text and headers; (6) avoiding the use of the colors in the green-blueviolet range, which are difficult for older adults to see; (7) avoiding the use of novelty typefaces; (8) using Helvetica or a sans serif typeface that is medium or bold weight; (9) presenting the text in caps and lower case and headers in all caps; (10) avoiding single spacing and reducing the number of characters per page; and (11) using nonjustified paragraph formatting (see Echt, in press; Hartley, 1999). SPRY Foundation has published a practical *Guide for Web Site Creators* that explains these recommendations and provides examples. The guide is available on their Web site: www.spry.org.

In brief, these findings, as well as the recommendations just listed, indicate that a Web site can be constructed that addresses age-related declines in cognition and vision. These innovations might well increase the use of the Web by older adults.

Issues on Web-Based Health Information

Although there are extensive health-related resources currently available on the Web, little systematic research has been conducted on how older adults might use the Web. A literature review located only 1 systematic study and 2 surveys on Web use in older adults. Mead, Spaulding, Sit, Meyer, and Walker (1997) examined the effects of age and type of training on efficiency and preferences in a Web search activity. Their results indicated that older adults were able to complete most of the Web search tasks, but they performed more procedures to find the required information than younger adults did. Bow, Williamson, and Wale (1996) surveyed adults over the age of 50 to determine how receptive they were to using the Web. Some of their participants were also observed using the Web. Although their respondents reported in general that they did not think the Web would be useful, their findings suggested that if the individuals in this age group were able to overcome mouse management problems, they became very positive about using the Web. Morrell and his colleagues surveyed young-old and old-old adults on their use of the Web. They found that individuals in these age groups were also enthusiastic about using the Web, and one of their primary goals was to use the Web to seek health information.

In addition, there are other critical issues that must be discussed. Much concern has been expressed about the validity of the information on current health Web sites. There is no mechanism in place to assure browsers that the information that they are viewing is current and/or reliable. Although health-related *telecommunications systems* are in use, little research has been conducted on these systems. The few results that have been reported are limited in evaluating the potential benefits and weaknesses of the systems (Scheerhorn, Warisse, & McNeilis, 1995). Finally, research is needed on how to make the Web user-friendly and accessible to older adults who are in low socioeconomic status categories, illiterate, or cognitively impaired. Finally, the issue of confidentiality in using the Web is also of major importance. Some Web sites currently sell their membership information.

Conclusion

In this article, we have described 4 important issues that concern older adults and their access to health information. First, the need for health information by older individuals, their caregivers, and their health service providers will increase dramatically in the 21st century. Traditional methods of health information delivery may not be enough to meet the demand. Second, the Web may be an additional option for providing health information to, older adults, their caregivers, and their health service providers. Third, older adults have shown substantial interest in using the Web, and they can learn and retain computer skills. Fourth, Web sites can be designed that take into consideration age-related declines in cognition and vision, which might ultimately increase the use of the Web for health information for older adults, their caregivers, and health service providers, as well as younger individuals. Caution must be taken, however, in the manner in which health information is currently presented on the Web. Clearly, more systematic research is needed on how best to present "new" health information over the Web in ways that facilitate learning, decision making, and maintenance in older adults.

RUSSELL E. MORGAN, JR.
ANN BENBOW
ROGER W. MORRELL

See also
Health Care: Financing, Use, and Organization
Internet Applications

References

Balas, E. A., Jaffrey, F., Kuperman, G. J., Boren, S. A., Brown, G. D., Pinciroli, F., & Mitchell, J. A. (1997). Electronic communication with patients: Evaluation of distance medicine technology. *Journal of the American Medical Association, 278,* 152–159.

Bow, A., Williamson, K., & Wale, K. (1996, October). *Barriers to public access.* Paper presented at Communications Research Forum, Melbourne, Australia.

Doyle, D. J., Ruskin, K. J., & Engel, T. P. (1997). The Internet and medicine: Past, present, and future. *Yale Journal of Biology and Medicine, 69,* 429–437.

Echt, K. W., Morrell, R. W., & Park, D. C. (1998). The effects of age and training modality on the acquisition of basic computer skills in older adults. *Educational Geronotology, 24,* 3–24.

Echt, K. W. (2002). Health information on the World Wide Web and older adults: Visual considerations and design directives. In R. W. Morrell (Ed.), *Older adults, health information, and the World Wide Web.* Mahwah, NJ: Lawrence Earlbaum Associates.

Hartley, J. (1999). What does it say? Text design, medical information, and older readers. In D. C. Park, R. W. Morrell, & K. Shifren (Eds.), *Processing of medical information* (pp. 233–248). Mahwah, NJ: Lawrence Earlbaum Associates.

Martindale, D. (2000, May). From power lines to pantyhose. *Scientific American.*

Mizsur, G. (1997, August). Helping patients find support on the Internet. *Nursing,* p. 28.

Mallory, C. (1997). What's on the Internet? Services for women affected by HIV and AIDS. *Health Care for Women International, 18,* 315–322.

Mead, S. E., Spaulding, V. A., Sit, R. A., Meyer, B., & Walker, N. (1997). Effects of age and training of World Wide Web navigation strategies. *In Proceedings of the Human Factors and Ergonomics Society 41st annual meeting* (pp. 152–156). Santa Monica, CA: Human Factors and Ergonomics Society.

Morrell, R. W., & Echt, K. V. (1997). Designing instructions for computer use by older adults. In A. D. Fisk & W. A. Rogers (Eds.), *Handbook of human factors and the older population* (pp. 335–361). San Diego, CA: Academic Press.

Morrell, R. W., Mayhorn, C. B., & Bennett, J. (2002). A survey of World Wide Web use in middle-aged and older adults. In R. W. Morrell (Ed.), *Older adults, health information, and the World Wide Web.* Mahwah, NJ: Lawrence Earlbaum Associates.

Patel, V. L., & Arocha, J. F. (1999). Medical expertise and cognitive aging. In D. C. Park, R. W. Morrell, & K. Shifren (Eds.), *Processing of medical information* (pp. 127–144). Mahwah, NJ: Lawrence Earlbaum Associates.

Post, J. A. (1997, Fall). Internet resources on aging. *Generations,* pp. 69–70.

Rogers, W. A., Cabrera, E. F., Walker, N., Gilbert, D. K., & Fisk, A. D. (1996). A survey of automatic teller machine usage across the life span. *Human Factors, 38,* 156–166.

Scheerhorn, D., Warisse, J., & McNeilis, K. D. (1995). Computer-based telecommunication among an illness-related community: Design, delivery, early use, and the functions of HIGHnet. *Health Communications, 7,* 301–325.

Widman, L. E., & Tong, D. A. (1997). Requests for medical advice from patients and families to health care providers who publish on the World Wide Web. *Archives of Internal Medicine, 157,* 209–212.

HEALTH INSURANCE

The Structure of Insurance

Health insurance, like all insurance, is intended to partially financially insulate one from bad events.

Plan elements commonly include a premium, deductible, co-pay or coinsurance, and a maximum out-of-pocket, among other specifics. The upfront cost (price) of a policy is called the *premium.* The *deductible* is a set dollar amount that must be satisfied before the health plan begins making payments on claims. A *co-payment* is a per occurrence patient payment (e.g. $20 to visit a primary care physician) while co-insurance is a percentage the patient is responsible for on a given insurance claim. The maximum *out-of-pocket* is the most a patient must pay themselves (not paid for by the insurance plan).

By definition, insurance benefits the high cost/unhealthy more and thus, all else equal, an insurance firm's customers are "adversely selected" to be higher cost. In recognition of this, insurers pursue 2 profitable strategies: they design their policies to encourage a predictable sorting and, when allowed, they carefully underwrite policies to adjust for observable signals concerning the customer's health. Predictable pools allow insurers to better anticipate claims. Primarily because of large employer's natural pool of low and moderate health cost workers, most non-elderly adults now receive health insurance through their employer. The history and future of health insurance is affected by the aforementioned insurer practices and risk pooling concerns.

History

The *health insurance industry* in the United States did not flourish until the middle of the 20th century, although there were numerous early attempts to protect against the costs of medical care. In the late 18th and 19th centuries, individuals formed mutual aid societies that paid cash to aid families on the death of their breadwinner. Due to poor understanding of actuarial concepts, many went bankrupt. Occasionally, employers in hazardous industries supplemented the costs of their employees' medical care. In 1917 Washington state passed the *Medical Act,* which required equal employer and employee contribution to defray the costs of medical care for accidents and injuries. This and other early workmen's compensation laws spurred several employers to finance non-injury-induced medical services.

Prior to 1930, most health insurance was actually "sickness" insurance, providing income replacement in the event of disability, illness, or accident. This made sense then because most patients were treated in their homes by family members, such that lost wages were the major cost. Medical technological advancements in the 1920s led to rising and more variable medical costs. Prompted by medical and public health leaders, the *Committee on the Costs of Medical Care* was created in 1926. Then, in 1929, Dallas teachers approached Baylor University Hospital and negotiated an arrangement where each teacher who paid $6 annually would be eligible for hospitalization of up to 3 weeks. The plan was later known as *Blue Cross.* A few months after the committee's final report in 1932 which argued strongly for some form of medical care prepayment insurance, Blue Cross began operation. The *American Hospital Association* (AHA) established a set of guidelines to eliminate inter-hospital competition and by 1937 all AHA-approved plans were enveloped in the Blue Cross name. In response, physicians developed their own plans under the name of *Blue Shield.* These plans required free choice of physicians.

In 1940, 1.3 million people had some form of hospital insurance, 49% of which were issued by *Blue Cross and Blue Shield.* Unlike commercial companies which experience rated, the Blues were non-profit so were often tax-exempt and required to community rate–charge the sick and healthy the same insurance premium. Commercial companies' relaxed pricing restrictions resulted in successful employee group bids. By 1951, commercial firms had more subscribers than both Blue Cross and Blue Shield.

A major change in government tax policy greatly increased the spread of group policies. An Internal Revenue Code in 1954 clarified and expanded eligibility of the 1943 administrative tax ruling stating that employers' contributions for their employees' group medical and hospitalization premiums were tax exempt. In general, the tax exemption, effectively a government subsidy, reduced after-tax insurance premiums enough to encourage the healthiest employees to enroll. In this way, sustainable risk pools were formed and group policies became more attractive to insurance companies.

Public insurance was greatly expanded with the establishment of Medicare and Medicaid in the *Social Security Act* of 1965. Medicare extended health coverage to almost all Americans aged 65 and older.

TABLE 1 National health expenditures per capita and percent distribution by source of funds: 1960–2002

	Percent of Gross Domestic Product		Percent of Total NHE				Per Capita (1)				
Year	National Health Expenditures	Public NHE	Private	Total	Public Federal	State and Local	National Health Expenditures	Private	Total	Public Federal	State and Local
2002	14.9	6.8	54.1	45.9	32.5	13.4	$5,439.9	$2,940.9	$2,499.0	$1,767.9	$731.1
2001	14.1	6.5	54.1	45.9	32.4	13.5	$5,021.3	$2,715.8	$2,305.5	$1,626.8	$678.7
2000	13.3	6.0	54.6	45.4	31.8	13.6	$4,670.1	$2,549.5	$2,120.6	$1,483.5	$637.1
1995	13.4	6.2	53.9	46.1	32.6	13.6	$3,697.8	$1,992.6	$1,705.1	$1,203.9	$501.2
1990	12.0	4.9	59.4	40.6	27.7	12.9	$2,738.4	$1,627.1	$1,111.3	$758.1	$353.3
1985	10.1	4.1	59.1	40.9	28.6	12.3	$1,764.7	$1,042.8	$721.9	$505.1	$216.8
1980	8.8	3.8	57.3	42.7	29.0	13.6	$1,066.6	$611.6	$455.0	$309.5	$145.5
1975	7.9	3.3	57.6	42.4	27.8	14.5	$589.6	$339.9	$249.7	$164.0	$85.8
1970	7.0	2.6	62.2	37.8	24.1	13.7	$347.6	$216.2	$131.4	$83.7	$47.7
1965	5.7	1.4	75.1	24.9	11.4	13.5	$205.2	$154.2	$51.1	$23.4	$27.7
1960	5.1	1.3	75.2	24.8	10.6	14.2	$143.3	$107.8	$35.5	$15.2	$20.3

(1) Census resident-based population less armed forces overseas and less the population of outlying areas.
Source: Centers for Medicare and Medicaid Services, Office of the Actuary: Data from the National Health Statistics Group.

In 1972, *Medicare* was expanded to include disabled persons and persons suffering from end-stage renal disease. In 2003, the *Medicare Prescription Drug, Improvement and Modernization Act* created a provision for prescription drugs, now referred to as *Medicare Part D*. About 19 million beneficiaries enrolled in 1965. Currently, Medicare provides coverage to approximately 40 million Americans and by 2030 it is estimated to serve 77 million Americans.

Medicaid was created in 1965 to provide health care services to low-income children, their parents, older adults, the blind, and individuals with disabilities. It expanded the existing federal-state welfare structure for the poor. In 1986, Medicaid was expanded to cover pregnant women, and, in 1990, the Medicaid prescription drug rebate program was enacted. In 1996, the current welfare system, or *Aid to Families with Dependent Children* (AFDC), was replaced by *Temporary Assistance for Needy Families* (TANF), which ended the automatic Medicaid enrollment and termination for those receiving or losing welfare cash assistance. In 1997, the *State Children's Health Insurance Program* (SCHIP) was created to expand coverage to near-poor children. Today, Medicaid and SCHIP together cover 15.7 million adults and 17.5 million children.

Recent Trends

As shown in Table 1, the nation spent 5.1% of its gross domestic product on health in 1960. Today, we spend close to 15% of GDP, over $5,000 annually per capita. Technological advancements in medicine account for a substantial portion, but certainly not all, of this cost increase. While out-of-pocket payments have risen, the federal government also now pays a considerably larger share of health expenses, tripling from 1960, to approximately 30%.

Today, about 61% of Americans are covered by an employer-sponsored health insurance policy. Each year of this century, these premiums had double-digit growth, unlike relatively stagnant wages, to an annual average of $3,383 for single coverage and $9,068 for family coverage.[1] Workers pay an average of 16% of their premium costs for single policies and 27% for family policies, with the remainder picked up by the employer. *Preferred provider organizations*, which have grown steadily in enrollment since 1996, now enroll about half of covered workers. *Health maintenance organization* enrollment, which dropped throughout the late 1990s, remains

[1] Average premiums and other employer sponsored insurance statistics are reported in Kaiser Family Foundation's 2003 annual survey of employer health benefits.

strong in the West and comprises one-quarter of covered workers nationally.

In general, those who do not expect medical costs to be high enough to warrant the premium choose to forgo health insurance. As the real costs of insurance has risen, so has the number of uninsured. In 2002, 44 million Americans (15.2%) were uninsured, up from 12.9% in 1987. Not surprisingly, most of the uninsured are lower income and spend very little on health care. Expansions to Medicaid and SCHIP have reduced the number of uninsured children. During the same period, the number of non-elderly uninsured adults has increased 4.5 percentage points. Largely due to Medicare, over 99% of the 65 and older population is currently insured. Public debate continues as to the true societal cost of uninsurance.

Elise Gould
Alexandra Minicozzi

See also
Medicare

HEALTH MAINTENANCE ORGANIZATIONS

Health maintenance organizations (*HMOs*) date to the 1930s when specific industry groups collected prepaid health insurance premiums in exchange for health care services by local providers. Forty years later, HMOs became associated with the *Health Maintenance Act* of 1973, enacted to stimulate the development of more prepaid practices primarily as a way to control escalating health care costs while maintaining high-quality care. HMOs are types of *managed care plans* and can be compared to other types of managed care plans, such as *preferred provider organizations* (PPOs) and *point of services plans* (POSs) or traditional *fee-for-service (FFS) plans*.

Traditional *health insurance* is often characterized by freedom of choice of providers by patients and provider autonomy for care that contributes to high costs for care and high premiums associated with overuse of health care services. By contrast, HMOs have less choice and usually low premiums. Members choose a primary care physician from a subset of community providers, or network, who provide direct patient care and act as *gatekeepers* by controlling inappropriate referrals to more expensive specialty care physicians and hospitals. PPOs increase patient choice and allow self-referrals, eliminating gatekeeper functions, but patients incur higher premiums than HMOs and predetermined out of pocket costs. POSs attempt to blend the structures of HMOs and PPOs by selecting a network primary care provider but permitting self-referrals out of network for increased out-of-pocket costs or deductibles.

Since their inception, HMOs have grown rapidly. In 1977, HMOs served approximately 8 million subscribers. By 1985, there were slightly over 20 million enrollees; this doubled to 40 million by 1992 and doubled again by 2000. However, by 2003 HMO enrollees had decreased to 72 million. A shift in type of plan by enrollees began to change noticeably in the late 1990s. In 1996, of health plans for covered workers, HMOs accounted for 31%, PPOs accounted to 28%, POSs accounted for 14%, and traditional plans accounted for 27% of the covered population. By 2001, HMOs accounted for 23%, PPOs accounted to 48%, POSs accounted for 22%, and traditional plans had dropped to 7% of the covered population (Gable, et al., 2001).

These changes are traced to demographics, technology, increased health insurance benefit costs for employers and major changes in health policy. The 1970s were characterized by high demand for services, hospital capacity expansion, increased use of high technology and uncontrolled health care costs. The early 1980s showed no signs of decreases in demand for services or cost increases, causing employers to encourage use of HMOs as a mechanism to control costs. The 1990s are characterized by consumer backlash to restrictions in choice and persist in today's market.

Although there is constant reorganization within the different types of plans, the following 5 types of models are commonly described: the *staff model HMOs* employ physicians and other providers directly, the *group model HMOs* contract with 1 or more group practices, *individual independent practice associations* (IPAs) contract with many individual physicians or providers who care for enrollees in their own offices, and *network model HMOs* contract not only with individuals but also with groups of physicians (Retchin, Brown, Yeh, Chu, & Moreno, 1997), and *mixed model HMOs* are a combination of any of the above models. In general, between 1980 and 2000, staff model HMOs have decreased considerably in enrollees, compared to sizable increases in IPA and mixed models (Institute for the Future, 2003).

Effects of HMOs on Older Adults

For older persons, Medicare provides nearly universal but limited coverage for health care. Medicare has substantial deductibles and co-payments. HMOs resisted enrolling older people primarily because of unfavorable cost-based reimbursement policies. The struggle between CMS and plans over reimbursement rates and premiums continue. In 1993, only 9% of Medicare beneficiaries were enrolled in Medicare fee-for-service coverage. Seventy-one percent had either employer-based or individually purchased supplemental FFS coverage, 13% were dually enrolled in Medicaid and Medicare programs, and 7% had enrolled in HMOs (Health Care Financing Administration, 1996). Between 1985 and 1996, the rates of Medicare HMO risk-contract enrollments more than doubled (Managed Care Online, 1999). In 1985, 38% of Medicare enrollees were enrolled under risk-contract HMOs. As of March 1996, 84% of Medicare enrollees were risk-contract HMOs. Under the 1997 Balanced Budget Act, Congress greatly expanded the ability of Medicare enrollees to join health maintenance organizations by creating the *Medicare+Choice program.*

Medicare contracts with the HMOs either through cost-based contracts or risk-based contracts. In cost-based contracts, the HMO bills Medicare based on services rendered. In a risk-based contract, *Medicare* pays a fixed premium to the plan, which is equivalent to the expenses for Medicare FFS beneficiaries in the local area (Luft, 1998). In 1996, 95% of the risk-contract HMOs offered coverage for an annual physical examination (this is not covered under *Medicare FFS*). Immunizations were offered by 86% of the HMOs, and 60% of the HMOs offered outpatient prescription drug coverage. Thus, a majority of older HMO enrollees are receiving a much broader range of health care coverage at a lower price than they could receive from Medicare FFS alone or supplemental insurance.

HMOs, operating under the system of *capitation*, tend to reduce use of resources and reward providers for "doing less." Elderly populations, on the other hand, tend to use health care services at higher rates than younger and healthier populations. Unlike employer-based enrollments in HMOs, Medicare beneficiaries in HMOs may disenroll within 30 days of enrollment. These policies by Medicare produce adverse risk selection by HMOs by restricting access to subspecialists for high-risk older enrollees, or making use of resources difficult for such enrollees, thus encouraging them to revert to *fee-for-service plans* (Luft, 1998).

Quality of Care in HMOs for Older Adults

Evidence from recent literature on quality of care is mixed. In a review of literature based on data collected earlier than 1994, Miller and Luft (1997) failed to find a clear verdict in support of or against the proposition that health maintenance organizations provide inferior quality of care for the elderly compared with fee-for-service plans. In terms of use of available health care resources, they found that HMOs use fewer resources than traditional FFS plans. For acute clinical conditions, outcomes for HMO plan enrollees were better than those in the FFS plans, but evidence was equivocal for services for chronic and long-term care for older adults. Analysis of data from the Medical Outcomes Study has shown that elderly patients with chronic illnesses under managed care tend to fare worse in their physical and health scores (Ware, Bayliss, Rogers, Kosinski, & Tarlov, 1996). An analysis of 4-year data from an HMO census on primary care staffing and access to care has shown that, among older adults, access to primary care providers is better with the HMOs than with the fee-for-service system. However, neither processes of care nor outcomes of care were found to be different between the 2 systems (Wholey, Burns, & Lavizzo-Mourey, 1998). The latest population report comparing traditional Medicare versus Medicare managed care (Landon, et al., 2004) indicated that Medicare managed care delivered better preventive services than traditional Medicare, but traditional Medicare was superior relative to access and overall beneficiary experiences.

Projections

Several emerging issues in care for older persons related to HMOs deserve mention. First, the debates on the quality of care will continue despite the studies of HMOs that have failed to show any significant difference in quality of care for the elderly. Second, Medicare has begun to provide a new prescription drug benefit to offset imports of less expensive prescriptions from other countries. Third, liability reform will continue to play a role in the evolution of services offered by HMOs. Fourth, the demand for cost-effective care will not decrease the attractiveness of HMOs and other forms of managed care for older populations.

The Institute for the Future (2003) proposes that 3 types of insurance plans are likely to develop based on employment status and household wealth. The "*carriage trade*" will consist of traditional FFS coverage and PPOs, including traditional Medicare. This group accounted for 53% of the population in 1997 and is expected to decrease to 33% in 2010. "*HMO descendants*" will represent the largest group, comprising traditional HMOs and PPOs characterized by low co-payments and deductibles for in-plan use of providers, with self-referrals costing more as either co-payments, deductibles, or reimbursement rates. In 1997 this group accounted for 27% of the population and in 2010 it is expected to increase to 50% of the population. Finally, the "*low tier*" will include the poor—Medicaid recipients and the uninsured—accounting for 20% in 1997, but decreasing to 17% in 2010. Wildcards that may affect the larger health insurance market and thus enrollment into type of coverage include: protracted recessions that shift enrollees from one type of plan to another; taxable status of health benefits causing employers to stop providing benefits; legislative changes that affect HMO enrollments; universal health insurance that would eliminate barriers to care access for the uninsured; and national health insurance that would either eliminate or virtually eliminate private-sector sponsored health insurance plans.

James C. Romeis

References

Gabel, J., et al. (2001). Job-based health insurance in 2001: Inflation hits double digits, managed care retreats. *Health Affairs*, *20(5)*, 180–186.

Health Care Financing Administration. (1996). *Profiles of Medicare*. Washington, DC: U.S. Department of Health and Human Services.

Institute for the Future. (2003). *Health and health care 2010* (2nd ed.). San Francisco: Robert Wood Johnson Foundation, Jossey-Bass.

Landon, B. E., et al. (2004). Comparison of performance of traditional Medicare vs Medicare managed care. *Journal of the American Medical Association*, *291*, 1744–1752.

Luft, H. S. (1998). Medicare and managed care. *Annual Review of Public Health*, *19*, 459–475.

Managed Care Online. (1999). *Medicare HMO enrollment* (On-line). Available: http://www.mcol.com/mcfact2.htm.

Miller, R. H., & Luft, H. S. (1997). Does managed care lead to better or worse quality of care? *Health Affairs*, *16*, 7–25.

Retchin, S. M., Brown, R. S., Yeh, S. C., Chu, D., & Moreno, L. (1997). Outcomes of stroke patients in Medicare fee for service and managed care. *Journal of the American Medical Association*, *278*, 119–124.

Ware, J. E., Jr, Bayliss, M. S., Rogers, W. H., Kosinski, M., & Tarlov, A. R. (1996). Differences in 4-year health outcomes for elderly and poor, chronically ill patients treated in HMO and fee-for-service systems: Results from the Medical Outcomes Study. *Journal of the American Medical Association*, *276*, 1039–1047.

Wholey, D. R., Burns, L. R., & Lavizzo-Mourey, R. (1998). Managed care and the delivery of primary care to the elderly and the chronically ill. *Health Services Research*, *33*, 322–353.

HEALTH-RELATED QUALITY OF LIFE

See
Quality of Life

HEARING

Hearing is mediated by the human *auditory system* and is critical in establishing and maintaining a person's relationship with the sociophysical environment. According to the latest National Health Interview Survey (2004), annual age-adjusted rates of some *hearing impairment* ranged from 11.0% to 12.7% in whites and 5.9% to 8.5% in African Americans. Rates of severe bilateral hearing impairment in these race groups were 0.7% to 1.1% and 0.1% to 0.5%, respectively. Reported rates of hearing impairment remained relatively stable in the United States from 1986 to 1995. The most common

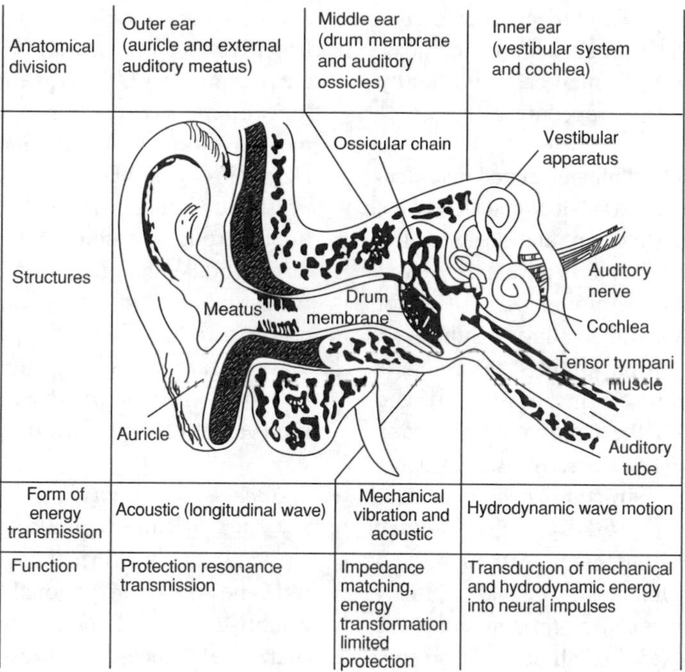

FIGURE 1 A schematic representation of the three anatomical divisons of the human ear, with their associated structural and functional characteristics. From Willard R. Zemlin, *Speech and Hearing Science: Anatomy and Physiology* (4th ed.). Copyright © 1998 by Allyn & Bacon. Reprinted with permission.

auditory disorder in older adults, affecting 13% of Americans older than age 65 years, is *presbycusis*, the bilateral loss of hearing capacity associated with normal physiological aging of the auditory system.

The Stimulus for Hearing

The adequate stimulus for normal human hearing is mechanical energy in the form of acoustic waves generated by a vibrating body and transmitted in a gaseous, liquid, or solid medium with a fundamental frequency between 20 and 20,000 Hz. *Auditory stimuli* include pure tones, complex tones, speech, and noise.

Figure 1 is a schematic representation of the 3 anatomical divisions of the human ear, with their associated structural and functional characteristics. The vestibular apparatus mediates equilibrium and does not pertain to hearing.

Age-Related Changes in the Human Auditory System

Outer Ear. With age, hair growth tends to increase within the folds of the pinna. The *pinna* may increase in length and breadth by several millimeters, and the supporting walls of the external *meatus* may show atrophic changes. *Cerumen* is found normally in the external canal. Approximately one-third of the elderly exhibit excessive and impacted cerumen. This common ear problem may appear as a *hearing loss*.

Middle Ear. Aging produces a thinning of the *tympanic membrane* and atrophy of the tensor tympani muscle. Arthritic changes occur in the incudomalleal and incudostapedial joints of the ossicular chain. In *otosclerosis*, a common condition more prevalent in women than men, new bone forms in the cochlear capsule and tends to immobilize the footplate of the shapes in the oval window.

Stapedial otosclerosis and other conditions, in which sound waves are unable to travel properly through the outer and *middle ear*, produce a *conductive hearing loss*. The progression of this loss, which never exceeds 60 dB, may be prevented by medical therapy or surgical procedures.

Inner Ear. Four classes of age-related disorders occur in the inner ear (Schuknecht & Gacek, 1993): (1) *sensory presbycusis* (atrophy and degeneration of hair cells and supporting cells in the extreme basal coil of the cochlea), (2) *neural presbycusis* (loss of neurons in the cochlea and the auditory pathways), (3) *strial presbycusis* (atrophy of the stria vascularis and corresponding deficiencies in the bioelectric and biochemical properties of the endolymphatic fluids), and (4) *cochlear conductive presbycusis* (atrophic changes in the vibratory structures of the cochlear partition). Each class of *presbycusis* is characterized by specific audiometric outcomes. Although the 4 types of presbycusis often occur in isolation, many hearing losses are evidenced as mixtures of these types. However, about 25% of all cases of presbycusis have indeterminate histologic characteristics.

Auditory Pathways and the Brain. In the retrocochlear region of the auditory system, a loss of *neurones* appears with age in the ventral cochlear nucleus. Also, the size and shape of the ganglion cells are altered in the medial geniculate body, the superior olivary nucleus, and the inferior colliculus. Atrophy occurs in the eighth cranial nerve, and the number of neuronal cells in the auditory pathway is reduced. The cortex of the temporal lobes of the brain retains normal stratification, but there is a bilaterally symmetrical loss of ganglion cells. The relationship between decreased *auditory processing* in presbycusis and the probable reduction in neurochemical/neurotransmitter functions within the *auditory system* (including brain stem, auditory cortex, and association areas) needs further study.

Basic Psychophysical Functions

Sensitivity for Pure Tones. The minimal sound pressure required to elicit an auditory response 50% of the time defines the absolute threshold for that particular stimulus under a given set of testing conditions. Reference threshold levels (audiometric zero) have been published by the American National Standards Institute. The relation between age and *pure tone thresholds* is now well established (Brant & Fozard, 1990). As frequency increases above 1,000 Hz, hearing becomes increasingly poorer as a function of age. Age held constant, men have poorer hearing than women above 1,000 Hz. Below 1,000 Hz, *women have poorer hearing*. Presbycusis changes in auditory thresholds are continual throughout adulthood but are most marked after age 60. With aging, hearing loss tends to spread from higher to lower frequencies. Frequency discrimination thresholds for pure tones and *complex tones* are also negatively affected by age. The International Organization for Standardization has specified values of normal hearing by frequency and age.

Speech Sensitivity. The minimal amount of acoustic pressure required for the *intelligibility of speech* in quiet defines the speech reception threshold. The American National Standards Institute has established 19-dB sound pressure level as the normal speech reception threshold for young adults tested on spondaic words. The *speech reception threshold* increases markedly with advancing age. This increase has been attributed to elevated frequency thresholds that increase at an accelerating rate between ages 50 and 90 years.

Speech Discrimination. The intelligibility of words presented at suprathreshold levels in quiet or noise is a measure of *speech recognition*. When hearing level is controlled across age groups, no differences in speech discrimination occur from age 55 to 84 years (Dubno, Lee, Matthews, & Mills, 1997). Under adverse listening conditions (e.g., noise, overlapping words, excessive reverberation, and temporally distorted speech), older persons exhibit disproportionately greater speech discrimination deficits than younger listeners, even when hearing levels are controlled. These findings suggest that neural and cortical processing functions beyond the peripheral level are implicated in age-related deficits in auditory communication. This is of critical importance because central auditory dysfunction has been related to cognitive dysfunction and senile dementia (Gates, Cobb, Linn, Rees, Wolf, & D'Agostino, 1996).

Temporal Discrimination and Summation. The monaural ability to hear the temporal separation between 2 successive noise segments or tones is a measure of temporal resolution. The minimal gap detection threshold for noise is 2 to 3 msec. *Auditory temporal summation* involves a reciprocal relationship between stimulus intensity and stimulus duration (up to 200 to 300 cosec) to produce a threshold response. Temporal resolution and temporal summation decline with age, even with hearing level controlled. The threshold interaural time difference for clicks at a low sound level is approximately twice as large for older than young listeners. Accordingly, older listeners show a decreased ability in sound lateralization and localization. Whether the reduction in temporal processing can account for the speech-understanding problems of older adults requires further investigation.

Rehabilitation of Impaired Hearing

Conventional Hearing Aids. Deteriorated hearing often may be improved by means of an electronic hearing aid. The optimal interface between hearing aid and hearing loss will depend on the degree and nature of the loss. Hearing aids vary in initial cost, acoustic efficiency, durability, operating expense, service availability, and physical attractiveness. Hearing aid selection will also be influenced by the physical and psychological characteristics of the listener, particularly in older adults. Whenever feasible, hearing devices should be fitted binaurally for maximal hearing advantage.

Hearing aids provide high-fidelity electronic enhancement of acoustic signals, by analog or digital processing. Types of hearing aids include body-worn, eyeglass, behind the ear, on the ear, and partially or completely in the ear canal. Some hearing aids include a programming function that allows the listener to set the electroacoustic parameters for maximal hearing in particular situations.

Assistive Listening Devices. The listening needs of older individuals cannot be successfully addressed with hearing aids alone. Assistive listening devices (ALDs), either solely or in conjunction with the use of personal hearing aids, can facilitate listening in various sound environments. Listening situations that are especially problematic even with hearing aids, such as listening in large groups, on the telephone, in restaurants and at concerts and movies are ideally suited for ALD use. ALDs can reduce the impact of hearing loss and also ensure safety for older individuals. These include the following categories:

Security and Alarm Systems. This includes safety devices that warn of the possibility of emergency situations, and signaling devices designed to alert individuals of common sounds, like doorbells or a ringing phone. Examples include smoke/fire detectors, alarm clocks, vibrating or flashing light signalers and telephone signalers.

Telephones and Accessories. This includes *amplified telephones*, cordless/speaker phones, amplified receiver handset, portable telephone amplifiers, and *telecommunications device for the deaf* (TDD-formerly called TTY), which are visual typewriters that send messages over the phone.

Listening Devices for Television, Theater, or Group Situations. Personal listening devices such as infrared listening devices and Personal FM Listening Devices make many situations more enjoyable for both the individual with the hearing loss and the people around them. The volume level of the television, radio, or stereo can be at normal levels if a listening device is used, therefore avoiding a situation where others cannot tolerate the high volume level needed for the individual with the hearing loss.

Implantable Hearing Aids. For patients with intractable conductive disorders and adequate cochlear reserve, hearing devices that circumvent some of the limitations of conventional hearing aids are available. The most widely used is the *bone-anchored hearing aid* (BAHA), a device anchored to the temporal bone that can provide better hearing than conventional hearing aids especially when fitting of the latter is hindered by anatomical abnormalities or chronic ear disease. The use of these devices has been recently extended for rerouting of sound signals in people with profound unilateral or asymmetric hearing loss.

Other implantable devices are available or under development. These devices directly stimulate the tympanic membrane, the ossicular chain or the cochlea. For certain listeners and testing conditions (e.g., speech in noise), an implanted temporal bone device can provide better hearing than a conventional bone-conduction or air-conduction hearing aid.

Cochlear Implants. In certain kinds of nearly total deafness, the cochlea is nonfunctional, but the auditory nerve remains essentially intact. Thus, implants with 1 to 20 or more electrodes can be inserted into the cochlea of adults and children to provide direct electrical stimulation of functional nerve fibers. The neural patterns generated by the cochlear implant will depend on the encoding strategy designed into the sound processor. In *multichannel implants*, the encoded information relates to the intensity, temporal characteristics, and frequency of the incoming sound. As the perception of sound through a cochlear implant is markedly different than that in normal hearing, training programs must be provided before the salient features of speech and environmental sounds can be recognized and properly interpreted in their neurally encoded form. Nevertheless, even in cases of pre-lingual deafness and congenital deafness due to cochlear malformations, multichannel implants can provide substantial improvements in hearing for speech and music. Postsurgical risks of a cochlear implant are always present and include degeneration of surviving auditory nerve fibers, facial nerve damage with paralysis, intracochlear infections, and increased tinnitus.

Education and Training Programs. Other technological advances are also available to assist hearing-impaired persons. Various kinds of amplifying systems can enhance speech signals, speech-visual interactive systems can improve speech-reading, auditory to tactile conversion devices can encode speech information, and *radio transmission systems* are useful in group situations (Corso, 1985). However, hearing-impaired persons should receive an appropriate educational orientation with counseling for a particular type of aid. Unless there is full participation in a well-developed rehabilitation program, maximal hearing benefits most likely will not be attained from any assistive device.

Emad Massoud

References

Brant, L. J., & Fozard, J. L. (1990). Age changes in pure tone thresholds in longitudinal study of normal aging. *Journal of the Acoustical Society of America*, *88*, 813–820.

Corso, J. F. (1985). Communication, presbycusis, and technological aids. In H. K. Ulatowska (Ed.), *The aging brain* (pp. 33–51). San Diego: College Hill Press.

Dubno, J. R., Lee, F. S., Matthews, L. I., & Mills, J. H. (1997). Age-related and gender-related changes in monaural speech recognition. *Journal of Speech, Language, and Hearing Research*, *40*, 444–452.

Gates, G. A., Cobb, J. L., Linn, R. T., Rees, T., Wolf, P. A., & D'Agostino, R. B. (1996). Central auditory dysfunction, cognitive dysfunction and dementia in older people. *Archives of Otolaryngology: Head and Neck Surgery*, *122*, 161–167.

National Health Interview Survey. (2004). *Journal of Gerontology Series A Biological Sciences and Medical Sciences*, *59*(11), 1186–1190.

Schuknecht, H. F., & Gacek, M. R. (1993). Cochlear pathology in presbycusis. *Acta Otolaryngology, Rhinology, and Laryngology*, *102*, 1–16.

HEMISPHERIC ASYMMETRIES

Definition and Nature

Prior to the 19th century, the 2 halves of the human brain were assumed to be mirror images: symmetrical in structure and function. The seeds of modern interest in hemispheric asymmetries, which are anatomical, physiological, and behavioral differences between the left and right sides of the brain, were sown with published observations of speech loss after left *brain injury* (Broca, 1865; translated by Berker, Berker, & Smith, 1986).

More than 2 centuries later, myriad other left *brain-right brain differences* have been documented, and many dichotomies proposed to characterize them. One of the earliest such dichotomies described the *left brain* as dominant for verbal (language, speech) and the *right brain* for nonverbal (spatial, musical) performance. This contrast fell out of favor as it was learned, for example, that the left hemisphere is crucially involved in processing temporal dimensions of music (Hellige, 2001) and the right hemisphere in lexical-semantic, pragmatic, and prosodic aspects of language comprehension (Brownell, 2004). Examples of later proposals include attributions of analytic and local cognitive operations to the left hemisphere realm, and holistic and global operations to the right. It is important to note that at present, such contrasts typically are taken to refer to each hemisphere's presumed primary involvement in or capacity for the denoted cognitive operations, rather than as true dichotomies. In any case, controversy continues to surround most such characterizations (Hellige, 2001), and much current work aims to determine the complementary contributions of the 2 hemispheres in various domains of function.

The likely origins of hemispheric asymmetries are evolutionary, hereditary, developmental, experiential, and pathologic (Hellige, 2001; Toga & Thompson, 2003). Brain asymmetries are not static, being modified by both exogenous and endogenous factors, such as task demands and, apparently, aging.

Changes in Hemispheric Asymmetries with Age

Anatomical Asymmetries. Recent MRI data from a large cross-section of highly educated adults provides little evidence of major change in asymmetries in regional *brain volumes over the life span* (Raz, Gunning-Dixon, Head, Rodrigue, Williamson, & Acker, 2004). In older individuals, decreased volume in the lateral prefrontal cortex was most prominent, with hippocampal reduction by the mid-50s. Each of the 11 other regions of interest evidenced essentially linear declines with age. Limitations of cross-sectional design and generalizability aside, microstructural analyses (e.g., cytoarchitectonic profiling, Amunts, Schleicher, Ditterich, & Zilles, 2003; assessment of cortical columnar structure and connectivity, Hutsler & Galuske, 2003) may be more sensitive to potential age-related changes. Raz and colleagues (2004) identified another particular challenge for research on anatomical asymmetries: as in other reports, these investigators found individual differences in both the size and direction of observed asymmetries. Also, the connection between anatomy and behavior may be elusive. A recent meta-analysis, for example, indicated a surprisingly weak association between hippocampal size and *episodic memory* performance in older adults (Van Petten, 2004).

Neurochemical Asymmetries. Age-associated reductions in *dopamine* transporters in humans are nearly linear (Van Dyck, Seibyl, Malison, Laruelle, Zoghbi, Baldwin, et al., 2002), but this may not be the case for other neurotransmitter systems. For example, recent work with Wistar rats indicated a reduction in laterality of high-affinity choline uptake in the *hippocampus* for aging males (Kristofikova, Stastny, Bubenikova, Druga, Klaschka, & Spaniel, 2004). Human investigation is clearly needed to determine the generalizability of this report, and to ascertain the nature and extent of age-related asymmetry change in other neurochemical systems.

Brain-Asymmetry Accounts for Cognitive Aging. In the 1980s, several groups of investigators proposed that the right hemisphere ages more rapidly than the left, and that this asymmetrical decline could account for behavioral patterns that typify adults who are ostensibly aging normally, such as preserved verbal but reduced performance IQs (e.g., Goldstein & Shelly, 1981). This "*right hemisphere aging*" hypothesis continues to be investigated in presumed right-hemisphere domains such as face processing (Harvey & Butler, 2004) and comprehension of emotional intonation (Orbelo, Testa, & Ross, 2003). It is not always clear in such research whether age-related processing difficulties (e.g., central auditory processing deficit; Purdy, 2001) or even more basic sensory changes have been taken into account.

Recently, functional neuroimaging evidence has suggested age differences in asymmetries along a different cerebral dimension. Tasks that elicit left-right asymmetries in prefrontal activation for younger adults often show more extensive and bilateral prefrontal activity in older adults (Reuter-Lorenz, Jonides, Smith, Hartely, Miller, Marshuetz, et al., 2000). According to Dolcos and colleagues (2002) this prefrontal "hemispheric asymmetry reduction in older adults" (HAROLD) (Cabeza, 2002) has been documented for episodic and *semantic memory*, *working memory*, *perception*, and *inhibitory control*; evidence consistent with HAROLD also was recently reported for *problem-solving in arithmetic* (El Yagoubi, Lemaire, & Besson, 2005). Cabeza and colleagues (2002) determined that HAROLD applied to high-performing but not low-performing older adults, whose activation patterns mirrored those of younger adults; similarly, Nielson and colleagues (2002) reported that HAROLD was connected with older subjects' success in inhibitory control. Cabeza and colleagues attribute such findings to efforts by higher-performing older adults to compensate for age-related declines.

Dolcos and colleagues (2002) note that the right hemisphere aging and *HAROLD hypotheses* are not mutually exclusive, suggesting that perhaps the former applies to brain regions outside the prefrontal cortex. However, this proposal is inconsistent with recent evidence of asymmetry reductions in other areas of the *aging brain*, as documented by fMRI in humans (Meulenbroek, Petersson, Voermans, Weber, & Fernandez, 2004) and neurochemical analysis in (male but not female) Wistar rats (Kristofikova, et al., 2004).

The right hemisphere aging hypothesis, focusing as it does on an entire brain hemisphere or relatively gross regions within that hemisphere, at present limits its potential explanatory value. While the HAROLD proposal is quite new, the same is true for it: prefrontal brain regions are vast and highly differentiated. Another problem for the HAROLD hypothesis is that in some experiments, older adults exhibit paradoxical prefrontal asymmetries (e.g., only left or right activation in working memory conditions that elicit right or left activation in younger adults; Reuter-Lorenz, et al., 2000) rather than reduced asymmetries. Future work will need to aim for a principled account of the existence, nature, and/or direction of more finely specified prefrontal hemispheric asymmetry changes in older individuals.

Issues in Investigation and Interpretation

There are varied challenges ahead for investigating age-related changes in hemispheric asymmetries. Among them are general difficulties related to clarifying and characterizing the existence and extent of asymmetries in young adults, to drawing longitudinal conclusions from cross-sectional data, and to cataloguing and controlling for myriad individual difference factors that may modulate observed relationships in both younger and older individuals. The strictly correlational nature of age-group comparison research is also problematic. A host of general issues needs to be solved in relation to interpreting evidence from neuroimaging work, as well. Among the most obvious is determining what activation and activation differences really reflect in terms of the brain circuitry that is engaged in any particular task. More work is required, too, to develop *a priori* predictions about the nature and locales of changes in hemispheric asymmetry that should characterize older adults, on the road to developing testable models with specific, falsifiable hypotheses. And as suggested above, another major goal will be to link observed asymmetries to varied indices of performance.

Connie A. Tompkins
Victoria L. Scharp

References

Amunts, K., Schleicher, A., Ditterich, A., & Zilles, K. (2003). Broca's region: Cytoarchitectonic asymmetry and developmental changes. *Journal of Comparative Neurology, 465*(1), 72–89.

Berker, E. A., Berker, A. H., & Smith, A. (1986). Translation of Broca's 1865 report. Localization of speech in the third left frontal convolution. *Archives of Neurology, 43*(10), 1065–1072.

Broca, P. (1865). Sur la faculte du langage articule. *Bulletin de la Societe d'Anthropologie, 6,* 337–393.

Brownell, H. H. (2004). Right hemisphere language and communication functions in adults. In R. D. Kent (Ed.), *The MIT encyclopedia of communication disorders* (pp. 291–294). Cambridge, MA: The MIT Press.

Cabeza, R. (2002). Hemispheric asymmetry reduction in older adults: The HAROLD model. *Psychology and Aging, 17*(1), 85–100.

Cabeza, R., Anderson, N. D., Locantore, J. K., & McIntosh, A. R. (2003). Aging gracefully: Compensatory brain activity in high-performing older adults. *Neuroimage, 17*(3), 1394–1402.

Dolcos, F., Rice, H. J., & Cabeza, R. (2002). Hemispheric asymmetry and aging: Right hemisphere decline or asymmetry reduction. *Neuroscience Biobehavioral Reviews, 26*(7), 819–825.

El Yagoubi, R., Lemaire, P., & Besson, M. (2005). Effects of aging on arithmetic problem-solving: An event-related brain potential study. *Journal of Cognitive Neuroscience, 17*(1), 37–50.

Goldstein, G., & Shelly, C. (1981). Does the right hemisphere age more rapidly than the left? *Journal of Clinical Neurology, 3*(1), 65–78.

Harvey, M., & Butler, S. H. (2004). Aging affects perceptual and eye-movement biases apparent in chimeric face processing. Available: http://www.perceptionweb.com/perception/ecvp04/0225.html

Hellige, J. (2001). *The asymmetrical brain: What's left and what's right* (2nd ed.). Cambridge, MA: Harvard University Press.

Hutsler, J., & Galuske, R. A. (2003). Hemispheric asymmetries in cerebral cortical networks. *Trends in Neurosciences, 26*(8), 429–435.

Kristofikova, Z., Stastny, F., Bubenikova, V., Druga, R., Klaschka, J., & Spaniel, F. (2004). Age- and sex-dependent laterality of rat hippocampal cholinergic system in relation to animal models of neurodevelopmental and neurodegenerative disorders. *Neurochemical Research, 29*(4), 671–680.

Meulenbroek, O., Petersson, K. M., Voermans, N., Weber, B., & Fernandez, G. (2004). Age differences in neural correlates of route encoding and route recognition. *Neuroimage, 22*(4), 1503–1514.

Nielson, K. A., Langenecker, S. A., & Garavan, H. (2002). Differences in the functional neuroanatomy of inhibitory control across the adult life span. *Psychology and Aging, 17*(1), 56–71.

Orbelo, D. M., Testa, J. A., & Ross, E. D. (2003). Age-related impairments in comprehending affective prosody with comparison to brain-damaged subjects. *Journal of Geriatric Psychiatry and Neurology, 16*(1), 44–52.

Purdy, J. K. (2001). Hearing loss associated with aging. Available: http://www.healthyhearing.com/library/article_content.asp?article_id=73

Raz, N., Gunning-Dixon, F., Head, D., Rodrigue, K. M., Williamson, A., & Acker, J. D. (2004). Aging, sexual dimorphism, and hemispheric asymmetry of the cerebral cortex: Replicability of regional differences in volume. *Neurobiology of Aging, 25*(3), 377–396.

Reuter-Lorenz, P. A., Jonides, J., Smith, E. E., Hartely, A., Miller, A., Marshuetz, C., et al., (2000). Age differences in the frontal lateralization of verbal and spatial working memory revealed by PET. *Journal of Cognitive Neuroscience, 12*(1), 174–187.

Toga, A. W., & Thompson, P. M. (2003). Mapping brain asymmetry. *Nature Reviews Neuroscience, 4,* 37–48.

Van Dyck, C. H., Seibyl, J. P., Malison, R. T., Laruelle, M., Zoghbi, S. S., Baldwin, R. M., et al. (2002). Age-related decline in dopamine transporters. Analysis of striatal subregions, nonlinear effects, and hemispheric asymmetries. *American Journal of Geriatric Psychiatry, 10*(1), 36–43.

Van Petten, C. (2004). Relationship between hippocampal volume and memory ability in healthy individuals across the lifespan: Review and meta-analysis. *Neuropsychologia, 42*(10), 1394–1413.

HIP FRACTURES

Hip fractures are increasingly common injuries in older persons and have a profound effect on morbidity and mortality. They often result in prolonged hospitalization and institutionalization. The incidence of hip fractures virtually doubles with each decade over age 50, and women have 2 to 3 times the rate of hip fracture as men. There is increased mortality within the first year following a hip fracture, and it is greatest in the first 4 to 6 months, with up to 30% of patients with hip fractures dying in the first year of related comorbidities. With an aging population complicated by multiple comorbidities, patients with hip fractures are an increasingly common group to use hospital resources, especially when their hospital stays are prolonged.

Optimal *management of hip fractures* in older people requires a coordinated, multidisciplinary approach. This includes optimizing related illnesses, prioritizing who should have which types of surgical intervention, and providing aggressive rehabilitation. Ideally these patients should have their hip fractures surgically addressed within 24 to 48 hours of admission. The goal of management is to reduce pain, optimize function, and return patients to their pre-morbid ambulatory status.

Diagnosis

The hip sits at the end of the long bone of the leg (femur) which has a rounded ball end that fits into a socket (acetabulum) formed by the bones of the pelvis (Figure 1). The diagnosis of a hip fracture is usually evident when a patient presents with the inability to bear weight after a slip and fall event. Pain is usually directed to the groin or anterior thigh with active range of motion or passive movement by the physician. If the fracture is displaced, the patient will be in the "down and out" posture with the affected leg shortened and externally rotated.

Radiographs taken in the 2 planes (AP and lateral) are generally sufficient to confirm the diagnosis (Figure 2). In suspected cases that cannot be confirmed with plain radiographs, MRI imaging may be necessary. Technician bone scanning is less sensitive, requiring 2 to 5 days post-injury to become diagnostic, but is sometimes still used, especially if access to MRI is difficult.

Initial Management

Once the diagnosis of hip fracture is established (Figure 3), a general medical assessment is required to document and manage related illness. These commonly are present, because while hip fractures

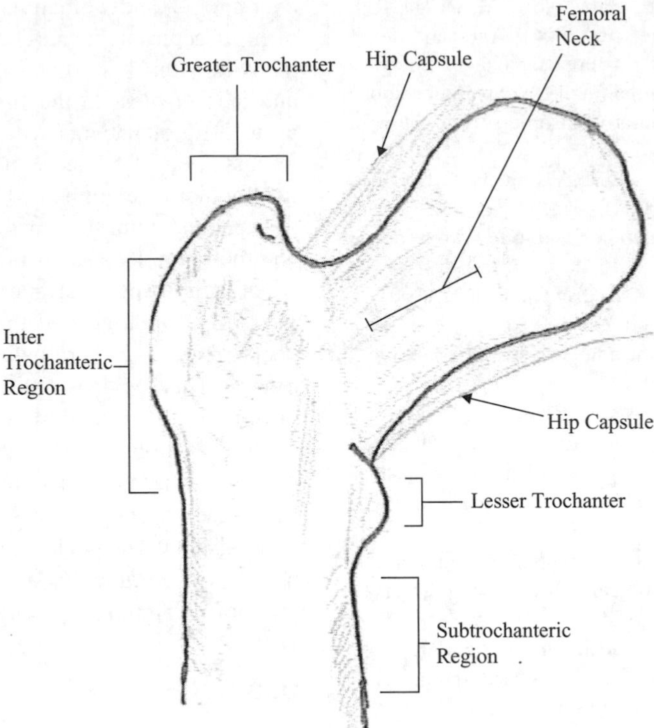

FIGURE 1 Hip Anatomy

can be incurred by vigorous old people (e.g., a fall while jogging), the great majority of older people who break their hips are frail and thus have multiple and interacting medical (and social) problems. Establishing the mechanism of injury is important—for example, to rule out a syncopal episode (faint) that might require further investigation. The past medical history and functional inquiry should focus on whether cancer might be present, as metastatic disease in a so-called "*pathologic*" *hip fracture* may be the initial presentation. Careful review of the radiographs to assess irregular lucency, associated soft tissue mass, or transverse fracture pattern is of utmost importance, as these characteristics may all be suggestive of a metastatic pathologic fracture.

Pain management with frequent low titrated doses of narcotic is required. Formal traction is not required, but splinting the leg to the unaffected one reduces pain if transport is necessary.

Non-operative management should only be considered in very select patient groups. Patients who present with stable impacted hip fractures, who after a fall present with hip pain but have walked on the affected side, have preserved active and passive range of motion with minimal discomfort, and have a radiographically impacted femoral neck fracture may be considered for non-operative management.

Patients who do not exhibit significant pain, who can walk from bed to chair, or are medically unstable or cognitively impaired may be treated non-operatively. Non-operative management, however, is fraught with complications of "*fracture disease*." These include increased pain, hypoventilation, atelectasis, pneumonia, urinary tract infections, thromboembolic disease, and decubitus ulcers. In consequence, surgical treatment usually preferred.

Classification

There are 2 major groups of hip fractures (Figure 4):

- ***Intracapsular fractures***, which are fractures occurring through the femoral neck. These can be further subclassified as *(a) displaced* or *(b) undisplaced.*

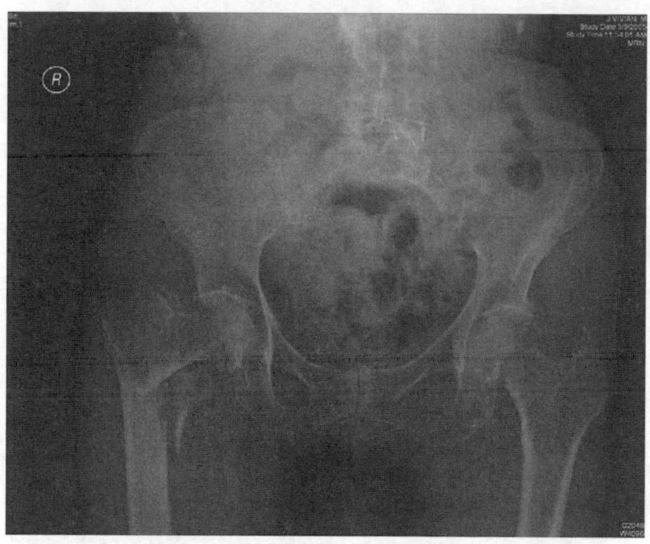

FIGURE 2 Intertrochanteric Fracture, Right Hip

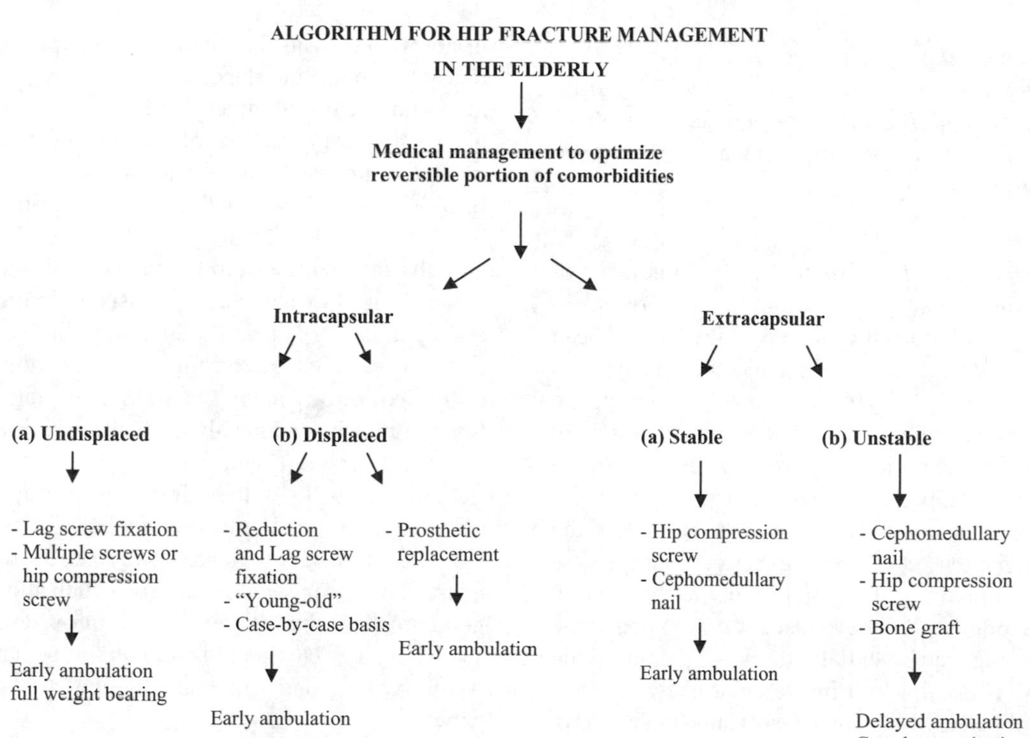

FIGURE 3 Algorithm for Hip Fracture Management in the Elderly

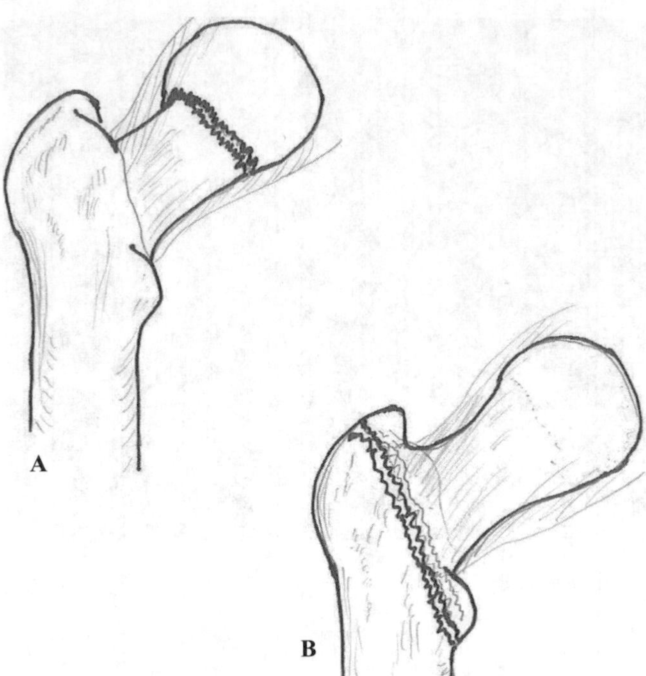

FIGURE 4 (A) Subcapital Hip Fracture (B) Intertrochanteric Hip Fracture

- ***Extracapsular fractures***, which include *intertrochanteric fractures*, *basicervical hip fractures* and *subtrochanteric fractures*. These fracture patterns can be subclassified as *(a) stable* or *(b) unstable*.

Intracapsular Hip Fractures. The relevance of distinguishing intracapsular hip fractures relates to the anatomy of the blood supply of the femoral head (Figure 5). In an adult, the major blood supply is retrograde, primarily from branches of the medial femoral circumflex artery. These vessels pass from the intertrochanteric region proximally and around the back and top, along the femoral neck. These vessels are subsynovial (i.e. within the capsule of the hip). A *femoral neck fracture* thus can disrupt these vessels, impairing the blood supply to the femoral head. Additionally, the *heamarthrosis* (blood in the hip capsule) can potentially further impair the blood supply. This can result in avascular necrosis of the femoral head, which can cause a subchondral fracture and collapse with potentially intractable hip pain. This is much more likely to occur in displaced fractures. As well, once the fracture is stabilized with lag screw fixation, the femoral neck is bathed in normal synovial fluid and this can impair healing at the bony interface of the fracture, leading to nonunion. If the intracapsular fracture is undisplaced, both complications of avascular necrosis and nonunion are less likely. Therefore, surgical stabilization of the fracture with lag screw compression is selected.

If the intracapsular hip fracture is displaced the complications of avascular necrosis and nonunion are significantly higher. Additionally, in displaced femoral neck fractures, comminution of the bone occurs posteriorly along the neck. Thus, lag screw fixation may be technically difficult to achieve stability at the fracture site.

For the majority of these fractures, prosthetic replacement is used. There are a number of prosthetic options. More recent trends have been to use cemented, *modular hemi-prosthesis*, which allows for good prosthetic bone fixation and improved soft tissue balancing. This should facilitate immediate full weight-bearing and hence earlier ambulation for the patient.

Total *hip arthroplasty* may be considered in patients with a history of *rheumatoid arthritis* or the rare patient who has coexisting hip osteoarthritis and sustains a hip fracture. Other prosthetic options are

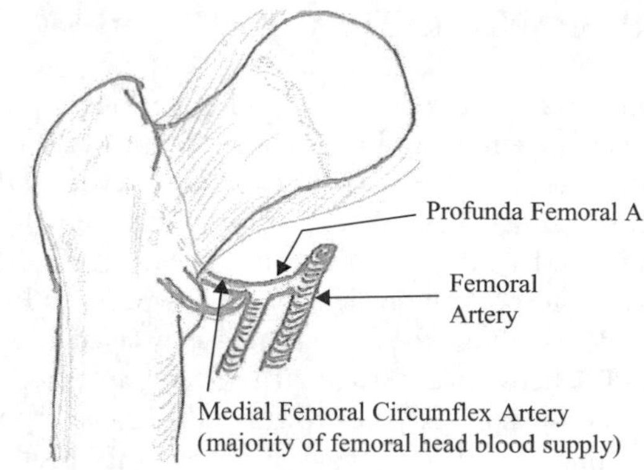

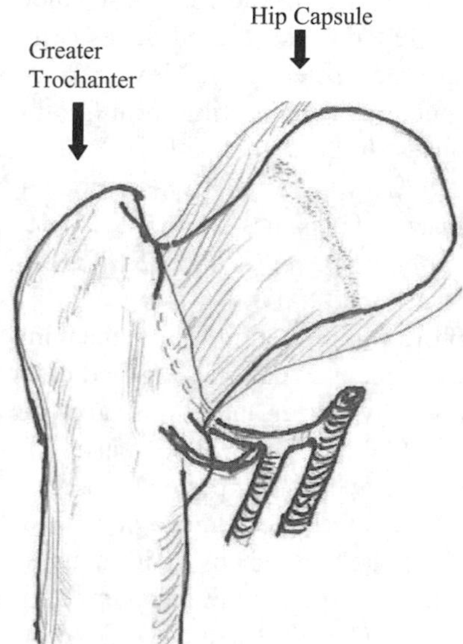

FIGURE 5 Hip Capsule and Blood Supply

a *unipolar prosthesis* (such as *Austin Moore prosthesis*) or a *bipolar prosthesis*. Each has their own advantages and disadvantages for use, and the surgeon's preferences may vary.

Post-operative management should aim for full weight-bearing. In cases of prosthetic replacement, dislocations can be minimized particularly in patients with neuromuscular disorders, such as Parkinson's disease or previous stroke, by using anterolateral or direct lateral hip surgical approaches.

Extracapsular Hip Fractures. Hip fractures that occur outside the capsule consist of intertrochanteric fractures and subtrochanteric fractures. Additionally, fractures can occur at the base of the femoral neck, which are outside of the capsule and are called *basicervical fractures.*

Intertrochanteric Fractures. Intertrochanteric fractures have specific complications including fixation failure as well as malunion such as *varus angulation*, shortening, or malrotation. Reduction and fixation is often further compromised by osteoporosis and *comminution*. The postero-medial portion of the calcar region just superior to the lesser trochanter is key. This area of the bone is structurally important for load bearing. Thus, if this area of the bone is injured, the fracture is unstable.

Intertrochanteric fractures require operative stabilization with *cephalomedullary and intramedullary nails* or *hip compression screws*. In unstable fracture patterns, reduction of the fractures can be challenging; reconstruction of the *medial calcar* is particularly important with hip compression screws. *Intramedullary devices* have the mechanical advantage of being a load-sharing device, and the implant is closer to the center of axis of rotation, thus able to withstand various bending forces. Either device has technical aspects, and not all fractures can be rendered stable with these implants.

The goal is for stable fixation and early ambulation of the patient. In older people who are frail, neuromuscular coordination often prevents patients from partial weight-bearing, so obtaining stable fixation is critical to enable full weight-bearing for early ambulation and maximal rehabilitation.

Subtrochanteric Fractures. Fractures occurring in the subtrochanteric region of the femur (i.e.: 5 cm below the lesser trochanter) are commonly unstable with significant risks of nonunion and hardware failure. There are multiple contributing factors including osteoporotic bone, comminution (multiple bone fragments), and intertrochanteric extension of the fracture. Additionally, mechanical factors include large bending moments in this area of the femur and unopposed muscle pull of the hip abductors and *iliopsoas tendon.*

Improved fixation techniques have lessened the failure rates with *cephomedullary nails* with a lag screw that transfixes the *intramedullary nail* into the femoral head. This is advantageous as it is a load-sharing device, with improved biomechanics that decreases the bending moment on the hardware. These are the least common (45%) but patients who sustain subtrochanteric fractures often experience more pain than with other hip fracture patterns. They also tend to bleed more with this pattern, both preoperatively and intraoperatively.

Prevention

Identification of people who are at high *risk for hip injury* is important. They include people with neuromuscular impairment as well as those with risk factors for osteoporosis. Caucasian females of a slight build are at increased risk for osteoporosis. Additional risk factors include smoking, excessive alcohol use, caffeine use, and decreased physical activity. A history of previous frailty fractures (previous wrist fracture, vertebral body compression fracture, or hip fracture) constitutes a significant risk. Attention needs to be based on prevention of these hip fractures. Simple measures to be taken include avoiding polypharmacy, particularly any kind of benzodiazepine-type hypnotics in older patients, as well as minimizing risks at home such as by removing throw rugs and having homes outfitted with grab rails and night lights.

Other preventative measures for longer term include medical *management for osteoporosis*, including the use of calcium and vitamin D and medications such as *didrocal* or *fosamax* for use in high-risk group patients. For institutionalized patients, use of *hip protectors* has been shown to reduce the incidence of hip fractures. The hip fractures presenting in older adults will continue to be a complex challenge for the health care system to provide optimal treatment.

Conclusion

Hip fractures continue to be a significant challenge for management. These patients present with many other things wrong, thus limiting treatment options, but also placing a high premium of fixing the hip quickly and definitively. Quickly allowing stable fixation is imperative for reducing pain, promoting early ambulation, and minimizing complications. This often takes a multidisciplinary approach from geriatricians, anaesthetists, orthopaedic surgeons, and rehabilitation specialists, as well as a comprehensive team of physical and occupational therapists, nurses, social workers, and other health care professionals.

PETER R. ROCKWOOD

See also
Osteoporosis

HISPANIC ELDERLY

In 2000, there were 32.8 million persons of Hispanic origin living in the United States, 12.0% of the total population (U.S. Census Bureau, 2001); it is estimated that this group will increase to 43.7 million by 2010 (U.S. Census Bureau, 2000). The Hispanic population increased 56.2% between 1990 and 2000. It is expected to increase by an additional 300% between 2000 and 2070, over 4 times as fast as non-Hispanics. The growth of the Hispanic population in the United States is primarily the result of high fertility and immigration rates. The vast majority of immigrants entering the United States come from Latin America, especially from Mexico. However, increasing numbers are arriving from Central American countries. In 2004, native-born Hispanics comprised 55.3% of the total Hispanic population and foreign-born Hispanics comprised 44.6% of the *Hispanic population in the United States* (Fry, Kochhar, Passel, & Suro, 2005).

As a result of prior immigration waves, the number of Hispanic people who are 65 years and older increased significantly during the 1980s, growing by 12% between 1990 and 2000 (U.S. Census Bureau, 2001). Their numbers are expected to increase from just over 5% of the total elderly population in 2000 to approximately 16.4% by 2050, a higher rate of growth than that of elderly of other ethnic or racial groups (U.S. Census Bureau, 2001). About 6% of Hispanics elderly (defined as aged 65 and older) were 85 years or older in 2000 (U.S. Census Bureau, 2001). By 2050, approximately 20% of Hispanic elderly will be aged 85 and older (U.S. Census Bureau, 2001), signaling a 12% increase from 2000 (U.S. Census Bureau, 2001). The growth in the number of the *oldest-old Hispanics* has serious implications pertaining to health care, long-term care, and caregiving (Angel & Hogan, 2004).

This population shift is the result of complex political, social, and economic forces, many of which are beyond the control of most immigrants. Mexicans seek economic opportunities and family reunification. The long and protracted civil wars in Central America, specifically Guatemala, Nicaragua, and El Salvador, prompted a different migration and therefore different adjustment issues. Although there are significant and visible differences based on class, race/ethnicity, education, and financial and legal supports provided by the U.S.

government, there are certain similarities among early Cuban and new *Central American political refugees*. Leaving the country of origin, with all its familiar places, relationships, culture symbols, and traditions, often results in a deep sense of isolation, even alienation, due to a loss of community, economic, and emotional supports.

Adjustment issues related to disruption of the cultural continuum are aggravated when the society the immigrant enters does not value cultural, linguistic, racial, and ethnic diversity. A deep sense of loss is often expressed in depression anxiety, as well as constant longing for the country of origin and familial roots. For *Mexican immigrants*, both recent ones and those whose families have been here for generations, travel back and forth to Mexico has developed into a "revolving door" and/or cultures of migration that, together with access to the Spanish-speaking media, reinforces culture and language time and time again, passing it from generation to generation. The result is an elderly population of Mexican descent that often functions in this country much as it did back home.

Just as there are marked cultural and socioeconomic differences between elderly people who are direct descendants of 16th-century Spanish settlers, those who came during and immediately after the *Mexican Revolution*, and Puerto Ricans who came to the mainland after annexation of the island by the United States, there are also marked similarities. The notion of "*Hispanidad*" and the Spanish language, regardless of speaking proficiency, becomes the glue that binds together the different cultural, racial, and ethnic threads found throughout this hemisphere.

Most recent elderly Central American and Mexican immigrants and those who have been here for decades reside in large urban settings, even though they arrive in the country with a rural orientation, little or no knowledge of the English language, and few marketable work-related skills. Many of those who were in the labor force for some time were in unskilled occupations that provided few if any benefits, such as health insurance and pensions, and have less opportunity to accumulate wealth (Fry, Kochhar, Passel, & Suro, 2005). Most *Hispanic elderly*, especially those of Mexican origin, depend on small Social Security benefits and related benefits from Supplemental Security Income (SSI) for economic support and on Medicare and Medicaid for health care. Social Security constitutes over half of the income of 76% of older Hispanics and keeps many individuals from falling into poverty (Social Security Administration, 2000).

Because of limited income, poverty rates are high. In 1998, 25.6% of all Hispanic households lived under 100% of the poverty line. Although Hispanics comprise the second-largest group of workers (behind whites), in the third quarter of 2004 their overall unemployment rate was 6.8%, higher than that of whites (4.3%) but lower than that of blacks (10.9%) (Fry, Kochhar, Passel, & Suro, 2005). When the 2000 average poverty threshold for a family of 4 was $17,603, in 2000, 8.4% of Hispanic households had incomes below $10,000, compared with 4% of white households and 11.7% of black households. According to 2000 income figures, almost two times more Hispanic families and individuals fell below 100% of the *poverty level* compared with non-Hispanics. In 1998, Hispanics aged 65 years and older were twice as likely to live in poverty (21%) than the average for all those aged 65 years and older of all races (10.5%).

Most Hispanic elderly receive neither a private pension nor Social Security and are less likely than non-Hispanic whites to live alone; nearly one-third live with children and other relatives (Angel & Hogan, 2004). Presently, the *Supplemental Security Income* (SSI) participation rate of Hispanics is lower than African American participation but greater than that of other racial/ethnic categories (U.S. Census, 1996). Without eligibility for SSI, access to Medicaid and food stamps decreases; without Social Security, access to Medicare is limited. A significant number of problems faced by Hispanic older adults are derivatives of poverty, such as poor health and nutrition status, lack of access to avenues of information, hunger, and lack of adequate and affordable housing. Because health status is so interrelated to poverty and lack of access to adequate services, health problems are a major concern. 2001 data indicate heart disease (23.9%) and cancer (19.7%) are the leading causes of death among Hispanics, followed by injuries and stroke (8.4% and 5.7%, respectively). Twice as many Hispanic elderly as non-Hispanics die of diabetes. As with other groups, cancer affects people aged 65 and older more frequently than any other age group (National Vital Statistics, 2004). Hispanic women, at any age, are more likely to be unaware or uninformed about breast and cervical cancer risks and what they can do (National Cancer Institute and the Centers for Disease Control, 1994). The largest source of *cancer deaths among Hispanics* is breast cancer, despite the fact that incidence of breast cancer is lower among Hispanics than among other races.

Despite the vulnerability of Hispanic elderly, lack of accessibility and underutilization of much-needed services continue to be issues for which effective solutions are yet to be found. No single cause in and of itself appears to be sufficient to account for it; rather, it is the result of several factors that affect different groups at different times under different conditions. Among the factors more often attributed as explanations of low service use are discrimination, lack of bilingual and/or bicultural personnel, inadequate outreach agency policies and procedures that discourage use of services, insensitivity to different cultural and linguistic factors, and issues related to class and education. The complexity of the relationship of these factors tends to create a situation that is difficult to change, particularly if each is approached separately and individually.

Research could increase understanding of the multiple factors that determine the well-being of the various Hispanic elderly groups. Yet research is inadequate, and most available research reflects limited aspects of the *Mexican-American* experience that often cannot be generalized to other Hispanic groups (Markides, Rudkin, Angel, & Espino, 1997). Narrow definitions of family, information networks, community relationships, and perceptions of well-being leave out important configurations that could define the different life experiences of this most varied population group.

JACQUELINE ANGEL

See also

Ethnicity

Minority Populations: Recruitment and Retention in Aging Research

References

Angel, J., & Hogan, D. P. (2004). Population aging and diversity in a new era. In K. E. Whitfield (Ed.), *Closing the gap: Improving the health of minority elders in the new millennium* (pp. 128–139). Washington, DC: Gerontological Society of America.

Centers for Disease Control. (2004). Health disparities experienced by Hispanics—United States. *MMWR Weekly, 53*(40), 935. Available: http://www.cdc.gov/mmwr/preview/mmwrhtml/mm5340a1.htm#tab

http://www.omhrc.gov/healthgap2003/diabetes.htm

http://iccnetwork.org/cancerfacts/cfs4.htm

Fry, R., Kochhar, R., Passel, J., & Suro, R. (2005). Hispanics and the Social Security debate. Pew Hispanic Center. Available: http://pewhispanic.org/files/reports/43.pdf

(34991753-31241831)/31241831

Markides, K. S., Rudkin, L., Angel, R. J. & Espino, D. (1997). Health status of Hispanic elderly. In L. G. Martin & B. J. Soldo (Eds.), *Racial and ethnic differences in the health of older Americans* (pp. 285–300). Washington, DC: National Academies Press.

U.S. Census Bureau. (1998). *Current population survey*, Table 2. Age, sex, household relationship, race and Hispanic origin by ratio of income to poverty threshold.

http://www.census.gov/hhes/poverty/threshld/thresh00.html

http://www.census.gov/prod/2003pubs/02statab/pop.pdf p. 41

http://www.census.gov/prod/2003pubs/p70-94.pdf p. 22.

U.S. Census Bureau. (2000). Census summary file 1; 1990 Census of population, general population characteristics, United States (1990 CP-1-1). (Table 1. Population 65 years and over by age: 1990 and 2000.)

U.S. Census Bureau. (2000). NP-T4-C projections of the total resident population by 5-year age groups, race, and Hispanic origin with special age categories: Middle series: 2006–2010. Population Projections Program. Available: http://www.census.gov/population/projections/nation/summary/np-14-c.txt

(32.8–21)/21

(132,493–32,800)/32,800

(463,639–274,087)/274,087

U.S. Census Bureau. (2000). NPT4-G projections of the total resident population by 5-year age groups, race, and Hispanic origin with special age categories: Middle series, 2050–2070. Available: http://www.census.gov/population/projections/nation/summary/np-14-t4-g.txt

U.S. Census Bureau. (2001). *Current population survey, March 2000*. (Table 1. Population by age, sex, race and Hispanic origin.) Available: http://www.census.gov/population/socdemo/age/ppl-147/tab01.txt.
U.S. Bureau of the Census. (1998).

HMOs

See

Health Maintenance Organizations

HOME EQUITY CONVERSION

Currently, nearly 80% of adults aged 65 and older in the United States are homeowners, with three-quarters of them owning their homes without *mortgage* debt. Home equity—the current market value of the house minus an existing mortgage if any—on average represents nearly half of an older adult's net worth. A house is an illiquid or a frozen asset, however, because it does not yield cash income to the owner. Furthermore, property taxes and maintenance costs represent a demand for cash that the older homeowner may not have. Hence, this creates a "house-rich, cash-poor" predicament for some. Converting home equity into cash while still being able to live in the house may resolve the dilemma (Chen, 1967; Scholen & Chen, 1980).

To alleviate the problem of demand on cash, some state and local governments in the United States offer property tax exemptions for older low-income homeowners, or deferred-payment loans for *property taxes* or for home improvements, postponing payment of these loans on owner-occupied houses until the homeowner dies or the house is sold. These tax concessions and deferred-payment loans may be regarded as one form of *home equity conversion*.

Another form of home equity conversion advances cash to the homeowner. It is the *reverse mortgage*, under which the lender pays cash periodically to the borrower (homeowner), while the borrower makes no repayment to the lender until the end of the loan, when a lump sum repayment is due. With this feature, older homeowners (usually the minimum age to qualify is 62) can borrow without fear of involuntary displacement or foreclosure. Upon the borrower's death or a voluntary move-out, the property is sold to pay off the debt. If the sale proceeds are more than needed to pay the debt, including interest, the remaining cash usually belongs to the borrower or his or her estate. If the sale proceeds are insufficient, the lender absorbs the loss. Some reverse mortgages come with a government guaranty of full repayment, in which case the lender will be reimbursed for any deficiency.

Dominant in the U.S. market for reverse mortgages in recent years has been a government guaranty program called the *Home Equity Conversion Mortgage* (HECM), which was introduced by the U.S. Department of Housing and Urban Development (HUD) in 1989 and made permanent in 1998 by an act of Congress. The HECM program, also known as the *Federal Housing Administration reverse mortgage*, has been successful in encouraging private lenders to offer this type of loan, having recently broken through the ceiling of 100,000 contracts. The cost of the government guaranty under the HECM program is borne collectively by borrowers who pay an insurance premium to HUD.

With government backing, lenders could offer more attractive terms than they could without the guaranty. Thus, the HECM program, which historically has received bipartisan support in Congress, has given the United States a new financial instrument that can help alleviate poverty among the house-rich, cash-poor older adults, and help middle-income seniors liquefy their otherwise-frozen asset, thereby helping to maintain their lifestyle into retirement.

A major problem with reverse mortgages is the high borrower cost, attributable in part to high premiums for mortgage insurance. High insurance premiums reflect the fear of adverse selection that reverse mortgage borrowers would stay in their homes or survive longer than elderly homeowners in the general population. Using data from the first 8 years of the HECM program, McConaghy (2004) has established that, contrary to lenders' original fears, HECM borrowers do not appear to reside in their homes longer, or to have better mortality experience, than their elderly home-owning counterparts in the general population (except those aged 90 or above). Nor did borrowers refinance their loans in large numbers (refinancing in times of low interest rates or after the home had appreciated in value would allow many borrowers to increase their borrowing power significantly). Taken together, these findings suggest that adverse selection does not play a strong role in the HECM borrower population, as some feared.

The HECM program allows borrowers to choose among many payment options. Cash may be received as: (1) a lump sum received at the time of the loan; (2) monthly payments for as long as the borrower resides in the house (called tenure payments); (3) higher monthly payments for a fixed period of time (called term payments), after which borrowers may continue to reside in the house and defer repayment; (4) a line of credit with which borrowers may vary the amounts and timing of payments up to a maximum; and (5) some combination of all of the above. In addition, borrowers may switch any unused credit from one payment option to another at any time for only a small administrative processing fee. The high degree of flexibility in selecting and modifying payment options may be important to older borrowers, whose life circumstances can change rapidly.

Most borrowers select the *line of credit* payment option and the median line of credit borrowers take out is 75% of their available credit lines. While married line of credit borrowers repay much more slowly than single borrowers in the first few years of the loan, couple's repayment rates increase more rapidly as the loan ages, to the point where little difference between singles and couples can be observed for the most mature loans; this may be due to intervening death of one spouse as much as changing repayment behavior of couples. All loans display a 2- to 3-year "seasoning period" starting at inception where repayment rates are exceptionally low. Noteworthy are the low repayment rates of borrowers in their 90s, relative to what one would expect given their high mortality and increased need for institution-based supportive services (McConaghy 2004).

Rapid growth of the HECM program began in 2001, with annual doubling of the number of new loans issued. This was attributable in part to the removal in 2000 of legal restrictions on reverse mortgages in Texas, and in part to sharp declines in the rates paid by banks on certificates of deposit, lowering the incomes of many home-owning older adults. A third factor has been the growth of loans to non-needy elders for "luxury" purposes, such as vacations, cruises, and home improvements, a market not contemplated by the original designers of the program (McConaghy, 2004).

Fannie Mae, a private company with a public charter, is currently a key player in the reverse mortgage market. Widely known for providing mortgage funds to the traditional home mortgage market, Fannie Mae has a lesser-known operation that buys virtually all HECM loans from the original lenders, freeing up their cash to make more HECM loans. Furthermore, Fannie Mae operates a conventional reverse mortgage product, called *Home Keeper*, which has many features similar to HECM but has no government guaranty. Some other purely private lenders offer reverse mortgages without either HUD or Fannie Mae participation.

Although some forms of home equity conversion involve the government (e.g., property tax concessions), all forms of home equity conversion are voluntary for the older homeowner. Home equity conversion may appeal only to those who prefer to receive more current income without relinquishing the house. Home equity conversion could even complement long-term home care (as compared to institutionalization) when home care is feasible and desired (Feinstein, Gornick, & Greenberg, 1980; Chen, 1980; Firman, 1983; Jacobs, 1985).

The conceptual foundation of home equity conversion should be understood in the context of the retirement income system in the United States, which frequently has been characterized as a 3-legged stool: *Social Security* is designed to provide a basic income protection, with private pensions and individual savings providing supplements to it.

The role of individual *savings* remains modest, however, because of the typically small or insignificant value of the older person's financial assets that are to varying degrees liquid. (Voluntary savings, even with tax incentives, do not appear substantial.) Another problem is the illiquid nature of home equity. To enhance the income status of many older adults by means of savings, we need to tap into the income potential of homeownership.

Although home equity conversion could bring current income to many elderly homeowners, this financial option has not met with immense popularity. Several reasons may account for it. Despite its logic, converting one's home equity into cash remains a novel idea for many. Some older people loathe the idea of going into debt in later years. Others are concerned about reducing the size of the estate for their heirs. To an individual, home equity conversion thus may present a difficult choice between (1) resigning to a low-income status so as to ensure a bequest, and (2) using home equity to increase retirement income to avoid burdening children or society. For future cohorts of homeowners, the choice may not be as difficult, because the current elders are products of the Great Depression, which may have strongly biased their attitudes against incurring debts.

Some public policy actions likewise pose a quandary. For example, if property taxes are excused for some older homeowners, other taxpayers will be paying more taxes (unless government expenditures are reduced commensurately with tax exemptions), thus making it possible for the exempt homeowners to preserve their bequests.

Reverse mortgage schemes also exist in other, primarily English speaking, countries. The *Canadian Home Income Plan* (CHIP) has offered reverse mortgages since 1986. Owned by a real estate investment trust, CHIP offers lump-sum reverse mortgages of up to $500,000 CD. The United Kingdom, which saw several wildly speculative home equity release programs come and go in the 1970–1980s, now has the widely offered "equity release mortgage," many of which conform to the *Safe Home Income Plans* (SHIP) ethics developed by a consortium of lenders. Varied financing plans available in the United Kingdom include line of credit loans, loan/annuity combinations, shared-appreciation, and "shared ownership."

Lenders in both Australia and New Zealand are now offering reverse mortgages. In addition, the Australian federal government offers a pension loans scheme to supplement the public, means-tested Australian age pension for retirees with low incomes but significant home equity (Howe, 2004). Elsewhere, a pure term (payment due at the end of the term) loan is available in Singapore, and the news media have recently reported efforts in Hong Kong to develop a reverse mortgage product. The Toyota Motor Company has introduced the reverse mortgage to Japan by offering them to empty-nesters aged 60 and older who purchased their homes from its subsidiary Toyota Home.

YUNG-PING CHEN
RICHARD W. MCCONAGHY

References

Chen, Y.-P. (1967). Potential income from homeownership: An actuarial mortgage plan. In *A compendium of papers, part II: The aged population and retirement income programs* (pp. 303–311). Subcommittee on Fiscal Policy, Joint Economic Committee, 90th Congress, First Session. Washington, DC: U.S. Government Printing Office.

Firman, J. (1983, Spring). Reforming community care for the elderly and disabled. *Health Affairs*, 66–82.

Howe, A. L. (2004). Communication to the authors. September 24, 2004.

McConaghy, R. W. (2004). *Mortality, moveout and refinancing as factors in HECM reverse mortgage payoffs*. Doctoral dissertation. Boston: University of Massachusetts.

HOMELESSNESS

Although the literature has included a wide array of age demarcations, there has been a general consensus that "*older homeless*" should be defined as age 50 and older (Cohen, 1999). This is because at this age many homeless persons look and act 10 to 20 years older. Similarly, there are differing definitions of what constitutes "homelessness." Typically in the aging literature, homeless includes those persons sleeping in shelters or public shelters as well as persons living in "skid row"-type flophouses. Older homeless persons often seem invisible to service providers and governmental agencies, which have focused on younger homeless people or subcategories of the homeless in which older persons may be subsumed but unacknowledged, such as veterans or women.

Using diverse methods and age demarcations, surveys have produced estimates of the number of older homeless persons ranging from 2.5% to 27.2% (Cohen, 1999). Since 1980 the proportion of older persons among the homeless has declined, although their absolute number has grown. The proportion of older homeless persons can be expected to increase dramatically as more baby boomers turn 50: the number of older homeless persons can be expected to increase in tandem with the anticipated doubling of the aged 50 and older population over the next 25 years. Thus, the older homeless population can be expected to rise from its current national level of 60,000 to 400,000, to around 120,000 to 800,000 persons, depending on the sampling methods that are used (Cohen, 1999).

We have developed a model of aging and homelessness that has 4 postulates (Cohen, 1999; Cohen, Ramirez, Teresi, Gallagher, & Sokolovsky, 1997):

1. There are individual risk factors that accumulate over a lifetime. These include individual early

background and demographic risk factors, and risk factors that occur in middle and later life. With the exception of extremely vulnerable individuals, homelessness is not likely to occur unless several individual risk factors coexist.

2. Systemic factors—e.g., the availability of low-cost housing and income to pay for housing—play a critical role and interact with individual risk factors. The systemic factors are thought to be the principal determinants of the community prevalence of homelessness found among older persons.
3. Enculturation factors—i.e., a person's adaptation to the street or shelter—further sustain and prolong homelessness.
4. Service interventions—their timeliness, quality, and availability—can prevent or terminate homelessness.

The principal *individual* risk factors (Barak & Cohen, 2003; Cohen, 1999; Crane, 1999; Hecht & Coyle, 2001) that have been found to increase vulnerability to homelessness among older individuals when contrasted with their age peers in the general population are: male gender (ratio of 4:1); being in the "*young-old*" age category (age 50 to 64 years); being *African American*; disproportionately more unskilled or semi-skilled occupations; a family history of poverty; experiencing more childhood disruptive events such as death of parents or placement in foster care; prior imprisonment; a high prevalence of alcoholism; higher levels of physical illness; having experienced high rates of *victimization*, such as robbery and rape; having social networks that are smaller and that include more material exchanges (e.g., food, money, or health assistance) but fewer intimate and family ties; higher levels of unmarried status; greater prevalence of mental illness with psychosis more common among women (about two-fifths of women versus one-tenth of men) and depression equal or slightly more prevalent among men (about one-third); slightly higher levels (10% to 34%) of cognitive impairment (generally mild to moderate); and a prior history of homelessness.

Evolution into long-term homelessness involves an *enculturation* process in which the individual learns to adapt and survive in the world of shelters or streets. Several factors promote enculturation (Cohen, 1999): (1) "shelter-ization," in which the group style organization of *shelters* may replicate earlier military or prison experiences for men, while others develop a type of "*learned helplessness*"; (2) rational choice based on safety and stability, especially for women; (3) a new social support system—more than one-third of shelter linkages are considered "intimates." Certain subgroups of older persons such as men, the mentally ill, and those with prior homeless episodes, are more apt to remain homeless for extended periods, most likely reflecting barriers at the personal and systems levels to rehousing.

The 2 principal *systemic* factors that create homelessness are low income and the lack of affordable housing. In cities where there may be adequate *housing supply*, high levels of poor-quality jobs, unemployment, and low incomes make most housing unavailable to the poor (Burt, 1992). Conversely, in cities where incomes may be higher and jobs are more plentiful, tight rental markets stemming from middle-class pressure and escalating living costs also makes housing less available to lower-income persons. Both these conditions can push some people over the edge into homelessness. There is now ample evidence that *deinstitutionalization of mental hospitals* does not exert a direct effect on homelessness; however, mental illness may contribute to homelessness, especially among older women (Cohen, 1999). Nevertheless, the reason for there being disproportionately more *homeless mentally ill* persons is likely due to systemic factors such as the nonavailability of appropriate housing and inadequate entitlements for this population.

Programmatic factors that affect interventions for older homeless persons include: (1) a limited availability of housing alternatives or in-home services for disabled older adults, (2) agency staff who lack motivation or skills to assist older persons, and (3) absence of outreach programs that target older adults.

In older persons, the decline to the state of homelessness often involves a cumulative series of events or risk factors in which one final event serves as the trigger into homelessness. Sullivan's (1991) study in New York City found that older women had experienced an average of 3 life events or crises over a period of 1 to 5 years preceding their homelessness. The direct "triggers" of homelessness among older persons depend largely upon at what age the person first becomes homeless (Crane, 1999). For those older persons who first became homeless in early adulthood, it may be precipitated by disturbed family homes, or upon being discharged from orphanages or the armed services, whereas for those who first became homeless in mid-life, triggers include the death of a parent, marital breakdown, and a drift to less secure transient work and housing. Finally, late-life homeless may follow widowhood, marital breakdown, retirement, the loss of accommodation tied to employment, or the increasing severity of a mental illness. Women are more apt to become homeless from failures or crises in family life, while men typically become homeless because of occupational failures. Older homeless persons are a heterogeneous population, and in Britain, Warnes and Crane (2000) identified 7 different subtypes of older homeless persons based on their housing patterns, their psychiatric state, use of alcohol, and occupational status.

Intervention Strategies

Despite demographic shifts that presage a dramatic increase in aging homeless persons, various statutory and service initiatives can potentially obviate this dire outcome. There are several key points with respect to devising intervention strategies:

1. Because the older homeless population is perhaps the most heterogeneous of homeless subgroups—there are broad differences, for example with respect to health, cognitive status, length of homelessness—interventions must be even more individualized than in younger populations.
2. Interventions are possible at any point in our model: at the distal level (early- and mid-life risk factors), the proximal level (more immediate causes of homelessness), and subsequent to becoming homeless.
3. In contrast to the self-sufficiency model used for younger persons—moving from transitional supported residential situations to independent living—it may be more profitable to consider various types of permanent supported living arrangements for more vulnerable older persons.
4. Legislation is needed to enhance the safety net for persons aged 50 and 64 years, who are much more vulnerable to homelessness than persons aged 65 and older (Cohen, Sokolovsky, & Crain, 2001). The former have difficulty securing employment if they are laid-off or have many physical problems, and they are more apt to experience widowhood and losses in close social ties. However, they are ineligible for many of the entitlements that become available at age 65.
5. Greater emphasis must be placed on *preventing homelessness* by identifying at an early stage and helping people who are vulnerable and at risk of becoming homeless (Keigher, 1991). Effective support systems need to be in place that enable people to manage in independent or supported housing, and which discourage people from either relinquishing tenancies or being evicted. Also, many older homeless persons need assistance in securing the benefits that they are entitled to by law.
6. With respect to specific service strategies, age-segregated drop-in/social centers coupled with outreach programs with strong medical and psychiatric components have been shown to be useful, and recent studies have suggested that case managers can help with securing benefits and rehousing older persons (Barak & Cohen, 2003; Levy & O'Connell, 2004; Warnes & Crane, 2000).

CARL I. COHEN

References

Barak, Y., & Cohen, A. (2003). Characterizing the elderly homeless: A 10-year study in Israel. *Archives of Gerontology and Geriatrics*, *37*, 147–155.

Burt, M. R. (1992). *Over the edge: The growth of homelessness in the 1980s*. New York: Russell Sage.

Cohen, C. I. (1999). Aging and homelessness. *Gerontologist*, *39*, 5–14.

Cohen, C. I., Ramirez, M., Teresi, J., Gallagher, M., & Sokolovsky, J. (1997). Predictors of becoming redomiciled among older homeless women. *Gerontologist*, *37*, 67–74.

Cohen, C. I., Sokolovsky, J., & Crain, M. (2001). Aging, homelessness, and the law. *International Journal of Law and Psychiatry*, *24*, 167–181.

Crane, M. (1999). *Understanding older homeless people*. Buckingham: Open University Press.

Hecht, L., & Coyle, B. (2001). Elderly homeless. A comparison of older and younger adult emergency shelter seekers in Bakersfield, California. *American Behavioral Scientist, 45*, 66–79.

Keigher, S. M. (1991). *Housing risks and homelessness among the urban elderly*. New York: Haworth Press.

Levy, B. D., & O'Connell, J. J. (2004). Health care for the homeless. *New England Journal of Medicine, 350*, 2329–2332.

Sullivan, M. A. (1991). The homeless older woman in context: Alienation, cutoff, and reconnection. *Journal of Women and Aging, 3*, 3–24.

Warnes, A., & Crane, M. (2000). *Meeting homeless people's needs. Service development and practice for the older excluded*. London: King's Fund.

HOME MODIFICATIONS

The strongest preference of older adults in regard to housing is to remain in their homes and neighborhoods as long as possible. However, most housing contains barriers that make remaining at home restrictive and even hazardous. Home modification refers to converting or adapting the environment to make performing tasks easier, reduce accidents, and support independent living. The goal is to reestablish equilibrium between a person whose capabilities have declined and the demands of their environment (Lawton & Nahemow, 1973). Home modification includes: (1) removing hazards, such as clutter or throw rugs, (2) adding special features or *assistive devices*, such as *grab bars* or *ramps*, (3) moving furnishings, (4) changing where activities occur, such as sleeping on the first instead of the second floor, and (5) renovations, such as installing a *roll-in shower*.

There are several benefits of home modifications. First, a supportive and accessible environment makes it easier to carry out tasks such as cooking and cleaning as well as other major life activities. Second, adequate space and features facilitate caregiving by relatives and the formal service system (Newman, Struyk, Wright, & Rice, 1990). For persons with dementia, a home modification intervention can help with IADL difficulty and behavioral problems as well as improve the *self-efficacy* of caregivers (Gitlin, Corcoran, Winter, Boyce, & Hauck, 2001). Third, the addition of supportive features in the home may minimize the need for more costly personal care services and delay institutionalization. Fourth, home modifications play a role in multifactorial interventions to prevent falls (e.g., risk assessment, exercise, home modification educational materials and programming, and follow-up) (Shekelle, Maglione, Chang, Mojica, Morton, Wu, & Rubenstein, 2002).

Incidence and Need for Modifications

According to the 1995 American Housing Survey, 3.4 million or 38% of households with at least 1 member with a permanent physical activity limitation had home modifications present. In conventional homes and apartments, grab bars and *shower seats* are the most common home modification at 23%, followed by wheelchair access inside the home, such as wide hallways (9%), special railings (8%), and ramps at street level (5%) (Tabbarah, Silverstein, & Seeman, 2000).

However, a study by the Joint Center for Housing Studies at Harvard University has found that a large number of older people who report problems with physical abilities live in housing without adaptive features. Over 5 million older households have 1 household member with a functional limitation. Of these households, 2.1 million express the need for home modifications to function independently, but only 1.14 million of these households have the modifications they desire (Joint Center for Housing Studies, 2000).

Functional Improvement and Injury Prevention

A number of studies have indicated the efficacy of home modification in improving independence, safety, caregiving, and functioning. For example, *bathroom modifications* such as grab bars and shower seats have been found to increase ease of bathing among persons aged 70 and older and those with high degrees of functional disability (Kutty, 2000; Gitlin, Miller, & Boyce, 1999). A study involving older persons in a controlled intervention involving assessment by an occupational therapist, home care services, and home modification reduced home health costs and delayed institutionalization of those in the treatment group (Mann, Ottenbacher, Fraas, Tomita, & Granger, 1999).

There is ample evidence that home modifications have an important role to play in *fall prevention*.

Studies indicate that the home environment is implicated in 35% to 40% of falls of older persons (Josephson, Febacher, & Rubenstein, 1991). For example, a study of persons identified in the emergency room as having fallen who were provided with detailed assessments (i.e., medical, functional, environmental), counseling about safety, and home modification reported significantly reduced numbers of falls compared with those in a control group (Close, 1999). Similarly, a controlled trial that included home assessment, home visits by an occupational therapist, and minor home modification reduced by 36% the proportion of people who fell compared with those in the control group. The effect occurred, however, only for those who had fallen in the prior year (Cumming, Thoma, Szonyi, Salkeld, O'Neill, Westbury, et al., 1999). Several other studies, however, have found weaker relationships between the presence of environmental hazards and falls, indicating the difficulty of isolating extrinsic factors such as scatter rugs and worn carpet from intrinsic factors such as balance, strength, and reaction time (Anemaet & Moffa-Trotter, 1999). Accordingly, the overall consensus is that the best approach is to include home modification in a multifactorial strategy of fall prevention (Shekelle, Maglione, Chang, Mojica, Morton, Wu, & Rubenstein, 2000).

Barriers to Home Modifications

Why don't more older persons who need home modifications have them? Several interrelated factors contribute to the problem. First, a lack of awareness of problems in the physical environment and the effectiveness of home modifications reduce the demand for adaptations. Studies suggest that older persons often adapt to their environment rather than change their settings to meet their needs. Even professionals such as doctors or case managers may overlook the role of the environment in supporting frail older persons.

A second barrier is the unattractiveness of some products. Older persons do not want their own homes to look institutional and therefore may only make adaptations after having experienced an accident or a disabling condition that threatens their independence.

Third, the service delivery system is a patchwork of providers, few of which are well trained in assessing the environment or in specifying appropriate solutions (Pynoos, Overton, Liebig, & Calvert, 1997). An effective *home modification delivery* system should be easy to access with skilled providers able to assess problems and make appropriate adaptations. Consumers report, however, that lack of access to providers is a major reason that they do not make additional home modifications that they report needing (AARP, 2000). The different providers that potentially play a role in home modifications include case managers, occupational therapists, remodelers, and social service agencies. Until recently, home modification services existed primarily in the public and non-profit sector. The development of a private sector home modification industry has been hindered by the modest nature of many modifications, the need for specialized skills, the low income of many potential clients, and consumer fears about the trustworthiness of private providers. However, there has recently been a slow but steady increase in for-profit home modification companies.

Fourth, because there is no entitlement program for home modifications, programs use a variety of sources, such as *Community Development Block Grants*, *Older Americans Act Title III* funds, special state and local funds, and increasingly, *Medicaid waiver* funds. Traditional *Medicare* pays little in the way of home modification. Medicaid pays for some home modification as long as they do not require permanent changes to the home. The use of multi-funding sources can present problems, as programs differ in terms of eligibility requirements, how much can be spent per client, and the types of repairs and modifications that can be made. Overall, programs operate on relatively small budgets that are insufficient to meet the needs of older persons and generally restrict them to a specific geographic area.

Fifth, some home modifications are costly and may be unaffordable to low and moderate income individuals. Over three-quarters of home modifications are paid for out of pocket. The cost of home adaptations ranges from less than $100 for the purchase and installation of a simple handrail or grab bar to more than $2,000 for a roll-in shower or a stair lift. Costs, however, remain a serious impediment to obtaining home modifications, especially for those who are low income or who require expensive features or major modifications to their dwelling units. According to a recent AARP (2000) survey, lack of funding is a major reason that people do not make home modifications.

Future Directions

The importance of home modifications can be expected to increase as the elderly population older than age 75 continues to expand rapidly and as policy emphasizes keeping older persons in their homes for as long as possible. Due to the increasing need and potential benefits of home modifications, further action is needed to promote its availability.

First, efforts should be made to increase awareness through public education programs that inform consumers on the benefits of home modifications. Training programs are also needed for case managers, occupational therapists, and remodelers on assessing the environment and making recommendations. Second, suppliers need to provide more attractive products that blend well into the home setting. Already, some products such as grab bars come in different colors, textures, and finishes. Third, centralized referral systems are needed that furnish provider references and the estimated costs of modifications. In addition, replication is needed of exemplary home modification programs, so new endeavors can avoid pitfalls and develop more rapidly. Fourth, Medicare and Medicaid should continue to pay for equipment and assistive devices and begin to reimburse for home modifications. It would also help if expenditure caps on the Medicaid Waiver programs, which can pay for a broader range of home modifications than traditional Medicaid, were raised. Managed care, which is based on a philosophy of prevention, could also play a role in home modifications. Health plans could provide its members with educational materials about home modifications and include home assessments as part of treatment plans. Fifth, *fall prevention programs* should include a home assessment and home modifications as a key component of the intervention.

More broadly, the future would ideally consist of homes and communities that are supportive, accessible, and elder-friendly. Toward this end, a universal design movement has been advocating for accessible housing that benefits both older persons and those with disabilities (Christenson, 1999). These homes would be accessible to persons in wheelchairs, persons with sight or hearing impairments, and other limitations. Although somewhat more costly initially, universal design, as applied to housing, will ultimately reduce later expenditures necessary for remodeling or retrofitting.

At a minimum, housing units of all types would include the features enumerated in the *Fair Housing Amendments Act* (FHAA) of 1988, such as accessible entrances, hallways, bathrooms, and kitchens; raised electrical outlets; and plywood backing in bathrooms for installing grab bars. In the United States, there has been progress in this direction with the adoption of "*visitability" codes* in localities such as Atlanta, Austin, Urbana, Illinois, and Pima County, Arizona and states such as Vermont, Georgia, and Texas. *Visitability* is a narrower concept that requires entrances and the first floor of single-family homes to be accessible. Such advances, however, continue to be resisted by developers who argue that mandates will increase the cost of housing and require buyers to purchase features they do not want. Builders prefer voluntary programs or incentives that waive building permit fees. Progress in this area therefore requires an educated group of consumer advocates who are convinced enough about the benefits of visitability to address the concerns of the building industry.

Beyond accessible homes, the creation of *elder-friendly communities* has received increasing attention across the nation. Such communities would consider the location of stores, churches, or parks, the adequacy of sidewalks, and the legibility of signage as important determinants to maintaining independence. The goal is to help older adults remain mobile and connected to the community. Future planning and policy initiatives must recognize the importance of the physical environmental context in the home and community as key to aging-in-place.

Jon Pynoos
Christy M. Nishita

See also
Environmental Assessment
Housing

References

AARP. (2000). *Fixing to stay: A national survey on housing and home modification issues*. Washington, DC: AARP.

Anemaet, W. K., & Moffa-Trotter, M. E. (1999). Promoting safety and function through home assessments. *Topics in Geriatric Rehabilitation*, *15*, 26–51.

Christenson, M. A. (1999, November 8). Embracing universal design. *OT Practice*, 12–15, 25.

Close, J., Ellis, M., Hooper, R. et al. (1999). Prevention of falls in the elderly trial (PROFET): A randomized controlled trial. *Lancet*, *353*, 93–97.

Cumming, R. G., Thoma, M., Szonyi, G., Salkeld, G., O' Neill, E., Westbury, C., & Frampton, G. (1999). Home visits by an occupational therapist for assessment and modification of environmental hazards: A randomized trial of falls prevention. *Journal of the American Geriatrics Society*, *47*, 1397–1402.

Gitlin, L. N., Corcoran, M., Winter, L., Boyce, A., Hauck, W. W. (2001). A randomized controlled trial of a home environmental intervention: Effect on efficacy and upset in caregivers and on daily function of persons with dementia. *Gerontologist*, *41*(1), 4–14.

Gitlin, L., Miller, K. S., & Boyce, A. (1999). Bathroom modifications for frail elderly renters: Outcomes of a community-based program. *Technology and Disability*, *10*, 141–149.

Joint Center for Housing Studies. (2000). *The State of the Nation's Housing 1999*. Boston, M. A.: Joint Center for Housing Studies of Harvard University.

Josephson, K., Febacher, D., & Rubenstein, L. Z. (1991). Home safety and fall prevention. *Clinical Geriatric Medicine*, *7*, 707–731.

Kutty, N. (2000). The production of functionality by the elderly: A household production function approach. *Applied Economics 32*, *10*, 1269–1280.

Lawton, M. P., & Nahemow, L. (1973). Ecology and the aging process. In C. Eisdorfer and M. P. Lawton (Eds.), *Psychology of adult development and aging*. Washington, DC: American Psychological Association.

Mann, W. C., Ottenbacher, K. J., Fraas, L., Tomita, M., & Granger, C. V. (1999). Effectiveness of assistive technology and environmental interventions in maintaining independence and reducing home care costs for the frail elderly. *Archives of Family Medicine*, *8*, 210–217.

Newman, S., Struyk, R., Wright, P., & Rice, M. (1990). Overwhelming odds: Caregiving and the risk of institutionalization. *Journal of Gerontology: Social Sciences*, *45*(5), S173–S183.

Pynoos, J., Overton, J., Liebig, P., & Calvert, E. (1997). The delivery of home modification and repair services. In J. Hyde & S. Lanspery (Eds.), *Housing adaptations to meet changing needs: Research, policy, and programs*. Amityville, NY: Baywood Publishing Company.

Shekelle, P., Maglione, M., Chang, J., Mojica, W., Morton, S. C., Wu, S. Y., & Rubenstein, L. Z. (2002). Falls prevention interventions in the Medicare population. *RAND-HCFA Evidence Report Monograph*, HCFA Publication #HCFA-500-98-0281—, 201.

Tabbarah, M., Silverstein, M., & Seeman, T. (2000). A health and demographic profile of non-institutionalized older Americans residing in environments with home modifications. *Journal of Aging and Health*, *12*(2), 204–228.

HOMEOSTASIS

History and Definition

Homeostasis embraces the belief of biologists that living organisms universally have internal processes and behavioral repertoires to assure, within limits, their continued operations and/or propagation in variable environments. If challenged, stressed, or perturbed so they are forced away from their normal state, they can and will eventually recover, closely, their original conditions and capabilities in the initial environment, or will adapt and find a new steady-state in a changed environment. Thus homeostasis may be thought of as expressing "the wisdom of the body" (Cannon, 1932). Cannon invented and defined homeostasis (homeo = same; stasis = condition) and provided examples of its physiological mechanisms in a now-classic article (1929). He recognized that homeostasis invites a *stability theory* for an organism, and found antecedents in the works and conjectures of Pflüger (1872), Bernard (1878), Fredericq (1885), and Richet (1900) (see Cannon, 1929, for sources). From a medical viewpoint, health equals stability. The concept of homeostasis does not imply or require that internal variables be kept constant by living systems—their stability is dynamic, not static, and admits variations within a regulation band.

The detailed history of this great stability concept, which some biologists have suggested almost matches evolution in grandeur and power in biological sciences, can be found in Wolfe and colleagues (2000). Although homeostasis was introduced as a formal, technical concept, it is now universally and loosely used by biologists in a degraded, metaphoric sense that specifies anything the user thinks is "good" for the organism.

Updating Homeostasis as a Stability Theory

Because homeostasis suggests the need for a stability theory for organisms, all of which are complex by our technological standards, attempts have been made to update Cannon's original ideas, which he claimed pertained to physiological and not physical mechanisms, by taking advantage of modern developments in nonlinear dynamics (including chaos and fractals) and the explosive growth of computation, artificial intelligence, system theory, control theory, cybernetics, and the sciences of complexity (Soodak & Iberall, 1978; Yates, 1982, 1987, 1994; Rosen, 1991). The homeostatic competence of an organism was initially assessed quantitatively in terms of gains of (approximately) linear negative feedback models, as a first approximation (Riggs, 1963). However, deep appreciation of the essential nonlinear character of life's processes demanded a more sophisticated, physical approach, one version of which has been called *homeodynamics* (Yates, 1994), that goes beyond simple notions of *constancy*, equilibria or steady-states, to concepts of dynamic regulations and controls invoking multiple entailments among internal, cyclic thermodynamic processes. These modern extensions of homeostasis preserve the original notion that living systems can experience and survive a certain range of perturbations from fluctuational internal and external environments, without losing their defining structures and functions after transients have subsided. They emphasize that the order shown by living systems is not particularly high by ordinary physical entropic measures, because it is not primarily structural. Instead, biological order is chiefly functional.

Senescence as Hierarchical and Heterarchical Losses of Homeodynamic Competence

The physiology of a human being is based on structures and functions at many scales. Aging (senescence) causes disintegration both hierarchically and heterarchically. From the hierarchical perspective (up-down interactions across levels) redundancies in structures on large scales lower their susceptibility to degradation and allow for some repair by replication of existing structure through lower-level processes. In contrast, the finer-scale structures and their operations are more susceptible to degradation through conventional thermodynamic, physico-chemical processes, including damage from metabolically produced free radicals. As damage at one scale accumulates over time, the scale of the total damage increases and becomes part of larger scale behavior. When the scale of the total damage reaches that of the organism as a whole, fragility or death results through loss of homeodynamic competence.

The extension of degradation from finer scales to larger scales is observed in various multi-scale subsystems, such as vascular and neuronal systems, that are themselves hierarchically organized and therefore likely to manifest the progression. Smaller scale structures whose behaviors are amplified are especially likely to cause system failure. Two examples are: (1) *DNA*, whose structural contributions are amplified in processes of copying, transcription, translation, protein splicing, and the alterations of gene expression by variable methylation, acetylation, and ubiquitination of their histone wrappings, and (2) the *heart*, whose timing mechanism behavior is amplified to create flow dynamics the effects of which are further amplified by widespread distributions to the exchange beds that support metabolism everywhere. However, it must be appreciated that complex systems can have failure modes peculiar to their organization, not always assignable to a particular level.

The heterarchical perspective (side-to-side interactions at same level) can be conceptualized as a network of nodes and connections among them, where a *node* is a local functional cooperative and its supporting structures, and a *connection* is an information flow path between nodes. Homeodynamic competence requires that nodes and connections both be operable within the normal limits that initially defined the health of the mature organism. Heterarchically, senescent damage to that competence can impinge on nodes, on connections, or on both. A resultant tendency is structural and behavioral simplifications (Lipsitz & Goldberger, 1992). Simplifications are essential manifestations of natural aging and ultimately lead to the inability of an old organism to act homeodynamically in responding to fluctuations in external or internal environments.

Senescence as Thermodynamically Inevitable

The senescent loss of *homeodynamic competence* occurs inevitably in any complex, self-organizing system whose constructive dynamic degrees of freedom have been frozen out by progressive development and maturation. In living multicellular systems, during development the metabolic energy throughput required for operation (e.g. life) finds fewer and fewer outlets because differentiations successively create new dynamic constraints that, at first, support increasing complexities of form and function, but later close out (constrain) further options for new energetic transformations. (For resolution of the seeming paradox that constraints can simultaneously both restrict and enrich possibilities, see Medawar, 1974.) Byproducts of metabolic activity continually attack these constraints, leaving debilitating thermodynamic residues as weakened nodes and connections (Yates & Benton, 1995). The organism becomes fragile.

F. Eugene Yates

See also
Senescence and Transformation

References

Cannon, W. B. (1929). Organization for physiological homeostasis. *Physiological Reviews, 9*, 399–431.

Cannon, W. B. (1932). *The wisdom of the body*. New York: W.W. Norton.

Lipsitz, L. A., & Goldberger, A. L. (1992). Loss of complexity with aging: Potential applications of fractals and chaos theory to senescence. *Journal of the American Medical Association, 267*, 1806–1809.

Medawar, P. (1974). A geometric model of reduction and emergence. In F. J. Ayala & Dobzhansky (Eds.), *Studies in the philosophy of biology* (pp. 57–63). Berkeley, CA: University of California Press.

Riggs, D. S. (1963). *The mathematical approach to physiological problems* (pp. 95–104). Boston: The MIT Press.

Rosen, R. (1991). *Life itself: A comprehensive inquiry into the nature, origin, and fabrication of life*. New York: Columbia University Press.

Soodak, H., & Iberall, A. S. (1978). Homeokinetics: A physical science for complex systems. *Science, 201*, 579–582.

Wolfe, E. L., Barger, A. C., & Benison, S. (2000). *Walter B. Cannon: Science and society* (pp. 144–165). Cambridge, MA: Harvard University Press.

Yates, F. E. (1982). Outline of a physical theory of physiological systems. *Canadian Journal of Physiology and Pharmacology, 60*, 217–248.

Yates, F. E. (Ed.) (1987). *Self-organizing systems: The emergence of order*. New York: Plenum.

Yates, F. E. (1994). Order and complexity in dynamical systems: Homeodynamics as a generalized mechanics for biology. *Mathematical and Computer Modeling, 19*, 49–74.

Yates, F. E., & Benton, L. A. (1995). Loss of integration and resiliency with age: A dissipative destruction. In E. J. Masoro (Ed.), *Handbook of physiology: Section 11—Aging* (pp. 591–610). New York: Oxford University Press/American Physiological Society.

HOMOCYSTEINE

Plasma homocysteine levels increase with age. High plasma homocysteine levels contribute to the development of *atherosclerotic vascular disease* by promoting arterial endothelial dysfunction. Increased plasma homocysteine levels are independently related to isolated systolic hypertension in older persons. Other mechanisms of homocysteine contributing to atherosclerotic vascular disease include enhancement of *thromboxane* A_2 formation and platelet aggregation, proliferation of smooth muscle cells, increased activation of *factors V and X*, increased *fibrinogen* levels, decreased serum *antithrombin* activity, and increased binding of lipoprotein (a) to fibrin. By increasing *oxidative stress*, impairing vascular endothelial function, inducing a prothrombotic state, impairing vascular smooth muscle cell function, and changing extracellular matrix structure and function, homocysteine may cause atherosclerotic vascular disease.

Coronary Artery Disease

Many studies have demonstrated that increased plasma homocysteine levels are associated with an increased prevalence of coronary artery disease (CAD) and an increased incidence of new coronary events. In a population of 347 women and 153 men, mean age 81 years, plasma homocysteine was a significant independent risk factor for the prevalence of CAD, with an odds ratio of 1.21 for each 1 μmol/L increase in plasma homocysteine (Aronow & Ahn, 1997). Elevated plasma homocysteine levels (>17.0 μmol/L) were present in 43% of men with CAD versus 18% of men without CAD and in 37% of women with CAD versus 12% of women without CAD (Aronow & Ahn, 1997). At 31-month follow-up of this elderly population, plasma homocysteine was a significant independent predictor of new coronary events (myocardial infarction or sudden cardiac death) in persons with prior CAD (risk ratio = 1.07 for each 1 μmol/L increase) and in persons without prior CAD (risk ratio = 1.11 for each 1 μmol/L increase) (Aronow & Ahn, 2000).

In postmenopausal women in the Women's Health Study, the adjusted relative risk for myocardial infarction or stroke for women in the top quartile of plasma homocysteine level was 2.2 compared with the lowest quartile (Ridker, Manson, Buring, et al. 1999). At 9- to 11-year follow-up of 1,788 men and women, mean age 65 years, living in Jerusalem, plasma homocysteine was a significant risk factor in men and women for all-cause mortality, cardiovascular mortality, and CAD mortality (Kark, Selhub, Adler, et al., 1999).

At 4.6-year median follow-up of 587 men and women, mean age 62 years (15% 70 years and older), with angiographically documented CAD, *plasma homocysteine levels* were a strong predictor of mortality (Nygard, Nordrehaug, Refsum, et al., 1997). The mortality ratios were 1.0 for patients with homocysteine levels of <9 μmol/L, 1.9 for homocysteine levels of 9.0 to 14.9 μmol/L, 2.8 for patients with homocysteine levels of 15.0 to 19.9 μmol/L, and 4.5 for patients with homocysteine levels of $\geq$20.0 μmol/L (Nygard, Nordrehaug, Refsum, et al., 1997).

In men and women who had coronary angiography performed, plasma homocysteine level was significantly associated with the presence of CAD and with the severity of CAD. In patients with *myocardial infarction* or unstable *angina pectoris*, high plasma homocysteine levels were associated with an increased intracoronary thrombus burden and with increased myocardial injury.

In a study of 440 patients with acute myocardial infarction (n = 236) or unstable angina pectoris (n = 204) (94 patients older than 70 years and 154 patients aged 60 to 70 years), patients with homocysteine levels in the upper 2 quintiles (>12.2 μmol/L) had a 2.6 times increase in the risk of a new coronary event at 2.5-year follow-up (Stubbs, Al-Obaidi, Conroy, et al., 2000). A high plasma homocysteine level was also an independent risk factor for new coronary events in patients undergoing dialysis.

Of 553 patients, mean age 63 years, undergoing coronary angiography, patients were randomized to receive *folic acid* 1 mg daily, vitamin B_{12} 400 μg daily, and vitamin B_6 10 mg daily or placebo for 6 months (Schnyder, Roffi, Flammer, et al., 2002). At 11-month follow-up, the composite endpoint of death, nonfatal myocardial infarction, and need for repeat coronary revascularization was significantly reduced 32% by *homocysteine-lowering therapy* with folic acid, *vitamin* B_{12}, and *vitamin* B_6 (Schnyder, Roffi, Flammer, et al., 2002).

Until the results of ongoing intervention trials in progress are completed, general screening for homocysteine levels is not currently recommended. However, persons with CAD without conventional risk factors and those at high risk for plasma homocysteine levels, including persons with impaired renal function, malnutrition, malabsorption, pernicious anemia, systemic lupus erythematosus, recurrent deep vein thrombosis, hypothyroidism, and those taking certain drugs, such as nicotinic acid, theophylline, L-dopa, methotrexate, tamoxifen, anticonvulsants, bile acid sequestrants, and fibric acid derivatives, should have a fasting plasma homocysteine level determined. An optimal level for plasma homocysteine is thought to be <10 μmol/L.

All persons should have an adequate intake of folate, vitamin B_6, and vitamin B_{12} by eating vegetables, fruits, fish, and fortified grains and cereals. High-risk persons may warrant supplemental vitamins with folic acid, vitamin B_6, and vitamin B_{12}.

Stroke

Four studies (2 performed in older persons) have also shown that increased plasma homocysteine is an independent *risk factor for stroke*. The *Framingham Study* demonstrated that plasma homocysteine was a significant independent risk factor for new stroke in 1,947 men and women, mean age 70 years (Bostom, Rosenberg, Silvershatz, et al., 1999). Compared with persons in the lowest quartile of plasma homocysteine level, the relative risk of new stroke was 1.82 for the highest quartile of plasma homocysteine, 1.44 for the second highest quartile of plasma homocysteine, and 1.32 for the third highest quartile of plasma homocysteine (Bostom, Rosenberg, Silvershatz, et al. 1999). At 31-month follow-up of 500 men and women, mean age 81 years, plasma homocysteine was a significant independent risk factor for new stroke (risk ratio = 1.08 for each 1 μmol/L increase of plasma homocysteine) (Aronow, Ahn, & Gutstein, 2000).

Extracranial *Carotid Arterial Disease*

Two studies have documented that plasma homocysteine is a risk factor for extracranial carotid arterial disease (ECAD) in older persons (Selhub, Jacques, Bostom, et al., 1995; Aronow, Ahn, & Schoenfeld, 1997). In 1,041 older persons in the Framingham Study, the odds ratios for ECAD were 2.0 in persons in the highest quartile of plasma homocysteine and 1.6 in persons in the second highest quartile of plasma homocysteine compared with persons in the lowest quartile of plasma homocysteine (Selhub, Jacques, Bostom, et al., 1995).

In 400 men and women, mean age 81 years, an increased plasma homocysteine level was associated with an increased risk of ECAD in men and women (Aronow, Ahn, & Schoenfeld, 1997). Increased plasma homocysteine levels were found in 45% of men with 40% to 100% ECAD, versus 20% of men with 0% to 39% ECAD, and in 40% of women with 40% to 100% ECAD, versus 18% of women with 0% to 39% ECAD (Aronow, Ahn, & Schoenfeld, 1997).

Peripheral Arterial Disease

Studies have shown that increased plasma homocysteine is a risk factor for peripheral arterial disease (PAD). In 520 persons, mean age 81 years, plasma homocysteine was a significant independent risk factor for PAD in men and women (Aronow & Ahn, 1998). The odds ratio for the prevalence of PAD was 1.13 for each 1 μmol/L increase in plasma homocysteine in this study (Aronow & Ahn, 1998). Increased plasma homocysteine levels were found in 49% of men with PAD versus 18% of men without PAD, and in 46% of women with PAD versus 15% of older women without PAD (Aronow & Ahn, 1998).

Aortic Atherosclerosis

Increased plasma homocysteine levels were significantly and independently correlated with the degree of atherosclerosis in the thoracic aorta measured with transesophageal echocardiography in 156 patients, mean age 69 years (Konecky, Malinow, Tunick, et al., 1997). Increased plasma homocysteine levels were also a marker of severity of thoracic atherosclerosis diagnosed by transesophageal echocardiography.

Deep Vein Thrombosis

Increased plasma homocysteine levels are also a risk factor for deep vein thrombosis. The association between increased plasma homocysteine levels and deep venous thrombosis is stronger among women than among men and increases with age.

Dementia and *Alzheimer's Disease*

At 8-year follow-up of 667 women and 425 men, mean age 76 years, without dementia in the Framingham Study, an increased plasma homocysteine level was a strong independent risk factor for the development of dementia and for the development of Alzheimer's disease (Seshadri, Beiser, Selhub, et al. 2002). In a study of 200 patients, mean age 78 years, patients with dementia with and without atherosclerotic vascular disease had a significantly higher mean plasma homocysteine level than patients with no atherosclerotic vascular disease or dementia (Storey, Suryadevara, Aronow, et al., 2003).

Hip Fractures

Increased plasma homocysteine levels have also been shown to be an important risk factor for osteoporotic fractures in older men and women (McLean, Jacques, Selhub, et al., 2004; van Meurs, Dhonukshe-Rutten, Pluijm, et al., 2004). In 825 men and 1174 women, mean age 70 years, men and women in the highest quartile of plasma homocysteine had a significantly greater risk of hip fracture than those in the lowest quartile (4 times increased for men, and 1.9 times increased for women) (McLean, Jacques, Selhub, et al., 2004).

Therapy

Randomized trials are in progress investigating whether *multivitamin therapy* to lower plasma homocysteine levels will decrease cardiovascular disease. If these trials demonstrate that reduction of increased plasma homocysteine levels by a combination of folic acid, vitamin B_{12}, and vitamin B_6 are effective in reducing cardiovascular disease, we will have a safe, inexpensive, easily administered treatment to reduce cardiovascular disease.

A potential *hazard of folic acid therapy* is progressive neurological damage (subacute combined degeneration of the spinal cord) in patients with subclinical vitamin B_{12} deficiency, in whom treatment with folic acid may mask the development of the hematological signs of *vitamin B_{12} deficiency*. This can be avoided by supplementing folic acid therapy with at least 400 μg daily of vitamin B_{12}. The minimum effective daily dose of folic acid for maximally reducing plasma homocysteine levels is 400 μg daily. Moderate hyperhomocysteinemia should also be treated with vitamin B_6, 10 to 50 mg daily.

WILBERT S. ARONOW

References

Aronow, W. S., & Ahn, C. (1997). Association between plasma homocysteine and coronary artery disease in older persons. *American Journal of Cardiology*, *80*, 1216–1218.

Aronow W. S., & Ahn, C. (1998). Association between plasma homocysteine and peripheral arterial disease in older persons. *Coronary Artery Disease*, *9*, 49–50.

Aronow, W. S., & Ahn, C. (2000). Increased plasma homocysteine is an independent predictor of new coronary events in older persons. *American Journal of Cardiology*, *86*, 346–347.

Aronow, W. S., Ahn, C., & Gutstein, H. (2000). Increased plasma homocysteine is an independent predictor of new atherothrombotic brain infarction in older persons. *American Journal of Cardiology*, *86*, 585–586.

Aronow, W. S., Ahn, C., & Schoenfeld, M. R. (1997). Association between plasma homocysteine and extracranial carotid arterial disease in older persons. *American Journal of Cardiology*, *79*, 1432–1433.

Bostom, A. G., Rosenberg, I. H., Silvershatz, H., et al. (1999). Nonfasting plasma total homocysteine levels and stroke incidence in elderly persons: The Framingham study. *Annals of Internal Medicine*, *131*, 352–355.

Kark, J. D., Selhub, J., Adler, B., et al. (1999). Nonfasting plasma total homocysteine level and mortality in middle-aged and elderly men and women in Jerusalem. *Annals of Internal Medicine*, *131*, 321–330.

Konecky, N., Malinow, M. R., Tunick, P. A., et al. (1997). Correlation between plasma homocyst(e)ine and aortic atherosclerosis. *American Heart Journal*, *133*, 534–540.

McLean, R. R., Jacques, P. F., Selhub, J., et al. (2004). Homocysteine as a predictive factor for hip fracture in older persons. *New England Journal of Medicine*, *350*, 2042–2049.

Nygard, O., Nordrehaug, J. E., Refsum, H., et al. (1997). Plasma homocysteine levels and mortality in patients with coronary artery disease. *New England Journal of Medicine*, *337*, 230–236.

Ridker, P. M., Manson, J. E., Buring, J. E., et al. (1999). Homocysteine and risk of cardiovascular disease among postmenopausal women. *Journal of the American Medical Association*, *281*, 1817–1821.

Schnyder, G., Roffi, M., Flammer, Y. et al. (2002). Effect of homocysteine-lowering therapy with folic acid, vitamin B12, and vitamin B6 on clinical outcome after percutaneous coronary intervention. The Swiss Heart Study: A randomized controlled trial. *Journal of the American Medical Association*, *288*, 973–979.

Selhub, J., Jacques, P. F., Bostom, A. G., et al. (1995). Association between plasma homocysteine concentrations and extracranial carotid-artery stenosis. *New England Journal of Medicine*, *332*, 286–291.

Seshadri, S., Beiser, A., Selhub, J., et al. (2002). Plasma homocysteine as a risk factor for dementia and Alzheimer's disease. *New England Journal of Medicine*, *346*, 476–483.

Storey, S. G., Suryadevara, V., Aronow, W. S., et al. (2003). Association of plasma homocysteine in elderly persons with atherosclerotic vascular disease and dementia, atherosclerotic vascular disease without dementia, dementia without atherosclerotic disease, and no dementia or atherosclerotic vascular disease. *Journal of Gerontology Medical Sciences*, *58A*, 1135–1136.

Stubbs, P. J., Al-Obaidi, M. K., Conroy, R. M., et al. (2000). Level of plasma homocysteine concentration on early and late events in patients with acute coronary syndromes. *Circulation*, *102*, 605–610.

van Meurs, J. B. J., Dhonukshe-Rutten, R. A. M., Pluijm, S. M. F., et al. (2004). Homocysteine levels and the risk of osteoporotic fracture. *New England Journal of Medicine*, *350*, 2033–2041.

HOMOSEXUALITY

Gay, *lesbian*, *bisexual*, and *transgender* (GLBT) older persons are as diverse as any other groups of older persons in terms of education, income, health, race, and other relevant variables. Some have children and grandchildren, some have long-term companions, and some have lived alone for many years. They have, however, often had different life experiences than exclusively heterosexual elders. For example, one gay man aged 90 wrote in the University of Chicago alumni magazine: "I'm gay, and I've known since I was 12; I didn't have a steady companion until I was 70, and I didn't come *out of the closet* until I was 85. I did propose to a woman on New Year's Eve, in 1945. Seven months into our marriage, I realized I had fallen in love with my wife. After suffering terribly from diabetes, she committed suicide about 12 and three-quarters years later. My male companion is now in an Alzheimer's care unit in this building. I visit him every day." (Rusterholtz, 1999).

There are significant issues of aging that differ for gay, lesbian, and bisexual elders. Because of the "*Defense of Marriage Act*" passed by the U.S. Congress and signed into law, Social Security and other federal programs will not pay spouse benefits or recognize surviving spouses in *same-gender relationships*, despite the availability of civil unions in Vermont and *same-sex marriages* of uncertain legal standing in Massachusetts and other U.S. jurisdictions. In most states, medical care decisions, hospital and nursing home visitation, inheritance taxes and rights, funeral arrangements, and even the right to continue living in a rental apartment are legally based on family relationships superseding the rights of a long-term, unmarried same-sex companion. Unless the (past) employer had a "*domestic partner*" policy, long-term *same-gender couples* may not have health insurance and other benefits that are received by married spouses of retirees.

In the absence of legal marriage, or its equivalent, skilled legal assistance is required to provide appropriate durable powers of attorney, health care directives, wills, and property ownership and division agreements (Dubois, in press). Tax experts are needed to prevent one's own property and belongings being *taxed as inheritance* when one's partner (who owned the property in common) dies. Financial consultants are needed to ensure that joint accounts, pensions, and investments are appropriately arranged so that maximum benefits go to the intended person or purpose, as tax laws are written with married spouses, but not friends, exempt from inheritance tax and able to roll over pretax accounts (Blevins & Werth, in press).

Often it is incorrectly assumed that if one is no longer sexually active, or in a committed relationship, sexual orientation does not exist. Organizations such as *SAGE* (*Services and Advocacy for GLBT Elders*, Inc.) in New York City offer a wide range of programs for older lesbians, gay men, bisexuals, and transgender persons that are important regardless of the individual's sexual life, such as friendly visiting, dances, support groups for a variety of topics, and many social activities (www.sageusa.org).

In general, open lesbians and gay men do not feel welcome in regular senior centers, which assume heterosexuality. Retirement housing is typically designed for married couples and heterosexual widows; however, some projects have been designed for lesbian, gay, bisexual, and transgender elders (Adelman, Gurevitch, deVries, & Blando, in press). Nursing homes typically do not consider the *sexual orientation* of their residents. In-service training on sexual orientation issues, gay-affirmative services, and lesbian/gay retirement centers are emerging in the United States. Generally, persons working with older adults should not make any assumptions about sexual orientation, but should inquire about significant persons and relationships; those must be respected as fully as possible, while recognizing that openness may lead to stigmatization (Kimmel, 1995; 2002).

Until recent years, lesbians, gay men, bisexuals, and transgender persons have been stigmatized by mental health professions, churches, and the legal system. Many older persons who lived openly with a same-gender companion have experienced and coped with social stigma. For most, it has left some residue of secrecy and fear about being vulnerable; it has often also strengthened their ability to confront oppression and be assertive individuals (Morrow, 2001). Ethnic minorities, however, often see the *gay movement* as important primarily for white men and may not identify with it (Adams & Kimmel, 1997)—despite the presence of towering figures such as James Baldwin, Audre Lorde, Bayard Rustin, and Bessie Smith, whose sexual orientation was well-known. The challenges of aging provide unique patterns for lesbians, because of issues involving gender as well as sexual orientation (Gabby, 2002). Bisexuals may progress through alternating periods of same-gender and other-gender relationships, entering late life with a same-gender orientation for the first time since their youth; conversely, some bisexuals find a partner of the other gender after a life of same-gender attractions. Such patterns can be confusing to children and family members (Dworkin, in press). Transgender persons face exceptional stigma, since their physical bodies may not conform to their gender identity; for this reason, they may avoid medical services and face ridicule and humiliation in hospital or nursing home settings (Cook-Daniels, in press; Donovan, 2001; Witten, 1999).

Health and mental health issues reflect past life experiences more than *stereotypes about sexual orientation* (D'Augelli, Grossman, Hershberger, & O'Connell, 2001; Grossman, D'Augelli, & O'Connell, 2001). Some lesbian and gay persons may be inhibited from seeking medical care, or being open with their physician (Stein & Bonuck, 2001). People who are infected with *HIV* are at risk for a range of difficulties (Meris, 2001); and the long-term effects of the disease when it is controlled by medications are very complex (Burgoyne, Rourke, Behrens, & Salit, 2004; New York State Department of Health *AIDS* Institute, 2004; Volberding, 2003). Greater life stress and greater gay-related stress have each been found to be related to symptoms of depression (Lewis, Derlega, Griffin, & Krowinski, 2003). Social oppression may increase the risk of *substance abuse*, including tobacco use, and suicidal behavior (Fergusson, Horwood, & Beautrais, 1999; Lock & Steiner, 1999). There may be late-life consequences of these risks, for example, alcohol and drug abuse (Satre, in press). A careful life history, including information about sexual orientation and practices, is always important to understand the person's particular risks and strengths, regardless of age.

Counseling and self-help *support groups* can be important for a variety of issues. In addition, older lesbians and gay men may appreciate groups or counseling for bereavement support, finding new relationships in late life, relationship issues and changes (perhaps related to health or dementia), and retirement adjustment. Such groups and counselors should be knowledgeable about the gay, lesbian, and bisexual community (and perhaps have single-gender groups) and be gay-affirmative in their personal philosophy and techniques (Baron & Cramer, 2000; Langley, 2001; Nystrom & Jones.

Many educational videotapes and written materials are available in libraries, bookstores, and local gay, bisexual, and lesbian centers. The *Lesbian and Gay Aging Issues Network* (LGAIN) is an interest group within the American Society on Aging (www.asaging.org) and can be contacted through that organization.

DOUGLAS C. KIMMEL

See also
Sexuality

References

Adams, C. L., Jr., & Kimmel, D. C. (1997). Exploring the lives of older African American gay men. In B. Greene (Ed.), *Ethnic and cultural diversity among lesbians and gay men* (pp. 132–151). Thousand Oaks CA: Sage.

Adelman, M., Gurevitch, J., deVries, B., & Blando, J. A. (in press). Openhouse: Community building and research in the LGBT aging population. In D. Kimmel, T. Rose, & S. David (Eds.), *Research and clinical perspectives on lesbian, gay, bisexual, and transgender aging*. New York: Columbia University Press.

Baron, A., & Cramer, D. W. (2000). Potential counseling concerns of aging lesbian, gay, and bisexual clients. In R. M. Perez & K. A. DeBord et al. (Eds.), *Handbook of counseling and psychotherapy with lesbian, gay, and bisexual clients* (pp. 207–223). Washington, DC: American Psychological Association.

Blevins, D., & Werth, J. L., Jr. (in press). End-of-life issues for lesbian, gay, bisexual and transgendered older adults. In D. Kimmel, T. Rose, & S. David (Eds.), *Research and clinical perspectives on lesbian, gay, bisexual, and transgender aging*. New York: Columbia University Press.

Burgoyne, R. W., Rourke, S. B., Behrens, D. M., & Salit, I. E. (2004). Long-term quality-of-life outcomes among adults living with HIV in the HAART era: The interplay of changes in clinical factors and symptom profile. *AIDS and Behavior, 8*, 151–163.

Cook-Daniels, L. (in press). Transgender aging. In D. Kimmel, T. Rose, & S. David (Eds.), *Research and clinical perspectives on lesbian, gay, bisexual, and transgender aging*. New York: Columbia University Press.

D'Augelli, A. R., Grossman, A. H., Hershberger, S. L., & O'Connell, T. S. (2001). Aspects of mental health among older lesbian, gay, and bisexual adults. *Aging and Mental Health, 5*(2), 149–158.

Donovan, T. (2001). Being transgender and older: A first person account. *Journal of Gay and Lesbian Social Services: Issues in Practice, Policy & Research, 13*(4), 19–22.

Dubois, M. (in press). Legal concerns of lesbian, gay, bisexual, and transgendered elders. In D. Kimmel, T. Rose, & S. David (Eds.), *Research and clinical perspectives on lesbian, gay, bisexual, and transgender aging*. New York: Columbia University Press.

Dworkin, S. (in press). Aging bisexuals. In D. Kimmel, T. Rose, & S. David (Eds.), *Research and clinical perspectives on lesbian, gay, bisexual, and transgender aging*. New York: Columbia University Press.

Fergusson, D. M., Horwood, L. J., & Beautrais, A. L. (1999). Is sexual orientation related to mental health problems and suicidality in young people? *Archives of General Psychiatry, 56*, 876–880.

Gabby, S. G. (2002). Lesbian aging: Review of a growing literature. *Journal of Gay and Lesbian Social Services: Issues in Practice, Policy and Research, 14*(3), 1–21.

Grossman, A. H., D'Augelli, A. R., & O'Connell, T. S. (2001). Being lesbian, gay, bisexual, and 60 or older in North America. *Journal of Gay and Lesbian Social Services: Issues in Practice, Policy and Research, 13*(4), 23–40.

Kimmel, D. C. (1995). Lesbians and gay men also grow old. In L. A. Bond, S. J. Cutler, & A. Grams (Eds.), *Promoting successful and productive aging* (pp. 289–303). Thousand Oaks, CA: Sage.

Kimmel, D. C. (2002). Aging and sexual orientation. In B. E. Jones & M. J. Hill (Eds.), *Mental health issues in lesbian, gay, bisexual, and transgender communities* (pp. 17–36). Washington, DC: American Psychiatric Publishing.

Langley, J. (2001). Developing anti-oppressive empowering social work practice with older lesbian women and gay men. *British Journal of Social Work, 31*, 917–932.

Lewis, R. J., Derlega, V. J., Griffin, J. L., & Krowinski, A. C. (2003). Stressors for gay men and lesbians: Life stress, gay-related stress, stigma consciousness, and depressive symptoms. *Journal of Social and Clinical Psychology, 22*, 716–729.

Lock, J., & Steiner, H. (1999). Gay, lesbian, and bisexual youth risks for emotional, physical, and social problems: Results from a community-based survey. *Journal of the American Academy of Child and Adolescent Psychiatry, 38*, 297–304.

Meris, D. (2001). Responding to the mental health and grief concerns of homeless HIV-infected gay men. *Journal of Gay and Lesbian Social Services: Issues in Practice, Policy and Research, 13*(4), 103–111.

Morrow, D. F. (2001). Older gays and lesbians: Surviving a generation of hate and violence. *Journal of Gay and Lesbian Social Services: Issues in Practice, Policy and Research, 13*(1–2), 151–169.

New York State Department of Health AIDS Institute. (2004). Criteria for the medical care of adults with HIV infection: Long-term complications of antiretroviral therapy. Available: http://www.hivguidelines.org/public_html/a-longterm/a-longterm.htm

Nystrom, N. M., & Jones, T. C. (2003). Community building with aging and old lesbians. *American Journal of Community Psychology, 31*, 293–300.

Rusterholtz, W. (1999, December). Interview by C. Snow (Ed.), Lifelong Chicagoans. *University of Chicago Magazine, 92*(2), 20–27.

Satre, D. D. (in press). Use and misuse of alcohol and drugs. In D. Kimmel, T. Rose, & S. David (Eds.), *Research and clinical perspectives on lesbian, gay, bisexual, and transgender aging*. New York: Columbia University Press.

Stein, G. L., & Bonuck, K. A. (2001). Physician-patient relationships among the lesbian and gay community. *Journal of the Gay and Lesbian Medical Association, 5*(3), 87–93.

Volberding, P. A. (2003). HIV therapy in 2003: Consensus and controversy. *AIDS, 17*(Suppl. 1), S4–S11.

Witten, T. M. (1999). Transgender aging: Introduction to an emerging field. *Gerontologist, 39*, 79–80.

HORMONE REPLACEMENT THERAPY (HRT)

Estrus refers to the regularly recurring periods of maximal sexual receptivity in female mammals. The word is derived from the Greek *oistros,* "the gadfly," an insect whose sting instigates a frenzy in cattle. In gynecology, estrus refers to the cycle of changes in the female genital tract induced by ovarian hormonal activity. Estrogen is the generic term coined for hormonal substances that induce estrus in female mammals. It is a combination of "estro" denoting estrus, plus "gen" from the Greek, gennao, "I bring forth" (Haubrich, 1984).

At the time of *menopause*, a woman's estrogen levels fall as secretion from the ovaries comes to an end. The symptoms of *estrogen deficiency* that may develop in this population include: hot flashes, night sweats, insomnia, difficulty concentrating or remembering, fatigue, dysuria, vaginal dryness, painful sexual intercourse, depression, nervousness, emotional lability, headaches, bloating, swelling of the hands and feet, and heart palpitations. Estrogen may be administered systemically, usually as a pill or a patch, for the symptomatic postmenopausal woman. Although this form of *estrogen replacement therapy* (ERT) is capable of relieving these symptoms in the majority of treated individuals, it does simulate proliferation of the uterine lining cells. When administered to a postmenopausal woman with a uterus, estrogen administration alone has been associated with an increased incidence of uterine (endometrial) cancer. This increased *risk of uterine cancer* is nullified by the administration of *progesterone* in addition to estrogen. The combination of estrogen and progesterone is called hormone replacement therapy (HRT). A woman whose uterus has been removed (hysterectomy) does not require progesterone, and may be treated for symptomatic relief with estrogen only (ERT).

In addition to symptom relief, studies published during the last 20 years (most of them observational) appear to support long-term *benefits of ERT* and HRT. A 1993 review of the literature (Bluming, 1993) found that HRT (using estrogen alone for women with *hysterectomies*, and *estrogen-progestin* for women without hysterectomies) resulted in:

1. A 50% decreased risk of atherosclerotic heart disease and a 28% decreased risk of death from heart disease.
2. A 50% *decreased risk of osteoporotic hip fracture*.

A hypothetical, population-based 1994 analysis concluded that the health *benefits of postmenopausal estrogen replacement* exceeded the health risks. In the analysis, 50-year-old women were assumed to take ERT for 25 years, with health outcomes extrapolated to age 75. In a cohort of 10,000 women using estrogen for 25 years, 574 deaths would be prevented. Women using estrogen would gain 3.95 quality-adjusted life-years compared with women not using it (Gorsky, Koplan, Peterson, 1994).

A 1997 decision analysis concluded that up to 99% of the current U.S. postmenopausal population would benefit from taking HRT as measured by decreased morbidity and improved longevity (Col, Eckman, Karas, et al., 1997). A review by Burkman and colleagues (2001) reported that HRT administration is associated with: (1) a 34% decreased risk of colon cancer, (2) a 20% to 60% decreased risk of Alzheimer's disease.

These conclusions, however, have not been supported by a series of prospective randomized studies of ERT, known as the *Women's Health Initiative*. This was a prospective, controlled primary prevention trial of 16,608 postmenopausal women randomized between HRT and placebo (if they had a uterus) and between ERT and placebo (if their uterus had been surgically removed) In general, these Women's Health Initiative studies showed that *conjugated equine estrogen* used for an average of almost 7 years, while decreasing the risk of hip fracture also increased the risk of stroke, and did not affect coronary heart disease. A possible *reduction in breast cancer* risk was noted, but in general the burden of incident disease events was equivalent in the estrogen and placebo groups, which indicated no overall benefit (Anderson, Limacher, Assaf, and the Women's Health Initiative Screening Committee, 2004). A largely similar profile was seen with the use of *estrogen plus progestin*, with similar adverse effects, against a positive *benefit on bone* mineral density and hip fractures (Cauley, Robbins, Chen, et al., 2003). Importantly, too, the Women's Health Initiative reported net adverse effects of the use of conjugated equine estrogen on cognition (Espeland, Rapp, Shumaker, et al., 2004; Shumaker, Legault, Kuller, et al., 2004); this effect was also seen to some degree with estrogen plus progestin. (Shumaker, Legault, Rapp, et al., 2003; Rapp, Espeland, Shumaker, et al., 2003). While postmenopausal estrogen use is effective for short-term treatment of hot flashes, it does result in common side effects such as breast tenderness and atypical vaginal bleeding (Nelson, 2004). Of note, in the Women's Health Initiative studies, *atypical vaginal bleeding* resulted in more *endometrial biopsies*; the investigators thus concluded that while it did not increase the risk of endometrial cancer, "The increased burden of endometrial biopsies [from estrogen plus progestin] required to assess vaginal bleeding further limits the acceptability of this regimen." (Anderson, Judd, Kaunitz, et al., 2003).

Why controversy still persists (Bluming, 2004) is perhaps best illustrated over the interpretation of the concern that ERT may facilitate or increase the risk of breast cancer development. This concern has not been supported by the majority of observational studies (Bluming, 1993). Nevertheless, reported conclusions from some of these studies have indicated such an association even though the data generated from them have not supported this conclusion. For example, the Nurses' Health Study, a prospective, observation analysis of 121,700 female registered nurses followed from 1976 through 1992, found no increased risk of breast cancer among women who used ERT (even for over 10 years) when compared to women who never used it (Colditz, Hankinson, Hunter, et al., 1995). The authors did, however, report an increased risk of breast cancer, but only for a minority of the women under study, and only after applying retrospective substratification, a statistical analytic tool that can sometimes be misleading (Smith, 2002; Kassirer, 2002). To evaluate an *increased risk of breast cancer* associated with estrogen ingestion, the investigators divided the population of women exposed to estrogen into those who had taken it and stopped, and those who were still taking it at the time of the most recent analysis, without offering an explanation for this retrospective stratification. They isolated a group of women who were postmenopausal, thin, having taken estrogen for over 5 years, and who were still taking it as the population in whom an increased risk of breast cancer was demonstrated. This relatively small, retrospectively identified group of women constituted a minority of those who had been taking estrogen. While this retrospective analysis could be used to generate a hypothesis that might be tested in a subsequent prospective study, these authors used this result as a conclusion rather than as a hypothesis.

The Women's Health Initiative was planned to run for 8.5 years and was expected to help resolve the question of ERT or HRT and breast cancer development. The HRT arm was prematurely halted after a mean follow-up of 5.2 years because "the test statistic for invasive breast cancer exceeded the stopping boundary for this adverse effect and the global index statistic supported risks exceeding benefits." (Roussouw, Anderson, Prentice, et al., 2002).

In fact, the increased risk of breast cancer reported was not statistically significant, nor was the risk of breast cancer found among women with hysterectomies who received only ERT at the time that part of the study was prematurely terminated 2 years later (Anderson, Limacher, Assaf, and the Women's Health Initiative Screening Committee, 2004). The Women's Health Initiative study has additionally challenged the previous reported benefits of ERT on ERT associated improvements in quality of life. (Anderson, Limacher, Assaf, and the Women's Health Initiative Screening Committee, 2004; Bluming, 2004).

In a time of headlined breakthrough announcements, the physician is still advised to formulate and update a benefit/risk assessment for every treatment prescribed, to stay current with recent literature which should be critically analyzed, and to remember, as Allan Hammond, AAAS president in 1980, advised: "In today's news-conscious world, there is an enormous emphasis on breakthroughs. But with rare exceptions, science is a process, not an isolated event. Conveying the way science really works—the interplay of persistence and luck, the painstaking accumulation of evidence, the clash of proponent and critic, the gradual dawning of conviction—demands a look behind the headlines."

AVRUM Z. BLUMING

References

Anderson, G. L., Judd, H. L., Kaunitz, A. M., et al. (2003). Effects of estrogen plus progestin on gynecologic cancers and associated diagnostic procedures: The Women's Health Initiative randomized trial. *Journal of the American Medical Association, 290*(13), 1739–1748.

Anderson, G. L., Limacher, M., Assaf, A. R., and the Women's Health Initiative Screening Committee. (2004). Effects of conjugated equine estrogen in postmenopausal women with hysterectomy: The Women's Health Initiative Randomized Controlled Trial. *Journal of the American Medical Association, 291*, 1701–1712.

Bluming, A. Z. (1993). Hormone replacement therapy: Benefits and risks for the general postmenopausal female population and for women with a history of previously treated breast cancer. *Seminars in Oncology, 20*, 662–674.

Bluming, A. Z. (2004). Hormone replacement therapy. The debate should continue. *Geriatrics, 59*, 30–37.

Burkman, R. T., Collins, J. A., & Greene, R. A. (2001). Current perspectives on benefits and risks of hormone replacement therapy. *American Journal Obstetrics and Gynecology, 185*, S13–23.

Cauley, J. A., Robbins, J., Chen, Z., et al. (2003). Effects of estrogen plus progestin on risk of fracture and bone mineral density: the Women's Health Initiative randomized trial. *Journal of the American Medical Association, 290*, 1729–1738.

Col, N. F., Eckman, M. H., Karas, R. H., et al. (1997). Patient-specific decisions about hormone replacement therapy in postmenopausal women. *Journal of the American Medical Association*, *277*, 1140–1147.

Colditz, G. A., Hankinson, S. E., Hunter, D. J., et al. (1995). The use of estrogens and progestins and the risk of breast cancer in postmenopausal women. *New England Journal of Medicine*, *332*, 1589–1593.

Espeland, M. A., Rapp, S. R., Shumaker, S. A., et al. (2004). Conjugated equine estrogens and global cognitive function in postmenopausal women: Women's Health Initiative Memory Study. *Journal of the American Medical Association*, *291*(24), 2959–2968.

Gorsky, R. D., Koplan, J. P., Peterson, H. B., et al. (1994). Relative risks and benefits of long-term estrogen replacement therapy: A decision analysis. *Obstetrics and Gynecology*, *83*, 161–166.

Haubrich, W. S. (1984). *Medical meanings. A glossary of word origins*. San Diego: Harcourt Brace Jovanovich.

Kassirer, J. P. (2002). Reflections on medical journals: Has progress made them better? *Annals of Internal Medicine*, *137*, 46–48.

Nelson, H. D. (2004). Commonly used types of postmenopausal estrogen for treatment of hot flashes: Scientific review. *Journal of the American Medical Association*, *291*(13), 1610–1620.

Rapp, S. R., Espeland, M. A., Shumaker, S. A., et al. (2003). Effect of estrogen plus progestin on global cognitive function in postmenopausal women: The Women's Health Initiative Memory Study: A randomized controlled trial. *Journal of the American Medical Association*, *289*(20), 2663–2672.

Roussouw, J. E., Anderson, G. L., Prentice, R. L., et al. (2002). Risks and benefits of estrogen plus progestin in healthy postmenopausal women: Principal results from the Women's Health Initiative randomized controlled trial. *Journal of the American Medical Association*, *288*, 321–333.

Shumaker, S. A., Legault, C., Kuller, L., et al. (2004). Conjugated equine estrogens and incidence of probable dementia and mild cognitive impairment in postmenopausal women: Women's Health Initiative Memory Study. *Journal of the American Medical Association*, *291*(24), 2947–2958.

Shumaker, S. A., Legault, C., Rapp, S. R., et al. (2003). Estrogen plus progestin and the incidence of dementia and mild cognitive impairment in postmenopausal women: The Women's Health Initiative Memory Study: A randomized controlled trial. *Journal of the American Medical Association*, *289*(20), 2651–2662.

Smith, G. D. (2002). Data dredging, bias or confounding. *British Medical Journal*, *325*, 1437–1438.

HOSPICE

The hospice reemerged in the modern era with the establishment of *St. Christopher's Hospice* outside London in 1967, but its origins date from the Middle Ages, when a hospice was a resting place for pilgrims on their way to the Holy Lands. However, even in modern times numerous institutions offered palliative care to the dying before Dame *Cicily Saunders* opened St. Christopher's. She first learned techniques in pain control at St. Luke's Hospital in London, where she worked as a volunteer after World War II. Founded in 1893 as a home for the dying poor, it specialized in caring for those dying of cancer and tuberculosis. In the United States, similar institutions existed, generally of a secular nature. For example, the *Home of the Holy Ghost* in Cambridge, Massachusetts, was known as a nursing home "devoted to the care of the incurable patient, particularly those dying of cancer" (Dunphy, 1976).

Thus, by the time Saunders established St. Christopher's Hospice in 1967, a well-formulated philosophy of hospice care existed, emphasizing *control of pain* and symptoms and the psychological needs of patients and their families. It was not long before this philosophy found fertile soil in the United States, initially with the establishment of an oncology unit in a Massachusetts chronic disease hospital and subsequently in the founding of *Hospice, Inc.*, in New Haven, Connecticut, in 1974. The first hospice standards of care were formulated in 1974 by a committee of the *International Work Group on Death and Dying*, led by Saunders and others (Kastenbaum, 1975). Concurrently, the hospice was emerging in Canada, with the establishment of the *Palliative Care Unit* at the Royal Victoria in Montreal under the direction of Dr. *Balfour M. Mount*. This program consisted of an inpatient unit, a home care service, and a consultation service that served other parts of the hospital.

The *hospice movement* in the United States grew out of a convergence of 2 popular trends; disenchantment with the unfulfilled promise of curative medicine, and a new sensitivity to *death and dying* (*Kubler-Ross*, 1969). These, in turn, were fueled by the demographic transition that began in the late-19th century and the rapid increase in life expectancy, which lead to a transformation in who was dying, and from what: from children with infectious diseases, to older persons burdened by multiple chronic illnesses. Saunder's original vision of the hospice was somewhat transformed in the United States by an emphasis on a "homelike" environment that was consistent with the U.S. perspective on deinstitutionalizing health care. The hospice movement in the United States was founded at a time when deinstitutionalization was prominent and home and community-based care had begun to grow. Strong support for the hospice movement in the United States led to the formation of the *National Hospice Organization* (NHO) in 1977, which advocated for the hospice philosophy of care for the dying, educated the public, and provided a resource and structure for information exchange among the burgeoning number of hospices throughout the United States.

The emergence of hospices in the United States was aided by governmental initiatives and not-for-profit foundation funding. In 1978 the National Cancer Institute awarded grants to 3 hospices, and shortly thereafter Congress mandated the Health Care Financing Administration to initiate a demonstration project to examine the costs, benefits, and feasibility of having Medicare pay for hospice care. (Mor, Greer, & Kastenbaum, 1988; Mor & Masterson-Allen, 1987). Around the same time, the W. K. Kellogg Foundation awarded a grant to the Joint Commission on the Accreditation of Hospitals in 1981 to develop standards that were ultimately transformed into legislation creating a Medicare-funded hospice benefit.

Creating a new covered service under Medicare was a coup for advocates given the cost-cutting orientation of the Reagan administration. However since a Congressional Budget Office study asserted that hospices would reduce costs relative to conventional care, it was introduced as part of cost-saving legislation (Mor & Masterson-Allen, 1987).

The legislation, subsequent regulations, and the reimbursement scheme reinforced the home-based nature of the program. Provisions included requiring a physician-certified survival prognosis of 6 months or less, a cap on the average annual reimbursement per patient, limitation of coverage beyond 210 days, a stipulation that reimbursement for inpatient care be limited to an aggregate of 20% of all hospice patient days, and that the hospice maintain financial and clinical control over all care provided to the patient, regardless of setting. Although there have been some modifications of these provisions, including an increase in their per diem reimbursement rate to hospices, the most important one has been the elimination of the 210-day coverage limit.

The hospice is one of the few innovative health care services introduced in the United States that was extensively evaluated. The largest such study was the *National Hospice Study*, an evaluation of the impact of the hospice demonstration program introduced by the Health Care Financing Administration. Another study, funded by the Veterans Administration, evaluated the impact of an inpatient hospice program in a single Veterans Administration hospital by using a randomized trial approach (Kane, Wales, Bernstein, Leibowitz, & Kaplan, 1984). Other studies, relying on available data, examined special issues such as cost differences experienced by hospice and nonhospice patients.

The National Hospice Study found that hospice patients used less hospital care and less costly and intensive diagnostic and therapeutic services in the last weeks of life than did comparable conventional care patients (Mor, Greer, & Kastenbaum, 1988). By and large, there were few differences in the quality-of-life or symptom-control domains of measurement between hospice and nonhospice patients, a National Hospice Study finding that was supported by the randomized study conducted by Kane and his colleagues in the Veteran's Administration health care system (1984).

Cost savings attributable to hospice were found to occur primarily in the last months of life and were very sensitive to patients' average time under hospice care. In the home care hospice model, savings from avoided inpatient costs were sufficient to offset higher costs incurred by long-staying patients. Patients served in hospital-based hospices incur home-care costs in addition to already high levels of inpatient use; however, since they consume relatively low levels of intensive therapy services while in a hospital, they had lower per diem hospitalization costs relative to conventional care, yielding costs that were relatively comparable to those incurred by conventional-care patients in the last year of life (Mor & Kidder, 1985).

The results of the National Hospice Study, as well as the VA randomized study, suggested that good hospice programs had outcomes comparable to good conventional-care treatment, and thus the individual and his or her family should be able to choose the style of care they preferred. Because the home-care style of hospice relies extensively on the support of family members, providing daily, round-the-clock care of individuals at home, the total societal costs might even be higher for the home-care approach; however, it is clear that this style of care is preferred by a reasonable number of people with terminal disease.

Even before the passage of the hospice legislation in 1982, there were a growing number of agencies claiming to provide hospice care. The U.S. General Accounting Office identified 59 operational hospices in 1978; by 1981 the Joint Commission on the Accreditation of Hospitals received 650 responses to a national survey of hospices, and in 1982 the NHO had 464 provider program members. After a slow start following the creation of the Medicare Hospice benefit, growth in the number of certified hospices increased as well. According to the 1993 National Home and Hospice Care Survey, 70.6% of the 1,000 participating *hospices were Medicare*-certified. In 1996 349,229 Medicare beneficiaries were enrolled in hospice care; in certain areas upwards of 25% of all cancer decedents were served by hospice. Based upon a series of recently completed analyses of Medicare claims data covering hospice stays throughout 1996, 37% have a noncancer diagnosis, over 80% of patients are served for less than the first benefits period of 90 days, and only 8.8% exceed 2 benefit periods or greater than 180 days (Gage & Dao, 2000).

An emerging phenomenon is the expanding role of hospice care delivered to residents of nursing homes. Petrisek and Mor (1999) found that in the mid-1990s over 30% of all nursing homes in the United States had at least 1 resident receiving hospice services on any given day, constituting about 6% of all nursing home residents. By matching data on nursing home residents with Medicare hospice data, Miller and colleagues estimated that between 25% and 35% of all *Medicare hospice* beneficiaries in 1996 were cared for in nursing homes, a considerable increase over the estimated 8.4% of hospice admissions preceded by stays in nursing homes that was observed in 1990. By 2000, Miller and Mor (2004) estimate that 76% of nursing homes have contracts with hospices to provide services to their dying residents, and an estimated 18% of nursing home residents received hospice services before dying.

The U.S. hospice movement has moved in a different direction from that in Canada, the United Kingdom, and the rest of Europe. The U.S. hospice movement has focused on *home care*, dehospitalization, and a shift in the care-taking responsibility from the institution to the family. Furthermore, most would agree that since the advent of Medicare/Medicaid coverage, hospice care, which began as a social movement, has evolved into yet another specialty care provider of third-party reimbursable health care services. Although the "hospice industry" is still dominated by not-for-profit providers, increasingly there are inroads made by the proprietary home care sector. How for-profit medicine mixes with the voluntary tradition of hospice remains to be seen.

SUSAN ALLEN
Updated by VINCENT MOR

See also
End-of-Life Care
Palliative Care

References

Dunphy, J. E., (1976). Annual discourse. On caring for the patient with cancer. *New England Journal of Medicine, 295*(6), 313–319.

Gage, B., & Dao, T. (2000). Medicare's hospice benefit: Use and expenditures. Division of Disability, Aging and Long-Term Care, Office of the Assistant Secretary for Planning and Evaluation, U.S. Department of Health and Human Services. Washington, DC.

Kane, R. L., Wales, J., Bernsteinz, L., Leibowitz, A., & Kaplan, S. (1984). A randomized controlled trial of hospice care. *Lancet, 1*(8382), 890–894.

Kastenbaum, R. (1975). Toward standards of care for the terminally ill: Part 1. What standards exist today? *Omega, 6,* 289–290.

Kubler-Ross, E. (1969). *On death and dying*. New York: Macmillan.

Miller, S. C., & Mor, V. (2004). The opportunity for collaborative care provision: The presence of nursing home/hospice collaborations in the U.S. *Journal of Pain Symptom Management, 28,* 537–547.

Mor, V., Greer, D. S., & Kastenbaum, R. (Eds.). (1988). *The hospice experiment*. Baltimore: Johns Hopkins University Press.

Mor, V., & Kidder, D. (1985). Cost savings in hospice: Final results of the National Hospice Study. *Health Services Research, 20*(4), 407–421.

Mor, V., & Masterson-Allen, S. (1987). *Hospice care systems: Structure, process, costs, and outcome*. New York: Springer.

Petrisek, A., & Mor, V. (1999). Hospice in nursing homes: A facility-level analysis of the distribution of hospice beneficiaries. *Gerontologist, 39*(3), 279–290.

HOSTILITY

Although some authors differ in their use of terminology, *hostility* as defined here includes a complex of cognitive, affective, and behavioral tendencies that foster interpersonal *antagonism*. The cognitive component includes cynical beliefs and mistrust of others. *Anger* is the most frequently discussed example of the affective component, but more subtle emotions such as *contempt* and disgust may be equally important. Overt *aggression* is the most obvious behavioral manifestation of hostility, but this can also be expressed more indirectly. For example, one can respond to a question in a friendly or aggressive manner depending on the vocal stylistics used. The 3 components of hostility are clearly interrelated. *Mistrust* of others fosters attributions of hostile intent, which leads to anger and sometimes to behavioral expressions of antagonism.

Much of the importance of the study of hostility stems from the demonstrations that high levels are associated with adverse health outcomes, including coronary heart disease, early mortality, and poor health habits. However, hostility has remained a significant predictor of mortality and coronary events after controlling for health habits.

Measures of hostility have taken many forms, most dealing with the individual components of the construct. The most widely used measure in health psychology is the *Cook-Medley scale*, which was originally devised to identify teachers who had conflicts with students but has been shown to be an effective predictor of a variety of health outcomes. It reflects all components of hostility, but emphasizes cynicism and mistrust. Measures that rely on observations of behavior during structured interview situations have also been informative. They have been related to coronary artery disease severity in cross-sectional studies of both patient and asymptomatic samples and have been shown to predict coronary events in community samples. Their special value may be due to tendencies for hostile people to be unaware of their behavior or unwilling to admit their feelings on self-report questionnaires. Observations of trained observers may overcome these biases.

These associations have been demonstrated in several societies, but there are differences in average hostility scores across cultures and subcultures. In particular, hostility scores are highly correlated with indicators of socioeconomic position, with more hostility reported by those with lower socioeconomic status. This is especially true in minority groups. Indicators of trust in others are important components of social capital, a construct thought to contribute to the collective health of communities.

Age trends in both cross-sectional and prospective studies have shown high hostility levels in adolescence and young adulthood that decrease by middle age. Both baseline hostility in adolescence and changes from baseline to midlife have been found to predict health behaviors such as smoking, drinking patterns, and body mass. Some aspects, particularly *cynicism*, appear to be higher in older age groups than in those who are middle-aged. Despite these trends in mean levels, the test-retest correlations in adults indicate remarkable stability in hostility scores across periods of up to 10 years.

There are some suggestions that the adverse *health effects of high hostility* are more apparent in younger adults. Effect sizes tend to be larger in studies of younger adults and the association of hostility with the mortality of cardiac patients appears to be stronger in those less than 60 years old. This may be a matter of selective survival, with the effects of hostility most visible in those who are the most vulnerable. In keeping with this hypothesis, interview-based hostility measures have been found to be most predictive of future events in those who have prior signs of coronary disease.

JOHN C. BAREFOOT

See also
Personality

References

Barefoot, J. C., Beckham, J. C., Haney, T. L., Siegler, I. C., & Lipkus, I. M. (1993). Age differences in hostility among middle-aged and older adults. *Psychology and Aging, 8*, 3–9.

Kawachi, I., & Berkman, L. (2000). Social cohesion, social capital, and health. In L. Berkman, & I. Kawachi (Eds.), *Social epidemiology* (pp. 174–190). Oxford: Oxford University Press.

Matthews, K. A., Gump, B. B., Harris, K. F., Haney, T. L., & Barefoot, J. C. (2004). Hostile behaviors predict cardiovascular mortality among men enrolled in the Multiple Risk Factor Intervention Trial. *Circulation, 109,* 66–70.

Siegler, I. C., Costa, P. T., Brummett, B. H., Helms, M. J., Barefoot, J. C., Williams, R. B., Dahlstrom, W. G., Kaplan, B. H., Vitaliano, P. P., Nichaman, M. Z., Day, R. S., & Rimer, B. K. (2003). Patterns of change in hostility from college to midlife in the UNC Alumni Heart Study predict high-risk status. *Psychosomatic Medicine, 65,* 738–745.

Siegman, A. W., & Smith, T. W. (Eds.). (1994). *Anger, hostility, and the heart.* Hillsdale, NJ: Lawrence Erlbaum Associates.

Smith, T. W., & Ruiz, J. M. (2002). Psychosocial influence on the development and course of coronary heart disease: Current status and implications for research and practice. *Journal of Consulting and Clinical Psychology, 70,* 548–568.

HOUSING

"Housing" describes the physical structures and services, governmental and economic influences, and the symbolic characteristics associated with where one lives. Minimally, housing is the setting in which persons sleep and prepare meals. Housing is an important consideration within aging, since much of the literature suggests that older adults in many countries spend the majority of their time where they are housed (Gitlin, 2003; Golant, 2003). We distinguish "housing" from "*living arrangements*" and "*home*." "Living arrangements" describe household composition, that is, with whom one lives, such as with a spouse, alone, with a family member, or in a non-family home (Mutchler & Burr, 2003). A large percentage of older adults in many developed countries prefer to live independently, although what comprises "*independent living*" may differ (Kim, Kim, & Kim, 2003; Rowles, Oswald, & Hunter, 2004; Van Den Heuvel, 1997; Wahl & Lang, 2004). "Home" describes "a phenomenon composed of essential meanings and experiences that may be unrelated to a particular physical setting" (Gitlin, 2003). Nevertheless, the creation of a home or the maintenance of a long-occupied home are of fundamental interest to the aged, as is the process of "breaking up" a long-occupied home and moving to smaller quarters, often consequent to a major life event such as widowhood or a significant medical episode. Home is a subjective notion that may indicate such conditions as comfort, support, protection, intimacy, privacy, and authority. Housing and the notion of home do not necessitate one another. One can live in a place that he or she does not consider to be a home.

Symbolic Characteristics

Nevertheless, housing may gain a symbolic and meaning-laden significance. Symbolic characteristics include place attachment, autonomy, and independence (Evans, Kantrowitz, & Eshelman, 2002; Foley, 1980; Gitlin, 2003; Newman, 2003; Rubinstein, 1989). Many of the symbolic characteristics fall under the purview of personal environments, which also include satisfaction and pride and can be considered a symbol of personhood.

In the United States, the majority (more than 80%) of adults aged 65 and older live independently in apartments or in single-family homes (Gitlin, 2003; Mutchler & Burr, 2003; Rowles, et al., 2004). In Germany, about 93% of those aged 65 and older live in a noninstitutional community setting. In Japan, elders tend to live with a son's family. In many village societies, elders may share a household or live close by, in an adjacent house or compound. Recent trends in Western countries show increasing percentages of older residents living alone, many of whom are women (Rowles et al., 2004).

Housing Types and Related Services

To present an overview of housing structures from a global perspective, we use 3 loosely based categories: *independent housing* within the general community, *age-segregated housing*, and housing based on need for medical care. These are not meant to be discrete categories but rather a way to conceptually group and consider the wide range of housing. In addition to overall housing type, it is important to consider the structural, spatial, and temporal dimensions of housing. The temporal aspect of housing describes housing needs at a particular time, with the understanding that needs undergo frequent reevaluation due to changes, such as an individual's or spouse's health, neighborhood safety, income, family needs, and others (Golant, 2003).

Independent Housing within the General Community

Our first category describes housing types not specifically designed for older residents but where they may reside. These include the person's own home, the home of a relative, and *naturally occurring retirement communities* (NORCs) (Newman, 2003; Pine & Pine, 2002). In the United States, the predominant form of housing for the aged is the independent, free-standing house or apartment with no special amenities, or amenities added by local service programs that help maintain the person at home. Important characteristics of such residences include familiarity, a "home-like" feeling, autonomy, and the ability to make one's own decisions. Residence with a relative, while important in many instances, is much less frequent than residence in an independent home. However, *African American* elders are more likely to reside within complex households composed of *kin* and non-kin residents than live alone or in institutions (Mutchler & Burr, 2003). Further, NORCs are residential housing complexes such as apartments where residents have gradually aged (Pine & Pine, 2002) as opposed to planned age-segregated communities. As the building or community ages, services must be added to allow persons to continue in their own homes.

Abroad, the trend in Sweden has been for older adults in the community to receive health services within their homes from government health programs (Malmberg, Ernsth, larsson, & Zarit, 2003). Data from a recent national survey comprising 4,000 adults aged 70 to 85 years in Germany revealed an average of 31.6 years lived in the same apartment and 50.3 years lived in the same town (Rowles et al., 2004).

While the thought of living independently in the community is attractive, it is important to note some of the down sides and difficulties if one's abilities begin to diminish. Rubinstein and colleagues (1992) point to financial strain of home upkeep, environmental barriers within the home such as stairs, changes in neighborhoods, and vulnerability to crime as additional difficulties to living independently within the community.

Age-Segregated Housing

Age-segregated housing describes housing built specifically for older adults living independently. This includes *government-subsidized congregate housing*, such as *Section 202 Supportive Housing* for the Elderly programs provided through the U.S. Department of Housing and Urban Development (HUD) and private-pay congregate housing such as retirement villages, independent living apartments in continuing care in retirement communities, veterans retirement communities, and others (Konchera, 2001; Parmelee & Lawton, 1990; Sheehan & Oakes, 2003). Recent changes in laws governing federally sponsored housing for the aged have made this setting available to other special needs populations, thus increasing the age range of residents. Increasingly, age-segregated housing is privately constructed by for-profit businesses in the form of senior (age 55 and older) retirement communities oriented toward leisure and assisted living, an increasingly significant sector of housing for the elderly (see below).

Early studies showed that elderly persons preferred age-segregation in special housing to age-integration. Regardless of whether this is still the case, age-segregated housing provides many amenities that come either as part of a residential "package" or as independently obtainable through purchase. There are many advantages to age-segregated housing that include the benefits of age-peer relations and the residue of similar life-course experiences. However, many such residents would see the absence of co-residential younger people as a disadvantage.

Housing Based on Need for Medical Care

Housing based on need for medical care describes institutional housing such as *nursing homes* and medically oriented independent living. In the United States, nursing homes are defined as: "A residence that provides a room, meals, and help with activities of daily living and recreation. Generally, nursing home residents have physical or mental problems that keep them from living on their own. They usually require daily assistance" (CMS, 2004). Increasingly, there may be difficulties in making distinctions between heavily serviced types of assisted living and nursing homes.

Although *assisted living* is often described as the fastest-growing type of senior housing (Hawes, Phillips, Rose, Holan, & Sherman, 2003), definitions differ. The Centers for Medicare and Medicaid Services (CMS) defines assisted living as: "A type of living arrangement in which personal care services such as meals, housekeeping, transportation, and assistance with activities of daily living are available as needed to people who still live on their own in a residential facility. In most cases, the 'assisted living' residents pay a regular monthly rent. Then, they typically pay additional fees for the services they get." In short, assisted living provides less care than a skilled nursing facility, has various levels of regulations depending on the state, is predominantly privately paid, and is generally considered unaffordable for those with moderate or lower incomes (Hawes, Phillips, Rose, Holan, & Sherman, 2003). In addition, assisted living claims to provide the symbolic goods of "independence, choice, risk, and privacy" (Carder & Hernandez, 2003).

ROBERT L. RUBINSTEIN
KATE DEMEDEIROS

See also
Home Modifications

References

Binstock, R. H., & Cluff, L. E. (2000). Home care advances. New York: Sage.

Carder, P. C., & Hernandez, M. (2004). Consumer discourse in assisted living. *Journal of Gerontology Social Sciences*, *59B*(2), S58–S67.

Center for Medicare and Medicaid Services. (2004). Available: http://www.cms.hhs.gov/glossary.

Evans, G. W., Kantrowitz, E., & Eshelman, P. (2002). Housing quality and psychological well-being among the elderly population. *Journal of Gerontology Psychological Sciences*, *557B*(4), P381–P383.

Foley, D. L. (1980). The sociology of housing. *Annual Review of Sociology*, *6*, 457–478.

Gitlin, L. N. (2003). Conducting research on home environments: Lessons learned and new directions. The Gerontologist. *43*(5): 628–637.

Golant, S. M. (2003). Conceptualizing time and behavior in environmental gerontology: A pair of old issues deserving new thought. *Gerontologist*, *43*(5): 638–648.

Hawes, C., Phillips, C. D., Rose, M., Holan, S., & Sherman, M. (2003). A national survey of assisted living facilities. *Gerontologist*, *43*(6), 875–882.

Kim, S., Kim, H., & Kim, W. G. (2003). Impacts of senior citizens' lifestyle of their choices of elderly housing. *Journal of Consumer Marketing*, *20*(3), 210–226.

Konchera, A. (2001). Section 202 supportive housing for the elderly. AARP. Available: http://research.aarp.org/il/f265r_housing.html.

Malmberg, B., Ernsth, M., Larsson, B., & Zarit, S. (2003). Angels of the night: Evening and night patrols for homebound elders in Sweden. *Gerontologist*, *43*(5), 761–765.

Mutchler, J. E., & Burr, J. A. (2003). Living arrangements among older persons: A multilevel analysis of housing market effects. *Research on Aging*, *25*(6), 531–558.

Newman, S. (2003). The living conditions of elderly Americans. *Gerontologist*, *43*(1), 99–109.

Parmelee, P. A., & Lawton, M. P. (1990). The design of special environments for the aged. In J. E. Birren, & K. Warner Schaie (Eds.), *Handbook of the psychology of aging* (3rd ed., pp. 464–488). San Diego: Academic Press.

Pine, P. P., & Pine, V. R. (2002). Naturally occurring retirement community-supportive service program: An example of devolution. *Journal of Aging and Social Policy*, *14*(3/4), 181–193.

Rowles, G. D., Oswald, F., & Hunter, E. G. (2004). Interior living environments in old age. In Wahl, H., Scheidt, R. J., & Windley, P. G. (Eds.), *Annual review of gerontology and geriatrics* (vol. 23, p. 167). New York: Springer Publishing.

Rubinstein, R. L. (1989). The home environments of older people: A description of the psychosocial processes linking person to place. *Journal of Gerontology: Social Sciences*, *44*(2), S45–S53.

Rubinstein, R. L., Kilbride, J. C., & Nagy, S. (1992). Elders living alone: Frailty and the perception of choice. New York: Aldine de Gruyter.

Sheehan, N. W., & Oakes, C. E. (2003). Bringing assisted living services into congregate housing: Residents perspectives. *Gerontologist*, *43*(5): 766–770.

Van Den Heuvel, W. (1997). Policy towards the elderly: Twenty-five years of Dutch experience. *Journal of Aging Studies*, *11*(3): 251–259.

Wahl, H., & Lang, F. R. (2004). Aging in context across the adult life course: Integrating physical and social environmental research perspectives. In Wahl, H., Scheidt, R. J., & Windley, P. G. (Eds.), *Annual review of gerontology and geriatrics* (vol. 23, pp. 1–33). New York: Springer Publishing.

HUMAN FACTORS ENGINEERING

By the year 2030, about 66 million people in the United States will be older than age 65, with many of these people belonging to the over-85 group. Not only are people living longer but they are also remaining more active, productive, and independent into older age. These changes in demographics present challenges and opportunities for society. Generally, increased age is associated with changes in perception, cognition, and movement that can make it difficult for some older people to perform everyday tasks such as driving, using technology, or remembering to take medications. Furthermore, older people are more likely to suffer from some type of chronic disease such as arthritis, high blood pressure, or dementia. Older people with chronic conditions often require assistance with basic activities such as preparing meals, bathing, or finding their way. Aging is also associated with positive changes such as increased *wisdom*, knowledge, and experience, and thus older people represent an extremely valuable resource to the community, workplace, and the family. There are numerous examples, such as senior mentoring, of how older adults continue to make productive contributions to society. In fact, many industries are now turning to older people to fill employment gaps.

The challenge confronting researchers, designers, and policy makers is to develop strategies to maximize the ability of older people to reach their potential and remain healthy and productive. In addition, strategies are needed to help older people who are frail or disabled receive needed care and support. Human factors engineering, the multidisciplinary science that focuses on user-centered design, can make valuable contributions toward accommodating an aging population. The concepts and methods of human factors engineering offer a natural framework to study problems encountered by older adults in the use of technology. The emphasis in human factors is on designing products, tasks, and environments to "fit" user populations. Furthermore, it encompasses both research and application for a wide range of topics such as work design, equipment/product design, environmental design, and training. Therefore, human factors offers a broad range of knowledge to apply to problems of aging, design, and everyday task performance. Relevant applications of human factors include: *housing design*, transportation, *product design*, and work. The intent of this text is to demonstrate how human factors engineering can enhance the daily lives of older adults. An overview of the field will be presented, followed by examples of human factors solutions to problems encountered by older people.

Definition

Human factors engineering is the study of human beings and their interactions with products, environments, and equipment in the performance of tasks and activities. The field of human factors is interdisciplinary encompassing the disciplines of engineering, psychology, computer science, physiology, and biomechanics. The focus of *human factors research* is the study of human capabilities, limitations, and characteristics in relation to real-world activities and systems. The overall objective of human factors is to improve the "fit" between people and the designed environment so that performance, safety, comfort, and user satisfaction are maximized. To achieve these goals human factors engineers use a *systems approach to design*. Using this approach the capabilities and limitations of the user are evaluated relative to the demands generated by products and tasks. An example of this approach would be evaluating the skill requirements necessary to operate a blood glucose monitor relative to the cognitive abilities and experience of the intended user population.

The focus on *user-centered design* makes human factors engineering a natural discipline to address the issues of older adults and help them retain and enjoy independence into their later years. Using the techniques and methods of human factors we can understand the impact of age-related changes in abilities on the performance of everyday tasks and activities, identify areas where problems and difficulties arise, and discover solutions to address them (Fisk, 1999). These solutions might include: redesign of equipment or environments, interface design solutions, training solutions, or suggestions for the development of new products or technologies.

The challenge for the human factors community is to identify the needs and specific types of problems encountered by older adults in everyday tasks and environments, so that appropriate solutions can be identified. For example, older people may require more light and larger font sizes to enhance their ability to read text such as medication labels or signage. Similarly due to changes in cognition older adults may need more time to learn something new or may benefit from some type of memory aid. The following sections will provide examples of how human factors engineering can be used to improve the lives of older people. Areas addressed include: mobility/transportation, living environments, work environments, and use of everyday technologies.

Mobility and *Transportation*

It is fairly well known that many older people, because of difficulty walking, using stairs, driving, or using public transportation, have difficulty getting from place to place. Problems with mobility often make it difficult for older people to get to stores, banks, and physicians' offices, participate in community activities, or maintain contact with family and friends. These problems are exacerbated for older adults who live in suburban or rural communities where public transportation is often minimal or nonexistent and driving is the only option. It is well known that *driving* is problematic for many older adults. In fact, this is a topic of great interest to policy makers, researchers, and the elderly themselves.

In this regard, issues related to the safety and mobility of older drivers have received considerable attention within the human factors community. This research has been directed toward understanding the difficulties experienced by older drivers and the reasons for these difficulties, as well as identifying potential design solutions. Several researchers have found that problems with driving are related to deficits in vision and aspects of cognition (Ball & Owsley, 1991). It is also known that certain tasks such as *left-hand turns* (U.S. Department of Transportation, 1994) or certain environments such as driving in construction zones are difficult for older people. Many older people also report difficulty adjusting to changes in automobile design (Rogers, Meyer, Walker, & Fisk, 1998).

Proven areas of effective intervention include redesign of *roadway signs* and warnings, modifications in the *design of the automobile*, and training. It has been shown, for example, that providing older people with training on abilities important to driving, such as visual attention, offers the potential of improving driving performance. Strategies such as increasing the contrast of roadway signs so that they are easier to read (Lambert & Fleury, 1994) or providing drivers with additional signs about upcoming traffic or roadway demands (Staplin & Fisk, 1991) can help also enhance the safety of *older drivers*.

Other important areas of human factors intervention include identifying solutions, such as modifications in *public transportation* systems to make them more easily available, so that the need for driving is reduced. Older people commonly report problems using *buses* or *subways* due to inefficient design. Common problems include: difficulty getting on and off, crowding, lack of security, and lack of availability of transportation systems (Rogers, Meyer, Walker, & Fisk 1998). Other problems relate to understanding schedules and maps. Many of these problems are amenable to human factors solutions.

Living Environments

Another area where human factors engineers can make important contributions is the *design of living environments*. Contrary to popular belief, most older people live in the community alone or with a relative. Many older people also spend a great deal of time at home (Lawton, 1990). However, living at *home* is often challenging for older adults, and they find it difficult to perform tasks such as bathing, cooking, and cleaning. The rate of home *accidents* is also high among older people (Czaja, 1990). Problems with home activities and home safety are often linked to inappropriate housing design.

Falls among the elderly are common and represent a frequent cause of *accidental injury* and death. Furthermore, many older people restrict their activities because of *fear of falling*. Reasons for falls among older persons include losses in vision, balance, reaction time, and changes in *gait*. Common locations/sources of falls include: stairs and steps, bathtubs and showers, ladders and stools, and tripping or slipping on throw rugs, runners, or carpets (Czaja, 1990). Understanding the reasons for these falls will help uncover design solutions. Many falls on stairways occur because older people, due to declines in vision, fail to perceive the first or last step. This problem might be addressed by installation of more lighting in stairways and highlighting through the use of color the beginning and ending of steps. *Handrails* will also help remedy the problem. A more radical solution is to design housing without stairs or in a way that minimizes the need for people to go up and down stairs. Strength and *balance training* has also been shown to reduce the risk of falls among older individuals and reduce the consequences if a fall should occur. In all of these examples, the goal is to help ensure a match between the capabilities of the older person and the demands of the task and the environment.

Work Environments

Recent demographic trends underscore the importance of designing *work environments* and work tasks to accommodate both younger and older workers. Because of a number of factors, such as the aging of the *baby boomers* and changes in retirement policies and benefits, the number of older workers will increase substantially over the next 2 decades. Clearly most businesses and industries now need to develop strategies to accommodate an aging workforce. To making work environments "age friendly" requires understanding: (1) the characteristics of *older workers*, (2) the potential implications of aging for work, and (3) the demands and skill requirements of current jobs.

Common myths about older people are that they are less productive, less reliable, less able, less interested in work, and less willing than younger people to learn new skills. The facts are that older adults are healthier, more diverse, and better educated than previous generations. They are also more interested in remaining engaged in some form of productive work. With respect to productivity, there is little support for the assertion that older people are less productive than younger people. With respect to other measures of job behavior, the findings, while limited, are more conclusive. Regarding accidents, older workers tend to have lower accident rates than younger workers; however, older workers tend to remain off the job longer if they are injured. Absenteeism and turnover rates also appear to be lower for older adults. Older workers are also willing and able to learn new tasks and skills.

Although there is a great deal of information about aging as a process, there is limited data on the practical implications of aging for work activities. There are a number of changes in abilities associated with normal aging that have implications for work. For example, the application of general *ergonomic principles* to the *design of workplaces* and jobs is particularly important for older people. Training programs and instructional materials are designed to accommodate age-related changes in perceptual and cognitive abilities. Overall, it is important to identify specific components of jobs that are challenging or limiting for older adults and to target areas where workplace interventions could best be used to enhance the ability of older people to meet job requirements. These interventions might include changes in job design, workplace and equipment redesign, or the development of new and innovative training strategies. Human factors engineers can play a critical role in making work environments "age friendly" and helping to ensure that older adults remain productive.

Technology and *Information Systems*

Currently, all forms of technology, including computers, communication, safety, and health monitoring devices, are being used to perform routine tasks and activities. Use of technology has become an integral component of work, education, communication, and entertainment. Technology also is being increasingly used within the health care arena for service delivery, in-home monitoring, interactive communication (e.g., between patient and physician), transfer of health information, and peer support. Use of automatic teller machines, interactive telephone-based menu systems, cellular telephones, and VCRs/DVDs is also quite common. Furthermore, telephones, television, home security systems, and other communication devices are becoming more integrated with computer network resources, providing faster and more powerful interactive services. To function independently and successfully interact with the environment, people of all ages need to interact with some form of technology.

Despite popular stereotypes older adults are interested and willing to use new technologies, and use of *technology among older people* is increasing. However, data also indicates that because of a lack of familiarity with technology, lack of training, and systems that are difficult to use, technology is often a source of frustration for many older adults, and the potential benefits of technology for this population are not realized. Not being able to use technology puts older adults at a disadvantage in terms of their ability to live and function independently and successfully negotiate the built environment. Furthermore, the full benefits of technology may not be realized by older populations. Technology holds great potential for improving the quality of life for older people. However, unless we have an understanding of why older adults have difficulty adapting to new technologies, and they are perceived as active users of technology by system designers, successful use of technology will continue to be a challenge for future generations of older people. This is another area where human factors engineers can and do make significant contributions.

Conclusion

Human factors engineering can be used to help design tasks, products, equipment, and environments to help accommodate an aging population. Research in this area has demonstrated the importance of attending to the needs of older people in system design and also that training and design solutions can be beneficial for older people. The basic premise of human factors is that successful performance results from user-centered design and a fundamental understanding of user capabilities, needs, and preferences. Improving the health and quality of life of older people requires that knowledge of aging be applied to the design of products and environments.

SARA J. CZAJA
CHIN CHIN LEE

See also
Industrial Gerontology

References

Ball, K., & Owsley, C. (1991). Identifying correlates of accident involvement for the older driver. *Human Factors, 33*, 583–595.

Czaja, S. J. (1990). *Human factors research for an aging population*. Washington, DC: National Research Council, National Academy of Science Press.

Fisk, A. D. (1999). Human factors and the older adult. *Magazine of Human Factors Applications, 7*, 8–13.

Fisk, A. D., Rogers, W. A., Charness, N., Czaja, S. J., & Sharit, J. (2004). Designing for older adults: Principles and creative human factors approach. Boca Raton, FL: CRC Press.

Lambert, L. D., & Fleury, M. (1994). Age, cognitive style, and traffic signs. *Perceptual and Motor Skills, 78*, 611–624.

Lawton, P. (1990). Aging and the performance of home tasks. *Human Factors, 32*, 527–536.

Rogers, W. A., Meyer, B., Walker, N., & Fisk, A. D. (1998). Functional limitations to daily living tasks in the aged: A focus group analysis. *Human Factors, 40*, 111–125.

Staplin, L., Fisk, A. D., (1998). A cognitive engineering approach to improve signalized left-turn intersections. *Human Factors, 33*, 559–571.

U.S. Department of Transportation. (1994). *Traffic safety facts*. Washington, DC: National Center for Statistics and Analysis.

HUMAN IMMUNODEFICIENCY VIRUS

See
AIDS/HIV

HUMANITIES AND ARTS

Cognitive psychologist *Jerome Bruner* (1986) asserts that there are 2 modes of thought by which we make sense of our world: *paradigmatic* and narrative. The former predominates in the natural sciences and leads to good theory, tight analysis, logical proof, and empirical discovery governed by reasoned hypothesis. The latter is the principal mode of the arts and humanities and, argues Bruner, of the way we experience life itself. *Narrative thought* deals with the multiple dimensions of reality, the uncertainties of human intention, and contributes to good stories, gripping drama, and believable historical accounts. How does Bruner's distinction apply to the humanities and arts as they add to our understanding of aging and later life?

As both a qualitative method for capturing research data in the form of stories and an expressive/descriptive method for conveying the lived experience of aging and later life, narrative renders life experiences, as *John Dewey* put it, "more luminous," and our dealing with them "more useful." Narrative makes its primary home in the humanities, the humanistic social sciences, and in the arts, including its history, criticism, production, and performance. Scientific gerontology is heavily influenced by clinical goals in pursuing knowledge leading to instrumental control over the adverse aspect of aging. In contrast, the humanities and arts help us appreciate the meaning and value of aging and later life while questioning the conditions under which a longer life can also be a qualitatively enhanced one.

The appearance of the *Handbook of the Humanities and Aging* (Cole, Van Tassel, & Kastenbaum, 1992), as well as its second edition (Cole, Kastenbaum, & Ray, 1999), bears out Bruner's distinction. These handbooks constitute a historic landmark confirming the rich and varied contributions to gerontology from scholars engaging in *humanistic interpretations of aging*, those exploring aging through *artistic expression*, and those developing programs to actively involve older adults in furthering personal growth, social awareness, and possibilities for meaning and belonging in the later years. The second edition adds emphasis on interdisciplinary approaches to aging, recognizing that the fast pace of social change around the conditions and perceptions of later life necessitate "crossing academic borders" to achieve a more comprehensive view of later life.

The 3 major U.S. gerontological handbooks—of biology, psychology, and the social science—have already gone through multiple editions.

How, then, should we assess the role played by the relative latecomers, the humanities and arts, in relation to scientific and human service contributions to aging, as achievements in their own right, and with regard to their capacity to enrich the lives of older adults and members of other generations?

The following discussion will answer these questions by examining: (1) the complementary, sometimes critical, role of the humanities and arts in relation to the growth of other professional discourses in gerontology; (2) applications of humanistic *and* artistic ways of knowing to practice (e.g., older adult education and participation in the arts); (3) connection to the spiritual dimensions of aging and to intergenerational relationships; and (4) prospects for the future.

Humanistic Scholarship

The humanities include the disciplines of language and literature, history, philosophy, religious studies, jurisprudence, and those aspects of the social sciences that emphasize describing, interpreting, explaining, and appreciating the contexts in which, and relationships through which, human beings fashion a world and try to understand it. *Humanistic disciplines* have subject matters and methods uniquely suited to deepening our knowledge of aging and later life. To the scientist's penchant for causal explanations (e.g., genetic, neurological, and cellular) and verifiable experiments, the humanities add a search for the meaning of aging and later life, values attributed to the experience of growing older, and the shaping influence on later life of historic events, cultural change, ethnic identity, gender, spiritual orientation, and artistic embodiment.

Whereas scientific gerontology and the human services have tended to focus on aging as a set of problems resulting from physical and mental decline and concomitant dependencies (the "failure model of aging"), the orientations of the humanities and arts has been to stress the strengths of aging (attainment of mature insight, practical wisdom, humility, and other virtues) or, at least, to challenge rigidly uniform views whether negative or positive.

An important analytic type of humanistic inquiry into aging, "*critical gerontology*," has built on the European philosophical schools of existentialism, phenomenology, hermeneutics, and critical theory to formulate assessments of research findings and policy developments that presume factual, empirical foundations but that, on closer analysis, reveal biases interwoven with social science methodologies or presuppositions based on the narrow view that aging is an irreversible and uniform process of cumulative decline (Cole, Achenbaum, Jakobi, & Kastenbaum, 1993).

Humanities scholars have also examined topics such as representations of old age in literature, the late style of aging artists, the character of wisdom, perspectives on aging in different religious and cultural traditions, values inherent in scientific theories of life course development, ethical issues in health care and end-of-life decisions, and the older person's legacy to the young as reflected in personal narratives, both written and spoken. Some of this work has had direct application to practitioners and policy makers. For example, the significant work on reconceptualizing the function and meaning of *reminiscence* (Kaminsky, 1984; Sherman, 1991) has led to changes, even reversals, in the way social workers and mental health specialists now regard the life review process as an important adaptive, potentially creative, process among seniors. Research on the history of the *Social Security Act* of 1935 (Graebner, 1980; Gratton, 1993) has provided policy makers with a better understanding of the multiple motives of the original legislation, and how age-based income supports influence the social construction of retirement, family relationships, and the need for older worker retraining programs. Broadly speaking, the contributions of the humanities also serve as responses to an unprecedented question made possible by a longer and healthier lifetime: Having added years to life, how do we add life to years? The humanities and arts speak to quality-of-life issues in maturity.

Humanistic scholars have helped improve the quality of later life by dispelling negative stereotypes and encouraging older adults to insist on dignified treatment and to project a more audible voice in determining their own destiny. Sometimes this takes the indirect form of interviews with courageous and innovative older people who become role models and mentors. Works of this type range from Berman and Goldman's (1992) interviews with older *artists* and other *creative* people, *The Ageless Spirit*, or from anthologies of modern and contemporary literary works that convey enduring passions, paradoxes, and points of view of older characters—for example, Sennett's *Full Measure: Modern Short Stories on Aging* (1988) and Fowler and McCutcheon's *Songs of Experience* (1991). At other times, these contributions take a more direct communicative form, as in Moody's (1988) philosophical critique of policies concerning aging and human development or Cole's (1992) critical analysis of the cultural history of aging in the United States.

Interpretation and practice of the arts play similar indirect and direct roles in helping us appreciate the nuances and textures of later life. This can take the form of examining changes in artists' self-portraits as they reflect theories of life stages. Interpretations may also differ as, for example, scholarly examination of the concept of "*late style*" has led some to postulate a set of predictable characteristics in artworks such as musical compositions and painting produced in old age—as in the "swan song" motif (Munsterberg, 1983; Simonton, 1998), whereas others have pointed to a multiplicity of counterexamples that defy stylistic classification (Kastenbaum, 1992).

That artistic works might reflect something about how the artist experiences and scrutinizes aging and later life is well documented for painting by McKee and Kauppinen (1987), for poetry by Woodward and Schwartz (1986), and for the novel by Wyatt-Brown and Rossen (1993). In addition, the expressive life of extraordinary ordinary people (i.e., nonartists) has been shown in diaries and journals (Berman, 1994). Creativity has also been linked to successful aging (Adams-Price, 1998).

Older Persons' Involvement in the Humanities and Arts

Not only are older adults the subject matter of humanities and arts discourses, they may become participants and practitioners. Recognizing that seniors would benefit from participation in humanities-focused reading and discussion groups, the National Council on the Aging (NCOA) established its *Senior Center Humanities Program* (later renamed *Discovery Through the Humanities*) in 1975 with major funding from the National Endowment for the Humanities (NEH). For 20+ years the program involved tens of thousands of both well and frail elderly in sites such as senior centers, public libraries, and nursing homes utilizing 17 different theme-based large-print anthologies accompanied by audiotapes, leader's guides, and publicity materials. The NCOA humanities program ended operations in 1999, but its resource materials were dispersed to lending centers across the United States.

The same year the NCOA program was established saw the birth of Elderhostel, a college-level educational program for people aged 60 and older that enables over 300,000 yearly to travel to campuses, conference centers, parks, and even volunteer service sites, where they participate in a wide variety of classes with heavy concentration on the humanities and arts. Again, in 1975, an in-store senior center-type program with emphasis on humanities and arts programming was launched by the May Company department store chain. The *Older Adult Services and Information System* (OASTS) institutes spread from 1 to, currently, 29 locations.

Another community-based educational program that invites seniors to engage in the study of the humanities and arts are the *Shepherd's Centers*, sponsored by some 100 coalitions of churches and synagogues, with their *Adventures in Learning* programs. Shepherd's Centers frequently draw on their members to plan and organize curricula and to teach classes. This peer-learning and peer-teaching modality represents a major trend in older adult education as seniors themselves take possession of their own learning goals, decision making, curricula, and methods of instruction.

Perhaps the fastest-growing informal network of older learner programs is known by the generic term *Institutes for Learning in Retirement* (ILRs). The first ILR-type program, the Institute for Retired Professionals, was established in 1962 at the New School for Social Research in New York. But it was not until the mid-1980s that the ILR movement accelerated with the establishment of ILR programs at colleges and universities across the country. Nationally, more than 300 programs provide substantive courses in humanities and arts topics, as well as studio work. A membership organization, the *Elderhostel Institute Network* (EIN), under the direction of *Elderhostel*, provides workshops for new ILR programs, convenes regional conferences, and distributes a newsletter among some 300 institute member organizations. Other organizations promoting networking in older adult education where humanities and arts programming flourish are the *Life Enrichment and Renewal Network* (LEARN), sponsored by the American Society on Aging; the National University Continuing Education Association (NUCEA); NCOA, with its humanities and arts board committee; and the Gerontological Society of America, with its arts and humanities committee—although the latter is primarily devoted to promoting scholarly endeavors among its members, some of whom are teachers of the humanities and arts.

Programs with a strong arts orientation range from *Liz Lerman*'s intergenerational dance troupe, *Dancers of the Third Age*, to the *Senior Neighbors* of Chattanooga's drama ensemble, the *Ripe and Ready Players*. *Senior theater*, in general, has seen rapid expansion of amateur performance groups and even a yearly conference. Political and cultural challenges to sentimental views of aging and the elderly are emerging in performance art involving older women, individuals suffering from dementia, and mixed gender senior performing groups (Basting, 1998). Some arts programs mix creative dramatics with a therapeutic orientation, such as the New York-based *Elders Share the Arts* (ESTA) organization, which works with living history theater, or design creative movement programs that are both expressive and therapeutic. A visual arts education program designed specifically for the institutionalized frail elderly, the Washington, DC-based *Museum One*, has provided art education classes while demonstrating how staff can utilize the arts to promote better communication among residents.

Well-known writers are continuing their careers into later life, often focusing on intergenerational relationships (e.g., Anne Tyler's 1998 novel, *A Patchwork Planet*), whereas other writers are emerging in the later years (e.g., Alison Lurie's 1998 novel, *The Last Resort* and poet Virginia Hamilton Adair's 1996 volume, *Ants on the Melon: A Collection of Poems*). A full discussion of these and other works can be found in Anne Wyatt-Brown's "The Future of *Literary Gerontology*," found in the second edition of the *Handbook* (Cole, Kastenbaum, & Ray, 1999).

Bringing the humanities and arts to older Americans, especially those in institutions, is the work of the New York City-based *Hospital Audiences*, Inc. (HAI), which has enabled over 7 million people to experience first-rate music, theater, and other types of performances.

For surveys of humanities and arts programming, see Mackintosh's *Humanities Programming for Older Adults* (1988) and the annotated bibliography of aging and the humanities, *Where Do We Come From? What Are We? Where Are We Going?* (Polisar, Wygant, Cole, & Perdomo, 1988). For a comprehensive review of research on older adult education, see Manheimer, Snodgrass, and Moskow-McKenzie (1995).

Spirituality and Intergenerational Aspects

Not only do the humanities and arts enrich intellectual and emotional aspects of personal development, they foster growth in spiritual experience and understanding. Contributions to a deeper understanding of how religious traditions help people find meaning and guidance in the face of finitude and frailty come from studies in comparative religion (see the chapters in the first edition of the *Handbook of the Humanities and Aging*, Part II Aging, Spirituality, and World Religion, and Robert Atchley's essay, "Spirituality," in the second edition), philosophy of religion, cultural history of religion (Cole, 1992), and comparative religion (Moody & Caroll, 1997). The role of the arts in enhancing *spiritual growth in old age* takes the form of *guided autobiography groups* (Ray, 2000), *drawing* as a mode of spiritual awareness, writing and performing plays, and scholarly inquiry, such as reflections on spiritual attainment as reflected in the late style of great artists (e.g., Rembrandt and Beethoven).

The humanities and arts have also served as portions of core curricula for dialogue between generations. Works of the humanities, such as anthologies from NCOA's humanities program, have been used in classes bringing older adults together with high school or college students. Intergenerational theater and music groups have been formed around the country. Some of the theater groups focus on relationships between young and old or similarities in the lives of old and young in contemporary society.

Prospects for the Future

Critical issues in gerontology and the trend in the United States, Europe, and parts of Asia of population aging suggest that the humanities and arts will have an increasingly important role in contributing to multifaceted understanding of aging and later life. Empirical studies of aging and the human life course cannot avoid questions about values, meanings, and portrayals of aging—the central preoccupations of the humanities' and arts. Increasingly, people want to know not only what to expect from normal aging but what ideals and possibilities are available to them (Manheimer, 1999). The spirit of possibility is captured in the term Third Age, which has come to stand for the individual period and outlook of a longer, healthier, and more active later life, as well as a collective phenomenon of societies that have the means to increase the length and quality of longevity. This situation calls for an ongoing, open-ended, interpretive process that can be communicated to a broad public. The humanities and arts, in partnership with the sciences and human services, have the potential to offer holistic views of life course development and possibilities of achieving an age-integrated society.

RONALD J. MANHEIMER

See also
Gerontology

References

Adams-Price, C. (Ed.) (1998). *Creativity and successful aging: Theoretical and empirical approaches*. New York: Springer Publishing.

Basting, A. D. (1998). *The stages of age: Performing age in contemporary American culture*. Ann Arbor: University of Michigan Press.

Berman, H. J. (1994). *Interpreting the aging self: Personal journals of later life*. New York: Springer Publishing.

Berman, P. L., & Goldman, C. (1992). *The ageless spirit*. New York: Ballantine.

Bruner, J. (1986). *Actual minds, possible worlds*. Cambridge: Harvard University Press.

Cole, T. R. (1992). The journey of life: A cultural historian's perspective. *Social Science and Medicine*, *29*, 377–383.

Cole, T. R., Achenbaum, A. W., Jakobi, P., & Kastenbaum, R. (Eds.). (1993). *Voices and visions in aging: Toward a critical gerontology*. New York: Springer Publishing.

Cole, T. R., Kastenbaum, R., & Ray, R. E. (Eds.) (1999). *Handbook of the humanities and aging* (2nd ed.). New York: Springer Publishing.

Cole, T. R., Van Tassel, D. D., & Kastenbaum, R. (Eds.). (1992). *Handbook of the humanities and aging*. New York: Springer Publishing.

Fowler, M., & McCutcheon, P. (1991). *Songs of experience*. New York: Ballantine.

Graebner, W. (1980). *A history of retirement: The meaning and function of an American institution*. New Haven, CT: Yale University Press.

Gratton, B. (1993). The creation of retirement: Families, individuals and the social security movement. In K. W. Schaie & W. A. Achenbaum (Eds.), *Societal impact on aging* (pp. 45–73). New York: Springer Publishing.

Kaminsky, M. (1984). *The uses of reminiscence*. New York: Haworth Press.

Kastenbaum, R. (1992). *The psychology of death*. New York: Springer Publishing.

Mackintosh, E. (1988). *Humanities programming for older adults*. Washington, DC: Federation of State Humanities Councils.

Manheimer, R. (1999). *A map to the end of time: Wayfarings with friends and philosophers*. New York: Norton.

Manheimer, R. Snodgrass, D., & Moskow-McKenzie, D. (1995). *Older adult education: A guide to research programs and policies*. Westwood, CT: Greenwood Press.

McKee, P., & Kauppinen, H. (1987). *The arts of aging: A celebration of old age in Western art*. New York: Human Sciences Press.

Moody, H. R. (1988). *Abundance of life*. New York: Columbia University Press.

Moody, H. R., & Carroll, D. (1997). *The five stages of the soul*. New York: Anchor Books.

Munsterberg, H. (1983). *The crown of life: Artistic creativity in old age*. New York: Harcourt Brace Jovanovich.

Polisar, D., Wygant, L., Cole, T., & Perdomo, C. (1988). *Where do we come from? What are we? Where are we going*? Washington, DC: Gerontological Society of America.

Ray, R. E. (2000). *Beyond nostalgia: Aging and life-story writing*. Charlottesville: University of Virginia Press.

Sennett, D. (1988). *Full measure: Modern short stories on aging*. St. Paul, MN: Graywolf Press.

Sherman, E. (1991). *Reminiscence and the self in old age*. New York: Springer Publishing.

Simonton, D. K. (1998). Age and outstanding achievement: What do we know after a century of research? *Psychological Bulletin, 104*, 251–267.

Wyatt-Brown, A. M., & Rossen, J. (Eds.) (1993). *Aging and gender literature: Studies in creativity*. Charlottesville: University Press of Virginia.

HUMOR

Humor about aging can have several functions (Freud, 1905/1960; Nahemow, McClusky-Fawcett, & McGhee, 1986). It may reduce the anxieties or fears about growing older. It may be a way of dealing with an otherwise taboo subject, such as aging and death. It can defuse touchy situations, expose pretensions, and be a form of social criticism. It may make oneself feel superior to older people who are worse off than you are. It can express hostility or solidarity. It can make fun of oneself or others. It often reveals negative attitudes about aging that people may not want to admit. Insofar as it reinforces negative stereotypes about aging, it is a common form of ageism (Palmore, in press). However, according to some, it can even enhance health (Seltzer, 1993).

Analysis of humor about aging can be used to investigate how widespread negative attitudes are toward aging, what kinds of *fears about aging* seem to be most prevalent, which aspects of aging produce more negative feelings, and how attitudes toward aged men differ from those toward aged women. The analysis of *jokes about aging* began in 1971 (Palmore, 1971); since then there have been several other analyses of jokes, as well as cartoons, greeting cards, the media, and even jokes told by older people (Nahemow, McClusky-Fawcett, & McGhee, 1986; Richman & Tallmer, 1976). Despite the diversity of content and methods, the following findings are fairly consistent.

Negative Attitudes

Most humor about aging reveals negative attitudes and *stereotypes*, such as the saying: "Old age: the time when the mind forgets, but the mirror reminds." Other humor is ambivalent, and some shows positive attitudes. An example of the rare positive joke is about the 80-year-old woman who gets a physical checkup because she notices she is losing her sexual desire. When asked by her doctor when she first noticed this, she replies, "Last night and then again this morning."

However, the humor of even "positive" jokes such as this one usually depends on contradicting some negative stereotype (such as loss of sexual desire).

Common Themes

The most common themes are longevity (or lack of it), physical ability and appearance, sexual ability (or lack of it), age concealment (most about women), retirement, and loss of memory. These themes reveal considerable anxiety about the topics of aging and death, illness and disability, sexual decline, and senility.

Gender Differences

Humor about older women tends to be more negative than humor about older men. This suggests a *double standard* in our society, whereby older women are viewed more negatively than older men. Specifically, there is much negative humor about "old maids" but not about "old bachelors;" and much humor about age concealment among women but not among men (with the exception of Jack Benny).

Vitulli and Parman (1996) found that both older men and women agreed that humor is an important quality for men, but only the women thought humor is important for women.

Solomon (1996) found that older men used more humor than older women, were quicker to catch on to jokes, and were more likely to see themselves as humorous.

Changes with Age in Sense of Humor

There has been considerable speculation about how the sense of humor may change with aging. Seltzer (1993) speculates that with adult development the complexity of what one appreciates as humor increases, the sources of humor proliferate, creativity of the individual's humor grows, and sophistication in the sense of humor increases.

However, a recent Canadian study (Shammi & Stuss, 2004) found that while appreciation and *reactiveness to humor* does not change with aging, the ability to comprehend more complicated forms of humor does tend to diminish in later years. The researchers speculated that the decline in comprehension of complex humor is caused by declines in complex cognitive function such as abstract reasoning, mental flexibility, and working memory.

The fact that several famous comedians continued their humor late in life such as Bill Cosby, George Burns, and Bob Hope (both into their 90s), is dramatic evidence of the persistence of humor in old age.

Ageism

Some have suggested that negative humor about the aged should be avoided, just as *sexist and racist humor* should be avoided, because an effect of such jokes is to reinforce negative *stereotypes about aging* (Davies, 1977; Palmore, 1999). Others (Weber & Cameron, 1978) point out that what seems negative to one observer may not seem negative to others, and that even negative humor may have certain desirable functions, such as release of repressed fears and reinforcement of certain values associated with youth (vigor, sexuality, and competence).

A test of whether a joke about aging is ageist or not is to try telling the joke without an age reference. If it is still funny, it would be safest to tell it without the age reference. If it is no longer funny, it probably does depend on some ageist stereotype, and telling it with the age reference will tend to reinforce ageism.

Therapeutic Humor

Some studies have found therapeutic effects of humor on older persons. Tennant (1986) found that patients recovering from cataract surgery who scored highest on a "humor survey" had the fastest rate of recovery. He also found in a later study (1990) that such comedy series as *I Love Lucy* and *The Honeymooners* enhanced morale in a sample of older residents in an apartment complex.

Schultes (1997) described how humor can be used by home health care and hospice nurses to provide more cost-effective and holistic care. Houston et al (1998) found that nursing home residents who participated in a humorous activity had reduced levels of anxiety and depression.

Cousins (1976) claimed that *laughing* at old comedy movies helped cure him of a degenerative spinal condition.

Most of these studies were not well designed and are open to various interpretations. Clearly, more research is needed to test whether "laughter is the best medicine."

In summary, humor about aging may have a wide variety of effects, ranging from reinforcing ageism to being enjoyable and therapeutic.

ERDMAN B. PALMORE

See also
Ageism

References

Cousins, N. (1976). *Anatomy of an illness*. New York: W.W. Norton.

Davies, L. (1977). Attitudes toward old age and aging as shown by humor. *Gerontologist, 17*, 220.

Freud, S. (1960). *Jokes and their relation to the unconscious*. In J. Straches (Ed.), *The complete psychological works of Sigmund Freud* (Vol. *8*). London: Hogarth Press. (Originally published in 1905).

Houston, D., McKee, K., Carroll, L., & March, H. (1998). Using humour to promote psychological well being in residential homes for older people. *Aging and Mental Health, 2*, 328–332.

Nahemow, L., McClusky-Fawcett, K., & McGhee, P. (Eds.) (1986). *Humor and aging*. New York: Academic Press.

Palmore, E. (1971). Attitudes toward aging as shown by humor. *Gerontologist, 11*, 181.

Palmore, E. (1999). *Ageism: Negative and positive* (2nd ed.). New York: Springer Publishing.

Palmore, E. (in press). Humor. In E. Palmore, L. Branch, & D. Harris (Eds.), *The encyclopedia of ageism*. New York: Haworth Press.

Richman, J., & Tallmer, M. (1977). *The foolishness and wisdom of age. Gerontologist, 17*, 210.

Schultes, L. (1997). Humor with hospice clients. *Home Healthcare Nurse, 15*, 561.

Seltzer, M. (1993). Humor. In R. Kastenbaum (Ed.), *Encyclopedia of adult development*. Phoenix: Oryx Press.

Shammi, P., & Stuss, D. (2004). Reported at www.seniorjournal.com/NEWS/Aging/3-08-25joke.htm.

Solomon, J. (1996). Humor and aging well. *American Behavioral Scientist, 39*, 249–271.

Tennant, K. (1986). The effect of humor on the recovery rate of cataract patients. In L. Nahemow, K. McCluskey-Fawcett, & P. McGhee (Eds.), *Humor and aging*. New York: Academic Press.

Tennant, K. (1990). Laugh it off: The effect of humor on the well-being of the older adult. *Journal of Gerontological Nursing, 16*, 11.

Vitulli, W., & Parman, D. (1996). Elderly persons' perception of humor as a gender-linked characteristic. *Psychological Reports, 78*, 83–89.

Weber, T., & Cameron, P. (1978). Humor and aging—a response. *Gerontologist, 18*, 73.

HYPERTENSION

Hypertension is the most common treatable cardiovascular disorder in older adults. *Systolic blood pressure* increases with age in Westernized countries. It is therefore not surprising that hypertension is common in older adults. In the *Health Survey for England* (2000–2001), 78% of men and 83% of women aged 65 or older had a blood pressure of 140/90 mmHg or more on a single occasion (Primatesta & Poulter, 2004). Data from the National Health and Nutrition Examination Survey (NHANES) (1999–2000) suggests that since 1988 in the United States prevalence of *hypertension in those aged* 60 or older has increased by 7.5% (Hajjar & Kotchen, 2003). With the increase in age of the general population, hypertension and its control is an important public health concern.

Risk of *Hypertension in Older Persons*

Hypertension is not a disease in itself but a risk factor for other diseases, such as coronary heart disease, stroke, heart failure, renal failure, peripheral vascular disease, and dementia. With regard to stroke, it is the most important modifiable risk factor. The risk of *hypertension in older adults* exceeds that of cholesterol and cigarette smoking and rivals diabetes (Cupples & D'Agostino, 1987). In terms of absolute risk, hypertension is a more potent risk in the over-65 age group than in middle age.

Previously, clinicians have concentrated on *diastolic blood pressures* when making decisions regarding treatment. However, as a result of increasing arterial stiffness with age, the type of hypertension most commonly seen in older adults is that of *isolated systolic hypertension* (ISH). This subtype accounts for about 65% to 80% of hypertension seen in those aged 60 or older (Franklin, Jacobs, Wong, L'Italien, Lapuerta, 2001). Over age 60, systolic pressure rather than diastolic is the better predictor of cardiovascular mortality and morbidity. In individuals aged 60 or older, a 10 mmHg *increase in systolic blood pressure* is associated with a 10% increase in the risk of all fatal and non-fatal complications except for coronary events (Staessen, Gasowski, Wang, Thijs, Den Hond, Boissel, et al., 2000). Data from the *Framingham Heart Study* has recently suggested that *pulse pressure* is the most important risk factor, and this finding is consistent across gender or whether individuals are treated or untreated (Haider, Larson, Franklin, & Levy, 2003).

Treatment

Non-Pharmacological Treatment. Non-pharmacological methods are a constant feature of recommendations in the *management of hypertension*. Most of the evidence for this comes from trials in middle age. The few trials in older adults suggest interventions to be at least as effective. The *Trial of Non-pharmacological Interventions in the Elderly* (TONE) showed an approximately 30% reduction in the need for *antihypertensive medication* by reducing average sodium intake by about 40 mmol per day (Appel, Espeland, Easter, Wilson, Folmar, & Lacy, 2001). However, age-related changes such as a decrease in taste bud sensitivity, increased rates of depression, anxiety, and a reluctance to change an established daily routine make changes to dietary intake more difficult to initiate in older adults. Additional comorbidities, such as osteoarthrosis, Parkinson's disease, and dementia make increasing exercise difficult. Salt reduction, weight loss, and an increase in physical activity are the areas that should initially be considered. Stopping smoking should also be encouraged to reduce overall cardiovascular risk.

Pharmacological Treatment. There is overwhelming evidence that antihypertensive treatment in individuals up to age 80 is beneficial. There have been several well conducted randomized controlled trials published over the last 20 years (Amery, Birkenhäger, Brixko, Bulpitt, Clement, Deruyttere, et al., 1985; Coope & Warrender, 1986; Dahlof, Lindholm, Hanson, Schersten, Ekbom, & Wester, 1991; SHEP Cooperative Research Group, 1991; Medical Research Council Working Party, 1992; Staessen, Fagard, Thijs, Celis, Arabidze, Birkenhäger, et al., 1997; Liu, Wang, Gong, Liu, & Staessen, 1998).

They have shown similar results with a *reduction in stroke* events of 25% to 47%, of cardiac events of 13% to 27% and all cardiovascular events of 17% to 40%. These benefits also have been reported in meta-analyses (Sanderson, 1996; Thijs, Fagard, Lijnen, Staessen, Van Hoof, & Amery, 1992). Subjects recruited to these trials represent older populations from Europe (East and West), the United States, Australia, and China with ISH, diastolic and systo-diastolic hypertension. There is a high benefit to risk ratio. The number needed to treat (NNT) for 5 years to prevent 1 adverse event for all stroke is 22 and for all coronary heart disease is 45 in older adults. This is much lower than the NNT for younger hypertensive individuals (Sanderson, 1996).

Recent data also raises the possibility that antihypertensive medication may reduce the incidence of both vascular and Alzheimer's dementias. The *Systolic Hypertension in Europe* trial (*Syst-Eur*) found that treatment based on the calcium channel blocker (CCB) *nitrendipine* reduced incidence dementia by 50%. (Forette, Seux, Staessen, Thijs, Babarskiene, Babeanu, et al., 2002) It should be pointed out however, that the numbers involved were small. Also other studies have not shown a clear benefit (SHEP Cooperative Research Group, 1991; Prince, Bird, Blizard, & Mann, 1996). Results from the *Perindopril Protection Against Recurrent Stroke Study* (PROGRESS) did not show a clear benefit from treatment based on an ACE-inhibitor regime on the overall risk of dementia (Tzourio, Anderson, Chapman, Woodward, Neal, MacMahon, et al., 2003) It did, however, show that treatment reduced the risk of the composite endpoint "dementia with recurrent stroke" by 34% (95% confidence interval [CI] 3–55) and of "cognitive decline and recurrent stroke" by 45% (95% CI 21–61). No benefit with regard to the risk of dementia was seen in those who were hypertensive, although with regard to cognitive decline there was a relative risk reduction of 21% (95% CI 0–38). With the high prevalence of dementia in older adults, especially age 75 or older, such benefits may have large implications. However, more data is required before any firm conclusions can be made.

A few caveats are worth mentioning. Firstly, individuals recruited to these trials were a select older group. They were less likely to have angina, diabetes, heart failure, dementia, depression, or limitations in their activities of daily living when compared to individuals of a similar age in the general population. Secondly, the level of blood pressure at entry for these trials was always 160 mmHg systolic or above. No trial to date has shown benefit from treating older adults with systolic blood pressures in the range 140–159 mmHg. Thirdly, individuals with *orthostatic hypotension* were under-represented in these trials, and it may be that when this group is treated, symptoms of orthostatic hypotension increase as well as the incidence of falls, a significant cause of mortality and morbidity in those age 75 and older.

Fourth, the number of patients older than age 80 recruited to these trials was small. There is data to suggest that in the *very old a high blood pressure* is associated with a better outcome (Mattila, Haavisto, Rajala, & Heikinheimo, 1988). This probably reflects a well preserved cardiac function rather than an actual protective effect of high blood pressure and a lack of comorbidities such as cancer or dementia, which are associated with a decrease in blood pressure. A meta-analysis of patients aged 80 or older recruited to these trials showed a reduction in stroke and heart failure but an increase in total mortality (Gueyffier, Bulpitt, Boissel, Schron, Ekbom, Fagard, et al., 1999). This suggests that the benefit to risk ratio may be different in the very old. The *Hypertension in the Very Elderly* (HYVET) pilot trial has recently showed a similar trend, although the results of the main trial will be required before a more definitive answer can be obtained (Bulpitt, Beckett, Cooke, Dumitrascu, Gil-Extremera, Nachev, et al., 2003).

It can be argued that those not included in these trials are at a greater risk, as they have a greater prevalence of risk factors and thus would gain more benefit from treatment. Equally, the greater prevalence of comorbidity might make them more susceptible to side effects. It is likely that at some stage the benefit is lost due to co-morbidity resulting in death before any benefit is obtained. Where that line is crossed is uncertain. What one can say is that older adults without significant co-morbidity up to the age of 80 with sustained blood pressures above 160 mmHg systolic or 90 mmHg diastolic should be treated. The aim should be to lower their pressure to 140/90 mmHg. This target would be consistent with the trial results. Diabetic patients in these trials have been shown to have greater benefit and lower targets for treatment should be aimed for. With regards to those with significant comorbidities, a more individualistic approach is required.

Choosing a Drug

The major placebo-controlled trials of antihypertensive treatment in older adults have used either *thiazide diuretics*, *beta-blockers*, or *dihydropyridine CCBs*. There is overwhelming evidence for the use of low-dose diuretics as the first line treatment of choice for uncomplicated hypertension and long-acting CCBs in isolated systolic hypertension. Although extensively used in the earlier trials, the benefit of beta-blockers is now felt to be less than previously suggested, and their use is no longer supported as first line treatment in uncomplicated hypertension (Messerli & Grossman, 1999). However, when hypertension is complicated by angina or the patient has previously sustained a myocardial infarction, the use of a beta-blocker is prudent and logical.

Data on the comparison of *ACE-inhibitors* against placebo comes from patients selected on the basis of their cardiovascular risk or presence of diabetes rather than blood pressure per se. In the *Heart Outcomes Prevention Evaluation* (HOPE) study, where 47% of the 9,297 patients recruited were known to have hypertension at baseline, there was a significant relative reduction in the primary endpoint (myocardial infarction, stroke or death from cardiovascular causes) of 22% with the ACE-inhibitor *ramipril* compared to placebo (Heart Outcome Prevention Evaluation Study Investigators, 2000). This beneficial effect was noted to be greater in those aged 65 or older compared to those younger than 65, and in those with a history of hypertension compared to those without, although not significantly so. Data on the use of *angiotensin II receptor blockers* (ARBs) comes from the *Study on Cognition and Prognosis in the Elderly* (SCOPE) (Lithell, Hansson, Skoog, Elmfeldt, Hofman, Olofsson, et al., 2003). This reported a benefit in preventing nonfatal strokes but not major cardiovascular events with the use of *candesartan*. Unfortunately, the placebo arm of the trial was changed to allow active treatment during the course of the trial, which may explain why significance was not achieved. It also reported that cognition did not appear to deteriorate.

Several comparative trials have provided data regarding differences between different drug regimes. They have compared ACE-inhibitor, CCB (all 3 subtypes) and ARB based treatment against conventional treatment based on diuretics, beta-blockers or both, as well as ACE-inhibitor against CCB (Hansson, Lindholm, Niskanen, Hedner, Niklason, Luomanmäki, et al., 1999; Hansson, Lindholm, Ekbom, Dahlöf, Lanke, Scherstén, et al., 1999; Hansson, Hedner, Lund-Johansen, Kjeldsen, Lindholm, Syvertsen, et al., 2000; Brown, Palmer, Castigne, de Leeuw, Mancia, Rosenthal, et al., 2000; ALLHAT Officers and Coordinators for the ALLHAT Collaborative Research Group, 2002; Pepine, Handberg, Cooper-DeHoff, Marks, Brunner, Ekman, et al., 2004). All except the Australian National Blood Pressure 2 study (ANBP2) (Wing, Reid, Ryan, Beilin, Brown, & Jennings, 2003) and the Losartan Intervention for Endpoint reduction in hypertension study (LIFE) (Dahlöf, Devereux, Kjeldsen, Julius, Beevers, de Faire, et al., 2002) have shown no difference in the primary composite endpoints that usually incorporated cardiovascular and cerebrovascular outcomes. ANBP2 reported an advantage in ACE-inhibitor based treatment against conventional treatment in the composite endpoint of all cardiovascular events or death from any cause that was just significant—hazard ratio 0.89 (95% CI 0.79–1.00; p = 0.05). LIFE showed a relative risk reduction in the primary endpoint of cardiovascular death, stroke, and myocardial infarction of 13% (95% CI 2–23; p = 0.02) in favor of the ARB *losartan* against *atenolol*. The individual trials have shown some differences in cause-specific outcomes, particularly heart failure.

The stopping of the *doxazosin* arm in the *Antihypertensive and Lipid Lowering Treatment to prevent Heart Attack Trial* (*ALLHAT*) has raised doubts about the use of beta-blockers (ALLHAT Collaborative Research Group, 2000). In the trial there was a borderline significant excess of stroke in the doxazosin arm, although poorer blood pressure control might explain this. However, there was a twofold increased risk of heart failure when compared to *chlorthalidone*. This does not mean that doxazosin is worse than placebo in treating hypertension, but simply that it is not as effective as diuretic-based treatment. In light of these results doxazosin should probably be avoided in patients with established heart failure.

Despite the differences in individual trials a meta-analysis of these trials has shown that there is no difference with any commonly used regimen regarding the reduction in risk of total major cardiovascular events (Blood Pressure Lowering Treatment Trialists' Collaboration, 2003). It also showed that larger *reductions in blood pressure* produce larger reductions in risk. A caveat about which drug to use firstline: to achieve the recommended targets for blood pressure treatment, 50% of patients will require more than 1 drug, and nearly 30% will need 3 or more. It is worth remembering that older patients often find it difficult to comply with complicated treatment regimens, particularly if they involve multiple drugs and multiple doses. If they live alone, have problems with concentration, understanding, and memory, or are mildly demented or depressed, compliance with such regimens becomes difficult. Treatment regimens must be kept simple. The old adage of "start low, go slow" (Bennet, 1994) remains good advice.

At present the treatment and control of hypertension is poor, irrespective of the country one considers, with control being lowest in older individuals. The NHANES (1999–2000) survey shows that in those aged 60 or older, 62% of those detected were treated and the control rate was lowest in this age group at 43% (Hajjar & Kotchen, 2003). Using the same definition of hypertension (140/90 mmHg or higher) and control (below 140/90 mmHg), data from the Health Survey for England (2000–2001) showed 56% of hypertensives aged 65 or older were treated and only 19% controlled (Primatesta & Poulter, 2004). Globally more needs to be done to develop strategies to implement the available trial evidence. Improved detection, treatment, and control for older individuals with hypertension will translate into a significant and welcome reduction in the cardiovascular burden in this age group.

RUTH PETERS
NIGEL BECKETT

References

ALLHAT Collaborative Research Group. (2000). Major cardiovascular events in hypertensive patients randomized to doxazosin vs. chlorthalidone: The antihypertensive and lipid-lowering treatment to prevent heart attack trial (ALLHAT). *Journal of the American Medical Association*, *283*, 1967–1975.

ALLHAT Officers and Coordinators for the ALLHAT Collaborative Research Group (2002). Major outcomes in high-risk hypertensive patients randomized to angiotensin-converting enzyme inhibitor or calcium channel blocker vs diuretic: The Antihypertensive and Lipid-Lowering Treatment to Prevent Heart Attack Trial (ALLHAT). *Journal of the American Medical Association*, *288*(23), 2981–2997. [Erratum: *Journal of the American Medical Association* (2003), *289*(2), 178; *Journal of the American Medical Association* (2004), *291*(18), 2196.]

Amery, A., Birkenhäger, W. H., Brixko, P., Bulpitt, C., Clement, D., Deruyttere, M., et al. (1985). Mortality and morbidity results from the European Working Party on High Blood Pressure in the Elderly trial. *Lancet*, *1*, 1349–1354.

Appel, L. J., Espeland, M. A., Easter, L., Wilson, A. C., Folmar, S., & Lacy, C. R. (2001). Effects of reduced sodium intake on hypertension control in older individuals: Results from the Trial of Non-pharmacologic Interventions in the Elderly (TONE). *Archives of Internal Medicine*, *161*(5), 685–693.

Bennet, N. E. (1994). Hypertension in the elderly. *Lancet*, *344*(8920), 447–449.

Blood Pressure Lowering Treatment Trialists' Collaboration. (2003). Effects of different blood-pressure-lowering regimens on major cardiovascular events: Results of prospectively designed overviews of randomized trials. *Lancet*, *362*, 1527–1535.

Brown, M. J., Palmer, C. R., Castigne, A., de Leeuw, P. W., Mancia, G., Rosenthal, T., et al. (2000). Morbidity and mortality in patients randomized to double-blind treatment with a long-acting calcium-channel blocker or diuretic in the International Nifedipine GITS study: Intervention as a Goal in Hypertension Treatment (INSIGHT). *Lancet*, *356*, 366–372.

Bulpitt, C. J., Beckett, N. S., Cooke, J., Dumitrascu, D. L., Gil-Extremera, B., Nachev, C., et al. (2003). Results of the pilot study for the Hypertension in the Very Elderly Trial. *Journal of Hypertension*, *12*, 2409–2417.

Coope, J. N., & Warrender, T. S. (1986). Randomized trial of hypertension in elderly patients in primary care. *British Medical Journal*, *293*, 1145–1151.

Cupples, L. A., & D'Agostino, R. B. (1987). Some risk factors related to the annular incidence of cardiovascular disease and death using polled repeated biennial measurements: The Framingham study 30-year follow-up. *DHHS Pub. No. NIH 83-2703*. Springfield, VA: U.S. Department of Commerce, National Technical Information Service.

Dahlof, B., Lindholm, L. H., Hanson, L., Schersten, B., Ekbom, T., & Wester, P.-O. (1991). Morbidity and mortality in the Swedish trial in old patients with hypertension (STOP-Hypertension). *Lancet*, *338*, 1281–1285.

Dahlöf, B., Devereux, R. D., Kjeldsen, S. E., Julius, S., Beevers, G., de Faire. U., et al. (2002). Cardiovascular morbidity and mortality in the Losartan Intervention for Endpoint reduction in hypertension study (LIFE): A randomized trial against atenolol. *Lancet*, *359*, 995–1003.

Franklin, S. S., Jacobs, M. J., Wong, N. D., L'Italien, G. J., & Lapuerta, P. (2001). Predominance of isolated systolic hypertension among middle-aged and elderly U.S. hypertensives: Analysis based on National Health and Nutrition Examination Survey (NHANES) III. *Hypertension*, *37*(3), 869–874.

Forette, F., Seux, M. L., Staessen, J. A., Thijs, L., Babarskiene, M. R., Babeanu, S., et al. (2002). The prevention of dementia with antihypertensive treatment: New evidence from the Systolic Hypertension in Europe (Syst-Eur) study. *Archives of Internal Medicine*, *162*(18), 2046–2052. [Erratum: *Archives of Internal Medicine* (2003), *163*(2), 241.]

Gueyffier, F., Bulpitt, C., Boissel, J.-P., Schron, E., Ekbom, T., Fagard, R., et al. (1999). Antihypertensive treatment in very old people: A subgroup meta-analysis of randomised controlled trials. *Lancet*, *353*, 793–796.

Haider, A. W., Larson, M. G., Franklin, S. S., & Levy, D. (2003). Systolic blood pressure, diastolic blood pressure, and pulse pressure as predictors of risk for congestive heart failure in the Framingham Heart Study. *Annals of Internal Medicine*, *138*(1), 10–16.

Hajjar, I., & Kotchen, T. A. (2003). Trends in prevalence, awareness, treatment, and control of hypertension in the United States, 1988–2000. *Journal of the American Medical Association*, *290*(2), 199–206.

Hansson, L., Lindholm, L. H., Niskanen, L., Hedner, T., Niklason, A., Luomanmäki, K., et al. (1999). Effect of angiotensin-converting enzyme inhibition compared with conventional therapy on cardiovascular morbidity and mortality in hypertension: The Captopril Prevention Project (CAPPP) randomised trial. *Lancet*, *353*, 611–616.

Hansson, L., Lindholm, L. H., Ekbom, T., Dahlöf, B., Lanke, J., Scherstén, B., et al. (1999). Randomized trial of old and new antihypertensive drugs in elderly patients: cardiovascular mortality and morbidity, the Swedish Trial in Old Patients with Hypertension–2 study. *Lancet*, *354*, 1751–1756.

Hansson, L., Hedner, T., Lund-Johansen, P., Kjeldsen, S. E., Lindholm, L. H., Syvertsen, J. O., et al. (2000). Randomized trial of effects of calcium antagonists compared with diuretics and beta-blockers on cardiovascular morbidity and mortality in hypertension: The

Nordic Diltiazem (NORDIL) study. *Lancet, 356*, 359–365.

Heart Outcome Prevention Evaluation Study Investigators. (2000). Effects of an angiotensin-converting enzyme inhibitor, ramipril, on cardiovascular events in high-risk patients. *New England Journal of Medicine, 342*, 145–153.

Lithell, H., Hansson, L., Skoog, I., Elmfeldt, D., Hofman, A., Olofsson, B., & et al. (2003). The Study on Cognition and Prognosis in the Elderly (SCOPE): Principal results of a randomized double-blind intervention trial. *Journal of Hypertension, 5*, 875–886.

Liu, L., Wang, J. W., Gong, L., Liu, G., & Staessen, J. A.; for the Systolic Hypertension in China (Syst-China) Collaborative Group. (1998). Comparison of active treatment and placebo in older Chinese patients with isolated systolic hypertension. *Journal of Hypertension, 16*, 1823–1829.

Mattila, K., Haavisto, M., Rajala, S., & Heikinheimo, R. (1988). Blood pressure and survival in the very old. *British Medical Journal, 296*, 887–889.

Medical Research Council Working Party. (1992). MRC trial of treatment of hypertension in older adults: Principal results. *British Medical Journal, 304*, 405–412.

Messerli, F. H., & Grossman, E. (1999). Beta-blockers and diuretics: To use or not to use. *American Journal of Hypertension, 12*, 157S–163S.

Pepine, C. J., Handberg, E. M., Cooper-DeHoff, R. M., Marks, R. G., Kowey, P., Messerli, F. H., et al. (2003). A calcium antagonist versus a non-calcium antagonist hypertension treatment strategy for patients with coronary artery disease. The International Verapamil-Trandolapril Study (INVEST): A randomized controlled trial. *Journal of the American Medical Association, 290*(21), 2805–2816.

Primatesta, P., & Poulter, N. R. (2004). Hypertension management and control among English adults aged 65 years and older in 2000 and 2001. *Journal of Hypertension, 6*, 1093–1098.

Prince, M. J., Bird, A. S., Blizard, R. A., & Mann, A. H. (1996) Is the cognitive function of older patients affected by antihypertensive treatment? Results from 54 months of the Medical Research Council's trial of hypertension in older adults. *British Medical Journal, 312*(7034), 801–805.

Sanderson, S. (1996). Hypertension in the elderly: Pressure to treat? *Health Trends, 28*, 117–121.

SHEP Cooperative Research Group. (1991). Prevention of stroke by anti-hypertensive drug treatment in older persons with isolated systolic hypertension. *Journal of the American Medical Association, 265*, 3255–3264.

Staessen, J. A., Fagard, R., Thijs, L., Celis, H., Arabidze, G. G., Birkenhäger, W. H., & et al. (1997). Randomized double-blind comparison of placebo and active treatment for older patients with systolic hypertension. *Lancet, 350*, 757–764.

Staessen, J. A., Gasowski, J., Wang, J. G., Thijs, L., Den Hond, E., Boissel, J. P., & et al. (2000). Risks of untreated and treated isolated systolic hypertension in the elderly: Meta-analysis of outcome trials. *Lancet, 355*(9207), 865–872. [Erratum: *Lancet* (2001), *357*(9257), 724.]

Thijs, L., Fagard, R., Lijnen, P., Staessen, J., Van Hoof, R., & Amery, A. (1992). A meta-analysis of outcome trials in elderly hypertensives. *Journal of Hypertension, 10*, 1103–1109.

Tzourio, C., Anderson, C., Chapman, N., Woodward, M., Neal, B., MacMahon, S., et al. (2003). Effects of blood pressure lowering with perindopril and indapamide therapy on dementia and cognitive decline in patients with cerebrovascular disease. *Archives of Internal Medicine, 163*(9), 1069–1075.

Wing, L. M., Reid, C. M., Ryan, P., Beilin, L. J., Brown, M. A., & Jennings, G. L. (2003). Second Australian National Blood Pressure Study Group. A comparison of outcomes with angiotensin-converting enzyme inhibitors and diuretics for hypertension in the elderly. *New England Journal of Medicine, 348*(7), 582–583.

I

ICIDH

See
Disability

IMMUNE SYSTEM

One of the hallmarks of aging is the *decline in immune function*. The increased severity and duration of infections caused by pneumococcus, influenza, and respiratory syncytial virus, the frequent reactivation of latent infections such as tuberculosis and herpes zoster, and the more rapid progression to *AIDS in older persons* infected with HIV are all considered to be outcomes of *age-associated changes in immunity*. The decline in *immune function during aging* has also been implicated in the *reduced response to vaccines* intended to prevent infection, as well as in the increased incidence of cancer. The biological significance of immune system competence with respect to life span is underscored by studies of *centenarians*, most of whom have well-preserved immune function (Franceschi, Monti, Sansoni, & Cossarizza, 1995). Conversely, longitudinal studies on 80-year-olds have identified a cluster of immune parameters (the so-called *immune risk phenotype*) that is correlated with early all-cause mortality (Pawelec, Akbar, Caruso, Effros, Grubeck-Loebenstein, & Wikby, in press).

Components

The immune system consists of innate and adaptive components, which complement each other in protecting humans from pathogens and cancer. *Innate (natural) immunity* is the early defense system that responds rapidly and somewhat non-specifically to foreign pathogens. This early response provides a bridge until the *adaptive (acquired) immune response* can take over.

The major cell types involved in innate immunity are the *neutrophils*, *monocyte/macrophages*, *dendritic cells* (DC), and *natural killer (NK) cells*. Neutrophils are among the first cells to respond to infection, producing bacteriocidal products and factors that influence the adaptive immune system. *Macrophages*, which arise from circulating *monocytes*, migrate into tissues throughout the body and recognize pathogenic microorganisms through cell surface receptors that are able to distinguish between pathogen and host. Macrophages engulf bacteria and secrete a variety of proteins called *cytokines* that communicate with other cell types and initiate the process of inflammation. DC are specialized phagocytic cells that are long-lived and migrate from the bone marrow to peripheral lymph nodes, where they can degrade bacteria or viruses into *antigenic peptides* that they then present to cells of the adaptive immune system. *NK cells* circulate in the blood and, if activated by certain macrophage-derived cytokines, can bind to and kill infected or tumor target cells by releasing cytotoxic granules.

The major cellular components involved in adaptive immunity are T and B *lymphocytes*, cells that derive from *hematopoietic stem cells* within the bone marrow. The intricate genetic mechanism by which *lymphocyte antigen receptors* are generated allows a limited number of *immunoglobulin* (Ig) and *T cell receptor* (TCR) genes to create an immune system with an enormous range of specificities. Briefly, during a lymphocyte's development, one member of a set of gene segments is joined to other gene segments by an irreversible process of DNA recombination. This random series of juxtapositions forms a sequence of gene segments, thereby yielding a receptor molecule that is unique to that cell. The consequence of this mechanism is that just a few hundred different gene segments can combine in a variety of ways to create thousands of receptor chains. This diversity is further amplified by the pairing of 2 different chains, each encoded by distinct sets of gene segments, to form a functional *antigen receptor*. Each lymphocyte bears many copies of its antigen receptor, and once generated, the receptor specificity of a lymphocyte does not change. The exquisite specificity of each lymphocyte results in the ability of the organism to respond to the nearly infinite number of foreign antigens that could be encountered over a lifetime (Janeway & Travers, 1997).

The *B cell response* is initiated when antigenic determinants on a pathogen are recognized by the surface Ig receptor on certain *B cells*. Those B cells proliferate to form a clone of identical cells, each of which produces antibodies identical to the original Ig receptor on the founder B cell. B cell stimulation by most antigens requires interaction with certain *helper T cells*, which in turn depend on antigen presentation by dendritic cells and macrophages. Once generated, soluble antibody molecules secreted into the serum can bind the pathogens, which results either in the direct inactivation of viruses and toxins, or, when combined with other serum proteins, in the lysis of bacteria. *Antibodies* can also cause bacteria to adhere to cells that subsequently engulf and degrade the bacteria (*opsonization*).

The second major component of the adaptive immune system is the T cell. Unlike B cells, *T cells* cannot recognize free antigen, but rather only portions of an antigen that are expressed on the surface of other cells. These peptides are "presented" on the cell surface in the context of cell surface molecules called *major histocompatibility (MHC) antigens* (Doherty & Zinkernagel, 1975). The so-called *cytotoxic (CD8) T cells* recognize peptide antigens derived from viruses, which are synthesized within the cell and presented in the context of MHC Class I molecules. Upon antigen recognition, *CD8 T cells* proliferate and acquire the capacity to lyse the infected cells. The second type of T cells, the CD4, or helper T cells, recognize peptides derived from degraded or ingested antigens, in this case presented on MHC Class II molecules. Helper T cells proliferate once they become activated, and release a variety of cytokines that facilitate immune responses of both CD8 T cells and B cells.

Age-Related Changes

During aging, alterations are observed in nearly every aspect of immunity, but the most dramatic changes are seen within the T cell compartment. A key step in the development and maturation of T cells occurs in the *thymus*, an endocrine gland that undergoes progressive involution over the life span, beginning at birth. Although the thymus retains the ability to orchestrate normal T cell development even late in life (Jamieson et al. 1999), the proportion of naïve T cells does decrease with age. This decrease and the concomitant increase in the proportion of *memory T cells* is one of the signature changes of aging. Furthermore, within the memory T cell compartment, one of the striking characteristics is the presence of oligoclonal expansions (Nociari, Telford, & Russo, 1999). The predominance of these expansions within the CD8 versus CD4 T cell subset most probably relates to the stronger, more persistent nature of the antigenic drive for CD8 T cells responding to chronic systemic intracellular pathogens, in contrast to the more discrete localization of extracellular pathogens recognized by CD4 T cells (Maini, Casorati, Dellabona, Wack, & Beverley, 1999). Indeed, there are high frequencies of specific CD8 T cell clonal populations in humans who are chronically infected with *cytomegalovirus*, human immunodeficiency virus (*HIV*), and *Epstein-Barr virus* (Maini, Casorati, Dellabona, Wack, & Beverley, 1999).

An intriguing aspect of the CD8 T cell clonal expansions in humans is that they contain high proportions of cells that lack expression of the CD28 co-stimulatory molecule and have shortened telomeres, suggesting that some of these cells may have reached an end stage phenotype associated with *replicative senescence* (Effros, 2000). Interestingly, these putatively senescent CD8 T cells are resistant to apoptosis, so that once generated, they persist. Cells with this senescent phenotype have been associated with suppressor functions as well as with *reduced antibody response* to vaccines (Cortesini, LeMaoult, Ciubotariu, & Cortesini, 2001; Saurwein-Teissl, Lung, Marx, Gschosser, Asch, Blasko et al., 2002). An indirect outcome of the increasing proportions of *oligoclonal expansions* with age is that the remaining naïve repertoire will be narrowed.

Within the helper T cell compartment, there is a general shift from Th1 to Th2 cytokines, a change implicated in the increased production of *autoantibodies* and concomitant reduction in cellular immunity. Reduced IL-2 production during aging is not restricted to memory or replicatively senescent cells: naïve T cells from old mice also produce significantly less *IL-2*, and even when the initial expansion defect is corrected by the addition of exogenous IL-2, the memory cell progeny resulting from this manipulation also show reduced IL-2 production, (Haynes, Eaton, & Swain, 1999). In humans, immunity to infection, which is critically dependent on a Th1 response pattern, may be reduced in older adults due to increased levels of the Th2 cytokines produced by activated PBMC (Lio, D'Anna, Scola, Di Lorenzo, Colombo, Listai, et al., 1999; Castle, Uyemura, Wong, Modlin, & Effros, 1997).

One of the hallmarks of aging is a qualitative change in the *B cell immune response*, so that even in cases where the *quantity* of antibody production to specific antigens remains robust, the antibodies are *functionally* insufficient. While many of the alterations in the antibody response during aging can be traced to the influence of helper T cells, there are also several striking changes that are intrinsic to the B cells. For example, the half-life of mature B cells in the spleen has been estimated to increase severalfold during aging (Kline, Hayden, & Klinman, 1999). The progressive increase in longevity of mature B cells with age is accompanied by an approximately 10-fold decrease in the proportion of recent bone marrow emigrés in the spleen as well as a reduction in the number of pre-B cells (Sherwood, Blomberg, Xu, Warner, & Riley, 1998). The proliferation and migration of activated B cells to splenic follicles, the so-called "*germinal center*" *reaction*, is markedly altered in older mice, a change that is due, in part, to defects in the CD4 T cells. Additional qualitative changes in the antibody response also may be due to altered expression of costimulatory molecules (Zheng, Han, Takahashi, & Kelsoe, 1997).

The *B cell compartment*, like the T cell compartment, is characterized by age-associated oligoclonal expansions. Interestingly, the clonal populations are predominantly within the CD5+ B cell population, a subset that increases in proportion during aging and which is responsible for the majority of autoantibodies produced in older mice. Although the increased autoantibody response generally has not been associated with pathophysiological consequences, the B cell clonal populations have been proposed as the precursors of 2 types of neoplasms that are dominated by CD5+ B cells or plasma cells—B cell chronic lymphocytic leukemia and multiple myeloma, respectively (LeMaoult, Manavalan, Dyall, Szabo, Nikolic-Zugic, & Weksler, 1999).

The innate immune system also undergoes age-related changes (Plackett, Boehmer, Faunce, & Kovacs, 2004). Neutrophils, which are recruited to tissue sites in response to inflammation or infection, normally release oxygen free radicals and proteolytic enzymes. During aging, the sustained capacity of neutrophils to produce these products is reduced, in part due to their *premature apoptosis*. The reduced ability of aged neutrophils to be rescued from death may be related to their increased sensitivity to certain cytokines and growth factors that enhance their survival during younger ages. Additionally, neutrophils from older individuals show alterations in migration and adhesion, properties that are integral in their trafficking from the blood to sites of infection.

Macrophages and DC, which link the innate and adaptive immune systems, also show age-related changes. In older humans, the proportion and function of alveolar macrophages is decreased, possibly contributing to the increased risk of pulmonary infections in the elderly (Zissel, Schlaak, & Meuller-Quernheim, 1999). Macrophages also show reduced production of reactive oxygen species and nitrogen intermediates. Monocytes from older donors show reduction in their IL-1 secretion, cytotoxicity, and protein kinase translocation (McLachlan, Serkin, Morrey, & Bakouche, 1995). Many of the macrophage changes may relate to the age-related reduced expression of Toll-like receptors, the specialized receptors required for recognizing common components of bacteria and parasites (Renshaw, Rockwell, Engleman, Gewirtz, Katz, & Sambhara, et al., 2002). Dendritic cells from older donors are inferior in terms of Class II and CD54 upregulation and triggering a *Th1 response to influenza* (Wick & Grubeck-Loebenstein, 1997). Certain aspects of antigen presentation by DC may be due to the reduced capacity of *proteasomes* to generate antigenic peptides in antigen-presenting cells.

The function of *NK cells* also undergoes certain changes during aging. In addition to a decrease in toxicity, NK cells from the elderly are unable to proliferate properly in response to IL-2. The combined effects of reduced lytic function and diminished proliferative potential may contribute to the age-related delayed recovery from infections and the decreased ability to rid the body of tumor cells.

The *Immune System and Diseases of Aging*

There is increasing evidence that immune system changes may contribute to some of the major pathologies of aging. *Cancer*, for which old age is the greatest risk factor, has been linked theoretically to altered immune surveillance, with some experimental validation documented in prostate and skin cancer (Alexander, Brady, Leffell, Tsai, & Celis, 1998; Galvaao, Sotto, Kihara, Rivitti, & Sabbaga, 1998). In *Alzheimer's disease*, there is increasing evidence that interactions between the proinflammatory *cytokine IL-6* and *beta amyloid* may play an active role in the development of its neuropathology. Other proteins, such as IL-1 and those of the classical complement pathway, are closely connected with beta-amyloid deposits, and high plasma concentration of TNF α is associated with *dementia in centenarians* (Bruunsgaard, Andersen-Ranberg, Jeune, Pedersen, Skinhj, & Pedersen, 1999). There is also evidence of T cell infiltration into the diseased tissue and a difference in T cell reactivity to beta amyloid between persons with Alzheimer's disease and age-matched controls (Trieb, Ransmayr, Sgonc, Lassmann, & Grubeck-Loebenstein, 1996).

Data from both epidemiological and experimental sources suggest immune involvement in *cardiovascular disease* as well. The presence of T cells in atherosclerotic lesions (Seko, Sato, Takagi, Tada, Matsuo, Yagita, et al., 1997; Schmitz, Herr, & Rothe, 1998) and the demonstrated interaction of CD40 on T cells with vascular endothelial cells, smooth muscle cells, and macrophages (Mach, Scheonbeck, Sukhova, Bourcier, Bonnefoy, Pober, et al., 1997) strongly implicate cell-mediated immune involvement in cardiovascular disease. *Chronic infections* have been hypothesized to increase the risk of cardiovascular disease by causing systemic inflammation, or by triggering autoimmunity, for example by cross-reactivity of hsp 60 with bacterial antigens (George, Harats, Gilburd, & Shoenfeld, 1996). Indeed, clinically healthy volunteers with sonographically documented carotid artery atherosclerosis have significantly increased antibody titers to hsp 65 compared to controls with no lesions, and in follow-up studies those with highest titers showed highest mortality (Xu, Kiechl, Mayr, Metzler, Egger, Oberhollenzer, et al., 1999). An increasing body of epidemiological evidence links immune reactivity, *Chlamydia pneumoniae*, and cytomegalovirus with cardiovascular disease. Further research is necessary to more precisely define the relationship between *immunosenescence* and some of the pathologies of aging.

RITA B. EFFROS

See also
AIDS/HIV

References

Alexander, R. B., Brady, F., Leffell, M. S., Tsai, V., & Celis, E. (1998). Specific T cell recognition of peptides derived from prostate-specific antigen in patients with prostate cancer. *Urology*, *51*, 150–157.

Bruunsgaard, H., Andersen-Ranberg, K., Jeune, B., Pedersen, A. N., Skinhj, P., & Pedersen, B. K. (1999). A high plasma concentration of TNF-alpha is associated with dementia in centenarians. *Journals of Gerontology. Series A, Biological Sciences and Medical Sciences*, *54*, M357–M364.

Castle, S., Uyemura, K., Wong, W., Modlin, R., & Effros, R. B. (1997). Evidence of enhanced type 2 immune response and impaired upregulation of a type 1 response in frail elderly nursing home residents. *Mechanisms of Ageing Development*, *94*, 7–16.

Cortesini, R., LeMaoult, J., Ciubotariu, R., & Cortesini, N. S. (2001). CD8+CD28- T suppressor cells and the induction of antigen-specific, antigen-presenting cells-mediated suppression of Th reactivity. *Immunology Review*, *182*, 201–206.

Doherty, P. C. & Zinkernagel, R. M. (1975). H-2 compatibility is required for T-cell-mediated lysis of target cells infected with lymphocytic choriomeningitis virus. *Journal of Experimental Medicine*, *141*, 502–507.

Effros, R. B. (2000). Costimulatory mechanisms in the elderly. *Vaccine*, *18*, 1661–1665.

Franceschi, C., Monti, D., Sansoni, P., & Cossarizza, A. (1995). The immunology of exceptional individuals: The lesson of centenarians [see comments]. *Immunology Today*, *16*, 12–16.

Galvaao, M. M., Sotto, M. N., Kihara, S. M., Rivitti, E. A., & Sabbaga, E. (1998). Lymphocyte subsets and Langerhans cells in sun-protected and sun-exposed skin of immunosuppressed renal allograft recipients. *Journal of the American Academy of Dermatology*, *38*, 38–44.

George, J., Harats, D., Gilburd, B., & Shoenfeld, Y. (1996). Emerging cross-regulatory roles of immunity and autoimmunity in atherosclerosis. *Immunologic Research*, *15*, 315–322.

Haynes, L., Eaton, S. M., & Swain, S. L. (1999). The defects in effector generation associated with aging can be reversed by addition IL-2 but not other related gamma-c receptor binding cytokines. *Vaccine* (*in press*).

Jamieson, B. D. et al. Generation of functional thymocytes in the human adult. *Immunity, 10*, 569–575.

Janeway, C. A., & Travers, P. (1997). *The immune system in health and disease*. NY: Garland Publishing Inc.

Kline, G. H., Hayden, T. A., & Klinman, N. R. (1999). B cell maintenance in aged mice reflects both increased B cell longevity and decreased B cell generation. *Journal of Immunology*, *162*, 3342–3349.

LeMaoult, J., Manavalan, J. S., Dyall, R., Szabo, P., Nikolic-Zugic, J., & Weksler, M. E. (1999). Cellular basis of B cell clonal populations in old mice. *Journal of Immunology*, *162*, 6384–6391.

Lio, D., D'Anna, C., Scola, L., Di Lorenzo, G., Colombo, A., Listai, F., et al. (1999). Interleukin-5 production by mononuclear cells from aged individuals: Implication for autoimmunity. *Mechanisms of Ageing and Development*, *106*, 297–304.

Mach, F., Scheonbeck, U., Sukhova, G. K., Bourcier, T., Bonnefoy, J. Y., Pober, J. S., et al. (1997). Functional CD40 ligand is expressed on human vascular endothelial cells, smooth muscle cells, and macrophages: Implications for CD40-CD40 ligand signaling in atherosclerosis. *Proceedings of the National Academy of Sciences of the United States of America*, *94*, 1931–1936.

Maini, M. K., Casorati, G., Dellabona, P., Wack, A., & Beverley, P. C. (1999). T-cell clonality in immune responses. *Immunology Today*, *20*, 262–266.

McLachlan, J. A., Serkin, C. D., Morrey, K. M., & Bakouche, O. (1995). Antitumoral properties of aged human monocytes. *Journal of Immunology*, *154*, 832–843.

Nociari, M. M., Telford, W., & Russo, C. (1999). Postthymic development of CD28-CD8+ T cell subset: Age-associated expansion and shift from memory to naive phenotype. *Journal of Immunology*, *162*, 3327–3335.

Pawelec, G., Akbar, A., Caruso, C., Effros, R. B., Grubeck-Loebenstein, B., & Wikby, A. (in press). Role of persistent Herpes viruses in configuring T cell immunity in the elderly. *Trends in Immunology*.

Plackett, T. P., Boehmer, E. D., Faunce, D. E., & Kovacs, E. J. (2004). Aging and innate immune cells. *Journal of Leukocyte Biology*, *76*, 291–299.

Renshaw, M., Rockwell, J., Engleman, C., Gewirtz, A., Katz, J., & Sambhara, S. (2002). Cutting edge: Impaired Toll-like receptor expression and function in aging. *Journal of Immunology*, *169*, 4697–4701.

Saurwein-Teissl, M., Lung, T. L., Marx, F., Gschosser, C., Asch, E., Blasko, I., et al. (2002). Lack of antibody production following immunization in old age: Association with CD8(+)CD28(−) T cell clonal expansions and an imbalance in the production of Th1 and Th2 cytokines. *Journal of Immunology*, *168*, 5893–5899.

Schmitz, G., Herr, A. S., & Rothe, G. (1998). T-lymphocytes and monocytes in atherogenesis. *Herz*, *23*, 168–177.

Seko, Y., Sato, O., Takagi, A., Tada, Y., Matsuo, H., Yagita, H., et al. (1997). Perforin-secreting killer cell infiltration in the aortic tissue of patients with atherosclerotic aortic aneurysm. *Japanese Circulation Journal*, *61*, 965–970.

Sherwood, E. M., Blomberg, B. B., Xu, W., Warner, C. A., & Riley, R. L. (1998). Senescent BALB/c mice exhibit decreased expression of lambda5 surrogate light chains and reduced development within the pre-B cell compartment. *Journal of Immunology*, *161*, 4472–4475.

Trieb, K., Ransmayr, G., Sgonc, R., Lassmann, H., & Grubeck-Loebenstein, B. (1996). APP peptides stimulate lymphocyte proliferation in normals, but not in patients with Alzheimer's disease. *Neurobiology of Aging*, *17*, 541–547.

Wick, G., & Grubeck-Loebenstein, B. (1997). Primary and secondary alterations of immune reactivity in the elderly: Impact of dietary factors and disease. *Immunological Reviews*, *160*, 171–184.

Xu, Q., Kiechl, S., Mayr, M., Metzler, B., Egger, G., Oberhollenzer, F., et al. (1999). Association of serum antibodies to heat-shock protein 65 with carotid atherosclerosis: Clinical significance determined in a follow-up study [see comments]. *Circulation*, *100*, 1169–1174.

Zheng, B., Han, S., Takahashi, Y., & Kelsoe, G. (1997). Immunosenescence and germinal center reaction. *Immunological Reviews*, *160*, 63–77.

Zissel, G., Schlaak, M., & Meuller-Quernheim, J. (1999). Age-related decrease in accessory cell function of human alveolar macrophages. *Journal of Investigative Medicine*, *47*, 51–56.

IMMUNIZATIONS

Aging and Infection

Aging is associated with an increase in the frequency and severity of a number of infections, including *influenza*, *pneumonia*, *nosocomial infections*, and recrudescent latent infections such as *varicella zoster virus* (*shingles*) (Smith, Roccaforte, & Caly, 1992). Overall, infection is the fifth leading cause of death in elderly Americans. *Immunosenescence*—a state of dysregulated immune function evident with aging—leads to defects in both cellular and humoral immunity and a concomitant increase in the production of inflammatory *cytokines*, and is felt to be an important contributor to this increased risk of infection (Burns & Goodwin, 1997).

Active immunization refers to the ability of the immune system to produce specific antibodies and memory cells in response to stimulation with *antigen*. Unfortunately, *primary prevention of infection* in older individuals is incomplete, even for infections against which a vaccine exists, because response to vaccination requires intact *cell-mediated immunity* to drive the *humoral response* and that is clearly diminished in this population (Burns & Goodwin, 1997). Despite this, several vaccinations have been shown to decrease morbidity and mortality in older persons and are recommended for routine use; much research has focused on strategies to improve the immune response to currently used vaccines and to develop new vaccines against other infections of epidemiologic significance in the older population.

Influenza

Epidemiology. Influenza is an acute *respiratory viral illness* caused by infection with *influenza type A or B virus*. Each year, hundreds of thousands of excess hospitalizations, tens of thousands of excess deaths, and billions of dollars in health care costs can be attributed to influenza and its complications. Although attack rates are highest in the young, morbidity and mortality are highest in the elderly. More than 80% of influenza-associated hospitalization and death occurs in persons older than 65 years (Glezen, Keitel, Taber, et al., 1991).

Influenza Immunization. Influenza vaccination represents the safest, most cost-effective means of prevention of morbidity and mortality from the influenza virus. Current guidelines recommend the use of influenza vaccine yearly in all individuals older than 65 years, all residents of long-term care facilities, children or adults with chronic pulmonary or cardiovascular illness, children requiring chronic *aspirin therapy*, and women who are pregnant during influenza season. A *yearly influenza vaccine* is also recommended for health care workers, employees of long-term care facilities who come in contact with patients, and home care providers or household contacts of high-risk individuals.

At present, an injectable, *trivalent (influenza A H1N1, H3N2, and influenza B), inactivated vaccine* is used. This vaccine has been shown to reduce the incidence of confirmed influenza, influenza-like illness, all respiratory infections, exacerbations of cardiopulmonary disease, hospitalization, and death in both community-dwelling elderly and in residents of long-term care facilities (Gross, Quinnan, Rodstein, LaMontagne, Kaslow, Saah, et al., 1988). Although the vaccine has only 30% to 40% efficacy in preventing *influenza infection in residents of long-term care facilities*, severe illness, hospitalization, and death are significantly reduced (Gross, Quinnan, Rodstein, LaMontagne, Kaslow, Saah, et al., 1988; Bradley, 1999). High vaccination rates among residents reduce the chances of an outbreak occurring in a long-term care facility significantly, and should an outbreak occur, vaccination will decrease hospitalizations by 50% to 60% and mortality by as much as 80% (Gross, Quinnan, Rodstein, LaMontagne, Kaslow, Saah, et al., 1988).

Because the influenza vaccine provides incomplete protection in older adults, it is important that efforts be made to reduce exposure to the virus. *Immunization of health care workers in long-term care facilities* has been shown to reduce the risk of *influenza outbreaks* (Stevenson, McArthur, Naus, Abraham, & McGeer, 2001) and to decrease all-cause mortality and pneumonia-associated mortality among residents (Potter, Stott, Roberts, Elder, O'Donnell, Knight, & Carman, 1997). In fact, the beneficial effect of immunizing staff exceeds the benefit of immunizing residents and is, therefore, critical to the reduction of influenza-associated morbidity and mortality in this high-risk group (Potter, Stott, Roberts, Elder, O'Donnell, Knight, & Carman, 1997). A newly developed but not yet licensed *cold-adapted, live-attenuated trivalent intranasal influenza vaccine* has been shown to increase serum, mucosal, and cell-mediated immunity when given in combination with the currently available intramuscular vaccine and may represent a future strategy for increasing protection from influenza in older adults.

Streptococcus Pneumoniae

Epidemiology. Streptococcus pneumoniae is the leading bacterial cause of *meningitis* and *pneumonia* in the United States, resulting in 175,000 hospitalizations and up to 12,500 deaths annually (Centers for Disease Control and Prevention, 1997). The elderly, the very young, the immunocompromised and persons who smoke are at increased risk of *pneumococcal disease*. Rates of pneumococcal pneumonia, bacteremia, and mortality all increase with advancing age and S. *pneumoniae* is the leading bacterial cause of infection among residents of long-term care facilities (Centers for Disease Control and Prevention, 1997). The case-fatality rate for invasive pneumococcal disease is approximately 20% for those aged 65 years or older and as high as 40% for those aged 85 and older (Centers for Disease Control and Prevention, 1997).

Pneumococcal Immunization. Given the increased rate of pneumococcal infection and its associated morbidity, mortality, and cost in older adults, the National Advisory Committee on Immunization (NACI) in Canada and the Advisory Committee on Immunization Practices (ACIP) in the United States recommend universal pneumococcal vaccination for persons older than 65 years. Despite these recommendations, controversy exists over the efficacy of *polysaccharide pneumococcal vaccine* (PPV). Many physicians still doubt the vaccine confers meaningful protection on older persons for whom it is primarily indicated, a factor contributing to the suboptimal vaccination rates seen in most studies. Observational studies have demonstrated that the 23-valent PPV is 50% to 70% effective in preventing invasive pneumococcal disease in older adults (Centers for Disease Control and Prevention, 1997; Shapiro, Berg, Austrian, Schroeder, Parcells, Margolis, Adair, & Clemens, 1991). Based upon this reduction in invasive disease, universal immunization of persons over age 65 with PPV has been shown to be cost-effective and even, in some studies, provide cost savings (Ament, Baltussen, Duru, Rigaud-Bully, de Graeve, Ortqvist, et al., 2000; Sisk, Moskowitz, Whang, Lin, Fedson, McBean, et al., 1997). Unfortunately, the impact of PPV on other outcomes, most notably all-cause *community-acquired pneumonia* and *pneumonia-associated mortality*, has not been seen. Five published meta-analyses have confirmed the protective efficacy of PPV against invasive disease but have failed to demonstrate reduction in the incidence of non-bacteremic pneumonia or death in adults over age 65 receiving PPV (Fine, Smith, Carson, Meffe, Sankey, Weissfeld, et al., 1994; Hutchison, Oxman, Shannon, Lloyd, Altmayer, & Thomas, 1999; Moore, Wiffen, & Lipsky, 2000; Cornu, Yzèbe, Léophonte, Gaillat, Boissel, & Cucherat, 2001; Watson, Wilson, & Waugh, 2002).

Conjugate pneumococcal vaccines, in which pneumococcal polysaccharide antigens are covalently linked to immunogenic carrier proteins, offer several potential advantages over PPV in older adults. Conjugation of *polysaccharide antigens* to proteins results in stimulation of a T-cell dependent immune response, leading to the induction of memory B cells and an improved B cell response when compared to polysaccharide antigen administration alone. Despite the obvious potential benefits of pneumococcal conjugate vaccines and the clinical and public health need for more effective pneumococcal vaccines in older adults, few studies have examined the immunogenicity of pneumococcal conjugate vaccines in this population (Powers, Anderson, Lottenbach, & Mink, 1996; Shelly, Jacoby, Riley, Graves, Pichichero, & Treanor, 1997). Improved response to pneumococcal conjugate vaccines has been demonstrated in otherwise healthy adults who fail to mount a response to PPV (Musher, et al. 1998; Zielen, Buhring, Strnad, Reichenbach, & Hofmann, 2000), in renal transplant recipients (Kumar, Rotstein, Miyata, Arlen, & Humar, 2003) and in patients with Hodgkin disease (Chan, Molrine, George, Tarbell, Mauch, Diller, et al., 1996).

Conjugate pneumococcal vaccines represent the most promising new advance in the prevention of morbidity, mortality, and cost associated with pneumococcal infections among older adults. Robust data on the immunogenicity of conjugate vaccines and the ability of conjugate vaccines to prime the immune system prior to a booster dose of PPV are urgently needed. Ongoing vaccine development efforts should focus on the development of adult-specific conjugate vaccines with broader serotype representation based upon adult *seroepidemiology*.

Tetanus and *Diphtheria Vaccines*

Although rare in the United States, the risk of *tetanus* and tetanus-associated mortality increases with advancing age, probably due to waning immunity following the primary vaccination series in childhood (Bardenheier, Prevots, Khetsuriani, & Wharton, 1998). A serologic survey in the United States revealed that the prevalence of *tetanus immunity* was 28% among persons older than age 70 compared to 80% among younger people (Gergen, McQuillin, Kiely, et al., 1995). Universal immunization with *diphtheria toxoid* in the United States has virtually eliminated diphtheria. More than 90% of cases of diphtheria occur in adults susceptible to infection because of waning immunity, lack of exposure to diphtheria, and failure to receive booster immunizations. Protection of adults from tetanus and diphtheria can be achieved by the administration of *tetanus-diphtheria toxoid* (Td); following the primary series in childhood, all adults should receive a Td booster every 10 years. Wound prophylaxis with Td should be given if the primary series is incomplete or the last booster was more than 10 years prior.

Because there is mounting evidence that the incidence of *pertussis* is increasing in adults and that adults may serve as a reservoir for infection in susceptible children, the routine *Td booster* in adults may be replaced with new adult-formulation combined *Td acellular pertussis* (Tdap) vaccines in the future (Campins-Marti, Cheng, Forsyth, et al., 2001). Studies assessing the safety and immunogenicity of Tdap in older adults, as well as detailed evaluation of age-specific morbidity and health care use associated with pertussis in adults of all ages, are critical to inform policy decision-making on the different potential targeted and universal adult acellular pertussis vaccination strategies.

Varicella Zoster Virus Vaccine

Varicella immunization is recommended for all adults who have no history of primary varicella infection (*chickenpox*). *Varicella vaccine* has been shown to boost cell-mediated immunity to varicella zoster virus in older persons (Levin, Barber, Goldblatt, Jones, et al., 1998). Because *herpes zoster* (*shingles*) occurs with increasing frequency as people age, probably owing largely to waning immunity, it is hoped that boosting of the immune response against varicella zoster virus by immunizing older adults with varicella vaccine will reduce the frequency and severity of shingles and its associated complications, particularly *post-herpetic neuralgia*. Results of a large-efficacy trial of varicella vaccine in 37,000 persons older than age 60 are expected soon.

SHELLY A. MCNEIL

See also
Immune System
Influenza

References

Ament, A., Baltussen, R., Duru, G., de Rigaud-Bully, C., de Graeve, D., Ortqvist, A., Jonsson, B., Verhaegen, J., Gaillat, J., Christie, P., Cifre, A. S., Vivas, D., Loiseau, C., & Fedson, D. S. (2000). Cost-effectiveness of pneumococcal vaccination of older people: A study in 5 western European countries. *Clinical Infectious Diseases*, *31*, 444–450.

Bardenheier, B., Prevots, D. R., Khetsuriani, N., & Wharton, M. (1998). Tetanus surveillance—United States, 1995–1997. *Morbidity and Mortality Weekly Report*, *47*, 1–13.

Bradley, S. F., et al. (1999). Prevention of influenza in long term care facilities. *Infection Control and Hospital Epidemiology*, *20*, 629–637.

Burns, E. A., & Goodwin, J. S. (1997). Immunodeficiency of aging. *Drugs and Aging*, *5*, 374–397.

Campins-Marti, M., Cheng, H. K., Forsyth, K., et al. (2001). International consensus group on pertussis immunization: Rationale and strategies for consideration. *Vaccine*, *20*, 641–646.

Centers for Disease Control and Prevention. (1997). Prevention of pneumococcal disease: Recommendations of the Advisory Committee on Immunization Practices (ACIP). *Morbidity and Mortality Weekly Report*, *46*(RR-08), 1–24.

Chan, C. Y., Molrine, D. C., George, S., Tarbell, N. J., Mauch, P., Diller, L., Shamberger, R. C., Phillips, N. R., Goorin, A., & Ambrosino, D. M. (1996). Pneumococcal conjugate vaccine primes for antibody responses to polysaccharide pneumococcal vaccine after treatment of Hodgkin's disease. *Journal of Infectious Diseases*, *173*, 256–258.

Cornu, C., Yzèbe, D., Léophonte, P., Gaillat, J., Boissel, J. P., & Cucherat, M. (2001). Efficacy of pneumococcal polysaccharide vaccine in immunocompetent adults: A meta-analysis of randomized trials. *Vaccine*, *19*, 4780–4790.

Fine, M. J., Smith, M. A., Carson, C. A., Meffe, F., Sankey, S. S., Weissfeld, L. A., et al. (1994). Efficacy of pneumococcal vaccination in adults. A meta-analysis of randomized controlled trials. *Archives of Internal Medicine*, *134*, 2666–2677.

Gergen, P. J., McQuillin, G. M., Kiely, M., et al. (1995). A population-based serologic survey of immunity to tetanus in the United States. *New England Journal of Medicine*, *332*, 761–766.

Glezen, W. P., Keitel, W. A., Taber, L. H., et al. (1991). Age distribution of patients with medically-attended illnesses caused by sequential variants of influenza A/H1N1: Comparison to age-specific infection rates, 1978–1989. *American Journal of Epidemiology*, *133*, 296–304.

Gross, P. A., Quinnan, G. V., Rodstein, M., LaMontagne, J. R., Kaslow, R. A., Saah, A. J., et al. (1988). Association of influenza immunization with reduction in mortality in an elderly population. A prospective study. *Archives of Internal Medicine*, *148*, 562–565.

Hutchison, B. G., Oxman, A. D., Shannon, H. S., Lloyd, S., Altmayer, C. A., & Thomas, K. (1999). Clinical effectiveness of pneumococcal vaccine. Meta-analysis. *Canadian Family Physician*, *45*, 2381–2393.

Kumar, D., Rotstein, C., Miyata, G., Arlen, D., & Humar, A. (2003). Randomized, double-blind, controlled trial of pneumococcal vaccination in renal transplant recipients. *Journal of Infectious Diseases*, *187*, 1639–1645.

Levin, M. J., Barber, D., Goldblatt, E., Jones, M., et al. (1998). Use of a live attenuated varicella vaccine to boost varicella-specific immune responses in seropositive people 55 years of age and older: Duration of booster effect. *Journal of Infectious Diseases*, *178*(Suppl. 2), S109–S112.

Moore, R. A., Wiffen, P. J., & Lipsky, B. A. (2000). Are the pneumococcal polysaccharide vaccines effective? Meta-analysis of the prospective trials. *BMC Family Practice*, *1*, 1.

Musher, et al. (1998). IgG responses to PCV in persons who are genetically incapable to responding to unconjugated polysaccharides. *Clinical Infectious Diseases*, *27*, 1487–1490.

Potter, J., Stott, D. J., Roberts, M. A., Elder, A. G., O'Donnell, B., Knight, P. V., & Carman, W. F. (1997). Influenza vaccination of health care workers in long-term-care hospitals reduces the mortality of elderly patients. *Journal of Infectious Diseases*, *175*, 1–6.

Powers, D. C., Anderson, E. L., Lottenbach, K., & Mink, C. M. (1996). Reactogenicity and immunogenicity of a protein-conjugated pneumococcal oligosaccharide vaccine in older adults. *Journal of Infectious Diseases*, *183*, 1014–1018.

Prevention and control of influenza: Recommendations of the Advisory Committee on Immunization Practices. (1998). *Morbidity and Mortality Weekly Report*, *47*(R-6), 1–26.

Shapiro, E. D., Berg, A. T., Austrian, R., Schroeder, D., Parcells, V., Margolis, A., Adair, R. K., & Clemens, J. D. (1991). The protective efficacy of polyvalent pneumococcal polysaccharide vaccine. *New England Journal of Medicine*, *325*, 1453–1460.

Shelly, M. A., Jacoby, H., Riley, G. J., Graves, B. T., Pichichero, M., & Treanor, J. J. (1997). Comparison of pneumococcal polysaccharide and CRM197-conjugated pneumococcal oligosaccharide vaccines in young and elderly adults. *Infection and Immunity*, *65*, 242–247.

Sisk. J. E., Moskowitz, A. J., Whang, W., Lin, J. D., Fedson, D. S., McBean, A. M., Plouffe, J. F., Cetron, M. S., & Butler, J. C. (1997). Cost-effectiveness of vaccination against pneumococcal bacteremia among elderly people. *Journal of the American Medical Association*, *278*, 1333–1339.

Smith, P. W., Roccaforte, J. S., & Caly, P. B. (1992). Infection and immune response in the elderly. *Annals of Epidemiology*, *2*, 813–822.

Stevenson, C. G., McArthur, M. A., Naus, M., Abraham, E., & McGeer, A. (2001). Prevention of influenza and pneumococcal pneumonia in Canadian Long Term Care Facilities: How are we doing? *Canadian Medical Association Journal*, *164*, 1413–1419.

Watson, L., Wilson, B. J., & Waugh, N. (2002). Pneumococcal polysaccharide vaccine: A systematic review of clinical effectiveness in adults. *Vaccine*, *20*, 2166–2173.

Zielen, S., Buhring, I., Strnad, N., Reichenbach, J., & Hofmann, D. (2000). Immunogenicity and tolerance of a 7-valent pneumococcal conjugate vaccine in nonresponders to the 23-valent pneumococcal vaccine. *Infection and Immunity*, *68*, 1435–1440.

IMPLICIT MEMORY AND LEARNING

Implicit memory occurs when performance reveals the effects of prior experiences (usually individual items or events), even in the absence of conscious recollection of those experiences. *Implicit learning* refers to acquiring information about the structural properties of relations among objects or events in the absence of either the intent to learn, or the awareness of what has been learned. Implicit forms of learning and memory differ from their explicit counterparts in that they obey different principles of operation, rely on distinct brain areas, are differentially sensitive to brain injury, and serve different functions (Frensch & Ruenger, 2003). For example, although being distracted during an initial encounter with a stimulus usually hurts explicit memory for that stimulus, it often does not hurt implicit memory. And although patients suffering from *amnesia* have profound impairments of *explicit memory* and learning, their performance on some implicit tests is often indistinguishable from that of healthy controls. Because implicit memory and learning differ from each other in important ways, they are considered in turn below.

Implicit Memory

Explicit tests of memory require conscious recollection. Explicit memory is called upon when people attempt to recall an event from their childhood, to *recall* which words occurred on a list encountered in the laboratory, or to decide whether or not a particular word or face occurred in a particular context. In all these cases, memory requires that the person be aware that some event occurred in the past. In contrast, implicit tests do not require such conscious recollection, such awareness of remembering. For example, implicit memory for a word is demonstrated if that word is read more rapidly on its second presentation than its first, even in the absence of explicit memory for the earlier encounter; such facilitation is called priming.

Typically, to compare implicit and explicit memory, researchers attempt to hold all aspects of a *memory test* constant, varying only the kind of instructions people are given at the time of the test. For example, people might first encounter a list of words (e.g., PROPANE) during an initial presentation period, and then later they would be given a memory test in which word stems are presented (e.g., PRO_). For an explicit test, people would be asked to complete the stems to form words that had been presented in the original list (word-stem cued recall), but for an implicit test, they would be asked to complete the stems to form the first words that come to mind (word-stem completion). Implicit memory for the earlier list would be inferred if people complete the stems to form words from the earlier list (e.g., PROPANE) more often than they do in a control condition in which the words had not been encountered earlier.

Of course, *implicit tests* can be influenced by conscious recollection, as when people who are told to complete the stems with "the first word that comes to mind" nonetheless attempt to complete them to form words they studied earlier. And explicit tests can be influenced by unconscious memory, as when people think they are guessing on a *cued recall test*, but their earlier encounter with a stimulus leads them (unknowingly) to "guess" it correctly. To overcome these complications, Hay and colleagues have introduced a *process-dissociation procedure* in which recollective (explicit) and automatic (implicit) components of memory are distinguished, not by comparing implicit and explicit tests, but rather by pitting them against each other in a single task (1999).

Dissociations between implicit and explicit memory occur in the course of healthy aging (Fleischman & Gabrieli, 1998; Light, Prull, LaVoie, & Healy, 2000; Prull, Gabrieli, & Bunge, 2000). Although substantial age-related deficits occur on almost all *explicit tests of memory*, age differences are usually smaller or absent on implicit tests. These small age-related deficits on implicit tests might be due to true age-related changes in some implicit memory processes that occur for most individuals, to deficits in a small proportion of older people who are in the early stages of as-yet undiagnosed dementia, or to the undetected influence of *conscious recollection*. Evidence favoring the latter interpretation comes from studies using the *process dissociation procedure*, and also from studies in which explicit contamination is monitored rigorously (Mitchell & Bruss, 2003) and brain correlates such as ERPs and fMRI offer converging evidence (Lustig & Buckner, 2004; Wegesin, Ream, & Stern, 2004).

The limits of this relative *age-constancy of implicit memory* remain unclear. There are many different memory implicit tasks, and although there is as yet no agreed upon taxonomy nor an adequate theoretical account, it is clear that these tasks do not all tap the same underlying cognitive processes. Some *implicit tests of memory* require that new associations be formed, whereas others do not. Some implicit tests seem to reflect the continuing activation of perceptual processes, whereas others are more conceptually based, reflecting the activation of a conceptually or semantically organized memory. So far, there is no consistent evidence that any of these categories of implicit memory are more likely than others to be impaired by healthy aging (Light, Prull, LaVoie, & Healy, 2000).

Implicit Learning

Implicit forms of learning are at least as diverse as their implicit memory counterparts. Implicit learning, which is often called *procedural learning*, includes *classical conditioning*, *skill learning* (of both cognitive and motor skills), learning of *stimulus covariations*, *sequence learning*, learning of *artificial grammars*, and learning in control of complex systems. As in the case of memory, it is difficult to separate implicit from explicit learning, because both often occur simultaneously. To make generalizations yet more difficult, the *aging of implicit learning* has been studied less than that of implicit memory. So far, some types of implicit learning have revealed age-related deficits, at least under certain conditions, whereas others have not. For example, classical conditioning is reduced in older people, and implicit learning of sequential patterns also shows age-related deficits when the patterns are complex and subtle. In contrast, the learning of spatial contexts and simultaneous covariations appears to be spared in healthy aging (Howard, Howard, Dennis, Yankovich, & Vaidya, 2004; Schmitter-Edgecombe & Nissley, 2002; Woodruff-Pak & Jaeger, 1998). These different patterns of aging for various forms of implicit learning likely reflect differential aging of their underlying neural substrates.

Implications

In general, research on the aging of implicit memory and learning serves as a reminder that implicit processes differ, calling on different cognitive and neural systems. Therefore, it is not possible to make general statements about the aging of all implicit processes. Nonetheless, even though implicit forms of learning and memory are not completely spared the ravages of age, at least some forms do seem to be less severely impaired than most forms of explicit learning.

The demonstration of the relative *age-constancy of implicit memory* and learning has presented new challenges for theories of *cognitive aging*, and has encouraged researchers to compare the patterns of savings and loss seen in amnesia, healthy aging, and dementia, such as Alzheimer's disease. The relative sparing of some forms of implicit memory and learning also is important for everyday life, because implicit processes exert subtle, usually unnoticed, influences on common activities. For example, implicit memory affects the likelihood that particular ideas will come to mind. It also affects the meaning people assign to stimuli they encounter. Implicit learning and memory influence the ease and accuracy with which people perceive external stimuli, as well as the preferences, impressions, and stereotypes they form. Implicit learning is involved in adapting to new environments and people, in learning the syntax of unfamiliar languages, and in learning to use new technologies such as computers. In addition, the fact that some forms of implicit memory and learning are relatively age-constant suggests that they take on an even more central role, compared to explicit forms, as people get older. This relative age-constancy also implies that the effectiveness of cognitive interventions might be improved if memory remediation programs for healthy older persons, as well as for amnesia and dementia patients, attempted to build on implicit memory, and if rehabilitation programs for stroke victims took advantage of relatively preserved implicit learning abilities.

DARLENE V. HOWARD

References

Fleischman, D. A., & Gabrieli, J. D. (1998). Repetition priming in normal aging and Alzheimer's disease: A review of findings and theories. *Psychology and Aging, 13*, 88–119.

Frensch, P. A., & Ruenger, D. (2003). Implicit learning. *Current Directions in Psychological Science, 12*, 13–18.

Hay, J. F., & Jacoby, L. L. (1999). Separating habit and recollection in young and older adults: Effects of elaborative processing and distinctiveness. *Psychology and Aging, 14*, 122–134.

Howard, J. H., Jr., Howard, D. V., Dennis, N. A., Yankovich, H., & Vaidya, C. J. (2004). Implicit spatial contextual learning in healthy aging. *Neuropsychology, 18*, 124–134.

Light, L. L., Prull, M. W., LaVoie, D. J., & Healy, M. R. (2000). Dual-process theories of memory in old age. In T. J. Perfect & E. A. Maylor (Eds.), *Models of cognitive aging* (pp. 238–300). Oxford: Oxford University Press.

Lustig, C., & Buckner, R. L. (2004). Preserved neural correlates of priming in old age and dementia. *Neuron, 42*, 865–875.

Mitchell, D. B., & Bruss, P. J. (2003). Age differences in implicit memory: Conceptual, perceptual, or methodological? *Psychology and Aging, 18*, 807–822.

Prull, M. W., Gabrieli, J. D. E., & Bunge, S. A. (2000). Age-related changes in memory: A cognitive neuroscience perspective. In F. I. M. Craik & T. A. Salthouse (Eds.), *Handbook of aging and cognition* (2nd ed.). Mahwah, NJ: Lawrence Erlbaum.

Schmitter-Edgecombe, M., & Nissley, H. M. (2002). Effects of aging on implicit covariation learning. *Aging Neuropsychology and Cognition, 9*, 61–75.

Wegesin, D. J., Ream, J. M., & Stern, Y. (2004). Explicit contamination contributes to aging effects in episodic priming: Behavioral and ERP evidence. *Journals of Gerontology B: Psychological Sciences and Social Sciences, 59*, P317–P324.

Woodruff-Pak, D. S., & Jaeger, M. E. (1998). Predictors of eyeblink classical conditioning over the adult age span. *Psychology and Aging, 13*, 193–205.

INDIVIDUAL RETIREMENT ARRANGEMENTS (IRAs)

An individual retirement arrangement—commonly known as *individual retirement account*, with the same acronym IRA—is a tax-favored saving and investment mechanism for individuals and their spouses intended to encourage people to save to supplement Social Security and employment-based pensions for their retirement years.

There are several types of IRAs. The *Employee Retirement Income Security Act* of 1974 (ERISA) created the traditional *IRAs*, and the *Revenue Act of 1978* created *employer-sponsored IRAs* (*SEP IRAs*). The *Tax Reform Act of 1986* created *SAR-SEP IRAs*. The *Small Business Job Protection Act* of 1996 created *SIMPLE IRAs*. Finally, the *Taxpayer Relief Act of 1997* created *Roth IRAs*.[1]

For *deductible IRAs*, a maximum of $3,000 for 2002–2004 (to increase to $4,000 for 2005–2007, and to $5,000 for 2008, with adjustments for inflation thereafter of $500 increments) of earned income per year may be deducted by each person under age 70 1/2, if neither the person nor the spouse actively participates in an employer-sponsored retirement plan (employer plan). A nonworking spouse may also contribute the deductible IRA limit if the couple has earned income of at least the combined contributed amount. If the person is a participant in an employer plan, the maximum deductible amount is phased out (for the year 2004) between adjusted gross income (AGI) of $45,000 to $55,000 for single taxpayers and between $65,000 to $75,000 for married couples filing a joint return. The *Economic Growth and Tax Reconciliation Act* of 2001 permitted additional *"catch-up contribution" amounts* for those aged 50 or older of $500 per year for 2002–2005, and of $1,000 per year for 2006 and thereafter. Under the 2001 act, these AGI phase-out limits are scheduled to increase in 2005 and thereafter to $50,000 to $60,000 for single taxpayers, and in 2007 to $80,000 to $100,000 for married filing jointly.

For traditional nondeductible IRAs, there are no income limits. However, the maximum limit on annual contributions (of earned income) applies to a person's combined IRAs (plus the spouse's eligible amount). Earnings on a traditional nondeductible IRA are not taxable until withdrawn. Amounts in a deductible IRA, including earnings, are not taxable until withdrawn.

For Roth IRAs, contributions are not deductible and earnings are not currently taxable. Earnings withdrawn from Roth IRAs are tax-free if the amounts remain in the account for at least 5 years and beyond age 59 1/2. The maximum annual contribution amount for a Roth IRA is phased out for single taxpayers with AGI between $95,000 and $110,000 and for married couples filing a joint return with AGI between $150,000 and $160,000.

All taxable *withdrawals from an IRA* are taxed as ordinary income in the year withdrawn. Taxable withdrawals from an IRA prior to *age 59 1/2* (except for death or disability) are generally subject to an additional 10% *early withdrawal tax*. However, certain withdrawals are not subject to the additional tax: periodic payments (e.g., an annuity); for medical expenses of the person or spouse or dependents in excess of 7.5% of AGI; for medical insurance of certain unemployed persons (and spouse and dependents); for qualified education expenses; and for first-time homebuyer expenditures up to $10,000.

IRA assets are similar to defined contribution pension plan assets. Thus, the individual is subject to the risk of gains and losses on the IRA investments. IRA amounts generally may be invested as the individuals decide, except that IRAs may not be invested in life insurance or collectibles (other than certain coins). Also, IRAs generally may not be invested in assets in which the IRA owner has an interest. IRAs cannot accept amounts in excess of the annual limit, except for amounts "rolled over" from another IRA or pension plan.

[1] The 1997 Act also created special savings accounts, originally called *Education IRAs*, which are now known as *Coverdell Education Savings Accounts* (*ESAs*), whereby taxpayers may contribute up to $2,000 per year (for a child under age 18 when the account is established) to such savings accounts for college education expenses and may withdraw the savings tax-free if used for qualified college expenses. The ESA contribution amount is nondeductible, and is phased out for taxpayers with modified adjusted gross between $95,000 and $110,000 for single taxpayers and between $190,000 and $220,000 for married couples filing joint returns.

TABLE 1 Participation in Deductible IRAs, 1979–1996

Year	Returns claiming IRA deduction (Millions)	Percentage of all returns	Deductions claimed ($ Billions)
1979	2.5	2.6%	3.2
1980	2.6	2.7	3.4
1981	3.4	3.6	4.8
1982	12.0	12.6	28.3
1983	13.6	14.1	32.1
1984	15.2	15.3	35.4
1985	16.2	15.9	37.8
1986	15.5	15.1	38.2
1987	7.3	6.8	14.1
1988	6.4	5.8	11.9
1989	5.8	5.2	10.8
1990	5.2	4.6	9.9
1991	4.7	4.1	9.0
1992	4.5	3.9	8.7
1993	4.4	3.8	8.5
1994	4.3	3.7	8.4
1995	4.3	3.6	8.3
1996	4.4	3.6	8.6

Source: Internal Revenue Service, *Statistics of income* (various years) and Joint Committee on Taxation, U.S. Congress, *Present Law and Background Relating to Tax Incentives for Savings* (JCX-7-99), February 23, 1999.

When the IRA holder reaches age 70 1/2, a minimum percentage of the amount in the IRA (other than for a Roth IRA) must be withdrawn each year, based on the life expectancy of the IRA holder or the joint life expectancy of the IRA holder and spouse. IRA holders may recalculate their life expectancies annually and adjust withdrawals accordingly.

Participation in IRAs

Taxpayer participation in IRAs increased dramatically in 1982–1986, after the 1981 legislation to permit persons in employer plans to also have deductible IRAs (Table 1). The percentage of tax returns claiming IRA deductions increased from 2.6% in 1979 to a peak of 15.9% in 1985. After 1986 legislation limited IRA eligibility rules, participation in IRAs declined to 6.8% in 1987 and to 3.6% in 1996. *Deductions claimed for IRAs* increased dramatically from $3.2 billion in 1979 to $28.3 billion in 1982, after the 1981 legislation, and increased further each year until a peak of $38.2 billion in 1986. IRA deductions declined sharply to $14.1 billion in 1987, with further declines each year to $8.3 billion in 1995.

Subsequently, deductible IRAs were claimed on 3.9% of individual returns in 1999, 4.6% in 2000, and 4.5% in 2001, with IRA deductions totaling $7.9 billion in 1999, $7.5 billion in 2000, and $7.4 billion in 2001 (Sailer & Holden, 2004).

Participation in deductible IRAs tends to increase as taxpayers' income rises. Tables 2 and 3 show the relative participation in IRAs by AGI class for 1985 and 1996, respectively. In 1985, the percentage of tax returns reporting IRA contributions was 2.3% for AGI under $10,000, rising to 76.1% for AGI over $100,000. Data for 1996 tax returns showed a marked difference in relative participation in IRAs by AGI class. The percentage of tax returns with earned income reporting IRA contributions was 1.1% for AGI under $10,000. It rose to 6.9% for AGI between $30,000 and $50,000, dropped to 3.5% for AGI between $50,000 to $75,000, and then increased to 6.6% for AGI over $100,000.

Under a *graduated income tax*, the amount of taxes saved (resulting from tax deduction for IRA contributions and tax deferral for IRA earnings) increases as the income tax rate bracket increases. For example, for the tax year 2005, a taxpayer in the 15% tax bracket will save $600 in tax on a $4,000 IRA

TABLE 2 Deductible IRA Participation by AGI Class, 1985

	Returns reporting IRA contributions		
AGI class	Number (Millions)	Percent of eligible returns	Amount of contributions ($ Billions)
Under $10,000	0.6	2.3%	1.1
$10,000 to $30,000	5.1	13.6	9.7
$30,000 to $50,000	5.7	32.9	13.5
$50,000 to $75,000	3.0	56.5	8.7
$75,000 to $100,000	0.9	74.1	2.7
Over $100,000	0.8	76.1	2.6
All AGI classes	16.2	17.8	38.2

Source: Internal Revenue Service, *1985 Statistics of Income*, and Joint Committee on Taxation, *Ibid.*

TABLE 3 Deductible IRA Participation by AGI Class, 1996

	Returns reporting IRA contributions		
AGI class	Number (Millions)	Percent of returns with earned income	Contributions ($ Billions)
Under $10,000	0.3	1.1%	0.4
$10,000 to $30,000	1.6	4.3	2.8
$30,000 to $50,000	1.4	6.9	2.4
$50,000 to $75,000	0.5	3.5	1.1
$75,000 to $100,000	0.2	4.5	0.7
Over $100,000	0.4	6.6	1.1
All AGI classes	4.4	4.1	8.6

Source: Internal Revenue Service, *1996 Statistics of Income*, and Joint Committee on Taxation, *Ibid.*

TABLE 4 IRA Assets by Types, End of Year Value, 1997–2001 ($ billions)

Type of IRA	1997	1998	1999	2000	2001
Traditional	1,637.0	1,975.0	2,417.5	2,406.6	2,394.9
SEP	84.7	115.4	146.1	134.0	131.4
SIMPLE	0.6	2.8	7.1	10.4	13.6
Roth	—	44.2	74.2	77.6	79.3
Educational	—	0.1	0.2	0.3	0.2
Totals	**1,722.4**	**2,150.1**	**2,651.2**	**2,628.9**	**2,619.4**

Source: Sailer, P., & Holden, S. (2004). Use of individual retirement arrangements to save for retirement—Results from a matched file of tax returns and information documents for tax year 2001. Presented at the 2004 American Statistical Association Meetings. Sailer, P., Gurka, K., & Holden, S. (2003). Accumulations and distributions of retirement assets, 1996–2000. Results from a matched file of tax returns and information letters. Presented at the 2003 American Statistical Association Meetings. Sailer, P., & Nutter, S. E. (2004, July). Accumulation and distribution of individual retirement arrangements, 2000. Statistics of income spring bulletin. Internal Revenue Service.

TABLE 5 Fair Market Value of all IRAs, by Age of Taxpayer, 2000

Age	Amount ($ Billions)	Percentage	Average ($)
Under 30	$14.5	0.55	$4,541
30–39	138.5	5.27	18,536
40–49	410.7	15.62	36,613
50–59	700.2	26.63	64,701
60–69	835.9	31.79	106,044
70+	529.4	20.14	93,144

Source: Sailer, P., Gurka, K., & Holden, S. (2003). Accumulations and distributions of retirement assets, 1996–2000. Results from a matched file of tax returns and information letters. Presented at the 2003 American Statistical Association Meetings.

deduction, and a taxpayer in the 28% tax bracket will save $1,120 in tax.

Participation in all IRAs in 2001 generally increased as incomes rose: 3.8% of eligible taxpayers with AGI under $25,000; 8.7% for AGI between $25,000 to $50,000; to 11.5% for AGI between $50,000 to $75,000; 14.6% for AGI between $75,000 to $100,000; 20.7% for AGI between $100,000 to $200,000; 21.1% for AGI between $200,000 to $500,000; and 20.5% for AGI between $500,000 to $1,000,000; participation is 16.9% for AGI of $1,000,000 and above (Sailer & Holden, 2004).

Participation in all IRAs in 2001 generally increased by age (up to 64): 2.6% for ages under 20; 4.3% for ages 20 to 24; 8.0% for ages 25 to 34; 9.6% for ages 35 to 44; 12.2% for ages 45 to 54; 14.6% for ages 55 to 64; 11.8% for ages 65 to 70; and declining to 2.3% for age 70 and older (due to the mandatory distribution rule beginning at age 70 1/2) (Sailer & Holden, 2004).

IRA Assets

As shown in Table 4, the fair market value of all IRAs increased from $1.72 trillion in 1997 to $2.15 trillion in 1998 and $2.65 trillion in 1999, before declining slightly (due to lower stock market valuations) to $2.63 trillion in 2000 and to $2.62 trillion in 2001. Traditional IRAs increased from $1.64 trillion in 1997, to $1.97 trillion in 1998 and $2.42 trillion in 1999, and also declined slightly to $2.41 trillion in 2000 and to $2.39 trillion in 2001. Roth IRAs increased in asset value from $44.2 billion in 1998, to $74.2 billion in 1999, $77.6 billion in 2000, and $79.3 billion in 2001, due to increased popularity of Roth IRAs. In 2001, traditional IRAs represented 91.4% of the asset value of all IRAs; Roth IRAs accounted for 3% of IRA asset value; and education (Coverdell) IRAs were a negligible amount and percentage. SEP and SIMPLE IRAs accounted for 5.5% of the total IRA asset value in 2001.

As indicated in Table 5, the fair market value of all IRA assets in 2000 generally increased with age (up to age 70): $14.5 billion for under age 30; $138.5 billion for ages 30 to 39; $410.7 billion for ages 40 to 49; $700.2 billion for ages 50 to 59; $835.9 billion for ages 60 to 69; and $529.4 billion for age 70 and older.

LEON W. KLUD
Updated by YUNG-PING CHEN

References

Sailer, P., & Holden, S. (2004). Use of individual retirement arrangements to save for retirement—Results from a matched file of tax returns and information documents for tax year 2001. Presented at the 2004 American Statistical Association Meetings.

Sailer, P., Gurka, K., & Holden, S. (2003). Accumulations and distributions of retirement assets, 1996–2000. Results from a matched file of tax returns and information letters. Presented at the 2003 American Statistical Association Meetings.

Sailer, P., Weber, M. J., & Gurka, K. S. (2002). Are taxpayers increasing the buildup of retirement assets? Preliminary results from a matched file of tax year 1999 tax returns and information returns. Paper presented at the 2002 National Tax Association Proceedings: Federal Tax Issues: Recent Research at IRS.

Sailer, P., & Nutter, S. E. (2004, July). Accumulation and distribution of individual retirement arrangements,

2000. *Statistics of income spring bulletin*. Internal Revenue Service.

INDUSTRIAL GERONTOLOGY

Industrial gerontology is the *study of aging and work*, focusing on the adaptation of middle-aged and older workers to employment and their transition to retirement. Major areas include career progressions and development, succession planning, motivational factors and organizational design, job design and redesign, training and retraining, obsolescence, social policy and law, stereotypes of the older worker, selection, job performance and appraisal, reentry workers, alternative work patterns, early buyouts, layoffs, and decisions related to planning for retirement (Sterns & Hurd-Gray, 1999). Over 6 decades ago, industrial gerontology in Great Britain began to address issues in *aging and work*. Research was motivated by concern regarding the effects of technological change and automation on the older worker (Sterns & Sterns, 2005).

The negative *stereotype of the older worker* has been a major concern for several decades. The social impact of this stereotype is substantial when maintained by an employer and creates even greater problems when held by older persons themselves. A major finding in industrial settings is that employers encourage older workers to take early retirement buyouts, and they are reluctant to hire or offer training to persons older than age 40 or to train or retrain those already employed. Many middle-aged and *older workers* have been affected by layoffs, downsizings, and plant closings; however, many of these same companies are hiring individuals into new positions. Career patterns are now more likely to be interrupted and may involve dramatic changes in job skills. More frequent and intensive periods of education will be required to remain effective in the workforce.

Characteristics of Older Workers

Older workers have developed fine work records, indicating that they are healthy, dependable, and productive and have low accident rates. Performance of older workers is highly individual and not necessarily different from that of younger workers. Performance often depends on level of motivation, self-reliance, recognition, workplace climate, experience, and job demands. (Sterns & Hurd-Gray, 1999).

Age Discrimination in Employment Act

The Age Discrimination in Employment Act (ADEA) of 1967, revised in 1978 and 1986, defines older workers as individuals aged 40 and older. By law, persons aged 40 and older working in businesses with more than 20 employees cannot be limited, segregated, or classified in any way that would restrict their employment opportunities or otherwise adversely affect their status as employees.

The law recognizes that age may sometimes be a "*bona fide occupational qualification*," reasonably necessary for the normal operations of a particular business. Currently, occupations such as commercial airline pilot and actor are covered by such an exception. Also, businesses are allowed to follow the terms of a bona fide seniority system or any bona fide benefit plan, such as a retirement, pension, or insurance plan. Executives in major leadership positions or high policy-making employees with sizable pension benefits can be required to retire at age 65 (Sterns, Doverspike, & Lax, 2005).

Performance Appraisal

Supervisors use performance appraisals to determine which individuals will be selected for promotion, training, transfer, demotion, or layoff. Such judgments are often made by a supervisor and based on formal subjective ratings. Major issues in such ratings are rater error and rater bias; training of raters is necessary to minimize bias against the older worker. Stereotypes about aging may influence the subjective *appraisal of an older worker* and not accurately reflect that worker's job performance. Studies comparing older and younger workers, using performance appraisal techniques based on job-relevant behaviors, have shown that many *older workers perform* as well as or better than younger workers. (Schaie & Schooler, 1998)

Selection

Older workers may find themselves competing with younger individuals for job placement by participating in extensive selection and assessment procedures. There is some evidence justifying a concern about age discrimination in testing. It has been found that although older subjects had significantly lower scores on a predictor battery, their performance on the job was equal to that of a younger group. The adverse impact of selection batteries on capable older workers is, therefore, a matter of some concern.

Training and Retraining

A major issue in the *training of older workers* is the balance between responsibility for self-management and assuring equitable access to training opportunities. Training policies and practices may reflect informal age restrictions, standards, and assumptions that may exclude older employees. In an era of extended work life, training and retraining provide older workers with opportunities to strengthen their knowledge and skills (Sterns & Sterns, 2005).

Highly *productive older workers* ran the risk of not being included in training opportunities. Their involvement in important ongoing projects makes supervisors reluctant to spare them. The problem faced by workers of any age is that if they do not engage in *retraining*, they grow further and further out of touch with new information, technology, and processes. Rapid technological changes create obsolescence of knowledge among all age groups. The need for retraining is shared by people in their 20s to age 70 and beyond. Training techniques have been developed to meet the special needs of the older worker. Older workers often take longer than younger workers to learn a new task; however, with sufficient time, older people perform as well as younger workers after training.

Demographic Changes and the Workplace

The U.S. Bureau of Labor Statistics projects that the U.S. labor force will grow from 151 million in 2005 to 165 million in 2020, an increase of approximately 9%. Workers aged 55 and older represented 15% of the entire labor force in 2000 and will represent 25% in 2020.

Over the 2000 to 2020 period, total employment is projected to increase by 17%, or 24 million. The labor force cohort aged 45 to 64 years will grow faster than that of any other age group as the baby-boom generation (born 1946–1964) continues to age. Older workers, those aged 40 and older, will make up more than half the workforce through the year 2020 (Fullerton, 2005).

The number of men aged 65 to 69 in the labor force has been increasing and is a change from historical declines over the last 4 decades. Currently, the participation rate stands at 33%. Increases for older women working have been even larger than those for men, although the total number of women working aged 65 to 69 is currently 23% (Federal Interagency Forum on Aging–related Statistics, 2004).

Once *older workers lose their jobs*, they stay unemployed longer than younger workers do, suffer a greater earnings loss in subsequent jobs than do younger workers, and are more likely to give up looking for another job. The average duration of unemployment in 2003 was 25.5 weeks for older jobseekers and 18.4 weeks for their younger counterparts. Just over 800,000 persons aged 55 and older who were not in the labor force reported that they wanted a job in 2003. Rix (2003) estimates that around 75,000 older adults can be considered discouraged workers not seeking a job but who would work if they found one.

In Europe, a number of countries including the United Kingdom, France, and Germany are reconsidering their emphasis on *early retirement*. Typically those in civil service positions can retire as early as age 55 in many European countries. In addition a number of countries are considering age discrimination in employment legislation to encourage those individuals who can work longer to do so.

HARVEY L. STERNS
ANTHONY A. STERNS

See also
Employment
Human Factors Engineering
Older Workers

References

Committee on Economic Development. (1999). *New opportunities for older workers—a statement on national policy by the Research and Policy Committee.* New York: Committee on Economic Development.

Federal Interagency Forum on Aging-related Statistics (2004). Older American 2004: Key indicators of well-being. Washington, DC: U.S. Government Printing Office.

Fullerton, H. N. Jr., (2005). The workforce of tomorrow. In P. T. Beatty & R. Visser (Eds.), *Strategies for organizational and systemic change.* Melborne, FL: Krieger Publishing.

Rix, S. (2003). Update on older workers: 2003. Public Policy Institute Data Digest. Washington, DC: AARP.

Schaie, K. W., & Schooler, C. (Eds). (1998). *Impact of work on older adults*. New York: Springer Publishing.

Sterns, H. L., Doverspike, D., & Lax, G. (2005). The age discrimination in employment act. In F. Landy (Ed.), *Employment discrimination litigation: Behavioral, quantitative, and legal perspectives* (pp. 256–293). San Francisco: Jossey-Bass.

Sterns, H. L., & Hurd-Gray, J. (1999). Employment and potential mid-life career crisis. In I. H. Nordhus, G. R. VandenBos, S. Berg, & P. Fromholt (Eds.), *Clinical geropsychology* (pp. 147–153). Washington, DC: APA Books.

Sterns, H. L., & Sterns, A. A. (2005). Training and careers: Growth and development over fifty years. In P. T. Beatty & R. Visser (Eds.), *Strategies for organizational and systemic change.* Melborne, FL: Krieger Publishing.

Sterns, H. L., & Subich, L. M. (2005). Counseling for retirement. In S. Brown & R. Lent (Eds.), *Career development and counseling* (pp. 506–521). Hoboken, NJ: Wiley.

INFLATION

The *impact of inflation* relative to aging can be viewed from 2 perspectives: its effects on individuals, especially its differential impacts on subgroups of older adults; and, more broadly, on society as a whole. Its impact also differs depending on whether its levels are high (e.g., 6% to 7% and above) or low (e.g., 1% to 3%) and on the type of inflation (general, medical, housing). Triggered by the unprecedented and sustained double-digit inflation of the 1970s and early 1980s, aging advocates decried the disproportionately adverse impact of *inflation on older adults*, the largest population with fixed incomes. In response, a number of special programs (*Medicare, Supplemental Security Income* [SSI], *Section 202 housing*, *Section 8 rental assistance*) were enacted or expanded to assist poor elderly individuals and older adults in general to cope with inflation more effectively. More importantly, Social Security benefits were increased and then indexed (adjusted upward) through automatic *cost-of-living adjustments* to compensate for the negative effects of high inflation. This public policy response to inflation is generally credited with raising substantial numbers of older adults above the poverty line (Moon & Mulvey, 1996; Clark, Burkhauser, Moon, et al., 2004).

Measurement of Inflation

Of the 3 customary measures employed to gauge the state of the economy (*Consumer Price Index* [CPI], *Producer Price Index*, *GNP deflators*), the *CPI* is used most often because it is specifically designed to measure the average consumer's purchasing power. The Bureau of Labor Standards makes some adjustments for quality improvements but does not take into account asset price inflation (residential and nonresidential real estate) (Davis, 1991). The CPI affects *cost-of-living adjustments for Social Security*, SSI, military and government employee pensions, and veterans' benefits. Rental rate increases, federal and state income tax brackets and deductions, and eligibility standards also are tied to this measure, thereby affecting old and young alike. Under the 1987 amendments to the *Older Americans Act*, the Bureau of Labor Standards was instructed to compile an experimental index (the *CPI-E*) for persons aged 62 and older. Although flawed, this 6-year study showed that older adults consistently experience higher inflation, with medical care expenditures accounting almost entirely for this difference (Amble & Stewart, 1994).

Differential Impacts of Inflation

High and low levels of inflation affect different subgroups of the aged in disparate ways. For example, high levels have disadvantaged recipients of employer-provided pensions, which generally are not indexed for inflation (except in the public sector) or only minimally so, usually on an ad hoc basis. A 5% inflation level erodes the value of unindexed pensions by 22% in 5 years. Furthermore, although SSI payments like Social Security are pegged to the CPI, the assets test was not similarly indexed, resulting in fewer older poor being eligible for that program over time (Clark, Burkhauser, Moon, et al., 2004). Conversely, during the 1970s, 1980s, and 1990s, those older adults with substantial assets benefited from or kept pace with inflation and the prevailing standard of living, as the value of their homes rose and their savings and stocks earned high rates of return. However, during the 1970s and 1980s, the somewhat regressive nature of the payroll tax, high inflation, and high rates of unemployment led to a drop in the purchasing power of some younger age groups. Thus, both the young and older poor (and particularly the near poor, or "*tweeners*" [Smeeding, 1986]), were especially hard hit.

Since 1987, the U.S. economy has enjoyed a period of disinflation (Steindel, 1997). However, although general inflation has been characterized by relatively low levels, the same has not been true for medical and housing inflation, as discussed below. Furthermore, except for the years 1998, 1999, and 2002, the *rate of inflation* has been higher than 2%. Still, even low rates of inflation can have negative impacts. Over a 10-year period, 1% inflation leads to an erosion of $1 by 10.5% to 90 cents, and in 20 years by 22% to 82 cents, due to compounding. Even a 4% rate of inflation, often considered moderate, shrinks the value of $1 to 68 cents in 10 years and to 8 cents in 20 years. Given the greater longevity of the older population, this *erosion of purchasing power* especially affects the well-being of the oldest old. The swings in inflation levels over the past several decades described above have led to proposals for different remedies.

Societal Effects of Compensating for Inflation Impacts

In the 1970s and 1980s, the longer-range effects of policies designed to cushion older individuals against inflation were examined in depth by leading economists, many of whom focused on the *overindexation of Social Security* benefits and its negative effects on financing the system, capital formation, and savings behavior. Other economists emphasized the cost burdens of retirement benefits and health care in an aging society, an issue that persists as the baby boom generation nears retirement. These views were heightened by contrasting the decreasing poverty rates of older adults with those of children (Preston, 1984), accompanied by perceptions of an *intergenerational equity gap*. As a result, aging advocates found themselves on the defensive amid calls for reducing or freezing Social Security benefits or cost-of-living adjustments, despite the identification of high poverty rates among women, the old-old, and minority elders.

During the 1990s and into the early 21st century, more far-reaching proposals—especially privatization and managed care—were generated to reform Social Security, Medicare, and other programs to reduce overall costs. Among the proposed remedies was a revision of the CPI itself. The Advisory Commission to Study the CPI was convened to determine if the CPI overstated the rate of inflation, a position held by many economists, including *Alan Greenspan*, the head of the Federal Reserve Bank. The commission report issued in 1996 determined that the *CPI overstates the rate of inflation* by an average of 1.1% annually. Its recommendation to adjust for this problem, however, was not enacted, despite the interest of Washington policymakers in reducing federal outlays. Had the proposal become law, recipients of Social Security, military, and government employee pensions would receive lower benefits because of the CPI's effects on initial benefit amounts and cost-of-living adjustments. Similarly, Medicare reimbursement rates to doctors and hospitals, also CPI-calibrated, would drop, thereby reducing expenditures for retirees and those with long-term disability.

Medical Inflation

Perhaps the most severe advocacy battles have centered on rapidly escalating levels of *inflation for medical services*. From 1982–1994, average annual medical price inflation was markedly higher than general inflation; only in the late 1970s was the reverse true (Driscoll, Jensen, & Raetzman, 1994). In the late 1990s, medical inflation increases were more in line with general inflation, partly due to managed care approaches. In 2003, however, *health care premiums increased* by 13.9%, in contrast with a 2.2% increase in general inflation, and by 11.2% in 2004, compared to a general inflation rate of 2%. In 2003 and 2004, facing budget deficits, states continued to *cut back on Medicaid* spending by trimming benefits and restricting eligibility, at a time when Medicaid rolls were increasing due to joblessness and a rise in the number of *uninsured Americans*.

Out-of-pocket costs for services not covered by Medicare and for *Medigap* insurance also have been driven by high rates of medical inflation, and *Medicare Part B* premiums have escalated since 2000. In 2004, premiums were raised by 13.5%, and in 2005 by 17%, the largest increase in the 40 years of the program's existence. Deductibles also were increased by 10%. A 2.1% increase in Social Security benefits was insufficient to offset these costs to older consumers. In 2000, Medicare expenses were 14% of an individual's Social Security check, a figure projected to rise to 37% in 2006. Those retirees without employer-provided post-retirement benefits—usually women, minorities, and low-income elders—have been and are particularly disadvantaged by these rising Medicare costs, although somewhat less so if they are covered by Medicaid or the special low-income Medicare programs, or are able to afford Medigap insurance.

Inflationary *prices of prescription drugs* have constituted a major factor in medical inflation, and in the 59% increase in health care premiums between 2000 and 2004 (Menn & Rosenblatt, 2004). *Prescription drug costs* also accounted for 11% of all state Medicaid outlays in 2004 (King & Gordon, 2004). In particular, prices for brand name drugs rose by at least 3 times the rate of inflation in 2003; for almost 200 such drugs, increases averaged 27.6% from 2000 to 2003 (AARP, 2004). The extent to which the Medicare prescription drug benefit will reduce out-of-pocket costs for most older adults is uncertain, as its initial implementation begins in 2006. However, the inability of Medicare to bargain for drug prices—unlike state Medicaid programs—will make it more problematic to rein in such costs. Similarly, medical inflation has affected the costs of long-term care and long-term care insurance. Consumers have recognized the need for inflation protection in such policies; however, such a provision adds significantly to their cost.

Housing Inflation

Similar to the impact of medical inflation, housing inflation and deflation are also insidious for older adults, in part because less attention is paid to this domain. Home ownership is generally a senior household's largest asset, while rent is typically the largest single reoccurring living expense for non-homeowners. In the 1990s and beyond, average U.S. *housing prices* rose steadily, as falling interest rates stimulated housing sales. Some localities experienced years of double-digit inflation, associated with demand from new and upgrading home buyers, regional economic expansion, or the in-migration of house-rich retirees. Conversely, housing deflation in other geographic areas led to smaller retirement nest eggs for many older homeowners and landlords.

The effects of housing inflation on homeowners and renters are distinctly different, a prime example of *intragenerational inequity* (Liebig, 1998). Some aging homeowners benefit from high housing demand and inflated prices. Some new or prospective retirees sell greatly appreciated homes and use the tax-sheltered gains to fund retirement moves, finance new homes, or generate income-producing assets. Some use the inflated value of their homes for executing *reverse mortgages* to pay for long-term care, home modifications to promote aging in place, or other expenditures. The dark side of housing inflation for older homeowners is the accompanying increase in *property taxes*, insurance, and maintenance costs that can make home ownership a bigger drain on income, even if there is no mortgage payment.

Older renters, many of whom are women and the oldest old, face different inflationary challenges. Strong housing demand and higher inflation trigger rent increases, often leading investors to sell rental properties to realize capital gains. The consequent removal of rental units from the market contributes to yet higher rents, rental housing shortages, and migration to lower cost, often less safe communities. Rising rents and lack of affordable rental housing also can result in older renters paying considerably in excess of the standard 30% of income, or can prevent them from living near their family members or in desirable, elder-friendly communities.

Thus, the impact of inflation on aging has continued to be a two-edged sword. On the one hand, unprecedented and relatively high levels of inflation from the mid-1960s through the mid-1980s, coupled with the generally low income levels of the aged, led to policy changes and compensatory mechanisms that raised the overall economic well-being of older adults. When general inflation abated and the costs of these anti-inflationary measures were seen as unfair and burdensome, cutbacks in income maintenance, health care, affordable housing, and many social services were enacted. Some of these were fairly severe, especially given the growth in absolute numbers of the older population and the continued economic vulnerability of poor older persons and the "tweeners." Thus, the relative levels of inflation, whether high or low, clearly have played a role in changing the philosophy and substance of elderly entitlements and are likely to do so in the future. Perhaps more important, greater awareness of the economic diversity of the elderly requires more focus on how different rates and types of inflation affect different groups of older adults. Given the strains of the federal deficit and the costs of the baby boomers in their retirement years, cutbacks in public programs over the next several decades will be attractive to policy makers, even if inflation levels continue to be low. Proposals to *revise the CPI* also are likely to resurface. Constructing politically and economically feasible policies that consider the economic diversity of older adults will require extraordinary skill.

PHOEBE S. LIEBIG
SUSAN J. JELONEK

References

AARP. (2004, September). Trends in manufacturer prices of brand-name prescription drugs used by older Americans–First quarter 2004 update. Washington, DC: AARP Public Policy Institute.

Amble, N., & Stewart, K. (1994, May). Experimental price index for elderly consumers. *Monthly Labor Review*, 11–16.

Clark, R. L., Burkhauser, R. V., Moon, M., et al. (2004). *The economics of an aging society*. Oxford, UK: Blackwell Publishing.

Davis, R. G. (1991, Summer). Inflation: Measurement and policy issues. *FRBNY Quarterly Review*, 13–24.

Driscoll, L., Jensen, D., & Raetzman, S. (1994). Beyond medical price inflation (Issue Brief #18). Washington, DC: AARP Public Policy Institute.

King, M., & Gordon, D. (2004, March). Medicaid: 10 fixes that work. *State Legislatures*, 14–18.

Liebig, P. S. (1998). Housing and supportive services for the elderly: Intragenerational perspectives and options. In J. S. Steckenrider & T. M. Parrott (Eds.), *New directions in old-age policies*. Albany, NY: SUNY Press.

Menn, J., & Rosenblatt, S. (2004, September 10). Health care premiums up. *Los Angeles Times*, A1, A23.

Moon, M., & Mulvey, J. (1996). *Entitlements and the elderly: Protecting promises, recognizing realities*. Washington, DC: The Urban Institute.

Preston, S. (1984). Children and the elderly: Divergent paths for America's dependents. *Demography*, *21*, 435–457.

Smeeding, T. M. (1986). Nonmoney income and the elderly: The case of the "tweeners." *Journal of Policy Analysis and Management*, *5*, 707–724.

Steindel, C. (1997). Are there good alternatives to the CPI? *Current Issues in Economics and Finance*, *3*(6), 1–6.

INFLUENZA

Epidemiology

Influenza is an acute respiratory viral illness caused by infection with *influenza type A* or B virus that typically occurs in outbreaks over a 5- to 6-week period each winter. Each year, hundreds of thousands of excess hospitalizations, tens of thousands of excess deaths, and billions of dollars in health care costs can be attributed to influenza and its complications. Attack rates may be as high as 10% to 40% in the community, and examination of influenza epidemic curves typically reveals a bimodal pattern, with attack rates highest in the young but morbidity and mortality highest in older persons (Glezen, 1982; Glezen, Keitel, Taber, et al., 1991). In most series, elderly persons comprise as much as 80% of those patients suffering serious *complications of influenza*, such as hospitalization and death (Lui, & Kendal, 1987; Advisory Committee on Immunization Practices, 1998).

Influenza can be a particularly difficult problem in elderly residents of long-term care facilities, where attack rates may exceed 40%, case fatality rates may exceed 5%, and up to 22% of infected residents develop complications resulting in hospitalization (Coles, Balzano, & Morse, 1992; Libow, Neufeld, Olson, Breuer, & Starer, 1996; Meiklejohn, Hoffman, & Graves, 1989; Gross, Quinnan, Rodstein, LaMontagne, Kaslow, Saah, et al., 1988; Gravenstein, Miller, & Drinka, 1992).

Clinical Findings

Influenza is typically characterized by abrupt onset of fever, chills, headaches, severe myalgias (muscle pains), malaise, and loss of appetite after an incubation period of 1 to 2 days. Dry cough, sore throat, and nasal discharge are usually also present but may be overshadowed by the systemic complaints. Fever typically resolves after approximately 3 days, but cough, sore throat, and hoarseness may persist for 3 to 4 more days. It is important to remember that in older adults, disease presentation may be atypical. Older individuals may present only with fever, lack of energy, and confusion without any evidence of respiratory illness. Influenza should be considered in any elderly person with an illness characterized by fever during influenza season.

Older patients and patients with high-risk medical conditions, including chronic lung or heart disease, kidney disease, problems with the immune system, cancer, or other chronic medical problems are at risk for developing complications from influenza. *Pneumonia caused by influenza* virus itself and secondary bacterial pneumonia are the most common and serious complications of influenza. Patients with *influenza pneumonia*, a complication which is fortunately quite rare, will present with typical signs and symptoms of influenza but go on to develop severe cough, shortness of breath, and cyanosis. Mortality is high even with prompt antiviral therapy.

Secondary *bacterial pneumonia* is indistinguishable from *community-acquired pneumonia* in the absence of influenza except that it occurs typically in older patients or patients with chronic heart or lung problems after recovery from a classic influenza illness. Patients usually will describe recurrence of fever, cough, and sputum production 4 to 14 days after their initial recovery from influenza. Gram stains of the sputum may reveal a predominance of a bacterial pathogen, most often *Streptococcus pneumoniae* or *Haemophilus influenzae*. *Staphyloccocus aureus* is seen less frequently now than in the past. Treatment of community-acquired pneumonia as a secondary complication of influenza infection is not different than in any other setting.

Although much less common, nonpulmonary *complications of influenza* can also occur. These rare complications include inflammation of the skeletal muscles, heart, and pericardium, *toxic shock syndrome*, and possibly *Guillain-Barré syndrome*. *Reye syndrome*, a syndrome of encephalopathy and hepatitis following exposure to *acetylsalicylic acid* (aspirin) in the setting of influenza or varicella infection, is now exceedingly rare.

Diagnosis

Influenza virus can be readily isolated from nasal swabs, nasal washes, nasopharyngeal swabs, throat swabs, and sometimes sputum. Throat swab alone is less sensitive than nasopharyngeal swabs or nasal washes, and the use of throat swabs is generally discouraged. As nasal washes are difficult to obtain in older, debilitated persons, nasopharyngeal swabs are preferred. Specimens should be placed into containers of viral transport medium and transported to the laboratory for viral culture. Two-thirds of positive cultures will be detected within 72 hours, with the remainder by 5 to 7 days. Particularly in the setting of influenza detection in long-term care facilities, faster methods of detection are needed to allow rapid implementation of preventative strategies. A variety of rapid detection methods exists that detect viral antigens by *immunofluorescence* in as little as 1 hour with reasonable sensitivity and specificity. If available, *reverse transcription-polymerase chain reaction* (RT-PCR) provides the most sensitive, rapid diagnostic option.

Treatment and Chemoprophylaxis

In otherwise healthy children and adults with uncomplicated influenza infection, antiviral therapy is not generally warranted. Bed rest, adequate fluid intake, and treatment with antipyretics, analgesics, cough suppressants, and decongestants may improve symptoms. Aspirin should not be used in children with influenza due to the risk of Reye syndrome.

In patients at significant risk for the development of influenza complications or in those with influenza pneumonia, the use of antiviral medications may decrease morbidity and mortality. Until recently, therapy for influenza typically involved the use of *amantadine* or *rimantadine*, *antiviral drugs active against influenza* A. Most studies examining the efficacy of these drugs have shown a reduction in clinical symptom scores, a faster resolution of fever, and a decrease in level and duration of virus shedding when compared with placebo (Hayden, & Monto, 1986). Most authorities support the use of amantadine in the treatment of complicated influenza A virus infection, even late in the course of illness. Treatment with antiviral medications is also generally recommended in the setting of outbreaks of influenza A virus infection in long-term care facilities, although few studies have been done to examine the impact of these drugs on prevention of illness, relief of symptoms, or reduction of duration of illness or complications in this setting. Use of amantadine and rimantadine in older persons can lead to significant complications. Confusion, delirium, seizures, falls, insomnia, or fractures occur in 22% to 47% of residents of long-term care facilities treated with amantadine, and drug resistance develops readily (Bradley, 1999). Side effects can be reduced in older persons by reducing the dose of amantadine to 100 mg or less daily in the presence of renal insufficiency. Central nervous system side effects are less problematic with rimantadine than with amantadine.

The neuraminidase inhibitors *zanamivir* and *oseltamivir* are a new class of antiviral medications with activity against both influenza A and B virus. Although resistance to these agents has been reported, it is not yet a significant problem. These agents are expensive but are better tolerated in older persons than amantadine, and therefore represent an important option for prophylaxis and treatment in this population. Although data regarding the efficacy of these agents in the elderly are limited, both drugs have been shown to prevent naturally acquired infection in healthy adults and to reduce duration of illness in both young and elderly adults. Oseltamivir, if started within 36 to 48 hours of onset of illness, has been shown to decrease influenza-associated pneumonia and hospitalizations. The experience with prophylactic use of zanamivir and oseltamivir in long-term care facilities is limited but encouraging (Bradley, et al., 1999; Peters, Gravenstein, Norwood, et al., 2001). Available studies of oseltamivir prophylaxis in residents of long-term care facilities demonstrate up to a 92% reduction in laboratory-confirmed influenza and a reduction in influenza-related complications and death (Bradley, et al., 1999; Peters, Gravenstein, Norwood, et al., 2001). Although more expensive than amantadine, oseltamivir has been shown to be more cost effective for prophylaxis because it is more efficacious and associated with less adverse events (Riseborough, Bowles, Simor, et al., 2005). It is likely that the *neuraminidase inhibitors* will become the primary agents used for the management of influenza in long-term care facilities in the near future.

Prevention

Influenza vaccination represents the safest, most cost-effective means of prevention of morbidity and mortality from influenza virus. Current guidelines recommend the use of influenza vaccine yearly in all individuals older than age 65, all residents of long-term care facilities, children or adults with chronic pulmonary or cardiovascular illness, children requiring chronic aspirin therapy, and women in the second or third trimester of pregnancy during influenza season. Yearly *influenza vaccine* is also recommended in health care workers, employees of long-term care facilities who come in contact with patients, and home care providers or household contacts of high-risk individuals.

At present, a *trivalent (influenza A H1N1, H3N2, and influenza B) inactivated vaccine* is currently used. This vaccine has been shown to reduce the incidence of confirmed influenza, influenza-like illness, respiratory infections, exacerbations of cardiopulmonary disease, hospitalization, and death in both community-dwelling elderly and in residents of long-term care facilities (Bradley, et al., 1999). Although the vaccine has only 30% to 40% efficacy in preventing influenza in residents of long-term care facilities, severe illness, hospitalization, and death are significantly reduced (Advisory Committee on Immunization Practices, 1998; Libow, Neufeld, Olson, Breuer, & Starer, 1996; Meiklejohn, Hoffman, & Graves, 1989; Gross, Quinnan, Rodstein, LaMontagne, Kaslow, Saah, et al., 1988; Gravenstein, Miller, & Drinka, 1992; Bradley, et al., 1999). High vaccination rates among residents significantly reduces the chance of an outbreak occurring in a long-term care facility, and should an outbreak occur, vaccination will decrease hospitalizations by 50% to 60% and mortality by as much as 80% (Gross, Quinnan, Rodstein, LaMontagne, Kaslow, Saah, et al., 1988; Bradley, et al., 1999). To maximize the effectiveness of the vaccine in the prevention of influenza-associated morbidity and mortality in residents of long-term care facilities, it is critical that high staff vaccine rates be maintained in hopes of reducing and delaying introduction of influenza into long-term care facilities. A newly developed but not yet licensed cold adapted, live-attenuated trivalent intranasal influenza vaccine has been shown to increase serum, mucosal, and cell-mediated immunity when given in combination with the currently available intramuscular vaccine.

SHELLY A. MCNEIL

References

Advisory Committee on Immunization Practices. (1998). Prevention and control of influenza: Recommendations of the Advisory Committee on Immunization Practices. *Morbidity and Mortality Weekly Report, 47*(R-6), 1–26.

Bowles, S. K., Lee, W., Simor, A. E., et al. (2002). Use of oseltamivir during influenza outbreaks in Ontario nursing homes, 1999–2000. *Journal of the American Geriatrics Society, 50*(4), 608–616.

Bradley, S. F., et al. (1999). Prevention of influenza in long-term care facilities. *Infection Control and Hospital Epidemiology, 20,* 629–637.

Coles, F. B., Balzano, G. J., & Morse, D. L. (1992). An outbreak of influenza A (H3N2) in a well immunized nursing home population. *Journal of the American Geriatrics Society, 40,* 589–592.

Glezen, W. P. (1982). Serious morbidity and mortality associated with influenza epidemics. *Epidemiologic Reviews, 4,* 24–44.

Glezen, W. P., Keitel, W. A., Taber, L. H., et al. (1991). Age distribution of patients with medically-attended illnesses caused by sequential variants of influenza A/H1N1: Comparison to age-specific infection rates, 1978–1989. *American Journal of Epidemiology, 133,* 296–304.

Gravenstein, S., Miller, B. A., & Drinka, P. (1992). Prevention and control of influenza A outbreaks in long-term care facilities. *Infection Control and Hospital Epidemiology, 13,* 49–54.

Gross, P. A., Quinnan, G. V., Rodstein, M., LaMontagne, J. R., Kaslow, R. A., Saah, A. J., et al. (1988). Association of influenza immunization with reduction in mortality in an elderly population. A prospective study. *Archives of Internal Medicine, 148,* 562–565.

Hayden, F. G., & Monto, A. S. (1986). Oral rimantadine hydrochloride therapy of influenza A virus H3N2 subtype infection in adults. *Antimicrobial Agents and Chemotherapy, 29,* 339–341.

Libow, L. S., Neufeld, R. R., Olson, E., Breuer, B., & Starer, P. (1996). Sequential outbreak of influenza A and B in a nursing home: Efficacy of vaccine and amantadine. *Journal of the American Geriatrics Society, 44,* 1153–1157.

Lui, K. J., & Kendal, A. P. (1987). Impact of influenza epidemics on mortality in the United States from October 1972 to May 1985. *American Journal of Public Health, 77,* 712–716.

Meiklejohn, G., Hoffman, R., & Graves, P. (1989). Effectiveness of influenza vaccine when given during an outbreak of influenza A/H3N2 in a nursing home. *Journal of the American Geriatrics Society, 37,* 407–410.

Peters, P. H., Gravenstein, S., Norwood, P., et al. (2001). Long-term use of oseltamivir for the prophylaxis of influenza in a frail older population. *Journal of the American Geriatrics Society, 49*(8), 1025–1031.

Riseborough, N. A., Bowles, S. K., Simor, A. E., et al. (2005). Economic evaluation of oseltamivir phosphate for post-exposure prophylaxis of influenza in long-term care facilities. *Journal of the American Geriatrics Society, 53*(3), 444–451.

INFORMATION-PROCESSING THEORY

In much of the first half of the 20th century, behaviorism was the dominant paradigm in psychology and the emphasis was on a science of psychology based on observable behavior. Because mental events could not be directly observed, behaviorists excluded them from psychology and mental processes were derided as "black box psychology." Cognitive psychologists found this to be far too limiting and thus developed the information-processing approach as a group of methods designed to "peer into the black box."

Cognitive psychologists believed that behavior could not, in principle be accounted for by the proximal stimulus in the environment as proposed by Stimulus-Response behaviorism, because without additional "cleaning-up" by mental processing in the cognitive system, the stimulus typically contains too little information to be identified (the "**poverty-of-the-stimulus**" argument). Taking inspiration from the "**Turing machine**" (Turing, 1936) in applied mathematics, early cognitive psychologists viewed the cognitive system as a general-purpose problem solver, sharing important characteristics with the newly developing digital computer. (See Lachman, Lachman, and Butterfield [1979] for a detailed description of the paradigm shift from behaviorism to the information-processing framework in psychology and Salthouse [1991] for an analogous discussion applied to aging research).

Early models of the mind became increasingly sophisticated, culminating in Atkinson and Shiffrin's (1968) model consisting of metal structures, including sensory memory, short-term memory, and long-term memory; and mental processes acting on the structures, such as selective attention (what to pay attention to), rehearsal (how to keep information active in short-term memory), storage (keeping information in long-term memory), and retrieval (moving memories from passive long-term memory into active short-term memory). Models have become increasingly complex, although for many purposes a simplified approximation has been found to be useful. This simple model views cognitive processing as proceeding through roughly five stages–stimulus encoding (forming a representation of the stimulus), template matching (comparing the represented stimulus to codes stored in memory in an attempt to find a match), stimulus decision (making a final match decision that results in stimulus identification), response decision (selecting a response for a given stimulus) and response execution (carrying out the response). Processing in these stages requires the mental structures proposed in Atkinson and Shiffrin's model.

Stage/Process Logic

Using innovative tasks, variables, and manipulations, the aim of information processing methods is to isolate a single stage of processing. Performance differences are then inferred to be due to the process or processes critical at that stage. For example, Sternberg (1969) investigated memory search by varying the number of remembered items in a same/different task. He found that each additional remembered item added about 40 msec to response time and inferred that memory search in short-term memory takes about 40 msec per item searched.

Key dependent measures in the information processing approach are **accuracy** and **response time**. Time is especially important, because mental operations occur in real time; under the right circumstances, task variations can provide direct information about the number or duration of mental events. Age differences in processing can be understood by comparing the increases in response times for young and old that are due to increases in processing requirements.

The focus on change in performance as a function of task variables is important, because overall differences in older and younger adults' performance can be difficult to interpret. When older adults are found to be slower than young, the locus might be at any of the five main processing stages. One generalization has been attempted – the **Complexity Hypothesis** (Cerella, Poon, & Williams, 1980; Cerella, 1985). As tasks become more complex, performance decreases (lower accuracy and/or longer response times); and importantly, age differences are often magnified by increasing task complexity. A primary question is whether the Complexity Hypothesis can account for age differences in general. If it can, detailed information processing analyses would not be required to understand cognitive aging.

Cerella (1985) reviewed a large number of studies, separating peripheral or sensory-motor (encoding and response execution) processes from central (template matching and decision) processes. He found greater age-related central-process than peripheral-process slowing. One might argue that complexity explains age differences in central processes based upon Cerella's work, but his inclusion of separate slowing for peripheral and central processing stages is more consistent with **process-specific slowing**. Indeed, in a number of studies age differences are not always predictable by task complexity alone. Information processing analyses are needed to detect which mental processes are most affected by aging and which are largely spared.

Process-Specific Slowing

Salthouse (1984) decomposed transcription typing into its simpler components, including choice reaction time (type a presented letter as quickly as possible) and motor speed (type "f" and "j" alternately as quickly as possible). He found clear age differences in speed on the components, but not with the more complex transcription typing task itself. In addition, with skill controlled, older typists were found to look slightly farther ahead as they typed than younger typists. Salthouse suggested that because of their very high levels of practice in transcription typing, older typist may be able to compensate for component slowing by more effectively overlapping their processing. In this study, increasing task complexity clearly does not produce larger age differences.

Allen, Madden, Weber, and Groth (1993) reported a series of experiments in which older and younger adults decided whether or not letter strings formed real English words. This lexical decision task involves semantic memory (knowledge). A manipulation of complexity in these studies was word frequency – more common words are recognized more quickly and easily than rarer words. Although younger adults respond more quickly, overall, than older adults, the increment in response time due to word frequency was actually less in old than young in some studies and about the same in others. Other manipulations with the lexical decision task (involving encoding and response selection difficulty) do show larger effects on old than young (Allen et al., 1993). This pattern suggests that some stages of mental processing clearly favor the young, but the stage of processing tied to word frequency (lexical access—a type of template matching) may actually favor the old. Complexity theory cannot account for the lack of age-related slowing for lexical access.

Is this pattern an anomaly occurring only for lexical access? No. The same pattern of data is obtained with the problem size effect in mental math studies. Problem size (e.g., "$2 \times 2 = 4$" is a small problem and "$7 \times 8 = 56$" is a large problem) can be manipulated in addition, multiplication, and subtraction. It takes longer to verify the correct answer on larger than smaller arithmetic problems, so this is our measure of complexity. Allen, Ashcraft and Weber (1992, multiplication), Geary and Wiley (1991, addition), and Geary, Frensch, and Wiley (1993, subtraction) all found that the problem size effect on reaction time to be no greater in old than young. Likely due to life-long experience with arithmetic, processing at the template matching stage appears to be spared in older adults for semantic tasks.

On the other hand, older adults do perform more poorly on the template matching stage when episodic memory (remembering specific information in time) rather than semantic memory (knowledge without context) is examined. For example, Allen, Sliwinski, and Bowie (2002) found age differences in template matching on four different episodic memory tasks (memory search and hybrid visual search with words and digits), but not with four semantic tasks (two lexical decision tasks that varied word frequency and two multiplication verification tasks that varied problem size). In contrast, with encoding, older adults showed a consistent decrement across all eight tasks (both semantic and episodic). Once, again, process-specific rather than complexity-based age effects are observed.

Do violations of the complexity rule occur in only one stage of processing? Apparently, not. Allen, Lien, Murphy, Sanders, Judge, and McCann (2002) conducted a study in which younger and older adults performed two tasks more or less simultaneously. Evidence for efficient parallel processing is obtained when individuals can complete stimulus decision processing on Task 2 before Task 1 processing is complete. Allen et al. (2002) found that older adults showed more efficient parallel processing than younger adults. Here again, older participants performed better than expected based on a complexity view.

A very different method to test complexity theory involves the use of structural equation modeling. Data from a large number of tasks given to the same people are modeled. The key question asks whether age differences can be accounted for by a single underlying factor. If so, a general slowing/complexity explanation is supported. If a number of underlying factors are required, a process-specific view of age differences would best account for the data. Allen, Hall, Druley, Smith, Sanders, and Murphy (2001) re-analyzed several sets of data that Salthouse and colleagues (e.g., Salthouse & Czaja, 2000) had previously claimed were best described by a common factor (complexity) model. The re-analysis by Allen et al. showed that there were process-specific age effects for all of the experiments analyzed by Salthouse. Similarly, Schmiedek and Li (2004) showed that the data from the Berlin Longitudinal Aging Study also exhibited process-specific age effects rather than just common-factor effects.

Conclusion

While older adults do slow down in performing most tasks, we see compelling evidence that, particularly with semantic memory, processing at some stages is spared or even improves. Therefore the aging process is not comprised simply of cognitive decline. Information processing analyses provide detailed process-level understanding, which opens the possibility for interventions to help older adults compensate in domains that do show age-related decline.

PHILIP A. ALLEN
BARBARA BUCUR
MARTIN D. MURPHY

References

Allen, P. A., Ashcraft, M. H., & Weber, T. A. (1992). On mental multiplication and age. *Psychology and Aging*, *7*, 536–545.

Allen, P. A., Hall, R. J., Druley, J. A., Smith, A. F., Sanders, R. E., & Murphy, M. D. (2001). How shared are age-related influences on cognitive and noncognitive variables? *Psychology and Aging*, *16*, 532–549.

Allen, P. A., Lien, M-C., Murphy, M. D., Sanders, R. E., Judge, K., & McCann, R. (2002). Age differences in overlapping-task performance: Evidence for efficient parallel processing in older adults. *Psychology and Aging*, *17*, 505–519.

Allen, P. A., Madden, D. J., Weber, T. A., & Groth, K. E. (1993). The influence of age and processing stage on visual word recognition. *Psychology and Aging*, *8*, 274–282.

Allen, P. A., Sliwinski, M., & Bowie, T. (2002). Differential age effects in semantic and episodic memory, Part II: Slope and intercept analyses. *Experimental Aging Research*, *28*, 111–142.

Cerella, J. (1985). Information processing rates in the elderly. *Psychological Bulletin*, *98*, 67–83.

Cerella, J., Poon, L. W., & Williams, D. M. (1980). Age and the complexity hypothesis. In L. W. Poon (Ed.), *Aging in the 1980s*. Washington, DC: American Psychological Association.

Geary, D. C., & Wiley, J. G. (1991). Cognitive addition: Strategy choice and speed of processing differences in young and elderly adults. *Psychology and Aging*, *6*, 474–483.

Geary, D. C., Frensch, P. A., & Wiley, J. G. (1993). Simple and complex mental subtraction: Strategy choice and speed-of-processing differences in younger and older adults. *Psychology and Aging*, *8*, 242–256.

Lachman, R., Lachman, J. L., & Butterfield, E. C. (1979). Cognitive psychology and information processing. Hillsdale, N. J.: Lawrence Erlbaum Associates.

Salthouse, T. A. (1991). Theoretical perspectives on cognitive aging. Hillsdale, N. J.: Lawrence Erlbaum Associates.

Salthouse, T. A. (1984). Effects of age and skill in typing. *Journal of Experimental Psychology: General*, *113*, 345–371.

Salthouse, T. A., & Czaja, S. J. (2000). Structural constraints on process explanations in cognitive aging. *Psychology and Aging*, *15*, 44–55.

Schmiedek, F., & Li, S.-C. (2004). Toward an alternative representation for disentangling age-associated differences in general and specific cognitive abilities. *Psychology and Aging*, *19*, 40–56.

Sternberg, S. (1969). Memory scanning: Mental processes revealed by reaction-time experiments. *American Scientist*, *57*, 421–457.

Turing, A. M. (1936). On computable numbers, with an application to the Einscheidungs problem. *Proceedings of the London Mathematics Society (Series 2)*, *42*, 230–265.

INJURY

The U.S. *population is aging* rapidly. Currently 35 million adults—1 in 8—are aged 65 or older; by 2020 this number is expected to reach 77 million, or 1 in 6. The *aging process* typically involves changes in body systems, such as the brain and the nervous, cardiovascular, and sensory systems. These changes, in turn, may cause a reduction in functional abilities including decreased muscle strength and endurance, delayed reaction times to different types of stimuli, and slower recovery after exertion or stress. Such physiological changes can make older adults particularly susceptible to injuries, which are a leading cause of disability and premature mortality. The following provides an overview of injuries among people aged 65 and older, with particular emphasis on falls, which are the main cause of both fatal and nonfatal injuries among older adults.

Epidemiology

Injuries are a serious public health problem. In 2002, injuries were the ninth leading *cause of death* among people aged 65 and older, and were responsible for 42,000 deaths. The most common were *falls* (30%), *motor vehicle accidents* (18%), *suicide by firearm* (10%), *suffocation* (8%), and fire or *burns* (3%) (Centers for Disease Control and Prevention, 2004). Across causes, the numbers of injuries and injury rates increased with age. From age 65 to age

85 and older, fatality rates increased almost sixfold. Men's rates exceeded women's rates for all ages.

For each *injury death*, approximately 64 nonfatal injuries were treated in hospital emergency departments (CDC, 2005.) In 2002, 2.7 million older adults were treated in emergency departments for nonfatal injuries, and about 500,000 of those treated were subsequently hospitalized (CDC, 2004). The great majority of these injuries were caused by falls (61%). The second leading cause of *emergency department visits* was motor vehicle crashes (7%), followed by being struck by or against an object (7%), *overexertion* (6%), and cut/pierce injury (4%). These 5 injury mechanisms accounted for 85% of nonfatal *injuries among older adults*.

Injuries also are costly both to individuals and to society. In 2000, 17% of people age 65 and older reported needing treatment for at least 1 injury, and the percentage was higher for women (19%) than for men (14%) (Centers for Disease Control and Prevention, 2004.) Medical treatment for these injuries cost $29 billion, approximately 9% of total U.S. medical expenditures.

Prevention

A model proposed by Haddon (1980) clarifies the processes by which injuries occur and can be prevented. This model contains 3 time periods: the time prior to the injury event, the time at which the injury occurs, and the time immediately following the injury. In the context of each time period, the model describes 3 factors. First is the host or person affected by the injury, with host characteristics including age, sex, education, physical condition, and mental state. Second is the agent, defined in terms of energy transferred to the host, which includes mechanical, thermal, chemical, and electrical energy. An example of the agent would be the transfer of mechanical energy to the host by impact with an automobile. Third is environment, which encompasses both physical and social dimensions. It includes elements that contribute to the occurrence of an injury such as weather, temperature, environmental hazards, and social norms. Injuries can be prevented if the characteristics of the host, agent, and/or environment can be modified. For example, in a hip fracture from a fall, a host factor may be osteoporosis, an agent may be the force of the impact, and an environmental factor may be an icy sidewalk. Each of these may be preventable or modifiable.

Falls

Among older adults, falling is a frequent occurrence. More than one-third of people aged 65 and *older fall* each year (Hornbrook, Stevens, Wingfield, Hollis, Greenlick, & Ory, 1994; Hausdorff, Rios, & Edelber, 2001) and *fall-related injuries* cause significant mortality and morbidity. Of those who fall, 20% to 30% suffer moderate to severe injuries that result in decreased functional abilities, loss of independence, and early admission to nursing homes (Alexander, Rivara, & Wolf, 1992; Sterling, O'Connor, & Bonadies, 2001; Tinetti &Williams, 1997). In 2002, falls were responsible for 12,800 deaths and 1.64 million hospital emergency visits for nonfatal injuries. Both fatal and nonfatal fall injury rates increased sharply with advancing age (CDC, 2004).

Community-dwelling older adults spend the majority of their time at home, so it is not surprising that between one-half and two-thirds of all falls, and 60% of fatal falls, occur in or around the home (Nevitt, Cumming, Kidd, & Black, 1989; Wilkins, 1999). Most fall injuries are caused by falling on a level surface or from a standing height (for example, by tripping while walking) rather than from falling down stairs or off ladders (Ellis & Trent, 2001). Compared to older adults living in the community, *nursing home residents* tend to be older, frailer, and more cognitively impaired. People in nursing homes are particularly susceptible to falling, and the rate of *falls among nursing home residents* is 2 to 3 times the rate for community-dwelling counterparts (Rubenstein, 1997).

Fracture is among the most prevalent injury outcome from a fall. Each year 360,000 to 480,000 older adults sustain *fall-related fractures* (Centers for Disease Control and Prevention, 1996). The most serious and disabling fall-related fracture is *hip fracture*. In 2001, there were about 327,000 hospital admissions for hip fracture, with 248,000 (76%) among women. Up to 20% of patients die within a year following a hip fracture (Leibson, Tosteson, Gabriel, Ransom, & Melton III, 2002) and those who survive often experience significant disability, limited mobility, and reduced quality of life (Wolinsky, Fitzgerald, & Stump, 1997; Hall, Williams, Senior, Goldswain, & Criddle, 2000). Many hip fracture patients are discharged to nursing homes, and as many as a quarter of formerly independent older adults remain institutionalized for at least a year (Magaziner, Hawkes, Hebel, Zimerman, Fox, Dolan, et al., 2000).

Fall risk factors can be categorized as personal or environmental. Personal risk factors include characteristics of the individual such as age, a past history of falls, being female, level of functional abilities and/or impairments, and having chronic conditions. For older adults living in community settings, environmental factors most often concern *fall hazards* in and around their home and include *tripping* hazards such as *throw rugs* and clutter, lack of stair railings or grab bars, slippery surfaces, unstable furniture, and poor lighting (Northridge, Nevitt, Kelsey, & Link 1995; Connell, 1996; Gill, Williams, Robison, & Tinetti, 1999.) The risk of falling increases with the number of risk factors present (Tinetti, Speechley, & Ginter, 1988) and the occurrence of many risk factors increases with age.

Because falls frequently are caused by a complex interaction between the individual and environment, effective interventions generally include multiple components that address a variety of risk factors (Tinetti, Baker, McAvay, Claus, Garrett, Gottschalk, et al., 1994). In particular, prevention strategies should focus on those risk factors that potentially are amenable to change such as lower-body weakness (Graafmans, Ooms, Hofstee, Bezemer, Bouter, & Lips, 1996), problems with walking and balance (American Geriatrics Society, 2001), medication use (especially psychoactive medications such as tranquillizers and sedatives) (Ray & Griffin, 1990; Cumming, 1998), and being visually impaired (Lord & Dayhew, 2001). In terms of the *Haddon matrix*, these *fall-prevention strategies* focus on host factors, but a number of other strategies also address environmental factors, such as assessing homes and reducing hazards, installing railings and *grab bars*, and improving lighting. (Hornbrook, Stevens, Wingfield, Hollis, Greenlick, & Ory, 1994; Carter, Campbell, Swanson-Fisher, & Redman, 1997; Close, Ellis, Hooper, Glucksman, Jackson, & Swift, 1999; Cumming, Thomas, Szonyi, Salkeld, O'Neill, Westbury, et al., 1999; McMurdo, Millar, & Daly, 2000; Day, Fildes, Gordon, Fitzharris, Flamer, & Lord, 2002; Nikolaus & Bach, 2003; Clemson, Cumming, Kendig, Swann, Heard, & Taylor, 2004).

There are many effective strategies to reduce injuries and injury risks to older adults. Among them are those to *reduce falls and fall injuries*. To reduce the burden of fall-related injuries, effective interventions need to be more widely disseminated. In addition, new and promising interventions need to be developed, implemented, and tested to benefit the growing older adult population.

JUDY A. STEVENS

References

Alexander, B. H., Rivara, F. P., & Wolf, M. E. (1992). The cost and frequency of hospitalization for fall-related injuries in older adults. *American Journal of Public Health, 82*(7), 1020–1023.

American Geriatrics Society, British Geriatrics Society, and American Academy of Orthopedic Surgeons Panel on Falls Prevention. (2001). Guideline for the prevention of falls in older persons. *Journal of the American Geriatrics Society, 49*(5), 664–672.

Carter, S. E., Campbell, E. M., Swanson-Fisher, R. W., & Redman, S. (1997). Environmental hazards in the homes of older people. *Age and Ageing, 26*, 195–202.

Centers for Disease Control and Prevention. (2002). Web-based injury statistics query and reporting system (WISQARS). Available: http://www.cdc.gov/ncipc/wisqars.

Centers for Disease Control and Prevention. (2004). Medical expenditures attributable to injuries—United States, 2000. *Morbidity and Mortality Weekly Report, 53*, 1–4.

Centers for Disease Control and Prevention. (1996). Incidence and costs to Medicare of fractures among Medicare beneficiaries aged ≥65 years—United States, July 1991–June 1992. *Morbidity and Mortality Weekly Report, 45*(41), 877–883.

Clemson, L., Cumming, R. G., Kendig, H., Swann, M., Heard, R., & Taylor, K. (2004). The effectiveness of a community-based program for reducing the incidence of falls in the elderly: A randomized trial. *Journal of the American Geriatrics Society, 52*, 1487–1494.

Close, J., Ellis, M., Hooper, R., Glucksman, E., Jackson, S., & Swift, C. (1999). Prevention of falls in the elderly trial (PROFET): A randomized controlled trial. *Lancet*, *353*, 93–97.

Connell, B. R. (1996). Role of the environment in falls prevention. *Clinics in Geriatric Medicine*, *12*(4), 859–880.

Cumming, R. G. (1998). Epidemiology of medication-related falls and fractures in the elderly. *Drugs and Aging*, *12*(1), 43–53.

Cumming, R. G., Thomas, M., Szonyi, G., Salkeld, G., O'Neill, E., Westbury, C., et al. (1999). Home visits by an occupational therapist for assessment and modification of environmental hazards: A randomized trial of falls prevention. *Journal of the American Geriatric Society*, *47*, 1397–1402.

Day, L., Fildes, B., Gordon, I., Fitzharris, M., Flamer, H., & Lord, S. (2002). Randomised factorial trial of falls prevention among older people living in their own homes. *British Medical Journal*, *325*(7356), 128–133.

Ellis, A. A., & Trent, R. B. (2001). Do the risks and consequences of hospitalized fall injuries among older adults in California vary by type of fall? *Journal of Gerontology: Medical Sciences*, *56A*(11), M686–M692.

Gill, T. M., Williams, C. S., Robison, J. T., & Tinetti, M. E. (1999). A population-based study of environmental hazards in the homes of older persons. *American Journal of Public Health*, *89*(4), 553–556.

Graafmans, W. C., Ooms, M. E., Hofstee, H. M. A., Bezemer, P. D., Bouter, L. M., & Lips, P. (1996). Falls in the elderly: A prospective study of risk factors and risk profiles. *American Journal of Epidemiology*, *143*, 1129–1136.

Haddon, W. (1980). Advances in the epidemiology of injuries as a basis for public policy. *Public Health Reports*, *95*, 411–421.

Hall, S. E., Williams, J. A., Senior, J. A., Goldswain, P. R., & Criddle, R. A. (2000). Hip fracture outcomes: Quality of life and functional status in older adults living in the community. *Australian and New Zealand Journal of Medicine*, *30*(3), 327–332.

Hausdorff, J. M., Rios, D. A., & Edelber, H. K. (2001). Gait variability and fall risk in community-living older adults: A 1-year prospective study. *Archives of Physical Medicine and Rehabilitation*, *82*(8), 1050–1056.

Hornbrook, M. C., Stevens, V. J., Wingfield, D. J., Hollis, J. F., Greenlick, M. R., & Ory, M. G. (1994). Preventing falls among community-dwelling older persons: Results from a randomized trial. *Gerontologist*, *34*(1), 16–23.

Leibson, C. L., Tosteson, A. N. A., Gabriel, S. E., Ransom, J. E., & Melton, J. L. III. (2002). Mortality, disability, and nursing home use for persons with and without hip fracture: A population-based study. *Journal of the American Geriatrics Society*, *50*, 1644–1650.

Lord, S. R., & Dayhew, J. (2001). Visual risk factors for falls in older people. *Journal of the American Geriatrics Society*, *49*, 508–515.

Magaziner, J., Hawkes, W., Hebel, J. R., Zimerman, S. I., Fox, K. M., Dolan, M., et al. (2000). Recovery from hip fracture in eight areas of function. *Journal of Gerontology: Medical Sciences*, *5A*(9), M498–M507.

McMurdo, M. E. T., Millar, A. M., & Daly, F. (2000). A randomized controlled trial of fall prevention strategies in old peoples' homes. *Gerontology*, *46*, 83–87.

Nevitt, M. C., Cumming, S. R., Kidd, S., & Black, D. (1989). Risk factors for recurrent nonsyncopal falls: A prospective study. *Journal of the American Medical Association*, *261*(18), 2663–2668.

Nikolaus, T., & Bach, M. (2003). Preventing falls in community-dwelling frail older people using a home intervention team (HIT): Results from the randomized Falls-HIT trial. *Journal of the American Geriatrics Society*, *51*(3), 300–305.

Northridge, M. E., Nevitt, M. C., Kelsey, J. L., & Link, B. (1995). Home hazards and falls in the elderly - the role of health and functional status. *American Journal of Public Health*, *85*(4), 509–515.

Ray, W., & Griffin, M. R. (1990). Prescribed medications and the risk of falling. *Topics in Geriatric Rehabilitation*, *5*, 12–20.

Rubenstein, L. Z. (1997). Preventing falls in the nursing home. *Journal of the American Medical Association*, *278*(7), 595–596.

Sterling, D. A., O'Connor, J. A., & Bonadies, J. (2001). Geriatric falls: Injury severity is high and disproportionate to mechanism. *Journal of Trauma*, *50*(1), 116–119.

Tinetti, M. E., Baker, D. I., McAvay, G., Claus, E. B., Garrett, P., Gottschalk, M., et al. (1994). A multifactorial intervention to reduce the risk of falling among elderly people living in the community. *New England Journal of Medicine*, *331*, 821–827.

Tinetti, M. E., & Williams, C. S. (1997). Falls, injuries due to falls, and the risk of admission to a nursing home. *New England Journal of Medicine*, *337*, 1279–1284.

Tinetti, M. E., Speechley, M., & Ginter, S. F. (1988). Risk factors for falls among elderly persons living in the community. *New England Journal of Medicine*, *319*, 1701–1707.

Wilkins, K. (1999). Health care consequences of falls for seniors. *Health Reports*, *10*(4), 47–55.

Wolinsky, F. D., Fitzgerald, J. F., & Stump, T. E. (1997). The effect of hip fracture on mortality, hospitalization, and functional status: A prospective study. *American Journal of Public Health*, *87*(3), 398–403.

INSTITUTIONALIZATION

Characteristics of *Institutionalized Older Persons*

Institutionalization of older adults represents a central concern of gerontological researchers and service professionals alike, and the processes and consequences of institutionalization will comprise the focus of this discussion. Long-term care facilities represent extensive financial investments by U.S. society toward care of the frail. There is also concern about the potentially high *human costs of institutionalization.* It has been argued that vulnerable older persons entering institutions are particularly susceptible to adverse environmental conditions (Lawton, 1980). Typically, older persons have little influence on the decision to be institutionalized, and many enter nursing homes against their will (McAuley & Travis, 1997). Often institutionalization is used not as a treatment of choice but rather as a comprehensive approach to deal with multiple frailties and lack of personal and social resources. Typically *older persons entering institutions* have experienced declining physical and/or psychological resources, along with deficits in social support. Accordingly, it must be recognized that even where competent and state-of-the-art care is provided, therapeutic effects are likely to be limited (Kahana, Kahana, & Chirayath, 1999).

About 5% of the U.S. population older than age 65 lives in long-term care institutions at any given time, with 75% of those *institutionalized being women* (National Center for Health Statistics, 1997). It is estimated that over 40% of the elderly will spend time in a nursing home at some point in their lives (Murtaugh, Kemper, & Spillman, 1990). After age 85, an individual can expect to live in a nursing home for close to half of the remaining life span (Liang, Liu, Tu, & Witelaw, 1996). The problem of institutionalization for older persons is likely to grow in importance as more and more Americans live to be very old.

The overriding cause of placement in a long-term care institution remains poor health and frailty of the patient and burden of the caregiver. Other factors that can lead to institutionalization include widowhood, solitary living, economic deprivation, and interpersonal conflicts (Bauer, 1996). Lack of community alternatives, burden experienced by caregivers, and advice of health care professionals have also been found to contribute to entry decisions (Dwyer, Barton, & Vogel, 1994; Yaffe, Fox, Newcomer, Sands, Lindquist, Dane, et al., 2002). *Institutional placement of an older individual* involves complex family processes of planning and decision-making, and is typically accompanied by urgency and a sense of turmoil for family members. *Institutionalization of a spouse* often results in new role demands for the community-residing spouse who typically visits often and may experience psychological distress, particularly if the *institutionalized spouse* suffers from dementia (Schulz, Belle, Czaja, McGinnis, Stevens, & Zhang, 2004). Although caregiving hours provided by families diminish after institutionalization of a parent, frequent visitation and attachments remain the norm. The majority of older adults move to long-term care facilities from acute-care hospitals or other institutional settings. Most suffer from multiple impairments and have significant functional limitations (National Center for Health Statistics, 1997). Nevertheless, many elderly persons who have functional impairments as severe as those who are institutionalized continue to function in the community (Morris, Sherwood, & Mor, 1984). Although there are generally recognized placement criteria, there is evidence that many older persons placed in long-term care facilities could be treated appropriately at lower levels of care (Spector, Reschovsky & Cohen, 1996). Furthermore, close to one-fourth of institutional admissions are discharged back to the community (National Center for Health Statistics, 1997). Ultimately, it is the interaction between personal vulnerability and loss or inadequacy of social supports that is most likely to bring about institutional placements. Research conducted in Hong Kong confirms the dual influence of functional limitations and absence of adequate social support as the major determinants of *late-life institutionalization* (Woo, Ho, Yu, & Lau, 2000). Research in Canada also has indicated that older adults who are unmarried, had less economic resources, or were of poor health are more likely to be institutionalized (Payette, Coulombe, Boutier, & Gray-Donald, 2000).

Older persons with mental illness and those suffering from *Alzheimer's disease* increasingly comprise a major subgroup of nursing home dwellers. Prospective studies of this group indicate that white older adults, those living alone, those with greater cognitive and activities-of-daily-living limitations, and those with more burdened caregivers are most likely to be institutionalized (Yaffe, Fox, Newcomer, Sands, Lindquist, Dane, et al., 2002). Surveys place the range of significant mental disorders among institutionalized older adults as between 65% and 90% (Smyer, Shea, & Streit, 1994). Yet only a very small percentage, estimated at less than 10%, receive any form of mental health services, at least in part due to the absence of a trained workforce to address such needs (American Geriatrics Society and American Association for Geriatric Psychiatry, 2003). Reports of successful integration of mental health care in long-term care facilities come from European countries (Depla, Pols, de Lange, Smits, de Graaf, & Heeren, 2003). Special care units represent one service trend aimed at enhancing quality of life for patients with Alzheimer's disease and other forms of dementia.

During the era of managed care, it has been recognized that both patient preferences and staff characteristics (such as workload of case managers) impact the likelihood of institutionalization (Degenholtz, Kane, Kane, & Finch, 1999). It is also increasingly evident that specific nursing home placements are often affected by cost and personal resource factors, facility availability, and organizational characteristics ranging from the facility's reputation to its resident selection (McAuley & Usita, 1998). *Waiting lists for nursing home placement* are common, particularly in European countries such as Belgium (Devroey, Van Casteren, & De Lepeleire, 2001). In the United States, macro-level variables related to characteristics of the state health care system, such as Medicaid spending on home- and community-based services, and the number of home health agencies in a given state also exert a significant impact on the likelihood of institutionalization of frail elders (Miller, Prohaska, Runer, Freels, Brody, & Levy, 1998).

Nursing homes now collect uniform information on all patients, referred to as *Minimum Data Sets* (Hawes, Mor, Phillips, Fries-Brant, Morris, Steel-Friedlob, et al., 1997). Since many Western countries now collect such baseline information, cross-national comparisons are possible concerning transitions between home, hospital, and long-term care settings. Patterns of admission and likelihood of discharge back into the community appear to vary widely among countries. In comparison to U.S. older adults, persons living in Japan are far more likely to be admitted to nursing homes from other long-term care settings, while elderly in Denmark are more likely to be admitted from their homes. Return of nursing home residents back to the community is far more likely in the Netherlands (27%) than in the United States (10%) (Frijters, Mor, DuPaquier, Berg, Carpenter, & Ribbe, 1997).

Demographic trends shape the characteristics of *nursing home populations*, resulting in marked changes in the racial and ethnic composition of nursing homes over time. Accordingly, the ratio of *institutionalized blacks* relative to whites has grown from .65 in 1982 to .85 in 1989 (Clark, 1997). Nevertheless, it is important to recognize that among older blacks relatively lower rates of institutionalization still exist and are complemented by higher use of paid home care, informal care, and no care.

In recent years, there have been important changes in the types of services offered by nursing homes. These changes reflect both the increasing diversity of institutionalized persons and the changing characteristics of the health care system. Nursing homes have expanded the spectrum of services they offer to include hospice care and post-acute or rehabilitation services.

The *Impact of Institutionalization*

The methodological challenges of determining the effects of institutionalization are considerable. The problems of attributing post-institutional changes in residents to the impact of institutional environments have been noted by Thorson and Davis (2000). Even when longitudinal data is available, often the effects of relocation, environmental change, and illness-related changes are difficult to distinguish from those of institutionalization. Furthermore, few populations can serve as true control groups in studies that consider the impact of institutionalization. Nevertheless, valuable information may be gleaned by considering evidence from diverse studies, even with their methodological limitations, regarding the experiences of institutionalized older persons and the impact of institutionalization on these individuals. Major empirical studies of institutionalization using sophisticated designs are needed to further elucidate processes and outcomes of institutional placement of older adults.

Institutionalization poses many discontinuities in relation to customary lifestyles in a community setting. Even when institutions provide high-quality health care, residents are likely to experience changes in their customary ways of living and their patterns of social interaction. Patients typically experience a loss of independence, privacy, and familiarity upon entry to an institution (Savishinsky, 1991). Interaction with friends and family members may be minimized, organizational involvements are curtailed, and customary social activities are altered. Institutionalized older persons have been found to show loss of self-esteem, withdrawal, and depressive symptoms (Kane, 1995–1996). Evidence has been found for a *"failure to thrive" syndrome*, akin to that manifested by institutionalized children, among elderly nursing home residents (Braun, Wykle, & Cowling, 1988). There is a high mortality rate among residents during the initial 3 months after institutionalization (Thorson & Davis, 2000).

The negative and dehumanizing effects of institutional living have been documented in qualitative studies of single institutions using participant observation and field study approaches (Diamond, 1992; Gubrium, 1993). Goffman's (1961) classic study of the career of the institutionalized mental patient presents a prototype for accounts by anthropologists (Savishinsky, 1991) and gerontologists (Gubrium, 1993). These accounts depict the "stripping," humiliation, loss of freedom, dignity, and deprivation of choice, which are experienced by "obsolescent" human beings (Henry, 1963) who have been placed in institutional settings. However, they also document valiant and often creative efforts of institutionalized older persons to adapt to their environment and create meaning in their lives.

Some confirmation of the negative effects of institutionalization has come from research using more quantitative approaches. Such research has indicated that isolation and loss of personal control (which may result from dependency-inducing behavior of staff) lead to learned helplessness among institutionalized elderly (Baltes, 1996). Resident inactivity and neglect by staff have been observed in institutional facilities (Gottesman & Bourestom, 1974). Confirming the adverse effects of institutional life on the self, some studies report more negative self-care reports and lower levels of self-esteem among institutionalized older adults even in other cultures such as Italy (Antonelli, Rubini, & Fassone, 2000).

Counterbalancing these reports is a smaller body of research that has failed to confirm the negative impact of institutional living (Patchner & Blagopal, 1993). High levels of resident satisfaction, improved family relations, and positive adaptations to life in long-term care settings have been observed by some researchers (Joiner & Freudiger, 1993; Kahana, Kahana, & Young, 1985). There is evidence that for some people at least, institutionalization may present positive alterations in lifestyles. Improved nutrition and medical care, availability of activities, and opportunities to be exposed to social interaction as well as cognitive stimulation enhance the lives of institutionalized older persons (Kahana, Kahana, & Chirayath, 1999). Recent exposition of ecologically based enhancements of institutional living, referred to as the Eden alternative, have suggested positive results when the institutional milieu has been oriented to building on residents' continuing capacity for growth (Thomas, 1996). Similarly, advances in the physical characteristics of nursing homes, utilizing enhancements in the built environment such as improved negotiability, have been shown to benefit institutionalized older adults (Calkins, 2003).

Special initiatives to enhance quality of life in nursing homes have been reported to yield success (Kahana, Kahana, & Chirayath, 1999). These initiatives include widely used restraint reduction programs, as well as interventions to improve nutritional status among residents. Programs reflecting psychosocial orientations include intergenerational programs that introduce contacts with children and young adults, as well as interventions aimed at enhancing environmental control and autonomy. Recent Montessori-based therapeutic efforts have targeted the large and growing number of cognitively impaired residents in institutions (Camp & Mattern, 1999).

The Americans With Disabilities Act also opened up far-reaching potentials for protection of older adults in nursing homes (Gottlich, 1995). Alternative dispute resolution techniques including mediation and nursing home ombudsman programs (Kahana, 1995) also have contributed to advocacy for the institutionalized elderly. With increasing numbers of cognitively impaired residents in institutions, attention has also been directed toward decision-making in long-term care (Schimer & Kahana, 1992). Questions have been raised about the impact of the widespread use of cognitive testing as a means of relocating residents to special care units within long-term care facilities and determining their competency for medical decision-making (Kane, 1993). Apparently contradictory data about the impact of institutionalization on older clients may be better understood when the complexities of the phenomena under study are considered; changes in well-being of the elderly are a function of environmental influences on the one hand, and individual differences in human adaptations on the other. Much of the research emphasizing negative aspects of institutional life focused on adverse environmental influences. In contrast, the focus of studies documenting positive post-institutional outcomes has often been on human resiliency and adaptability (Kahana, Kahana, & Young, 1985). Whereas earlier research tended to treat institutions as if they had a global or unitary effect on residents, more recent efforts have been directed at identifying the conditions of both the person and the environment that maximize well-being (Soth, 1997).

The congruence between personal preferences and environmental characteristics has been found to influence resident morale and satisfaction, in addition to effects attributable to personal or environmental characteristics alone (Kahana, Liang, & Felton, 1980). Research has also called attention to personal coping strategies as important mediators of the stress of institutionalization (Kahana, Kahana, & Young, 1985).

Additionally, research findings have shed new light on long-held assumptions about the functioning of institutions. Staff members have been observed to portray positive attitudes toward patients and to treat patients as equals (Kahana & Kiyak, 1984). The expectation of long-term institutionalization for all of those entering the facilities has been found to be incorrect, with significant numbers now returning to community living. Persons without diagnoses of dementia and with first-time nursing home admissions are most likely to be discharged into the community (Engle & Graney, 1993). After entry into institutions, levels of health among residents appear to hold up. Major shifts in health status among nursing home residents only occur during their last 4 to 6 weeks of life (Kiely, Morris, & Morris, 1997).

As research and conceptual approaches to institutionalization become more sophisticated, there have been calls to focus research on processes that occur in the course of institutionalization and on the dimension of time implicit in studies of change (George, 1984). The recognition of the potential influence of existential variables, such as maintenance of goals or meaning in life and spirituality, also present promising approaches to future research (Reker, 2001-2002). An important challenge in this area is the linking of institutional input variables to patient outcomes and satisfaction. It is now also recognized that the institutional setting must be considered in a community and social context. The potentially useful role of focusing involvement in residential long-term care also represents an area of inquiry with great heuristic value (Gaugler, Anderson, Zarit, & Pearlin, 2004). Experts suggest that development of incentives for care to improve provision and outcomes of institutional services may be useful (Kane, Bell, Riegler, Wilson, & Keeler, 1983). Changing characteristics of the elderly, in the direction of more native-born, more educated, and more sophisticated consumers, are also likely to lead to changing expectations of future consumers of institutional care and even to demands for greater options and more self-determination. At the same time, the unique needs of minority populations requiring long-term care must be recognized, as greater diversity is acknowledged among the elderly. There are also indications of major impending changes in financing, organization, and delivery of long-term care in the near future, with group trends toward community-based care (Rowland, Burns, Schafft, & Randolph, 1997). These changes are likely to result in more diversified services provided in alternative settings, altering the meaning of institutionalization and requiring multidimensional approaches to assessing its role and impact in the spectrum of services that comprise long-term care.

EVA KAHANA

References

American Geriatrics Society and American Association for Geriatric Psychiatry. (2003). Recommendations for policies in support of quality mental health care in U.S. nursing homes. *Journal of the American Geriatrics Society, 51*, 1299–1304.

Antonelli, E., Rubini, V., & Fassone, C. (2000). The self-concept in institutionalized and non-institutionalized elderly people. *Journal of Environmental Psychology, 20(1)*, 151–164.

Baltes, M. M. (1996). *Many faces of dependency in old age*. Cambridge: Cambridge University.

Bauer, E. (1996). Transitions from home to nursing home in a capitated long-term care program: The role of individual support systems. *Health Services Research, 31(3)*, 309–326.

Braun, J. V., Wykle, M. H., & Cowling, W. R. (1988). Failure to thrive in older persons: A concept derived. *Gerontologist, 28*, 809–812.

Camp, C., & Mattern, J. (1999). In D. Beigel & A. Blum (Eds.), *Innovations in practice and service delivery across the lifespan* (pp.). New York: Oxford University Press.

Calkins, M. (2003). Powell Lawton's contributions to long-term care settings. In R. Scheidt & P. Windley (Eds.), *Physical environments and aging: Critical contributions of M. Powell Lawton to theory and practice* (pp. 67–84). New York: Haworth Press.

Clark, D. (1997). U.S. trends in disability and institutionalization among older blacks and whites. *American Journal of Public Health, 87(3)*, 438–440.

Degenholtz, H., Kane, R., Kane, R., & Finch, M. (1999). Long-term care case managers' out-of-home placement decisions. *Research on Aging, 21(2)*, 240–274.

Depla, M., Pols, J., de Lange, J., Smits, C., De Graaf, R., & Heeren, T. (2003). Integrating mental health care into residential homes for the elderly: An analysis of six Dutch programs for older people with severe and persistent mental illness. *Journal of the American Geriatric Society, 51*, 1275–1279.

Devroey, D., Van Casteren, V., & de Lepeleire, J. (2001). Revealing regional differences in the institutionalization of adult patients in homes for the elderly and nursing homes: Results of the Belgian network of sentinel GPs. *Family Practice, 18*, 39–41.

Diamond, T. (1992). *Making gray gold: Narratives of nursing home care*. Chicago: University of Chicago Press.

Dwyer, J., Barton, A., & Vogel, W. (1994). Area of residence and the risk of institutionalization. *Journals of Gerontology, 49(2)*, S75–S84.

Engle, V. F., & Graney, M. J. (1993). Predicting outcomes of nursing home residents: Death and discharge. *Journals of Gerontology, 48(5)*, S269–S275.

Frijters, D., Mor, V., DuPaquier, J., Berg, K., Carpenter, G., & Ribbe, M. (1997). Transitions across various continuing care settings. *Age and Ageing, 26(2)*, 73–76.

Gaugler, J., Anderson, K., Zarit, S., & Pearlin, L. (2004). Family involvement in nursing homes: Effects on stress and well-being. *Aging and Mental Health, 8(1)*, 65–75.

George, L. (1984). Institutionalized. In E. Palmore (Ed.), *Handbook on the aged in the United States* (pp. 339–354). Westport, CT: Greenwood Press.

Goffman, E. (1961). *Asylums: Essays on the social situation of mental patients and other inmates*. Garden City, NY: Doubleday.

Gottesman, L., & Bourestom, N. (1974). Why nursing homes do what they do. *Gerontologist, 14(6)*, 501–506.

Gottlich, V. (1995). Protection for nursing facility residents under the ADA. *Generations, 4(4)*, 43–47.

Gubrium, J. (1993). *Speaking of life: Horizons of meaning for nursing home residents*. Hawthorne, NY: Aldine de Gruyter.

Hawes, C., Mor, V., Phillips, C. D., Fries-Brant, E., Morris, J. N., Steel-Friedlob, E., Greene, A. M., & Nennstiel, M. (1997). OBRA-87 nursing home regulations and implementation of the Resident Assessment Instrument: Effects on process quality. *Journal of the American Geriatrics Society, 45(8)*, 977–985.

Henry, J. (1963). *Culture against man*. New York: Vintage.

Joiner, C. M. & Freudiger, P. T. (1993). Male and female differences in nursing home adjustment and satisfaction. *Journal of Gerontological Social Work, 20(3-4)*, 71–85.

Kahana, E., Kahana, B., & Chirayath, H. (1999). Innovations in institutional care from a patient-responsive perspective. In D. Beigel & A. Blum (Eds.), *Innovations in practice and service delivery across the lifespan* (pp. 249–275). New York: Oxford University Press.

Kahana, E., Kahana, B., & Young, R. (1985). Social factors in institutional living. In W. A. Peterson & J. Quadango (Eds.), *Social bonds in later life: Aging and interdependence* (pp. 389–419). Beverly Hills, CA: Sage.

Kahana, E., & Kiyak, A. (1984). Attitudes and behavior of staff in facilities for the aged. *Research on Aging, 6*, 395–416.

Kahana, E., Liang, J., & Felton, B. (1980). Alternative models of person-environment fit: Prediction of morale in three homes for the aged. *Journal of Gerontology, 35*, 584–595.

Kahana, J. S. (1995). Reevaluating the nursing home ombudsman's role with a view toward expanding the concept of dispute resolution. *Journal of Dispute Resolution, 2*, 217–234.

Kane, R. A. (1993). Ethical and legal issues in long-term care: Food for futurist thought. *Journal of Long-Term Care Administration, 21(3)*, 66–74.

Kane, R. A. (1995—96). Transforming care institutions for the frail elderly: Out of one shall be many. *Generations, 4*, 62–68.

Kane, R., Bell, R., Reigler, S., Wilson, A., & Keeler, E. (1983). Predicting the outcomes of nursing home patients. *Gerontologist, 23(2)*, 200–206.

Kiely, D., Morris, J., & Morris, S. (1997). The effect of specific medical conditions on function decline. *Journal of the American Geriatrics Society, 45*, 1459–1463.

Lawton, M. P. (1980). *Environment and aging*. Monterey, CA: Brooks/Cole.

Liang, J., Liu, X., Tu, E., & Witelaw, N. (1996). Probabilities and lifetime durations of short-stay hospital and nursing home use in the United States, 1985. *Medical Care, 34(10)*, 1018–1036.

McAuley, W., & Travis, S. (1997). Positions of influence in the nursing home admission decision. *Research on Aging, 19(1)* 26–45.

McAuley, W., & Usita, P. (1998). Conceptual model for the mobility patterns of nursing home admissions. *Gerontologist, 38(6)*, 726–734.

Miller, S., Prohaska, T., Runer, S., Freels, S., Brody, J., & Levy, P. (1998). Time to nursing home admission for persons with Alzheimer's disease: The effect of health care system characteristics. *Journals of Gerontology, 53B(6)*, S341–S353.

Morris, J., Sherwood, S., & Mor, V. (1984). Assessment tool for use in identifying functionally vulnerable persons in the community. *Gerontologist, 24(4)*, 373–379.

Murtaugh, C., Kemper, P., & Spillman, B. (1990). The risk of nursing home use in later life. *Medical Care, 28*, 10.

National Center for Health Statistics. (1997). An overview of nursing homes and their current residents: Data from the 1995 National Nursing Home Survey. *Advance Data from Vital and Health Statistics, No. 280*. Bethesda, MD: National Center for Health Statistics.

Patchner, M. A., & Balgopal, P. R. (1993). *Excellence in nursing homes*. New York: Springer Publishing.

Payette, H., Coulombe, C., Boutier, V., & Gray-Donald, K. (2000). Nutrition risk factors for institutionalization in a free-living functionally dependent elderly population. *Journal of Clinical Epidemiology, 53*, 579–587.

Reker, G. (2001—2002). Prospective predictors of successful aging in community-residing and institutionalized Canadian elderly. *Ageing International, 27(1)* 42–64.

Rowland, M., Burns, B., Schafft, G., & Randolph, F. (1997). Innovative services for elderly populations. In S. Henggeler & A. Santos (Eds.), *Innovative approaches for difficult-to-treat populations* (pp. 289–310). Washington, DC: American Psychiatric Press.

Savishinsky, J. S. (1991). *The ends of time: Life and work in a nursing home*. New York: Bergin and Garvey.

Schimer, M. R., & Kahana, J. S. (1992). *Legal issues in the care of older adults*. Cleveland, OH: Western Reserve Geriatric Education Center, CWRU School of Medicine.

Schulz, R., Belle, S., Czaja, S., McGinnis, K., Stevens, A., Zhang, S. (2004). Long-term care placement of dementia patients and caregiver health and well-being. *Journal of the American Medical Association, 292(8)*, 961–967.

Smyer, M., Shea, D., & Streit, A. (1994). The provision and use of mental health services in nursing homes: Results from the National Medical Expenditure Survey. *American Journal of Public Health, 84*, 284–287.

Soth, N. B. (1997). *Informed treatment: Milieu management in psychiatric hospitals and residential treatment centers*. Lanham, MD: Medical Library Association/Scarecrow Press.

Spector, W., Reschovsky, J., & Cohen, J. (1996). Appropriate placement of nursing-home residents in lower levels of care. *Milbank Quarterly, 74(1)*, 139–160.

Thomas, W. (1996). *Life worth living: How someone you love can still enjoy life in a nursing home. The Eden alternative in action*. Acton, MA: VanderWyk and Burnham.

Thorson, J., & Davis, R. (2000). Relocation of the institutionalized aged. *Journal of Clinical Psychology, 56(1)*, 131–138.

Woo, J., Ho, S., Yu, A., & Lau, J. (2000). An estimate of long-term care needs and identification of risk factors for institutionalization among Hong Kong Chinese aged 70 years and over. *Journals of Gerontology Series A Biological Sciences and Medical Sciences, 55*, M64–M69.

Yaffe, K., Fox, P., Newcomer, R., Sands, L., Lindquist, K., Dane, K., & Covinsky, K. (2002). Patient and caregiver characteristics and nursing home placement in patients with dementia. *Journal of the American Medical Association, 287(16)*, 2090–2097.

INSTRUMENTAL ACTIVITIES OF DAILY LIVING

See
Activities of Daily Living

INTELLIGENCE

Maintaining intellectual competence assumes major importance for the quality of life of many older persons. Assessment of intellectual competence is often required to provide information relevant to questions of retirement for cause (in the absence of mandatory retirement at an early age), sufficient competence for independent living, or for the control and disposition of an individual's property.

Changes in competence that represent actual intra-individual decrement must be differentiated from performance that has remained stable over time but that is now below the average performance of today's younger persons. The latter finding would not represent an older person's decline, but instead reflects the obsolescent functioning of older cohorts when compared to younger peers. Researchers and practitioners want to know at what age *developmental peaks in intelligence* occur in the level of performance and rate of age change, and why some individuals show *intellectual decrement in early adulthood* while others maintain or increase their level of functioning on some ability variables well into old age.

The intellectual processes required for the acquisition of cognitive structures and functions in childhood are not necessarily relevant to the maintenance of functions and the reorganization of structures that may be needed to meet the demands of later life. However, certain basic concepts relevant to the understanding of intelligence in childhood retain relevance throughout life, while the manner in which observable behaviors *(phenotypes)* express such constructs (*genotypes*) may change with age in pattern and organization.

Intellectual Development in Old Age

Most data on *adult intellectual development* is based on work with the *Wechsler Adult Intelligence Scale* (*WAIS*; Matarazzo, 1982) or with Thurstone's *Primary Mental Abilities* test. Studies with the WAIS have focused upon a so-called classical pattern that shows a plateau reached in the 20s age cohort, with maintenance of performance on verbal subtests such as vocabulary and comprehension until the 60s, but early adult decline on performance tests such as block design or object assembly. More recent studies, however, suggest that in healthy individuals WAIS performance may hold up well into old age (Busse, 1993).

Age comparisons on the WAIS are compromised by the finding that the factorial structure of that battery changes from early adulthood to old age (Cohen, 1959). By contrast, it has been established that the structure of the primary mental abilities remains rather stable across adulthood (Schaie, Maitland, Willis, & Intrieri, 1998). Data for the PMA indicate continued gains for most abilities until the persons reached ages of late 30s or early 40s. Thereafter a plateau is maintained until the early 60s, with the exception of the highly speeded measure of word fluency (vocabulary recall) that shows significant decline in the 50s. Gender differences have been reported that suggest earlier decline for spatial ability in men and word fluency in women. The average magnitude of *intellectual decline*, however, is quite small during the 60s and early 70s and is probably of little significance for the competent behavior of the young old. However, substantial average decline for most abilities are observed once the 80s are reached (Schaie, 1996, 2004).

Individual Differences in Adult Intellectual Development

The data on average age changes tend to conceal a most important item. It might indicate to the casual observer that intellectual decrement in old age is universal and unavoidable. Data from the *Seattle Longitudinal Study* (Schaie, 2004) argues to the contrary. Only about one-third of individuals studied declined reliably over a 7-year period from age 60 to 67, and about 40% declined from age 67 to 74. Even by age 81, about 50% of the members of the longitudinal panels maintained their functional level over a 7-year period.

What accounts for these individual differences in intellectual change over time? In addition to factors that might be genetic in nature, other attributes characterize individuals who do not decline in old age; (1) they are free of cardiovascular and other chronic disease, (2) their *perceptual speed* has declined less than average, (3) they have at least average socioeconomic status, (4) they exhibit a stimulating and engaged life style, and (5) they describe themselves as having flexible attitudes and behaviors at mid-life (Schaie, 2004).

Can Intellectual Decrement be Reversed?

In studies related to optimal or adaptive intellectual functioning, it has been recognized that older adults can be disadvantaged in at least 2 different ways. First, some age-related decline may occur through disuse, whether by personal choice or environmental restrictions. Second, some people may be disadvantaged because of rapid sociocultural and technological change. Cross-sectional *cognitive training* research has strongly suggested the modifiability of older adults' performance on a number of intelligence dimensions. However, the cross-sectional nature of this research made it impossible to examine one fundamental question: to what extent did training procedures result in remediation of age-related decline versus the acquisition of new performance levels in subjects experiencing no decline?

Within the context of a longitudinal study it has been found that reliably documented 14-year decrement could be reversed in approximately 40% of subjects undergoing a cognitive training program and significantly reduced in an additional 25% of participants (Schaie & Willis, 1986). Performance levels were enhanced also in substantial numbers of persons whose performance had remained stable. The effects of training were maintained over as long as 14 years (Schaie, 2004; Willis, 2001). The data suggests that for many older persons intellectual decline or cohort-related disadvantage (compared to younger peers) may be largely experiential in nature and can be modified by modest intervention efforts.

Intelligence in the Everyday World

Attention has turned to the question of how traditional measures of intelligence relate to performance in real-life circumstances. Measures of so-called *practical intelligence* often appear to assess situation-specific competence rather than basic components of intelligence that would be widely generalizable. Hence, the application of intelligence to everyday situations will always require different combinations of more basic intellectual abilities. For an examination of practical intelligence from various points of view, see Schaie & Willis (1999).

K. Warner Schaie

References

Busse, E. W. (1993). Duke longitudinal studies of aging. *Zeitschrift für Gerontologie*, *26*, 123–128.

Cohen, J. (1959). The factorial structure of the WAIS between early adulthood and old age. *Journal of Consulting Psychology*, *21*, 283–290.

Matarazzo, J. D. (1972). *Wechsler's measurement and appraisal of adult intelligence*. Baltimore: Williams and Wilkins.

Schaie, K. W. (1996). *Intellectual development in adulthood: The Seattle Longitudinal Study*. New York: Cambridge University Press.

Schaie, K. W. (2004). *Developmental influences on adult intelligence: The Seattle Longitudinal Study*. New York: Oxford University Press.

Schaie, K. W., Maitland, S. B., Willis, S. L., & Intrieri, R. L. (1998). Longitudinal invariance of adult psychometric ability factor structures across seven years. *Psychology and Aging*, *13*, 8–20.

Schaie, K. W., & Willis, S. L. (1986). Can intellectual decline in the elderly be reversed? *Developmental Psychology*, *22*, 223–232.

Schaie, K. W., & Willis, S. L. (1999). Theories of everyday competence. In V. L. Bengtson & K. W. Schaie (Eds.), *Handbook of theories of aging*, (pp. 174–195). New York: Springer Publishing.

Willis, S. L. (1996). Everyday cognitive competence in elderly persons: Conceptual issues and empirical finding. *Gerontologist*, *36*, 595–601.

Willis, S. L. (2001). Methodological issues in behavioral intervention research with the elderly. In J. E. Birren & K. W. Schaie (Eds.), *Handbook of the psychology of aging* (5th ed., pp. 78–108). San Diego, CA: Academic Press.

INTERFERENCE

Interference is a general term for the disruptive effects of *irrelevant information*. This irrelevant information may come from *environmental distractors*, or it may be internally generated, such as currently irrelevant thoughts or memories or "strong but wrong" *habitual responses* that are inappropriate for the current situation. Interference is said to occur when such irrelevant information reduces the accuracy of or slows response. As a general rule, older adults are more susceptible to interference effects than young adults (Hasher & Zacks, 1988; Hasher, Zacks, & May, 1999; McDowd, Oseas-Kreger, & Filion, 1995).

Older adults' vulnerability to interference from environmental distraction can be seen on a variety of tasks including visual search, reading, problem-solving, and categorization. Age differences in distractor interference are especially large when there are many distractors, and when it is difficult to distinguish the distractors from the target. For example, when searching for a target in a visual display, older adults may not be more impaired than young adults by the presence of a single distractor, but are increasingly affected as the number of distractors is increased (Foster, Behrmann, & Stuss, 1995; Hommel, Li, & Li, 2004; Madden & Langley, 2003; Plude & Hoyer, 1986; Scialfa, Esau, & Joffe, 1998).

Age differences in *vulnerability to interference* are sensitive to the similarity between the relevant and irrelevant information. For example, on visual search tasks, *age differences in distractor interference* can be reduced by making the distractors easy to distinguish from the targets (e.g., Zeef, Sonke, Kok, Buiten, & Kenemans, 1996), or by having them appear in predictable locations (see Madden & Plude, 1993, for a discussion of sparing factors). Conversely, age differences in distractor interference are especially large if the distractors are related to the targets.

Age differences and the influences of target-distractor similarity are apparent on both simple and complex tasks. Both younger and older adults are slower to decide which category a word belongs to if it is surrounded by words from competing categories compared to when it is flanked by words from the same category, but this difference is especially large for older adults (Shaw, 1991). Likewise, in the *Remote Associations Test*, in which participants need to generate a word that creates a link between 3 otherwise unrelated words (e.g., ship, crawl, outer: SPACE) older adults are more influenced than younger counterparts by both leading (rocket, atmosphere, attic) and misleading (ocean, inner, floor) distractors (May, 1999). When reading paragraphs, *older adults' reading times* are more slowed than young adults' by distracting words scattered throughout the text, and older but not young adults are further slowed if the distractor words have meanings related to the passage (Carlson, Hasher, Connelly, & Zacks, 1995; Connelly, Hasher, & Zacks, 1991; Duchek, Balota, & Thessing, 1998; Dywan & Murphy, 1996; Li, Hasher, Jonas, Rahhal, & May, 1998). Thus, on both simple and complex tasks, older adults are more affected by environmental distractors than are young adults. These age differences in distractor interference appear to increase with the number of distractors and with the difficulty of distinguishing between targets and distractors.

Interference can also come from internally generated sources, such as *irrelevant thoughts and memories*. Some studies suggest that older adults may be more distracted by thoughts and concerns about their performance, to the point that this distraction impairs their performance on the task (Hess, Auman, Colcombe, & Rahhal, 2003; Rahhal, Hasher, & Colcombe, 2001). Interference is also widely considered to be a primary factor in forgetting, a major concern for older adults.

Interference in memory is classically studied using procedures designed to create either proactive or retroactive interference. *Proactive interference* occurs when a previous but now irrelevant memory impairs memory for a newly relevant item; for example, it can be difficult to remember exactly where in the lot the car is parked because now-irrelevant memories for previous parking spots interfere. *Retroactive interference* is the opposite phenomenon: newer information impairs memory for things that occurred further in the past. As reviewed in previous entries (Kane & Hasher, 1995; Lustig & Hasher, 2001), the evidence generally supports the idea that older adults are more susceptible than younger counterparts to both types of interference. The few age-comparative studies of interference on *delayed memory tests* since then are consistent with this conclusion (Hasher, Chung, May, & Foong, 2002; Jacoby, Debner, & Hay, 2001; Persad, Abeles, Zacks, & Denburg, 2002).

The roles of proactive and retroactive interference on short-term or working memory tests have recently become a focus of research. With rare exception (Tehan & Hauff, 2000), these studies overwhelmingly find older adults to be more susceptible to both types of *interference on working memory* tasks, although there is some controversy as to the reason (Andres, Van Der Linden, & Parmentier, 2004; Bowles & Salthouse, 2003; De Beni & Palladino, 2004; Hedden & Park, 2003; Lustig, May, & Hasher, 2001; May, Hasher, & Kane, 1999).

Other studies examine age differences in mechanisms underlying interference, and in some cases manipulate these mechanisms to improve the *memory performance of older adults*. Competition between items is a major mechanism of interference, and can be investigated by varying the number of items associated with a *memory cue*. As more items are associated with the cue, the retrieval of any 1 item becomes slower and less likely to succeed. For example, learning 3 facts about an object, (e.g., "The potted palm is in the lobby," "The potted palm is in the laundromat," "The potted palm is in the stairwell" makes retrieval of any 1 of those more difficult as compared to when only 1 fact is learned about an object (e.g., "The pay phone is in the hall.") Older adults are more susceptible to this "fan effect," or the increase in difficulty as more facts "fan off" the memory cue. However, presenting multiple pieces of information in a way that allows their integration into a single scene or mental model (e.g., "The potted palm is in the lobby," "The pay phone is in the lobby," "The wastebasket is in the lobby") reduces competition and fan effects for both young and old adults (Radvansky, Zacks, & Hasher, 1996).

For young adults, identifying irrelevant information as such and telling participants to forget it reduces both memory for the irrelevant information and its interference with the relevant, to-be-remembered information. Older adults usually show less of a "*directed forgetting*" effect (Andres, Van der Linden, & Parmentier, 2004; Dulaney, Marks, & Link, 2004; Earles & Kernsten, 2002; Zacks, Radvansky, & Hasher, 1996). There have been some reports of age equivalence in directed forgetting, but these may result from manipulations that make it difficult for young adults to forget the irrelevant information, thus reducing their directed forgetting effect to that of older adults (Earles & Kersten, 2002; Gamboz & Russo, 2002).

Strong or habitual responses can also be a source of interference. A classic example is the *Stroop task*, which consists of color words printed in conflicting ink colors (e.g., the word "red" printed in blue ink). When attempting to name the ink color, older adults are typically more vulnerable to the competing effects of the word information than are young adults (Davidson, Zacks, & Williams, 2003; but see Verhaegen & De Meersman, 1998). Likewise, older adults usually have more difficulty with "go/no-go" tasks and stop signal tasks, both of which require rapid responses to most stimuli, but withholding responses to certain rarely occurring stimuli (Kramer, Humphrey, Larish, Logan, & Strayer, 1994; May & Hasher, 1998). Furthermore, if the rules of a task change, older adults are more likely to persist using the now incorrect, outdated response than are their younger counterparts (Kramer, Humphrey, Larish, Logan, & Strayer, 1994).

The term interference has also been applied to *dual-task* (also known as *divided attention*) situations, in which participants are asked to perform 2 tasks at the same time. Interference in this case refers to the reduced performance on either task compared to doing only 1 of those tasks. The evidence for age differences in dual task interference is mixed, and may be more evident on measures of reaction time than of accuracy (Verhaegen, Steitz, Sliwinski, & Cerella, 2003). Age studies of *dual-task interference* are complicated by the potential relevance of both tasks (rather than 1 being relevant and the other irrelevant), and young and older adults may differ in the priorities they assign to each (Li, Lindenberger, Freund, & Baltes, 2001). Assigning young adults to a dual-task condition is a classic method of attempting to reduce their performance to the level of older adults' in a single-task situation (Craik & Byrd, 1982; Fernandes & Moscovitch, 2003).

A major question is the degree to which these different forms of interference—disruption from environmental distraction, strong responses, previous memories—reflect the operation of same versus different processing mechanisms. Large, latent-variable studies with young adults suggest partial independence (Friedman & Miyake, 2004). Biologically based studies with both younger and older adults generally support this view, and further suggest that age effects may vary with the mechanisms involved. For example, the size of age differences in interference varies with circadian arousal. Older adults are generally more vulnerable to interference in the afternoon across a range of tasks, including those with interference from environmental distraction, strong responses, and previous memories (May, 1999; May & Hasher, 1998; Hasher et al., 2002. However, at least 1 study suggests that the form of age-circadian interactions may differ for the different types of interference (West, Murphy, Armilio, Craik, & Stuss, 2002). Measurements of brain activity, including event-related potentials (ERPs), position emission tomography (PET) and functional magnetic resonance imaging (fMRI) generally concur in finding age differences in *brain activation related to interference* (Langenecker, Nielsen, & Rao, 2004; Milham, Erickson, Banich, Kramer, Webb, Wszalek, et al., 2002; West & Alain, 2000). Recent fMRI studies with young adults also support the idea of both shared and distinct brain networks involved in different types of *interference processing* (Sylvester, Wager, Lacey, Hernandez, Nichols, Smith, et al., 2003; Nelson, Reuter-Lorenz, Sylvester, Jonides, & Smith, 2003). The overall research on the question of same versus different mechanisms for interference processing is preliminary, but the active, multi-technique state of research in this area promises important insights to come.

In summary, older adults are typically more vulnerable than younger persons to interference from irrelevant information, whether internally or externally generated. Age differences in interference—and in overall performance—can often be reduced and occasionally even eliminated by reducing competition, the major mechanism of interference. Age differences in interference vulnerability have a biological basis, as reflected in their sensitivity to circadian arousal and in measures of brain activity. The degree to which different forms of interference are mediated by the same or different processing mechanisms is an active and exciting area of research.

CINDY LUSTIG
LYNN HASHER

See also
Cognitive Processes

References

Andres, P., Van der Linden, M., & Parmentier, F. B. R. (2004). Directed forgetting in working memory: Age-related differences. *Memory, 12*, 248–256.

Bowles, R. P., & Salthouse, T. A. (2003). Assessing the age-related effects of proactive interference on working memory tasks using the Rasch model. *Psychology and Aging, 18*, 608–615.

Carlson, M. C., Hasher, L., Connelly, S. L., & Zacks, R. T. (1995). Aging, distraction, and the benefits of predictable location. *Psychology and Aging, 10*, 427–436.

Connelly, S. L., Hasher, L., & Zacks, R. T. (1991). Age and reading: The impact of distraction. *Psychology and Aging, 6*, 533–541.

Craik, F. I. M., & Byrd, M. (1982). Aging and cognitive deficits: The role of attentional resources. In F. I. M. Craik & S. E. Trehub (Eds.), *Aging and cognitive processes* (pp. 191–211). New York: Plenum Press.

Davidson, D. J., Zacks, R. T., & Williams, C. C. (2003). Stroop interference, practice, and aging. *Aging Neuropsychology and Cognition, 10*, 85–98.

De Beni, R., & Palladino, P. (2004). Decline in working memory updating through ageing: Intrusion error analyses. *Memory, 12*, 75–89.

Duchek, J. M., Balota, D. A., & Thessing, V. C. (1998). Inhibition of visual and conceptual information during reading in healthy aging and Alzheimer's disease. *Aging Neuropsychology and Cognition, 5*, 169–181.

Dulaney, C. L., Marks, W., & Link, K. E. (2004). Aging and directed forgetting: Pre-cue encoding and post-cue rehearsal effects. *Experimental Aging Research, 30*, 95–112.

Dywan, J., & Murphy, W. E. (1996). Aging and inhibitory control in text comprehension. *Psychology and Aging, 11*, 199–206.

Earles, J. L., & Kersten, A. W. (2002). Directed forgetting of actions by younger and older adults. *Psychonomic Bulletin and Review, 9*, 383–388.

Fernandes, M. A., & Moscovitch, M. (2003). Interference effects from divided attention during retrieval in younger and older adults. *Psychology and Aging, 18*, 219–230.

Foster, J. K., Behrmann, M., & Stuss, D. T. (1995). Visual attention deficits in Alzheimer's disease: Simple versus conjunctive feature search. *Neuropsychology, 13*, 223–245.

Friedman, N. P., & Miyake, A. (2004). The relations among inhibition and interference control functions: A latent-variable analysis. *Journal of Experimental Psychology: General, 133*, 101–135.

Gamboz, N., & Russo, R. (2002). Evidence for age-related equivalence in the directed forgetting paradigm. *Brain and Cognition, 48*, 366–371.

Hasher, L., Chung, C., May, C. P., & Foong, N. (2002). Age, time of testing, and proactive interference. *Canadian Journal of Experimental Psychology/Revue Canadienne De Psychologie Experimentale, 56*, 200–207.

Hasher, L., & Zacks, R. T. (1988). Working memory, comprehension, and aging: A review and a new view. In G. H. Bower (Ed.), *The psychology of learning and motivation* (vol. 22, pp. 193–225). New York: Academic Press.

Hasher, L., Zacks, R. T., & May, C. P. (1999). Inhibitory control, circadian arousal, and age. In D. Gopher, & A. Koriat (Eds.). *Attention and performance* (Vol. 17, pp. 653–675). Cambridge, MA: MIT Press.

Hedden, T., & Park, D. C. (2003). Contributions of source and inhibitory mechanisms to age-related retroactive interference in verbal working memory. *Journal of Experimental Psychology-General, 132*, 93–112.

Hess, T. M., Auman, C., Colcombe, S. J., & Rahhal, T. A. (2003). The impact of stereotype threat on age differences in memory performance. *Journals of Gerontology Series B-Psychological Sciences and Social Sciences, 58*, P3–P11.

Hommel, B., Li, K. Z. H., & Li, S. C. (2004). Visual search across the life span. *Developmental Psychology, 40*, 545–558.

Jacoby, L. J., Debner, J. A., & Hay, J. F. (2001). Proactive interference, accessibility bias, and process dissociations: Valid subjective reports of memory. *Journal of Experimental Psychology-Learning Memory and Cognition, 27*, 686–700.

Kane, M. J., & Hasher, L. (1995). Interference. In G. Maddox (Ed.), *Encyclopedia of aging* (2nd ed., pp. 514–516). New York: Springer Publishing.

Kramer, A. F., Humphrey, D. G., Larish, J. F., Logan, G. D., & Strayer, D. L. (1994). Aging and inhibition. Beyond a unitary view of inhibitory processing in attention. *Psychology and Aging, 9*, 491–512.

Langenecker, S. A., Nielson, K. A., & Rao, S. M. (2004). fMRI of healthy older adults during Stroop interference. *Neuroimage, 21*, 192–200.

Li, K. Z. H., Hasher, L., Jonas, D., Rahhal, T. A., & May, C. P. (1998). Distractibility, circadian arousal, and aging: A boundary condition? *Psychology and Aging, 13*, 574–583.

Li, K. Z. H., Lindenberger, U., Freund, A. M., & Baltes, P. B. (2001). Walking while memorizing: Age-related differences in compensatory behavior. *Psychological Science, 12*, 230–237.

Lustig, C., & Hasher, L. (2001). Interference. In G. Maddox (Ed.), *Encyclopedia of aging*, (3rd ed., pp. 553–555). New York: Springer-Verlag.

Lustig, C., May, C. P., & Hasher, L. (2001). Working memory span and the role of proactive interference. *Journal of Experimental Psychology-General, 130*, 199–207.

Madden, D. J., & Langley, L. K. (2003). Age-related changes in selective attention and perceptual load during visual search. *Psychology and Aging, 18*, 54–67.

Madden, D. J., & Plude, D. J. (1993). Selective preservation of selective attention. In J. Cerella, J. Rybash, W. Hoyer, & M. L. Commons (Eds.), *Adult information processing: Limits on loss* (pp. 273-300). San Diego, CA: Academic Press.

May, C. P. (1999). Synchrony effects in cognition: The costs and a benefit. *Psychological Bulletin and Review, 6*, 142–147.

May, C. P., & Hasher, L. (1998). Synchrony effects in inhibitory control over thought and action. *Journal of Experimental Psychology-Human Perception and Performance, 24*, 363–379.

May, C. P., Hasher, L., & Kane, M. J. (1999). The role of interference in memory span. *Memory and Cognition, 27*, 759–767.

McDowd, J. M., Oseas-Kreger, D. M., & Filion, D. L. (1995). Inhibitory processes in cognition and aging. In F. N. Demster & C. J. Brainerd (Eds.), *Interference and inhibition in cognition* (pp. 363–401). San Diego: Academic Press.

Milham, M. P., Erickson, K. I., Banich, M. T., Kramer, A. F., Webb, A., Wszalek, T., & Cohen, N. J. (2002). Attentional control in the aging brain: Insights from an fMRI study of the Stroop task. *Brain and Cognition, 49*, 277–296.

Nelson, J. K., Reuter-Lorenz, P. A., Sylvester, C. Y. C., Jonides, J., & Smith, E. E. (2003). Dissociable neural mechanisms underlying response-based and familiarity-based conflict in working memory. *Proceedings of the National Academy of Sciences of the USA, 100*, 11171–11175.

Persad, C. C., Abeles, N., Zacks, R. T., & Denburg, N. L. (2002). Inhibitory changes after age 60 and their relationship to measures of attention and memory. *Journals of Gerontology Series B-Psychological Sciences and Social Sciences, 57*, P223–P232.

Plude, D. J., & Hoyer, W. J. (1986). Age and the selectivity of visual information processing. *Psychology and Aging, 1*, 4–10.

Radvansky, G. A., Zacks, R. T., & Hasher, L. (1996). Fact retrieval in younger and older adults: The role of mental models. *Psychology and Aging, 11*, 258–271.

Rahhal, T. A., Hasher, L., & Colcombe, S. J. (2001). Instructional manipulations and age differences in memory: Now you see them, now you don't. *Psychology and Aging, 16*, 697–706.

Scialfa, C. T., Esau, S. P., & Joffe, K. M. (1998). Age, target-distractor similarity, and visual search. *Experimental Aging Research, 24*, 337–358.

Shaw, R. J. (1991). Age-related increases in the effects of automatic semantic activation. *Psychology and Aging, 6*, 595–604.

Sylvester, C. Y. C., Wager, T. D., Lacey, S. C., Hernandez, L., Nichols, T. E., Smith, E. E., & Jonides, J. (2003). Switching attention and resolving interference: fMRI measures of executive functions. *Neuropsychologia, 41*, 357–370.

Tehan, G., & Hauff, H. M. (2000). Proactive interference effects on ageing: Is inhibition a factor? *Australian Psychologist, 35*, 249–254.

Verhaegen, P., & De Meersman, L. (1998). Aging and the Stroop effect: A meta-analysis. *Psychology and Aging, 13*, 120–126.

Verhaegen, P., Steitz, D. W., Sliwinski, M. J., & Cerella, J. (2003). Aging and dual-task performance: A meta-analysis. *Psychology and Aging, 18*, 443–460.

West, R., & Alain, C. (2000). Effects of task context and fluctuations of attention on neural activity supporting performance of the Stroop task. *Brain Research, 873*, 102–111.

West, R., Murphy, K. J., Armilio, M. L., Craik, F. I. M., & Stuss, D. T. (2002). Effects of time of day on age differences in working memory. *Journals of Gerontology Series B-Psychological Sciences and Social Sciences, 57*, P3–P10.

Zacks, R. T., Radvansky, G., & Hasher, L. (1996). Studies of directed forgetting in older adults. *Journal of*

Experimental Psychology-Learning Memory and Cognition, 22, 143–156.

Zeef, E. J., Sonke, C. J., Kok, A., Buiten, M. M., & Kenemans, J. L. (1996). Perceptual factors affecting age-related differences in focused attention: Performance and psychophysiological analyses. *Psychophysiology, 33*, 555–565.

INTERGENERATIONAL EQUITY

The concept of intergenerational equity, encompassing issues of fairness in the distribution of resources and obligations among age groups, is relatively new. In the United States, it arose in the late 1970s. Prior to that time, during the 4 decades dating from the enactment of *Social Security* in 1935, U.S. society incrementally created an old-age welfare state nourished by compassionate *stereotypes of older person* in public discourse (Binstock, 1983). Older persons tended to be stereotyped as poor, frail, socially dependent, objects of discrimination, unable to help themselves, and above all "deserving." For 40 years U.S. society accepted this compassionate ageism, the oversimplified notion that all older persons are essentially the same, and all worthy of governmental assistance. By the late 1960s and 1970s, almost every issue or problem that advocates for the aging identified as affecting at least *some* older persons was adopted as a governmental responsibility.

The Construction of "Intergenerational Equity"

Starting in 1978 in the United States and somewhat later in other countries, (Walker, in press) the long-standing compassionate stereotypes of older persons began to undergo an extraordinary reversal. Older people came to be portrayed as one of the more flourishing and powerful groups in U.S. society and yet attacked as a burdensome responsibility. Throughout the 1980s and 1990s and into the 21st century, the new stereotypes, readily observed in popular culture, have depicted *older persons as a new elite*—prosperous, hedonistic, politically powerful, and selfish (Gibbs, 1980).

A dominant theme in such accounts of older Americans was that their selfishness was ruining the nation. The *New Republic* highlighted this motif with an unflattering caricature of older persons depicted on the cover, accompanied by the caption "greedy geezers." The table of contents "teaser" for the story that followed announced that "The real me generation isn't the yuppies, it's America's growing ranks of *prosperous elderly*" (Fairlie, 1988). This theme was echoed widely, and the epithet "greedy geezers" became a familiar adjective in journalistic accounts of federal budget politics (Salholz, 1990). In the early 1990s *Fortune* magazine declaimed that "the tyranny of America's old" is "one of the most crucial issues facing U.S. society" (Smith, 1992). Two elements contributed to this reversal of stereotypes: dramatic improvements in the aggregate income status of older Americans, in large part due to the impact of Social Security, Medicare, and other federal programs; and the tremendous growth in the amount and proportion of federal dollars expended on benefits to aging citizens which, for the first time had come to be comparable in size to expenditures on national defense (Hudson, 1978).

In this unsympathetic climate of opinion older adults emerged as a scapegoat for an impressive list of American problems, and the concept of so-called intergenerational equity—often promulgated in terms of intergenerational *inequities*—became prominent in public dialogue. At first, these issues of equity were propounded in a contemporary dimension.

The Contemporary Dimension. Demographers and advocates for children, noting the total and growing proportion of expenditures on benefits to older persons, blamed the political power of elderly Americans for the plight of youngsters who had inadequate nutrition, health care, education, and insufficiently supportive family environments (Preston, 1984). One children's advocate even proposed that parents receive an "extra vote" for each of their children, in order to combat older voters in an *intergenerational conflict* (Carballo, 1981). A former Secretary of Commerce (Peterson, 1987) suggested that a prerequisite for the United States to regain its stature as a first-class power in the world economy was a sharp reduction in programs benefiting older Americans. Widespread concerns about spiraling U.S. health care costs were redirected in part from health care providers, suppliers, administrators, and insurers—the parties that were responsible for setting the prices of care—to the elderly persons for whom health care is provided. A number of academicians and public figures expressed concern that *health care expenditures on older persons* would soon absorb an unlimited amount of national resources, and crowd out health care for others as well as various worthy social causes. Some of them even proposed that old age-based health care rationing would be necessary, desirable, and just (e.g., Callahan, 1987; Daniels, 1988; Smeeding, Battin, Francis, & Landesman, 1987).

By the end of the 1980s, the themes of intergenerational equity and conflict had been adopted by the media and academics as routine perspectives for describing many social policy issues (Cook Marshall, Marshall, & Kaufman, 1994). They had also gained currency in elite sectors of U.S. society and on Capitol Hill. For instance, the president of the prestigious American Association of Universities asserted, "[T]he shape of the domestic federal budget inescapably pits programs for the retired against every other social purpose dependent on federal funds" (Rosenzweig, 1990).

Indeed, the construct of intergenerational inequity had gained such a strong foothold in the thinking of many policy elites that they took it for granted as they analyzed U.S. domestic policy issues. For example, in 1989 a distinguished "executive panel" of U.S. leaders convened by the Ford Foundation designated older persons as the only group of citizens that should be responsible for financing a broad range of social programs for persons of all ages. In a report entitled *The Common Good: Social Welfare and the American Future*, the panel recommended a series of policies, costing a total of $29 billion (Ford Foundation, 1989). The panel proposed that this $29 billion be financed solely by *taxing Social Security benefits*; in fact, every financing alternative considered in the report assumed that older people should be the exclusive financiers of the panel's package of recommendations for improving social welfare in the nation. The Ford panel apparently felt that the reasons for this assumption were self-evident; it did not even bother to justify its selections of these financing options, as opposed to others (Beatty, 1990).

The Aging of the Baby Boom: Older People versus Society. The construct of intergenerational equity also has a future dimension, focusing on changes in the age structure of American society that will be brought about by the aging of the large baby boom birth cohort—76 million persons born between 1946 and 1964. One aspect of this issue was highlighted by the "*intergenerational accounting*" analyses of economist Kotlikoff (1992) which, although controversial (see Haveman, 1994), have continued to receive considerable attention. He suggested that future generations of older people will do less well than contemporary older people in terms of the relationship between payroll taxes they pay during their working years to finance Social Security and Medicare and the subsequent lifetime benefit payments they will receive through these programs.

Concerns about the economic consequences for society of sustaining the old-age welfare state in the 21st century was initially highlighted by the efforts of *Americans for Generational Equity* (AGE). Formed as an interest group in 1985, with backing from the corporate sector as well as a handful of congressmen who led it, AGE recruited some of the prominent "scapegoaters" of older people to its board and as its spokespersons. According to its annual reports, most of AGE's funding came from insurance companies, health care corporations, banks, and other private sector businesses and organizations that are in financial competition with Medicare and Social Security (Quadagno, 1989).

Since the mid-1980s, anxieties about the societal consequences of an aged baby boom have been expressed in an apocalyptic fashion. For instance, biomedical ethicist Callahan, concerned about future health care expenditures for older people, characterized the *elderly population as "a new social threat*" and a "demographic, economic, and medical avalanche . . . one that could ultimately (and perhaps already) do [sic] great harm" (1987). Accordingly, he proposed that Medicare reimbursement for lifesaving care be categorically denied to anyone aged 80 and older. Economist Thurow (1996) saw baby boomers and their self-interested pursuit of government benefits as a fundamental threat to the U.S. political system.

Intergenerational Equity in the 21st Century

In the early years of the 21st century, concerns about intergenerational equity have spread from elite circles to younger age groups in the broader U.S.

population. These concerns are an artifact of the way that Social Security is financed. A number of polls consistently revealed that younger workers, paying payroll taxes to support benefits for today's retirees, doubt that they will receive retirement benefits when they reach old age. This followed repeated official projections that there will be a shortfall in Social Security's capacity to pay full benefits several decades hence.

At the same time, the intergenerational equity themes developed in the 1980s and 1990s persist. Scholars who advocate for the well-being of children, for instance, attempt to plead the justness of their cause by pointing out the comparatively large expenditures on older persons, now more than 33% of the federal budget (Pati, Keren, Alessandrini, & Schwarz, 2004). And a commentary (Chapman, 2003) on legislation in 2003 that provided some prescription drug coverage under Medicare was entitled "*Meet the Greedy Grandparents*." Undoubtedly, policy debates will continue to be framed by issues of intergenerational equity, as baby boomers increasingly join the ranks of old age.

ROBERT H. BINSTOCK

See also
Intergenerational Relationships

References

Binstock, R. H. (1983). The aged as scapegoat. *Gerontologist, 23,* 136–143.

Beatty, J. (1990). A post-cold war budget. *Atlantic Monthly, 256*(2), 74–82.

Callahan, D. (1987) *Setting limits: Medical goals in an aging society.* New York: Simon and Schuster.

Carballo, M. (1981). Extra votes for parents? *Boston Globe, December 17,* 35.

Chapman, S. (2003, December 10). Meet the greedy grandparents. *Slate*. Available: http://slate.msn.com/id/2092302/%20.

Cook, F. L., Marshall, V. M., Marshall, J. E., & Kaufman, J. E. (1994). The salience of intergenerational equity in Canada and the United States. In T. R. Marmor, T. M. Smeeding & V. L. Greene (Eds.), *Economic security and intergenerational justice: A look at North America* (pp. 91–129). Washington, DC: Urban Institute Press.

Daniels, N. (1988). *Am I my parents' keeper? An essay on justice between the young and the old.* New York: Oxford University Press.

Fairlie, H. (1988). Talkin' 'bout my generation. *New Republic, 198,* 19–22.

Ford Foundation, Project on Social Welfare and the American Future. (1989). *The common good: Social welfare and the American future*. New York: Ford Foundation.

Gibbs, N. R. (1980). Grays on the go. *Time, 131*(8), 66–75.

Haveman, R. (1994). Should intergenerational accounts replace public budgets and deficits? *Journal of Economic Perspectives, 8,* 95–111.

Hudson, R. B. (1978). The "graying" of the federal budget and its consequences for old age policy. *Gerontologist, 18,* 428–440.

Kotlikoff, L. J. (1992). *Intergenerational accounting: Knowing who pays, and when, for what we spend.* New York: Free Press.

Pati, S., Keren, R., Alessandrini, E. A., & Schwarz, D. F. (2004). Generational differences in U.S. public spending, 1980–2000. *Health Affairs, 23*(5), 131–141.

Peterson, P. G. (1987). The morning after. *Atlantic Monthly, 260*(4), 43–49.

Preston, S. H. (1984). Children and the elderly in the U.S. *Scientific American, 251*(6), 44–49.

Quadagno, J. (1989). Intergenerational equity and the politics of the welfare state. *Politics and Society, 17,* 353–376.

Rosenzweig, R. M. (1990). Address to the president's opening session, 43rd Annual Meeting of the Gerontological Society of America, Boston, MA. November 16: 16.

Salholz, E. (1990). Blaming the voters: Hapless budgeteers single out "greedy geezers." *Newsweek,* October 29, 36.

Smeeding, T. M., Battin, M. P., Francis, L. P., & Landesman, B. M. (Eds.). (1987). *Should medical care be rationed by age?* Totowa, NJ: Rowman & Littlefield.

Smith, L. (1992). The tyranny of America's old. *Fortune, 125*(1), 68–72.

Thurow, L. C. (1996). The birth of a revolutionary class. *New York Times Magazine,* May 19, 46–47.

Walker, A. (2006). Aging and politics: An international perspective. In R. H. Binstock & L. K. George (Eds.), *Handbook of aging and the social sciences* (6th ed.). San Diego, CA: Academic Press.

INTERGENERATIONAL RELATIONSHIPS

Family relationships are critical in the aging process and in the lives of older individuals. Understanding relationships among members of different *generations within families* is a focal area of research for scholars in the field of aging. Intergenerational relationships are between members of a family who share a common lineage, such as parents and their children or grandparents and their grandchildren. Intergenerational relationships in families are distinct from relationships between age groups (cohorts) in society. *Intercohort relations* occur at the macro level of society, while intergenerational relations involve micro-level social interactions. *Intergenerational family relations* are characterized by varying degrees of solidarity that reflect different levels of affection, interaction, shared values, norms of familial obligation, exchanges of help and support, and conflict, as well as differences in family structures (Silverstein & Bengtson, 1997). Together, these are the ties that bind generations in a family and influence the nature and quality of their relationships across the life course. With global population aging, people now spend more of their lives in intergenerational relationships than at any time in the past; co-survivorship of generations means a *wider family network*, and these *extended family relations* remain strong and are increasingly important (Bengtson, 2001; Bengtson, Lowenstein, Putney, & Gans, 2003; Vollenwyder, Bickle, Lalive d'Epinay, & Maystre, 2002).

Intergenerational solidarity (Bengtson & Schrader, 1982) comprises 7 dimensions:

1. Affection—the sentiments and emotional evaluations, both positive and negative, of a relationship with a parent, child, or grandparent;
2. Association—the type and frequency of interaction between 2 family members of different generations;
3. Consensus—how closely the generations within a family agree on values, opinions, and orientations;
4. Functional exchanges—material, instrumental, and social support and assistance between generations;
5. Familial norms—expectations about intergenerational support and filial obligations;
6. Structural arrangements—the opportunities the generations have for interaction based on the number, gender, and geographic proximity of intergenerational family members;
7. Conflict—the tensions, hostilities, disagreements, and feelings of ambivalence that occur between parents and adult children or grandparents and grandchildren.

Studies of *intergenerational families* from around the world show that bonds of *affection* between parent and child generations in most families are quite strong (Bengtson, Lowenstein, Putney, & Gans, 2003; Lowenstein, Katz, Mehlhausen-Hassoen, & Prilutzsky, 2003; Lye, 1996). Nonetheless, in a small minority of families (less than 10%) estrangement, "cutoffs" (Ungar & Mahalingham, 2003), "drifting apart" (Szydlik, 2002), or "long-term lousy relationships" (Mabry, Bengtson, & Tagaki, 2002) occur between adjacent generations. The nature of adult intergenerational relationships often reflects patterns begun much earlier in life (Ahrons & Tanner, 2003; Schmeeckle & Giarrusso, 2002; Yoshihara, 2003). In *grandparent-grandchild relationships*, affection and overall quality is largely mediated by the middle (parent) generation. The nature of parents' relationships with their own parents influences children's relationships with grandparents, and affects the amount of contact a child has with a grandparent, both key determinants of grandparent-grandchild relationship quality (Brown, 2003).

Interestingly, members of different generations assess their relationships differently. Children and grandchildren typically report lower levels of affection and relationship quality than parents and grandparents typically do, a fact known as the *intergenerational stake phenomenon* (Giarrusso, Feng, Silverstein, & Bengtson, 2001; Shapiro, 2004). Younger generations typically are eager to create separate identities, families, and legacies of their own, while older generations usually have a greater stake in the intergenerational relationship due to the intensive investment and legacy that their children and grandchildren represent. Investment in the intergenerational relationship declines with greater distance between generations, from parents to grandparents to great-grandparents (Drew & Silverstein, 2004). Still, older generations enjoy an invaluable return on their investment in younger generations in that aging parents' bonds of affection with adult children enhance their well-being and decrease their mortality risks (Wang, Silverstein, & Bengtson, 1999).

Association, or the interaction and contact between members of different generations, is vital to solidarity maintenance. For many *extended families, association* is facilitated by proximity, as most older adults live within 30 minutes' drive of an adult child (Crimmins & Ingegneri 1990). Even if not living nearby, most parents have weekly contact by phone or in person with adult children (Bengtson & Harootyan, 1994). Another generational difference in perceptions of the intergenerational relationship is evident in each generation's account of contact: adult children report more frequent contact with parents than parents report with children (Shapiro, 2004). *Coresidence of multiple generations*, a situation that typically necessitates high levels of association, is waning as today's workforces of younger adults are increasingly mobile and government provisions for the aged make independent living feasible for many retirees (Chen & Silverstein, 2000; Someya, 2003). Although living greater distances apart increases the danger of generations drifting apart (Szydlik, 2002) and limits opportunities for exchanging help (Pelaez & Martinez, 2002), most families use modern communication and transportation to bridge these new circumstances. However, because *coresidence* is an important form of family *caregiving* (Peek, Coward, & Peek, 2000), declines in coresidence may be problematic in areas where there are few or no formal services available.

How much *consensus* in values and attitudes is there between older parents and their adult children? Is there a "*generation gap*," as people have supposed since the social upheavals of the 1960s? Scholars have returned to this question a number of times and each time the answer to the question is, generally speaking, no: there is not much in the way of a generation gap (Bengtson, 1970, Occhionero, 2000). While parents and children have their differences (particularly during the teenage years), parents remain highly successful at transmitting values, beliefs, attitudes, and aspirations to their children through the process of socialization (Bengtson, Biblarz, & Roberts, 2002). While parents and adult children share many values, values from broader culture change over time, and those changes can be seen in a modest but consistent intergenerational change in values over time (Occhionero, 2000).

Families provide *functional* support in the forms of financial, material, emotional, social, and practical assistance. Although older persons are typically thought of as depending upon younger family members for help and support, a wealth of research suggests that most family elders are active exchange partners to younger family members, and older generations often provide more help than they receive. Even in societies with strong norms concerning filial obligation, as found in many Asian and Latin cultures, the majority of older parents provide assistance to their children and grandchildren in various forms ranging from childcare to financial transfers (Agree, Biddlecom, Chang, & Perez, 2002; Kalaycioglu & Rittersbergertilic, 2000; Palma, 2001). Following the *norm of reciprocity*, older family members are most satisfied when both giving and receiving help and support (Chen & Silverstein, 2000; Jang, Haley, & Reynolds, 2000; Kim & Kim, 2003). Parents especially appreciate expressions of affection and emotional support from their adult children, but are less satisfied when they receive informational support from them (Lang & Schutze, 2002). *Intergenerational exchange patterns* change across the life course along with changes in members' social and health statuses (Litwin, 2004). Positive memories of early-childhood relationships with their parents are associated with greater concern and support for aging parents by adult children (Silverstein, Parrot, & Bengtson, 1995). However, few *adult children* provide high levels of assistance to both their own parents and their parents-in-law simultaneously (Shuey & Hardy, 2003). In addition, the greater economic security of today's aging cohorts makes it possible for older family members to provide instrumental support to younger family members in need. These new links may strengthen older adults' roles within the family, while bolstering the younger generation and family cohesion (Kohli, 1999).

Norms concerning family obligations for the care of elderly members are prevalent in most countries of the world. And, by far, families are the most prevalent source of care to aging individuals. Variations exist, however, in the extent to which caring for older adults is seen as a voluntary duty or a social obligation, as well as in the preferred balance of family care versus services, with many non-Eastern societies reflecting a higher preferences for services (Daatland & Herlofson, 2003). Norms within a family regarding what members of different generations should expect from one another are shaped by broader social norms (Ward, 2001), just one link between families and larger social forces.

Broad social factors also affect the *structure of intergenerational families*. Greater longevity, lower birth rates, trends in divorce, and diverse family forms mean the structure of intergenerational families is changing. Intergenerational relations depend on who is in the family—the family structure or form. Traditionally, the *structure of families* looked like a pyramid, with few older members at the top and many young members at the bottom. Today, families increasingly look more like a bean pole with relatively equal numbers of members in each generation. A number of social changes occurring in much of the world toward the end of the 20th century profoundly affected the structure of families, such as women's widespread workforce participation, cohabitation and nonmarital childbearing, and increases in divorce, single-parent families, and blended or step-family formations (Bengtson, 2001; Bengtson et al., 2003). *Changes in family structures* and cultural norms surrounding family life contribute to greater ambiguity in intergenerational relations. Ambiguity results from the array of undefined roles and uncertain expectations of new types of relationships, such as contemporary step-parent/step-children relations (Boss, 1999). Given the structural diversity of families today, scholars face the challenge of devising new conceptual approaches for understanding modern intergenerational relations.

Conflict is not an uncommon element of human social interaction, and so conflict is not uncommon in intergenerational family life. Conflict includes disagreements, arguments, tension, criticism, and/or violence. Families typically embody elements of both positive affective bonds and conflict, rather than extremes representing either harmony and refuge or anger and abuse. Adult children and their parents tend to disagree on a variety of issues. Six general sources of *intergenerational conflict* between aging parents and adult children are: (1) communication and interaction style; (2) habits and lifestyles; (3) childrearing practices and values; (4) politics, religion, and ideology; (5) work orientation; and (6) household maintenance (Clarke, Preston, Raskin, & Bengtson 1999). Disagreement, competition, and conflict often coexist with order, stability, and cooperation within the family and between generations (Bengtson, Rosenthal, Burton, 1995). An interesting question, then, is how many people manage those mixed feelings.

Although both affection and conflict are integral parts of intergenerational relations, understanding how people navigate mixed feelings, or *ambivalence*, in the context of ongoing intergenerational relationships is of growing scholarly interest (Pillemer & Luscher, 2004). Family relations commonly produce conflicting roles, like being a mother of children and being a caregiver of aged parents, or being an independent adult who relies on an adult child for chore help (Luscher & Lettke, 2004). Ambivalence arises both at the psychological level, where people experience contradictory feelings, motivations, and thoughts, and at the sociological level, where social norms, roles, and statuses come into conflict in intergenerational relations (Luscher & Pillemer, 1998). Ambivalence stems from tensions between autonomy and connection (Spitze & Gallant, 2004), dependency and obligations (Pillemer & Suitor, 2002), transition to the "sick" or "dependent" role (Phillips, Ray, & Ogg, 2003), and poor parent-child relations earlier in life; it is more common in dyads of women (Willson, Shuey, & Elder, 2003). Strategies to cope with *ambivalence* include minimizing dependency, rationalizing unmet expectations, maintaining clear relationship boundaries, resisting efforts to assert control in the relationship, and relying on others for social support (Spitze & Gallant, 2004). Adult child-parent relationships are not necessarily the most ambivalent, however, as this relationship changes across the life course (Fingerman & Hay, 2004). Family members tend to be fairly adept at managing ambivalence, which is one reason that the study of coping with *ambivalence in intergenerational relationships* has escaped the attention of researchers until recently (Plakans, 2004).

Intergenerational relationships involve solidarity and conflict, positive and negative feelings, tensions and uncertainties. Rather than being either very close or distant, families vary considerably. Five general *types of intergenerational relationships* occur between adult children and their parents: (1) tight-knit, with high levels on all dimensions of solidarity; (2) sociable, with high degrees of interaction, shared values, and closeness, but not frequently exchanging support; (3) obligatory, with frequent contact and exchanges of assistance, but lacking closeness and shared values; (4) intimate-but-distant, characterized by closeness and shared vales, but without frequent contact or exchanges of assistance; and (5) detached, with children and parents not engaged on any dimension of solidarity (Silverstein & Bengtson 1997). Some past research and popular portrayals depict the family either as harmonious and idyllic or as dysfunctional and abusive. These extremes are *caricatures of family life* that ignore the diversity and complexities of families around the globe. A challenge for future research on aging is to incorporate the multiple facets of family life, their transformations over time, and their effects on intergenerational relationships.

VERN L. BENGTSON
J. BETH MABRY

See also
Intergenerational Equity

References

Agree, E. M., Biddlecom, A. E., Change, M. C., & Perez, A. E. (2002). Transfers from older parents to their adult children in Taiwan and the Phillipines. *Journal of Cross-Cultural Gerontology, 17*, 269–294.

Ahrons, C. R., & Tanner, J. L. (2003). Adult children and their fathers: Relationship changes 20 years after parental divorce. *Family Relations, 52*, 340–351.

Bengtson, V. L. (1970). The "generation gap": A review and typology of social-psychological perspectives. *Youth and Society, 2*, 7–32.

Bengtson, V. L. (2001). Beyond the nuclear family: The increasing importance of multigenerational relationships in American society. *Journal of Marriage and Family, 63*, 1–16.

Bengtson, V. L., Biblarz, T. J., & Robert, R. E. (2002). *Why families still matter: A longitudinal study of youth in two generations*. New York: Cambridge University Press.

Bengtson, V. L., & Harootyan, R. (Eds.). (1994). *Intergenerational linkages: Hidden connections in American society*. New York: Springer Publishing.

Bengtson, V. L., Lowenstein, A., Putney, N., & Gans, D. (2003). Global aging and the challenges to families. In V. L. Bengtson & A. Lowenstein (Eds.), *Global aging and challenges to families* (pp. 1–24). Hawthorne, NY: Aldine de Gruyter.

Bengtson, V. L., Rosenthal, C. J., & Burton, L. M. (1995). Paradoxes of families and aging. In R. H. Binstock & L. K. George (Eds.), *Handbook of aging and the social sciences* (4th ed., pp. 253–282). San Diego: Academic Press.

Bengtson, V. L., & Schrader, S. S. (1982). Parent-child relations. In D. Mangen & W. Peterson (Eds.), *Handbook of research instruments in social gerontology* (vol. 2, pp. 115–185). Minneapolis: University of Minnesota Press.

Boss, P. (1999). *Ambiguous loss: Learning to live with unresolved grief*. Cambridge, MA: Harvard University Press.

Brown, L. H. (2003). Intergenerational influences on perceptions of current relationships with grandparents. *Journal of Intergenerational Differences, 1*, 95–112.

Chen, X., & Silverstein, M. (2000). Intergenerational social support and the psychological well-being of older parents in China. *Research on Aging, 22*, 43–65.

Clarke, E., Preston, M., Raskin, J., & Bengtson, V. L. (1999). Types of conflicts and tensions between older parents and adult children. *Gerontologist, 39*, 261–270.

Crimmins, E. M., & Ingegneri, D. G. (1990). Interaction and living arrangements of older parents and their children. *Research on Aging 12*, 3–35.

Daatland, S. O., & Herlofson, K. (2003). Family responsibility norms in European countries: Contrasts and similarities. *Retraite et Societe, 38*, 18–47.

Drew, L. M., & Silverstein, M. (2004). Intergenerational role investments of great-grandparents: Consequences for psychological well-being. *Ageing and Society, 24*, 95–111.

Fingerman, K. L., & Hay, E. (2004). Intergenerational ambivalence in the context of the larger social network. *Contemporary Perspectives in Family Research, 4*, 133–151.

Giarrusso, R., Feng, D., Silverstein, M., & Bengtson, V. L. (2001). Grandparent-adult grandchild affection and consensus: Cross-generational and cross-ethnic comparisons. *Journal of Family Issues, 22*, 456–477.

Jang, Y., Haley, W. E., & Reynolds, S. L. (2000). Mutual exchange of support and intergenerational relationships in Korean families. *Hallym International Journal of Aging, 2*, 135–147.

Kalayciouglu, S., & Rittersbergertilic, H. (2000). Intergenerational solidarity networks of instrumental and cultural transfers within migrant families in Turkey. *Ageing and Society, 20*, 523–542.

Kim, I. K., & Kim, C. S. (2003). Patterns of family support and the quality of life of the elderly. *Social Indicators Research, 62–63*, 437–454.

Kohli, M. (1999). Private and public transfers between generations: Linking the family and the state. *European Societies*, *1*, 81–104.

Lang, F. R., & Schutze, Y. (2002). Adult children's supportive behaviors and older parents' subjective well-being: A developmental perspective on intergenerational relationships. *Journal of Social Issues*, *58*, 661–680.

Litwin, H. (2004). Intergenerational exchange patterns and their correlates in an aging Israeli cohort. *Research on Aging*, *26*, 202–223.

Lowenstein, A., Katz, R., Mehlhausen-Hassoen, D., & Prilutzky, D. (2003). A comparative cross-national perspective on intergenerational solidarity. *Retraite et Societe*, *38*, 54–75.

Luscher, K., & Lettke, F. (2004). Intergenerational ambivalence: Methods, measures, and results of the Konstanz Study. *Contemporary Perspectives in Family Research*, *4*, 153–179.

Luscher, K., & Pillemer, K. (1998). Intergenerational ambivalence: A new approach to the study of parent-child relations in later life. *Journal of Marriage and the Family*, *60*, 413–425.

Lye, D. N. (1996). Adult child-parent relationships. *Annual Review of Sociology*, *22*, 79–102.

Mabry, J. B., Bengtson, V. L., & Tagaki, E. (2002). Long-term lousy relationships: A life course perspective on intergenerational relationships. Boston: 55th Annual Scientific Meetings of the Gerontological Society of America.

Occhionero, M. F. (2000). Generations and value change across time. *International Review of Sociology*, *10*, 223–233.

Palma, J. L. (2001). Family support: Transference by and for the older population inside or outside the household. *Demos*, *14*, 40–41.

Peek, M. K., Coward, R. T., & Peek, C. W. (2000). Race, aging, and care: Can differences in family and household structure account for race variations in informal care? *Research on Aging*, *22*, 117–142.

Pelaez, M., & Martinez, I. (2002). Equity and systems of intergenerational transfers in Latin America and the Caribbean. *Pan American Journal of Public Health*, *11*, 439–443.

Phillips, J., Ray, M., & Ogg, J. (2003). Ambivalence and conflict in aging families: European perspectives. *Retraite et Societe*, *38*, 80–103.

Pillemer, K., & Luscher, K. (2004). Ambivalence in parent-child relations in later life. *Contemporary Perspectives in Family Research*, *4*, 1–19.

Pillemer, K., & Suitor, J. J. (2002). Explaining mothers' ambivalence toward their adult children. *Journal of Marriage and Family*, *64*, 602–613.

Plakans, A. (2004). Intergenerational ambivalences in the past: A sociohistorical assessment. *Contemporary Perspectives in Family Research*, *4*, 63–82.

Schmeekle, M., & Giarrusso R. (2002, July). Diverse perceptions of family ties: Adult children's perception of step, ex-step, and biological parents. Brisbane, Australia: Meetings of the International Sociological Association.

Shapiro, A. (2004). Revisiting the generation gap: Exploring the relationships of parent/adult-child dyads. *International Journal of Aging and Human Development*, *58*, 127–146.

Silverstein, M. S., & Bengtson, V. L. (1997). Intergenerational solidarity and the structure of adult child-parent relationships in American families. *American Journal of Sociology*, *103*, 429–460.

Silverstein, M. S., Parrot, T. M., & Bengtson, V. L. (1995). Factors that predispose middle-aged sons and daughters to provide social support to older parents. *Journal of Marriage and Family*, *57*, 465–475.

Shuey, K., & Hardy, M. A. (2003). Assistance to aging parents and parents-in-law: Does lineage affect family allocation decisions? *Journal of Marriage and Family*, *65*, 418–431.

Someya, Y. (2003). Changing relationships between the elderly and their adult children. *Japanese Journal of Family Sociology*, *14*, 105–114.

Spitze, G., & Gallant, M. P. (2004). The bitter with the sweet: Older adults' strategies for handling ambivalence in relations with their adult children. *Research on Aging*, *26*, 387–412.

Silverstein, M. S., & Bengtson, V. L. (1997). Intergenerational solidarity and the structure of adult child-parent relationships in American families. *American Journal of Sociology*, *103*, 429–460.

Szydlik, M. (2002). When generations drift apart. *Zeitschrift fur Soziologie der Erziehung und Socialisation*, *22*, 362–373.

Ungar, L. R., & Mahalingam, R. (2003). We're not speaking anymore: A cross-cultural study of intergenerational cut-offs. *Journal of Cross-Cultural Gerontology*, *18*, 169–183.

Vollenwyder, N., Bickle, J. F., Lalive d'Epinay, C., & Maystre, C. (2002). The elderly and their families, 1979–94: Changing networks and relationships. *Current Sociology*, *50*, 263–280.

Wang, H., Silverstein, M. S., & Bengtson, V. L. (1999). The linkage between parent-child relations and the mortality risk of older parents: Evidence from a longitudinal study over 13 years. San Francisco: 52nd Annual Scientific Meeting of the Gerontological Society of America.

Ward, R. A. (2001). Linkages between family and societal-level intergenerational attitudes. *Research on Aging*, *23*, 179–208.

Willson, A. E., Shuey, K. M., & Elder, G. H. (2003). Ambivalence in the relationship of adult children: Aging parents and in-laws. *Journal of Marriage and Family, 65*, 1055–1072.

Yoshihara, C. (2003). Sibling relationships in an aging society: Activation and its factors. *Japanese Journal of Family Sociology, 15*, 37–47.

INTERNATIONAL ASSOCIATION OF GERONTOLOGY

The International Association of Gerontology (IAG) was founded at the *First International Congress of Gerontology* in Liege, Belgium, in 1950. The founder of IAG, Shock (1988), believed that "the primary accomplishment of the IAG has been to establish gerontology as a visible scientific discipline dedicated to the study of aging with roots in biology, medicine, and social science." Additionally, Busse (1988) called attention to the interdisciplinary nature and role of IAG.

IAG promotes and assists in arranging the International Congress of Gerontology (*World Congress of Gerontology*), now quadrennial, with topics in biology, medicine, behavioral and social sciences, and social research and planning. Past congresses are as follows: Liege, Belgium, 1950; St. Louis, 1951; London, 1954; Merano, Italy, 1957; San Francisco, 1960; Copenhagen, 1963; Vienna, 1966; Washington DC, 1969; Kiev, 1972; Jerusalem, 1975; Tokyo, 1978: Hamburg, 1981; New York, 1985; Acapulco, Mexico, 1989; Budapest, 1993; Adelaide, Australia, 1997; Vancouver, Canada, 2001. At present, future congresses are planned in Rio de Janeiro in 2005 and Paris in 2009.

In accordance with its bylaws, IAG has 4 regional committees: Asia-Oceania, European, Latin American, and North American. Regional congresses are organized in the periods between the world congresses of gerontology.

In recognition of outstanding work in gerontology, the following awards have been presented by IAG at the world congress meetings: presidential awards; *Busse Research Awards*; the *Sandoz* (later *Novartis) Prize* for *Gerontological Research* (discontinued in 1999); the *Chinoin Award for Young Scientists* and the UN Testimonial Award to IAG in 1993.

IAG has consultative status with the United Nations and the World Health Organization. It is member of the UN Committee of Non-governmental Organizations and the Committee on Aging.

In 2000 IAG celebrated the 50th anniversary of its founding in Salsomaggiore, Italy, during which the association discussed its support of development, achievements, education, research, and practice of national and global activities in the 21st century (Andrews, 2000). In 2002, the *Valencia Forum* endorsed the "Research Agenda for the 21st Century" (RAA-21) prepared by IAG to support the *UN Program on Aging*; the UN General Assembly welcomed adoption of RAA-21 (Gutman, 2003).

The IAG plays an important role in research on gerontology throughout the world. Fourteen countries took part in the first IAG congress in 1950. The association now has 66 member societies from 63 countries. The increasing number of the aging population has resulted in growing interest in gerontology.

EDIT BEREGI

See also
Organizations in Aging

References

Andrews, G. (2000). Strategic directions for IAG. *IAG Newsletter* [50th Anniversary], *6*, 1–2.

Busse, E. W. (1988). The history of gerontology and interdisciplinary research. In M. Bergener, M. Ermini, & H. B. Stahelin (Eds.), *Crossroads in aging*. London: Academic Press.

Gutman, G. M. (2003). Expanding our international profile. *IAG Newsletter, 17*, 1.

Shock, N. W. (1988). The International Association of Gerontology 1950–1986: A chronicle. New York: Springer Publishing.

INTERNATIONAL CLASSIFICATION OF FUNCTIONING, DISABILITY, AND HEALTH

The need for standardization of the concepts and terminology used in research and clinical communications is increasing. The International Classification of Functioning, Disability, and Health (*ICF*) (World

Health Organization, 2001) aims at providing a scientific basis for the understanding and study of health and health-related conditions, determinants, and outcomes, and establishing a common language for describing health and health-related conditions in order to improve communication among different stakeholders, including health care workers, researchers, policy-makers, and people with disabilities. It also aims at allowing for comparisons of data across countries, health care disciplines, services, and time by providing a systematic coding scheme.

The ICF is part of the international classification family (such as the *International Classification of Disease*, version 10, or ICD-10) developed by the *World Health Organization* (WHO). It was endorsed by the World Health Assembly in 2001 as a successor classification to the *International Classification of Impairment, Disability, and Handicap* (ICIDH).

The ICF classifies functioning and disability as components of health. By contrast, ICD-10 was developed to describe the etiological bases of diseases. Therefore, ICF and ICD-10 are complementary systems providing for meaningful description of the health of individuals and populations.

ICIDH used concepts of impairment, disabilities, and handicaps to describe the state of health as a consequence of a disablement process and in relation to the social role of the individual. The ICF is more neutral with regard to etiology; the conceptual terms of the ICIDH, which contained negative perspectives, are replaced by more neutral components, namely body functioning, body structure, and activity and participation. However, beyond these components, contextual influences are also stressed, namely environmental factors and personal factors. The ICF emphasizes the interaction of its various components with these contextual factors in determining the health status of an individual.

In the ICF, body functioning is defined as the physiological functioning, including the psychological functioning, of body systems. Body structures are the anatomical parts of the body, such as organs, limbs, and their components. Impairments are defined in the ICF as problems of body function or structure that represent a significant deviation or loss.

The activities and participation component describes human functioning from both an individual and a societal perspective. Activity is the execution of a task or action by an individual, and activity limitations are the difficulties an individual may have in executing such tasks. Participation is involvement in life situations, and participation restrictions are problems an individual may experience for involvement in life situations.

Disability in the ICF therefore is an umbrella term for impairments, activity limitations, and participation restrictions.

Environmental factors are features such as products, support, and other services and systems that impact the individual's state of health, whether as barriers or facilitators. This conceptualization has developed based on the *Quebec model of ICIDH* application (Fougeyrollas, 1995).

Personal factors are the particular background features of an individual's life and living conditions, and comprise factors that are not demographically related to a health condition or status, such as gender, race, and age. These factors are constituents of the basic interaction framework of the ICF, but are not included as codes because of their large social and cultural variance.

Codes and Qualifiers in the ICF

The *ICF codes* are composed of one alphabet letter followed by numerical codes. The letters *b*, *s*, *d* and *e* indicate body functions, body structures, activities and participation, and environmental factors components, respectively. They are followed by hierarchically arrayed numeric codes that signify chapter number with the first digit, and more detailed second to fourth levels of categorization, each with one digit.

For the first digit level of description, the maximum number of codes per person is 34. The number of codes at second digit level is 362. WHO urges use at this level for surveys and clinical classification. At more detailed levels, possible codes number up to 1,424. These detailed codes are required for specialist services, such as rehabilitation outcomes and geriatrics.

The ICF codes can be used meaningfully only in the presence of a qualifier, which denotes a degree in the level of health, or the severity of the problem. Qualifiers have the same structure for all components of the ICF, using the same 5-point scale ranging from 0 to 4 to represent a percentage range that denotes the severity or level of presence of the problem: 0 indicates no problem (0–4%),

1 indicates a mild problem (5–24%), 2 indicates a moderate problem (25–49%), 3 indicates a severe problem (50–95%), and 4 indicates a complete or total problem (96–100%).

In the activity and participation component, WHO recommends the use of 2 qualifiers, namely, the *performance qualifier* and the *capacity qualifier*. The performance qualifier describes what an individual can do in his or her current environment, with the implication that the individual's performance may alter if the environment changes. By contrast, the capacity qualifier describes the highest possible level of functioning that a person is able to attain in a given domain at a given moment, such as in a rehabilitation room with training equipment. Thus, capacity reflects the environmentally adjusted ability of the individual, and it must be standardized by reference to a uniform environment to permit statistically meaningful comparison. The difference between an individual's capacity and performance is considered to be a reflection of environment. Removal of environmental factors that act as barriers should lift the performance level of an individual in the direction of his or her capacity level.

Application of the ICF

The innovative characteristic of the ICF, compared to the ICIDH, is its recognition of the role of environmental factors in health, which allows for a change in the locus of a problem—and hence the focus of intervention—from the individual to the environment in which the individual lives (Schneidert, Hurst, Miller, & Ustun, 2003). An intervention that removes barrier environmental factors may improve an individual's performance level. This view has been adopted generally in many countries, as well as in specific health care settings.

Numerous projects have been initiated to adapt the ICF for use in research and national surveys. Some projects have the goal of translating the results of extant research into an ICF format, so that the researcher can use existing data in an ICF context (Granlund, Eriksson, & Ylven, 2004; Weigl, Cieza, Harder, Geyh, Amann, Kostanjsek, et al., 2003). National *surveys based on ICF* concepts are also underway (Madden, Choi, & Sykes, 2003; McDougall & Miller, 2003; Roussel & Barral, 2003).

However, the adaptation of ICF codes to specific populations, such as to the geriatric care setting, is still ongoing. Further work is required to reach a consensus on how each code and qualifier should be related to a specific population. A given code may have different implications in different care settings. Because ICF aspires to be a universal model suitable for all populations regardless of age, culture, and the like, a broad range of validity and reliability studies will be required to establish measurement settings in specific areas. An example of such an attempt is the development of ICF core sets for specific medical conditions, by linking to relevant extant measures (Stucki, Ewert, & Cieza, 2003). Another possible methodology is to apply item response theory and item banking methods, which allow comparisons between scales accommodating their differing stringencies (Wolfe, 2000).

For further information, see the ICF and ICF checklist, which is a practical tool composed of salient items within the ICF codes, and a recent update of research at www3.who.int/icf/icftemplate.cfm.) Recent research on the ICF in North America and other countries is available from the research conference of the North American Collaborating Center meeting (North American Collaboration Center of ICF, 2004). *Pictograms developed for each ICF* code for use in geriatric care settings are also available, from the *ICF illustration library* (Takahashi, 2003).

JIRO OKOCHI

See also
Disability

References

Fougeyrollas, P. (1995). Documenting environmental factors for preventing the handicap creation process: Quebec contributions relating to ICIDH and social participation of people with functional differences. *Disability and Rehabilitation, 17(3-4)*, 145–153.

Granlund, M., Eriksson, L., & Ylven, R. (2004). Utility of International Classification of Functioning, Disability and Health's participation dimension in assigning ICF codes to items from extant rating instruments. *Journal of Rehabilitation Medicine, 36(3)*, 130–137.

Madden, R., Choi, C., & Sykes, C. (2003). The ICF as a framework for national data: The introduction of ICF into Australian data dictionaries. *Disability and Rehabilitation, 25(11-12)*, 676–682.

McDougall, J., & Miller, L. T. (2003). Measuring chronic health condition and disability as distinct concepts in national surveys of school-aged children in Canada: A comprehensive review with recommendations based on the ICD-10 and ICF. *Disability and Rehabilitation, 25(16)*, 922–939.

North American Collaboration Center of ICF. (2004). *10th North American Collaborating Center Conference on ICF. Advancing a research agenda for ICF*. Available: http://www.icfconference.com/presentations.shtml

Roussel, P., & Barral, C. (2003). Reference to ICIDH in French surveys on disability. *Disability and Rehabilitation, 25(11-12)*, 659–664.

Schneidert, M., Hurst, R., Miller, J., & Ustun, B. (2003). The role of environment in the International Classification of Functioning, Disability and Health (ICF). *Disability and Rehabilitation, 25(11-12)*, 588–595.

Stucki, G., Ewert, T., & Cieza, A. (2003). Value and application of the ICF in rehabilitation medicine. *Disability and Rehabilitation, 25(11-12)*, 628–634.

Takahashi, T. (2003). *ICF illustration library*. Available: http://www.tokyo.image-lab.or.jp/icf/ill/english/

Weigl, M., Cieza, A., Harder, M., Geyh, S., Amann, E., Kostanjsek, N., et al. (2003). Linking osteoarthritis-specific health-status measures to the International Classification of Functioning, Disability, and Health (ICF). *Osteoarthritis and Cartilage, 11(7)*, 519–523.

Wolfe, E. W. (2000). Equating and item banking with the Rasch model. *Journal of Applied Measurement, 1(4)*, 409–434.

World Health Organization. (2001). *International classification of functioning, disability and health: ICF*. Geneva: World Health Organization.

INTERNATIONAL FEDERATION ON AGEING

The International Federation on Ageing (IFA) is an international non-government organization founded in 1973, whose mission is to inform, educate, and promote policy and practice to improve the quality of life of older people around the world. Through its members the federation represents over 45 million older people across 62 countries. Its primary responsibility is to build, facilitate, and strengthen bridges between government, non-government, and the corporate sectors concerned with ageing and age-related issues. Toward this end the IFA has formal working relations with the United Nations, the World Health Organization, the U.N. Educational, Scientific, and Cultural Organization, the International Labour Organization, and the U.N. Economic and Social Commission for Asia and the Pacific.

Ageing issues and leading practice are promoted through policy and community-based research and disseminated through regular and special IFA publications, regional forums, seminars, and biannual conferences. Poverty, health and well being, abuse and neglect, discrimination and ageism, and gender are key areas of attention and interest. The journal *Global Ageing: Issues and Action* carries accounts of innovative programs for older persons from all over the world, encouraging cross-cultural and cross-national adaptation. The monthly publication *Intercom: Ageing in Focus* features actions from local and community perspectives that highlight the power of leading practice in the field of NGOs and industry.

The federation's *Biannual Global Conferences on Ageing* provide a unique global stage for issues and concerns of ageing and foster the development of associations and agencies that serve or represent older people.

Full IFA membership is reserved for non-government organizations that represent or serve older persons. Government, corporate, and individual involvement is extended through associate membership.

JANE BARRATT

See also
Organizations in Aging

INTERNATIONAL LONGEVITY CENTER

The International Longevity Center (ILC) is a nonprofit, non-partisan, independent organization (with 501(c)(3) status) devoted to the *study of population aging* and longevity, and their impact on society. The ILC is international, interdisciplinary and intergenerational. Its mission is to help societies prepare for aging in positive and productive ways, and its priorities are the promotion of a productive work life and an active (healthy) life expectancy through education, research, and policy initiatives.

The ILC was co-founded in 1990 by *Robert N. Butler* in the United States (ILC-USA) and

Shigeo Morioka in Japan (ILC-Japan). It now includes sister organizations in France, Great Britain, India, and the Dominican Republic. Future plans include the development of new centers in selected nations.

The ILC-USA's research program focuses on such studies as: the future contributions of older adults in paid and unpaid sectors of the economy; the role of annuities in financing postretirement years; the affordability and quality of housing for older people globally; the influence of family and community ties on the demand for reverse mortgages; and the effect of universal health care coverage on disparities in health among older adults.

The *Economic Status of Older Persons database* (ESOP), developed by ILC research co-director *Charlotte Muller*, enables researchers from across the globe to use this comparative tool in their own studies. In addition, the *World Cities Project* studies health care and social services delivery to children and older persons in Tokyo, London, Paris, New York, and Santo Domingo.

Communication and education programs encompass a variety of areas. Highlights include the *Age Boom Academy*, which is an annual intensive 1-week seminar on aging issues for journalists co-sponsored by the New York Times Company Foundation, and ILC publications, which are available electronically on the center's Web site or in print. A visiting scholars program draws scholars from diverse academic disciplines, such as labor and health economics, epidemiology, the humanities, and ethics, to spend a sabbatical period at the center for research on population aging.

In 2003, *International Longevity Centers* in the United States, the United Kingdom, and France expanded their international focus with the creation of The *Alliance for Health and the Future*. Its mission is to combine research, education, and policy efforts to promote good health and productivity throughout the life course by advancing knowledge and providing training, skills, and systems to help individuals and society realize a healthy future. Operating as a division of the International Longevity Center, the Alliance secretariat is in Paris with additional offices in London and New York.

ROBERT N. BUTLER

See also
Organizations in Aging

INTERNET APPLICATIONS

The Internet is a collection of networks linking computers to computers and serves as a transport vehicle for information. The term Internet is not synonymous with the World Wide Web. Whereas the *Internet is the physical medium* used to transport information, the *World Wide Web is a collection of protocols* used to access information. Using the Internet and the World Wide Web it is possible to retrieve documents, view images, animation, and videos, listen to sound files, speak and hear voice, and view a wide variety of programs. Originally designed to transmit text and numeric data, the Internet now has a variety of types of information (e.g. travel, health, business, financial) and offers a wide variety of services (communication, on-line support, shopping, bill paying). Furthermore, technical advances such as high-speed transmission and affordable computer systems and modems have made Internet access possible to large numbers of people, many of whom do not have technical skills. Use of the Internet has become an integral part of daily life and is used increasingly in most settings, including the home. In 2003, 63% of U.S. adults used the Internet, an increase of 47% from the year 2000. The most *common on-line activities* include communicating via e-mail or chat rooms, information seeking, financial and transaction-based activities (e.g., on-line banking and shopping), and hobby or entertainment activities (Pew Internet and American Life Project, 2003).

Benefits of the Internet for Older People

There are a number of ways that Internet may be beneficial to older people, especially those who live alone, in rural environments, or have some type of mobility restriction. The Internet can facilitate linkages between older adults and health care providers and communication with family members and friends, especially those who are distant, since it is quite common within the United States for family members to be dispersed among different geographic regions. Also, about 30% of noninstitutionalized older people live alone, and the number of older people who live alone increases with age.

A number of studies (Czaja & Rubert, 2002) have shown that computer networks may prove beneficial for *family caregivers* of older relatives.

Currently about 21% of adults in the United States are involved in some type of caregiving. (National Alliance for Caregiving & AARP, 2004). Access to the Internet may enhance the ability of caregivers to access information and resources and *communicate with health care professionals*, distant family members, and other caregivers. Many caregivers often have trouble utilizing available resources and participating in support groups due to logistic problems associated with providing care.

The Internet also is having a pronounced impact on health care delivery and personal health behavior. Interactive health communication, or "*e-health*," generally refers to the interaction of an individual with an electronic device or communication technology (such as the Internet) to access or transmit health information, or to receive or provide guidance and support on a health-related issue (Robinson, Patrick, Eng, & Gustafson, 1998). The scope of e-health applications is fairly broad but mostly encompasses searching for health information, participating in support groups, and consulting with health care professionals. Currently there are more than 70,000 Web sites that provide health information, and in 2003 77 million U.S. adults searched the Internet for health information (Pew Internet and American Life, 2003). E-health applications may prove to be particularly beneficial for older adults, since as the prevalence of chronic conditions and disease increases with age, older adults are more likely to need some type of health-related support or continued care. Many older adults have difficulty accessing needed care due to logistic problems or mobility restriction. Technologies such as the Internet may enhance the likelihood that older people who are ill or disabled are able to remain in their homes and live with a greater degree of autonomy. A recent survey (Morrell, Mayhorn, & Bennett, 2000) found that older adults are particularly interested in learning how to use the World Wide Web to locate information on health-related topics.

However, there are some potential pitfalls and perils that need to be considered within the domain of interactive health, especially for older consumers. Access to this wide array of health information can overload both patient and physicians, disrupt existing relationships, and lead to poor decision making on the part of consumers. For example, a major concern is the lack of quality control mechanisms for health information on the Internet. Currently, consumers can access information from credible scientific and institutional sources (e.g., Medline Plus) as well as unreviewed sources of unknown quality. Other concerns relate to the ability of nonspecialists to integrate and interpret the wealth of information that is available, and the ability of health care providers to "keep pace" with their patients. Finally, some consumers may find health information difficult to access because of design features that result in usability problems, lack of training, or limited access to technology.

The Internet can also be used by *older people for continuing education*. Web sites and software programs are available on a wide variety of topics. There are also formal *on-line degree programs* and opportunities to be connected to classrooms via videoconferencing and networking facilities. The *AARP* has begun to offer several *on-line courses*. These opportunities can enable older adults to remain intellectually engaged and active, especially those who have difficulty accessing more traditional classroom-based adult education programs. The imminent availability of the next-generation Internet and interactive multimedia programming will further expand the education experiences available to individuals and enable information to be tailored to the specific needs and characteristics of users. This may be particularly beneficial to older adults, who often learn at a slower pace than younger people and need more instructional support.

Access to computers and the Internet may expand *employment opportunities for older people*. Computers and the Internet make working from home a more likely option. *Telecommuting*, which refers to working from a location other than a traditional office and interacting with the workplace using some form of technology, is rapidly increasing. In 1995 at least 3 million Americans were telecommuting for work, and this number is expected to increase by 20% per year (Nickerson & Landauer, 1997). Telecommuting may be particularly appropriate for older adults, as they are more likely than younger people to be "mobility impaired" or engaged in some form of caregiving. Telecommuting also allows for more flexible work schedules and autonomy and is more amenable to *part-time work*–job characteristics which are general preferred by older people. A recent study (Sharit, Czaja, Hernandez, Yang, Perdomo, Lewis, et al., in press) found that older adults are interested in performing telecommuting work for the flexibility offered by this type of work arrangement.

Web pages also are increasingly being developed for seniors. For example *FirstGov for Seniors* (www.firstgov.gov) is a comprehensive collection of links to government resources, such as social security and retirement planning, geared toward the needs of seniors. The administration on aging has also developed a web directory for seniors (www.aoa.gov/aoa/webres/craig.htm) and the National Institutes on Aging (NIA) has an on-line resource directory available for seniors. In addition, NIA has recently published a compendium of scientific research and design guidelines related to the Internet and older adults (Morrell, Dalley, Feldman, Mayhorn, & Echt, 2001).

Access and Usability Issues

Although access to information and the Internet is generally desirable, effective use of the Internet may represent a challenge for many people, especially those who have had limited exposure to technology. The National Research Council (1997) recently issued a report suggesting that although the usability of systems has improved substantially, current interfaces still exclude many people from effective Internet access, such as those who are older or people with disabilities. Although Internet use is rapidly increasing among adults aged 65 and older, it is still low compared to other age groups. In 2003 only 20% of Americans over age 65 were on-line compared to 56% of those aged 30 to 49 years and 36% of those in the 50 to 64 age group. Seniors who access the Internet tend to be male, highly educated, and relatively affluent. Furthermore, people with a disability, such as impaired vision or problems with manual dexterity, are only half as likely to use computers and the Internet as those without a disability (U.S. Department of Commerce, 2002).

Although most older people are receptive to using new technologies, they often encounter difficulties when attempting to adopt these systems. Barriers to successful adaptation of technology are largely related to a failure on the part of system designers to perceive older adults as active users of technical systems. Overcoming these barriers depends on training and design solutions that accommodate age-related declines in perceptual, cognitive, and motor abilities; this might involve software modifications, alternative input devices, or redesign of instructional manuals. The development of these solutions requires an understanding of the needs, preference, and abilities of older people. To design interfaces for information systems so that they are useful and usable for older people it is important to understand: (1) why technology may prove difficult to use, (2) how to design technology for easier and effective use, and (3) how to effectively teach people to use and take advantage of technologies.

Although design issues related to the Internet have received attention within the human-computer interaction literature, available data on this topic is limited for older people. The topic of the *Internet and older adults* is important and needs attention within the research and design communities, given the aging of the population and the increased reliance on network technologies such as the Internet for information dissemination and communication.

SARA J. CZAJA

References

Czaja, S. J., & Rubert, M. (2002). Telecommunications technology as an aid to family caregivers of persons with dementia. *Psychosomatic Medicine*, *64*, 469–476.

Morrell, R. W., Dailey, S. R., Feldman, C., Mayhorn, C. B., & Echt, K. V. (2001). *Older adults and information technology: A compendium of scientific research and Web site accessibility guidelines*. Washington, DC: National Institute on Aging.

Morrell, R. W., Mayhorn, C. B., & Bennett, J. (2000). A survey of World Wide Web use in middle-aged and older adults. *Human Factors*, *42*, 175 –182.

National Alliance for Caregiving & AARP. (2004). Caregiving in the U.S. Washington, DC: National Alliance for Caregiving and AARP.

Nickerson, R. S., & Landauer, T. K. (1997). Human-computer interaction: Background and issues. In M. G., Helander, T. K., Landauer, & P. V., Prabhu. *Handbook of human-computer interaction* (2nd ed., pp. 3 –32). Amsterdam, The Netherlands: Elsevier.

Pew Internet & American Life Project. (2003, December 22). *America's online pursuits: The changing picture of who's online and what they do*. Available: http://www.pewinternet.org/reports/toc.asp? Report=106.

Robinson, T. N., Patrick, K., Eng, T. R., & Gustafson, D. (1998). An evidence-based approach to interactive health communication: A challenge to medicine in the information age. *Journal of the American Medical Association, 288*, 1264–1269.

Sharit, J., Czaja, S. J., Hernandez, M., Yang, Y., Perdomo, D., Lewis, J., Lee, C., & Nair, S. (in press). An evaluation of performance by older persons on a simulated telecommuting task. *Journal of Gerontology: Psychological Sciences, 59*, 2305–2316.

INTERPERSONAL PSYCHOTHERAPY

Interpersonal psychotherapy (IPT) was developed as a time-limited *treatment for major depression* by Weissman and colleagues (2000). IPT has an interpersonal focus, because a large body of research has documented that interpersonally relevant issues precede or are concurrent with depression. IPT is delivered in 3 phases of treatment that usually last a total of 16 weeks. In the initial sessions, the diagnosis of depression is made and discussed with the patient, significant current and past relationships are reviewed, major *interpersonal problem* area(s) are identified, and a *treatment contract* is made. During the middle sessions, treatment focuses in 1 or 2 areas: *interpersonal role disputes* (conflict with a significant other), *grief* (complicated bereavement), *role transitions* (major life change), or *interpersonal deficits* (persistent difficulty in initiating or sustaining relationships). Goals and strategies for each of the 4 problem areas have been delineated. During the termination phase, the end of treatment and associated feelings are discussed, progress in treatment is reviewed, and encouragement to the patient for independent functioning after the end of treatment is provided.

One of the earliest and most notable uses of IPT was in the large, multisite *National Institute of Mental Health treatment of depression* collaborative research program, where IPT was found to be an effective treatment for unipolar major depression (Elkin, Shea, Watkins, Imber, Sotsky, Collins, et al., 1989). In the years since its development, IPT has proven to be an extremely versatile therapy. In randomized, controlled clinical trials, IPT has been successfully applied to different age groups (adolescent, adults, older adults), clinical populations (depressed HIV-positive men, primary care patients), other psychiatric disorders (bulimia, bipolar disorder), and in different formats (group, conjoint for marital disputes, maintenance treatment). IPT has international appeal and has been adopted by researchers and clinicians in North and South America, Europe, Australia/New Zealand, and other regions. Notably, IPT was successfully used in the group treatment of Ugandan adults with major depression in the first randomized, controlled clinical trials of psychotherapy in Africa (Bolton, Bass, Neugebauer, Verdeli, Clougherty, Wickramaratne, et al., 2003).

IPT researchers recognized early that the *psychotherapy* may have utility in the treatment of *late-life depression*. Historically, gerontologists have had concern about the social and emotional well-being of older adults who confront a range of age-related social and interpersonal losses. Although studies document that the majority of older adults experience satisfactory social and emotional well-being, *late-life psychosocial problems* have been associated with increased risk for depression including major depression (Bruce, 2002; George, 1994). Studies also document that social and interpersonal factors are tied to the outcome of major depression in older adults (Bosworth, McQuoid, George, & Steffens, 2002).

Two pilot studies suggested that IPT may be effective in the treatment of major depression, but a definitive, randomized controlled clinical trial of IPT for the acute treatment of IPT has yet to be done. The largest study of IPT for older adults was completed at the University of Pittsburgh (Reynolds, Frank, Perel, Imber, Cornes, Miller, et al., 1999). The goal of the study was to determine which treatment or treatments were most useful in preventing or delaying the recurrence of major depression in older adults. This was a continuation/maintenance study of a large group of persons aged 60 years and older with a diagnosis of recurrent major depression. They were initially treated with both weekly IPT and *nortriptyline* and then randomized to 4 study groups: nortriptyline and IPT, nortriptyline and medication clinic (brief visits for review of symptoms and side effects), IPT and placebo, and placebo and medication clinic. In the maintenance phase of the study, IPT-treated older adults received only monthly sessions of IPT. Study subjects were followed for up to 3 years or until they relapsed into another episode of major depression. Of those older adults treated with weekly IPT and nortriptyline, 78% achieved remission from the episode of major depression-rates that were comparable to those of younger adults in a parallel treatment study. Recurrence rates during the maintenance phase of the study were the following: nortriptyline plus IPT, 20%; nortriptyline plus medication clinic, 43%; IPT plus placebo, 64%; medication clinic plus placebo (90%). The frequency of different IPT problem areas were role transitions (43%), interpersonal disputes (37%), grief (19%), and interpersonal deficits (1.9%). More than half of the subjects (57%) had a second IPT problem focus.

Like many other empirically supported treatments, dissemination into general clinical practice has been slow. However, there are reports that IPT can be readily applied to the treatment of *late-life depressive syndromes* in outpatient clinical practice. Older adults find the collaborative, time-limited format of IPT appealing, and there are few treatment dropouts. Alone or in combination with antidepressant medication, three-quarters of older adults appear to have favorable clinical outcomes that mirror those of research studies. With careful supervision, graduate and postgraduate students in clinical psychology can successfully apply IPT with depressed older adults (Hinrichsen, 1999).

GREGORY A. HINRICHSEN

See also
Psychotherapy

References

Bolton, P., Bass, J., Neugebauer, R., Verdeli, H., Clougherty, K. F., Wickramaratne, P., Speelman, L., Ndogoni, L., & Weissman, M. (2003). Group interpersonal psychotherapy for depression in rural Uganda: A randomized controlled trial. *Journal of the American Medical Association*, *289*, 3117–3124.

Bosworth, H. B., McQuoid, D. R., George, L. K., & Steffens, D. C. (2002). Time-to-remission from geriatric depression: Psychosocial and clinical factors. *American Journal of Geriatric Psychiatry*, *10*, 551–559.

Bruce, M. L. (2002). Psychosocial risk factors for depressive disorders in late life. *Biological Psychiatry*, *52*, 175–184.

Elkin, I., Shea, M. T., Watkins, J. T., Imber, S. D., Sotsky, S. M., Collins, J. F., Glass, D. R., Pilkonis, P. A., Leber, W. R., Docherty, J. P., Fiester, S. J., & Parloff, M. B. (1989). National Institute of Mental Health treatment of depression collaborative research program: General effectiveness of treatments. *Archives of General Psychiatry*, *46*, 971–982.

George, L. K. (1994). Social factors and depression in late life. In L. S. Schneider, C. F. Reynolds, B. D. Lebowitz, & A. J. Friedhoff (Eds.), *Diagnosis and treatment of depression in late life* (pp. 131–154). Washington, DC: American Psychiatric Press.

Hinrichsen, G. A. (1999). Treating older adults with interpersonal psychotherapy of depression. *Journal of Clinical Psychology/In Session*, *55*, 949–960.

Reynolds, C. F., III, Frank E., Perel, J. M., Imber, S. D., Cornes, C., Miller, M. D., Mazumdar, S., Houck, P. R., Dew, M. A., Stack, J. A., Pollock, B. G., & Kupfer, D. J. (1999). Nortriptyline and interpersonal psychotherapy as maintenance therapies for recurrent major depression: A randomized controlled trial in patients older than 59 years. *Journal of the American Medical Association*, *281*, 39–45.

Weissman, M. M., Markowitz, J. C., & Klerman, G. L. (2000). *Comprehensive guide to interpersonal psychotherapy*. New York: Basic Books.

INTROVERSION

In Jungian (1923) psychology, the term introversion is used to mean an inward, subjective orientation, a concern for and interest in the self rather than the environment. But contemporary personality psychologists understand introversion as the opposite of *extraversion*—a broad dimension of *personality traits* that include sociability, adventurousness, assertiveness, activity, and cheerfulness. In this sense, the introvert is reserved, cautious, unassertive, low-keyed, and sober (Costa & McCrae, 1992a).

It is widely believed that *introversion increases with age*; an evaluation of that claim requires attention to the 2 different meanings of introversion. Inner orientation in the Jungian sense is not easily measured. Using the *Thematic Apperception Test*, a projective instrument in which individuals are asked to create a story to fit a picture presented to them, Neugarten (1964) reported that older respondents evidenced a greater preoccupation with inner life, less emotional attachment to the world, and a movement from active to passive mastery.

Introversion as the opposite of social extraversion can be more easily studied using standard personality inventories. Longitudinal studies show more evidence of stability than change (McCrae & Costa, 2003). However, cross-sectional studies, which can cover a larger portion of the adult life span, often detect small increases in social introversion (McCrae, Costa, de Lima, Simões, Ostendorf, Angleitner, et al., 1999).

Individual differences in introversion/extraversion are highly stable in adulthood. Leon and colleagues (1979), for example, found a stability coefficient of .74 for the *MMPI Social Introversion scale* over a period of 30 years in a group of 71 men initially middle-aged. Peer ratings of extraversion over a 7-year interval showed retest correlations of .78 for men and .81 for women (Costa & McCrae, 1992b). Introverts remain introverts and extraverts remain extraverts across the adult life span. Intervention programs aimed at providing social opportunities for older adults should recognize that there are stable individual differences in the desire for social contact. Not all older men and women enjoy socializing, nor should they be expected to.

ROBERT R. MCCRAE

See also
Personality

References

Costa, P. T., Jr., & McCrae, R. R. (1992a). *Revised NEO Personality Inventory (NEO-PI-R) and NEO Five-Factor Inventory (NEO-FFI) professional manual.* Odessa, FL: Psychological Assessment Resources.

Costa, P. T., Jr., & McCrae, R. R. (1992b). Trait psychology comes of age. In T. B. Sonderegger (Ed.), *Nebraska Symposium on Motivation: Psychology and aging* (pp. 169–204). Lincoln, NE: University of Nebraska Press.

Jung, C. G. (1923). *Psychological types*. London: Routledge & Kegen Paul.

Leon, R. R., Gillum, B., Gillum, R., & Gouze, M. (1979). Personality stability and change over a 30 year period—middle age to old age. *Journal of Consulting and Clinical Psychology, 23,* 245–259.

McCrae, R. R., & Costa, P. T., Jr. (2003). *Personality in adulthood* (2nd ed.): A Five-Factor Theory perspective. New York: Guilford.

McCrae, R. R., Costa, P. T., Jr., de Lima, M. P., Simões, A., Ostendorf, F., Angleitner, A., Marusic, I., Bratko, D., Caprara, G. V., Barbaranelli, C., Chae J.-H., & Piedmont, R. L. (1999). Age differences in personality across the adult life span: Parallels in five cultures. *Developmental Psychology, 35,* 466–477.

Neugarten, B. L. (1964). Summary and implications. In B. L. Neugarten (Ed.), *Personality in middle and late life* (pp. 188–200). New York: Atherton Press.

ISOMERIZATION

Ribosomal protein synthesis links aspartic acid (Asp) to other amino acid residues only through its alpha-carboxyl group. This places the side chain beta-carboxyl group in the precise orientation needed for the proper structure and function of the protein. As a protein ages, however, it can undergo a spontaneous chemical reaction involving the nucleophilic attack of the adjacent backbone nitrogen on the side chain carbonyl carbon of both Asp and asparaginyl (Asn) residues, forming a 5-membered cyclic succinimide (Figure 1). This succinimide ring is spontaneously opened by the attack of water on either of the carbonyl carbons, resulting in the formation of anormal Asp residue or an isomerized "isoaspartyl" (isoAsp) or "beta-aspartyl" linkage, in which the peptide backbone goes through the beta-carboxyl group (Figure 1).

The kinetics of these reactions have been extensively studied in vitro. The half-life (t,/2) of *succinimide* formation in synthetic peptides under physiological conditions (37°C, pH, 7.3–7.5) ranges from as little as 0.24–1.4 days for Asn-Gly and 41 days for Asp-Gly sequences to more than 200 days when the Asn/Asp (Asx) residue is adjacent to bulky hydrophobic residues (Brennan & Clarke, 1995). In proteins, however, constraints imposed by secondary or tertiary structure can stabilize some Asx residues so that no degradation at all is seen at those sites (Clarke, 1987). Local flexibility, the presence of small or hydrophilic adjacent residues, and increases in temperature or pH all promote succinimide formation. The succinimide itself is quite unstable, hydrolyzing with a t1/2 of only 2.4 hours under physiological conditions (Geiger & Clarke, 1987). Interestingly, this hydrolysis generates the isoAsp product 3 to 4 times more often than the Asp product under a variety of conditions.

Two other reactions are associated with *succinimide formation*. First, the succinimide is prone to *racemization* (inversion of the chiral alpha-carbon); the L-succinimide in one hexapeptide was found to racemize to the n-succinimide with a tl/2 of 19.5 hours, much faster than occurs in the open-chain Asp and isoAsp forms (Geiger & Clarke, 1987). D-Asp and D-isoAsp residues are therefore likely to be found whenever a succinimide-linked mechanism is involved. Second, Asa-containing peptides can undergo a reaction in which the side-chain nitrogen

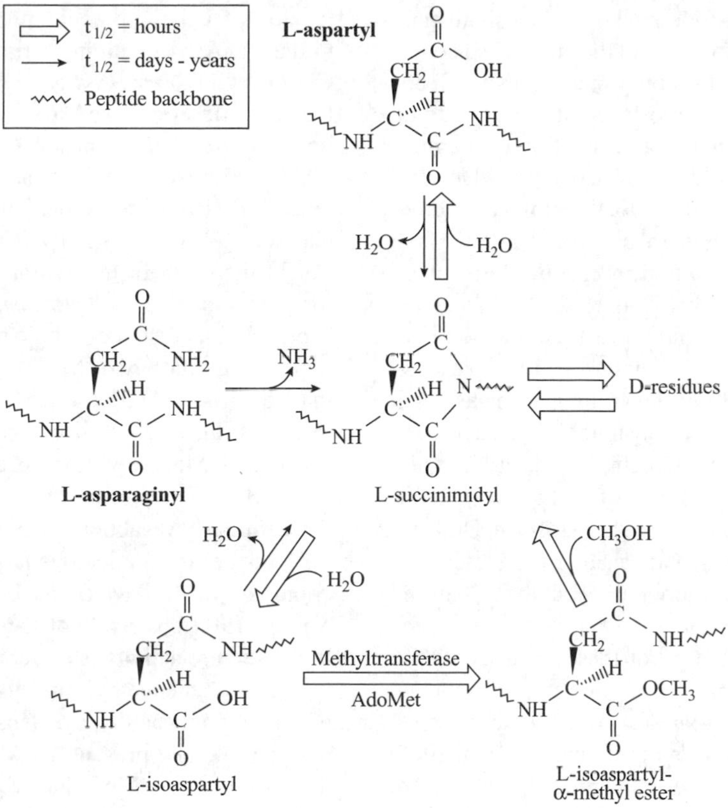

FIGURE 1 Mechanisms of degradation and methyltransferase-linked repair of protein L-aspartic acid and L-asparagine residues.

attacks the backbone carbonyl carbon and cleaves the peptide bond, leaving a C-terminal succinimide on one of the peptide fragments. This reaction is significant in synthetic peptides when the residue to the carboxyl side of the Asn is bulky and hydrophobic and is predominant in Asn-Pro sequences (Geiger & Clarke, 1987; Tyler-Cross & Schirch, 1991). These succinimide-linked reactions have also been observed in in vivo-aged proteins in eye lens and brain (Fujii, Ishibashi, Satoh, Fujino, & Harada, 1994; Roher, Lowenson, Clarke, Wolkow, Wang, Cotter, et al., 1993; Voorter, deHaard-Hoekman, van den Octelaar, Bloemendal, & de Jong, 1988).

Given these in vitro reaction rates, it seems likely that *isoAsp* formation would be a significant problem within physiological systems. *Spontaneous deamidation* of proteins in vivo is widely recognized and easily detected by the increase in negative charge that accompanies the conversion of Asn to Asp or isoAsp residues (Wright, 1991). The $t_{1/2}$ of *deamidation* of an Asn-His sequence in the rabbit muscle aldolase is just 8 days in vivo, indicating that, at least in this case, the reaction rate is similar to those measured with small peptides in vitro. It must be noted, however, that Asn deamidation in some proteins may proceed through succinimide-independent mechanisms and thus not form isoAsp residues (Wright, 1991). The conversion of Asp to isoAsp residues in proteins slightly alters their net charge but is more easily detected by using the enzymatic methylation assay described below. Asp residues in human erythrocyte calmodulin (Ota & Clarke, 1990) and brain beta-amyloid (Roher, Lowenson, Clarke, Wolkow, Wang, Coffer, et al., 1993) are known to undergo succinimide formation in vivo, and similar results have been seen in a variety of native and recombinant proteins in vitro.

What are the effects of isoAsp residues on protein function? The transfer of a methylene group from a side-chain to the peptide backbone is a significant change, but except for the fact that all isoAsp bonds are resistant to digestion by proteases, their effects should vary with the importance of that residue in maintaining the structure and function of the protein. The presence of just 1 or 2 isoAsp residues, for example, can decrease by 80% the biological activity of recombinant human epidermal growth factor (George-Nascimento, Lowenson, Borissenko, Calderon, Medina-Selby, Kuo, et al., 1990) and the ability of bovine calmodulin to activate calmodulin-dependent protein kinase (Johnson, Langmack, & Aswad, 1987), can limit the affinity of chicken egg lysozyme for its chitin substrate (Yamada, Ueda, Kuroki, Fukumura, Yasukochi, Hirabayashi, et al., 1985), can alter the affinity of calbindin D9k for calcium (Chazin, Kordel, Thulin, Hofman, Drakenberg, & Forsen, 1989), and can alter the angiogenic properties of human angiogenin (Hallahan, Shapiro, Strydom, & Vallee, 1992).

The detrimental nature of these residues within living cells is supported by the existence of an L-isoaspartate (D-aspartate) o-methyltransferase that specifically catalyzes the transfer of a methyl group from s-adenosylmethionine (AdoMet) to damaged Asp residues, initiating their "repair" back to the normal L-Asp form. This enzyme is present in bacteria, fungi, plants, and all human tissues thus far examined (Johnson, Ngo, & Aswad, 1991). Methylation of the alpha-carboxyl group of an L-isoAsp residue can increase the rate at which it forms a succinimide 10^3- to 10^4-fold; the net result of methylation, succinimide formation, and succinimide hydrolysis is the conversion of L-isoAsp to L-Asp residues, with the slow accumulation of racemized residues (Figure 1). Mammalian methyltransferases also recognize D-Asp residues, but with lower affinity than for L-isoAsp residues (Lowenson & Clarke, 1992). L-IsoAsp residues in many peptides and proteins are methylated by the human enzyme with high affinity (K_m values of 0.5–20 μM) and comparable velocities; only constrained higher order structure and a few sequence elements can inhibit the reaction (Lowenson & Clarke, 1991). With radiolabeled AdoMet, the methyltransferase can be used in an assay sensitive enough to detect less than 200 fmol of L-isoAsp residues. It cannot, however, restore deamidated Asn to its original form.

The repair pathway described above has been demonstrated in vitro with the up to 80% conversion of L-isoAsp-containing synthetic peptides to their L-Asp-containing forms (Johnson, Murray, Clarke, Glass, & Aswad, 1987). Furthermore, the activities of L-isoAsp-containing deamidated bovine *calmodulin* (Johnson, Langmack, & Aswad, 1987) and deamidated E. *cols* phosphocarrier protein HPr (Brennan, Anderson, Jia, Waygood, & Clarke, 1994) are partially restored upon incubation in vitro with the methyltransferase and AdoMet. Mice lacking the *methyltransferase* have recently been developed, and cytosolic proteins in these animals accumulate two- to six-fold more L-isoAsps than do normal mice, establishing that repair of these residues has physiological importance (Kim, Lowenson, MacLaren, Clarke, & Young, 1997). Although born and weaned at the expected frequency, these mice have abnormal cortical activity about 50% of the time and suffer fatal seizures at an average age of 42 days (Kim, Lowenson, Clarke, & Young, 1999). The role of L-isoAsp accumulation in the seizure activity is as yet undetermined.

Although the methyltransferase remains fully active in aging healthy eye lens and brain, it cannot completely prevent isoAsp accumulation as these tissues age (McFadden & Clarke, 1986; Man, Fisher, Payan, Cadilla-Perezrios, Garcia, Chemburker, et al., 1987; Johnson, Shirokawa, Geddes, Choi, Kim, & Aswad, 1991), perhaps because of limited protein turnover or because succinimide formation is increased in denatured proteins. Expression of the enzyme appears to be lower in human *cataractous eye lens*, which contains abundant L-isoAsp residues in aggregated crystallins (Kodama, Mizobuchi, Takeda, Torikai, Shinomiya, & Ohashi, 1995), but higher in Alzheimer's disease brain (Kondo, Shirasawa, Itoyama, & Mori, 1996). Furthermore, the methyltransferase activity can be significantly inhibited in diseases like uremia, in which the s-adenosylhomocysteine level is elevated (Perna, Ingrosso, De Santo, Galletti, & Zappia, 1995). The accumulation of isoAsp residues in cellular proteins with age may also contribute to the loss of self-tolerance in autoimmune diseases such as systemic lupus erythematosus (Mamula, Gee, Elliott, Sette, Southwood, Jones, et al., 1999).

Extracellular proteins are not subject to the repair pathway. In fact, about 75% of the *beta-amyloid peptides* found in dense extracellular plaques (Roher, Lowenson, Clarke, Wolkow, Wang, Cotter, et al., 1993) and much of the *tau protein* from paired helical filaments (Watanabe, Takio, & Ihara, 1999) in *Alzheimer's disease brains* contain one or more isoAsp residues. Immunohistochemistry using antibodies specific for L-isoAsp-containing beta-amyloid have identified older plaques that are correlated with dementia severity (Fonseca, Head, Velazquez, Cotman, & Terrier, 1999). In addition, antibodies against an L-isoAsp-containing fragment of aged collagen are being used to diagnose certain bone diseases (Fledelius, Johnsen, Cloos, Bonde, & Qvist, 1997). Whether damaged Asp residues contribute to the pathology of these diseases or are simply a consequence of the long-term stability of selected proteins is as yet unknown.

JONATHAN D. LOWENSON

See also
Racemization

References

Brennan, T. V., Anderson, J. W., Jia, Z., Waygood, E. B., & Clarke, S. (1994). Repair of spontaneously deamidated HPr phosphocarder protein catalyzed by the L-isoaspartate-(D-aspartate) o-methyltransferase. *Journal of Biological Chemistry, 269,* 24586–24595.

Brennan, T. V., & Clarke, S. (1995). Deamidation and isoaspartate formation in model synthetic peptides: The effects of sequence and solution environment. In D. W. Aswad (Ed.), *Deamidation and isoaspartate formation in peptides and proteins* (pp. 65–90). Boca Raton, FL: CRC Press.

Chazin, W. J., Kördel, J., Thulin, E., Hofmann, T., Drakenberg, T., & Forsen, S. (1989). Identification of an isoaspartyl linkage formed upon deamidation of bovine calbindin D9k and structural characterization by 2D 1H NMR. *Biochemistry, 28,* 8646–8653.

Clarke, S. (1987). Propensity for spontaneous succinimide formation from aspartyl and asparaginyl residues in cellular proteins. *International Journal of Peptide and Protein Research, 30,* 808–821.

Fledelius, C., Johnsen, A. H., Cloos, P. A. C., Bonde, M., & Qvist, P. (1997). Characterization of urinary degradation products derived from type I collagen. Identification of a beta-isomerized Asp-Gly sequence within the C-terminal telopeptide (alpha 1) region. *Journal of Biological Chemistry, 272,* 9755–9763.

Fonseca, M. I., Head, E., Velazquez, P., Cotman, C. W., & Tenner, A. J. (1999). The presence of isoaspartic acid in beta-amyloid plaques indicates plaque age. *Experimental Neurology, 157,* 277–288.

Fujii, N., Ishibashi, Y., Satoh, K., Fujino, M., & Harada, K. (1994). Simultaneous racemization and isomerization at specific aspartic acid residues in alpha B-crystallin from the aged human lens. *Biochimica et Biophysica Acta, 1204,* 157–163.

Geiger, T., & Clarke, S. (1987). Deamidation, isomerization, and racemization at asparaginyl and aspartyl residues in peptides. *Journal of Biological Chemistry, 262,* 785–794.

George-Nascimento, C., Lowenson, J., Borissenko, M., Calderon, M., Medina-Selby, A., Kuo, J., Clarke, S., & Randolph, A. (1990). Replacement of a labile aspartyl residue increases the stability of human epidermal growth factor. *Biochemistry, 29,* 9586–9591.

Hallahan, T. W., Shapiro, R., Strydom, D. J., & Vallee, B. L. (1992). Importance of asparagine-61 and asparagine-109 to the angiogenic activity of human angiogenin. *Biochemistry, 31,* 8022–8029.

Johnson, B. A., Langmack, E. L., & Aswad, D. W. (1987). Partial repair of deamidation-damaged calmodulin by protein carboxyl methyltransferase. *Journal of Biological Chemistry, 262,* 12283–12287.

Johnson, B. A., Murray, E. D., Jr., Clarke, S., Glass, D. B., & Aswad, D. W. (1987). Protein carboxyl methyltransferase facilitates conversion of atypical L-isoaspartyl peptides to normal L-aspartyl peptides. *Journal of Biological Chemistry, 262,* 5622–5629.

Johnson, B. A., Ngo, S. Q., & Aswad, D. W. (1991). Widespread phylogenetic distribution of a protein methyltransferase that modifies L-isoaspartyl residues. *Biochemistry International, 24,* 841–847.

Johnson, B. A., Shirokawa, J. M., Geddes, J. W., Choi, B. H., Kim, R. C., & Aswad, D. W. (1991). Protein L-isoaspartyl methyltransferase in postmortem brains of aged humans. *Neurobiology of Aging, 12,* 19–24.

Kim, E., Lowenson, J. D., Clarke, S., & Young, S. G. (1999). Phenotypic analysis of seizure-prone mice lacking L-isoaspartate (D-aspartate) o-methyltransferase. *Journal of Biological Chemistry, 274,* 20671–20678.

Kim, E., Lowenson, J. D., MacLaren, D. C., Clarke, S., & Young, S. G. (1997). Deficiency of a protein-repair enzyme results in the accumulation of altered proteins, retardation of growth, and fatal seizures in mice. *Proceedings of the National Academy of Sciences, U.S.A., 94,* 6132–6137.

Kodama, T., Mizobuchi, M., Takeda, R., Torikai, H., Shinomiya, H., & Ohashi, Y. (1995). Hampered expression of isoaspartyl protein carboxyl methyltransferase gene in the human cataractous lens. *Biochimica et Biophysica Acta, 1245,* 269–272.

Kondo, T., Shirasawa, T., Itoyama, Y., & Mori, H. (1996). Embryonic genes expressed in Alzheimer's disease brains. *Neuroscience Letters, 209,* 157–160.

Lowenson, J. D., & Clarke, S. (1991). Structural elements affecting the recognition of L-isoaspartyl residues by the L-isoaspartyl/D-aspartyl methyltransferase: Implications for the repair hypothesis. *Journal of Biological Chemistry, 266,* 19396–19406.

Lowenson, J. D., & Clarke, S. (1992). Recognition of D-aspartyl residues in polypeptides by the erythrocyte L-isoaspartyl/D-aspartyl protein methyltransferase. *Journal of Biological Chemistry, 267,* 5985–5995.

Mamula, M. J., Gee, R. J., Elliott, J. I., Sette, A., Southwood, S., Jones, P. J., & Blier, P. R. (1999). Isoaspartyl post-translational modification triggers autoimmune responses to self-proteins. *Journal of Biological Chemistry, 274,* 22321–22327.

Man, E. H., Fisher, G. H., Payan, I. L., Cadilla-Perezrios, R., Garcia, N. M., Chemburkar, R., Arends, G., & Frey, W. H., II. (1987). D-aspartate in human brain. *Journal of Neurochemistry, 48,* 510–515.

McFadden, P, N., & Clarke, S. (1986). Protein carboxyl methyltransferase and methyl acceptor proteins in aging and cataractous tissue of the human eye lens. *Mechanisms of Ageing and Development, 34,* 91–105.

Ota, I. M., & Clarke, S. (1990). Multiple sites of methyl esterification of calmodulin in intact human crythrocytes. *Archives of Biochemistry and Biophysics, 279,* 320–327.

Perna, A. F., Ingrosso, D., De Santo, N. G., Galletti, P., & Zappia, V. (1995). Mechanism of erythrocyte accumulation of methylation inhibitor s-adenosylhomocysteine in uremia. *Kidney International, 47,* 247–253.

Roher, A. E., Lowenson, J. D., Clarke, S., Wolkow, C., Wang, R., Cotter, R. J., Reardon, I. M., Zurcher-Neely, H. A., Heinrikson, R. L., Ball, M. J., & Greenberg, B. D. (1993). Structural alterations in the backbone of β-amyloid core protein may account for its deposition and stability in Alzheimer's disease. *Journal of Biological Chemistry, 268,* 3072–3083.

Tyler-Cross, R., & Schirch, V. (1991). Effects of amino acid sequence, buffers, and ionic strength on the rate and mechanism of deamidation of asparagine residues in small peptides. *Journal of Biological Chemistry, 266,* 22549–22556.

Voorter, C. E., de Haard-Hoekman, W. A., van den Oetelaar, P. Bloemendal, H., & de Jong, W. W. (1988). Spontaneous peptide bond cleavage in aging alpha-crystallin through a succinimide intermediate. *Journal of Biological Chemistry, 263,* 19020–19023.

Watanabe, A., Takio, K., & Ihara, Y. (1999). Deamidation and isoaspartate formation in smeared tau in paired helical filaments. Unusual properties of the microtubule-binding domain of tau. *Journal of Biological Chemistry, 274,* 7368–7378.

Wright, H. T. (1991). Nonenzymatic deamidation of asparaginyl and glutammyl residues in proteins. *Critical Reviews in Biochemistry and Molecular Biology, 26,* 1–52.

Yamada, H., Ueda, T., Kuroki, R., Fukumura, T., Yasukochi, T., Hirabayashi, T., Fujita, K., & Imoto, T. (1985). Isolation and characterization of 101-beta-lysozyme that possesses the beta-aspartyl sequence at aspartic acid-101. *Biochemistry, 24,* 7953–7959.

J

JOB PERFORMANCE

See
Productivity

K

KIDNEY AND URINARY SYSTEM

The 2 kidneys normally are located in the back just below the rib cage, although anatomic variations in number and location are common. The *nephron* is the kidney's functional unit, and each kidney contains many thousands of them. The nephron consists of a *glomerulus* that acts as a filter for blood and tubules that selectively reabsorb and secrete filtered molecules and water. The glomerulus filters the large quantities of blood circulating through the kidneys, allowing fluid and small molecules (but not large molecules, such as protein) and cellular structures such as red and white cells and platelets to enter the tubular system. In the tubules, molecules that the body needs to conserve, such as sodium, potassium, and glucose, are reabsorbed back into the bloodstream, and waste products of the body metabolism, such as *creatinine* and *urea*, can be excreted in the urine. This way the body's fluid and electrolyte content can be carefully regulated, varying the rates of reabsorption and secretion as necessary.

Ureters connect the 2 kidneys to the bladder (detrusor) made up of smooth muscle. This serves as a reservoir for urine until a time is convenient for emptying, when the urine leaves the *bladder* through the urethra. The filling and emptying of the bladder are under the control of the autonomic (sympathetic, parasympathetic) nervous system and voluntary (cortical) nervous system. Between the bladder and urethra are 2 sphincters (valves) that *control urination*—internal and external sphincters. Sympathetic stimulation allows the *filling of the bladder* by relaxing bladder musculature and closing the internal sphincter. When the bladder fills to a certain pressure (volume), the *micturition reflex* alerts the individual of the need to urinate. This reflex can be facilitated or inhibited by centers in the brain stem and cerebral cortex (brain stem *micturition center*) that control the external sphincter. This sphincter is under voluntary control and can initiate, prevent, or interrupt urination. Parasympathetic stimulation (*Valsalva maneuver*) promotes the opening of the internal sphincter and contraction of bladder musculature, initiating urination (micturition). Whereas interruption of the sympathetic nervous system has no effect on micturition, interruption of the parasympathetic nervous system (spinal cord injury) results in complete *bladder dysfunction*. In males, the prostate gland, normally walnut size, encircles the start of the urethra. With age, this tends to increase in size, so it may cause difficulty in the passage of urine and even obstruct urine flow.

Aging and the Kidney

Although kidney function often declines substantially with age, it usually remains sufficient to remove all waste products of metabolism (urea, creatinine, phosphorus), and to regulate the volume and composition (sodium and potassium) of body fluids. A decrease in the capacity for filtering the serum or plasma component of blood (*glomerular filtration rate*, or GFR) is the most easily measured and important functional defect caused by age-related anatomic and physiologic changes. The GFR can be measured by determining a *creatinine clearance* through collection of a timed urine sample and serum sample. This measure is stable in the normal young adult at 100–120 ml/min until age 30 to 40 years, after which the mean value decreases at a rate approaching 1 ml/min/year. Kidney function also is estimated for clinical purposes by measuring serum creatinine (normally 0.6–1.2 mg/dl) or serum *urea nitrogen* (normally 6–22 mg/dl) concentrations. These values exceed these levels only after some pathological process affects the kidneys to reduce their function to below one-third of normal. Because the creatinine in serum comes from muscle metabolism and because muscle mass decreases with age, the creatinine clearance may decrease substantially with age without any appreciable increase in the serum creatinine concentration. This is important to recognize when using serum creatinine concentrations to establish dosages for drugs cleared totally or partially by the kidney (digoxin and certain antibiotics, such as gentamicin). The early *Cockroft-Gault formula* for estimating creatinine clearance from serum creatinine concentration in older individuals has been improved upon using data from the *Modification of Diet in Renal Disease* (MDRD) study group (Levey, Bosch, Lewis, Greene, Rogers, & Roth, 1999).

Longitudinal studies show that *aging's effect on the kidney* (serial creatinine clearances in individuals) varies substantially. In a study of healthy, upper-middle class volunteers (*Baltimore Longitudinal Study of Aging*), one-third of older individuals showed no decrease in clearances over periods up to 20 years or more (Lindeman, Tobin & Shock, 1995). This finding suggests that the decline in renal function observed with age is due to underlying pathology, such as atherosclerosis, rather than any inevitable aging process (senescence).

Other *functions of the kidney* (ability to concentrate and dilute urine, excrete acids, reabsorb sugars, and secrete organic acids) decrease with age at rates closely paralleling changes in GFR. Leakage of protein (*proteinuria*) does not normally increase with age; its appearance in the urine generally is due to some disease process.

Common *Disorders of the Kidney*

The most common kidney disorders in older adults are similar to those seen at younger ages, although the frequency tends to vary. These include: (1) *nephrotic syndrome*, (2) *glomerulonephritis*, (3) partial or complete *blockage of a renal artery* or arteries, and (4) acute and chronic *renal failure* (insufficiency).

Nephrotic syndrome is due to loss of protein in the urine (greater than 3 gm/day) with generalized edema and susceptibility to infections. Diabetes mellitus is the most common cause, but it can also be seen with a variety of other immunologic and systemic disease processes.

Glomerulonephritis (diffuse inflammatory changes in the glomeruli) can be acute in onset following a variety of infections (post-infectious glomerulonephritis), or more chronic, often associated with systemic immunological diseases such as lupus erythematosus. Symptoms and findings include blood and protein in the urine, edema, and hypertension.

Partial (*renal artery stenosis*) and total occlusion (thrombosis, embolism) of one or more arteries in older persons are usually atherosclerotic in origin. They cause hypertension and loss of renal function. Cholesterol emboli are unique to older adults.

Acute renal failure (ARF) is characterized by rapidly rising serum urea nitrogen and creatinine concentrations, and can be ischemic or toxic in origin. Ischemic ARF results from inadequate perfusion of the kidneys due to dehydration, heart failure, and/or hypotension. Prolonged periods of poor perfusion, especially during major surgery, can result in injury to the renal tubules (*acute tubular necrosis*). Toxic ARF can result from administration of certain antibiotics and other medications, anesthetics, or diagnostic agents, or release of hemoglobin or myoglobin into the blood (*rhabdomyolysis*). It is important to rule out *urinary tract obstruction*, such as *prostate hypertrophy* or stricture, when *urine flow ceases* or is scant, as this is readily reversible if appropriately diagnosed.

Chronic renal failure is the end result of a wide array of pathological processes that reduce kidney function to the point where dialysis or transplantation is necessary for survival. In-center and home *hemodialysis* and chronic ambulatory *peritoneal dialysis* are options for the older person with end-stage renal disease. Most older adults do well on dialysis; problems arise primarily from comorbidity, such as accelerated atherosclerotic disease. *Renal transplantation* is increasingly being utilized in persons older than 60 years, but there remains a reluctance to allocate a scarce resource (the donor kidney) to those with a limited life expectancy. Nevertheless, older adult transplant patients matched with dialysis patients by age, underlying diagnosis, and comorbidities have 5-year survival rates of 81% versus 51% (Schaubel, Desmeules, Mao, Jeffery, & Fenton, 1995). Further descriptions of these conditions in older adults are reported elsewhere (Kelleher & Lindeman, 2002).

Urinary Incontinence, Infections, Tumors, and Stones

Urinary incontinence can result from inadequate closure of the sphincters between the bladder and urethra (*stress incontinence*), from hyperactive bladder musculature (*urge incontinence*), or a combination of both (*mixed incontinence*). It can also result from excessive filling of the bladder due to obstruction (*prostate hypertrophy*, *urethral stricture*) or loss of bladder stimulation (*diabetic neuropathy*) causing overflow incontinence.

Another common problem affecting the bladder of older persons is recurrent infection. Females are particularly prone to this, presumably because their short urethra facilitates bacterial access. Symptoms and findings include a need to urinate frequently, pain on urination (*dysuria*), and blood (*hematuria*) and white blood cells (*pyuria*) in the urine. Fever is often low grade or absent. High fevers and back (flank) pain generally indicate that the infection has involved the kidneys (*pyelonephritis*). Short courses of antibiotics usually clear *bladder infections*; more aggressive antibiotic therapy is needed for *kidney infections*. Older persons often have permanent bacterial colonization without symptoms (*asymptomatic bacteriuria*). Treatment of this condition is generally unnecessary.

Kidney cancers (*hypernephromas*) often are widely disseminated before detection. Blood in the urine is the most common first symptom, but unexplained fever, or low (anemia) or high (*polycythemia*) blood hemoglobin concentrations also may be clues. Bladder cancers are common in older adults and usually present with blood in the urine. The diagnosis can be made by viewing the inside of the bladder with a *cystoscope* inserted through the urethra. Treatment with surgical removal and/or radiation therapy usually controls the cancer.

Kidney stones occur at any age. Stone collection and analysis help to determine the type of stone, so that further stone formation may be prevented with appropriate medical management. Intense flank pain and blood in the urine are the primary manifestations. Many small stones pass spontaneously; larger stones, often associated with recurrent infections or blockage of urine flow, tend to require surgical removal or destruction with ultrasound (*lithotripsy*).

ROBERT D. LINDEMAN

References

Kelleher, C. L., & Lindeman, R. D. (2002). Renal diseases and disorders. In E. L. Cobbs, E. H. Duthie, & J. B. Murphy (Eds.), *Geriatric review syllabus: A core curriculum in geriatric medicine* (5th ed., pp. 374–384). Malden, MA: Blackwell Publishing/American Geriatric Society.

Levey, A. S., Bosch, J. P., Lewis, J. B., Greene, T., Roger, N., & Roth, D. (1999). A more accurate method to estimate glomerular filtration rate from serum creatinine: A new prediction equation. Modification of Diet in Renal Disease Study Group. *Annals of Internal Medicine*, *130*, 461–470.

Lindeman, R. D., Tobin, J., & Shock, N. W. (1985). Longitudinal studies on the rate of decline in renal function with age. *Journal of the American Geriatrics Society*, *33*, 278–285.

Schaubel, D., Desmeules, M., Mao, Y., Jeffery, J., & Fenton, S. (1995). Survival experience among older adults end-stage renal disease patients. A controlled comparison of transplantation and dialysis. *Transplantation*, *60*, 1389–1394.

INDEXES

SUBJECT INDEX

Note: Boldface page numbers indicates pages on which articles appear.

CONTRIBUTOR INDEX